shakespearean criticism

Mr. WILLIAM SHAKESPEARES

COMEDIES, HISTORIES, & TRAGEDIES.

Published according to the True Originall Copies.

Martin Droeshout sculpsit London.

LONDON

Printed by Isaac Iaggard, and Ed. Blount. 1623.

Frontispiece to the First Folio (1623). By permission of the Folger Shakespeare Library.

ISSN 0883-9123

Volume 79

shakespearean criticism

Criticism of
William Shakespeare's Plays and Poetry,
from the First Published Appraisals
to Current Evaluations

Michael LaBlanc
Project Editor

GALE®

THOMSON

GALE

Detroit • New York • San Diego • San Francisco • Cleveland • New Haven, Conn. • Waterville, Maine • London • Munich

Shakespearean Criticism, Vol. 79

Project Editor
Michael L. LaBlanc

Editorial
Jessica Bomarito, Jenny Cromie, Kathy D. Darrow, Elisabeth Gellert, Julie Keppen, Jelena O. Krstović, Michelle Lee, Thomas J. Schoenberg, Marie Toth, Lawrence J. Trudeau, Russel Whitaker

Permissions
Peg Ashlevitz

Imaging and Multimedia
Robert Duncan, Lezlie Light, Kelly A. Quin

Composition and Electronic Capture
Kathy Sauer

Manufacturing
Stacy L. Melson

LIBRARY OF CONGRESS CATALOG CARD NUMBER 86-645085

ISBN 0-7876-7009-X
ISSN 0883-9123

Printed in the United States of America
10 9 8 7 6 5 4 3 2 1

Contents

Preface vii

Acknowledgments xi

SC Contents, by Volume xiii

Literary Criticism Series Advisory Board xvii

Preface

*S*hakespearean Criticism (*SC*) provides students, educators, theatergoers, and other interested readers with valuable insight into Shakespeare's drama and poetry. A multiplicity of viewpoints documenting the critical reaction of scholars and commentators from the seventeenth century to the present day derives from hundreds of periodicals and books excerpted for the series. Students and teachers at all levels of study will benefit from *SC,* whether they seek information for class discussions and written assignments, new perspectives on traditional issues, or the most noteworthy of analyses of Shakespeare's artistry.

Scope of the Series

Volumes 1 through 10 of the series present a unique historical overview of the critical response to each Shakespearean work, representing a broad range of interpretations.

Volumes 11 through 26 recount the performance history of Shakespeare's plays on the stage and screen through eyewitness reviews and retrospective evaluations of individual productions, comparisons of major interpretations, and discussions of staging issues.

Volumes 27 through 56 in the series focus on criticism published after 1960, with a view to providing the reader with the most significant modern critical approaches. Each volume is ordered around a theme that is central to the study of Shakespeare, such as politics, religion, or sexuality. The topic entry that introduces each volume is comprised of general essays that discuss this theme with reference to all of Shakespeare's works. Following the topic entry are several entries devoted to individual works.

Beginning with volume 57 in the series, *SC* provides a works-based approach; each of the four entries contained in a regular volume focuses on a specific Shakespearean play or poem. The entries will include the most recent criticism available on the works, as well as earlier criticism not previously included in *SC.* Select volumes contain topic entries comprised of essays that analyze various topics, or themes, found in Shakespeare's works. Past topic entries have covered such subjects as Honor, Jealousy, War and Warfare, and Elizabethan Politics.

Until volume 48, published in October 1999, *SC* compiled an annual volume of the most noteworthy essays published on Shakespeare during the previous year. The essays, reprinted in their entirety, were recommended to Gale by an international panel of distinguished scholars.

Organization of the Book

An *SC* entry consists of the following elements:

■ The **Introduction** contains background information that introduces the reader to the work or topic that is the subject of the entry and outlines modern interpretations of individual Shakespearean topic, plays, and poems.

■ Reprinted **Criticism** for each entry consists of essays arranged chronologically under a variety of subheadings to facilitate the study of different aspects of the play, poem, or topic. This provides an overview of the major areas of concern in the analysis of Shakespeare's works, as well as a useful perspective on changes in critical evaluation over recent decades. The critic's name and the date of composition or publication of the critical work are given at the beginning of each piece of criticism. Unsigned criticism is preceded by the title of the source in which it appeared. Footnotes are reprinted at the end of each essay or excerpt. In the case of excerpted criticism, only those footnotes that pertain to the excerpted texts are included.

■ A complete **Bibliographical Citation** of the original essay or book precedes each piece of criticism.

- Critical essays are prefaced by **Explanatory Notes** as an aid to students using *SC*. The explanatory notes summarize the criticism that follows.

- Each volume includes such **Illustrations** as reproductions of images from the Shakespearean period, paintings and sketches of eighteenth- and nineteenth-century performers, photographs of modern productions, and stills from film adaptations.

- An annotated bibliography of **Further Reading** appears at the end of each entry and suggests resources for additional study. In some cases, significant essays for which the editors could not obtain reprint rights are included here.

Indexes

A **Cumulative Character Index** identifies the principal characters of discussion in the criticism of each play and nondramatic poem.

A **Cumulative Topic Index** identifies the principal topics in the criticism and stage history of each work. The topics are arranged alphabetically, by topic.

A **Cumulative Topic Index, by Play** identifies the principal topics in the criticism and stage history of each work. The topics are arranged alphabetically, by play.

Citing *Shakespearean Criticism*

When citing criticism reprinted in the Literary Criticism Series, students should provide complete bibliographic information so that the cited essay can be located in the original print or electronic source. Students who quote directly from reprinted criticism may use any accepted bibliographic format, such as University of Chicago Press style or Modern Language Association (MLA) style. Both the MLA and the University of Chicago formats are acceptable and recognized as being the current standards for citations. It is important, however, to choose one format for all citations; do not mix the two formats within a list of citations.

The examples below follow recommendations for preparing a bibliography set forth in *The Chicago Manual of Style,* 14th ed. (Chicago: The University of Chicago Press, 1993); the first example pertains to material drawn from periodicals, the second to material reprinted from books:

Morrison, Jago. "Narration and Unease in Ian McEwan's Later Fiction." *Critique* 42, no. 3 (spring 2001): 253-68. Reprinted in *Shakespearean Criticism,* Vol. 72, edited by Michael L. LaBlanc, 212-20. Detroit: Gale, 2003.

Brossard, Nicole. "Poetic Politics." In *The Politics of Poetic Form: Poetry and Public Policy,* edited by Charles Bernstein, 73-82. New York: Roof Books, 1990. Reprinted in *Shakespearean Criticism,* Vol. 73, edited by Michael L. LaBlanc, 3-8. Detroit: Gale, 2003.

The examples below follow recommendations for preparing a works cited list set forth in the *MLA Handbook for Writers of Research Papers,* 5th ed. (New York: The Modern Language Association of America, 1999); the first example pertains to material drawn from periodicals, the second to material reprinted from books:

Morrison, Jago. "Narration and Unease in Ian McEwan's Later Fiction." *Critique* 42. 3 (spring 2001): 253-68. Reprinted in *Shakespearean Criticism.* Ed. Michael L. LaBlanc. Vol. 72. Detroit: Gale, 2003. 212-20.

Brossard, Nicole. "Poetic Politics." *The Politics of Poetic Form: Poetry and Public Policy.* Ed. Charles Bernstein. New York: Roof Books, 1990. 73-82. Reprinted in *Shakespearean Criticism.* Ed. Michael L. LaBlanc. Vol. 73. Detroit: Gale, 2003. 3-8.

Suggestions are Welcome

Readers who wish to suggest new features or topics to appear in future volumes, or who have other suggestions or comments are cordially invited to call, write, or fax the Project Editor:

Project Editor, Literary Criticism Series
The Gale Group
27500 Drake Road
Farmington Hills, MI 48331-3535
1-800-347-4253 (GALE)
Fax: 248-699-8054

Acknowledgments

The editors wish to thank the copyright holders of the excerpted criticism included in this volume and the permissions managers of many book and magazine publishing companies for assisting us in securing reproduction rights. We are also grateful to the staffs of the Detroit Public Library, the Library of Congress, the University of Detroit Mercy Library, Wayne State University Purdy/Kresge Library Complex, and the University of Michigan Libraries for making their resources available to us. Following is a list of the copyright holders who have granted us permission to reproduce material in this volume of *SC*. Every effort has been made to trace copyright, but if omissions have been made, please let us know.

COPYRIGHTED MATERIAL IN *SC,* VOLUME 79, WAS REPRODUCED FROM THE FOLLOWING PERIODICALS:

COPYRIGHTED MATERIAL IN *SC,* VOLUME 79, WAS REPRODUCED FROM THE FOLLOWING BOOKS:

PHOTOGRAPHS APPEARING IN *SC*, VOLUME 79, WERE RECEIVED FROM THE FOLLOWING SOURCES:

SC Contents, by Volume

Literary Criticism Series Advisory Board

Henry V

For further information on the critical and stage history of *Henry V,* see *SC,* Volumes 5, 14, 30, 49, and 67.

INTRODUCTION

The concluding drama of Shakespeare's second historical tetralogy, *Henry V* was first performed in 1599 and likely written in the same year. The play recounts the reign of celebrated English monarch Henry V, centering on his successful military campaign against France in the early fifteenth century. Shakespeare based his play on numerous works, including Raphael Holinshed's *Chronicles of England, Scotland, and Ireland* (1577), Edward Hall's *The Union of the Two Noble and Illustre Families of Lancaster and York* (1548), and *The Famous Victories of Henry the Fifth,* an anonymous play of the 1580s. Although generally perceived as an adulatory piece that commemorates the exploits of its historical protagonist, the drama has elicited considerable scholarly controversy, much of it in regard to the precise nature of Shakespeare's depiction of King Henry. Overall, critics remain divided as to whether Henry should be regarded as an ideal king whose war with France is justified, or as a brutal, Machiavellian leader. While most critics acknowledge that Shakespeare probably intended to present a patriotic valorization of a legendary national hero, contemporary scholarly studies and theatrical interpretation have tended to stress the ambiguous nature of Henry's character.

Recent assessments of *Henry V* have continued the scholarly tradition of evaluating Shakespeare's characterization of King Henry as the central and defining element of the play. In his survey of the drama, C. W. R. D. Moseley (1988) underscores Shakespeare's rendering of Henry as an ideal hero drawn from Christian and classical estimations of an effective and just leader. Thus, Moseley sides with those critics who eschew ironic readings of the English king, instead emphasizing Henry's fortitude, faith, martial élan, and efficacy as a peacemaker. Pamela K. Jensen (1996) similarly suggests that Shakespeare sought to present a flattering portrait of King Henry in his drama, one that would appeal to English audiences. She evaluates the king's status as a skilled decision maker whose actions reflect his concern with political expediency and general avoidance of domestic responsibilities in favor of the prospects for glorious military victory abroad. For Jensen, Henry's inspirational qualities and charismatic leadership on the battlefield at Agincourt solidify his appeal, even if the play's Elizabethan viewers would likely have realized that his spectacular historical accomplishments would not outlast his own lifetime. Richard Corum (1996) offers an alternative take on King Henry's personality by exploring the "homosocial" dynamics of the drama. Corum claims that far from rendering a simple and laudatory portrait of the English king, Shakespeare's *Henry V* conceals a multitude of obscured historical motivations, which are made manifest when studied in terms of Henry's displaced homoerotic and phallic desires. Camille Wells Slights presents a historicist view of his character in her 2001 study. Concentrating on Henry's internalization of the Reformation notion of conscience, she suggests that Shakespeare dramatized the monarch as a fervent instrument of God's will, an individual embodiment of divine providence guided by his private sense of moral responsibility.

For the vast majority of its stage history, *Henry V* has been treated as a straightforward celebration of the king who would become England's foremost military hero. Since the second half of the twentieth century, however, many directors have tended to stress the play's ambiguous nature. Summarizing this trend, Robert Shaughnessy (1998) examines the postmodern inspiration for British productions of *Henry V* since the 1960s, observing the ways in which directorial interest in ambiguity, intertextuality, interpretive dissonance, and the cultural myths of the postwar era have informed performances. In a complementary study, Kathy M. Howlett (see Further Reading) considers Kenneth Branagh's 1989 film version of *Henry V* as an intriguing interpretation of the drama that draws attention to its own ironic and ambivalent handling of history. Critics have also surveyed recent individual stage productions of *Henry V.* Ruth Morse reviews the Parisian staging of the play directed by Jean-Louis Benoit in 2000, the first ever French-language theatrical production. Noting its stylized form, apolitical tone, and self-conscious theatricality, Morse finds this performance inventive, humorous, and altogether well-realized. Russell Jackson's review of the 2000 production of *Henry V* at Stratford-upon-Avon, directed by Edward Hall, emphasizes its unspecified wartime setting and cynical, rather than heroic, tone. War was the central visual component of the 2001 staging at Canada's Stratford Festival, attended by critic Kevin Nance. In his review, Nance highlights designer Dany Lyne's eclectic gathering of wartime models— from medieval Agincourt to the military conflicts of the twentieth century—and the production's generalized antiwar sentiment. Alvin Klein comments on actress Nance Williamson's compelling performance as the Chorus in Terrence O'Brien's 2002 *Henry V* for the Hudson Valley Shakespeare Festival. Aside from Williamson's deft interpretive interludes, however, Klein finds this production more concerned with pageantry and the pursuit of contemporary relevance than with meaningful characterization. Lastly, Markland Taylor negatively reviews the limited cast and extensive directorial intervention of the 2002 Shakespeare & Co. production directed by Jonathan Epstein.

Contemporary studies of *Henry V* oriented toward genre and theme have placed particular emphasis on the political and historical meaning of the work as either a tacit celebration or subtle critique of Henry's rule, as well as its ambivalent generic status as either historical romance or tragicomedy. Paul Dean (1981) argues that in *Henry V* Shakespeare manipulated the conventions of the chronicle history play by juxtaposing elements of romance, thus introducing a distinctive ambiguity into the thematic fabric of the play. W. M. Richardson (1981) maintains that the world of *Henry V* is a hopelessly cynical one. Calling the drama "a classic portrait of the modern state," he asserts its thematic dissociation from moral sensibility and evocation of a worldview in which the ethical significance of the ordinary individual has been radically diminished. In a contrasting assessment, Richard Levin (1984) questions the relevance of such ironic readings of *Henry V,* including those that portray Henry as an inauspicious or corrupt ruler, suggesting that these are blunt misinterpretations of Shakespeare's text. Historiography and genre are key elements in Marsha S. Robinson's (1996) evaluation. Robinson considers *Henry V* as part of a romantic cycle of fraternal conflict, reconciliation, and redemption, examining its spiritualized conception of English history passing through tragic interludes of isolation, dislocation, and violent disruption. Joan Lord Hall (1997) surveys multiple themes in the text, such as a social and cosmological concern with order and chaos, a complex evocation of war from the violent horrors of battle to the heroic glory of victory, and its central theme of kingship, including the justness of Henry's rule, the conscience of the king, and his political legitimacy. Finally, Alison Thorne (2002) concentrates on the political world of *Henry V,* maintaining that the work demonstrates an ambivalent relationship to the traditional ideological tenets of the English chronicle history play. Thorne concludes that in this play Shakespeare examined class relations and questioned the view that "the common subject can participate on an equal footing in the creation of a national community that continues to be defined in the interests of a ruling elite."

OVERVIEWS AND GENERAL STUDIES

Paul Dean (essay date spring 1981)

SOURCE: Dean, Paul. "Chronicle and Romance Modes in *Henry V." Shakespeare Quarterly* 32, no. 1 (spring 1981): 18-27.

[*In the following essay, Dean suggests that the structure of* Henry V *is a combination of two dramatic forms ("chronicle" history and "romance" history), highlights Shakespeare's sophisticated characterization of King Henry V, and explores the dynamic relationship of the drama's main plot and subplots.*]

It is customary to divide plays written during the Elizabethan period upon subjects related to English history into two groups: "chronicle" histories, which draw their source-material, in the main, from the work of non-dramatic prose or verse historiographers, and "romance" or "pseudo" histories, which incorporate characters from history within a completely imaginary, usually comic, plot. It is further agreed, by the principal authorities, that only the "chronicle" histories had any important influence on Shakespeare's contribution to the genre.[1] There are grounds for questioning this assumption, which cannot be discussed in detail here;[2] an interesting case-study of an individual play has, however, been provided by Anne Barton in an important article on *Henry V* (1599).[3] Relating Shakespeare's play to earlier "romance" histories—such as *George a Greene, the Pinner of Wakefield* (1587-1593), Peele's *Edward I* (1590-1593), Heywood's *1 Edward IV* (1592-1601) and *Fair Em, the Miller's Daughter of Manchester* (1598-1601)—which, like *Henry V,* make use of the motif of the disguised king who mingles unrecognized among his subjects, Barton argues that Shakespeare took the opportunity to re-examine the tradition, not without a certain cold detachment. The "nostalgic but false romanticism"[4] of the earlier plays, with their Utopian dream of a world in which King and commoner could meet on equal terms,[5] is, in Barton's view, rejected by Shakespeare, for whom "*Henry V* seems to have marked the end of his personal interest in the tragical history. He had virtually exhausted the form, at least in its English version."[6]

Mrs. Barton's alignment of *Henry V* and "romance" histories affords a long-overdue acknowledgment that it was not only in his comedies that Shakespeare explored the conventions of romantic pastoral. Nonetheless, her argument illuminates only parts of the play. If it incorporates "romance" elements, to speak of it as an example of "the tragical history" seems too narrow: as does the alternative category of comic history.[7] Its tone of disillusionment with an ideal of social democracy, for example, is at odds with the confident, "chronicle" history nationalism apparent (embarrassingly so to our age) elsewhere, in Henry's speeches. Critical disagreements about the play and its eponymous hero have, indeed, centered upon questions of tone and attitude; but such qualities are notoriously elusive, and it is my contention that we shall do better to concentrate on the play's structure, about which it is possible to arrive at more definite conclusions. For, ultimately, we are not dealing with a contrast of tones, but of modes.

I

The main structural components of *Henry V* are the Choruses, the main plot and the subplot; the relationship between them has caused much discussion. It has been maintained, for example, that the Choruses provide the popular conception of Henry which is contradicted by his actions in the play;[8] that this contradiction is resolved in Act V;[9] that the Choruses are to be regarded as no more than a conventional Epic device.[10] Again, it is debated whether the subplot characters act as foils to the King, who appears even greater when compared to them,[11] or whether the parallels of incident, character, and language reduce Henry to the clowns' level.[12] Yet again, the play is obviously indebted to a tradition of heroic drama inaugurated by *1 Tamburlaine* (1587-1588),[13] but are we to see Henry as a figure parallel to Tamburlaine,[14] or as an ironic contrast?[15]

The most thorough and persuasively-argued structural analysis (although, as I shall argue, it is ultimately unsatisfactory) is that of Richard Levin, and it is convenient to begin from his account of the relationship between the plots, which is designed to justify the conclusion that "Everything in the subplot points unambiguously to its function as a foil to contrast with, and so render still more admirable, the exploits of the 'mirror of all Christian kings.'"[16] He cites in support a series of striking contrasts: between the English forces, hierarchically organized and embracing the entire British Isles (Gower, Fluellen, Macmorris, Jamy) as well as the ranks of common soldiery (Bates, Court, and Williams) subordinated to the unifying monarch, on the one hand, and, on the other, the autonomous, freelance, "fringe" militia (Nym, Bardolph, Pistol); between Henry's aim of conquest and the clowns' aim of filching; between Henry's unimpeded good fortune, ending in a marriage consummating national and international harmony, and the cumulative decline in the clowns' fortunes, from the loss of Falstaff (II.i, II.iii) to their cowardliness at Harfleur (III.ii) to the deaths of Nym and Bardolph and the final departure for England of the bereaved Pistol (V.i)—all emphasized by the scornful choric comments of the Boy (III.ii.28-57, IV.iv.69-80); between Henry's victories against immense odds and

Kenneth Branagh in the title role of his 1989 film version of Henry V.

the clowns' verbal menaces which are never put into action; between Henry's resolution of the quarrel with Williams, where the King's honor forbids his personal engagement but matters are settled amicably (IV.viii), and Fluellen's quarrel with Pistol, which the latter neglects to prosecute out of cowardice and in which he is ignominiously beaten (V.i). Levin concludes that "the negative analogies have been consistently deployed to augment the seriousness and elevation of the main action."[17]

Attractive though these antitheses may be, there is much, not so unambiguously to Henry's credit, which they pass over in silence. A closer study of the text reveals a number of parallels which seem to draw King and clowns, and also King and Frenchmen, together. Before these can be examined, however, the character of Henry must be set against a "romance" history tradition to which Shakespeare makes definite allusions.

In Act I of the play we see Henry in the role of warlord; in Act V, in that of lover. Elizabethan dramatists, including Shakespeare, had made a commonplace of this conjunction and had explored it metaphorically (by using the language of one of the activities to talk about the other) and in terms of character (by examining the adverse effects upon the monarch's military prowess of the enfeebling sickness of love). Some of the most important "romance" histories in which Mars and Venus are at odds are Lyly's *Campaspe* (1580-1584),[18] Marlowe's *1 Tamburlaine*,[19] Greene's *Friar Bacon and Friar Bungay* (1590-1594) and *James IV* (1590-1591) and the anonymous *Edward III* (1590-1595). By 1599, therefore, a dramatist could assume that the love/war link would be understood, and there is no need to insist on a specific precedent for *Henry V*. Nonetheless, there are indications that Shakespeare had *Edward III* particularly in mind (and, it is worth remembering, his connections with that play may have extended to part-authorship).[20] Direct references are limited to Canterbury's assertion that the Scottish King was sent to France "to kill King Edward's fame with prisoner kings" (I.ii.162), which derives from the earlier play and not from any extra-dramatic historical account; and to the possibility that *Henry V*, III.vii.150-54 echoes *Edward III*, III.iii.159-62.[21] References to events dramatized in *Edward III* are, however, more frequent. Canterbury, for instance, encourages Henry:

> Go, my dread lord, to your great-grandsire's tomb,
> From whom you claim; invoke his war-like spirit,
> And your great-uncle's, Edward the Black Prince,
> Who on the French ground play'd a tragedy,
> Making defeat on the full power of France;
> Whiles his most mighty father on a hill
> Stood smiling to behold his lion's whelp
> Forage in blood of French nobility.
>
> (I.ii.103-10)

The incident of Edward III's refusal to save the Black Prince from danger (*Edward III*, III.iv; note the theatrical image of "play'd a tragedy" above) is also referred to by the French King (II.iv.53-62), whose admonition to fear one descended from such hardy stock is exactly the advice subsequently given to the French by Exeter (II.iv.91-95). The victory at Crecy is, finally, recalled by Fluellen ("as I have read in the chronicles") after Agincourt (IV.vii.94-98).

It seems then that Henry is presented as challenging comparison with Edward III. In the earlier play, Edward demonstrates his princely virtue by resisting the temptation to seduce the Countess of Warwick, and his victory in this amorous struggle is echoed in the lists of war by his son's triumph (also unaided) against apparently overwhelming numbers of Frenchmen. What Shakespeare's predecessor had seen as two separate though analogous trials requiring two separate though analogous characters, Shakespeare conflates into the single character of Henry in his dual aspects of warlord and wooer.[22]

It is the King's personal equilibrium which is emphasized at the outset of the play. His "two bodies,"[23] his public and private selves, we are assured, are completely at one, and this harmoniousness is conventionally reflected by that of his court and his kingdom, whose various parts "keep in one consent, / Congreeing in a full and natural close, / Like music" (I.ii.181-83). Yet Canterbury is shortly advising him to "Divide your happy England into four" (I.ii.214), and the simile quoted above recurs with ambiguous effect when, in trying to win over the coy Katharine, Henry demands, "Come, your answer in broken music" (V.ii.256-57). The order celebrated at the play's beginning does not necessarily persist to its close, and the references to Edward III may be intended as a discomforting contrast rather than as an admiring parallel. In combining into Henry the roles of Edward III and the Black Prince,[24] Shakespeare at least made his King a more complex character, and the nature of that complexity needs further examination.

I shall now take up again the question of the relationships between the plots.

II

It is generally agreed that Pistol is in certain respects a parody of Henry. His "On, on, on, on, on! to the breach, to the breach!" (III.ii.1) blatantly echoes "Once more unto the breach, dear friends, once more" (III.i.1), although Pistol, as usual, does nothing to follow up his encouragement, and the phrase is also used by Fluellen (III.ii.21) and echoed by Macmorris (III.ii.111 ff.). More substantially, the references to throat-cutting first made by Nym (II.i.22-24, 69 ff.) and Bardolph (II.i.91 ff.) are taken up by Pistol in his catch-phrase "Couple a gorge!" (II.i.71, IV.iv.37). According to the Quarto of the play (1600), he also speaks these words at the end of IV.vi, just after Henry's order to his troops to kill the French prisoners (IV.vi.37), which is repeated, with the specification of throat-cutting, at IV.vii.65. The Quarto is an unauthorized text, and the Folio omits Pistol's parting shot; but, as William Empson argues, the other occurrences of the phrase allow us to take it seriously as associating Henry's action with the coarse vindictiveness of Pistol.[25] Again, critics have commonly found difficulty in accepting what seems to be gratuitous ranting on Henry's part at Harfleur (III.iii.1-14); the New Arden editor's assurances that the King is "precisely and unswervingly following the rules of warfare as laid down by Vegetius, Aegidius Romanus and others"[26] do not seem an adequate explanation. When we connect Henry's behavior here with the throat-cutting incident, and with his exposure, through an elaborate trick, of the traitors Cambridge, Scoop, and Grey (II.ii)[27]—a trick which deliberately mocks them despite Henry's verbal professions of sympathy—we cannot but feel uneasy.

Henry is also associated with the subplot characters through his supporters, who are by no means so united as Richard Levin claims. We may not feel inclined to attach much weight to the charges of Nym and the Hostess, that the King has virtually murdered Falstaff (II.i.88, 121-26), but Williams' retorts to him in IV.viii (considered below) are more serious criticisms (as are the soldiers' arguments in IV.i). Again, the quarrel between Macmorris and Fluellen in III.ii parallels that between Nym and Pistol in II.i; whilst the encounter between Fluellen and Pistol in V.i has been anticipated by Fluellen and Williams in IV.viii, and by Henry and Williams in IV.i. I am suggesting, in short, that *Henry V* may not be a straightforward double-plot play with a clown subplot acting as foil, but what Levin calls an "equivalence plot" play;[28] and, at the risk of appearing unduly schematic, I further propose that the parallels of character, implied by the parallels of incident given above, may be transcribed, using Levin's own system, into a series of proportional relations, thus:

Henry:Williams::Fluellen:Williams::Fluellen:Pistol.

If we eliminate the common factors in this equation, we have

Henry:Williams:Pistol,

which brings the King into comparison with both a member of the acceptable common people, and a wholly unacceptable rogue. This sequence may not be mathematically exact, but it is dramatically suggestive and excludes the possibility of placing Henry on a level of his own in which every bad action committed by other characters somehow makes him seem more admirable.

His behavior toward Williams, in particular, casts interesting light on the claims made for him in I.i as the complete man and the complete King. In disguise he declares that "The King is but a man, as I am . . . His ceremonies laid by, in his nakedness he appears but a man" (IV.i.100 ff., 105 ff.). Anne Barton sees ironic scrutiny of the "romance" history motif here; her point can be developed by observing that, in "romance" history, the King's disguise and the equality it provides are possible only because the King *is* the King; his condescension is in itself an aspect of his royal magnanimity, so that ultimately there is no Utopia at all. Henry illustrates this point too: he appears to be denying that he is any different from his subjects, but the phrase "as I am" is an escape clause: to be a man as Henry is is not to be a man in the normal sense. Subsequently Henry pulls rank in telling Williams, "It was ourself thou didst abuse" (IV.viii.50; note the change from "I" to "we"). But Williams is not to be cowed:

> Your majesty came not like yourself: you appeared to me but as a common man; witness the night, your garments, your lowliness; and what your highness suffered under that shape, I beseech you, take it for your fault and not mine: for had you been as I took you for, I made no offence; therefore, I beseech your highness, pardon me.
>
> (IV.viii.51-58)

It is true that he asks forgiveness, but his attitude is quite unlike the abject terror of, for example, Hobs in *1 Edward IV* when he discovers the real identity of his erstwhile boon companion. Williams' common-sense defense of his actions, his readiness to suggest that the King is at fault, discomfort Henry by reducing him to the level of "a common man" at a time, and in a place, where it does not suit his convenience. He evades a direct reply (as he did in IV.i.150-92, when Williams asked about the King's personal guilt for the deaths of his soldiers in battle) by the obligatory distribution of largesse: "Here, uncle Exeter, fill this glove with crowns . . ." (IV.viii.59), and by reducing Williams to the status of "this fellow" (IV.viii.60). But when Fluellen tries to imitate the King by offering Williams a shilling, the latter's irritation explodes: "I will none of your money" (IV.viii.70). Fluellen's gesture reflects back upon Henry's, cruder though it is; we have witnessed a gap between Henry as King and as man which has involved him in, to say the least, inconsistent behavior.

The Williams episode affects its subsequent analogues. Fluellen's offer of money to Williams is repeated to Pistol (V.i.60 ff.), who, appropriately to his lower status, gets a groat rather than a shilling but, like Williams, refuses it. Additionally, the glove given by Henry to Williams as a gage has its comic counterpart in the leek sported by Fluellen and eaten by Pistol.[29] Even though we may be reluctant to accept R. W. Battenhouse's view that the leek episode is a parody of Henry's marriage to Katharine,[30] still the symbols link Henry to Pistol, and Fluellen's anger toward Pistol, which even Gower condemns as excessive ("Enough, captain: you have astonished him," V.i.40), recalls Henry's overbearing treatment of Williams. Fluellen, has, moreover, already been established as a substitute-Henry by his observation that the King, like him, wears the leek on St. David's day, and by Henry's explanation that "I wear it for a memorable honour; / For I am Welsh, you know, good countryman" (IV.vii.108-9).

Fluellen is also the means of furnishing another comparison for Henry's rule. Following Henry's claim that the English are descended from a race of Alexanders (III.i.19), he is himself compared to "Alexander the Pig" by Fluellen (IV.vii.14-55), who has earlier proved himself a master of inapt analogy in equating the valor of Pistol with that of Mark Antony (III.vi.12-16). As a commentator on this episode remarks, the references to Antony and Alexander "precede questionable ethical actions by the two men [i.e., Pistol and Henry] which belie the classical designations or, ironically, reflect them, and through contrast undercut the apparently heroic images."[31] It is tempting to think, in the "romance" history context, that memories of Lyly's Alexander in *Campaspe* are surfacing in Shakespeare's mind here, and that the character joins Edward III as a pattern of the integrated self in comparison with whom Henry fares badly.[32]

I have so far been trying to establish comparisons between the mainplot and subplot worlds which imply an equivalence, and not a contrast, between them, and accumulate to qualify radically our approval of the King. I now turn to the resemblances between Henry and the French, which are less explicit but nonetheless significant.

The opening of the play establishes a pattern of religious references in which England and France are placed at opposite ends of the ethical scale. As a "true lover of the holy Church" (I.i.23), one whose reform of his life was so sudden as to be almost miraculous, Henry is living testimony to the power of God, "in whose name," he charges the French ambassadors, "tell you the Dauphin I am coming on" (I.ii.291). In opposing Henry the French are, in effect, siding with the Devil, as are their undercover agents at the English court. The actions of these traitors seem to Henry to constitute "another fall of man" (II.ii.142); he denounces Scroop as an "inhuman creature" (II.ii.95), the seduction of whom—to thoughts of treason and murder, those "two yoke-devils sworn to either's purpose" (II.ii.106)—represents a triumph for the forces of darkness:

> . . . whatsoever cunning fiend it was
> That wrought upon thee so preposterously
> Hath got the voice in hell for excellence:
> . . . . .
> If that same demon that hath gull'd thee thus
> Should with his lion gait walk the whole world,
> He might return to vasty Tartar back,
> And tell the legions: "I can never win
> A soul so easy as that Englishman's."
>
>   (II.ii.111-13, 121-25)

This way of viewing rebellion is a wholly conventional one, but it is given special prominence by the insistence on Henry's personal piety: moreover, it reappears more explicitly in the clown scene which separates I.ii from II.ii. There we hear Nym boasting that "I am not Barbason; you cannot conjure me" (II.i.53), Barbason being, as the editor notes, the name of a devil. The association becomes more marked when the Boy refers to Pistol as "this roaring devil i' the old play" (IV.iv.73-74). In their desire for self-interest, their indifference to moral standards, and their isolation from the order of Henry's court, the subplot characters are inimical to the King's religious conception of his own person and mission, and so are to be allied mentally with the French as agents of disruption and wickedness.

This conjunction of the French and the clowns, and their joint association with the Devil, apparently forms a group of characters, and a body of values, to which Henry can figure as a splendid contrast. But the play's moral values are not so straightforward. Perhaps the King's old tutor had something to teach him yet; Falstaff on his deathbed, we are told, stigmatized women as "devils incarnate" (II.iii.32), and in his courtship of Katharine, Henry himself is drawn into the magic circle. Henry's first words after kissing her are "You have witchcraft in your lips, Kate" (V.ii.292); he later admits to Burgundy, "I cannot so conjure the spirit of love in her, that he will appear in his true likeness" (V.ii.306-8), to which Burgundy replies, "If you would conjure in her, you must make a circle" (V.ii.310-11). Various extenuating explanations of this language can be offered—that it is a light-hearted conventional metaphor for falling in love, or that it is part of Shakespeare's purpose to show Henry as an adept courtier. Katharine is not a "witch" in the same way as Joan of Arc or Margaret in Shakespeare's *Henry VI* trilogy. Yet the equation of the power of beauty with the power of black magic had been established in "romance" history since *Friar Bacon and Friar Bungay*.[33] and, taken together with the other references to devils given above, these uses of the metaphor cannot be dismissed as mere badinage. They seem to reflect the parallelisms of character discussed earlier in this essay, casting doubt on Henry's judgment and actions. Furthermore, his courtship is conducted partly in bawdy terms which we have previously heard from Katharine (in the language-lesson in II.iv) and the Dauphin. Lamenting his amorous ineptitude in the approved soldierly fashion, he claims that

> If I could win a lady at leap-frog, or by vaulting into my saddle with my armour on my back, under the correction of bragging be it spoken, I should quickly leap into a wife. Or if I might buffet for my love, or bound my horse for her favours, I could lay on like a butcher and sit like a jack-an-apes, never off.
>
>   (V.ii.138-45)

Compare with this the obsession with horses characteristic of the Dauphin in III.vii, in particular this exchange on the subject of his own horse:

DAU.

> . . . I once writ a sonnet in his praise and began thus: "Wonder of nature,"—

ORL.

> I have heard a sonnet begin so to one's mistress.

DAU.

> Then did they imitate that which I composed to my courser; for my horse is my mistress.

ORL.

> Your mistress bears well.

DAU.

> Me well; which is the prescript praise and perfection of
> a good and particular mistress.
>
> (III.vii.41-48)

Henry in the wooing scene allies himself, through the use of a specific sexual image as well as of a bawdy tone (the references to "conjuring in" Katharine carry the same suggestiveness), with the French and, implicitly, with the subplot characters—the enemies of England and of God.[34]

It may be argued against this that, again, bawdy may be innocent or merely to be expected in wooing. But Henry's behavior with Katharine cannot be seen apart from the accumulation of details to which I have related it, and, taken together with them, it becomes profoundly disquieting. The kinds of unity achieved by the marriage—the national and international peace which it cements—are ambiguous. As in *Campaspe* and *Edward III*, the activities of war and love are imaged in terms of each other as if to emphasize a final harmony. Henry admits that, although he is the conqueror, he "cannot see many a fair French city for one fair French maid that stands in my way" (III.ii.335-37), and the French King comments, "Yes, my lord, you see them perspectively, the cities turned into a maid; for they are all girdled with maiden walls that war hath never entered" (V.ii.338-41). From this point of view Henry's union with Katharine is one between equals who are complete in themselves yet complementary. Yet the key word is "perspectively"—point of view is important, and mutable.[35] There is a disjunction between Henry as man and as King; Katharine's high social position does not shield her from suspicions of black magic. From such a union we can hardly expect permanence, and, as the final Chrous reminds us, Henry's successors "lost France and made his England bleed" (l. 12). The peace purchased by Agincourt was, after all, dearly bought.

III

I have sought to indicate Shakespeare's debt, in *Henry V*, to other aspects of the "romance" tradition than those noted by Anne Barton, and in doing so to mediate between the critical disagreements outlined at the beginning of section II. If the play is viewed "perspectively," it becomes more complex than is generally allowed. It shows us *both* the Henry of popular esteem, the undaunted, unsophisticated, all-conquering patriot, expecting that he and Katharine will beget another such conqueror (V.ii.215-20), *and* an imperfect man, sometimes hasty, sometimes brutal; both an Epic Prince and a private person; both a triumph of unification and a failure to perpetuate it. The subplot acts as both foil to, and critique of, the main plot; the Choruses make just claims for the King's achievement and also caution us against a blind endorsement of his success.

Henry V demonstrates an equilibrium of a kind which makes irrelevant the academic distinction between "chronicle" and "romance" history with which this essay began: indeed, it contains both kinds within itself. The materials of the story derive from Hall, Holinshed, and other chronicles,[36] but the story is not the same thing as the plot; and the plot turns upon conventions of romance such as the King disguised and the King in love. Shakespeare's handling of these conventions, however, is such as to hint at his dissatisfaction with their representations of reality. The world of *Henry V* is not a place where the contest between good and evil is straightforward, or where the values of the English establishment are wholeheartedly endorsed: nor is it one where there is not virtue extant—the positives for which Henry stands really are positive It is, rather, a world of profound ambiguities, as I have tried to show: a world where the juxtaposition of "chronicle" and "romance" visions of political action (the one encouraging a sober realization of the responsibilities of power, the other a light-hearted appreciation of its privileges) stretches the history-play genre to its limits. It is worth remembering that Shakespeare's next history-play, of any kind, was to be what the Folio firmly called the tragedy of *Julius Caesar.*

Notes

1. See, e.g., E. M. W. Tillyard, *Shakespeare's History Plays* (London: Chatto and Windus, 1944); Lily B. Campbell, *Shakespeare's "Histories": Mirrors of Elizabethan Policy* (San Marino, Cal.: The Huntington Library, 1947); Hardin Craig, "Shakespeare and the History Play," *Joseph Quincy Adams Memorial Studies,* ed. Brander Matthews and Ashley H. Thorndike (Washington, D.C.: Folger Shakespeare Library, 1948), pp. 55-64; F. P. Wilson, *Marlowe and the Early Shakespeare* (Oxford: Clarendon Press, 1953), pp. 105-8; Irving Ribner, *The English History Play in the Age of Shakespeare* (Princeton: Princeton Univ. Press 1957; rev. ed., London: Methuen, 1965); Kenneth Muir, "Source Problems in the Histories," *Shakespeare Jahrbuch,* 96 (1960), 49; F. P. Wilson, "The English History Play," in *Shakespearian and Other Studies,* ed. Helen Gardner (Oxford: Clarendon Press, 1969), pp. 1-53.

2. I am preparing a full discussion in another article.

3. "The King Disguised: Shakespeare's *Henry V* and the Comical History," in *The Triple Bond: Plays, Mainly Shakespearean, in Performance,* ed. J. G. Price (University Park: Penn. State Univ. Press, 1975), pp. 92-117.

   Terminal dates for plays follow S. Schoenbaum's revision of Alfred Harbage's *Annals of English Drama 975-1700* (London: Methuen, 1964).

4. Barton, p. 99.

5. Not exactly equal, as I point out below.

6. Barton, p. 117.

7. Even A. P. Rossiter, who brilliantly explored this sub-genre, failed to notice the connections between the plots: "There are fine things in *Henry V;* but much of the comedy has lost touch with the serious matter" (*Angel with Horns,* [London: Longmans, 1961], p. 58).

8. H. C. Goddard, *The Meaning of Shakespeare* (Chicago: Univ. of Chicago Press, 1951), p. 218.

9. W. Babula, "Whatever Happened to Prince Hal?: An Essay on *Henry V,*" *Shakespeare Survey,* 30 (1977), 47-59.

10. J. H. Walter, ed. New Arden edition (London: Methuen, 1954), pp. xiv-xvii and note on I.i.1. All subsequent references to *Henry V* are cited to this edition.

11. Richard Levin, *The Multiple Plot in English Renaissance Drama* (Chicago: Univ. of Chicago Press, 1971), p. 116.

12. R. W. Battenhouse, "*Henry V* as Heroic Comedy," *Essays on Shakespeare and Elizabethan Drama in Honor of Hardin Craig,* ed. Richard Hosley (Columbia: Univ. of Missouri Press, 1962), pp. 169-80.

13. See David Riggs, *Shakespeare's Heroical Histories: "Henry VI" and its Literary Tradition* (Oxford: Oxford Univ. Press, 1972).

14. R. Egan, "A Muse of Fire: *Henry V* in the Light of *Tamburlaine,*" *Modern Language Quarterly,* 29 (1968), 275-82.

15. R. W. Battenhouse, "The Relation of *Henry V* to *Tamburlaine,*" *Shakespeare Quarterly,* 27 (1974), 71-79.

16. Levin, *Multiple Plot,* p. 116.

17. Ibid., p. 119.

18. *Campaspe* is not an English history play, but its inclusion in the list is justified since it provided the basic "romance" history structure, it is referred to in *1 Henry IV* (see A. Davenport, "Notes on Lyly's *Campaspe* and Shakespeare," *Notes and Queries,* 199 [1954], 18-20, and A. R. Humphreys' New Arden ed. [London: Methuen, 1960], note on II.iv.402-9), and, as I suggest below, we may be meant to recall it in *Henry V* also.

19. Also not an English history play, but central to the tradition (cf. above, note 13).

20. The debate is summarized by Kenneth Muir, *Shakespeare as Collaborator* (London: Methuen, 1960), pp. 31-55. See further 1. Koskenniemi, "Themes and Imagery in *Edward III,*" *Neuphilologische Mitteilungen,* 65 (1964), 446-80.

21. See New Arden *Henry V ad loc.*

22. The extent to which a "romance" conception colors *Edward III* is indicated by the fact that the historical Edward raped the Countess of Salisbury. (I am grateful to John W. Velz of the *SQ* Editorial Board for pointing this out.)

23. Cf. Ernst Kantorowicz, *The King's Two Bodies* (Princeton: Princeton Univ. Press, 1957).

24. There are striking similarities between the portrayal of the Black Prince and both the Hal and Hotspur of *1 Henry IV.*

25. "Falstaff and Mr. Dover Wilson," *Kenyon Review,* 15 (1953), 241-43 (but the whole article repays close study).

26. New Arden ed., p. xxv. For criticisms of Henry, see the comments by G. Gould and D. A. Traversi reprinted in *Henry V: A Casebook,* ed. Michael Quinn (London: Macmillan, 1968).

27. Compare the machinations of Richard II in II. ii of the anonymous play now generally called *Woodstock* (1591-1595; ed. A. P. Rossiter [London: Chatto and Windus, 1946]). He manipulates the accepted Court custom of petitioning the King as a sardonic method of ending Woodstock's protectorship and claiming the crown. (Once again it is interesting to note possible connections between *Woodstock* and *1 Henry IV:* see R. Helgerson, "*1 Henry IV* and *Woodstock,*" *Notes and Queries,* 221 [1976], 153 ff.).

28. See *Multiple Plot,* chapter 5.

29. Noted by Levin, pp. 118 ff. Anne Barton, "The King Disguised," p. 117, compares the treatment of Kendal's emissary in *George a Greene, the Pinner of Wakefield,* and that of the Summoner in *1 Sir John Oldcastle* (1599), which may be indebted to *Henry V.*

30. Article cited above, note 12.

31. R. P. Merrix, "The Alexandrian Allusion in Shakespeare's *Henry V,*" *English Literary Renaissance,* 2 (1972), 333.

32. Merrix provides detailed discussion of Elizabethan attitudes to Alexander. Interestingly, in *1 Henry IV,* III. ii, Shakespeare may well have drawn some details for Henry's advice to Hal from a recent translation of a pseudo-Aristotelian work in which Alexander is similarly counseled: See T. P. Harrison, "The Folger *Secret of Secrets, 1572,*" in *Joseph Quincy Adams Memorial Studies,* pp. 609 ff. (Once again, I owe this reference to John W. Velz.)

33. See William Empson, *Some Versions of Pastoral* (London: Chatto and Windus, 1935; 2nd ed. 1966),

p. 33, and W. Towne, "'White Magic' in *Friar Bacon and Friar Bungay?*", *Modern Language Notes,* 67 (1952), 9-13.

34. Paul A. Jorgensen, "The Courtship Scene in *Henry V,*" *Modern Language Quarterly,* 11 (1950), 183ff., inaptly compares the scene to King William's wooing of Mariana in *Fair Em,* but sees no derogation of Henry here.

35. On perspectives as a symbol for relativist perception see *Richard II,* II. ii. 19-20. The whole subject is illuminatingly surveyed by A. Shickman, "The 'Perspective Glass' in Shakespeare's *Richard II,*" *Studies in English Literature,* 18 (1978), 217-28.

36. See New Arden ed., pp. xxxi-xxxiii, and the relevant chapter in Kenneth Muir, *The Sources of Shakespeare's Plays* (London: Methuen, 1977).

C. W. R. D. Moseley (essay date 1988)

SOURCE: Moseley, C. W. R. D. "This Sceptred Isle: *Henry V.*" In *Shakespeare's History Plays* Richard II *to* Henry V: *The Making of a King,* pp. 147-70. London: Penguin Books, 1988.

[In the following excerpt, Moseley describes the principal characters and plot structure of Henry V, *emphasizing thematic elements in the drama associated with the heroic role of Henry.]*

In *Henry V* there are so many references back in time to the events dramatized in the previous plays that, while the play is, naturally, able to stand quite independently, it gains enormously from being seen against the well-known events of the reigns of Richard II and Henry IV. Even more does it gain when seen against the background of the discussion of rule and the ruler in Shakespeare's treatment of those historical events.

In watching the movement of Hal from Eastcheap towards the crown, a redefinition of his self, and an acceptance of the implications of his role, we have been constantly reminded (not least by Henry IV) of the movement of Richard away from the crown to his discovery of a new self in his new nonentity. The careers of both—and of Henry IV too—centre round their possession, or not, not only of legitimate title to the throne, but also of the Cardinal Virtues of Prudence, Justice, Temperance and Fortitude. In *Henry V* these virtues are seen for the first time united with legitimate possession of the throne; the earlier plays demonstrated how necessary they are to a ruler by showing men engaged in power struggles who possessed them only partially or not at all. Richard, for example, lacked both justice and temperance, and was imprudent to a degree; in his fall he learned fortitude and, when it was too late, the three divisions of prudence—*memory* of his own misdeeds, *understanding* of what was happening to him, and *foresight* of what would happen to his realm.[1]

Henry Bolingbroke's fortitude we can take for granted; he possessed a sense of justice and was temperate, but he was led into a course of events whose outcome he did not foresee and whose consequences dog his reign with unhappiness and rebellion. In the *Henry IV* plays, Henry tries hard to understand and foresee his problems, but ultimately is a responder to events rather than a controller of them; his sympathetic portrait is neatly set against that of the unlikeable political schemer Worcester, who possesses almost a parody of prudence. (Worcester is also contrasted with Northumberland—a vacillating man, given to misjudgement.) Hotspur has a complete lack of the virtue of prudence—he has no policy or forethought, can control neither his tongue nor his actions, and lacks the broadness and generosity of mind that is essential to justice. Falstaff's cunning is shortsighted, working on assumptions we know to be false, and takes no thought for the time that will come when no man may work. He shies away from prudent consideration of the ultimate end of man when he tells Doll not to speak like a death's-head, a *memento mori,* to him (Part 2, II.iv.229-30ff.). In his lechery and gluttony he is a very figure of intemperance; he is mean and unjust in his treatment of the Hostess, his soldiers, and—had he been able—would have been so to Shallow and Silence. The idea of connecting fortitude with Falstaff is ludicrous, and the nearest the Eastcheap group come to a perception of fortitude is in the ridiculous posturing of Pistol—which hides a deep cowardice.[2]

Against all these is set Hal. He has prudence in full measure; his behaviour throughout Parts 1 and 2 indicate an awareness of his family history, an understanding of public opinion and people as well as political reality, and a foresight that allows him to turn his possession of the throne into a mark for later ages to aim at. This quality is also shown in his examination of the evidence in the council in Act 1 of *Henry V,* before committing himself to war. That council also shows his concern for a cause that is just; and his justice is shown not only in the treatment of Scroop and Cambridge but also of Bardolph, who is caught robbing a church. He is fair and just to both the Hostess and Hotspur.

The justice that Hal comes to exemplify is neatly underlined when he plays the part of his own father giving judgement in Part 1, II.iv (a picture deliberately set against the icon of misrule we have just seen in Falstaff), and in the confirmation in his speech to the Lord Chief Justice of the visible symbols of justice, the sword and the scales (which still surmount the Old Bailey). The mercy (of which more later) that goes with justice is shown in his treatment of Falstaff and his companions. His fortitude in battle and hardship is obvious, and we have seen how in the midst of intemperance in Part 1 he remained temperate. Henry in *Henry V* is thus not only a legitimate king, but also a good man.

He is also a Christian. The emphasis on this in *Henry V* is very noticeable, and the play examines, among other things, the implications of a deeply held personal Christianity for the ruler. The Prayer for the Church in the First (1549) and Second (1552) Prayer Books is virtually identical to that in the 1662 Book of Common Prayer; it beseeches God to

> defend all Christian Kings, Princes and Governors; and specially thy servant Elizabeth our queen; that under her we may be godly and quietly governed: And grant unto her whole Council, and to all that are put in authority under her, that they may truly and indifferently minister justice, to the punishment of wickedness and vice, and to the maintenance of thy true religion and virtue.

The prayer stresses the powerlessness of the ruler without God's help, his duty of good government, and of impartial justice. These are exactly the issues that the play deals with in the series of tableaux framed by the Choruses, and furthermore it scrutinizes what is involved in being a Christian prince. Henry in this play has to blend his role as a conqueror and legitimate ruler with his inward, personal Christianity. The tension has the potential for tragedy, but through it Henry discovers his true identity and reaches a triumphant synthesis.

The first act of *Henry V* is so structured as to bring these issues into consideration. Shakespeare often uses in his political plays a big Court scene at or near the beginning to introduce us to the issues the play will raise, and to the persons involved. The staging of such a scene necessarily reminds us of the hierarchy in the state that mirrors the *ordo* in the universe; we have seen this at the beginning of *Richard II* and *1 Henry IV*. Frequently too (but not invariably) he structures these scenes so that we have a short introduction by some minor characters who prepare us for what we are about to witness, then the big state entry, then a third division commenting on some of the implications of what has happened.[3]

Act 1 opens with Canterbury and Ely talking about the king. They both agree he is 'full of grace and fair regard' and 'a true lover of the holy Church' (I.i.22-3), and Canterbury goes on to enumerate his perfections. The inevitable reference to his reformation is couched in terms specifically religious, echoing the Baptism Service of the Prayer Book of 1560; the prince's 'consideration' (repentance) has, as it were, undone the Fall and left a perfect man, the proper abode for the

Holy Spirit. (It is noteworthy that already we have, as we did in Gaunt's complaint about Richard's mistreatment of England, reference to the Garden of Eden and that other garden, the Paradise of the blessed.) His character is more than just reformed. He can understand the subtler points of theology (ll. 38-40); he is skilled in civil law (ll. 41-2); he can speak eloquently on the art of war (ll. 43-4);[4] he is an expert in statecraft or 'policy', and can by reason solve problems that would have driven even an Alexander to use his sword.[5] He speaks with all the admired arts of rhetoric, and has married the 'theoric' and 'practic' sides of life as a good Renaissance prince should. What is being described is nothing less than the Renaissance ideal of the *uomo universale* we see in Sidney or Castiglione, a man who is mater of himself and master of the pleasure that would corrupt other men (l. 51; cf. above, p. 141). Ely—who holds a bishopric that, as we know from *Richard III,* has something of a reputation for strawberries—replies with garden/cultivation images (the strawberry thriving under the useless nettle, and so on) to suggest that there may have been an organic connection between the king's early wildness and his present excellence.

After this prologue comes the state entry. We should envisage a stage crammed with people—even if we only allow two attendants per noble (mean by Renaissance standards) there would be twenty-one people on stage before Canterbury and Ely enter. This company obviously must have been organized as nearly as possible in a pattern like that of the Elizabethan Parliament. Henry's opening of the matter of his claim to the French throne shows exactly those qualities Canterbury has enumerated: mastery of the legal issues, eloquence, a readiness to defend his right by battle, a recognition that the king bears a heavy responsibility under God for his actions. He is a king who is far from trigger-happy, but cares deeply about justice. He is aware that the rightness of his cause is not one he alone can decide (I.ii.10-12) and warns Canterbury not to 'fashion, wrest, or bow [his] reading' to suit what he thinks Henry wants to hear. A far cry from the flattering counsellors of Richard! Canterbury's reply is to be taken seriously, however difficult we find it to do so; it emphasizes the justness of Henry's claim and the legitimacy of his decision to pursue it by war if negotiation fails.[6] Henry is adamant on this point: 'May I with *right and conscience* make this claim?' This careful weighing of the legal and moral rights shown by Henry is highlighted by the parallel with his father, for although Bolingbroke had right and law on his side, this careful consideration never crossed his mind. He was pulled by the logic of his own actions into rebellion and the deposition of an anointed king.

Ely supports Canterbury, and caps the latter's roll-call of English heroes and his reminiscence of the well-known story of the Black Prince at Crécy with a call to

Henry to live up to their valiant example.[7] Prophetic; for Agincourt was, like Crécy, a desperate throw against huge odds, and Edward and Henry did, in 1356 and 1415, 'forage in blood of French nobility'. A lesser king would immediately be swayed by such a volume of ecclesiastical agreement; but Henry still holds back. The 'policy' Canterbury described is exemplified in his concern to protect his realm from the incursions of the Scots. But, as his counsellors agree, here is no Irish expedition of a King Richard; this realm is properly and harmoniously organized, and Canterbury's memorable speech about the mutual interdependence of the commonwealth of the bees finally convinces Henry of what he should do.

Yet this part of the scene is not quite so simple as this makes it sound. For a start, the support of two senior bishops is pretty powerful; and we ought to remember that Bolingbroke's actions to seek the throne were strongly opposed by Carlisle, and his continuance on it by the Archbishop of York. Both appealed to divine sanction for their opposition; but Canterbury and Ely represent such a sanction *supporting* Henry. The contrast with his predecessors could hardly be more powerful. Secondly, Canterbury's speech about the bees holds up an analogy to the well-ordered state, an ideal to be worked for, rather than offering a description of what actually *is*. There is an implied conditionality in his lines,

> I this infer,
> That many things, having full reference
> To one consent, may work contrariously
>
> (ll. 204-6)

which reinforces his earlier suggestion that 'obedience' (i.e. this interdependence in the state) (l. 187) is 'an aim or butt' to be worked for. It may not yet have been achieved, and the achievement may be temporary. The confidence—and it is a real confidence—of this scene is set off by the recognition that the ideal is not automatically achieved; the details of the hive of England are, in fact, examined in subsequent scenes. Henry has to be the 'sad-eyed justice' delivering over to execution, at whatever personal cost, those who break his trust and their own faith.

But that painful act of self-control is still in the future. A more pressing one is immediate. To highlight Henry's nature, Shakespeare made a significant change to his sources at this point. In the sources the Dauphin's insult arrives *before* the decision is taken to press Henry's claim. Here it is clear that the decision has been reached in fair and open concert of the prince with his counsellors, working together like the commonwealth of the bees, and that the Dauphin's insult does not affect the issue one way or another. What it now serves to do is to underline that, as the ambassadors report (II.iv.29ff.),

the rest of Europe must take note of the change in Henry as his own country has had to do in *2 Henry IV.*

The ambassadors enter with a good deal of trepidation. Henry reassures them:

> We are no tyrant but a Christian king,
> Unto whose grace our passion is as subject
> As in our wretches fettered in our prisons
>
> (I.ii.242-4)

—a reply which not only endorses the law of nations, but reminds us of the standards of kingship we are to apply to Henry and of the justice in him that controls both his subjects and his own passions. His own passions need that self-control, for he is clearly deeply offended and angry at the Dauphin's joke. He contains his anger, even turns it into a series of bitter puns and images, but it is clear that the irresponsibility of the Dauphin, a more foolish Hotspur, must bear a good deal of the blame for the decision to refuse Henry's demands, and thus for the war that will devastate France. Five times in the last twenty-five lines of the first act Henry emphasizes that he is acting in God's name and that his cause is just, and there is no reason to suspect any irony on his or Shakespeare's part. After all, the historical tradition attributed to Henry V a piety and seriousness about religious issues that there is no reason to doubt; he is known to have had long and earnest theological arguments with Oldcastle to win him back to the orthodox religion so that he could save him from execution. Shakespeare has already made Canterbury endorse this, and the whole of Act I has been focused on demonstrating what qualities make him a credible 'mirror of all Christian kings' (II,Chorus,6). Shakespeare could have left the matter there and merely taken Henry off to a gung-ho expedition to bash the French. But he does something much more interesting. He shows Henry developing those qualities in action that the mere statement by Canterbury might not be enough to convince us he possessed, and developing a piety and humility that reflect, perhaps, Richard's later consciousness of his place in God's sight. Henry grows and develops in this play not only as a ruler but as a man conscious of his huge moral responsibility, at the cost of his own personal feelings. The justice Canterbury speaks of is shown not only in the patient searching of his own title to the French throne, where he stands to gain a good deal, but also in the extremely painful and wounding confrontation with the conspirators in II.ii.

He clearly knows all about the treason of Scroop, Grey and Cambridge before he asks them their opinion about the treatment of the wretch who committed *lèse-majesté*. Those who themselves would have betrayed him advise severity—the advice of flatterers who say what they think he wants to hear. But he shows the wretch the royal prerogative of mercy; and their own mouths have denied the conspirators the chance of mercy for their more heinous crime. All their betrayals are bad enough; but the one that is particularly wounding is that of Scroop, for clearly Henry loved the man. He is given a long speech of reproach (II.ii.79-144) in which the tones of the public man give way to the broken cadences of a betrayed friend. The most common grammatical structure is a pained, reproachful question; the second person singular (signalling the intimacy of the reproach) dominates, and the imagery moves from money to extortion (l. 99), to devils tempting a man to fall, then to the devils' ability to deceive with fair-seeming, and finally to the open mention of what had been more and more insistent in the subtext: the Fall itself. Like Adam, Scroop has fallen from grace, and has committed the sin of Judas in betraying his master. The reminiscence of Richard is inescapable in this, the last betrayal, as that of Richard was the first. The speech is full of the tones, even the very rhetorical patterns (ll. 127ff.), of Richard; yet their positions are antithetical. Richard was powerless against his betrayers, and had to fall to learn what being a king meant; Henry knows what being a king entails, and has to use his power to punish, however unwillingly. Against the desires and pain of the private man they must be punished. Henry assumes again the royal plural in their sentence, for this is a necessary act of policy. His passions are indeed in prison. We may applaud so just a prince, but we are made aware of the cost to the man.

Memory of the other plays again highlights this moment. When Bolingbroke indicts and condemns Green and Bushy (*Richard II,* III.i), there is more than a hint of personal animus in what purports to be justice; and neither of them accepts either his authority or the justice of his condemnation. Worcester, when condemned by Henry IV (*1 Henry IV,* V.v), can merely 'embrace this fortune patiently', and does not accept Henry's right though he must accept his power. Mowbray and the Archbishop of York (*2 Henry IV,* IV.ii) are also indignant at Prince John's stratagem—which is not, incidentally, so unlike his brother's here. But these traitors not only accept Henry's justice and right, not only repent of their crimes and ask for God's pardon, but also applaud his action. There could be no stronger endorsement of Henry's kingship than this, from those who would have destroyed him.

Scene ii extends the private self-control of I.ii into public action. The world is having to notice this prince who indifferently ministers justice. The contrasting comic scenes, II.i and II.iii (of which more later) give some idea of the sort of people for whom Henry has responsibility; even there, as Falstaff lies dying, his heart 'fracted and corroborate' by the king's rejection, Nym accepts 'the King is a good king'. In II.iv the news of the formidable nature of this prince reaches France. Here is another of those visual parallels Shakespeare used so often; the court of England in I.ii, presided over in harmony by Henry, is contrasted with that of the France he claims. Here is no country acting in concert. In the face of external threat, the counsellors disagree. The Dauphin shows a foolish and imprudent disregard of Henry as a monarch, and speaks with the contemptuousness of a Hotspur, while the Constable urges that the ambassadors' report of his excellence must be taken seriously. King Charles wisely agrees, remembering Crécy and the tree of which this prince is a shoot. When Exeter and his train are announced, again the Dauphin foolishly butts in, implicitly comparing the English to a pack of dogs and the French to the noble deer; the irony of which he is unconscious is that the deer is hunted and pulled down by the dogs (II.iv.69-70). Exeter's message to the king reveals a good deal about Henry. He is not entering on this war lightly, and, like the French king himself just before, is terribly aware of the horror of war and its insatiable appetite (ll. 104-5;109). He beseeches Charles 'in the bowels of the Lord' whom they both acknowledge (l. 102) to deliver up the crown to save the suffering of the innocent. To the Dauphin he sends back insult in the same terms as he received it; and that foolish young man desires nothing more than the arbitrament of war without thought of the cost. His folly, over-confidence and silly pride masquerading as honour keep alive in this play, as a coarsened and distorted reflection, the memory of Hotspur whose character was strongly contrasted with the inner honour of Prince Hal.

In Act III, war has arrived. Henry's physical courage, fortitude and prowess does not need exploring in this play; had Shakespeare wished to do so, he could have dramatized the famous and historical combat with the Duc d'Alençon he found in his sources—he alludes to it in some detail at IV.vii.150ff. What is explored as the play goes on is his inheritance, and more, of his father's gift of inspiring and leading men. The speech before Harfleur (III.i), the favourite old warhorse of anthologists, would never have acquired that status had it not been indeed inspiring. It belongs to a recognized genre for which Shakespeare and his generation must have known a plethora of classical precedents—'the general's address to his soldiers before the battle'—and a masterpiece of rhetoric was obligatory, particularly in an 'epic' play. Its first half centres round a striking image: a peaceful human face physically distorted by rage into the mask of 'grim-visaged war', nostrils flared, teeth set, eyes staring. The second half appeals to pride of family and of country, to a consciousness of national worth about to be tested, before Henry's own face distorts in the roar of the battle-cry. The material on which he must bring his inspiration to bear is immediately underlined by the next scene. Shakespeare obviously cannot—as he keeps reminding us through the Chorus—show the siege of Harfleur, but he can illustrate the responses of the combatants. Bardolph's first line is a broken, comic reminiscence of Henry's own—quite serious, though; but the old sweats and bravos of Eastcheap, Nym and Pistol, are finding things too hot for their liking, and the poor Boy would rather have a pot of ale than any amount of glory. (There is more than an echo of Falstaff here) Fluellen enters in high rage and drives them on, leaving the Boy behind. Alone, he outlines his contempt for their cowardice and their thieving—and their silliness in both. It is such men that Henry has to turn into heroes.

But Fluellen, Captain Jamy and Captain Macmorris are another matter, comic as they are. (There were stage Welshmen, Irishmen and Scotsmen in Elizabethan theatre, as there are in our own.) Their disputes are comic and longwinded, but they are about the art of war and the serious matter in hand—unlike the ludicrous quarrel of Nym and Bardolph in II.i; here are representatives of the whole of Britain uniting in the king's service and sinking their pride and difference in a common purpose.

Shakespeare has not given Henry a simple attitude to war. Henry has been convinced his war is just, and we ought to accept that the audience would have agreed, whatever our own feelings. Shakespeare shows him proceeding on the course that he lays out for him very carefully and thoughtfully—even cautiously. If his claim to the throne of France is just, then the war the French engage in by rejecting his claim is a civil war—'impious war', as he calls it at III.iii.15. He is therefore acting according to Elizabethan ideas with every bit as much—and more—justice and legitimacy as Henry IV did in putting down the rebellions of his reign. His ambassadors gave the French a chance to agree, and warned them of the consequences; by refusing, they accepted the graphically realized horrors of an invasion. So Henry proceeds to his first campaign at Harfleur. But before committing his troops to the sack of the town, he stops, and gives the Governor another chance to acknowledge his lordship. His speech at III.iii.1ff. is imperious, frightening; he spells out what happens when a city is sacked—something Elizabethans knew all about, from the upheavals in the Low Countries. It is not a nice picture. The images of violence, pain, fire, devils and monsters swirl in and out of the speech to make a picture that chills the blood. The soldier whose blood is up is like a hunting-dog, 'fleshed', mowing down without remorse children and young girls, deflowering[8] them even while they shriek and their old fathers have their brains knocked out against the walls. This hellish picture is further intensified by images that send us back to the Mystery play of the Massacre of the Holy Innocents—babies spitted and jerking on the swords and spears of Herod's men while their mothers look on.[9]

Henry does not want this to happen—he is himself horrified by the picture—but he has the wisdom to know the limits of command: no general, in wars from Troy to Vietnam, has ever been able to control his troops in victory. And he is trapped; he cannot raise the siege and end the war now, for what is done cannot be undone. He has to play the role of king through to the end. The only way out of this horrible fate is for the town to acknowledge his lordship. When it does, instead of the punishment it might deserve for resisting in the first place he commands Exeter to 'Use mercy to them all'. For mercy becomes the throned monarch better than his crown.

The daring juxtaposition of this tense moment and the little scene with Katherine (III.iv) works interestingly. The scene is charming. After the noise and heat of battle that the language has conjured up, there follows this picture of peace and quiet and innocence, with a delicate play of cross-language bawdy. The violent rapes of Henry's imagination give way to hints of peaceful and willing dalliance. The scene serves a particular purpose: it shows us the future Queen of England, whose femininity will complement and complete the manhood of her king. But a darker side shows in this symbol of the innocence that war might have destroyed. The war, however just, is a terrible risk, and might destroy the very thing it sought to win.

However glorious and admirable as a war-leader Henry may be, therefore, Shakespeare has not presented us with a simplistic view either of human conflict or of the man himself. Throughout the four plays, from Richard's and Carlisle's prophecies onwards, the horror of war has constantly been realized. The little people do suffer in the conflicts of the mighty, and the vulnerable and guiltless new growth is uprooted by its terrible storm. The question must be asked: how can a war be just, fought (as Henry's is) in the name of a just and merciful God, and yet perpetrate such unjust cruelty? The answer, which the play faces squarely, lies in the very nature of man in his fallen state. . . . God gave man not only a nodal position in the chain of being, but free-will so that he could be a responsible moral person and not a mere automation. That freedom necessarily entails the possibility of refusing to do God's will, and this means that man's decisions will have effects far beyond himself. Man fell in Eden and the whole earth subject to him inevitably suffered, not for any sin of its own but because its governor had failed in his responsibility to it. In his mercy, as Augustine said, God instituted states and law to contain the effects of the Fall, but the Fall could not be undone, nor could the intimate connection between man's actions and the world he lived in be severed. Strife became a condition of man's existence. War was a consequence not of God's will but of man's refusal to obey it; and when the mighty disobeyed the right, their subjects suffered because of the structure of the world and society within it. The king thus shoulders a frightful responsibility, and Henry is agonizedly aware of it. Hence his caution on starting the war and in conducting it, and his appeals to the French to reconsider their disobedience; hence the responsibility for the suffering of the innocent lies on those who refuse, as the devils refused, the right. But if war is a consequence of the disorder caused by human sin, God's providence can nevertheless use it to punish the guilty and redress the disorder of the world into a temporary balance—before the next round of sin caused by man's fallen state. 'War is His beadle' (IV.i.164)—that is, his policeman: the idea is not far from that which Marlowe gives to Tamburlaine, who causes cruel havoc by his conquests, seeing himself with huge pride as 'the scourge of God'. War, however horrible, is thus somehow purging and cleansing; it is also a necessary consequence of human freedom and the love God showed for man in giving him that freedom.

But while Henry accepts his own, and King Charles's, peculiar responsibility, there are limits to it. The issue is discussed acutely in the conversation with Bates and Williams (IV.i). The peasant sense of Williams is sceptical of the disguised Henry's assertion of the 'king's cause being just and his quarrel honourable' (ll. 123-4): 'That's more than we know.' Bates sees, however, that they are not qualified to judge the issue, and that if they as individual soldiers behave as good subjects even in a bad cause, they are guiltless of that cause's guilt. Williams rejoins that if the cause is not good, the king must bear a 'heavy reckoning' (l. 131) for leading men to their deaths before they could put their own souls in order—that is, he must carry not only the responsibility for his own misjudgement but for the damnation of those who might die in sin. With careful logic Henry demonstrates that this cannot be so (ll. 143ff.) and the individual soldiers must be responsible for their own moral conduct as individuals in so far as it is based on their own choice and actions—this the king cannot take on himself: 'Every subject's duty is the king's; but every subject's soul is his own' (ll. 171-2). War is no excuse for conduct that would be evil and immoral in peace, even in the heat of the sack of a town like Harfleur. The effective argument convinces Williams and Bates,[10] and is yet another demonstration of Henry's power of leadership and his possession of that inspiring common touch that can make a ruler not just obeyed but loved. (When Henry later reveals himself to Williams in IV.viii, he does so with such grace, humour and generosity that the 200-year-old tradition of Henry as an exceptional king of men becomes credible indeed.)

Henry's reaction to this conversation (ll. 218ff.) is his only soliloquy in the play (it is briefly interrupted by Erpingham, recalling Henry to his public duties), and that alone is enough to signal its significance. He reveals

as nowhere else in the play the deepest elements in himself; and the speech shows him not only as a philosopher who understands the burden of rule, but also as an honest man. He explores more deeply the attitude to the crown we glimpsed in his reaction to his father's sickness in *2 Henry IV* (and Henry IV himself, in his guilt, observed: 'Uneasy lies the head that wears a crown'; cf. *2 Henry IV*, III.i.4-31 and IV.v.22ff.). He is no longer an observer, though; he wears it himself and knows its cost. He is lonely; the king is separated by his role from his subjects, yet he is a man as they are, and his crown cannot cure his ills. The common labourer knows delights of rest and sleep and simple honest work the king can only envy, and the king must take responsibility, at great personal cost, for providing the conditions in which the peasant can sleep in peace (ll. 272ff.). The king must bear, too, the blame the commons put upon him without thought. In this moment of stillness in the play, before the great clash of Agincourt, Henry has found himself and accepted the full implications of the hard condition of a king, on whose decisions rest both peace and war. As his prayer confirms (ll. 283ff.), he has not only committed his cause to God but also accepted his own sinfulness and his inheritance of guilt. His pious acts cannot undo that primal Fall, be it Richard's murder or the Fall of man. He, like his subjects, is under judgement, dependent on the mercy of God. The Chorus opening this act reminded us of the terrible tension between the public face on whose confidence and courage everyone depends, and the pain and fear felt by the inner man. We have seen both in action in this scene.

The depth and thoughtfulness of Henry's understanding of his role and conduct is illuminated by the contrast with the French reactions to his campaign. In III.v, after the quiet delicacy of the scene with Katherine, the French Court—thirty nobles on stage at once, nearly all to be killed at Agincourt—explodes in anger and hurt pride, at once mystified by the success of the enemy and scornful of them. The Dauphin is particularly strident. The French do not pray; they merely swear. Here is no policy, merely folly. The Constable, against all the warnings of the siege of Harfleur, wishes the enemy stronger so that the *personal* glory of defeating them might be the greater.[11] There is strong contrast with the (comic) pride in their mastery of the practical arts of war that Fluellen and Macmorris have shown in III.ii and the quiet dignity and efficiency of Henry. When Henry receives the insulting message insultingly delivered by Montjoy (III.vi.116ff.), his self-control shows in his firm and courteous reply. There is no Dauphin-like bravado; he is aware that his army is small, tired, sick, yet—'God before' (l. 154)—he will advance. Gloucester's trepidation (l. 166; cf. IV.i.1ff.) only elicits once more Henry's confidence that his cause is 'in God's hand' (l. 167).

In the scene that takes place the night before Agincourt, Shakespeare has shown us the king understanding, in his isolation, the burden he must bear; the same scene also shows us an army tense, serious, yet united by the personality of Henry. Against this is set, in point for point contrast, the other, deliberately parallel, night scene in the French camp (III.vii). While the English are serious, tense, fearful, the French nobles are longing for the night to pass. Henry visits his soldiers and understands them; the Dauphin is insufferable, boastful, praising his horse—it is not even a proper war-horse!—to a ludicrous degree. He is insulting to the Constable, and there is an undertone of mere quarrelsomeness for its own sake that only the Constable's good humour prevents from flaring into open anger. This is not the sensitivity to the real issue of the king's trustworthiness that lies behind the ironic comedy of Williams's quarrel with Henry—just the sort of thing that might happen in moments of such tension—which is rapidly smoothed by Bates. The Dauphin and Rambures are stupidly over-confident, holding their enemy in derision. Yet the Constable, far more sensible and experienced than the others, suggests that the Dauphin's courage and abilities are strictly limited (ll. 89ff.). The picture is not a flattering one, and in the Dauphin we see what royalty should not be. The contrast with Henry's attitude to war could hardly be greater.[12]

We see the same qualities in IV.ii. The Constable's speech (ll. 13ff.), another 'general's address to his soldiers', obviously contrasts with Henry's before Harfleur. Its over-confidence and contempt for the enemy is not simply ironic—for we know that Henry will win the battle; it illustrates a godless tempting of Providence, a regret that the slaughter will not be greater. Set against this the humanity, humour, true honour, generosity and courage of Henry's rallying call to his army in IV.iii, where the idea of the king as leader of a united *country* is brought vividly to life. This is where all the discussions of honour in the Henry IV plays reach their climax; the very tones of Hotspur—a Hotspur who, unlike the Dauphin, has grown up—are heard in

> But if it be a sin to covet honour,
> I am the most offending soul alive.[13]
>
> (ll. 28-9)

Montjoy's second arrival (IV.iii.79) reminds us of Henry's appeal to the Governor of Harfleur to surrender; but the only mention of mercy is ironic—a suggestion that the soldiers make a good confession before their inevitable deaths. Henry's reply is gallant and even manages humour; but underneath, as the hypermetric line (l. 128) musingly reveals, he knows their plight is dangerous.

The success of Henry—beautifully conveyed by the verbal slapstick of IV.iv, where even Pistol, the comic simulacrum of soldierly valour, wins a prisoner—throws the French into angry and horrified confusion (IV.v). Even the Dauphin at last recognizes the real nature of the enemy. The reaction is to lead a counter-attack to retrieve 'honour' by a pointless death—not the honourable and noble death of York, recounted by Exeter (IV.vi.7ff.), but an attack that is far from noble. Its fruit is the killing of the unarmed boys of the baggage train. Fluellen, from whom we hear of it first, is horrified by this breach of the law of arms (IV.vii.1ff.). Gower's anger leads him to applaud Henry's reported order for an action that would be equally horrific: to cut the throats of the prisoners (ll. 8-10). But Henry, angry and shocked as he is, is no butcher; he is prepared to do this only if the French—the Dauphin and others, who did not take part in the attack—do not join the fight, or leave the battlefield (ll. 56-7). Even here, in the heat of battle, the motive is to limit further slaughter.

Casualty lists are never pretty reading. But the size of the English victory, emphasized by the roll-call of the great names of France fallen in this field (IV.viii.75ff.), had a central place in the Elizabethans' myth of their own history, just as their defeat of the Armada had for later generations. Shakespeare could have shown Henry here simply as the glorious and triumphant king and got away with it. In fact he makes him turn right away from any pride, ascribing the honour and glory to God alone. His first thought is of humble gratitude and of his own littleness in the eye of Providence. The seriousness of the faith of this mirror of all Christian kings has been tested in the furnace, and God has vindicated him. He is a holy monarch. In line 106 he quotes the first verse of what is now Psalm 115 in the English Prayer Book, and later orders it to be sung in thanksgiving (l. 122); it is one of the psalms of celebration of God's deliverance of his chosen people Israel from their enemies, and in the Vulgate Latin text is part of Psalm 114, which begins: 'When Israel came out of Egypt, and the House of Jacob from among a strange people'. The link in Henry's—and the audience's—mind between the English army defended by God from the power of the French and the Israelites' escape across the Red Sea from Pharaoh's army is quite open. Then and in later times, many Englishmen (in particular the Puritans) saw their nation as a holy country in whose affairs Providence frequently took a hand, as God had intervened in the politics of Israel. Such a country needs a monarch who will be both a David and a Solomon.[14] Henry is shown to have been both, and a mirror for future monarchs.

So far we have only seen Henry at war, or preparing for it. The arts of peace belong to a monarch too, and Act V concentrates on these. Before taking us on in time (five years) to the final peace, the Chorus to Act V describes the return to London in a triumphal procession quite proper to a conqueror, but here again the emphasis is on Henry being 'free from vainness and self-glorious pride'. Once more there is a heightening comparison—this time to Julius Caesar, another of the Nine Worthies.[15]

But a conqueror must be judged not just by the battles he has fought but the peace he concludes, and it is that which constitutes the business of this final act. The complex tableau of the peacemaking is preceded by the lightness of V.i, where Pistol gets his comic come-uppance at the hands of the delightful Fluellen. It is not mere diversion; symbolically it is integral to what follows, for here, in the comic mode, the proper ruler shows up the fake for the deceit and silliness it is. As Henry re-establishes England and the crown, so Fluellen cleanses the English camp of the fakes and the cheats and the rogues. We have had plenty of time to observe both Fluellen and Pistol in the play, and the similarities between them emphasize a deep contrast. Both of them maul the language to the point of occasional incomprehensibility; both are proud to a fault; both love Henry (Pistol may be taken as sincere in IV.i.44ff.); but Fluellen is a real soldier and an honest man, not the mere appearance of both that Pistol has attempted (sometimes with success) to sustain. (In III.vi.12ff. it is clear that he managed to fool Fluellen himself for a time.) The scene is important, since it dramatizes in Fluellen's punishment of Pistol the final rejection and discomfiture of all false honour and pretence. Pistol's grotesque language is a mere extension to nonsense of the hyperbolic posturing that heroes, in and out of plays, are often given to. His connection with the *miles gloriosus* of Roman comedy should not blind us to his connection with the selfish, sterile, hyperbolic honour of Hotspur and the Dauphin, while his capture of Monsieur le Fer must remind us of Falstaff's similar capture—by illusion—of Colevile of the Dale. Real honour appropriate to his rank is shown by the honest, frank, not frightfully eloquent, touchy Fluellen—who, indeed, in his love for and pride in Henry, signals to us one very important standard of assessment.[16]

But the world is not cleansed finally; it will always have its Pistol. He sets off for a new career as bawd, thief and professional Old Soldier, who fakes wounds and scars in order to beg the better. (The number of vagrant old soldiers—genuine or not—begging in this way was one of the scandals of Shakespeare's age, incidentally.) Falstaff, at the end of *1 Henry IV,* merely did the same thing on a larger and more barefaced scale. Eastcheap will always be with us.

The second scene divides into three parts: the full Court scene, the wooing of Katherine by Henry, and the final conclusion of the peace. In the first section the dominating speech is that of Burgundy, the peacemaker, but before he speaks the queen gives a striking reminiscence of Henry's own conceit before Harfleur—of the face distorted by anger into that of 'grim-visaged war' (V.ii.14ff.); now, the 'venom of such looks . . . / have lost their quality'. Burgundy, as I have said above (p. 110), pulls together all the garden/farming images of the four plays in a formal and exhaustive catalogue of the disorder in the kingdom—a disorder caused by the war against her true master. Vines, hedges, fields and meadows all need tending, the weeds must be uprooted, and the tide of blood must be turned back by a proper gardener. The whole catalogue is governed by the personification of peace that introduces it:

> Why that the naked, poor, and mangled peace,
> Dear nurse of arts, plenties, and joyful births,
> Should not in this best garden of the world,
> Our fertile France, put up her lovely visage?
>
> (ll. 34-7)

The pathos of this personification of peace as vulnerable, abused femininity focuses the images of rape and sexual violence that have been insistent accompaniments to the war. (Interestingly, the French when invaded saw their honour as somehow sexually connected: cf. III.v.5ff., 27ff.; IV.v.15-16.) As the delegates leave to discuss the treaty, Peace herself puts up her lovely visage. For just as the delicacy of the earlier scene with Katherine—which on the personal level more than suggested her interest in King Henry—made visible the femininity that war could debauch and destroy, this part of the scene works both as a delicate wooing of the two persons, with all the charm of Henry's soldierly gaucheness, and also uses Katherine as a symbol of that peace that will be restored in the marriage of the two kingdoms. She is, as Henry says, 'our capital demand' (l. 96). But philosophers like Erasmus had stressed that a marriage merely for the sake of an alliance was likely to lead to further strife. Shakespeare is at pains to show us, within the conventions of the stage, that this is a love-match too.

The switch to prose signals a drop to intimacy and privacy after the publicity of the Court. It shows Henry in a most attractive, entirely new, light. He is, we know, witty and fond of word-play, but in the Henry IV plays that wit had been at someone else's expense. Here it is at his own. He is eloquent, yet his long prose speech is uncomfortable in its rhythms, embarrassed and confused in its argument, lacking in any of the devices of the stage wooer. For a moment we are reminded of the curiously attractive clumsiness of Hotspur with Lady Percy. And his conclusion is that 'a good heart, Kate, is the sun and the moon—or rather, the sun, and not the moon; for it shines bright and never changes, but keeps his course truly'. This is what this sun-like king is offering. The scene is completely convincing and suddenly makes the hero entirely human and believable. The 'silken dalliance' the youth of England left in the wardrobe for the war (II, Chorus, l. 2) is worn again.

The divorce of king from country symbolized by the separation of Richard from Isabel is healed; these lovers, unlike Glendower's daughter and Mortimer, can understand each other despite the barrier of language. . . .

The return of the rest of the Court confirms, as expected, Henry's title to France. Peace is concluded. But before that announcement is made, Shakespeare includes a striking prose passage between Henry and Burgundy, the imagery of which is of the greatest importance. The marriage of Katherine and Henry, the male aggressive and the female receptive, is of course a symbol of the equilibrium of balanced opposites that constitutes the best peace man can hope for; Katherine is France and Henry England. But Shakespeare draws in other ideas through a chain of sexual word-play. 'Conjure up the spirit of love' (ll. 284-5) has an obvious play on 'spirit', and Mercutio uses virtually this phrase to Romeo; 'conjure', though, introduces ideas of *magia,* which Burgundy picks up. The spirit of love, Cupid, will be called up 'naked and blind', which leads into other plays on 'wink', 'yield', 'do', 'stands', 'girdled', 'walls', 'will', and so on. Now this joyous playing with the idea of sexual intercourse transposes into the major key the subtheme in the imagery throughout, of war as *violently* sexual; it has a last echo here (ll. 355-8). This congress is willing and willed without destroying proper feminine modesty. But the aim of the magus was the 'alchemical marriage' of opposites in a balance that would be healing and harmonious, and go some way towards restoring the image of Eden on earth. The imagery delicately suggests this hope for Katherine and Henry, perhaps even suggests the necessity for this in Elizabethan politics. Moreover, the symbolism of Katherine is underlined both by her lover, 'who cannot see many a fair French city for one fair French maid that stands in [his] way', and by her father in his response: 'Yes, my lord, you see them perspectively,'[17] the cities turned into a maid; for they are all girdled with maiden walls, that war hath never entered.' The obvious reference to virginity hides from us another neat visual allusion. Cities were often depicted allegorically as women, crowned with a crown of walls. Katherine 'is' these cities of France that she will bring with her as her dowry to her lord.

And so in the mystery of marriage the just war is over, the rebellion quenched, the effects of the fall stayed for an interim. The land can be cultivated once more, and the gardener knows his job. In one sense the ending of *Henry V* is comic *at this point,* for the ideal king has found himself and his role, is married to his kingdom in a harmony that reminds us of that costly harmony at the end of some of Shakespeare's comedies. But the cost, public and private, has been huge, and payment will continue to be exacted till the day of doom. For the play does not end with peace and the marriage; it closes

with the Chorus predicting, in a regular Shakespearean sonnet, what the audience knew had actually happened—the loss of all that Henry had won.

The choice of a sonnet is itself of interest. Sonnets, to most of us, are just sonnets; but the Elizabethans recognized several different types which did specific jobs. Shakespeare's choice of the sonnet form (as in the first meeting of Romeo and Juliet) is therefore a signal to the audience, at the very least of a serious and aphoristic overview of the experience of the play. It begins and ends with the difficulties of the medium—a favourite idea, the inadequacy of words or vision to compass reality. This is, indeed, how the play began. But in the third quatrain, which builds up to the conventional emphatic pause before the final couplet, the Chorus looks forward to the loss of France by Henry VI. 'So many had the managing' of his state that Henry V's achievement was undone, and, in a last and striking return of the images of *Richard II* and the opening of *1 Henry IV,* 'made his England bleed'. This is history, and the material of Shakespeare's own popular *1 Henry VI;* but it is also a deliberate and open warning. If the state is not united in counsel, as in the 1590s England was not, if the wrong counsellors have the prince's ear, then England will bleed again. The ideal monarch is but a man, and men die. Elizabeth had not yet named an heir, and was obviously nearing her end.

We must therefore return briefly to that picture of the monarch Shakespeare has given us. He is a just prince and a good man, who understands his people, be they Pistol who bumps into him (significantly, in the dark), or Fluellen, or Williams; he understands his father too. We have in him a deliberate conflation of the ideal of a Christian man whose every act is felt to be in God's eye, and the classically derived 'Aristotelian mean'— the man in whom passions are felt but controlled, who knows himself for what he is and avoids excess in any particular. Then add to this the ideal of Christian kingship, where king, people and Church act in concert: the play shows Henry harnessing not only the support of the Church and his nobles to the cause, but also that of the common people, down to the very rogues. Finally, Henry is linked to the great conqueror Alexander, but surpasses him. Fluellen's delicious attempt to find parallel incidents in the lives of the two men (IV.vii.12-51) is highly comic. Pedant that he is, versed (not very well) in the ancients, he constructs in the proper rhetorical manner a 'comparison' between the two. He compares the places where they were born, seeking similarities between the Monmouth he knows and the Macedon he does not, and then moves on to look for parallel events in the lives of the two. All he can manage is the dissimilarity between Alexander killing Cleitus when drunk and (significant!) a sober Hal turning

Kenneth Branagh as Henry V in his 1989 film version of the play.

away Falstaff. Behind the humour is something serious; Henry is actually superior to the great Alexander, for he is a Christian and not a pagan prince.

The true hero knows when to fight and when to seek peace, when to beat the ploughshare into the sword and when to return to the field. Before Harfleur his imagery, particularly his pun on 'metal', kept alive the notion of an England of farmers suddenly and exceptionally called to labour in a different field:

> And you, good yeomen,
> Whose limbs were made in England, show us here
> The mettle of your pasture,
>
> (III.i.25-7)

who sold their pasture to buy their warhorses (II, Chorus, ll. 3-5). But summoning up the blood must have an end and the fields must be ploughed after the blood has been shed for another harvest. Behind the glory of the figure and the reign of Henry, Shakespeare lets us see the shadows. And they will not go away. All flesh is grass, the grass withereth, and the flower thereof

fadeth away. Here is no abiding city, and there will never be peace on earth, for man is fallen.

And so man—all men—can only throw themselves on God's mercy. They must work, labour in the vineyard in the heat of the day, for that is a condition of existence, but in the end it is God's mercy that will save or not. The prince, as God's vice-gerent, needs that mercy too, but is also in peculiar need of the quality of mercifulness. This is the attribute of power that validates all the others; it is in this that a king may be called, as with unconscious irony the Duchess of York calls Bolingbroke, 'a god on earth':

> The quality of mercy is not strain'd,
> It droppeth as the gentle rain from heaven
> Upon the place beneath: it is twice blest,
> It blesseth him that gives and him that takes,
> 'Tis mightiest in the mightiest; it becomes
> The throned monarch better than his crown.
> His sceptre shows the force of temporal power,
> The attribute to awe and majesty,
> Wherein doth sit the dread and fear of kings;
> But mercy is above this sceptred sway,
> It is enthroned in the hearts of kings,
> It is an attribute of God himself;
> And earthly power doth then show likest God's
> When mercy seasons justice . . .
> . . . in the course of justice, none of us
> Should see salvation: we do pray for mercy,
> And that same prayer doth teach us all to render
> The deeds of mercy.
>
> (*The Merchant of Venice,* IV.i.180ff.)

Notes

1. This threefold division is a medieval and Renaissance cliché. The interdependence of these qualities is well demonstrated in Titian's 'Allegory of Prudence'.

2. Pistol's dramatic ancestors include the *miles gloriosus* ('boastful soldier') of Roman comedy, a stock figure who appeared regularly on the Elizabethan stage. The number of quotations from Marlowe Shakespeare buries in his speech suggests he was less than impressed by the hyperbolic heroics Marlowe gives his royal figures, particularly Tamburlaine, to speak.

3. For example, cf. *King Lear.* Sometimes, as in *Henry V,* Shakespeare uses what are marked in the text as separate scenes to build up this structure (cf. *Julius Caesar,* I.i, I.ii; and *Hamlet,* I.i, I.ii).

4. We ought not to let our perfectly proper horror of war blind us to the fact that our ancestors saw it as potentially glorious, an activity that called for nobility and self-sacrifice, and an art utterly desirable for the true ruler to possess.

5. This reference to Alexander's 'unloosing' the Gordian knot, of which it is prophesied that he who undid it would rule the world, is quite important,

and anticipates Fluellen's linking—comic in expression, but to be taken quite seriously—of Henry to Alexander. The link cannot be openly made without overstatement, but it can be suggested with force; and Alexander was one of those Nine Worthies who set up a standard for all other military men. These were the three Jews (Joshua, Gideon and Judas Maccabaeus), three pagans (Hector, Alexander and Julius Caesar) and three Christians (Arthur, Charlemagne and Godfrey de Bouillon who captured Jerusalem from the Saracens in 1099).

6. Which raises the issue of the *Just War.* The theology of this idea ultimately derives from Augustine. In the thirteenth century St Thomas Aquinas laid down three conditions in which arms may be taken up: it must be on the authority of the sovereign, the cause must be just, the belligerents must have a rightful intention—for example, to prevent a greater evil. (Some thinkers also added that it was a good idea to make sure you had a good chance of winning.) Henry's war is made out to be just on these terms; and likewise the French, resisting their lawful sovereign, are fighting an unjust one. The issue is a topical one, in which the Elizabethans were much interested.

7. The imagery is of lions. We recall Henry's own call before Harfleur to 'imitate the action of the tiger'—a royal and noble beast, but violent and destructive. Note the imagery below—the Scots are doggy, wolfish, weasels, mice; the English eagles, lions, cats.

8. The imagery is extremely complex in lines 13-14. We think of death as a reaper of all flesh, which, as the Bible says, is grass; but superimposed on this is a strange and grotesque mixture of sexuality (death was often at this time pictured as a grotesque lover) and springlike growth unnaturally destroyed. Indeed, once again Virgilian agricultural images come into play, but Virgil never achieved this astonishing denseness of reference.

9. A stained glass in St Peter Mancroft, Norwich, shows this scene from the cycle of plays. Dolls would be used, of course, which could be made to jerk realistically by shaking the sword.

10. In III.vi.104-7 we saw Henry putting it into practice when he condemned Bardolph for behaving as soldiers all too often do: 'We would have all such offenders so cut off: and we give express charge, that in our marches through the country there be nothing compelled from the villages, nothing taken but paid for . . .' Bardolph receives the same impartial justice as the traitors. War is no suspension of the moral imperatives.

11. Henry in his victory gave the glory to God, and was glad his army was so small: the risk to his country was so much less (IV.iii.18ff.).

12. Shakespeare has neatly avoided a tricky problem here. He has to have an opponent to Henry who will contrast with him in almost every way—in attitude to honour, humility, relations with his fellows, lack of policy, and so on. And we have to dislike him. But he could not portray King Charles like this, as he needed to keep him reasonably credible as a future party to the peace and father-in-law of Henry. So he carefully keeps Charles in the background and pushes the Dauphin forward.

13. The speech looks forward to a future that is the Elizabethan past, where Agincourt is a legend of a monarch and people united in a common and glorious purpose.

14. This issue is too complex to go into in detail, but the evidence for this assertion is manifold. It can be found in quotations from the Bible, especially the Psalms, in prints like that of the defeat of the Armada, in Christian names (particularly of Puritans), and in the literary use of biblical history as a cover for discussion of English affairs, for example in Dryden's *Absalom and Achitophel* or Milton's *Samson Agonistes.* One specific example of the Puritan vision of England's troubles must suffice: in 1646, John Hancock published a print entitled 'Englands [*sic*] Miraculous Preservation Emblematically Described', where the Civil War is seen in terms of the successful weathering of a storm by an Ark—an Ark, doubtless, of the Solemn League and Covenant!—in which, with unconscious comedy, are the House of Commons, the Lords, and the Assembly of the Church of Scotland. Various royal and royalist figures float in the waves.

15. Lines 29ff. refer to what was hoped of Essex; the topicality might extend a good deal—and dangerously—further.

16. Notice how his feelings almost get the better of him in IV.vii.90ff. Henry's replies to him are very gentle, and the little vignette heightens the emotions felt in the moment of success by, as it were, defusing them.

17. The word has changed its meaning. A perspective could mean a distorted picture that, viewed from a different angle, suddenly became lifelike. There are many Renaissance examples—the famous portrait of Edward VI, for example, or the skull in Holbein's 'The Ambassadors', that was designed to be seen from the side and above. (The painting was meant to hang at the foot of a staircase.)

Pamela K. Jensen (essay date 1996)

SOURCE: Jensen, Pamela K. "The Famous Victories of William Shakespeare: *The Life of Henry the Fifth.*" In *Poets, Princes, and Private Citizens: Literary Alternatives to Postmodern Politics,* edited by Joseph M. Knippenberg and Peter Augustine Lawler, pp. 235-69. Lanham, Md.: Rowman & Littlefield Publishers, Inc., 1996.

[*In the following excerpt, Jensen presents an overview of* Henry V *from the point of view of politics, concentrating on Henry's rhetorical appeal to English audiences. The critic contends that with this play Shakespeare sought to render "a king worthy of our admiration both for his unflinching realism and for his righteousness."*]

INTRODUCTION

To defend the claim that Shakespeare's plays are appropriately treated as political texts, it may be helpful to indicate what Shakespeare's poetry has in common with such students of politics as Plato, Aristotle, Machiavelli, and Rousseau. These thinkers equate the study of politics and what is at the heart of how people live; in their view politics establishes the fundamental opinions of a society and shapes human aspirations accordingly. Shakespeare agrees with this orientation and, thus, sees an intimate connection between his characters and the political contexts in which he places them. His characters live in various political settings, with events in their lives subject to influences that could only arise in those settings. Because the plays depict political principles in concrete or applied rather than theoretical form, we can observe and compare the effects of different political arrangements on human beings. By entering imaginatively into the characters' lives, we can learn more about how to evaluate various political alternatives, an enterprise in which we must engage in order to see our own situation clearly. Further, by considering the choices made by the characters, we can refine our own ability to make sound political judgments, which are always constrained by circumstances and always occur within a particular time and place. I will demonstrate in just one case, *The Life of Henry the Fifth,* how Shakespeare contributes to our political education, by discussing some of the things he leads us to think about when we read or see the play.[1]

I know of no other Shakespearean play whose commentators are as concerned about the author's political judgment as this one. Virtually all the principal *dramatic* questions raised by *Henry V* resolve themselves into *political* questions. Above all, they ask, what does Shakespeare think about the king he portrays? And, as a related question, what ought *we* to think about him? Claims about Shakespeare's assessment range from the view that he intended to glorify an icon of English history to the view that he meant ironically to subvert the king. Some say that Shakespeare's artistic freedom was restricted at the outset—by the theatrical medium, by the need to defer to his queen's Welsh forebears, or, generally, by the Elizabethan cultural context.[2]

The major episodes of Henry's life were well known in Shakespeare's time, its legendary outline already drawn. Shakespeare had as sources a number of Elizabethan accounts: the anonymous, crudely drawn comic play called *The Famous Victories of Henry the Fifth* (1598), Samuel Daniel's patriotic poem *The First Fowre Bookes of the Civile Warres* (1595), and the stately historical chronicles of Holinshed and Hall.[3] In the play, the various episodes in Henry's life roll by us like a series of tableaux appropriate to epic, punctuated and strung together by a personified chorus, but they roll by in a uniquely altered form. It is true that Shakespeare's fidelity to Raphael Holinshed's *Chronicles* extends even to the repetition of Holinshed's errors. And there are numerous close parallels between the structure of Shakespeare's plays about Henry and *Famous Victories,* particularly in its juxtapositions of court and tavern and its seamless commingling of chronicled fact and comic fiction. But in both cases, what is derivative in *Henry V* only throws Shakespeare's originality into greater relief. His reinterpretation of the story produces a different kind of king from either the chronicles or popular legend. Shakespeare's refashioning of his source material evinces the desire both to represent for his audience the actual politics of medieval England and to supplant other accounts of the king.[4] Rather than imitating, Shakespeare's representation rivals the accounts of those whose labor he employs. He blends deference to history with creative self-assertion. I will show that Shakespeare seeks neither to debunk Henry's high reputation nor to sentimentalize his portrait, but to make a king worthy of our admiration both for his unflinching realism and for his righteousness.

Shakespeare levels his judgment on Henry V in light of the two kings—Richard II and Henry IV—who preceded him, and whose lives he presented in the three earlier plays in the so-called second tetralogy (*Richard II* and the two parts of *Henry IV*). Henry V combines the strengths of both his predecessors without the weaknesses of either.[5]

As prince, Henry made himself invisible, obscuring attentiveness to his royal responsibilities "beneath a veil of wildness" (I.i.63-64).[6] Notwithstanding Henry's love of playacting, *Henry V* makes clear that hard political necessities prompted his counterfeit of his true nature. Especially vulnerable to those who would have sacrificed him—the heir and first-born son—in his father's quarrels, Henry hid himself "as gardeners do with ordure hide those roots / That first shall spring and be most delicate" (II.iv.39-40). Likening him to the founder of the Roman republic, who was called "Bru-tus" because he seemed stupid, the French constable insists that Henry wore "a coat of folly," the better to conceal his prudence (1.38). To avoid becoming embroiled in his father's self-destructive quarrels, the prince sacrificed his father's friendship during his father's lifetime and took up with Falstaff, his surrogate father.[7] Consorting with Falstaff's crowd at Eastcheap conferred positive political benefits on Henry as well, foremost among them the advantage to be gained from an adjustable political lens. Unlike kings who simply look down, Henry has also seen the high from below and the low at eye level.

As king, Henry proves to need the same talents he displayed as the "nimble-footed madcap prince of Wales": his ability to hide in plain sight, both to capture the hearts of his friends and to baffle his enemies (I.ii.266-68; II.iv.26-29). Shakespeare takes some pains to remind us of Henry's versatility as a player; his prodigious skill in changing his nature. He can be fox as well as lion, has eyes in the back of his head, and can even parade in sheep's clothing. Since the first two acts of *Henry V* depict conspiracies directed by those nearest the king and various sorts of masked men throughout, we can say that *the* political virtue for a king who knows how to deceive by appearances is how not to *be* deceived (III.vi.79-81). The paramount question in Shakespeare's *Henry V* is whether or not Henry see his enemies clearly.

ACTS I AND II: FRIENDS AND ENEMIES AT HOME

WAR DELIBERATIONS

We bring to the play the principle that foreign war is the condition of civil peace. As the play opens, England's war with France, which makes up the whole action of the play, is virtually a foregone conclusion. Especially in light of the deathbed advice of Henry's father that he "busy giddy minds with foreign quar-rels,"[8] King Henry's own hesitancy is especially strik-ing. He must be assiduously exhorted on all hands, even cajoled into the war. The deliberations occupying most of Act I acquire their particular character from this fact. Henry is punctilious on all points of right and extraordinarily cautious on all points of policy. On behalf of the church, the archbishop of Canterbury and Bishop Ely volunteer to overcome the king's resistance; they vouch for both the justice and the feasibility of war. Only after Henry's scrupulous sense of rectitude has been satisfied and his mind eased on the potential Scottish menace does he commit himself. Thus, the overwhelming impression conveyed by the *speeches* in Act I is that it is not Henry at all, but the church most definitely that wants this war, and that the clergy has ef-fectively manipulated the king to do its bidding. Ap-pearances notwithstanding, Henry's hesitancy concern-ing the war with France is dissembled.

Shakespeare retains from Holinshed the clergy's determination to promote war with France in order to forestall consideration of a parliamentary bill to take away its so-called "temporal," that is, nonchurch, lands. On this hint, Shakespeare draws the bishops as decid-edly worldly men, ready to wield their mighty spiritual influence in order to safeguard their wealth.[9] With heavy irony, the "spiritualty" is the explicit spokesman in the play for men's bodies and money (I.i.79-81; ii.130-35). In the absence of foreign war, in order to throw Parlia-ment off the scent, these clerics would not scruple to foment civil war (I.i.3-5), in which case they could likely count on the aid of France or Scotland. If the clergy were to declare that Henry V was not the legitimate king of England, for instance, it might incite the nobles into open rebellion against him. Even in less extreme circumstances, there could be no bold or vigor-ous war effort without the church's support. To insure the friendship with the church that is so necessary to his designs, Shakespeare's Henry gives the bishops the illusion that they exert the influence over him—the power to "impawn" him—that they actually wield in Holinshed. The intense orthodoxy and chivalry of the king in the chronicles make him guileless and pliant in the clergy's hands, subject to their leadership and to their limitations. By contrast, Shakespeare's King Henry allows his ostensible reluctance to be overcome by Can-terbury and Ely, but only on the grounds he establishes and in a setting he completely orchestrates.[10]

Canterbury has sounded Henry out on the parliamentary bill in private and, perceiving him to hesitate on the question, makes an unprecedentedly generous offer of support in the imminent war to the king in order to win him over. While appearing in the main favorably disposed, Henry does not actually confirm to the archbishop whether the offer was persuasive, prompting him to up the ante. Just at the point at which Canter-bury was about to lay before Henry his "true title" to the French crown, presumably to tantalize him into battle, Henry breaks off the interview because the French ambassador demands a hearing. In the next scene, however, as Canterbury and Ely go themselves to the court to hear the French ambassador, we find that Henry is calling for Canterbury. The French ambas-sador has been left outside cooling his heels until the archbishop resolves for Henry "some things of weight," pertaining to his claims on the crown of France. This is the very same conversation that Canterbury sought to have with him earlier. We must conclude, then, that Henry broke off the private conversation solely that it might be resumed in public, that is, before the as-sembled nobility. Henry's hesitation on the parliamen-tary bill in private insures that the archbishop will press Henry's claims with the utmost vigor in public. Above all, in a very adroit move, Henry transforms the archbishop's willingness to make a private bribe into the necessity that the church accept full responsibility for starting the war. By contrast to Holinshed's prelates, who were content to stay in the background, Shakespeare's bishops are thrust into the limelight: "For God doth know how many now in health / Shall drop their blood in approbation / Of what *your reverence* shall incite us to" (I.ii.18-20; emphasis added).[11]

Deft evasion of public responsibility is Henry's typical mode of rule throughout the play.[12] This invisible command, an extension of his actions as prince, situates Henry between Richard II, whose notorious irresponsibility brought him down, and Henry's father, whose palpable and unrelenting efforts to protect the crown only heightened his vulnerability further; such that every step he took to strengthen himself had the opposite effect.

In view of the awful gravity of Henry's opening speech to the clergy, what is most striking about the ensuing discussion is that, by his design it brings to light only legal and political questions that are patently easy to answer, while shrouding in deep silence every real difficulty. There is a belabored consideration of the traditional objections to English forays into France that, as such, have well-known and well-worn responses. The assembly's focus on them draws all attention away from Henry's real problems. As in Holinshed, Canterbury proves the impeccable credentials of King Henry as claimant to the French throne by demonstrating the groundlessness of the Salic Law; an ancient French statute that disallows claims to the crown made through the female line, which is the source of the claim to France of Henry's great-grandfather, Edward III. Henry actually *confines* the discussion of his legal claims to the interpretation of the Salic Law, and it is very easy for Canterbury to prove its irrelevance because there have been so many French violations of it in their own dynastic history. However freely one grants the point though, Henry's legal difficulties remain. Edward III may have laid claim to France with impunity. The real legal-political question, which is pointedly circumvented, is whether Henry V is the rightful heir to Edward III in *England*. England's claim to the French throne is in fact better established than Henry's claim to the English throne. The first claim is, so to speak, an English tradition, while the rule of Henry's family is not, and was indeed hotly contested in the civil wars that flared up after his death. By enforcing concentration on irregularities in the French royal lineage, Henry deflects attention from irregularities in the English royal lineage.

As Canterbury justifies Edward III's claim to France in his long, tedious speech (I.ii.33-95;98-114), he is forced to acknowledge tacitly, without equivocation or question, that Henry is Edward III's rightful heir. It is this public attestation to his legitimacy that Henry seeks above all to extract from Canterbury. This is the prize

he needed most to win. The clerics thus note Henry's rock-solid link to his most illustrious forebears, Edward III and his son Edward: "You are *their* heir, you sit upon *their* throne" (1.117; emphasis added). But the names of his immediate predecessors Richard II (Edward III's grandson) and Henry IV are nowhere publicly mentioned in the play; instead, they are expunged from the historical record, as if they and the fatal quarrel between them never even existed.

The public silence Henry purchases from the church serves the cause of domestic peace. He does not take the public suppression of the questions, however, as a cue to walk away from "the fault / My father made in compassing the crown," as he will later reveal in private (IV.1.294-305).

Indeed, for the priests to call Henry "a true lover of the holy Church" says more than they realize. Henry's righteousness, not theirs, supplies the model for piety and rectitude in the realm. Not only does a sense of right enhance his soldier's' readiness to fight for the cause, Henry's strict preoccupation with justice also inspires their trust.[13] As in the self-government or "grace" he shows the French ambassador (I.ii.241-45), at every opportunity Henry communicates his freedom from arbitrary or capricious actions. "We are no tyrant, but a Christian king" (1.241). The ideal of medieval chivalry, which Shakespeare first brings to light by showing Richard II's betrayal of it, conjoins valor and righteousness; this combination of qualities depends on self-government—keeping one's passions as subject "as our wretches fett'red in our prisons" (1.3). A man as watchful over himself as over others can be trusted to reward and punish evenly.[14] By contrast to his predecessors, Henry wins support by his example, expecting nothing of others except what he embodies in himself.

To assess the justice of Henry's claim to France—whether he really goes forth with "rightful hand in a well-hallow'd cause" (1.293)—we may note, in addition to French provocation, long-standing English tradition.[15] However remote, Henry's claim to France arises with Edward III. He makes use of that claim, but does not invent it.

In the deliberations, Henry also appears to be as unconcerned about domestic problems as he is about his title in England. The sole practical problem he worries over is Scotland. Far from seeking to busy giddy minds with foreign quarrels, Henry seems hard-pressed to stop thinking about England's "giddy neighbor" Scotland (1.145). By fastening tenaciously on the matter of Scottish incursions into England, a problem that admits of easy resolution on traditional grounds, Henry is able once again to obfuscate the real issues and to avoid pointing to his real vulnerabilities. Henry's actual fears about the domestic danger he might incur by leaving home are allayed in the discussion led by Canterbury.[16]

Once having satisfied the demands for justice and prudence in this war, Henry reassures "the noble sinews of our power" that there is room now for all men of merit—those with sufficient courage—to thrive in the realm: the "empery" over which England will rule in Europe is "large and ample"; the dukedoms that are up for grabs are "(almost) kingly" (11.222-27). Even if there remain some disgruntled nobles in the audience, however, they now know the church will not help them. If Henry succeeds, he will be stronger than the clergy or nobility ever imagined; his aims as well as his achievements extend farther than his great predecessors'. If his plans miscarry, the clergy will bear the brunt of the inevitable criticism (1.97). The clergy has given him a great deal. He has given them nothing more tangible than the impression that he is on their side.

The efficacy of the war with France to curtail domestic rivalries and submerge them temporarily in a common cause is underscored in the conversation among Falstaff's followers in the following scene, a comic reenactment and recapitulation of the events of Act I. The "home-bred broils" over who has rightful possession of Hostess Nell Quickly arising in Falstaff's band of confederates, are prorogued without bloodshed by the promise of better trade in France. Bardolph intercedes between Nym, who was engaged to Nell, but never had her, and Pistol, who usurped Nym's title with her willing complicity. Nym's cowardice and susceptibility to Pistol's verbal virtuosity make is easy for Bardolph to convince them that the new quarrel will be better than the old. Like the church, Nym is ready to forgive and forget—forgive Pistol and forget Nell—in return for eight shillings, a small enough recompense as it stands. Under the spell of Pistol's cleverly evasive speech, however, Nym is placated by the ephemeral promise of even less currency, to be extracted in some vague future, and Pistol's current friendship (II.i.105-10).

THIEVES

The final domestic impediment to Henry's designs abroad, the English traitors who have ostensibly been suborned by French gold, is eliminated in the second scene of Act II. The traitors corroborate the effectiveness of Henry's strategy with the clergy. Since they cannot color rebellion against Henry as a righteous cause sanctioned by the church, they must confine their efforts to a covert assassination plot. Their sole chance is to reconcile the country to a *fait accompli*. The donnybrook at Eastcheap makes the appropriate segue to this scene; moving us smoothly from a low band of thieves of "crowns" to a highly placed one. Depending on how it is read, Henry's disposition of the three traitors either signifies an apparent success that obscures a real failure, or a real success that is deliberately hidden from view. The difficulty arises from the fact that at least one of the traitors, the earl of Cambridge, disguises his real motives; admitting as much in his cryptic allusion to having motives other than money (II.ii.155-57). Since Henry does not expose the ruse, nor even appear to notice it, the question arises, as in Act I, whether Henry sees his enemies clearly or is instead deceived by appearances.

On the surface, the episode is a resounding success. Henry publicly unmasks the traitors in such a way as to deter imitators. Further, by making an example of traitors, he turns back on them their own supposedly well-meaning advice that he should make an example of wrongdoers (11.79-83). They can thus seem to be responsible for their own demise, not the king; to be hoist on their own petard. Having discovered this plot by mysterious means unknown to anyone at court (11.6-7), Henry's efforts to rule remain inscrutable.

The event vividly displays Henry's boldness and his uncanny ability to ferret out secrets, as well as his impartial but implacable justice.[17] And Henry's excoriation of his best friend and, hence, the worst traitor, Scroop, serves notice on the other nobles in the most memorable way that, henceforth, Henry will on principle distrust the outward appearance of chivalry or loyalty. Since the false knight has been exposed, the true knights will be assumed to be false (11.138-41). Once again, in addition to inspiring fear, Henry's vigilance regarding friend and enemy, and the exquisite precision with which he draws the line between justice and vengeance (1.174), inspires trust. Shakespeare confirms the reputation Henry has in the chronicles for giving people exactly what they deserve—the exact inverse of Richard II and Henry IV, whose maltreatment of both friends and enemies was their chief failing. Henry's friends and enemies know exactly where they stand: they can rise by merit, but not by flattery; and no one falls from grace owing either to the king's willfulness or his morbid anxiety.[18]

From every angle, then, Henry appears to have orchestrated the whole unpleasant event to his utmost advantage, turning, as only a "good wit" can, and in true Falstaffian fashion, something bad to something good; as Falstaff would say, turning "diseases to commodity" (*2 Henry IV,* I.ii.248): "We doubt not of a fair and lucky war, / Since God so graciously hath brought to light / This dangerous treason lurking in our way" (II.ii.184-6). In the traditional accounts of this episode, however, it is actually Henry's victory here that is merely apparent. Just as Henry seems in the chronicles to be at least the intended pawn of the church, so is he portrayed there as the dupe of his chief enemy's dissimulation.[19]

Cambridge, who is executed along with the other traitors, only counterfeits an interest in French crowns when his real object is the English crown. Because the king did not *see* Cambridge's motives, it is alleged that he missed an opportunity to secure himself and his own heirs from danger.[20] It is likely that an Elizabethan audience familiar with Shakespeare's other plays about Henry V would have recognized the true crime lurking beneath the false one. Here, however, Shakespeare offers nothing about Cambridge's true motive beyond a tantalizing hint. As he had done earlier with respect to the English royal genealogy, however, by skirting the issue, he may point up its importance.

The poet Daniel says that the source of Henry's failure to see this plot clearly was his "unsuspicious magnanimite"; a quality that is part and parcel of the king's own chivalry, leading him to focus concertedly on the opportunity for glorious action abroad to the exclusion of the court intrigue.[21] By contrast, Shakespeare's Henry may be perfectly equal to the task of dealing with the likes of Cambridge. If he is foiled in doing so, the fault may not be failure to foresee the danger of the earl's enmity (see 11.86-89), but failure—if it can be called such—to foresee his own untimely death.[22]

Henry *seems* to take almost no notice at all of Cambridge in this scene, being bewildered and shocked at the revelation of Scroop's personal treachery. Moreover, the interposition of the scene with Scroop between the two scenes in the play occupied with the death of Falstaff, for which his followers hold the king responsible, indicates that the two events are somehow interconnected. Falstaff's staunchest supporters might allege that Shakespeare explicitly juxtaposes the two parallel betrayals here (since Henry renounced Falstaff's friendship when he became king), and find a kind of justice in the fact that, having proven to be a false friend himself, Henry is shown to suffer the pain of having one (11.93-104).

The evidence of the play itself supports exactly the opposite view, suggesting that Henry is neither the dupe of appearance, nor the false friend to Falstaff, man to man. This scene, a kind of reenactment of incidents at Eastcheap, does after all show the extent of Henry's debt to Falstaff; on whom he practiced exposing liars and from whom he learned how to get out of tight spots. Henry's greatest pleasure as prince seems to have been to expose Falstaff as a boasting thief, and then watch with mock-indignation how Falstaff would try to wriggle out of paying for what he had done.[23] Henry's association with Falstaff is thus a dress rehearsal for the most serious business he has as king. In the extensive speech about Scroop occupying most of the scene, moreover, we can detect an artful silence on a real enemy joined to an artful silence on a real friend.

The bulk of Henry's speech to the "ingrateful, savage, and inhuman" Scroop is an extended enumeration of his putative virtues. Now it is impossible to imagine that Henry could so elaborately rehearse Scroop's false virtues without thinking fondly on Falstaff's true faults. Henry's list is a perfect counter to—the inversion of—a well drawn portrait of Falstaff. Outwardly, Scroop looked eminently to be dutiful, grave, learned, well born, and religious; the very model of discipline and grace, that is, Falstaff's opposite: "Or, are they *spare in diet,* / Free from gross passion, or mirth or anger, / Constant in spirit, not swerving with the blood, / Garnish'd and deck'd in modest complement, / Not working with the eye, without the ear, / and but in purged judgment trusting neither?" (11.131-36; emphasis added).

In view of the presence of Falstaff's spirit in this act, Henry's deeply moving renunciation of apparent chivalry has a double meaning. The very falseness of Scroop's chivalry vindicates the falseness of Falstaff's—whose name is literally and symbolically false (the real king had no companion named *Fals*-taff).[24] Falstaff perpetually tries to be something he is not. He is the false knight who, consequently, lacks the flaws of the lean and hungry Scroop and who is, therefore, despite his falseness, true. Although Falstaff is laid low by sins from which Scroop is exempt, he was not liable to the sins of the traitors. With one notable exception—when he pretends to be dead—Falstaff is a terrible liar.[25] His colossal corporeality tells *against* him—he is a walking confession of the sins of the flesh—but also *for* him. He is an open book.

The speech against Scroop serves, and its placement suggests that it is meant to serve, as the king's secret eulogy of the dying Falstaff. There may be no express place for Falstaff in Henry's public world but Henry gives full play to Falstaffian sentiments as king. What Henry appears to forget, he does not forget. In addition to everything else, Falstaff's very material and very mortal presence is important to remember because it deters kings from being deceived by outward appearances—by the forms and ceremonies of their office—and teaches them to recognize their own human vulnerability. Both Richard II and Henry IV forgot the flesh and blood man beneath the dazzling crown—leading the first to commit crimes as king and the second to commit crimes to become king. But it is hard to be beguiled by *form* next to the living exemplar of *substance,* matter itself, this "mountain of flesh," this "tun of man."

Now, if Henry is silent about his friend, he may also be silent about his enemy. Henry's concentration on Scroop would be a perfectly effective feint to deflect attention away from Cambridge. And Henry may need to obscure the conspirators' motivations more than they do. To be forced to take note of a rival claimant to the throne is to lend, by the very fact of shedding publicity on it, credibility to that claim. If Henry cannot eliminate his enemies, he must at least prevent them from showing themselves as enemies in public. As with the clergy, Henry must discover new ways of coping with them that do not require him to expose their counterfeits. He confounds his enemies best then by appearing not to see them. As Henry had satisfied without appearing to see the mercenary motives of the church, so in the case of the traitors, he appears to see only mercenary motives.

So much for Henry's potential enemies. To break the cycle of hostilities coming from the traditional quarters—church and nobility—Henry must, in addition, also create new friends; a feat his father could not perform. As Henry diminishes the power of the church by supplanting it as the exemplar of righteousness, so he tempers the political priority of the nobility by raising the common man. He seeks in fact to establish the commonwealth of England on an altogether new foundation; one that will at least fully incorporate the commons into the realm. His aims are visible in Shakespeare's treatment of the war with France.

Acts III and IV: Friends and Enemies Abroad

The Dauphin and the French

It is clear that Shakespeare emphasizes the inferiority of the French to the English in certain fundamental respects—for instance, orderliness and discipline, deference to authority, modesty, gravity, and cohesion. As perfect counterparts of the English, the French are the foil setting off the English more clearly by contrast. The weaknesses in the French army emanate directly from court, where the dauphin, the heir apparent, sets the tone. The contrast between him and Henry reprises the earlier contrast between Richard II, just before his political fall, and Henry Bolingbroke, at the moment of his greatest ascendancy.

The arrogance of the dominant elements in the French court is about to undo them. When the dauphin has his ambassador give Henry a box of tennis balls as a present, to say nothing of the contemptuous greeting he attaches to it (I.ii.249-57); when the French disdain to show up in force to defend the besieged city of Harfleur—being utterly scornful of their adversary (III.iii.43-46); when the nobles shoot dice before Agincourt to decide who will get the ransom on the prisoners they expect to capture—we can see they are readying for a fall.[26] While acting through British agents, moreover, the French are behind the attempt to assassinate Henry V. This move is not only shocking and provocative, but also reckless with respect to their own king's security; it makes regicide a thinkable crime.

Along with their boastfulness, an uncritical attachment to feudal aristocratic tradition lures the French to defeat themselves. Indeed, the theme of self-defeat is another carry-over from the earlier plays in this series; a reminder first of Richard's and then of Henry IV's debilities.

While the French forces vastly outnumber the English—the odds are five to one—their numerical superiority is worth less than it seems.[27] The haughty aversion of the French aristocrats to the common soldier rends their army in two, canceling out their overwhelming advantage in numbers. A mounted French knight could not brook being beholden to or seconded by a man of low degree (IV.ii.25-28).[28] The French nobles, like Richard II before them, refuse to recognize the humanity they share with their commons. In their own minds, far more important than the numbers in their army are the names. The unity that the French fail to achieve for the sake of victory is the punishment inflicted on them in defeat. Ten thousand Frenchmen, lying in jumbled heaps, litter the field at the close of the battle of Agincourt. This final commingling of aristocrats and commoners may be more humiliating to the French than the grim body count itself (IV.vii.74-81).

The class consciousness of the French nobles, their desire to distinguish themselves from their own commons and from the English, is confined to externals or forms. They are imprisoned by what is weighty and palpable to the eye. Preoccupied with gilding the body, they altogether ignore the soul or the inner man. As a consequence, like Richard II's and Henry IV's seduction by outward regal trappings, they are deceived by appearances; this is the characteristic French vice in the play.

Overall, the French are victims at Agincourt of a self-imposed double deception. Judging by externals, they misperceive both English strengths and French weaknesses. They assume that the English are not men to be reckoned with essentially because they do not look the part. And they assume that their own mere presence in glistening battle regalia will suffice to defeat the English. "Do but behold yond poor and starved band, / And your fair show shall suck away their souls, / Leaving them but the [shells] and husks of men" (IV.ii.16-18). Against such hollow, counterfeit men only a counterfeit valor—valor's "vapor"—is needed (11.18-24). As it is, until it is too late, the French bring only apparent valor, a "fair show," and nothing more, to bear.

Henry and the English

When the two armies meet, the French are at the peak of their form while the English are at the lowest ebb of theirs. To this point the English have not seriously tested themselves against the French; they are engaged by the French when Henry's sick and famished army is retreating to Calais for the winter (III.vi).

The play suggests that in the absence of Henry's leadership of the English at Agincourt, French self-confidence would have been very well founded. The resplendent and formidable outward appearance of the French, on which they themselves rely, *is* the one thing that can defeat the English. Despite their own weaknesses therefore, the French army possesses the power to unnerve and paralyze the English, in effect defeating them in advance, before a single arm is lifted. The English, too, are in danger of becoming their own worst enemy. To avoid what is essentially *their* own self-defeat, then, the English must be made proof against appearances. Henry can insure that they do not make the French mistake only by making them literally blind to what they see (IV.i.290-91). For Henry and his friends, this is the real battle at Agincourt.

To confound or over rule their senses, Henry must steel their hearts. Since the body *is* merely the outside or skin of a man, the mere shell or "husk," we may say that nature cooperates with Henry's effort. Henry muses, "when the mind is quick'ned, out of doubt, / The organs, though defunct and dead before, / Break up their drowsy grave, and newly move / With casted slough and fresh legerity" (IV.i.18-23).[29] The soul can rally, even resurrect, the body.

Historical accounts of the war with France often stress the unique resources of the English. By and large, however, they emphasize English weaponry and the mode of warfare, in particular, the prominence in the English army of the long bow and, hence, of the archers, who were commoners, over the mounted knights or nobles.[30] In *Henry V,* Shakespeare is silent on all such matters.[31] Indeed, the greatest peculiarity of this play organized around war is that there is no actual warfare in it.

Shakespeare may want to show that the cause of the English victory is not discernible in weapons or combat tactics at all, but is, on the contrary, entirely a matter of hearts and minds. As Henry himself insists: "All things are ready, if our minds be so" (IV.iii.71). On the English side, the cause of victory is manifest therefore in Henry's speeches to his men before battle. From these speeches we can conclude that Agincourt does indeed represent a departure from tradition; not because of the new preponderance of the common man's weapons, but because of the new preponderance of the common man's heart. This is not to say that King Henry is a democrat in disguise. From Henry's actions we can, however, infer his recognition of the common humanity underlying all social and political distinctions.

As Shakespeare presents it, the war provides the opportunity not only to cover up or postpone the old quarrels, but also to begin to eradicate their cause. The secure allegiance of the commons establishes a bulwark for the crown missing in previous reigns. Henry's actions imply, therefore, a more far-reaching and revolutionary design than anything conceived by his father. As he also sets about to reconstruct England's past, Henry sets about to construct the English nation, to make a whole out of the disparate parts.[32] To achieve genuinely national goals, Henry must put amity where there might otherwise be distrust and mutual respect where there could be contempt.[33]

With his speeches, Henry aims to kindle a zeal for the common cause within which the differences between nobles and commons can merge and, for a time, dissolve themselves. He seeks both to ameliorate the traditional aristocratic impulses toward an aloof and segregated existence, and to encourage the common soldiers to catch some of the fire that more easily inflames the nobles; *or,* if not rendering them ardent, at least making them obedient. In the first place, to achieve these two purposes Henry does not so much denounce the thirst for distinction that underlies the hereditary aristocracy as to nurture that pride on a new basis. As much as the French nobility, but in a novel way, Henry ostentatiously flaunts good breeding. England herself and not a few old, established families is now hailed as the progenetrix of the best men. "And you, good yeomen, / Whose limbs were made in England, show us here / The mettle of your pasture; let us swear / That you are worth your breeding, which I doubt not; / For there is not one of you so mean and base / That hath not noble lustre in your eyes" (III.i.25-30). Further, the new upper class, the rarefied fraternity to which Henry invites his little "band of brothers," is all-inclusive with respect to those who participate in the engagements in France and who partake of the common danger, but is reserved for them alone; an exclusive club in which membership is earned by valiant service. "For he today that shed his blood with me / Shall be my brother; be he ne'er so vile, / This day shall gentle his condition" (IV.iii. 38-39; 59-61).

At the deepest level, however, and contrary to what one might expect, the task Henry has to weld English hearts together in a single whole demands that he stay alive to the real heterogeneity and indeed the inequality of his men. If the concentration on the body democratizes men by reducing them to the lowest common denominator, which is the tendency—against their will—of the French, the focus on souls expresses a genuinely aristocratic impulse. To make Englishmen out of all his men does not require that Henry seek to obliterate the natural distinctions between them, but that he bring them by different routes, "contrariously," to a common goal (I.ii.205-6).

Henry speaks to his soldiers as if he spoke to two natural classes of men.[34] The natural nobles seek honor and can even be made to prefer it to life, and the natural commoners would trade all of the martial fame in the world, since it belongs to dead men, for the page boy's pipe dream: "a pot of ale and safety" (II.i.12-13). To speak well to each of these types of men, Henry must meet their real concerns, while being free of their self-deceptions or delusions. Henry cannot shore up the nobles' flagging spirits by appearing to be anything less than the foremost exemplar of chivalric virtue; as if he embraces entirely Harry Percy's intrepid, even reckless zeal for outward glory (Harry Percy is called "Hotspur") and does not share at all in Falstaff's immunity to it.[35] "But if it be a sin to covet honor, / I am the most offending soul alive" (IV.iii.28-29). He cannot shore up the commoners' hearts by being king at all, and so he disguises himself as a common man. As in his jests with Falstaff that had no apparent purpose beyond themselves, to achieve his deadly serious purposes as king, Henry bestows himself so that he may serve as the touchstone to the souls of the other men while hiding his own. As Chorus tells us, the famous "little touch of Harry in the night," enables "mean and gentle all" to derive support from the king's example "as may unworthiness define," that is, each according to his own limits (1V.i.45-47). There is, moreover, a central trick or paradox in each of the two main speeches Henry delivers on the eve of the battle at Agincourt that reveals how well he knows his men.

To treat the second of Henry's audiences first: Henry's prebattle speech to the nobles is apparently very traditional. To overcome their fear of death, Henry appeals to their thirst for honor. The stark imbalance in the sizes of the two armies is thus no disadvantage: "The fewer men, the greater share of honor" (IV.iii.22).[36] What the soldier sees so clearly with his mind's eye—the honor that will be his—can make him ignore the things he apprehends with his senses. Death itself can be made to disappear from view.

Thus, Henry anticipates for the nobles the accolades that will be heaped upon them after the battle. In the most vivid, intoxicating way, Henry commemorates the victory attained at Agincourt before it is won.[37] There is no reverential invocation of the ancestors in Henry's speech as there had been earlier in England and at Harfleur. The knights who face the French at Agincourt are no mere latecomers or *epigoni*. On the contrary, the achievements of those who have come to France before slip into oblivion. "This day is call'd the feast of Crispian . . . / And Crispin Crispian shall ne'er go by, / From this day to the ending of the world / But *we* in it shall be remembered" (11.40,57-59; emphasis added).

The celebration Henry lovingly depicts for his men weaves perfectly together an acknowledgment and a forgetting of their mortality. Given the inevitability of death at *some* time, the deliberate choice of a noble

death is more compelling: "He that outlives this day, *and* comes safely home, / Will stand a' tiptoe when this day is named," and, "he that shall see this day, *and* live old age, / Will yearly on the vigil feast his neighbors" (11.41-45; emphasis added). Nevertheless, the overriding impression conveyed by Henry's speech is one of high-spirited vitality, camaraderie, and warm good cheer. The portrait of the celebrants of Agincourt is so lifelike, its hearers can place themselves in the imagined scene, subtly obscuring the fact that in Henry's foreshadowing, they are not actually there. Henry has made clear that all names of note must be earned by valiant service. Barely perceptible in his picture, however, is the fact that *all* that remains of the men to whom he is speaking is their names. The seductive, imaginary commemoration takes the place of the real ones, which they are not to enjoy. Inconspicuously but definitely embedded in the promise of undying honor, so to speak, as its escort, is the promise of death. Henry's immortal speech to his nobles is their funeral oration.[38] . . .

Notes

1. All citations are to *The Riverside Shakespeare* (Boston: Houghton Mifflin, 1974). I wish to thank Lauren Weiner, Diana Schaub, and Fred Baumann for their assistance, and Mary Nichols, Ernest Fortin, and Lee and Joseph Knippenberg for enabling me to present earlier versions of this essay. I also thank the Earhart Foundation for fellowship aid.

2. See Herschel Baker's "Introduction" in the *Riverside Shakespeare* for a summary of critical positions, 930-34. See also Ken Adelman, "The Blast of War," in *Policy Review* no. 52 (spring 1990), 80-83; Lily Campbell, *Shakespeare's "Histories": Mirrors of Elizabethan Policy* (San Marino, Calif.: Huntington Library, 1947); Jonathan Dollimore and Alan Seinfeld, "History and ideology: the instance of *Henry V*," in *Alternative Shakespeares,* ed. John Drakakis (London and New York: Methuen, 1985), 206-27; Stephen Greenblatt, "Invisible Bullets: Renaissance Authority and Its Subversion, *Henry IV* and *Henry V*," in *Political Shakespeare: New Essays in Cultural Materialism* (Ithaca and London: Cornell University Press, 1985), 19-47; Harry M. Geduld, *Filmguide to Henry V* (Bloomington and London: Indiana University Press, 1973), 55-69; Lawrence Olivier, "The Making of *Henry V,*" *Classic Film Scripts* (London: Lorrimer Publishing, 1984), 1; Robert Ornstein, *A Kingdom for a Stage* (Cambridge: Harvard University Press, 1972); Norman Rabkin, "Rabbits, Ducks and *Henry V,*" *Shakespeare Quarterly* vol. 28 no. 3 (summer 1977); 279-96; E. M. W. Tillyard, *Shakespeare's History Plays* (New York: Macmillan Press, 1946); Derek Traversi, *Shakespeare from Richard II to Henry V* (Stanford,

Calif: Stanford University Press, 1957); and Gunter Walch, "*'Henry V'* as Working-House of Ideology," in *Shakespeare Survey* 40, (1987): 63-68. On the general approach I am employing, see Allan Bloom with Harry Jaffa, *Shakespeare's Politics* (New York: Basic Books, 1964); and Catherine Zuckert, *Natural Right and the American Imagination: Political Philosophy in Novel Form* (Savage, Md: Rowman & Littlefield, 1990).

3. All references to Shakespeare's sources are to Geoffrey Bullough, *Narrative and Dramatic Sources of Shakespeare's Plays,* vol. 4 (New York: Columbia University Press, 1960), 299-434. See also Graham Holderness, "*Henry V,*" in *Shakespeare: The Play of History,* ed. Graham Holderness, Nick Potter, and John Turner, (Iowa City: University of Iowa Press, 1987), 62-82.

4. See Paul Cantor, *Shakespeare's Rome: Republic and Empire* (Ithaca and London: Cornell University Press, 1976), 7-18; Friedrich Nietzsche, *Beyond Good and Evil,* trans. Walter Kaufmann (New York: Vintage, 1996), section 224 (pp. 151-3).

5. See *Richard II,* I.i.104; III.iii.108; V.vi.43; and Pamela K. Jensen, "Beggars and Kings: Cowardice and Courage in Shakespeare's *Richard II,*" *Interpretation,* vol. 18, no. 1, (fall 1990): 111-44.

6. See Holinshed, in Bullough, *Narrative and Dramatic Sources,* 280-88; *Famous Victories,* in Bullough, *Narrative and Dramatic Sources* 1.480, 313; 11.550-51,570-72, 315; Bullough, *Narrative and Dramatic Sources,* 354 ff; *1 Henry IV* (I.ii.195-217); and *2 Henry IV* (V.ii.122-29). *Narrative and Dramatic Sources* is hereafter referred to as *N-and D-S-*.

7. See Bullough, *N- and D-S-,* 216-17; *Famous Victories,* 1.480, 313; 11. 550-51,750-52, 315; *1 Henry IV,* V.iv.49-52.

8. *2 Henry IV,* IV.v. 202-20; *1 Henry IV,* I.i.18-28.

9. Holinshed speaks of the "sharpe invention" of the church to support the war in order to set aside the commons' bill. Shakespeare preserves from Holinshed the fact that this wealth was "devoutlie given," but refrains from repeating Holinshed's phrase that it was also "disordinately spent" (Bullough, *N- and D-S-,* 377-78; see also 356).

10. By contrast to Holinshed's *Chronicles* and *Famous Victories,* in the play it is Henry rather than the clergy who introduces the possible objections of the Salic Law and Henry rather than either the clergy or the nobles who introduces and presses home the objections that could be made about Scotland. Both of Shakespeare's sources present

an actual debate on, especially, the latter question. Canterbury in *Famous Victories* and Westmoreland in the *Chronicles* raise questions about Scotland, which are duly answered in the former case by Oxford (1. 770-75, 779;. 331-32), and in the latter by Exeter, whose "earnest and pithie persuasions" entirely carry the day, "according as the archbishop had mooved" (379-80). See also Holinshed, in Bullough, *N-and D-S-,* 377-81, 407; Winston Churchill, *A History of the English Speaking Peoples* (New York and London: Cassell and Company Ltd., 1956), Volume I, 292-94; *1 Henry VI,* I.i.35-36; see also III.i.

11. See Holinshed, in Bullough, *N- and D-S-,* 407.

12. I.ii.21-22; 281-88; II.ii. 79-82; 184-87; III.iii.39-40; IV.i.155-56; V.ii.68-71.

13. *2 Henry IV,* II.ii, 79-82.

14. *Richard II,* II.1.15-16, 28-29,70; Jensen, 113, 120.

15. The attack that the English make on what they call "the borrowed glories" of France (II.iv.78-79) is matched in Shakespeare's play *King John,* where the French ambassador tells the English king to lay down the "borrowed majesty" he holds in the English crown (I.i.4). The battles at Crécy (1346) and Poitiers (1356) (II.iv.50-55) took place during the lifetime of the sitting French king, making the war seem like a renewal of a quarrel, which Henry's predecessors had to forgo (*Famous Victories,* 1.768). Richard II had, however, married a French queen, inaugurating a kind of truce that lasted into Henry's reign.

16. Given the clergy's unanimity on the war question, the editorial attributions of the speech at I.ii.166 to Ely and that at 1.174 to Exeter, might be misattributions, and perhaps transposed.

17. Holinshed, in Bullough, *N- and D-S-,* 407.

18. Calling Henry "a severe justicer" who was both loved and obeyed, Holinshed says he left "no offense unpunished, nor freendship unrewarded" (Bullough, *N- and D-S-,* 406).

19. Holinshed reports that Cambridge "rather confessed . . . monie" as his motive than reveal his true purposes because he desired "rather to save his succession than himself," a situation that, had Henry "either doubted or foreseene," would not have come to pass (Bullough, *N- and D-S-,* 385-6). *Famous Victories* does not treat the conspiracy.

20. Nominally, Cambridge acts on behalf of Mortimer, earl of March, Richard II's designated heir, who is not mentioned in the play. Because Mortimer had no son, however, Cambridge harbored the not unfounded hope that the crown would devolve on

his own heirs. After Henry's death, Cambridge's son, Richard Plantagenet, does initiate the claims against Henry VI that start the dynastic wars. See *1 Henry VI*, II.vi.91-95; II.v. 23-33, 55, 63-97.

21. Daniel's Henry "for being good, hates to be ill." See stanzas 34-35, in Bullough, *N- and D-S-*, 428-29.

22. See Machiavelli, *The Prince*, trans. with intro. Harvey C. Mansfield, Jr. (Chicago: University of Chicago Press, 1985), chap. 14, 60. See also Chaps. 3, 12; 14, 60; 18, 25, esp. at 100.

23. *1 Henry IV*, I.ii.186-90; II.iv; III.iii.163; *2 Henry IV*, II.ii.169-70.

24. In *1 Henry VI*, I.i.131, Shakespeare uses the name "Sir John Falstaff" for the cowardly knight Sir John Fastolfe; he originally gave the name Oldcastle to the prince's companion. (*2 Henry IV*, Epilogue, 1.32; and *Riverside*, 843).

25. *2 Henry IV*, IV.iii.18-23.

26. Holinshed reports that before the battle at Agincourt, the French built a chariot at the site, to be used to parade Henry through French streets, "little weening (God wot) how soone their brags should be blowne awaie" (Bullough, *N- and D-S-*, 394).

27. Holinshed reports odds of six to one, in Bullough, *N-and D-S-*, 392.

28. It may have been to justify their fighting alongside lesser men rather than to call forth more gallant service from them, that the French court created five hundred new knights just before the battle at Agincourt (IV.vii.85-86).

29. See *2 Henry IV*, I.ii.193-201.

30. Dupuy and Dupuy, *The Encyclopedia of Military History* (New York: Harper and Row, 1870), 330-35, 414-15; Winston Churchill, 294-296; Michael Howard, *War in European History* (Oxford: Oxford University Press, 1976), 1-19; Theodore Ropp, *War in the Modern World* (London: Collier Macmillan, 1959), 19-25.

31. To enhance the effectiveness of the archers, Henry employed a device that is nearly as famous as the battle itself, one made into a picturesque part of the battle scenes in both the Olivier and Branagh film versions of the play. To protect the archers compromising the vanguard, Henry planted tall sharpened stakes in the ground in front of them; in order to gore the horses of any assaulting Frenchmen who survived the initial shower of arrows. The importance of this arrangement is attested to by Holinshed. *Famous Victories* essentially incorporates his description as part of the order of battle (11.1160-80), in Bullough, *N- and D-S-*, 39 and 332-33. In *1 Henry VI*, the inability to employ this particular device is adduced as a factor in England's defeat when the war with France is renewed (I.i.115-19). It is all the more curious then to note that no reference to it, or to the order of battle or tactics at Agincourt, or even archers, occurs in *Henry V*.

32. Moving the aristocracy away from French, the historical Henry was the first king of England to write his field dispatches in English. See Churchill, 299.

33. The night before Agincourt, the French nobles dissipate their own considerable eloquence and facility with language, which might have been used to muster courage in the army, in sophisticated and lascivious wordplay having to do with horses and mistresses and taking the one for the other. The ridiculous lengths to which the dauphin goes to celebrate his horse ("his neigh is like the bidding of a monarch") is also telling because, judging from the way he—the heir apparent—is treated by his closest associates, "the prince of palfreys," receives more deference than the prince himself (III.vii.10-40). The dauphin inspires a senseless, frivolous competition in the nobility, which prevents the men from helping one another or from wanting to help him (III.vii.72-123). As the model for the realm as a whole, the order that is missing in his own life infects the army. At the most crucial moment, the horrified nobles recoil at the disorder that has defeated them by a veritable panegyric on disorder. In deference to chivalry, the best they can do is to attempt to escape disgrace by embracing death (IV.iv.6-22).

34. Harvey Mansfield, "Machiavelli's Political Science," *American Political Science Review* 75, no. 2 (June 1981): 293-306.

35. The contrast between Falstaff and Percy is made in *1 Henry IV*, V.iv.

36. Holinshed merely reports at this point "a right grave oration," culminating in "manie words of courage." The point of the speech as he describes it, moreover, is: the fewer men, the less damage to England. An additional advantage to having so few men is that the soldiers will not ascribe the victory to themselves, but to God. His Henry also makes a disdainful reference to the French (Bullough, *N- and D-S-*, 393-4; Churchill, 295).

37. Strictly speaking, as is true of the Battle of Gettysburg, for example, the commemoration of valor at Agincourt is independent of the attainment of victory.

38. The peculiarity of Henry's speech as a pre- rather than a postbattle oration, as well as something of

the universality of the sentiments it expresses about tales soldiers tell "in their flowing cups" is captured in General Norman Schwarzkopf's address to the departing troops after the success of Desert Storm in Bahrain on 8 March, 1991. "I can hear the war stories now. Over Lone Star beer, over Colorado Kool-aid, over some great German beer, a firewater or two, and what you drink the most, that Diet Pepsi and Coca-Cola. I know what glorious war stories they are going to be": (Richard Pyle, *Schwarzkopf: The Man, the Mission, the Triumph* (New York: Signet, 1991), 255-56.

CHARACTER STUDIES

Richard Corum (essay date 1996)

SOURCE: Corum, Richard. "Henry's Desires." In *Premodern Sexualities,* edited by Louise Fradenburg and Carla Freccero, pp. 71-97. New York: Routledge, 1996.

[*In the following essay, Corum offers a "homosocial" reading of Henry's character in* Henry V, *analyzing phallic desire as a motivating force in the play.*]

> . . . not the physical past whose existence is abolished, nor the epic past as it has become perfected in the work of memory, nor the historic past in which man finds the guarantor of his future, but the past which reveals itself reversed in repetition.
>
> —Jacques Lacan

Let me begin with a brief account of the materials on one's desk when one sits down to work on Shakespeare's *The Life of King Henry the Fifth.* First, the figure Henry. Too visible after the fact, and altogether unrecoverable as a fact, Henry, "like himself," is by 1415 already a legendary figure inherently vulnerable and inescapably defensive, a vanishing point in the real not to be separated from the imaginary/symbolic orders which constructed him nor to be untangled from those imaginary and symbolic orders which unfold from him.[1] Then, the various pre-Shakespearean, post-Henrician textualizations of this figure: chronicle histories, earlier plays, poems.[2] Despite destabilizing genealogical differences, these texts construct Henry as a miraculously reformed Prince "applyed . . . unto all vyce and insolency [who became] a majestie . . . that both lived & died a paterne in prince-hood, a lode-starre in honour, and mirrour of magnificence." As an object of government control, censorship, containment, Henry's life is a site for the production of an official history that registers

and adjudicates competing points of view in order to speak with "full mouth" of the figure it holds up as a "paterne" for, and of, those who wield power.[3] In the face of this official historiographical project, another group of representations/valuations comes quickly to mind: those dissenting knowledges and voices that this official, totalizing, and territorializing narrative of perfection was constructed to make illegitimate and inaudible; subversive points of view and antithetical judgments of Henry, that is, which, despite state power "descending to the most recalcitrant fibers of society," have nevertheless been to a degree recovered— "nomadic" valuations (to use Deleuze and Guattari's term) which neither idealize Henry, nor praise him (Foucault 1982, 795; Deleuze and Guattari 1987).[4]

When we place Shakespeare's play(s)—three quartos and a folio; Globe and Jacobean Court performances—in the context of this official history/unofficial histories binary, we realize that for a common actor-playwright to write and produce, not just *a* life, but *The Life of King Henry the Fifth* in early modern England was a risky undertaking to the extent that his *Life* did not reproduce the official version. So it is (and long has been) of considerable interest, reading the folio and the sources, to see that although the play gives us the official life, it also supplements this life with extensive additions, changes and omissions. What can be said with complete confidence about this Folio text is that there is nothing in it (given the dangers, there could be nothing in it) that can conclusively prove that Shakespeare was not wholly committed to the official version of Henry's life, and much to suggest that he was. On the other hand, there is also nothing in this text which conclusively proves that Shakespeare was committed to this official version, and much to suggest that he was not. If in dramatizing the official version Shakespeare added a parallel, unofficial and destabilizing version/ valuation of Henry's life and actions, this version, by the logic of censorship, would have had to be officially invisible, however unofficially accessible.[5]

When we turn to the extensive critical/performative materials surrounding Shakespeare's play, it is not surprising to discover that, apart from those who found the play a disappointment, critics and producers have been sharply divided into three principal groups: first, those who read the sources, the stage tradition and the play, and see no significant difference between the official Henry and Shakespeare's Henry except that the latter serves the state as a more powerful ideological vehicle than the chronicles or the earlier dramatizations; second, those who read the sources and the play and perceive a profound difference between the official representation of Henry as ideal and the play's ironic rerepresentation of Henry as a manipulative, conscienceless autocrat who masked his will to power and consequent predations under a carefully constructed "godlie" image. For this group, Shakespeare's semiotic excess, voicing subversive knowledge and transgressive values, radically negates the official version of Henry's sovereign ideality which of necessity it must also articulate. Thus Shakespeare stands, not as a self-effacing handmaid of the state, but as a powerfully articulate subversive who brought text/performance critically to bear against a dominant formation of power, its construction of identity and subjectivity, its apparatuses of representation and dissemination, its appropriations of theatre and so on. In brief, a second Henry, a second Shakespeare and a second logic: not the official logic of sovereign ideality supplemented by Shakespeare's dramatic genius, but an unofficial, deconstructive logic of Shakespearean supplementarity identifying a fissure between dominant myth and historical fact.[6] Finally, there are those who argue, in an attempt to mediate this longstanding controversy, that Shakespeare's text gives us both an eagle Henry *and* a hyena Henry because, as Kantorowicz argued, kings have two bodies (1957). The text, Norman Rabkin asserted, is indeterminate, and although there are those who will insist on determining it one way or another, the wiser critic will step back and see that the play gives both views of Henry in tension, and that Shakespeare's text, far from taking one or the other side of this difference, is caught up, as Shakespeare and his culture were caught up, in what Anthony Brennan and Graham Bradshaw term the "complex multiplicity" of sovereignty itself.[7]

What general observation can we make about this controversy, and what role can we say postmodern theory, particularly queer theory, plays when it enters the space of this debate? The *Henry V* controversy has not been primarily about Shakespeare's Henry. Instead Henry has long functioned as a particularly charged archaeological site where English-speaking cultures have recorded, layer upon layer, their deeply contestatory attitudes towards one or another manifestation of masculine aggressive sovereignty. As Rabkin (1981) implicitly understood, the controversy has always had a powerful displacement effect. When Henry ceased being useful as an object for Tudor and pre-Tudor discussions of monarchical sovereignty itself, he became a site for discussions of the value of human (as opposed to divine) monarchical sovereignty in a Protestant state; then, with the decline of monarchy, the value of bourgeois England's nationalistic opportunisms in, and imperial aggressions against a radically expanding Third World; and, more recently, after the partial decline of two English-speaking empires, the value of masculine authority in a variety of domestic spheres, particularly, on this side of the Atlantic, patriarchal institutions (Congress, the Supreme Court, the military, the family, marriage) and professions, including, of course, the profession of English itself.[8] From 1415 to the present, the debate about Henry has been a debate about the

value of various forms of masculine sovereignty and has been fueled in part by the need to enlist the foremost literary genius of the culture on one or the other side of one of the most important issues of the last several hundred years: absolute patriarchal sovereignty and its monopolizations of identity, rule, aggressivity, logic, and representationality.

When postmodern theorists entered this deeply layered and massively contested field, they did so, in the main, to further destabilize dominant masculine sovereignties as well as the subjectivities and memory constructs (the "histories") such dominance has produced. Postmodern theorists engaged in this analytical/deconstructive enterprise work to prevent the return of such sovereignties and their sociopolitical consequences, and to understand and represent (as well as legislate against) the culture's long attraction to, its dependencies on, its identifications with, and its endless imitations of patrilogosovereignties. One could say, in brief, that postmodern theories are the most recent powerfully articulate return of those intellectual/cultural activities that absolute patriarchal sovereignties have long repressed. Thus, whereas among other things, new historicists and cultural materialists decenter "Shakespeare" as an effect of cultural appropriation in order to reposition a rehistoricized Shakespeare on the subversive/transgressive margins of Elizabethan/Jacobean culture, and whereas deconstructionists and feminists decenter Henry as an effect of essentialist and misogynistic cultural formations, queer and psychoanalytic theorists decenter Henry as an effect of desire and the unconscious, political or otherwise.[9]

As a general theorization of sexuality and the cultural production and use of sexualities, queer theory makes visible the private parts, so to speak, of the language that constitutes a textual/theatrical phenomenon like *Henry V.* Queer theory interrogates Henry's, Shakespeare's, critics', directors', editors', and audiences' sexualities—their libidinal, erotic investments, their desires and pleasures—as a function of their knowledge/power/unconscious and its production of actions, texts, performances, critical representations, cultural constructions, and pedagogical interventions. For example, Jonathan Goldberg's "Desiring Hal" section of *Sodometries* addresses (among numerous other issues) a question raised a century and a half ago by Hazlitt: "How then do we like [Ha]?"[10] Working from the rich resources of postmodern queer theory (particularly the work of Foucault, Bray, and Sedgwick) as well as alongside Lacan's mirror stage and aggressivity papers, Goldberg's answer is that those critics and audiences who like Hal do so (to put a complex argument very briefly) because they desire Hal, identify with him, and construct themselves after his "paterne" in order to manifest his ideal Christian, heterosexual image while acting out the homophobic, misogynistic repressions this image necessitates and disguises. That is, dazzled by an "imaginary . . . identification" with Henry "that founds the ego in its desire for sovereignty," those who endorse Hal "as the very locus of [their] identity" do so to *be* Hal, and to blind themselves, as Hal does, to the homonarcissistic foundations of this identification (Goldberg 1992, 147).

In this paper, queer theory is again brought to bear on *Henry V*, but the question I address concerns Henry's desires as these desires are articulated by the language of the play. My argument assumes that Shakespeare's theatrical resources are not limited to an official historicization of Henry's life and actions as a public figure; rather, *Henry V* is seen as a particularly brilliant historicization of a subjectivity whose "deep truth" (to use Foucault's phrase) is its sexuality.[11]

To plot the actions by which Henry traverses homosocial space is not to repeat the history *Henry V* is ostensibly telling us; rather, it is to articulate an alternative history that Shakespeare's text is showing us. This unofficial history (to borrow a sentence from Harry Berger, Jr.'s discussion of *Lear*) is not the history Henry prefers to hear about himself, but an account of his life, as I read it, "which strikes closer to home and which [Henry] would find harder to bear," though how hard will not become fully clear until the third section of this paper (Erickson and Kahn 1985, 210-29).[12]

Having lingered outside homosocial space (as we know from *2 Henry IV*, if not from the chronicles) as an associate of prostitutes, thieves and a dissolute, ex-homosocial man, Falstaff, in whose company he has been addicted "to courses vain," Henry has lost phallic stature except in name.[13] In this exterior space he has become, in effect, penile, and, content to be little more than penile, he has enjoyed the sodomitical pleasures afforded by the penis.[14] Thus his position at the death of his father (that is, at the end of *2 Henry IV*) is a precarious one. Neither his homosocial God—the Phallus— nor his homosocial lords can be pleased with his performance, though his defeat of Hotspur at Shrewsbury (in *2 Henry IV*) proved an exception to his dissoluteness. Thus, at the beginning of *Henry V*, most of Henry's lords do not respect or fear him. Probably none of them love him, and several love his cousin, Mortimer, a man who has a better claim to the throne than Henry. No doubt others also desire to take his place. In this position Henry has options. He can stay "outside" and die, since if he does not come in, one of his cousins—Mortimer, Cambridge or York—will take his place and he will be too dangerous to be allowed to live. Or he can "come in." But because there are doubts ("Can I/he possibly be/come phallic?"), and because there are desires ("I/he can be/come phallic"), Henry must quickly and thoroughly phallicize himself if he is to survive and rule.

How does Henry do this? First, at the end of *2 Henry IV*, he reestablishes homosocial space by re-drawing its boundary with "himself" inside. In Holinshed's account, he banishes his "misrulie mates of dissolute order and life . . . from his presence . . . inhibiting them upon a great paine, not once to approoch, lodge, or sojourne within ten miles of his court or presence" (280). For Henry to have brought any of these sodomitical outsiders inside would have violated a fundamental rule of homosocial space and would have destroyed him as surely as such behavior destroyed Edward II and Richard II.

Once back inside (and prior to the beginning of *Henry V*), Henry labors to purge himself of his penile habits, desires, pastimes, vices. To quote Canterbury's account of this "mortification," this "scouring [of] faults," we are to understand that:

> Consideration like an angel came
> And whipped th'offending Adam out of him,
> Leaving his body as a paradise
> T'envelop and contain celestial spirits
>
> (1: 2, 28-31)

Rather than an "offending" sodomitical vessel containing mortal spirits (sperm/alcohol/money), Henry's body, given a clean new mythic interiority, is reimagined as an Edenic "paradise," a granary, to be filled only with celestial, phallic seed.

Thus, having emptied himself of "th'offending Adam," Henry must now fill his paradisical body with celestial spirits, and he must prove to his homosocial God that it is so filled, so that this God will embrace, love, empower, and protect him. Of the available technologies for interiorizing the phallus—cannibalism, necrophagy, positive and negative predation, inheritance, self-sacramentalization, education—it seems, from Ely's account (1:1, 38ff.), that Henry's first attempt is to fill himself with knowledge.[15] This gives him some phallic status ("when he speaks, / The air, a chartered libertine, is still, / And the mute wonder lurketh in men's ears / To steal his sweet and honeyed sentences"), but not enough to suffice. In *2 Henry IV* Henry had also turned to positive predation, trading some of his dark, wet, penile stains for Hotspur's hot and dry phallic fame and glory; but clearly, only limited resources of this sort are available to him in England. Nor is reliance on his inheritance a sure solution, since his father was a usurper and a murderer, and one of his cousins has a better claim to his throne than he does. Given these obstacles, Henry must go to war. Aggressivity, in the ancient form of trial by combat/trial by ordeal, is the only viable way Henry can weed out his rivals, regain his legacy in France, and achieve phallic dominance.

Henry's next problem is how he is going to persuade his lords to follow him into battle. It does not seem likely that homosocial men will be eager to wage war under the direction of a young man who has been lingering outside, who lacks the phallus, and whom, as a consequence, they cannot fear, respect or love. Clearly, Henry will have to manipulate them into making him wage war. But how will he do this? From what the first two scenes of the play give us, we can infer (if we have not been blinded by official representations of Henry as ideal, "godlie" sovereign) that before the action of the play begins, Henry has sent ambassadors to France insultingly and arrogantly demanding his properties there, and that he has also reintroduced a bill from his father's reign, which, if passed, would empty half of the church's coffers and massively reduce its power and influence. With this threat in his hands, we can also infer that Henry then lets it be known to Canterbury that if he does not produce a compelling argument to accomplish Henry's desire, Henry will prosecute this bill. Henry waits to convene council until the French reply to his demand is in his anteroom. Then, in council (as the second scene of *Henry V* documents), Henry, presenting himself as a pious young king facing a difficult crisis, first humbly and dutifully seeks the advice of his spiritual lord by asking Canterbury, on the life of Canterbury's soul, what he should do about the French matter, as if this matter had just come to his attention, and then summons the French ambassadors so his temporal lords may hear their reply, knowing that the insults and arrogance he sent to France will have provoked sufficient insults and arrogance in turn to provoke his temporal lords. In response to the urgings of these lords, Henry declares his intention of going to war if his property in France is not returned immediately, a demand he knows will be refused. Thus, although Henry seems to follow textbook protocol (faced with a difficult problem, a young king requests, listens to, and accepts sage advice), Henry is in fact manipulating his lords into creating the political fiction and the war it entails that he needs if he is to phallicize himself.

Having declared war, Henry must figure out how to win it, and the solution he adopts is (to use Lacan's phrase) to make his desire the desire of the phallic Other, by constructing the war he is about to wage not as his war, but as his God's war. And since this intolerant phallic God wants a pure and unified homosocial England, one with an unstained, phallic identity (just as he wants Henry to have a pure, unstained, phallic identity), Henry will use war as a way of doing to England and France what he is doing to himself. As God's angel, Henry will whip "th'offending Adam" out of the body of England (a body symbolized by his army), making England a "paradise / T'envelop and contain celestial spirits." He will also use war to whip "th'offending Adam" out of England's other "garden," France, making it, too, a paradise to envelop and contain his celestial spirit.

Who are these offending Adams whom Henry must whip out if he is to rewrite England as a perfect homosocial paradise? Needless to say, they are the French, who wrongfully penetrated and sodomitically fill what was once England's "paradise" with thousands of offending, penile Adams, and, among these thousands, most particularly a Dauphin who loves, who writes sodomitical verses to, a horse that is his "mistress" (3:7, 42). Needless to say, too, they are also the Eastcheap occupants: Falstaff, Bardolph, Pistol, Nym and Mistress Quickly, those very uncelestial spirits fouling the interiority of England. And, among others, they are Cambridge, Scroop, and Gray, traitors to Henry and to homosociality itself.

If in personal terms, then, war allows Henry to invert his status as sodomitical object of homosocial law into scouring agent of such law, and if in narrative terms the plot of the play is Henry be(com)ing the chosen, only begotten, phallic son whose homosocial identity is no longer obnubliated by any sodomitical stain whatsoever, the other plot of this play is the construction of England as a pure homosocial space. The objective of Henry's weeding, pruning, limbing, lancing, and burning is not to steal or destroy France, but to create for England a *national* homosocial identity, and thus the kind of unity, purity, maturity, and completeness which will enable Henry and England not only to be "the mirror of all Christian kings" and all Christian states, but also to be the mirror in which Henry's God will see nothing but his own "ideal image." The objective here is not just that Henry, having rid his God's England of penile, sodomitical difference, will surely be chosen and blessed by this God; it is also that Henry's kingship will be a sacrificial ritual of purification: those homosocial men who survive Agincourt will have proved themselves to be the celestial spirits who alone will be enveloped and contained by the English paradise Henry's God is creating through the instrumentality of Henry's acts. And this is the tableau we witness at the play's end: a happy band of celestial brothers occupying a homosocial Christian paradise, with Henry the most celestial, the most phallic, the most homosocial, standing on top of an enormous pile of dead sodomites who had to be pruned from the sacred tree in order for Henry and England to blossom. In short, Henry "like himself" is one of the chief architects, if not the chief architect, of that reactionary rise of intolerance which radically reshaped English homosociality in early modern England.[16]

We are now in a position to analyze specific aspects of Henry's reactionary homosocialization and homonationalization of himself and England as these are illuminated by the play. Of the numerous scenes, episodes and passages about which questions have been asked and answers given, there is space here to look at only three: why Henry takes only one quarter of his army to France, why he orders his soldiers to kill their prisoners at Agincourt, and why he hangs Bardolph. These scenes are important to address because they typify the textual detail which tends to be ignored or simplified in modernist discussions and productions of this play, erasures that have the effect of deleting Henry's subjectivity/sexuality from the play's historiographical project.

The official explanation for the first of these is that Henry must leave three quarters of his army in England to deal with the unruly Scots: "We must not only arm t'invade the French, / But lay down our proportions to defend / Against the Scot . . ." (1: 2, 136-37). The way "proportion" is argued in council makes it seem that Henry is doing what he can under the circumstances: he would take a larger proportion if he could. From the perspective of homosociality, however, we realize that Henry's purpose for taking only one quarter of his army is that Henry *chooses* to reduce the size of his army, despite the fact that if a military leader is facing two opponents one of which is three times larger than the other, he ought to put one quarter against the lesser threat, Scotland, the rest against the greater, France, other things being equal. Henry, a man schooled in military strategy, knows this, yet he does exactly the opposite. What, then, is Henry's strategy, if this action seems calculated to lose the very war he must win? The answer is that the war Henry must win is not the war we see him fighting on the ground. Henry has to find out if and prove that his God is on his side, and the only way he knows to do this—the only way he knows to make his God reveal his choice—is to make his English army so small that it cannot possibly win without his God's blessing and help. In short, Henry takes one quarter of his army to effect a religious miracle. If he wins with an army too small to have a chance of winning in its own right, he will know beyond doubt that his God has forgiven him. War is his God's instrument of judgment, and Henry is determined to prove himself "straight" in its crucible: "be he ne'er so vile [Agincourt] shall gentle his condition" (4:3, 62-63). Knowing that "the man whose mind is backward" will perish in war (4:3, 72), Henry has good reason to insist that the victory at Agincourt is "none but [God's]": "be it death proclaimed through our host / To boast of this [victory], or take that praise from God / Which is his only" (4:8, 109-111). A victory that is not God's would be useless to him because it would not prove what Henry must prove, namely, that he is no longer a sodomite. Agincourt, that is, is Henry's way of writing himself as exemplary, and France is the fatted calf Henry's God slaughters to honor his rephallicized prodigal.

Of course, there is also a practical, manipulative side to this matter of proportions. What Henry needs to produce is a victory he can retroactively represent as (and, to the extent he can dominate representation, *will* be read as) a divine blessing/gift. So Henry studies history, not the myths of England's legendary past, but the practical military history of numbers, positions, probabilities: how Edward III won at Crécy. So Henry learns exactly how many men he will need, exactly where to put his archers, exactly how far his lines will have to be from the French (and how muddy it will have to be) to slow the French advance to an exhausted crawl, and exactly how much to reduce his own army to get it stuck in just a tight enough corner to insure that his soldiers will fight in phallic fashion or die. But this manipulative aspect of Henry's behavior should come as no surprise. Henry at war, like Henry in the council scene, is staging a theatrical show, *The Miracle of Agincourt*. Playwright, producer, set designer, chief actor—what role is Henry not performing? And although the "new man" whom this victorious war produces has seemed to many to be a complete transformation of Henry's prodigal adolescence into solid Christian/homosocial maturity, it is necessary to recognize that this war, this victory, this new man are no less theatrical productions than the prodigal Hal we saw in Eastcheap, except that here Henry, not Falstaff, is writing the script, and that here the script Henry writes is a homosocial masque, not the antihomosocial antimasque Falstaff wrote in the past. To set aside childish things for adult things is, for Henry, setting aside apprenticeship in one kind of transgressive theatricality for a sovereign appropriation of theatricality itself. And though the official view is that this appropriation produces a noble, mature, complete Henry as Henry's aggressive, manipulative performance plays itself out in the real, it would be more accurate to say that Henry assumes (and has been contained by) the despotic structure of power that he and Falstaff had previously mimically subverted.

Critics have long been troubled by Henry's reasons for ordering his soldiers to cut their prisoners' throats.[17] The official version, worked out in the chronicles and in modernist criticism/performances against doubts about the morality of such an action, is that Henry gives this order either because a fresh attack by the French would overwhelm an English army heavily burdened with prisoners, or because Henry's rage requires revenge for the slaughter of his baggage boys. From a homosocial perspective, however, what Henry sees as playwright and director when he looks over his battlefield is that men like Pistol are contemplating how rich they will become when their prisoners are ransomed. The only way Henry can put an end to this theft of his inheritance ("France is mine," he is saying to himself, "and it is not penile money; it is my phallic wealth/inheritance"), the only way he can keep penile men like Pistol from getting rich at his expense, and prevent them from penilizing his war, is to force them to kill their prisoners. To phallicize his men rather than merely enrich them—to get the phallus inside them rather than French gold in their pockets—Henry orders this castration of the penile, sodomitical other. What this act also means, of course, is that if the English are captured they will be killed, not ransomed. So, by forcing his men to kill their prisoners, Henry powerful induces them to stop thinking about making money and to start turning themselves into aggressive, celestial spirits capable of whipping the French.

A third incident queer theory is in a position to illuminate is Bardolph's execution (3.6). In defiance of Henry's edict against plunder, Bardolph has stolen a pax from a French church. He is tried, found guilty, and hanged. Why does Henry not pardon his old friend? One pro-Henry answer is that Henry needs to send a strong message to his soldiers or run the risk of having his decrees trifled with in a situation where trifling could destroy his chance of victory, and what stronger message could Henry send than the one being sent by the execution of Bardolph? From a homosocial perspective, however, Bardolph, a man with no phallic essence, is penile, and, worse, a man immune to phallic penetration: his ears do not take in Henry's edict against plundering. What Bardolph perceives as stealing a piece of gold from a French altar in order to enrich himself in a base, material, nonhomosocial manner is in fact a blasphemous misperception of a synecdochical piece of the phallus as a source of monetary profit. Moreover, since this small piece of France is part of Henry's phallic inheritance, Bardolph is stealing Henry's legacy in order to engross himself financially outside, and at the expense of, an economy of homosocial aggressivity. This mistake is, of course, the same mistake Bardolph and his associates made in the past with respect to Hal. They took the prince to be a means of profit and were unable to perceive that, despite his stains, Hal was part of the phallus. Hanging Bardolph restores this theft, revenges this misrecognition, reconstructs this eroded difference, and thus marks Henry as an extension of the omnipotent Phallus.

Hanging Bardolph also functions in another register of Henry's imaginary. To prove that he has moved from outside to inside, from prodigal son to phallic leader of the chosen people, Henry must consistently produce greater and greater differences between the past and the present—differences he can then record as history, differences which he can use official "history" to reify as fact. In the present theatre of Agincourt, he needs a band of happy brothers, whereas in the past theatre of Eastcheap, he needed a ragtag, stained band of happy rogues. Thus, given his needs at Agincourt, he cannot allow a homosocial army to plunder the countryside in the manner his Eastcheap's army had plundered Gadshill in the past. To allow such a sameness would be to let his stained past stain his present, collapsing the boundary between outside and inside, past and present, and thereby to destroy the binary differences (phallus/penis) he has worked hard to construct. To execute Bardolph, then, is to execute the past, construct a difference, and transform a former penile "love" into a phallic/aggressive love. It would be a mistake, however, not to see that, both at Gadshill and at Agincourt, Henry's script satisfies the same will to power in the same theatrical fashion. The reason Henry must compulsively enforce with repetitive acts of violence the difference he is trying to construct is that the difference between these two wills to power inevitably keeps collapsing into a terrifying sameness: his repetitively repressed sodomitical stains keep returning no matter how many times he whites them out. Thus, no matter how many times he whips those offending Adams out of his domains, they have an uncanny way of returning, a return (a sameness) against which Henry defends by writing a history of his life and actions in which a deeply wished-for perfection fictively triumphs over the real.

In much the same way that Troilus' Cressida "is, and is not Cressida," Shakespeare's *Henry V* is, and is not a homosocial history, because it records not only the phallic, but also the penile, truth of Henry's life. And (if I may state my thesis before presenting supporting documentation) the penile truth about Henry's life is not just that Henry was an adolescent sodomite in his "bed-pressing" moments with Falstaff and others outside homosocial space, but that, as England's sovereign, he remains a sodomite *inside* this space. Fueling Henry's actions is the fact that although Henry presents himself (and must present himself) as a person who is free of the offending Adam, he knows this whipping has failed in one fundamental respect: his body is still full of sodomitical desires. The "barbarous license" (1: 2, 272) rumored about his past and officially declared to be a thing of a juvenile past is not just a thing of the past. And though everything Henry does in public appears to validate the claim that his desire has been entirely subjected to the desire of his phallic Christian God, in fact Henry's desire is not, and cannot be, the desire of this Other. He cannot scour this stain from his homosocial identity because it *is* his identity. As a result, he is no doubt terrified. He knows that (like Pistol) "he is not the man that he would gladly make show to the [w]orld he is" (3: 6, 81-82). He knows homosocial law condemns him. He knows that to *be* a sodomite (as Goldberg writes with respect to Edward II and Piers Gaveston) is "to be damned, a being without being." But "it is just such 'being' that [Henry] has" (Goldberg 1992, 121-22). Sodomy, in short, is Henry's treasonous subjectivity. To be Henry "like himself" is to be his God's and culture's worst traitor.[18]

As the French Ambassador's initial speech makes clear, the French know this to be the case:

> . . . the prince our master
> Says that you savor too much of your youth,
> And bids you be advised: There's naught in France
> That can be with a nimble galliard won;
> You cannot revel into dukedoms there.
> He therefore sends you, meeter for your spirit,
> This tun of treasure. . . .

KING:

> What treasure, uncle?

EXETER:

> Tennis balls, my liege.

(1: 2, 250-56, 259)

Tennis balls are "meeter for [Henry's] spirit" because, as the Dauphin's tun insinuates, Henry's body is gendered (in homosocial terms), not with lethal, phallic "gun stone" testicles, but with sodomitical "tennis balls": "You, Henry, are this tun, and what is inside this tun is, symbolically speaking, inside you; thus we present you with the truth of your sexuality in the form of tennis balls, and we do so as a mockery of your present homosocial, phallic pretensions." In short, a tun of French treasure has the effect of outing Henry not just as a former sodomite, but also as a present one, and does so in front of Henry's entire homosocial court.[19]

Henry tries to "wash [this sodomitical] mote out of his conscience" (4: 1, 169-70) by, for example, fighting and killing Hotspur. By rooting a too-hot political spur out of the body of England, Henry can be seen as trying, in displaced fashion, to root a too-hot libidinal spur out of his own body. Likewise, one could argue that, taken in and by itself, the fact that Henry digs up Richard II's body and reinters it in Westminster Abbey need suggest nothing more than guilt with respect to his father's usurpation, anxiety about his legitimacy, and a penitential effort to put things as right as he can; but in conjunction with a second curious fact, that Henry brings Richard II's body to Westminster and reinters it there with the body of Richard's wife, Anne, does suggest an attempt not only to compel Richard to assume his proper heteronormative identity after the fact, but to map onto Richard's royal body the same reheterosexualization that Henry must enact on his own.

But the task proves impossible. To Henry's despair, his homosocial desire to destroy his sodomitical desire fails. So, filled with fear, guilt, anxiety, he must have told himself that he was finished; that like Edward II, he, too, would lose his crown; that he, the son of the man whom God used to execute sodomitical Richard II, would be struck down; that he, the man who wanted to be, not sodomitical Edward II, but homosocial Edward

III, is Edward II. In desperation, urgent to be Edward III, Henry desires to be straight, but because of his desires, he cannot be straight. Not just a problem, this doubleness poses an insoluble dilemma, since as homosocial king it is Henry's duty to destroy sodomites—to train lethal gun stones (to use the play's imagery) against tennis balls—wherever he finds them. Henry's problem, then, is that he is, and yet he cannot be, a sodomite, and the plot as we have it, I am suggesting, traces Henry's compulsively repetitive attempts to "solve" this endlessly recurring, permanently insoluble problem without seeming to be solving any such problem at all. What applications of denial, repression, splitting, and projection will ensure the ongoing fantasy that his homosocially constructed desire not to be a sodomite will be able to make invisible, unconscious, and nonexistent his sexual desire to be a sodomite? By what means, that is, can Henry bring homosociality's lethal apparatuses of power to bear absolutely, and yet not bear at all, on his actual self? As we shall see, one effect of this doubleness is that every signifier attached to Henry has two signifieds; another is that every question a critic can ask about Henry's behavior has at least two contexts of explanation—a homosocial one and a sodomitical one.[20]

Consider Henry's remarks after declaring war against France:

> Either our history shall with full mouth
> Speak freely of our acts, or else our grave,
> Like a Turkish mute, shall have a tongueless mouth,
> Not worshipped with a waxen epitaph.

(1: 2, 231-34)

At first glance this claim that history will loudly and freely proclaim Henry a hero if he wins his war or forget him if he does not seems conventionally heroic, if oddly perturbed. Given a second, queer look, however, this boast also is stating a promise that Henry will control what is said about himself, and will do so by silencing anyone who could say anything other than what the official version shall speak with "full mouth." We may understand the "full mouth" / "Tongueless mouth" binary not only, that is, in the apparent sense noted above, but also as a defense against the anxieties bred by Henry's fear of exposure: Henry will literally remove the tongue from (will Turkishly "mute") any mouth which is in a position to expose him. And, by symbolic extension, Henry's act will ensure that never again will "tongues" (that is, penises) be in "mouths" (that is, orifices). In short, Henry's signifiers, oddly perturbed by the multiplication of their unsuspected signifieds, allow Henry to announce the "barbarous license" he must pursue under the guise of glorious war he will pursue. Henry wages war, that is, not only to become phallic (the homosocial and speakable context of his discourse), but to hide under the exigencies of

Pistol and Fluellen in Act V, scene i of Henry V.

honorable war the murder of anyone who could destroy this assumption of phallic stature (the sodomitical and unspeakable context). Henry's confidence is that no one will be able to see these homicides because, disguised as sovereign martial necessities, they will be wholly invisible. Thus, were we to ignore the perturbations by which Shakespeare's unspeakable history disturbs Henry's history of "Henry," Henry's "full mouth" would be the only mouth speaking his history (though not, thanks to the ironists, the only mouth valuing the consequences and effects of this history), and Shakespeare's unofficial history would become a tongueless mouth, *his* text a "Turkish mute."[21]

Whom does Henry murder? First Falstaff, as Nell ("the King has killed his heart") and Fluellen tell us:

FLUELLEN:

> I think it is in Macedon where Alexander is porn. I tell you, captain, if you look in the maps of the orld, I warrant you sall find, in the comparisons between Macedon and Monmouth, that the situations, look you, is poth alike. There is a river in Macedon, and there is also moreover a river at Monmouth. It is called Wye at Monmouth; but it is out of my prains what is the name of the other river. But 'tis all one; 'tis alike as my fingers is to my fingers, and there is salmons in poth. If you mark Alexander's life well, Harry of Monmouth's life is come after it indifferent well; for there is figures in all things. Alexander, God knows and you know . . . did, in his ales and his angers, look you, kill his best friend, Cleitus.

GOWER:

> Our King is not like him in that. He never killed any of his friends.

FLUELLEN:

> . . . As Alexander killed his friend Cleitus, being in his ales and his cups, so also Harry Monmouth, being

in his right wits and his good judgments, turned away the fat knight with the great pelly doublet. . . .

(4: 7, 31ff.)

What did Henry kill? A man who was to Henry what Cleitus, Alexander's sodomitical lover, was to Alexander. Homosocial critics like Richard Levin have enjoyed ridiculing Fluellen's method of comparison—the logical inconsequentiality of his comparison of "salmons" and "rivers"; but, of course, literal salmons and rivers and a literal comparison between them is not the point of Fluellen's wobbling exposition. By the logic of double signification operating in this text, salmons and rivers become simultaneously an innocent way of talking about two geographical regions, Monmouth and Macedon, *and* an extremely graphic way ("there is salmons in both") of talking about what Alexander had in Cleitus, and Henry in Falstaff, or vice versa—"Harry of Monmouth's life com[ing] after [Alexander's] indifferent well" (4: 7, 29-30). How did Henry kill Falstaff? By cutting him off cold. "I put my hand into the bed," Nell Quickly tells us, "and felt [Falstaff's feet], and they were as cold as any stone. Then I felt to his knees, and so upward and upward, and all was as cold as any stone" (2: 3, 21-24). Without desire, without love, the corpulent embodiment of sodomitical love becomes in death a symbol of what (from the perspective of homosocial space) it ought to have been in life, "as cold as any stone," just as Henry, in turning the fat knight away, himself becomes as cold as a stone. What Nell almost tells us, but does not, is that Falstaff's warm "tennis ball" testicles have also become cold stones. What she might have told us, had she lived, is that, in killing Falstaff, Henry creates the first of many "tongueless mouths."

Henry is stone cold nowhere more obviously than during the hanging of Bardolph. Here again (if we add the sodomitical to the homosocial context) a single signifier, hanging Bardolph, asserts two signifieds, Henry's official and his unofficial objectives. "We would have all such offenders so cut off," Henry asserts (3:6, 103). The official homosocial objective of this execution (as we saw above) is to cut Bardolph off as an "offending [thief] Adam"; the unofficial homicidal one is to cut Bardolph, like Falstaff, off as an "offending [sodomitical] Adam." But why "cut off" Bardolph by hanging him, and why the dark humor about his large red bulbous nose: "His face is all bubukles and whelks, and knobs, and flames o' fire, and his lips plows at his nose, and it is like a coal of fire, sometimes plue and sometimes red; but his nose is executed, and his fire's out" (3: 6, 99-103)? Officially, Bardolph is hanged because hanging is standard for thieves; but unofficially Bardolph's punishment, like Falstaff's, is symbolic in another register of signification. So if a homosocial Henry is satisfied to see Bardolph hanged as a thief, a defensively sodolethal Henry needs to see Bardolph's mortal, penile body grow stiff, his "head" become engorged with blood, his nose become even more penile than it was before.[22] It is not that Henry needs to see Bardolph executed; rather, he needs (as the text specifically asserts) to see that Bardolph's "nose is executed" as a symbolic surrogate for the erect, sodomitical penis itself. He needs to see the "sometimes [b]lue and sometimes red" head of an orgasmically twitching penile man snapped and turned cold, its fire put out, its mouth made "tongueless," its orifices "mute."

Scroop is a more difficult mouth for Henry to make tongueless, because Scroop is a more recent, a more visible "bedfellow" with standing inside homosocial space, and thus a more dangerous opponent, a mouth that could speak a more damning sodomy than Falstaff's or Bardolph's. For Henry to ask how he is going to hide the murder of Scroop is to ask how he is going to implicate Scroop in a plot along with Cambridge and Grey, so that the three can be exposed as traitors, and leave no one with grounds to suspect that, though three die as traitors, one also dies because he was Henry's lover.[23] It is also to ask how, in implicating Scroop, Henry made sure that Scroop would not prove rash enough to add slander to treason. Scroop's death is also a symbolic execution: Henry must see the stained homosocial head literally cut off, to see that same castration physically inflicted on another, on three others, which he, in a sense, is having to inflict psychically on himself: neither he nor Scroop will ever use his "head" again for pleasure. Without a head, Scroop becomes yet one more sodomite struck down by homosocial justice, one more "tongueless mouth" that cannot speak Scroop's or Henry's real name. It can be objected that all traitors of rank are beheaded, and thus that Scroop's beheading has no unusual symbolic significance. But this is exactly Henry's objective, to leave no trace: the invisible signifieds which Henry is concealing under the visible ones, treason/(sodomy), execution/(murder), escape detection because Henry makes the signifier of the closeted signified virtually identical to the signifier of the uncloseted one. In Shakespeare's text, however, a trace, a difference, is in fact left: Gary Taylor tells us that Henry's reaction to Scroop's betrayal is "so prolonged and excessive that it has almost never been performed in full" (1982, 45). My suggestion is that Henry's execution/(murder) of Scroop's treason/(sodomy) is almost never performed in full because to perform it in full would allow a scene to leave a trace which, when not performed in full, plays altogether straight.

Falstaff, Bardolph and Scroop are not, of course, the only sodomites destroyed in Henry's purge. Consider the boys who are killed guarding the baggage: "Kill the poys and the luggage?" asks Fluellen. "'Tis expressly against the law of arms. 'Tis as arrant a piece of knavery, mark you now, as can be offert" (4:7, 1-3).

Did retreating French soldiers kill these baggage boys, as the official version maintains? The French are in retreat, fleeing for their lives. Perhaps it is believable that terrified French soldiers might stop long enough and be cowardly enough to slaughter baggage boys as revenge, but would they have been able, under the circumstances of chaotic retreat, to kill *every* single boy even if they had wanted to do so? "'Tis certain," Gower tells us, "there's not a boy left alive" (4:7, 5). Henry, on the other hand, has a powerful motive to have every boy killed. If he is to disguise, as a French atrocity, the murder of the boy he knew in his Eastcheap life, and thereby create yet one more "tongueless mouth," one more "Turkish mute," Henry would have had to be absolutely certain that not a single boy survived, since a survivor's tongue could wag in the direction of English, rather than the alleged French, assassins. Henry's objective in staging such an atrocity is not just, however, that there would be no boy left to speak his crime; it is also that there would be no more boys to tempt him, or make him suffer unendurable pangs of desire for what he cannot any longer enjoy, or pollute his band of celestial brothers. For further evidence of Henry's involvement, consider the subsequent scenic juxtapositioning: Fluellen's and Gower's discussion of the slaughtered boys turns directly to a discussion of whether Henry killed Falstaff as Alexander killed Cleitus.[24]

At (4:3, 129-30), the Duke of York—next in succession once Mortimer dies—petitions Henry: "My lord, most humbly on my knee I beg / The leading of the vaward [vanguard]." At (4:8, 98-100), we learn that "Edward the Duke of York, the Earl of Suffolk, Sir Richard Ketly, [and] Davy Gam" are the only English dead "of name"—York and Suffolk being the only dead English nobility. So the play invites us to ask "why York and Suffolk are the *only* English nobility who die at Agincourt." And the play is constructed, I suggest, to provide an answer at 4: 6, 10ff., where we learn that by York's "bloody side, / . . . The noble Earl of Suffolk also lies":

> Suffolk first died; and York, all haggled over,
> Comes to him, where in gore he lay insteeped,
> And takes him by the beard, kisses the gashes
> That bloodily did yawn upon his face,
> And cries aloud, 'Tarry, my cousin Suffolk!
> My soul shall thine keep company to heaven. . . .'
> So did he turn, and over Suffolk's neck
> He threw his wounded arm and kissed his lips;
> And so, espoused to death, with blood he sealed
> A testament of noble-ending love.

This quotation, a considerably abbreviated version of Shakespeare's lengthy addition to Holinshed, is, I suggest, a test case of Alan Bray's thesis that it is not possible to tell the difference between male-male friend/lovers and male-male sex/lovers in early modern

England (1990). So we can ask: Is it merely a coincidence that the only two noble English dead "of name" are York and Suffolk? And is it a coincidence that it is York who petitioned Henry to lead the vanguard, or may we assume that York's desire became the desire of the royal Other as a result of the same sort of manipulative coercion which shaped Canterbury's desire to Henry's martial desire in Act One, and which will shape Katherine's desire to Henry's heteronormative desire in Act Five? To be sure, it is not possible to conclude with certainty that York and Suffolk were sex/lovers, or that they are being represented as such in this passage.[25] In the context of Henry's war, however, given that anyone who dies is a sodomite (since, by definition, phallic men do not die), York and Suffolk are nonetheless what Henry needs them to be: two more "tongueless mouths," two more dead lovers who will not remind Henry of his identity, and two more who, far from being "celestial spirits," will not populate/pollute Henry's English paradise or be included in Henry's "band of brothers."

In killing Falstaff, Scroop, Bardolph, the boy, York, and Suffolk, as well as the thousands of soldiers and prisoners who die (and a Dauphin who disappears) at Agincourt, Henry's motive is not just to purify England, not just to project his own sodomitical desire onto others so he can obliterate this desire in the obliteration of the sodomitical other, not just to remove temptations and witnesses, nor just to make impossible any history of his life other than his official one; Henry's motive is also to "prove" to himself that sodomites die—to "prove" that the homosocial God means exactly what he says ("no sodomite can suceed"). How can Henry persuade himself not to be what he is except by causing to happen to numerous sodomitical others that very fate which he fears will be imposed on him if he is not what he must be? It is in this respect that we understand why a victory that is not his God's would be valueless: such a victory could not "prove" what Henry needs to prove, that he is straight and that, among others, York and Suffolk are sodomites.

Critics have often pondered what Henry is doing during the night he waits for trial by combat/ordeal to prove his phallic identity. So we may also ask whether queer theory is able to illuminate Henry's disguised encounter with three common soldiers, Williams, Court, and Bates, or the briefer bracketing scenes, also frequently cut from performance, between Henry and Pistol, Pistol and Fluellen. At the outset of Act Four, the Chorus tells us:

> . . . O, now, who will behold
> The royal captain of this ruined band
> Walking from watch to watch, from tent to tent. . . .
> For forth he goes and visits all his host,
> Bids them good morrow with a modest smile. . . .
> That every wretch, pining and pale before,
> Beholding him, plucks comfort from his looks. . . .

> His liberal eye doth give to every one,
> Thawing cold fear, that mean and gentle all
> Behold, as may unworthiness define,
> A little touch of Harry in the night.

> (4: Cho., 28ff)

As numerous commentators have observed, we do not in fact behold any of this. Virtually everything that happens in the scenes that immediately follow this official account of Harry in the night contradicts the picture the Chorus paints. What we do behold is a disguised Henry who, going off (he says) to be alone, comes into contact first with Pistol, and then with three common soldiers, Williams, Court, and Bates. After a lengthy argument with the latter three turns into a heated quarrel, Williams and a disguised Henry each agree to wear the other's glove in his hat until they can meet and settle their differences. In a subsequent scene Henry asks Fluellen to wear William's glove in his hat. In a third scene, Williams challenges Fluellen, thinking him to be the disguised stranger he argued with in the night. Henry intervenes, acknowledging that he was the soldier with whom Williams quarreled, and rewards Williams by filling Williams's glove with gold.

These episodes are complicated enough to cause many directors to cut them, and many critics to wonder why Shakespeare filled his fourth act with such obscure material. If we set aside the content of Henry's and Williams's lengthy political/ethical argument as not irrelevant but secondary to the action taking place, and look instead at the relations of power and sexuality structuring the action of these scenes, we discover, I suggest, that Henry is out at night wandering among his troops for two contradictory reasons. This might be the last night he will be alive and, in his loneliness and anxiety, he is, I suggest, longing for illicit male companionship; he is also deeply worried that his men might be longing for the same thing ("a little touch of Henry in the night"). Henry has a terrible need for what he is afraid he will find: men, like himself, who are succumbing to the temptations of the penile body symbolized, in Henry's case, by the fact that he confronts these men not "like himself" but disguised by a cloak.[26] However, for his miraculous victory to transpire the next day, Henry must eradicate any possibility of penile weakness (anxiety, fear, doubt), and, more importantly, any possibility of sodomitical pleasures taking place between his men, as well as between himself and his men. So, when Henry encounters Williams, arguably a handsome enough young soldier for Henry to dally with (in contrast to the very brief, earlier exchange he has with Pistol), Henry must, if he is to live, transform his and Williams's powerful libidinal attraction to each other into homosocial anger and aggression (just as Katherine's libido is translated into aggression in the English lesson and wooing scenes). Hence the quarrel. Then, as a way of permanently fixing this translation of libido into anger and aggressivity, Henry symbolically reifies it. He moves Williams's glove—a symbolic surrogate for bodily orifices that fingers and penises may penetrate, as well as a symbolic surrogate for such penetrating appendages—from Williams's waist to his own cap, and he simultaneously moves his own glove, similarly symbolic, from his waist to Williams's cap. In this way, penile/sodomitical libidos and their bodily organs are sublimated and territorialized by being rewritten as tokens of exchange within that highly aggressive homosocial ritual, the challenge. In order to further defend against sodomitical desire, Henry then fills Williams's glove, not with semen, but with gold (here symbolic of phallic power) in order to transform penetration and filling from sodomitical to phallic acts. In short, the three scenes with Williams act out the ritualistic processes of phallicization that structure homosocial space itself. And by reenacting these constitutive formulae the night before Agincourt, Henry (in Foucault's formulation) *produces* aggressive homosocial bonding out of sodomitical libido. So if Henry is "thawing cold fear" as the Chorus proclaims, it is Henry's own fears and anxieties that are being thawed; and if anyone is getting "a touch of Henry in the night," Henry is making sure that it is an aggressive, and not a sodomitical one.[27]

But because desire is strong and repression "endlesse worke," Henry's sublimational alchemy must be compulsively repeated. In fact, the scene with Williams is already a repetition of numerous earlier instances of this process, particularly the first scene of this fourth act. Prior to meeting Williams, Henry plays out a brief version of this sublimational process with Pistol (a character, like Hotspur, whose name and "character" create dangerously incoherent conflations of penis and phallus). Rather than recognition, friendship or nostalgia at what may be the last meeting between these two Eastcheap friends, there must now be nothing but the safe lubricants of nonrecognition and aggression, as Pistol's cudgeled head learns yet one more time in 5:1, where Pistol is forced to play out this process in far more violent fashion with Henry's surrogate, Fluellen, a scene in which Pistol's eating of Fluellen's leek (a symbolic staging of fellatio) is visually translated into Pistol's symbolic submission to Fluellen's phallic correction, and in which a penis surrogate (a leek held at Fluellen's waist) is translated into a phallic surrogate (a leek in Fluellen's cap).

We are now in a position to ask why Shakespeare adds four captains—an Englishman, a Scot, an Irishman, and a Welshman—to the Henrician legend, given that none of these four are to be found in any of the chronicle sources. If these captains, like Henry's Eastcheap associates, disappear in criticism and in performance (as they disappear in Olivier's and Branagh's films) into a quotidian military mass, there is no point for Shakespeare's addition except to supply proof that support for Henry's war comes from every ethnic part of an allegedly unified nation. But if three of these captains are beautiful young men, then there is a powerful point to their diversity, their exoticism, their difference. Why would Henry not want to surround himself, at the moment he submits to homosocial law, with the most handsome *speci-men* in uniform he can find from the four quarters of his empire?[28] To love all and to be loved by all of his homosocial subordinates is the least he deserves in repayment for his suffocated desire. So why should not his "band of brothers" be an especially aesthetically pleasing lot, given that Gower, Jamy, and Macmorris, and the Welshman, Fluellen, are homosocial replacements in Henry's life for Bardolph, Nym, Pistol, and Falstaff? The question to ask, I suggest, is who is acting the part of Fluellen? And if the answer is Will Kempe, the actor who presumably played Falstaff, then the transformation of this actor's role from Henry's sodomitical to Henry's homosocial father figure is a particularly vivid theatrical visualization of the sublimational logic dominating Henry's behavior, a logic which transforms sodomitical libido not only into homosocial aggression but also into homosocial aestheticism. Of course, these captains can also be said to be evidence of a desperate hope surviving somewhere deep in Henry's psyche that the universal *sameness* demanded by homosocial Christianity might still have some room in it for heavily fissured differences, despite the necessity of having to be marked as same.[29]

From the perspective of those who do not want to witness, celebrate, or identify with Henry's victorious Christian/homosocial/heteronormative absolutism, Shakespeare's *The Life of King Henry the Fifth* is a tragedy, though, of course, it is also a "comedy" for those who, standing in homosocial space, need precisely to see, celebrate, and identify with such a victory. From a nonhomosocial perspective, the answer to the question, "Why is this history tragic?" is simple. Because thousands are dead. Because Henry, more and more threatened by every noncathected tongue, becomes more and more dependent on violence to perform his hyperideal identity. And because, as a result of this dependency, Henry's economy, psychic and otherwise (not to mention England's economy under Henry), inevitably degenerated into an economy of waste and decline which seemed to prosper only when it was at war, which is why Henry spent the rest of his life fighting "himself" in the fields of France.

Given such consequences, one must interrogate the cause of such a tragedy. Is it the fact that Henry is a sodomite? Would things have been different, that is, if Henry had been straight? If by "straight" one means homosocial heteronormativity, no doubt English homosociality would have gone on, nevertheless, in its own direction, and Henry would have been one more monarch hiding under his phallic identity a subjectivity riddled by autoeroticism, voyeurism, adultery, rape, pederasty, fornication, or some other sodomitical activity tolerable when hidden. But if by "straight" one means heteroromantic/reciprocal love/sex, then Henry would also have been in trouble. To be sure, had Henry simply been discovered as being straight in this sodomitical sense he would not have been executed, as Edward II was, with a red hot poker inserted into his anus, but he hardly could have commanded the respect, fear, and love of, nor could he have assumed or exerted sovereign authority over his homosocial peers. So to have kept his crown, a straight Henry (in this sense of "straight") would also have had to engage in something like the endlessly repetitive dissimulations of desire in which Henry is so thoroughly trapped.

But the larger point is that Henry's sexuality *per se* is not the cause of this tragic waste; Henry's sodomitical desire is not correctable, nor is sodomitical desire the problem Shakespeare's play is interrogating. The cause of the tragedy that is Henry's life is the cultural demand/ introject, "Be straight or die," and the homosocial formation which necessitates such a demand/introject. This cause *is* correctable, and it is the problem Shakespeare's text is analyzing. The solution to Henry's problem, that is, is not the sodolethal apparatus of power Henry brings to bear upon his desire displaced onto the other, but the removal of homosociality itself, its "Be straight or die" demand/introject, its identities, aggressivities, sexual roles, protocols, relations of power, monopolies, and histories. To solve Henry's problem, a culture must be created in which a person like Henry might do something more valuable with his energies and intelligence than construct himself as a celestial spirit, England as a fascist paradise and English culture as a happy band of Christian/homosocial brothers, and something more pleasurable with his sodomitical desires than make them fodder for sadomasochistic purgation or fuel for sadistic purifications. So, though it is true that homosocial productions and homosocial readings of *Henry V*—caring more for Henry and homosociality than they do for the thousands of lives they happily sacrifice on the altars of Henrician perfection—do "draw their audiences irresistibly toward the celebration of . . . power [based on] force and fraud";[30] it is also true that Shakespeare's *Henry V* was designed to draw its audiences away from "mighty men . . . in little room . . . mangling . . . their glory" (Epi., 3-4), and draw them toward that revisionistic assault on such power, force, and fraud which we now call democracy.

In *Misrepresentations,* Graham Bradshaw argues that "history never tells us what Henry's motives were, because it can't; in this simple but important sense a history play that pretended to make Henry's motives clear would be historically irresponsible" (1993, 46-

47).[31] I have been arguing, on the contrary, that Shakespeare's play makes a way to Henry's motives available, if not clear. There is in this text that which functions, in censorial circumstances, as evidence—a collocation of traces, coincidences, displacements, repetitions, overdeterminations, and juxtapositionings which register on a nonhomosocial audience. I have catalogued some of this collocation—this semiotic excess that Shakespeare added to his chronicle sources. That Olivier, Branagh, and others have had to cut so much of this excess in order to produce their versions of *Henry V* as homosocial masterpieces—and their Henries as sovereignty's best piece of poetry—suggests just how much of Shakespeare's play is irresponsible in Bradshaw's sense. Shakespeare's *Henry V* is and is not irresponsible, but, paradoxically, it is its irresponsibility that makes it so useful to some as history, just as it is its thoroughly coerced responsibility that makes it so useful to others as homosocial History.

Notes

1. Cho. 5; all citations of this play are from *The Life of King Henry the Fifth* (*Henry V*), Shakespeare (1972). I would like to thank the editors of this volume, Louise Fradenburg and Carla Freccero, for their careful editorial attention to the argument that follows.

2. Chronicle histories: Hall (1548); Fabyan (1559); Holinshed (1587); Stow (1580). Poems: *The Battle of Agincourt* (c. 1530); Baldwin (1575); Daniel (1595). For a discussion of the earlier Henry V plays, especially *The Famous Victories of Henry the Fifth* (1598), see Taylor (1982, 3-4).

3. Holinshed (1587), in Bullough (1962; 280, 408). For discussions of Tudor chronicles as history and the complexity of Tudor representations of Henry, see: Levy (1967); Kelly (1970); Smith (1976 3-26); Patterson (1989, 71-92); Hunter (1990); Rackin (1990); and Bradshaw (1993).

4. For a recent account of Henry's life, see Hibbert 1975; for an earlier account, see Wylie, 1914- 1929.

5. On quarto/folio differences see: Taylor (1982, 12- 26); Patterson (1989); Graham Holderness, *et al.* (1988); Holderness and Loughrey (1993). On censorship, see: (Hill 1986, 32-71); (Clare 1990). For a discussion of Shakespeare's relation to his chronicle sources, see Tomlinson (1984); Taylor; Walter (1954); and Bullough (1962). Taylor relates the critical controversy to the quarto/folio differences: unlike the 1623 Folio, the 1600 Quarto "removes almost every difficulty in the way of an unambiguously patriotic interpretation of Henry and his war" (12). Brennan 1992 shows that a longstanding stage tradition in which productions

are generally as heavily cut as the 1600 Quarto has had much the same jingoizing effect. In other words, the play's critics have *seen* remove from the play most of what Shakespeare added to the chronicle accounts.

6. Among those attracted to Henry: Wilson (1943); Walter (1954); Humphrey (1968); Aoki (1973); Sanders (1977); Berg (1985). Among those repelled: Gould (1919), (1969); Doren (1939); Goddard (1951); Rossiter (1961); Richmond (1967); Gurr (1977); and Barber and Wheeler (1986, 198-236).

7. Rabkin (1981). Rabkin was anticipated, in the play itself, by Pistol ("I love the lovely bully"); Nym ("the King is a good King . . . but the King hath run bad humors on the knight [Falstaff]"); Hazlitt (1817), who termed Henry an "amiable monster" [cited in Quinn (1969, 37)]; Traversi (1957); and Hapgood (1963, 9-16). Rabkin's lead was followed by Salomon (1980, 343-56); (Pye 1990, 13-42); Brennan (1992); and Bradshaw (1993).

8. As Rabkin (1981) implicitly recognized, the long-standing debate about *Henry V* was not so much a crisis created by ironic readings of *Henry V* as a crisis within the profession occasioned by the new discourses being used to produce such readings. Thus Rabkin's effort to negotiate a solution to the *Henry V* controversy was implicitly an attempt to resolve a methodological problem which was proving increasingly divisive to the profession.

9. The theoretical work on *Henry V* to which I am particularly indebted is that of Williamson (1975); Greenblatt (1981); Mullaney (1983); Dollimore and Sinfield (1985); Erickson (1985); Wilcox (1985); Czerniecki (1988); Leggatt (1988); Berger (1989); Rackin (1990; 1991, 323-45); Newman (1991); Helgerson (1992); and Traub (1992a).

10. Goldberg (1992, 145-75). Quinn (1969) cites the relevant passage from Hazlitt (1817, 37).

11. To read Shakespeare's text as sexualizing, materializing, and thus as historicizing its central character is not to read Shakespeare's Henry as a person; rather, it is to perceive Shakespeare's Henry as a theatrical analysis of an historical subject who is recognized as having been embedded in and conditioned by social processes that produced his sexuality as a function of his cultural identity.

12. In addition to Goldberg's, the queer theory to which I am indebted includes: Foucault (1976/ 1980); Irigaray (1977/1985); Hocquenghem (1978); Cixous (1981); Bray (1982 and 1990); Sedgwick (1985 and 1990); Butler (1990); Bredbeck (1991); Smith (1991); and Traub (1992b).

13. In *1 Henry IV*, Falstaff mocks Hal as a "dried neat's-tongue," "a bull's pizzle," a "stock-fish"— euphemistic expressions, David Bevington's glosses at 2: 4, 240-42 tell us (1987), which are designed to point out Hal's "genital emaciation"; Falstaff's larger objective, however, as Goldberg notes, is to "point to the phallus Hal lacks" (1992, 174).

14. Holinshed quotes Christopher Ocklund's (1580) *Anglorum Praelia. Ab anno Domini 1327 usque ad annum Domini 1558* (R. Neuberie for H. Bynneman): *"Ille inter iuvenes paulo lascivior ante"* [translated by Bullough (1962) as "Previously he has been somewhat wanton among the young men" (280)].

15. For an anthropological analysis of these predatory/ incorporative technologies, see Bloch (1982a), and Bloch and Perry (1982b, 1982c, 211-30).

16. It is not necessary here to outline the rise of intolerance which Boswell 1980 locates in thirteenth- and fourteenth-century Europe; Boswell's account is brilliant and well-known. It is necessary, however, to note that English homosociality became increasingly intolerant as the crown of England passed from Richard Coeur de Lion (1189-1199), to Edward II (1307-1327), Richard II (1377-1399), and to Henry V (1413-1422).

17. For recent alternative discussions of this matter, see Barber and Wheeler (1986, 227); Brennan (1992, 92-95); Bradshaw (1993, 294n26).

18. After Foucault (1976/1980) and Bray (1982), it has become conventional to distinguish between late modern homosexual *identities* and early modern sodomitical *acts*—the former category confining sodomy to an essentialized subset of the culture, the latter regarding it as a sin everyone is capable of committing. Recently, however, this distinction has been questioned by Bruce R. Smith, who observes that in Renaissance satire "the sodomite was a distinct type rather than a universal figure" (1991, 75-76).

19. Many critics of this scene conclude that the Dauphin is simply in error about Henry's present situation because he has not yet heard about Henry's miraculous reformation. However, the unofficial history we are watching encourages us to recognize that the Dauphin is not in error, that he knows the official myth articulating the pastness of Henry's past but simply does not believe it. The obvious reason, apart from needing something to carry them in, that the French Ambassador presents the tennis balls in a tun (*OED*, s. v. tun: a large vessel in general; a tub or

vat; a chest; Holinshed writes, "a barrel of Paris balls" [545]) is to get an insulting tub-equals-Henry analogy in the King's face. Much of the force of this insult is lost, however, if Shakespeare's tun is turned (as it is in the Branagh production) into a small, elegant box.

20. A particularly striking example of this double semiotic is Henry's relation to Salic Law. Why, we may ask, is Henry so troubled by a law that says "'*In terram Salicam mulieres ne succedant*'; / 'No woman shall succeed in Salic land'" (1: 2, 38-39)? The official answer is that if Salic law stands, Henry's claims on ancestral lands in France are invalid. But to recognize only this official, homosocial explanation would be to miss the less visible function of Salic Law in this text. In reading Salic law, Henry finds himself reading the handwriting on the wall, because for him this law bars possession of his inheritance in a sense quite different from the bar being asserted in public. For Henry, Salic Law is seen to stand as a restatement of the divine injunction against sodomy: "no sodomite shall succeed in homosocial land." Thus, for Henry to circumvent the visible law is, magically, to circumvent the less visible one. Moreover, to circumvent the invisible law is to put himself in the position, as we have seen above, of enforcing it: Henry will now ensure that "no sodomite shall succeed in homosocial space."

21. "Tongueless mouth" has, of course, other registers of signification. This passage alludes to the myth of Tereus and Philomela in Book Six of *The Metamorphoses of Ovid* (1955). The more obvious connection is a narrative one—Tereus, having raped Philomela, his wife's sister, responds to her threat—"I shall come forward before your people, and tell my story. If I am to be kept shut up in the woods, I shall fill the forests with my voice, and win sympathy from the very rocks that witnessed my degradation"—by turning Philomela into a tongueless mouth—"But even as she poured out her scorn . . . he grasped her tongue with a pair of forceps, and cut it out with his cruel sword" (162-163). The less obvious connection is the performative aspect of this barbarity: "The very acts which furthered [Tereus's] wicked scheme made people believe that he was a devoted husband [to Procne], and he was praised for his criminal behaviour" (160). A second subversive connection to *Henry V* lies in a common historiographical project: as Philomela, unable to speak Tereus' tyranny, weaves a tapestry which tells her story ("Cunningly she set up her threads on a barbarian loom, and wove a scarlet design on a white ground, which pictured the wrong she had suf-

fered" [163]), so Shakespeare's *Henry V,* unable to proclaim Henry's barbarity, weaves a text which tells Henry's victims' stories.

22. In the place of the conventional terms, *homophobic/homophobia,* I will be using *sodolethal.* I do so because a friend of mine asked why a term which voices the anxieties and fears of the aggressor should be used to mark the violent effects of these fears on the aggressor's victims.

23. For a valuable discussion of this scene, see Wentersdorf (1976). For discussions of the commonplace linkage of treason and sodomy, see Bray (1982, 70-80), and Smith (1991, 41-53). For a discussion of the sodomitical puns in the scene (as throughout *Henry V* and *1 & 2 Henry IV*), see Rubenstein (1984). Among the numerous entries Rubenstein indexes (324-25), see, in particular, "Bungle(hole), bungle Anus. . . . *Henry V.*" One part of this complex discussion must stand for the whole: a "'demon' (homosexual) . . . 'gull'd' (buggered) Scroop . . . (who, in turn, buggered Henry)" (39-40). The brunt of the entry in the *Dictionary of National Biography*—SCROPE, HENRY le, third Baron Scrope of Masham (1376?-1415 [11 years older than Henry])—is that Scrope's "complicity . . . in the plot . . . caused general surprise. It seemed strangely inconsistent with his character as well as his past career. He himself pleaded that he had become an accessory in order to betray the conspiracy (*Rot.Parl.iv.66)*" (1077). Is it possible, in other words, that Henry drew Scroop into this plot by "asking" his "bedfellow" to become an accessory, in much the same way that he had "asked" Canterbury to support war and Katherine to accept marriage, and then charged Scroop as an accomplice?

24. Henry also, of course, derives military value from this atrocity. What better way to redouble his soldiers' efforts at a moment of potential defeat than throw a war atrocity in their faces? Henry has already used one tactic to shore up their phallic valor—making them kill their prisoners—so by killing the boys he not only provides a justification for this command but also translates fear into outraged violence.

25. It is possible, for example, that Henry's imaginary constructs York and Suffolk as sodomites in order to justify killing York, a successor to the throne.

26. For antecedents for Henry's disguise, see Barton (1975). One antecedent Barton does not discuss is the Christian one. In Henry's homosocial space the chief paradigm for the ritualistic productivity of disguise is, of course, Christ. Coming disguised as the man Jesus into the night of the fallen world, Christ puts on, like a cloak, the penile condition

of man as a preface to the technologies of rephallicization by which he will rehomosocialize himself and the penile other through various forms of aggressivity against self and other. For a medieval parallel, see Fradenburg (1991, 240-41).

27. These scenes are also working in at least two other ways: Henry is making it absolutely impossible for himself to remain "disguised," and he is proleptically rehearsing during the night the transformation from disguised penile sodomite to victorious phallic sovereign he intends to actualize the following morning.

28. Four geographically distinct captains call to mind the imperial habit of articulating homosocial monuments with nude women, one for each corner of the empire: the Albert Memorial in London, for example, or the figures presently outside the Musee d'Orsay in Paris, or, earlier, the title-pages of Renaissance texts. The homosocial message is that empire harnesses sexuality as a means of producing civilization, even though this message is purposefully transgressed by an illicit exploitation of the colonialized subjects' sexualities. Equally relevant is the recognition that these sculpted nudes offer an illicit reward to the imperial gaze—i.e., dominance over the subjected other's sexual body. Cp. also the figures of Emetreus and Lygurge in Chaucer's "Knight's Tale."

29. Henry is so compulsive about transforming sodomitical libido into homosocial identity that he seems to have arranged events so that his miracle of Agincourt would take place on October 25, "the Feast of Crispian" (4:3, 40), a feast day celebrating two brothers, Crispianus and Crispinus, who, martyred A.D. 287, became the patron saints of shoemakers. But why this feast day? One answer, I suggest, is that in Henry's imaginary this day could be seen as celebrating penile brothers who become saintly brothers by containing their penile names ("-anus" and "-pinus") within their saintly phallic names (Crispianus and Crispinus) through the mediation not so much of their martyrdom as of their fetishized craft role, shoemaking. As saints, that is, one brother becomes an asexual cover (a "shoe") for the foot taken as a fetish substitution for the penis, while the other becomes an asexual surrogate for the anus taken as a fetishized receptacle (a "shoe") for the fetishized foot. As 'shoes' they no longer have a (visible) "-pinus" or "-anus."

30. Greenblatt (1988, 20). On "territorialization" see Deleuze and Guattari (1983).

31. Bradshaw is echoing Maynard Mack on the subject of motivation. To quote Berger "the essence of Mack's argument . . . is that since

characters are not only imaginary persons but also emblems, archetypes, and exemplars, motivation is beside the point" (1985, 224).

Works Cited

Aoki, Keiji. 1973. *Shakespeare's "Henry IV" and "Henry V": Hal's Heroic Character and the Sun-Cloud Theme.* Kyoto: Showa Press.

Baldwin, W., ed., 1575. *A myrroure for magistrates* . . . London: Thomas Marsh.

Barber, C. L. and Richard P. Wheeler. 1986. *The Whole Journey: Shakespeare's Power of Development.* Berkeley: University of California Press.

Barton, Anne. 1975. "The King Disguised: Shakespeare's *Henry V* and the Comical History," in *The Triple Bond,* ed. Price. 92-117.

The Battle of Agincourt. c. 1530. London: John Skot.

Berg, Kent T. van den. 1985. *Playhouse and Cosmos: Shakespearean Theater as Metaphor.* Newark: University of Delaware Press.

Berger, Harry, Jr. 1985. "Text against Performance: The Gloucester Family Romance," in *Shakespeare's "Rough Magic,"* ed. Erikson and Kahn, 210-29.

———. 1989. "What Did the King Know and When Did He Know It? Shakespearean Discourses and Psychoanalysis." *The South Atlantic Quarterly* 88: 842-62.

Berman, Ronald, ed. 1968. *Twentieth Century Interpretations of Henry V.* Englewood Cliffs, NJ: Prentice-Hall.

Bevington, David, ed. 1988. *Henry V.* New York: Bantam Books.

———. 1987. *Henry V.* Oxford: Oxford University Press.

Bloch, Maurice. 1982a. "Death, Women and Power," in *Death and the Regeneration of Life,* ed. Bloch and Perry. 211-30.

Bloch, Maurice and Jonathan Perry. 1982b. "Introduction: Death and the Regeneration of Life," in *Death and the Regeneration of Life,* ed. Bloch and Perry. 1-44.

Bloch Maurice and Jonathan Perry. 1982c. *Death and the Regeneration of Life.* Cambridge: Cambridge University Press.

Boswell, John. 1980. *Christianity, Social Tolerance, and Homosexuality: Gay People in Western Europe from the Beginning of the Christian Era to the Fourteenth Century.* Chicago and London: University of Chicago Press.

Bradshaw, Graham. 1993. *Misrepresentations: Shakespeare and the Materialists.* Ithaca and London: Cornell University Press.

Bray, Alan. 1982. *Homosexuality in Renaissance England.* London: Gay Men's Press.

———. 1990. "Homosexuality and the Signs of Male Friendship in Elizabethan England." *History Workshop Journal* 29: 1-19.

Bredbeck, Gregory. 1991a. *Sodomy and Interpretation: Marlowe to Milton.* Ithaca and London: Cornell University Press.

———. 1991b. "Constructing Patroclus: The High and Low Discourses of Renaissance Sodomy," in *The Performance of Power,* ed. Case and Reinelt. 77-91.

Brennan, Anthony. 1992. *Twayne's New Critical Introductions to Shakespeare: Henry V.* New York: Twayne Publishers.

Bullough, Geoffrey, ed. 1962. *Narrative and Dramatic Sources of Shakespeare.* London: Routledge and Kegan Paul.

Butler, Judith. 1990. *Gender Trouble: Feminism and the Subversion of Identity.* New York and London: Routledge.

Candido, Joseph and Charles R. Forker. 1983. *Henry V: An Annotated Bibliography.* New York: Garland.

Case, Sue Ellen and Janelle Reinelt, eds. 1991. *The Performance of Power: Theatrical Discourse and Politics.* Iowa City: University of Iowa Press.

Charnes, Linda. 1993. *Notorious Identity: Materializing the Subject in Shakespeare.* Cambridge: Harvard University Press.

Cixous, Hélène. 1981. "The Laugh of the Medusa," in *New French Feminisms,* ed. Elaine Marks and Isabelle de Courtivron. Brighton: Harvester Press. 245-55.

Clare, Janet. 1990. *"Art Made Tongue-Tied by Authority": Elizabethan and Jacobean Dramatic Censorship.* Manchester: Manchester University Press.

Czerniecki, Krystian. 1988. "The Jest Digested: Perspectives on History in *Henry V,*" in *On Puns,* ed. Jonathan Culler. Oxford: Basil Blackwell. 62-82.

Daniel, S. 1595. *The first fowre books of the civile warres betweene the two houses of Lancaster and Yorke.* London: Simon Watterson.

Deleuze, Gilles and Félix Guattari 1983. *Anti-Oedipus: Capitalism and Schizophrenia,* trans. Robert Hurley, Mark Seem and Helen R. Lane. Minneapolis: University of Minnesota Press.

———. 1987. *A Thousand Plateaus: Capitalism and Schizophrenia,* trans. Brian Massumi. Minneapolis: University of Minnesota Press.

Dollimore, Jonathan and Alan Sinfield. 1985. "History and Ideology: The Instance of *Henry V,*" in *Alternative Shakespeares,* ed. Drakakis. 206-27.

Doren, Mark Van. 1939. *Shakespeare.* New York: Henry Holt.

Drakakis, John, ed. 1985. *Alternative Shakespeares.* London: Methuen.

Dutton, Richard. 1990. "The Second Tetralogy," in *Shakespeare,* ed. Wells. 337-80.

Erikson, Peter. 1985. *Patriarchal Structures in Shakespeare's Drama.* Berkeley: University of California Press.

———and Coppélia Kahn, eds. 1985. *Shakespeare's "Rough Magic": Renaissance Essays in Honor of C. L. Barber.* Newark: University of Delaware Press.

Fabyan, Robert. 1559. *The Chronicle . . .* 4th ed. London: Jhon Kyngston.

The Famous Victories of Henry the Fifth. 1589. London: T. Creede.

Feifel, Herman, ed. 1959. *The Meaning of Death.* New York: McGraw-Hill.

Foucault, Michel. 1969/1972. *The Archaeology of Knowledge,* trans. A. M. Sheridan-Smith. New York: Harper and Row.

———. 1976/1980. *The History of Sexuality, Vol. I: An Introduction,* trans. Robert Hurley. New York: Vintage Books.

———. 1982. "The Subject and Power." *Critical Inquiry* 8: 777-95.

Fradenburg, Louise O. 1991. "The Wild Knight," in *City, Marriage, Tournament: Arts of Rule in Late Medieval Scotland.* Madison: University of Wisconsin Press.

Goddard, H. C. 1951. *The Meaning of Shakespeare.* Chicago: University of Chicago Press.

Goldberg, Jonathan. 1992. *Sodometries: Renaissance Texts, Modern Sexualities.* Stanford: Stanford University Press.

Gould, Gerald. 1919. "A New Reading of *Henry V.*" *The English Review* 29: 42-55. Reprinted in Quinn, 81-94.

Greenblatt, Stephen. 1981. "Invisible Bullets: Renaissance Authority and its Subversion, *Henry IV* and *Henry V.*" *Glyph* 8: 40-61. Revised and reprinted in *Shakespearean Negotiations,* 21-65.

———. 1988. *Shakespearean Negotiations: The Circulation of Social Energy in Renaissance England.* Berkeley: University of California Press.

Gurr, Andrew. 1977. "*Henry V* and the Bee's Commonwealth." *Shakespeare Survey* 30: 61-72.

Hall, Edward. 1548. *The vnion of the two noble and illustre famelies . . .* London: Richard Grafton.

Hapgood, Robert. 1963. "Shakespeare's Delayed Reactions." *Essays in Criticism* 13: 9-16.

Hazlitt, William. 1817. *Characters of Shakespear's Plays.* London: C. H. Reynell for R. Hunter: reprint London: Oxford University Press, 1966.

Helgerson, Richard. 1992. *Forms of Nationhood: The Elizabethan Writing of England.* Chicago: University of Chicago Press.

Hibbert, Christopher. 1975. *Agincourt.* London: Batsford.

Hill, Christopher. 1986. *Collected Essays of Christopher Hill.* Brighton: Harvester Press.

Hocquenghem, Guy. 1978. *Homosexual Desire,* trans. Daniella Dangoor. London: Allison & Busby.

Holderness, Graham. 1988. *Shakespeare: The Play of History.* London: Macmillan Press.

————and Brian Loughrey, eds. 1993. *The Chronicle History of Henry the Fift with his battell fought at Agin Court in France.* Lanham: Barnes & Noble.

Holinshed, Raphael. 1587. *The third volume of chronicles . . .* London: Henry Denham.

Humphrey, A. R. 1968. *Henry V.* Harmondsworth: Penguin Books.

Hunter, G. K. 1990. "Truth and Art in History Plays." *Shakespeare Survey* 42: 15-24.

Irigaray, Luce. 1977/1985. *This Sex Which Is Not One,* trans. Catherine Porter. Ithaca: Cornell University Press.

Kantorowicz, Ernst H. 1957. *The King's Two Bodies: A Study in Mediaeval Political Theory.* Princeton: Princeton University Press.

Kelly, Henry Ansgar. 1970. *Divine Providence in the England of Shakespeare's Histories.* Cambridge: Harvard University Press.

Leggatt, Alexander. 1988. *Shakespeare's Political Drama: The History Plays and the Roman Plays.* London: Routledge.

Levin, Richard. 1979. *New Readings vs. Old Plays: Recent Trends in the Reinterpretation of English Renaissance Drama.* Chicago and London: University of Chicago Press.

Levy, F. J. 1967. *Tudor Historical Thought.* San Marino: Huntington Library.

Marcuse, Herbert. 1959. "The Ideology of Death," in *The Meaning of Death,* ed. Feifel. 64-76.

Mullaney, Steven. 1983. "Strange Things, Gross Terms, Curious Customs: The Rehearsal of Cultures in the Late Renaissance." *Representations* 3: 53-62.

Newman, Karen. 1991. "Englishing the Other: '*Le tiers exclu*' and Shakespeare's *Henry V,*" in *Fashioning Femininity and English Renaissance Drama.* Chicago: University of Chicago Press. 95-108.

Ovid. 1955. *The Metamorphoses of Ovid,* trans. Mary M. Innes. Baltimore: Penguin.

Patterson, Annabel. 1989. *Shakespeare and the Popular Voice.* Cambridge: Basil Blackwell.

Price, Joseph G., ed. 1975. *The Triple Bond: Plays, Mainly Shakespearean, in Performance.* University Park: Pennsylvania State University Press.

Pye, Christopher. 1990. "Mock Sovereignty: *Henry V,*" in *The Regal Phantasm.* London: Routledge. 13-42.

Quinn, Michael, ed. 1969. *Shakespeare, Henry V: A Casebook.* London: Macmillan Press.

Rabkin, Norman. 1981. *Shakespeare and the Problem of Meaning.* Chicago: University of Chicago Press.

Rackin, Phyllis. 1990. *Stages of History: Shakespeare's English Chronicles.* Ithaca: Cornell University Press.

————. 1991. "Genealogical Anxiety and Female Authority: The Return of the Repressed in Shakespeare's Histories," in *Contending Kingdoms,* ed. Marie Rose Logan. 323-45. Detroit: Wayne State.

Richmond, H. M. 1967. *Shakespeare's Political Plays.* New York: Random House.

Rossiter, A. P. 1961. "Ambivalence: The Dialectic of the Histories," in *Angels with Horns.* New York: Theatre Arts Books. 40-64.

Rubenstein, Frankie. 1984. *A Dictionary of Shakespeare's Sexual Puns and Their Significance.* London and Basingstoke: Macmillan Press.

Salomon, Brownell. 1980. "Thematic Contraries and the Dramaturgy of *Henry V.*" *Shakespeare Quarterly* 31: 343-56.

Sanders, Norman. 1977. "The True Prince and the False Thief: Prince Hal and the Shift of Identity." *Shakespeare Survey* 30: 29-34.

Sedgwick, Eve Kosofsky. 1985. *Between Men: English Literature and Male Homosocial Desire.* New York: Columbia University Press.

————. 1990. *Epistemology of the Closet.* Berkeley: University of California Press.

Shakespeare, William. 1972. *The Life of King Henry the Fifth,* ed. Alfred Harbage. Middlesex: Penguin.

Smith, Bruce R. 1991. *Homosexual Desire in Shakespeare's England: A Cultural Poetics.* Chicago and London: University of Chicago Press.

Smith, Gordon Ross. 1976. "Shakespeare's *Henry V:* Another Part of the Critical Forest." *Journal of the History of Ideas* 37: 3-26.

Stow, John. 1580. *The Chronicles of England . . .* London: Ralphe Newberie.

Taylor, Gary, ed. 1982. *Henry V.* Oxford: Clarendon.

Tillyard, E. M. W. 1944. *Shakespeare's History Plays.* London: Chatto & Windus.

Tomlinson, Michael. 1984. "Shakespeare and the Chronicles Reassessed." *Literature and History* 10: 46-88.

Traub, Valerie. 1992a. "Prince Hal's Falstaff: Positioning Psychoanalysis and the Female Reproductive Body," in *Desire and Anxiety: Circulations of Sexuality in Shakespearean Drama.* London: Routledge. 50-70.

———. 1992b. "The (In)significance of Lesbian Desire in Early Modern England," in *Erotic Politics,* ed. Zimmerman. 150-69.

Traversi, Derek. 1957. *Shakespeare: From "Richard II" to "Henry V."* Stanford: Stanford University Press.

Walter, J. H., ed. 1954. *Henry V.* London: Arden.

Wells, Stanley, ed. 1990. *Shakespeare: A Bibliographical Guide, New Edition.* Oxford: Clarendon Press.

Wentersdorf, Karl P. 1976. "The Conspiracy of Silence in *Henry V.*" *Shakespeare Quarterly* 27: 264-87.

Wilcox, Lance. 1985. "Katherine of France as Victim and Bride." *Shakespeare Survey* 17: 61-76.

Williamson, Marilyn L. 1975. "The Courtship of Katherine and the Second Tetralogy." *Criticism* 17: 326-34.

Wilson, John Dover. 1943. *The Fortunes of Falstaff.* Cambridge: Cambridge University Press.

Wylie, J. H. 1914-1929. *The Reign of Henry the Fifth.* 3 vols. Reprint 1968. New York: Greenwood Press.

Zimmerman, Susan ed. 1992. *Erotic Politics: Desire on the Renaissance Stage.* New York: Routledge.

Camille Wells Slights (essay date winter 2001)

SOURCE: Slights, Camille Wells. "The Conscience of the King: *Henry V* and the Reformed Conscience." *Philological Quarterly* 80, no. 1 (winter 2001): 37-55.

[*In the following essay, Slights probes the historical context of Henry's conscience in* Henry V, *including his mediation between personal judgment and social obligation as King of England.*]

Since the celebrations of Shakespearean characters as portrayals of universal human nature have been largely silenced by scholarly attacks on the universalizing of the bourgeois subject, analyses of early modern representations of human life have risked an equally ahistorical projection of a postmodern fragmented subject onto early modern texts and have sometimes avoided attributing all meaning to originary subjects only by effacing human agency altogether. If we assume that reality is grasped through language, that there is no pre-linguistic knowledge, then we need to be wary of how we use our own vocabulary in analyzing early modern subjectivities and to look carefully at historical linguistic practice. As Anne Ferry has shown, sixteenth-century English had yet to develop a vocabulary for the analysis of internal experience. Such terms as "super-ego," "unconscious," and "emotions" are relatively recent developments, and words like "self" and "subject" were used in ways different from ours.[1] As Ferry observes, the closest term for continuous internal awareness available in sixteenth-century vocabulary was "conscience."[2] Thus when William Fenner advises, *"Let a man examine himself,* that is, his conscience," the appositional construction assumes that the self is the conscience.[3] Conscience was usually defined as the part of practical understanding that applies inherent knowledge of the basic principles of good and evil to particular actions, judging past actions and legislating future ones. According to the influential preacher and theologian, William Perkins, conscience "is (as it were) a little God sitting in the middle of men[s] hearts, arraigning them in this life as they shal be arraigned for their offences at the tribunal seat of the everliving God in the day of judgement."[4] Thus, in contrast to contemporary psychoanalytic discourse, which assumes a pre-moral psyche, Fenner assumes the inherently moral nature of the self.

While conscience signified moral self-awareness, it was also the efficient cause of political action. For example, John Speed observed of the Elizabethan settlement that "many that had fled the Realm in case of conscience, returned,"[5] and the plethora of books published during the 1640s and 50s with such titles as *The Ancient Bounds, or Liberty of Conscience* (1645) and *Against Universall Libertie of Conscience* (1644) demonstrates that, by the time of the civil war, "conscience" had become a code word for political controversy. In early modern England, then, conscience was a site where subjectivity and politics, ideas of salvation and of nationhood, were inextricably entangled. The representations of conscience in theological, legal, political, and literary texts provide significant access to the self-understanding of early modern selves and their social relations. By focusing on conscience in William Perkins's *Discourse of Conscience,* James VI and I's *Basilicon Doron,* and Shakespeare's history plays, particularly *Henry V,* I hope to illuminate tensions between individual judgment and obligations to authority within the concept of conscience that give us more precise understanding of religious and national identity in early modern England.

In Shakespeare's history plays, conscience is the nexus where internal self-awareness and external political action, the obligations of obedience and the authority of personal judgment converge. In *Richard III,* it performs a unifying function both structurally and politically. In the ruthless world Richard of Gloucester bustles in, most characters attempt to maintain or to acquire power and do so in defiance of their consciences. From Richard's sardonic announcement that he is "determined to prove a villain" (1.1.30), through his gleeful boast that he has seduced Anne with "God, her conscience, and these bars against me" (1.2.234), to the murderer's decision not to "meddle with it [conscience], it makes a man a coward" (1.4.134-35), the play directs our attention to characters' choosing to act against their own understanding of moral goods.[6] But, as Perkins warns, although sinning against one's conscience is common, finally the judgment of conscience is unavoidable: "as God cannot possibly be overcome of man, so neither can the judgment of Conscience being the judgement of God be wholly extinguished" (3). In *Richard III,* attempts to ignore conscience are futile. In Clarence's dream, the men he has betrayed return to accuse him. His murderer discovers that his conscience will not stay neatly packed away "in the Duke of Gloucester's purse" (1.4.128) and repents "this most grievous murther" (1.4.273). The murderers of the princes flee "with conscience and remorse" (4.3.20). King Edward, Hastings, Buckingham, and Lady Anne all face the accusations of their guilty consciences and repent shortly before death. Only Richard continues to deny his conscience. Lady Anne's report of his "timorous dreams" (4.1.84) alerts us that the "worm of conscience" has been gnawing at his soul as Margaret's curse predicted (1.3.221), and on Bosworth field Richard's guilty conscience is performed on stage as his victims haunt his dreams. But even as he acknowledges that "My conscience hath a thousand several tongues, / And every tongue brings in a several tale, / And every tale condemns me for a villain" (5.3.193-95), he dismisses conscience as "but a word that cowards use . . . to keep the strong in awe" and determines to let "Our strong arms be our conscience, swords our law" (5.3.309-11). Yet his desperate determination to carry on "pell-mell; / If not to heaven, then hand in hand to hell" (312-13) fulfills the curses to "Despair and die!" of his conscience-stricken dream. Richard's reckless despair, as well as the pattern of sin and repentance, illustrates Perkins' admonition that conscience cannot be extinguished. Those who "goe on in their owne waies against conscience," he warns, "after the last judgement, shall have not onely their bodies in torment, but the worme in the soule and conscience shall never die" (3).

At the end of the first tetralogy, then, the conscience that brings murderers to repentance and troubles Richard's dreams is the clear voice of God's judgment,

manifested in external events as well as in the individual soul. The psychic division of Richard's guilty conscience ("I love myself. . . . Alas, I rather hate myself' [5.3.187, 189]) epitomizes the condition of the nation itself, an England torn apart by the rivalry of York and Lancaster, "Divided in their dire division" (5.5.28). On Bosworth field, Richard is defeated and killed by Richmond, who has slept the sleep of the just, and by an army in which "Every man's conscience is a thousand men" (5.2.17). Richmond's final speech announcing the uniting of the houses of York and Lancaster and praying for lasting peace tells us that the clear consciences of Richmond and his army have been the means through which God's providence will heal the divisions of the nation.[7]

In *Henry V,* the end of the second tetralogy, conscience is again a central issue, but its presentation is more complicated and ambiguous. Instead of a pattern of parallels and contrasts, in which several characters are defined in terms of their adherence to their consciences, the conscience of Henry himself commands the audience's attention. While in *Richard III* political problems are treated as the consequences of sin, of individuals acting against their consciences, in *Henry V,* an opaque political world is the given, the field in which moral decisions must be made.

When King Richard just before the battle of Bosworth Field dismisses "coward conscience" (*R3,* 5.3.179), his echo of the second murderer's equation of conscience and cowardice reminds us of the universality of the moral economy: the decisions of king and hired thug are basically homologous. All people have consciences that tell them to do good and avoid evil, and for all the differences in rank and power and severity of sin, the rejection of conscience is a rejection of God and a maiming of self by king and commoner alike. In contrast, *Henry V* directs our attention to the differences between Henry's moral responsibilities and those of his subjects. He is not primarily a symbol of his country, the product and cause of its guilt, nor an Everyman working out his individual salvation. As a person, Henry has a conscience that directs and judges his actions as he moves towards salvation or damnation. As a king, he is supreme political authority whose decisions have direct life-and-death consequences for his subjects and a moral authority with responsibility for the spiritual health of his country. In the year that *Henry V* was first performed, James VI of Scotland published *Basilicon Doron,* dedicated to his son and instructing him in "*all the points of his calling, aswell generall, as a Christian towards God; as particular, as a King towards his people.*"[8] According to James, conscience is "the conseruer of Religion, . . . nothing else, but the light of knowledge that God hath planted in man," and he advises Prince Henry, "Above all . . . labour to keepe sound this conscience" by carefully examining it daily

(17). *Henry V* similarly focuses on a monarch's dual responsibilities as a Christian and a king. In *Richard III,* an England guilty of rebellion and regicide has produced and suffers under the guilty ruler it deserves, and with Richard's death exorcizes its guilt and produces a king who will heal the nation morally as well as materially. *Henry V* demystifies this symbiotic relationship, scrutinizing the conscience of a king who would also be his country's conscience.

From his first appearance, where Henry questions the justness of his claims in France, to his soliloquy the night before the St. Crispin's Day battle, where he struggles with a sense of guilt for his father's usurpation of the crown, Henry's conscience is troubled. Such doubts and anxieties are signs of an active, rather than an evil, conscience, and demand resolution before action. Perkins repeatedly warns that *"Whatsoever is not of faith,* that is, whatsoever is not done of a setled perswasion in judgement and conscience out of Gods word, however men judge of it, *is sinne"* and thus *"Whatsoever is done with a doubting conscience is a sinne"* (41). Henry refuses to proceed against France until he is fully persuaded that he may "with right and conscience make this claim" (1.2.96). And he does not announce himself "well resolv'd" (222) until he is assured that England will be securely protected in his absence. Similarly, in his restless anxiety the night before the battle at Agincourt, Henry does not, like Richard before Bosworth, recklessly reject his conscience in guilt and despair, but thoughtfully analyzes his moral responsibilities in debate with common soldiers. When the disguised Henry claims, "I will speak my conscience of the King" (4.1.118-19), the Riverside gloss of *conscience* as "honest opinion" does not fully register its self-reflexive force. As Perkins explains, when men use such expressions as,

> *In my conscience I never thought it . . .* they signifie that they thinke something or they thinke it not, & that their consciences can tell what they thinke. . . . For there be two actions of the understanding, the one is simple, which barely conceiveth or thinketh this or that: the other is a *reflecting* or doubting of the former, whereby a man conceives or thinks with himselfe what he thinkes. And this action properly pertaines to the conscience. . . . By it I conceive and know what I know.
>
> (7-8)

When Henry says, "Methinks I could not die any where so contented as in the King's company, his cause being just and his quarrel honorable" (4.1.126-28), the audience is to understand that he has examined his conscience and is at peace with himself.

The establishment of Henry as a king with an active conscience begins even before he appears on stage. In the play's first scene, the bishops of Ely and Canterbury describe the radical transformation of madcap prince into gracious king:

> The breath no sooner left his father's body,
> But that his wildness, mortified in him,
> Seem'd to die too; yea, at that very moment,
> Consideration like an angel came
> And whipt th'offending Adam out of him,
> Leaving his body as a paradise
> T'envelop and contain celestial spirits.
> Never was such a sudden scholar made;
> Never came reformation in a flood
> With such a heady currance, scouring faults.
>
> (1.1.25-34)

The emphasis here is on the intellectual nature of the virtue Henry has acquired—"Consideration" has effected the change and produced a "scholar"—and on the sudden totality of his conversion. These emphases signal that the king's sobering experience is not merely grief at his father's death but enlightenment and rectification of his understanding. Also, as Gary Taylor observes in his note to *reformation* in line 33, "The Protestant Reformation must surely have influenced the nuance of this word for Elizabethans."[9] Henry has acquired not only a reformed, but a proto-Reformation conscience.

While the concept of conscience was pervasive, it was also unstable. English Protestant treatises on conscience by William Perkins, William Ames, Robert Sanderson, and Jeremy Taylor all define conscience and its workings, substantially as Aquinas had done, as the human mind operating morally, but Reformation emphasis on salvation by faith alone and on the individual's unmediated relation to God modified the understanding of conscience. While Catholic theologians held that the conscience derives its authority from God and insisted that acting against one's conscience is sinful, they also emphasized that an individual conscience may be wrong, and dealt with the troublesome problems of "erroneous" or "doubting" consciences by maintaining that they should be corrected and resolved by the guidance of the church. In contrast, Reformed theologians insisted that conscience is subject only to God's word as revealed in Scripture. And, though they accepted the traditional view that all humans have consciences, they also insisted that only regenerate consciences are good consciences and that a regenerate conscience requires a conversion through faith. According to Perkins, "Regenerate conscience is that which beeing corrupt by nature, is renewed and purged by faith in the blood of Christ. For to the regenerating of the conscience, there is required a conversion or change; because by nature all mens consciences since the fall are evill, and none are good by grace. The instrument serving to make this change is faith" (44). The implication for Protestant thought of this linking of conscience and faith is that conscience functions not only to apply knowledge of God's law to particular actions, as it does in scholastic thought, but to judge the person as a whole.[10] As the sphere of conscience expanded from ethics to salvation,

Kenneth Branagh as Henry V and Ian Holm (far right) as Fluellen in Branagh's 1989 film version of Henry V.

its emotional dimension became more important—for Luther, as important as the rational dimension, according to Michael Baylor.[11] Perkins echoes Luther's understanding of the judgment of conscience as corresponding to God's judgment of the individual as a whole, and, while he defines conscience as a cognitive faculty, he too emphasizes its emotional effects—the shame, sadness, and terror of an accusing conscience and the confidence and joy of a clear conscience (39-41). Thus Huston Diehl's description of the Protestant conscience as an internalized self-disciplinary spectator should be qualified with acknowledgment of its empowering force. As she correctly observes, frequently "metaphors of sight and spectatorship . . . convey the inner workings of conscience,"[12] but metaphors of conscience as precious jewel, guide, compass, book, ship, and physician are also common. On a single page, for example, Perkins calls an evil conscience sergeant, jailor, witness, judge, hangman, and hellfire, and figures a good conscience as man's best friend, a continual feast, and an earthly paradise (74). Perhaps most significantly, he claims that "two notable effects" of a regenerate conscience are boldness and confidence and

echoes Luther in citing Proverbs 28:1 as a description of a regenerate conscience: *"The righteous are bold as a lyon"* (41).[13]

In *Henry V,* what David Kastan calls Henry's "characteristic idiom of moral certainty"[14] suggests the boldness of a regenerate conscience as described by Protestant theologians. But Henry is also specifically a medieval Christian, "a true lover of the holy Church" (1.1.23), according to the Bishop of Ely. In the course of the play, Henry moves from a position as a medieval king consulting ecclesiastical authorities on political policy to one as an English Protestant king who recognizes no higher political or religious authority. By portraying this change, *Henry V* explores the moral and political implications of the emergent Protestant conscience in sixteenth-century England.

One aspect of Henry's development is increasing independence. At the beginning of the play he is a young king accepting the moral and political direction of the church. In Act 2, stung by the betrayal of trusted friends, he manipulates them to condemn themselves. By Act 3 he is a battle-hardened warrior making agonizingly difficult moral choices—to fight on with his exhausted army, to refuse to set a ransom for himself, to agree to the execution of his old friend, and in Act 4 to order the killing of the French prisoners—and making them alone. With this growth in independence comes a display of interiority. When Henry in his first scene has "some things of weight / That task our thoughts" (1.2.5-6), he sends for advisers. In Act 4, he looks for solitude: "I and my bosom must debate a while, / And then I would no other company" (4.1.31-32). His sardonic reference to the vastly larger enemy forces as "our outward consciences" because they serve as reminders "That we should dress us fairly for our end" (4.1.8, 10) calls attention to the inwardness of his examination of his conscience in the two soliloquies that follow. In the first, Henry complains about, but does not consider shirking, the responsibilities of kingship. Although his description of the mindless complacency of his subjects is obviously inaccurate and unfair as a description of the men he has just been talking with, his analysis of the discrepancy between the king's two bodies—his physical vulnerability and mental anguish as a man and his power as a king—is tough-minded and accurate. His analysis of the emptiness of ceremony, as Norman Rabkin has pointed out, is as clear-sighted as Falstaff's of honor.[15] But the crucial difference is that, while Falstaff rejects honor, Henry does not reject ceremony. His attitude toward the ceremonies of monarchy reflects the Protestant attitude toward religious ceremonies: they have their uses but should not be idolized. King James advises his son to "learne wisely to discerne betwixt points of saluation and indifferent things, betwixt substance and ceremonies" (19) and to remember that "this glistering worldly glorie of Kings, is giuen them by God, to teach them so to pre-asse so to glister and shine before their people" (13). Similarly, Henry scoffs at ceremony as superstition—as an idol, a god eliciting adoration—but also understands that in social reality ceremony is "place, degree, and form, / Creating awe and fear in other men" (4.1.246-47), and he has no intention of rejecting "place, degree, and form" or the responsibilities they entail.

In his second soliloquy, Henry takes his problems of conscience directly to God, without the intervention of priestly authority explicating French law. Praying to the "God of battles" (4.1.289) to give his soldiers courage and confessing his inherited guilt from his father's usurpation, he illustrates the basic paradox of the emotional workings of the early modern Protestant conscience, the simultaneous presence of buoyant certainty and abject fear. Protestants stress the confidence of the regenerate conscience, but they also insist on its total humility. Luther, for example, argues that faith produces confidence that "the works which you do are acceptable and pleasing to God, whatever they may turn out to be," but also insists, "you can have the

confidence . . . when you realize that through these works you are nothing in His sight."[16] Within this frame of reference, Henry is bold and decisive at Agincourt *because* he knows that "all that I can do is nothing worth, / Since that my penitence comes after all / Imploring pardon" (4.1.303-5).

This internalization of conscience is expressed in a developing sense of nationhood. Henry's ambitions in France, which in the opening scenes are discussed in terms of family lineage and inherited right, by the battle at Agincourt have become a matter of national honor, transcending linguistic and class differences and uniting "a band of brothers" (4.3.60) in a common cause. Moreover, in assuming the moral authority of the church, Henry assumes responsibility to act as moral as well as military leader. According to James, God has made a king "a little GOD to sit on his Throne, and rule ouer other men" (12). Just as a king can learn "all the things necessarie for the discharge of [his] duetie, both as a Christian, and as a King" by looking to God, "seeing in him, as in a mirrour, the course of all earthly things, whereof hee is the spring and only moouer" (13), so a king should act as "a mirrour to [his] people . . . that therein they may see, by [his] image, what life they should leade" (34). A "King is not *mere laicus* [a mere layman]"(52); as conscience is "the light of knowledge that God hath planted in man" (17) so a king should be "a lampe and mirrour . . . giuing light to [his] seruants to walke in the path of venue" (42). As James recommends, Henry serves as a model to others: he inspires his army with his own courage, keeps his word to refuse to set a ransom for himself, applies the law impartially, and insists on attributing the English victory to God.[17] When scrupulous Fluellen, whose tag phrase is "in my conscience," wistfully asks whether boasting a bit about the body count is allowable, Henry agrees with a condition: "with this acknowledgment, / That God fought for us" (4.8.119-20). In Fluellen's response, "Yes, my conscience, he did us great good" (4.8.121), "my conscience" ambiguously both registers that in his *own* conscience he has accepted that human actions themselves are "nothing worth" and addresses Henry *as* his conscience.

But if the king was, as Kevin Sharpe says, "the conscience of the commonweal,"[18] Henry also clearly distinguishes individual consciences. In addition to his exemplary courage, integrity, and humility, the characteristic form Henry's moral leadership takes is the urging of others to examine their consciences. Even in submitting his own case of conscience to the bishops, he warns them that his trust that "what you speak is in your conscience wash'd / As pure as sin with baptism" (1.2.31-32) involves them in responsibility for the consequences of their advice. A similar motive to guide his subjects in the path of virtue can explain his stratagem to trick the traitors, Cambridge, Scroop, and Grey, to condemn themselves out of their own mouths and to repent their perfidy. Insistence on personal moral responsibility also informs his charges against the French enemy. He sends word to the Dauphin that "his soul / Shall stand sore charged for the wasteful vengeance" (1.2.283) and to King Charles that "the widows' tears, the orphans' cries / The dead men's blood" are "on your head" (2.4.105-7) and warns the men of Harfleur, "you yourselves are cause" of the threatened horrors (33.19). Most notably, he rejects the charge from his own soldiers that the king is responsible for the souls of the men he leads into battle: "Every subject's duty is the King's, but every subject's soul is his own. Therefore should every soldier . . . wash every mote out of his conscience" (4.1.17680). Henry is not merely evading responsibility and blaming the victim, but insisting that every person has a conscience accountable to God.[19]

Shakespeare's representation of the Protestant conscience is far more sympathetic than, say, Jonson's satiric portrait of Zeal-of-the-Land-Busy. From the perspective of the Reformation conscience, Henry's combination of self-righteous certainty and self-effacing humility, which has proved so disturbing to modern critics, does not appear as Machiavellian hypocrisy.[20] As king, Henry scrupulously examines his conscience, acts only when he has resolved his doubts, articulates profound awareness of the terrible consequences of his actions in innocent suffering, performs his duties zealously, administers the law justly, and inspires his subjects with a sense of national purpose. But without undercutting Henry's good intentions, the play also raises questions about the decisions themselves and the devious and violent means by which they are carried out and thus about the implications of the transfer of moral authority from the universal church to the sovereign state. Henry's assumption that he can both respect the individual consciences of his subjects and yet command their obedience exemplifies, as Kevin Sharpe observes, "the central problem of the early modern state: if conscience were the foundation of the duty of obedience to princes, yet conscience informed some subjects that the ruler acted 'directly against God', how could monarchy and the commonweal survive?"[21]

The most direct challenge to Henry's image as his country's conscience comes from the soldier Michael Williams the night before the battle of Agincourt. Williams is skeptical about the justice of the war and imagines the judgment the king would face for wasting lives for an unjust cause: "if the cause be not good, the King himself hath a heavy reckoning to make, when all those legs, and arms, and heads, chopp'd off in a battle, shall join together at the latter day and cry all, 'We died at such a place'" (4.1.134-38). More disturbing for Henry, however, Williams goes on to hold the king

morally responsible for placing his soldiers in a situation where they are unable to prepare themselves for death and judgment:

> I am afeard there are few die well that die in a battle; for how can they charitably dispose of any thing, when blood is their argument? Now, if these men do not die well, it will be a black matter for the King that led them to it; who to disobey were against all proportion of subjection.

> (4.1.141-46)

Henry presents two arguments to defend himself. First, by drawing an analogy linking king, master, and father, he argues that authorities are not responsible for the unintended consequences of their orders: "The King is not bound to answer the particular endings of his soldiers, the father of his son, nor the master of his servant; for they purpose not their death when they purpose their services" (4.1.155-58). His second argument is that each soldier is morally responsible for himself: "Besides, there is no king, be his cause never so spotless, if it come to the arbitrement of swords, can try it out with all unspotted soldiers . . . every subject's soul is his own" (4.1.158-77).

Henry's argument that he is not responsible for other men's souls provides the theoretical foundation for his speech at the siege of Harfleur, where he not only charges the consciences of the men of Harfleur with guilt for the terrible consequences of resistance, but by invoking the image of a soldier "With conscience wide as hell, mowing like grass / Your fresh fair virgins and your flow'ring infants" (3.3.13-14), he implicitly distances his own conscience from the savage latitude of his soldiers' in the heat of battle. By acknowledging the independent consciences of his soldiers and the capacity of the fallen human conscience to embrace hellish acts, he also admits limits to his moral authority and acknowledges that he does not embody a collective English conscience. Indeed he emphasizes his inability to exercise moral authority over his troops:

> We may as bootless spend our vain command
> Upon th' enraged soldiers in their spoil,
> As send precepts to the leviathan
> To come ashore. . . .

> (3.3.24-27)

Henry's speech at Harfleur, then, is consistent with his emphasis on each soldier's moral independence in his reply to Michael Williams, but it also reveals the inadequacy of his response to the problems Williams raises, revealing the oversimplification of his primary argument that a king is morally responsible only for the results he consciously intends. His analogy linking king, master, and father is familiar. Citing Cicero, James uses it to contrast a "good King," who is like a "naturall father and kindly Master," with a tyrant, who is like "a step-father and an uncouth hireling" (20). In both cases the analogy obscures important differences among political, familial, and economic relationships. First, Henry's claim of innocent intentions is simplistic. Although Henry may "purpose not their death" when he sends men into battle, he makes clear that he fully intends the "waste and desolation" (3.3.18) they commit. Of course, he does not actually subject the city's inhabitants to the savage violence he threatens. The violence of his language, in fact, is a successful tactic for avoiding the horrors he describes. Yet if Henry distinguishes his repugnance for "murther, spoil, and villainy" from the ferocity of "th' enraged soldiers in their spoil" (32, 25), he also insists that the decision to cause the "waste and desolation" is his to make and that he will make it without regret. After Agincourt he attributes victory to God, but when the crucial battles are yet to be won, he does not rely on the "God of battles," nor does he, like Richmond at Bosworth field, suggest that his forces will win because their hearts are pure and their cause just. He uses the threat of rape and rapine as a military tactic and announces his willingness to use them in fact. Far from being "the mirror of all Christian kings" (2.6), in which his people can see themselves in an image of virtue, Henry deliberately sets up "the blind and bloody soldier with foul hand" (3.3.34) as the mirror in which he sees himself: "I am a soldier, / A name that in my thoughts becomes me best" (5.6).

The play's foregrounding of the clash between Henry's image of himself at Harfleur releasing "the flesh'd soldier" to range "in liberty of bloody hand" (3.3.11-12) with his image of himself before Agincourt keeping watch "to maintain the peace" (4.1.283) dramatizes not the hypocrisy of a callous manipulator but the inadequacy of a concept of conscience as wholly internal good intentions. While the clergymen who advise Henry that his cause is just in order to protect the financial interests of the church show the limitations of a consequentialist morality, Henry illustrates the dangers of an intentionalist morality. The play presents him as genuinely convinced of the rightness of his cause and appalled by the horrors of war but unaware that, as Jeremy Taylor says in his monumental work on conscience written after the civil war, there are "social crimes, in which a man's will is deeper than his hand" and people are responsible for the crimes others commit in their name with their approval.[22] According to Taylor, although sin always involves some degree of choice, responsible choice includes diligent consideration of the consequences of one's actions, and people are responsible for the sins they foresee and cause but commit involuntarily.[23] Although Henry's defense relies on the concept of intention, Michael Williams has argued that the king is morally responsible for the unintended consequences of his actions, for imperiling the souls of his subjects: "if these men do not die well, it will be a black matter for the King that led them to it" (4.1.144-45). Like King James, Henry assumes that a king is responsible for promoting the spiritual as well as the material well-being of his subjects, but, although he acknowledges responsibility for the physical suffering and death consequent on his decision to invade France, he fails to accept responsibility for the moral and spiritual consequences for his men of his decision to fight at Agincourt against overwhelming odds. His advice that "every soldier in the wars [should] do as every sick man in his bed, wash every mote out of his conscience" (4.1.178-80) rings hollow after his vivid description of the bloodlust of "enraged soldiers" with "conscience wide as hell" (3.3.25, 13).

Henry's debate with his soldiers raises troubling questions about the moral responsibilities of subjects as well as of the king. Williams is unconvinced by the disguised king's self-defense and continues to express skepticism about his trustworthiness, but since he never argued that the sins of the soldiers who die unrepentant are somehow transferred to the king, he easily agrees that "every subject's soul is his own" and that no one can avoid God's judgment: "'Tis certain, every man that dies ill, the ill upon his own head, the King is not to answer it" (4.1.186-87). And he apparently concurs with John Bates's opinion that common soldiers are not responsible for judging the justice of the cause they fight for: "we know enough, if we know we are the King's subjects. If his cause be wrong, our obedience to the King wipes the crime of it out of us" (4.1.131-33). But Williams's pessimism about the possibility of virtue on the battle field and his belief that "to disobey were against all proportion of subjection" (4.1.145-46), opinions he shares with Henry, show soldiers in an impossible moral dilemma and reveal how attenuated the concept of volition is within an ethic of unquestioning obedience. Theorists of conscience present the same impasse, agreeing both that conscience dictates obedience to human rulers and that the law of God supersedes human authority. Perkins, for example, indignantly condemns "notorious rebels . . . that beeing borne subjects of this land, yet choose rather to die then to acknowledge (as they are bound in conscience) the Kings Majestie to bee supreame governour under God in all causes and over all persons" (37-38), and he is equally adamant that if human authority commands "things that are evill and forbidden by God, then is there no bond of conscience at al; but contrariwise men are bound in conscience not to obey" (34). Citing the locus classicus on obedience, Romans 13.5, *yee must bee subject not only for wrath, but also for conscience sake,* he comments, "Magistracie is indeede an ordinace of God to which wee owe subjection, but how farre subjection is due, there is the question" (26).

No one in the debate in Act 4 questions the extent of subjection, but the play raises the issue obliquely through the figure of the Boy. Shamed and disgusted by the antics of the "three swashers," Bardolph, Pistol, and Nym, the Boy concludes his catalogue of their cowardice and thievery with a complaint about their requirements of him and a decision to leave their service:

> They would have me as familiar with men's pockets as their gloves or their handkerchers; which makes much against my manhood, if I should take from another's pocket to put into mine; for it is plain pocketing up of wrongs. I must leave them, and seek some better service. Their villainy goes against my weak stomach, and therefore I must cast it up.
>
> (3.2.47-53)

In deciding to leave his masters, the Boy faces a case of conscience much like Launcelot Gobbo's dilemma of whether to flee from Shylock's service and the one Prince Hal poses to Francis. Launcelot Gobbo, who thinks of his decision as a psychomachia with his conscience advocating obedience to authority and "the fiend" encouraging flight, is irremediably caught between two evils, since his conscience tells him to stay with "the Jew my master, who . . . is a kind of devil" and "the fiend . . . is the devil himself" (*MV* 2.2.22-27). When Prince Hal challenges Francis, he puts the question in terms of courage and cowardice rather than of good and evil but also points the paradox involved in renouncing the service of a lawful master: "darest thou be so valiant as to play the coward with thy indenture, and show it a fair pair of heels and run from it?" (*1H4* 2.4.46-48). Like Prince Hal, the Boy sees the decision as a question of valor and, like Launcelot Gobbo, he understands it as a moral choice. But only the Boy is unequivocal that he must "seek some better service." None of these plays invites the audience to endorse the actual repudiation of a lawful master. Shylock willingly agrees to negotiate Launcelot Gobbo's change of service, and poor Francis does not understand the question much less attempt to act on the suggestion. The Boy presumably is killed in the French slaughter of the boys guarding the luggage before he can act on his decision, but his response to the "plain pocketing up of wrongs" raises the possibility of disobedience as a moral duty.

Henry V portrays with remarkable fullness the understandings of conscience current at the end of the sixteenth century. The Chorus's descriptions present conscience as the voice of God manifested in Henry as "the mirror of all Christian kings" shaping human history; soliloquies dramatize conscience as the fallible capacity for self-reflection in the individual soul's relation to God; and scenes of dialogue and debate dramatize, in the circumstantial particularities of human interaction, the conflicts arising from the tension between a concept of conscience as God's will always and everywhere the same and a concept of conscience

as private and individual. The play does not attempt to harmonize the unsettling resonances between Bates's principle that subjection removes moral responsibility and the Boy's visceral decision that he can no longer stomach following villainous orders. Similarly it does not reconcile the mercifulness of Henry's order to treat French civilians leniently and respectfully with the ruthlessness of his command to kill all the French prisoners, nor does it mitigate the emotional impact of the application of the order against looting in the execution of Bardolph. The primary effect of these unresolved problems, I think, is not to render the figure of Henry ambiguous but to engage the consciences of the audience with these doubtful cases. Gary Taylor suggests that the pattern of audience response in Henry's decision to invade France, to threaten Harfleur, and to kill the prisoners is to raise our suspicions and then to allay them, emotionally at least.[24] I would argue rather that in each case the play directs us to understand Henry's conscientious decisions but neither to condemn nor to endorse them. While Henry resolves his doubts, the play stimulates doubt in the audience. Joel Altman has demonstrated that imaginative participation in Henry's on-stage war allowed original audiences to play out the emotional ambivalences of the off-stage Irish war and to embrace the imperialist venture even while questioning its values.[25] Although Altman's analysis brilliantly accounts for the play's emotional power, I am skeptical that the theatrical sacralizing of violence he describes silences the questions the play raises, either about Henry's decisions or about their application to other times and places. That is, the interplay of choric commentary, soliloquy, and debate activates the consciences of the audience without offering clearly right answers to specific cases; the imaginative participation the play invites includes the engagement of our moral reason.

In particular, Henry's sense of monarchal duty, Fluellen's rigid adherence to law and precedent, Williams's stubborn integrity, and the Boy's planned rebellion suggest that the concept of the authority of the individual conscience may undermine national cohesiveness in a hierarchical social structure. His subjects' conscientious performance of duty, which is the foundation of Henry's power, is a potential threat to that power. Through his trick with the glove, Henry finds a way to enable Williams to keep his word and thus satisfy his conscience without violating hierarchical principle. But while this representational strategy allows the plot to move to harmonious resolution, it does not conceal the deviousness of Henry's stratagem or the suggestion that differences among individual consciences may create conflicts that cannot be reconciled. The Epilogue reminds the audience of the fortuitousness of Henry's victories—"Fortune made his sword" (6)—and of the bloodshed that follows in his son's reign when "so many had the managing" (11) of the state. That is history, already performed on the stage. It also reminds us, though not the play's original audiences, that in the future, within fifty years, England will bleed again when Royalists and Parliamentarians fight for conscience's sake.

Notes

1. Anne Ferry, *The "Inward Language": Sonnets of Wyatt, Sidney, Shakespeare, Donne* (U. of Chicago Press, 1983), Chapter 1.

2. Ferry, 45.

3. William Fenner, *The Souls Looking-glasse . . . With a Treatise of Conscience* (Cambridge: Roger Daniel for John Rothwell, 1640), 38.

4. William Perkins, "A Discourse of Conscience" in *William Perkins, 1558-1602,* ed. Thomas F. Merrill (Nieukoop: B. DeGraaf, 1966), 9.

5. John Speed, *The History of Great Britaine* (London, 1611), 832.

6. *The Riverside Shakespeare,* ed. G. Blakemore Evans et al., 2nd ed. (Boston: Houghton Mifflin, 1997).

7. I discuss conscience in *Richard III* in more detail and from a different perspective in *The Casuistical Tradition in Shakespeare, Donne, Herbert, and Milton* (Princeton U. Press, 1981), 68-79.

8. Basilicon Doron in *King James VI and I: Political Writings,* ed. Johann P. Sommerville (Cambridge University Press, 1994), 2.

9. *Henry V,* ed. Gary Taylor, The World's Classics (Oxford U. Press, 1994) 1.1.34n. In "The Hybrid Reformations of Shakespeare's Second *Henriad,*" *Comparative Drama* 32 (1998): 176-206, Maurice Hunt discusses attempts at reformation in *Henry IV, 1* and *2* and *Henry V* as Shakespeare's melding of Protestant and Catholic elements.

10. See Michael G. Baylor, *Action and Person: Conscience in Late Scholasticism and the Young Luther, Studies in Medieval and Reformation Thought,* vol. 20 (Leiden: E. J. Brill, 1977), Chapter 6.

11. Baylor, 209.

12. Huston Diehl, *Staging Reform, Reforming the State: Protestantism and Popular Theater in Early Modern England* (Cornell U. Press, 1997), 202.

13. Cf. *Luther's Works,* ed. Jaroslav Pelikan and Helmut T. Lehmann, 55 vols. (Saint Louis: Concordia, 1955-76), 25:400.

14. David Scott Kastan, *Shakespeare and the Shapes of Time* (University Press of New England, 1982), 64.

15. Norman Rabkin, *Shakespeare and the Problem of Meaning* (U. of Chicago Press, 1981), 47-48

16. Works, 360.

17. I am not suggesting, of course, the direct influence of *Basilicon Doron* on *Henry V.* The reference to the Irish expedition in the fifth chorus suggests dating the play in the Spring of 1599. James's treatise was written in 1598 in Middle Scots, and in 1599 an English version was printed in a very limited edition of seven copies. It did not become widely available in England until 1603 with the publishing of a revised English edition with an added preface. Sommerville, "Introduction" xviii. Also see Jenny Wormald, "James VI and I: *Basilikon Doron* and *The Trew Law of Free Monarchies:* The Scottish Context and the English Translation" in *The Mental World of the Jacobean Court,* ed. Linda Levy Peck (Cambridge U. Press, 1991), 36-54.

18. Kevin Sharpe, "Private Conscience and Public Duty in the Writings of James VI and I" in *Public Duty and Private Conscience in Seventeenth-Century England,* ed. John Morrill, Paul Slack, and Daniel Woolf (Oxford: Clarendon Press, 1993), 80.

19. Henry's evasion of responsibility is stressed by W. L. Godshalk in "Henry V's Politics of Non-Responsibility," *Cahiers Elisabethains* 17 (1980): 11-20 and by Richard Helgerson in *Forms of Nationhood: The Elizabethan Writing of England* (U. of Chicago Press, 1994), 231, 232. Dennis Kezar argues convincingly that *Henry V*'s distribution of guilt uses theological concepts to explore metadramatically questions of authorial function and responsibility. "Shakespeare's Guilt Trip in *Henry V,*" *MLQ* [*Modern Language Quarterly*] 61.3 (2000): 431-61.

20. Condemning Henry, as Harry Berger says, "is currently considered a sign of liberal chic." I want to demonstrate that focusing on Henry's conscience—its earnest humility as well as its self-righteous evasions—precludes the reductiveness of both sides in what Berger describes as "a tedious squabble . . . between Harry-lovers and Harry-haters." *Making Trifles of Terrors: Redistributing Complicities in Shakespeare* (Stanford U. Press, 1997): 250.

21. [See note 18].

22. Jeremy Taylor, *The Whole Works,* ed. Reginald Heber, rev. C. P. Eden (Oxford, 1854), 10:570.

23. Taylor, 10:611-16

24. "Introduction," 38.

25. Joel B. Altman, "'Vile Participation': The Amplification of Violence in the Threater of *Henry V,*" *SQ* [*Shakespeare Quarterly*] (1991): 1-32.

PRODUCTION REVIEWS

Robert Shaughnessy (essay date May 1998)

SOURCE: Shaughnessy, Robert. "The Last Post: *Henry V,* War Culture and the Postmodern Shakespeare." *Theatre Survey* 39, no. 1 (May 1998): 41-61.

[*In the following essay, Shaughnessy surveys stage and film versions of* Henry V *from the postwar period, evaluating the ways in which the interpretative principles of postmodernism increasingly informed these productions.*]

"Marketing, that mysterious part of the theatre industry, can produce surprising effects,'" observes Peter Holland in his recent book on Shakespearean production in Britain during the 1990s.[1] Discussing the material constraints on the repertory of the Royal Shakespeare Company, Holland cites the promotion of the 1994 production of *Coriolanus* as it transferred to the Barbican, which, knowingly addressed a "youth" market versed in the work of Oliver Stone and Quentin Tarantino. The RSC poster displayed a blood-soaked Toby Stephens in the title role, accompanied by the slogan "A natural born killer too." For an even more surprising and mysterious example of optimistically modish marketing, consider the tactics of the newspaper advertisement announcing the 1996 season at Stratford-upon-Avon. Avoiding any direct mention of Shakespeare, his plays, or theatre, it pictured an ominously darkened cloudscape, with slogans projected onto it, almost like skywriting. These posed a question, "Virtual reality?" and a riposte: "Try the real thing." This intriguing solicitation aptly summarized the RSC's current perception of its position as an organization dedicated to the production of Shakespeare's plays within the global multi-media cultural economy. On the face of it, this was a none-too-subtle attempt to expand and rejuvenate the RSC's audience base. Closer inspection reveals an antithesis between the virtual and the real that rehearses a well-entrenched opposition between the insubstantial, possibly worthless, even narcotic products of technological mass culture, characterized by banality and nerdish triviality on the one hand, and high theatrical culture, centered, inevitably, on Shakespeare on the other. It is equally evident that the exhortation to "try the real thing" evokes the qualities of immediacy, relevance, even danger, as well as those of authority and authenticity that have traditionally informed the company's work and provided its *raison d'etre.* The advertisement also offers a point of departure for a consideration of the relations between contemporary RSC Shakespeare and postmodernism. The opposition also implicitly differentiates between the modernist and postmodernist modes of cultural production or between

a conception of theatre as high art that (notwithstanding the populist aspirations of successive RSC administrations) has held sway at Stratford since the early 1960s, and what Fredric Jameson has famously termed the "cultural logic of late capitalism"; the logic, that is, of "consumer society, media society, information society, electronic society or high tech, and the like."[2] Much virtue in "virtual."

There is, however, some irony in this particular instance of RSC self-promotion. Even if we ignore the not-so-faint echoes of the slogan of the Coca Cola Company (purveyor of perhaps the central component of globalized culture), and leave aside the Pirandellian question of how theatrical performance has become the "real thing," it has become evident in recent years that the RSC's repertoire is no longer (if it ever was) separable from mass and media culture. Viewed within the frame of high culture, of course, the postmodern theatrical Shakespeare has begun to attract some critical attention.[3] Dennis Kennedy identifies the key characteristics of this latest phase of Shakespearean production toward the end of his history of Shakespearean stage performance in twentieth-century Europe and America. Contemporary Shakespearean production is, he argues, mesmerized by the rhetoric of the image, and what he terms "neo-pictorialism" is dominant. This mode is characterized by self-consciousness, intertextuality, baroque ornamentation, eclecticism, quotation, hybridity, and pastiche. It is typified by the Shakespeare productions of figures as diverse as Peter Zadek in West Germany, Ariane Mnouchkine at the Theatre du Soleil in Paris, Robin Phillips at Stratford, Ontario, and Adrian Noble at Stratford-upon-Avon. Kennedy observes that the *lingua franca* of late twentieth-century Shakespearean stage production carries the distinguishing marks of the postmodern, signaled by "a clear preference for the metaphoric over the metonymic" and "a trans-historical or anti-historical use of eclectic costuming and displaced scenery, creating, through irony, a disjunction between the pastness of Shakespeare's plays and the ways we now receive them."[4] In this essay I wish to explore further some of the effects of this pervasive sense of irony, displacement, and disjunction, first by offering a brief overview of the RSC's work in the 1980s and early 1990s, and then by means of a more extended discussion of a recent postmodern production, the 1994 revival of *Henry V,* directed by Matthew Warchus.

As a self-reflexive, stylistically eclectic and contradictory text, *Henry V* is already easily readable as a presciently postmodern work; it has, moreover, also become increasingly problematic in terms of its cultural politics. If Kennedy's sense of the "pastness" of the play can be extended to include not only the evidently archaic qualities of language, characterization, and ideology but its specific cultural histories, the pastness of *Henry V* is partly constituted by its contribution to the shaping of British national identity in terms of military conquest. As Kennedy notes, the postmodern Shakespeare is not simply a repertoire of stylistic devices, but operates within the context of postcolonial and intercultural Shakespeare, where, Barbara Hodgdon writes, the yoking of "divergent cultural materials and identities into pastiche, collage, and bricolage, is oppositional to the grand literary and theatrical narratives that would draw national and cultural boundaries around 'Shakespeare' and manage 'his' meanings."[5] But the 1994 *Henry V* demonstrates that, in the case of the RSC, the postmodern Shakespeare is constituted by relations between text and *mise-en-scene* that are governed and administered within national and cultural boundaries, themselves rather less secure than they might at first appear.

MOVING PICTURES

Before beginning a detailed discussion of this production, however, I need to establish its broader critical and theatrical context. In order to recognize the distinctive features of the postmodern RSC Shakespeare, it is necessary to set it against its modernist antecedents. The late 1970s were both a defining moment in Shakespearean performance criticism and a period of significant transition for the English Shakespearean theatre. If "neopictorialism" has become the dominant mode in the last decade-and-a-half, it was certainly not the future imagined for Shakespeare, particularly within performance criticism twenty years ago. In 1977, J. L. Styan proclaimed a "revolution" in both criticism and performance, and, declaring that "the straining towards a psychological and pictorial realism for Shakespeare" was "all in the past," confidently prophesied the revival of "the half-apprehended mystery of a supremely non-illusory drama and theatre."[6] This was apparently confirmed by RSC practice. The 1970s saw celebrated non-illusionist productions such as Peter Brook's *A Midsummer Night's Dream* in 1970, John Barton's ritualistic *Richard II* in 1973, and, on a smaller scale, Buzz Goodbody's *Hamlet* and Trevor Nunn's *Macbeth* in The Other Place in 1975 and 1976, respectively. Much of this was seen in another definitive RSC event of the 1970s, Terry Hands's 1975 production of *Henry V*. In 1977, RSC director Barry Kyle confidently declared that "there's a new simplicity, director's theatre is dead."[7] As almost everybody recognized at the time, the move towards the "poor Shakespeare"[8] of scenic austerity was more the product of a progressive squeeze on the company's funding than an application of the methods of Poel, Granville-Barker, Guthrie, Brecht, Grotowski, or Brook; nonetheless, the work of this period was in a tradition of twentieth-century Shakespearean performance which operated within the paradigm that Hugh Grady has identified as the "modernist Shakespeare" in that it aimed to offer "a

critical and Utopian alternative to instrumental reason and capitalist discipline."[9] The empty-space aesthetic of the 1970s was recognizably modernist, insofar as it was founded upon a metaphysics of presence, and upon the unity and hermetic self-sufficiency of both text and performance. The productions of the 1970s demonstrated a close convergence of theatrical and literary values, as the eschewal of illusion and spectacle appeared to be coextensive with respect for or trust in the text; these maneuverings, in turn, derived their immediate impetus from the rich (but also unstable) combination of E. M. W. Tillyard, F. R. Leavis, and Jan Kott that provided the critical and theoretical rationale for much of the RSC's work.[10]

But in the early 1980s it all changed. At the turn of the decade, the RSC took stock of its position in the cultural market-place and, as Terry Hands recalled (in terms which suggest a diversification of a portfolio of investments), "took a policy decision to go into spectacle."[11] Initially, the change of direction was signaled in Trevor Nunn's 1981 production of *All's Well that Ends Well,* which located the play in what Nicholas Shrimpton described as an "explicitly and persuasively Edwardian" social world.[12] The setting provided a context for a notoriously difficult play, offering a persuasive rationale for both Bertram's rejection of Helena and what emerged as her proto-feminist assertiveness. In retrospect, however, the scrupulous historicity of this production seemed more like an elegiac tribute to a vanished era of realist pictorialism (and hence, in itself a postmodern strategy of stylistic pastiche) than a clue to the future direction of the RSC. This kind of actualization of social settings as complete, coherent, and comprehensible reflects a positivist historiographical perspective which is in turn a product of enlightenment rationality. It declares a certain faith in the *grand recits* of history in that it attempts to substantiate the motives and behavior of Shakespeare's characters and to contextualize the action of the plays. A year later, however, the main-stage debut of director Adrian Noble and designer Bob Crowley established a different kind of postmodern pictorialism as the dominant form. In their 1982 *King Lear,* the specificity of historical reference that had underpinned *All's Well* was supplanted by a freewheelingly anachronistic and eclectic *mise-en-scene.* This appeared to range from the Austro-Hungarian empire to the nineteenth-century English music hall to contemporary Beirut, from the world of Edward Bond's *Lear* to that of Beckett's *Endgame.* It featured, Shrimpton recorded, "everything from Russian soldiers with sandbags to Japanese kendo fighters." Although Shrimpton thought this merely "whimsically diverse"[13] (the *Shakespeare Quarterly* reviewer similarly described it as a "hideous visual muddle"[14]), the production could be seen as staging the postmodern fragmentation and commodification of history itself as, to quote Jameson again, "a vast collection of images, a multitudinous photographic simulacrum," fueling the fantasies of "a society bereft of all historicity, one whose own putative past is little more than a set of dusty spectacles."[15] *King Lear* was followed, in 1984, by a *Measure for Measure* which, although apparently set in an eighteenth-century Vienna, featured an electric chair for the prison scenes and depicted Mariana's moated grange as "a Jazz Age villa on the French Riviera."[16] A "post-Falklands" *Henry V* followed in which fifteenth-century French aristocrats in black velvet and golden armor went to battle with an English army in anonymous combat fatigues which "inevitably prompted associations with the First World War."[17] Bill Alexander's *A Midsummer Night's Dream,* in 1986, "placed the court of Theseus in 1930s Mayfair, took the mechanicals from a 1950s beatnik espresso bar, and (despite lip-service to Arthur Rackham) based the fairy scenes on Cicely M. Barker's saccharine *Flower Fairies.*"[18] The culmination of this trend was John Caird's exuberant, and, as Stanley Wells put it, "brilliantly clever, consistently postmodern"[19] production of *A Midsummer Night's Dream* at the end of the decade, which treated the conjuncture of play and production as a huge metatheatrical joke. In this production, which trawled shamelessly through Anglo-American popular and high culture, as well as through the stage and screen history of the play, the stage was filled with scrapyard junk, delinquent fairies were dressed in heavy boots and shoddy gauze wings, and Puck was portrayed as a combination of "Just William, Bugs Bunny, Olivier's Richard III, Ken Dodd, Biggles, Groucho, Batman."[20] This was not only theatre about theatre; it was also a richly anarchic celebration of the relations between Shakespearean tradition and pulp culture.

Placed in its broader theatrical context, the neo-pictorial RSC Shakespeare of the 1980s and 1990s may well reflect the influence, not only of Euro-Shakespeare, but of the postmodern theatrical *avant-garde,* typified by the work of Robert Wilson, where, as Nick Kaye summarizes, the "gradual transformation and development of images which reflect and fold into each other . . . continually invites and at the same time seeks to displace particular readings."[21]

I would suggest, in addition, that the RSC's mutating house style owes as much to the influence of cinema. The mixing of styles, genres and periods is reminiscent of a number of postmodern cult movies of the 1980s and 1990s, such as Ridley Scott's *Blade Runner* and Terry Gilliam's *Brazil,* as well as of the "art house" films of Peter Greenaway (most obviously, the "neo-Jacobean" *The Cook, The Thief, His Wife, and Her Lover* and, of course, *Prospero's Books*) and Derek Jarman (*The Tempest* and *Caravaggio*). In the RSC's productions of the history plays, in particular, the juxtaposition of disparate periods deliberately confused the mythical past, fragmented present and imagined future, produc-

ing a weird hybrid of costume drama and science fiction. In Noble's *Henry V*, which has already been mentioned, the French appeared at Agincourt "on a gleaming, pennant-hung gallery which beams down on the stage with spaceship lights."[22] The awesome armor and weaponry of *The Plantagenets* (Noble's 1988 adaptation of the First Tetralogy) suggested a kind of medieval cyberpunk, recalling the milieu of *The Terminator* and *RoboCop.* In *The Plantagenets,* especially, the re-presentation of the Elizabethan "world picture" as baroque technological spectacle provided an analogue for the cyberpunk worldview characterized by Jameson as a vision of "the labyrinthine conspiracies of autonomous but deadly interlocking and competing information agencies . . . the impossible totality of the contemporary world system."[23] Increasingly, during the 1980s, Shakespeare's texts were read and presented in cinematic terms—the borrowings from, and references to, film culture proliferated, and stage productions drew upon its repertoire of images of the past as if these were the substance of history itself. Bob Crowley said of *Henry V* that "it was as though Shakespeare had composed the very first film script."[24] Maria Bjornson's monochrome design for the 1984 *Hamlet* depicted "a Jacobean film noir."[25] A world of movie gangsters and detectives was also evoked in the same season's *Measure for Measure,* according to Nicholas Shrimpton, with prison scenes conjuring "the State Pen circa 1930—a wall of grey bricks and an electric chair."[26] In Bill Alexander's *Merry Wives of Windsor* (1985), set in the 1950s, the cinematic references were even more overt: "characters rushed about . . . to incidental music in the manner of the Ealing Comedies . . . Dr. Caius became (to very good effect) a medical equivalent of Peter Sellers's Inspector Clouseau"; Nicky Henson's disguised Ford appeared "dressed in a Hollywood tough guy's trench coat"[27] (like Harrison Ford in *Blade Runner*). In Ian Judge's 1990 production of *The Comedy of Errors,* cinematic intertextuality activated the various layerings of illusion and artifice: the first scene "began in police-cell monochrome" for Egeon's narrative, but moved "at once from black and white to the Technicolor of Mark Thompson's shamelessly vivid set . . . the transformation to this surreal dreamscape was rather like that in the film of *The Wizard of Oz.*" (Peter Holland also caught hints of the Beatles' *Yellow Submarine.*[28]) Whereas during the 1970s, the square box of the Royal Shakespeare Theatre had aspired to the condition of the Wooden O, it now seemed to want to transform itself into the silver screen.

This sustained preoccupation with film culture on the part of the RSC during the 1980s and 1990s is one of the most visible ways in which the company's work has become postmodernized, and may well reflect increasingly pressing (although rarely openly articulated) concerns about the changing status of the theatre within media culture. Working upon the fair assumption that the bulk of the RSC audience will command a degree of cine-literacy which is likely to be considerably higher than their knowledge of literary, theatrical, or art history, easy-to-spot references to the film canon now function rather like Peter Brook's use of Watteau in his 1946 *Love's Labour's Lost,* or of Beckett in his 1962 *King Lear.* It is also important that the heyday of Styan's Shakespearean revolution, which supposedly saw specifically *theatrical* production situated at the center of Shakespeare studies, coincided with the arrival of the cheap video technology that decisively moved the teachings and criticism of Shakespeare-in-performance from the domain of the theatre into that of film and television. This has involved a shift from live performance towards a new set of texts—whether these are the canonical film versions of Olivier, Kurosawa, and Branagh, the dull but reliable BBC Television Shakespeares, or the more user-friendly animated Shakespeares. As public perceptions of the plays are increasingly shaped by their screen versions (which present their own hierarchies of definitive and variant readings), live performance seems to carry less and less conviction as the true or natural home of Shakespeare.

I suggest, moreover, that the combination of postmodern scenography and cinematic intertextuality is beginning to have a significant impact upon the way the text-performance relationship is perceived, and hence signals a significant shift in the RSC's use of Shakespeare. The old imperatives of faithfulness to the text and topicality, a conjuncture which Alan Sinfield has labeled "Shakespeare-plus-relevance,"[29] have given way to irony, knowingness, and, in some instances, to camp. If the half-empty spaces of the 1970s aimed to reveal the essential Shakespeare by stripping away what was extraneous and inorganic, the productions of the 1980s and 1990s reversed this process by situating the plays amidst a ludic proliferation of images, quotations, and associations. Increasingly, Shakespeare's texts might be said to be quoted rather than spoken; the act of interpretation is foregrounded. Rather than being located "in" performance (as in the modernist paradigm), the "text" of the postmodern Shakespeare is suspended alongside it in wry quotation marks. What this involves is a desanctification of the formerly empty stage itself—no longer evacuated and hermetically sealed from history, the Royal Shakespeare Theatre now acknowledges its permeable boundaries, acknowledges that it is as likely to register the traces of the mass media as any other cultural space. Even more disconcertingly, the typically postmodern playful refusal of depth, origin, and foundation may also threaten to dismantle the humanist subject of modernist Shakespearean performance. Benedict Nightingale observed of the 1982 *King Lear* that its visual inventiveness risked "substituting theatricality for truth of feeling." Robert Smallwood voiced similar doubts about the 1989 *Dream,* arguing that the relentless theatrical virtuosity eradicated both

character and genuine feeling: "the audience applauded a performer as they might applaud a magician doing his turn." Peter Holland criticized the 1990 *Comedy of Errors* in much the same terms. Appraising the production's essentially cinematic (or televisual) tactic of having the sets of twins each played by a single actor, he concluded that the inventiveness and ingenuity of the staging became far more important than the action of the play: "the history of the characters is replaced by the history of the performance."[30] This displacement itself signifies a postmodern rupture, between a depth model of self/character and a performative account of subjectivity.

A LITTLE TOUCH OF LARRY

There is much at stake here, I suggest: not only the "humanity" of Shakespeare in the broad sense, but, more narrowly and perhaps (for some) even more troublingly, Englishness itself as recurrent anxieties about the self-referential virtuosities of director's and designer's Shakespeare coupled with the perennial issue of the quality of verse speaking, reflect a deeper unease over the changing status of the Shakespearean text, and over the continuing viability of the cultural and national values that it supposedly embodies. It is here that we may turn to *Henry V,* a text whose own stage and screen history in the British Isles demonstrates the close relations between the reproduction of Shakespearean drama, the military adventures of the English/British, and the fashioning of national identities. The play's political significance lies not simply in its ostensible "relevance" to the historical and political situations in which it has been read, quoted, staged and screened, but also in its capacity actively to produce national history and patriotic myth. As Tom Healy observes, "whether extended by spectacle or depleted by cuts, the play has come to constitute the actual history of national comradeship which it purports merely to be culturally celebrating."[31] The most important twentieth-century version of *Henry V,* in this respect, is Laurence Olivier's 1944 film; and because they are central to the 1994 production, the implications of the dominance of this film text over the play's subsequent stage history need to be briefly addressed. Martin Banham has commented that "when thinking of *Henry V* many of us think first of the play as a film—Laurence Olivier's famous version"; Ralph Berry refers to the film's "dominant grip on the public consciousness." Both comments point to the profoundly ideological nature of its role within postwar culture.[32] As Berry has demonstrated, every stage version of the play since the war has taken its bearings from Olivier, especially, from the 1960s onwards, in the form of anti-heroic counter-readings, set in conspicuous opposition to Olivier's heroic and celebratory account of Henry and of Agincourt. The best-known instance of this is Kenneth Branagh's 1989 film of *Henry V,* which, as has been shown by a number of commentators, is locked into what Peter Donaldson characterizes as an Oedipal "intertextual rivalry"[33] with Olivier's film text; and which, Branagh declared, sought to liberate the play "from jingoism and World War Two associations."[34]

The point is that these associations are specifically focused upon Olivier's film. What I wish to emphasize here is the remarkable convergence of the cinematic strategies deployed in the film, the film's continuing ideological role within British culture, and the post-war stage history of *Henry V* itself. It is well known that the most spectacular (that is, the most purely cinematic as well as extra-textual) elements of Olivier's film (notably the setpiece battle scenes) have been the key factor in its particular potency in its first instance and its popularity ever since; and it has been recognized that this is where the film most clearly evidences "its patriotic application of the play to the current national crisis" and where it celebrates "the confident, militaristic emotions of 1944."[35] But as a number of commentators have argued, the film's ideology is less cohesive than it appears—in particular, the opening scenes at the Globe complicate (and possibly even subvert) the patriotic project. Of particular relevance here is Graham Holderness's emphasis upon the disruptive potential of the first, "theatrical" part of the film, which, he argues, "distance[s] the art of film from reality, displaying the artificiality of the medium in such a way as to qualify (though not, ultimately, to dispel) the passionate conviction of the patriotic emotion."[36] Importantly, this qualification, and the ambivalence which it articulates, are mediated through an interplay between the theatre and the cinematic medium (which itself is divided into variegated strata of realism and artifice, ranging from the non-naturalistic painterly codes of the French scenes to the epic treatment of Agincourt).

Yet this is not how Olivier's version has generally been received, and if it is the most spectacularly cinematic aspects of the film that have afforded it its enduring ideological potency, these have also been the source of its contentiousness. The lasting appeal of the film, particularly within the British context, lies in its continuing capacity to mobilize nostalgia for the Second World War itself (for which Agincourt is a surrogate), and for the ideals of national unity and purpose that supposedly obtained during that period, in the context of the dissolution of empire and declining military and economic power. This is what the post-war performance history of the play has had to contend with. And if this history of *Henry V* has operated within the framework of a dialectic between heroic and anti-heroic readings which are identified with and against Olivier respectively, then this history is also readable as a succession of exchanges not just with Olivier, but also between the cinematic and theatrical modes of Shakespearean production. This has been evident in the three previous RSC productions of the play. Working through the

related binary oppositions of heroic versus anti-heroic, depth versus surface, illusion versus non-illusion, myth versus realism, the productions of 1964, 1975, and 1984 all engaged with Olivier, to a greater or lesser extent, as a means of contending with the larger spectacular and patriotic theatrical, cinematic, and nationalist traditions that his film is held to embody, and, importantly, in order to assert the primacy of theatre over cinema. With the Vietnam War in mind, Peter Hall and John Barton's production of 1964 combated Olivier on various intertextual fronts: casting Ian Holm against romantic type as Henry ("his style is contemporary, there is nothing statuesque or declamatory about him," wrote Hugh Leonard); battle scenes which, according to Gareth Lloyd Evans, were "bloody, clobbering and unpleasant;" and signs of authenticity in the shape of smoke and mud, and dirty grey and khaki costumes. Juxtaposed with all this, however, was a Chorus who appeared to have just stepped out of Olivier: a "miniature by Nicholas Hilliard," as Robert Speaight put it, and dressed (like Leslie Banks's Chorus) in vivid yellow, he was conspicuously at odds with the rest of the production, and according to John Russell Brown, "was allowed to orate and make flourishes about a quite different play, as if the directors thought that all he said had to be ironically wrong."[37] Here was the myth, the rhetoric, the world of film; there was the reality, the world of the stage. The implication was that the theatre is more real, more true, more authentically Shakespearean than the cinema could ever hope to be. Rather than framing the world of the play, this Chorus was ironized by the insistent authenticity of the stage production. If this production evoked Olivier's patriotic iconography in order to dispute it, Terry Hands's 1975 production was both more detached and more conciliatory, even as it emphasized the ultimate superiority of live performance. As Hands saw it, Olivier had (necessarily, in the circumstances) suppressed the "doubts and uncertainties" in the play which his production sought to restore; more crucially, Hands aimed to reclaim the text from Olivier by taking "Shakespeare's theatre play par excellence" on its own terms, which meant that he could "abandon the artistic strictures of 'naturalist' theatre, with its cinematic crowds and group reactions."[38] But if Hands's approach repudiated the vocabulary of stage illusion (significantly elided with cinema here), aspects of his production actually seemed to reproduce Olivier's tactics. The most important of these was the decision to start the play in modern dress and in a mock "rehearsal-room" situation and then gradually, and partially, let it take on the trappings of illusionist representation. This removed the opening-out process in Olivier's film, particularly when considered in conjunction with Guy Woolfenden's musical score (that in places pastiched William Walton's score for Olivier), which provided a quasi-cinematic accompaniment to the action. The depiction of the French as figures trapped within highly formalized settings modeled on medieval miniatures was another obvious nod toward Olivier, and here articulated the opposition between the enemy and the English as an antithesis between pictorial artifice and three-dimensional theatricality. The French were afforded a similar treatment in Adrian Noble's 1984 "post-Falklands" production, which featured Kenneth Branagh in the title role, and which, as noted earlier, the designer Bob Crowley approached as a film script. I have already noted that in the staging, the French army appeared just before Agincourt as if on a descending spacecraft out of *Close Encounters of the Third Kind*. The night before Agincourt was even more memorably staged. The French aristocrats lounged upstage in glistening bronze armor, behind a trellis of golden spears, while the khaki and grey English huddled on the forestage. As Roger Warren observed, the moral "was absolutely clear: visual splendor must automatically be distrusted, while drabness must reflect the grim reality underneath the glittering surface of war, and the price in human terms to be paid for it."[39] The relative scarcity of overt references to Olivier in this production did not, however, mean that it was free of his spell. Ian McDiarmid's skeptical Chorus, who with blue bomber jacket and white scarf looked like an RAF bomber pilot, might well have been one of the "airborne troops" to whom the 1944 film was dedicated. But more significantly, a number of reviewers evoked Branagh's predecessor as the absent Other against which his portrayal of the king was to be defined. Francis King, for example, mused that, physically, he was "far removed from the romantic hero-king best exemplified by Olivier;" B. A. Young recorded that he was "no dashing hero leading his army into victory with Churchillian periods;" and Sheridan Morley wrote that "Branagh's Henry remains in some doubt about the wisdom of going once more into the breach, and his doubts are what inform much of the rest of an intelligently low-keyed reconsideration of a play that is in fact a great deal darker than Olivier's Technicolor version allowed."[40] Thus the anti-heroic made sense in relation to the heroic: because the terms do not negate each other but are interdependent.

DON'T MENTION THE WAR

Turning now to the 1994 production of *Henry V,* directed by Matthew Warchus and with Iain Glen in the title role, it is possible to see elements of this pattern repeating themselves. Comparisons were again drawn with Olivier. Nicholas de Jongh wrote that Glen "cuts a convincing new interpretative line" on a figure "whom Laurence Olivier made into a symbol of confident warrior glory," while Chris Peachment felt that, in the final scene, Glen (who in the battle scenes was like "an early Errol Flynn") "suddenly reveals a gauche, awkward man, far removed from Olivier's smooth seducer." More widespread, however, were the comparisons with Branagh (the film rather than the stage version): Benedict Nightingale concluded that Glen "avoids both Olivier's triumphalism and the post-Falklands ennui of Branagh;" Charles Spencer reckoned that he was "far sexier than Branagh;" while a more skeptical Russell Jackson felt that Glen's "straightforwardly heroic and fundamentally dissatisfying" performance "did not tell a story (as did Noble's stage production and Branagh's film) of Henry's personal journey to maturity and what the war cost him."[41] While it is the business of reviewers to draw such comparisons, the postmodern orientation of the Warchus production actively encouraged this through its tactics of pastiche, quotation, and reflexivity. There were many echoes of previous stage and screen versions of the play, but once again the most significant intertext was Olivier's film, seen in such elements as its overall color scheme—with azure skies and impossibly yellow fields recalling Olivier's Technicolor landscapes—the *Book of Hours* iconography utilized at Harfleur, the pennants fluttering overhead before Agincourt, and the woosh of arrows during the battle itself. One important opening-out in Olivier, the account of the death of Falstaff, was reworked. Whereas Olivier depicts the death of the knight in poignant detail, with Olivier as Prince Hal declaring his rejection in voice-over; Warchus juxtaposed the Hostess's description with a spotlight on Henry's face, "as if he knew telepathically what was occurring."[42] This was a rather cinematic touch, a flash-sideways rather than a flashback, which switched the focus from Falstaff's memory of his own rejection to Henry's prescient imagining of Falstaff's death. If, in Olivier's film, the demise of Falstaff marks the point of transition from theatrical to cinematic space, this juxtaposition afforded Glen's Henry a temporary panoptical authority over his subjects and over the stage world. The associative and disjunctive scenography tended on the whole to work in a manner akin to that of cinematic montage—this was appropriate enough, given that the vocabulary of the war movie continues to provide a primary means of structuring public perceptions of war itself. As in Branagh's film, the recurrent nods towards Olivier served to interrogate the film's martial and heroic rhetoric, although to a less emphatically "anti-heroic" effect. The key difference was that while Branagh countered Olivier with a fierce insistence upon the "reality" of political chicanery, of the blood and squalor of battle, Warchus appeared content to leave the ethical and political questions open.

I have suggested that the continuing appeal of Olivier's *Henry V* lies in its capacity to activate a kind of double nostalgia: for the fairy-tale feudalism it celebrates, but also for the wartime history which permeates the film, from the opening dedication to the troops onwards. In 1944, Olivier revisited Agincourt to anticipate the invasion of Europe, representing, as fantasy, what contemporary warfare ought to be. Viewed from the vantage point of 1964, 1984, or 1994, his *Henry V* shows us, again at the level of myth, dream, or fantasy, a nostalgic re-enactment of how it should have been. Re-viewing the film text as a historical document in the 1990s adds another dimension to an already intricate temporal structure. Warchus's 1994 production was well placed to address the nostalgia for the Second World War which has acted as such a powerful force in post-war British culture. The fiftieth anniversary of the D-Day landing was marked by ceremonials and media retrospectives on an unprecedented scale, and the business of collective commemoration figured very prominently in the production. The first image was of Tony Britton as Chorus, depicted, wrote Carole Woddis, as "a bluff old Remembrance Day Colonel, complete with fawn cavalry overcoat, walking stick and medals." With the house lights still up, he delivered the opening lines ("in the long-fossilised style of British Movietone News," wrote Irving Wardle), and then (following the gesture of Derek Jacobi's Chorus in Branagh's film) threw a heavy wall-mounted switch that plunged the auditorium into darkness and brought up the lights on the first scene. Audiences saw a medieval regal robe draped over a tailor's dummy, surrounded by poppies and enclosed behind low rope barriers, like a museum exhibit, or, Russell Jackson suggested, a film studio.[43] The juxtaposition of the historic and the contemporary, while a familiar tactic of postmodern pictorialism, was particularly resonant in this instance, because it established a concern with the function of history, and of historical myth within the present. As Peter Holland read the production, it "investigated the play as a series of overlays of history."[44] The broadly postpositivist approach to history was underlined in the production program, which contained a note on the play's cultural history by the historian John Ramsden declaring that "we are all relativists, reconstructing myths of the past for our own age." The temporal and stylistic juxtapositions which are generic to the postmodern Shakespeare here worked to emphasize the mythical and imaginative function of this representation of history—the modern-dress Chorus was set against the medieval figures of the English and French, a distinctly Dickensian Eastcheap gang, and a silent cohort of women and children in 1940s dress (the home front—Olivier's audience). For a few reviewers, the anachronisms simply suggested the universality of the play's concerns. As David Nathan put it, the staging conveyed "the eternal sameness of slaughter."[45] More intriguingly, the specific characterization of the Chorus had the effect of rendering the status of the events unfolding on stage teasingly ambiguous, with the Chorus supplying a frame which called the truth of the representation into question without offering a judgment upon it. Depending upon how you were disposed toward the play, its subject-matter, and old soldiers, the ensuing action could be read as a celebration, as an act of remembrance, as a dream, as false memory, as a patriotic fantasy which could be endorsed,

qualified or rejected; it could also be seen as an exploration of the functioning of the Agincourt myth within the national psyche.

This use of multiple time-frames produced one particularly fine, startling effect, which attracted little critical comment, oddly enough. During the climactic scene of the battle of Agincourt, depicted as a brutal and unwieldy slog on a steeply raked stage, Iain Glen as Henry slipped, almost fell and caught the end of the walking stick helpfully thrust forward by the Chorus, who had stood as a silent witness throughout. For a couple of beats medieval king and twentieth-century veteran stared at each other, frozen as icons, locked in an indecipherable tryst. History, memory, and fantasy collided in the moment, and the spectator was left to read this Wilfred Owenite "strange meeting" at whatever realistic, fantastic, or metaphoric level he or she wished.[46] Who was imagining whom here? Was it a timeless image of bonding and comradeship, Henry's premonition of an endless future of conflict, a miraculous intervention in history? Or was it a romantic re-imagining of the Chorus's own personal experience, alerting us to the ways that the myth of Agincourt has both mediated and been mediated through subsequent conflicts? The encounter could be read sentimentally, as an affirmation of universal comradeship. Alternatively, it could be seen as a radically disruptive moment, for the intervention which ensured Henry's survival actually secured the course of the history which the Chorus was now commemorating: the Chorus was actively making history happen. While the convergence of reminiscence and re-enactment is strongly evocative of another memory play dealing with warfare, Frank McGuiness's *Observe the Sons of Ulster Marching Towards the Somme* (which was, coincidentally, revived by the RSC in 1996), this impossible exchange between past and present has resonance which, perhaps rather unexpectedly, can be located in the wider context of popular film culture. The Chorus's anachronistic intervention in history aligns the production with an entire science-fictional subgenre of time-travel movies which began in the 1980s, from *The Terminator* through *Back to the Future* and its various sequels, *Bill and Ted's Excellent Adventure,* to *Twelve Monkeys*. With its implicit suggestion that this particular history of Henry V was a kind of self-sustaining loop, Warchus's staging of the encounter between King and Chorus offered an oedipal juncture reminiscent of the situation in *The Terminator,* where the time-traveling hero must ensure the survival of the child who is to become a future hero, or in *Back to the Future,* where the central character races to prevent his own extinction by securing the union of his parents. These are not entirely facetious parallels. As a number of commentators have pointed out, the time-travel genre articulates widely-held millennial anxieties about the supposed End of History itself, with progress, linearity, and purpose apparently evaporating—leaving, as I. Q. Hunter remarks of the genre, "no underlying pattern, only the unintended consequences of ambiguously intended acts."[47] In Warchus's *Henry V*, it was the integrity of the past, rather than of the future, that seemed to be at stake.

This scene of the battle was one of the most memorably staged, in a production that fluently combined the picturesque, the emblematic, and the metonymic. The raked-stage section upon which Henry's army battled with the French, at claustrophobically close quarters as if on the Raft of the Medusa, resembled a huge memorial stone. On it was carved the dates 1387-1422: the enactment of history co-existed with its commemoration as myth. Extras planted red poppies on the flat stage surrounding this platform while scraps of armor and weaponry hung overhead like dismembered bodies. This was typical of what Jackson called the production's "scattershot of associations." For the siege of Harfleur, similarly, "the stage became a noisy military building site" in front of a metal roller blind; after Henry's ultimatum this was raised "to reveal a stylized Gothic townscape out of a book of hours."[48] As The final scene was coolly framed within a pavilion-like open box. As this scene ended, everyone on stage froze in place, the Chorus returned to throw the switch again, arresting a moment of history as a *tableau vivant*. Such spatial disjunctions are, as Jameson observes in a different context, characteristic not only of the postmodern hyperspace of the city and the shopping mall, but, in a "new and virtually unimaginable quantum leap in technological alienation,"[49] of postmodern warfare itself.

The production displayed considerable sensitivity to the sentiments underpinning the D-Day anniversary celebrations, and in political terms it seemed to achieve the subtly nuanced even-handedness which had been sought in every RSC production of *Henry V* since the 1960s. As the instance of the encounter between King and Chorus indicates, the metatheatrical structure made it difficult to ascribe to the production any singular or determinate view of the play, its hero or its subject matter. For many reviewers (largely in the right-wing press), ignoring the more disruptive implications of the production's self-reflexive subtleties (which was easily done) allowed for a fairly straightforward reading of the play and production as exhibiting a "balance" between the heroic and the realistic. Nicholas de Jongh's view was that the text was played "as an epic of regal neurosis in the face of warfare rather than as complacent royalist propaganda;" Charles Spencer was glad that "having reminded us of the modern parallels, Warchus's production doesn't deprive us of the clanking armour and Plantagenet pageantry that are such an enjoyable part of the play"; and John Peter concluded that both play and production "should appeal to the disillusioned 1990s as well as the more solid certainties of the older generations." As always, much relied upon the portrayal

of the king, and most reviewers praised what they saw as Glen's thoughtful, charismatic, and complex Henry, which reconciled the oppositions informing both the play and our divided responses to it. This was aptly described by John Peter: "His heroism, his frank, manly behaviour with his soldiers, is the conduct of a born commander, but also of the cool politician. . . . His spontaneity is infectious; and yet there is also a deliberateness and a hard remoteness about him." This Henry adopted a monkish habit for his pre-Agincourt walkabout, carried out the execution of the French prisoners onstage, and yet was both ruthless and engagingly gauche in the "wooing" of Katherine. More worryingly, the production also provided the opportunity for the *Daily Telegraph* reviewer to dismiss "modish directors who hijack the show to demonstrate the horrors of war" and for David Nathan to take a swipe at "politically correct lecturers teaching peace studies at a polytec—oops!—I meant to say 'university.'" Although such comments simply epitomize the tendency of reviewers to find what they want to find in productions (Carole Woddis, conversely, saw the production as "a deeply moving lament of pacifist persuasion"), they also highlight the political ambivalence of the postmodern Shakespeare.[50] Adopting the characteristic tactic of foregrounding the processes of representation, the production might have displayed the political and ethical ambivalence which has been a critical issue in postmodern cultural theory; but as these comments indicate, it could be readily appropriated for a reactionary agenda.

Perhaps reflecting this, not all the notices were so favorable. For the *Guardian*'s Michael Billington, the production offered a dazzling array of visual effects but lacked both "a controlling vision" and a stable and coherent characterization of Henry himself: "each big speech becomes a distinct solo aria so that the terrifying address at Harfleur is treated as pure rhetoric and the inward meditation on ceremony is delivered with belting fortissimo." This view of Glen's performance may be difficult to square with the more positive accounts offered by other reviewers, but a more important point is that it shares with them a set of well-entrenched assumptions about Shakespearean performance that the move towards the postmodern may well call into question. Billington's criticism (which recalls the doubts about the 1989 *Dream* and the 1990 *Comedy of Errors* that I have already cited) rests upon a depth model of performance which is situated within the humanist tradition of characterization, and which, partly as a legacy of the modernist theatrical Shakespeare, views conspicuous stage spectacle as always potentially meretricious. The logic of the postmodern Shakespeare, however, suggests otherwise. It may well be that Glen's discontinuous and, in Billington's terms, superficial and effect-driven performance was, in the context of the production's visual iconography, entirely appropriate. In postmodern terms, after all, everything may (or may not) have quotation marks attached. Similar objections were voiced by Irving Wardle, who found Glen's Henry a "mechanical three-note performance," and who read the scenic juxtapositions as incoherent: the contrasts between "a heroic upstage picture" and "the down-to-earth floor" invited "a dialogue between the rhetoric and reality of war. But no such dialogue takes place."[51] These are familiar critical oppositions. A recurrent feature of reviews of the play during the post-war period has been the attempt to arbitrate the pro- and anti- views of Henry, of Agincourt, and of war in general by means of a distinction between the "rhetoric" and the "reality" of conflict—the one identified with the posturing of the Chorus, the other with the mud and blood of the battlefield. It is this distinction that informs the differing tactics of Olivier and Branagh. Warchus's production, however, dismantled this simple binary, so that the spectator was presented with (at least) two rhetorics of warfare—the rhetoric of heroism and the rhetoric of realism—with neither term privileged over the other. In this sense, the production was more concerned with the representation of war than with "war itself." Indeed, in the postmodern epoch, these terms have become increasingly difficult to disentangle. In an era of military actions so technologized, so highly mediated, so transformed into spectacle and virtual reality that, in Jean Baudrillard's controversial formulation, the 1991 Gulf War had not really taken place, being "a process of the extermination of war, an operational stage set of a fact, war . . . "realized" by sophisticated technical means,"[52] this distancing of the conflict itself had a certain cruel logic. Furthermore (as John Peter reflected in his *Sunday Times* review, citing "Edward Heath, Denis Healey, Enoch Powell and Tony Benn" as "the last generation of politicians whose experiences and beliefs were shaped by a great war"), the direct experience of conflict which has been a key factor in post-war political history has become the preserve of a dwindling (and now professionalized) minority. As a consequence, the relation of actors, audiences and critics to the subject matter of *Henry V* have become more vicarious than ever before. As direct experience of war has diminished, so too have the moral certainties and priorities associated with it. In the context of international peacekeeping, no subsequent conflict has enabled the English so unproblematically to render their own war-making as an affirmation of sovereignty, an act of national self-definition based on moral right.

If this is another (perhaps the primary) reason why the Second World War has retained its central symbolic importance within English culture for so long, then it is also a key factor in the history of *Henry V* in the same period. Perhaps this production, like the anniversary celebrations themselves, may come to be seen as marking a turning point. More than any previous production at Stratford, it was more concerned with nostalgia, memory, myth, and representation than with the physical realities of warfare. Although the anniversary celebrations of 1994-95 provided the opportunity yet again to recycle the cultural myths, they also may have signaled the beginning of the end of the "post-war" epoch itself. In the era of global capitalism, as the traditional boundaries of the British nation-state have, in economic terms, largely ceased to function, the mechanisms which have combined the integrity of the nation with the moral right of victory are no longer sustainable; it remains to be seen how *Henry V* can be (and of course will be) adjusted to this new situation.[53] If British cultural and national identities during the second half of the twentieth century have operated within the parameters generated by the events and aspirations of the wartime period, successive appropriations of *Henry V* have played a considerable part in keeping memories of that time alive. By drawing attention to the mechanisms that have maintained this nostalgia for so long, the 1994 *Henry V* may be seen not only as a postmodern production of the play, but as perhaps the RSC's first post-postwar engagement with it.

Notes

1. Peter Holland, *English Shakespeares: Shakespeare on the English Stage in the 1990s* (Cambridge: Cambridge University Press, 1997), 10.

2. Fredric Jameson, *Postmodernism, or, The Cultural Logic of Late Capitalism* (I.mdm: Verso, 1991), 3.

3. See, for example, Andreas Hofele, "A Theater of Exhaustion? 'Posthistoire' in Recent German Shakespeare Productions," *Shakespeare Quarterly* 43 (1992), 80-86; Johannes Birringer, *Theatre, Theory, Postmodernism* (Bloomington and Indianapolis: Indiana University Press, 1993), Michael Hattaway, Boika Sokolova, and Derek Roper, eds., *Shakespeare in the New Europe* (Sheffield: Sheffield Academic Press, 1994); Susan Bennett, *Performing Nostalgia: Shifting Shakespeare and the Contemporary Past* (London: Routledge, 1996); James C. Bulman, *Shakespeare, Theory, and Performance* (London: Routledge, 1996); W. B. Worthen, *Shakespeare and the Authority of Performance* (Cambridge: Cambridge University Press 1997).

4. Kennedy, *Looking at Shakespeare: A Visual History of Twentieth-Century Performance* (Cambridge: Cambridge University Press, 1993).

5. Barbara Hodgdon, "Looking for Mr. Shakespeare after 'The Revolution': Robert Lepage's Intercultural Dream Machine," in Bulman, *Shakespeare, Theory, and Performance,* 81.

6. Styan, *The Shakespeare Revolution: Criticism and Performance in the Twentieth Century* (Cambridge: Cambridge University Press, 1977), 232-33.

7. Quoted in Jim Hiley, "A Company with Direction," *Plays and Players,* October 1977.

8. See Peter Thomson, "Towards a Poor Shakespeare: The Royal Shakespeare Company at Stratford in 1975," *Shakespeare Survey* 29 (1976), 151-56.

9. Grady, *The Modernist Shakespeare: Critical Texts in a Material World* (Oxford: The Clarendon Press, 1991).

10. Accounts of the critical influences upon the RSC's work are given by Alan Sinfield, "Royal Shakespeare: Theatre and the Making of Ideology," in Jonathan Dollimore and Alan Sinfield eds., *Political Shakespeare: New Essays in Cultural Materialism* (Manchester: Manchester University Press, 1985), 158-81; Christopher J. McCullough, "The Cambridge Connection: Towards a Materialist Theatre Practice," in Graham Holderness, ed., *The Shakespeare Myth* (Manchester: Manchester University Press, 1988), 1, 12-21; and Robert Shaughnessy, *Representing Shakespeare: England, History and the RSC* (Hemel Hempstead: Harvester Wheatsheaf, 1994).

11. Quoted in Michael Coveney, "Terry Hands, Adrian Noble and Peter Hall, Masters of the RSC, Talk Theatre," *Observer,* 28 June 1992.

12. Nicholas Shrimpton, "Shakespeare Performances in Stratford-upon-Avon and London, 1981-82," *Shakespeare Survey* 36 (1983), 149.

13. Ibid, 152.

14. Roger Warren, "Shakespeare in Stratford and London, 1982," *Shakespeare Quarterly* 34 (1983), 85.

15. Jameson, *Postmodernism,* 18.

16. Shrimpton, "Shakespeare Performances in Stratford-upon-Avon and London, 1983-4," *Shakespeare Survey* 38 (1985), 202.

17. Ibid, 204.

18. Shrimpton, "Shakespeare Performances in London, Manchester and Stratford-upon-Avon 1985-," *Shakespeare Survey* 40 (1988), 173.

19. Wells, "Shakespeare Production in England in 1989," *Shakespeare Survey* 43 (1990), 200.

20. Robert Smallwood, "Shakespeare at Stratford-upon-Avon, 1989 (Part I)," *Shakespeare Quarterly* 41 (1990), 109.

21. Nick Kaye, *Postmodernism and Performance* (Basingstoke: Macmillan, 1994), 68-69.

22. Martin Cropper, *The Times,* 15 May 1985.

23. Jameson, *Postmodernism,* 38.

24. Quoted in "Set Pieces That Release the Forces of Darkness," *Guardian,* 17 April 1984.

25. Kennedy, *Looking at Shakespeare,* 294.

26. Shrimpton, "Shakespeare Performances 1983-4," 202.

27. Shrimpton, "Shakespeare Performances in London and Stratford-upon-Avon 1984-5," *Shakespeare Survey* 39 (1986), 197-99.

28. Smallwood, "Shakespeare at Stratford-upon-Avon, 1990," *Shakespeare Quarterly* 42 (1991), 348; Holland, "Shakespeare Performances in England, 1989-90," *Shakespeare Survey* 44 (1991), 176.

29. Sinfield, "Royal Shakespeare," 159.

30. Nightingale, *New Statesman,* 1 June 1982; Smallwood, "Shakespeare at Stratford upon-Avon, 1989," 108; Holland, "Shakespeare Performances in England, 1989-90," 176.

31. Healy, "Remembering with Advantages; Nation and Ideology in *Henry V,*" in Hattaway et al., *Shakespeare in the New Europe,* 181.

32. Banham, "BBC Television's Dull Shakespeares," *Critical Quarterly* 22, 1 (1980), 31; Berry, *Changing Styles in Shakespeare* (London: Allen and Unwin, 1981), 67.

33. Donaldson, "Taking on Shakespeare: Kenneth Branagh's *Henry V,*" *Shakespeare Quarterly* 42 (1991), 61.

34. Quoted in *The Times,* 5 October 1989.

35. Graham Holderness, *Shakespeare Recycled: The Making of Historical Drama* (Hemel Hempstead: Harvester Wheatsheaf, 1992), 184.

36. Ibid, 185.

37. Leonard, *Plays and Players,* August 1965; Lloyd Evans, "Shakespeare, the Twentieth Century and 'Behaviourism,'" *Shakespeare Survey* 20 (1967), 139; Speaight, "Shakespeare in Britain," *Shakespeare Quarterly* 15 (1964), 387; Brown, "Three Kinds of Shakespeare: 1964 Productions in London, Stratford-upon-Avon and Edinburgh," *Shakespeare Survey* 18 (1965),151.

38. Hands, "Introduction to the Play," in Sally Beaumann, ed, *The Royal Shakespeare Company's Centenary Production of Henry V* (Oxford: Pergamon Press, 1976), 15-16.

39. Warren, "Shakespeare in Britain," *Shakespeare Quarterly* 36 (1985), 81.

40. King, *Sunday Telegraph,* 19 May 1985; Young, *Financial Times,* 17 May 1985; Morley, *Punch,* 29 May 1985.

41. De Jongh, *Evening Standard,* 11 May 1994; Peachment, *Sunday Telegraph,* 15 May 1994; Nightingale, *The Times,* 12 May 1994; Spencer, *Daily Telegraph,* 12 May 1994; Jackson, "Shakespeare at Stratford-upon-Avon, 1994-95," *Shakespeare Quarterly* 46 (1995), 345.

42. Ibid., 343.

43. Woddis, *What's On,* 18 May 1994; Wardle, *The Times,* 15 May 1994; Jackson, "Shakespeare at Stratford-upon-Avon," 342.

44. Holland, "Shakespeare Performances in England, 1993-1994," *Shakespeare Survey* 48 (1995), 208.

45. Nathan, *Jewish Chronicle,* 20 May 1994.

46. There was an analogous moment in the 1984 *Henry V* when Branagh's Henry and McDiarmid's Chorus unexpectedly encountered one another on the eve of Agincourt, and, in Holderness's account, "miming a surprised double-take of near-recognition"; for a brief moment, as in the 1994 production, "we saw the fictional world of the dramatic action suddenly enter the fictional activity of the Chorus" (*Shakespeare Recycled,* 200). In 1984, the surprise meeting was played for comic effect, whereas in 1994 it was strangely moving

47. I. Q. Hunter, "Capitalism Most Triumphant: Bill and Ted's Excellent History Lesson," in Deborah Cartmell; I. Q. Hunter, Heidi Kaye and Imelda Whelehan, eds., *Pulping Fictions: Consuming Culture across the Literature/Media Divide* (Landon: Pluto Press, 1996), 122.

48. Jackson, "Shakespeare at Stratford-on-Avon, 1994-95," 342-43.

49. Jameson, *Postmodernism,* 45.

50. De Jongh, *Evening Standard;* Spencer, *Daily Telegraph;* Peter, *Sunday Times,* 15 May 1994; Nathan, *Jewish Chronicle;* Woddis, *What's On.*

51. Billington, *Guardian,* 12 May 1994; Wardle, *Independent on Sunday,* 15 May 1994.

52. Quoted in "This Beer Isn't a Beer: Interview with Anne Laurent," in Mike Gane, ed, *Baudrillard Live: Selected Interviews* (London: Routledge, 1993), 185.

53. As a postscript to the above, the 1994 *Henry V* was followed, with unusualness, by a brash and poorly-received production at Stratford three years later. It is also worth noting that the inaugural

production at the Bankside Globe the same year was a self-consciously Elizabethan, all-male *Henry V,* directed by Olivier's son.

Ruth Morse (review date 18 February 2000)

SOURCE: Morse, Ruth. "Review of *Henry V.*" *Times Literary Supplement,* no. 5055 (18 February 2000): 19.

[*In the following review, Morse comments favorably on director Jean-Louis Benoit's stylized, comedic, and nonpolitical 2000 French-language staging of* Henry V.]

Although the imported films of Welles, Olivier and Branagh have been extremely popular in France, this *Henry V* is the first French theatrical production. Understandably, perhaps. It was briefly seen last summer at the Avignon festival, in the star position of the great outdoor courtyard, and televised live, to scathing reviews. Transferred now to one of the more intimate theatres at the former arsenal in Vincennes (whose surrounding woods, after the devastating storms at Christmas, are looking too much like a war-torn landscape), its virtues are wholly apparent.

Above all, by taking advantage of the play's calls to its own theatricality, the director, Jean-Louis Benoit, avoids the risk of offending French nationalist sensibilities. The costumes and sets recall Olivier's make-believe Middle Ages, with a painted castle, tricks of perspective out of manuscript illustration, and a pretty landscape constructed of doll's-house-sized villages and rolling hills which turns out to be a huge rug, rolled back to reveal the dead soldiers (and dead horse) of *l'après Azincourt.* From the beginning, a Chorus in a bright orange wig and twentieth-century gamin costume (Laure Bonnet) emphasizes the use of a wooden wheel lying flat stage centre, a literal "Wooden O" on to which characters step out of the action to address us directly. And there is need to address us, to recruit us into filling out "the swelling scene", since the cast numbers only fifteen. Not only the Chorus, but the Heralds, are women, cross-dressed. The need to double—and treble—adds to the artifice, and taxes the strength and staying power of the energetic, mainly young, cast, with the inequalities of playing which that implies. Jean-Pol Dubois is outstanding five times: as a pedantic, calculating Archbishop of Canterbury, plotting to finesse the young king into a war order to protect Church revenues; as one of the conspirators; as the Duke of York; as the English soldier, Williams and as a feeble and tottering Charles VI, a mannikin out of Ionesco's *Le Roi se meurt.*

Using another of the imaginative, risk-taking translations of Jean-Michel Déprats, the story proper opens with a pseudo-Shakespearean scene in the Boar's Head tavern, to introduce the calculating Prince of Wales and his dissolute companions (including "Sir Falstaff"—the name by which plump Jack is known from *Falstaff,* the French title of Welles's *Chimes at Midnight*), whose further adventures (or lack of them) *Henry V* recounts. The playing style is broad, making cartoon characters of the old English enemy. One can hardly take them seriously, let alone hate them. The same can be said of the French, played in the Olivier style of silliness, so that one cannot identify with, let alone love, them.

It is this heavily stylized ensemble against which Philippe Torreton as the English King defines himself. He is in a different play, and remains there through five acts, accompanied only by his brothers. Yet he is alone, and that is the emphasis and interpretation of this production. Torreton is a great actor, capable of changing his style to suit Tartuffe at the Comédie Française or the eponymous Captain Conan of Bertrand Tavernier's recent war film. The trend of the director's cut intensifies Harry's solitude: this Harry sees Falstaff's coffin, sees and suffers the condemnation of Bardolph. Gone, as might have been expected in a French production, is the forging of a nation; the joke about the Irishman, the Scotsman and the Welshman has disappeared, as has, to all intents and purposes, the "little touch of Harry in the night". Gone is most of the King's interchange with Bates, the common soldier; here, he feels the weight of his responsibility and distance, with none of the redeeming joke about Bates's wager with him after the battle. This monarch is tired, and he is ill. He knows he has to play the king, but sometimes it is too much. Henry's long—some would say excessively long—speech over his betrayal by the traitor, Scrope, gives Torreton the occasion to diagnose his condition. He can trust no friend, because he can have none. Benoit's production is neither a celebration of Britishness nor a study of the costs of war. Against the usual wisdom of the difference between Continental interpretations of Shakespeare and English ones, it is less, rather than more, political.

And it is very funny. The emphatic self-consciousness of the play opens the way to a brilliant solution to the Princess Katherine's English lesson by reversing the languages: the women speak English and call it French; French and call it English. Marie Vialle has a fine gift for comedy, and a ravishing neck. For the improper puns, Déprats offers "gown/con" and "foot/foutre". His language jokes become wildly more mixed in the wooing scene: Torreton and Vialle move from English to French so quickly that the audience are whirled from one pretence to the other. Which language are they pretending is which? Only here, with his Kate, does Harry seem outmatched. By now, however, with the audience in the palm of his princely hand, the romantic interlude becomes an ironic send-up of romantic

interludes (only the Dauphin's disappointment spoils the fun). This kind of theatricality is not just what the theatre does best, it is what only the theatre can do.

Russell Jackson (review date spring 2001)

SOURCE: Jackson, Russell. "Review of *Henry V.*" *Shakespeare Quarterly* 52, no. 1 (spring 2001): 107-32.

[*In the following review, Jackson details the somber wartime setting and cynical mood of Edward Hall's 2000 production of* Henry V *at Stratford-upon-Avon.*]

Edward Hall's production of *Henry V,* with designs by Michael Pavelka, was a story told in a time of war by modern soldiers. When the audience entered the theater, men and women in gray fatigues and tee shirts, all wearing metal identity tags, were sitting or wandering around the stage in a state of half-busy, half-idle expectancy. Some were checking equipment, others writing letters home. At the back of the stage, in front of a sheer brick wall, was a gantry resembling a dockside crane. A clutter of gray ammunition and equipment boxes occupied the downstage area, which was covered with a gray silk cloth, a red cross at its center. A mobile phone rang just as the houselights were dimming, causing some amusement and annoyance until it turned out to be in the backpack of one of the soldiers. He found it, switched it off, and turned to ask the audience to make sure all their pagers and mobiles were also turned off. (A rhyming prologue to the *Comedy of Errors* had ended with the same request, usually made from front of house.) The Chorus's first speech, each sentence taken by a different cast member, ended with the cloth being pulled up and shaken, scattering what had become a shower of poppies onto the floor. This was now revealed as a war memorial inscribed with the names of those who had fallen at Agincourt, with three larger inscriptions "To The Glory of God," "I Have Fought a Good Fight," and "I Have Finished My Course." The gray boxes were cleared back to form an altar, and two actors then enrobed as bishops—and the play began.

The use of an unspecified twentieth- (or twenty-first-) century conflict, the adaptation of the choruses as part of a Brechtian story-telling technique, and the onstage evocation of a war memorial are devices familiar from recent productions of the play. This particular combination of them displaced the heroism of the campaign and the monarch onto the achievement (against the odds) of telling the story, making palatable an otherwise unflinchingly patriotic tale by conjuring up the cynicism of the "poor bloody infantry." This attitude, famously compatible with the desire to "do one's bit," is voiced during the otherwise-unconvincing attempts of the disguised king to argue his case on the eve of Agincourt: now it was as though the likes of Bates and Williams were presenting the whole play. The production did not suggest specific recent conflicts as analogies for Henry's opportunistic and aggressive campaign but proposed that the state of being at war produces contradictions and stresses that the Elizabethan play can speak to. No production of *Henry V* will ever be as acute about the particular politics and horrors of modern warfare as *Das Boot, Platoon,* or *Saving Private Ryan.* However, the play's celebratory dimensions (real enough for Olivier's film to be "faithful" to its original) are notoriously offset by the space it allows for doubt and cynicism. Cutting removed one layer of metahistorical ambiguity, however: Fluellen's discussion with Gower of the comparison between Henry and Alexander was excised, together with its notable failure on the part of the play's amateur historian to recall Falstaff's name.

Within this framework, the story of Henry's arrival at responsibility was developed in a way at once chilling and satisfying. He could *handle* being a king. He showed his athleticism and energy as well as rhetorical prowess at Harfleur, both before and after the siege. (The gantry moved downstage like a terrifying war machine, lights flashing and siren blaring, and scaling ladders were raised against the front of the dress circle.) Forced to witness the execution of Bardolph, Henry showed none of the signs of pity and self-reproach evident in Kenneth Branagh's Henry (at Stratford in 1984 and in his 1989 film). He was simply left contemplating the hanging figure while the troops formed up and marched off through the audience, singing of their desire to fight for the king. (The only one not singing was Pistol, who turned to look at Henry and Bardolph.) Unlike David Troughton's Henry IV, the fifth monarch of that name had little trouble in putting the crown on his head: he treated it as a symbol of office and responsibility, rather than a mystical and desired extension of his personality. He donned it to meet the Dauphin's messenger but wore appropriate military headgear (uniform cap or helmet) as necessary. To deal with the traitors, Henry wore "undress" uniform and even put on spectacles to read dispatches. This was a scene set up as a council of war which turned into an informal court martial—at the end of which the guilty men were taken to the back and shot against a brick wall. Exeter, bespectacled and punctilious, was a career officer. Henry's coolness was manifested in the matter of the tennis balls: the gift consisted of a pair of balls rotating in a music-box casket, and Henry's reply was to have the stage showered with tennis balls from above. When the last one had bounced to rest, and only then, he uttered his mirthless "Ha, ha."

The king's adoption of battle fatigues and weaponry was not a sudden transformation of accomplished courtier into G. I. Joe but a "natural" extension of

Henry's versatility and effectiveness in this brutal conflict. This sense of an unglamorous, warlike existence was aided by the general absence from the production of the other usual signs of royal pageantry or symbolic assertion. There were no robes of state, no orbs or scepters. The French court was well dressed but not foppish. There was some mockery in their treatment by the story-telling soldiers—the second part of the play began with Katherine reading a large French-English dictionary while a band played "Thank heaven for little Girls." Alice walked in through the audience, and the princess gave a game rendition of "La Vie en Rose." The fleur-de-lis was seen only on a parachute-silk backdrop (rather tattered by the end of the campaign), and the French king wore a *képi* rather than a royal crown. In the final scene Henry hung his crown on the back of a chair to conduct his wooing, picking it up hastily at "Here comes your father" (as usual now, a laugh line.) When he asked the French king for his daughter's hand, Henry held the crown in his own. He allowed himself (what actor would not at the end of a long and noisy evening?) the geniality of the comic wooing, but the opposition of Katherine was formidable and the ultimate result uncomfortable. At the very end of the play, as Henry and Katherine faced each other, the Union Jack that had been unfurled behind the tableau fell to the ground. Burgundy's frank mirth was cut from the scene, as was the character of Queen Isabel. Burgundy was played as a sober diplomat, and much of his emotive speech about the condition of France was also cut. After the joining of their hands, Katherine lifted the crown from Henry's head and he simply walked down to the front of the stage and out through the audience.

Kevin Nance (review date December 2001)

SOURCE: Nance, Kevin. "Review of *Henry V.*" *Stage Directions* 14, no. 10 (December 2001): 42-5.

[*In the following review of the 2001* Henry V *at the Stratford Shakespeare Festival in Canada, Nance concentrates on stage and costume design, particularly its contribution to this production's multifaceted wartime setting.*]

As the United States and its allies are discovering in their fight against terrorism, all wars are not created equal. Each has its own iconic leaders, its own weapons, its own look. And each has its particular emotional resonance for the participants.

Similar thoughts about the vagaries of war, and the way we view wars of various historical periods, were roiling in Toronto designer Dany Lyne's mind as she approached Shakespeare's *Henry V,* which would grow into the boldest, most visually striking production of the Stratford Festival of Canada's 2001 season.

Lyne's eclectic design incorporated an abstract set (complete with a backdrop on which prerecorded and live video images were projected) and costumes inspired by military uniforms from four distinct historical periods: 1414, the year of the actual Battle of Agincourt; 1914, the dawn of World War I; 1945, during the last days of World War II; and 1999, the era of the sleek black uniforms of the British Special Air Service (SAS), known for their appearances in the Persian Gulf War and the ongoing conflict in Northern Ireland.

The combination of all of those visual styles on the same stage sounds chaotic, but at Stratford's Avon Theatre the various facets of the production design blended easily, coherently and with devastating impact. It was a daring artistic gamble that paid off spectacularly, mainly because it was conceived with great care by Lyne, director Jeannette Lambermont and the sound and video designer Wade Staples.

They began the process with the Bard's great history play itself, viewing it not as an inquiry into the nature of heroism, as it's often interpreted, but as an anti-war statement. "I wanted it to sit in the realm of the great anti-war films, such as *Apocalypse Now* and especially *All Quiet On The Western Front,* which stopped me dead in my tracks," says Lyne, an award-winning designer who has created sets and costumes for numerous plays and operas at Stratford and throughout Canada. The question immediately became: How do we set *Henry V* in a context where the ambience of war would reach the audience in a very real way? And we felt we just couldn't serve that purpose by staying in the play's historical period.

The problem, she felt, was that period costume distances audiences so much that battle scenes can seem more like a fairy tale than actual combat. "A bunch of guys going at each other with swords doesn't resonate with today's audience as a particularly violent act," Lyne says, "It's almost more like a ballet than real [fighting]."

. . . This sent the production hurtling exactly 500 years forward, helped in part by the texts's references to mines and trenches. "Say the word 'trench' and immediately World War I comes to mind," she says. "So the original idea was to take 1414 and 1914 and put them in a blender at high speed."

But after drafting several designs, Lyne came to feel that the blender didn't contain enough ingredients to create the visceral dish of wartime horror that she envisioned. "We did stick with 1914 quite a while, but it still didn't have the edge that we wanted," she says. "It didn't seem close enough and frankly, violent enough. Once I did the preliminary design, in which I had only 1914, there was still that sense of distance. It didn't have that punch I was after."

And so Lyne went shopping in history. It was to her a natural leap from World War I to World War II, and from there to the SAS soldiers of the 1990s. Quickly she began to perceive visual connections between the various periods of battle garb. For example, the quilted leather undergear that Henn, and his soldiers would have worn beneath their armor at Agincourt bore a striking resemblance to the bulletproof vests of the SAS. "Once we started mixing periods, I began looking at pants, jackets and boots as words," she says. "They became a vocabulary, and I was eventually going to form those words into sentences and paragraphs." The unique syntax of the show extended to the sound design, which included both medieval and 20th-century wartime noises, as well as a cellist who played live music onstage throughout the show; to the set, a series of bare diagonal platforms and parallelogram shapes; and even to a series of video images on a giant backdrop.

Staples assembled a montage of moody location images, many of them shot with a handheld camcorder by actor Graham Abbey (who played the title role) on a trip tracing the historical Henry V's path through northern France. All of the images were turned into grainy black-and-white, then played using a stuttering effect that made them look like newsreel footage from the first two world wars, as well as CNN videotape of more recent conflicts.

Staples also developed what he came to call "the honor roll"—a series of ghostly, silent, prerecorded video portraits of the individual cast members that are played before, during and after the play. "At the beginning, you're seeing the cast, and at the end, you're seeing the faces of the dead," he says. There so much desolation, death and destruction in war, and the video images were there to convey that in a very contemporary context using contemporary technology."

Particularly up-to-date was Staples' use of live video at various points. Young actor Paul Dunn, who played a boy wandering through the battlefields, carried a video recorder throughout the production. At one point he lay flat on the floor and delivered a monologue directly into its lens, his smudged, tear-stained face looming huge on the upstage screen.

"The idea was to bring the audience into the psyche of this young boy caught in the midst of this turmoil," Staples says. "That was amazingly well received, especially by younger audiences. You're touching on subject matter and time periods that most of these kids have no knowledge of, and using multimedia like that brings the material within their realm of understanding. It was powerful."

During the design phase, however, both Lyne and Staples had fears about how all the conceptual elements would fit together. There was a real risk, they both knew, of producing an attention-grabbing effect that might detract from the story rather than serve it. "It's a difficult balance to strike, between the requirements of emotional/psychological realism and the fact that those requirements can't always be accomplished with what's naturalistic," says Lyne. "What's important is to give the play a context in which it can find its truest and fullest expression for a contemporary audience. If you have to change the actual words of the text to fit the design and start interfering with the work itself, then the design concept becomes too heavy-handed and whacks people over the head. You find yourself falling into the pits of the Grand Canyon. But we didn't feel we were doing that."

Stratford's Artistic Director Richard Monette had concerns along similar lines. He joked to a Stratford audience that when the creative team had promised an authentic period design, "I wasn't expecting four different periods." Says Lyne, "I do think he was worried. But he was also intrigued by the direction we were going in, and he didn't step in at any time. I thought about the risk, too, but it never occurred to me to mitigate my ideas, because I felt so passionately about them." In the end, Staples happened to be standing near Monette after the opening-night performance and overheard him exclaim, "No, I liked it!"

But perhaps one audience member's comments following a performance showed most clearly that the design scheme had worked perfectly: "War is war," he said.

Alvin Klein (review date 23 June 2002)

SOURCE: Klein, Alvin. "Review of *Henry V.*" *New York Times* (23 June 2002): 8.

[*In the following review of Terrence O'Brien's* Henry V *for the 2002 Hudson Valley Shakespeare Festival, Klein praises Nance Williamson's excellent work as the Chorus, but otherwise finds the project "misguided" in its depiction of King Henry.*]

Everyone knows that Shakespeare is summertime's No. 1 theatrical sport, but it's the comedies and tragedies, 28 in all, that leap to mind. Only the most intransigent devotee will miss the histories, which add up to seven.

For most of us, there is plenty of Shakespeare to go around without having to bone up on royal French and English genealogy, such study invariably involving an immersion in politics, in religion and in the military, for through the ages, nobility thrived on the glory and the spoils of warfare.

From the Hudson Valley Shakespeare Festival's founding artistic director, Terrence O'Brien, comes this statement: "War is always relevant." But it somehow lacks

the power to persuade us that the most interesting and accessible festival in the metropolitan region should be drawn to *Henry V,* its first history play in 16 years.

Happily, often deliriously so, the festival has put an indelible imprint, on many productions, even on the impossible *Titus Andronicus.*

But on *Henry,* no.

Granted, it is impossible to resist the heady rendering of the famous line, "A little touch of Harry in the night" by the Chorus of the occasion, and Mr. O'Brien's staging does not stint on levity, the abandon and the accessibility that defines the festival's inimitable style. But the complexity of the title character—he is many shaded and conflicted, but he is not great—and the grave undercurrents of an imperfect play are out of reach here.

Traditionally played by one actor, the Chorus warms up the audience, eager to report news from the battlefield, sometimes with cannon fire as accompaniment, promising to take us to mighty places. And once the word is out that the scintillating Nance Williamson is the welcoming Chorus here, it's likely that haters of plays historical will flock to this one.

Talk of welcoming. "O for a muse of fire, that would ascend / The brightest heaven of invention," is the Chorus' first utterance, and with that Ms. Williamson has you hooked. When Ms Williamson, wearing her black trenchcoat as if it were the must-have coat of summer, implores the audience ("On your imaginary forces work," "Piece out our imperfections with your thoughts" and "Gently to hear, kindly to judge our play"), she lifts a problematical play to a universal statement about the mind's possibilities and theater's power to enliven them.

But then, Ms. Williamson radiates the generosity of spirit that lifts the company, one of those ineffable gifts possessed by some performers who are themselves possessed by the magic of theater.

Note too that Ms. Williamson makes a brief appearance as Montjoy, a French herald.

But when it comes to ripening a King Henry "into noble manhood," the transformation is out of the hands of a Chorus. While Harrison Long evokes shades of the carousing Prince Hal of his former days, the actor relies on political savvy at the expense of substance and the inner turmoil of a man who is determined to hold onto honor in defiance of the seductiveness of war and power that could overtake his sense of responsibility. The affable side of Henry is perceptible; his monster side is either unconvincing or too well concealed.

Mr. Long and the flirtatious, bewildered and altogether winning Natasha Piletich as the French and French-speaking Princess Katherine are fun in their courtship scenes, in which neither much understands what the other is talking about. The festival's customary aura of fun, irreverence and musical anachronism is minimally effective here and the choreographed swordplay from the fight director Ian Marshall is overly extended, landing in a pretentious muddle.

It remains for the ever-dependable Chorus to tell us, at the very end, how the horror, the brutality of war was all for nothing, "confining mighty men / Mangling by starts the full course of their glory."

With that, one can understand Mr. O'Brien's sense of the play's contemporary importance. But the director's concentration on an incompletely realized portrait of one man learning a painful lesson is misguided. Pageantry is a conventionally handy compensation for dramatic flaws, but the festival's resources do not encompass such essential embellishment. We must expend extra effort when Ms. Williamson commands us to "grapple your minds . . . work, work your thoughts."

Markland Taylor (review date 5-11 August 2002)

SOURCE: Taylor, Markland. "Review of *Henry V*." *Variety* 387, no. 11 (5-11 August 2002): 30.

[*In the following review of the 2002 Shakespeare & Co. production of* Henry V *directed by Jonathan Epstein, Taylor observes that gratuitous stage business, comic nonsense, and an overall lack of directorial cohesion defined this deeply flawed staging of the play.*]

For the first time in its 25 years, Shakespeare & Co. has staged *Henry V,* which joins *Macbeth* in the Founders' Theater through Sept. 1. It isn't as bad as the *Macbeth,* how could it be? But its still below-par Shakespeare and continues to suggest S&Co. has an enormous way to go before it begins to live up to its new Lenox campus and its first real theater, the Founders.

Having just 10 actors to perform *Henry V* is a problem to begin with, and a reading of the playbill makes it look as though many characters must have been excised. But that is not necessarily the case, as the company turns its hand to a multitude of roles, English, French and Welsh, high- and low-born. When the archbishop of Canterbury is supposed to enter immediately after the prologue, the actors look around the stage and out into the audience for him and then decide to dress up the straw soldier at center stage and have one of them pop his head up above it in an impersonation of the archbishop. Similar expediencies follow.

The more or less set-less production opens with a child singing off-stage; then a penny whistle is heard, then neighing. Allyn Burrows as Henry is revealed plunging his sword into the straw soldier (sculpted by Michael Melle) as a variety of voices urge him, "For God's sake go not to these wars." Eventually we get to Shakespeare's opening "O for a muse of fire" prologue.

Jonathan Epstein's main directorial conceit is to turn the entire company into clowns. He does so by having them wear red noses on strings, which they don and doff throughout. In theory this aims to suggest that every human being, whether king or lowest of subjects, is a clown at times. In practice it's meaningless.

Epstein also sees the play as "25 one-act plays that are connected thematically." Yet in this production, scene after scene is incomprehensible and no theme is discernible. If Epstein wanted to suggest that war is just one big, stupid, messy boondoggle, he could be said to have succeeded.

There are some moments of relief, such as Ariel Bock as Mistress Quickly actually touching the emotions as she delivers her epitaph to the dead Falstaff. But they are far too few.

The title role is a demanding part that needs an actor of real stature and presence. Burrows does contribute some physical glamour (he looks like Robert Redford), but he doesn't have sufficient histrionic heft; at times his approach is too conversational, and his voice often sounds strained.

As is too often the case in Shakespearean productions, the comics are tiresome, though Tony Simotes' Nym does have an amusing cockiness. And, most unfortunately, far too many of the actors have been allowed to bellow, bluster and shout, to the great detriment of the text.

The charming English-lesson scene between French princess Katherine (Susanna Apgar) and her attendant Alice (Bock) is marred by too much physical business—the two women are on Melle's sculptured half-horses carried by other cast members. There's also too much clambering around and sliding down the theater's scaffolding.

The costumes are a motley mix often taken out of onstage trunks, including outsize wigs for the French royals. For no good reason, Katherine is at one point seen in a '50s cocktail dress and, finally, in what looks like a debutante's ball gown.

Performance seen was astonishingly poorly attended. Let's hope S&Co. heeds the warning.

THEMES

Brownell Salomon (essay date autumn 1980)

SOURCE: Salomon, Brownell. "Thematic Contraries and the Dramaturgy of *Henry V*." *Shakespeare Quarterly* 31, no. 3 (autumn 1980): 343-56.

[*In the following essay, Brownell affirms the unified design of* Henry V *by presenting a scene-by-scene analysis of the drama in relation to its theme of "private cause" versus "public good."*]

That *Henry V* provokes radically different responses from its modern interpreters is well known. For every critic willing to accept the play at face value as heroic drama, there is another determined to find it an ironic satire of Machiavellian militarism. But controversy fails to daunt Shakespeareans who are newly attracted to the play, each intent upon developing an interpretation that reasonably accounts for the largest measure of evidence. No exception, I here offer my own view that *Henry V* is a coherent dramatic work, an imaginative unity with a form totally integral with its meaning.

This is not to obscure the fact that the play is also one segment of a four-play historical sequence. Yet that particular fact should not be given more than its just due—as too often, I believe, it is. Extra-textual evidence, usually from the other plays of the Lancastrian tetralogy, may corroborate details in *Henry V,* but it cannot be relied upon to uphold a full reading. As Edgar Allan Poe neatly phrased the axiom, "Every work of art should contain within itself all that is requisite for its own comprehension." We are, then, the more likely to gain practical understanding by scrutinizing the play itself for evidence of its formally controlling purpose. Above all, one looks for clues to an underlying idea, some organizing principle that governs all the characters and the configuration of all the parts.

I

To date, the clearest insight into the overall structure of *Henry V* is that provided by Richard Levin.[1] Approaching the work as one type of Renaissance double-plot play, Professor Levin shows that Pistol and his cronies afford a near-perfect illustration of the "clown subplot" that serves as a foil to (as distinguished from a parody of) the main-plot actions. He finds the foil relationship to be most fully developed through a number of negative analogies. For example, Henry's impassioned urging of his army at the siege of Harfleur (III.i) is formally opposed to the succeeding scene in which Fluellen must drive the unwilling clown-foils into battle. ". . . Everything in the subplot," argues Levin, "points

unambiguously to its function as a foil employed to contrast with, and so render still more admirable, the exploits of the 'mirror of all Christian kings'" (p. 116). Because plot-subplot analysis of this kind embraces a play's central elements, it offers a persuasive structural account of *Henry V.*

But an even more comprehensive explicative method is available to the student of Renaissance dramaturgy: analyzing the principles of design by which individual scenes are aggregated into the play as a whole. That approach is only now coming into its own, and will surely find wider use in future studies of Renaissance drama. A few years ago, Alfred Harbage noted that "It is one of the curiosities of Shakespearean criticism that it has offered so little analysis of scenic structure as compared with analysis of characters in the last century, and of images in the present one. Perhaps the reason is that the subject has lain fog-bound in the exhalation of the phantom 'acts' which have diverted or baffled inquiry."[2] In his fine recent study of Shakespeare's dramaturgy, Mark Rose agrees, declaring the matter of disputed act divisions "a scholarly red herring" that "discourage[s] us from seeing the plays as they really are."[3] As Professor Rose demonstrates, the basic structural unit of Shakespearean drama in particular and late Tudor drama generally is the cleared-stage scene.

One may account for this fact by the uniquely pictorial, visual sensibility of Shakespeare and his contemporaries. The Renaissance tendency to fuse the sister arts of poetry and painting in the spirit of the Horatian dictum, *ut pictura poesis* ("poetry is like painting") is illustrated in many genres, but nowhere more clearly than in the remarkable popularity of the emblem book—a collection of spatially discrete "speaking pictures." But if Renaissance aesthetic notions of spatial form and multiple unity are influences upon the emblem book, they also figure importantly in the symmetry and schematic organization of long poems like Spenser's *Faerie Queene* and *Epithalamion,* and Marlowe's *Hero and Leander.* So, likewise, do the aggregate scenes of a Shakespearean play comprise, in effect, an integral series of speaking pictures. Shakespeare tailors his scenic design to his drama of ideas; he makes conscious use of patterning for thematic purposes. To relate the independent scenes to their controlling idea, Shakespearean dramaturgy characteristically employs such formal means as frame scenes, diptych scenes (for example, the opening scene of *Romeo and Juliet* as divisible "hate" and "love" segments), ironic juxtapositions, and parallels and liaisons between scenes.

It is in light of these known Shakespearean methods that I offer the following scene-by-scene analysis, endeavoring to show that *Henry V*'s individual scenes are organically interconnected, unified by a single conceptual framework. That framework consists in two rival ethical attitudes, whose prevalence oscillates in successive scenes or groups of scenes throughout the play until at last the favored attitude overrules. Specifically, the idea of the play's structure is embodied in two thematic contraries: private cause versus public good.

II

Crystallized in that antinomy is an essential tenet of sixteenth-century political morality: namely, that the needs of the commonwealth take precedence over the welfare of private citizens. So often did that sentiment find expression in Tudor literature that it attained proverbial status. From Morris Tilley's compilation of Elizabethan proverbs only two of many examples contemporaneous with Shakespeare's play need be cited: "private welfare is not to be preferred before common-weale," from Nicholas Ling's *Politeuphuia. Wits Common Wealth* (London, 1597); and "private cause must yield to public good," from George Chapman's (George Peele's?) *Alphonsus, Emperor of Germany,* I.ii.26 (London, 1594).[4] In Shakespeare's own work, the private/public antinomy has major ethical and thematic relevance in the tragic poem, *The Rape of Lucrece* (1594). There, as in *Henry V,* "private" is equated with negative, solipsistic values, and "public" with the positive, societal values imperiled by Tarquin's crime:

> 'Thy secret pleasure turns to open shame,
> Thy private feasting to a public fast,
> . . . . .
> 'Why should the private pleasure of some one
> Become the public plague of many moe?
> . . . . .
> For one's offence why should so many fall,
> To plague a private sin in general?
>
> (*Luc.,* ll. 891-92, 1478-79, 1483-84)[5]

In *Henry V,* to be sure, the private/public polarity is somewhat less obvious, taking the form, by and large, of a unifying structural concept rather than a verbalized motif. Yet it is an ideational conflict that remains constant and pervasive in the play. The mode of opposition among particular scenes may variously be expressed as solipsism vs. altruism, self-love vs. public spiritedness, special pleading vs. the communal welfare, selfhood vs. the polity, parasitism vs. social benefaction, egoism vs. fellow feeling, partiality vs. mutuality, the subjective code vs. the objective ethos, opportunism vs. patriotism, and so forth.

In the analysis that follows, every scene will be considered except for the brief Prologue and Epilogue. These are excluded from the analysis because they function as mood-setting, presentational frame scenes that lead the audience into and out of the drama proper, which is thus formally set apart.

III

The opening scene (I.i) is flatly concerned with advancement of a private cause. From the first line on, we hear that the main problem for the Archbishop of Canterbury and the Bishop of Ely is to defend the Church's lands against an impending parliamentary bill of expropriation: "If it pass . . . We lose . . . half of our possession" (ll. 7-8). Of course, the bishops assert only the highest charitable motives for wanting to hold on to the property that parliament would "strip from us" (l. 11). But there is little doubt that narrow group interests take precedence over those of the commonwealth when we learn that Canterbury has cynically moved to incline King Henry to their cause by offering a great sum of money (ll. 75-81) in support of the tentative French invasion.

With the ceremonial entry of the King and his attendants (I.ii) we are instantly shifted to the arena of public interest. Once the question of England's just claim to France has been legally and morally resolved by Canterbury's discourse on the Salic Law, and ratified by the English lords, that policy is then extolled in the most glowing terms. The French expedition is thus unmistakably affirmed as a collective, national endeavor, not a strategy for the monarch's personal glory. Exeter invokes a traditional analogy to express their common solidarity: "For government, though high, and low, and lower, / Put into parts, doth keep in one consent, / Congreeing in a full and natural close, / Like music" (I.ii.180-83). With an equally traditional metaphor, Canterbury descants for 39 lines on the correspondence between England's national unity-in-diversity and that of the beehive (ll. 183-221). Though at the same time the King's courage and honor are enlarged upon ("I will dazzle all the eyes of France"), his virtues are never isolatedly his own, but rather meld with the nation's destiny: "I am coming on . . . to put forth / My rightful hand in a well-hallowed cause" (ll. 293-94). Henry's is a collaborative enterprise that allies the entire cosmic hierarchy: God, himself, and his subjects ("by God's help / And yours, . . ." ll. 223-24). His half-dozen allusions to God in this scene are no mere index of personal piety, therefore, but thematic affirmations of the lofty, communal sanction of the venture. As though in direct response to Henry's call to action in the tag line of this scene, the Chorus enters to announce that the royal imperative has been translated forthwith into a single-minded, national effort: "Now all the youth of England are on fire, / . . . / Following the mirror of all Christian kings / With winged heels" (II. Chor. 1, 6-7).

Displacing the show of public unanimity just witnessed, the scene following (II.i) presents a speaking picture of utterly different behavior: the petty contentiousness of Nym and Ancient Pistol. The cause of their grudge is a third party, Nell Quickly, who has faithlessly revoked her trothplight to the one in order to marry the other. That fact only makes the blustering exchanges of oaths and threats between the two former friends seem the more perverse and solipsistic. Even their comic diction negatively accents the trivial, *personal* ("solus") nature of their quarreling, which keeps them (ll. 86-88) from responding to their public duty in France:

NYM

I would have you solus.

PISTOL

"Solus," egregious dog? O viper vile!
The "solus" in thy most mervailous face!
The "solus" in thy teeth, and in thy throat, . . .

(II.i.43-46)

Another iterative word in this scene, and in the play thereafter, is Nym's catchword, "humour." In contemporary usage the word was, of course, a synonym for any personal whim, crotchet, quirk, or idiosyncrasy—as in Nym's phrase beginning at line 52, "I have an humour to knock you." Both "solus" and "humour" are thematic words, connoting verbally what Nym and Pistol's repeated drawing and sheathing of their swords symbolize visually throughout the scene. They are the gestes of private indulgence that derogate from the public interest.

Act II, scene ii again presents the contrary side of the equation. Bedford and Exeter's opening dialogue reveals that the conspiracy of Scroop, Cambridge, and Grey is known to the King, and that the traitors "shall be apprehended by and by" (l. 2). Since the first eleven lines foretell how this scene must end, its purpose is obviously not to build suspense as to the conspirators' identities. It is, rather, to dramatize the ascendancy of the public welfare over that most despicable of all private crimes against the social order, treason. By way of reinforcing the dramatic irony, Henry reminds the dissembling conspirators where true allegiance ought to lie, with the martial task that has the nation's whole-hearted support: "we are well persuaded / We carry not a heart with us from hence / That grows not in a fair consent with ours" (ll. 20-22). As the traitors are handed their orders of arrest, Henry berates them as "English monsters" who "Join'd with an enemy proclaimed, and from his coffers / Receiv'd the golden earnest of our death" (ll. 85, 168-69). The rigor of the law must be imposed, he says, not because it revenges the attempt against his person (l. 174), but because of the public chaos their capital crime would have produced. They would have sold the King's "princes and his peers to servitude, / His subjects to oppression and contempt, / And his whole kingdom into desolation" (ll. 171-73).

With the shift of locale to the Boar's Head Tavern (II.iii), we again revert to the world of selfish opportunism. For a few moments, the grieving of Pistol, the

Hostess, and their friends at the news of Falstaff's death is allowed to evoke our sympathy and amusement (at the Hostess' malapropisms and Pistol's alliterations). But not for long, because the scene closes with Pistol reaffirming his self-serving, parasitic motives: "Let us to France, like horse-leeches, my boys, / To suck, to suck, the very blood to suck!" (II.iii.50-51). Ironically, his words recall the earlier-mentioned depredations of a proclaimed national enemy, "the weasel Scot" who "sucks her princely eggs" (I.ii.170-71). At the French court in the next scene (II.iv) self-centeredness also prevails, but in a different modality. While the French King and the Constable recommend caution and national preparedness against the English invasion, the Dauphin speaks slightingly of Henry, and would put private enmity and spite above public policy: "Say, if my father render fair return, / It is against my will; for I desire / Nothing but odds with England" (II.iv.127-29). As his advice to his father shows, the Dauphin virtually incarnates self-regarding hauteur: "Self-love, my liege, is not so vile a sin / As self-neglecting" (ll. 74-75).

Stirringly, the Chorus at the beginning of Act III recalls us to the arena of public-spirited action. We the audience become vicarious participants in the sailing of Henry's "brave fleet" toward the great national mission at Harfleur: "who is he . . . that will not follow / These culled and choice-drawn cavaliers to France?" (III.Chor.22-24). The imperative mood is employed all-pervasively in this speech ("Suppose . . . Play . . . behold . . . think . . . follow, follow! / Grapple"), as though to compel *our* allegiance to the common cause. This is the same rhetorical mode that Henry will use with his troops in the famous speech in the following scene: "imitate the action of the tiger: / Stiffen the sinews, summon up the blood, . . . On, on, . . ." (III.i.6 ff.). Henry's inspiring presence before Harfleur is the apotheosis of communal values in action: "Cry 'God for Harry! England and Saint George!'" (III.i.34).

Act III, scene ii divides into two episodes, before and after line 23, the two segments of the diptych representing contrary ethical priorities. Nym, Pistol, Bardolph, and the Boy have heard the King's order to the breach, but choose rather to evade the call to heroic warfare: "The knocks are too hot. . . . The humour of it is too hot" (ll. 2-4). Nym's "humour" is again the verbal high sign of solipsism, of the elevation of private cause over public welfare.

But immediately afterward, the anti-social motivations of his cohorts are pointedly censured in the Boy's soliloquy. Pistol is a coward, and Nym and Bardolph are shirkers and downright thieves: "They will steal anything, and call it purchase" (III.ii.38). The Boy repudiates such practices ("Their villainy goes against my weak stomach," l. 48) and expresses his intention to leave their service. The entire speech is choric in tone,

Emma Thompson as Katherine in Kenneth Branagh's 1989 film version of Henry V.

stressing that its condemnation of parasitism is the play's ethical position directly confided to the audience. And to emphasize that Pistol and his friends are untypical of English soldiery, there follows an episode showing that bravery, dependability, and loyalty to the common welfare are in fact the dominant social values (ll. 50-130). Symbolizing the national unity-in-diversity are captains Gower, Fluellen, Macmorris, and Jamy, who set aside their respective regional loyalties (English, Welsh, Irish, and Scottish) to embrace a public duty that could well involve the ultimate self-sacrifice. Jamy's sentiments speak for all: "ay'll de gud service, or ay'll lig i' th' grund for it! ay, or go to death!" (ll. 106-7). An honorable band whose efforts are socially productive, they are in stark contrast to the ignoble fraternity of Nym and Bardolph, "sworn brothers in filching" (ll. 40-41).

In Act III, scene iii Henry addresses the besieged Governor of Harfleur and brings about the French town's immediate surrender. Using a rhetorical strategy designed to provoke fear of his soldiers' reprisals,

Henry gains his objective without additional bloodshed. The victory, however, is shown to belong to the English forces collectively rather than to the King alone; he is but the self-effaced embodiment of the national will. Henry's sole concerns are for the vanquished ("Use mercy to them all") and for his soldiers' health and well-being (ll. 54-56).

The "language lesson" scene (III.iv) featuring Princess Katherine and her gentlewoman might seem to signal an alternation to merely personal values, but this is not the case. Though the scene serves several dramatic functions at once, the key phrase relating to the private/public antithesis is Katherine's assertion that she must learn the English language: "il faut que j'apprends à parler" (ll. 4-5). That English is felt necessary ("il faut") for a French princess is, in effect, an acknowledgment of France and England's cultural parity. More important, it foreshadows England's later political and cultural transcendence. Even the Princess' blushing allusions to the obscene words that are the French sound-alikes of the English words *foot* and *gown* are more than instances of local humor. They are dramatic expressions of the Princess' sexual awareness, and by extension her nubility, which will have important social implications in the play's final scene. The present scene takes place in France and deals with personal matters; but paradoxically, its main reason for being is as a reverberation of Henry's victory for English communal values in the preceding scene.

With Act III, scene v comes a regression to egotistic motives. It is noteworthy that the French forces, who have met to plan their defense against the English, are represented by only the narrowest upper stratum of aristocrats. Unlike the English, whose cause energizes social cohesiveness ("Now all the youth of England are on fire"), the French response is actuated only incidentally by the threat to the nation as a whole. What preoccupies the French nobles is the confined interest of their class. They wish to avenge the loss of *self*-esteem occasioned by the English invasion. What lip service they give to patriotism is couched in terms of wounded personal honor: "shall our quick blood, spirited with wine, / Seem frosty? O, for honor of our land, / Let us not hang like roping icicles . . ." (ll. 21-23). The notion of honor echoes throughout the scene, but always in the sense of a private punctilio which must be vindicated rather than an internalized public ethic: "with spirit of honor edged . . . hie to the field . . . now quit you of great shames" (ll. 38-39, 47; cf. l. 27). Most stinging of all to the French is the affront to their pride and manhood: "Our madams mock at us and plainly say / Our mettle is bred out" (ll. 28-29).

In the scene following (III.vi), the play's ethical alternatives confront one another, to the esteem of public values. Pistol attempts to persuade Fluellen to intercede with the Duke of Exeter in behalf of Bardolph, who is to be hanged for stealing that "pax of little price" (l. 44). Fluellen refuses Pistol's special pleading, saying that he would want his own brother executed if he were guilty, "for discipline ought to be used" (l. 55). Minutes later, King Henry informs Fluellen that maintaining orderly conduct is not just a military necessity but, because they are on enemy soil, a socio-political one as well (ll. 103-9). In his attempt to raise private expediency above obligation to the community, which Fluellen and the King exemplify, Pistol is once more shown up as the very embodiment of egoism: "a rogue, that now and then goes to the wars to grace himself" (ll. 66-67). The King, on the other hand, takes the occasion humbly to reaffirm the dependence of his army upon a suprapersonal reality, God (ll. 145, 151, 164).

The next scene (III.vii) is a vignette wholly concerned with the French nobles' vanity and frivolousness on the eve of the battle of Agincourt. As they banter about the relative merits of their armor and horses, not the slightest heed is given to the battle's wider implications. The narcissistic Dauphin's boastfulness is only slightly more conspicuous than the others', but it makes him the easy target of the Constable's taunts. Without exception, every speaking character in this scene is given to vaunting French superiority. But the primary focus here is not upon real versus apparent valor, but rather upon the utter self-absorption of these aristocrats, which points up the flaccid social bond underlying their cause. French defeat is a foregone conclusion.

The impression of social divisiveness in the previous scene, expressed through the belittling, sarcastic exchanges among the French leaders, is contrasted in the Chorus to Act IV by an impression of unity and fellow feeling on the English side. The rapport between Henry and his soldiers is not the product of their mutual danger, but of Henry's ability to instill a sense of personal co-identification, of shared participation in their national mission: "with a modest smile / . . . [he] calls them brothers, friends, and countrymen" (IV. Chor. 33-34). Unlike the inwardly preoccupied French nobles, the outer-directed Henry upholds a demotic, communal goal. By his visits among his men ("A little touch of Harry in the night," l. 47), he makes co-partnership of every rank the object of personal concern: "A largess universal, like the sun, / His liberal eye doth give to every one" (ll. 43-44).

Act IV, scene i involves the subtlest expression of the private/public dialectic in the play. This is the scene of Henry's incognito conversation with his soldiers, Bates and Williams, on the eve of the battle. For the first time there is a hint of possible contradiction between Henry's avowed public intention not to allow himself to be ransomed if he were captured by the French, and what

action he might actually take. By refusing ransom, the King has magnanimously set aside a royal prerogative which would serve his private advantage, choosing instead to tie his own fate to that of his army. Henry's third-person self-deprecations in this scene ("the king is but a man . . . his senses have but human conditions," ll. 98, 100) both humanize him and enhance his credibility. Clearly, the King's private thoughts and public enactments are identical. Nevertheless, Williams is entitled to his skepticism. Henry's display of valor could be but a false mask for cowardice: "He may *show* what *outward* courage he will" (l. 109; italics mine). Unlike the common soldier, moreover, the King might revert with impunity to self-regard: "when our throats are cut, he may be ransomed, and we ne'er the wiser" (ll. 183-84). Henry's certain knowledge that he would keep his public promise never to be ransomed is unprovable, for the special privilege he enjoys as a king exempts him from being held to such a pledge: the validity of his oath as a private person is mooted by the royal prerogative. The frustration this causes Henry is not self-created, but inheres in the medieval and Renaissance legal sanction of his office, which distinguished between the king's two bodies, the private and the public: "O hard condition, / Twin-born with greatness" (ll. 219-20).[6] Williams' incredulousness piques Henry, then, because it calls his private as well as his public oath into question. By way of postponing their altercation to a more fitting time, Henry gets Williams to agree to exchange gloves, with both to wear them in their respective headgear for later identification (ll. 197-202).

Our every observation of the play to this point argues against interpreting this episode as mere psychological realism, as a scene intended to depreciate Henry's maturity as a king.[7] The scene is preeminently of emblematic significance. For, notwithstanding its unfriendly tone, the act of exchanging "gages" (l. 197), or pledges, symbolizes the reciprocity and mutuality existing between Henry and his men. Their shared public allegiance creates a genuine brotherhood, a human parity that transcends the disparity in rank. As Henry later puts it, "he to-day that sheds his blood with me / Shall be my brother" (IV.iii.61-62; cf. IV. Chor. 34). Viewed in anthropological terms, the exchange of gloves is a social-bonding ritual. It is a "rite of incorporation" exactly as the inter-tribal marriage, the exchange of visits or gifts, the communal feast, or the peace-pipe ceremony are for primitive peoples.[8] Such a rite puts one or both of its participants under a constraint. By giving over his glove to one of his ordinary soldiers, then, all the while continuing to hide his elevated status, Henry symbolically reaffirms his earlier vow that self-interest shall defer to the body politic.

The Dauphin and three other French peers then blusteringly take the stage, at once displaying their narcissism.

As in III.vii, they are absorbed by externals, the "fair show" (IV.ii.17) of their horses and dress:

ORLEANS

The sun doth gild our armor. Up, my lords!

DAUPHIN

Monte, cheval! My horse, varlet lacquais! Ha!

ORLEANS

O brave spirit!

DAUPHIN

Via les eaux et terre!

The four men are then joined by a fifth, the Constable. Though staging calls for the group to stand before the audience in a line, the impression conveyed is one of mutual isolation and detachment—the very opposite of group solidarity. The fragmentary nature of the opening lines also confirms an aura of divisiveness, of obliviousness to everything but private concerns ("our honors," l. 32). To observe how well Shakespeare has used structural means to contrast public-spirited with egocentric values here, consider the way Henry's final line in the previous scene creates a liaison with this one. Henry's words, "The day, my friends, and all things wait for me" (IV.i.296), had emphasized his commitment to obligations outside himself. Juxtaposition of those words with the light-minded bravado of the Frenchmen heightens the play's central ethical opposition.

King Henry's "Crispin's day" speech is the rhetorical high point of IV.iii and of the play. But more important, the speech makes explicit the King's almost sacramental identification of himself and his men with their unanimous, high purpose: "We few, we happy few, we band of brothers; / For he to-day that sheds his blood with me / Shall be my brother" (ll. 60-62). The sense of community among Henry's officers had already been depicted at the beginning of the scene in their exchange of affectionate epithets—"noble," "good," "kind," "full of valor," "princely" (ll. 8-16). This camaraderie and devotion to public responsibility, in spite of the "fearful odds" (l. 5), may be contrasted with the endless self-congratulations of the Frenchmen in the preceding scene.

Pistol's capture of Monsieur le Fer in IV.iv is an episode that is humorous only on the surface. Though we may smile at Pistol's punningly tortured French, the chilling purpose of the scene is to remind us that Pistol and his "yoke-fellows in arms" became soldiers for predatory, not patriotic, reasons: "like horse-leeches . . . to suck!" As Pistol leads off his captive, whose life has been spared by the promise to pay 200 crowns in ransom, the

Boy soliloquizes on Pistol's self-serving hypocrisy and cowardice: "I did never know so full a voice issue from so empty a heart . . . 'The empty vessel makes the greatest sound'" (IV.iv.66-68). As Derek Traversi rightly observes, "The chief quality of Pistol is *emptiness,* a bombastic show that wordily covers vacancy."[9] Pistol, his lately-hanged confederates Nym and Bardolph, and the boastful French nobles are all types of the "hollow men" envisioned by T. S. Eliot in the poem of that name. And significantly, all of these self-centered, spiritually vacuous characters are later defeated or humiliated by characters who represent the good of the commonweal.

The next scene (IV.v) finds the French army in disarray and facing imminent defeat. In their concern with private stigma ("O perdurable shame! Let's stab ourselves. . . . Shame, and eternal shame! nothing but shame! / Let us die in honor," IV.v.8, 11-12), the Dauphin and his colleagues are oblivious to the national danger. The operative word in this brief, 24-line scene is *shame;* it occurs no less than six times. As in the preceding scene, personal interests transcend public ones, though for the last time in the play. From IV.vi through to the end, every scene magnifies the ideal of community.

In scene vi of Act IV, a mirror inversion of the previous scene, King Harry hears Exeter describe the noble battlefield deaths of Suffolk and York. Although both scenes are virtually equal in length (24 lines in IV.v, 36 in IV.vi) and deal with the fortunes of war, their emphases are antithetical. Whereas in IV.v the French were engrossed with private honor, York's dying words in IV.vi refer selflessly to his public commitment: "'Commend my service to my sovereign'" (l. 23). There follows yet another exemplary resolution of the private/public antinomy. Upon Exeter's admission that he was moved to tears by York's death, Henry too gets "mistful eyes" (l. 34). At that precise moment the French sound an alarum (l. 34 s.d.) signifying their intention to rally. Henry is compelled instantly to respond to that tactical disadvantage by ordering the French prisoners executed. Predictably, critics who opt for an ironic reading of the play interpret this action as heinous or unnecessarily cruel.[10] But the manifest function of the incident is to make a razor-sharp juxtaposition: Henry as capable of feeling the deepest private compassion, yet able to stanch that emotion utterly when public danger threatens. For this episode Shakespeare even adapts his sources—in both Hall and Holinshed—in a way calculated to enhance our impression of Henry as a model of social responsibility, not the private avenger of the murdered luggage boys.[11]

After the English victory, Montjoy the herald seeks King Henry's permission to allow the French to bury their dead. The herald makes a special point of the need

"To sort our nobles from our common men" for ". . . our vulgar drench their peasant limbs / In blood of princes" (IV.vii.69, 72-73). The class partiality of the living is now to be reimposed upon the dead. By contrast, among Fluellen and his other comrades of high and low estate, King Henry reaffirms the mutuality that continues to unify all levels of the English social hierarchy (ll. 89-173). His mock-serious teasing of Williams in the next scene—his pretended indignation at the "bitter terms" he endured while incognito in IV.i, and his desire for "satisfaction"—ends good-naturedly with the presentation of the glove filled with crowns (IV.viii.53-54). Henry's gift-giving assuages Williams' honor, and, like their earlier exchange of gloves, functions as a rite of incorporation, re-establishing parity in their interdependent social relationship. Like the glove-exchange, the gesture has little psychological interest, being above all emblematic social symbolism.[12]

From the Chorus we learn of Henry's triumphal return to England. For reasons of modesty, the King refuses to display tokens of his personal heroism, "Being free from vainness and self-glorious pride; / Giving full trophy, signal, and ostent / Quite from himself to God" (V. Chor. 20-22). Henry's piety remains a conspicuous thematic idea throughout the play, and this emergence of it echoes his own words in the previous scene: "O God, . . . to thy arm alone, / Ascribe we all!" (IV.viii.101-3). And yet its very obviousness arouses suspicion in several modern commentators, who refuse to take Henry's virtue at face value.[13] To be sure, Henry refers to God oftener than any other Shakespearean character, even more frequently than the Henry whose deeds Holinshed records. But never, in any of its dramatic contexts, does the trait smack in the least of personal righteousness. Instead, it functions as a socio-ethical motif, connoting the alliance with Providence that rewards champions of the general welfare.

The critics who insist upon reading the two scenes of Act V as the concluding segment of a traditional five-act structure are almost always disappointed. Samuel Johnson, for example, held that "the poet's matter failed him in the fifth act, and he was glad to fill it up with whatever he could get."[14] That the historical actions of the last act take place five years after the heroic battle of Agincourt inevitably strikes Shakespeare's detractors as the worst kind of anticlimax. But if the two scenes comprising Act V are analyzed *scenically,* in terms of their significant bearing upon the private/public thematic paradigm, the organic purpose of the last act becomes manifest. While every scene after IV.v vindicates communal values, the two scenes of Act V together form a diptych that provides the public ethos with its final, closural affirmation. With these two scenes, the conceptual opposition that informs the entire play is climactically resolved. Scene i, in the satiric mode, presents the exemplary defeat or nullification of private expediency;

scene ii, on the other hand, is in the mode of festive comedy, and celebrates personal and socio-political harmony on an international scale.

Each scene is dominated by an emblematic, ritual action which has the reverse implications of that in the other scene. In scene i, that action is Fluellen's belaboring Pistol with a leek until he falls stunned to his knees (V.i.32-34). On the literal level, as farce, the gesture signifies revenge for Pistol's having insulted the Welshman for wearing the leek on St. Davy's day. But as dramatic symbolism, Pistol's humiliation betokens the play's wider repudiation of the kind of self-love that undermines responsibility to the community at large. By reason of his cowardice and opportunism, Pistol has been an exemplar of anti-social behavior; he is thus the play's comic villain. His punishment figures forth society's retributive action: the ritual expulsion of the scapegoat who personifies hated taboo values. With both Fluellen and Gower "officiating," Pistol's rites take the form of abusive name-calling ("scurvy, lousy . . . counterfeit cowardly knave," etc.), physical degradation (being pummeled with and forcefed the leek), and finally explicit banishment ("God bye you. . . . Go, go. . . . Fare ye well"). Shakespeare is careful to emphasize that Pistol is no mere victim of personal vengeance, but the object of collective derision. For the leek is unequivocally a social symbol, a totem of British patriotic virtue which even King Henry himself wears as an "honorable padge" (IV.vii.96-100). It is thus an index of Pistol's self-absorption that he grows "qualmish at the smell of leek" (V.i.19), being given only to "mock at an ancient tradition, begun upon an honorable respect and worn as a memorable trophy of predeceased valor" (ll. 63-65). His ignominy lacks even a shred of pathos. But though now a declared pariah, the unrepentant Pistol will yet maintain his leech-like relation to society: "To England will I steal, and there I'll steal" (l. 79). That he also intends to become a bawd (l. 78) expands his associations with social outlawry and sterility—a fact that establishes a significant liaison with the next scene, as will be apparent shortly.

Whether primitive or advanced, every society employs special ceremonies to mark its members' crucial changes of life. Rites of banishment, expulsion, or excommunication are one type of what Arnold van Gennep has called rites of passage, and initiatory rites of incorporation are seen as their counterpart (van Gennep, pp. 113-15). And whereas an expulsion ritual was found to be the underlying form of V.i of *Henry V,* Act V, scene ii involves the converse symbolic action, a rite of incorporation. Anticipatory rites of incorporation had occurred earlier in Act IV, scenes i and viii, when the King gesturally affirmed a bond of mutuality with his soldiers. But the betrothal of Henry and Princess Katherine solemnizes a full-scale personal and national incorporation. In the opening moments there are semiological expressions of divisiveness: the French and English parties make ceremonial entries from opposite doors, and take up positions on either side of a wooden bar (V.ii.27) that divides the stage.[15] The scene concludes, however, with a summary enactment of the new "incorporate league" (l. 350) of France and England. A ceremonial trumpet flourish accompanies Henry's kiss of the Princess (l. 342 s.d.), magnifying that gesture into a national rite of unification.

Even the numerous sexual references and innuendoes in this scene relate to the ascendancy of public over private values in the play. For unlike the brutal sexuality associated with Pistol in the last scene, the sexual nuances attending Henry's betrothal to the French princess have socially beneficial connotations. As the royal pair embodies political unity ("Combine your hearts in one, your realms in one!" l. 344), so their sexuality is directed toward communal, national-evangelical goals ("Shall not thou and I . . . compound a boy, half French, half English, that shall . . . take the Turk by the beard?" ll. 200-203). Such sexual allusions as this and the remarks of the quibbling Duke of Burgundy ("If you would conjure in her, you must make a circle," ll. 282-83; cf. ll. 136-41, 200) have both thematic and anthropological relevance. They are metonyms for the life-force necessary to rejuvenate the French nation, once a "garden of the world, / Our fertile France" (ll. 36-37), but now made moribund and infertile by war ("nothing teems / But hateful docks, rough thistles, kecksies, burrs," ll. 51-52). And just as indecency worked as vestigial fertility symbolism in Greek Old Comedy, surviving as a saturnalian element in Shakespearean festive comedies like *Love's Labor's Lost* and *Much Ado About Nothing*,[16] so it functions with like effect in *Henry V.* Surely it was for this purpose that the Princess' sexual sophistication was established in III.iv, when she acknowledged to her gentlewoman her awareness of the obscene puns. That incident not only revealed Katherine's humanity but suggested her latent sexuality, foreshadowing the role that her procreativeness would eventually play in the dynastic and sociopolitical union of France and England. The play ends with the marriage in immediate prospect, and the wedding party departs in a festal procession—an analogue of the *kommos* of Attic comedy, and the canonical ending of all comedy. When one considers the important question of genre, then, necessarily a side issue in the present essay, the cumulative structural and stylistic evidence makes it clear that *Henry V* is as much a festive comedy or a heroic romance as a history play.[17]

IV

The foregoing scene-by-scene analysis confirms what many recent studies of Shakespearean structure have demonstrated: that act division plays no part at all in the design of the plays; that their basic dramatic unit is the scene; that there is a conscious design in the internal organization of the scenes, as in the schematicism of *A Midsummer Night's Dream* or the symmetry of *The Winter's Tale;* and that the scenes are individually molded compositions which are part of an organically unified pattern.[18] This is true of *Henry V,* whose individual scenes or integral groups of scenes severally depict two contrary sets of values, values which alternate in prominence throughout the play.

There is, however, a wide disparity in the structural emphasis given the two sets of contraries. If we let the total number of lines in support of each ethical alternative stand as a rough index of relative importance, then *communitas* is preferred to egoism by nearly three to one, 2541 lines (73.6%) as compared with 880 (26.4%).[19] But more important is the fact that the climactic last half-dozen scenes of the play present a sustained triumph of the public ethos. In other words, the overall pattern of scenes organizes the positive and negative values not merely as oscillating, paradigmatic categories, but as an emerging temporal sequence wherein social mores progressively transcend anti-social ones.[20] It is emphatically a moral structure.

Expressed diagrammatically, the fortunes of characters who variously represent self-interest, such as Pistol and the French chivalry, begin a diagonal descent to repudiation and defeat almost from the beginning of the play. Intersecting that downward vector is the upward diagonal that represents the justification and growing success of King Henry and like-minded supporters of communal goals. A comprehensive analysis of scenic structure not only reveals the unifying conceptual design of *Henry V,* but also verifies the majority understanding of the play as one whose nature is exemplary rather than ironic or satiric.

Notes

1. Richard Levin, *The Multiple Plot in English Renaissance Drama* (Chicago: Univ. of Chicago Press, 1971), pp. 116-19.

2. Alfred Harbage, gen. ed., *The Complete Pelican Shakespeare* (Baltimore: Penguin Books, 1969), p. 32.

3. Mark Rose, *Shakespearean Design* (Cambridge, Mass.: Belknap Press of the Harvard Univ. Press, 1972), p. 21 et passim; the remarks immediately following are indebted to this book. On the "speaking-picture" aspect of Renaissance visual epistemology, mentioned next, see also Forrest G. Robinson, *The Shape of Things Known: Sidney's Apology in Its Philosophical Tradition* (Cambridge, Mass.: Harvard Univ. Press, 1972), chaps. 2 and 3.

4. Morris Palmer Tilley, *Elizabethan Proverb Lore in Lyly's* Euphues *and in Pettie's* Petite Palace *with Parallels from Shakespeare,* Univ. of Michigan Publications, Language and Literature, 2 (New York: Macmillan, 1926), item 505. Unaccountably, the proverb and its many examples are omitted from Tilley's expanded version of this work, published posthumously in 1950.

5. Citations are to *The Complete Pelican Shakespeare,* op. cit.

6. See E. F. J. Tucker, "Legal Fiction and Human Reality: Hal's Role in *Henry V,*" *Educational Theatre Journal,* 26 (1974), 308-14; Ernst H. Kantorowicz, *The King's Two Bodies: A Study in Mediaeval Political Theology* (Princeton: Princeton Univ. Press, 1957), p. 8 et passim.

7. See Marilyn L. Williamson, "The Episode with Williams in *Henry V,*" *Studies in English Literature, 1500-1900,* 9 (1969), 280-81; cf. Anne Barton's view, that the quarrel and Henry's allegedly patronizing generosity contradict the romantic, ballad tradition ("The King Disguised: Shakespeare's *Henry V* and the Comical History," in *The Triple Bond: Plays, Mainly Shakespearean, in Performance,* ed. Joseph G. Price [University Park: Pennsylvania State Univ. Press, 1975], pp. 100-101).

8. Arnold van Gennep, *The Rites of Passage,* trans. Monika B. Vizedom and Gabrielle Caffee (Chicago: Univ. of Chicago Press, 1960), pp. 131-33.

9. Derek Traversi, *Shakespeare from* Richard II *to* Henry V (Stanford: Stanford Univ. Press, 1957), p. 193. Note, too, that Pistol's trumpery in this scene is stylistically isolated by his use of stilted blank verse, while the Boy and the Frenchman converse ingenuously in prose.

10. E.g., Norman Rabkin condemns the act as an illegitimate "response to the fair battlefield killing of some English nobles by the French" ("Rabbits, Ducks, and *Henry V,*" *Shakespeare Quarterly,* 28 [1977], 292), but fails to mention the French alarum that prompted it; H. M. Richmond considers the English as "guilty of barbarities" as the French (*Shakespeare's Political Plays* [New York: Random House, 1967], p. 198).

11. Holinshed, "The Third Volume of Chronicles: Henry V," *Narrative and Dramatic Sources of Shakespeare,* ed. Geoffrey Bullough, IV (1962; rpt. London: Routledge & Kegan Paul, 1975), 397.

12. See van Gennep, pp. 131-33.

13. For a debunking of this refutative critical technique, which has been used specifically to question Henry V's piety, see Richard Levin, "Refuting Shakespeare's Endings. Part II," *Modern Philology,* 75 (1977), 139-40. See also Traversi, cited above.

14. *The Yale Edition of the Works of Samuel Johnson,* Vols. VII and VIII, *Johnson on Shakespeare,* ed. Arthur Sherbo (New Haven and London: Yale Univ. Press, 1968), VIII, 565. J. M. Maguin observes that Act V is structurally coextensive whether the act division of the First Folio or of modern editions is used, making V.i-ii by either scheme a depressing "continuation of a deliberately descending curve" ("Shakespeare's Structural Craft and Dramatic Technique in *Henry V,*" *Cahiers Elisabethains,* 7 [1975], 59). For an affirmative approach to Act V, differing from my own, see George Walton Williams' argument that its scenes "are thematically united in presenting peace and order, at home and abroad. They are also thematically unified by references to language and to the garden" ("The Unity of Act V in *Henry V,*" *South Atlantic Bulletin,* 40 [1975], 5).

15. The semantic value of gesture, movement (including stage grouping), and decor is discussed in my essay, "Visual and Aural Signs in the Performed English Renaissance Play," *Renaissance Drama,* NS 5 (1972), 154-57.

16. See C. L. Barber, *Shakespeare's Festive Comedy: A Study of Dramatic Form and its Relation to Social Custom* (Princeton: Princeton Univ. Press, 1959), pp. 7-8, citing Francis MacDonald Cornford, *The Origins of Attic Comedy* (1914; rpt. Garden City, N.Y.: Doubleday Anchor, 1961), see esp. pp. 38-39.

17. Barber's classic study approaches two other history plays, *1* and *2 Henry IV,* in terms of festive comedy, but not *Henry V.* Significantly, in its bawdiness the latter more typifies Shakespearean comedy; it was designated "the obscenest of the Histories" by the authority on such matters, Eric Partridge (*Shakespeare's Bawdy: A Literary and Psychological Essay and a Comprehensive Glossary* [1947; rev. rpt. London: Routledge & Kegan Paul, 1968], p. 45).

18. See Rose, esp. pp. 1-26; Hereward T. Price, "Mirror-Scenes in Shakespeare," in *Joseph Quincy Adams Memorial Studies,* ed. James G. McManaway, et al. (Washington, D.C.: Folger Shakespeare Library, 1948), pp. 101-13; and Wildred T. Jewkes, *Act Division in Elizabethan and Jacobean Plays 1583-1616* (Hamden, Conn.: Shoe String Press, 1958). See also Emrys Jones, *Scenic Form in Shakespeare* (Oxford: Clarendon Press, 1971). A precursor of the extended scenic-structural reading is Hereward T. Price's analysis of *1 Henry VI*

in *Construction in Shakespeare,* Univ. of Michigan Contributions in Modern Philology, 17 (Ann Arbor: Univ. of Michigan Press, 1951), pp. 24-37.

19. Lineation used is that of Charlton Hinman's facsimile edition of the First Folio (New York: W. W. Norton, 1968). For the reason given earlier, the fifty lines of the combined Prologue and Epilogue are excluded from the count.

20. For other uses of oscillation analysis in Shakespeare studies, see Elemér Hankiss' report on the Investigative Committee on New Research Methods in *Shakespeare 1971: Proceedings of the World Shakespeare Congress, Vancouver, August 1971,* ed. Clifford Leech and J. M. R. Margeson (Toronto: Univ. of Toronto Press, 1972), p. 274.

W. M. Richardson (essay date winter 1981)

SOURCE: Richardson, W. M. "The Brave New World of Shakespeare's *Henry V* Revisited." *Allegorica* 6, no. 2 (winter 1981): 149-54.

[*In the following essay, Richardson claims that* Henry V *features Shakespeare's depiction of a cynically modern and amoral state.*]

By modern political criteria, the medieval world was confused and chaotic. Men's loyalties and duties were divided among the often conflicting claims of the Church, the crown, and their feudal overlords; and it was largely due to these divided loyalties that Malory's Arthur's dream of an England united in the fellowship of the Round Table failed. By the time Malory's *Morte D'arthur* ends, feudal loyalties, the Grail quest and other claims of the Church, clan loyalties, and the obligations of the Courtly Love tradition have broken the ties of brotherhood so precariously united in the Round Table; and both Arthur and his dream are dead.

However, it is doubtful that the political confusion resulting from the varying claims of these institutions more seriously complicated life for the generality of men than the later emergence of a unified state under a powerful central government. Because Church, crown, and overlord were often in competition with one another, their demands on the individual were ultimately less oppressive than those of the all-powerful state. Moreover, the options available to most men may have been enhanced, giving the individual more freedom to choose his own priorities rather than those assigned him by the state.

Certainly the world of Malory, like that depicted by Chaucer in *The Canterbury Tales,* is a broader, more comprehensive world than that which exists at the end of Shakespeare's *Henry V* trilogy. For by the end of the trilogy, everything—man, the Church, even God—has been reduced to the narrow expediency of the state as embodied in Shakespeare's Hal. To pass from Arthur's dream to Hal's reality is to pass into a shrunken world, a world of diminished possibilities. The transformation of England from a medieval society to a modern state is the larger theme of Shakespeare's trilogy, and much more is at stake than simply Hal's own humanity. Before the end of *Henry V* Falstaff, the symbol of warm, lusty, unregenerate life for its own sake, is banished and dead. Hotspur, the ostensible personification of the chivalric ideal, has been used and betrayed by the practitioners of the new politics and is finally killed by its most successful practitioner, who desires only the appearance of chivalry. The Church, trying desperately to protect its resources from the crown, has become an accomplice to Hal's morally and legally dubious war against France; and Bardolph and Nym have been sentenced to death for a relatively trivial crime by a man whose hands are red with the blood of thousands—a man who is shortly to order the massacre of large numbers of helpless prisoners.

Even the feudal injunction requiring the loyalty and obedience of the vassal only as long as they are not in conflict with basic Christian values has been abrogated. In his dialogue with the common soldier Williams, this consummate politician manages to place the blame for the wrongs committed in the service of the king or state upon the shoulders of its humblest instruments. They, with God, must share the joint responsibilities for the bloody acts of the state.

The radical dissociation of moral sensibilities so characteristic of the modern state and, indeed, of modern man has already taken place.[1] And, for Hal, the dissociation is convenient. Hal can forgive his would-be assassins for their plot on his person but can order them executed for their conspiracy against him as the state. As the state, he can blackmail the Church into sanctioning his war on France and make it God's war as well as his. As the state, he can threaten the recalcitrant citizens of Harfleur with the rape of their daughters, the slaughter of their elders, and the spitting of their infants upon pikes. And after his exchange with the soldier Williams on the eve of Agincourt, this politic aggressor, this most warlike of kings, can speak with terrible sincerity of the terrible burdens of kingship, of

> What watch the King keeps to maintain the peace,
> Whose hours the peasant best advantages.
>
> (*Henry V,* IV, i)[2]

Nearly all the contents of the Pandora's box of evils that modern man has opened are present in the trilogy—not only the split between the private and public sphere of human action but also the dreadful consequences of a narrow and parochial nationalism. When one considers the context of the foregoing speech and Hal's motives in invading France: to busy "giddy minds with foreign quarrels," the peace he speaks of can only be the domestic peace of England. For that, another peaceful kingdom must be laid waste, helpless prisoners slaughtered, and men killed in thousands. It is a familiar gambit, an act of short-term expediency. The French, like William Perkins' poor, are expendable in a good cause, "a cursed generation," who are, in contrast to the English, denied the promise of God's kingdom and belong to "no civill societie," but are as "rotten legges and arms, that drop from the body." Thus Christianity, with its larger obligations and its promise of a larger brotherhood, is now confined within national boundaries and, like man, suffers from diminution in Hal's brave new world.

That Shakespeare provides a classic portrait of the modern state and its rulers in the trilogy is undeniable. That Hal has generally been considered Shakespeare's ideal king is perhaps due to the acquiescence of modern man in his own diminution and the corresponding shrinkage of his moral perspective. That Shakespeare encourages us to see Hal's limits, his moral obliquity, is, I think, obvious. In Henry IV, Part I, he places Hal in the shadow of Hotspur and Falstaff; in Part II, he shows him cruelly rejecting Falstaff and eagerly seizing his father's crown. Further, he gives us little evidence that Hal is either a good or responsible king, or that he considers England any more than an extension of himself.

Many critics have been taken in by Hal's wit and rhetorical skills, but the soldiers who, with the French civilians, are the initial victims of his policies are under no illusions about him. Pistol knows that the English are going to France "like horse leeches . . . to suck, to suck, the very blood to suck." Hal evades rather than answers the charges of the loyal Williams, and the comparison of Hal and "Alexander the Pig" by Gower and Fluellen after hearing of the order to kill the French prisoners is devastating in its irony:

Gow.

.. the King, most worthily, hath caused every soldier to cut his prisoner's throat. O, 'tis a gallant King!

Flu.

Aye, he was porn at Monmouth, Captain Gower. What call you the town's name where Alexander the pig was born?

Gow.

Alexander the Great.

Flu.

Why, I pray you, is not pig great? The pig, or the great, or the mighty, or the huge, or the magnanimous, are all one reckonings, save the phrase is a little variations.

This rather pointed exchange, which also involves parallels drawn between Alexander's Cleitus and Hal's Falstaff, ends with Fluellen exclaiming "I'll tell you there is good men porn at Monmouth" (*Henry V*, IV, vii).

Those who believe that the larger theme of the trilogy shows a tragic Hal reluctantly surrendering his humanity to the importunities of kingship overlook the fact that Hal is the only unchanging factor in the trilogy. Only his outward circumstances change. Hal is, in the end, as he was in the beginning, the shrewd, unscrupulous, politician using people as tools for his own ends, whether they be to astound the world with his reformation, as factors "to engross up glorious deeds" in his behalf, or to fill up breaches in the walls of Harfleur. Most damaging is Hal's brutal rebuttal of the troubled Williams' assertion that if Hal's soldiers "do not die well, it will be a black matter for the king that led them to it, whom to disobey were against all proportion of subjection." Hal answers:

> The King is not bound to answer the particular endings of his soldiers . . . for they purpose not their death when they purpose their services. Besides, there is no king, be his cause never so spotless, if it come to the arbitrement of swords, can try it out with all unspotted soldiers. Some peradventure have on them the guilt of premeditated and contrived murder; some, of beguiling virgins with the broken seals of perjury; some, making the wars their bulwark, that have before gored the gentle bosom of peace with pillage and robbery. Now if these men have defeated the law and outrun native punishment, though they can outstrip men, they have no wings to fly from God. War is His beadle, war is His vengeance, so that here men are punished for before-breach of the King's laws in now the King's quarrel. . . . Then if they die unprovided, no more is the King guilty of their damnation than he was before guilty of those impieties for the which they are now visited. Every subject's duty is the King's, but every subject's soul is his own.
>
> (*Henry V*, IV, i).

The speciousness of Hal's logic here is stunning.

Samuel Johnson said of Homer that neither nations nor time has been "able to do more than transpose his incidents, newname his characters, and paraphrase his sentiments." Most certainly this is true of nations in the twentieth century with regard to Shakespeare. Hal's sentencing of Bardolph and Nym and his specious reply to Williams have, in our day, been echoed at Nuremberg and the Lieutenant Calley trial. The cry of "Once more unto the breach" has echoed continually since Hal's time, and uncounted millions have rushed forth in their youth to fill one breach or another. Still the breaches become larger and the cries shriller and more urgent.

Surely the larger tragedy and theme of the *Henry V* trilogy is not Hal's alone but humanity's as well. To be sure, that medieval order, of which Hotspur and Falstaff

Christian Bale as Falstaff's Boy, Ian Holm as Fluellen, and Daniel Webb as Gower in Kenneth Branagh's 1989 film version of Henry V.

are in their own differing ways representative, was decadent. It was an order whose decadence was reflected in the venality of the churchmen in *Henry V* as well as in the excesses of both Hotspur and Falstaff. Clearly, a change was needed, and Shakespeare was not engaged in whitewashing the past at the expense of the present. But a world lacking the qualities embodied in a Falstaff or Hotspur, however much they need tempering, is surely a poorer world. A world in which religion and the chivalric ideal have value only as instruments of policy is a poorer world. As Hal reduces all to his narrow exigencies, the range of human choice becomes more and more limited until, in the end, there is only the state. Arthur's dream would have united the conflicting loyalties and institutions of his world into a partnership and directed them toward a common and loftier secular end. Hal's reality subordinates or destroys them in pursuit of its own questionable ends. One feels that Arthur would have rejoiced in a Hotspur and a Falstaff even as he sought to curb their excesses, but Hal destroys them.

The larger promises implicit in Hal's soliloquy in *Henry IV,* Part I, beginning

I know you all, and will a while uphold
The unyoked humor of your idleness,

are made quite explicit by the end of *Henry V;* and Falstaff's cry "Banish plump Jack and banish all the world" has been prophetic because only the state blindly pursu-.ing its own purposeless destiny remains. Despite his wit and his moments of insight, Hal remains, beneath his stolen mantle of chivalry, a sort of political Flem Snopes. He has pursued power as blindly as and to no more discernible purpose than Flem pursued wealth, and therein lies the tragedy for both Hal and humanity. If Flem is Faulkner's equivalent of Max Weber's capitalist man—one who rationally exploits other human beings for profit pursued as an end in itself—then Hal is his political equivalent: one who rationally exploits people for power pursued as an end in itself. And the emergence of both Hal and Flem in the modern age has given an added touch of horror to a world already horrible enough in its reality. Both exploit and manipulate men for ends that are incomprehensible in terms of normal human motivation, ends that are, in fact, ahuman. We can comprehend the motivations of Flem's predecessors, the Compsons, Sutpens, and Sartorises even as we deplore them, just as we can comprehend those of a Falstaff and Hotspur and his fellow conspirators even as we deplore them. With both Hal and Flem man's sublunary predicament has come to mirror his predicament in the larger universe he inhabits. Man's own world which had, with the traditional consolations of religion, provided him with some relief from the hell of life in an indifferent and incomprehensible universe has become as indifferent to his needs and as incomprehensible to him as that larger universe. Therein lies, I think, the peculiar horror of Hal and the modern state of which he is Shakespeare's exemplar

There are critics who are fond of speaking of Shakespeare's dark period, but I submit that the *Henry V* trilogy is the blackest work Shakespeare ever did. The implications of Hal's brave new world are too sad, too horrible for satire, cynicism, or railing; and the sympathy of Shakespeare must finally embrace Hal, even as that of Faulkner embraces Flem. It is for these reasons that so much critical confusion exists about Shakespeare's intention with regard to Hal and what he represents. The dreary truth of the emergence of the modern state and its consequences for man can only be treated in the tones of restraint that sorrow and utter hopelessness engender. Shakespeare's apprehensions concerning the new political order which Hal represents have become a frightening reality today; and virtually the only voices one hears in our literature are those of frightened, impotent little men vainly protesting that they want to live. But our Hals in their madness do not hear and still ready themselves and their peoples to prevail or die to no purpose on some field of Agincourt. Their world, like Hal's,

> Hath really neither joy, nor love, nor light,
> Nor certitude, nor peace, nor help for pain.

After writing his trilogy, it would have been redundant, I feel, for Shakespeare to have exclaimed like Conrad's Kurtz over the horror of it all.

Notes

1. Nor is this radical separation of the private sphere from the public with regard to morality restricted to politicians like Hal. One is almost inescapably reminded of R. W. H. Tawney's comment on the Puritan tendency to regard "religion as a thing privately vital but publicly indifferent." Historically, it was the middle class, puritanical in nature before Calvin, who joined with the monarchy to found modern England; and if one can give credence to his critics, the Puritan was as pathologically concerned as Hal to conceal this schism.

2. All quotations from Shakespeare are taken from G. B. Harrison's *Shakespeare: The Complete Works.* (New York, 1952).

Richard Levin (essay date summer 1984)

SOURCE: Levin, Richard. "Hazlitt on *Henry V,* and the Appropriation of Shakespeare." *Shakespeare Quarterly* 35, no. 2 (summer 1984): 134-41.

[*In the following essay, Levin argues that contemporary ironic readings of* Henry V—*those that generally suggest that Shakespeare's dramatic presentation of King Henry is unfavorable—have tended to "appropriate" the work rather than properly interpret it.*]

What used to be called the new ironic reading of Shakespeare's *Henry V* is of course no longer new, since it has been espoused by a growing number of studies of the play over the past three decades, and therefore does not require any extended explanation. Although these studies differ among themselves on matters of detail and emphasis, and sometimes add special qualifications of their own, they generally follow the basic line laid down in Harold Goddard's essay, published in 1951, which is still the most elaborate and probably (as later references to it would indicate) the most influential statement of this position.[1] Its fundamental premise is that Shakespeare designed the play to convey two contradictory meanings—an apparent or surface meaning (usually explained as a sop to the less intelligent members of his audience) which seems to present Henry as a great national hero, the "mirror of all Christian kings," but which is undercut by a pervasive and subversive irony (aimed at the wiser few) that embodies the real meaning and reveals that Henry is actually a cynical hypocrite, a cold-blooded Machiavellian, a brutal butcher, and so forth.

To judge from a quick survey of recent publications, this is now the dominant view of the play, and is well on its way to becoming the new orthodoxy. As early as 1970, Laurence Michel could say that it was not necessary to spend much time arguing for his ironic interpretation because "most of this exegesis has been done already, and I can merely reiterate," which he proceeds to do in a brief summary; and eight years later Ralph Berry began his essay by asserting that "the ironic reading of *Henry V,* which has received some outstandingly able advocacy, seems to me unanswerable. But I shall assume at least a general acquiescence on that score."[2] I have presented my answers to this reading elsewhere,[3] and have no desire to reiterate them here, since I would like to examine instead a different but closely related new reading that has emerged alongside this one and is now also on its way to achieving orthodox status—namely, the reading of William Hazlitt's essay on *Henry V,* published in 1817 in his *Characters of Shakespear's Plays,* as an ironic interpretation and hence as a forerunner of Goddard, Michel, Berry, and the rest. I believe that this is a serious misunderstanding of Hazlitt which should be rectified, but that is not my only motive, because I also believe that an examination of this misunderstanding will vindicate one of my own arguments against the ironic reading of *Henry V* that has been challenged, and at the same time shed some light on the nature of the reasoning that underlies such readings of this play and of many others as well.

I

The earliest suggestion of this view of Hazlitt known to me appears in 1962 in a study by Roy Battenhouse which he introduces as "a basic extension" of the Goddard position that *Henry V* is constructed as a "double-edged" play:

> It will allow some spectators, blinded by a surface patriotism, to admire as their own ideal its particular heroism. But it will permit others to discern, as various modern critics have, . . . a suspicious fulsomeness in the rhetoric, and a kind of heroism in Henry more suggestive of "a very amiable monster" (Hazlitt's phrase), or of "some handsome spirited horse" (Yeats's phrase), than of a truly human being.[4]

It is made clearer a few years later in Ronald Berman's assertion that Hazlitt regarded the play "as a satire on the *ancien régime,* and applauded anything in it which seemed to undercut hierarchy, feudalism, and Christian politics."[5] In 1970 Herbert Coursen explicitly equates Hazlitt's interpretation with Goddard's: "Harold Goddard and others . . . have filled in Hazlitt's outline and have read the play as a *condemnation* of its principal character"; and in 1978 he calls this "the Hazlitt-Goddard thesis."[6] Michael Manheim, writing in 1973, cites two recent ironic readings of the play and explains that they "follow a long tradition of Hal-haters, notably among literary figures: Hazlitt, Swinburne, Masefield, Yeats, and Mark Van Doren."[7] And in his 1978 essay Ralph Berry proposes to show that

> the mode of *Henry V* is the dubious or fallacious argument. If the arguments so constantly advanced in *Henry V* are generally sound [he of course will prove that they are not], then the play is a Meissonier canvas of a Great Patriotic War, Carlyle is right and Hazlitt is wrong, and modern critics have been wasting their time in peering for ironies where none exist.[8]

Several other statements of this sort were evoked by my assertion, in *New Readings vs. Old Plays,* that the earliest ironic reading of *Henry V* I could find was Gerald Gould's article of 1919,[9] and that before then there was a general consensus of opinion that the play was not ironic. In their reviews of the book, Roy Battenhouse objects: "Is there really a consensus of response? Hazlitt, we may recall, considered Henry V an 'amiable monster'"; while E. A. J. Honigmann claims that Gould's reading "has an honourable ancestry before 1919 in the work of Hazlitt, Watkiss Lloyd, Yeats, and others. There are really two traditions where *Henry V* is

concerned."[10] And Coursen criticizes me for "overlook-[ing] Hazlitt's violent exception to 'consensus' in 1845, a predictable republican reaction to be reiterated by the Quaker, Harold Goddard, a century later."[11]

II

To see that this view of Hazlitt's position is clearly wrong, we need go no further than the first two sentences of his essay. He begins:

> Henry V. is a very favourite monarch with the English nation, and he appears to have been also a favourite with Shakespear, who labours hard to apologise for the actions of the king, by shewing us the character of the man, as "the king of good fellows." He scarcely deserves this honour.[12]

And the essay itself faithfully follows the logic of this double thesis. The first section draws up an indictment of Henry (which appears to be directed more at the historical personage than at the dramatic character) in order to show that he does not deserve the honor Shakespeare has bestowed on him, so it is obviously presented as Hazlitt's own indictment and not the play's. Then comes the transition: "So much for the politics of this play; now for the poetry" (p. 286). The remainder of the essay is devoted to a series of "splendid quotations," almost all of which contribute directly to the favorable portrayal of Henry and his cause. Hazlitt often expresses his admiration for the "strength and grace" or "beautiful rhetorical delineation" or "heroic beauty" of these passages, although he also occasionally indicates his disapproval of the values they embody[13]—a disapproval which presumably accounts for his resistance to that favorable portrait, and for his judgment that this "is but one of Shakespear's second-rate plays" (p. 289).

Thus, while it is perfectly clear that Hazlitt condemns Henry, there is no suggestion that he thinks the play does so. In fact, in the first section he admits that

> We like him in the play. There he is a very amiable monster, a very splendid pageant. As we like to gaze at a panther or a young lion in their cages, . . . so we take a very romantic, heroic, patriotic, and poetical delight in the boasts and feats of our younger Harry, as they appear on the stage.
>
> (p. 286)

And in the second section he says that

> The behaviour of the king, in the difficult and doubtful circumstances in which he is placed, is as patient and modest as it is spirited and lofty in his prosperous fortune.
>
> (p. 291)

Nor is there any suggestion that Hazlitt finds anything that might be called satire or irony in Shakespeare's treatment of Henry. I think we must conclude, therefore, that far from being an ancestor (much less an "outline") of Goddard's reading of *Henry V,* Hazlitt's is exactly the opposite: he interprets the play as a straightforward and very positive presentation of Henry that fails, whereas Goddard interprets it as an ironic and very negative presentation of him that succeeds (that is, for the wiser few, a group to which Hazlitt obviously does not belong).

III

We would also have to conclude, as a logical consequence, that Hazlitt's reading is not an exception to the consensus of opinion I spoke of, but is in fact part of it. For I was referring to a consensus in the *interpretation* of the play, not in the *evaluation* of it or its protagonist. We all know, of course, that the prevailing estimates of Renaissance characters and plays (and even of Renaissance drama as a whole) fluctuated widely over the years, because of changes in taste and in the theatre itself, and also in political and social attitudes, as Hazlitt demonstrates. What I maintained, however, was that the basic interpretation of most of these plays—that is, the perception of their intended effect, broadly defined—has remained quite constant from the earliest recorded responses, which often go back to the seventeenth century,[14] down to the advent of the new ironic readings in our own day. In this sense, then, the consensus on *Henry V* includes both Hazlitt and Carlyle, since they agree in their interpretation of Shakespeare's intention (to present Henry as an object of admiration), although they disagree sharply in their judgments of Henry (on whether he "deserves this honour") and hence of the play (on whether it realizes that intention). One could even argue that; in proving the existence of this consensus, Hazlitt's position is more significant than that of Carlyle and the many other admirers of Shakespeare's protagonist, for his disapproval of Henry should have made him especially sensitive to any indications of a similar attitude in the play itself. Therefore, the fact that he sees no such indications—that, despite his own feelings, he still believes that Henry was "a favourite with Shakespear, who labours hard to apologise" for him—must be considered a very impressive confirmation of the consensus, like the corroborative testimony of a hostile witness in court.

The same can be said, moreover, of several of the other "Hal-haters" named by the critics quoted earlier. Swinburne, Masefield, and Van Doren may question the merits of Henry (and of the play), but they never suggest that Shakespeare's portrayal of him is meant to be ironic or negative.[15] Their readings, in other words, belong to the same general class as Hazlitt's rather than Goddard's, which places them within this basic interpretive consensus. Watkiss Lloyd is different, since he argues that there are deliberate ironies in the play's

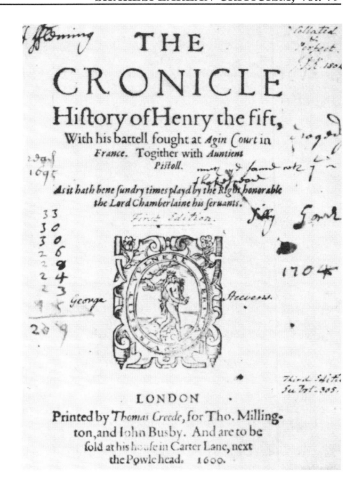

Title page of the First Quarto of Henry V *(1600).*

presentation of Henry; however, he regards them as "reservations" which are designed to qualify but not to cancel out the overall impression favorable to him and his enterprise, and so stops far short of claiming that the play as a whole is ironic.[16]

Yeats is the only one of those named who makes such a claim; he concludes that Shakespeare could not have admired Henry, and "watched [him] not indeed as he watched the greater souls in the visionary procession, but cheerfully, as one watches some handsome spirited horse, and he spoke his tale, as he spoke all tales, with tragic irony."[17] Although that is scarcely the kind of irony that Gould and Goddard and their followers find in the play, which is supposed to produce an emphatic condemnation of Henry, I probably should have cited this essay, rather than Gould's, as the earliest ironic reading and hence the first real break in the consensus on *Henry V.*

I may of course have overlooked other nineteenth-century ironic readings, but I do not see how there could be many of them, or how they could constitute a "tradition" of ironic interpretation, as Manheim and Honigmann suggest. If such a tradition existed, Gould was certainly not aware of it, since he titles his article "A New Reading of *Henry V*," and begins it with the assertion that "None of Shakespeare's plays is so persistently and thoroughly misunderstood as *Henry V*," after which he announces, in italics, that *"The play is ironic,"* as if he had made a major discovery. Indeed, Gould is even careful to distinguish his reading from Hazlitt's: "He detested Henry, and said so: but he made the mistake of supposing that that detestable character was a 'favourite' character of Shakespeare's" (p. 42).[18] Moreover, Gould seems to have had no discernible effect on the non-ironic consensus, which prevailed for at least thirty more years, even among those "Hal-haters," as we found in the case of Van Doren.[19] So far as I can ascertain, the ironic tradition did not really get under way (if that is what traditions do) until the studies of Goddard and Gilbert in the 1950s.

IV

It is not enough, however, to correct this erroneous conception of Hazlitt's essay (and of its relationship to the consensus), because we still have to ask why it has become so widespread. Since the critics quoted earlier could not have been deliberately misrepresenting Hazlitt, they must have been misreading him. And the nature of their misreading is quite clear: they failed to distinguish his view of Henry from his view of Shakespeare's view of Henry. They seem to have assumed, in other words, that his attitude toward the protagonist would also be the attitude he attributed to the play. And this assumption is by no means limited to them; it reappears, for instance, in several recent discussions of *Henry V* which divide the critics into those who admire Henry and those who dislike him, as if that were the crucial distinction which would necessarily determine their interpretations of the play.[20] But we have just seen that this is not true—that it is possible (or, at least, used to be possible) for critics to dislike Henry and yet believe that Shakespeare admired him and intended to present him non-ironically as an object of admiration. Such critics, we might say, disagree with the play.

Should we then ask if there are any examples of the reverse disagreements of critics who admire Henry but think that Shakespeare disliked him and meant to portray him ironically as an object of detestation? The question itself seems absurd, since it is obvious that all of the critics who read the play as an ironic condemnation of Henry also condemn him themselves. They never disagree with the play, because the attitude they find in it turns out to be identical with their own. This may help to explain why they have assumed that the same would be true of Hazlitt. And it may also raise the suspicion that they, unlike Hazlitt, are projecting their

attitude into *Henry V*, that with their ironic reading they are appropriating the play—to adopt Alan Sinfield's phrase[21]—so that it will mean what they want it to mean.

If we go on to consider why they should do this, it is not difficult to find explanations (I am not of course implying any conscious intention to distort the play). Projection is, after all, a natural tendency to which we are all subject in our responses to art as well as to life. It is also natural enough to take pleasure in discovering that, in the attitudes involved here, we are on the same side as our greatest cultural hero (which means proving that *he* is on *our* side). But the primary motive for these ironic readings would seem to be the desire to vindicate the play and its author. Critics like Hazlitt and Van Doren, who disliked Henry but thought that Shakespeare did not, tended to downgrade the play; their disagreement with it became, in effect, an adverse judgment of its values. But such a judgment is apparently inconceivable to the modern ironic critic. He sees it as his task to prove that the play's values are right (that is, that they coincide with his own), so if they seem to be wrong he must show, by means of an ironic reading, that they are only the "apparent" values and that the "real" ones are above reproach. (As Sinfield put it, he "attempt[s] to juggle the text into acceptability.") Goddard, for instance, is quite open about this; he begins his chapter on *Henry V* by stating that he will clear Shakespeare of the "charge" of jingoism (p. 216). And the fact that Gould's essay appeared in 1919 would suggest that he wanted to absolve Shakespeare of the sentiments associated with militarism, which now seemed so abhorrent.

Nor has this rescue operation been limited to *Henry V*. It is the underlying cause, I believe, of our many new ironic readings of *The Taming of the Shrew* and *The Merchant of Venice* (probably the two plays of the canon whose "apparent" values are most unacceptable today), which set out to demonstrate that we are really meant to condemn Petruchio's taming of Kate (or else to conclude that she was never really tamed after all), and that Portia and Antonio are really shown to be at least as bad as Shylock, if not much worse. Indeed, this conception of interpretation as exoneration is now so widely accepted that I have even heard the suspicion voiced (though I have not yet seen it in print)[22] that those who do *not* read these plays ironically may themselves be guilty of male chauvinism and antisemitism. From the perspective of the ironic critics this seems quite logical, because they always try to prove that a play embodies values which they believe in, and therefore expect that others will do so too. This is the same kind of reasoning, I suggested, which led them to assume that, if Hazlitt disliked Henry, he would read the play ironically in order to find it echoing his own attitude. That is what they would have done in his place.

V

It is also easy to understand why they would want to claim that Hazlitt's reading is ironic. For most of the critics quoted at the outset are themselves committed to the ironic interpretation of *Henry V,* and are therefore faced with the embarrassing fact that the "real" meaning they have discovered in the play does not seem to have been noticed for three hundred years by spectators or readers, including some of the most insightful commentators on Shakespeare, who have all interpreted the play in the opposite way (which is what the nonironic consensus means). This would indicate that there must be something radically wrong with the play, since it had obviously failed to communicate its meaning. But these critics cannot accept such a judgment, for we saw that their purpose was to vindicate the play—in fact they usually insist that it is brilliantly successful.[23] And that is why they feel the need to deny the consensus, and to recruit "an honourable ancestry" in Hazlitt and others. In order to protect their ironic reading of Shakespeare, they must go on to produce ironic readings of earlier readings of Shakespeare. Things bad begun make strong themselves by ill.

Now it may not matter very much if we misinterpret Hazlitt's little essay, which can scarcely be considered one of the treasures of our literary heritage. But I hope it is not necessary to argue that it matters a great deal if we misinterpret Shakespeare. And that will happen, inevitably, whenever we set out to prove that our own attitudes and values are mirrored in his plays. I may be entirely wrong, of course, in suggesting that this is what the new readings of the ironic critics amount to. But if I am, there is a very simple test that they can take to acquit themselves and refute me. All they have to do is tell us some significant respects in which their view of Henry's victory, or Kate's taming, or Shylock's trial differs from the view they attribute to Shakespeare. They certainly should be able to do this, because it is hardly possible that an author writing almost four centuries ago, in a culture which was in so many ways quite unlike ours, would have exactly the same attitudes on war and women and Jews (not to mention the more general social and moral values involved) as a critic living today. It seems perfectly fair, therefore, to ask them to state some of these differences in attitude. If they cannot, it seems fair to conclude that they are not really interpreting Shakespeare but appropriating him.

Notes

1. *The Meaning of Shakespeare* (Chicago: Univ. of Chicago Press, 1951), chap. 17.

2. *The Thing Contained: Theory of the Tragic* (Bloomington: Indiana Univ. Press, 1970), p. 65; *The Shakespearean Metaphor: Studies in Language and Form* (Totowa, N. J.: Rowman & Littlefield, 1978), p. 48.

3. *The Multiple Plot in English Renaissance Drama* (Chicago: Univ. of Chicago Press, 1971), pp. 116-19; *New Readings vs. Old Plays: Recent Trends in the Reinterpretation of English Renaissance Drama* (Chicago: Univ. of Chicago Press, 1979), chap. 3 passim.

4. "*Henry V* as Heroic Comedy," *Essays on Shakespeare and Elizabethan Drama in Honor of Hardin Craig,* ed. Richard Hosley (Columbia: Univ. of Missouri Press, 1962), pp. 165, 168.

5. Introduction, *Twentieth Century Interpretations of* Henry V (Englewood Cliffs, N. J.: Prentice-Hall, 1968), p. 14.

6. "Henry V and the Nature of Kingship," *Discourse,* 13 (1970), 283; Review of *The Triple Bond* (ed. Joseph Price), *Shakespeare Quarterly,* 29 (1978), 302. See also *The Leasing Out of England: Shakespeare's Second Henriad* (Washington, D. C.: University Press of America, 1982), p. 155.

7. *The Weak King Dilemma in the Shakespearean History Play* (Syracuse: Syracuse Univ. Press, 1973), p. 194. The two recent ironic readings cited are John Bromley, *The Shakespearean Kings* (Boulder: Colorado Associated Univ. Press, 1971), chap. 6, and C. H. Hobday, "Imagery and Irony in *Henry V,*" *Shakespeare Survey,* 21 (1968), 107-13.

8. *Shakespearean Metaphor,* p. 50.

9. "A New Reading of *Henry V,*" *English Review,* 29 (1919), 42-55.

10. *Comparative Drama,* 14 (1980), 237; *Yearbook of English Studies,* 12 (1982), 246.

11. *Exchange,* 5 (1979), 54 (he is responding to an earlier article where I made the same point). Hazlitt died in 1830, and Goddard was not a Quaker.

12. I quote from *The Complete Works of William Hazlitt,* ed. P. P. Howe (London: J. M. Dent, 1930-34), IV, 285-91.

13. See especially p. 288: "It is worth observing that in all these plays, which give an admirable picture of the spirit of the *good old times,* the moral inference does not at all depend upon the nature of the actions, but on the dignity or meanness of the persons committing them. . . . Might was right, without equivocation or disguise, in that heroic and chivalrous age."

14. The earliest comments known to me which could indicate an interpretation of *Henry V* are in Thomas Heywood's *An Apology for Actors* (1612), sig. B4ʳ, and Margaret Cavendish's *CCXI Sociable Letters* (1664), pp. 245-46 (Letter 123), and they both would belong to the consensus I am referring to.

15. Algernon Charles Swinburne, *A Study of Shakespeare* (London: Chatto & Windus, 1880), pp. 112-15; John Masefield, *William Shakespeare,* Home University Library of Modern Knowledge (London: Williams and Norgate, 1911), pp. 120-23; Mark Van Doren, *Shakespeare* (New York: Henry Holt, 1939), pp. 170-79.

16. William Watkiss Lloyd, *Critical Essays on the Plays of Shakespeare* (1856; rpt. London: George Bell, 1875), pp. 251-67: "Thus much in reservation, or thus much in vindication of the poet, who must not be lightly misconstrued as exhibiting a dazzling display of military heroism to take and astonish the world by its dash and brilliancy, while he overlooks or forgets to hint at the basenesses that are compatible with glories of this class. . . . Apart, however, from the question of the cause that calls them forth, the qualities that achieve military success are in themselves truly honourable and admirable. . . . While, therefore, the poet does not conceal the qualifications they are subject to, he addresses the national military spirit distinctly enough, and excites our esteem" (pp. 255-56). He concludes with a warning against "giv[ing] applause unmingled with any reservation to the successful bravery and ambition of Henry" (p. 267). Schlegel also finds some ironic elements in the play which qualify its presentation of "Shakespeare's favourite hero in English history"—see *A Course of Lectures on Dramatic Art and Literature* (1809-11), trans. John Black (London: Bohn, 1846), pp. 428-32.

17. William Butler Yeats, "At Stratford-on-Avon," *Ideas of Good and Evil* (London: A. H. Bullen, 1903), pp. 154-64.

18. See also Alan Gilbert, whose ironic reading is more tentative than Gould's: "Are we, going further even than Hazlitt, to interpret the work as a satire on a hypocrite whose ambition disregards the misery he causes?" ("Patriotism and Satire in *Henry V,*" *Studies in Shakespeare,* ed. Arthur Matthews and Clark Emery [Coral Gables, Fla.: Univ. of Miami Press, 1953], p. 62).

19. Further evidence can be found in the surveys of criticism in John Dover Wilson's introduction to the New Cambridge edition (Cambridge: Cambridge Univ. Press, 1947), and Paul Jorgensen's "Accidental Judgments, Casual Slaughters, and Purposes Mistook: Critical Reactions to Shakespeare's *Henry the Fifth,*" *Shakespeare Association Bulletin,* 22 (1947), 51-61. Neither of them mentions Gould, or seems to be aware of an ironic interpretation of the play.

20. Manheim's list of "Hal-haters," quoted above, is part of such a division based on the critics' own feelings. See also the division in Larry Champion, *Perspective in Shakespeare's English Histories* (Athens: Univ. of Georgia Press, 1980), p. 211, which lumps together on the anti-Henry side ironic readings like Bromley's and non-ironic ones (including Hazlitt's). Ronald Berman runs into a greater problem in *A Reader's Guide to Shakespeare's Plays* (rev. ed., Glenview, Ill.: Scott, Foresman, 1973), pp. 73-74, with his classification of "three groups of critics: those who hate the play and its hero; those who admire both; those who attempt to remain neutral." The first group includes Hazlitt, Swinburne, Van Doren, and Battenhouse, among others. But Battenhouse—to adopt this terminology—hates Henry and admires the play, since he thinks the play hates Henry too. And this would also apply to Hazlitt, if what Berman said about him in the passage quoted earlier (that he regarded the play "as a satire on the *ancien régime*") were true.

21. "Against Appropriation," *Essays in Criticism,* 31 (1981), 181-95; see also the briefer comments by Maynard Mack, *Rescuing Shakespeare* (Oxford: International Shakespeare Association, 1979), pp. 4-5; and Joanne Altieri, "Romance in *Henry V,*" *Studies in English Literature,* 21 (1981), 238-40.

22. René Girard comes quite close in "'To Entrap the Wisest': A Reading of *The Merchant of Venice,*" *Literature and Society* (Selected Papers of the English Institute, 1978), ed. Edward Said (Baltimore: The Johns Hopkins Univ. Press, 1980), p. 109. See also Edna Krane, "Literary Criticism and Theological Anti-Semitism," *Midstream,* 30 (1984), 47-50.

23. Berry, for instance, says that Shakespeare's ironic strategy "calls for sleight-of-hand of the highest order, for the disparity between the two versions [i.e., the apparent and real meanings] has to be indicated discreetly yet unmistakably" (p. 48), which leads one to wonder why it was in fact mistaken for all those years.

Marsha S. Robinson (essay date 1996)

SOURCE: Robinson, Marsha S. "Mythoi of Brotherhood: Generic Emplotment in *Henry V.*" In *Shakespeare's English Histories: A Quest for Form and Genre,* edited by John W. Velz, pp. 143-70. Binghamton N.Y.: Medieval and Renaissance Texts and Studies, 1996.

[In the following essay, Robinson examines Shakespeare's manipulation of English historiography in Henry V *through a thematic evocation of fraternal conflict and reconciliation, and generic blending of tragedy and comedy.]*

In the English history plays, Shakespeare's generic choices are often expressed in a symbolic language indigenous to English historiography. The form of *Henry V* reflects the interplay of several traditions of historiographic practice, each of which appropriates the mythoi of fraternal strife and fraternal reconciliation to articulate the generic shape of the past. Shakespeare's repeated allusions to brotherhood, which are particularly significant in the complementary generic dynamics of *Richard II* and *Henry V,* are more than thematic; they are, in fact, a way of articulating form and genre.

This relationship between the figurative representation of historical content in the historian's narrative and the generic form implicit in any account of the past is illuminated by Hayden White's characterization of historical narratives as "verbal fictions" which "mediate" between "past events and processes" and the "story types that we conventionally use to endow the events of our lives with culturally sanctioned meanings."[1] White thus argues that historical discourse is generically "emplotted" as comedy, tragedy, romance or satire: the chronicle facts, which are "value-neutral" and could serve as the components of several kinds of stories, "are encoded by the use of the figurative language in which they are characterized, in order to permit their identification as elements of the particular story type to which *this story* belongs."[2] The historical narrative, then, can best be described as a *"complex of symbols"* which "points in two directions simultaneously: *toward* the events described in the narrative and *toward* the story type or mythos which the historian has chosen to serve as the icon of the structure of events."[3] White's explanation of the operation of historical discourse invites us to read the figures of brotherhood used to encode the facts of English historiography as signs of the generic story types apart from which the past is incomprehensible. Moreover, White's comment that "history-writing thrives on the discovery of all the possible plot structures that might be invoked to endow sets of events with different meanings"[4] illuminates the exploratory and provisional character of Shakespeare's quest for historiographic form.

Shakespeare's English history plays, like all histories, "mediate among . . . the *historical field,* the unprocessed *historical record, other historical accounts* and an *audience.*"[5] Therefore, it is imperative that we not isolate these dramatic works from their historiographic heritage, but that we consider in some detail the generic strategies for "emplotting" the past which inform the historical accounts on which he drew. Such an approach requires that we entertain historical narratives, "the contents of which are as much *invented* as *found,*"[6] not merely as sources of historical content or fact, but as "literary artifacts," which as generic emplotments of the past provided Shakespeare with conceptual models against which he undertook his own rewriting of the English past. Thus Shakespeare's use of fraternal conflict as an informing principle in his English history plays reiterates not merely the thematic content, but the shape of both Christian and classical accounts of the past.[7] In these accounts secular history was often perceived as a fraternal contest for power and glory and expressed in formal patterns that counterposed the tragedy of fraternal strife with the comedy of brotherly reconciliation.[8]

One model for such accounts is St. Augustine's *De Civitate Dei,* in which the Cain and Abel story is assigned an explanatory and seminal role. Augustine's vision of history not only influenced Christian historiography; his articulation of the tragicomic form of the history of salvation as well as his "political realism" shaped the ideology and the generic structure of the medieval mystery cycles.[9] Augustine's selective fashioning of biblical history provided a generic model for the formulation of secular history, one which Augustine applied in his analysis of the Roman empire, one which the English writers of the cycle plays invoked in their localization of biblical history and one which Shakespeare tested as he sought to create a dramatic model of English history.

Augustine, following Genesis 4:17-22, designates Cain, a fratricide, as the founder of the earthly city.[10] He thus identifies recurring fraternal conflict as the definitive pattern which informs secular history, a pattern often obscured by the mask of political cooperation. The counterpart of the earthly city is the heavenly city, the citizens of which are the symbolic heirs of Abel and his successor, Seth. The earthly city, driven by egotism and power, "glories in itself"; the heavenly city glories in God.[11] Just as Cain's enmity toward his brother represents, Augustine argues, the hatred of the earthly city for the heavenly city, so the fraternal strife between Romulus and Remus, founders of Rome, symbolizes the enmity among members of the earthly city itself.[12] Attributing the conflict between brothers to the unwillingness of one partner to diminish his glory by sharing it with the other, Augustine characterizes the history of the earthly city as an account of "wars, altercations and appetites of short-lived or destructive victories" in which self-interest directs the pursuit of fame and honor.[13]

For St. Augustine history is linear and progressive and has a definite end. As literary fictions, endings as well as beginnings serve to encode Augustine's narrative as a particular genre.[14] The tragic history of the earthly city, destined to suffer its final end—damnation, culminates in the Last Judgment. On the other hand, the citizens of the heavenly city, sharing the communion of the saints and united by their love for God, enjoy eternal life. While the tragedy of fraternal strife is limited to time, the comedy of salvation, begun in time, is fulfilled in an apotheosis in which history is transcended and the members of the heavenly city share in the final triumph of the Church. It is this tragicomic pattern which informs the medieval mystery cycles in which "the role of Cain and Abel remains immensely significant, for it confirms the pattern of the Fall which will resonate through the entire series of plays until finally the 'two classes' of people will be separated on the Last Day of history."[15] In the typological structure of the Corpus Christi cycles, Abel's tragic death as a martyr anticipates Christ's death and the comedic redemption of history.[16]

Another widespread influence on English historiography, the representation of internecine conflict in classical histories, provided a distinctive model of the past. Tragic or ironic, the generic shape of these accounts is essentially at odds with the linear and progressive form of Christian history with its tragicomic vision of time.[17] The past is represented as a cyclic alternation of unity and internecine discord in which typical sequences of behavior repeat themselves as part of an irreconcilable duality which is never supplanted. For example, Thucydides presents the Peloponnesian War as a tragic record of recurrent intestine factionalism motivated by a self-aggrandizement and ambition which turned Greek against Greek.[18] In these accounts of the devastating reverses of circumstance to which the city state is subject, Thucydides comments that blood proves a weaker tie than party, which violently divides classes and families. Not only does the father kill the son, but foreigners are invited by partisans to prey upon their fellow citizens. On the other hand, moments of human achievement are described in terms of the communal cooperation of citizens who with oaths of reconciliation unite in the face of immediate difficulty. History is thus represented as a continuous struggle between men and circumstances in which "human reason" is "defeated and crushed by the forces of irrationality."[19]

Although Shakespeare's formulation of history as fraternal conflict may well draw on the ultimately Augustinian historiography of the mystery plays, English historians themselves, incorporating both classical and Christian strategies of representation, fashioned the past as a story of fraternal discord. The Anglo-Norman chroniclers of the twelfth century, for example, many of whom serve as sources for the Tudor chroniclers, repeatedly represent the past as a story of fraternal discord. Their narratives illustrate the process of historical selection. The factual field is the object not of reduction but "distortion": the historian "'displaces' some facts to the periphery or background and moves others closer to the center, encodes some as causes and others as effects, joins some and disjoins others. . . ."[20] The resulting emplotment takes the form of a cycle in which tragic internecine conflict alternates with periods of comedic reconciliation: brothers prey upon brothers with impunity, periodically uniting to defeat their mutual enemies. Commenting that William of Normandy "did not even spare his own brother," Henry of Huntingdon, like his fellow historian, William of Malmesbury, invokes this cycle in his emplotment of the reigns of William the Conqueror and his sons and heirs—William II, Henry I, and Robert Duke of Normandy.[21] Unlike Augustine, who refuses to identify the heavenly city with political entities, Henry of Huntingdon implicitly designates the English as the party of Abel and interprets the internecine fierceness of the Cain-like Normans as evidence of their role as God's scourge, sent to "humble" the English nation.[22]

Speaking through the voices of the Norman lords, the historian Ordericus Vitalis even more self-consciously reflects the tragic pattern which he ascribes to Anglo-Norman history, perceiving it as inherent in the past itself. His text clearly demonstrates the way in which the invocation of a motif or figurative symbol—"brothers"—encodes the facts as a component of a particular kind of story. For example his query, "What happened to the Thebans under the two brothers, Eteocles and Polyneices?," summarizes in miniature the course of Anglo-Norman history and informs it with the shape of tragedy. Comparing the nation to a woman continually "suffering the pangs of labor" and "Cruelly harassed by [her] own sons," he uses a language of internal division to signal the generic shape of the past.[23] Like the other historians, he depicts a cycle of fraternal violence and mutual support: "But as discord makes divisions among them, and fatally arms them against each other, while they are victorious in foreign lands they are conquered by themselves and cut each others throats without mercy. . . ."[24] Drawing on a classical use of fratricide to encode accounts of internecine conflict, Ordericus, like Augustine, presents fraternal conflict as unnatural—the mark of the immorality of secular history. Moreover, his juxtaposition of tragic and comedic emplotments, exemplified in the very language of this passage, demystifies communal cooperation. Because such reconciliations, as Augustine remarks, give rise to the kind of self-interested concord exhibited by a band of pirates,[25] Ordericus represents them as ironic inversions of the comedic reconciliation of brothers.

It is Geoffrey of Monmouth in his *History of the Kings of Britain,* however, who most clearly articulates the pattern, projecting onto a fictitious British past the generic outlines of Anglo-Norman accounts of the past.[26] The distinctive feature of his narrative is its formal unity. The unique details of historical discourse which populate the literal surface of historical narratives and which often defy formal coherence are supplanted by the "figurative element." The generic form of the past, which in most historical narratives recedes to "the interior of the discourse," is foregrounded.[27] In each successive reign the ruling heir is challenged or even deposed by an ambitious brother (sometimes one with whom he jointly shares the throne), cousin or other relative.[28] For example, Mempricius and Malim, the great-grandsons of Brute, contest the throne, struggling for possession of the island, and Mempricius murders his brother in a meeting ostensibly planned to forge "concord betwixt them."[29] The threat of internecine destruction is further dramatized in a second scenario—the return of the exiled brother (sometimes accompanied by a foreign army) to reclaim his patrimony. Both of these scenarios anticipate Shakespeare's representation of the English past in which "brothers" are displaced and then return, as do Henry Bolingbroke and the Earl of Richmond, to displace their rivals. Treating his material from an almost secular perspective, Geoffrey does not condemn the brothers in his history as Cains, but with the detachment which also anticipates Shakespeare, he presents their often disastrous choices as representatives of forces of personal desire and individual destiny, forces at odds with the political relationships which determine national unity.[30]

Geoffrey's tragic scenarios are juxtaposed with interludes of reconciliation in which hierarchy is reaffirmed as the brothers become one in unity or acknowledge differences in lineal rank.[31] The motif of two becoming one—the effacement of all difference, encoded even in the alliterative names of pairs—figuratively represents the comedic ending which generically identifies these stories. Exiled brothers are restored to their patrimony, and the nation is united. Such reconciliation inspires foreign conquests as reunited brothers, typified by Belinus and Brennius, venture forth to conquer the Franks and finally Rome itself.[32] In this formulation fraternal strife is temporarily supplanted by a spirit of unity. History gives way to romance as a tragic or ironic model of the past is displaced by a model of what should be.

Geoffrey presents such moments as "exemplary" history: "the end of fraternal strife restores civil harmony and paves the way for the conquest of foreign lands."[33] These scenarios, however, do not ultimately provide comedic closure, for Geoffrey's cyclic history has no "ending."[34] His classical and secular vision of history as a contest of irreconcilable forces casts an ironic shadow on these moments of success; the empowering of the nation incites ambition and issues in or is inextricably linked with the resurgence of national crisis in which personal ambition reasserts itself as civil conflict.[35] In Geoffrey's formulation of history the unity of brothers anticipates not an ending, but the renewal of a pattern of fraternal hostility and thus ironically defies generic expectations.

The Tudor historian Edward Hall, in contrast, invokes the conflict of brothers to articulate a tragicomic formulation of the past in which English history is a chapter in the history of salvation, the ending of which anticipates Christian apotheosis. In his *The Vnion of the Two Noble and Illustre Famelies of Lancastre and Yorke,* Hall sets forth the conflict between heirs as a manifestation of the tragic "intestine deuision" between "the brother and the brother" as one instance of the factionalism which had shaped the history of European realms.[36] Commenting in his introduction that unity cannot be comprehended apart from division, Hall represents the record of warring brothers as both a tragic story of suffering and death and a prelude to the restoration of concord enacted in the marriage of Henry VII and Elizabeth of York. Hall's opening analogy between marriage and Christian redemption, part of an ode to unity, becomes an identification in the conclusion of his account, in which he celebrates this union as a succession of the "ioy" by which "peace was thoughte to discende oute of heauē into England. . . ."[37]

Hall's articulation of the Tudor view of the state as a redemptive agency is, however, destabilized by a political realism inherent in any detailed chronicling of fact. The past as an account of warring brothers is represented in a modality which is at odds with and thus ignores providential design.[38] Hall's tragicomic emplotment—unity born out of division—is divested of its informing power and disengaged from the text. For although Hall finally describes the Tudor dispensation "as a thynge by God elected and prouided," he immediately proceeds to record Henry's continuing preoccupation with the suppression of "dyuision" and "dissencion."[39] His generic model of tragic conflict superseded by providential apotheosis gives way to a continuing pattern of conflict.

In his English histories, Shakespeare more self-consciously enlists the conventional plot scenarios of fraternal conflict and cooperation, testing their iconic power to inform the past and deconstructing familiar patterns. Just as the form of *Richard II* is, for example, articulated in terms of the biblical paradigm of fraternal conflict, so *Henry V* dramatizes the comedic or romantic resolution of that cycle—brotherly reconciliation and redemption.[40] The play's comedic or romantic emplotment is dramatized not only by recurring references to brotherhood but by iconic and exemplary strategies which create the play's "ceremonial" representation.[41] Supporting a vision of unity, these strategies enforce the unity of the text itself.

The play's reenactment of these modes is counterpointed by its denial of the complementary tragic phase of this cycle, expressed in its suppression and isolation of tragedy and its displacement of violence. The comedic voice of the play, a voice of denial, ironically evokes a "tragic emplotment" of events which challenges the very form of the play. As White explains, "The same set of events can serve as components of a story that is tragic *or* comic, as the case may be, depending on the historian's choice of the plot structure that he considers appropriate for ordering events of that kind so as to make them into a comprehensible story."[42] Shakespeare's creation of dual emplotments is a characterizing feature of sophisticated historical texts, which are "always written as part of a contest between contending poetic configurations of what the past *might* consist of."[43] Mediating between contending emplotments,[44] Shakespeare qualifies Henry's comedic vision of reconciliation with a tragic model of events.

The form of *Henry V* is illuminated by the generic dynamics of *Richard II,* which, in its representation of fraternal conflict, appears to be the tragic counterpart of the comedy of reconciliation. In *Richard II* Shakespeare juxtaposes the tragic conflict of Cain and Abel and an ironic version of that story in which secular history is distanced from redemptive history. Challenging Mowbray, Bolingbroke covertly identifies Richard as his uncle's murderer, a figurative Cain who

> Sluic'd out his innocent soul through streams of
>   blood—
> Which blood, like sacrificing Abel's, cries,
> Even from the tongueless caverns of the earth,
> To me for justice and rough chastisement.
>
>   (I.i.103-6)

He assigns himself the role of avenger on behalf of Gloucester, whose identity as sacrificing Abel (104) is reinforced by the Duchess of Gloucester's entreaty addressed to Gaunt—an appeal to "brotherhood" and a protest against the desecration of a sacred heritage symbolized by the Plantagenet blood of her murdered husband (I.ii.9-36). Ostensibly defending the old dispensation, symbolized by the anointed blood of Edward III, against unnatural violation, Bolingbroke assumes the role of Abel's champion. He implicitly aligns himself with England, whose bloodstained "earth" is metaphorically identified as the temporal locus of the heavenly city. Richard, in turn, associates his adversary, whom Shakespeare significantly casts in the role of a brother—"Were he my brother, nay, my kingdom's heir, / As he is but my father's brother's son" (I.i.116-17)— with the heartless and violent power of Cain (III.ii.111).

Exposing the moral posturing, Shakespeare anamorphically conflates his Cains and Abels in their shifting relationship to power and right. Although Cain's exile, the biblical anticipation of the separation of the heavenly city from the earthly city, is repeatedly invoked by the participants as a God-ordained punishment for the apostasy of rebellion, exile in fact dramatizes shifting relations of power in the earthly city (I.iii.198-203), much as it does in Geoffrey's account of the past. Moreover, it foreshadows the recurrence of violence as brothers return to claim their patrimony. Thus Bolingbroke, Mowbray (Richard's surrogate), Richard, and finally Exton (Bolingbroke's surrogate), each forced into "exile" by a "brother," are condemned by

their enemies as apostate violators of the body politic— "With Cain go wander through shades of night" (V.vi.43; I.iii.176-77). Each, on the other hand, identifies himself with Abel. Bolingbroke portrays himself as Abel's defender. Richard, in his martyr-like role as Cain's victim, is implicitly compared to Abel and fashions himself as Abel's typological counterpart, Christ (IV.i.170-72). Even Mowbray and Exton belie their roles as Cains; a crusader, the exiled Mowbray serves Christ in the very capacity which Bolingbroke repeatedly covets for himself and later dies in Venice, yielding up his soul to Christ (IV.i.93-101); in contrast, Bolingbroke's death in the Jerusalem Room at Westminster, not the Holy Land (*2 Henry IV* IV.v.232-40), ironically signifies his Cain-like exile in the earthly city. Exton, Richard's murderer, believes he serves Henry in his role as the Lord's Anointed.

Although in *Richard II* the struggle between brothers is fashioned by the contestants as a conflict between Abel and his apostate enemy Cain, Shakespeare, like Augustine, challenges myths of legitimacy which support the power of worldly empires. The identification of England as the heavenly city—the inheritance of Abel—is counterpointed with a vision which undermines the assumptions of a whole tradition of Christian historiography in which the state is a "monument to God's ordering of history," and the "political or social hero" is informed with the "nature of both Christ and Caesar."[45] The tragic demise of Richard as the Lord's Anointed and thus Abel's representative is emplotted as an ironic struggle for power among the descendants of Cain, whose pretensions to moral legitimacy belie the true foundations of the earthly city—power and self-interest. A play in which successive monarchs assume the role of Cain (V.vi.45-46), *Richard II* enacts the shape of history as recurring fraternal conflict.

Because *Henry V* is a self-conscious work of historiography, the play itself calls attention to the problematic relationship of genre and history. The selective processes by which the facts of history take on generic form are often transparent; the past is clearly a text subject to the shaping of the historian. In *Henry V,* generic fashioning becomes evident in what the historian leaves out as much as in what he includes.[46] One of many such incidents which allude to the recurrence of fraternal violence, the Southampton plot (II.ii) illustrates Shakespeare's use of selective strategies to invoke one generic formulation and suppress an alternative representation.

The operation of the selective process becomes clear when one examines the chroniclers' attempts to place this event in the larger pattern of historical change. Assuming the retrospective view of the historian, Tudor chroniclers generally represent the Southampton plot as an anticipation of the Wars of the Roses. Recounting Henry's discovery of the conspiracy and his efficient dispatch of the perpetrators, Hall, for example, proceeds to place the event in the broader historical continuum, identifying it as a prologue to the eventual demise of the house of Lancaster:

> But if he [Henry] had cast his eye to the fyre that was newly kindled, he should haue surely sene an horrible flame incesed against the walles of his owne house and family, by the which in conclusion his line and stocke was cleane destroyed and consumed to ashes, which fire at that very tyme paradvuenture might haue bene quenched and put out.[47]

In the works of Hall and Holinshed this tragic interlude is juxtaposed in chronicle fashion with heroic accounts of Henry's reign; the poet-historian Samuel Daniel, however, attempts to present a coherent generic model of the past. Emplotting his *The Civil Wars* as tragedy, he foregrounds the Southampton plot as smoldering evidence of "the lowe depressed fire, / Whose after-issuing flames confounded all" (5.1).[48] Daniel self-consciously reflects on the tensions arising from his generic emplotment. He must eschew the "intermedled good report" characteristic of chronicle accounts in which inclusiveness supplants generic formulation (5.13). Having committed himself to a tragic account of the past—"'Nothing but blood-shed, treasons, sinne and shame'" (5.6)—he can "onely tell the worst of euerie Raigne" (5.13).[49] Given his program of selection, the representation of Henry's reign, as Daniel acknowledges, becomes problematic. He must subordinate "this so happy a meanewhile" (5.33)—an allusion to Henry's enlightened policies of national reconciliation—as a mere parenthesis in a tragic discourse, in which, he laments, the glorious battle of Agincourt has no place (5.13).

The chroniclers and Daniel not only identify the Southampton plot as part of a tragic formulation of the past, they disclose the motives of Cambridge, Grey and Scroop, the king's would-be assassins. Hall, for example, questions the motive of greed confessed by the conspirators, who according to some reports had been bought by the French:

> diuerse write that Richard earle of Cambridge did not conspire with the lorde Scrope and Sir Thomas Graye to murther kyng Henry to please the Frenche kyng withal, but onely to thentent to exalte to the croune his brotherinlawe Edmonde earle of Marche as heyre to duke Lyonel.[50]

Revealing that the conspirators were supporters of Lyonel's heir, the descendant of an elder brother, Hall redefines the plot as a recurrence of fraternal conflict and so discloses its tragic configuration: hierarchical differences are effaced as king and subject are identified as rival kinsmen, contenders for the crown and near equals in their rights and claims.

Although the conspiracy in fact challenges the success of the policy of reconciliation and reinstatement by

which Henry sought to control and re-assimilate his father's enemies, particularly the Yorkist claimants (II.ii.25-31),[51] in *Henry V* this plot against the king, discovered on the eve of Henry's embarkation to France, appears strangely transformed. Shakespeare divests the conspiracy of the tragic identity assigned to it by the chroniclers and Daniel. Instead, he uses iconic strategies of representation to divorce the incident from the historical continuum, and thus he contains it.[52] First of all, this account of the insurrection is detached from the past and future to which it implicitly points, offering no analysis of political cause and effect. It is presented as neither a replay of the Ricardian conspiracies which plagued Henry IV nor a reciprocal reenactment of the familial bloodshed of the past—specifically the murder of Richard II.[53] Moreover, it is distanced from the anticipation (in the Epilogue) of the fraternal conflict between the Lancastrian and Yorkist parties which "made his England bleed."

Ignoring the questions of precedent and outcome essential to historical discourse, Shakespeare not only isolates the event from its temporal context but obscures its motivation.[54] Henry seizes upon the conspirators' confession that they acted out of greed, appearing to accept this motive at face value (II.ii.88-91) despite Cambridge's ambiguous disclaimer (155-56). In addition, the particular historical details which would disclose factionalism are effaced; Shakespeare is silent about the genealogical facts or political alliances which might reveal the reciprocity of the adversaries and identify the assassination plot as a manifestation of fraternal enmity.[55]

Here, as elsewhere in the play, it is Henry who rewrites events, collaborating with the Chorus, an "official historian."[56] In this scene the tragedy of fraternal discord is effaced and finally supplanted in a coherent and self-contained drama which evokes the Last Judgment. Depoliticizing and universalizing the conspiracy, Henry in fact stages a biblical drama of sin and judgment in which he assumes a God-like role as the embodiment of an impartial justice (II.ii.174)—righteous, inclined to mercy, but implacable in the face of sin.[57] Attributing the conspiracy to unfathomable human depravity, he characterizes the defection of his intimate friend, Scroop, as "Another fall of man" (II.ii.142). He thus magnifies the conspirators' treason as a type of the spiritual apostasy of both Adam and Cain, whose rebellion is structurally represented as a second fall in the medieval cycle plays.[58] Interestingly, this moral emplotment echoes the medieval account commissioned by Henry, in which the conspirators, condemned as "Judas-like," are implicitly linked with Cain, Judas' typological counterpart in the cycle plays.[59] Evoking history's final drama in which justice triumphs over sin, Henry dissociates himself from motives of revenge (174) and identifies himself with both law (143, 176-77) and mercy. He thus denies his reciprocal relationship with his opponents. They in turn, "rejoic[ing]" (159, 161) in the providential discovery of their betrayal, assume the roles of penitents and suppliants, signaling their subordination to the king.

In concert with Henry, the Chorus pursues the theme of betrayal; "English monsters" (II.ii.85) and a "nest of hollow bosoms" (II.pro.21), Cambridge, Scroop and Grey are demonized (II.ii.111-25) as unnatural "children" (II.pro.19). Moreover, their violence and disloyalty are displaced upon the French enemy with whom they are linked (II.ii.88-90, 100). Ironically belying insurrection, this fiction preserves the play's affirmation of "one consent" (I.ii.181, 206; II.ii.20-24). A moralized vision of English unanimity is invoked as a standard for exposing the immorality and unEnglish otherness of the conspirators (II.ii.126-40). The tragic dimensions of the Southampton plot are thus exorcised in a generic metamorphosis by which tragedy, a mere prelude to the reaffirmation of divine order, corroborates the play's insistent declaration of unity. Tragedy is subsumed by and anticipates the romance of brotherly reconciliation.

Henry's generic representation of the conspiracy is characteristic of the political fashioning of history in *Henry V.* Holinshed suggests that the official account of the conspiracy was in fact a fabrication: "their [the conspirator'] purpose was well inough then perceiued, although happilie not much bruted abroad, for considerations thought necessarie to haue it rather husht and kept secret."[60] Shakespeare allows us to witness the fashioning of this event, dramatizing the process which began in Henry's court. The suppression of brotherly conflict is of course clearer to the modern reader with access to documents which suggest that the motive of greed was apparently the invention of Walsingham, a Lancastrian apologist, as was the identification of Scroop as the intimate of the king.[61] Both fictions obscured the grievances of the dispossessed Earl of March, whom Henry had forced to pay a huge marriage fine, and of Richard, Earl of Cambridge, who in keeping with Henry's program of reconciliation with his enemies, had been given a title, but had never been awarded any source of income.[62] These facts, excluded from official accounts, disclose the continuation of brotherly discord. Henry's manipulation of the Lyonel faction through economic strangulation was in fact interpreted by the Earl of March, who feared that the king would "undo him," as an act of metaphorical violence.[63]

Most of these facts were probably not available to the Tudor chronicles or to Shakespeare. He plays on the ambiguity of the confession as well as the fictitious character of the indictments for treason, confirmed, in this case, by the retrospective acknowledgment (made official by Yorkist claimants) that the "traitors" were never legally convicted (*1 Henry VI* II.iv.96-97).[64] Although the conspirators (except Scroop) confessed to a plan to elevate the Earl of March by taking him into Wales and proclaiming him king, those who wrote the indictment, in their effort to win a conviction for treason, charged the conspirators with having plotted to assassinate the king and his brothers. This fiction was designed to substantiate the conventional charge, derived by implication, of "imagining and compassing the king's death."[65] Shakespeare's allusion to unvoiced motives activates the dissonance between medieval accounts, which invoke this event to affirm national unity, and the Tudor perspective, in which it figures as a continuation of and motive for the feud between brothers, inspiring the revenge of Richard Plantagenet, Cambridge's son. The Southampton plot ironically anticipates the demise of Lancastrian fortunes and the reinstatement of the Yorkist faction in the person of Edward IV, grandson of Richard, Earl of Cambridge. In a reversal of roles in which Cains and Abels change places, the three Lancastrian kings would in 1460 be declared usurpers, and the perpetrator of this treason, Richard of Cambridge, would later by parliamentary decree lose the name of traitor.[66]

Henry represents his violent repression of fraternal conflict as a type of the Last Judgment and thus disengages this confrontation from the familiar tragic emplotment which encodes acts of internecine conflict. Henry's celebration of the battle of Agincourt is, in contrast, fashioned in terms of the comedy of brotherly reconciliation and Christian redemption. Henry implicitly compares the communal cooperation of his soldiers to the transcendent fellowship of the heavenly city. Like Christ who calls his obedient followers his brothers, Henry promises that "he today that sheds his blood with me / Shall be my brother" (IV.iii.61-62) and styles himself as one of a "happy few, we band of brothers" (60). Framed as prognostication, Henry's account of the yearly commemoration of the battle of Agincourt (IV.iii.39-67) anticipates the end to which Christian history points; national history becomes a type of the history of salvation in which tragedy is eclipsed and history redeemed.

Evoking the spiritual and eschatological connotation of brotherhood, Henry, in fact, transforms English history to national hagiography—an account of the suffering and triumphs of the heavenly city as a brotherhood of saints. Just as the hagiographer exhorts the brotherhood of the faithful to endure by reminding them of the Christian's ultimate consolation—the promise of eternal life—[67]so Henry exhorts his men to endure by envisioning for them the consolation promised to national heroes—historiographic fame (51-59). And just as hagiographic literature celebrates death in the company of Christian brothers—one's fellow martyrs—as a privilege and an honor,[68] so Henry's anticipatory account of

English history celebrates the felicity of death in the company of fellow Englishmen—a select brotherhood of national saints. Henry distinguishes this new nobility from that nobility conferred by blood (61-63). Elevating achievement over inheritance, he honors a perseverance and self-sacrifice motivated by a secular faith—patriotism.

Henry completes the spiritualization of English history by transforming the future commemoration of the battle of Agincourt into a secular feast day memorializing those martyrs who gave their lives for the faith.[69] Unifying the observance of the martyrdom of Sts. Crispinus and Crispianus, whose feast day it is, with the annual remembrance of the heroism of this band of brothers, Henry reinforces the image of a sacred brotherhood. Crispinus and Crispianus, brothers and wealthy heirs to a secular patrimony, succeed to a more transcendent brotherhood as heirs of Christ. They embrace the Christian faith and live as humble shoemakers, sharing the gospel in the face of persecution.[70] As martyred brothers, not only do they embody Henry's vision of his band of brothers, but their conversion to the Christian faith metaphorically echoes the historic change implicit in Henry's fashioning of events: the subordination of patriarchal and aristocratic notions of allegiance to a new concept—allegiance to country. In creating a new brotherhood of secular saints, Henry forges bonds of communal allegiance, honoring those who are willing to subordinate individual ambition to public goals.

As members of the happy band of brothers, the four Captains—the Welsh Fluellen, the Irish Macmorris, the Scots Jamy and the English Gower—are actors in a comedy of brotherly reconciliation. Foils to the quarrelsome, unsoldierly French, they courteously and generously pay tribute to one another's valor and professionalism and enjoy the comradery of yokefellows committed to a mutual task (III.ii.63-65, 75-81). The ethnic and national divisions dramatically voiced in the distinctive dialects of these officers are discounted by Gower, who rebukes Pistol's xenophobic contempt for Fluellen: "You thought, because he could not speak English in the native garb, he could not therefore handle an English cudgel" (V.i.73-75).

The play's comedic vision of the English past—its denial of ethnic differences—is, of course, at odds with the audience's awareness of a continuing history of ethnic rebellion. For as the play elsewhere indicates, in 1599 the English audience awaits news of the subjection of Ireland (V.pro.29-34). Thus, ethnic animosities surface even in the midst of a supportive communal dialogue. For example, the outraged "What ish my nation?" (III.ii.121) with which Captain Macmorris responds to Fluellen's innocent allusion to "many of your nation" (120) fiercely contests the dehumanization

of the Irish by their English oppressors. Stigmatized as "a villain, and a bastard, and a knave, and a rascal" (121-22), the Irishman was of course excluded from both the contest of brothers, a story of near equals, and the comedy of fraternal reconciliation. Hardly candidates for brotherhood, the Irish, like the French before them, were "the other"—the victims of the imperialism which brotherhood inspires. Intimations of tragedy, the deep and irreconcilable divisions articulated by this Irish voice, like the voices at Southampton, must, of course, be muted and transfigured as they are in this scene: "Gentlemen both, you will mistake each other," cautions Gower (133).

Because England's politically sensitive relationships with a rebellious Ireland and an independent Scotland do not support an English story of fraternal reconciliation, Shakespeare selectively foregrounds Fluellen, a shadow of the Welsh-born Henry, as a symbol of the spirit of patriotic unity—a corporate nationalism which in the world of the play transcends these ethnic differences.[71] Playing the stranger, Henry, the first among Englishmen, disguises himself as Henry Le Roy, "a Welshman" and proclaims to a hostile Pistol that he is Fluellen's countryman, friend "And his kinsman too" (IV.i.51-59). Henry not only acknowledges the power of bonds based on ethnic and national identity, he at once enacts the effacement of the differences he celebrates. Henry—king and commoner, Welshman and Englishman—becomes all things to all people to win them to his cause, forging fraternal bonds which permeate social, ethnic and national boundaries.

The comedy of reconciliation is enacted on the field of Agincourt itself where the king's identification of himself as a Welshman and Fluellen as his "good countryman" (IV.vii.104) is reciprocally acknowledged by Fluellen: "I am your Majesty's countryman" (110). However, shared nativity, Fluellen realizes, is but a material bond, and thus his kinship with Henry, like the brotherhood of the four Captains in the play, is a spiritual one, a shared integrity. For Fluellen will confess their relatedness "so long as your Majesty is an honest man" (IV.vii.118-19). Just as Henry fashions the battle of Agincourt, so Fluellen proceeds to rewrite Welsh history as a comedy of fraternal cooperation. Shakespeare's allusion to Holinshed's tragic record of atrocities done in 1399 by the monstrous Welsh women on the bodies of dead Englishmen in *1 Henry IV* is succeeded in *Henry V* by Fluellen's record of "good service" in a French garden of leeks, where the Welsh reappear as brothers-in-arms to the English (97-98).[72] Conflating a Welsh St. David's day victory, sometimes identified as a Celtic defeat of the Saxons, with the Black Prince's victory at Crécy, Fluellen creates an account of "St. Davy's day" which both validates Welsh nationalistic pride and is ironically refashioned to serve "English purposes" (II.pro.15). Connecting the past with the present, this narrative places the battle of Agincourt in the broader context of English history as a continuing comedy of fraternal reconciliation intrinsically connected to the staging of a foreign war. Incorporated into the fabric of English history, St. David's day—a memorial to Welsh valor—anticipates and is subsumed by St. Crispin's day. A celebration of brotherly cooperation, it commemorates the reconciliation of ethnic differences which like "many arrows, loosed several ways, / Come to one mark" (I.ii.207-8). The generic impulse of comedy—incorporation—is thus enacted again and again in the representation of ethnic brothers. The embodiment of this incorporation, Fluellen, the king's kin, countryman and double, collaborates with Henry to create an incorporative history of English fraternity, which honors difference while invoking an inclusive English brotherhood as the earthly model of the fellowship that epitomizes the heavenly city.

Henry's fashioning of the past and future as a comedy of reconciliation conflates the history of redemption with the triumphs of the earthly city. Shakespeare, in contrast, distances the earthly city from its heavenly counterpart by destabilizing Henry's emplotment, in which tragedy is averted and transformed. The comedic unity of the play is, in fact, constantly under siege as inverse accounts of fraternal discord surface. For example, the tragic outlines of the Southampton plot and the intimations of ethnic hostility emerge displaced onto another fraternal triumvirate, the fictional conspirators, Bardolph, Nym and Pistol, "three sworn brothers" (II.i.12). The Southampton plot is, in fact, the centerpiece in a dramatic triptych, the flanking panels of which reenact the classical emplotment of history as a tragic or ironic cycle of fraternal violence and reconciliation. A parodic version of Henry's comedic representation of the conspiracy, Act II, scene i burlesques the quarrel of brothers. Nym and Pistol draw swords; their mutual threats of murder reenact the discord among brothers disguised by the official account of the Southampton plot (II.i.35-73). Vying for the hand of Mistress Quickly, who is married to Pistol but was contracted to Nym, they openly contest a reductive version of the competing claims which remain unspoken in Henry's encounter with his co-claimant. Suspending this quarrel, the announcement of Falstaff's death with the explanation "the King has kill'd his heart" (II.i.88) not only restages Henry's own betrayal by his intimate friend, Scroop, but also implicates Henry himself in the reciprocal economy of fraternal hostility.

A reenactment of the historiographic comedy of affiliation, the third scene (II.iii) in this triptych counterpoints the first. Echoing Henry's assurance that "every rub is smoothed" (II.ii.188), Pistol's promise to Nym that "friendship shall combine, and brotherhood" (II.i.109) anticipates an alternate story, one which will supplant the conflict of brothers played out in this scene. The reconciliation is, however, an ironic and starkly realistic version of the idealized national unity Henry constructs for the audience in scene ii. Brotherly unity is achieved by the repression of differences which still fester (Nym cannot kiss the hostess goodbye); confederacy is merely a redirection of predatory self-interest: "Yoke-fellows in arms, / Let us to France, like horse-leeches, my boys, / To suck, to suck, the very blood to suck!" (II.iii.53-55). The thievish ambitions of Pistol, Nym, and Bardolph, "sworn brothers in filching" (III.ii.43-44), expose both the ambitions of another triumvirate—the would-be usurpers of the crown—and the imperial ambitions of Henry himself. Enclosing Henry's comedic and self-contained staging of history, this parodic reenactment of the historiographic fictions of fraternal violence and brotherly reconciliation reformulates the past in both a tragic and ironic mode. Generically transformed, Henry's story is subsumed as part of a continuing pattern of internecine violence which informs Anglo-Norman accounts of the English past. Just as the Anglo-Normans, driven by self-interest, destroy their brothers and then turn their mutual hostility against their enemies, so the English unite to prey upon the French.

Shakespeare, in fact, interrogates Henry's model of national brotherhood—a fellowship of saints bound together by mutual love—invoking an alternative model of community, a sworn brotherhood of thieves. Shakespeare's critique of the pragmatic bonds which support national unity echoes Augustine's depiction of the earthly city as a confederation of thieves:

> Set justice aside then, and what are kingdoms but fair thievish purchases? For what are thieves' purchases but little kingdoms, for in theft the hands of the underlings are directed by the commander, the confederacy of them is sworn together, and the pillage is shared by law amongst them? And if those ragamuffins grow up to be able to keep forts, build habitations, possess cities, and conquer adjoining nations, then their government is no more called thievish, but graced with the eminent name of a kingdom, given and gotten, not because they have left their practice, but now because they may use them without danger of law.[73]

Just as Augustine, citing Alexander the Great, effaces the distinction between the emperor and the thief, so Shakespeare counterpoints Henry's band of brothers with a band of thieves, exposing the basis of communal cooperation rooted in egotism and material ambition.

Henry's vision of brothers reconciled and redeemed from obscurity by the power of the historiographic record "From this day to the ending of the world" (IV.iii.58) informs time with a comedic closure and implicitly anticipates the redemption of history. Analogy becomes identity as English history, rewritten in the form of redemptive history, becomes one with

Christian history. Shakespeare, however, questions the relationship between the record of history and the record of eternity, creating alternative "endings" which reformulate the story of Henry's reign. Henry's identification of secular history with the history of the heavenly city and his depiction of the state as a redemptive agency is countered by Williams' anticipation of "the latter day":

> But if the cause be not good, the King himself hath a heavy reckoning to make, when all those legs and arms and heads, chopp'd off in battle, shall join together at the latter day and cry all, "We died at such a place"— some swearing, some crying for a surgeon, some upon their wives left poor behind them, some upon debts they owe, some upon their children rawly left. I am afeard there are few die well that die in battle; for how can they charitably dispose of anything, when blood is their argument?

(IV.i.133-42)

In this vision of the Last Judgment, Shakespeare recreates the alternative ending of Christian history; the comedic apotheosis of the saints is rewritten as the tragedy of damnation. If the play's presentation of the body politic in a language of unanimity exemplified by "one consent" (I.ii.181, 206; II.ii.22-23), "all," (II.pro.1), "one" (I.ii.208-9, 212; V.ii.357-58) and in images of harmony—the beehive (I.ii.187-204) and the happy band of brothers—insistently encodes its story as a comedy, the shocking image of dismembered body parts, brutally dissevered, signals a contending version of Henry's seamless story of "one consent." In this apocalyptic anticipation of the "heavy reckoning" due to men engaged in amoral conquest, the earthly city is envisioned as a dissevered body and the material basis of its unity is disclosed. Contrasting the "argument" or sign which identifies men who live and die by violence—blood—with the mark of the heavenly city— charity—Williams calls into doubt the sanctification of a band of brothers united not by justice, but by blood. Williams's severing of the history of conquest from the history of the heavenly city echoes Augustine's division between the party of Cain and the party of Abel: "that boasts of ambitious conquerors led by the lust of sovereignty: in this all serve each other in charity. . . ."[74] Ironically, Williams's anticipation of time's ending subverts the transcendent implications of Henry's anticipation of a temporal apotheosis. It also subjects Henry himself to the "heavy reckoning" which he invokes in condemning his fraternal enemies in his own drama of sin and judgment.

The demythologized accounts of the band of brothers as a confederacy of thieves and an assembly of severed body parts figure forth an alternative story, reiterating the generic tensions which give shape to *Henry V.* Shakespeare discloses the artifices—both political and aesthetic—which fabricate a vision of unanimity. He

thus reveals the fictive character of the comedic closure created by Henry's rewriting of the Southampton plot as a triumphant Last Judgment and his fashioning of the story of Agincourt as its redemptive counterpart. The comedic mode is sustained by a conjuring effort expressed in pleas, promises and acts of imagination. These voices deny, rebuke or transcend the reverse story—history as an account of fraternal enmity. Ironically, these voices at once demystify the English historiographic assumption that foreign conquest reflects or enhances national unity.[75] For example, Bardolph's plea for reconciliation between Pistol and Nym, "Come, shall I make you two friends? We must to France together" (II.i.90-93), juxtaposed with the tragic alternative—"knives to cut one another's throats"—is echoed by Bates's plea, "Be friends, you English fools, be friends" (IV.i.219). Henry's promise of eternal brotherhood is adumbrated by the material vision of Pistol's promise to Nym. Just as his assurance that "friendship shall combine, and brotherhood" (II.i.109) anticipates the literal profits of that union, so Henry's promises serve his imperial ambitions. Not only do the characters persuade one another, but the Chorus in a language of unanimity ("all," "every," "solely" [II.pro.1-4]) also directs us in the romantic project of imagining the unity of "English purposes" (II.pro.15). Although the Chorus enjoins the audience to accept its poetic figuration as history, "submitting the shows of things to the desires of the mind,"[76] the conjuring mode discloses that we are witnessing not history itself but the ceremonial fashioning of an historical text.

While the interior play, Henry's play, imitates the comedic form of redemptive history, all but overpowering dissenting voices which, like that of Williams, invoke the tragedy of damnation, a third "ending" is proposed in the play's epilogue. Recalling the historical continuum, signaled by references to the succession and the future, Shakespeare reframes the past. The Chorus supplants the ending of Henry's story with the record of recurring civil violence. One becomes "many" (Epi.11, 12) as Henry's brothers vie for control of the realm and its young heir.[77] Shakespeare counters a comedic myth of transcendence with a secular vision of history similar to Geoffrey of Monmouth's ironic or realistic emplotment of British history, in which fraternal enmity and reconciliation are part of a continuous and inescapable cycle. Distancing history's amoral conflicts and its temporary and pragmatic reconciliations from the history of the heavenly city, Shakespeare represents this cyclical interplay of tragic and comedic scenarios as a parodic counterfeit of the tragicomic form of redemptive history.

Shakespeare, then, explores the generic configurations of the past by reenacting in alternative emplotments the interplay of fraternal strife and brotherly reconciliation, a familiar model for medieval drama and English historiography. The discourse of *Henry V* is, in fact, marked by "a dialectical tension" between generic models. Such a tension, as Hayden White argues, is the mark of "the element of critical self-consciousness present in any historian of recognizably classical stature."[78] Shakespeare dramatizes Henry's own effort to rewrite history, exorcising the tragic aspects of the mythic configuration of English historiography and institutionalizing the divine comedy of brotherly reconciliation. The play itself presents an ironic view of history's comedies and tragedies. Like an anamorphic image, brotherhood figures forth the "alternative emplotments" which endow a set of historical events, which in themselves have no story, with "all the possible meanings" accessible to Shakespeare's audience.[79] The comedy or romance of brotherly reconciliation is sustained by the non-mimetic strategies of the Chorus and of Henry's moral emplotment, designed to evoke what should or might have been. Nevertheless, neither moral exhortation nor appeals to the imagination succeed in exorcising the tragedy of fraternal enmity which reappears in mimetic representation of violated brotherhood. Shakespeare, thus, invokes generic patterns common to English historiography to recreate history's shifting perspectives and to test those formulations against the witness of the record.

Notes

1. Hayden White, "The Historical Text as Literary Artifact," in his *Tropics of Discourse: Essays in Cultural Criticism* (Baltimore: Johns Hopkins Univ. Press, 1978), 82, 88.

2. White, "Historicism, History, and the Figurative Imagination" in his *Tropics,* 109; White defines "emplotment," a term which I borrow (along with its cognates, "emplot" and "emplotted"), as "the encodation of the facts contained in the chronicle as components of specific *kinds* of plot structures, in precisely the way that Frye has suggested is the case with 'fictions' in general" ("Historical Text," 83).

3. White, "Historical Text," 88.

4. White, "Historical Text," 92.

5. Hayden White, *Metahistory: The Historical Imagination in Nineteenth-Century Europe* (Baltimore: Johns Hopkins Univ. Press, 1973), 3.

6. White, "Historical Text," 82.

7. See Clyde Kluckhohn, "Recurrent Themes in Myth and Mythmaking," in *Myth and Mythmaking,* ed. Henry A. Murray (New York: G. Braziller, 1960), 52. For a discussion of tragedy as fraternal violence see René Girard, *Violence and The Sacred,* trans. Patrick Gregory (Baltimore: Johns Hopkins Univ. Press, 1972).

8. For a discussion of the representation of power in medieval drama see John D. Cox, *Shakespeare and the Dramaturgy of Power* (Princeton: Princeton Univ. Press, 1989), 23-25.

9. Cox xi; V. A. Kolve, *The Play Called Corpus Christi* (Stanford: Stanford Univ. Press, 1966), 57-67.

10. St. Augustine, *The City Of God,* trans. John Healey, 2 vols. (1945; repr. New York: E. P. Dutton, 1973), 2:64.

11. Augustine, 2:59. See Gail Kern Paster, *The Idea of the City in the Age of Shakespeare* (Athens: Univ. of Georgia Press, 1985). Paster identifies the archetype of opposed cities as an ancient one, which appears in classical as well as scriptural sources, and is "always deeply involved with the notion of historical time" (2-13). She discusses the "bipolar image" of the city as it appears in Renaissance tragedy, masque and city comedy.

12. Augustine 2:64.

13. Augustine 2:63.

14. White, "Historical Text," 98.

15. Clifford Davidson, *From Creation to Doom* (New York: AMS Press, 1984), 46.

16. Davidson, 46-47; Kolve, 66-67.

17. Charles Norris Cochrane, *Christianity and Classical Culture: A Study of Thought and Action from Augustus to Augustine* (Oxford: Oxford Univ. Press, 1957), 471.

18. Cochrane, 473; Thucydides, *The Peloponnesian War,* trans. Richard Crawley, Modern Library College Editions (Modern Library: New York, 1951), 3.80-86.

19. Cochrane, 473.

20. White, "Historicism," 111-12.

21. *The Chronicle of Henry of Huntingdon,* trans. Thomas Forester (1853; repr. New York: AMS Press, 1968), 217; *William Malmesbury's Chronicle of the Kings of England* (London, 1889), 331-33.

22. Huntingdon, 216.

23. Ordericus Vitalis, *The Ecclesiastical History of England and Normandy,* trans. Thomas Forester, 4 vols. (1854; repr. New York: AMS Press, 1968), 2:433; 4:156-57.

24. Ordericus, 4:156-57.

25. Augustine, 1:115; Cochrane, 489.

26. Robert W. Hanning, *The Vision of History in Early Britain: From Gildas to Geoffrey of Monmouth* (New York: Columbia Univ. Press, 1966), 139.

27. White, "Historicism," 115.

28. Hanning, 142-43.

29. Geoffrey of Monmouth, *History of the Kings of Britain,* Sebastian Evans translation revised by Charles W. Dunn (New York: E. P. Dutton, 1958), 32-33.

30. Hanning, 125-26, 142, 159-60. Geoffrey is the source for Thomas Norton and Thomas Sackville's *Gorboduc* (1562). A forerunner of the Marlovian and Shakespearean history play (Irby B. Cauthen, Jr., ed., *Gorboduc or Ferrex and Porrex* [Lincoln: Univ. of Nebraska Press, 1970], xiv), this drama didactically portrays fraternal strife as the tragic sequel to any deviation from "single rule." The play's polarized iteration of this historiographic pattern provided the Elizabethan auditor with a model for interpreting the present and future, a model which foregrounds issues of unity, authority and succession.

31. Geoffrey, 61-63.

32. Geoffrey, 51-56.

33. Hanning, 125-26, 145.

34. Hanning, 140.

35. Hanning, 148-49.

36. Edward Hall, *Hall's Chronicle* (London, 1809), 1.

37. Hall, 1-2, 425.

38. Henry Ansgar Kelly, *Divine Providence in the England of Shakespeare's Histories* (Cambridge, Mass.: Harvard Univ. Press, 1970), 122-23.

39. Hall, 425.

40. *The Complete Works of Shakespeare,* ed. David Bevington (Glenview, Ill.: Scott Foresman, 1980). All quotations follow this edition.

41. Herbert Lindenberger, *Historical Drama: The Relation of Literature to Reality* (Chicago: Univ. of Chicago Press, 1975), 78-82.

42. White, "Historical Text," 84.

43. White, "Historical Text," 98.

44. Hayden White, "The Fictions of Factual Representation," in *Tropics,* 129.

45. Hanning, 31-43; Cox, 12-15. Augustine's skepticism of the political order sets him at odds not only with classical idealism but with the assumptions of Christian historians for whom the history of the Christian state is synonymous with the history of the heavenly city.

46. White ("Historical Text," 90-1), discusses Levi-Strauss's theory that "the coherence" of the historian's "story" is achieved by the exclusion of "one or more of the domains of facts."

47. Hall, 61.

48. Samuel Daniel, *The Civil Wars,* ed. Laurence Michel (New Haven: Yale Univ. Press, 1958).

49. White ("Historicism," 111-2) describes generic formulation as a selective process which is not a reduction but a "distortion of the factual field."

50. Hall, 61.

51. See G. L. Harriss, "The King and His Magnates," in *Henry V: The Practice of Kingship,* ed. G. L. Harriss (Oxford: Oxford Univ. Press, 1985), 31-51. Harriss discusses the Southampton plot as a renewal of the rebellion against Henry IV (36-37).

52. James R. Siemon, *Shakespearean Iconoclasm* (Berkeley and Los Angeles: Univ. of California Press, 1985), 103-4. Siemon argues that, despite Henry's allegorical shaping of this scene as a symbol of his magnanimity, it "pushes into the realm of history, where at each moment disorder and discrepancy force one to take up the burden of interpretation, to consider before and after, origin and end, purpose and conclusion without any promise of satisfying certainty to come." I would suggest that the scene itself successfully represses such inquiry except at one point—the concession of motive—although, as I argue below, other parts of the play contest the generic representation of this scene, reidentifying it as a story of re-emergent civil conflict.

53. Karl P. Wentersdorf, "The Conspiracy of Silence in *Henry V,*" *Shakespeare Quarterly* 27 (Summer 1976): 272-74.

54. Jonathan Dollimore and Alan Sinfield, "History and Ideology: The Instance of *Henry V,*" in *Alternative Shakespeares,* ed. John Drakakis (London: Methuen, 1985), 220.

55. Wentersdorf, 271, 274.

56. Emmon Grennan, "'This Story Shall the Good Man Teach His Son': *Henry V* and the Art of History," *Papers on Language and Literature* 15 (Fall 1979): 371.

57. See John H. Walter, ed. *King Henry V,* the Arden Shakespeare (1954; repr. London: Methuen, 1979). Interpreting Henry as an emblematic figure—the ideal Christian prince—he reads this scene as an exemplum of kingly justice, clemency (xviiii) and magnanimity (xvi) and argues that Henry is, like "pius Aeneas," an agent of God's plan (xxv). Dollimore and Sinfield, in contrast, comment on the universalizing of this defection (220) as a political strategy. The dual emplotment allows us to entertain Henry as both an emblem of justice and an astute politician adept at rewriting events and staging his own Doomsday pageant.

58. *Gesta Henrici Quinti: The Deeds of Henry V,* trans. and ed. Frank Taylor and John S. Roskell (Oxford: Clarendon Press, 1975), 19; Kolve, 85.

59. Dollimore and Sinfield, 217.

60. Raphael Holinshed, *Holinshed's Chronicles of England, Scotland, and Ireland,* 6 vols. (London, 1807), 3:72.

61. T. B. Pugh, *Henry V and the Southampton Plot of 1415* (London: Alan Sutton, 1988), 156, 109.

62. Pugh, 97-102.

63. Harriss, 46.

64. Pugh, 129.

65. Pugh, 129-30. See also John G. Bellamy, *The Tudor Law of Treason: An Introduction* (Buffalo: Univ. of Toronto Press, 1979), 9-11.

66. Pugh, 133-35, 129.

67. Helen C. White, *Tudor Books of Saints and Martyrs* (Madison: Univ. of Wisconsin Press, 1963), 8-9. White identifies the address "of consolation and encouragement to the faithful in time of persecution" as one of the most significant "hagiographic genres."

68. Helen C. White, 9-10.

69. Helen C. White, 14. The "afterlife" of the martyr is historical as well as transhistorical. In conflating the celebration of Agincourt with the yearly commemoration of a saint's day, Henry invests historical deeds with the kind of transcendence reserved for the sacrifices of Christian martyrs.

70. *Butler's Lives of the Saints,* ed. Herbert Thurston and Don Atwater (New York: P. J. Kenedy, 1956), 4:197-98.

71. Joan Rees, "Shakespeare's Welshmen," in *Literature and Nationalism,* ed. Vincent Newey and Ann Thompson (Savage, Md.: Barnes & Noble Books, 1991), 29.

72. Rees, 22; 33-34. Weighing the documentary support for Fluellen's account, Rees discusses the conflicting accounts of this Welsh victory and the origins of the Welsh celebration of St. David's day.

73. Augustine, 1:115.

74. Augustine, 2:59.

75. Dollimore and Sinfield, who argue that the play is not "'about' unity" but about insurrection (216), contend that the notion that foreign wars distract from internal conflict and enforce unity is demystified (215-18). If so, Shakespeare is implicitly challenging an assumption which is reiterated (and sometimes questioned) in English historiography.

76. Sir Francis Bacon, *The Advancement of Learning,* in *The Works of Francis Bacon,* ed. James Spedding, R. L. Ellis, and D. D. Heath, 3 vols. (Philadelphia, 1842), 1:192. The play's comedic or romantic enactment of an idealized version of brotherly reconciliation and its ceremonial exorcising of the tragic witness of fact recalls Bacon's distinction between poetry and history, in which poetry idealizes by "submitting the shows of things to the desires of the mind," while history, like reason, "doth buckle and bow the mind unto the nature of things."

77. Dollimore and Sinfield, 220.

78. White, "Historical Text," 94.

79. White, "Historical Text," 84, 92.

Joan Lord Hall (essay date 1997)

SOURCE: Hall, Joan Lord. "Themes." In Henry V: *A Guide to the Play,* pp. 77-93. Westport, Conn.: Greenwood Press, 1997.

[*In the following essay, Hall highlights the complexities of* Henry V's *principal themes: order versus disorder, the nature of warfare, and the requirements of kingship.*]

Image patterns are often a clue to a play's underlying concerns. In *Henry V* the garden metaphor sets ordered fertility against disorderly chaos; images of blood (symbolizing both familial ties and violent destruction) project a multifaceted concept of war; and the extended personification of "ceremony" in the King's troubled soliloquy before Agincourt expands on the key issue of kingship. These three central themes—the importance of order in the nation, the ambivalence of war, and the challenging nature of kingship—emerge from the play's development of plot and character as well as its language.

As might be predicted in a play that Shakespeare wrote only a year or two before *Hamlet,* the treatment of these themes is complex; *Henry V* offers no straightforward celebration of the King and his military mission. The play raises questions rather than providing clear answers. Is it possible to achieve lasting unity in the state of England, or do currents of disorder inevitably destabilize this society? Can war against another nation ever be justified, and is it always a mixture of the vile and the heroic? What is the nature of kingship? Must the successful monarch combine the expediency of a Machiavel with the virtues of a Christian? These issues develop in dialectical fashion.

ORDER AND DISORDER

While the key dramatic topics are clear enough—order, war, and kingship—readers or directors of the play may differ in their interpretation of how these topics are handled in the drama, and thus how they build into fully articulated themes. "Order" is a case in point. The topic is introduced very deliberately in I. ii, where Exeter first develops a musical analogy to evoke the harmony of a well-ordered kingdom:

> For government, though high, and low, and lower,
> Put into parts, doth keep in one consent;
> Congreeing in a full and natural close,
> Like music.
>
> (I. ii. 180-84)

Then the Archbishop of Canterbury elaborates a parable on how the honeybees "by a rule in nature teach / The act of order to a peopled kingdom." The speech, a rehearsing of a fable that had classical and Renaissance precedents,[1] is often cited by earlier critics as a key to the play's central theme; J. H. Walter terms it a "reflection of Shakespeare's concern with unity of action in the structure of the play,"[2] and A. R. Humphreys thinks it "is meant as a genuine celebration of national harmony."[3] Deconstructive critics . . . have been more skeptical, discovering in the speech a propaganda pitch for the dominant Elizabethan ideology of social order through submission to authority. In its context it is certainly a piece of special pleading by the clergymen—a reminder to Henry that he can achieve the throne of France if his subjects who are left at home cooperate obediently. Social harmony is thus promoted a little too stridently. Canterbury expounds the parallel between the beehive's "rule in nature" and the well-ordered kingdom, where all levels of society (magistrates, merchants, and soldiers) work for the good of the ruler. Yet the bees' monarch, described as "busied in his majesty," is strangely passive, content merely to survey the labors of his underlings—the pillaging soldiers and the toiling porters. The progression of the imagery suggests that order at home is easily achieved. Canterbury buttresses the concept of unity in diversity—"That many things, having full reference / To one consent, may work contrariously"—with a series of images from nature (fresh streams meeting in one salt ocean) and human culture (arrows flying to one mark, lines converging in the dial's center). This takes him smoothly to the main point at issue, the military campaign:

> So may a thousand actions, once afoot,
> End in one purpose, and be all well borne
> Without defeat. . . .
>
> (211-13)

Yet beneath this ideal of harmonious order in the state lurk rebellious segments, barely kept in check; the Scots are threatening to pour into England "like the tide into a breach" and suck the "princely eggs" of "eagle" England (149, 169-71). In a sense, too, Canterbury's speech deconstructs the premise of order, since its powerful rhetoric is finally in the service of a divided rather than a strongly unified kingdom. The prelate is urging Henry to partition England in four and to trust that the commonwealth will continue to run smoothly in his absence, so that he can deploy one-quarter of the male population in his war against France. Ironically it turns out that Canterbury's paradigm of a unified state, all parts interlocking, is at odds with much of what we see in the play: the conspiracy of Cambridge, Scroop, and Grey; the fraternity of thieves (Pistol, Bardolph, and Nym) defying Henry's decree that nothing be stolen from France; and Williams' muted threat of insubordination when he challenges the King's "cause." There is even the slight possibility, up to the very end of the play, that Princess Katherine might sabotage Henry's plans for unifying the two kingdoms by failing to exercise her womanly duty and conform to his grand design.

Do we interpret the theme here as the necessity for order in the commonwealth, or the difficulty of maintaining it?[4] The specious way in which Canterbury's speech sets up the "act of order" as an assured achievement, masking disorder, may undercut its viability. It is clear that the play presents social unity under a strong monarchy as preferable to anarchy (or the cut-throat rivalry of the so-called brotherhood of Eastcheap), but this theme is not presented simplistically. The stability and order of the kingdom partly depend on Henry's proving his qualities as a strong leader (unified in himself),[5] so that the theme of order and disorder is linked to that of kingship. Moreover, war may temporarily unite England, but it creates havoc and disorder in France; the images of the wasted garden do more to convince the audience of the importance of a unified kingdom than does Canterbury's complacent speech. In particular, Burgundy's dignified exposition of what happens to civilization in wartime, when "hateful docks" and "rough thistles" stamp out the "cowslip, burnet, and green clover" (V. ii. 49-52), drives home in realistic detail the disorderly "savagery" in a society where peace is "mangled."

WAR

Henry V has been described as the "anatomy of a war."[6] Anatomy is an appropriate term: The play presents different aspects of warfare for our inspection, and we are left to decide whether war is a heroic enterprise or one that brings out the worst in its participants. If the theme can be summed up at all, it is that war has many faces. Filmgoers conditioned by Olivier's movie may think that *Henry V* glorifies war. But the text provides no stirring battle after the call to arms at Agincourt, only a scene in which the mercenary-minded Pistol captures the cowardly Le Fer. We simply do not see much of the "pride, pomp, and circumstance of glorious war" (*Othello*, III. iii. 354); the heroism of York and Suffolk, for instance, is reported, not shown.[7] War in this play is frankly the means to an end—a way of unifying the country and extending England's boundaries—but the means is often sordid and always costly.

Because Henry revives an old, somewhat tenuous claim to the throne of France, the war is not strictly necessary. Only by sleight of hand can he turn the French into the initiators; the campaign is more a political opportunity for him to prove his prowess as a leader and a conqueror. Nevertheless, Henry is not depicted as an aggressive warmonger. It is Canterbury who, for pragmatic reasons, urges Henry to "unwind your bloody flag" while Exeter reminds him to emulate his ancestors, the "lions" of his "blood." Acknowledging both the "waste" and the responsibility incurred, Henry's vision of war is sober:

> For never two such kingdoms did contend
> Without much fall of blood, whose guiltless drops
> Are every one a woe, a sore complaint
> 'Gainst him whose wrongs gives edge unto the swords
> That makes such waste in brief mortality.
>
> (I. ii. 24-28)

The King's speech personifies drops of blood as bitter complainants, but Williams goes further in imagining how the dismembered body parts of those killed in war will rise up in protest on the Day of Judgment:

> all those legs and arms and heads, chopped off in a
> battle, shall join together at the latter day and cry all,
> "We died at such a place," some swearing, some crying
> for a surgeon, some upon their wives left poor behind
> them, some upon the debts they owe, some upon their
> children rawly left.
>
> (IV. i. 137-43)

The speech is a graphic reminder of the cost of war in terms of human lives and relationships. Williams also illuminates the corrupting nature of war, the inevitable clash between moral sensibilities and concentration on killing, when he ponders, "I am afeard there are few die well that die in a battle; for how can they charitably dispose of anything when blood is their argument?" Blood, as the Eastcheap Boy remarks, is "unwholesome food" (II. iii. 58). This theme of moral coarsening through an obsession with blood (as murder) is echoed in Burgundy's description of how France is affected by the war. Even the children, suffering from the devastating aftereffects of Henry's military campaign, "grow like savages—as soldiers will / That nothing do but meditate on blood" (V. ii. 59-60).

It is at Harfleur that the "savagery" of war is delineated most clearly. In a passage that again focuses on blood and extends into rape, Henry envisages how, if the town refuses to surrender, "the fleshed soldier, rough and hard of heart, / In liberty of bloody hand shall range /

With conscience wide as hell" (III. iii. 11-13). Despite this human ferocity, the vision of war becomes curiously impersonal, for the images that follow show abstractions, rather than people, taking the initiative: "Impious war" is personified and compared to the "prince of fiends," Satan himself; "licentious wickedness" races downhill; and "murder, spoil, and villainy" are envisaged as natural phenomena, "filthy and contagious clouds." Once the war machine grinds into gear, it generates its own horrors, so that the "enraged" warriors are somehow not held morally accountable. Indeed, to be a soldier at all means cultivating a tough impersonality, as Henry makes clear when he backs up his exhortations at the breach—"Disguise fair nature with hard-favor'd rage" (III. i. 8)—with images of the eye as a brass cannon and the brow as a rock lashed by the sea. In contrast to the Roman warrior Coriolanus, depicted in battle as a "thing of blood, whose every motion / Was tim'd with dying cries" (*Coriolanus,* II. ii. 109-10), Henry never becomes an inhuman war machine. Nor does he indulge in the mindless fury parodied in Macmorris's "so Chrish save me, I will cut off your head!" (III. ii. 135). He can, nevertheless, be ruthless in military strategy, prepared to use "bloody constraint" in fighting for the French Crown (II. iv. 97) and to kill the prisoners when his dominance on the battlefield is threatened.

The apparent contradictions in Henry's response to war—compunction coupled with sublime indifference or even callous acceptance—point to a central ambivalence in the way that war is presented. The question of the King's responsibility for lives lost in war, introduced in Act I, resurfaces in Act IV. Henry cannot completely argue away his nagging sense of shedding "guiltless drops" of blood by separating the state of the individual's soul from his "duty" to go to war for his king, as he attempts to do in his conversation with Williams. And the idea that death in battle can serve as the scourge of God—"War is his beadle, war is his vengeance" (IV. i. 173-74)—may come across as a convenient rationalization too. On the other hand, the King at Harfleur accurately points out the inexorable momentum of war, where the "blind and bloody soldier," swept up in battle fury, acts like an automaton. Such momentum, Henry argues, is out of his control and therefore beyond his jurisdiction. These perspectives on war in the play remain antithetical; they cannot be reconciled.

There is a tension, too, between the creative energy of being transformed into an effective soldier ("bend up every spirit / To his full height!" is phallic, as are other images connected with storming the breach) and the repulsive acts of destruction engendered by this ferocity: rape, carnage, and mortal combat leading to the stench of corpses on the battlefield. Exhilaration is counterbalanced by grotesque detail in the exhortation at the breach, which A. R. Humphreys defines as "desperate, appalling, and inspiring at once."[8] War in *Henry V* is envisaged as a test of manhood, ranging from the images of virility at Harfleur ("Stiffen the sinews, conjure up the blood" [III. i. 7]) to the Dauphin's lament that French "mettle is bred out" (III. v. 29). To be on the losing side of the war game is to experience impotence or sexual dishonor, as when Bourbon feels an overwhelming "shame" at seeing the broken ranks of the French. Refusing to return to the fray, says Bourbon, is equivalent to being a "base pander" who watches his daughter being raped by a "slave" (IV. v. 15-17). And war lust is always yoked to death, as suggested in the erotic image of York and Suffolk embracing as they die on the battlefield (IV. vi).

The theme of war in *Henry V* encompasses more than heroic excitement and violent bloodshed. Hard work and drudgery are also required in any military campaign. With his consternation that the mines at Harfleur are not "according to the disciplines of the war" and his pride at the "excellent discipline" of his compatriot Exeter at the bridge, Fluellen represents the military man's meticulous attention to detail. War is exhausting, too. Branagh's movie adds to the text by showing the slog through mud and rain as part of the campaign's horrors; but a simple stage direction in Shakespeare's play, "Enter the King and his poor Soldiers" (III. vi. 90), is enough to convey the total enervation of the army as they march toward Calais. Exhaustion, as well as resolve, emerges from the halting rhythms and monosyllabic weight of the speech in which Henry addresses Montjoy at the end of this scene. What at first glance appears to be flat, even repetitive verse gives a clue to Henry's underlying emotions: He is bracing himself, presenting a bold front to the French despite being terribly weary. He admits that "My people are with sickness much enfeebled, / My numbers lessened" but continues:

> If we may pass, we will; if we be hind'red,
> We shall your tawny ground with your red blood
> Discolor; and so, Montjoy, fare you well.
> The sum of all our answer is but this:
> We would not seek a battle as we are,
> Nor, as we are, we say we will not shun it.
>
> (168-73)

In *Henry V* the different dimensions of war—its exhilaration and opportunities for courage, juxtaposed with its horrors, grinding weariness, and inhumanity—build into a complex vision, a questioning of whether war can ever be fully justified. King Henry does harness the military venture to his advantage and to the glory of England, for the war effort makes possible not only national unity in the abstract sense but the strongly forged brotherhood felt in the Crispin's Day speech. What is more, the speed with which Shakespeare turns from this heroic speech to Pistol's capture of Le Fer,

and from Montjoy's somber request to collect the French corpses to the comic interlude between Fluellen and Williams (IV. viii), may discourage too prolonged a questioning of war's bleakness. Darker nuances remain, however, in the unheroic thievery of the Eastcheap men, sucking the blood of France, and the vision of atrocities that the "blind and bloody" soldier may at any moment perpetrate. And although the English are granted a relatively bloodless victory (few of their men are killed), the war, as Burgundy points out, is disastrous for the fertile garden of France. While a performance of *Henry V* with a totally anti-war message would be a distortion of the text (and run counter to the energy Henry inspires as a military leader), stage productions in the second half of the twentieth century have taken up hints from the play script and delivered some critique of the war. The Royal Shakespeare Company's 1984-85 version, for instance, did not allow the audience to forget the cost of the French campaign. Even as the marriage between Henry and Katherine was being sealed, "the battlefield, with candles glimmering beside corpses, was seen through a gauzy traverse curtain behind the tableau of Henry's triumphant diplomatic wedding."[9] Branagh's film . . . reveals more of the contradictions of war than does Olivier's, with its firmer emphasis on the pageantry and patriotism of the military endeavor. As *Henry V* itself continues to insist, war is both terrible *and* energizing.

KINGSHIP: THE PLAY AS THE TESTING OF A MONARCH

The central theme of *Henry V* is kingship; in terms of both plot and character, the play unfolds as the testing of a monarch. Henry cannot rely on the sacred "name" of king that Richard II invoked, since divine right has been cancelled by his father's act of usurping the throne. As a de facto rather than a de jure ruler, Henry IV struggles to maintain his authority throughout the *Henry IV* plays, and Henry V, once he is King of England, must also prove his fitness to rule through appropriate choices and actions. A long list of "king-becoming graces," helpful in defining the ideal monarch, appears in *Macbeth* when Malcolm is addressing Macduff. The future king specifies

> . . . justice, verity, temp'rance, stableness,
> Bounty, perseverance, mercy, lowliness,
> Devotion, patience, courage, fortitude . . .
>
> (IV.iii. 92-94)

Arguably Henry exemplifies most of these Christian qualities during the course of the play; yet, like Malcolm disguising his true nature from Macduff in order to test him, he is also capable of deviousness, even machiavellianism. As Robert Egan comments, there is an inevitable "dichotomy between conqueror and Christian"[10] in *Henry V.* Strong leadership, Shakespeare implies, requires cunning as well as open "courage"—the combination that Machiavelli outlines when he advises the prince to be both "fox" and "lion."[11] And far from being a straightforward demonstration of kingship, with Henry displaying various facets of the royal persona in a fairly static way,[12] the play allows for undercurrents of uneasiness or doubt, moments of possible failure as Henry refines his roles as monarch.

Before we see him, Henry is projected as a kingly paragon; Canterbury expresses wonder at this new king's attributes in the opening scene. As well as being a great orator, Henry excels in four areas: he can "reason in divinity," he is an expert in "commonwealth affairs," his "discourse of war" is highly impressive, and he can expound on "any cause of policy" (i.e., argue about politics). What is more, Henry goes beyond the rhetorician who theorizes on abstract propositions, for he has put into practice an active rather than a contemplative virtue:

> . . . the art and practic part of life
> Must be the mistress to this theoric.

(I. i. 51-52)

King Henry has much to live up to. Can he establish himself as an accomplished orator, a pious man of God, a statesman-politician, and a military leader? All of these roles are manifested, to some degree, as the play progresses, and most of them are touched on in Henry's opening scene.

When Henry first appears on stage, in I. ii, he is very much on trial. Not only is this the first time that the theater audience sees him, but he is still a relatively new king—and a young one, historically only twenty-five—who needs to make a strong initial impression on the inner circle of noblemen. As a decisive ruler he must take command of the situation and display his control publicly. The key term here is "resolved." Almost Henry's first words, referring to the legitimacy of his title in France, are "We would be resolved," and once Canterbury's explanations are complete and the King is ready to call in the Dauphin's ambassadors, he closes the debate with "Now are we well resolved" (I. ii. 222). Not only has the issue been clarified, enabling him to proceed, but he is fully determined ("resolved") to go ahead with his military campaign. In addition, Henry projects himself as both responsible and pious before he allows Canterbury to launch into his discussion of Salic law. Concerned with the "truth" of his claim, he urges the Archbishop to expound the case "justly and religiously." In effect the King adopts the role of spiritual authority (the "prelate" who can "reason in divinity") when he warns Canterbury

> Under this conjuration, speak my lord:
> For we will hear, note, and believe in heart

> That what you speak is in your conscience washed
> As pure as sin with baptism.

(29-32)

At the end of the Archbishop's speech Henry checks again, in front of witnesses, that his own "conscience" will not be sullied by pursuing a title that is specious:

> May I with right and conscience make this claim?

(96)

Showing his skill in "commonwealth affairs," he cuts through Canterbury's rousing talk of heroic royal ancestors to discuss instead practical steps to "defend / Against the Scot" while the English troops are away in France. Shrewdly Henry recalls how the Scots invaded England while Edward III was away campaigning in France, but Canterbury, also a politician, caps this by reminding Henry how England under Edward III not only defended itself adequately against the Scots but also captured the Scottish King. The King listens carefully to his counselors; he is persuaded by their pragmatic arguments that one-quarter of the English forces can win the war in France while the rest defend their own country.

Once Henry is "resolved," he is ready to act decisively: "France being ours, we'll bend it to our awe, / Or break it all to pieces" (224-25). Whatever Henry's other possible motives (desire for a heroic enterprise to unify England or the need to busy "giddy minds with foreign wars" as his father advised), it is clear that winning France is also a personal quest for him—a means of proving his prowess as king. The sentiment that he expresses more openly at the end of II. ii, "No king of England, if not King of France!", is registered here in his extremist attitude to the enterprise. Either he will succeed magnificently and rule France "in large and ample empery," or he will die in obscurity with no memorial tomb, his deeds uncelebrated. Achieving France will be, as Robert Ornstein comments, "an ultimate proof" of his "kingliness."[13]

The arrival of the French ambassador and his entourage presents Henry with another opportunity to demonstrate his royal command of the situation. In assuring them that they may deliver their message from the Dauphin "freely," Henry contends

> We are no tyrant, but a Christian king,
> Unto whose grace our passion is as subject
> As is our wretches fett'red in our prisons. . . .

(241-43)

Henry is promising to behave temperately; because he is gracious (Canterbury respects him as "full of grace" [I. i. 22]), he is not prey to outbursts of anger or tyrannical behavior. Although highly provoked by the

Dauphin's references to his earlier frivolity ("galliard" and "revel") and by the demeaning present of tennis balls, the King keeps his promise. The English court, as shown in Branagh's movie, may be watching keenly. How exactly *will* Henry react? He keeps his temper under control, converting anger into irony and rousing rhetoric:

> And tell the pleasant prince this mock of his
> Hath turned his balls to gunstones. . . .
>
> (281-82)

Again, he is aware that the campaign will test him, enabling him to display to both nations the "practic part of life":

> But tell the Dauphin I will keep my state,
> Be like a king, and show my sail of greatness,
> When I do rouse me in my throne of France.
>
> (273-75)

"Be like a king" is significant. The opening Chorus regrets that the stage lacks resources to show "the warlike Harry, like himself," but here Henry goes one better; he promises to "dazzle all the eyes of France" with his intrinsic "greatness." Although this is kingship in quest of national glory, his heroic impulse is always tempered by rational control. In planning the French campaign Henry judiciously recommends an "expedition" (punning on military invasion and speed) that will progress with "reasonable swiftness" rather than reckless haste.

In Act II Henry faces a more probing test: how to deal with the traitors in a way that proves he understands when "mercy" must give place to just punishment. His related dilemma—can a king be powerful *and* popular?—is pointed up by Cambridge's hypocritical tribute, "Never was monarch better feared and loved / Than is your Majesty" (II. ii. 25-26). As Machiavelli comments in *The Prince*,[14] it is difficult to inspire both emotions equally, and more important for the strong leader to be respected than adored. In an ideal society, the king could rely on "hearts create of duty, and of zeal" (31). But Henry learns by hard experience that his "bedfellow" Scroop appeared to love him only to take advantage of his friendship. Holinshed captures some of the precarious balance between being "loved" and "feared" when he describes Henry as "so severe a justicer" that "his people both loved and obeyed him"; he left "no offence unpunished nor friendship unrewarded" and proved a "terror to rebels, and suppressor of sedition."[15] In the Southampton scene Henry does not hand out rewards for friendship (although he promises "quittance of desert and merit / According to the weight and worthiness" [34-35]), but we do see him firmly administering punishment, acting the part of "severe . . . justicer" so that he can effectively crush sedition.

The scene opens with Bedford's reassurance that "the king hath note" of all that the traitors "intend." This ensures that the audience can savor the dramatic irony, knowing that Henry is orchestrating the situation toward disclosure and that what appears to be naive overconfidence in his subjects ("We carry not a heart with us from hence / That grows not in a fair consent with ours" [21-22]) is actually a tactic for unmasking his enemies. Admittedly the King's strategy is machiavellian. But he is using deception (the pointed irony of referring to the traitors' "too much love and care" of him [52-53]) to expose hypocrisy; one might view him, in John F. Danby's terms, as the "machiavel of goodness,"[16] doing what the cunning leader must do to establish his authority. He shows magnanimity in pardoning a drunken man for verbal abuse, even when Grey, damning himself in advance, urges the "taste of much correction." (In a parallel sequence in IV. viii, Fluellen advocates "martial law" for Williams, whereas Henry pardons him because, as Williams explains, "All offenses . . . come from the heart" and his heart has remained loyal to the King.) For the traitors, however, there can be no mercy. Henry perhaps speaks as a man in his long speech where he deeply regrets the perfidy of Scroop, who has "infected / The sweetness of affiance" (126-27). But his voice is that of a responsible monarch who puts the safety of his kingdom first when he declares:

> Touching our person, seek we no revenge,
> But we our kingdom's safety must so tender,
> Whose ruin you have sought, that to her laws
> We do deliver you.
>
> (174-77)

At Harfleur the King's challenge is to prove himself a military giant, displaying the qualities of "courage" and "fortitude" as a warrior-king. Strong leadership, Shakespeare suggests, is a matter of playing the role convincingly and encouraging others to do the same—to become what they act:

> In peace there's nothing so becomes a man
> As modest stillness and humility;
> But when the blast of war blows in our ears,
> Then imitate the action of the tiger.
>
> (III. i. 3-6)

The aggressive soldier must "Disguise fair nature with hard-favor'd rage" and assume the properties of a war machine or a predatory animal. By the time he speaks to the Governor (III. iii), Henry has completely appropriated the persona of the soldier, calling it "A name that in my thoughts becomes me best" (6). His threatening speech is thus predicated on a total divorce between the sensitive mortal who is bound to feel "pity" for violated women and butchered babies and the hardened military leader who would fatalistically let his soldiers run amok. If Henry actually allowed this brutality to

Battle scene in Kenneth Branagh's 1989 film version of Henry V.

take place, could he remain a respected ruler, full of "king-becoming graces"? Again there is a tenuous balance between the monarch's ruthlessness[17] (a kind of "justice," if Harfleur breaks the rules of war that Henry outlines here) and "mercy." It is possible, though not certain, that the blood-chilling threats are merely a clever tactic to coerce surrender, so that once the Governor has capitulated Henry can "Use mercy to them all" (54). There is a similar conflict between the King's "lenity" and "cruelty" toward an individual when Henry, while insisting on treating the French with respect and not stealing from their land because "the gentler gamester is the soonest winner," nevertheless approves Bardolph's execution (III. vi. 112). He reveals no regret over the death of an old comrade for theft. The expedient military leader clearly cannot afford to be sentimental.

Michael Goldman comments astutely on how *Henry V* reveals "the effort of greatness" and "the demands on the self that being a king involves."[18] In Act IV Henry as king faces several challenges: keeping up the morale of his soldiers before and during battle, and justifying his cause (while in disguise) to his men. The Chorus

paints a glowing picture of Henry as the "royal captain" who rallies his troops the night before battle with his resilience and "sweet majesty." Indeed when we first see him at the beginning of IV. i, he is succeeding admirably in cheering up his comrades. He makes the best of a bad situation, "gathering honey out of the weed" by turning adversity to advantage:

> For our bad neighbor makes us early stirrers,
> Which is both healthful, and good husbandry.
>
> (IV. i. 6-7)

Even the mind, he argues, is "quick'ned" by harsh conditions. It is quite possible, judged by his later "I and my bosom must debate a while" (31), that the King is experiencing anxiety on a deeper level; yet he projects a "cheerful semblance"—the king-becoming grace of "stableness"—so convincingly that we believe in his fundamental optimism and, most important, in his ability to transmit a positive outlook to his subordinates.

The sequence where the King is in disguise points up the ultimate irony: Henry is unable to shed the royal persona and its responsibilities. The price of kingship is isolation from other people, even though Henry is eager to present himself to the commoners (Bates, Court, and Williams) as an ordinary human being: "I think the King is but a man, as I am. . . . His ceremonies laid by, in his nakedness he appears but a man; and though his affections are higher mounted than ours, yet when they stoop, they stoop with the like wing" (103-10). He does not appear to convince them. Indeed, whatever emotions he may be feeling, Henry must remain committed to the public role of "outward courage" in order to rally his subjects; as he goes on to explain, "no man should possess [the king] with any appearance of fear, lest he, by showing it, should dishearten his army" (112-14). For a king, the appearance of strength is paramount. Yet Henry continues to defend the King's private self and his "conscience," maintaining that the King's cause is "just" and his quarrel "honorable." Whereas Bates expresses unquestioning loyalty, Williams probes the implications, the "heavy reckoning" at the Day of Judgment, if the cause is not "good." Sensitive on the issue of the King's responsibility for so many lives lost in battle, Henry concentrates on separating the "duty" of the subject, which belongs to the King, from the "soul" of the subject, which is that person's own concern, regardless of whether or not he has been sent to war on a valid pretext. The long speech (150-90) is perhaps a Pyrrhic victory for the King's position. It convinces Williams that "the king is not to answer" for the sins of individual subjects but leaves him suspicious of the King's "word," his promise that he will never be ransomed: "Ay, he said so, to make us fight cheerfully; but when our throats are cut, he may be ransomed, and we ne'er the wiser" (197-99). Henry's defense of kingship, so coherent on one level, has confirmed the wide chasm—the lack of complete trust, the sense of operating by different standards, the inability to communicate frankly—between the monarch and his subjects.

Henry's meditation on "ceremony" bitterly explodes the mystique of kingship: its dependence on empty forms, which calls into question its genuine substance. Suddenly the emperor is admitting that he has no clothes. Whatever authority the King possesses he must forge for himself, since "place, degree, and form" have no creative or healing powers. No wonder that Henry deeply resents the "ceremony" that both insulates him from his subjects and traps him in a web of anxieties and public responsibilities. Inevitably he romanticizes the lives of the private man (as "infinite heart's-ease") and the peasant (who "Sleeps in Elysium"), just as he exaggerates the "hard condition" of being a king. On a deeper level, though, he faces up to the implications of his title. When he prays that God will take from his men the "sense of reck'ning" he refers literally to the soldiers' ability to count the huge number of the French enemy, but he also touches on the somber meaning that Williams has introduced just before: a "reckoning" on the Day of Judgment.

The two soliloquies crystallize the King's dilemma; he must accept the penalties of his role if he is to play it successfully on the following day. Acknowledging and coming to terms with his solitary burden (that he alone must "bear all") releases fresh confidence in his public persona. His oratory before Agincourt demonstrates the positive side of kingship, for it is not only a superb display of his own "courage" and "fortitude" but of the king-becoming grace of "perseverance" in building the same confidence in his followers. To Westmoreland, desperate for ten thousand more fighting men, Henry responds, "What's he that wishes so?" Again turning adversity to advantage, he stresses, "The fewer men, the greater share of honor" and projects a Hotspur-like persona who thirsts for glory in battle when he describes himself as "the most offending soul alive" in coveting "honor." But whereas Hotspur wanted no "corrival" in the honor stakes (*Henry IV, Part i*, I. iii. 207), Henry inspires others to join him in a fellowship of heroic feats. The Crispin's Day speech is the ultimate proof of Henry's strength as a leader. Gone is the defensiveness that made communication with the three commoners difficult; paradoxically, in his public address to the army he can reach out to his men on personal terms, abandoning the royal "we" for the "we" of shared enterprise as he forges English brotherhood on French soil:

> We few, we happy few, we band of brothers
>
> (IV. iii. 60)

The apocalyptic overtones of "The day, my friends, and all things stay for me" (IV. i. 315) have dissolved into the absolute conviction that he and his men together have the necessary mental fortitude: "All things are ready, if our minds be so" (IV. iii. 71). No longer fearing the infamy or silence of a failed campaign, Henry proudly tells Montjoy that even those Englishmen who die this day will "draw their honors reeking up to heaven" and be remembered for the terrible plague they bred in France. Valiant as ever, the King again swears that the French will never ransom his living body. Moreover, Henry projects confidence without appearing boastful; he takes pride in his "warriors for the working day," but his fundamental humility, his submission to the will of God, is underlined in the proviso that they will win the battle only "if God please" (120). This humility (the "lowliness" outlined by Malcolm in *Macbeth*) is most fully revealed in his conclusion, after he reads the brief list of English dead at Agincourt, that "O God, thy arm was here!" (IV. viii. 108). Regardless of the underlying reasons for Henry's piety, what matters is that he manifests it appropriately, and, by making it a capital offense to "boast" of victory, he deflects his army from the kind of arrogance that has undermined the French.

This is a superb display of practical kingship. The scenes that follow, presenting the King in action at Agincourt, are less clear in their intention—in particular, Henry's order to kill the French prisoners followed by a second threat to cut the throats of all those captured by his soldiers is confusing.[19] Shakespeare may be trying to encompass too much here—presenting Henry as a shrewd leader who is coldly ruthless when he foresees danger for his army but also as a furious, spontaneous avenger of the slaughter of the boys in the camp, to the point where he is no longer required to be temperate or magnanimous: "And not a man of them that we shall take / Shall taste our mercy" (IV. vii. 66-67). At any rate, Henry's royal magnanimity is again tested when he has the chance to punish Williams for his "bitter terms" the previous night. Instead of doing so, he graciously accepts Williams' entreaty to "take it for your own fault, and not mine" and rewards the man for his honest heart: "Here uncle Exeter, fill this glove with crowns, / And give it to this fellow" (IV. viii. 58-59). This gesture may serve as an example of Henry's generosity (or the King rewarding his loyal friends); yet it has the effect of patronizing Williams, who is now addressed as "fellow" and not as the "brother" of the Crispin's Day speech. And it is ironic that Henry thinks it appropriate to reward Williams—possibly to buy his loyalty—by giving him gold, even though he himself has spurned wealth in favor of "honor."

The ambivalence here points to the complexity of Shakespeare's treatment of the theme of kingship. On one level the sequence illustrates Henry's "bounty" as one of the king-becoming graces, just as Henry has displayed "temperance" to the Dauphin's messengers, "justice" to the traitors, "devotion" to God, and "courage" and "fortitude" in battle. But the King's justice is sometimes akin to ruthlessness and his honesty undercut by deviousness or cunning, although these too (the play suggests) may be necessary attributes of kingship. *Henry V* reflects what Michael Manheim terms the Renaissance "acceptance of deception and intrigue and violence as legitimate instuments of political behavior."[20] And for Henry the dark side of royalty is its utter isolation—the king, vulnerable to betrayal, can have no close friends—as well as its deceptive appearance of glory. Since the "ceremony" of monarchy is merely symbolic, the king must work on his own initiative, with talents honed through trial and risk, to win solid achievements for his country.

Notes

1. The fable of the bees was developed by both Virgil (*Georgics,* Book IV) and Pliny (*Natural History,* Book XI). Shakespeare might have found it in the Renaissance authors Erasmus (*Institutio Principis Christiani*) and Lyly (*Euphues*); see Andrew Gurr, "*Henry V* and the Bees' Commonwealth," *ShS,* [*Shakespeare Survey*] 30 (1977), 61-72.

2. *Henry V* (ed.), *The Arden Shakespeare* (1954), p. xvi.

3. *Henry V* (ed.), *The New Penguin Shakespeare,* p. 11.

4. Derek Traversi, *Shakespeare: From* Richard II *to* Henry V (Stanford, Calif.: Stanford University Press, 1957), decides that "the principal theme of *Henry V* . . . is the establishment in England of an order based on consecrated authority and crowned successfully by action against France" (166). Conversely, Jonathan Dollimore and Alan Sinfield, "History and Ideology: The Instance of *Henry V,*" in John Drakakis (ed.), *Alternative Shakespeares* (London and New York: Methuen, 1985), single out "insurrection" as the play's "obsessive preoccupation" (216).

5. Rose A. Zimbardo, "The Formalism of *Henry V*" (1964), in Michael Quinn (ed.), *Shakespeare,* Henry V: *A Casebook* (London: Macmillan, 1969), pp. 163-70, pushes this idea to its ultimate conclusion, arguing that the play is a formal celebration of how "the ideal king embodies in himself and projects upon his state the ideal metaphysical order" (164).

6. Alexander Leggatt, *Shakespeare's Political Drama: The History Plays and the Roman Plays* (London and New York: Routledge, 1988), p. 114.

7. See Anthony Brennan, "'Mangling by Starts the Full Course of That Glory': The Legend and the Reality of War in *Henry V,*" in *Onstage and Offstage Worlds in Shakespeare's Plays* (London and New York: Routledge, 1989), p. 196.

8. *Henry V* (ed.), p. 34.

9. Russell Jackson and Robert Smallwood (eds.), *Players of Shakespeare 2* (Cambridge: Cambridge University Press, 1988), p. 5.

10. "A Muse of Fire: *Henry V* in the Light of *Tamburlaine,*" *MLQ,* [*Modern Language Quarterly*] 29 (1965), 15-28, 26.

11. *The Prince,* trans. George Bull (Harmondsworth: Penguin Books, 1961), Chapter 18, pp. 99-100.

12. As Moody E. Prior concludes in *The Drama of Power: Studies in Shakespeare's History Plays* (Evanston, Ill.: Northwestern University Press, 1973), p. 323.

13. *A Kingdom for a Stage* (Cambridge, Mass.: Harvard University Press, 1972), p. 185.

14. Chapter 17, p. 96.

15. *Chronicles,* in J. R. Brown (ed.), *Henry V, The Signet Classic Shakespeare* (1965; 1988), p. 208.

16. This is the term he uses for Prince Hal, in *Shakespeare's Doctrine of Nature* (London: Faber and Faber, 1949), p. 91.

17. Ronald S. Berman, "Shakespeare's Alexander: Henry V," *CE*, [*College English*] 23 (1962), 532-39, explores the "dark side of Henry's majestic purposefulness" (537).

18. "*Henry V:* The Strain of Rule," in *Shakespeare and the Energies of Drama* (Princeton: Princeton University Press), p. 73.

19. John Arden, *To Present the Pretence* (London: Eyre Methuen, 1977), calls it a "part-justified, part unmotivated moment of horror" (206).

20. *The Weak King Dilemma in the Shakespearean History Play* (Syracuse, N.Y.: Syracuse University Press, 1973), p. 13.

Alison Thorne (essay date 2002)

SOURCE: Thorne, Alison. "'Awake Remembrance of These Valiant Dead': *Henry V* and the Politics of the English History Play." *Shakespeare Studies* 30 (2002): 162-87.

[*In the following essay, Thorne concentrates on the political world of* Henry V, *maintaining that the work demonstrates an ambivalent relationship to the traditional ideological tenets of the English chronicle history play.*]

'A propaganda-play on National Unity: heavily orchestrated for the brass" was how A. P. Rossiter summed up *Henry V* in 1954.[1] The assumption that this play is complicit with the promonarchical, nationalist rhetoric of the Chorus, and with the particular myth of Englishness it propounds, has persisted. In recent years the most cogent articulation of this view has come from Richard Helgerson, who sees the play as the culmination of Shakespeare's gradual tightening of his "obsessive and compelling focus on the ruler" during the writing of his English history cycle, at the cost of occluding the interests of the ruled. In contrast to the historical dramas staged by the rival Henslowe companies, which, he argues, were less concerned with the "consolidation and maintenance of royal power" than with the plight of the socially inferior "victims of such power," Shakespeare's chronicle plays exorcised the common people from their vision of the nation with increasing ruthlessness: It is as though Shakespeare set out to cancel the popular ideology with which his cycle of English history plays began, as though he wanted to efface, alienate, even demonize all signs of commoner participation in the political nation. The less privileged classes may still have had a place in his audience, but they had lost their place in his representation of England.[2]

Helgerson explains this exclusionary process as part of a policy of self-gentrification pursued by Shakespeare and the Lord Chamberlain's Men—a determination to remove themselves as far as possible from the humble, "folk" origins of the theater they served. According to his reading, the banishment of Falstaff at the end of *2 Henry IV,* along with the popular carnivalesque values he stands for, symbolically enacts this desire to be cleansed of the taint of vulgarity associated with the public stage. And in *Henry V* the purgation is completed. Despite the monarch's populist credentials earned in the Eastcheap tavern, the last play in the cycle confirms the "radical divorce . . . between the King and his people," riding roughshod over the "dream of commonality, of common interests and common humanity, between the ruler and the ruled" that had figured so prominently in the popular imagination.[3]

On the face of it, *Henry V* offers ample evidence to validate the proposition that, of all Shakespeare's chronicle plays, this one is "closest to state propaganda," and that such proximity denies the "less privileged classes" a significant place in the nation. One need only cite the near-unanimous commitment to Henry's cause expressed by nobility and commoners alike (in a striking departure from the aristocratic factionalism and popular insurgence that had dominated the preceding plays in the cycle); the curiously muted treatment of those few dissenting voices that do make themselves heard; the play's protective attitude to its royal protagonist, whom it shields from overt inquiry into the legitimacy of his claim to the English as well as the French throne; and, last but not least, the decision to excise Falstaff, whose iconoclastic wit could, on past form, be trusted to play havoc with the nationalistic pieties and chivalric ideals promulgated in *Henry V.* In each of these respects, the play appears to be fully implicated in the Chorus's campaign to "coerc[e] the audience into an emotionally undivided response" in favor of the English monarch.[4] As the play's critical history attests, however, the pressures exerted by its patriotic rhetoric have not precluded more sceptical responses. What might be called the "Machiavellian" reading, first formulated by Hazlitt in 1817, has tended to focus on the gaps between Henry's laboriously constructed public image as "the mirror of all Christian Kings" and his manifest brutality and political opportunism, between the aggrandizing rhetoric of king and Chorus and what is actually shown on stages.[5] Latterly, cultural materialists have argued that, in the act of rehearsing various discourses of national unity, the play unconsciously discloses the faultlines inherent in them.[6]

This essay concurs with such readings in arguing that *Henry V* distances itself from the Chorus's brand of patriotism, but it contends that the play does this not so much by incorporating vocal dissent or through inadvertent self-exposure, as by means of the ironic self-referentiality of its dramatic form.[7] As he reached the end of a period of working intensively within a given genre, Shakespeare habitually turned a searching eye on the structural conventions governing that genre. The last play in his second tetralogy is no exception. From beginning to end, *Henry V* is informed by an acute "metadramatic self-consciousness," which entails a close scrutiny of the discursive modes and conventions associated with the English chronicle play.[8] Through a process of internal mirroring, the ideology of this particular form is opened up to critical inspection in ways that expose both the latent ambiguities and the coerciveness implicit in its discourse of native heroism. The play also invites scrutiny of the rhetorical usage of history ascribed to the genre, by showing how the past is deployed to manipulate audiences (both on- and offstage) into identifying with a political enterprise founded upon a value system and material interests that must, in many cases, have been fundamentally at odds with their own. It is this provocative mixture of reflexivity and self-contradictoriness in the play's modes of address, I argue, which allows scope for a more complex, more divided affective response than that solicited by the Chorus. Indeed it is here that we should perhaps locate the primary source of the play's ideologically ambivalent effects.[9]

As it has become customary to note, the rhetorical energies of King Henry and the Chorus are ultimately directed at producing a collective sense of national identity. The linguistic ploys used in seeking to achieve this will be examined more closely in the second half of this essay. First, though, we need to consider what sorts of problems would have to be imaginatively negotiated when evoking the effects of nationhood on the public stage. It has long been accepted that the outpouring of historiographic texts, including chronicles and plays dealing with English history, in the closing decades of Elizabeth's reign played a crucial part in fostering national selfawareness. The late sixteenth-century vogue for historical drama is said to have "incited patriotic interest in England's past and participated in the process by which the English forged a sense of themselves as a nation"; more specifically, it "provided a 'myth of origin' for the emerging nation," whose people "learned to know who they were by seeing what they had been."[10] In *Henry V* the appeal to history as a means of exciting jingoistic fervor is made unusually explicit. But which version of the nation does the play invite us to endorse? And should we assume the efficacy of its patriotic appeal as given in advance, bearing in mind that the play's success depended on its capacity to engage all sections of the socially heterogeneous audiences that patronized the public playhouses of the period, not merely a privileged minority?[11] For what must be emphasized at the outset is the integral involvement of the lower orders in the "cultural project of imagining an English nation." So far from being ef-

faced, demonized, or even confined to mere tokenism (as Helgerson and others claim), popular participation is shown by Shakespeare's English history cycle to be an essential component in the making of the modern political nation. *Henry V,* in particular, vividly discloses the extent to which the monarchy's imperialistic exercise in nation-building depends upon the active collaboration of the common populace—in the context not only of the dramatic fiction itself but of the theater in which that fiction was staged and consumed.

Twentieth-century political theorists and historians of nationalism are generally agreed that the emergence of the modern nationstate presupposed the existence of a broad popular mandate, though they differ sharply in their dating of this event.[12] Expanding on his influential definition of the nation-state as an "imagined community," Benedict Anderson relates the rise of this sociopolitical formation to the decline of the "divinely-ordained, hierarchical dynastic realm" and its displacement by a horizontal sense of community strong enough to engender feelings of kinship between complete strangers and across existing social divisions. The nation is thus

> imagined as a community, because, regardless of the actual inequality and exploitation that may prevail in each, the nation is always conceived as a deep, horizontal comradeship. Ultimately it is this fraternity that makes it possible . . . for so many millions of people, not so much to kill, as willingly to die for such limited imaginings.[13]

Others have echoed Anderson's insistence that the mere fact of social stratification need be no hinderance to conceiving of the nation as a community of free and essentially equal individuals with the right, in principle at least, to participate in political decision-making. Arguing specifically for the sixteenth-century origins of English nationhood and nationalism in general, Liah Greenfeld finds that this grew out of an alliance of interests between the monarchy and the common people—the very alliance that, in the civil upheavals of the next century, it would help to destroy. As "an important symbol of England's distinctiveness and sovereignty," the crown provided an initial focus for nationalist sentiment; conversely, the Tudor monarchs, who "were time and again placed in a position of dependence on the good will of their subjects," found it expedient to support this burgeoning national consciousness.[14] Claire MacEachern similarly holds that the Tudor system of monarchical government was not incommensurable with a genuine belief in a "corporate political identity." Existing as an affective utopian structure, this belief, she suggests, was rooted in a sense of intimacy or fellow-feeling between the populace and the personified institutions of the state, concentrated in the person of the monarch himself.[15]

Yet we scarcely need press the point that nations are never as integrated in reality as our myths of national identity would have us believe. The meaning of the nation is continually being contested by different social and ethnic groupings in ways that are liable to expose the fractures within its ideal unity. As Anthony D. Smith remarks, "deep within what appears to the outside as a unifying myth, are hidden many tensions and contradictions, which parallel and illuminate the social contradictions within most communities." Moreover, although as a general rule national loyalties, once established, tend to override local allegiances and sectional interests, this is not always the case.[16] In *Henry V* the contradictions embedded in the myth of corporate identity are registered primarily through the fluctuating boundaries (both geographic and demographic) of the nation, which are constantly being redrawn. As recent investigations of the play's colonial context have reminded us, the question of whether England's Celtic neighbors should be excluded from, or absorbed within, the "pale" of an expanded English or proto-British polity was never wholly resolved under successive Tudor and Stuart administrations.[17] Hence the Irish and the Scots are sometimes stigmatized in this play as inveterate enemies of the English state to be kept at a distance (1.2.166-73; 5.0.30-34). At other times—notably in the scene (3.3) bringing together the four captains from each of the constituent countries of the British isles—they are figured as loyal servants of the Lancastrian crown. A similar prevarication can be traced in the play, as I shall try to show, over the entitlement of the common people (and of other subordinate groups, including women) to be counted as members of the nation's imagined community. How far the king and Chorus choose to recognise the people's contribution in bringing that community into being varies sharply according to the political exigencies of the moment. The likelihood of the tussle between class-based and broader national identities enacted in *Henry V* being replicated in the experience of the play's first audiences is also considered in the conclusion to this essay. Owing to its ideological multivalency and the social inclusiveness of its clientele, the popular theater of the Elizabethan and early Jacobean era has been widely regarded as an authentically national institution, one of the key sites where a sense of collective identity was forged.[18] Yet insofar as they represented a "heterocosm" of the nation, the public playhouses were also bound to reflect its underlying social divisions, and such deep-seated differences among those present at performances (whether as players or spectators) may well have proved easier to activate than appease.

Shakespeare's second tetralogy charts a shift in political episteme remarkably like that described by Anderson. That is, it stages a process of transition from the feudal, hierarchically organised realm of Richard II, putatively authorized by the principle of divine right, to a recognizably more modern prototype of the nation-state under Bolingbroke and his heir, which, though still centred on the monarchy, acknowledges the need for popular legitimation. Like his father, Henry V is acutely mindful of the necessity of compensating for the loss of sanctified authority, consequent upon the usurpation and murder of the annointed king, by winning popular approval. His adroit manipulation of the royal image to make it "show more goodly and attract more eyes" (*1 Henry IV*, 1.2.214) is wholly directed to that end. Contrary to Helgerson's suggestion, the demotic touch Henry learns in the tavern is not discarded on entering political adulthood; rather, as Joel Altman remarks, such "vile participation" is consistently the "distinguishing feature of Harry's princely career as Shakespeare represents it."[19] No mere short-term "fix" imposed on him by a perilous situation, the rhetoric of crossclass fraternity he invokes on the battlefield of Agincourt is central to his fashioning of the nation's self-image. Hence he figures his army (in whom that nation is synecdochically represented) as "warriors for the working day" (4.3.110), who draw their strength from their broad social origins in contrast to the aristocratic hauteur and effeteness of the French. But even among those who fully appreciate the political capital to be made from such "vile participation," the social interdependency it implies may well inspire ambivalent feelings as a potential source of shame and inevitable dilution of royal sovereignty. Equally, the appearance of new forms of national consciousness did not signal the instantaneous demise of the dynastic realm, whose modes of thought and social organization retained a hold on men's minds long after they had lost their absolute political hegemony. Henry's oratory testifies to the ideological fluidity that characterized ideas of the commonwealth at the turn of the sixteenth century. In his speeches, the embryonic discourse of national solidarity collides repeatedly with older self-definitions based on aristocratic codes of behavior, the desire to "pluck allegiance from men's hearts" with the desire to withdraw his royalty from the defiling contacts this entails. And similar tensions, as we shall find, shape the Chorus's dealings with the theater audience.

The compromises demanded by this redefining and opening up of the monarchically governed state to allow for greater popular participation are inscribed in the two best-known contemporary accounts of the English chronicle play. In Thomas Nashe's *Pierce Penniless* (1592) and Thomas Heywood's *Apology for Actors* (printed in 1612, but probably also written during the 1590s), a shared ideological agenda is sketched out for this dramatic genre. For both these writers, the chief function of the history play was to resurrect "our forefathers valiant actes" by reenacting their "memorable exploits" with such "lively and well-spirited action" that the spectator would be induced to emulate their example.[20] One reason for emphasising the exemplary nature of historical drama, we may surmise, was to sustain a sense of continuity between the present and England's glorious past in ways that appealed to, and helped to bolster, the nation's growing self-confidence.[21] Yet in his legendary account of the origins of the genre, Heywood dwells on the exclusively "noble," even quasi-divine, derivation of this historical tradition:

> In the first of the Olimpiads, amongst many other active exercises in which Hercules ever triumph'd as victor, there was in his nonage presented unto him by his Tutor in the fashion of a History, acted by the choyse of the nobility of Greece, the worthy and memorable acts of his father Jupiter. Which being personated with lively and well-spirited action, wrought such impression in his noble thoughts that in meere emulation of his fathers valor . . . he perform'd his twelve labours: Him valiant Theseus followed, and Achilles, Theseus. Which bred in them such hawty and magnanimous attempts, that every succeeding age hath recorded their worths, unto fresh admiration.[22]

And so it goes on: a dramatic reconstruction of Achilles' part in the fall of Troy made so great an impression on Alexander the Great that "all his succeeding actions were meerly shaped after that patterne," just as Julius Caesar's actions were patterned on those of Alexander. Heywood imagines the principle of dramatic imitation engendering its own eminent genealogy of valor, as each performance begets a new generation of royal heroes, from Hercules down to the present: "Why should not the lives of these worthyes, presented in these our dayes," he inquires, "effect the like wonders in the Princes of our times . . . ?"

When he turns to "our domesticke hystories," however, Heywood is forced to modify this discourse of aristocratic heroism in order to accommodate the socially mixed clientele of the public playhouses. That the Elizabethan history play was targeted primarily at the ordinary citizens in its audience is strongly implied by Heywood's citing, among his justifications for the theater, that it "hath taught the unlearned the knowledge of many famous histories, [and] instructed such as cannot read in the discovery of all our English Chronicles."[23] It is presumably this plebeian presence that dictates the insinuation of a calculated imprecision, a politic ambiguity, into Heywood's language: "To turne to our domesticke hystories, what English blood seeing the person of any bold English man presented and doth not hugge his fame, and hunnye at his valor. . . . What coward to see his contryman valiant would not bee shamed of his owne cowardise?" By refusing to locate the grammatical subject in terms of the social categories insisted upon earlier in the Apology, Heywood manages to create the impression that any Englishman, whatever his class origins, is capable of being "inflam'd" by the spectacle of native valor, and so "may be made apt and fit for the like atchievement."[24] Nationality, coming of

"English blood," has replaced narrower status definitions as the criterion for participating in this heroic tradition. Comparable efforts to broaden the appeal of the English chronicle play, to render its elitest discourse more flexibly inclusive, are made on Nashe's side. In return for the patriotic sentiments it would elicit, he hints, this type of historical drama offers its audiences a stake in the "right of fame that is due to true nobilitie deceased." Hence the chief bait it "propose[s] to adventurous minds, to encourage them forward" is the prospect of sharing, at some unspecified level, in the "immortalitie" normally bestowed by the chronicle play on such dead English heroes as "brave Talbot," Edward III, or Henry V.[25] Underlying both texts is a suggestion that the malleable spectator, who allows images of the past to act upon him in this way and "fashion [him] to the shape of any noble or notable attempt," will be rewarded by being joined with the valiant dead in what Nashe calls "one Gallimafry of glory" that transcends class differences.

If the heroic vision of Englishness projected by the chronicle play is seen here as dependent for its very force and validation on the involvement of the common spectators, what precisely was expected of them? It is clear from Nashe and Heywood's vivid descriptions of the reception given to such plays that the contribution sought was primarily of an imaginative kind. Both writers ascribe a "bewitching" power to the genre that derives, firstly, from its ability to impart a living presence to the dead (who are "raysed from the Grave of Oblivion, and brought to pleade their aged Honours in open presence") and, secondly, from the power of dramatic impersonation to make audiences experience in themselves the full immediacy of the emotions enacted on stage (known in rhetoric as ethopeia). Indeed, it is the unmatchable reality effects made possible by the theatrical medium, according to Nashe, that renders the history play a far more effective instrument for inculcating patriotic values than "worme-eaten bookes" of chronicles. At one point he asks:

> How would it have joyd brave Talbot (the terror of the French) to thinke that after he had lyne two hundred yeare in his toomb, he should triumph againe on the Stage, and have his bones new embalmed with the teares of ten thousand spectators at least . . . who in the Tragedian that represents his person, imagine they behold him fresh bleeding.[26]

This illusion of presence, combined with the powerful affects it stirs in the spectators, solicits an imaginative identification with what is witnessed on stage so complete that the distinction between dramatic fiction and historical reality, between the actor and the part he plays, is temporarily erased.[27] In much the same vein, Heywood asserts that audiences, "seeing the person of any bold English man presented," will be irresistibly impelled to "hugge his fame, and hunnye at his valor, pursuing him in his enterprise with [their] best wishes . . . as if the Personator were the man Personated."[28] In the context of the popular commercial theater, then, it would appear that the mimetic desires aroused by a dramatic reenactment of the past are no longer regarded chiefly as a means of calling forth heroic deeds. Instead their function is to secure the spectator's acquiescence in, and identification with, the nationalist ideologies staged by the play.

Benedict Anderson repeatedly poses the question of why the imagined community of the nation should command such deep emotional attachments that even its most oppressed or disenfranchised members are prepared to sacrifice their lives for this idea. For an explanation of how such identifications are produced, however, we may find it more useful to turn to Louis Althusser's now-classic account of interpellation: that is, the procedures whereby ideology addresses the individual subject in a manner that ensures his or her cooperation with the existing sociopolitical formation.[29] Echoing Jacques Lacan's emphasis on the importance of the "mirror phase" in the psychic construction of identity, Althusser argues that interpellation always takes a specular form. Individuals are invited to recognize themselves in the image of authority in whose name a given ideology exists, and to identify with the roles, or subject positions, designated for them within that ideology. Crucially, interpellative techniques operate through rhetorical manipulation, not force. By persuading us to accede to the fictive representation of actual social relationships it reflects back at us, ideology masks our subjection to the dominant order and ensures that we will freely give of our own labor—or, as Althusser puts it, that we work by ourselves. Theatrical experience, because of the ways it is structured, is peculiarly well adapted to producing such specular effects. In its exemplarity the chronicle play capitalizes on that potential by urging spectators to discover their own image in—and transform themselves into—the heroic models it sets before them. Its success in fostering such identifications may partly explain why Nashe and Heywood chose to focus on this particular dramatic genre when defending the theatre against the endlessly reiterated charge that it promoted sedition and civil unrest.[30] The use of historical exemplars as an incitement to patriotic behavior, they believe, offers the strongest proof that "stage-plaies" are, in fact, a "rare exercise of venue," instrumental in deflecting rebellious impulses and fashioning compliant subjects who willingly defer to the rule of constituted authority.

Henry V, I would argue, stands in a profoundly ambivalent relationship to these sixteenth-century definitions of the English chronicle play and its politico-moral functions. On the one hand, it cannot be denied that Shakespeare's play exploits the strong affective charge generated by identification with dead English heroes—as the regularity with which it has been either performed or invoked at times of national crisis confirms.[31] Yet it does so in ways that seem to discourage, rather than invite, an uncritical acceptance of the imaginary versions of the nation articulated within the play. This paradoxical effect, I suggest, is achieved largely by self-reflexive means. In particular, the play insistently foregrounds the interpellative techniques used with fearsome efficiency by various characters, laying open its own ideological stratagems in the process. Thus Henry is shown addressing his common soldiers as "so many Alexanders" in the making as he endeavors to mould them into a redoubtable fighting force in 2.1 and 4.3, while the Chorus's appeals to the theater audience position them as the king's loyal camp followers who embrace his trials and tribulations as their own (cf. 3.0.17-24). Concomitantly, the normally dissembled purposes for which such techniques are deployed are also made visible. Summoning up the idea of a harmoniously integrated commonwealth in 1.2, the Archbishop of Canterbury reflects knowingly on its effectiveness in "setting endeavour in continual motion; / To which is fixed, as an aim or butt, / Obedience" (lines 186-88). A similar observation is made by Henry as, preparing to set himself up as an inspirational model to his troops, he extols the power of "example" to "quicken" the mind and cause the bodily organs to "move with casted slough and fresh legerity" (4.1.1823).[32] Whether the king is demanding extraordinary physical efforts from his soldiers, or the Chorus is urging the audience to "work, work [their] thoughts," their characteristic modes of address are quite blatantly directed at getting others (mostly representatives of the lower orders) to labor on behalf of the king's cause.

Superficially, *Henry V* also appears to reaffirm the populist agenda ascribed to the English chronicle play to the extent that both Henry and the Chorus strive to invoke a socially inclusive model of history. Replicating Nashe and Heywood's tactics, they manage this by putting a more egalitarian "spin" on the patrician ideals of martial heroism associated with the genre. But even as the play celebrates the king's ability to enlist every stratum of society in his imperialist enterprise, uniting them in "one purpose" through a charismatic appeal to "mean and gentle all" (cf. 4.0.2847), it discloses the anxieties, strains, and contradictions attendant on this project. All Henry's rhetorical dexterity cannot smooth away the class tensions inherent in the goal of national unification that, ironically, are thrown into greater prominence by his attempts to reconfigure aristocratic idioms for popular consumption. Cumulatively, these reflexive devices seem designed to provoke us into questioning the fundamental, if tacit, claim underpinning contemporary defences of the genre: that the common subject can participate on an equal footing in the creation of a national community that continues to be defined in the interests of a ruling elite.

Within the play, the coercive use of historical exempla as a means of "setting endeavour in continual motion" is reflected on three different levels: in the analogous modes of address employed by the king's counselors towards him, by the king to his troops, and by the Chorus to the audience. The Archbishop of Canterbury sets the tone in 1.2 with his convoluted exposition of the Salic law, which shamelessly manipulates historical precedent in the hope of inciting Henry to pursue his hereditary claim to the French throne and so divert him from implementing a bill that would strip the Church of the "better half of [its] possession." With the same end in view, the archbishop proceeds to invoke the "tragedy" enacted on French soil by Henry's "mighty ancestors" at the battle of Crecy nearly seventy years before:

> Look back into your mighty ancestors.
> Go, my dread lord, to your great grand-sire's tomb,
> From whom you claim; invoke his warlike spirit,
> And your great-uncle's, Edward the Black Prince,
> Who on the French ground played a tragedy,
> Making defeat on the full power of France,
> Whiles his most mighty father on a hill
> Stood smiling to behold his lion's whelp
> Forage in blood of French nobility.
>
> (1.2.100)

Other counselors take up this exhortation to emulate past greatness, urging the king to "awake remembrance of those valiant dead, / And with [his] puissant arm renew their feats" (1.2.115).

Conscious of the obligations this heroic lineage imposes, Henry accepts their challenge, and the terms of his acceptance reveal what is personally at stake for him:

> Or there we'll sit,
> Ruling in large and ample empery
> O'er France and all her almost kingly dukedoms,
> Or lay these bones in an unworthy urn,
> Tombless, with no rememberance over them.
> Either our history shall with full mouth
> Speak freely of our acts, or else our grave
> Like Turkish mute, shall have a tongueless mouth,
> Not worshipped with a waxen epitaph.
>
> (1.2.225)

The dialectical structure of this speech implicitly equates military victory with fame; for Henry occupying France is, first and foremost, a route to securing his place in history. By reenacting the drama of imperial conquest performed by his ancestors in this land, he will ensure that his exploits too are preserved from oblivion in their turn, and that "history" will "speak freely of [his] acts" to future generations.[33] Without such forms of official "remembrance," Henry admits, he would be reduced to the impotent condition of a "Turkish mute," lacking any influence in shaping the national destiny.

In staging the council scene as a contest in deliberative oratory, Shakespeare takes his cue from Holinshed, who narrates the "earnest and pithie persuasions" employed by Henry's advisors to "induce" him to adopt the course of action they prescribe.[34] But Shakespeare infuses this rhetorical occasion with an ironic self-consciousness largely absent from his source, and thereby makes provision for a more skeptical appraisal of the practice of resorting to an exemplary past. The archbishop's figuration of the Black Prince's victory at Crecy in 1346 in terms of a dramatic mise-en-scene (cf. 2.4.53-62) pointedly calls attention to the role of the theater as a site where such national traditions are not simply commemorated but actively manufactured. Phyllis Rackin has argued that such metadramatic allusions can produce "a kind of alienation effect," pushing the audience into adopting a critically detached position relative to the action, especially when combined (as they are here) with anachronism.[35] For it should not be forgotten that the idealized chivalric past evoked by the name of Crecy existed at a double historical remove from the audiences who first saw *Henry V* in 1599. As we noted earlier, the ethos of the English chronicle play was epitomized for Nashe by the figure of "brave Talbot," whose death wrung tears from "ten thousand spectators at least." Nashe's remark has been taken as an allusion to Shakespeare's *1 Henry VI* (which is usually, though not conclusively, dated to 1590-91), where the discourse of ancestral valor, kept alive by funerary monuments to the "valiant dead" and by the aristocracy's self-sacrificing feats of bravery, is firmly centred on Talbot and his son. But even in the earlier play the values upheld almost singlehandedly by the Talbots are represented as a throwback to a vanishing chivalric world (associated ironically with the memory of Henry V's French conquests), whose passing leaves them vulnerable to the machinations of a more secular, pragmatic age. And by the time *Henry V* was staged roughly a decade later, this discourse had become still more conspicuously outmoded, more jarringly at odds with the context of *realpolitik* in which it is invoked.[36] In such circumstances, it would have been hard for an audience not to register the competing political interests that motivate the characters' appeals to "bygone valour," or to overlook the way that past is being manipulated as a means of mobilizing and channeling activity in the present.[37]

In the following acts Henry redirects the rhetorical strategies used so effectively on him at the plebeian subject, with the aim of eliciting superhuman exertions from his troops. For that purpose he seeks to assimilate the rank-and-file to the loftily aristocratic vision of English heroism conjured up in 1.2 by giving this a more demotic inflection. His celebrated oration before the walls of Harfleur, which first holds out the possibility of an egalitarian partnership that suspends class differences, is deeply and ineluctably ambiguous. Henry prefaces the speech with an oblique acknowledgment that wartime situations such as this license the violation of normal social decorums, according to which "there's nothing so becomes a man [especially, it is implied, the low-born man] / As modest stillness and humility" (3.1.3). The self-transformative action Henry calls for in exhorting his soldiers to "bend up every spirit / To his full height" (line 16) is nevertheless accompanied (as Michael Goldman has shown) by a terrible sense of strain, as though betraying his belief in the grotesque unnaturalness of aspiring to transcend one's allotted place in the social hierarchy.[38] The troops are then urged to authenticate their mythologized ancestry by fighting bravely:

> On, on you noblest English,
> Whose blood is fet from fathers of war-proof,
> Fathers that like so many Alexanders
> Have in these parts from morn till even fought,
> And sheathed their swords for lack of argument.
> Dishonour not your mothers; now attest
> That those whom you called fathers did beget you.
> Be copy now to men of grosser blood,
> And teach them how to war. And you good yeomen,
> Whose limbs were made in England, show us here
> The mettle of your pasture; let us swear
> That you are worth your breeding—which I doubt not,
> For there is none of you so mean and base
> That hath not noble lustre in your eyes.
>
> (3.1.17)

Essentially Henry faces the same problem here as Heywood did in the Apology: he has to find a way of negotiating the uncomfortable gap between an elitest tradition of martial valor and its popular reenactments. Not surprisingly, he too hits upon the solution of subsuming social demarcations in an ambiguously inclusive discourse of nationhood. Henry's speech is addressed first to "you noblest English," the nobility whose duty is to "by copy [i.e., an example] to men of grosser blood / And teach them how to war," before turning to the "good yeomen," who are admonished to model their behavior on that of their military leaders. But these sharply differentiated designations are offset by his skillful playing upon the indeterminacy of words such as "noble," "base," and "mean," which, though they originated as status terms, were increasingly used in this period to denote relative moral worth. A similar slippage occurs in his references to "blood" and "breeding"; initially defined in a hereditary context as coming of noble parentage or blood, having the required breeding is later broadened to include anyone born and raised on English soil. Through such rhetorical sleights-of-hand, Henry contrives to suggest that all Englishmen, irrespective of class origins, are eligible to participate in his exalted "fellowship," provided their actions prove them worthy of it.

The incipient contradictions in Henry's interpellation of the soldiers make his vision of a socially inclusive partnership highly vulnerable to contestation.[39] And in 4.1 the implication (reinforced by the Chorus at the beginning of the act) that "mean and gentle all" can become equal participants in this imagined community is duly challenged. As has often been observed, Henry's disguised encounter with three of his common foot soldiers, in which he tries unsuccessfully to convince them that "the King is but a man" of their sort, serves only to expose the "complete lack of rapport," the ineradicable differences of perspective, separating him from them.[40] In disputing Henry's claims to ordinariness, Soldier Williams and his companions drive a wedge into the self-serving myth that the monarch and his common subjects are bound together not so much by political expediency as by their shared humanity and commonality of interests. The humiliation inflicted on the king in this debate provokes a backlash in his ensuing soliloquy. Where once he courted the approval and loyal cooperation of his subjects, he now laments the "hard condition" that subjects his own "greatness" to "the breath / Of every fool, whose sense no more can feel / But his own wringing" (4.1.221-3). His rhetorical energies also undergo a radical reorientation, as he seeks to reestablish his distance from the multitude; no longer addressed as "brothers, friends, countrymen," the common soldiers are now reclassified in terms of aristocratic contempt as "lackey[s]," "wretched slave[s]," and ignorant "peasants" (lines 255-72). But with his army teetering on the brink of a catastrophic defeat, Henry is again compelled by circumstances to seek assistance from those whose social consequence he dismissed a short while before.

Accordingly, his prebattle address to the troops resorts once more to the rhetoric of brotherhood. Previous hints that the ordinary conscript, "be he ne'er so vile," will "gentle his condition" by his valiant deeds and earn the right to partake of the fame normally reserved for patrician warriors, are restated more baldly in an attempt to bribe him into action. With this we see a return to the same fudging tactics, the same ambiguities and inconsistencies, that allow Henry to construct the image of an egalitarian national community, but that simultaneously threaten to unravel that fantasy. His reiterative use of the first-person plural hovers between the royal and the collective "we," between the exclusive and inclusive senses of that pronoun. (Cf. "If we are marked to die, we are enough / To do our country loss" [4.3.20]; or "We would not die in that man's company / That fears his fellowship to die with us" [line 38]). Yet, in one sense, there is no contradiction here, since the community envisaged turns out to be little more than an expansion of the regal persona. For as Henry's rallying cry—"the fewer men, the greater share of honour"— should remind us, the fame promised the soldiers is predicated on a feudal cult of honour and ancestral pride that is, by definition, jealously individualistic. The nearest approximation to genuine fellowship this aristocratic code of honor admits is the blut-bruderschaft of Suffolk and York, whose deaths in battle are invested, in Exeter's elegiac narrative (4.6.627), with the full panoply of chivalric values once bestowed on Talbot or Hotspur. To attempt to found a modern nation-state on such an inherently elitest and anachronistic code is self-evidently untenable. That Henry winds up the speech by drawing the parameters of his imagined brotherhood in relation not to the foreign enemy but to the significant proportion of his subjects it excludes among whom are numbered not only "grandsires, babies, and old women" (3.0.20) but all "those men in England that do no work today" (4.3.64-67)—merely underscores the problem.

The second half of the speech leaps forward to a hypothetical future perfect where the "Feast of Crispian" has become a day of national commemoration honoring the English triumph at Agincourt. Henry's ingenious manipulation of his audience's temporal perspective fulfils various purposes. On one level, it mimics the peculiar motivational logic of the chronicle play; treating a yet-to-be-accomplished victory as something long since achieved and sanctified by memory enables the soldiers to be inspired by their own historical example and, by spurring them into action, ensures that the day will indeed be won. But it also offers assurance that the fraternal cross-class community forged on the battlefield will be maintained into futurity through the observance of collective forms of remembrance. Imaginatively projecting this annual event as a popular domestic scene, combining the functions of an aural history lesson with a convivial feasting of the neighborhood, is another brilliant touch, in that it presents an image, at once homely and heroic, with which the common soldier can hardly fail to identify. Yet this carefully crafted vision of shared national rituals cannot entirely dispel the social tensions latent within it. In a recent essay highlighting the importance of memory in the play, Jonathan Baldo notes that, although the Elizabethan establishment was no less intent on orchestrating the collective memory in the pursuit of national unity than Shakespeare's *Henry V,* the act of remembering continued to be a potential site of division and resistance.[41] The same holds true here:

> Old men forget; yet all shall be forgot,
> But he'll remember, with advantages,
> The feats he did that day. Then shall our names,
> Familiar in his mouth as household words
> Harry the King, Bedford and Exeter,
> Warwick and Talbot, Salisbury and Gloucester
> Be in their flowing cups freshly remembered.
> This story shall the good man teach his son,
> And Crispin Crispian shall ne'er go by
> From this day to the ending of the world
> But we in it shall be remembered,
> We few, we happy few, we band of brothers.
>
> (4.3.49-60)

At the same time that the personal recollections of the Agincourt veterans are granted a central role in perpetuating the fame of that legendary victory, it is archly insinuated that their memories will play them false, leading them not only to embellish "feats [they] did that day," but (by extension) to exaggerate the degree of intimacy they once enjoyed with the "great commanders," whose names are "familiar in [their] mouths as household words."[42] This nostalgic fantasy of brotherhood will be belied even as they speak by the fact that the names immortalised through their reminiscences are confined to the aristocratic titles of their leaders. (Again, the fluctuating use of the first-person plural at once encodes and masks this shift: "our names" are syntactically opposed to "their flowing cups" in lines 51-55, the pronoun only recovering its inclusive meaning at line 60.) While Henry thus concedes the need for popular involvement in establishing such national traditions, he cynically anticipates that the ordinary veterans will be denied the honorable place promised them in the official (and unofficial) historical records. This is confirmed after the battle when, reading from the roll call of the English dead, he lists several casualties among the ranks of the nobility and gentry, concluding "none else of name, / And of all other men, / But five-and-twenty" (4.8.103). Significantly, these lines closely paraphrase Holinshed, who rarely bothers to identify individual foot soldiers by name in his chronicling of Henry's French campaigns.[43]

Both Henry's methods of galvanizing his troops into action and the ambiguities inscribed in those methods are paralleled in the Chorus's repeated exhortation of the play's audience. From the outset, the Chorus helps to construct a reflexive, metacritical framework for the dramatic action by foregrounding the difficulties posed by historical representation and the theatrical medium through which the past must be brought back to life. Initially, like Heywood, he fantasizes about an exclusively royal performance, "a kingdom for a stage, princes to act, / And monarchs to behold the swelling scene" (1.0.13), before ruefully conceding that this ideal is unrealizable on the public stage where common players masquerade as kings. Conversely, he displays none of Heywood or Nashe's confidence in the theater's ability to produce a compelling recreation of ancient prowess by means of powerful reality effects. On the contrary, he assumes that this can only be achieved if the playhouse's inadequate technical resources are supplemented by the spectators' cerebral activity. It is their "thoughts," he urges them, that "now must deck our kings," their laboring imaginations that must give impetus to Henry's campaign. The Chorus's apparent readiness to defer to the "imaginary puissance" of the humbler sections of the audience—as implied by the artisanal metaphor of "the quick forge and working-house of thought" (5.0.23)—making them co-partners in his theatrical enterprise, has led some critics to find an expression therein of the communal ethos of the Elizabethan theater.[44] But while his entreaties to the audience to "eke out our imperfections with your mind" certainly confirm (once again) the indispensability of popular participation, they also reveal this recognition of dependency to be fraught with tension and anxiety. Often accepted at face value as a token of (quasi-authorial) modesty, the Chorus's apologetic references to the "imperfections" of the stage can more plausibly be seen, I suggest, as rehearsing a familiar set of anxieties regarding the subversive potential of the popular commercial theater. As Stephen Orgel (among others) has argued, a recurrent concern of the theater's opponents in this period was that the "great image of Authority" would be undermined and debased by being staged to the common view, a fear that greatness might be demystified in the very act of dramatizing it.[45] It is surely an echo of this social pathology that resonates in the Chorus's claim that "so great an object" as Henry's famous victory cannot be "cramm'd" within the walls of this "wooden O" without travestying its true magnitude (1.0.8-18), or in the apology he tenders in the epilogue for the playwright's "rough and all-unable pen," which has allegedly defaced the reputation of "mighty men," "mangling by starts the full course of their glory." For all his eagerness to recruit the spectator's "imaginary forces" to the service of the royal cause, the Chorus (like the king of whose image he makes himself custodian) betrays considerable nervousness at the thought of allowing a tradition of aristocratic heroism to be adulterated by being performed and intimately witnessed by low-born subjects—in this case, on the "unworthy scaffold" of the Curtain or the newly opened Globe.

Henry's pledge that his soldiers will be ennobled (in the moral if not social sense) by their participation is also echoed in the Chorus's practice of addressing the spectators as "gentles all" (1.0.8, cf. 2.0.35), who are entreated "gently to hear, kindly to judge our play" (1.0.34). The prospect of gentling their condition is itself conditional upon their willingness to collaborate in the construction of the play's heroic vision of Englishness, and is obviously intended to bind them into that vision. But it is, of course, an inescapable fact that a large proportion of the play's original audiences would have been drawn from the "base, common and popular" classes.[46] Exposing the actions of the monarchy to the gaze and judgment of the common multitude congregated around the platform stage was a risky and unpredictable affair—indeed the very fervency of the Chorus's appeals may perhaps indicate that they are designed to head off unsympathetic responses from that quarter. Given their predominantly modest social origins, however, we may reasonably infer that some spectators at least would have been more inclined to follow Soldier Williams's example in resisting the invitation to identify with the royal viewpoint. (It is

Williams, after all, who brings home to the king that there are limits to the power of interpellation, that he may command the "beggar's knee," but not necessarily his innermost thoughts [4.1.228-45]). Women, too, formed an important constituency within the theatergoing public of the day, and they are even more emphatically excluded by the chivalric, masculine terms in which Henry's confraternity is defined (cf. 3.0.17-24).[47] Should we assume that the manifold ironies in the exhortations of king and Chorus would have escaped the attention of these playgoers? The less privileged members of the play's audience may well have balked at being asked to overcome through their imaginative exertions deficiencies that are seen as arising directly from their own lowly status and that of the theater they patronised. Female as well as plebeian spectators may equally have resented attempts to coerce them into identifying with an imagined community that, overtly or not, defines itself in opposition to them.

This essay has argued for the need to reappraise Helgerson's generalizing and oversimplified account of the attitude to the common populace expressed by Shakespeare's English history plays. A careful analysis of the rhetoric of class in *Henry V* reveals that those beneath the rank of gentleman are not, as alleged, progressively erased from the play's ideological construction of the nation, but neither are they fully embraced as equal partners in its formation. Instead, a more complicated picture of class relations emerges in which the leveling dynamic inscribed in the newly formed discourse of nationalism interacts with an older status-defined politics of exclusion in complex and unpredictable ways. Similarly, there has been a critical tendency to homogenize the reception that its original audiences gave to Shakespeare's history cycle. Dissenting from the widely accepted premise that the response elicited by these plays was straightforwardly patriotic and must have functioned to solidify the spectators' sense of belonging to a larger national community, I have suggested that in all likelihood audience reactions varied markedly, depending on a number of factors. In the case of *Henry V* it seems probable that differences in social allegiance would have inflected the way each spectator related imaginatively to the ambiguous position assigned to the lower orders in the play's representation of the nation as a heroic fellowship incorporating both "mean and gentle."

Yet while there is every reason to suppose that the political significance of *Henry V* would have been contingent, in part, on the particular social make-up of its audiences along with other extratextual circumstances affecting its production and reception, we should not therefore deny Shakespeare's text a decisive role in determining its meaning and ideological effect. In the last analysis, as I have tried to show, it is the rhetorical mechanisms of that text which, by acting upon the emotional proclivities and class loyalties of individual spectators, create the conditions for a more complex and diverse response than the characters' patriotic effusions might seem to call for. For if, on the one hand, the play's modes of address, together with its rhetorical invocation of history, are framed to elicit an unquestioning commitment to the values inculcated by king and Chorus, on the other, its generic self-consciousness, by working to expose the coercive and contradictory aspects of such strategies, enables resistance to the process of interpellation. In adopting this paradoxical stance, *Henry V* makes available to the spectator (or reader) a range of possible subject positions. Like the disaffected conscripts of 4.1 who, despite being suspicious of Henry's fraternal rhetoric, resolve to "fight lustily" for him, we may thus move between—or even experience at one and the same moment—a critical distantiation from, and emotional identification with, the royal myth of Englishness.

Notes

1. A. P. Rossiter, "Ambivalence: The Dialectic of the Histories," rpt. in *Angel with Horns,* ed. Graham Storey (London and New York: 1961), 57.

2. Richard Helgerson, *Forms of Nationhood: The Elizabethan Writing of England* (Chicago and London: University of Chicago Press, 1994), 214.

3. Helgerson, *Forms of Nationhood,* 232.

4. Andrew Gurr ed., *Henry V,* New Cambridge ed. (Cambridge: Cambridge University Press, 1992), 7.

5. See William Hazlitt, *Characters of Shakespear's Plays,* ed. Ernest Rhys (London, 1906), 156-64. For a more recent Machiavellian reading, see H. C. Goddard, *The Meaning of Shakespeare* (Chicago: University of Chicago Press, 1951), 215-68.

6. See, e.g., Alan Sinfield and Jonathan Dollimore, "History and Ideology, Masculinity and Miscegenation: The Instance of *Henry V*," in Alan Sinfield, *Faultlines: Cultural Materialism and the Politics of Dissident Reading* (Oxford: Oxford University Press), 109-42.

7. All references to the play cited in this text are taken from the Oxford edition (1982), ed. Gary Taylor. The majority of the reflexive features identified below are present only in the Folio version, including all the Chorus's speeches, crucial parts of the council scene (1.2.115-35), 3.1, and the king's soliloquy (4.1.218-72). Critical opinion generally concurs with the view that the omission of these and other passages in the 1600 Quarto, whether theatrically or politically motivated, "simplif[ies] the play in order to make it more un-

complicatedly patriotic" (Oxford edition, 23; cf. Annabel Patterson, *Shakespeare and the Popular Voice* [Oxford: Oxford University Press, 1989)], 76-77).

8. The phrase is borrowed from Phyllis Rackin, *Stages of History: Shakespeare's English Chronicles* (Ithaca and London: Cornell University Press, 1990), 71. Previous critics have seen the dramatic self-reflexivity of *Henry V* as a vehicle for exploring the hazards of imposing dramatic unity on the chaos of history (James L. Calderwood, *Metadrama in Shakespeare's Henriad: "Richard II" to "Henry V"* [Berkeley: University of California Press, 1979], chap. 7), or for highlighting the performative basis of royal power (Rackin, Stages of History, 76-85).

9. Norman Rabkin's classic study of this ambivalence of effect invokes the model of a gestalt drawing, which can be seen either as a rabbit or a duck but never both at once, to argue that the play lends itself equally to being construed as a celebration of ideal kingship or a disillusioned study of Machiavellian imperialism ("Either/Or: Responding to *Henry V*," in *Shakespeare and the Problem of Meaning* (Chicago: University of Chicago Press, 1981). Where I part company with Rabkin is (firstly) in positing the play's rhetorical mechanisms and generic self-consciousness as the main source of this ambivalence, rather than characterization, plot, or dramatic sequencing, and (secondly) in arguing for the possibility of experiencing simultaneously conflicting responses to Henry's nationalist project.

10. See Jean Howard and Phyllis Rackin, *Engendering a Nation: A Feminist Account of Shakespeare's English Histories* (London and New York: Routledge, 1997), 18, and Philip Edwards, *Threshold of a Nation: A Study in English and Irish Drama* (Cambridge: Cambridge University Press, 1979), 68. For much of the twentieth century the rise of the English history play was directly attributed to the tide of patriotism and "exuberant national sentiment" that swept England in the wake of the defeat of the Spanish Armada in 1588. (On the history of this critical commonplace, see Lily B. Campbell, *Shakespeare's "Histories": Mirrors of Elizabethan Policy* (San Marino, CA: Huntington Library Press, 1947), chap. 2). Although recent writing on Shakespeare's history plays has tended to reject the more triumphalist and politically naive aspects of this theory, a causal connection between the emergence of the genre and a growing sense of nationhood is still widely postulated.

11. As Larry Champion observes of this patriotic reading, "the essential difficulty with such an approach is that it assumes both an audience basically

sympathetic to the monarchy and a universal perspective in plays that, in fact, are designed to appeal to, and engage the emotional interests of, as many spectators as possible" (*The Noise of Threatening Drum: Dramatic Strategy and Political Ideology in Shakespeare and the English Chronicle Plays* (Newark: University of Delaware Press, 1990), 9.

12. Many regard both nations and nationalism as a distinctively modern phenomenon, locating its origins in the revolutionary movements of the late eighteenth century along with the advance of industrialisation and capitalist economics, but this theory (as propounded by Hobsbawm, Gellner, and Anderson) has come under increasing pressure in recent years from those who believe that the antecedents of the modern nation-state are traceable back to the sixteenth century and beyond.

13. Benedict Anderson, *Imagined Communities: Reflections on the Origin and Spread of Nationalism* (1983; rev. ed., London: Verso, 1991), 7.

14. Liah Greenfeld, *Nationalism: Five Roads to Modernity* (Cambridge: Harvard University Press, 1993), chap. 1, esp. 50-51, 65.

15. Claire McEachern, *The Poetics of English Nationhood, 1590-1612* (Cambridge: Cambridge University Press, 1996), chap. 1. McEachern's thesis is extended, and subtly qualified, by her later analysis of *Henry V,* which she rightly considers to be "as vigilant in limiting the scope of common feeling as it is in encouraging it" (108).

16. Anthony D. Smith, *Myths and Memories of the Nation* (Oxford: Oxford University Press, 1999), 71, 86-88.

17. See, e.g., Michael Neill, "Broken English and Broken Irish: Nation, Language and the Optic of Power in Shakespeare's Histories," *Shakespeare Quarterly* 45 (1994): 1-32, and Christopher Highley, *Shakespeare, Spenser, and the Crisis in Ireland* (Cambridge: Cambridge University Press, 1997).

18. See, e.g., Robert Weimann, *Shakespeare and the Popular Tradition in the Theater,* ed. Robert Schwartz (Baltimore and London: Johns Hopkins University Press, 1978), 169-77, and Walter Cohen, *Drama of a Nation: Public Theater in Renaissance England and Spain* (Ithaca and London: Cornell University Press, 1985). Peter Womack argues further that, by involving audiences in the reconstruction of a collective "national"; past, the Elizabethan theater invited them "not merely to contemplate the 'imagined community' but to be it" ("Imagining Communities: Theatres and the English Nation in the Sixteenth Century," in *Culture and History 1350-1600: Essays on English Communities, Identities and Writing,* ed. David Ayers [New York and London: Harvester Wheatsheaf: 1992], p. 138).

19. Joel Altman, "'Vile Participation': The Amplification of Violence in the Theater of *Henry V,*" *Shakespeare Quarterly* 42 (Spring 1991): 7.

20. This formula basically sought to adapt received humanistic notions of historiography to a theatrical context. According to sixteenth-century authorities such as Thomas Lanquet and Thomas Blundeville, the writing and reading of history was profitable because it preserved the fame of great rulers and commanders of antiquity, thereby providing a storehouse of instructive exempla, both positive and negative, of the arts of governance and warfare that would "sturre [readers] to vertue, and . . . withdrawe them from vice." Of course such a theory is hardly able to encompass the diversity of approach that actually characterized English historical drama in this period; besides overlooking historical romances like Greene's James IV, it offers an inadequate definition of the chronicle play proper, which rarely followed such a straightforwardly didactic and hagiographic agenda.

21. According to A. D. Smith, the "myth of descent" is among the most potent of the ethnic myths, symbols, and traditions that constitute the bedrock of any nation. In invoking an heroic ancestry it provides the aspirant nation with a model of identity and a charter for "regenerative collective action," as its people seek to recreate the spirit of a "past golden age" (*Myths and Memories,* chap. 2).

22. Thomas Heywood, *An Apology for Actors* (1612), ed. Richard H. Perkinson, (New York: Scholars' Facsimile, 1941), B3r.

23. Heywood, *Apology for Actors,* F3r. Cf. the implied concession to the illiteracy of some sections of the audience in the opening lines of the chorus to act 5: "Vouchsafe to those who have not read the story / That I may prompt them" (5.0.1-2).

24. Heywood, *Apology for Actors,* F3r.

25. Pierce Pennilesse his supplication to the Divell (1612), (Menston, England: Scolar Press, 1969), H2,.

26. Pierce Pennilesse, H2'.

27. Cf. Pugliatti, *Shakespeare the Historian,* 60-62.

28. Heywood, Apology for Actors, B4r.

29. See "Ideology and Ideological State Apparatuses," in Louis Althusser, *"Lenin and Philosophy" and Other Essays,* trans. Ben Brewster (London:

1961), 121-76. Despite the usefulness of Althusser's theory of interpellation for my purposes, this essay stops short of subscribing to its deterministic and totalizing implications. As many critics have noted, by positing the subject as a simple effect of ideology, Althusser seemingly precludes the possibility of individual agencies resisting its operations. (See, e.g., Claire Colebrook, *New Literary Histories* [Manchester: Manchester University Press, 1997], 158-62). Drawing on recent work that critiques such monolithic narratives of ideology, culture, and the formation of self, I attempt to show how the contradictory ways in which characters and audience are interpellated in *Henry V* result in a proliferation of subject positions, thereby opening up a space for political contestation.

30. It cannot be coincidental that Heywood's comments on the instructive value of the history play are followed by a ringing affirmation of the ideological orthodoxy of the theatre in general: "Plays are writ with this ayme, and carryed with this methode, to teach the subjects obedience to their King, to shew the people the untimely ends of such as have moved tumults, commotions, and insurrections, to present them with the flourishing estate of such as live in obedience, exhorting them to allegeance, dehorting them from all trayterous and fellonious stratagems" (F3v, cf. Nashe, 1-12-H3T).

31. See Taylor's introduction to the Oxford edition, 11.

32. The play abounds in promises or exhortations to rouse oneself to action. In addition to the instances discussed below, cf. 1.2.122-4, 273-75, 309-10; 2.2.36-38; 2.3.3-5; 2.4.69-72; 3.0.17-18; 3.1.1-2; 3.2.1; 3.5.48-53; 4.5.16-17; 4.7.56-60; 5.0.8-9; 5.1.9-12.

33. One might assume that "history" refers here to the chronicles, twice cited in the play (1.2.163, 4.7.89), once by Fluellen, whose excessive reverence for, and comic misuse of, historical precedent is one of the ways in which the practice of invoking an exemplary past is ironized in the play. However, the personification of history as "speak[ing]," along with the allusions to funerary monuments, seems to encompass more popular (oral and visual) forms of historical commemoration.

34. Raphael Holinshed, *Chronicles of England, Scotland and Ireland,* rev. ed. (London, 1587), 3.546.

35. Rackin, *Stages of History,* 94.

36. The intervening figure of Hotspur, whose self-dedication to the obsolete code of "bright honour"

is represented as both laudable and ludicrous, is the clearest index of this shift of perspective.

37. For an excellent analysis of the ideological appropriation of heroic exemplars sanctioned by humanist tradition, see Timothy Hampton, *Writing from History: The Rhetoric of Exemplarity in Renaissance Literature* (Ithaca and London: Cornell University Press, 1990). As Hampton notes, Shakespeare's attitude to this practice is consistently sceptical (though he confines his study to the latter's handling of classical models): "[His] use of the exemplar theory of history works both to celebrate the power of the past and to undermine attempts to appropriate its authority for political ends. Shakespeare demystifies the relationship between politics and history and demonstrates the extent to which all use of the past in guiding public action is shaped by rhetoric" (206).

38. See Michael Goldman, *Shakespeare and the Energies of Drama* (Princeton: Princeton University Press, 1972), 58-73.

39. Such contrarieties emerge not only from the diction, imagery, and other rhetorical devices of particular speeches, but between speeches. A much less flattering image of the common soldier as an inhuman and immoral brute is delineated by Henry at 3.3.90-121, and 4.1.152-59.

40. See, e.g., Helgerson, *Forms of Nationhood,* 231, and Anne Barton, "The King Disguised: Shakespeare's *Henry V* and the Comical History" (1975), rpt. in *Essays, Mainly Shakespearean* (Cambridge: Cambridge University Press, 1994), 207-33.

41. Jonathan Baldo, "Wars of memory in *Henry V,*" *Shakespeare Quarterly* 47 (1996): 132-59.

42. Again we are alerted to the mystification of social relationships by the existence of alternative images. At 3.6.70-83, Gower offers a less romantic "take" on the veteran who exploits his supposed intimacy with the "great commanders" to defraud gullible "ale-washed wits." In actuality, the ordinary conscripts could expect to suffer acute social and economic hardship on their return from the wars (see Pugliatti, *Shakespeare the Historian,* 229-32).

43. For exceptions, see Holinshed, *Chronicles,* 3.551, 565. But, equally significantly, there is no equivalent in Holinshed for the exchanges between Henry and individual foot soldiers in 4.1 and 8, which (as with 3.2) do, briefly confer both an identity and a voice on the recalcitrant conscripts.

44. See, e.g., Weimann, *Shakespeare and the Popular Tradition,* 214-15.

45. See, esp., Stephen Orgel, "Making Greatness Familiar," in *The Power of Forms in the English Renaissance,* ed. Stephen Greenblatt (Norman: University of Oklahoma Press, 1982), 41-48, and David Scott Kastan, "Proud Majesty Made a Subject: Shakespeare and the Spectacle of Rule," *Shakespeare Quarterly* 37 (1986): 459-75.

46. Although the relative proportion of "priviliged" versus "non-privileged" spectators estimated to have attended the public playhouses in this period is still vigorously debated, Andrew Gurr's conclusion that the citizen and artisanal classes provided the staple audience has been widely accepted (see *Playgoing in Shakespeare's London* [Cambridge: Cambridge University Press, 1987], 64).

47. For the evidence of women frequenting the commercial theatres, see Gurr, *Playgoing,* 55-63. The question of how their experience of plays and playgoing might have been differently inflected by their gender is addressed by Jean Howard in *The Stage and Social Struggle in Early Modern England* (London: Routledge, 1994), 76-92, and (with Rackin) in *Engendering a Nation,* 32-36.

FURTHER READING

Criticism

Baldo, Jonathan. "Wars of Memory in *Henry V.*" *Shakespeare Quarterly* 47, no. 2 (summer 1996): 132-59.
　　Evaluates *Henry V* as a play primarily concerned with collective memory, forgetting, and the legitimization of the sovereign nation-state.

Cubeta, Paul M. "Falstaff and the Art of Dying." *Studies in English Literature 1500-1900* 27, no. 2 (spring 1987): 197-211.
　　Assesses the effectiveness of Shakespeare's indirect dramatization of Falstaff's death in the *Henriad.*

Erickson, Peter. "Fathers, Sons, and Brothers in *Henry V.*" In *Modern Critical Interpretations: William Shakespeare's* Henry V, edited by Harold Bloom, pp. 111-33. New York: Chelsea House Publishers, 1988.

Considers the tragic dimension of *Henry V* in its representation of strained masculine relations.

Granville-Barker, Harley. "From *Henry V* to *Hamlet.*" In *More Prefaces to Shakespeare,* edited by Edward M. Moore, pp. 135-67. Princeton N.J.: Princeton University Press, 1974.
　　Explores the dramatic disappointments of *Henry V* as part of the arc of Shakespeare's artistic development toward the achievement of *Hamlet.*

Howlett, Kathy M. "Framing Ambiguity: Kenneth Branagh's *Henry V.*" In *Framing Shakespeare on Film,* pp. 92-114. Athens: Ohio State University Press, 2000.
　　Examines the irony and ambiguity in Kenneth Branagh's 1989 film version of *Henry V.*

Kezar, Dennis. "Shakespeare's Guilt Trip in *Henry V.*" *Modern Language Quarterly* 61, no. 3 (2000): 431-61.
　　Suggests that *Henry V* delves into concepts of authorial responsibility and guilt as understood within the cultural context of Renaissance England.

Kohler, Michael. "Review of *Henry V.*" *Theatre Journal* 52, no. 2 (May 2000): 263-66.
　　Reviews a 1999 French production of *Henry V* performed at Avignon and directed by Jean-Louis Benoit, commenting on an overall flatness occasioned by its political neutrality.

McEachern, Claire. "*Henry V* and the Paradox of the Body Politic." *Shakespeare Quarterly* 45, no. 1 (spring 1994): 33-59.
　　Considers the ways in which *Henry V* treats the tension between the political hegemony of the nation-state and the human bonds that constitute a social community.

Sutherland, John, and Cedric Watts. "Henry V's Claim to France: Valid or Invalid?" In *Henry V, War Criminal? and Other Shakespeare Puzzles,* pp. 117-25. Oxford: Oxford University Press, 2000.
　　Argues that Henry's already suspect claim to the French throne is finally depicted as invalid and illegitimate at the conclusion of *Henry V.*

Tiffany, Grace. "Puritanism in Comic History: Exposing Royalty in the *Henry* Plays." *Shakespeare Studies* 26 (1998): 256-87.
　　Focuses on Falstaff in the *Henriad* as a carnivalesque inversion of the Puritan figure.

Othello

For further information on the critical and stage history of *Othello,* see *SC,* Volumes 4, 11, 35, 53, and 68.

INTRODUCTION

Othello (ca. 1604) is generally considered to be one of Shakespeare's finest dramatic works. The play, a character-driven domestic tragedy of jealousy and deception, is set in Venice and Cyprus and recounts how the Venetian general Othello falls victim to the treachery of his ensign Iago. Scholars have identified the principal source of the story as Cinthio's Italian novella *Hecatommithi* (1565), which features in broad outline the characters and incidents that Shakespeare adapted into his tragic drama. In Shakespeare's version, Othello, after blindly succumbing to the diabolic machinations of his trusted standard-bearer Iago, quickly descends into enraged jealousy, falsely believing that his lieutenant Cassio has had a sexual affair with Desdemona, his innocent wife. Othello later smothers Desdemona, and then falls on his own sword when Iago's nefarious scheming comes to light. Commentators, actors, and directors have generally been drawn to the fascinating figures of Iago, the quintessential Shakespearean villain whose murky motivations for evil have remained elusive; Desdemona, a complex amalgam of feminine submissiveness and willful determination; and Othello, possessed of intriguing qualities ranging from his status as an exotic "Other" to his tragic propensity for self-deception. These figures have largely shaped modern critical assessments of the drama.

Character-centered study of *Othello* has long been the centerpiece of scholarly interest, with each of the drama's three principal figures—Othello, Iago, and Desdemona—eliciting some share of critical examination. Twentieth-century criticism of Othello's character has commonly emphasized the Moor's status as an exotic "Other" within the contexts of the racially heterogeneous Venetian society depicted in Shakespeare's drama. Albert Gerard (1957) opts for a moral understanding of Othello that highlights his anti-intellectual or "barbarian" nature. According to Gerard, the Moorish general, although a noble figure, lacks the full capacity for self-knowledge and moral wisdom necessary to avert tragedy; thus he is the perfect victim of Iago's cynical intrigues. Gerard insists that even at the play's conclusion Othello fails to attain an adequate intellectual awareness of his moral deficiencies. Millicent Bell

(2002) concentrates on Othello's self-doubt as conditioned by the racialistic social world in which he exists. In Bell's view, Othello, as a black converted Christian recently married to a white woman, ultimately suffers from his inability to completely assimilate into a community that deems him a racial outsider. Turning to Iago, Leah Scragg (1968) maintains that the stage ancestry of this generally despicable character derives from dramatic representations of the Devil, rather than from the allegorical figure of Vice, a staple player in the medieval morality play tradition. Scragg argues that far from being an ambiguously motivated, amoral role, Shakespeare's consummate villain bears affinities to the Christian dark angel, a merciless seducer of souls driven by a cosmological desire for revenge. Addressing the last of the central triad of characters in *Othello,* Emily C. Bartels (1996) offers a feminist assessment of Desdemona's assertive qualities, explicating her impulse to question and destabilize the repressive hierarchy of patriarchal social order in the drama. According to Bartels, this defining aspect of Desdemona's character is one that traditional, male-oriented criticism of the play has tended to circumvent, obscure, or ignore.

Othello has had a sustained appeal among audiences, perhaps due to its decidedly human themes and potent, domestic intimacy, and remains one of Shakespeare's most frequently performed plays. The problem of successfully realizing its multifaceted characters and balancing the diverse issues raised in the play, however, has made the task of staging an entirely satisfying production an elusive one. Doug Hughes's 2001 production at New York City's Public Theater received mixed reviews. Ben Brantley (2001) finds the dramatic power of Liev Schreiber's near-psychopathic Iago to be the central element of this production and contends that no one else in the cast "comes close to matching Mr. Schreiber's playful interpretive intelligence." Barbara D. Phillips (2001) likewise praises Schreiber, and observes that his star performance as Iago tended to highlight the deficiencies of the remaining members of the cast, including those of Keith David, whose representation of Othello she deems less compelling. In another review of Hughes's production, Charles Isherwood (2001) offers a complementary estimation. Acknowledging the "confident grasp of Schreiber's bewitching Iago," Isherwood describes how the actor was able to draw audiences into a circle of complicity with his evil acts. The critic additionally stresses the manner in which stage and lighting effects served to illuminate Schreiber's mesmerizing power. Other commentators, however, found the emphasis on Othello's spiteful ensign less appealing. Michael Feingold (2001) records flashes of brilliance from Schreiber, but nevertheless finds that his impassive rendition of Iago "lacks credibility." Feingold deems Keith David's Othello the better of the two character interpretations, although he does contend that David could not sustain his stately, moving, and dignified performance evenly throughout the evening. John Simon (2001) offers the most negative review of the staging, suggesting that the responsibility for its limitations rests solidly with director Doug Hughes, whose casting and interpretive decisions, he claims, obscured the tragic grandeur of Shakespeare's drama, burying its loftier, philosophical qualities among the sordidness of domestic drama.

Contemporary assessments of the thematic issues raised in *Othello* have included the play's representation of race symbolized by Othello's dark skin, the elements of wonder and spectacle embodied in Desdemona's lost handkerchief, and the linguistic subversion found in Iago's masterful manipulation of language. Race and colonialism figure prominently in Thorell Porter Tsomondo's (1999) new historicist estimation of the drama, which underscores a narrative dislocation of Othello as "Other," an outsider displaced from Venetian norms by language, skin color, geography, and ideology. While exploring the racial dynamics at work in *Othello,* Edward Washington (1997) nevertheless focuses on the drama as a tragedy of misinterpreted signs, locating Othello's culpability for his own downfall in his reliance on a coded system of gestures and images, rather than on the underlying truths they represent. Paul Yachnin (1996) and Andrew Sofer (1997) concentrate on the symbolic and thematic resonance of Desdemona's handkerchief in *Othello.* Stolen by Iago and later produced as proof of her infidelity, the handkerchief is a fetishized commodity in Yachnin's reading, capable of eliciting wonder and ultimately violence. For Sofer, the handkerchief embodies a broad spectrum of thematic functions in the play, designating an interlocking chain of signification that includes witchcraft, sexuality, jealousy, revenge, murder, inconstancy, and falsified evidence. A prop as metaphor, the handkerchief ties together the drama's leading motifs as well as drawing attention to its own theatricality, Sofer concludes. Linguistic signification is the subject of Lucille P. Fultz's (1997) essay, which considers Iago's skillful manipulation of language to orchestrate the deaths of Othello and Desdemona. For Fultz, verbal seduction—a desire for power achieved through language—is a basic thematic component of the drama, one embodied by Iago in each of his relationships with fellow characters. Lastly, Thomas Moisan (2002) considers the role of the Venetian state in shaping the characters and tragic outcome of the play.

OVERVIEWS AND GENERAL STUDIES

Thorell Porter Tsomondo (essay date June 1999)

SOURCE: Tsomondo, Thorell Porter. "Stage-Managing 'Otherness': The Function of Narrative in *Othello.*" *Mosaic: A Journal for the Interdisciplinary Study of Literature* 32, no. 2 (June 1999): 1-25.

[*In the following essay, Tsomondo analyzes the narrative and dramatic strategies of* Othello, *concentrating on the construction of Othello as "Other" in terms of its implications within the play and for Shakespeare's canonical status in the postcolonial epoch.*]

New historicist and postcolonial research has lent to narratology's concern with voice and location of voice a heightened awareness of the sociopolitical as well as ideological functions of narrative discourse and the ways that literary texts inscribe and exploit these functions. In Hayden White's view, narrative is "not merely a neutral discursive form that may or may not be used to represent real events . . . but rather entails ontological and epistemic choices with distinct ideological and even specifically political implications" (ix). More concretely, Foucault's *Discipline and Punish,* and Said's *Culture and Imperialism,* draw critical attention not only to the sociopolitical and psychic dimensions of narrative discourse but to questions of power relations that inform narrative structures and practices.

Although Shakespeare's *Othello* is a dramatic rather than a narrative work—or perhaps because it is drama in which racially-turned narrative performance is conspicuously, structurally staged—the play offers a fascinating, if unusual, site for examining narrative production and use. The plot in itself is simple enough: Othello, a General in the Venetian army and a Moor, secretly weds Desdemona, the young daughter of a Venetian senator. Iago, Othello's ensign, beguiles him into believing that Desdemona has been adulterous with the lieutenant, Cassio, and in a jealous rage, Othello murders Desdemona. The period in which the play was written—the Elizabethan age of exploration and colonial expansion, a time of shifting geographic boundaries and of unprecedented cross-cultural transaction—has already attracted considerable attention on the part of theorists concerned with the constitution of institutionalized sociopolitical structures and the textualization of these structures, as well as those concerned with modes and processes of literary representation and the ideological and rhetorical tensions that it necessarily inscribes. What needs more attention, however, is how these features are concretely conjoined in a work like *Othello* and how this play makes a unique contribution to our understanding of the politics and poetics of the Elizabethan period.

Thus in the following essay, I want to focus on the significance of the narrative/dramatic strategies that Shakespeare employs in *Othello,* arguing that these strategies subtly distinguish and operate along the geographic, political, and cultural boundaries that the play's Renaissance world stage draws. With a view to showing how the contrastive interplay of these generic techniques enacts the ideological accountability of narrative functions in general as well as of Shakespeare's manipulation of these functions, I will first analyze Shakespeare's use of these formal literary devices in the play to create a thematics of absence/presence that comments tellingly on Othello's dubious identity in Renaissance society. Then, I will elaborate on Shakespeare's procedure by linking it to the dynamics of fiction-making in general, going on to explore what his particular construction of *Othello* reveals about his poetic agenda. Finally, I will expand my argument to explore relations of power in imperialist culture and the signs of this power in Shakespeare's art and canonic status. In this way, I wish to demonstrate not only how Shakespeare's schizoid casting of the Moor as, at once, central subject and marginalized object reflects colonial power relations but also how the play's colonializing instrumentality extends beyond the literary text and pertains to Shakespeare scholarship and criticism of the play as well.

In the last scene of *Othello,* the protagonist, aware of how he has been duped by Iago, is confined with the corpse of his wife whom he has just murdered; the time seems to have come finally for what Othello has not yet done: self-examination in the heroic tradition of Shakespearean tragedy. Though Othello's predicament is markedly different from that of Richard II, one might expect that like Richard he would study how to "compare this prison . . . unto the world," and engage in setting "the word itself against the word" (5.5.1-14). Given his knowledge of Desdemona's innocence—the sight of "the tragic loading of this bed"—and the realization that he has been nothing more than a comic actor in Iago's deadly play, one might have expected Othello to be teased into thoughts of the kind that Macbeth utters upon hearing of the death of his wife:

> She should have died hereafter;
> There would have been a time for such a word.
> . . . Out, out, brief candle!
> Life's but a walking shadow, a poor player,
> That struts and frets his hour upon the stage,
> And then is heard no more. It is a tale
> Told by an idiot, full of sound and fury,
> Signifying nothing.
>
> (5.5.17-28)

Macbeth's aside, indeed, captures the meaning that Iago has imposed on Othello's life and what must have seemed to Othello to be the significance of his life as he gazes on its deadly outcome.

Othello, however, has no capacity for reflection of this kind, either in personal or general humanistic terms. Faced with the tragic results of his poor judgment, he musters an audience and, predictably, tells another story: "I have seen the day / That with this little arm, and this good sword, / I have made my way . . ." (5.2.261-63). Earlier, goaded into believing that Desdemona is guilty of adultery, he disintegrated into apoplectic incoherence: "Lie with her? lie on her? We say lie on her, when they belie her . . . Handkerchief—confessions—handkerchief—. . . Pish! Noses, ears, and lips. . .' (4.1.36-42). When faced with similarly disillusioning circumstance, Hamlet (though it is highly unlikely that he could be tricked by Iago) protested:

> . . . O God, God,
> How [weary], stale, flat, and unprofitable
> Seem to me all the uses of this world!
> Fie on't, Ah fie! 'tis an unweeded garden
> That grows to seed, things rank and gross in nature
> Possess it merely. That it should come [to this]!
> But [two days married], nay, not so much, not two.
> Let me not think on't! Frailty, thy name is woman!
>
> (1.2.132-46)

Though one cannot applaud Macbeth's oblique assessment of his dilemma nor endorse Hamlet's misogyny, one is aware that their commentaries represent stages in their moral and intellectual delineation. The closest Othello comes to soliloquizing in the vein characteristic of Shakespeare's tragic heroes is in his paranoiac(ally) telescoped aside:

> Haply for I am black,
> And have not those soft parts of conversation
> That chambers have, or for I am declin'd
> Into the vale of years (yet that's not much),
> She's gone. I am abus'd and my relief
> Must be to loathe her.
>
> (3.3.236-68)

In these lines, Othello's insuppressible urge to tell his story points not inward to a heightened consciousness but outward to the narrative signs of his insecurity.

Othello (1604) was written four years after *Hamlet,* one year before *King Lear* and two years before *Macbeth,* the three plays with which it is usually ranked. Yet *Othello* is not invested with any of the self-searching, self-revelatory monologues that endow Shakespeare's tragic heroes with their special poignancy. Othello does not experience those ennobling moments when with lyric intensity the protagonist faces a personal crisis and gains and imparts insight into self and the vicissitudes of human life. In Shakespeare, the soliloquy is one means of bringing the hero closer to the audience; it magnifies and at the same time humanizes him. Lear's self-excoriating "unaccommodated man," Hamlet's benumbing "heartache and the thousand natural shocks

/ that flesh is heir to," Macbeth's sobering "brief candle," all involve their audiences in moments of intense moral reckoning and philosophic contemplation.

Notably, in *Othello,* instead of the Moor, it is Iago, his white ensign, who is given to self-communing and his primary role is to diminish, through calculated psychic violence, Othello's humanity. As part of this function, Iago's privileged soliloquizing installs him between the protagonist and the audience even as it signalizes his own impressive intellectual capabilities and psychological astuteness. With this edge, Iago interprets, manipulates, even forecasts the hero's thought and actions for the audience, flattening the character, rendering increasingly evanescent verbal profundities like those allowed to Hamlet and Lear. Othello himself, in contrast, is limited to retailing his history, telling stories about his past exploits.

The predominance of narrative in *Othello,* that is "the presence of a story and a storyteller" (Scholes & Kellog 4), distinguishes the play and, in turn, has prompted much critical dispute, which inevitably turns on Othello's verbal proclivities and therefore his character. In a well-documented critical dialogue, when A. C. Bradley defined Othello as a poetic romantic victimized by Iago's "absolute egoism" (179), T. S. Eliot and F. R. Leavis respectively responded by describing Othello as someone given to "dramatizing himself" (111) and as doomed by his own "noble," "brutal egoism" (146). More recently, Stephen Greenblatt has described Othello as self-fashioner of an "identity" that is dependent upon "constant performance . . . of his story" (81); Martin Elliott, in turn, has noted what he sees as a "habit of self-publication" (108), and Valerie Traub has argued that Othello essentially becomes a "signifier only of another signifier" (36). James Calderwood goes even so far as to suggest that Othello's preoccupation with storytelling comes close to jeopardizing the drama: "For a moment we seem on the edge of an *Arabian Nights* infinite regression of stories: Shakespeare's dramatic story yields to Othello's senatorial story, which disappears into stories of cannibals and Anthropophagy which might disappear into. . . . But fortunately they do not" (294). While these assessments accord with the play's own depiction of Othello's "bumbast circumstance / Horribly stuff'd with epithites of war" (1.1.13-14), in doing so they also point to a number of questions that need to be asked of *Othello* and its author. Why this yielding to the narrative impulse in this drama? Why in this play more than in any other is Shakespeare's dramatic art in danger of being upstaged by the characters' storytelling? What necessary dramatic function does narrative serve in *Othello?*

Drama and narrative are not, of course, mutually exclusive generic provinces, and Derrida's observation that a text may participate in more than one genre—thereby not belonging to any one specifically (61)—seems particularly applicable to Shakespeare. Harold Bloom, indeed, rates Shakespeare as one of the "great originals among the world's strongest authors" on the grounds that he "violates known forms": "Shakespeare wrote five-act dramas for stage presentation, yet Shakespeare wrote no genre. What . . . is *Troilus and Cressida?* It is comedy, history, tragedy, satire, yet none of these singly and more than all of them together" (18). While one could similarly ask whether *Othello* is drama or narrative singly or more than both combined, and while it is true that Shakespeare resists generic prescriptives, one also needs to bear in mind that "violation of forms" does not erase form, and that there can be no infringement where there are no boundaries. Todorov's solution is to regard theory of genre as "hypothesis" or proposition merely; he maintains that study of literary works from a generic viewpoint will "discover a principle operative in a number of texts rather than what is specific about each of them" and that the best procedure is to begin by "presenting our own point of departure" (1,19-20).

For my purposes, then, a helpful starting point is Robert Scholes's contrastive definition of the two genres: "drama is presence in time and space; narrative is past, always past" (206; emphasis mine). Because narrating can take place only in the "once upon a time" of the story that it relates, in the dramatic here and now of the play, the staged present of the tale that Othello tells about himself is not the events he recounts or the "self" he re-creates but the act of narration. This act or role directs attention to past events and to a protagonist (the hero of his narrative) whose experiences are framed in an earlier time than stage time, the time of the narrating, and in unfamiliar, distant locations. Interpreted in this context, Scholes's definition may be reworded thus: narrative is a sign of absence, whereas drama is a sign of presence. To some extent, then, drama and narrative could work at cross-purposes. And when, as in *Othello,* narrative is woven extensively into the dramatic work, the significance of Scholes's "time" and "space" translates into stage-time and stage-space and thereby into commentary on the play's dramatic representation.

In *Othello,* the "pastness" which narrative re-presents, functions as a "distancing" device which enables Shakespeare to locate the Moor or alien on the Elizabethan stage and by extension in the European community. Through juggling of narrative and dramatic devices, Shakespeare is able to manipulate stage time and space so that much of the action that defines the protagonist is located offstage, outside the cultural and geographical purviews of the Elizabethan audience, in revealing contradistinction to his central, heroic stage position. Thereby the playwright renders largely innocuous the threatening or "undramatizable" elements of his material he displaces them into the storied realms of distant lands and times. Just as within the play the Turks' diversionary military tactics are described as "a pageant / to keep us in false gaze" (1.3.18-19), so there may be something deceptively seductive about Shakespeare's recourse to narrative strategies.

In the terms used by critics to define Othello's self-expression—"self-fashioner," "self-publication," "signifier . . . of another signifier," "disappearing" stories, "bumbast"—one can detect a tacit articulation of a sense of lack or absence, and at the heart of this absence and lending it validity is Othello's blackness. It is this otherness that necessitates and gives impetus to his narrative "I am" and correspondingly to his individuated expansive rhetoric, just as conversely it is Shylock's otherness that induces his startlingly callous economy of speech. According to Greenblatt, "the telling of the story of one's life—the conception of one's life as a story—is a response to public inquiry: to the demands of the Senate sitting in judgment, or at least to the presence of an inquiring community" (42; emphasis mine). Othello's self-declarative stories, however, register less his presence than they do a palpable absence. This dilemma is due in part to the nature and utility of narrative itself. It is Othello's awareness of his cultural disconnectedness that makes his narrative performance necessary. At the same time, it is this awareness that further cultivates and intensifies the very sense of discontinuity that his story attempts to dispel—the story can be told from the beginning, his childhood, but only up to the point at which he is required to tell it. So, Othello must repeat his history later for Desdemona and later still for the Senate in a seemingly endless effort to establish an identity. In this light he is, for the most part, a potential presence only, his dramatic contextualization, his presence, being seriously undermined by his narrative (dis)position.

In an attempt to fix this problematic characterization, Leslie Fiedler makes a telling remark: "mythologically speaking, Othello is really black only before we see him; after his first appearance [on the stage], he is archetypally white, though a stranger still, as long as he remains in Venice: a stranger in blackface" (185). Since the dramatic tension throughout the work rests upon Othello's blackness, Fiedler's comment also raises questions about representation. Is the "lascivious Moor"—"the old black ram" with "thick lips"—of Scene 1 indeed transformed into and replaced by a disguised European in Scene 2? Does the audience, or rather can the audience, dispel the scathing image of blackness so pointedly drawn in the first scene when the disguised "white" Othello later enters the stage? Or does the audience, cognizant of the essential discrepancy, merely sit back and enjoy the power of dramatic irony?

What Fiedler reads as the substitution of identities—familiar for strange—is a strategic stage dislocation: a shift in the Moor's *figurenposition,* as Robert Weiman

terms "the actor's position on the stage and the speech, action, and degree of stylization associated with that position" (224). The shift in Othello's *figurenposition* is from a narrativised presentation in Scene 1 to a dramatic representation in Scene 2, in other words, from a figural absence to a symbolic presence. The play between these two modes of enactment creates the ironic illusion of the color-coded color blindness that Fiedler's statement describes: black and white being interchangeable, racial difference is neutralized; Shakespeare is vindicated. In the debate about Othello's color, Fiedler takes his place among those critics who abstract the sign of Othello's presence and name it "white." The early scenes of the drama invite this interpretation by splitting the character into competing fragments: a narrativised (alien) half and a dramatized (familiar) counterpart. Besides, this interpretation is necessary if the tragedy of a noble-mind-in-a-black-body corrupted by a black-mind-in-a-noble-body is to work.

The question of race continues to be a vexed one in *Othello* criticism. In her study, *Gender, Race, Renaissance Drama,* Ania Loomba points out that whereas there has been controversy about Othello's ethnicity, there has been no debate concerning the racial identity of Aaron the Moor of *Titus Andronicus;* Aaron, "unlike Othello," corresponds easily to "the stereotype of black wickedness, lust and malignity"—he, as well as other characters repeatedly link his intractably evil nature to his "physical features" (46). In an essay titled "Race," Kwame Appiah cautions against attributing such bias to Shakespeare's works since, he argues, in Elizabethan England Jews and Moors were hardly an "empirical reality"; stereotypes were based largely on the non-Christian standing of these ethnic groups, not on experience of them (277).

Some critics, however, see things differently, arguing that Elizabethans had access to much more than inherited theological beliefs. Eldred Jones, for example, marshals a wealth of research data to support his contention that factual information concerning peoples of Africa was available: classical historical documents, popular digests, and eyewitness "accounts of actual sea voyages and land travels" (1). Noting as well that black slaves were introduced into England as early as 1554, several years before John Hawkins's first voyage (15-16), Jones concludes that *Othello* derives from "conflicting material" from various sources (14). Similarly, Jack D'Amico traces a "Moroccan connection" of extensive trade and diplomacy between England and Morocco from circa 1550-1603; as he sees it, Othello represents the sum of Elizabethan images of the Moor as "everything" from the noble to the monstrous, and that in creating him Shakespeare explores the inherent contradictions (177-96).

In addition to "conflicting material" and complexity of issue, it is likely that, given his subject matter, Shakespeare had to deal also with his own divided impulses regarding Africans. His extended deployment of narrative in a dramatic work and the tension created by the dynamics of the two generic modes may be evidence of this division. Of course, shifting perspectives is nothing new in his art. John Keats lauds as "Negative Capability" this quality in Shakespeare. John Bayley sees as a mark of genius the irresolution and reserve that characterize the dramatist's works (15). Herman Melville identifies Shakespeare as a master "of the great Art of Telling the Truth" "not so much for what" the playwright "did do as for what he did not do, or refrained from doing" (65-66). However, unsettledness and reticence do not signify neutrality, and in the case of *Othello,* moreover, we have the kind of social and political baggage that has a charged ideological resonance in whatever context the subject appears and by whomever it is addressed.

Through the narrative/dramatic strategies that Shakespeare employs, *Othello* reveals, among divided impulses and motives, some instructive exclusions, emphases, and suppressions. Othello's initial introduction to the audience takes place in his absence and in the form of gossip between Iago and Roderigo. This gossip may be likened to the third person narrative point of view which voyeuristically creates the character it describes. Shakespeare's use of this means of introducing Othello is felicitous. The familiarity that is apparent in Iago and Roderigo's conversation, in the coarse language they use and in their interrelationship, is soon seconded by the concordant sentiments that their "concern" about Desdemona's elopement awakens in the socially and politically privileged senator and parent, Brabantio, who endorses Roderigo: "O would you had had her" (1.1.175). This breakdown of reserve between social classes and individuals signifies the existence of common cause with the Elizabethan audience; it articulates the society's deepest fears: sexual deviation and miscegenation. Already, before the audience sees him, Othello is guilty of a cultural transgression; he has seduced the senator's daughter, married her without parental consent. Iago, Roderigo, and Brabantio react within the bounds of a shared cultural understanding that makes Othello a threatening otherness. Aptly, therefore, their conversation locates him offstage, out of sight.

By contrast, in *Macbeth,* the absence of the protagonist and the use of a third person, formal narrative to introduce him, locates him centerstage. The sergeant's story of Macbeth's battlefield prowess and the king's response establishes the protagonist as defender, kinsman, hero whose past as well as destiny is also the community's. In this case, the distance that narrative signals is temporary only; the past, because it is shared, is retrievable. In a similar vein, Prospero's story of his past provides Miranda with a history, bridges the reserve

between father and daughter and preludes their return home. In these instances, narrative creates a sense of distance the better to dramatize presence and continuity.

This is not to say that narrative always works in the same way in Shakespeare or generally. The distance inherent in and implied by narrative performance varies in its schema and function. The form it takes will depend upon the relation between teller, story, and audience and what is at stake. For example, Caliban and Prospero tell similar stories of loss and dispossession but from different standpoints. Prospero's story subjects Caliban: "This thing of darkness I acknowledge mine" (5.1.275). And even if, as is commonly believed, Caliban is Prospero's psychological double, it takes a degree of "heroic" suzerainty to claim the "dark" or alien thing, whether one does battle with it like Ahab or, like Prospero, puts it to work. The encoding of removedness in the stories that characters tell or that are told about them, therefore, is determined largely by the text's discourse on power and power relations, whereby it is of some significance, then, that even when Othello is located physically in the presence of an audience—on the stage or in the Senate—his stories place him figurally elsewhere.

In Elizabethan drama, as John Draper observes, "the initial appearance of a character generally strikes a fundamental keynote in his nature" (91), or, to put it another way, in the way a figure is characterized. In addition to the symbolic significance of the subversive introduction of Othello and of his strategic location offstage in the opening scene, there is his problematic first actual appearance on the stage. His dignified response to Brabantio and the Senate tends to minimize the fact that he enters under siege, that he is on trial for a cultural infraction, and that the terms of Iago's devaluation of him are a central part of Brabantio's suit as well as of the outcome of the play.

Othello is on trial before the Senate, before all Venice and, simultaneously, before all audiences wherever the play is produced for as long as it continues to be acted or read. Ironically, the charges against him—"she [Desdemona] is abus'd, stol'n from me and corrupted. . . ." (1.3. 60-61)—as well as his defense are bound up with the very thing that marks his alienness, his history. His story chronicles "most disastrous chances" and "hairbreadth scape" involving cannibalism, threatening landscapes, human anomalies. These foreign, uncultivated, and therefore unreclaimable elements constitute a heritage and persona with which Venetians and Elizabethans can have little empathy. Later, this sign of (dis)location will be emphasized metonymically in the way that Desdemona's handkerchief, token of the bond between the lovers, also signifies spatial and temporal disjunction; in its Egyptian legacy of ancient magic, "prophetic fury" and mummy's dye it symbolizes the social gulf between the couple. Although Othello is aware, albeit subconsciously, of his disarticulation, he must nevertheless depend on the past to sway the Senate: "My services which I have done the signiory / Shall out-tongue his [Brabantio's] complaints" (1.2.18-19). They do.

Othello's exoneration, however, has been anticipated and subverted by Iago's declaration in Scene 1 that the State needs Othello "to lead their business" and cannot "with safety cast him" off (1.1147-53). Iago's unreliability notwithstanding, the implication that the Senate, like he, must "show out a flag and sign of love / which is indeed but sign" renders suspect the Duke's ready capitulation: "I think this tale would win my daughter too" (1.1.156-57). It also draws attention to the Duke's double-edged conciliatory advice to Brabantio: "Take up this mangled matter at the best; / Men do their broken weapons rather use / Than their bare hands: (1.3.173-75). This caution is more relevant to the Senate than to Desdemona's father; Othello is Venice's only weapon against the advancing Ottomites. Significantly, Brabantio leaves the Signiory to die of "pure grief"—Desdemona's "match [being] mortal to him" (5.2.205)—and his dissenting, estranged, and foreboding voice may be representative of the protesting attitudes of civilian Venice. Thus in 1693, Thomas Rymer was to cite Othello as "a caution to all Maidens of Quality, how without their parents' consent they run away with Blackamoors" (89).

Othello is distanced also by the manner in which he tells his story. Storytelling around the cottage hearth served an important social function in early modern Europe; it had the power to unite the community by bringing together its diverse elements. As Dennis Kay notes, Renaissance England, in particular, was not only a "storytelling culture," but also "a world of ritualized social narrative," which some of its writers exploited by interpreting and moralizing "the act of storytelling" in their art (209, 211). It is of particular interest, then, that Shakespeare's audience hears Othello's history at the trial and therefore at great remove from the domestic "ritualized" fireside setting in which Desdemona and her father would have heard it. By placing the domestic scene offstage, the dramatist conjures and rejects at once the familiarity that the retelling can only insinuate, whereby the Elizabethan ritualized social pastime becomes a means of identifying and excluding the Moor. Further, Othello recounts not his story but the story of his storytelling and its outcome. In the process, he locates himself in another place at an earlier time, telling a story that situates him in yet a more distant place and time in seemingly endless regression. In addition to denoting his receding *figurenposition,* the narrative retrogradation imbues Othello's speech with a more literary than spoken quality, thus proclaiming a lack of the full presence that drama by its very definition signi-

fies. The play of difference, spatial and temporal, within the mimetic cosmos of the dramatic stage provides a striking commentary on Othello's tenuous identity and place.

The series of narrative displacements inscribed in Othello's story also serves to move offstage another significant social ritual. The audience does not witness Othello's wooing of Desdemona but hears of it rather in the context of a trial in which the audience is being asked to judge. Interestingly, the tale that Othello relates on this occasion begins not with his courtship of Desdemona but, aptly, his relationship to Brabantio: "Her father loved me, oft invited me; / Still question'd me the story of my life" (1.3.128-29). In this public, male, juridical emplotment, Desdemona's love is the unforeseen, unsought outcome of a domestic travesty which implicates her father, who, in inviting the stranger to the hearth, unwittingly exposed her heart.

The significance of this situation becomes even clearer if we note that in *Romeo and Juliet* the wooing scene is by contrast an important dramatic exponent. The play resembles *Othello* in plot; both works test the boundaries of forbidden love. In the former play, however, Shakespeare's task is to reconcile coequals—"two houses both alike in dignity"—whereas in *Othello* his problem is more challenging; he must unite the irreconcilable. It is a tribute to the playwright's skill that in neither case does he espouse any easy solution, for while in *Romeo and Juliet* reconciliation does succeed, it is at great cost to the two houses. In that play, at first the stage bustles with energy, the possibility of and necessity for change taking place against the backdrop of habituation and impotence. The wooing, which lasts for an entire scene of approximately one hundred ninety lines, registers that energy with a whole gamut of emotions and impulses: rebellious idealism—"deny thy father and refuse thy name" (2.2.34); fascination/fear—"this contract tonight, / It is too rash, too unadvis'd, too sudden / Too like the lightening" (2.2.117-119); romantic optimism—"this bud of love / . . . may prove a beauteous flow'r when next we meet" (2.2.120-22). Ultimately, however, as *Romeo and Juliet* pledge their love in the moonlight, they also court and win favor with the audience. In contrast, the wooing scene in *Othello* is screened from view. Is it that the Moor is not easily integrated into the role of lover on the Elizabethan stage? And by way of answer here consider how, unlikely lover though he is, the diabolical Richard III, in the midst of a funeral procession and in full view of the audience, substitutes one ritual (wooing) for another (mourning) with the dramatic facility that only an insider could.

By narrativising where he might have dramatized Shakespeare also displaces Othello's much touted heroism with fairy-tale sleight of hand: "our wars are done;

the Turks are drown'd" (2.1.202). Provided with the equivalent of neither a Dunsinane nor a Bosworth Field, with no heraldic account of triumph and no heroic battle-scarred stage entry, Othello's martial courage remains a matter of repute. Besides, if Anthony Hecht is right, the "valor" with which Othello is credited may bear ironic implications:

An Elizabethan audience would not have been willing to grant Othello the unlimited admiration he receives from Cassio, Desdemona, the Duke, and his senate at the beginning of the play. He would have been recognized from the start as an anomaly, not only "an extravagant and wheeling stranger / of here and everywhere," who has no real home, and therefore no civic allegiance, but, far more suspiciously, one who, had things only been slightly different (and perhaps more normal) would have been fighting on the enemy side, with the Turks against the Venetians. (123)

And yet, unquestionably, Shakespeare invests Othello with regal bearing and dignity, particularly in the early scenes of the play. In Venice, he faces Brabantio's aggression with authoritative restraint and the Signiory with aplomb, and the positive aspects of his portrayal are especially evident in contrast to Shakespeare's other "black" characters who fare poorly with regard to cherished heroic tropes like valor, honor, and romantic love. Aaron is an "irreligious Moor," a self-styled "black dog" who instigates rape and mutilation and fathers a "tawny slave," even if later his courageous attempts to save his son earn him a measure of humanity; Caliban is a would-be rapist; the Prince of Morocco chooses in love as badly as Portia wishes that all those of his "complexion" would; Shylock is a shocking figure of inhumane greed. In comparison to the way that these characters are cast, Othello is not only hero of the play but initially his sterling reputation and his endearing tenderness with Desdemona bespeak the playwright's attempt to paint the Other in humanistic strokes.

It is significant, though, that the opportunities for dramatizing various features that would bolster Othello's heroic profile are transposed into narrative and, therefore, are not staged. Did Shakespeare experience a greater sense of division in treating Othello than he did with his other tragic heroes? He figurally displaces Othello even while ostensibly setting him at the center of the stage, through deft manipulation of narrative/ dramatic modes. This explains why the play is often interpreted from Iago's perspective. It also explains why the Moor is never a serious threat to the Venetian social order. The catastrophic ending of the drama is inscribed in the apprehensive beginning which, in turn, is validated by the violent conclusion. That is, the

Actually, Othello's subjection has bconcluding tableau—the "tragic loading" of the "bed" that "poisons sight" and must be "hid"—harks back to the opening of

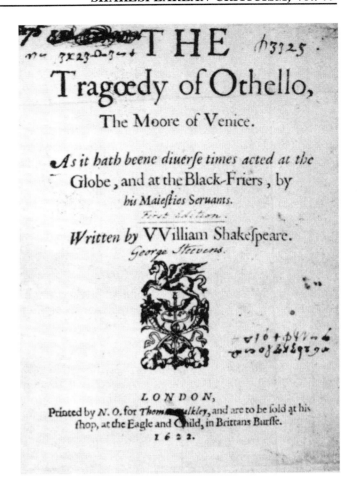

Title page from the 1622 edition of Othello.

the play or the fearful bed that Brabantio had tried to forestall: "the black ram . . . tupping your white ewe." By focusing on this loaded bed—ironically one of the rare "domestic frames" in this "domestic tragedy"—the play exposes that at its very center, the bedroom, there is the following proscription: "if such actions may have passage free, bondslaves and pagans shall our statesmen be" (1.2.98-99). Not surprisingly therefore, Othello's suicide is usually viewed as propitiatory: the protagonist's Christianized half destroys the Moorish part and Othello defers to Venetian society in a final attempt to (re)gain entry into the civilized world against which he has transgressed.

But far more than conciliation, Othello's suicide represents his final (dis)location. Othello's death occurs at a telling juncture; it coincides with, indeed impels the past ("in Allepo once") into the present ("I took . . . / And smote him thus"). In other words, as Othello stabs himself, narrative translates into drama, signifying his conscious emergence into the dramatic now. This coming forth, however, is insupportable in the world of the play; the Moor's psychic debut is synonymous with suicide. Othello dies into, and with, his story, to be re-created in Lodovico's narrative. But, unlike Hamlet who need only call upon Horatio's loyalty and intimate knowledge of his affairs to speak for him—"Absent thee from felicity a while / . . . To tell my story" (5.2.347-49)—Othello, outsider, feels distrustful; he pleads for fair accounting and anxiously attempts to dictate his own narrative terms: "Speak of me as I am; nothing extenuate, / Nor set down aught in malice" (5.2.342-43). Since Othello's audience is made up primarily of the Venetian deputation, the episode repeats the early trial scene in the Signiory, and implicitly indicts the protagonist even as he publicly executes himself. Othello's story will be recreated by Lodovico, therefore, in the only format possible for a Moor: Lodovico's story will be a Venetian narrative in and to which Othello is subject. een apparent to the audience, though not to him, from the moment Iago fabricates a tale with which "to abuse Othello's [ear] / That he is too familiar with his wife" (1.3.395-96). Iago's declared aim is to convince Othello that "he" (Cassio) is having an affair with Desdemona, but as Greenblatt notes, the use of the vague pronoun carries the implication that Othello's relationship with his own wife is also transgressive. Through Iago's ability and the privilege to fashion a story and the power to translate it into drama, he accomplishes what Othello cannot; within the given cultural context, Othello cannot locate his history and himself in the present, and therefore he also cannot exert control over his future. Because of the difference in their narrative trajectories, Iago is able to make Othello into the audience of a play in which the latter is unwittingly also the main actor; he makes Othello spectator to Othello's own life. In the process, Iago not only dramatizes but parodies Othello's dubious figuren-position, his figural absence, thereby baring the divide that invites and accommodates his (Iago's) plot.

Notwithstanding Iago's elaborate metaphor of conception and birth: "It [his scheme] is engend'red. Hell and night / Must bring this monstrous birth to the world's light" (1.3.403-05), his story is largely the appropriation and exploitation of one of the potential narratives that are inferable, given the immediate social scenario, from Othello's history up to the time that he himself can relate it. In her discussion of "Narrative Versions," Barbara Herstein Smith suggests the dynamic that functions here when she observes:

> For any particular narrative, there is no single basically basic story subsisting beneath it but, rather, an unlimited number of other narratives that can be constructed in response to it or perceived as related to it. . . . [For] basicness is always arrived at by the exercise of some set of operations, in accord with some set of principles, that reflect some set of interests, all of which are, by nature, variable and thus multiple. . . .

> Whenever these potentially perceptible relations become actually perceived, it is by virtue of some set of interests on the part of the perceiver.

> (217-18)

One may speculate, then, that had it suited Iago's purpose, he would have fabricated, in response to Othello's story, a very different "play." He could have produced, for example, an "and they lived happily ever after" romance. And so, of course, could Shakespeare. To examine the way that, instead of opting for some of the other potentially available stories, Iago construed from Othello's history a tale of sexual anxiety, lust, betrayal, and murder, is also to raise questions about Shakespeare's perceptions. Using Hernstein Smith's terms, we might ask what "set of operations," what "principles," what "interests" motivated the playwright to construct—out of the multiple other narratives open to him—this Othello?

By way of answering this question, it is instructive to consider the earlier narrative upon which Shakespeare based his tale. Generally, Shakespeare exercises great license in utilizing his sources, and in writing *Othello,* his use of the Italian novella from Cinthio's collection, *Gli Hecatommithi,* is no exception. In Cinthio's fiction, the Moor and "Disdemona" have been a happily married couple for some time when they set out for Cyprus, and Iago's motive for ensnaring them is clear: a jealous lust for Disdemona. In addition, as John Gilles points out, Disdemona and her unnamed Moorish spouse are both commoners and of equivalent age, whereas in Shakespeare's play, there is a discrepancy in their ages and both are of higher rank—Desdemona is the young daughter of a senator, Othello is a Venetian General "declined / Into the value of years." Paradoxically, however, Othello's military rank does not allay the unease that the biracial coupling fosters. Instead, Gilles further notes, "as in the myth of Tereus," Othello's position is presented as a "circumstantial anomaly, enabling a bizarre exception to the rule rather than legitimizing miscegenation per se"; these elements of the text added to Othello's "utterly black and physiologically Negroid" appearance make the marital pairing pointedly "transgressive" and therefore pointedly indecorous (26).

Mindful that the language of "racial difference" in the play is symptomatic of the embedded discourse of racial divide in the dramatist's culture, Virginia Mason Vaughan concludes that "when Shakespeare tackled Cinthio's tale of a moor and his ancient, he had no choice but to use this discourse" (*Contextual History* 70). I agree with Vaughan only partially. While the paradigmatic dimension of this discourse is not uniquely Shakespearean, the syntactic structure, the choice, combination, and sequence of vocabulary, statements, and concepts are the playwright's own. And it is also from this standpoint that Shakespeare's most inventive departure from Cinthio—his prescribing for the Moor a storytelling definition and role—makes most sense.

A number of issues bear emphasis here. First, in making Othello and Desdemona newlyweds, Shakespeare changes what in Cinthio's tale was an established relationship into a question about the possibility of such a marriage, while by interjecting a sense of "indecorum" he implies the "proper" response. Second, in making Iago's motive equivocal the playwright ensures that, at any given moment in the play, the audience has no stable ground on which to take a decided stand against the villain, as one is likely to do in the case of Edmund in *King Lear.* Rather, Iago inspires in the audience a deep fascination for his craft, a fascination that widens the distance between them and the protagonist since the latter's otherness is intensified by his facile surrender to Iago's subterfuge. The audience may feel pity for, but cannot empathize with, Othello. In effect, Shakespeare induces the audience's complicity in Othello's duping and thereupon communalizes Iago's "motives," subtly reinforcing the reservations voiced at the outset concerning the propriety of the fateful match. Finally, in making Othello the teller, audience, subject, and target of stories, Shakespeare circumscribes the protagonist in the narrative outskirts of the dramatic here and now. In so doing, he provides an acceptable, reassuring profile of the exotic barbarian and of the controlled, safely exploitable space that he does and must inhabit.

Narrative/dramatic space in *Othello* bears a strong kinship with Renaissance colonial plots; both are caught up in the politics of space. In many respects, therefore, both may be defined as what Foucault calls "disciplinary space," whose purpose is to "establish presences and absences," to categorize and "locate individuals" and groups, to "set up useful communications, to interrupt others" (143). Disciplinary space is "a procedure, therefore, aimed at knowing, mastering, and using" (193); it fabricates reality. Though these insights are based on Foucault's study of post Renaissance penal systems, they are crucial, as he himself makes clear, to understanding the structure and operation of other institutions such as education, religion, the military, as well as colonization and slavery, to name a few. On a general plane, Foucault's analysis probes the "technology of power" that produces, indeed fabricates, western society and that accounts for the kinds of individuals that comprise that society. Central to disciplinary space, according to Foucault, is an "apparatus of production"— commerce and industry marked by "conflict" and governed by "rules of strategy" (308), which include "techniques" and "methods" for the distribution and "control and use of men" (141). In the course of this mass location and exploitation of people, strategy becomes normalized and the distinction between the concocted and the real breaks down. In *Othello,*

"disciplinary space" aptly defines the organization of representational space; we might say that the play anticipates Foucault, exposing the common ground that dramatic representation shares with the colonialist enterprise: spatial politics and the construction of its machinery of production and control.

The case for viewing certain of Shakespeare's plays, most notably *The Tempest,* as a commentary on colonialism has a well documented history. Especially since the new historicists, it has also become commonplace to read *Othello* as, among other things, a discourse on the complex relationship between colonist and colonized. From this perspective, my critique of the "narrativising" process in *Othello* supports what Greenblatt defines as "the process of fictionalization," a procedure whereby "another's reality" is transformed into a "manipulable fiction" ("Improvisation and Power" 61). Such a "process" will betray, of course "some set of operations" and "principles" that both reflect and promote the colonizer's agenda. We will recall that Iago produces Othello's life by weaving into Othello's history a seemingly logical and predictable part. This sequel is dictated not by Othello's interests but by those of Iago and of the larger Venetian community. In Foucault's terms, "a real subjection is born mechanically from a fictitious relation" (202). Commenting on racial difference in this play, Loomba has observed:

Othello is valuable as a Christian warrior, or the exotic colonial subject in the service of the state. In the Senate scene, the Venetian patriarchy displays an amazing capacity to variously construct, co-opt and exclude its "others." Brabantio is certain that the Senate will back his opposition to Othello's marriage, and if it appears strange (or remarkably liberal) that they don't, we need only to recall their concern with the Turkish threat. Othello, the warrior is strategically included as one of "us" as opposed to the Turkish "they" (50).

Greenblatt regards the chameleon "ability to capitalize on the unforeseen and transform given materials into one's own scenario," as a form of "improvisation" which on a larger scale can be viewed as "a central Renaissance mode of behaviour" whereby "the Europeans . . . again and again . . . insinuate themselves into the preexisting political, religious, even psychic, structures of the natives and . . . turn those structures to their advantage (60,63,60). In this light, Greenblatt suggests, Shakespeare the "master improviser" is neither "rebel" nor "blasphemer"; he is a conservative Elizabethan extemporizing a part of his own within his culture's "orthodoxy" (90).

While Greenblatt's conclusion accords with my reading of *Othello* thus far, we still have to consider what all this means in Shakespeare criticism, including the way that my own conclusions, for example, seem to be drawn from arguments founded largely on assumptions that are binarily opposed—black/white, drama/narrative, one/other—and which, therefore, are suspect. This limitation raises questions about the nature and roles of our own "extemporizations" as literary critics, our recourse to ideological or "colonizing" narrative productions in the continuing process of fictionalization. Here, again, Greenblatt is helpful when he observes that in order to be successful, "improvisation" must mask itself, conceal its true purposes. So, "if after centuries" Shakespeare's "improvisation" has been revealed to us as embodying an almost boundless challenge to [his] culture's every tenet, a devastation of every source" (90; emphasis mine), that is hardly surprising.

Greenblatt's claim has far-reaching implications, and what I now wish to contend is that what Shakespeare's art "reveals" to us at any given critical juncture will depend largely on the kind of story that we have need to devise. If my contention has validity, then Greenblatt's further commentary—in "The Improvisation of Power," his 1987 version of his earlier 1978 "Improvisation and Power"—has a certain efficacy in Shakespeare criticism. In this updated version, he returns to a familiar issue: Shakespeare's elusive, because constantly shifting, point of view:

> If any reductive generalization about Shakespeare's relation to his culture seems dubious, it is because his plays offer no single, timeless affirmation or denial of legitimate authority and no central, unwavering authorial presence. Shakespeare's language and themes are caught up, like the medium itself, in unsettling repetitions, committed to the shifting voices and audiences, with their shifting aesthetic assumptions and historical imperatives, that govern a living theater.
>
> (58-59)

Greenblatt concludes, therefore, that "all that can be convincingly demonstrated, is that Shakespeare relentlessly explores the relations of power in a given culture" (59). Christopher Norris would agree; in Shakespearean criticism from Johnson to Leavis he detects "a certain dominant cultural formation," "an effort" to secure "ideological containment," and "harness the unruly energies of the text to a stable order of significance," whereas what is needed, he feels, is the recognition that Shakespeare's "meaning" cannot be reduced to suit notions of "liberal-humanist faith" nor of "pristine incorrupt authority" (66).

That Shakespeare's plays have an exploratory energy cannot be denied, and unquestionably it behooves the critic to avoid reductive generalizations. Yet one wonders whether insistence on and submission to what Norris calls "the lawlessness of Shakespeare's equivocating style" (55) is not another kind of "effort of ideological containment," an attempt to release the "unruly energies of the text" from implication in its own "ideological compulsions." Equivocation is open to analysis, and equivocation, as Shakespeare himself demonstrates through Iago and Macbeth, can also be the instrument by which "meaning" is insinuated and by which the individual is (mis)led. If we have reason for celebrating this "equivocating lawlessness," therefore, we also have reason for resisting it. What about those elements, social and historical, for instance, that are discernible among its shifting accents and which enter into its discourse? Criticism's "shifting aesthetic assumptions and historical imperatives" may highlight or background these elements from time to time, but they seem to persist.

If one may judge from *Othello* and from the socio/political climate of the 1990s, "race" and attitudes toward it have altered little since the Renaissance. In fact, racist attitudes of the kind that Iago represents have deepened in ways that affect people's lives as profoundly as they affect Shakespeare's fictional characters. Colonialism, too, became a force that shaped our world irrevocably. With respect to his handling of race and colonial discourse in *Othello*, Shakespeare's so-called challenges to his culture's "every tenet" are difficult to demonstrate when *Othello*'s narrative circumscription within the dramatic text is viewed not as the result of the character's peculiar rhetorical tendency but as the playwright's brilliantly devised stratagem. For then the burden of proof shifts from apprehension of the fictional character as a living volitional being to character as an ideologically crafted device.

Further, the claim that Shakespeare poses a challenge to his culture's "every tenet" and "every source" must be assessed against the culturally unchallenged ascendancy of the Shakespeare canon and the global role that it has played in the promotion and dissemination of his culture. To say that Shakespeare's art conceals multiple levels of meaning cannot satisfactorily explain why, for instance, in spite of the blatant racist language and stereotypes that they display, works like *Othello, Titus Andronicus, Merchant of Venice,* and *The Tempest* have been handed down uncritically from generation to generation of students on various levels, not only in the West but in the colonized areas of Africa, the African Diaspora, and Asia. Presented as works not concerned with race or even otherness, such plays have been lauded as dealing unequivocally with universal human issues such as jealousy, justice, greed, betrayal, good/evil, to name a few. Neither can the notion of Shakespeare's "elusiveness" explain why contemporary American students "do not readily recognize racism as an issue within *Othello*," as Vaughan observes in her 1991 introduction to "New Perspectives" on the play (22), and wherein she suggests that perhaps these students do not see racism as a concern in their own lives.

Of course much has happened since 1991 to draw national attention to racial discourse in American Society—the highly publicized Rodney King affair and the O. J. Simpson trial come to mind. At the same time, however, it would seem that Hollywood—that trendsetter in, as well as gauge of, the American cultural mass market—has not been sensitized. In spring of 1996, a film version of *Othello* was produced by Castle Rock, a subsidiary of Columbia Studios, in which Othello's otherness and its implication in the tragedy are dismissed, and it is the jealousy theme that is emphasized. Oliver Parker, scriptwriter and director, may have pursued this angle because it produces a comfortable, totalizing and commercially prudent narrative, but the general blindness to the sociopolitical issue in the text may also have something to do with Shakespeare's reputation. Readers and viewers tend to approach the playwright with reverence; his mammoth literary stature precludes what is, for them, a diminishing, if humanizing, factor. They are caught in the kind of "cultural trap" that Lawrence Levine experienced in writing *Highbrow/Lowbrow,* his study of Shakespeare's transformation from 19th-century American popular theater to 20th-century sacred author who warranted protection from the intellectually uninitiated and/or unsuitably appreciative. As Levine explains, before he could commence his study, he had to overcome an intimidating cultural "legacy": the belief that so formidable a talent as Shakespeare could be approached "only with great humility" (4-5).

One issue that thus becomes clear as one studies Shakespeare and the critical responses to his works is the extent to which criticism itself is a stratagem, a form of what Greenblatt terms "improvisation." Literary tradition has made of Shakespeare an institution and a cultural enterprise. Under the auspices of the literary dealers in cultural commerce, Shakespeare, like the Christian God, is made to embrace all—Jew and Christian, African and European, king and slave—with impartial, universal, cultural largesse. In fact, the Shakespeare canon has provided Britain with one of its most powerful and enduring colonizing commodities, second in its appeal perhaps only to the King James Bible. On the colonial front, Shakespeare (unlike Othello in Venice) is confidently cast. Billed, installed, and received centerstage, even when Shakespeare is perceived as historically Other, he is never regarded as strange, exotic or transgressive. His works, authorized on multiple levels, speak in the here-and-now of other cultures and times with the soliloquizing, "humanizing" comprehensiveness of a Hamlet or a Lear, while with the narrative inventiveness and chameleon dominion of an Iago they locate and direct alien players in their many parts.

This unexcelled canonical power may be measured in laudatory comments such as that by Caribbean artist, V.

S. Naipaul: "all literatures are regional; perhaps it is only the placelessness of a Shakespeare . . . that makes them less so" (29). Similarly, in *The Autobiography of an Unknown Indian,* Bengali writer Nirad Chaudhuri recalls: "our first notion of Shakespeare was of a man whose writings all grown-up persons were expected to discuss and, what was even more important, to recite" (99). The extent to which the Shakespeare canon served as a cultural catechismal text for Indians can also be seen in Chaudhuri's dedicatory epigraph:

> To the Memory of the
> British Empire in India
> Which conferred Subjecthood on us
> But withheld citizenship;
> To which yet
> Every one of us threw out the challenge
> "civis Britannicus sum"
> Because
> All that was good and living
> Within us
> was made, shaped and quickened
> By the same British rule.

The astonishing because unintentional irony in this 1951 eulogy comments forcefully on the phenomenon of cultural imperialism, a subject which prompted African writer, Ngugi wa Thiong'o, to protest in 1986 that "it is the final triumph of a system of domination when the dominated start singing its virtues" (20).

Discussing the effects of a colonial identity bound by a "logic . . . embodied deep in imperialism," Ngugi contends that "regardless of the extent to which the imported literature carried the great humanist tradition of the best in Shakespeare, Goethe, Balzac, Tolstoy, Gorky, Brecht, Sholokhov, Dickens," the point to be noticed and decried is the way that European history and culture became for the African the "center" of his universe (18). Eight years earlier, writing about Rhodesia during the war for independence, Shona artist and rebel, Dambudzo Marechera, had similarly chafed: "When I was a student I had discovered late that however much I tried to be objective in my criticism of Shakespeare . . . (in *Titus Andronicus, Othello,* and *The Tempest*) . . . there was always at the back of my mind a smouldering discontent which one day would erupt" (122). Not surprisingly, therefore, some of the fiercest academic battles waged in post-independence African schools and universities have been over Shakespeare: how to dislodge the canon from its curricular eminence to make room for the indigenous literature.

Naipaul's and Chaudhuri's testimonials, as well as Ngugi's and Marechera's apostasy, attest to the insidious nature and force of ideological domination and the part that literature may play. They also call attention to the reciprocally constituted position of the dominated in relations of power and in transmission of knowledge.

This reciprocity, indeed, is what leads Foucault to object to the use of negative terms—"it excludes," "it represses"—for describing the effects of power. As he sees it, "power produces reality; it produces domains of objects and rituals of truth" (194; emphasis mine). The individual, whether dominant or subjected, and whatever we know about him/her are the products of this transmission of knowledge.

The forever elusive, the non-partisan Shakespeare—or what, by another route is but a covert re-visioning of the placeless, timeless artistis a fictional construct, a product of cultural commerce and a means for ideological containment. Though Norris is right in maintaining that the narratives we write of Shakespeare's texts are but "partial and complicated stories of our own devising" (66), we need also to note that collectively these stories have erected a monument that is at its most powerful when it most insists on a Shakespearean canon that is voiceless in both the authorial and authorizing sense. But the literary text, like all criticism itself, is bound by the politics of space and cannot escape the "disciplinary" grammar of boundaries. It is within such a context, therefore, that I have attempted to show that Shakespeare's use of narrative/dramatic strategies in *Othello* reveals not only a great artist but also an Elizabethan who explores—at a time when Europe was redefining its geographical, economic, and psychic boundaries—a topical issue: the relationship between "civilization" and Other. In his narrative (dis)position of the hero, as I see it, the dramatist takes a distinctly conservative stand: he effects artistically and ideologically a spatial reserve that discourages the very kinds of cross-boundary communication that his society fears, and in the process defines the limits of the "barbarian" located within the European "economy of power."

To this end, the conclusion of *Othello* can be seen as one of Shakespeare's most trenchant. The irony in the protagonist's anxiously attempting to relinquish in death that which he unwittingly forfeited several scenes ago—that is, his power to control his history—demonstrates as forcefully as the playwright's worldwide appeal does today that power does create. These insights make palpable the at once fragile yet compelling utility of language, of narrative constructions and their commodification, and how they function both among individuals as well as among peoples.

Works Cited

Appiah, Kwame Anthony. "Race." *Critical Terms for Literary Study*. Ed. Frank Lentricchia and Thomas McLaughlin. Chicago: U of Chicago P, 1990. 274-87.

Bayley, John. *The Uses of Division: Unit and Disharmony in Literature*. London: Chatto, 1976.

Bloom, Harold. *The Book of J.* New York: Grove, 1990.

Bradley, A. C. *Shakespearean Tragedy*. New York: St. Martins, 1985.

Calderwood, James. "Speech and Self in Othello." *Shakespeare Quarterly* 38(1987):293-303.

Chaudhuri, Nirad C. *The Autobiography of an Unknown Indian*. Berkeley: U of California P, 1951.

Cinthio, Giovanni Giraldi. "Gli Hecatommithi." *Narrative and Dramatic Sources of Shakespeare*. Ed. Geoffrey Bullough. Vol. 7. New York: Columbia UP, 1973.

D'Amico, Jack. *The Moor in Renaissance Drama*. Tampa: U of South Florida P, 1991.

Derrida, Jacques. "The Law of Genre." Mitchell 51-77.

Draper, John W. "Monster Caliban." *Caliban*. Ed. Harold Bloom. New York: Chelsea, 1992. 89-94.

Eliot, T. S. "Shakespeare and the Stoicism of Seneca." *Selected Essays*. New York: Harcourt, 1932.102-20.

Elliott, Martin. *Shakespeare's Invention of Othello*. New York: St. Martin's, 1988.

Fiedler, Leslie A. *The Stranger in Shakespeare*. London: Croom Helm, 1972.

Foucault, Michel. *Discipline and Punish: The Birth of the Prison*. Trans. Alan Sheridan. New York: Random, 1979.

Gilles, John. *Shakespeare and the Geography of Difference*. New York: Cambridge UP, 1994.

Greenblatt, Stephen J. "Improvisation and Power." *Literature and Society: Selected Papers from the English Institute*. Ed. Edward W. Said. Baltimore: John Hopkins UP, 1978. 57-99.

Hecht, Anthony. "Othello." *Othello*. Ed Harold Bloom. New York: Chelsea, 1987.123-41.

Jones, Eldred D. *The Elizabethan Image of Africa*. Washington, D.C.: Folger Shakespeare Library, 1971.

Kay, Dennis. "'To hear the rest untold': Shakespeare's Postponed Endings." *Renaissance Quarterly* 37.2(1984):207-27.

Leavis, F. R. "Diabolic Intellect and Noble Hero." *The Common Pursuit*. London: Chatto, 1952.136-59.

Levine, Lawrence W. *Highbrow/Lowbrow: The Emergence of Cultural Hierarchy in America*. Cambridge: Harvard UP, 1988.

Loomba, Ania. *Gender, Race, Renaissance Drama*. New York: St. Martin's, 1989.

Marechera, Dambudzo. *The House of Hunger: A Novella and Short Stories*. New York: Pantheon, 1978.

Melville, Herman. "Hawthorne and His Mosses." *The Apple-Tree Table and Other Sketches*. New York: Greenwood, 1922. 53-86.

Mitchell, W. J. T. ed. *On Narrative.* Chicago: U of Chicago P, 1980.

Naipaul, V. S. "Jasmine." *The Overcrowded Barracoon and Other Articles.* New York: Knopf, 1973. 23-29.

Norris, Christopher. "Post-structuralist Shakespeare: Text and Ideology." *Alternative Shakespeare.* Ed. John Dukakis. New York: Methuen, 1985. 47-66.

Rymer, Thomas. *A Short View of Tragedy.* New York: Garland, 1974.

Said, Edward. *Culture and Imperialism.* New York: Random, 1994.

Scholes, Robert. "Language, Narrative, and Anti-Narrative." Mitchell 200-08.

Scholes, Robert, and Robert Kellog. *The Nature of Narrative.* New York: Oxford UP, 1966.

Shakespeare, William. *The Riverside Shakespeare.* New York: Houghton Mifflin, 1997.

Smith, Barbara Hernstein. "Narrative Versions, Narrative Theories." Mitchell 209-32.

Thiong'o, Ngugi wa. *Decolonizing the Mind: The Politics of Language in African Literature.* Portsmouth: Heinemann, 1986.

Todorov, Tzvetan. *The Fantastic: A Structural Approach to a Literary Genre.* Trans. Richard Howard. Ithaca: Cornell UP, 1973.

Traub, Valerie. *Desire and Anxiety: Circulations of Sexuality in Shakespearean Drama.* New York: Routledge, 1992.

Vaughan, Virginia Mason. *Othello: A Contextual History.* New York: Cambridge UP, 1994.

————. "Introduction." *Othello: New Perspectives.* Ed. Virginia Mason Vaughan and Kent Cartwright. Teaneck: Fairleigh Dickinson UP, 1991. 13-25.

Weimann, Robert. *Shakespeare and the Popular Tradition in the Theater.* Baltimore: Johns Hopkins UP, 1978.

White, Hayden. *The Content of the Form.* Baltimore: Johns Hopkins UP, 1987.

CHARACTER STUDIES

Albert Gerard (essay date 1957)

SOURCE: Gerard, Albert. "'Egregiously an Ass': The Dark Side of the Moor. A View of Othello's Mind." In *Aspects of* Othello: *Articles Reprinted from* Shakespeare Survey, edited by Kenneth Muir and Philip Edwards, pp. 12-20. Cambridge: Cambridge University Press, 1977.

[*In the following essay, originally published in 1957, Gerard evaluates Othello as a "barbarian" figure by considering the Moor's failure to intellectually assess his own flaws, which ultimately leads to his "tragedy of groundless jealousy."*]

> It is through the malice of this earthly air, that only by being guilty of Folly does mortal man in many cases arrive at the perception of sense.
>
> Herman Melville

There are three schools of *Othello* criticism. The most recent of these is the symbolic school, chiefly represented by G. Wilson Knight and J. I. M. Stewart, who have endeavoured to explain away the difficulties inherent in the traditional psychological interpretation of the Moor by turning the play into a mythic image of the eternal struggle between good and evil, embodied in the noble aspirations of Othello and the cunning cynicism of Iago.[1] This school arose in part as a reaction to an attitude mainly exemplified by Stoll, though already initiated by Rymer and Bridges, according to whom this tragedy ought to be treated as a purely dramatic phenomenon, created by Shakespeare for the sake of sensation and emotional effect.[2] The third school is the traditional school of naturalistic interpretation; it branches off into two main streams: the Romantic critics, from Coleridge to Bradley, take Othello at his own valuation, and seem to experience no difficulty in assuming that his greatness of mind should blind him to Iago's evil purposes; more recent students, however, tend to have a more realistic view of the Moor and to stress the flaws in his character: T. S. Eliot speaks of *bovarysme* and self-dramatization, while his homonym, G. R. Elliott, asserts that the main tragic fault in Othello is pride.[3]

One way to solve this crux of Shakespeare criticism is to use the inductive method recently advocated by R. S. Crane, and look for the "particular shaping principle (which) we must suppose to have governed Shakespeare's construction of the tragedy" through "a comparison of the material data of action, character, and motive supplied to Shakespeare by Cinthio's *novella* with what happened to these in the completed play".[4] By analysing the way Shakespeare used (or neglected) some of the data provided by Cinthio, the way he transmuted a vaudevillesque melodrama into one of the unforgettable tragedies in world literature, we may perhaps hope to gain a fresh insight into what he saw in it, why he was attracted by it and what he meant to do with it.

Erring Barbarian and Credulous Fool

This method is the one already applied by H. B. Charlton in his Clark Lectures at Cambridge, 1946-7.[5] According to Charlton, one of the most significant alterations made by Shakespeare to Cinthio's story consists in the strengthened emphasis upon the difference in manners and outlook between Desdemona and her husband. Though this motif is barely alluded to by Cinthio, Shakespeare seized on the hint and expanded it to meaningful proportions. The most conspicuous, though, admittedly, the most superficial, aspect of this difference is the complexion of the Moor. In the original tale, there is only one allusion to Othello's blackness. In the play, his black skin and thick lips are mentioned time and again. As it is obviously impossible to retain the Romantic view that Othello is not a real Negro,[6] we can safely assume that the blackness of the Moor, though it did not strike the Italian writer, appealed to the imagination of Shakespeare, who found it significant in a way that Cinthio, probably, could not even conceive.

Where is this significance to be found? I do not feel very happy about Charlton's suggestion that Shakespeare wanted to stress the physical and psychological antinomies between Othello and Desdemona because "the situation created by the marriage of a man and a woman who are widely different in race, in tradition and in customary way of life" was, at the time, "a particular problem of immediate contemporary interest". There does not seem to be any compelling evidence that such a problem was especially acute in the early seventeenth century, so that it may be worth while to try another line of interpretation.

In *The Dream of Learning*, D. G. James has made excellent use of the changes which Shakespeare introduced into the personality of Belleforest's Hamlet so as to make it plausible that this young Danish chieftain should appear to all ages as the embodiment of the man of thought, or, to use a more up-to-date expression, of the intellectual. Now, if Shakespeare turned Hamlet into an intellectual, it is equally true that he reversed the process in his handling of Othello. Not only does Iago call the Moor an "ass" and a "fool", not only does Othello concur with this unfavourable view in the last stages of the action, but the action itself is hinged upon Othello's obtuseness. This is quite palpable in III, iii, and we may be confident that if Partridge had seen *Othello* performed, he would have felt, at that moment, like jumping on to the stage and telling the Moor not to be an ass. Othello's muddle-headedness on this occasion is so extreme that critics like Rymer, Bridges and Stoll have indeed found it incredible and psychologically untrue. We might draw up a formidable list of Othello's glaring mistakes as exemplified in this scene. A few examples will suffice.

First, he must know that Iago wanted to become his lieutenant: he ought to be suspicious of his accusations against Cassio. Even though he believes, like everybody else, in Iago's honesty,[7] he must know that his Ancient has a vulgar mind, and he should not allow his imagination to be impressed by Iago's obscene pictures of Desdemona. It is also remarkable that he does not try to argue the matter with Iago; in the early stages of his evolution, he simply proclaims his faith in Desdemona's chastity, but he cannot find any sensible argument with which to counter Iago's charges. It is true that he asks for some material proof of his wife's treachery, but he never bothers to inquire about the value of the "evidence" produced by Iago. Finally, once he is convinced of Desdemona's unfaithfulness, surely the next step is to go and discuss things with her or with Cassio; this he never does. Few people would make such a hopeless mess of the situation.

Whereas Shakespeare had keyed Hamlet's intelligence to the highest possible pitch, he deliberately stressed Othello's lack of intellectual acumen, psychological insight, and even plain common sense. In the play, Othello's negroid physiognomy is simply the emblem of a difference that reaches down to the deepest levels of personality. If Hamlet is over-civilized, Othello is, in actual fact, what Iago says he is, a "barbarian" (I, iii, 363).

Othello's fundamental barbarousness becomes clear when we consider his religious beliefs. His superficial acceptance of Christianity should not blind us to his fundamental paganism. To quote again from Charlton's study, "when his innermost being is stirred to its depths", he has "gestures and phrases" which belong rather "to dim pagan cults than to any form of Christian worship". These primitive elements receive poetic and dramatic shape in the aura of black magic which at times surrounds Othello. Though Brabantio is wide of the mark when he charges the Moor with resorting to witchcraft in order to seduce his daughter, it is nevertheless true, as Mark Van Doren has said, that "an infusion of magic does tincture the play",[8] and it comes to the fore in the handkerchief episode. The magic in *Othello* results from his acquiescence in obscure savage beliefs. It is an elemental force at work in the soul of the hero. It helps to build up the Moor as a primitive type.

Here again, we wonder why Shakespeare was attracted by such a hero. A twentieth-century dramatist might be interested in the clash of two cultures, which occurs in the mind of Othello. But though this aspect of the situation is not altogether ignored by Shakespeare, his main concern lies in another direction. The fact is that this tragedy of deception, self-deception, unjustified jealousy and criminal revenge demanded such a hero.

The crime-columns of the newspapers teach us that the people who murder their wives out of jealousy are generally mental defectives. Ordinary sensible people simply cannot believe that such a crime should deserve such a punishment. It was impossible for Shakespeare to take a subnormal type as a hero for his tragedy. Tennessee Williams could do it, I suppose, but not Shakespeare, because the Renaissance tradition required that tragedy should chronicle the actions of aristocratic characters. He might have chosen as his hero some nobleman with an inflated sense of honour, but then he probably could not have made him gullible enough to swallow Iago's lies. *And it is precisely the gullibility that is essential.* Shakespeare was not intent on emulating Heywood's achievement of the year before in *A Woman Killed With Kindness. Othello* is not a tragedy of jealousy: it is a tragedy of *groundless* jealousy.

So, in Cinthio's tale, Shakespeare found reconciled with a maximum of credibility the requirements of Renaissance tragedy and the necessities of his own private purpose: a character with a high rank in society, with a noble heart, and with an under-developed mind. It seems therefore reasonable to suppose that if Shakespeare was interested in Othello, it was not primarily because he is a barbarian, but because this noble savage provided him with a plausible example, suitable for use within the framework of the Renaissance view of tragedy, of a psychological characteristic that makes Othello the very antithesis of Hamlet. Othello's intellectual shortcomings have not passed unnoticed by students of the play, but the importance of this feature for its total meaning has not received the attention it deserves. We may say without exaggeration that Othello's lack of intellectual power is the basic element in his character. It is a necessary pre-requisite for his predicament. It is essential to the development of the situation as Shakespeare intended it to develop. And it may also throw some light on the nature of Shakespeare's tragic inspiration.

Steps to Self-Knowledge

At the beginning of the play, Othello appears as a noble figure, generous, composed, self-possessed. Besides, he is glamorously happy, both as a general and as a husband. He seems to be a fully integrated man, a great personality at peace with itself. But if we care to scrutinize this impressive and attractive façade, we find that there is a crack in it, which might be described as follows: it is the happiness of a spoilt child, not of a mature mind; it is the brittle wholeness of innocence; it is pre-conscious, pre-rational, pre-moral. Othello has not yet come to grips with the experience of inner crisis. He has had to overcome no moral obstacles. He has not yet left the chamber of maiden-thought, and is still blessedly unaware of the burden of the mystery.

Of course, the life of a general, with its tradition of obedience and authority, is never likely to give rise to acute moral crises—especially at a time when war

crimes had not yet been invented. But even Othello's love affair with Desdemona, judging by his own report, seems to have developed smoothly, without painful moral searchings of any kind. Nor is there for him any heart-rending contradiction between his love and his career: Desdemona is even willing to share the austerity of his flinty couch, so that he has every reason to believe that he will be allowed to make the best of both worlds.

Yet, at the core of this monolithic content, there is at least one ominous contradiction which announces the final disintegration of his personality: the contradiction between his obvious openheartedness, honesty and self-approval, and the fact that he does not think it beneath his dignity to court and marry Desdemona secretly. This contradiction is part and parcel of Shakespeare's conscious purpose. As Allardyce Nicoll has observed, there is no such secrecy in Cinthio's tale, where, instead, the marriage occurs openly, though in the teeth of fierce parental opposition.[9]

Highly significant, too, is the fact that he does not seem to feel any remorse for this most peculiar procedure. When at last he has to face the irate Brabantio, he gives no explanation, offers no apology for his conduct. Everything in his attitude shows that he is completely unaware of infringing the *mores* of Venetian society, the ethical code of Christian behaviour, and the sophisticated conventions of polite morality. Othello quietly thinks of himself as a civilized Christian and a prominent citizen of Venice, certainly not as a barbarian (see II, iii, 170-2). He shares in Desdemona's illusion that his true visage is in his mind.

Beside the deficient understanding of the society into which he has made his way, the motif of the secret marriage then also suggests a definite lack of self-knowledge on Othello's part. His first step towards "perception of sense" about himself occurs in the middle of Act III. While still trying to resist Iago's innuendoes, Othello exclaims:

> Excellent wretch! Perdition catch my soul,
> But I do love thee! and when I love thee not,
> Chaos is come again.
>
> (III, iii, 90-2)

This word, "again", is perhaps the most unexpected word that Shakespeare could have used here. It is one of the most pregnant words in the whole tragedy. It indicates (*a*) Othello's dim sense that his life before he fell in love with Desdemona was in a state of chaos, in spite of the fact that he was at the time quite satisfied with it, and (*b*) his conviction that his love has redeemed him from chaos, has lifted him out of his former barbarousness. Such complacency shows his total obliviousness of the intricacies, the subtleties and the dangers of moral and spiritual growth. In this first anagnorisis, Othello realizes that he has lived so far in a sphere of spontaneous bravery and natural honesty, but he assumes without any further questionings that his love has gained him easy access to the sphere of moral awareness, of high spiritual existence. In fact, he assumes that his super-ego has materialised, suddenly and without tears. Hence, of course, the impressive self-assurance of his demeanour in circumstances which would be most embarrassing to any man gifted with more accurate self-knowledge.

This first anagnorisis is soon followed by another one, in which Othello achieves some sort of recognition of what has become of him after his faith in Desdemona has been shattered. The short speech he utters then marks a new step forward in his progress to self-knowledge:

> I had been happy, if the general camp,
> Pioners and all, had tasted her sweet body,
> So I had nothing known. O, now, for ever
> Farewell the tranquil mind! farewell content!
> Farewell the plumed troop, and the big wars,
> That make ambition virtue! O, farewell!
> . . . . .
> Farewell! Othello's occupation's gone!
>
> (III, iii, 345-57)

The spontaneous outcry of the first three lines results from Othello's disturbed awareness that the new world he has entered into is one of (to him) unmanageable complexity. He is now facing a new kind of chaos, and he wishes he could take refuge in an ignorance similar to his former condition of moral innocence. The pathetic childishness of this ostrich-like attitude is proportionate in its intensity to the apparent monolithic quality of his previous complacency.

What follows sounds like a *non sequitur*. Instead of this farewell to arms, we might have expected some denunciation of the deceitful aspirations that have led him to this quandary, coupled, maybe, with a resolution to seek oblivion in renewed military activity. But we may surmise that his allusion to "the general camp", reminding him of his "occupation", turns his mind away from his immediate preoccupations. The transition occurs in the line

> Farewell the tranquil mind! farewell content!

which carries ambivalent implications. The content he has now lost is not only the "absolute content" his soul enjoyed as a result of his love for Desdemona: it is also the content he had known previously, at the time when he could rejoice in his "unhoused free condition". This was the content of innocence and spontaneous adjustment to life. There is no recovering it, for, in this respect, he reached a point of no return when he glimpsed the truly chaotic nature of that state of innocence.

The fact that Othello starts talking about himself in the third person is of considerable significance. G. R. Elliott has noticed that the words have "a piercing primitive appeal: he is now simply a name".[10] Besides, in this sudden ejaculation, there is a note of childish self-pity that reminds one of the first lines of the speech. But the main point is that it marks the occurrence of a deep dichotomy in Othello's consciousness of himself. As he had discarded his former self as an emblem of "chaos", so now he discards the super-ego that he thought had emerged into actual existence as a result of his love. It is as if that man known by the name of Othello was different from the one who will be speaking henceforward. The Othello of whom he speaks is the happy husband of Desdemona, the civilized Christian, the worthy Venetian, the illusory super-ego; but he is also the noble-spirited soldier and the natural man who guesses at heaven. That man has now disappeared, and the "I" who speaks of him is truly the savage Othello, the barbarian stripped of his wishful thinking, who gives himself up to jealousy, black magic and cruelty, the man who coarsely announces that he will "chop" his wife "into messes", the man who debases his magnificent oratory by borrowing shamelessly from Iago's lecherous vocabulary.

Thus Othello, whom love had brought from pre-rational, pre-moral satisfaction and adjustment to life to moral awareness and a higher form of "content", is now taken from excessive complacency and illusory happiness to equally excessive despair and nihilism. These are his steps to self-knowledge. That they should drive him to such alternative excesses gives the measure of his lack of judgment.

No Marriage of True Minds

From the purely psychological point of view of character-analysis, critics have always found it difficult satisfactorily to account for Othello's steep downfall. That it would have been easy, as Robert Bridges wrote, for Shakespeare "to have provided a more reasonable ground for Othello's jealousy", is obvious to all reasonable readers.[11] The fact that Othello's destruction occurs through the agency of Iago has induced the critics in the Romantic tradition to make much of what Coleridge has called Iago's "superhuman art", which, of course, relieves the Moor of all responsibility and deprives the play of most of its interest on the ethical and psychological level. More searching analyses, however, have shown that Iago is far from being a devil in disguise.[12] And T. S. Eliot has exposed the Moor as a case of *bovarysme,* or "the human will to see things as they are not",[13] while Leo Kirschbaum has denounced him as "a romantic idealist, who considers human nature superior to what it actually is".[14]

For our examination of *Othello* as a study in the relationships between the intellect and the moral life, it is interesting to note that the ultimate responsibility for the fateful development of the plot rests with a flaw in Othello himself. There is no "reasonable ground" for his jealousy; or, to put it somewhat differently, Shakespeare did not chose to provide any "reasonable" ground for it. The true motive, we may safely deduce, must be unreasonable. Yet, I find it difficult to agree that the Moor "considers human nature superior to what it actually is": this may be true of his opinion of Iago, but Desdemona is really the emblem of purity and trustworthiness that he initially thought her to be. Nor can we justifiably speak of his "*will* to see things as they are not" (though these words might actually fit Desdemona); in his confusion and perplexity there is no opportunity for his will to exert itself in any direction. The basic element that permits Othello's destiny to evolve the way it does is his utter *inability* to grasp the actual. If we want to locate with any accuracy the psychological origin of what F. R. Leavis has called his "readiness to respond" to Iago's fiendish suggestions, we cannot escape the conclusion that his gullibility makes manifest his lack of rationality, of psychological insight and of mere common sense, and that it is a necessary product of his undeveloped mind.

Othello has to choose between trusting Iago and trusting Desdemona. This is the heart of the matter, put in the simplest possible terms. The question, then, is: why does he rate Iago's honesty higher than Desdemona's? If it is admitted that Iago is not a symbol of devilish skill in evil-doing, but a mere fallible villain, the true answer can only be that Othello does not know his own wife.

More than a century of sentimental criticism based on the Romantic view of Othello as the trustful, chivalrous and sublime lover, has blurred our perception of his feeling for Desdemona. The quality of his "love" has recently been gone into with unprecedented thoroughness by G. R. Elliott, who points out that the Moor's speech to the Duke and Senators (I, iii) shows that "his affection for her, though fixed and true, is comparatively superficial".[15] Othello sounds, indeed, curiously detached about Desdemona. His love is clearly subordinated, at that moment, to his soldierly pride. If he asks the Duke to let her go to Cyprus with him, it is because *she* wants it, it is "to be free and bounteous to her mind". In the juxtaposition of Desdemona's and Othello's speeches about this, there is an uncomfortable suggestion that his love is not at all equal to hers, who "did love the Moor to live with him", and that he is not interested in her as we feel he ought to be. At a later stage the same self-centredness colours his vision of Desdemona as the vital source of his soul's life and happiness: his main concern lies with the "joy" (II, i, 186), the "absolute content" (II, i, 193), the salvation (III, iii, 90-1) of his own soul, not with Desdemona as a woman in love, a human person. It lies with *his* love and the changes his

love has wrought in him, rather than with the object of his love. It is not surprising, then, that he should know so little about his wife's inner life as to believe the charges raised by Iago.

On the other hand, his attitude to Desdemona is truly one of idealization, but in a very limited, one might even say philosophical, sense. Coleridge wrote that "Othello does not kill Desdemona in jealousy, but in the belief that she, his angel, had fallen from the heaven of her native innocence".[16] But Coleridge failed to stress the most important point, which is that this belief is mistaken. Desdemona is *not* "impure and worthless", she has *not* fallen from the heaven of her native innocence. Othello is unable to recognize this, and his failure is thus primarily an intellectual failure.

His attitude to Desdemona is different from that of the "romantic idealist" who endows his girl with qualities which she does not possess. Desdemona does have all the qualities that her husband expects to find in her. What matters to him, however, is not Desdemona as she is, but Desdemona as a symbol, or, in other words, it is his vision of Desdemona.

In his *Essay on Man,* Ernst Cassirer has the following remark about the working of the primitive mind:

> In primitive thought, it is still very difficult to differentiate between the two spheres of being and meaning. They are constantly being confused: a symbol is looked upon as if it were endowed with magical or metaphysical powers.[17]

That is just what has happened to Othello: in Desdemona he has failed to differentiate between the human being and the angelic symbol. Or rather, he has overlooked the woman in his preoccupation with the angel. She is to him merely the emblem of his highest ideal, and their marriage is merely the ritual of his admission into her native world, into her spiritual sphere of values. Because he is identifying "the two spheres of being and meaning", he is possessed by the feeling that neither these values nor his accession to them have any actual existence outside her: his lack of psychological insight is only matched by his lack of rational power.

The Neo-Platonic conceit that the lover's heart and soul have their dwelling in the person of the beloved is used by Othello in a poignantly literal sense (IV, ii, 57-60). If she fails him, everything fails him. If she is not pure, then purity does not exist. If she is not true to his ideal, that means that his ideal is an illusion. If it can be established that she does not belong to that world in which he sees her enshrined, that means that there is no such world. She becomes completely and explicitly identified with all higher spiritual values when he says:

> If she be false, O! then heaven mocks itself!
>
> (III, iii, 278)

Hence the apocalyptic quality of his nihilism and despair.

The fundamental tragic fault in the Moor can therefore be said to lie in the shortcomings of his intellect. His moral balance is without any rational foundation. He is entirely devoid of the capacity for abstraction. He fails to make the right distinction between the sphere of meaning, of the abstract, the ideal, the universal, and the sphere of being, of the concrete, the actual, the singular.

When Othello is finally made to see the truth, he recognizes the utter lack of wisdom (V, ii, 344) which is the mainspring of his tragedy, and, in the final anagnorisis, he sees himself for what he is: a "fool" (V, ii, 323). The full import of the story is made clear in Othello's last speech, which is so seldom given the attention it merits that it may be well to quote it at some length:

> I pray you, in your letters,
> When you shall these unlucky deeds relate,
> Speak of me as I am; nothing extenuate,
> Nor set down aught in malice: then, must you speak
> Of one that loved not wisely but too well;
> Of one not easily jealous, but being wrought
> Perplex'd in the extreme; of one whose hand,
> Like the base Indian, threw a pearl away
> Richer than all his tribe; of one whose subdued eyes,
> Albeit unused to the melting mood,
> Drop tears as fast as the Arabian trees
> Their medicinal gum. Set you down this;
> And say besides, that in Aleppo once,
> Where a malignant and a turban'd Turk
> Beat a Venetian and traduced the state,
> I took by the throat the circumcised dog,
> And smote him, thus. (*Stabs himself*)
>
> (V, ii, 340-56)

One may find it strange that Shakespeare should have introduced at the end of Othello's last speech this apparently irrelevant allusion to a trivial incident in the course of which the Moor killed a Turk who had insulted Venice. But if we care to investigate the allegorical potentialities of the speech, we find that it is not a mere fit of oratorical self-dramatization: it clarifies the meaning of the play as a whole. There is a link between the pearl, the Venetian and Desdemona: taken together, they are an emblem of beauty, moral virtue, spiritual richness and civilized refinement. And there is a link between the "base Indian", the "malignant Turk" and Othello himself: all three are barbarians: all three have shown themselves unaware of the true value and dignity of what lay within their reach. Othello has thrown his pearl away, like the Indian. In so doing, he has insulted, like the Turk, everything that Venice and Desdemona stand for. As the Turk "traduced the State", so did Othello misrepresent to himself that heaven of which Desdemona was the sensuous image.

S. L. Bethell has left us in no doubt that the manner of Othello's death was intended by Shakespeare as an indication that the hero is doomed to eternal damnation.[18] Such a view provides us with a suitable climax for this tragedy. Othello has attained full consciousness of his barbarian nature; yet, even that ultimate flash of awareness does not lift him up above his true self. He remains a barbarian to the very end, and condemns his own soul to the everlasting torments of hell in obeying the same primitive sense of rough-handed justice that had formerly prompted him to kill Desdemona: it is a natural culmination to what a Swiss critic has aptly called "eine Tragödie der Verirrung".[19]

Notes

1. G. Wilson Knight, 'The *Othello* Music' in *The Wheel of Fire* (1930; fourth edition, 1949). J. I. M. Stewart, *Character and Motive in Shakespeare* (1949).

2. For a close discussion of the views of Rymer, Bridges and Stoll, cf. Stewart, *op. cit.* [*Character and Motive in Shakespeare* (1949)].

3. T. S. Eliot, 'Shakespeare and the Stoicism of Seneca', in *Selected Essays* (1932); G. R. Elliott, *Flaming Minister. A Study of Othello* (Duke University Press, Durham, 1953).

4. R. S. Crane, *The Languages of Criticism and the Structure of Poetry* (Toronto, 1953), p. 147. The quotations are taken from a discussion of R. B. Heilman's method in his 'More Fair than Black: Light and Dark in *Othello*', *Essays in Criticism*, 1 (1951), 315-35.

5. H. B. Charlton, 'Othello', in *Shakespearian Tragedy* (Cambridge, 1948).

6. Cf. Coleridge, *Lectures and Notes on Shakespere and Other English Poets* (1904), p. 386.

7. Levin L. Schucking, in *Shakespeare und der Tragödienstil seiner Zeit* (Bern, 1947) considers Othello's belief in Iago's honesty as "eine der Hauptschwächen in der Konstruction der Fabel", for, he says "es ist höchst unwahrscheinlich, dasz Othello nach so langem Zusammenleben im Kriegsdienst sich derart über den bösartigen Character seines Fahnrichs im unklaren geblieben sein sollte" (p. 68). The general consensus about Iago's honesty, carefully stressed by Shakespeare, should nullify this particular criticism.

8. Mark Van Doren, *Shakespeare* (New York, 1953), p. 196.

9. Allardyce Nicoll, *Shakespeare* (1952), p. 144.

10. G. R. Elliott, *op. cit.* [*Flaming Minister. A Study of Othello* (Duke University Press, Durham, 1953).] p. 130, n. 30.

11. R. Bridges, 'The Influence of the Audience on Shakespeare's Drama' in *Collected Essays,* 1 (1927).

12. Cf. G. R. Elliott, *op. cit. passim* [*Flaming Minister. A Study of Othello* (Duke University Press, Durham, 1953);] J. I. M. Stewart, *op. cit.* [*Character and Motive in Shakespeare* (1949)] p. 103; and F. R. Leavis, 'Diabolic Intellect and the Noble Hero', in *The Common Pursuit* (1952), p. 140.

13. T. S. Eliot, *op. cit.* ['Shakespeare and the Stoicism of Seneca', in *Selected Essays* (1932).]

14. In *ELH,* December 1944 (quoted by J. I. M. Stewart, *op. cit.* [*Character and Motive in Shakespeare* (1949)] p. 104.)

15. G. R. Elliott, *op. cit.* [*Flaming Minister. A Study of Othello* (Duke University Press, Durham, 1953).] p. 34.

16. Coleridge, *op. cit.* [*Lectures and Notes on Shakespere and Other English Poets* (1904)] pp. 393 and 529.

17. E. Cassirer, *An Essay on Man* (New Haven, 1944), p. 57.

18. S. L. Bethell, 'Shakespeare's Imagery: The Diabolic Images in *Othello*', pp. 29-47 of this volume.

19. R. Fricker, *Kontrast und Polarität in den Charakterbildern Shakespeares* (Bern, 1951).

Leah Scragg (essay date 1968)

SOURCE: Scragg, Leah. "Iago—Vice or Devil?" *Shakespeare Survey* 21 (1968): 53-65.

[*In the following essay, Scragg contends that Iago, who exhibits distinct affinities with the allegorical figure of Vice found in medieval mystery and morality plays, should more properly be said to derive from stage representations of the Devil.*]

For a considerable time critics have traced the characteristics displayed by Iago back to the Vice, the artful seducer of the Morality plays. Alois Brandl in 1898 included Iago among the descendants of the Vice, although apparently associating that figure with the Devil:

> If we follow the role of Vice in the other English tragedies of this period and the following decades, we still find Haphazard in 'Appius and Virginia' as well as Ambidexter in 'Cambyses' as representatives of the old Morality-type, i.e. as seducer and hypocrite. In Marlowe's Mephistopheles the original diabolic character

of this figure once more reaches full expression; in Marlowe's black Ithimor, Shakespeare's Aaron and Iago it is still strongly to be felt;[1]

and Cushman in 1900, while showing the utter disparity between the nature of Vice and Devil, explicitly endorses Brandl's derivation of Iago from the former and would add other Shakespearean villains to the list:

> Why not also add to these Edmund in *Lear,* Richard III, Don John in *Much Ado About Nothing* and Antonio in *The Tempest*?[2]

The most recent and convincing exponent of this view is Bernard Spivack (*Shakespeare and the Allegory of Evil,* New York, 1958), who examined the typical characteristics of the Vice, proved that figures displaying similar characteristics were found in a number of Elizabethan plays and having shown Iago possessed the same attributes, concluded that he was, in fact, a descendant of the Vice playing his traditionally motiveless role beneath a mask of motivated hostility. In this way, the difficulties encountered in the play, particularly the ambiguous nature of Iago's motivation, are seen as the result of an attempt to 'translate' the popular, but amoral, seducer of the Morality stage into realistic Elizabethan-Jacobean drama.

However, if the characteristics which are thought to be typical of the Vice, and which are used by these critics as a kind of hallmark to detect his literary progeny, were found before, during and after the period of the popularity of the Morality play in the figure of the Devil, it would be equally arguable that it is to the Devil, not the Vice, that Iago is indebted. In this case he would revert once more from the unmotivated seducer to the motivated antagonist—from the amoral to the immoral. In the first part of this article I shall therefore attempt to show that Vice-like characteristics are not restricted to amoral beings, and in the second to suggest that the evidence within *Othello* points to an association between Iago and the powers of darkness which at least confirms his moral nature, if not proving his derivation from a traditional stage presentation of the Devil.

I

The attributes which typify 'The Vice', the figure which emerged after 1500 from the group of vices engaged in the psychomachia of the early Morality plays, and which are said to characterize his descendants, are as follows.[3] He was a gay, light-hearted intriguer, existing on intimate terms with his audience, whom he invited to witness a display of his ability to reduce a man from a state of grace to utter ruin. He invariably posed as the friend of his victim, often disguising himself for the purpose, and always appearing to devote himself to his friend's welfare. He treated his seduction as 'sport' combining mischief with merriment, triumphing over his fallen adversary and glorying in his skill in deceit. So far the analogy with Iago is obvious. He provided for his audience both humour and homiletic instruction. Above all, he was an amoral being whose behaviour was completely unmotivated—he simply demonstrated the nature of the abstraction he represented. In this respect, as Spivack points out, the Devil and the Vice are completely distinct:

> The purposes of the Devil are those of a complex moral being. The whole purpose of the Vice is to illustrate his name and nature and to reflect upon the audience the single moral idea he personifies. The former acts to achieve his desires, the latter only to show what he is. Between the two no ethical continuity is possible because in the nature of a personification there is nothing that is subject to ethical definition.[4]

But although entirely disparate ethically, in their dramatic presentation the Vice and the Devil have much in common, those characteristics which I have outlined as typical of the Vice being found in the Devil of the Mystery plays over a hundred years before the emergence of the allegorical figure—as the motivated antagonist who leaped on to the stage at York, pushing the audience aside, reveals:

> Make rome be-lyve, and late me gang,
> Who makis here all þis þrang?
> High you hense! high myght ȝou hang
> right with a roppe.
> I drede me þat I dwelle to lang
> to do a jape.

(XXII, 1-6)[5]

This is the introduction to Satan's temptation of Christ in the wilderness, but the tones in which the Devil speaks are exactly those of the Vice, with his direct, familiar relationship with the audience, his vivacity and emphasis on what is to take place as a 'jape'. He too confides in the audience, relating the way in which he delights to bring men to eternal pain (XXII, 7-12), why he intends to tempt Christ—i.e. his motivation (XXII, 19-22), what he intends towards his victim (XXII, 39-42) and how he is going to attempt it (XXII, 43-8). In other words he invites us to witness a display of his boasted ability to bring men to sin. When he actually approaches Christ, he poses as his friend:

> Þou hast fasted longe, I wene,
> I wolde now som mete wer sene
> For olde acqueyntaunce vs by-twene,
> Thy-selue wote howe.
> Ther sall noman witte what I mene
> but I and þou.

(XXII, 61-6)

The Devil is naturally unsuccessful and his actions are limited by the necessity of following the Biblical narrative, but nevertheless, in this earliest surviving dramatic

presentation of a tempter on the English stage, the attitudes of the later Vice figure are already evinced. The intimacy with the audience, the self-explanatory, demonstrative role for homiletic effect, the attitude to the attack on the spiritual welfare of the victim as 'sport', the device of posing as the friend of the person to be betrayed, are all present. The only, and very significant, difference lies in the fact that the Devil is implicitly and explicitly motivated. Since the York cycle was first presented between 1362 and 1376 and was played until 1568[6] this kind of antagonist was seen on the English stage long before the emergence of the Vice after 1500 and continued to be seen throughout the period of the popularity of the Morality play.

The Chester cycle, which probably originated between 1377 and 1382 and which was played until 1575, does not present such a vivacious Devil as the York plays but elements which are to be typical of the Vice may be seen—notably the emphasis on disguise:

> A manner of an Adder is in this place,
> that wynges like a byrd she hase,
> feete as an Adder, a maydens face;
> her kinde I will take;

(II, 193-6)[7]

and the pose as the friend of the victim:

> Take of this fruite and assaie:
> It is good meate, I dare laye,
> and, but thou fynde yt to thy paye,
> say that I am false.

(II, 233-6)

Similarly the attitude to the temptation of Christ as a game is still present:

> a gammon I will assay.

(XII, 4)

The play of the Last Judgement in the Wakefield cycle (originated 1390-1410) also presents vivacious Devils eager to destroy their human victims. Their chief, Tutivillus, introduces himself on his first entrance, priding himself on his dexterity in entrapping the unwary (XXX, 211-21),[8] and commenting with cynical glee on the lasciviousness and general corruption of the times which give him his opportunity to win souls (XXX, 273-304). Although a Devil, Tutivillus does not comment in any way on the motive for his antagonism. He shows no cause for his hostility towards mankind—his whole being is involved in an attitude of merriment, almost glee, not hatred and resentment. His joyful, triumphant, imaginary welcoming of the sinners to hell is typical:

> ye lurdans and lyars / mychers and thefes,
> fflytars and flyars / that all men reprefes,

Spolars, extorcyonars / Welcom, my lefes!
ffals Iurars and vsurars / to symony that clevys,
   To tell;
hasardars and dysars,
ffals dedys forgars,
Slanderars, bakbytars,
   All vnto hell.

(XXX, 359-67)

He has the energy, life and homiletic function which are claimed to be typical of the Vice, together with his professional pride in his work:

I am oone of youre ordir / and oone of youre sons;
I stande at my tristur / when othere men shones.

(XXX, 207-8)

And like the Vice these Devils blend comedy and homiletics as they triumph over their fallen victims:

SECUNDUS DEMON:

   Where is the gold and the good / that ye gederd
      togedir?
   The mery menee that yode / hider and thedir?

TUTIUILLUS:

   Gay gyrdyls, iaggid hode / prankyd gownes, whedir?
   Haue ye wit or ye wode / ye broght not hider
   Bot sorowe,
   And youre synnes in youre nekkys.

PRIMUS DEMON:

   I beshrew thaym that rekkys! He comes to late that
      bekkys youre bodyes to borow.

(XXX, 550-8)

The Devil is beginning to appear on the stage with the motive for his antagonism taken for granted, while he simply exhibits his delight in evil and his dexterity in entrapping souls.

The Devil of the single pageant extant from the New-castle plays, which originated before 1462 and were played until 1567-8, has similar characteristics. He exists on intimate terms with his audience, confiding to them his plans to corrupt Noah's wife (lines 109-13).[9] He too exhibits a light-hearted approach to his deception and insinuates himself into the confidence of his dupe. His bland greeting to Mrs Noah, whom he hopes to destroy, 'Rest well, rest well, my own dere dame' (line 115), might well have been spoken by innumerable later Vice figures.

Quires N, P, Q, R, of the *Ludus Coventriae*[10] (originated *c*. 1400-*c*. 1450) probably had a separate existence before their inclusion in the cycle and the Devil of these sections is of a very different kind from the demon filled with overt hatred found in other parts. He shares the characteristics noted in earlier Devils, particularly the intimacy with the audience to whom he introduces himself (26, 1-2), recounts with pride his aim in the world:

I am Norsshere of synne · to þe confusyon of man
To bryng hym to my dongeon · þer in fyre to dwelle

(26, 5-6)

and recites his past triumphs and his skill in entrapping souls (26, 23-4). He also confides to them his plans for the destruction of Christ (26, 50-3), invites them to become his friends (26, 61-3) and finally departs with a declaration of alliance (with obvious homiletic significance) between himself and his listeners:

I am with 30w at all tymes · whan 3e to councel me
   call
But for A short tyme · my-self I devoyde.

(26, 123-4)

The Devil here has much in common with the Vice and clearly shows that Vice-like characteristics are not solely the province of amoral beings. The Devil, as Satan, also has a speech addressed directly to the audience at the opening of Play 31, in which, having introduced himself, he confides to the audience his fears about Christ, and outlines his plans for revenging the rebuff given to him by Christ when he tempted him in the wilderness:

Þat rebuke þat he gaf me · xal not be vn-qwyt
Som what I haue be-gonne · & more xal be do
Ffor All his barfot goying · fro me xal he not skyp
but my derk dongeon I xal bryngyn hym to.

(31, 486-9)

The Devil, the original motivated revenger of English drama addresses his audience here in tones very like those of innumerable self-explanatory villains of the Elizabethan stage. When the other Devils are appalled at the prospect of Christ coming to hell and Satan realizes that he has over-stepped himself, it is in terms of his 'sport' that he laments:

A · A · than haue I go to ferre
but som wyle help I haue a shrewde torne
My game is wers þan I wend here
I may seyn · my game is lorne.

(31, 507-10)

Once more the Devil anticipates the Vice.

All that remains of the Norwich Mystery cycle are two versions of the pageant of Adam and Eve where the Devil appears simply as the Serpent. However in the version composed after 1565 he shows his kinship with the traditional tempter—taking his audience into his confidence and revealing to them his intention to

Othello, Desdemona, Roderigo, Iago, Emilia, Cassio, Montano, Gentlemen, and attendants in Act II, scene i of Othello.

disguise himself to further the temptation (lines 38-41).[11] The motive for the antagonism displayed by the Serpent is not commented upon; like Iago he simply 'can yt nott abyde, in theis joyes they shulde be'. Antagonism from the Devil, in whatever form he appears, is understood.

Thus in three out of the four major Mystery cycles extant (if the Chester cycle is regarded as a partial exception), as well as in those pageants surviving from the Newcastle and Norwich plays, the Devil shows many of the characteristics which typify the Vice, and which have been identified by Brandl, Cushman and Spivack as vestigial traces of the Vice in the self-explanatory villains of the Elizabethan-Jacobean stage with their curious combination of malice and merriment. It seems fairly safe to assume that these Devils were typical of those in the Mystery plays as a whole, which originated before the emergence of the allegorical drama, were performed throughout the period when the Morality play enjoyed its popularity, and, judging from the number of copies made at the close of the

sixteenth century, would still have been familiar after they had actually disappeared from the stage.

However, the Devil was presented as the seducer of mankind in the Morality plays themselves before 'The Vice' as distinct from a number of vices, emerged into dramatic prominence. In the first complete Morality play extant, *The Castle of Perseverance* (1405-25), it is the Evil Angel, not the subsidiary vices, nor even The World or The Flesh, who is Humanum Genus's chief enemy. His method of seduction is the traditional one. He poses as man's friend supporting him against the 'bad' counsels of the Good Angel (IV, 340-8)[12] while instructing the vices on the means to be used to procure Humanum Genus's downfall (V, 547-51). But he is not simply the artful contriver of the hero's ruin—he also displays the irreverent humour and contempt for virtue shown by Spivack to be typical of the Vice, for example:

> 3a! whanne þe fox prechyth, kepe wel 3ore gees!
> he spekyth as it were a holy pope.

goo, felaw, & pyke of þe lys
  þat crepe þer up-on þi cope!

(VI, 804-7)

—a speech addressed to the Good Angel! When Humanum Genus finally dies in sin, he triumphs over him as the Vice is to triumph over his victim and as Iago is to triumph over the fallen Othello.

Similarly, in *Mankind*[13] (1465-70), the second complete Morality play extant, it is not the vices—Nought, New-Guise and Now-a-days—who are Mankind's most potent adversaries, for he is easily able to repel them by beating them away; it is their cunning chief, Titivillus, who brings about his downfall. Mr Spivack devotes a long section to Titivillus (*op. cit.* pp. 123-5) showing, step by step, how his actions and speeches provide a pattern for the behaviour of a Vice,[14] but in fact, as Spivack barely notices, he is not a Vice at all. The playwright makes his nature perfectly clear when he declares, 'propy[r]lly Titiuilly syngnyfyes the fend of helle' (III, 879). He is not an unmotivated amoral figure representing an inner moral frailty, he is the motivated antagonist of Mankind, the moral being devoted to his spiritual destruction. It is true that the role he plays is soon to be taken over by the Vice because, as Mr. Spivack rightly observes, the Devil 'is not a personification but an historical figure out of Christian mythology and folklore, and an illogical intrusion, therefore, into the drama of abstraction' (*op. cit.* p. 132), but the dramatic qualities the Vice comes to represent are surely derived from him.

The Devil also acts as seducer in the third of the so-called Macro-morals, *Mind, Will and Understanding* (1450-1500). Here he enters immediately after Mind, Will and Understanding have been presented and in typical manner quickly takes the audience into his confidence, revealing who he is:

I am he þat syn be-gane

(line 332)[15]

and what has motivated his animosity:

My place to restore,
  God hath mad a man.

(lines 327-8)

In Vice-like manner he boasts of his cunning (lines 341-2) and then proceeds to share with the audience his intention to corrupt Mind, Will and Understanding, thus bringing the soul to damnation (lines 365-70). Most significantly, however, he disguises himself before proceeding to the temptation, showing once more that the disguise motif, associated with the pose as the friend of the victim, originated with the Devil:

For, to tempte man in my lyknes,
yt wolde brynge hym to grett feerfullness,
I wyll change me in-to bryghtnes,
  & so hym to be-gy[le].

(lines 373-6)

In the role of well-wisher, he then dupes the trio into believing that a life of prayer and contrition is not pleasing to God, brings them from piety to depravity and triumphs to his intimates, the audience, on his good success, while he proceeds, Iago-like, to tell the ultimate goal of his operation:

That soule, God made in-comparable,
To hys lyknes most amyable:
I xall make yt most reprouable,
  Ewyn lyke to a fende of hell.
At hys deth I xall a-pere informable,
Schewynge hym all hys synnys abhomynable,
Prewynge hys soule damnable,
  So with dyspeyer I xall hym qwell.

(lines 536-43)

Similarly in *Mary Magdalene* (*c.* 1480-1520), a curious combination of Mystery and Morality, it is the Devil, as Satan, who is once more the cause of the central character's downfall. He enters in the seventh scene to confide to the audience both the motive for his hatred of mankind and his desire for their destruction (lines 366-71).[16] It is he who initiates the attack on Mary Magdalene, inviting the help of The World and The Flesh, and his is the principal triumph and joy at the news of her downfall ('a! how I tremyl & trott for ȝese tydynges!'). It is he who severely punishes his agents when Mary escapes his clutches and he who, with the Seven Deadly Sins under his command, provides the combination of temptation and comedy associated with the Vice.

John Bale's anti-catholic Mystery play *The Temptation of Our Lord and Saviour Jesus Christ by Satan* (1538) also gives a picture of a Satan who is a fitting heir to the traditional archetypal adversary of the Mystery stage. He enters immediately after Christ's first speech and proceeds to explain his name and function to the audience in the manner typical of the Vice. The only difference lies in the motivated hostility displayed:

I am Satan, the common adversary,
An enemy to man, him seeking to destroy
And to bring to nought, by my assaults most crafty.
I watch everywhere, wanting no policy
To trap him in a snare, and make him the child of
  Hell.

(p. 155)[17]

He then confides his fears of Christ's coming (p. 155) and reveals his purpose towards him. He intends to deceive him by guile and will adopt a disguise frequently used by Vices for the same purpose:

I will not leave him till I know what he is,
And what he intendeth in this same border here:
Subtlety must help; else all will be amiss;
A godly pretence, outwardly, must I bear,
Seeming religious, devout and sad in my gear.
If he be come now for the redemption of man,
As I fear he is, I will stop him if I can.

(pp. 155-6)

He then disguises himself as a hermit, approaches Christ
and poses as one well-disposed towards him (p. 156).
Having insinuated himself into his company, he begins
to flatter him, to seem solicitous for his welfare, while
at the same time trying to instil doubts into his mind
beneath the cloak of friendship—just as Iago is later to
plant seeds of doubt in the mind of his victim:

Now, forsooth and God! it is joy of your life
That ye take such pains; and are in virtue so rife
Where so small joys are to recreate the heart:

(p. 156)

—compare his exclamation on hearing how long Christ
has fasted:

So much I judged by your pale countenance.

(p. 156)

In his attempt to persuade Christ to change the stones
to bread, he emphasizes that his sole thought is upon
the well-being of his friend:

My mind is, in this, ye should your body regard;
And not, indiscreetly, to cast yourself away.

(p. 157)

His attitude throughout the temptation is that of an honest man showing his friend the 'folly' of his behaviour.
He is the man of the world, offering his knowledge of
things to the unrealistic idealist—the analogy with Iago
is obvious:

I put case: ye be God's son—what can that further?
Preach ye once the truth the bishops will ye murther.

(p. 157)

Compare:

Alas! it grieveth me that ye are such a believer:

(p. 164)

and

If I bid ye make of stones bread for your body,
Ye say man liveth not in temporal feeding only.
As I bid ye leap down from the pinnacle above,
Ye will not tempt God, otherwise than you behove.
Thus are ye still poor; thus are ye still weak and
    needy:

(p. 164)

and the supreme counsel of the down-to-earth man of
the world, the counsel Iago gives Othello: renounce
your faith, it is foolish:

Forsake the belief that ye have in God's word,
That ye are His son, for it is not worth a turd!
Is he a father that see his son thus famish?
If ye believe it, I say ye are too foolish.
Ye see these pleasures—if you be ruled by me,
I shall make ye a man: to my words, therefore, agree.

(p. 164)

Defeated, Satan, the eternal antagonist, like Iago, vows
eternal defiance:

I defy thee . . . and take thy words but as wind.

(p. 166)

This Devil with his pose of friendship, his man of the
world attitude and his subtlety, is a direct pointer to the
kind of Devil Iago is.

The Devil continued to appear, sporadically, as the
antagonist of mankind throughout the history of the
Morality play. He was the chief enemy of Youth in
Lusty Juventus (1547-53), he had a less important role
as Satan in *All For Money* (1559-77) when the transition from allegorical to literal drama had begun, and,
while the Morality play was foundering in the closing
decades of the century, he took new life as Mephisto-
philis in *Dr Faustus* (1588-92).

Thus not only did the Devil possess many of the
characteristics of the Vice long before the emergence of
the latter figure (such Devils as Titivillus anticipating
the Vice in every respect), he continued to appear on
the stage as tempter throughout the history of the Morality play. Moreover, a number of plays show that in fact
a certain confusion between the respective roles of Vice
and Devil existed in the minds of at least some Tudor
dramatists. In *The World and The Child* (1500-22),
when Conscience hears that Manhood has been seduced
by the Vice, Folly, he exclaims:

Lo, sirs, a great ensample you may see,
The frailness of mankind,
How oft he falleth in folly
Through temptation of the fiend:

(p. 267)[18]

which suggests that even if Folly does not partake of
the nature of the Devil, he somehow acts under his
guidance. Similarly, in Bale's *Three Laws of Nature,
Moses and Christ* (1538), Natural Law exclaims to the
Vice, Infidelity,

I defy thee, wicked fiend.

(p. 15)[19]

This Vice is called 'fiend' more than once in the course of the action and Natural Law declares that he shuns his company as he would 'the devil of hell' (p. 16). Confusion of this kind is most apparent in the 1578 edition of *All For Money*. In addition to the usual stage directions this edition provides elaborate instructions for the costumes of the various characters, including:

> Here commeth in Gluttonie and Pride dressed in deuils apparel.
>
> (B iii r)[20]

Later in the same play we are told that 'Here all the deuilles departe' (B iiii r) when it is clear that Satan, Gluttony and Pride have gone out. Ethically disparate as they undoubtedly are, the Vice and the Devil have a similar function and share a fund of common characteristics which makes confusion between their dramatic roles possible.

Finally, the Devil was still seen on the Elizabethan and Jacobean stage long after the decline of both Mystery and Morality play—*Grim the Collier* (1600), *The Merry Devil of Edmonton* (1599-1604), *If it Be Not Good, The Devil is in it* (1611-12), *The Birth of Merlin* (1597-1621), etc., all testifying to the perennial popularity of the figure of the supreme antagonist. For, ultimately, it is the Devil who, in Christian myth, and thus in Christian drama, is the implacable enemy of mankind. The Vice, the allegorical representation of an inner moral frailty, takes over the role of seducer in the Morality play, but he continues to show the traditional attitude to the part—the intimacy with the audience, the self-revelation, glee, irreverence, triumph over the fallen victim, etc. Freed from the confines of the Biblical narrative and the limitations of a narrowly defined moral status, he is able to develop these characteristics to a more marked degree, and by virtue of his amoral demonstrative nature and consequent detachment from the fate of his victims, he is able to pass naturally and easily, as Spivack has shown, into non-allegorical farce. But, fundamentally, the operation of the Vice is the operation of the Devil adapted to fulfil the needs of the dramatized psychomachia, and it is as the Devil that the figure passed into Elizabethan and Jacobean drama. If, therefore, the characteristics Iago displays were derived from an earlier figure, it seems extremely likely that it is to the Devil rather than the Vice that he is indebted, and that far from being a basically motiveless, amoral figure, he is a motivated being, engaged in the pursuit of some kind of revenge.

II

There is much evidence in *Othello* to confirm the suggestion that Iago is related, in some way, to the powers of darkness, and critics have long commented upon the diabolism that surrounds the figure of the 'villain' and invests the imagery of the play. Coleridge called Iago 'a being next to devil, and only not quite devil',[21] Bradley disputed the point[22] and modern critics continue to argue the question. Among those who support the view (in one way or another) that Iago partakes of the nature of the Devil, Stoll has pointed to the ambiguity of his motivation:

> None of the motives at which Iago glances—the grievance in the matter of the promotion, or his lust for Desdemona, or his fancy that Othello or Cassio may have played him foul with Emilia—is sufficient for the vast villainy of his nature . . .

and concluded that:

> He is a son of Belial, he is a limb of Satan.[23]

Wilson Knight has seen the play as a cosmic battle for the soul of man with Iago as a 'kind of Mephistopheles',[24] Maud Bodkin sees Iago as an archetype of the Devil, defining 'Devil' as 'our tendency to represent in personal form the forces within and without us that threaten our supreme values',[25] and S. L. Bethell analysing the distribution of the diabolic imagery in the play concludes that:

> The play is a solemn game of hunt the devil, with, of course, the audience largely in the know. And it is in this game that the diabolic imagery is bandied about from character to character until the denouement: we know the devil then, but he has summoned another lost soul to his side.[26]

Heilman, discussing Iago's loss of humanity and the function of the serpent imagery in this respect, has suggested the way in which Iago's diabolism functions in the play:

> As Iago's diabolism thus emerges distinct from the interwoven texture of action and language, we see how the myth of the devil enters into the play—not as a formula which squeezes out the individuality of Iago, nor as a pure idea of which the dramatic parts are an allegorical projection, but as an added dimension, a collateral presence that makes us sense the inclusiveness of the fable.[27]

But against this view stands Dr Leavis with his famous pronouncement that Iago is no more than 'a necessary piece of dramatic mechanism' designed to trigger off Othello's jealousy,[28] and Marvin Rosenberg who emphasizes Iago's humanity (showing him to be a recognizable psychological type) and repudiates his fiendishness[29] in spite of the fact that his study of the stage history of the play shows that Iago's role is most powerful when played, as Macready played it, as 'a revelation of subtle, poetic, vigorous, manly, many-sided devilry'.[30]

To attempt to analyse the diabolic element in the play when this has been done so fully by the critics cited would be superfluous, but for the purpose of this article it is necessary to summarize very briefly the evidence in support of the view that the myth of the Devil does enter, at some level, into the play. From the very opening of the action, Iago's relationship with the powers of darkness is continually emphasized—it is towards hell that he looks constantly for inspiration, hell and the Devil are for ever in his mouth, continually invoked by him; compare

> Hell and night
> Must bring this monstrous birth to the world's light
>
> (I, iii, 397-8)

with:

> Divinity of hell!
> When devils will the blackest sins put on,
> They do suggest at first with heavenly shows,
> As I do now:
>
> (II, iii, 339-42)

and

> I do hate him as I do hell pains
>
> (I, i, 155)

where his very tones suggest familiarity with the pains he speaks of. Examples could be multiplied. As Heilman has shown, when Othello falls a victim to Iago's temptation, he catches from him not only his debased view of life but his field of reference:

> Damn her, lewd minx! O, damn her, damn her!
> Come, go with me apart; I will withdraw
> To furnish me with some swift means of death
> For the fair devil.
>
> (III, iii, 479-82)

> Naked abed, Iago, and not mean harm!
> It is hypocrisy against the devil.
>
> (IV, i, 5-6)

> Fire and brimstone!
>
> (IV, i, 228)

The word 'devil' is passed constantly from mouth to mouth. Much of the action of the play seems to take place in the darkness and horror of hell itself—the confusion and darkness of the night scene before Brabantio's house, the quarrel during the night watch, the attempted murder of Cassio—scenes of darkness and mischief over which Iago presides like an evil genius. But it is the final scene of the play that provides the most convincing evidence for Iago's diabolism when the accumulated reference of the play is finally crystallized and centred on him as Othello, in a moment of terrible clarity, realizes the truth:

> I look down towards his feet—but that's a fable.
> If that thou be'st a devil, I cannot kill thee.
>
> (V, ii, 289-90)

His failure to do so and Iago's derisive reply,

> I bleed, sir; but not kill'd
>
> (V, ii, 291)

surely provide a comment on Iago's ultimate nature. Othello, at least, has no doubts about the nature of the deception that has been practised on him.

> Will you, I pray, demand that demi-devil
> Why he hath thus ensnar'd my soul and body?
>
> (V, ii, 304-5)

Indisputably Iago is engaged in the elaborate seduction of a representative of mankind and the destruction of the values that he represents. But although he undertakes this attack with joy, almost light-heartedness, he reveals that, however gleeful he is in pursuing the downfall of his victim, his hatred of him, of the virtues he possesses, is malevolent in the extreme. Note the intensity of the hatred in the following:

> I follow him to serve my turn upon him.
>
> (I, i, 42)

> So will I turn her virtue into pitch;
> And out of her own goodness make the net
> That shall enmesh them all.
>
> (II, iii, 349-51)

> If Cassio do remain,
> He hath a daily beauty in his life
> That makes me ugly.
>
> (V, i, 18-20)

These are not the tones of an amoral figure acting under the necessity imposed by dramatic convention to demonstrate his own nature, but the accents of a moral being impelled by a burning desire to feed fat a consuming hatred with revenge.[31]

But if Iago is to be regarded on one level (Heilman's 'added dimension') as a Devil rather than a Vice, his famous motives may no longer be regarded as the realistic trappings designed to cloak his allegorical origins, and fit him for the literal stage. They must be organic rather than functional. The proposition that Iago is a Devil in some sense of the word[32] implies that it is his nature to envy those whose character or situation is in any way superior to his own, to suffer from a sense of injured merit and to seek to destroy anything which by its very superiority threatens his self-love. Hence, locally, he feels he has been slighted by Othello in the promotion of Cassio, he asserts that Othello and Cassio have cuckolded him from his conviction that they cannot be as virtuous as they appear, and from his diseased belief that he is being constantly slighted. His 'love' for Desdemona is his desire to possess that object which is clearly highly desirable and belongs to someone else. But the ultimate motive for his hatred of Othello, Desdemona, and Cassio is his denial of the values they affirm, his fixed opposition to the virtues they represent. It is the hatred of Satan for the sanctity of Adam and Eve, the hatred of a being who is forced to recognize a virtue he cannot share and constantly desires. Hence the 'daily beauty' of the lives of Othello, Cassio, and Desdemona is a constant affront to him. The myth of Satan depicts him as falling from heaven from a sense of being undervalued; he tempted Adam and Eve both because they were superior to him, and therefore an object of envious hatred, and because he desired to avenge a supposed injury. Iago's motivation is very similar. At the close of the play, when he has corrupted Othello's mind, destroyed both him and Desdemona, when, for them, Paradise has been lost, Iago is dragged away to the tortures that are his element. He does not die at the end of the play, he is not to be put rapidly to death. He is to linger in pain like the powers of whom he is the instrument. Iago follows the pattern laid down in the garden of Eden and repeated over and over again in Christian literature by the archetypal adversary of mankind. Antagonistic to all forms of virtue, obscurely envying a state he constantly denies, he is the inveterate opponent of virtue, the seducer of mankind, who reduces his victims by guile from their original state of bliss to grief, death and hell.

It is clear that the characteristics displayed by Iago could well have been derived from the Devil rather than the Vice and that this proposition is reinforced by the emphasis on devilry in the play and the nature of Iago's attitude to his victims. But it would be overstating the position to assert categorically that Iago's characterization is *necessarily* derived from a traditional stage presentation of the Devil. All that can be claimed is that the Devil's claim to be Iago's forefather is at least as good as that of the Vice, and is supported by evidence in the play. Thus, while the Devil cannot be proved to be Iago's ancestor, his contradictory claim clearly invalidates the view that Iago *must* be regarded as a descendant of the Vice because of the dramatic characteristics he displays. Literary origins make dubious discussion at best, and it would be highly lamentable for Iago to be deprived of his motivation on the grounds that he is an amoral survivor from the psychomachia, roughly clad in the garments of realism, when the very characteristics which have reduced him to this exigency, together with the corroborative evidence from the play, suggest that he is not a Vice but a Devil.

Notes

1. *Quellen des weltlichen Dramas in England vor Shakespeare* (Strassburg, 1898), p. xciv.

2. 'The Devil and The Vice in the English Dramatic Literature before Shakespeare', *Studien zur englischen Philologie,* Heft VI (Halle A. S., 1900).

3. This summary is drawn from Mr Spivack's analysis of the figure.

4. Spivack, *op. cit.* p. 134.

5. References are to *York Plays,* ed. Lucy Toulmin Smith (Oxford, 1885).

6. The dates of all plays are those given in *Annals of English Drama 975-1700,* by Alfred Harbage, revised by S. Schoenbaum (1964).

7. References are to *The Chester Plays,* Part I, ed. Hermann Deimling, E.E.T.S. *E.S.* LXII (1892).

8. References are to *The Towneley Plays,* ed. George England and Alfred W. Pollard, E.E.T.S. *E.S.* LXXI (1897).

9. References are to the text of this play included in *The Non-Cycle Mystery Plays,* ed. Osborn Waterhouse, E.E.T.S. *E.S.* CIV (1909).

10. References are to *Ludus Coventriae* or *The Play called Corpus Christi,* ed. K. S. Block, E.E.T.S. *E.S.* CXX (1922).

11. References are to the text included in *The Non-Cycle Mystery Plays* (see n. 9 above).

12. References are to the text in *The Macro Plays,* ed. F. J. Furnivall and Alfred W. Pollard, E.E.T.S. *E.S.* XCI (1904).

13. A text of this play may be found in *The Macro Plays* (see n. 12 above).

14. Cp. 'The pivotal action of the allegorical drama, repeated as many times almost as there are plays, is a more sophisticated version of just such a demonstration and such a lecture' (Spivack, *op. cit.* p. 125).

15. References are to the text of the play included in *The Macro Plays* (see n. 12 above).

16. References are to the text of the play in *The Digby Mysteries,* ed. F. J. Furnivall, The New Shakespeare Society (1882).

17. References are to *The Dramatic Writings of John Bale,* ed. John S. Farmer, Early English Drama Society (1907).

18. References are to *Dodsley's Old English Plays,* vol. I, ed. W. Carew Hazlitt (4th ed. 1874).

19. See n. 17 above.

20. Cp. *All For Money,* Old English Drama, Students Facsimile Edition (1910).

21. *Notes and Lectures upon Shakespeare,* ed. Mrs H. N. Coleridge (1849), I, p. 262.

22. Lecture VI (Othello), *Shakespearean Tragedy* (St Martin's Library, 1957), pp. 185-6.

23. *Art and Artifice in Shakespeare* (Cambridge, 1933), p. 97.

24. Cp. 'The Othello Music' in *The Wheel of Fire* (1930).

25. Cp. *Archetypal Patterns in Poetry* (Oxford Paperbacks, 1963), p. 223.

26. Cp. 'Shakespeare's Imagery: The Diabolic Images in *Othello*', *Shakespeare Survey 5* (1952), p. 72.

27. Cp. *Magic in the Web* (Lexington, 1956), p. 96.

28. Cp. 'Diabolic Intellect and the Noble Hero' in *The Common Pursuit* (Peregrine Books, 1962), p. 138.

29. Cp. *The Masks of Othello* (Berkeley and Los Angeles, 1961), pp. 170-1.

30. *Ibid.* p. 124.

31. Rosenberg's study of the stage history of *Othello* is again illuminating here, for he shows that Iago's role is unsatisfying when played as Vice rather than Devil. Thus an Iago of 1912 'tended to be impish rather than devilish . . . the real venom . . . seldom emerged' (p. 156) and Maurice Evans failed in the part because 'young, open of countenance, light and gay of speech and step' as his Iago was, his evil lost its point, was 'too much akin to *irresponsible mischief making*' (my italics). He was clearly amoral rather than immoral.

32. He has been variously regarded as a Devil on the metaphysical level, as a Devil incarnate, as a man possessed, and as a man in the process of becoming a Devil by the denial of the basic facts of his humanity.

Emily C. Bartels (essay date spring 1996)

SOURCE: Bartels, Emily C. "Strategies of Submission: Desdemona, the Duchess, and the Assertion of Desire." *Studies in English Literature, 1500-1900* 36 (spring 1996): 417-33.

[*In the following essay, Bartels offers a feminist assessment of Desdemona's assertive qualities, explicating her impulse to question and destabilize the repressive hierarchy of patriarchal social order in* Othello.]

Chaste, silent, shamefast, and obedient—these have become the buzz words in feminist discussions of early modern women: the dictates of an anxious patriarchal network, intent on regulating inevitably unruly female voices and bodies; the signs that women, continually accosted by sermons, marriage tracts, conduct books, communal rituals, and laws espousing these terms, really could not have had a renaissance.[1] Renaissance women seem to have known it too. Why is it that Queen Elizabeth, visibly the most powerful woman in England from the mid-sixteenth to early seventeenth century, "speak(s) a discourse of apparent abjection," alternately adjuring her femaleness and acknowledging its weaknesses?[2] Why is it that "Jane Anger" (probably a pseudonym for an English gentlewoman) begins her proto-feminist "Protection for Women" (1589) with a letter to "the Gentlewomen of England" "crav(ing) pardon" for speaking out "rashly"?[3] Why is it that Aemilia Lanyer introduces her bold poetic defense of women, *Salve Deus Rex Judaeorum* (1611), by critiquing the "powers of ill speaking" exhibited "unadvisedly" by "some women"?[4] Why is it, that is, that even the most outspoken women of the early modern period reiterate the terms that would prevent women from "inhabiting their own subjectivity"?[5]

The easy—and recently, automatic—answer is, of course, containment, brought into currency not only by New Historicists, whose preoccupation with power marginalized the subject of women, but also by feminists themselves. The necessary project of exposing the long-ignored but long-standing oppression of women has almost destined us, when we focus on women, to focus on their circumscription. Couple that to a tradition of representation in which rebellious, outspoken, or desiring women habitually end up married, muted, or dead, and there seems to be no escape, even for those subjects who show remarkable autonomy before they go. Yet women such as Lanyer and Anger (literally) were making names for themselves. And if we continue to read their acts of compliance as signs of limitation, we ourselves put serious limits on their agency, subjectivity, and voice.

Part of the problem is our hesitancy to think of early modern women—who, after all, had no place on the stage—as actors. Recent work has begun to uncover multiplicity and conflict within established positions of those in and out of power, but we still tend to take women's voices, whether represented or real, at face value.[6] Men get to play all the parts, to fashion states, society, selves, and even femininity.[7] Since, in this period, self-making is an activity of the public sphere, we do not expect women (other than the queen) to do it—at least not with the same self-consciousness, manipulativeness, and control. They fill, rather than construct, roles. By and large, we recognize only the most exceptional or "unruly" figures as exceptions—

figures such as *As You Like It*'s Rosalind (1599-1600) or Thomas Middleton and Thomas Dekker's "roaring girl" (1608-10?), who mastermind strategic, self-serving if not self-affirming, fictions, albeit through male voices and bodies and sometimes in male drag.[8] Even then, we allow more license to fictive characters than to "real" disorderly women, and we privilege punishments over "crimes" which sometimes evidence impressive autonomy.[9] In any case, these stories predestine us to see female agency only in and as resistance, itself delimited (whether contained or not) by the challenged terms.

Indeed, when these or other women play by the rules, into obedience, chastity, shamefastness, and silence, we routinely assume them either constrained or restrained, despite histories that suggest otherwise.[10] When aggressively outspoken women such as Jane Anger apologize for their rashness, we have read their gestures as a sign that they "accepted silence as a feminine ideal" or, at best, "felt constrained" to comply with it.[11] Less consistently aggressive figures fare even worse. Although Desdemona has the audacity to elope with a Moor and follow him to Cyprus, that she is "so good a wife" (V.ii.234) makes us lose faith in her daring.[12] She becomes "the perfect wife," who "remains perfectly submissive to the end" and whose "very self consists in not being a self, not being even a body, but a bodiless obedient silence."[13]

Wives, like Desdemona, are particularly susceptible to this kind of critical circumscription, perhaps because they were among the most (if they were not themselves the most) vigorously regulated of early modern women. Yet, as historians have shown, across the classes they had substantial power within their households.[14] Consider, for example, the case of Margaret Ferneseede, a one-time prostitute and bawd, who apparently "'barred' her husband '"of the possession and command" of their (legally his) home, who lived prosperously (probably with her lover) on her own, and who, upon her husband's death, openly mocked him, saying she scarcely expected to "hear so well of him."'[15] Margaret was ultimately condemned for murdering her husband, largely on the grounds that she showed such "slight regard" for him in life and such "careless sorrow" at his death (p. 355). As her case suggests, what wives lacked was not power, but authority, terms which Constance Jordan has usefully separated.[16] At home wives could take charge, make decisions, and act on them. But in the world at large, that power gave them no authority, no means to legitimate their capacities or agendas outside those compatible with a patriarchal scheme. With power and not authority, Margaret Ferneseede was surely doomed.

According to Jordan, contemporary defenses of women (most authored by men) offered a wife only two strategies for validating her worth: either she could "reaffirm the value of her duties as her husband's subordinate," or she could "reject the grounds upon which she ha(d) been assigned her role and discover others that provide(d) her with greater scope."[17] The cost in each case is self-sacrifice: either the wife remains fully subordinate (though she elevates the value of her subordinate part), or she risks incrimination (as a scold or worse) for options that, if legal, may have been only theoretically available.

There is, however, a middle ground that proffers the safety of the first option with the radicality of the second and allows women to be actors: to speak out through, rather than against, established postures and make room for self-expression within self-suppressing roles. Under the cover of male authority, women could modify its terms and sanction their moves without direct resistance. They could be good wives and desiring subjects, obedient and self-assertive, silent and outspoken. In *Julius Caesar* (1599), Portia is unable to gain her husband's confidence by appealing to "the right and virtue of (her) place" (II.i.269) as wife and trying to give that place a "greater scope." But when she recasts herself as subordinate—when she kneels before Brutus, "grant(s)" that she is an implicitly inferior "woman" (II.i.292), and gives herself value in terms of men, as a woman nobly "father'd" and "husbanded" (II.i.297)—she gets what she wants, Brutus's promise to disclose to her "the secrets of (his) heart" (II.i.306).

Portia's role and desires become subordinated as the action moves back to its hyper-male spheres, but elsewhere on the stage, where only men had the chance to act out modes of self-presentation, women's capacity to perform and construct strategic selves emerges as a central subject. Importantly, what figures there as a key device for radical self-expression is the posture of obedience. I want to look here at two examples, John Webster's *The Duchess of Malfi* and William Shakespeare's *Othello,* whose female leads seem to be at opposite ends of the spectrum of behavior: the one (the duchess) a willful and defiant actor, and the other (Desdemona) a self-effacing and compliant victim. Yet the stories they tell are similar. For in each, gestures of submission paradoxically enable the expression of desire, showing female figures who inhabit their subjectivities, who are able to seem as well as be and, consequently, be as well as seem.

The Duchess of Malfi is ostensibly a story of resistance of a willful widow who actively defies her brothers' wishes and refuses to be constrained by (male) authority. While her brothers, Ferdinand and the Cardinal, "would not have her marry again" (I.i.265), she immediately sets out to do so, declaring: "If all my royal kindred / Lay in my way unto this marriage, / I'd make them my low footsteps" (I.i.348-50).[18] When she does marry (soon after), she not only marries in secret, she also marries out of class, choosing Antonio Bologna, her household steward. Before we know it, she has also had several children—provocative signs to her brothers (who have little room to talk) of a sexuality gone wild. Her actions peg her as a woman willing and eager to fight back, to prevent anyone (even her new husband, who is already her subordinate) from taking charge of her body and desires.[19] She does have grounds for asserting such authority. She is, after all, an aristocratic widow with claims on a duchy and with autonomy so legitimate that her brothers must use clandestine means to restrain her.[20] Yet at stake in the play is not merely the question (or problem) of a widow's unique rights, independence, and power and how they can or cannot be contained by male authority. At issue too is the prospect of female self-fashioning and the kind of voice and agency it carries. Though in part *The Duchess of Malfi* dramatizes what men can do to women, at its core is rather what women can do to men.

That the duchess will act on her will comes as no surprise, given her initial asides. What is puzzling, and revealing, however (especially since she seems to have married as much to exhibit her autonomy as to satisfy herself), is that she does so through submission. On the one hand, she dares "old wives" to report that she "winked, and chose a husband" (I.i.355-6). On the other, she keeps her move into marriage and sexuality under close cover. When the "deadly air" (III.i.56) of a "scandalous report" (III.i.47) actually approaches her, her honor, and her brothers, she proclaims her innocence. In the face of the suspecting Ferdinand, she denies the truth and assures him that she will marry only "for (his) honor" (III.i.44). Pretending to be deeply troubled by rumors "touching (her) honor" (III.i.48) and helpless to intervene, she leaves the remedy in his hands. It is only later, when he overhears her speaking of her closeted sex life (she thinks to Antonio), that she confesses to her marriage. Yet when she does, she strategically hides her husband's identity and his problematic social standing and underplays the implications of all her secrecy, insisting: "I have not gone about, in this, to create / Any new world, or custom" (III.ii.111-2).

To some degree, the duchess's posture of "innocency" (III.i.55) is a matter of survival, forced upon her by a family and society intent on keeping the widow under wraps. At the end of the play, when her secret is out, her time to live is up. Importantly, however, hers is not a simple case of co-optation, a forced relinquishing of her desires. Instead, her ostensible compliance marks a move into will and desire, giving her significant leverage to do as she pleases, to have her cake and eat it too in a society that would have no more cakes and ale.[21]

Her gains are truly extraordinary, at least for a female character on the early modern stage, and the play amplifies their significance by underscoring the pressures that surround her. By the end of act II, the duchess's reputation is under siege and her life threatened. Ferdinand, an early modern Wolfman, vilifies her as "a notorious strumpet" and is ready to "purge" her "infected blood" (II.iv.26) and, even to the Cardinal's horror, "(hew) her to pieces" (II.iv.31). At the beginning of act III, her infamy has spread to the "common rabble," who, according to Antonio, "do directly say / She is a strumpet" (III.i.25-6). Yet in the meantime, during a leap of two children and several years, this "excellent / Feeder of pedigrees" (III.i.5-6) is living and producing heirs at liberty. And her brothers, the representatives of church and state, have not said a word, at least not one that stops her. To some degree, the play smooths over this gap in time and plot, unprecedented in Jacobean tragedy, by having characters talk about it, about how time and children fly. Nonetheless, it remains so jarring that critics have questioned the text's authority and coherence. But whatever its textual origins, the break works dramatically to underscore the duchess's unprecedented freedom, to highlight the remarkable, though invisible, license that comes with visible compliance. Secretly autonomous, she is overtly submissive to her brothers' constraints; overtly submissive, she seems at once untouched and untouchable. Under the cover of patriarchal authority, she can act on her will.

In the end, of course, the duchess is caught, confined, tormented by madmen, and turned into "a box of worm seed" (IV.ii.124) at the murderous hands of Bosola, Ferdinand's righthand man. Yet tellingly, when her subjugation becomes reality, a matter of force rather than choice, she no longer complies. When there is nothing left to gain from submission, she asserts her will directly, making clear the uncompromised and uncompromising nature of her voice. As long as there is hope for release, as long as Ferdinand (as Bosola pretends) will entertain reconciliation, the duchess displays "a behavior so noble / As gives a majesty to adversity" (IV.i.5-6), and asks for her brother's pardon, still (if Bosola is right) "passionately apprehend(ing) / Those pleasures she's kept from" (IV.i.14-5). But once Ferdinand himself gives up his guise of innocence and betrays his undaunted aggression, so also does she. When he brings her the hand of (he pretends) Antonio and denounces her children as "bastards" (IV.i.36), she lambastes him for denying the legitimacy of her marriage and "violat(ing) a sacrament o' th' Church" (IV.i.39)—once again invoking a patriarchal authority to authorize herself, but this time openly against him. It is then that she "account(s) this world a tedious theater" where she "play(s) a part . . . 'gainst (her) will" (IV.i.83-4), and then that she refuses to play it. It is also then that she resists Bosola's efforts to dominate and destroy her, and then that she declares herself "Duchess of Malfi still" (IV.ii.142).

In locating this, her signal moment of self-assertion, in the midst of her confinement and immediately before her death, Webster may be underscoring the vacuity of such expression in an era only beginning to come to terms with interiority, as some have argued.[22] But he may also be dramatizing what he has been showing throughout—the possibility of self-assertion within circumscription. Even if the self in question is not yet fully interiorized, articulated, or defined, the duchess's claim is neither vacuous nor defeating. For it is she who ultimately gets the last word.[23] After her death, her voice reverberates from the grave, echoing warnings to Antonio that could (if this were not Jacobean tragedy) save his life. And at the end of the play, we hear that one of her and Antonio's sons will inherit the duchy—importantly, through his "mother's right" (V.v.113). She is "Duchess of Malfi still."

Significantly, it is from a position as wife and not widow, the ruled rather than the unruly, that the duchess has established her "right"; through marriage and not widowhood that she has acted on her desires. In Elizabethan drama, when marriage figures as a means to power, it is predominantly as a means to male power—a means for men to safeguard (male) society from oversexed and overactive women, to manipulate, appropriate, traffic in, and otherwise dominate women. Yet in *The Duchess of Malfi* and plays emerging in the surrounding decades, when the debate about women is also in full and vigorous swing, the illusion (probably always an illusion) that women could be contained through marriage is seriously challenged.[24] Indeed, in Middleton's *Women Beware Women* (ca. 1620), Isabella (who has pledged herself to the doltish Ward in order to have an incestuous affair with her uncle) celebrates marriage as "the only veil wit can devise / To keep our (illicit) acts hid from sin-piercing eyes" (II.i.237-8)—a veil for her use, protection, and pleasure.[25]

In the cases of Isabella and the duchess of Malfi, of female figures who let us in on their secrets and come out fighting from the start, it is easier to see compliance for the strategy that it, in these cases, is. But what about wives or would-be wives who do not talk to us? who are less transgressive at the beginning and less assertive at the end? What about "so good a wife" as Desdemona?

Although Desdemona seems much less a player than the duchess of Malfi, she is, in some ways, more—so much so that she has continually eluded our critical grasp. Desdemona gives us, in effect, two selves to choose from: the one, a fully sexual "woman capable of 'downright violence'" (I.iii.249); and the other, "'A maiden, never bold'" (I.iii.94), as Peter Stallybrass has argued.[26] The first escapes her father's "guardage" (I.ii.70) to elope with a Moor and insists on accompanying her husband to Cyprus—a military outpost in the

play and the locus of Venus and "very wanton" women in classical and other contemporary accounts—a dangerous place for a new wife to be on both counts.[27] Too, this first self notices, while undressing, that "Lodovico is a proper man" (IV.iii.35). The second, that "perfect wife" and "bodiless obedient silence" mentioned above, emerges primarily in the play's second half and stands passively by as her husband destroys her reputation and her life. She then takes responsibility for the deed and clears his name.

When Hamlet, the prince of players, moves in and out of madness, inertia, and love, we readily entertain the possibility that he indeed knows "seems," that he is a man of many masks (if not all mask and no interior). When Desdemona, the good wife, shows two ostensibly incompatible sides, our tendency has been to treat them as a dramatic or characterological disruption, as something that impedes rather than enables her emergence as a subject. Attempting to resolve the problem of these dueling personas, critics have either argued for one at the expense of the other or located a gap within the characterization, a moment (in the middle of act III) when type A Desdemona becomes type B.[28] Or they have displaced the conflict onto culture: Desdemona becomes a site of ideological production and supports the normative "sex/race system" even as she "deviate(s)" from its "norms," or unwittingly threatens it just by being sexual and female.[29] As astute as many of these readings are, what they occlude is the possibility that Shakespeare creates a Desdemona who, like her male or more rebellious female counterparts, stages different selves.

It is clear from the start that Desdemona is an actor, as adept as Iago, Othello's second wife, at manipulating the system from within. When Othello wants to exonerate himself from charges of bewitching Desdemona, he writes her into his narrative of exoticism, portraying her as a vicarious adventurer, hungry to hear of his "disastrous chances" (I.iii.134) and frustrated by "house affairs" (I.iii.147). When Desdemona herself testifies, she—to the contrary and better advantage of both—stresses her conventionality and cloaks her unprecedented marital choices in social and familial precedent. Paying due respect to her "noble father" (I.iii.180), she acknowledges that she is "bound" to him "for life and education" (I.iii.182), that he is "the lord of duty" (I.iii.184), and that she is "hitherto (his) daughter" (I.iii.185). She then insists that her marriage fulfills her "duty" to turn from father to husband, as daughters must and as her mother did, "preferring (Brabantio) before her father" (I.iii.187). Significantly, in aligning herself with her mother, she strategically glosses over two factors that make her own marriage radically different and socially taboo: that she has eloped and eloped with a Moor. She further deflects attention from the incriminating specifics of her case by finding fault with society for assigning women an impossible "divided duty" (I.iii.181) to both fathers and husbands. In her hands, acts of filial disobedience and miscegenation (brilliantly) become not only acceptable but also expected behavior. Brabantio, the one protesting against those acts, has no choice but to give up and in, as indeed he does.

Similarly, when Desdemona seeks permission from the duke to go to Cyprus rather than, as he suggests, stay with Brabantio, she presents her plan as better for her father, whom she would otherwise put "in impatient thoughts / By being in his eye" (I.iii.242-3), and then humbly begs assistance for her "simpleness" (I.iii.246). Not surprisingly, one scene later, she is in Cyprus, welcoming her "dear Othello" to the shore (II.i.182).[30]

In these instances, Desdemona's interventions do not markedly disturb the political system, since what she wants (to be in Cyprus as Othello's wife) does not alter what the Venetian court wants (to have Othello there, wife or no wife). Yet on the domestic front, as critics have argued, her desires do go beyond Othello's, who is determined to keep Cupid's "lightwing'd toys" from blunting his "speculative and offic'd (instruments)" (I.iii.268, 270) and housewives from making "a skillet of (his) helm" (I.iii.272). When she acts on those desires, albeit to enhance rather than subvert her marital relations, she, in effect, counters the terms of those relations. In these cases, the stakes in her staging of submission are higher. For through it she not only gets what she wants; she also challenges the very system that makes what she wants taboo.[31]

Desdemona's most blatant expression of her desires comes as she mediates for Cassio, under the patriarchally sanctioned authority of his voice.[32] She (and Shakespeare) make clear from the outset that, while the agenda is Cassio's, at issue is her will and her right to voice it. When agreeing to intercede, she promises (in the space of less than thirty lines):

> Be thou assur'd, good Cassio, I will do
> All my abilities in thy behalf.
>
> (III.iii.1-2)

> Do not doubt, Cassio,
> But I will have my lord and you again
> As friendly as you were.
>
> (III.iii.5-7)

> Do not doubt . . .
> I give thee warrant of thy place. Assure thee,
> If I do vow a friendship, I'll perform it
> To the last article.
>
> (III.iii.19-22)

And perform she does, in ways that license her self-expression and desire at the expense of male authority.

Her performance exploits and collapses the two male fantasies that most define early modern wives: the one, negative, of the shrew, and the other, the ideal of the submissive subordinate. Lest we believe the stereotypes and think Desdemona truly shrewish, she announces that she will play the shrew—that she will "talk (Othello) out of patience" (III.iii.23), "intermingle every thing he does / With Cassio's suit" (III.iii.25-6), make his bed "a school" and "his board a shrift" (III.iii.24), and assault him verbally at every turn until he again embraces the lieutenant. True and alert to form she does so, hounding Othello to meet with Cassio "shortly," "to-night at supper," "To-morrow dinner," "to-morrow night," and so on (III.iii.56-60). Othello responds as if she were indeed a shrew, overstepping the proper bounds of female speech. Although he insists "I will deny thee nothing" (III.iii.76), his acquiescence serves to cut her off at the pass. In response, Desdemona outdoes his own illusory submission and rewrites her outspokenness as part of, and not subversive to, her duty as wife, as a gesture that neither threatens his position nor advances hers. "Why, this is not a boon," she tells him:.

> 'Tis as I should entreat you wear your gloves,
> Or feed on nourishing dishes, or keep you warm,
> Or sue to you to do a peculiar profit
> To your own person.
>
> (III.iii.76-80)

When Othello misses the point, again asserts "I will deny thee nothing" (III.iii.83), and asks to be left "but a little to myself" (III.iii.85), Desdemona reiterates the submissiveness of her pose. "Shall I deny you?" she asks, echoing Othello's own denial of denial, and answers with a firm "No" (III.iii.86). She then assures him, "Be as your fancies teach you; / What e'er you be, I am obedient" (III.iii.88-9)—presenting an assertive "I am" boldly in line with obedience.

In merging the postures of good wife and shrew, Desdemona indirectly challenges the presumption of their difference enforced in marriage handbooks, homilies, church courts, misogynist pamphlets, and the like. Her performance highlights what that discourse masks: that to be a shrew is, in fact, to follow the rules, to be obediently disobedient, to fill a role created by (male) authorities who needed shrews in order to contain, by criminalizing, female speech. Conversely, Desdemona also places outspokenness within the perimeters of appropriate wifely behavior, insisting that to speak out against her husband (and his refusal to see Cassio) is to "do a peculiar profit to" him.

While Othello uses acquiescence to repress, Desdemona uses it to assert herself, to sanction the expression of her own desires.[33] After declaring that what she seeks is "not a boon," she warns Othello that someday she may seek one:

> when I have a suit
> Wherein I mean to touch your love indeed,
> It shall be full of poise and difficult weight,
> And fearful to be granted.
>
> (III.iii.80-3)

Although she only promises here to make "fearful" and "difficult" personal demands in the future (notably a "when" and not an "if"), she claims the right to do so now, to be a desiring subject, to command Othello's love, and to "mean." It is no wonder that Othello tries to curtail their interchange or that, immediately after (and not before), he begins to pick up on Iago's incriminating hints that Desdemona has been untrue. For Desdemona's message comes through loudly and clearly; her "meaning has a meaning" that is decidedly her own.[34]

What then are we to do in the play's second half when, as the going gets rough, Desdemona seems to fall apart at the seams and slide into a fatal passivity, the woman capable of "downright violence" subsumed by the "maiden never bold" whom she has staged? What happens to the space Desdemona and Shakespeare have opened for her voice? We still see hints that Desdemona will stand her ground under the cover of obedience. When Othello strikes her in public, for example, she both protests that she has "not deserv'd this" (IV.i.241) and then withdraws, as Lodovico notes, like an "obedient lady" (IV.i.248). Later, in the face of Othello's mistrust, she declares that she is "honest" (IV.ii.65) while addressing herself to his "will" and "pleasure" (IV.ii.24-5). Like the duchess of Malfi, she also calls on heaven—on the fact that she is a Christian and "shall be sav'd" (IV.ii.86)—to support her stance, using male authority to dispute Othello's. Yet by and large, in the last acts of the play, Desdemona's interactions with her husband show her to be increasingly silent and submissive and her desires increasingly at bay. Although she promises to mediate further for Cassio, she gives up speaking for herself, admitting that, for his case, "What I can do, I will; and more I will / Than for myself I dare" (III.iv.130-1). Presenting herself as "a child to chiding" (IV.ii.114) who cannot negotiate for herself, who "cannot tell" how it is with her (IV.ii.111) or whether or not she is "that name," whore, that Othello has called her (IV.ii.118), she enlists Iago to help her "win my lord again" (IV.ii.149).

Yet in her case as in the duchess's, what has changed is not Desdemona but the circumstances which surround her—circumstances that force her, not to give up her voice, but to redirect it. Once Othello decides that she is a whore, her gestures of obedience cease to have any

meaning and any power to safeguard her speech. Desdemona, of course, does not know the whole story, does not know, that is, what drives Othello's "strange unquietness" (III.iv.133). Even after he has accused her repeatedly of being false, she continues to ask "What's the matter?" (V.ii.47). But she is aware that she has a husband she "nev'r saw . . . before" (III.iv.100), one whose erratic responses give her no readable text to play into. And two things more are clear: outspokenness may hurt her and obedience will not help her. In the face of Othello's distraction, Desdemona senses that her "advocation is not now in tune" (III.iv.123) and admits for the first time that she has "stood within the blank of (Othello's) displeasure / For (her) free speech" (III.iv.128-9). She twice evokes the possibility that she could be "beshrewed"—telling Emilia, at one point, to "beshrew me much" (III.iv.150) for "arraigning (Othello's) unkindness with my soul" (III.iv.152) and, at another, to "beshrew" her if she were ever to be unfaithful (IV.iii.78)—as if she now understands speech as dangerous. Othello also makes all too clear to her that submissiveness is no antidote. After Lodovico has praised her obedience, Othello harshly mocks it, retorting (to Lodovico):

> Ay, you did wish that I would make her turn.
> Sir, she can turn, and turn; and yet go on
> And turn again; and she can weep, sir, weep;
> And she's obedient, as you say, obedient;
> Very obedient.—Proceed you in your tears.—
> Concerning this, sir—O well-painted passion!—
>
> (IV.i.252-7)

Obedience, the very thing that has made her self-assertions safe, now leaves them and her defenseless, blurring into her tears as a "well-painted passion."

Importantly, though, while Desdemona does become less willing to assert her desires in Othello's presence, she continues to define herself as a desiring subject and to set the terms in which she is to mean. While she seems, to feminists' dismay, to defend Othello to the end (and even after) at her own expense, she actually exonerates herself and implicates him. She presents herself as a loyal wife, willing to sacrifice herself for love. But registered within her narrative of self-sacrifice is what we have been waiting desperately for her to produce—testimony of her fidelity and Othello's error. She vows in front of Emilia and Iago: "Unkindness may do much, / And his (Othello's) unkindness may defeat my life, / But never taint my love" (IV.ii.159-61). She uses the story of her love to render his "unkindness" questionable. As she prepares herself for the bed that (as she too anticipates) will be her deathbed, she recounts the tragedy of her mother's maid Barbary and, through it, sets herself in the context of other women who suffered or died wrongly at the hands of their lovers. Recent interest in issues of race has brought the seemingly digressive tale into currency for its evocation of Africa. As significant as that context is in a play about a Moor, that Barbary is a woman, and a woman wronged in love, is, I think, more significant still, at least as far as the representation of Desdemona is concerned. For Barbary's story and song provide a crucial model for Desdemona's own self-fashioning and a critical key for our interpretation of it.[35]

The story itself is simple: Barbary "was in love" with one who "prov'd mad / And did forsake her"; as a result, she died, singing "a song of 'Willow,'" "an old thing" that "express'd her fortune" (IV.iii.27-9). That song (which Desdemona admittedly cannot get out of her mind and so sings) tells of a woman, "I," who "sat (sighing) by a sycamore tree" (IV.iii.40), mourning a lover, and declaring: "'Let nobody blame him, his scorn I approve'" (IV.iii.52). Her approval, however, seems more strategic than sincere. When Desdemona reaches this final line, she notices that "that's not next" (IV.iii.53) and inserts what should have preceded, what explains the speaker's acquiescence—the possibility that she herself will be slandered:

> I call'd my love false love; but what said he then?
> Sing willow, willow, willow;
> If I court moe women, you'll couch with moe men.—
>
> (IV.iii.55-7)

In refusing to blame her lover, the speaker (followed by Barbary) keeps blame from herself. For as the male voice within the ballad threatens, her incriminations of him will only lead to his recriminations against her: if she accuses him for courting more women, then he will accuse her of "couching" with more men. Admittedly, by loyally "approving" his scorn, she seems to be subdued by her husband. But by exposing the circumstances that surround her submission, she exposes also the falseness and vacuity of his position.

And so it is with Desdemona. When direct attempts to modify the system promise only recrimination, she turns to indirection and tells, rather than acts out, her story. Yet even though at the end she is forced to play defense rather than offense, she continues to play, to creative a submissive counternarrative that challenges and changes the order of things. In the final act, when she speaks after death, she breaks through the code of silence expected of the dead as of women and not only declares her death "guiltless" (V.ii.122) and herself "Oh falsely, falsely murder'd" (V.ii.117), but also, enigmatically, insists that "Nobody; I myself" (V.ii.124) killed her. Her "nobody" points suggestively back to the Willow Song, to the speaker's directive that "nobody" blame her lover, and reiterates the loyalty that has defined the speaker, Barbary, and Desdemona. Although critics have routinely heard the "nobody" rather than the "I" and turned her into a "bodiless obedient silence," Desde-

mona has both voice and body here. Given the dramatic context surrounding her assertion, and her characterization throughout, the real enigma here is that we take her answer, literally the lie direct, at face value, her performance as passivity.

In fact, the onstage audience hears her. And her dying voice destabilizes the master narrative that has defamed her and puts incriminating words in Othello's mouth. Ironically, in order to prove her a liar (which is, to him, a whore) and to usurp the claim to truth, Othello confesses to the crime, insisting "'Twas I that kill'd her'" (V.ii.130), undoing himself in order to undo her. Her voice also licenses Emilia's revolt against Iago. It is only after Desdemona has spoken that Emilia questions her husband's honesty, vows to "ne'er go home" (V.ii.197), and dies testifying against him. Tellingly, as Emilia "speak(s) as liberal as the north" (V.ii.220) before she too dies at her husband's hand, she reinvokes the Willow Song and, as she says, "die(s) in music" (V.ii.248) like her lady—music that is the food not just of love but also of female affirmation.

Desdemona, Emilia, Barbary, and the ballad's anonymous speaker all submit and die, but not before speaking out through a male-authored narrative that would otherwise occlude their voices. Each, in effect, tells her own story, registering desires not suitable for women through postures of obedience that are. Singing "willow" under a sycamore tree, they turn "nobody" into "I." There are reasons that lead Othello to cry whore and Ferdinand to cry wolf—reasons that caution us against taking conventional postures, in general, and conventional female postures, in particular, as authentic rather than posed. Shakespeare, Webster, Jane Anger, and Aemilia Lanyer may have different reasons for staging female compliance. But however their representations promote, remodel, resist, or otherwise respond to the possibility of such performance, together they testify to a prominent cultural awareness that all the world was indeed a stage, and its men and women players.[36]

Notes

1. The signal essay is Joan Kelly-Gadol, "Did Women Have a Renaissance?", in *Becoming Visible: Women in European History,* ed. Renate Bridenthal and Claudia Koonz (Boston: Houghton Mifflin, 1977), pp. 137-64. Other important studies include: Constance Jordan, *Renaissance Feminism: Literary Texts and Political Models* (Ithaca: Cornell Univ. Press, 1990); Linda Woodbridge, *Women and the English Renaissance: Literature and the Nature of Womankind, 1540-1620* (Urbana: Univ. of Illinois Press, 1984); the introductory material in Katherine Usher Henderson and Barbara F. McManus, *Half Humankind: Contexts and Texts of the Controversy about*

Women in England, 1540-1640 (Urbana: Univ. of Illinois Press, 1985), pp. 3-130; and Suzanne W. Hull, *Chaste, Silent, and Obedient: English Books for Women, 1475-1640* (San Marino CA: Huntington Library, 1982), pp. 1-143. See also Gail Kern Paster, *The Body Embarrassed: Drama and the Disciplines of Shame in Early Modern England* (Ithaca: Cornell Univ. Press, 1993).

2. Barbara Hodgdon, "The Making of Virgins and Mothers: Sexual Signs, Substitute Scenes, and Doubled Presences in *All's Well that Ends Well*," *PQ* 66, 1 (Winter 1987): 47-71, 66. For full discussion of Elizabeth's self-representations, see Mary Thomas Crane, "'Video et Taceo: Elizabeth I and the Rhetoric of Counsel," *SEL* [*Studies in English Literature*] 28, 1 (Winter 1988): 1-15, and John M. King, "Queen Elizabeth I: Representations of the Virgin Queen," *RenQ* [*Renaissance Quarterly*] 43, 1 (Spring 1990): 30-74.

3. "Jane Anger, Her Protection for Women" (London, 1589), in Henderson and McManus, pp. 172-88, 173.

4. From Aemelia Lanyer's letter "To the Vertuous Reader" prefacing *Salve Deus Rex Judaeorum* (London, 1611). See also Hull, pp. 98-9.

5. Maureen Quilligan, "Staging Gender: William Shakespeare and Elizabeth Cary," in *Sexuality and Gender in Early Modern Europe: Institutions, Texts, Images,* ed. James Grantham Turner (Cambridge: Cambridge Univ. Press, 1993), p. 208. Quilligan is discussing Gayle Rubin's important essay, "The Traffic in Women: Notes on the Political Economy of Sex," in *Toward an Anthropology of Women,* ed. Rayna R. Reiter (New York: Monthly Review, 1975), pp. 156-210.

6. See, for example, *The Matter of Difference: Materialist Feminist Criticism of Shakespeare,* ed. Valerie Wayne (Ithaca: Cornell Univ. Press, 1991).

7. Ironically, Karen Newman's interesting study *Fashioning Femininity and English Renaissance Drama* (Chicago: Univ. of Chicago Press, 1991) focuses primarily on the ways men "fashion femininity."

8. Unruly women were also doing remarkable things in the street literature of the period. For a useful survey of it, see Joy Wiltenburg, *Disorderly Women and Female Power in the Street Literature of Early Modern England and Germany* (Charlottesville: Univ. of Virginia Press, 1992).

9. See the case of Margaret Ferneseede, discussed below.

10. One notable exception is Michael C. Schoenfeldt's intriguing essay on "Gender and Conduct in Paradise Lost," in Turner, pp. 310-38. Schoenfeldt

sees in Eve's "artful expression of blind obedience," not "the intellectual and ontological inferiority it ostensibly declares," but "impressive verbal dexterity" (p. 325). "Gestures of submission in Milton," he argues, "are at once static and dynamic, unquestioned declarations of one's place in a hierarchy and the necessary condition for rising," and *Paradise Lost* "uses the constrictions of courtesy literature to construct a space—albeit limited, and only sporadically inhabited—for the conception of active female virtue" (p. 336).

11. Henderson and McManus, p. 54.

12. All quotations from Shakespeare are from *The Riverside Shakespeare,* ed. G. Blakemore Evans (Boston: Houghton Mifflin, 1974).

13. Michael D. Bristol, "Charivari and the Comedy of Abjection in Othello," in *True Rites and Maimed Rites: Ritual and Anti-Ritual in Shakespeare and His Age,* ed. Linda Woodbridge and Edward Berry (Urbana: Univ. of Illinois Press, 1992), pp. 75-97, 92; Quilligan, p. 229.

14. Two central studies are Susan D. Amussen, "Gender, Family, and the Social Order, 1560-1725," in *Order and Disorder in Early Modern England,* ed. Anthony Fletcher and John Stevenson (Cambridge: Cambridge Univ. Press, 1985), pp. 196-217; and Keith Wrightson, *English Society, 1580-1680* (New Brunswick: Rutgers Univ. Press, 1982), esp. pp. 89-104.

15. "The Arraignment and Burning of Margaret Ferneseede" (1608), in Henderson and MacManus, pp. 351-9, 358, 354. Subsequent page references appear in the text.

16. Jordan, pp. 3-5.

17. Jordan, p. 13.

18. All quotations from the play come from *Drama of the English Renaissance II: The Stuart Period,* ed. Russell A. Fraser and Norman Rabkin (New York: Macmillan, 1976).

19. Compare Catherine Belsey, *The Subject of Tragedy: Identity and Difference in Renaissance Drama* (London: Methuen, 1985), pp. 206-7, who reads the marriage as an expression of romantic love.

20. See Lisa Jardine on how the duchess's widowhood affects her place (*Still Harping on Daughters: Women and Drama in the Age of Shakespeare* (1983; rprt. New York: Columbia Univ. Press, 1989), pp. 78-93).

21. Compare Jardine, who sees the duchess as a flagrant "strong woman," who "must be systematically taught the error of her ways" (pp. 68-102, 98).

22. See, for example, Belsey, pp. 35-41.

23. Compare Kathleen McLuskie, *Renaissance Dramatists* (Atlantic Highlands NJ: Humanities Press, 1989), p. 145, who argues that the duchess is overcome by her brothers' power. See also McLuskie, "Drama and sexual politics: the case of Webster's Duchess," in *Drama and Sexual Politics* (Cambridge: Cambridge Univ. Press, 1985), pp. 77-91.

24. Because of the prominence of this challenge, I would argue against the assumption that "misogyny is generally on the rise in the drama of late Elizabethan and early Jacobean years," reiterated most recently in Steven Mullaney, "Mourning and Misogyny: *Hamlet, The Revenger's Tragedy,* and the *Final Progress of Elizabeth I,* 1600-1607," *SQ* 45, 2 (Summer 1994): 139-62, 144.

25. Thomas Middleton, "Women Beware Women," in *Jacobean and Caroline Tragedies,* ed. Robert G. Lawrence (London: J. M. Dent, 1974).

26. Peter Stallybrass, "Patriarchal Territories: The Body Enclosed," in *Rewriting the Renaissance: The Discourses of Sexual Difference in Early Modern Europe,* ed. Margaret W. Ferguson, Maureen Quilligan, and Nancy Vickers (Chicago: Univ. of Chicago Press, 1986), pp. 123-42, 141.

27. The information about Cyprus comes from James F. Gaines and Josephine A. Roberts, "The geography of love in seventeenth-century women's fiction," in Turner, p. 292.

28. See Bristol, Quilligan, and Stallybrass, "Patriarchal Territories." For an excellent alternative, see also Michael Neill, "Unproper Beds: Race, Adultery, and the Hideous in *Othello,*" *SQ* [Shakespeare Quarterly] 40, 4 (Winter 1989): 383-412.

29. Karen Newman, "'And wash the Ethiop white': Femininity and the Monstrous in *Othello,*" in *Shakespeare Reproduced: The Text in History and Ideology,* ed. Jean F. Howard and Marion F. O'Connor (New York: Methuen, 1987), pp. 142-62, 153; see also Stephen Greenblatt, *Renaissance Self-Fashioning: From More to Shakespeare* (Chicago: Univ. of Chicago Press, 1980), pp. 222-54.

30. See also II.i., where Desdemona points to her role-playing, her plan to "beguile / The thing (she is) by seeming otherwise" (II.i.122-3).

31. For a powerful essay on the discourses that surround Desdemona, see Valerie Wayne, "Historical Differences: Misogyny and *Othello,*" in *The Matter of Difference,* ed. Wayne, pp. 153-79.

32. I have sketched out the beginnings of this argument in "Making More of the Moor: Aaron, Othello, and Renaissance Refashionings of Race," *SQ* 41, 4 (Winter 1990): 433-54, esp. 452-4.

33. Related is the instance of Kate in *The Taming of the Shrew,* which, if Quilligan is right, seems "to grant Kate the exercise of her own biologically gendered sexual desire at the moment of her most freely chosen obedience" (p. 223).

34. *The Jew of Malta,* IV.iv.106, from *Christopher Marlowe, The Complete Plays,* ed. J. B. Steane (London: Penguin Books, 1969).

35. Compare Stallybrass, who argues that as a "single" but doubly resonant "signifier," Barbary "slides between male and female" ("Transvestism and the 'body beneath: Speculating on the Boy Actor," in *Erotic Politics: Desire on the Renaissance Stage,* ed. Susan Zimmerman (New York: Routledge, 1992), pp. 64-83, 73).

36. I have presented versions of this paper at the Shakespeare Association of America Convention, Kansas City, April 1992, and to the Columbia Shakespeare Seminar, Columbia University, October 1992, and am indebted to the participants in both, especially to Rob Watson, Maurice Charney, and Jean Howard, as well as to the reader at *SEL.* Finally, very special thanks to Jim Siemon, whose comments and encouragement have been vital.

Millicent Bell (essay date spring 2002)

SOURCE: Bell, Millicent. "Shakespeare's Moor." *Raritan* 21, no. 4 (spring 2002): 1-14.

[*In the following essay, Bell explores the racial dynamics of Othello's character and contends that he ultimately suffers from his inability to completely assimilate into a community that deems him a racial outsider.*]

Othello's whole life seems to be shaped by a society—like Shakespeare's England—in which self-transformation as well as the transformations effected by the forces of social change, or even by mere accident, operate to alter what one is, shift one's very selfhood from one template to another. Before he became the hero who won the regard of the Venetian state and the love of Desdemona, he had been someone we can only dimly imagine. Somehow, his career had begun by exile from an origin we never see directly. We can merely suspect its vast difference from his present condition. What he might have been as a person of station in his native place we will never know.

We do not even know without doubt that he is a "blackamoor," a Negro from sub-Saharan Africa, like "raven-coloured" Aaron the Moor in *Titus Andronicus* who is described as having a "fleece of wooly hair" and whose child is called a "thick-lipped slave." Roderigo slurringly refers to Othello as "the thick lips," and he is called "black" throughout the play and says, himself, "Haply for I am black." But, perhaps, he is a "tawny Moor" from the Mediterranean rim, like the Prince of Morocco in *The Merchant of Venice,* or a Berber or "erring Barbarian," as Iago puns, or the "Barbary horse" who has "covered" Desdemona, as the same racist provocateur vulgarly tells Brabantio. Shakespeare does not remove all doubt, but he seems willing to let us visualize "a veritable negro," to use Coleridge's phrase for the Othello whose love for a white woman he found "something monstrous to conceive." Elizabethans might not have reacted as Coleridge would come to do. Othello was played as a black man on the stage in Shakespeare's own day and for over a century and a half after. And so again we feel that the part must be played today, though the nineteenth and a good portion of the twentieth century were able only to tolerate a sort of light-skinned Arab sheik to represent him.

But one way or another, his exact beginnings remain obscure to us. Though he has told Desdemona as well as her father "the story of [his] life / From year to year—the battles, sieges, fortunes / That [he] passed . . . even from [his] boyish days"—his summary to the signory of Venice is vague, and the "travailous history" he offers of wars and wanderings, of captures and escapes, and of encounters with monsters and cannibals is mythically Odyssean. One thing we know is that he had once experienced the ultimate degradation that had come when, "taken by the insolent foe," he had been "sold to slavery." Somehow, he found his freedom, and we can presume that he was converted from his original Muhammadanism, but we are ignorant of when or how. Already, when we first meet him, he is a Christian and a "self-made man" who has made the most of opportunity and his own genius and has overcome the handicaps of being foreign and black in the white Venetian world in which he has found a place. This stranger with an exotic, almost mythical otherness has acquired a place within the order of Venice by his own efforts on behalf of a colonial empire. And yet, in the end, he cannot sustain this new personhood, this transformed social being donated by altered occasion, forged by his own will.

The curtain rises for good reason on a discussion about jobs and how one is qualified for them. Iago's declared envy of Cassio's promotion is plausible, even though he expresses this resentment only in a single remark to Roderigo. It serves to relate the play to a new seventeenth-century social climate that gave rise to uncertainty about personal identity—and gives a historical meaning to the way Iago comes before us as the man who believes that one is only what one appears to be, what role one is able to personate successfully. Iago's most significant statement of this view is the skeptical declaration he makes to Roderigo—"'tis in ourselves that we are thus, or thus. Our bodies are gardens, to which our wills are gardeners"—which is almost sincerely his own philosophy, though it hardly serves the feckless Roderigo to whom it is addressed. Iago calls Cassio, just appointed lieutenant, a mere classroom soldier, "a great arithmetician . . . / That never set a squadron in the field / Nor the division of a battle knows / More than a spinster." Practical field experience is a legitimate requirement for the promotion Cassio has gained—and something different from the mere entitlement of class and even the textbook theory he has acquired. In contrast, Iago has served in battle, as he reminds Othello: "in the trade of war I have slain men." Iago professes to believe in promotion for merit and resents the arbitrary advancement of the candidate, like Cassio, who is part of an old boys' network. He also claims the earned rights of seniority rather than preferment gained by letters of recommendation from influential somebodies.

> Preferment goes by letter and affection
> And not by old gradation, where each second
> Stood heir to th' first.

But though he makes his claim by referring to a system of respect for service he calls "old gradation," he himself has tried to go up the ladder by the aid of "letter and affection" and secured the support of "[t]hree great ones of the city." He is one of the new breed of men who not only claim advancement by merit but will manipulate and scheme for advancement—and by either means expect to escape assignment to a fixed definition. That he has not received his deserved promotion and must prosper just the same is something he is prepared for as a master of Machiavellian elasticity. He deprecates title and position and even the old division into masters and followers that organizes society:

> We cannot be all masters, nor all masters
> Cannot be truly followed. You shall mark
> Many a duteous and knee-crooking knave
> That, doting on his own obsequious bondage,
> Wears out his time much like his master's ass
> For nought but provender, and when he's old, cashiered.
> Whip me such honest knaves!

Others, adapting to a new social climate, know the meaninglessness of the identities society assigns. Taking instruction from Machiavelli, they make the most of opportunity, and, though observing the old boundaries of outer behavior,

> trimmed in forms, and visages of duty,
> Keep yet their hearts attending on themselves
> And, throwing but shows of service on their lords,
> Do well thrive by them, and when they have lined
> their coats,

Desdemona, Duke of Venice, and Othello in a scene from Othello.

Do themselves homage; these fellows have some soul
And such a one do I profess myself.

But not all have Iago's confidence. In a mobile society, one is always likely to lose one's footing and become a nobody—that is, to cease to exist in a social sense. The play is full of implicit references to a milieu in which, as in today's corporate world, there is no longer a guarantee of tenure. Demotion breaks Cassio's heart. Othello remembers with grief how he had "done the state some service" before his replacement as general and administrator of Cyprus.

Unlike the aristocratic Cassio, Othello, who may once have been a prince, has been a mercenary soldier and before that even a slave in another world. But, as the play begins, he is in command of the Venetian forces in defense of Cyprus against the Turks. A Renaissance idea of fame, or of "making a name" for oneself, is invoked in the play, as is Iago's Machiavellian idea of "thriving." It is the heroic character Othello has made for himself that achieves his success in his wooing. He makes Desdemona put aside the prerequisites of class

and race assumed for her appropriate suitor. She says she "loved [him] for the dangers [he] had passed," though her father, who looks for inherited credentials he understands better in the sons of Venetian aristocracy, calls Othello's recounting of his history "witchcraft." And perhaps such self-fabrication, such transformation by which one of the colonized joins the military elite of a colonial power, is a kind of magic. For Brabantio, miscegenation is, classically, a threat of redefinition not to be made less threatening by proof of Othello's worthiness. "For if such actions may have passage free / Bond-slaves and pagans shall our statesmen be," he shouts in an outburst of class panic. Iago will remark a bit later to Cassio, "he to-night hath boarded a land carrack," implicitly comparing Othello's sexual conquest to the seizure of a Spanish or Portuguese treasure ship (a "carrack") by an English privateer—in other words, an act of social piracy.

Yet nothing can be more fragile than Othello's self-making, which has none of Iago's confidence in being whatever, for the occasion, he wills himself to be. His attempt to give rebirth to an ancient ideal of epic heroism is vulnerable to the spirit of the later time represented by Iago. As his nobility is erased by rage and despair in the middle of the third act, he mourns,

> O now for ever
> Farewell the tranquil mind, farewell content!
> Farewell the plumed troops and the big wars
> That make ambition virtue! O farewell,
> Farewell the neighing steed, and the shrill trump,
> The spirit-stirring drum, th' ear-piercing fife,
> The royal banner, and all quality,
> Pride, pomp, and circumstance of glorious war!
> And, O ye mortal engines, whose wide throats
> Th' immortal Jove's great clamours counterfeit,
> Farewell: Othello's occupation's gone.

The strangeness of this wonderful speech is seldom commented on. There is no real reason why Othello should say goodbye at this point to his soldier's profession, which has given him an epic selfhood. His terrible crime, for which he only escapes punishment by performing his own execution, is still ahead of him. But the collapse of personal being he is already experiencing is inseparable from the loss of occupation. Before he embraces his literal self-destruction at the last, he refers to himself in the third person, saying "Where should Othello go?" as though the man he was is no longer speaking. Afterwards, when Lodovico comes looking for him with "Where is this rash and most unfortunate man?" he replies, "That's he that was Othello? here I am." Then, he remembers his former self—the self created by his public career—as having once defended the Venetian State even as, at this ultimate moment of further transformation, he identifies himself with the "circumcised dog" he once killed. Critics are mistaken who have spoken of Othello's "recovery" in the final scene when he seems to become, again, a fearless soldier and romantic lover who dies by his own hand. It is hard to admire Othello uncritically once having read T. S. Eliot on this hero's famous final speech ("What Othello seems to me to be doing in making this speech is cheering himself up. He is endeavoring to escape reality"). But Eliot did not observe that what happens at this last moment is tragic acceptance rather than escape, an acceptance of his original status as a racial outsider, which neither his military achievements nor his marriage have succeeded in permanently altering.

His marriage has proved to be the theater in which the issues of self-realization, the issues that beset men in society at large, are acted out for Othello on the scale of intimate relations. Marriage to a woman of a rank above one's own has been a universally practiced means of male self-advancement throughout human history, of course, but the marriage of Othello to Desdemona has provided a precarious bridge over the gaps between them. Shakespeare hints that Othello's jealous anguish

and distrust of his own perceptions may be caused by the interracial character of his union with a daughter of his Venetian masters. All those reminders by Iago of the impossibility of establishing Desdemona's adultery—a privacy invisible directly—refer one back to a miscegenation over whose consummation a cloud of unknowableness also hangs. The real but equally transgressive relation of Othello and Desdemona is even less easily viewable than the adultery of Desdemona with Cassio that did not take place but was so vividly supposed. This marriage becomes, by implication, something not to be made "ocular," as though it is obscene, as though it can be fairly represented only by animalistic metaphor in Iago's description to the shuddering Brabantio at the beginning of the play: "Even now, now, very now, an old black ram / Is tupping your white ewe!" Just as he will cause Othello to hallucinate the false image of Desdemona and Cassio locked in naked embrace, Iago rouses her father with his wizard evocation, setting into the mind of the old man the animal coupling that represents their racial transgression as "making the beast with two backs," and figuring Othello as a black ram as well as a Barbary horse.

It seems probable that, at this early point, Othello and Desdemona have not yet had the opportunity of establishing the union they have secretly contracted. The newly married pair could not have enjoyed their nuptial rapture for long during their first night in Venice when a midnight summons from the Duke posts the bridegroom to the defense of Cyprus. But not only circumstances or conditions keep this marriage from being consummated. The play suggests that Othello himself is engaged in a deferral of this forbidden act. Othello portrays himself convincingly at his trial before the Venetian Duke and Senators as one more used to the "flinty and steel couch of war" than to the "downy" bed of love. This war-hardened soldier hasn't had much experience of love's soft delights. He confesses: "since these arms of mine had seven years' pith, / Till now some nine moons wasted, they have used / Their dearest action in the tented field." He is no Marc Antony. Though Desdemona will accompany him to Cyprus, he is at pains to remind the Duke how largely his military preoccupation will absorb him:

> And heaven defend your good souls that you think
> I will your serious and great business scant
> When she is with me. No, when light-winged toys
> Of feathered Cupid seel with wanton dullness
> My speculative and officed instrument
> That my disports corrupt and taint my business,
> Let housewives make a skillet of my helm.

He tells Desdemona, as he assumes his new assignment, "I have but an hour / Of love, of worldly matter and direction / To spend with thee. We must obey the time."

Desdemona may still be a virgin when they are reunited after separate crossings to Cyprus, and Othello says, "The purchase made, the fruits are to ensue. / The profit's yet to come 'tween me and you." He gives orders for a wedding party while he leads his wife to bed, but the party grows wild and brings Cassio into disgrace, and Othello and Desdemona are interrupted once more-after which Othello lingers on with the wounded Montano, saying to his wife, with some equanimity, "Come Desdemona: lis the soldiers' life / To have their balmy slumbers waked with strife." Shakespeare may have wanted us to wonder how well their lovemaking had gone or if it had even got under way, and to sustain the doubt in Iago's earlier question, "Are you well married?"

We may connect the jealousy aroused so readily in Othello with one of those postnuptial awakenings that come to men unprepared for the active sexuality of the women they marry. Was Desdemona too quick or he too slow? It has been evident from the start of the play that she can take the initiative. We recall that when she first heard Othello's narrative of his past exploits she told him that "she wished / That heaven had made her such a man"—a remark that either expresses her longing for masculine roles or her bold invitation to him to make himself hers. She prompted Othello by telling him that if he had a friend who loved her, he "should but teach him how to tell" such a story as his own, "and that would woo her." She herself admits to the Duke of Venice, "That I did love the Moor to live with him / My downright violence and scorn of fortunes / May trumpet to the world," and so she pleads to be allowed to accompany him to Cyprus rather than to be left behind, "a moth of peace." When Othello lands in Cyprus to find her already there waiting for him he greets her, "O my fair warrior!" Perhaps she already is what Cassio calls her, his "captain's captain." Her father may not have known the daughter he describes as "[a] maiden never bold, / Of spirit so still and quiet that her motion / Blushed at herself."

Her activeness may be sexual. She had insisted to the Duke that if she were left behind, "the rites for which I love [Othello] are bereft me." Later, convinced that she has made love to Cassio, Othello will come to say, under Iago's influence, "O curse of marriage / That we can think these delicate creatures ours / And not their appetites!" Iago will have laid the ground for such a disillusion by his suggestion that Desdemona had already been an awakened woman before her marriage, a "super-subtle Venetian": "In Venice they do let God see the pranks / They dare not show their husbands." Brabantio charged Othello before the Venetian signory with having bound Desdemona in "chains of magic"— for how, otherwise, could she, "so opposite to marriage that she shunned / The wealthy, curled darlings of our nation" and incurred "the general mock," have "run

from her guardage to the sooty bosom / Of such a thing"? But Othello knows he has used no witchcraft, and to him Iago suggests "a will most rank, / Foul disproportion; thoughts unnatural" in Desdemona. And with this disbelief in her genuine love for him, along with a suspicion of her too-ready sexual forwardness, he is lost. Perhaps he suspects a racial will to dominance in her sexual "appetite," which declares that she is not his but that he is hers as a slave belongs to his owner.

This, of course, is a counterpart to the white master's fear of the slave's rebellion, which expresses itself in the racist presumption of the dangerous lustfulness of the oppressed and repressed—the cliche of a primitive savagery more powerful than the white man's, a lust threatening white womanhood. Someone like the stupid Roderigo, who has failed to get Desdemona even to glance at him, will refer to the "gross clasps of a lascivious Moor" when he attempts to arouse Brabantio against Othello. Iago works this vein when he portrays Othello as someone of mere impulse. "These Moors," he says, "are changeable in their wills." He even claims to believe that "it is thought abroad" that his General's unbridled lust has extended to Emilia, and cuckolded him. "I do suspect the lusty Moor / Hath leaped into my seat," he says, and though he may not really think this possible, he repeats his half-belief in this suggestion that Othello had "done [his] office 'twixt [his] sheets," while confessing that he is only looking for specious causes for his animosity: "I know not ift be true, / But I, for mere suspicion in that kind, / Will do as if for surety." Perhaps the same promptness to such presumption has infected the minds of some of the plays readers ever since, despite Shakespeare's exposure of the motives of both Iago and Roderigo in seizing so readily upon the ancient stereotype of the "lusty Moor." A refined version of it has even been discovered in Othello by so distinguished a modern Shakespeare scholar as E. A. J. Honigmann, the editor of the latest Arden Edition of the play, who speaks of Othello's "exceptional sensuousness, though not necessarily 'racial'" to be found in some of Othello's tributes to Desdemona's effect upon him. Honigmann cites, particularly, Othello's swooning recall of her appeal to his sense of smell—as when he exclaims, in his culminating anguish, "O thou weed / Who art so lovely fair and smellst so sweet / That the senses ache at thee."

But, in fact, Othello himself, as Shakespeare shows, is quite the reverse of the stereotypical "lusty Moor." To respond to the call of arms, Othello delays his wedding-night happiness without hesitation, almost welcoming, in a curious way, as I have noted, the deferral of his bliss. Moreover, he himself goes so far as to deny the sensuality of his feelings for his beautiful bride. He supports her plea to accompany him to Cyprus with the odd observation to the Duke: "I . . . beg it not / To please the palate of my appetite / Nor to comply with heat, the young affects / In me defunct, and proper satisfaction, / But to be free and bounteous to her mind." This renunciation of sexual urgency almost removes his color for his grateful employers as though to refute the convention that attributes "savage" sexuality to the black man. "Your son-in-law is far more fair than black," the Duke tells Brabantio as Othello accepts his mission. It is Desdemona rather than himself who is to be suspected of illicit lust, as Iago will soon persuade him when he stresses the positive unnaturalness of her love for her husband instead of for a social and racial equal—knowing, rightly, how such a thought will promote that jealous insecurity he wishes to arouse. He responds to Othello's protest that Desdemona's betrayal would be an incredible case of "nature erring from itself" by suggesting that it is her marriage itself, her inclination for Othello, that is a perversity.

> Not to affect many proposed matches
> Of her own clime, complexion, and degree,
> Whereto we see, in all things, nature tends—
> Foh! one may smell in such a will most rank,
> Foul disproportion; thoughts unnatural.

We can imagine how these suggestions affect Othello, most especially the reference to "complexion." Paradoxically, Iago actually increases Othello's self-doubt when he suggests that Desdemona has not freed herself from her father's racism. Is not this borne out by a love that began with her vision of her lover's "visage in his mind"—rather than in the black face gazing at her? To match this, Othello's disclaimer to the Duke and Senators of Venice of his physical desire for his wife may be connected to his fear of their physical union stated in almost the same terms when he declares that all he looks forward to is "but to be free and bounteous to her mind."

So, Othello seems to suffer the insecurity of someone who has crossed the racial line yet feels reproved for it when his white wife is reclaimed by her social and racial world in her supposed affair with Cassio. Iago can count on the self-hating that afflicts the victim of prejudice who cannot, himself, believe that he is loveable to someone of the other race. He has been compelled to hallucinate her intimacy with a white man, but can hardly imagine his own union with her. She may be expected to retain an inclination for such a familiar species as Cassio. Only moments before she is murdered she will remark upon the Venetian nobleman to whom she is related by blood as well as class, "This Lodovico is a proper man." To which Emilia replies, woman-to-woman, "I know a lady in Venice would have walked barefoot to Palestine for a touch of his nether lip." For this is how, according to the code of Venice, a Venetian woman should feel; it is perfectly "natural." When Desdemona is called a "whore" by an Othello reduced to the racial enemy's language by his jealousy, Emilia exclaims, "Hath she forsook so many noble matches, / Her father, and her country, and her friends, / To be called whore?" But this is exactly what her social desertion must seem to white society, something more adulterous, indeed, than the affair with Cassio of which she is falsely accused.

Othello's collapse into murderous violence would seem to be an illustration of the way, according to the racist view, the coating of civilization must slide readily off the "savage" personality. But Shakespeare's readiness to admit the instability of personality—as though he is ready to entertain Iago's denial of intrinsic and permanent character—is apparent in all his tragedies. The Macbeth who is held by his wife to be too full of the milk of human kindness before his murder of Duncan is not the same as that "dead butcher" whose head is triumphantly carried onto the stage on the uplifted lance of Macduff at the end. Certainly, in Othello, the serene and just commander of himself and others we first meet is not the madman who shrieks, "I will chop her into messes," as he accepts the view that his wife has betrayed him. The play exhibits that mutability in the alteration of his very language from a majestic poetry that has been called the "Othello music" to a debased tone from which all music has gone. But this alteration is only temporary. The play does not justify the racist theory of the uneducable savage. Othello is always too noble even in his preposterous delusion and degradation, too superior to everyone else on the scene, for such a view. And yet, again, though many have seen in Othello's final end a full recovery of tragic greatness, Shakespeare's vision may be too pessimistic to allow that either.

There are no more romantic lovers in all of Shakespeare than the almost virginal warrior and the highminded virgin Lady whose love he wins by recital of his heroic past. But they also recall the May-December prototypes of farce; Othello feels his head for horns like the deluded old husband of a thousand comic tales. Despite the grimness of this tragic history, the comic foregrounding of sex, as in farce, is both invoked and obscured in a play in which so much of the time the marriage bed is at least present to mind even if offstage, just guessed at, though unseen, like the sexual union enacted there. Othello's sexual secret discloses itself, however—rather than being merely suspected or hinted—on the deathbed that has been laid with his and Desdemona's wedding sheets—"sheets" being an evasive metonymy for the bed and for the lovemaking that takes place upon it. When Iago claims to hate Othello because "twixt my sheets / He's done my office," or when he remarks to Cassio on Cyprus, "Well, happiness to their sheets!" the same figure of speech, along with the sniggering euphemism of "office," has been employed. Like Desdemona's honor, which Iago thinks of as "an essence that's not seen," her sexual union with Othello, though sanctified by marriage, has not been directly imaginable till now when it is revealed to the prurient gaze as the curtains of the marriage bed are drawn apart. "My mistress here lies murdered in her bed," Emilia announces, as though the bed of marriage, with its "tragic lodging" of dead bodies-one black, the other white, lying side by side-is what horrified vision must take in at last. "Lodging" even implies the living together, the cohabitation of the lovers. The change of the word to "loading" in the Folio version of the text recalls Iago's plundered "land carrack." When Lodovico says, "the object poisons sight, / Let it be hid," the horror he feels is for a forbidden union as much as for the deaths this union has caused. To intensify that horror and to further emphasize the perversity of their sexual relation, there is a hint of necrophilia in the implication that now, at last, their love is consummated. Othello tells his victim, "Be thus when thou art dead, and I will kill thee / And love thee after," and then, having done so, "I kissed thee are I killed thee. No way but this: / Killing myself to die upon a kiss," giving "die" its usual Elizabethan double sense as orgasm.

The play makes it seem, even if we are sure of the contrary, that only their deathbed unites their bodies in ultimate union. "Starcrossed" by racial difference, they resemble Romeo and Juliet, their prototypes in the enactment of a *Liebestod* climaxing a forbidden love, forbidden for both pairs of lovers even in marriages that constitute social adultery. We must recall that Othello's anticipations of bliss had prompted thoughts of death:

> If it were now to die,
> 'Twere now to be most happy; for I fear
> My soul hath her content so absolute
> That not another comfort like to this
> Succeeds in unknown fate.

It is one of those flights of Othello's hyperbole that suggests too much before the fact, and Desdemona herself reins him in with, "The heavens forbid / But that our loves and comforts should increase / Even as our days do grow." To think that one will reach the peak of happiness—and so be ready to die—is a traditional poetic extravagance, but here more sinister, forecasting as it does the death which will actually be the consequence of their love-and Desdemona's literalism seems to express an appropriate caution. And well it might, for in the calculus of their unanticipated difficulties Shakespeare has added something besides the uncertainty of the bridegroom, the too-readiness of the bride. In this play about love and jealousy, which shows how love is a moment's hazardous leap over vast distance, he has included the crippling prohibition of racial difference.

At the last, Othello surrenders himself to the prison of race he thought he had escaped. He is not able, in the end, to cast away the role and character which societal

convention prescribed to him at the beginning of his career in the white colonial world. He recalls an exploit of his adopted Venetian identity when he remembers how, "in Aleppo once," he had taken by the throat a "turbanned," that is, unconverted, Turk (wearer of what Shakespeare calls in *Cymbeline* an "impious turband") who "[b]eat a Venetian and traduced the state." He remembers how he "smote him-thus," as he turns his dagger toward himself. This has generally been taken as splendid coup de theatre—but it is more. Reenacting that killing of an infidel by his transformed Christian self, Othello becomes again what he was before his conversion and enlistment in the service of Venice. His magnificent self-making has been undone and he now kills, again, the irreversibly circumcised, unassimilable racial other that he is.

PRODUCTION REVIEWS

Ben Brantley (essay date 10 December 2001)

SOURCE: Brantley, Ben. "A Revolt against God with No Apology." *New York Times* (10 December 2001): E1, E4.

[*In the following review of* Othello *directed by Doug Hughes at the Joseph Papp Public Theater, Brantley observes the dominance of Liev Schreiber's Iago in the production.*]

The psychopath is running the asylum again. And isn't it wonderful to know that you're in such—shall we say—capable hands?

Playing the ultimate disgruntled employee in the fast-paced production of *Othello* that opened last night at the Joseph Papp Public Theater, the amazing Liev Schreiber presents a tic-ridden, sexually crippled Iago who is clearly as mad as a rabid raccoon.

Yet he also possesses the sort of gifts that are usually rewarded with keys to the executive washroom: charm, efficiency, discreet sycophancy, organization and excellent people skills, including an ability to plant an idea in someone else's head and make him think it's his own.

A pity about that motiveless evil thing. But if he lived in latter-day Manhattan instead of long-ago Cyprus, this Iago would be the head of a Fortune 500 company or perhaps be one of Broadway's few bankable directors. At least until someone discovered a body in one of his filing cabinets.

Anyone doubting that Mr. Schreiber has advanced to the top rungs of American stage actors need only check out his smart, flashy and extremely entertaining portrait of Shakespeare's most subtle destroyer of men. Last seen in New York in an exquisitely understated portrait of one of the cryptic adulterers in Harold Pinter's *Betrayal,* Mr. Schreiber here shifts into a more flamboyant mode.

But don't worry. The cool fireworks he sends off have been just as impeccably orchestrated as the elliptical silences of *Betrayal.* In Doug Hughes's swift and streamlined interpretation of Shakespeare's most relentless tragedy, Iago and the man playing him are unconditionally in charge.

Granted, this leads to a definite imbalance. No one else in the cast, led by the gifted Keith David as Othello, comes close to matching Mr. Schreiber's playful interpretive intelligence.

So Mr. Hughes really has no choice but to lead with the ace that is Mr. Schreiber, turning the whole evening into Iago's playground. For here is a Mephistopheles who was born, as he sees it, not just to rebel against God but to usurp his function.

Correspondingly, in ways beautifully enhanced by the staging and production design, all the world—or at least most of Cyprus—becomes Iago's stage. Mr. Hughes is expert in clearly configuring his cast members in the patterns of chess figures as seen through Iago's eyes.

Robert Wierzel's superb lighting takes us directly into the overheated workshop of Iago's mind, where we find him serenading his own shadow. And David Van Tieghem's sound design includes sinister bell noises that seem to signal those moments when Iago clicks another piece of his diabolical puzzle into place.

Even Neil Patel's minimal set, in which screens play an appropriately central role, and Catherine Zuber's costumes seem to feed into Iago's master plan. The mood is 18th-century rococo, recalling a time in which rank and class were elaborately stratified. In an inspired interpolative touch, Iago becomes Othello's valet cum dresser as well as his ensign. And who is more invisible than a valet?

Taking advantage of such handy camouflage, this Iago proceeds to write the script of the undoing of his charismatic boss, barely able to repress a murmur of delight when props, actors and scenery all conspire to fall into place. You'll often find him in an aisle of the theater, looking on like the archetypal nervous director, nibbling his fingers with a mixture of satisfaction and anxiety. He's like an evil urban twin of Prospero, the world-ordering wizard of *The Tempest.*

This Iago, for the record, is no bland-seeming, self-effacing functionary, which has become the fashion. The brilliant British actor Simon Russell Beale provided the last word in that vein in his landmark performance for the Royal National Theater several seasons ago.

Instead, Mr. Schreiber leaves no doubt that his Iago, addled by sexual resentment and class envy, is as bonkers as the serial killer played by Kevin Spacey in *Seven* or one of Thomas Harris's diabolical pleasure killers. This Iago knows he has to keep a somber mask over his enjoyment of the disasters he brings about, but every so often the mask slips in public. And there, fleetingly, in plain view are the compulsive flinches and twitches, that infernal smile of self-satisfaction.

The struggle to sustain the mask provides most of the real tension in this *Othello.* Mr. David's interpretation of the Moor scales down the usual majesty of presence. He's extremely composed and authoritative, a natural leader. But he doesn't have the hypnotic grandeur or the implicit force of passion that so famously won over Desdemona (Kate Forbes).

This means that when Othello does battle with that old green-eyed monster, he doesn't really have very far to fall. He suggests a self-involved businessman (too self-involved and self-confident to notice that his ensign Iago is subverting him at every turn). When he famously bids farewell to the "tranquil mind" and martial glory, it's as if he's saying goodbye to expense account lunches at "21."

Christopher Evan Welch's foppish, foolish Roderigo is perhaps too easy a characterization, but it works. And Mr. Schleiber is never so creepy as when pulling Mr. Welch into a comradely embrace that seems mighty close to a stranglehold. Jay Goede is fine as the handsome Cassio, especially when in his drunkenness he says exactly what he shouldn't say if he wants to stay in Iago's good graces. Becky Ann Baker, an excellent actress, anachronistically brings to mind a whiny Shelly Winters as Desdemona's handmaiden.

Ms. Forbes, once you get past the self-conscious plumminess of her diction, is a refreshingly plucky Desdemona. She's heartier and more self-assertive than most Desdemonas, and it makes sense that she would stand up both to her father (Jack Ryland, in an enjoyably distraught performance) and her husband. She also does beautifully by the melancholy, introspective scene that precedes her murder.

Mr. David incisively conveys the uxorious sensual pride that Othello takes in his wife. But in this *Othello* it's Iago's relationship with Desdemona that seizes our imagination. Watch this Iago venturing, ever so tentatively, to touch Desdemona's neck as she weeps, simultaneously registering impulses both erotic and homicidal.

He's such a fascinating creature that you at first shrug off that no one else reaches Mr. Schreiber's level. After all, isn't that sort of appropriate, given the upper hand that Iago sustains for most of the evening?

By the second half, however, you're forced to remember that the play's title is indeed *Othello*. And this Othello's descent into tragic rage just doesn't intrigue except as it gratifies Iago. Tellingly, the audience was chuckling away even when Desdemona was being strangled (instead of suffocated as usual), not a good sign.

All the same, it isn't often that a production of a play as well known as *Othello* tells you anything new. And Mr. Schreiber, working with Mr. Hughes, draws an intriguing and persuasive new diagram of Iago's pathological web. Now if only his victims presented slightly more of a challenge.

Barbara D. Phillips (essay date 12 December 2001)

SOURCE: Phillips, Barbara D. "Review of *Othello*." *Wall Street Journal* (12 December 2001): A15.

[*In the following review of the 2001 Public Theater staging of* Othello, *Phillips notes the "austere power" of director Doug Hughes's production, but laments the lack of a more compelling Othello to match Liev Schreiber's masterful Iago.*]

Othello is Shakespeare's most intimate tragedy, one in which the audience is made privy from the start to Iago's corrosive envy and hatred, his malign manipulations unrestrained by moral bounds. And it is the playwright's most concentrated drama, one in which the villain makes quick work of love, loyalty and honor as he destroys a forthright war hero and his innocent young bride using a stealthy arsenal of artful insinuation, pregnant pauses and a handkerchief embroidered with strawberries. The play, which opened Sunday at the Public Theater in a compelling production directed by Doug Hughes, and starring Keith David as Othello, the masterly Liev Schreiber as Iago and Kate Forbes as Desdemona, has its share of swordplay. But the true battlefield is one of wordplay—a personal realm in which language, well-aimed, is a powerful weapon.

Othello's soaring rhetorical gifts win the heart of his bride, Desdemona, who is entranced by his tales of far-off lands and courageous adventures. And they persuade the Duke, despite the anger of Desdemona's father, to give the couple his blessing. But this African prince, a foreign-born hero of the Venetian public realm, finds himself brought to ground by Iago, his low-born ensign, a gutter-fighter who can paint a lurid picture of Desdemona's supposed sexual deception with just a

few well-placed strokes. Iago creates an illusory world in which he is perceived as an "honest" friend by those he sees as enemies and is both director and playwright of their undoing.

Iago's self-justifying motives—fury at being passed over for promotion; contempt for Cassio, the higher-born man who got the job from Othello; suspicion that his own wife, Emilia, has slept with the Moor; lust for Othello's wife, Desdemona—never quite explain the intensity of his anger or the scope of his evil.

The Public's Anspacher Theater proves to be the perfect setting for this rapid descent into hell, where its thrust stage and steeply banked seats keep some 275 ticket-holders within spitting distance of Iago's devilry. And director Doug Hughes puts the action at even closer range, staging the play in the aisles as well.

This could be a painful proximity in a production less sure-footed than the Public's. But Mr. Hughes's American cast shows a rare ease with both the music and meaning of Shakespeare's language. (Messrs. David and Schreiber are both noted voice-of-God narrators of TV documentaries, as well as classical actors.) Just as important, their well-chosen gestures serve as narrative footnotes for the modern audience, conveying the intent of words and phrases that the past four centuries of linguistic change have obscured.

It is, however, Mr. Schreiber's show from the start, more *Iago* than *Othello*. There is something in the way he carries himself, in his slightly askew posture, twitchy movements and the hooded nature of his gaze, that makes the skin crawl. Yet Iago's ability to gull both the innocents and sophisticates around him is plausible. Thanks to Mr. Schreiber's finely calibrated performance, we see with horror—and a guilty thrill—how Iago, his own self-control always threatening to slip away, is able to prey upon the individual weaknesses of each of his victims and play on the instruments of their destruction, remaining in their deluded eyes (until his final unmasking) a trusted confidante.

Mr. David is a less compelling actor, lacking the charismatic fire needed to balance Mr. Schreiber's infernal flame. When proud Othello is pulled downward, caught in the sinkhole of Iago's lies and fetid imagery, as well as his own unworldliness in the private realm, we don't feel the full measure of the distance he has traveled. Still, this Othello's epileptic seizure is frighteningly real, as are the tender kisses he plants on the sleeping mouth of the bride he is about to strangle to death.

In Catherine Zuber's 18th-century costumes, Ms. Forbes projects a nubile innocence as young Desdemona, her breasts all but popping out of her tightly bodiced dresses—no wonder she attracts the attention of these soldiers. But there is a firm determination beneath her soft curves, as when she pleads her own case with her choleric father, Brabantio (Jack Ryland), and lobbies for Cassio (Jay Goede) with her husband. In the secondary role of Iago's wife, an earthy Becky Ann Baker (probably best known as the mom on *Freaks and Geeks*) makes the most of Emilia's horror at the unwitting role she has played in Iago's cruel and deadly schemes.

Robert Wierzel's dramatic lighting, David Van Tieghen's expressionistic sound and Neil Patel's spare but strong scenic design (moveable Gothic screens, hanging lanterns, African drums)—underscore the austere power of this *Othello*.

Charles Isherwood (essay date 17-23 December 2001)

SOURCE: Isherwood, Charles. "Review of *Othello*." *Variety* 385, no. 5 (17-23 December 2001): 42-3.

[*In the following review of the Public Theater's 2001* Othello, *Isherwood remarks on the weakening of the drama's tragic anguish caused by its focus on Iago as enacted by Liev Schreiber—a performance unmatched by Keith David's "respectable" Othello or those of the remainder of the cast.*]

Destruction is raised to the level of art in *Othello,* and audiences couldn't ask for a more captivating creator of chaos than the Iago of Liev Schreiber, the latest and finest in this exemplary young actor's growing gallery of Shakespeare performances for the Public Theater. Title notwithstanding, Shakespeare's tragedy is dominated on the page and often on the stage by its nihilistic antihero, and such is the case with Doug Hughes' clean-lined, efficient production. Keith David's performance as the manipulated Moor has many fine attributes, but it ultimately lacks the grandeur to wrest the play from the cool, confident grasp of Schreiber's bewitching Iago.

Schreiber, who has previously won major acclaim for his Iachimo (in *Cymbeline*) and his Hamlet in Public Theater productions, is the rare American actor of any generation who lives so comfortably inside the sound and sense of Shakespearean verse that centuries of developments in syntax, vocabulary and grammar seem to evaporate as soon as he opens his mouth. While some actors merely bellow fancy language at us (here Jack Ryland's overacted Brabantio is an egregious example), Schreiber seems to be whispering Iago's thoughts clearly into our ear.

That's a particularly happy aptitude for this inventive schemer, who makes the audience his unwilling confidante by way of some of Shakespeare's richest soliloquies. The role is significantly larger than Othello's, and one of the longest in the canon, but it's also multifaceted and mysterious, and the great achievement of Schreiber's Iago is that we can never pin him down.

At first he seems unhinged, as the show opens with a whirl of whispering voices inside his head (David Van Tieghem's aggressive sound design and electronic music have both effectively unsettling and overbearing moments). A certain twitchiness, a straining of the neck as if to escape the sufferings of his skin, arises when Iago speaks of his humiliation at being passed over in favor of Cassio for promotion by Othello, and he seems equally disturbed at the rumor of his wife's infidelity with the Moor, His eyes become slits, his voice takes on a seething, sullen tone when the subject of women arises.

But most of the time, Iago's cool as a cucumber, a puppeteer pulling strings and taking a cheeky, casually chilling pleasure in doing so. The scene in which Iago languidly plants the suggestion of Desdemona's unfaithfulness in Othello's gullible heart is brilliantly played here by both actors. Throughout, as Iago flits between a kind of seething incipient madness and nearly diffident manipulation—his famous avowal "I am not what I am" made manifest—Schreiber's seductive voice, his sly charm and sheer intelligence lend Iago's machinations more than enough of the malignant fascination that are necessary to keep us from recoiling; on the contrary, when he's offstage, and we're watching his plots unfold without his sardonic commentary, we miss him. (The production's sharp, expressionistic lighting design by Robert Wierzel also serves to emphasize the character's centrality: The play ends with the spotlight not on the doomed lovers but on the shivering figure of Iago, for instance.)

Poised in opposition to the negative energy of Iago is the love between Othello and Desdemona, of course, and the piteousness of the play comes from our discovery of how easily the match is won by Iago's wanton destructiveness. The play offers a sad commentary on the fragility of faith in the face of reason, of love when opposed by hate: Our hearts should break at the ease with which Othello's great love for Desdemona is undone by the insinuating arguments and feeble "proofs" Iago puts before him.

Here Hughes' production disappoints—it doesn't give rise to real anguish. For the play to acquire the tragic dimension it needs to transfer our engagement from the mind of Iago to the heart of Othello, the profundity of Othello's love and the paralyzing pain of its loss need to come across forcefully. It doesn't quite, here.

David is in many respects a fine, respectable Othello. He cuts a virile figure, and the sensual attraction between his Othello and Kate Forbes' serene, sensible and lovely Desdemona is palpably felt. He is an experienced, accomplished handler of Shakespearean verse, too, and has a baritone of supple richness to do it full musical justice.

Othello's jittery unease as Iago's poison works its way into his heart is effectively rendered, but as we listen to David's handsome voice rise in anger or drop suddenly to a smooth basso aside, it's often the sculpted phrases we hear, not the volcano of feeling behind them. The superficial nobility of the warrior and hero are here, but the greater nobility of the full-hearted lover, in which resides the character's grandeur and significance, is not. As a result, Othello's duping is a sad waste, but not quite tragic, so its consequences don't carry the horrific force they should, despite Forbes' fine work in the last scene.

The supporting cast, clad in Catherine Zuber's handsome if somewhat generic 18th-century garb, is competent. Becky Ann Baker's Emilia is surprisingly lacking in color, as is, less surprisingly, Jay Goede's Cassio (that's a reflection on the character, not the actor). The set design by Neil Patel is an odd mixture whose cement pillars and walls sometimes recall contemporary Venice, Calif., more than Venice, Italy, and Cyprus.

But the evening belongs to Schreiber's Iago, and he's no less fascinating at the conclusion than the start. The character's final lines, in answer to Othello's demand to know the cause of his hate, are among the most bluntly stunning in Shakespeare. "Demand me nothing. What you know, you know. / From this time forth I never will speak word." Iago's sudden silence is a rebuke to the comforting idea that human evil has a cause, and thus a cure. All we really know about Iago, in the end, is that he's awful and he's fascinating. And, thanks to the lucid complexity of Schreiber's performance, he's disturbingly real.

Michael Feingold (essay date 18 December 2001)

SOURCE: Feingold, Michael. "Less Is Moor." *Village Voice* 46, no. 50 (18 December 2001): 71.

[*In the following review of Doug Hughes's 2001* Othello *staged at New York City's Public Theater, Feingold acknowledges the overall merit of this production, but finds its passion "distressingly contained."*]

Greed is the drama critic's prevailing sin. Not greed for power or money—though none of us would complain if the artists all did exactly what we told them, and offered us bushels of cash to praise them for doing it—but greed for greatness. Offer me passable, I want good; give me good, I demand excellent; grant me excellent, and I say, "What ever happened to sublime?"

Take Doug Hughes's staging of *Othello*. It is a solid, handsome, intelligent, and skillfully acted production, at which I had a good time. And now I shall prove almost as ungrateful as Iago, who had a good job and hated his employer for not giving him a better one. *Othello* is such a good job that I want it to be great. It ought to be great; the people involved are capable of greatness, and some of them have occasionally demonstrated it. Why the show isn't great, I don't know. Whether it will be great in a few more weeks, I can't predict. Right now it is a good job; if you've never seen a great *Othello,* or great performances of the individual roles, and so have no yardstick by which to gauge its greatness, this solidly competent production will introduce the play to you very effectively.

I should add in fairness that great Othellos are not easily come by. The play is the most concentrated of Shakespeare's late tragedies, with virtually no spectacle or battle to distract from the central story. Its one perfunctory clown scene is always blessedly cut (most people don't even know it exists), and one of the few better-than-good things in the current production is Christopher Evan Welch's demonstration that Roderigo is a brave, albeit foolish, gentleman and not the usual pratfalling fop who provides alleged comic relief. This leaves, to interrupt the main characters' tragic conflict, only the party scene where Cassio gets drunk, staged here by Hughes with the same taut, abstemious lucidity as everything else. No, there's never a lot of diversion in *Othello*: Its pleasure lives in the acting and the word—music of two of the most arduous and complex roles in the canon (Iago is actually the longest role in Shakespeare), flanked by four supporting roles, all of which must also be played superbly for a production to take flight. Like you, I've never seen it happen, though I've seen sublime performances of all six roles individually.

Hughes's cast is a handsome one, astutely assembled. Before we even got to the meaty central acts, I liked Welch's clash of dignity and tempted gullibility; I liked Jack Ryland's tantrummy bulldog of a Brabantio; and I grinned with an old playgoer's satisfaction at George Morfogen's foxily soft-spoken Duke of Venice. But even in Venice, both Keith David's Othello and Liev Schreiber's Iago gave warning signs of acting trouble ahead. Or maybe one should say "lack-of-warning" signs, since the problem stalking this production seems to be that neither actor knows exactly who he is—a surprising letdown for Hughes, whose Delacorte *Henry V* was so good precisely because Andre Braugher's Henry knew more about himself, and made us learn more, with every scene. There a director and an actor reaffirmed the central reality of drama: It progresses through time and reveals over time. Schreiber and David have many colors to their acting, but the colors are laid intermittently, and sometimes not at all; they don't build over time to reveal a complete picture.

David fares the better of the two. Amiable and genteel at the beginning, he has moving bursts later of both rage and a pathos just this side of self-pity. At the end, he offers a fierce dignity—we see his power as a military commander best when he's with Desdemona— and a sense of loving desperation that, abetted by Kate Forbes's ripe sincerity, makes the familiar death scene deeply stirring. When David hits these high marks, the production seems fresh and electric. Catherine Zuber's handsome, somber-toned costumes put the play in the Regency era, evoking images of Lord Nelson or the Napoleonic Wars; they give David's African-sculpted good looks a Byronic touch.

But the beautiful touches in David's performance dissipate as quickly as they come. He has rage and tenderness, but not, apparently, the inner dynamic to produce both at once. Othello is a man riven by contradictions; one reason the play has such resonance for us is that he sees himself—like so many Americans, black and otherwise—as an outsider, who has won status in a society where he still feels alien, a poetically articulate man who apologizes for his rudeness of speech. Iago succeeds with him by playing on fears that are already there. Never wholly believing that Desdemona can love him, Othello lets himself be convinced that she doesn't. Under his early affirmations, we need to see the fears; under his late rages, the nagging doubts. With David, until the death scene, they come one at a time, or not at all.

Then there is the question of pomp. Othello's rage is often linked to his stature and power: Between the first and fifth acts, virtually everyone we see is under his command, and Shakespeare gives him plenty of word-music in which to affirm his grandeur. Giuseppe Verdi made the old way of playing the role as pure word-music unfeasible. Next to what he achieved with a heroic tenor voice and a full orchestra, even Paul Robeson, at least on record, pales by comparison. In the shadow of such competition, David and his director seem to have decided consciously to keep the role low-keyed. You would never know, hearing David, that the passage about the Propontic and the Hellespont was one in which all English-speaking actors used to dream of displaying their most vibrant tones, just as you wouldn't know, from his suavely gentle first act, why Salvini was described as playing it like "a smoldering volcano." For a play with so much fevered passion and blood in it, the performance is distressingly contained.

As is, even more distressingly, Schreiber's Iago. Here is an actor whose power in this realm was proved several years back, when he played what might be called the

junior version of the role (Iachimo is the diminutive of Iago) so gloriously in the Delacorte production of *Cymbeline*. Expecting the best, what we get here is merely all right. Even more complex than Othello, Iago is also a more elusive figure. Far from having no motive, his malignity has almost too many: Othello gave someone else the better job; he may have slept with Iago's wife; the fellow he gave the job to, Cassio, is unqualified. There is a class issue—Cassio is a gentleman, Iago a professional soldier—to go with the race issue. Modern eyes have seen a homosexual element in Iago's fixation on Othello's love life (Hughes's staging relocates his interest in Roderigo), and a degree of projection that suggests his desire to replace not Cassio but Othello. Two of Schreiber's most striking moments come when he nearly kisses Desdemona, and when, plotting Cassio's murder, the notion of taking command himself seems to cross his mind. Such moments are like lightning flashes of the great Iago Schreiber ought to be.

For the most part, though, what we get is solid, not quite stolid, impassivity. Like David avoiding the trumpet tones of pomp, Schreiber shuns the temptation to revel in his evil with shriek and rant, which has destroyed countless Iagos (the worst ever was Christopher Plummer's, so openly demented that even Roderigo would have had him put away). But in dodging the one trap, Schreiber falls into its opposite, enjoying his evil so little that it lacks credibility. The best Iago I ever saw, because the most convincingly scary, was Christopher Walken. You could see why the other characters accepted him as sane, though he was clearly unhinged; he rarely raised his voice, but it was easy to believe that he might want to kill any number of people. Schreiber dutifully declares that he hates the Moor; he goes efficiently through the motions of killing Roderigo and Emilia; but the person whose thoughts we've been privy to, through lines and lines of lucidly spoken soliloquy, doesn't appear to have any strong connection to these acts. You expect his alibi to be "The script made me do it." Mary McCarthy praised Jose Ferrer (playing opposite Robeson) for finding in the role the visionary "who makes his dream of evil come true on earth." Maybe that was more readily imaginable in the late 1940s, with Hitler just destroyed and Stalin still alive. But surely we have examples enough all around us today; bringing them to imaginative life, so that we can exorcise them from ourselves through the ritual of playgoing, is the difficult part.

As if trying hard not to steal the muted thunder of these centerpieces, Hughes's supporting actors often tend to come in just slightly under their best work. Even Forbes, a strong and beautiful Desdemona, occasionally gets too soft-spoken for the Anspacher's three-quarter stage. The good work by oldsters Ryland and Morfogen at the start is balanced, later on, by two appealing youngsters in tiny roles: Natacha Roi (Bianca) and Dan Snook (Lodovico). Jay Goede is a likable, slightly callow Cassio, and Becky Ann Baker a firm but oddly unincisive Emilia. Some of the limitation involved may come from Hughes, whose austere approach consciously leaves blank many moments that beg for supportive detail. Just as drama critics, getting the good, always beg for the better.

John Simon (essay date 24 December 2001)

SOURCE: Simon, John. "Moor is Less." *New York Magazine* 34, no. 49 (24 December 2001): 109.

[*In the following review of the 2001 Public Theater staging of* Othello *directed by Doug Hughes, Simon faults Hughes's casting and interpretive decisions, claiming that they obscured the tragic grandeur of Shakespeare's play, burying its loftier, philosophical qualities among the sordidness of domestic drama.*]

What a chance for timeliness was missed by Doug Hughes's staging of *Othello*! By reducing the play to domestic drama (which on one level it is), the Public Theater has deprived it of its political and metaphysical half: the war between civilized goodness (Venice, Christianity, order) and barbarous evil (the Turks, treachery, chaos). That may have cut too close to the bone and required a larger, grander production than the impoverished one here. But how sad to see a shatteringly relevant historical and philosophical clash shrunk to a chamber piece of mere personal conflict, and even that poorly executed.

The casting of the principals demands a keen aesthetic sensibility. Whereas it is right to give nearly central importance to Iago, he should not physically dominate Othello, yet the hulking Liev Schreiber as Iago does precisely that. By making Iago smaller and physiognomically more trustworthy, the power of unperspicuous, insidious evil is more graphically highlighted. Othello, though decently acted by Keith David, needs to be of more heroic stature, more purblind nobility, and, eventually, of more pitiable, poetic grandeur than mere competence can summon. An even greater problem is Desdemona, surely the most demanding female role in the Shakespeare canon, a role of feminine and human perfection, neither of which the visually and histrionically ordinary Kate Forbes can approximate.

It is a costly mistake to have a Roderigo (Christopher Evan Welch) more interesting than Cassio (Jay Goede); to turn Lodovico (Dan Snook) into an immature and prissily spoken hunk; to cast an Emilia (Becky Ann Baker) who looks more like Iago's sexless aunt than his jealousy-provoking wife; and to give us a Bianca (Natacha Roi) more desirable than Desdemona.

Schreiber does wring a good deal out of Iago, but much of it is literally and figuratively misdirected. Although lechery for Desdemona may be a minor cause of his intrigues, directing him to clasp, cradle, and fondle her consolingly is socially and dramatically unacceptable. And the final image of Iago—already reduced to cowering from a mighty blow of Othello's Notung-like sword—left standing tall above the three corpses of his making is absurd. What's called for is his being dragged off to punishment. For him to start twitching in what looks like remorse as the lights go down is even more preposterous.

Caryn James (essay date 21 January 2002)

SOURCE: James, Caryn. "Review of *Othello*." *New York Times* 151, no. 52005 (21 January 2002): E1, E5.

[*In the following excerpted review of a BBC television adaptation of* Othello *directed by Geoffrey Saxe in 2002, James emphasizes the film's contemporary, racially charged setting and overall merit, despite its flawed depiction of a simplified dramatic villain.*]

[I]nstitutional racism is the backdrop for [a televised] *Othello*, which entirely abandons Shakespeare's language. It cuts from a passionate scene of Othello in bed with Dessie (the cloyingly contrived name for Desdemona) to an episode in which the police beat a black suspect to death.

The film is richly photographed and stylized. Eamonn Walker, an English actor known for his utterly convincing role as the American Muslim Said in HBO's prison series, *Oz*, is Othello. He makes his name by standing outside his station house on the the night of the attack, raising his arms and declaring to an angry crowd that if the police acted badly they will be held responsible. Set against a dark sky and the glare of lights, this scene is one of many (directed by Geoffrey Saxe) that has an iconic, theatrical feel yet firmly reflects reality. Soon Othello is the new police commissioner, and Jago is incensed at being passed over.

[T]his film does not bludgeon viewers with social commentary. Instead, the story of Othello's love for and jealousy of Dessie, and of Jago's ambition and manipulation, is set against the backdrop of a racist, media-driven society. When Othello marries Dessie (Keeley Hawes), a white heiress who works as a journalist, they become media darlings. Michael Cass (Richard Coyle), the updated Cassio, is a police officer sent to protect Dessie after racist thugs throw stones through her window—the perfect setup for Jago to hint that Dessie and Cass are having an affair. Mr. Walker creates a convincingly strong, impassioned Othello, though at times he seems to sigh more than Al Gore at a political debate, reducing Othello's growing suspicions to simple exasperation.

This fascinating, multilayered film suffers from one central flaw, though. Jago's character, as written and as acted by Christopher Eccleston, is too transparent, so obviously slimy that it is hard to believe Othello would fall for his pretence at friendship. Characters in many other films written by Mr. Davies talk directly to the camera, as Jago needlessly does here.

"It was about love," he says at the start and again at the end of his story. "Don't talk to me about race, don't talk to me about politics—it was love, simple as that." By the end, he is more clearly alluding to his own love for Othello, but of course he is wrong about other things. . . .

THEMES

Paul Yachnin (essay date 1996)

SOURCE: Yachnin, Paul. "Magical Properties: Vision, Possession, and Wonder in *Othello*." *Theatre Journal* 48, no. 2 (1996): 197-208.

[*In the following essay, Yachnin interprets* Othello *as a theatrical evocation of the violent potentiality of wonder, embodied in Desdemona's fetishized handkerchief.*]

A specter is haunting new historicism—the specter of the aesthetic: the attributes of beauty and sublimity, the realm of wonderful objects and feelings of awe. From Louis Montrose's evocation of the uncanny connections between Simon Forman's dream of Queen Elizabeth and William Shakespeare's *A Midsummer Night's Dream* to Stephen Greenblatt's book, *Marvelous Possessions: The Wonder of the New World,* we can discern an investment in wonder among those whom we might have expected to be more attuned to the political dimensions of literature.[1] Of course, materialist criticism is entitled to examine the forms of wonder, since wonder is as much involved in the socio-political realm as is gender, rank, or race. But it is not merely a cool-headed interest in wonder that we find in new historicism; on the contrary, it is an undertaking to arouse amazement in the reader. For some practitioners, the attempt to awe their readers has to do with the cachet associated with the mystifying style of postmodernist French theory, but for lucid writers such as Montrose and Greenblatt, the attempt to arouse wonder has its roots in other ground. That ground is Shakespeare.

My focus is the operations of wonder in Shakespeare's playhouse, but I also will examine the differences between Renaissance versions of theatrical wonder and later forms in Shakespeare as literature. These versions are linked by their relationship with subjectivity, possession, and the nature of the object, but are produced in different ways and toward different ends—theatrical wonder is largely visual, processive, and collective; literary and critical wonder is "visionary," possessive, and directed toward the individual as individual. Roughly speaking, it is the difference between an outing to the circus and a morning in church; we tend to misinterpret the earthly pleasures of the former in light of the heavenly raptures of the latter.

Othello is an illuminating text for the purposes of my discussion because it is both wonderful in itself and critical of how "magical" properties can seduce the eye and mind. By analyzing *Othello*'s attempts to fetishize theatrical properties, we can begin to understand the fetishistic investments made by present-day readers and critics. This is not to suggest that the play is magically prescient. Rather its fictions of possession and wonder imply the conditions of its production and make the contradictions in that production visible as ideology. Pierre Machery tells us that "the book revolves around this myth [i.e., that the book is uncannily alive]; but in the process of its formation the book takes a stand regarding this myth, exposing it. This does not mean that the book is able to become its own criticism: it gives an implicit critique of its ideological content, if only because it resists being incorporated into the flow of ideology in order to give a *determinate representation* of it."[2] So while Shakespeare is the source of the specter haunting recent Shakespeare criticism, his play's "implicit critique of its ideological content" might nevertheless provide something like an exorcism.

Shakespeare's attempts to reconfigure playgoing as conversional wonder have meshed with the emergence of the aesthetic as a major cultural formation; however, it is unlikely that his drama in fact transformed the experiences of Renaissance playgoers.[3] They, no doubt, continued to expect recreation rather than re-creation. In *Othello,* Shakespeare maneuvers to make wonder out of the material he has to work with, which, among other things such as language and costume, includes the fabric of the handkerchief and the body of the boy actor who plays Desdemona. These two objects are constructed so as to enhance the cultural status of the play by raising it above the commercialism and materiality of actual play production. But if we can deploy a strategic resistance to the play's sublimity (a resistance that came more easily to the original audiences), then the ordinariness of these "wonders" and the particular ways in which they are presented will allow us critical insight into the mystifications of Shakespeare and Shakespeare criticism.

* * *

To move toward a historical understanding of Shake-spearean wonder, let us begin by considering two exemplary views—Northrop Frye's idea of *The Tempest* as a play where wonder leads to self-knowledge and Greenblatt's troubled but similar account of the effects of wonder. Of course, new historicism arose in opposition to approaches such as Frye's, but humanist and antihumanist forms of criticism share some surprisingly similar assumptions about the relationship between the literary text and the subject. Here is Frye, writing in 1959:

> [T]he play is an illusion like the dream, and yet a focus of reality more intense than life affords. The action of *The Tempest* moves from . . . reality to realization. What seems at first illusory, the magic and music, becomes real, and the *Realpolitik* of Antonio and Sebastian becomes illusion. . . . When the Court Party first came to the island "no man was his own"; they had not found their "proper selves." Through the mirages of Ariel, the mops and mows of the other spirits, the vanities of Prospero's art, and the fevers of madness, reality grows up in them from inside, in response to the fertilizing influence of illusion.[4]

Greenblatt in 1991 sees wonder as "the central figure in the initial European response to the New World"— "something like the 'startle reflex' one can observe in infants." Although his model of personhood is far more corporealized than Frye's, he nevertheless sees wonder as ineluctably inward:

> Someone witnesses something amazing, but what most matters takes place not "out there" or along the receptive surfaces of the body where the self encounters the world, but deep within, at the vital, emotional center of the witness. This inward response cannot be marginalized or denied, any more than a constriction of the heart in terror can be denied; wonder is absolutely exigent, a primary or radical passion. . . . The experience of wonder seems to resist recuperation, containment, ideological incorporation; it sits strangely apart from everything that gives coherence to Léry's universe [Jean de Léry, whose *History of a Voyage* (1585) Greenblatt is discussing here], apart and yet utterly compelling.[5]

Although connected with the violent harrowing of the self central to Christian visionary experience, Frye and Greenblatt generally understand wonder in terms of a modern idea of personhood, where wonder provokes what Frye calls "realization," the emptying out of the world and the concomitant expansion of the self. This view differs from Shakespeare's; Shakespeare usually shows how wonder violates or nullifies the self rather than how it precipitates the self's expansive fulfilment. We remember Horatio "harrow[ed] . . . with fear and wonder" (*Hamlet*, 1.1.45) or Cleomenes reduced to nothing by "the ear-deaf'ning voice o' th' oracle" (*Winter's Tale*, 3.1.9).[6] For Frye and Greenblatt, in contrast, our ability to grasp an authentic selfhood has

to do centrally with possessing and with being possessed by a fetishized text. "*The Tempest*," Frye says, "is a play not simply to be read or seen or even studied, but possessed."[7] At the beginning of *Marvelous Possessions*, Greenblatt too declares his investments in the marvels of narrative: "I remain possessed by stories and obsessed with their complex uses."[8]

To be sure, the idea of being possessed by theatrical spectacle was current in the Renaissance. In his *Apology for Actors* (1612), Thomas Heywood, reiterating Shakespeare's emphasis on the invasive power of spectacle, praises theatre's capacity to re-fashion the members of the audience: "so bewitching a thing is lively and well-spirited action that it hath power to new mold the hearts of the spectators and fashion them to the shape of any noble and notable attempt."[9] But among eyewitness accounts of the drama, there are far fewer indications of the formative power ascribed to it by Heywood. We remember that the actors normally performed in the cold light of day and did not have the scenic resources of the court masque. Thomas Platter, in 1599, writes of the "marvelous" dancing that followed a performance of *Julius Caesar;* about the play he notes only that it was "very well acted."[10] In 1613, Sir Henry Wotton recounts disapprovingly the tawdry spectacle Shakespeare's company made of the history of Henry VIII: "The King's Players had a new play called *All is True,* representing some principal pieces of the reign of Henry VIII, which was set forth with many extraordinary circumstances of pomp and majesty, even to the matting of the stage . . . sufficient in truth within a while to make greatness very familiar, if not ridiculous."[11] So while there were marvels in the theatre, they were usually greeted as something akin to mere showiness.

In accord with these views of theatrical spectacle, playgoers seem not usually to have been possessed by wonder.[12] The antitheatricalist writer and sometime dramatist Stephen Gosson writes scathingly about the fun audience-members have at the playhouse:

> In our assemblies at plays in London, you shall see such heaving and shoving, such itching and shouldering to sit by women. Such care for their garments that they should not be trod on, such eyes to their laps that no chips light in them, such pillows to their backs that they take no hurt . . . such tickling, such toying, such smiling, such winking, and such manning them home when the sports are ended that it is a right comedy to mark their behavior.[13]

Indeed, a considerable part of the thrill of playgoing had little to do with the plays themselves, but was involved instead with the erotic and social gratifications of seeing and being seen by other spectators. In 1613, Henry Parrot satirizes the practices of self-display characteristic of a theatre described by one antitheatricalist as "Venus' palace":[14]

When young Rogero goes to see a play,
His pleasure is you place him on the stage,
The better to demonstrate his array,
And how he sits attended by his page,
  That only serves to fill those pipes with smoke,
  For which he pawned hath his riding cloak.[15]

In view of the mirthful and eroticized atmosphere of Renaissance playhouses, it seems clear that the emphasis upon the conversional marvelousness of Shakespeare's plays must have been consequent upon their transformation into literature, a process that began in earnest only after Shakespeare's death. In the 1623 First Folio, Jonson lauds Shakespeare as "the wonder of our stage," but promotes his "book" as an embodiment of genius that makes an irresistible claim on all those who "have wits to read, and praise to give."[16] In the Second Folio (1632), Milton expresses similar "wonder and astonishment" at Shakespeare's "Delphic lines." In Milton's account, Shakespeare's astonishing book transforms the reader into a "livelong monument"—"thou our fancy of itself bereaving, / Dost make us marble with too much conceiving."[17] In commendatory verses prefixed to *Poems: written by Wil. Shake-speare* (1640)—twenty-four years after the playwright's death—Leonard Digges is able to remember "how the audience, / Were ravished, with what wonder they went hence," but invites the reader to look upon the "wit-fraught book, . . . whose worth / Like old-coined gold, . . . / Shall pass true current to succeeding age."[18] These tributes suggest that Shakespearean wonder, from the outset, was an experience which, while it might be imagined as the rapture of audience—members possessed by a bewitching spectacle, in fact belonged to readers who owned the text. "[Y]ou will stand for your privileges . . . to read, and censure," urge John Heminge and Henry Condell, the actors responsible for the publication of the First Folio. "Do so, but buy it first . . . whatever you do, buy."[19]

But while there are differences, there is also a historical line to be traced from the spectacles performed in Shakespeare's playhouse to the visionary wonders of the First Folio to the retailing of literary wonder in recent criticism. These versions of the marvelous are related to the broader development of what Georg Lukács calls "reified consciousness," the idea that persons become objects to themselves because of their traffic in fetishized commodities—goods onto which are projected the realities of human labor and relations, and for whose commodified value real persons exchange their own worth. In "Reification and the Consciousness of the Proletariat," Lukács develops an analysis of the alienating effects of commodity fetishism: "The essence of commodity-structure . . . is that a relation between people takes on the character of a thing and thus acquires a 'phantom objectivity,' an autonomy that seems so strictly rational and all-embracing as to conceal every trace of its fundamental nature: the rela-

tion between people." "The commodity character of the commodity, the abstract, quantitative mode of calculability shows itself here in its purest form: the reified mind necessarily sees it as the form in which its own authentic immediacy becomes manifest."[20]

When the commodity in question is literary wonder, and when such wonder is a possession that possesses and is the form in which the reader's mind finds its own "authentic immediacy," readerly investments will be both profound and unstable. A text like *Othello* will be to the engrossed reader as Desdemona is to her husband—an object whose capacity to arouse wonder in the beholder is seen to underwrite the beholder's selfhood. Kenneth Burke explains Othello's stake in Desdemona as "ownership in the profoundest sense of ownership, the property of human affections, as fetishtically localized in the object of possession, while the possessor is himself possessed by his very engrossment."[21] We want to bear in mind the differences between the spectacular marvels staged in the culturally lowbrow Shakespearean theatre and the visionary wonder produced in the highbrow province of Shakespeare as literature. We also should remember that a performance—unlike a book—cannot be owned. But we also want to consider the possibility that reading Shakespeare for his profound insights into the meaning of life, or writing about Shakespeare in ways calculated to arouse wonder in our readers, might constitute particular institutional transformations of spectacular, *commercial* theatricality.

* * *

In Shakespeare's London, Othello's handkerchief would have been marketable goods, a square of embroidered cloth in a nation whose primary industry was the production of textiles, a stage property in a theatre whose largest operating expense was the purchase of costumes and draperies. Othello's mystification of the handkerchief within the play is of a piece with Renaissance Londoners' investments, both financial and psychological, in what even Caliban recognizes as "trash"—the "glistering apparel" (*Tempest*, 4.1. 224, 193 [stage direction]) that advertised individuals' high social status in the real world and whose visual appeal in the theatre helped to make Shakespeare's drama so popular. The play's stake in the handkerchief registers the theatre's participation in English society's fetishized trade in textiles.

In the world of the play, all the characters except Othello view the handkerchief as marketable goods; he defines it as a magical talisman. The effect of this definitional contest is twofold. One, the handkerchief emerges as wondrous—an object of great emotional and sexual energy. The napkin's enhancement serves the institutional project of valorizing drama over against the theatre's degraded world of work and its trade in playtexts and textiles. Two, the intensity of Othello's investments in this square of cloth works to reveal the fetish character of commodities in general. Although everyone except Othello thinks of the handkerchief as an ordinary object, they fetishize it too. They turn it into a commodity, in Marx's sense: a thing that becomes "mysterious . . . simply because in it the social character of men's labour appears to them as an objective character stamped upon the product of that labour."[22] To understand the particular mystery the fetishized handkerchief evokes, however, we need to expand the field of labor and exchange to include the "work" of sex. That is necessary because the characters' projections of themselves onto the handkerchief run along lines determined by sex and gender. Moreover, to take sex and gender into account is to recognize their importance in the development of modern aesthetic fetishism. In this view, the art-object is the feminine beloved of the masculine owner—"a non-alienated object, one quite the reverse of a commodity, which like the 'auratic' phenomenon of a Walter Benjamin returns our tender gaze and whispers that it was created for us alone."[23]

For most of the characters, the handkerchief is reproducible, exchangeable, and has a certain cash value. Furthermore, although it circulates widely, everyone recognizes it as private property. Because it is private property, Emilia, Cassio, and Bianca all speak about making copies of it. In this regard, is it even clear that Emilia plans to keep it after having found it? She says, "My wayward husband hath a hundred times / Woo'd me to steal it . . . I'll have the work ta'en out, / And give 't Iago" (3.3.292-96). Does she intend to give Iago the original or the copy? Does she perhaps prefer robbing the handkerchief of its singularity to stealing the thing itself from Desdemona? For Desdemona, the handkerchief balances between the everyday and the sacred, becoming a hugely valued love token that is nonetheless commensurable with monetary value. "Where should I lose the handkerchief?" she asks, "Believe me, I had rather have lost my purse / Full of crusadoes" (3.4.23,25-26).

Cassio and Emilia each intend to have the handkerchief copied because they recognize it as property that will be wanted by its owner. The strawberry-spotted handkerchief bears the print of the owner's possessive desire for it as a singular object, even though it is not necessarily unique, but potentially only the first of a series. It could be reproduced endlessly for an endless number of owners. This contradiction is paralleled by Iago's jealous ownership of his wife. She bears the imprint of his possessive desire for her as a unique prize even though he discounts her, with a sexual quibble, as "a common thing": "You have a thing for me? It is a common thing" (3.3.302).

The handkerchief's properties are continuous with the properties of love. Were Desdemona an object like the handkerchief, Othello could possess her, but so could anyone else, and in any case she would then be a "common thing" like the handkerchief, certainly not the inimitable treasure for which Othello happily sacrifices his "unhoused free condition" (1.2.26). If she is not an object to Othello, then she is a subject—which is to say she is an object to herself. As self-possessed, she is free to give herself away to another. If she is her own private property, as Peter Stallybrass points out, then her defining attribute—her honor—becomes as detachable as her handkerchief:[24]

IAGO:

> But if I give my wife a handkerchief—

OTHELLO:

> What then?

IAGO:

> Why then 'tis hers, my lord, and being hers,
> She may, I think, bestow 't on any man.

OTHELLO:

> She is protectress of her honor too;
> May she give that?

> [4.1.10-15]

No possible permutation is able to unburden heterosexual love of the contradictions involved in the patriarchal ownership of women, who are also required to be owners of themselves.

The handkerchief figures possessive male desire for the female "common thing" in ways that legitimize jealousy in terms of the "phantom objectivity" of the gender system. The operation of this system seems invisible to the characters, and its effects cut across gender lines. Bianca returns the handkerchief to Cassio, refusing to "take out the work" since she thinks it was given to him by another woman. This other woman is a "hobbyhorse," while Cassio is allowed the agential attributes of desire and deceitfulness:

> What did you mean by that same handkerchief you gave me even now? I was a fine fool to take it. I must take out the work? A likely piece of work, that you should find it in your chamber, and know not who left it there! This is some minx's token, and I must take out the work? There, give it your hobby-horse.

> [4.1.148-54]

Given the invisible influence that the handkerchief wields in its travels through the play, the claims Othello makes about both its sacred, feminine origins and its magical power to bind husband to wife through male desire seem not to belong to an enchanted world entirely foreign to Venetian civility, but rather to constitute a somewhat outlandish explanation of the handkerchief's actual operations. The play opens to analysis the fetish character of the handkerchief with regard to all the characters who touch it. It does so through Othello's explanation of its quasi-magical powers, but more so by the way Othello convinces himself into accepting it as "ocular proof" (3.3.360) against his wife (since it falls to the stage in his presence and as a result of his action some 150 lines before Iago reports having seen Cassio wipe his beard with it). Othello uses the handkerchief to prove something against Desdemona that the desirable thingness of the handkerchief has already inscribed as inevitable in heterosexual relations—the "destiny un-shunnable" (3.3.275) of being made a cuckold. It is the fate of every man to invest his all in the vexed figure of Woman, she who is unique because she is a rare object and "common" because she is a subject. On this account, the vexing constitution of Othello's selfhood on the basis of heterosexual mutuality is no different from anyone else's—it is only that his terminology is strangely revealing.

But Othello's terms constitute more than an exotic account of the ordinary. In Othello's telling, the handkerchief is a different kind of thing—a wonder that possesses a particular history and a charismatic hold on its owner. Desdemona is reframed as just such a wonderful object. If she were like the handkerchief that Othello imagines, then he could possess her wholly yet she would become neither the "common thing" of marketplace exchanges nor the free trader of her own honor. Not, of course, that the handkerchief ever becomes convincingly magical. It is rather that its movements in the play suggest that there *could* be "magic in the web of it" (3.4.69). The handkerchief is held in hand after hand, but its significance is never grasped by any one possessor. Its power to generate an unseen network of connections over the heads of every character except Iago lends it a certain marvelousness. Even Iago cannot quite get hold of it. He is just lucky: it is surprising that Cassio is unacquainted with Othello's first and most valued gift to Desdemona, especially since Cassio went "a-wooing" with Othello "from first to last" (3.3.71,96). "Sure," Desdemona says, "there's some wonder in this handkerchief" (3.4.101). For the play's original spectators and for us, there is indeed some wonder since, as Douglas Bruster comments, "uncanniness arises as the result of an extended social order" that is apparent in the handkerchief but not visible to the characters.[25]

So while the play opens to examination the operations of commodity fetishism, it also works to fetishize the handkerchief in the wonderful terms of Egyptian charmers, sibylline prophetic fury, and "mummy . . . / Conserved of maidens' hearts" (3.4.74-75). In order to understand the theatre's apparent need to redescribe its most important material resource, we do not need to

follow Richard Wilson's spirited attack either on Shakespeare's theatre as "part of the apparatus of the English nation-state" or on Shakespeare as a proto-capitalist enemy of the artisanal class of clothworkers.[26] But perhaps we do need to consider that costumes in the commercial theatre, while expensive and often gorgeous, were also redolent of the theatre's participation in trade and manual labor. Some costumes could project the somewhat grubby aura that went with being aristocratic cast-offs, but those costumes had themselves passed through the pawnbrokers and the second-hand dealers' shops; and other costumes and all the rest of the cloth used in performances constituted at one level "ocular proof" of the theatre's material and class connections with the increasingly hard-pressed and riotous clothworkers. In this view, the play endeavors to "take out the work" from textiles in order to purge theatre of the manual labor that made theatre possible, aligning drama thereby with the ethos of courtliness that itself was an important factor in the theatre's commercial success.

* * *

In 1610, Henry Jackson, member of Corpus Christi College, witnessed a performance of *Othello* at Oxford. "They also had tragedies," he wrote,

> which they acted with propriety and fitness. In which [tragedies], not only through speaking but also through acting certain things, they moved [the audience] to tears. But truly the celebrated Desdemona, slain in our presence by her husband, although she pleaded her case very effectively throughout, yet moved [us] more after she was dead, when, lying on her bed, she entreated the pity of the spectators by her very countenance.[27]

Jackson was a serious and religious young man, and Oxford probably provided a more attentive audience than the Globe or even Blackfriars.[28] Yet his response to the boy actor, while deeply engaged, is equivalent to neither Frye's "realization" nor Greenblatt's "radical passion." In Jackson's account, the audience's response mirrors the shift within the play from the language-based relationship between the lovers at the outset to Othello's subsequent attempt to gain visual mastery over Desdemona. At first they woo each other through story-telling, hinting, and speaking (1.3.128-70); under Iago's instruction, however, Othello learns to "[w]ear" his eyes so as to be ever on the watch for signs of his wife's infidelity (3.3.198). As a consequence of this shift from an aural to an ocular axis of relationship, Desdemona is transformed into a spectacle of duplicity within Othello's theatre of the gaze. In similar fashion, the Oxford spectators are moved by the speaking and acting of the actors, but are more affected by the sight of the countenance of the dead Desdemona. Importantly, however, the audience resists the conversion of Desdemona into the iconic figure of purity exemplified by Othello's comparison of his wife to "such another world / Of one entire and perfect chrysolite" (5.2.144-45) or by A. C. Bradley's classic description—"her nature is infinitely sweet and her love absolute."[29] On stage at Oxford, not even death can transform her into the figure of "monumental alablaster" (5.2.5) envisioned by the text and by critics such as Bradley. Instead the murdered Desdemona remains like a speaking subject: her face "entreated the pity of the spectators" ("*spectantium misericordiam ipso vultu imploraret*").

Plays such as *Othello, King Lear, Pericles, The Winter's Tale,* and *The Tempest* work fetishistically to transform the bodies of the boy actors into sights of wonder. It is not surprising that Shakespeare and his theatre should use the actors in this way. The body as show-piece is simply more impressive than any other spectacular object—with the possible exceptions of the costly machines being developed by Inigo Jones for court masques or the fireworks or cannon-fire displays like the one that caused the destruction of the Globe in 1613. Yet however well woman-as-fetish works within the playtexts or in the context of the modern formation of aesthetic fetishism, it seems unlikely that the early modern audience would have agreed, for example, with Ferdinand's proprietary, already jealous awe at his first sight of Miranda: "My prime request, / . . . is (O you wonder!) / If you be a maid, or no?" (*Tempest,* 1.2.426-28).

* * *

Finally, let us consider the relationship between the handkerchief and Desdemona as well as the idea that the play's infusion of charisma into the body of Desdemona operates in relation to the Renaissance difference between movable property and land.[30] That Desdemona's body replaces the handkerchief (not to mention Othello's blackness) as an object of wonder makes good sense because bodies are more evocative than textiles, but what I want to suggest is that the play *trades* the handkerchief for Desdemona's body. To understand the wonder of Desdemona as the profit accruing from a sequence of exchanges within the spectacular economy of the play is to begin to grasp the production of woman-as-fetish and understand the Shakespearean fetish as continuous with ordinary life rather than as something sacred set over the ordinary.

Desdemona's amazing value is the culmination of a series of trades involving land, cash and movables, women, and status. Roderigo, very much like a number of young, landed gentlemen in Jacobean city comedy, converts his land into money in order to buy jewels in order to win the love of a woman, a treasure, who will bring him high status. But while Roderigo believes that Desdemona will confer greater sexual and social status

than his land, the play, like so many city comedies, suggests the ideal that landedness is the only true basis of high status. Land is different from commodities because, in this somewhat nostalgic view, land possesses the possessor, who must live on it in order to administer and preserve it. In medieval law, all land belongs in principle inalienably to the king; general unease with the system by which land becomes virtually as exchangeable as other commodities finds expression in John of Gaunt's lament for the shameful binding of the sacred "earth of majesty, . . . / This other Eden" within "inky blots, and rotten parchment" (*Richard II,* 2.1.41-42,64).[31] In the early seventeenth century, furthermore, the duties of landholders to their property and tenants was an acute social issue. The landed gentry flocked to London, leaving the rural population without governance, judicial supervision, or "hospitality"; some members of the gentry even lost their inherited estates while pursuing status in the spendthrift circles around the court.[32] Roderigo speaks for this group when he promises to invest everything he owns in the chase after Desdemona: "I am chang'd. . . . I'll sell all my land" (1.3.380,382). Since land itself has become a commodity like all others, Desdemona, "full of most bless'd condition" (2.1.249-50), takes its place (as the possession that possesses) in the conferring of social status and personal worth.

So Desdemona is not merely a treasure, but the treasure of land. With wicked irony, Iago says, "[Othello] tonight hath boarded a land carract. / If it prove a lawful prize, he's made for ever" (1.2.50-51). Desdemona is as solid and valuable as land, Iago insinuates, but she is also movable and leaky like a boat. That irony infects Othello. Only by killing Desdemona can he be cured of it. Only at the end can he settle into a view of Desdemona as the permanent, possessing possession that land ideally was for the Jacobeans. This construction of Desdemona is intensely tragic for Othello. That she is Othello's homeland means that her murder renders his personhood irredeemably homeless:

> Where should Othello go?
> Now—how dost thou look now? O ill-starr'd wench,
> Pale as thy smock! when we shall meet at compt,
> This look of thine will hurl my soul from heaven,
> And fiends will snatch at it.
>
> [5.2.271-75]

From the shattered viewpoint of Othello's impending damnation, Desdemona's body shines out wonderfully as the promised land forever out of reach. We should perhaps bear in mind Othello's scattered, destroyed personhood when we—following, indeed, the play's hint—undertake to transvalue *Othello,* making it into "a play not simply to be read or seen or even studied, but possessed."[33] We might also remember Othello's fate when we attempt to exchange the moving sight of Desdemo-

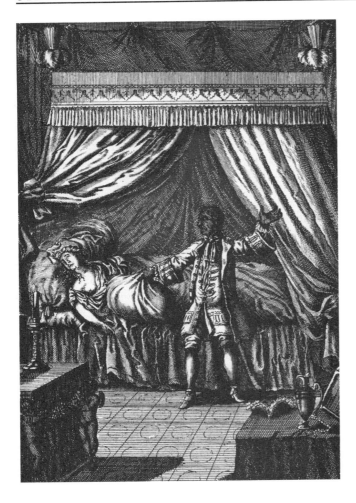

Othello and Desdemona in Act IV, scene ii of Othello.

na's body for a "magical property," a visionary possession of Desdemona in which we try to find manifested our own "authentic immediacy."

The eighteenth-century writer and lawyer Arthur Murphy once imagined himself at Parnassus. He saw that the land had been divided by Apollo among the great writers of the classical and modern canons. Among these figures he found Shakespeare:

> The great *Shakespeare* sat upon a cliff, looking abroad through all creation. His possessions were very near as extensive as *Homer*'s, but in some places, had not received sufficient culture. But even there spontaneous flowers shot up, and in the *unweeded garden, which grows to seed,* you might cull lavender, myrtle, and wild thyme. . . . Even *Milton* was looking for flowers to transplant into his own Paradise.[34]

Murphy's quaint description of Shakespeare as land and as landholder may remind us of the fetishistic investments readers and critics make when they attempt to inhabit and be inhabited by a text such as *Othello.* Like

the wandering Court Party on Prospero's Island or the wonder-struck conquistadors in the New World, we attempt to stake a claim to territories that seem able to restore us to ourselves. Instead of possessing and being possessed by *Othello,* however, we might do better to prize it for the multiplicity of its uses. As a useful rather than a sacred object, *Othello* would be, among other things, a work of literature, a script for actors, a text of some historical importance, and, by virtue of its implicit critique of ideology, a parable about the violence of wonderful representation.

Notes

1. Louis Adrian Montrose, "'Shaping Fantasies': Figurations of Gender and Power in Elizabethan Culture," *Representations* 2 (1983): 61-94; Stephen Greenblatt, *Marvelous Possessions: The Wonder of the New World* (Chicago: University of Chicago Press, 1991).

2. Pierre Machery, *A Theory of Literary Production,* trans. Geoffrey Wall (London: Routledge, 1989), 64.

3. On the emergence of the aesthetic, see Terry Eagleton, *The Ideology of the Aesthetic* (Oxford: Blackwell, 1990); on the conditions of production of conversional wonder in Shakespeare, see my "The Politics of Theatrical Mirth: *A Midsummer Night's Dream, A Mad World, My Masters,* and *Measure for Measure,*" *Shakespeare Quarterly* 43 (1992): 51-66.

4. Northrop Frye, "Introduction" to *The Tempest,* in *The Complete Pelican Shakespeare,* ed. Alfred Harbage (Baltimore: Penguin, 1969), 1370.

5. Greenblatt, *Possessions,* 14.

6. All Shakespeare quotations are from *The Riverside Shakespeare,* ed. G. Blakemore Evans (Boston: Houghton Mifflin, 1974). Subsequent references will be included parenthetically in the text.

7. Frye, "Introduction," 1372.

8. Greenblatt, *Possessions,* 1.

9. Thomas Heywood, *An Apology for Actors* (London 1612; facsimile reprint New York: Scholars' Facsimiles and Reprints, 1941), B4.

10. Thomas Platter, quoted in the *Riverside Shakespeare,* 1839. The *Riverside* prints both the original German text and the translation used here.

11. Sir Henry Wotton, quoted in the *Riverside Shakespeare,* 1842.

12. See Andrew Gurr, *Playgoing in Shakespeare's London* (Cambridge: Cambridge University Press, 1987), 44-48.

13. Stephen Gosson, *The Schoole of Abuse* (London, 1579; facsimile reprint New York: Garland, 1973), C1v.

14. Phillip Stubbes, *The Anatomie of Abuses* (London, 1583; facsimile reprint Amsterdam: Theatrum Orbis Terrarum, 1972), L7v.

15. Henry Parrot, *Laquei ridiculosi: or Springes for Woodcocks* (London, 1613), C6v.

16. Ben Jonson, *The Complete Poems,* ed. George Parfitt (Harmondsworth: Penguin, 1975), 264.

17. John Milton, *Complete Poems and Major Prose,* ed. Merritt Y. Hughes (Indianapolis: Odyssey Press, 1957), 63-64.

18. Leonard Digges, commendatory poem prefixed to "Poems: written by Wil. Shake-speare. Gent." (1640), quoted in the Riverside Shakespeare, 1846.

19. John Heminge and Henry Condell, "To the great Variety of Readers," facsimile reprint in the *Riverside Shakespeare,* 63.

20. Georg Lukács, *History and Class Consciousness: Studies in Marxist Dialectics,* trans. Rodney Livingstone (Cambridge: MIT Press, 1986), 83 and 93.

21. Kenneth Burke, "*Othello:* An Essay to Illustrate a Method," *Hudson Review* 4 (1951): 166-67.

22. Karl Marx, *Capital: A Critique of Political Economy,* ed. Frederick Engels, trans. Samuel Moore and Edward Aveling (New York: Modern Library, 1906), 83.

23. Eagleton, *Ideology,* 78.

24. Peter Stallybrass, "Patriarchal Territories: The Body Enclosed," in *Rewriting the Renaissance: The Discourses of Sexual Difference in Early Modern Europe,* ed. Margaret W. Ferguson et al. (Chicago: University of Chicago Press, 1986), 137.

25. Douglas Bruster, *Drama and the Market in the Age of Shakespeare* (Cambridge: Cambridge University Press, 1992), 84.

26. Richard Wilson, "'A Mingled Yarn': Shakespeare and the Cloth Workers," *Literature and History* 12 (1986): 169.

27. The original Latin text, along with the translation used here, is quoted in the *Riverside Shakespeare,* 1852; note that since the *Riverside* encloses the entire translation in brackets, its own internal editorial additions are enclosed in parentheses.

28. See *Dictionary of National Biography,* entry on Henry Jackson, for an account of his character and career.

29. A. C. Bradley, *Shakespearean Tragedy: Lectures on Hamlet, Othello, King Lear, Macbeth* (1904; reprint London: Macmillan, 1964), 145.

30. On woman as land, see Stallybrass, "Patriarchal Territories."

31. See Kenelm Edward Digby, *An Introduction to the History of the Law of Real Property* (Oxford: Clarendon Press, 1875).

32. See Felicity Heal, "The Crown, the Gentry and London: The Enforcement of Proclamation, 1596-1640," in *Law and Government under the Tudors,* ed. Claire Cross et al. (Cambridge: Cambridge University Press, 1988), 211-26.

33. Frye, "Introduction," 1372.

34. Arthur Murphy, *Gray's-Inn Journal* (London, 1786), quoted in Mark Rose, *Authors and Owners: The Invention of Copyright* (Cambridge: Harvard University Press, 1993), epigraph.

Andrew Sofer (essay date fall 1997)

SOURCE: Sofer, Andrew. "Felt Absences: The Stage Properties of *Othello*'s Handkerchief." *Comparative Drama* 31, no. 3 (fall 1997): 367-93.

[*In the following essay, Sofer examines the symbolic and thematic significance of the handkerchief in* Othello, *listing the varying qualities it represents, such as Desdemona's misused honor, Othello's "ocular proof," the powers of magic, the poetic notion of "felt absences," and the inescapable "charm of objects."*]

Desdemona's handkerchief makes its first appearance in Shakespeare's source, Giraldi Cinthio's *Hecatommithi.* According to Cinthio, it is "a handkerchief embroidered most delicately in the Moorish fashion, which the Moor had given her [Disdemona] and which was treasured by the Lady and her husband too."[1] Cinthio's handkerchief contains no magic in its web; it is, rather, a crude plot device whose utility depends upon a string of chance events.[2] By contrast, there is nothing coincidental in Shakespeare's dramatic embroidering of Cinthio's lurid pulp. In performance, Othello's handkerchief exerts an uncanny power over both characters and audience, and it propels the action as it repeatedly emerges in the right place at the wrong time. It seems almost to bend the characters to its own enigmatic will.

How do we account for the handkerchief's extraordinary grip on the audience's experience of *Othello?* Certainly no performance of the play can occur without it. When Iago tells Roderigo that "we work by wit and not by witchcraft," he may not, strictly speaking, be accurate.[3]

Without the magic handkerchief, Iago's lies would not stick; the drama would be literally and figuratively unstageable. In its three brief appearances, the handkerchief draws the six characters it touches—Othello, Desdemona, Emilia, Iago, Cassio, Bianca—into its own repetitive story, a story which begins in love and ends in death. As if to fulfill the sibyl's prophecy of doom, by the play's end the first three characters are dead, the fourth faces torture and death, the fifth is wounded, and the sixth is in prison, where (as a prostitute jailed under military law for the suspected murder of a high-ranking officer) her prospects for survival are dim.

In hindsight, Bianca's initial wariness regarding the handkerchief seems justified. But the phrase she uses to describe it is peculiar:

> O Cassio, whence came this?
> This is some token from a newer friend.
> To the felt absence now I feel a cause.
> Is't come to this? Well, well.
>
> (3.4.174-77)

In context we can understand this speech in two ways. Bianca interprets the handkerchief as an incriminating sign, concrete evidence of a woman for whose sake Cassio has been neglecting her ("some token from a newer friend"), but she speaks more truly than she knows. Bianca herself is the latest "cause"—the latest link in the chain—animating the handkerchief's "felt absence": its paradoxical ability to be at once present, felt, corporeal, yet also somehow absent, elusive, lost. We begin to disentangle the handkerchief's "magic in the web" (3.4.65) once we see that, from a phenomenological perspective, the peculiarity of stage properties is that they both are and are not themselves. Oscillating between sign and thing, props are "felt absences" that draw our attention simultaneously to their signifying function—Bianca's word "token" simply means a sign—and to their materiality ("felt" is of course a particular fabric). Thus the handkerchief is at once a token—a signifier which points to something absent, beyond itself, like Bianca's fictitious minx—and a talisman, an object that possesses (or seems to possess) magical qualities inherently bound up in its "work."[4]

The handkerchief's double status as sign and thing explains why, as Bert O. States has persuasively argued, we must supplement a purely semiotic approach to stage objects with a phenomenological one in "a kind of binocular vision" that allows us to see them both as signs for something else and as nothing but themselves.[5] Following States's lead, I wish to supplement the many accounts of the handkerchief's symbolism with a phenomenological description of its magic. Bracketing the question of whether the handkerchief's magic (or magic in general) exists outside the confines of the playhouse, I shall instead describe how the handkerchief

appears to consciousness—both that of the characters and of the audience—as the play unfolds in performance.[6] The handkerchief is not merely a sign but a performer in the play's action, and its physical movements and shifting emotional impact deserve as much attention as its symbolism.

That symbolism is relentlessly overdetermined. In a sort of semiotic juggling act, the play requires us to bear so many conflicting accounts of the handkerchief in mind—forehead binder, erotic toy,[7] "Trifle light as air" (3.3.323), "magic in the web" (3.4.65), "minx's token" (4.1.147), "recognisance and pledge of love" (5.2.213), "antique token" (5.2.215) that they ultimately collapse into a mute object which, like Posthumus's "[s]enseless linen," refuses to signify beyond itself.[8] While the characters ascribe greater and greater significance to the handkerchief which culminates in the fateful ocular proof, the actual square of cloth refuses coherent meaning and insists instead on its own phenomenal "charm," its lethal materiality in performance. Like a black hole, the handkerchief sucks the characters into its magic web, literally absorbing those who would reduce it to a mere sign (or "token") into the folds of its own uncopiable "work."[9] The handkerchief arrogates a dizzying number of significations only to repudiate them; to paraphrase Brabantio, the handkerchief "engluts and swallows other [signs] / And yet is still itself" (1.3. 57-58).

A phenomenological approach is thus justified partly because the handkerchief exhausts all attempts to pin down its meaning and partly because the characters themselves, confronted by the handkerchief's strange properties, face the same interpretive hurdle as the audience or critic. If we examine the handkerchief purely in the semiotic attitude, as almost all its critics have done, we risk misreading its magic as a sign or metaphor for something else and failing to account for its grip on us in the heat of performance. While audience members since Thomas Rymer have complained of the handkerchief's inanity as a plot device, the very fascination it holds for the characters seductively commands our attention in the playhouse.

More crucially, a close examination of the handkerchief's three appearances reveals the specific theatrical mechanism at the core of the play. Shakespeare stages the handkerchief as a series of imaginative "reductions" performed by the play's characters. At these key moments, the play—world is "bracketed" (or reduced) so that the handkerchief alone absorbs a character's attention in all its mystery. In performance, *Othello* likewise demands that we perform the same process of imaginative reduction as the characters who serially encounter the handkerchief in the play. Shakespeare asks his audience to suspend the skeptical attitude towards witchcraft exemplified by the Venetian senate in act 1 and consider this particular handkerchief—not as an object "out there," but as it seeps into our consciousness. The handkerchief's numinous properties, which accrete as the action unfolds, then color our perception of the surrounding play-world just as Othello's jealousy, once aroused, infects his interpretation of all subsequent events. The play's strategic repetitions ensure that we cannot get the handkerchief off our minds.

The scene in which Bianca takes the handkerchief from Cassio serves as a concrete example. Bianca has come upon her neglectful lover while he waits for Desdemona to press his suit for reinstatement to Othello. Cassio bears a strange handkerchief and demands that Bianca "[t]ake me this work out" (3.4.174).[10] The moment when the handkerchief changes hands is dramatically ironic, for the audience is by now aware of the magic in its web. While to Cassio it is merely a pleasing trinket he has found in his chamber, we have just heard Othello's "magic in the web" speech (3.4.51-71) and have witnessed his obsessive iteration of "The handkerchief!" together with Desdemona's ensuing panic: "Sure there's some wonder in this handkerchief; / I am most unhappy in the loss of it" (3.4.95-96). Magic or no, the handkerchief has become charged with dramatic value and danger.

When Bianca takes the handkerchief, however, we are invited to "bracket" what we have heard and seen about the handkerchief so far—not in order to disavow its magic, but to put it, as it were, on hold. As the handkerchief is "given" to Bianca's consciousness, we are invited to see it through her eyes as if for the first time. The handkerchief takes on a sharper outline as its "felt absence" etches itself into Bianca's awareness, doubling the pain of Cassio's neglect by adding insult to injury. If Bianca is not charmed by the magic into falling further in love with Cassio—for she returns to fling it back at 4.1.149—she is nevertheless seized by the conviction that she has been thrown over: "Is't come to this? Well, well" (3.4.177).

Cassio himself seems smitten by the handkerchief in another way. In answer to Bianca's reasonable question, "Why, whose is it?" he replies:

> I know not neither; I found it in my chamber.
> I like the work well. Ere it be demanded
> As like enough it will—I'd have it copied.
> Take it and do't, and leave me for this time.

> (3.4.182-85)

Cassio seems oblivious to the pain he has caused Bianca, and his peculiar assertion that "like enough" the handkerchief will be "demanded" is unlikely to render convincing his account of chancing upon it. The handkerchief here throws the couple's relationship into stark relief. Cassio is upset that Bianca has followed

him and that Othello might glimpse him with a prostitute—hardly auspicious, given his disgraced circumstances—and brushes her off, while Bianca's parting comment, "'Tis very good; I must be circumstanced" (3.4.195), shows that she is resigned to making the best of things as they are. Bianca is forced to take the handkerchief with her as a bitter reminder of her own subservient position and a galling sign that Cassio is "womaned" (3.4.189). The handkerchief thus imports quite different values, and incites virtually opposite emotions, in the two characters whose consciousness it absorbs for the duration of the scene.

In sum, I am arguing that at privileged moments in performance the handkerchief becomes a dramatic event unto itself. It is an object "given to" a person's consciousness while at the same time being constituted by that consciousness. Shakespeare calls this reduction of the external world to the contents of consciousness "magic." (Iago's word for the same mechanism is "jealousy," of which more later.) Shakespeare might just as easily have used the term "glamour," in the archaic sense of a spell; for it is the charm of objects apprehended in performance—their glamour, in fact—that is my subject here, just as it is Shakespeare's covert subject in *Othello*.

But with what sort of magic are we dealing? Critics, reluctant to take the handkerchief's magic seriously, have treated it as delusion or symbol. John A. Hodgson, for instance, asserts that "Othello lies . . . when he asserts that there is magic in the web of the handkerchief."[11] David Kaula dismisses Othello's belief in the handkerchief's magic as merely a psychic defense: "The magical associations of the handkerchief are temporary. They are symptoms of the delusion which grips the hero in the middle phase of the tragic action."[12] In a recent article, Paul Yachnin equates the handkerchief's spurious magic with that of commodity fetishism: Shakespeare at once fetishizes "magical" props so as to enhance his play's cultural status and unwittingly exorcises that magic by deconstructing the ideology behind it.[13] Linda Woodbridge more cautiously historicizes the play's magic as "a mental phenomenon that is part metaphor, part intellectual construct, part protection magic."[14]

To Robert B. Heilman, the handkerchief's "magic in the web" intertwines various strands of symbolic association and thus provides him with the title and subject matter of an influential book outlining "patterns of permanence" in the play's poetic language: a matrix of connections in which images echo and re-echo to forge a new kind of dramatic unity.[15] Heilman argues that the poetic language surrounding the handkerchief becomes mysteriously endowed with dramatic value and meaning, but his figurative account of the handkerchief's magic as a spiritualized symbol of love gives us only half the story. If we strip *Othello* of its literal magic, its power to reduce consciousness at will, we miss what the play is doing: using magic not as a metaphor for something else (love, reputation, commodity fetishism) but as a reflexive model of theater itself. The handkerchief not only symbolizes magic but enacts it by reducing its victims' consciousness to consciousness of itself. In other words, the handkerchief does to its victims in the play-world precisely what *Othello* does to its audience in the playhouse.

I am not claiming that the handkerchief's "magic" is real to any particular character or that members of Shakespeare's original audience (or indeed Shakespeare himself) identified the handkerchief with witchcraft.[16] Instead, I aim to clarify what kinds of magic are taken seriously by whom at which points in the play and to what dramatic purpose. My argument is that magic in *Othello* can be defined as self-authenticating, self-consuming emotion: once you believe it's real, it's real. Whether it "exists" independently of consciousness or not, magic is shown to work effectively wherever and whenever consciousness of magic is present. As Brabantio puts it, "'Tis probable and palpable to thinking" (1.2.76). Just as the handkerchief weaves its magic by reducing to itself the consciousness of each character with whom it comes into contact, so Iago reduces Othello's awareness to a groundless jealousy that engulfs him.

The very point of jealousy, in fact, is its groundlessness, for as soon as one suspects one might have cause to be jealous, one is. In Emilia's apt words:

> They are not ever jealous for the cause,
> But jealous for they're jealous. 'Tis a monster
> Begot upon itself, born on itself.
>
> (3.4.154-56)

Magic and jealousy thus mirror each other and model *Othello* as it works on its audience. Magic is the mechanism by which we come to accept an object before us (a handkerchief, a wife, a play) as "charmed," for good or ill; and as we follow its path through the action, the handkerchief models for us the glamorous process by which a thing becomes a charm, relentlessly accruing talismanic value beyond its mundane function as it is handled both by characters and in dialogue. When critics disagree over whether the handkerchief is "really" magical, they are in some sense missing the point. In performance, its charm is inescapable.

II

Desdemona produces her handkerchief at 3.3.289, the midpoint of the play's central scene. It is thus the pivot around which the play turns. Desdemona takes literally Othello's metaphorical reference to cuckoldry ("I have

a pain upon my forehead here" [3.3.286]) and offers to bind Othello's head. There is no hint as yet of the handkerchief's peculiarity, although blood-stained cloths recur in Shakespeare as signs of death and wounding that are open to misreading: Posthumus's bloody handkerchief in *Cymbeline,* like Thisbe's bloody mantle, misleadingly betokens the death of the heroine.[17] In this scene there is no actual blood, but it is possible that the strawberries later said by Iago to "spot" the handkerchief (3.3.436) are visible to the audience. There is nothing odd about the handkerchief at this point, however, except the virulence with which Othello rejects what is clearly a token of Desdemona's solicitude.

Yet the handkerchief's physical trajectory is unstable and resists precise plotting. The handkerchief must pass in the space of thirty lines from Desdemona to Othello, from Othello to Emilia, and from Emilia to Iago, but there is no textual indication as to how this stage minuet is to be executed. After Othello retorts, "Your napkin is too little," neither F nor Q1 provides a stage direction. Rowe's 1709 edition inserts the stage direction "She drops her handkerchief" (adopted by Ridley's Arden edition); Capell's 1768 edition adds "He puts the handkerchief from him, and she drops it" (adopted by Sanders); Alvin Kernan's Signet edition has "He pushes the handkerchief away, and it falls." Othello's next line is: "Let it alone. Come, I'll go in with you" (3.3.290), and, as Kernan notes, "it makes a considerable difference in the interpretation of later events whether this 'it' refers to Othello's forehead or to the handkerchief."[18] Both referents are consistent with the dialogue, but nothing in the spoken text precludes Emilia from seizing the handkerchief; she is on stage throughout the couple's exchange, and Shakespeare leaves unclear what she is doing. QI indicates that Desdemona leaves with Othello, possibly leaving the handkerchief on the ground for Emilia to pick up; F indicates that Othello storms out first, so perhaps Desdemona must choose between retrieving her handkerchief and following her husband. Yet a third possibility is that Emilia takes advantage of the lovers' quarrel to filch the handkerchief directly. Perhaps the handkerchief's precise trajectory is left open so as to occlude the motives of those who handle it.[19]

In the first of the handkerchief's imaginative reductions, the stage empties and the action contracts to Emilia's consciousness as she, turning the handkerchief over in her mind and hand, literally toys with its possibilities. Emilia's soliloquy clarifies her pleasure at discovering the handkerchief but obscures her reasons for keeping it:

> I am glad I have found this napkin:
> This was her first remembrance from the Moor.
> My wayward husband hath a hundred times
> Wooed me to steal it; but she so loves the token,

For he conjured her she should ever keep it,
That she reserves it evermore about her
To kiss and talk to. I'll have the work tane out
And give't Iago.
What he will do with it, heaven knows, not I:
I nothing but to please his fantasy.

(3.3.292-301)

Shakespeare's elision of the staging forces the actor playing Emilia to make choices that are left ambiguous by the text. Why should Emilia feel compelled to justify her actions here, and why offer the handkerchief to her "wayward" husband, a man she already has good reason to distrust, especially since she knows that it is her mistress's prized possession? Emilia accepts or feigns ignorance of Iago's intentions ("heaven knows, not I") even though she claims he is already obsessed with the handkerchief; at line 301, Q1 provides the even more suggestive "I nothing know, but for his fantasy." Is her nonchalance a piece of self-deception masking a need she herself may not fully fathom? Emilia's feigned ignorance of the handkerchief's whereabouts at 3.4.20 is especially puzzling if one assumes Emilia's motives towards Desdemona are benign.[20] Emilia's decision to "have the work tane out" before giving it to her husband is suggestive. The syntax is ambiguous as to which "work," the original or the duplicate, she intends to give him. Perhaps she wishes to keep the original for her own devices; perhaps she anticipates that it may give her some power over Iago. Whichever, Emilia's fascination seems motivated by the attractive "work" itself, just as Cassio's will be, rather than by any talismanic properties she ascribes to it.

Emilia's enumeration of the handkerchief's properties is intriguing, nevertheless. We learn that it was Othello's first gift to Desdemona and that she values it highly; perhaps that is the sole reason Iago covets it. In the first whiff of magic since act 1, Emilia notes that Othello "conjured" Desdemona to keep it (3. 3.296a word used by Shakespeare in two senses: to "[c]all upon solemnly, adjure" and to "[c]all upon, constrain (a devil or spirit) to appear or to do one's bidding by incantation or the use of some spell, raise or bring into existence as by magic."[21] This double meaning casts a grim retrospective irony on Brabantio's earlier accusation of witchcraft: "conjured" into accepting the magic handkerchief as her lover's first gift, Desdemona may have had no choice but to fall (or remain) in love.[22] Of course we have no inkling as yet that the handkerchief contains magic in its web—though the ambiguous "conjured" might have jarred a contemporary audience—but we are told that the handkerchief is of intense interest both to Iago and to Desdemona, who "so loves the token / . . . That she reserves it evermore about her / To kiss and talk to" (3.3.295, 297-98).

With these lines a new interior landscape emerges. Desdemona's child-like behavior in this regard marks a peculiar emotional regression from her apparent maturity and self-possession earlier in the text and invites a psychoanalytical interpretation. On the manifest level, the handkerchief is Desdemona's stand-in for Othello: a "token" that can substitute for kissing and stroking the true object of her affections, Othello's felt absence. But at an unconscious level, Desdemona treats her gift precisely as a child treats what psychoanalyst D. W. Winnicott calls a "transitional object." In Winnicott's scheme, a child adopts a bit of cloth, blanket, or hair-ribbon as a way of holding onto the absent mother at a crucial stage in its development when its own boundaries are still inchoate. "It is a first symbol, and it stands for confidence in the union of baby and mother based on the experience of the mother's reliability and capacity to know what the baby needs through identification with the baby."[23] Transitional objects become essential to the child's security and happiness—objects "created" by the baby even if they existed, as it were, before their creation. They are themselves felt absences, neither purely objective nor purely subjective but liminal, existing both "inside" and "outside" the baby. A handkerchief is an interesting choice in this regard: it is the repository of inner bodily matter, a prophylactic extension of the permeable borders of the body's surface which itself blurs the distinction between inner and outer.[24]

Desdemona has a father but no mother, and Brabantio in act 1 sees his daughter as property to be guarded from unwanted male attention until she can be married off to his advantage. By trading her father's protection for Othello's, Desdemona moves from one masculine domain to another. Disowned by her father, Desdemona is utterly at the mercy of a husband whose military life she has elected to share in a military outpost far out at sea, 1,300 miles from Venice. In legal terms, she is now her husband's property. Desdemona understandably imbues her handkerchief with the sympathetic qualities of her dead mother and treats it as a confidante, a feminized ally in a masculine stronghold. In Kristevan terms, the handkerchief operates both at the level of the "symbolic," as a token of heterosexual desire and commitment, and of the "semiotic," as a tie to the prediscursive maternal body.[25] Desdemona's mother never speaks and is mentioned only in passing (1.3.184), yet in act 4, scene 3, as Emilia prepares her for bed, Desdemona identifies herself with her mother's maid Barbary, abandoned by a lover who "proved mad" (4.3.26). Barbary died singing the "willow song" that Desdemona reprises and which itself retails Barbary's story in verse, even as the handkerchief re-stages it in death. Singing poor Barbary's song, Desdemona inserts herself into a weave of dead women abandoned by men and edged with madness.

The handkerchief, given to Desdemona by Othello and symbolizing his ownership of both, thus partakes of male and female economies simultaneously. It looks at once forward to Desdemona's sexual maturity and husband, and backward to her childhood and mother. It signals both Desdemona's readiness to enter into the patriarchal order of wifehood and motherhood and her unconscious resistance to adopting those subject positions. Desdemona's relation to the handkerchief is thus ambivalent from the outset and soon turns to panic when she discovers its absence. At the moment she loses possession of the handkerchief, Desdemona loses her self-possession along with her last link to her mother, and becomes herself possessed by a feeling of dread: "I had rather lose my purse / Full of crusadoes . . . it were enough / To put him to ill thinking" (3.4.21-25). The handkerchief has crossed over from the Kristevan "semiotic" to the "symbolic," has changed from token of female companionship to fetish of male jealousy and murderous revenge.

If this psychoanalytical account seems glib, that is partly the point. Seemingly casual revelations surrounding the handkerchief—in this case, a chance remark by Emilia easily generate intriguing psychological landscapes. By momentarily focusing all our attention on the handkerchief, Emilia's charged language weaves the handkerchief into a shifting pattern of felt absences, a network of significances that increases its charm—its emotional grip on us in performance—while obscuring the source of its mysterious power over the characters to which we are never privy. The fact that Desdemona fondles the handkerchief invites us to reevaluate her relationship to Othello, which in turn invites us to reevaluate the handkerchief's meaning as a "remembrance," and so forth ad infinitum. Emilia's monologue may occupy only a minute of stage time, but it posits a network of fraught emotional relationships ("he hath a hundred times . . ."). The monologue at once stresses the handkerchief's bewitching materiality and deepens its semiotic mystery. Emilia (and, perhaps, the actor playing her) knows why she wants the handkerchief, but this information is deliberately withheld from the audience even in soliloquy, the traditional place where obscure motives are revealed and clarified.

No sooner has the notion of taking out the work occurred to her than Emilia is left empty-handed: Iago appears, as if on cue, and acquires the handkerchief to plant in Cassio's lodging. Once again, the text does not indicate whether Iago grabs the handkerchief from Emilia or persuades her to relinquish it, leaving the couple's literal hold over each other open to directorial interpretation. In a bid for power, Emilia tries to use the precious object as a token of exchange ("What will you give me now / For that same handkerchief?" [3.3.307-08]) and offers a version of events which may or may not be true: "she let it drop by negligence, / And to th'advantage I being here took't up" (3.3.31314). As soon as Iago takes hold, Emilia feels the handkerchief's absence and demands it back: "Poor lady, she'll run

mad / When she shall lack it" (3.3.319-20). Iago dismisses her, and once again the stage empties to a solitary figure, alone with the suggestive piece of cloth.[26] It is the handkerchief which gives Iago the vague idea of implicating Cassio somehow, a strategy of which he is himself dubious: "I will in Cassio's lodging lose this napkin / And let him find it. . . . This may do something" (3.3. 322-25).[27]

Iago secretes the handkerchief just as his general reappears, Othello's own consciousness now entirely subdued to jealousy. Iago's improvised narrative at once creates and authenticates a past history of infidelity: when Iago tells Othello that he saw Cassio wipe his beard with "a handkerchief / Spotted with strawberries" (3.3.435-36), the very handkerchief that is hidden on Iago's person, Othello swears his revenge. One of the handkerchief's key stage functions, then, is to capture the imagination of those who intersect with it. In quick succession, Desdemona, Othello, Emilia, Iago, and Cassio are enmeshed in an emotional net Iago sees himself as controlling, but it is the handkerchief that allows Iago's improvisations to take root rather than vice versa. The handkerchief refuses to stay fixed in time or space; it must continually be "given over" to please another's "fantasy" before it can satisfy one's own.

III

Our fullest glimpse of the handkerchief's strange properties is offered by Othello as he admonishes the panicked Desdemona not to lose what is already, to her, a keenly felt absence. When Desdemona is unable to produce the handkerchief on demand, Othello launches into his story before an onstage audience of Emilia (who knows Iago has the handkerchief) and his alarmed wife (who does not). Whether Othello believes his own tale or not, its effect on Desdemona is palpable. The "magic in the web" speech puts her into a panic, and as we witness Desdemona's response via Emilia's mute presence, Emilia cues our reaction. The contagious (mimetic) structure of magic is thus triangulated through a third party. What is important here is not that Othello or Desdemona "really" believes in the charm—Othello may well be lying—but that they are seen to seem to believe in the moment of performance by Emilia, and this is what makes it "real enough" at this moment. For the space of Othello's speech, the audience's consciousness is altered. We are imaginatively drawn into a world of magic and death that eclipses the play's formerly skeptical attitude towards witchcraft, as evinced by the Venetian senate's dismissal of Brabantio's accusations in act 1.

Shakespeare reintroduces the theme of witchcraft, absent since Othello's trial, by reducing our imaginative attention to the effect of Othello's words on Desdemona; we see the handkerchief fill Desdemona's harried consciousness as it acquires an otherworldly history. Othello spins his narrative thread both backwards to include his parents, an Egyptian charmer, and the sibyl who sewed the work; and forwards, propelling the charm via Desdemona (and the mute Emilia) out to the audience in language that links the handkerchief to a supernatural domain:

> That handkerchief
> Did an Egyptian to my mother give:
> She was a charmer and could almost read
> The thoughts of people. She told her, while she kept it,
> 'Twould make her amiable and subdue my father
> Entirely to her love; but if she lost it
> Or made a gift of it, my father's eye
> Should hold her loathed and his spirits should hunt
> After new fancies. She dying gave it me,
> And bid me when my fate would have me wive,
> To give it her. I did so, and take heed on't:
> Make it a darling, like your precious eye.
> To lose't or give't away were such perdition
> As nothing else could match. . . .
> 'Tis true. There's magic in the web of it:
> A sibyl, that had numbered in the world
> The sun to course two hundred compasses,
> In her prophetic fury sewed the work;
> The worms were hallowed that did breed the silk,
> And it was dyed in mummy, which the skilful
> Conserved of maidens' hearts.
>
> (3.4.51-71)

The language surrounding the handkerchief adds an eerie supernatural coloring to the familiar landscapes of sixteenth-century Venice and Cyprus that have so far dominated the play. While it is true that the handkerchief is an "emblem of Othello's exotic genealogy and hence of his family's honor," its provenance is at once feminine and fey.[28] Othello's measured, dream-like cadences limn a pagan world inhabited by psychic soothsayers, two-hundred year old sibyls in the throes of prophetic ecstasy, and dye made from lovingly preserved hearts ripped from living virgins' bodies. This is a far cry from the ordered republic of Venice we have witnessed in act 1; but Cyprus, where the bulk of the action takes place, is a contested battleground in the process of shifting from the Christian sphere of Venice to the "heathen" sphere of the Ottomans.[29] Writing in about 1603, Shakespeare here followed contemporary history: Cyprus fell to the Turks in 1572 after a temporary reprieve by gales corresponding to the storm that disperses the Turkish fleet in 2.1. Cyprus itself would have constituted a recently felt absence, at least to Shakespeare's more educated audience, and Shakespeare here romantically associates Islam's exoticism with mummies, sybils, and love charms.

By invoking a pagan dimension to the world of the play, the handkerchief suggests also the historic association of Cyprus with the ancient rites of Venus, an association for which preparation has already been made by Desdemona's arrival on the island in 2.1. Arriving safely ashore, Cassio states:

> Tempests themselves, high seas, and howling winds,
> The guttered rocks and congregated sands,
> Traitors enscarped to clog the guiltless keel,
> As having sense of beauty do omit
> Their mortal natures, letting go safely by
> The divine Desdemona.
>
> (2.1.68-73)

According to legend, Aphrodite was born from the sea out of the genitals of Uranus, castrated by his son Cronos to avenge his oppression. The goddess of fertility, of love both pure and carnal, of beauty (and, especially relevant to 2.1, the protectress of sailors) then came ashore at Cyprus. The "divine Desdemona" becomes for a moment the genius loci, the goddess before whom Cassio bids the men of Cyprus kneel (2.1.84).[30] But this association has its sinister side. Paphos became the site of a temple where sacrifices took place during an annual festival, the Aphrodisia, and, according to Doros Alastos, "The ritual included mysteries, the character of which we do not exactly know."[31] These mysteries may well have included human sacrifice; certainly the cult of Aphrodite involved the ritual sacred prostitution of virgins before their wedding, and these rites of Venus, according to Frazer's *The Golden Bough,* incorporated Near-Eastern pagan rituals we can only guess at.[32]

Not coincidentally, there are clear textual indications that Desdemona is still a virgin on her death night. Iago interrupts Othello and Desdemona's nuptials between 1.1 and 1.2, and Othello sets sail next morning for Cyprus. Once there, Othello leads his wife to bed with the words "Come, my dear love, / The purchase made, the fruits are to ensue; / That profit's yet to come 'tween me and you" (2.3.8-10), which Iago glosses as "he hath not yet made wanton the night with her" (2.3.15-16). But this second intended night of pleasure is usurped by Iago's mutiny (2.3), and the action next day is continuous until Desdemona asks Emilia to put the wedding sheets on her bed (4.2.104), an action which implies that their marriage is never consummated.

"Divine Desdemona," then, provides a propitiatory virgin offering to her own divine image. Her handkerchief "[s] potted with strawberries" (3.3.436) becomes the emblem of a deflowering that, ironically, never takes place.[33] By refusing to shed Desdemona's hymeneal blood through consummating her marriage ("Yet I'll not shed her blood" [5.2.3]), and thus by refusing to stain her wedding sheets, Othello denies himself the only real ocular and tactile proof of Desdemona's chastity he could ever have.[34] In killing Desdemona, Othello is careful not to shed the virgin blood that was, by rights, to have been his but instead is consecrated to "yond marble heaven" (3.3.461).[35]

Once we break the spell of Othello's verse, however, the handkerchief's charm becomes impossible to quantify. In Othello's account, the charm passes down a human chain which to this point comprises the sibyl, the Egyptian charmer, Othello's mother, Othello, and Desdemona. What seems at first glance a simple repeated pattern of erotic binding is in fact so complex that it becomes very hard to say just when and how the magic is supposed to work, for the charm never acts in the same way twice. Rather than mechanically binding receiver to giver, the handkerchief adjusts its erotic valence to fit shifting circumstance.[36] No erotic link exists between the Egyptian charmer and Othello's mother, for instance, nor between the latter and Othello. The charm, first conferring desirability on Othello's mother, subdues her sexual partner. Its magic then lies dormant until Othello's "fate" decrees his marriage (3.4.60). This seems to imply that Desdemona is bound to Othello, her future husband; but for the handkerchief's charm to work the same way twice, Othello should have kept it, since that is how his mother subdued his father. Yet Othello cannot keep it, because his mother tells him that he must give it away in order for the charm to work at all.

Perhaps, Desdemona's telling admission that "My heart's subdued / Even to the very quality of my lord" (1.3.24647) notwithstanding, the magic subdues Othello to Desdemona rather than vice versa. Othello's "when my fate would have me wive" is ambiguous; we cannot tell if he himself controls the timing and direction of the charm, or if he is compelled by fate to give it up at the propitious moment (something of this ambiguity is caught in the variance between QI's "wive" and F's more passive "Wiu'd"). Logically, Desdemona's receipt of the handkerchief should confer desirability on her and not on Othello. This seems borne out by the fact that, once she loses it, Othello fulfills the dreaded prospect and "hold[s] her loathed" (3.4.58). Yet because Othello prevents the initial pattern from repeating itself, by giving the handkerchief away rather than keeping it, we can never be certain if Othello charms Desdemona by giving, or if Desdemona charms Othello by receiving, or both, or neither.

Thus far the handkerchief's magic seems selective according to the hidden direction of its own inscrutable fatedness. To complicate matters still further, it is impossible to say whether the handkerchief is inherently magical or is abruptly endowed with pseudo-magical properties by Othello's mesmerizing speech. In other words, we do not know if Othello is telling the truth or improvising the magic in order to spook Desdemona—that is, whether the handkerchief is a genuine charm (the magic inheres in and originates with the object itself) or a fetish (an ordinary object Othello chooses to endow with special significance). This latter possibility is especially evident given that, as we shall

see, Othello later revises his account of the handkerchief's origin and thus obscures its magical status still further. In either case, we must reevaluate the sardonic attitude towards magic that came so easily to Iago and the senators in act 1, the self-evident superiority of witcraft to witchcraft.

As the handkerchief tightens its grip on the characters' emotions, its dramatic function shifts from that of love charm to death fetish. Othello's love turns to raging jealousy, fulfilling the fate prophesied by the sibyl. Desdemona's desperate evasions only spur Othello's demands to produce the gift, and Othello's thrice-repeated "The handkerchief!" (3.4.88-92) threatens to break down communication altogether (as it will later, when Othello falls into his fit and misses a potentially decisive encounter with Cassio), substituting the brute sound of the words for the square of cloth they signify. Desdemona can only respond by accusing Othello for the first and only time—"I'faith, you are to blame" (3.4.92)—which only enrages him further. Emilia fatally ignores the opportunity to confess to stealing the handkerchief, and act 3 ends, as we have seen, with Bianca's receiving the handkerchief from Cassio in what is almost a burlesque of Othello and Desdemona's quarrel. Shakespeare cunningly conflates Cassio's prostitute and sewing-woman, separate in Cinthio, so as to stress the handkerchief's economy of movement. Bianca's resigned jealousy over the handkerchief is a pale echo of Othello's, but her pain is apparent. Cassio's displeasure at seeing her out of doors and his insistence she return home anticipate the claustrophobic shuttering of the other women in act 5 and the chilling confinement of the death chamber.

The handkerchief continues to sew dissension and heartache as, through Cassio and Bianca, it repeats its by now familiar dance of absent presence. Bianca initially accepts Cassio's demands to copy the work (again, the text leaves open when and how it changes hands), but its charm cools and she returns to fling it back: "wheresoever you had it. I'll take out no work on't" (4.1.148-49). The handkerchief, then, repeatedly inspires, yet refuses its own duplication; what is repeated instead is the pattern of human beings seeking to replicate its unique work.[37] Like a director, the handkerchief compels a repeat performance but one that is always slightly different from the previous one. In this case, the magic circuit fails (or perhaps its erotic current reverses): instead of making Bianca fall further in love with Cassio, the handkerchief turns her against him. It evidently has no romantic designs for Cassio and Bianca but uses them to provide a crucial tableau.

It is of course Iago who sets the stage for Othello's misprision of the "ocular proof," the handkerchief's final appearance in its brief stage career. Having reduced Othello to a state of furious jealousy, Iago stages a scene in which Othello observes Iago's interview of Cassio but mistakes the latter's object of scorn (Bianca) for Desdemona. By placing Othello out of earshot, Iago encourages him to loose his imagination just he has manipulated it all along by perversely framing the general's experience as a judicious phenomenological reduction, one that sets aside all subjective value judgments: "Look to your wife, observe her well with Cassio; / Wear your eyes thus: not jealous, nor secure" (3.3.199-200). As fate would have it, when Bianca unexpectedly erupts into the scene bearing the handkerchief, Othello glimpses the very ocular proof he has demanded of Iago and thus allows the latter once more to improvise: "she gave it him, and he hath given it his whore" (4.1.168). While Iago has staged a "reduction" whereby Othello can see but not hear—a recipe for misreading—once again it is the handkerchief that clinches the scene. Iago's lies have transformed the handkerchief into an emblem of Desdemona's faithlessness. Ironically, Othello is so intent on the handkerchief's function as a sign that he almost misses its material presence as an image: "Was that mine?" (4.1. 166). For Othello, the handkerchief now embodies the most palpable absence of all: Desdemona's honor.

The Egyptian charmer's gift is a double-edged sword, administering love and death in equal measure. For Cassio and Bianca, the handkerchief's eros and thanatos here cancel each other out. Considering its potentially lethal powers, the characters may be said to get off lightly, at least for now. Once Bianca gives it up (always the fatal error) we never see the handkerchief again, but her line "There, give it your hobby-horse" (4.1.148) leaves open the possibility that a dumbfounded Cassio simply takes it back and hence inadvertently starts a new cycle of love and death.[38] The handkerchief's felt absence is invoked one final time, however, which marks the collapse as well as the finale of its narrative. Once Montano, Gratiano, and Iago burst into the death chamber, Othello justifies Desdemona's murder to the aghast nobles by explaining that he saw Cassio with "an antique token / My father gave my mother" (5.2.215-16)—thereby revising his previous account of the handkerchief and, in effect, complicating its origins past all intelligibility. As we have seen, a "token" is not magical at all but is any object that has some significance for somebody—in other words, a sign. With one stroke, the play forces us to reevaluate Othello as an unreliable narrator. If Othello's father gave Othello's mother the handkerchief, the tale of the sibyl is mere invention, and all bets as to the handkerchief's magical properties are off.

Why does Othello revise his story? Faced with this crux, critics diverge. David Kaula notes, "Shakespeare provides no definite clue that he intends this [alteration] to be taken as the true account of the handkerchief's history and the former one as a fabrication," but on bal-ance he sees the "antique token" as "a more plausible love token than the horrific thing contrived by the superannuated sibyl in her prophetic fury."[39] Despite Othello's insistence that his magic fable is "most veritable" (3.4.72), Robert S. Miola takes him at his second word: the Moor's revision reveals "the more mundane truth" about the origins of the handkerchief.[40] John A. Hodgson, too, agrees that Othello's revision of his earlier "wild story" reveals its untruth; Michael C. Andrews, by contrast, argues that the magic is real for Othello but no longer of interest to Shakespeare.[41] Fernand Baldensperger and Mark Van Doren are also hesitant in rejecting Othello's belief in the charm.[42] One of the handkerchief's apparent abilities, then, is to obscure and efface its own origin. By the play's end, all we can say for certain is that the handkerchief is an "antique token"—but of what?

The handkerchief's elusive properties bring us back to the enigma of Desdemona herself. The handkerchief emerges from Desdemona's person to become an agent of her destruction, providing an odd mirror of her own "divine" powers. If in psychoanalytic terms Desdemona projects the emotional residue of her mother onto the handkerchief, in magic terms the handkerchief slyly absorbs Desdemona's symbolic essence just as it has literally introjected the victims whose "mummy" dyes its work.[43] Both Desdemona and the handkerchief share the same numinous quality, seeming at once to belong to and to transcend the frenzied masculine world of the play. Desdemona's consecration of her "soul and fortunes" to Othello (1.3.250) and her simple declaration that "I saw Othello's visage in his mind" (1.3.248) seem utterly at odds with her dogged (even shrewish) commitment to Cassio's reinstatement in 3.3. Miraculously flickering back to life, Desdemona's final words come as if from beyond the grave: "Commend me to my kind lord" (5.2.126). Her pardon of Othello marks a Christlike level of forgiveness that can only be deemed beyond the human. Like the handkerchief, she has possessed a lethal attractiveness: love of her has destroyed Brabantio and Roderigo as well as Othello and Emilia. Committing the final act of slaughter, Othello, providing the pagan gods with a final immolation, simultaneously tries and executes himself and thus acts as both faithful servant to the Venetian state and "turbaned Turk" (5.2.349); his act transforms the struggle between Venice and Constantinople into something primitive and frightening.

Like Prospero's, the sibyl's magic has drawn the characters to an island in order to involve them in a ritual action beyond their ken. From the moment Othello's mother "gave it [him] / And bid [him] when [his] fate would have [him] wive, / To give it her" (3.4.59-61), the handkerchief's fatedness has driven the plot forward. Desdemona produces the handkerchief to aid Othello; Iago happens upon Emilia just as she finds the handkerchief; Bianca returns it to Cassio just at the point when an eavesdropping Othello is close enough to recognize it. At each step the handkerchief inspires Iago to ever more lethal improvisation, and, shorn of the handkerchief in the play's last scene, he has nothing more to add. Yet the handkerchief is conjured once more in a final tableau: when Othello stabs himself and falls on the spotless wedding sheets, he replicates the pattern of the strawberry-spotted token, magnifying the play's central image in our consciousness before the bed-curtains are drawn (5.2.361). Othello's bloody climax is thus the handkerchief writ large.

IV

In tracing the handkerchief's felt absences, its oscillation between sign and thing, I have tried to show that *Othello* provides two seemingly incompatible perspectives on magic. In one, a mundane object such as a handkerchief accrues value and significance through the otherworldly meaning imputed to it; in the other, a thing is inherently magical and carries its charm wherever it goes. The handkerchief exhibits both properties, and the play's final irony is that these properties' effect is identical: the charm works because people believe in it. As in the case of Winnicott's transitional object, we need never ask if the charm exists independently of our consciousness of it. It suffices that something or someone appears to be magical (or unfaithful) for the magic (or jealousy) to work. Magic is mimetic-always caught, like an infection, from someone else.[44] Thus the fact that Othello seems to believe his "magic in the web" speech is enough to convince Desdemona, while the fact that she seems to believe him ("Then would to God that I had never seen't!" [3.4.73]) is enough to convince Emilia and the offstage audience—at least for the duration of the scene. In each case, the handkerchief is "magic enough" to produce real consequences.

The analogue of this ju-ju, by which something becomes real as soon as it is perceived, is jealously. Iago's success bears witness that this self-authenticating, self-consuming emotion need only be entertained as a possibility for it to become real. Iago himself is not inured to this infectious disease, which "gnaw[s] my inwards" (2.1.278). Contemplating the rumor that Emilia has slept with Othello, Iago unwittingly lays bare the mechanism at the heart of the play: "I know not if't be true / Yet I, for mere suspicion in that kind, / Will do as if for surety" (1.3.370-72). Iago admits that it does not matter to him whether Emilia slept with Othello or not; he has bracketed the question of reality (i.e., adultery) entirely, and his untrammeled jealousy soon includes Cassio (2.1.288).

Othello reveals that the effects of magic and jealousy are identical. Jealousy—or magic—becomes a self-fulfilling prophecy, like the sibyl's curse. It is as real as

we think it is, which is precisely what makes it dangerous. I have outlined this mechanism in detail because I believe the play can be understood as a cautionary fable about the phenomenological power of theater.[45] Just as the handkerchief invites its victims to bracket the world outside itself, with all its skepticism about magic-hence the play's Venetian prologue, a pageant of rationality to keep us in false gaze—so the theater invites us to bracket the world outside the playhouse and thus serves to reduce reality to the objects presently before our eyes. Magic is neither trick nor metaphor, *Othello* warns, but a psychic mechanism whose workings we ignore at our peril. The play implies that theater is a phenomenological rather than an epistemological endeavor: we go to the theater not because it represents things true but because it makes us feel things which we experience as true. *Othello* acknowledges the theatricality of its own magic but argues that theatrical magic should be taken seriously because it produces genuine emotions, and emotions have potentially lethal results—both in and out of the playhouse.

However opaque its moral, *Othello* does provide an object lesson in the dangers of hermeneutic tunnel vision. Taken to its extreme, the semiotic attitude yields an Othello-like obsession with an object's sign-function, a refusal to see the lost handkerchief as simply a lost handkerchief. Conversely, taken to its extreme, the phenomenological attitude yields Iago, a reductive ego gone berserk. Iago refuses to see the world except through the distorting lens of his own pathology, and he achieves a nightmarish solipsism in which love is lust, honor a word, marriage a farce. What remains once Iago performs his cynical reductions is not transcendence but pornography: a world of bodies without souls, "a lust of the blood and a permission of the will" (1.3.326). Iago embodies a monstrous Cartesian dualism, a mind reflecting coolly on the body's depravities. Instead of the transcendental, revelatory structures of the ego envisioned by Husserl, Iago's reductionism offers anarchy and chaos.[46]

The play's very topography is a metaphor for phenomenological reduction gone haywire. Venice in part represents a skeptical audience's "natural attitude" to sorcery, which is literally put on trial in act 1 as if to underscore the point. The senate is a model of rational deliberation, admirably suspicious of "pageant[s] / To keep us in false gaze" (1.3.18-19), and Brabantio is all but ridiculed for suggesting that Othello practiced charms on Desdemona. Once we reach Cyprus, however, "a town of war, / Yet wild" (2.3.194-95), the rational world of Venice is bracketed, and the passionate energies unleashed by the handkerchief engulf us. Othello's reductions on the emotional level are mirrored by reduction at the spatial level. The play forces upon us a series of near-concentric constrictions in spatial possibility—Venice, Cyprus, citadel, chamber, bed, sheets, bodies, blood—precisely to increase our sense of claustrophobic bracketing. Othello's self-stabbing, providing a visual reminder of the handkerchief, collapses everything to the dimensions of this central property.

Thomas Rymer famously derided "[s]o much ado, so much stress, so much passion and repetition about an Handkerchief!"[47] But from the handkerchief's perspective, *Othello* can be seen as a witty and disturbing mediation on the magical properties of props: their liminal status in performance as both themselves and other than themselves, objects as well as symbols. It is true that, as a "token" or gift, the handkerchief can be seen as a conveniently empty counter in a series of symbolic exchanges; but in performance the handkerchief stubbornly insists on its materiality over and above its referentiality and refuses to accede to an overdetermined symbolic "absence." In a startling reversal of a prop's usual function, Othello's handkerchief uses and discards its victims rather than vice versa. Instead of merely symbolizing its human couriers, the handkerchief absorbs and literally inscribes them as felt absences within its ghostly palimpsest. The "mummy" that forms its dye (3.4.70) is liquid drained from the embalmed bodies of its victims, an ironic parody of a handkerchief's mundane function as a repository of bodily waste. To the handkerchief, waste is all that the body is, and Othello's tragedy is merely an episode in its larger (offstage) life. The felt absence which the handkerchief embodies is Shakespeare's synecdoche for the theater itself: an alchemy whereby the word is briefly made flesh before being once more absorbed into the "work."

Notes

1. Giraldi Cinthio, *Hecatommithi,* in *Narrative and Dramatic Sources of Shakespeare,* ed. Geoffrey Bullough, 8 vols. (London: Routledge and Kegan Paul, 1973), 7:246.

2. The evil ensign (Shakespeare's Iago) steals the handkerchief directly from Disdemona and impulsively plants it in the bed of the captain (Shakespeare's Cassio). The captain decides to return it to Disdemona by the back door but runs away when the suspicious Moor reappears. Later, the ensign and the Moor happen to pass by the captain's lodging when the captain's woman is visible in a window duplicating the handkerchief's pattern—and thus providing the ocular proof of Disdemona's infidelity and sealing her doom at the men's hands with a sand-filled stocking.

3. *Othello,* 2.3.337; quotations from this play in my paper are from the *New Cambridge Shakespeare,* ed. Norman Sanders (Cambridge: Cambridge University Press, 1984).

4. According to Frances A. Yates, *The Art of Memory* (Chicago: University of Chicago Press, 1966), "The talisman is an object imprinted with an image which has been supposed to have been rendered magical, or to have magical efficacy, through having been made in accordance with certain magical rules" (154). Fernand Baldensperger, "Was Othello an Ethiopian?" *Harvard Studies and Notes in Philology and Literature* 20 (1938): 3-14, argues that "poor Othello's 'handkerchief' is an amulet—one of those powerful Ethiopian talismans, already alluded to in Heliodorus, which any specialist in superstitions ranks to-day among the most efficient of all the magic helpers of a credulous humanity" (13). Linda Woodbridge, in *The Scythe of Saturn: Shakespeare and Magical Thinking* (Urbana: University of Illinois Press, 1994), also will see Desdemona's handkerchief as an amulet, "a bodily protection against a magical weapon: the supernaturally powerful gaze of an enemy" (60) the "evil eye" passed from Iago to Othello to Desdemona.

5. Bert O. States, *Great Reckonings in Little Rooms: On the Phenomenology of Theater* (Berkeley and Los Angeles: University of California Press, 1985), 8. According to States, objects are constantly mutating (via language) into signs and then back into what States calls "images." In what could stand as an apt image of Desdemona's handkerchief, States calls the sign/image "a Janus-faced thing: it wants to say something about something, to be a sign, and it wants to be something, a thing in itself, a site of beauty" (10).

6. Obviously not every member of all audiences for every production will understand a theatrical moment in a definitive way. By repeatedly invoking "the (attentive) audience," however, I am trying to pinpoint moments when the text seems to demand specific effects in the theater, independent of any given production. The handkerchief itself, for example, like its own "work," cannot be "tane out" of the play (3.3.298). If I risk imposing my own staging ideas on *Othello,* I do so in the hope that my arguments will be suggestive enough to provoke the reader's own sense of the play's demands in performance.

7. Iago tells Emilia that he has "use" for the handkerchief (3.3.321) and Othello that he saw Cassio "wipe his beard" with it (3.3.439). For the erotic connotations of these terms, see David Kaula, "Othello Possessed: Notes on Shakespeare's Use of Magic and Witchcraft," *Shakespeare Studies* 2 (1966): 123.

8. *Cymbeline,* 1.3.7; quotations from *Cymbeline* in my paper are from *The Riverside Shakespeare,* ed. G. Blakemore Evans et al. (Boston: Houghton Mifflin, 1974).

9. We are told the handkerchief "was dyed in mummy, which the skilful Conserved of maidens' hearts" (3.4.70-71). The handkerchief's dye is thus derived from the embalmed bodies of its victims. See A. H. R. Fairchild, "'Mummy' in Shakespeare," *Philological Quarterly* 1 (1922): 143-46.

10. The phrase "take out" is ambiguous. To "take out" embroidery is an idiom that means to copy, but the phrase also suggests somehow removing the embroidery itself. If we are to equate this "work" with the handkerchief's strawberry-spotted pattern, this second meaning would imply restoring the handkerchief to a state of pure whiteness—an interesting concept if we link the handkerchief's pattern to Desdemona's virginity and to her (perhaps) spotless wedding sheets, which she bids Emilia place on her bed at 4.2.104. For a reading equating the handkerchief with wedding sheets and its strawberries with virgin blood, see Lynda E. Boose, "Othello's Handkerchief: 'The Recognizance and Pledge of Love',' *English Literary Renaissance* 5 (1975): 360-74.

11. John A. Hodgson, "Desdemona's Handkerchief as an Emblem of Her Reputation," *Texas Studies in Literature and Language* 19 (1977): 318.

12. Kaula, "Othello Possessed," 127.

13. Paul Yachnin, "Magical Properties: Vision, Possession, and Wonder in *Othello*," *Theatre Journal* 48 (1996): 197-208. Yachnin's claim that "[t]he play's stake in the handkerchief registers the theatre's participation in English society's fetishized trade in textiles" (202) is intriguing but proceeds from very different foundational assumptions than mine about the kind of "registering" audiences (and critics) do when confronted with objects on stage.

14. Woodbridge, *The Scythe of Saturn*, 67. Frances Teague, "Objects in *Othello*," in *Othello: New Perspectives*, ed. Virginia Mason Vaughan and Kent Cartwright (Rutherford: Fairleigh Dickinson University Press, 1991), notes that "the handkerchief has a range of potential meanings that are mutually exclusive: symbol of self or of jealousy, emblem of treachery, and literal magic token. The play denies none of these meanings, but it does not specify one either" (184).

15. Robert B. Heilman, *Magic in the Web: Action and Language in Othello* (Lexington: University of Kentucky Press, 1956), 17.

16. In "The 'Arts Inhibited' and the Meaning of *Othello*," *Boston University Studies in English* 1 (1955): 129-47, James A. S. McPeek makes the rare argument that Shakespeare's audience would have seen the handkerchief as "clearly a token of witchcraft" (143) and Iago as demonic. See also S. L. Bethell, "Shakespeare's Imagery: The Diabolic Images in *Othello*," *Shakespeare Survey* 5 (1952): 62-80. McPeek points out that the controversy over witchcraft's existence was at its peak in Shakespeare's day, and that James I had publicly weighed in on the side of belief in his *Daemonologie* (1597).

17. Compare Queen Margaret's handkerchief, stained with the blood of Rutland and used to torment York in *3 Henry VI*, and Orlando's "bloody napkin" in As You Like It which makes "Ganymede" swoon. In a gothic twist, Webster's *The Duchess of Malfi* features a handkerchief whose blood engulfs the initials of Antonio's name and presages his death. In Kyd's *The Spanish Tragedy*, Hieronymo displays a handkerchief besmeared in his son's blood that becomes a token of his revenge. J. L. Styan, *The English Stage: A History of Drama and Performance* (Cambridge: Cambridge University Press, 1996), remarks that for the Elizabethans "dipping a handkerchief in the victim's blood was a practice at public executions" (115).

18. Alvin Kernan, ed., *Othello,* by William Shakespeare (New York: New American Library, 1963), 103n.

19. It is as if Shakespeare has left it up to the handkerchief itself to choreograph the action. Mary Douglas, *Purity and Danger: An Analysis of Concepts of Pollution and Taboo* (New York: Frederick A. Praeger, 1966), indicates that "an external symbol can mysteriously help the coordination of brain and body. Actors' memoirs frequently recount cases in which a material symbol conveys effective power: the actor knows his part, knows exactly how he wants to interpret it. But an intellectual knowing of what is to be done is not enough to produce the action. He tries continually and fails. One day some prop is passed to him, a hat or green umbrella, and with this symbol suddenly knowledge and intention are realised in the flawless performance" (63). I am grateful to Judith Issroff for this reference.

20. The actor playing Emilia is given some scope here. Writing of a 1990 production at *The Other Place* in Stratford-upon-Avon, for instance, the editors of *Shakespeare in Performance* explain: "When Emilia denies to Desdemona any knowledge of what has happened to the handkerchief, it can be an uncomfortable moment inconsistent with loyal friendship, but for Zoe Wanamaker it read powerfully as a moment in which she was prepared to have Desdemona suffer a little of the marital

disharmony that for Emilia was habitual" (*Shakespeare in Performance*, ed. Keith Parsons and Pamela Mason [London: Salamander Books, 1995], 167).

21. C. T. Onions, *A Shakespeare Glossary* (Oxford: Clarendon Press, 1986), 56.

22. In "Honest Othello: The Handkerchief Once More," *Studies in English Literature* 13 (1973): 273-84, Michael C. Andrews exonerates Othello of the charge of witchcraft by begging the question: "[I]t is plain enough that Othello regards the handkerchief as ensuring the continuance of his love for Desdemona, not hers for him" (281-82). Nevertheless, the fact that Brabantio has earlier accused Othello of binding Desdemona "in chains of magic" (1.2.65) eerily resonates throughout the play.

23. D. W. Winnicott, "Living Creatively," in *Home is Where We Start From: Essays by a Psychoanalyst* (London: Penguin, 1986), 50.

24. For a discussion of how the handkerchief mediates between the operations of the body and its apertures and "[t]he transformation of the handkerchief from locus of privileged meaning to commonplace," see Peter Stallybrass, "Patriarchal Territories: The Body Enclosed," in *Rewriting the Renaissance: The Discourses of Sexual Difference in Early Modern Europe*, ed. Margaret W. Ferguson, Maureen Quilligan, and Nancy J. Vickers (Chicago: University of Chicago Press, 1986): 123-44, esp. 137-39.

25. See Julia Kristeva, *Revolution in Poetic Language*, trans. Margaret Waller (New York: Columbia University Press, 1984), esp. 25-30.

26. Both acts 1 and 2 end by shrinking the stage to Iago's solo figure, and the audience's attention is thus forcibly reduced to his malevolent consciousness. The handkerchief takes up this "spotlighted" function at the close of act 3. On Iago's own capacity "to reduce imaginatively all he contemplates," see Sanders's introduction to the New Cambridge edition, 30-34.

27. Shakespeare here follows Cinthio: "The wicked Ensign, seizing a suitable opportunity, went to the Corporal's room, and with cunning malice left the handkerchief at the head of his bed" (*Narrative and Dramatic Sources*, ed. Bullough, 7:247).

28. Stallybrass, "Patriarchal Territories," 137.

29. In his introduction to *Othello*, Sanders notes that for Shakespeare's contemporaries Janus-faced Venice itself "gazed in two directions: towards civilised Christianity and towards the remote eastern world of pagan infidels, the Turks, and the mighty power of Islam" (18).

30. William Davenant adopts this topos in scene 3 of *The Siege of Rhodes*, Part 1 (1656). Roxolana enters Rhodes, furious that Ianthe has "stolen" Solyman. Rustan comments, "You come from Sea as Venus came before; / And seem that Goddess, but mistake her shore." To this Pirrhus adds helpfully, "Her Temple did in fruitful Cyprus stand; / The Sultan wonders why in Rhodes you land" (*The Works of Sir William Davenant*, 2 vols. [1673; reprint London: Benjamin Blom, 1968], 2:14).

31. Doros Alastos, *Cyprus in History* (London: Zeno, 1955), 37.

32. James George Frazer, *The Golden Bough: A Study in Magic and Religion*, 9 vols. (1911-15; reprint New York: St. Martin's Press, 1990), Part IV, 1:31-36. Baldensperger, "Was Othello an Ethiopian?" asserts that "[i]t was quite in accord with the reputation of Cyprus, 'dedicated to Venus,' to have Bianca, a Venetian courtesan with a house in the island, welcoming young men from the metropolis" (6).

33. Jean Jofen, in "The Case of the Strawberry Handkerchief," *Shakespeare Newsletter* 21 (1971): 14, traces Shakespeare's association of strawberries with impotence and linen with innocence and also identifies the spotted handkerchief with "the successful culmination of the sexual act." Jofen sees a tension between the virginal innocence of the "handkerchief" derived from the mother and the "minx's token" of sexual promiscuity perceived by Bianca. In "The Meaning of Strawberries in Shakespeare," *Studies in the Renaissance* 7 (1960): 225-40, Lawrence J. Ross equates the strawberries with the handkerchief's "work" and explains that the strawberry emblem, classical in origin, was by Shakespeare's day ambiguous: it could represent both perfect righteousness and lurking moral corruption. Expanding Ross's insights, Kaula, "Othello Possessed," speculates that "[i]n view of the sacramental implications of the strawberry emblem, Iago's verbal abusing of the handkerchief, like his other conversions of caritas to lust, parallels one of the more lurid features of the Black Mass, the sexual defilement of the eucharist, the theoretical purpose of which was magically to reduce the power of the white god and transfer it to the black" (123-24). McPeek, "The 'Arts Inhibited'," suggests that the strawberries are symbols of maidens' hearts (145). The handkerchief's strawberries, worked into the folds of the handkerchief, are a fascinating emblem within an emblem whose significance clearly merits further discussion.

34. I am grateful to Grace Tiffany for this observation.

35. Shakespeare may here be referring to the faux-marble underside of the stage cover in the Globe Theater. In *Cymbeline,* Sicilius bids Jupiter "[p]eep through thy marble mansion" (5.4.87); and after Jupiter ascends Sicilius remarks, "The marble pavement closes, he is enter'd / His radiant roof' (5.4.120-21), presumably referring to a trap door in the stage cover itself. Both *Othello* and *Cymbeline* played at the Globe in Shakespeare's lifetime: *Othello* in April 1610, and *Cymbeline* in September 1611.

36. It is even somewhat misleading to characterize the handkerchief's intricate exchanges in terms of "givers" and "receivers" since Othello refuses the handkerchief (3.3.289); Iago apparently snatches it (3.3.317); and Cassio finds it in his lodging and lends it to Bianca (3.4.185), who tries (and possibly fails) to return it (4.1.149).

37. Hodgson, "Desdemona's Handkerchief as an Emblem," is thus mistaken in asserting that "[w]hile no one, as it happens, takes out the work of Desdemona's handkerchief, we must recognize that it would be quite possible for someone to do so" (318). Yachnin, too, misses the point when he claims that the handkerchief "is not necessarily unique, but potentially only the first of a series. It could be reproduced endlessly for an endless number of owners" ("Magical Properties," 203). In fact, the handkerchief's uniqueness reinforces States's crucial phenomenological distinction between signs and images: "Unlike the sign, the image is unique and unreproducible (except as facsimile); whereas the sign is of no value unless it repeats itself' (*Great Reckonings,* 25). States goes on to quote Derrida: "a sign which does not repeat itself, which is not already divided by repetition in its 'first time', is not a sign" (Jacques Derrida, "The Theater of Cruelty and the Closure of Representation," in *Writing and Difference,* trans. Alan Bass [Chicago: University of Chicago Press, 1978], 246, as quoted by States, 25).

38. Hodgson, "Desdemona's Handkerchief as an Emblem," muses that the handkerchief might appear one last time, when Bianca tends the wounded Cassio in 5.1, which "would be intriguingly evocative of the handkerchief s first appearance, when Desdemona tries to bind Othello's aching forehead with it" (319) but this is pure conjecture.

39. Kaula, "Othello Possessed," 126-27.

40. Robert S. Miola, "Othello Furens," *Shakespeare Quarterly* 41. (1990): 58.

41. Hodgson, "Desdemona's Handkerchief as an Emblem," 315; Andrews, "Honest Othello," 283.

42. Baldensperger, "Was Othello an Ethiopian?" excuses Othello's deliberate lie about the "antique token" by asking rhetorically, "Among so many enlightened people, how could he speak of the fatal abduction of an amulet?" (14). Mark Van Doren, *Shakespeare* (New York: Henry Holt, 1939), suggests that "in Othello's case an element of mystery and magic, native to his original environment and in the meantime only half-forgotten, would seem to have become operative again. His voice and his very clothes have brought the scent of it along" (229).

43. From a psychoanalytic perspective, we may say that the handkerchief identifies with its victims, given that "[i]dentification is a process in which the human subject 'introjects' attributes of other people and transforms them through the unconscious imagination. This identification with another is made a part of the subject by incorporation: the taking in of objects, either wholly or partially, to form the basis of an ego" (Anthony Elliott, *Psychoanalytic Theory: An Introduction* [Oxford: B. H. Blackwell, 1994], 13). In its bloodthirsty incorporations, the handkerchief may be said to take the Freudian model of ego-formation very much to heart.

44. In this, magic resembles desire, which is also mimetic in the play. Desdemona falls in love while eavesdropping on Othello recounting his adventures to Brabantio; Desdemona then tells Othello that the way to "woo" her would be to teach his story to a friend and have him tell it to her (1.3.163-65). Even Brabantio's conviction that Desdemona has been stolen is both instantiated and confirmed by a dream (1.141-42). Narrative, it seems, works like a charm.

45. As Bert O. States puts it in another context, "theatergoing in itself is a kind of bracketing, or epoche, in which we willingly, if not involuntarily, suspend our belief in the empirical world and attend to a half-reality already 'reduced' by the premeditations and manipulations of a series of prior and present artists" ("The Phenomenological Attitude," in *Critical Theory and Performance,* ed. Janelle G. Reinelt and Joseph R. Roach [Ann Arbor: University of Michigan Press, 1992], 371-72).

46. Edmund Husserl, *Cartesian Meditations,* trans. Dorion Cairns (The Hague: Martinus Nijhoff, 1977).

47. Thomas Rymer, "A Short View of Tragedy," in *The Critical Works of Thomas Rymer,* ed. Curt A. Zimansky (New Haven: Yale University Press, 1956), 160.

Edward Washington (essay date 1997)

SOURCE: Washington, Edward. "'At the Door of Truth': The Hollowness of Signs in *Othello*." In *Othello: New Essays by Black Writers,* edited by Mythili Kaul, pp. 167-87. Washington D.C.: Howard University Press, 1997.

[*In the following essay, Washington locates Othello's personal flaw in his tragic "dependence on image at the expense of truth, reality, and hope" and details the process of his downfall within the context of race.*]

Even in this time of diverse, sophisticated, and politically progressive critical methodologies, Kenneth Burke's formalist statements (144, 149) remain a valuable guide for critics of *Othello* who wish to avoid the dubious conclusions that ensue from ill-premised racist ideology. In the first detailed account of racism's influence on *Othello* scholarship, Martin Orkin exposes and denounces the long tradition of racist discourse that pervades even the highest echelons of *Othello* criticism. Several scholars have since taken up the issue of race in *Othello* seemingly in response to Orkin's implicit challenge to critics to construct unbiased (that is, reliable if not precisely "objective") evaluations of the drama's racial dimensions. Although most of these more recent essays strive to establish critical positions that eschew hasty racial prejudgments, no reading of the play has yet emerged that fully sets forth the semantic complexity of Othello's blackness.[1] There are two reasons for this. First, *Othello* scholarship has relied too heavily on historical and anthropological methodologies to explain the significance of Othello's blackness and has neglected available alternative meanings of blackness within the play.[2] Second, critics tend to evaluate Othello's motivations and actions from the delimiting (or delimited) gaze of the dominant white Venetian society, thereby precluding an unsentimentalized view of "the action as a whole" from Othello's perspective—that is, from the perspective of an "all sufficient" (IV.i.261) black figure ascribed a culturally marginal position by white "others." In the effort to address these two critical deficiencies, and to supply the interpretive lacuna regarding racial blackness in *Othello,* this essay will explore the relationship between the play's racial signifiers and the transmutations of convention in the text. More important, given the ways in which the authority of Shakespeare—and by extension that of his critics—continues to shape normative cultural values, this essay will also seek to determine the degree to which Shakespeare's *Othello* reconfigures, rather than confirms, conventional cultural stereotypes of blacks.

The difficulty in defining Othello's blackness as either a conventional or unconventional literary sign (or trope) is illustrated by the sharply varying opinions of critics who question its moral and aesthetic value. Thus, whereas Eldred Jones, Gwyn Williams, and Martin Orkin see Othello as admirable (that is, finally unstereotypical and unconventional) because of his intrinsic but tragically vulnerable honor and nobility, others such as Lemuel Johnson and Anthony Barthelemy see Othello's blackness as an artfully devised ironic mask, a black patina of virtue and nobility that obscures the more conventional meaning of the sign. And although cultural materialist Ania Loomba believes that Othello's "barbarity" is an "ideological construct" rather than a quality "natural" to blacks, she warns against glossing the faults in Othello that do in fact uphold insidious racial stereotypes. This variety of critical opinion leaves unresolved the question of whether blackness in *Othello* is good or evil, literal or symbolic, conventional or unconventional, stereotypical or typically human. As Elliot Tokson laments:

> Arguments have been raised both for and against the view of Othello as a noble Moor . . . and the problem of that nobility—or barbarism—unavoidably has turned attention to the question of Shakespeare's racial tolerance or bigotry. Some critics believe that Shakespeare was uninterested in the racial aspects of the tragic situation altogether while others hold that Shakespeare was so deeply concerned with Othello's blackness that to miss that theme is to miss the heart of the play. . . . Whether Shakespeare's imagination probed more deeply than any other writer of this period into the possibilities of the black man, or whether he basically followed the stereotyped pattern on which he traced the outline of Othello's character, or whether he combined popular notions with original perspective are gritty questions that one could more fruitfully pursue were there available some suitable materials with which *Othello* could be compared.
>
> (xi)

Tokson's frustration with the inconclusiveness of meaning inherent in Othello's blackness is, however, exactly the point: that is, the ambiguous mixture of virtues and deficiencies in Othello is what makes him both more mimetically "human," and tragically complex. This is not to suggest (as many have) that Othello's blackness is simply incidental (or coincidental) to the "larger" meanings in the play. On the contrary, although Othello's blackness is not a one-dimensional emblematic signifier, it does represent an essential element in his dramatic characterization—like Richard III's deformity, Shylock's "Jewishness," Falstaff's rotundity, or Lear's age. That is, blackness in Othello's character provides the rationale for why he thinks and acts the way he does in the given dramatic context.

I

Bernard Spivack, Mark Rose, and Howard Felperin (among others) draw attention to a metaphorical relationship that exists between the play's dramatic realities regarding race and the play's dramatization of blackness as an unconventional Shakespearean literary emblem. They see *Othello* as a struggle between two traditional literary genres—(chivalric) romance and morality drama—each vying with the other for ascendancy in the play.[3] To the extent that Othello knows his "cues" and can play his part "without a prompter" (I.iii.82-83), he would have us see the play as a romance: more particularly, I would argue, as his version of the romantic fairy tale "Beauty and the Beast." In this tale, Othello plays the part of the black prince, once thought to be beastly, but whose true beauty is revealed through the love of the fair woman whom he marries. Iago, on the other hand, in his role as playwright or stage director, prefers to have us see the play as a morality drama, with himself in the role of Chief Vice. Through deceit and innuendo, Iago seeks to destroy Othello's romance by turning the virtue of the would-be fairy tale into the pitch of tragedy. Taken together, Iago's lies and innuendos make up a false story, a parallel second plot that constitutes a morality drama test for the Beauty and Beast of Othello's plot. As the author of this false second story, Iago strongly resembles the dark tempter Archimago in Spenser's *Faerie Queene*. Like Archimago, Iago deceives his victim into believing that his love has been unfaithful to him. Like Archimago, Iago also achieves his goal by deluding his victim with falsehoods so realistic that the false seems truer than the true. Like the Redcrosse Knight, once Othello is taken in by these potent lies, he loses faith in real love.[4]

In the balance of the struggle between Iago and Othello hangs not only the play's tragic outcome but also the fate of the image that Othello has carefully built up of himself. That is, depending on the outcome of the struggle, Othello's reputation as an "all-sufficient" black soldier will be either furthered or destroyed. Similarly, on the level of metadrama, Othello's (or Shakespeare's) poetic image of unconventional black beauty either will be confirmed through romance or, should Iago prevail, will revert (as many critics argue it does) to stereotypical definitions of beastly blackness.

II

In spite of Othello's relatively secure situation in Venice, his role in the drama is circumscribed (more than has been generally recognized) by the social realities of race-centered marginalization, or racism. This racism is not always overt (Othello is held in high regard by many); rather it is most often a latent and muted hatred of blackness that surfaces suddenly with vituperative and sometimes destructive force, with or without the necessity of demonstrably "Moorish" behavior by Othello. For example, throughout the play, Emilia either implies or states outright that Othello is unfit for Desdemona because of his blackness; Roderigo glosses over

his own unsuitability for Desdemona by denigrating Othello as "the thick lips" or the "gross . . . lascivious Moor" (I.i.66, 126). Iago of course claims to hate the Moor for particular and perhaps for general reasons, and it is significant that he (and Roderigo) incite the ire of Brabantio, the "good" (that is, white) citizen and cheated father, by resorting to racebaiting.

Brabantio himself reflects most sharply the quite real and unpredictable nature of antiblackness in Venice, dangerous even to a black figure as well-situated as Othello. Having once been the charitable host to Othello, Brabantio suddenly becomes not simply a wounded father who has lost his daughter to an "unlawful" suitor but a racist demagogue who would brand Othello a conjuring black witch, to be imprisoned (and burned at the stake, we might imagine, should the accusations be sustained). Thus, although Othello has found some acceptance in Venice, his blackness is nevertheless susceptible to the dangers of white racism that erupt when he transgresses Venetian definitions of racial acceptability.

Although recent critics have begun to acknowledge the role of racism in the play, few have pursued in much depth the degree to which the play shows Othello himself to be keenly aware of forces that stand ready to reject his blackness at the least provocation. It is unlikely that Othello could have achieved the success he has over a period of years without being cognizant of the latent (and overt) racism in society. Despite the fair number of critics who maintain that Othello's tragedy results from his being an outsider in Venice, one wonders how Othello could have not only survived but thrived here, without having understood a good deal about this society's dangerous racial waters. I would suggest that Othello has survived Venice's latent racism by cultivating a reputation and respect strong enough to hold back the tide of antiblackness. The bedrock of this reputation is, of course, military prowess, but Othello is no mere brute soldier. He has the charisma of a commander, and he emphasizes the ceremonial aspects, the pomp and circumstance of the position he holds. But more than this, Othello has established himself socially in Venice: he is well liked, much respected, and welcomed into the homes of Venetian aristocrats like Brabantio. He inspires so much respect in fact that he is able to defuse, without much effort, the racial protest against a marriage that few dominant groups would allow to an outsider. (Even the Jewess Jessica in *The Merchant of Venice* must turn Christian in order to marry Lorenzo.)

Othello achieves this acceptance by his politic behavior. We see it in his conduct of military affairs: in the selection of the highly regarded Cassio as his lieutenant; in the way he halts the impending clash on the streets of Venice; in the "full liberty" he grants his men after the

Othello and Desdemona in Act IV, scene ii of Othello.

defeat of the Turks (and before they begin their new duties in Cyprus). We also see it in Othello's judicious handling of Cassio's drunken brawling on the island: Othello demotes Cassio, not because he believes him unworthy but rather to "make . . . an example" (II.iii.242) of him to the other soldiers. (As Iago says, the demotion is "a punishment more in policy than in malice" [II.iii.265-66]). We see it again in his timely reminders to Venice of how much it has benefited from his military service. Othello's politic abilities are not limited to war matters, however; in social situations, too, he uses his intelligence and his grandiloquence (G. Wilson Knight's "Othello music") in a manner that serves to distance him from conventional white notions

In a broader sense, Othello'of blacks as barbarians and beasts.[5] More than being simply articulate and sonorous, Othello is a consummate storyteller whose tales impress not only Desdemona but even the Duke, who observes that Othello's story "would win [his] daughter too" (I.iii.171). Othello's wondrous stories invariably draw attention to his stellar accomplishments—but in addition to presenting images of all sufficiency, they are infused with a pathos that gains him generous sympathy and tolerance from the Venetians.

There are times also when Othello goes to great lengths to efface himself, ingratiate himself, and evoke pity. Many critics have argued that Othello's excessive deference to the Venetians denotes a callow disavowal of his identity as a black outsider, and that this naivete about his "place" as a black in Venice explains why he is so easily duped by the lies of a "true" Venetian like Iago. This view of Othello leads Anthony Barthelemy to conclude that Othello, as a Shakespearean black character, "never possesses the power or desire to subvert civic and natural order" (161).

To this charge of co-optation or "Uncle Tomism" in Othello, I would respond that Othello uses ingratiation, purposely, to smooth his way in a racist Venice. His intent is to achieve success and humanization for his blackness in moderate fashion. Othello's mode of achieving change differentiates him from Aaron, who would avoid racial conflict by leaving Rome to return "home"; from the "dark lady," who seemingly never appears in public with her white lover; and from Caliban, who attempts to raise violent revolt against his oppressors. Most simply, the choice between militancy or moderation in the need for change is endemic to all political contexts in which weaker forces struggle against those with more power. (In black-white race relations, the best example of this conflict is the militancy of Malcolm X and the moderation of Martin Luther King, Jr.) Hence, Othello has not forgotten that he is black, nor does he forget his cultural heritage or his history of enslavement. Rather he has taken a moderate course as he seeks to achieve personal success through the politic "humanization" of his blackness in Venice. s deference to forces that have power over him is part of a larger issue of decorum and "place" in the play. That is, all the characters are very much concerned with their status in social hierarchies—whether in terms of public influence, like Brabantio; military rank, like Iago and Cassio; the proper place of fathers, daughters, wives, and "men"; or the proper "place" of a black in white Venice. Like Othello, the other characters are concerned with either maintaining their achieved "place" by any means they can or trying to improve their given status through some form of deference or ingratiation to those who have power to grant them what they seek. In one way or another, everyone has to be politic.

Thus, when Othello tells the Duke, "Rude am I in my speech . . . / And therefore little shall I grace my cause / In speaking for myself" (I.iii.81-89), we realize that this is far from true. And when Othello claims that "little of this great world can I speak / More than pertains to feats of broils and battles" (I.iii.86-87), we sense, likewise, that he exaggerates the extent to which his life has been "a flinty and steel couch of war" (I.iii.230). And after the bold fait accompli of his elopement with Desdemona, Othello is again politic—in deferring to the Duke's judgement, and by downplaying his sexual desires—thus refashioning the stereotype of blacks as lascivious beasts, which Iago and Roderigo have invoked to incite Brabantio (that is, the black ram tupping a white ewe). As Othello says:

> And heaven defend your good souls that you think
> I will your serious and great business scant,
> For she is with me; . . . no, when light-wing'd toys,
> And feather'd Cupid, foils with wanton dullness
> My speculative and active instruments,
> That my disports corrupt and taint my business,
> Let housewives make a skillet of my helm,
> And all indign and base adversities
> Make head against my estimation!
>
> (I.iii.266-74)

Although several critics have argued that these statements reveal the central patriarchal flaw in Othello's "love" for Desdemona, it seems to me that they are the finishing touches Othello gives to a muted image of black sexuality, an image that attempts to assuage conventional white fears of black lasciviousness.

This politic behavior determines, in part, Othello's unlikely marriage. Because Othello asks himself why he ever married (III.iii.246), we might presume that he had some reason for not marrying earlier. The most likely explanation for his extended bachelorhood is that the soldier's life has not allowed "skillets" to interfere with "service"; but it is interesting to speculate on the circumstances (beyond love) that lead him to marry this particular woman at this particular time, especially given the potential racial dangers of such a marriage.

After world travel, exploits, and wars, Othello has seemingly found a place for himself in Venice, even before his marriage to Desdemona. He is the Venetians' chief military officer; he speaks their language and is a Christian; he seems well connected socially and has loyal supporters; he has "fortunes" that revert to Venetian legal "relatives" on his death. Thus, despite his blackness, Othello is more integrated into the dominant community than are other Shakespearean black characters, and he is less socially isolated than Venice's own Shylock. Yet, although the cornerstone of black Othello's acceptance in Venice is his military indispensability, it is also true that this indispensability is subject to time. Being "no god" (III.iv.146), the strength of his mighty arm will decline as he ages—and Othello is already "getting older" at the start of the play. Thus, when we meet Othello, he is a man at the apex of his career and at a point in life where it would be plausible for him to be more open to the prospect of settling down. In this context, marriage to an admired and well-placed Venetian woman might bestow on him an ideal image of social (and human) sufficiency that would protect his blackness in Venice in his declining years.[6] This is not to suggest that Othello calculatingly

directs his life toward this end, nor to doubt that he "loves the gentle Desdemona" (I.ii.25) as he says he does. Rather, the dramatic givens of the play—racism, Othello's age, and later, the correlation Othello sees between a successful marriage and a successful military "occupation"—simply emphasize the further advantages of his marriage to Desdemona at present.[7] As in "Beauty and the Beast," she will be the beautiful wife who will help to reveal the full humanity in Othello's blackness.

In the light of the discussion thus far, it is not surprising that Othello's concern for his image, especially in the context of his marriage, becomes the vulnerable spot that Iago attacks when he selects the marriage as the vehicle through which he will destroy the Moor.

III

The beginning of Act II presents an Othello who has defended himself in a judicious and politic manner against each racist charge leveled against him, an Othello at the high point of his powers. His facile victory over the Turks only further confirms the security of his place in Venice. At this point, Othello's romance seems "well-shipped" (II.i.47).

But Iago perseveres in his Vice-like effort to discredit the Moor and to transform this blithe romance into a dark morality drama. In seeking to turn Othello's unconventional virtue into conventional pitch, he applies jealousy, a potent morality drama temptation that might cause anyone to miss a step. The jealousy that Iago grafts on Othello is, however, simply the catalyst that brings to the fore a more prominent vulnerability in Othello—a vulnerability of which not even Iago is fully aware and one that Othello can least defend himself against (as seems indicated by his swift, easy, and complete collapse): his fear of the loss of his image of "all in all" sufficiency in Venice. Thus, while the thought of Desdemona's unfaithfulness touches a raw nerve in Othello, it also raises the specter of a dashed opportunity (at a key point in his career) to preserve and even enhance the possibility of a safe and viable life in Venice—a city whose acceptance of blackness would seem to be contingent on his maintaining a flawless image of all-sufficiency.[8] Thus when Iago mounts his assault, the Moor loses rational control of a situation that, earlier in his life, he might have been able to control; or had Iago's evil not been quite so pernicious,[9] one he might have been able to ward off (as he does Brabantio's less potent challenge earlier on).

After what appear to have been years devoted to promoting an image of ideal blackness that allows him to claim his due and protect his place in Venice, Othello has, in fact, begun to reason and act on images of truth as if they were truth itself. His storytelling, for example, shows him using vivid and effective images of his past to win hearts and minds in Venice. These imagistic tales are essentially true but sound suspiciously similar to those titillatingly imagistic (but apocryphal) travel book stories so popular at the time. Even Othello's beautiful language is sprinkled with high-sounding neologisms (*provulgate, exsuffligate*) whose actual meaning and application are vague. Significantly, the things he cherishes most about his life as a soldier involve the outward trappings of war, the images of war rather than actual fighting:

> Farewell the plumed troop, and the big wars
> That makes ambition virtue; O farewell!
> Farewell the neighing steed, and the shrill trump,
> The spirit-stirring drum, the ear-piercing fife;
> The royal banner and all quality,
> Pride, pomp, and circumstance of glorious war!

> (III.iii.355-60)

Ironically, there is a vast discrepancy between the image and the reality—between Othello's gestures and the fact that there is little or no concrete action to back them up. Othello helps to keep the peace in Venice ("Keep up your bright swords, for the dew will rust 'em" [I.ii.58-59]), but no fighting actually occurs. In the ensuing sea battle with the Turks, strangely, a storm sinks the enemy ships, and Othello receives accolades without having fired a shot. Othello's scapegoating of Cassio on Cyprus saves him from having to "lift [his] arm" (II.iii.199) to quell further quarrels among his men.

The same dearth of substantive action prevails in situations occurring after Iago's lies about Desdemona have begun. For instance, the Moor's menacing threats against Iago in Act III and Emilia in Act V fall flat, as Iago slithers to safety and Emilia proclaims, "Thou hast not half the power to do me harm as I have to be hurt" (V.ii.163-64). Othello invokes black vengeance against Cassio but shuffles the job off onto Iago, and in the end, he sees the murder attempt fail. He is disarmed by Montano, and his final avenging lunge at Iago is ineffective. The only person he is physically violent with is Desdemona—and as Lodovico says, violence against a woman is not valorous. Othello does manage to take his own life—but this represents less an act of warlike power than the supreme gesture of powerlessness.[10]

The same empty gestures mark Othello's sexual power in the play. That is, despite all the talk about sexuality in *Othello,* there is little of it in the relationship between Othello and Desdemona. Although I disagree with those who suggest that Othello and Desdemona never consummate their marriage, the dramatic action of the play is orchestrated in a way that suggests that the couple's private time together suffers constant interruption. And after Iago's lies, sexual relations between the two seem simply unlikely. Also, although little reason exists to doubt that Othello loves Desdemona, many

have noted how Othello often speaks of her in idealized Petrarchan terms—revealing his sense of her as a wonderful "image" of womanhood rather than as a real woman to love. Thus, for Othello, Desdemona appears a "rose," a "perfect chrysolite," a "pearl" with skin as "white as snow" and as "smooth as alabaster"; his "soul's joy" to whom he would "deny nothing."

Given this tendency to objectify Desdemona as an "image" of beauty, and the way in which the play obscures real sexuality between them, Othello's reactions to Desdemona in the bedchamber scene just prior to her murder not only raise questions concerning his sexual power but also accentuate what lies at the heart of Othello's susceptibility to Iago's evil: his general propensity to treat abstract images as concrete realities. When Othello contemplates the sleeping Desdemona, with genuine ardor he murmurs words of Petrarchan praise and love. Then, when she wakens and invites him to bed, offering him, it seems, an opportunity to give his romance story a happy ending after all, the prospect of an enlivened and desirous Desdemona (as opposed to an alabaster figure) disorients Othello, and he draws back from the prospect of love made concrete and actual. Although it is easy enough to see Othello's withdrawal as the steeling of his resolve to carry out the execution, it also seems clear that it is not within the scope of his capabilities to move beyond an imagined view of love to its concrete reality. At the very end of the play, we do find Othello and Desdemona lying together on the bed; but the lifeless bodies only underscore the lost potential for real love—and even this final image of unity is disrupted by the presence of Emilia lying beside them.

IV

Othello's too-strong dependence on gestures and images—his taking them for truth—is the Achilles heel Iago exploits. Such gestures include the false images of Cassio's nonexistent dream, the misrepresenting dumb show of Cassio's cuckolding brag, and generally speaking, all circumstantial signs "which lead . . . to the door of truth" (III.iii.412-13). This dependence on image prevents Othello from seeing that the white antagonism he would defend himself against has undergone a change for the better—perhaps due to his own influence. That is, even with its dangers, Othello's Venice is not the antiblack and antilife "wilderness of tigers" that Aaron contends with in Titus's Rome; even the Venetians in *The Merchant of Venice* are more superciliously intolerant of cultural others, among them Moroccan princes and rich Jews, than is the case in *Othello.* In fact, given Renaissance England's and Renaissance drama's image of Italian cities as hotbeds of intrigue and sin, all in all, Othello's Venice seems remarkably civilized. This is not to suggest that Venetian society is ideal; however, in key ways, it is more tolerant and accepting of Othello than he realizes. Othello's inability to perceive this, however, makes it impossible for him to read the signs of hope that exist for him in Venice—positive signs that would allow him to resist the fearful images of lost love, lost marriage and lost occupation, painted by Iago.

The leaders of the State indicate this change and hope. They ferret out the truth and have a clear sense of justice—traits that bode well for a black man wary of racist stereotypes, assumptions, and prejudgments by whites. The best examples of the State's pursuit of truth occur during the War Room scene in Act I. The Duke and several other leaders receive a flurry of confusing and conflicting reports about the strength and strategy of the enemy Turks. Obviously, these false reports foreshadow the seemingly true falsehoods that Iago will unleash on Othello during the course of the play. Through patience and good judgment, however, the Venetian leaders uncover the truth about the Turks, seeing through the false report of Angelo, one who, like Iago, should be "honest" but is not. Later, the State, through the Duke, challenges and dismisses Brabantio's accusations against Othello as "thin habits and poor likelihoods" (I.iii.108) and finally adjudges Othello a suitable husband for Desdemona. Further, no leader in the State denigrates Othello; and even when the truth of Othello's crime is known, Lodovico responds more in sorrow than in anger.

Corroborating and extending the idea that these Venetians are more unconventionally accepting of Othello's blackness than he realizes are the suggestions that Othello is not the only "outsider" in Venice, a remarkably healthy political and religious state whose power and success derive from cultural heterogeneity rather than from narrow ethnocentrism. This sense of Venice as an expansive, inclusive, and fluid society comes to us in part from the many references to people, places, and things that originate outside the city's ethnic and geographical boundaries but that, nevertheless, seem integral to Venetian life and perspective. The characters, for example, allude to crusadoes, carracks, guineas, coloquintidas, and Spanish swords; they have some knowledge of monkeys, baboons, aspics, crocodiles, locusts, and Barbary horses; they have been to or know about Aleppo, Rhodes, Cyprus, Egypt, Mauritania (and Moors). Cited also are the Pontic, the Propontic, and the Hellespont, as well as England, Denmark, Germany, Holland, Rome, Sparta, and Verona. Venetian men are said to be partial to "foreign laps" (IV.iii.88), and the Venetian women would proverbially "walk barefoot to Palestine" (IV.iii.38-39) to find a good husband. All of these references connote a sense of cultural and geographic expansiveness. Then too, there is the well-known passage in which Emilia speaks to Desdemona at length about what she would do to gain "all the world": the "huge thing" of "great price" that she would

risk "purgatory for" if she could have it for her labor (IV.iii.65-75). Even here, Emilia's reference serves as the culminating epiphany to over thirty allusions to the "world" in this play—from Brabantio who wants to be judged by "the world" (I.ii.72) if his accusation of Othello is false, to Iago's desire to bring his monstrous evil "to the world's light" (I.iii.402), to the Clown who would "catechize the world" (III.iv.13) to find Cassio.

Admittedly, other Shakespearean plays allude to places outside of the immediate dramatic setting. In *Othello,* however, the Venetians are construed to be the leaders of a group of Christian "others" who join together to oppose, not non-Venetians, but rather nonbelievers—in this case the infidel Turks: Florentines, like Cassio; Greeks, like Marcus Luccicios; Cypriots, who are old friends; black Moors "of here and everywhere" (I.i.137) like Othello. In fact, as Venice's field general, it is Othello's "occupation" to unite Florentines, Greeks, Cypriots, and Venetians alike under the Christian banner of the Venetian State and to serve the State in places like Aleppo, Rhodes, Cyprus, and Mauritania.

This general acceptance of heterogeneity and of the Other is particularized in Desdemona. She is the center of moral rightness and truth in the play,[11] and it follows that her views on blackness provide the best instruction regarding its meaning in the play. At the beginning of the drama, we are told that Desdemona's love for Othello derives from having seen "his visage in his mind" (I.iii.252), thereby rendering Othello's racial blackness a moot issue in her affections for him. In Act III, after Desdemona discovers that she has misplaced the handkerchief, Emilia asks her if the Moor is jealous. Desdemona replies, "Who, he? I think the sun where he was born / Drew all such humours from him" (III.iv.26-27). Here, not only does Desdemona reject the conventional stereotype of black jealousy, but her speculation that Africa's hot climate is actually beneficial opposes the standard Renaissance view of Africa as the "foul furnace"[12] that turned Africans into hellish black devils. Futhermore, in a play that so earnestly questions whether the "best" women in a society ought not to marry their own kind, it is significant that, even after she has been called a "whore" and struck in public, Desdemona asserts that Othello's "[u]nkindness may do much, / And his unkindness may defeat my life, / But never taint my love" (IV.ii.161-63). When Desdemona affirms her love for Othello despite his behavior, the figurative sense of "unkind" as "unnatural" and thus "racially different" is heard as well, and Desdemona vows that—no matter what Othello has done, or why—she will not capitulate to the temptation to scapegoat his racial Otherness.

The idea of Othello's Venice as a heterogeneous state (and therefore more accepting of Othello than he realizes) is nevertheless confused by the racism and ethnocentrism that Iago advances in order to create a larger "place" or status for himself at the expense of an outsider. Moreover, although Roderigo, Brabantio, and (to a lesser degree) Emilia also foster racial divisiveness, these Venetians are as much under Iago's spell as Othello or Cassio.[13] It is Iago who sabotages the friendship, camaraderie, and love that has developed around, or in spite of, difference. He helps to poison the friendship between Brabantio and Othello and between Othello and Cassio; he tries to divide Cassio and Montano, the respective lieutenants of the newly combined Venetian and Cypriot forces. Most important, he poisons the love between Othello and Desdemona, in part by emphasizing their differences:

> Not to affect many proposed matches,
> Of her own clime, complexion and degree,
> Whereto we see in all things nature tends;
> Fie, we may smell in such a will most rank,
> Foul disproportion; thoughts unnatural.
>
> . . . . .
>
> I may fear
> Her will, recoiling to her better judgment,
> May fall to match you with her country forms,
> And happily repent.
>
> (III.iii.233-37; 239-42)

In general then, Iago seeks to turn fathers against daughters, husbands against wives, men against women, whites against blacks, and ultimately a heterogeneous Venetian society against itself.

Despite Iago's antiblackness, the play itself intentionally undercuts blackness as a signifier of evil by investing the white characters (even the more likable ones) with traits that are dark and sinister: Brabantio is exposed as a hypocrite and a racist; Roderigo is a fortune-hunter, a racist, and a would-be murderer; Emilia's loyalty and egalitarianism are diametrically counterposed by her slavishness, her deceit, and her bigotry; the suave Cassio has a nasty temper and a coarse side to his view of women. Even Desdemona seems to sway in the wrong direction when she attempts to redress Othello's demotion of Cassio. And Iago, of course, epitomizes the play's conversion of white to black as he plays the part of a Renaissance white devil. But the character who best exemplifies how the play transmutes the conventional meanings of black and white in *Othello* is Bianca.

Giving the name *Bianca* (that is, *white* in Italian) to a relatively substantial character in a play with a major black character is highly suggestive. As the character signifying whiteness, Bianca should, according to convention, be an ideal Petrarchan woman—which she is not. Yet, confusingly, a further reversal in Bianca's unconventionally "evil" whiteness occurs when she is said to be a whore in order to obtain the essentials of "bread and clothes" (IV.i.95). Also, in a play so

obsessed with fidelity, Bianca loves but one man (although her profession gives her license to "love" many [IV.i.97]), and like Desdemona with Othello, she remains devoted to Cassio despite his ill-treatment of her.

But Bianca's most positive aspect is her implied rejection of Iago's hypocrisy and falsehood. At the end of Act IV, she rebels against Iago's and Emilia's efforts to bewhore her and to implicate her falsely in the wounding of Cassio. Even more significant is Bianca's earlier refusal to make a copy of Desdemona's stolen handkerchief: in refusing to fall in line with Iago's surreptitious effort to create a second (morality drama) story of infidelity with the handkerchief, she refuses to fabricate a false signifier of Othello's and Desdemona's romance. Moreover, in declining to "take out the work" (that is, destroy through replication) of the true love token (IV.i.153), Bianca is the first to reject outright Iago's evil designs. Her defiance signals a major turning point in the play, the point where other manipulated characters begin to throw off Iago's influence, thus bringing his plot to light.

The point here is that the conventional forms of antiblackness in this play occur almost exclusively in the context of Iago's fabrications about Othello and Desdemona. The racist sentiments in the play are uttered either by Iago or by characters over whom he has gained power through an exploitation of their frailties. As such, Iago spins an Archimago-like illusion of racial intolerance that distorts a truer (though certainly not perfect) reality of Venice that Othello does not discern.

V

Despite any sympathy we might have for Othello's need to foster an ideal black image in Venice, and despite our awareness of Iago's potent malignity, Othello remains culpable. Although his culpability ensues neither from his emblematic blackness nor (up to a point) from his "human" susceptibility to error and sin, Othello may be held accountable for his failure to read and understand the unconventional signs of hope in Venice that could have allowed him to see through Iago's false images.

In a sense, the question of Othello's culpability ought to be resolved when he realizes that he has foolishly killed a faithful wife, and seeing his error, embarks on what appears to be a reconciling course of tragic resolution. With good tragic form, Othello confesses his mistakes and then takes his own life in order to atone for his tragic folly. Thus, although Othello fails in his attempt to remake "Beauty and the Beast," he does manage to rework his part to fit that of the hero in a tragic romance ("I will kill thee, / And love thee after" [V.ii.18-19]). After all, to die by one's own hand while in the arms of one's slain lover is the stuff of tragic romance in *Romeo and Juliet* and *Antony and Cleopatra*. The point, however, is that although Othello realizes that he has mistakenly killed a faithful wife, and that a scheming ensign has gulled him, he never recognizes how his own too-strong dependence on images has contributed to the crime he has committed. This lack of recognition reveals his inability, even at the end, to see the whole truth. Thus, Othello's noble reconciliation at the end of the play is more ambiguous than it initially appears, and there is much in Othello's last words and deed to suggest that the image of blackness in this play is not redeemed.

For example, something seems awry in Othello's perception of reality when he describes Montano, the soldier who has disarmed him, as a "puny whipster" (V.ii.245). He understates the soldierly abilities of Montano and overstates his own capabilities. Some lines later, he seems to come to terms with his actual powerlessness when he admits that his threat against Gratiano is but a "vain boast" (V.ii.265). Yet it is disquieting that Othello should define his lost power as his inability to "control . . . fate" (V.ii.266), since he is at least partly to blame in the death of Desdemona. Othello cannot have fully come to terms with his own failings if he can refer to the Desdemona he has murdered as an "ill-starr'd wench" (V.ii.273). Just a few lines further, Othello asserts that Desdemona's faultless spirit "will hurl [his] soul from heaven, / And fiends will snatch at it" (V.ii.275-76); but despite his genuine anguish, he again misses the point when he fails to acknowledge not only Desdemona's commitment to their conjugal love but also the forgiveness and redemption she offers when she assumes responsibility for his crime.

The most telling instances of ambiguity concerning Othello's redeemed vision occur in his very last speech. Although the tone of Othello's once again noble words is lofty, the words themselves raise many questions about the clarity of Othello's vision and his motivations at the end. That is, although Othello claims to be heart-stricken over the senseless loss of the woman he loves, he begins his final speech with, "Soft you, a word or two . . . / I have done the state some service, and they know't" (V.ii.339-40). We have seen how Othello has used this ploy, understandably but manipulatively, to defend his ideal black image from racist attacks; but here, Othello's reinvocation of an earlier politic defensiveness seems uncontritely self-serving and unredeemingly out of place, not only in the light of his contrition but also in the light of his culpability in Desdemona's death.

Shortly thereafter Othello almost literally spells out how his part in recent events should be represented, in writing, to the Venetian State. As he has done in the past, Othello idealizes the image of himself that he would have Venice remember. When he tells Lodovico to "speak of my deeds as they are; nothing extenuate" (V.ii.343), he should mean, "Don't spare the awful truth"—but he probably does not. Further, in instructing Lodovico not to "set down aught in malice" (V.ii.344), Othello seems to say, "Don't tone down anything about me (for I am great of heart), but also, don't say anything that suggests that you don't approve of me." Othello thus asks us to keep our image of him not only grand but also uncritical—for his errors are but the consequence of "unlucky deeds" (V.ii.342). He goes on to fashion his future storied image of himself as "one that lov'd not wisely, but too well: / Of one not easily jealous" (V.ii.345-46). But is he completely truthful when he claims to have loved Desdemona "too well"? Did he love her so well that he judged her guilty on evidence that even Iago called circumstantial? Did he love her too well when he denied her the right to prove herself innocent? Can we ever accept his view that in killing Desdemona quickly he has somehow been "merciful" (V.ii.88)? And can we accept, without question or qualification, his assertion that he is not easily jealous in the absence of all resistance on his part against the lies of Iago? To raise such questions is to deny neither Othello's love for Desdemona nor the pernicious evil of Iago, but rather to gauge the degree to which Othello fully sees, understands, admits to, and mends the weaknesses within himself that have allowed Iago to bring forth the hideous scene that lies before him.

In short, the other characters in *Othello* come to terms with the truth, confess their disastrous errors, and go on to gain either real or symbolic salvation. Although Othello appears to undergo a similar process, his continued posturing prompts us to question whether he has recognized how his dependence on image has contributed to the tragic events—and in turn, to wonder if in fact he redeems himself with his dramatic self-sacrifice. In questioning the soundness of Othello's tragic resolution, we must also question whether he has seen the avenues of hope before him that might have saved his wife, his life, and his soul in Venice. That is, has Othello understood that Desdemona accepted him, loved him, and then saved him with her forgiveness? Does Othello (despite his error) see the possibility of redemptive vindication at the hands of a clear-sighted, just, and tolerant white Venetian state? And, in the context of the play as a morality drama, has Othello faith enough to believe that he will receive grace despite his earthy trials and sins?

VI

The last half of Othello's last speech is an imagistic travelogue of his sojourns culminating in his story of the slaughtered infidel. Othello then transposes the image of the slain infidel into a metaphorical image that represents his own faithlessness and penitent suicide. Putting a knife to his own throat is Othello's last grand gesture. Yet Gratiano startles us with his deflating observation that Othello's ostensibly noble and redeeming act mars "all that's spoke" (V.ii.358).

In the context of morality drama, Othello's suicide (especially with the signs of change and hope in Venice) denotes his capitulation to the last and most subtle deception of Vice—despair—the hopelessness that blinds one to the grace of God. Hence, at the end of the play, we find Othello to be in much the same predicament as Spenser's Redcrosse as he nears the end of his trials. Like Othello, the image-bound Redcrosse struggles with his fiend in an effort to come to terms with his lack of faith in a faithful woman. Having seen his errors, Redcrosse, like Othello, would redress his sins by doing away with himself at knifepoint:

> [The fiend] to [Redcrosse] raught a dagger sharpe and
>   keene,
> And gave it him in hand: his hand did quake,
> And tremble like a leafe of Aspin greene,
> And troubled bloud through his pale face was scene
> To come, and goe with tydings from the hart,
> As it a running messenger had beene.
> At last resolved to worke his finall smart
> He lifted up his hand, that backe againe did start.

(I.ix.51)

But unlike Othello, in the end, Redcrosse remains open to the truth of Una's love and forgiveness and God's grace—and pulls back from the pit to gain his salvation:

> "Come, come away, fraile, feeble, fleshly wight,
> Ne let vaine words bewitch thy manly hart,
> Ne divelish thoughts dismay thy constant spright.
> In heavenly mercies hast thou not a part?
> Why shouldst thou then despeire, that chosen art?
> Where justice growes, there grows eke greater grace,
> The which doth quench the brond of hellish smart,
> And accurst hand-writing doth deface.
> Arise, Sir knight arise, and leave this cursed place."
>   . . . . .
> So up he rose, and thence amounted streight.

(I.ix.53; 54)

The trials of Redcrosse reflect the trials of morality drama protagonists generally; and to the degree that *Othello* is a play that incorporates the form and substance of morality drama, Othello's attempt to redeem himself through an otherwise noble suicide inadvertently leads him directly into the clutches of a hellish Vice. Thus, in the metadramatic struggle between genres, morality drama bests romance; for as Lodovico observes to Iago as the curtain is closed on the tragic bed, "[T]his is thy work" (V.ii.365).

My argument is that Othello's dependence on image at the expense of truth, reality, and hope (what the play calls "matter") is the "cause" of his downfall. More specifically, in the context of race, Othello continues to view his salvation in terms of his ability to build and live up to an ideal image—as valiant soldier, as fairy-tale husband, as the hero of a tragic romance—in order to redeem the integrity of his black humanity from denigration at the hands of conventionally hostile white "critics" (II.i.119) like Iago (or even those cited by Orkin). In this context of black survival, Othello's aims are fatal but not ignoble; consequently, his fall is more dramatically tragic than stereotypically evil—especially because the black image he strives to protect has found some measure of acceptance in Venice.

Notes

1. See Neill, Loomba, Newman, Braxton, Dollimore, Berry, Cantor, and Bartels. These critics, however, almost invariably discuss the issue of race in *Othello* in conjunction with a "related" subject, such as colonialism, Renaissance ideologies of gender, sexual mores of the audience, and psychosocial functions of perversion. In *Othello* criticism, the introduction of such "larger" issues tends to obfuscate rather than reveal fully the complexities of racial blackness in the play. In this regard, Loomba, Berry, and Bartels are more focused, and many areas of agreement exist between their arguments and my own.

2. Leah Marcus has outlined the essential problem of historical analyses of Shakespeare as follows: "What we call Shakespeare is somehow mysteriously different, impervious to history at the level of specific factual data, the day to day chronicling of events" (xi). See also Graham Holderness.

3. Spivack examines the play in relation to morality drama allegory; Rose presents a convincing case for his view of *Othello* as a chivalric romance; and more broadly, Felperin asserts that several literary forms (morality drama and romance inclusive) are showcased in *Othello*—varied forms that ensue from the tendency of most of the characters to present, and represent, themselves in an array of conventional literary roles. Most recently, Paul Cantor has described the play as a "generic . . . displacement . . . [of] martial epic . . . into Italian bedroom comedy" (297).

4. Rose cites this analogy (295).

5. The idea that Othello's way with words, his "music," is related to issues of race in the play would seem to be confirmed by *New York Times* editor Brent Staples, in his essay "Black Men in Public Space." In this essay, Staples discusses the problems of "image" encountered by people of color in U.S. cities today. He says: "Over the years, I learned to smother the rage I felt at so often being taken for a criminal. Not to do so

would surely have led to madness. I now take precautions to make myself less threatening. [For example] I whistle melodies from Beethoven and Vivaldi and the more popular classical composers. Even steely New Yorkers hunching toward nighttime destinations seem to relax, and occasionally they even join in the tune. Virtually everybody seems to sense that a mugger wouldn't be warbling bright, sunny selections from Vivaldi's Four Seasons." Staples's frequently anthologized essay first appeared in *Ms.* magazine, September 1986.

6. Othello is not enfeebled; however, we may note that the play encourages us to accept the idea of aging as a motif of some consequence. We know that Othello contemplates his own "declin[e] / Into the vale of years" (III.iii.270) as a possible reason for Desdemona's ostensible unfaithfulness. More to the point is Iago's suggestion that no matter how faithful a man's service to the state, "when he's old" he is sure to be unceremoniously "cashier'd" (I.i.48).

7. Felperin sums up this line of argument succinctly: "As the living symbol of high Venetian culture, Desdemona is not simply a wife to Othello but the legitimating agent of his acculturation" (78). Peter Stallybrass states more simply: "Desdemona is the active agent of Othello's legitimization" (272).

8. It should be underscored again that, although Othello's preoccupation with image makes him more vulnerable to Iago's lies, this vulnerability should not be construed as an attribute of "blackness" that confirms him to be a stereotypical racial emblem. Like other somewhat less than ideal qualities in Othello, the Moor's anxious concern to be seen as all-sufficient derives largely from his desire to achieve his deserved place in Venice: to defend himself against a race-based antiblackness that would deny him his just rewards.

9. The play encourages us to equate Othello's vulnerability to Iago's lies with Cassio's susceptibility to wine. Hence, like Cassio, Othello is imbued with a poisonous force powerful enough to swiftly and completely bring about the destruction of his better self and give rein to his weaknesses and fallibilities.

10. The absence of concrete military power in Othello might be seen to further confirm his need to look ahead to a time when he would no longer be able to sustain his ideal soldier's image: a good marriage would be a hedge against any resulting loss of place in Venice.

11. Despite Desdemona's Christian intention to mend evil with good, and her Christ-like sacrifice at the end, many critics have found fault with her as the voice of right reason in the play. Some have judged her to be a weak white foil who exists only for the purpose of dramatizing the black deeds of men; others have seen her as a beautiful, but naive and wayward romantic who wanders into dark and forbidden waters; still others have claimed that her Christ-like forgiveness of Othello is so ideal that it unfits her as a true sounding board for meaning in a mature Shakespearean tragedy. Notwithstanding these criticisms, Desdemona is the beacon of moral rightness in *Othello*, and her viability in this role is sustained in part by the fact that she is not the stock good angel of a morality drama or fairy-tale romance. That is, Desdemona is as prone to error and flaw as any character in the play; but, to a greater degree than all other characters, she has the ability to adapt and grow, and ultimately, through love and faith, to find out truth.

12. See Chapter 1 of E. Jones and pages 433-42 of Bartels for fuller treatments of sixteenth-century England's view of Africa.

13. In addition to hoodwinking both Othello and Cassio, Iago exploits Roderigo's desire for Desdemona and her "full fortune," Brabantio's paternal possessiveness, and Emilia's love for him.

Works Cited

Bartels, Emily C. "Making More of the Moor: Aaron, Othello, and Renaissance Refashionings of Race," *Shakespeare Quarterly, 41* (1990), 433-54.

Berry, Edward. "Othello's Alienation," *Studies in English Literature, 30* (1990), 315-33.

Braxton, Phyllis, "The Moor and the Metaphor," *South Atlantic Review, 55* (1990), 1-17.

Cantor, Paul A. "Othello: The Erring Barbarian among the Supersubtle Venetians," *Southwest Review, 75* (1990), 296-319.

Dollimore, Jonathan. "The Cultural Politics of Perversion: Augustine, Shakespeare, Freud, Foucault," *Genders, 8* (1990), 1-16.

Felperin, Howard. *Shakespearean Representation*, Princeton, Princeton UP, 1977.

Holderness, Graham. *Shakespeare's Histories*, New York, St. Martin's Press, 1985.

Jones, Eldred. *Othello's Countrymen: The African in English Renaissance Drama*, London, Oxford UP, 1965.

Loomba, Ania. *Gender, Race and Renaissance Drama*, Manchester, Manchester UP, 1989.

Marcus, Leah. *Puzzling Shakespeare*, Berkeley, U of California P, 1988.

Neill, Michael. "Unproper Beds: Race, Adultery, and the Hideous in *Othello*," *Shakespeare Quarterly, 40* (1989), 383-412.

Newman, Karen. "Femininity and the Monstrous in *Othello*," *Shakespeare Reproduced,* ed. Jean Howard & Marion O'Connor, New York, Methuen, 1987.

Rose, Mark. "Othello's Occupation: Shakespeare and the Romance of Chivalry," *English Literary Renaissance, 15* (1985), 293-311.

Spivack, Bernard. *Shakespeare and the Allegory of Evil,* New York, Columbia UP, 1958.

Stallybrass, Peter. "Patriarchal Territories: The Body Enclosed," *Othello: Critical Essays,* ed. Susan Snyder, New York, Garland, 1988.

Lucille P. Fultz (essay date 1997)

SOURCE: Fultz, Lucille P. "Devouring Discourses: Desire and Seduction in *Othello*." In Othello: *New Essays by Black Writers,* edited by Mythili Kaul, pp. 189-204. Washington D.C.: Howard University Press, 1997.

[*In the following essay, Fultz interprets* Othello *as a drama of linguistic subversion represented by Iago's desire to discursively seduce and manipulate Othello, Desdemona, and the other principal figures in the drama.*]

In her "Introduction" to *Othello: New Perspectives,* Virginia Mason Vaughan delineates the genealogy of *Othello* criticism, which according to her, "remained . . . a bastion of formalism and psychological analysis" well into the 1980s (13). Prior to this period, according to Vaughan, *Othello* critics were concerned with issues of textual history and authority, while debates swirled around issues of definitive editions and textual conflations. Vaughan maps the movement of criticism from controversies surrounding "which version was better" or "closer to Shakespeare's original text" to analyses of patterns of language and imagery, symbolism, and psychological motivations of characters. A major turning point in *Othello* criticism occurred in the 1980s with a shift toward feminist critique, deconstruction, and performance (14-18). Georgianna Ziegler, speaking of *Hamlet* criticism, contends that "in every age Shakespeare's text[s] [have] been subjected to the interests and the view of that generation" (1), and Jean E. Howard observes, "[W]e need more new readings of Shakespeare: readings which continue to bring to bear on these plays the human concerns which press on us now" (145). This is particularly applicable to *Othello* at present.

My own critique of *Othello* is situated in a postmodern moment that foregrounds discursivity as constitutive of the self and the worlds the self inhabits. Such a reading seeks to expose Iago's desire to locate power in discourse, a power that ultimately leads to Desdemona's murder and Othello's suicide. In other words, this study examines the ways in which Iago discursively problematizes Othello's marriage to Desdemona. To this end, Iago engages in what Michael Neill terms an "operation . . . principally aimed at converting the absent/present bed into a locus of imagined adultery by producing Othello's abduction of Desdemona as an act of racial adulteration" (391). Iago's campaign against the marriage begins in the opening scene and continues until he has ensnared Othello into his trap of "racial adulteration" by convincing him that Desdemona is unfaithful to him mainly because of his race. By opening the play with Iago's base commentary on Othello's marriage, Shakespeare foregrounds marriage as the thematic and discursive issue in the play. Commenting on Iago's influence and Othello's vulnerability as an alien in Venice, G. M. Matthews contends that despite his physical and cultural difference, Othello is "a great human being who . . . recognizes (within the limits of his social role) only universal humane values of love and loyalty," which he loses once he allows himself to become "vulnerable to irrational, unhuman forces, embodied in Iago" (123).

Othello offers an expansive view of the ways in which language works against certain speakers and is twisted and perverted in the mouth of a dishonest practitioner. By playing on the ambiguities and ironies inherent in language, Iago is able to use the seductive dimensons of discourse to achieve diabolical ends. Through a consciously selective use of language, Iago distorts reality and manipulates others so that they unwittingly play into his hands. In short, Iago listens for the spaces and slippages in discourse in order to play upon latent and manifest fears. As Kenneth Burke observes, "Iago, to arouse Othello, must talk a language that Othello knows as well as he, a language implicit in the nature of Othello's love as the idealization of his private property in Desdemona." Although Iago's language is the "dialectical opposite of Othello's," Burke continues, "it so thoroughly shares a common ground with Othello's language that its insinuations are never for one moment irrelevant to Othello's thinking" (414). Ultimately, Iago's double discourse destroys Othello and Desdemona by distorting their love and their most intimate relationship. I wish to argue that by analyzing Iago's control and manipulation of discourse, we can better understand Othello's downfall.

Othello is at one level a dramatization of the mechanism and failure of language, a dialectic between reality and "invention." Iago's diabolical, insatiable desire, bounded only by Desdemona's death, moves within a socially established discourse that feeds on itself and devours other discourses in its wake. Language in *Othello* is, then, not merely a dramatic vehicle or tool; language is the element of thematic concern. Language confirms, indicts, and convicts.

The marriage of Othello and Desdemona, with which the play opens, seems to suggest that deeply entrenched prejudices—suspiciousness of other races and cultures, of those who are "alien" and do not seem to belong—are about to be overcome and there is a possibility of social transformation. But such a possibility is challenged at the very moment of its inception, even before the marriage is consummated, because Iago insists—even in the face of Brabantio's acquiescence ("Gone she is, / And what's to come of my despised time / Is nought but bitterness" [I.i.159-61]) and the Duke's sanction of the marriage on the grounds of Othello's character ("If virtue no delighted beauty lack, / Your son-in-law is far more fair than black" [I.iii.285-86])—that marriage to a black man is not proper for a Venetian woman. Consequently, Iago jealously guards what is putatively now his exclusive sphere of influence in order to avenge himself on the Moor by challenging his humanity and coextensively his right to be wedded to Desdemona.

Through a shrewd insight into the desires and fears of others, and through a radical inversion of their discourses, Iago fulfills his own desire for revenge and control. Anthony Kubiak argues that Iago's "terrorist discourse" is far "more potent" than Othello's physical violence because it "operates through the *effect of discourse on seeing*." Such a *seeing*, Kubiak further states, "engenders the perjury and its vengeance" (63). Thus, in order to manipulate and/or forestall truth/proof, Iago constantly resorts to this terrorist discourse by substituting a "manifest discourse" (Baudrillard, 53) for ocularity and by positing a discourse that contradicts or delays verification. In short, Iago manipulates discourse as a medium of power.

Iago's desire constitutes and controls the dramatic movement of *Othello*. His conviction that Brabantio will object to his daughter's marriage on racial grounds provides Iago with the terms for a disruptive discourse, the first in a series of rhetorical gestures that jeopardize rather than undermine and dissolve Desdemona's marriage to the Moor. Iago intends not merely to call attention to "a sexual union represented as a form of pollution" (Tennenhouse, 89) but to destroy the partners in this union as well. As Michael Neill observes, Iago keeps the "real imaginative focus of the action always the hidden marriage-bed . . . within which [he] can operate as a uniquely deceitful version of the *nuntius*, whose vivid imaginary descriptions taint the vision of the audience, even as they colonize the minds of Brabantio and Othello" (396).

The structure of any play resides, in large measure, in the words of characters. The structure of *Othello* resides in the words of the character who simultaneously has control of her or his own discourse and the discourse of others. Both Desdemona and Iago evince their ability to expropriate other characters' discourses. But in the final analysis, Iago subverts Desdemona's linguistic power, not so much by dominating her discourse directly as by controlling the discourse of those in close communication with her.

It is interesting to note that near the opening of the play, Iago tells Roderigo to call up Brabantio, rouse and incense him with "timorous accent and dire yell" (I.i.74). Iago's directive is metalinguistic, one that announces Iago's awareness of language and its power to persuade, to excite and incite. He says as much in a soliloquy:

> When devils will the blackest sins put on,
> They do suggest at first with heavenly shows
> As I do now. For whiles this honest fool
> Plies Desdemona to repair his fortunes,
> And she for him pleads strongly to the Moor,
> I'll pour this pestilence into his ear.
>
> (II.iii.318-23)

The lines to Roderigo, then, indicate Iago's modus operandi. In order to "poison" Brabantio's "delight," Iago bombards him with gross images of Othello:

> Even now, now, very now, an old black ram
> Is tupping your white ewe. . . .
> . . . the devil will make a grandsire of you.
>
> (I.i.89-92)

Iago posits physicality and sexuality as the essential markers of the Moor's humanity and continues this line of discourse in the face of Brabantio's disbelief. But Iago's language and intent are so egregiously offensive that poetic discourse cannot accommodate them and gives way to debased prose:

> [Y]ou'll have your daughter cover'd with a Barbary horse, you'll have your nephews neigh to you, you'll have coursers for cousins, and jennets for germans.
>
> (I.i.111-13)

In notable contrast to Roderigo's discourse which invokes Othello's race ("thick lips," "lascivious," and "extravagant and wheeling stranger"), Iago's "diseased preoccupation" (Neill, 397) with Othello's sexuality results in a bestialization of the Moor and a devaluation of his marriage by making it *sound* obscene. His vision, as Kubiak points out, is "transformative and perjured" (24), a vision he imposes through language. Principally, Iago's aim is to control the discursive field. Such control resides in the hybrid nature of his discourse. Thus, *Othello* is as much about the ways in which one discourse is able to devour other discourses as it is about Iago's diabolical revenge on the Moor. In short, *Othello* is about the failure or fulfillment of desire through the loss or adroit use of discursive power.

Iago, as Margaret Ranald observes, is a "skillful opportunist who turns situations to his own account." His discursive power is cumulative; it relies on repetition and insinuation. He is aware of Desdemona's naivete about the "wickedness of the world outside" and knows "inexperience and decency blind her to the possibility that her motives might appear questionable and her actions capable of misconstruction" (136, 137). As Ranald further observes, Iago uses this naivete to undermine Desdemona's virtue and invert the "warm[th] and vital-[ity]" she evinces in her spontaneous espousal of Cassio's cause (144). She is, thus, caught in a web of words spun by Iago from the matrix of male domination, "the pernicious effects of chastity . . . a doctrine men impose upon women" (Snow, 387). To achieve his purpose of undermining Desdemona's chastity, Iago concludes that his most effective method would be "to abuse Othello's ear / That [Cassio] is too familiar with his wife," since Cassio has "a smooth dispose / To be suspected, framed to make women false" (I.iii.378-81). Although Othello is to be the dupe of Iago's performative gestures, it is clearly Desdemona who must suffer character assassination via the male order.

At this point, a review of Jean Baudrillard's theory of seduction might help us better articulate the theater of discourse in *Othello,* since his theory accommodates my reading. Baudrillard observes that "in seduction . . . it is manifest discourse—discourse at its most superficial—that turns back on the deeper order (whether conscious or unconscious) in order to invalidate it, substituting the charm and illusion of appearances" in contrast to *all meaningful discourse [which] seeks to end appearance.*" But, Baudrillard continues, "inexorably, discourse is left to its appearances, and thus to the stakes of seduction, thus to its own failure as discourse" (53-54). It is in this light that we might examine the use of discourse in *Othello,* especially discourse as manipulated and enjoyed by Iago, who, as Roy Roussel observes, shows the "seducer's fascination with the spectacle of his own manipulation and control" (725). In other words, Iago is seduced by his own ability to seduce. Baudrillard describes this autoseduction as the moment when "perhaps discourse is secretly tempted . . . by the bracketing of its objectives, of its truth effects which become absorbed within a surface that swallows meaning. . . . [I]t is the original form by which discourse becomes absorbed within itself and emptied of its truth in order to better fascinate others: the primitive seduction of language" (54).

Reading *Othello* in the context of Baudrillard's seduction theory permits us to examine discourse motivated by desire. To begin with, it is worth remarking that marriage between Desdemona and Othello stems from Desdemona's desire for knowledge about Othello and the seductive power of that desired knowledge. For example, when asked about his use of charms to win

Desdemona's affection, Othello argues that his narrative discourse was the charm, the power, he employed. Observing Desdemona's eagerness to hear him recount his exploits, Othello states that he:

> Took once a pliant hour and found good means
> To draw from her a prayer of earnest heart
> That would all my pilgrimage dilate
> Whereof by parcels she had something heard,
> But not intentively. I did consent.
>
> (I.iii.150-54)

Desdemona confirms the force of Othello's narrative discourse, its seductive power, by hinting that he propose marriage, by preferring him to men of her own race and class:

> I saw Othello's visage in his mind
> And to his honors and his valiant parts
> Did I my soul and fortunes consecrate.
>
> (I.iii.248-50)

"I saw Othello's visage in his mind" is the critical line because it simultaneously discloses Desdemona's awareness of Othello's race and her ready acceptance of his mind (his intellectual and narrative powers) above any thoughts of race. She insists that she has looked beyond the physical—which on the surface seems of no consequence to her—into the soul of the Moor and likes what she discovers. But her dismissal of his face underscores her recognition of the fact that Othello's race does matter. At the same time, she readily submits to his maleness as evinced by her unquestioned "duty" to him—a duty dictated by tradition and gender.

Desdemona's statement cannot be contradicted by Brabantio, but it is too much for him to accept. And he is prepared to lose his daughter rather than accept the Moor as an affine:

> I here do give thee [Othello] that with all my heart
> Which, but thou has already, with all my heart
> I would keep from thee.
>
> (I.iii.191-93)

Brabantio's pronouncement on his daughter's behavior in marrying Othello without permission is precisely the utterance that opens a space for Iago to work his will on the Moor and undermine the union that Iago himself finds most repugnant: "Look to her Moor, if thou hast eyes to see: / She has deceived her father and may thee" (I.iii.288-89), words Iago will later reiterate to Othello.

Othello and Desdemona use language to "deliver" what Baudrillard terms "real meaning," "truth," or honest discourse, in contradistinction to Iago's manifestly perjured discourse. If, as Baudrillard observes, seduction sports "triumphantly with weakness, making a game of it with its own rules," then we cannot rightly call Othello's narrative of his personal history, recited at Brabantio's and Desdemona's requests, a seductive act. Seduction robs discourse of its "sense and turns it from truth" by causing "manifest discourse"—the surface meaning—to "say what it does not want to say; it causes determinations and profound indeterminations to show through in manifest discourse." It is, then, the responsibility of interpretation to "break the appearance and play of the manifest discourse" (53). Interpretation is vital to a deeper understanding of the ways by which discourse operates in *Othello*, where, as Kubiak convincingly argues, "we can begin to see how the language of the theatre *within the theatre* is . . . always eminently terrorist because of language's failure to adequately state its intentions" (63). Yet early in *Othello*, language does achieve what Roland Barthes terms its "adequation of enunciation" (208) through Othello's and Desdemona's performative gestures.

For example, when Othello is accused of bewitching Desdemona, and thus marrying her without her "knowing" what was happening to her, he defends himself on discursive grounds: he argues from the force of his narrative, categorically stating that it was language's power to recreate the images of his exploits that merited Desdemona's affection. [Though he declares at one point that he is "rude" of speech "[a]nd little blessed with the soft phrase of peace" (I.iii.81-82), we are perhaps not meant to take the declaration seriously.] Othello won her father, too, initially:

> Her father loved me, oft invited me,
> Still questioned me the story of my life
> From year to year—the battles, sieges, fortunes,
> That I have passed.
>
> (I.iii.127-30)

Othello—like any "author" recognizing that his words have not merely conveyed their intentions but have moved to another level of meaning beyond their author's expectation—realizes that the more he reiterates his deeds of valor and his triumphs over adversities, the closer Desdemona is drawn to him:

> This to hear
> Would Desdemona seriously incline;
>   . . . . .
> She would come again, and with a greedy ear
> Devour up my discourse.
>
> (I.iii.144-49)

In other words, Othello tells the Venetians, Desdemona was moved by his deeds and seduced by his discourse:

> She thanked me,
> And bade me, if I had a friend that loved her,
> I should but teach him how to tell my story,
> And that would woo her.
>
> (I.iii.162-65)

In fact, Othello's rehearsal of the scene clearly reveals that Desdemona, not he, was the seducer:

> Upon this hint I spake:
> She [first] loved me for the dangers I had passed,
> And I [in return] loved her that she did pity them.
> This only is the witchcraft I have used.
>
> (I.iii.165-68)

Asked to corroborate Othello's testimony, Desdemona, like Othello, preempts her father's argument by taking the discursive initiative: she expropriates her father's discourse of "obedience" and, like Othello, demonstrates language's ability to state the bald truth as she understands it, a truth by which she lives. She brilliantly turns her father's discourse on duty back on him without hint of conscious irony, but rather by a conscious rhetorical gesture. Because she wants desperately to have his approval, she reaches for the best way to articulate that duty—by placing her duty on par with her mother's, a claim her father cannot gainsay:

> My noble father,
> I do perceive here a divided duty:
> To you I am bound for life and education;
> My life and education both do learn me
> How to respect you. You are lord of all my duty;
> I am hiterto your daughter. But here's my husband;
> And so much duty as my mother showed
> To you, preferring you before her father,
> So much I challenge that I may profess
> Due to the Moor my lord.
>
> (I.iii.178-87)

Both Desdemona and Othello demonstrate that "real meaning" and "manifest discourse" are not necessarily mutually exclusive, that they can operate simultaneously toward a mutual telos at this juncture. The tragedy occurs when the two pull in opposite directions and when Othello and Desdemona, especially Desdemona, lose the discursive advantage.

Iago's observation of Desdemona's "seduction" of Othello and her discursive power over her father, no doubt, warns Iago against a direct attempt to seduce her to leave Othello. Having seen her turn male discourse back on her father and the Senate in her resolve to remain with Othello by arguing that it was she, not Othello, who did the seducing and by requesting and obtaining from that august body permission to join Othello in Cyprus, despite the fact that it is a site of battle, Iago surely realizes that Desdemona can discursively match him. Witness, for example, her astute comparison of her decision to marry Othello to a battle and her boldness in trumpeting the implications of that decision to the world:

> That I did love the Moor to live with him,
> My downright violence and storm of fortunes
> May trumpet to the world.
>
> (I.iii.244-46)

Iago most surely observes that Desdemona belies what Teresa De Lauretis terms "the web of the male Oedipal logic" in which "the little girl has no other prospect but to consent and be seduced into femininity" (52). Desdemona preempts her father's traditional right to make a "proper" choice for her.

Iago's power to manipulate discourse, however, gives him the dramatic edge over Desdemona. The motivation for linguistic manipulation, and thereby manipulation of human beings, stems from Iago's perception—whether real or imagined—that he has been superseded by an inferior military man, namely Cassio, and that he has been cuckolded by Othello. Furthermore, he "smarts under neglect" by a general he deems racially inferior to himself. This conviction that he has been slighted, Harley Granville-Barker contends, is the "immediate spring" of Iago's desire to denigrate the Moor (125).

Lacking a sphere of influence within the civil and military hierarchy, Iago locates his power in the manipulation of discourse. And, ironically, in the final analysis, Othello is seduced by his own discourse because the language Iago employs to defame Desdemona and challenge Othello's manhood is Othello's, albeit perverted and polluted.

Iago plays upon what Philip McGuire terms the "deliberate disjunction of action and feeling" to accomplish his goal of turning Othello into an animal. In other words, Iago employs "rhetoric to undercut reason" (205). The play is, then, to borrow from McGuire again, "an imitation of an action of knowing and judging"; an "assay on the limits of intelligence and natural passion, deception deftly and most intelligently practiced" (209) through terrorist discourse. Kubiak adds to this when he states that Iago "terrorizes Othello with the most subtle shift of seeing refracted through an almost imperceptible misdirection of the eye—a misdirection effected through Iago's words" (63-64).

Roderigo and Othello challenge or try to circumvent such terrorist discourse when they ask Iago to substantiate his verbal claims with objective proof. They, especially Roderigo, recognize the tension between Iago's discourse and objective reality; yet ironically, they must rely on Iago, whose discourse they question, to resolve that tension. Although Othello is satisfied to have Iago supply the evidence, Roderigo threatens to see for himself—to confront Desdemona directly now that he has begun to "find [him]self fopped" (IV.ii.190). When threatened by Roderigo's decision to confront Desdemona, however, Iago proves that he still controls the discourse, which he quickly interposes between Roderigo's demand for proof and his own will to power. Moreover, according to Kubiak, Iago knows that "ocularity in which [Roderigo] seeks his truth is as much a failure as the language that directs it." Kubiak describes

the failure of ocular proof in *Othello* as the "violence of failed seeing—the desire to see, seeing desire, seeing what one has been told (not) to" and adds that "both seeing and speaking" in Othello are ensnared by a "falsely assumed empiricism" that relies not on proof but on Iago's capacity "to reproduce or rehearse 'the Same,' that impossibility" (66). If sight is not to be trusted, then discourse must bear the greater responsibility for proof, which should, therefore, be an incontrovertible proof that does not rely on but rather opposes and exposes seduction. Baudrillard formulates this opposition between ocularity and discourse: "All appearances conspire to combat and root out meaning (whether intentional or otherwise), and turn it into a game . . . one that is more adventurous and seductive than the directive line of meaning" (54).

Roderigo first challenges Iago's discourse in Act IV when he realizes that he has been duped: "I *heard* too much; for your words and performances are no kin together" (my emphasis). He protests Iago's failure to deliver on his promises and decides to "make [him]self known to Desdemona":

> If she will return my jewels, I will give over my suit and repent my unlawful solicitation; if not, assure yourself I will seek satisfaction of you.
>
> (IV.ii.193-96)

There will be no further deliberation on this issue, and Iago knows it. Now he must retreat from dilatory,[1] verbal strategy to direct action. Hence the fabrication about Cassio's delivering a message that will send Othello and Desdemona to Mauritania and the proposal to murder Cassio: "I will show you such a necessity in his death that you shall think yourself bound to put it on him" (IV.ii.231-32). Iago's "show" will, of course, be verbal.

Roderigo's recognition that Iago's words are at odds with his actions—promises without proof, discourse without substance—begins the ineluctable drive toward the failure of Iago's disruptive discourse. Roderigo's threat to confront Desdemona engenders a quick and strategic discursive move on Iago's part. Roderigo's suspicions coupled with Othello's desire for "ocular proof" sorely undermine Iago's discourse. Thus, discourse cannot serve Iago in this crisis of credibility and therefore must be "redeployed as action" (Baudrillard, 54). He must stage another scenario while he recovers the discursive ground, first, by praising Roderigo's decision and then by forestalling that decision. It is noteworthy that at this juncture, Iago shifts from poetic discourse to prose, a clear indication of his failure to control his best weapon, language, and of his diminishing power to manipulate Roderigo:

> Why, now I see there's mettle in thee, and even from this instant do build on thee a better opinion than ever

before. Give me thy hand, Roderigo. Thou has taken against me a most just exception; but yet I protest I have dealt most directly in thy affair.

Roderigo counters that he has seen no evidence to support Iago's claims: "It hath not appeared." Iago concedes as much but does not stop at mere concession: he inverts Roderigo's argument:

> I grant indeed it hath not appeared; and your suspicion is not without wit and judgement. But, Roderigo, if thou hast that in thee indeed, which I have greater reason to believe now than ever—I mean purpose, courage, and valour—this night show it. If thou the next night following enjoy not Desdemona, take me from this world with treachery, and devise engines for my life.
>
> (IV.ii.200-11)

Clearly, Iago is weakened by Roderigo's threat of intervention, a threat that not only will expose his machinations vis-à-vis Roderigo but also will expose Iago's entire charade. Iago skillfully diverts Roderigo from his failure to deliver on his promises. This scene brilliantly illustrates Baudrillard's observation that seduction stems from weakness, not power: "To seduce is to appear weak. To seduce is to render weak" (83). Iago is unquestionably the "seduced" in this scene because Roderigo has weakened Iago's ability to control him by words alone.

Othello is marked by a series of seductive gestures that lead to the untimely and unwarranted death of Desdemona. In *Othello,* the contours of desire are shaped by individual discourse and gestures of seduction. Iago's desire to bend Othello to his will is contingent upon his power of seduction. Iago's desire constitutes and controls the dramatic center, while Desdemona's position as object of male desire—her marriage to the Moor and Roderigo's desire for a sexual union with her—constitutes the thematic center of the drama. Iago's actions circulate around this marriage plot. Desdemona's elopement with a black man provides the basis for Iago's seduction of Roderigo, Brabantio, and Othello, while her position as Othello's wife provides the ground on which Iago's vengeance operates.

Iago recognizes power when he meets it. He recognizes the strength of Desdemona's resolve, which makes the Senate agree to her remaining with him even in Cyprus. Thus, Iago elects to work toward denying Desdemona her desires by manipulating those around her and by subterfuge, or what Baudrillard calls seduction or a turning "from one's own truth" or leading another "from his/her truth." It is precisely Iago's desire to lead Desdemona from the Moor's bed that results in her tragic death. Very early on, Iago insists to Roderigo that Desdemona will turn from Othello once his narrative becomes tiresome and she is forced to see him in racial

terms, that is, see him as black. He insists that Desdemona's violent love for the Moor, engendered by his "bragging and telling her fantastical lies" (II.i.213), will eventually be destroyed by ocularity: "Her eye must be fed. And what delight will she have to look on the devil?" (II.i.215-16). Being sated, Iago contends, Desdemona will see the physical reality of Othello:

> When the blood is made dull with the act of sport, there should be, again to inflame it and to give satiety a fresh appetite, loveliness in favour, sympathy in years, manners and beauties: all which the Moor is defective in. Now for want of these required conveniences, her delicate tenderness will find itself abused, begin to heave the gorge, disrelish and abhor the Moor.
>
> (II.i.216-22)

Iago articulates this thesis of Desdemona's "momentary" infatuation with the Moor and true attachment to the younger, handsome Cassio not only to Roderigo but to Othello as well. Only instead of stating it openly, he makes insidious suggestions—"Did Michael Cassio, / When you wooed my lady, know of your love?" (III.iii.93-94)—that force Othello to voice doubts about Desdemona's fidelity. The conversation proceeds with Iago's saying little by way of direct accusation but suggesting a great deal, insinuating his thoughts into Othello's psyche:

> By heaven, he echoes me,
> As if there were some monster in his thought
> Too hideous to be shown.
>
> (III.iii.109-11)

Finally, Othello, seduced into believing his wife has been unfaithful, becomes totally confused about his own thoughts. So muddled, in fact, is Othello at this juncture that he fails to note and pick up Iago's overt admission of treachery, "[O]ft my jealousy / Shapes faults that are not" (III.iii.148-49), or heed his warning, "O beware, my lord, of jealousy" (III.iii.167).

Othello, at first, defends Desdemona's virtue, her playful spirit and easy show of affection for others: "Where virtue is, these are more virtuous" (III.iii.188). He defends her honesty on the grounds that she chose him despite his race. But Iago returns to his discursive strategy by echoing Brabantio's warning:

> She did deceive her father, marrying you;
> And when she seemed to shake and fear your looks
> She loved them most.
>
> (III.iii.207-9)

Edward Snow brilliantly observes that the "decisive moment in Iago's seduction" occurs when Iago gets Othello to see Desdemona "in terms of Brabantio's warning" (399). Snow further argues that Othello's reference to Desdemona's reputation being as "black as

[his] own face" suggests that he is being manipulated by a language "calculated to *make* him despise himself because he is black" (401).

Subtly goaded by Iago, Othello admits, "I think my wife be honest, and think she is not, / I think thou art just, and think thou art not" (III.iii.385-86). But, Othello continues, Desdemona has made an unnatural match by marrying him, her "nature erring from itself" (III.iii.229), a point Iago seizes on to undermine Othello's faith in Desdemona's love and acceptance of him. He reminds Othello that Desdemona refused numerous "proposed matches / Of her own clime, complexion and degree" (III.iii.231-32), implying that Othello is not on the same human level as the Venetian suitors.

Doubting/trusting both his wife and Iago, Othello asks Iago for a "living reason," actual proof of Desdemona's infidelity. Iago obliges with a performance calculated to remove all doubt: Cassio's discourse of love ostensibly spoken during sleep. Iago cleverly reminds Othello that what he has reported is only a dream; Othello counters that it is "a foregone conclusion" (III.iii.429). At this juncture, Iago sets the discursive stage for the tragic conclusion. All that remains is ocular proof misdirected and interpreted by Iago. Finally, what Othello sees is infected by his desire, a desire informed through Iago's words. Othello's murder of Desdemona results from his own victimization by Iago. Iago is partially correct when he tells Emilia, "I told [Othello] what I thought, and told no more / Than what he found himself was apt and true" (V.ii.175-76).

The circulation of desire in *Othello* and the concomitant acts that affect desire provide an insight into Iago's decision to manipulate others discursively. Iago's narrative is directed toward a conclusion that satisfies his desire for power through discursive control, whereas Desdemona's narrative moves along an axis of desire for happiness through a shared experience. Iago's and Desdemona's interlocking desires collide through Iago's attempts to break Othello's hold on Desdemona and through Desdemona's efforts to influence Othello on Cassio's behalf. Out of this matrix of interlocking and conflicting desires comes Iago's seduction of Othello.

Iago's seductive power is situated in his ability to manipulate the sociolect,[2] a hybridization of a desire to manipulate and destroy Othello, who is for Iago the locus of misplaced power and the object of illegitimate desire. Iago's enterprise is, then, to desempower Othello, not by making Othello undesirable to Desdemona (which he realizes he cannot do) but by turning Othello against Desdemona.

To achieve this end, Iago employs another of his dramatic skills—acting. Granville-Barker observes that

Iago assumes a dual acting role—he his both the persona Iago of the play *Othello* and the character who exploits the role of actor to accomplish his desired goal:

> The medium in which Iago works is the actor's; and the crude sense of pretending to be what he is not, and in his chameleonlike ability to adapt himself to change of company and circumstance, we find him an accomplished actor.

(162)

Both the pleasure and the success of Iago's enterprise are contingent upon what Roussel terms the "seducer's fascination with the spectacle of his own manipulation and control" (725), while Baudrillard argues that seduction derives its "passion" and "intensity" not from an "energy of desire" but rather "from gaming as pure form and from purely formal bluffing" (82). "Gaming" and "purely formal bluffing" describe Iago's method precisely and completely.

The so-called "brothel scene" represents the triumph of Iago's gaming and bluffing. Iago's strategy proposes to expose Othello's gullibility and confirm his contention that Othello is not quite on the same human level with Desdemona and is therefore not a suitable mate for her. This strategic move by Iago clearly indicates that Othello is the object of Iago's seduction, not Desdemona. It is as though Iago seeks Othello's moral and mental downfall, in part, because he cannot match Othello's physical prowess and narrative skill. What he seeks, and what he succeeds in effecting, is the undermining of the Moor's intelligence and coextensively his humanity. The outcome of the play turns, then, on Iago's seduction of Othello and Othello's collusion in his own downfall, and that collusion becomes the ultimate sign of Iago's mastery of multiple discourses.

Notes

1. Patricia Parker notes that Iago gains power over Othello "at the threshold of the great temptation scene . . . through those pauses, single words and pregnant phrases which seem to suggest something secret or withheld, a withholding which fills the Moor with the desire to hear more" (54).

2. Michael Riffaterre notes that the socioelect is the site of "myths, traditions, ideological and esthetic stereotypes . . . harbored by a society," as well as the site of "ready-made narrative and descriptive models that reflect a group's idea of or consensus about reality." Iago refers to Othello in animalistic terms to play to the Venetian socioelect. His references to Othello as "an old black ram," "the devil," and "a Barbary horse" reveal Renaissance stereotypes and, more important, play upon the racial fears of the Western male (130).

Bibliography

Parker, Patricia. "Shakespeare and Rhetoric: 'Dilation' and 'Delation' in *Othello*," *Shakespeare and the Ques-*

tion of Theory, ed. Patricia Parker and Geoffrey Hartman, New York, Methuen, 1985.

Riffaterre, Michael. *Fictional Truth,* Baltimore, John Hopkins UP, 1990.

Thomas Moisan (essay date 2002)

SOURCE: Moisan, Thomas. "Relating Things to the State: 'The State' and the Subject of *Othello.*" In *Othello: New Critical Essays,* edited by Philip C. Kolin, pp. 189-202. New York: Routledge, 2002.

[*In the following essay, Moisan considers the role of the Venetian state in shaping the characters and tragic outcome of* Othello.]

> *Yea and some forrain men and strangers haue beene adopted into this number of citizens, eyther in regard of their great nobility, or that they had beene dutifull towards the state, or els had done unto them some notable seruice.*
>
> (Contareni, 18)

> *Men in Great Place, are thrice Seruants: Seruants of the Soueraigne or State; Seruants of Fame; and Seruants of Businesse. So as they haue no Freedome; neither in their Persons; nor in their Actions; nor in their Times.*
>
> (Bacon, "Of Great Place," 42)

From "honest" to "dilate," from "what's the matter?" to "My husband?" *Othello* has been shown to be home to a number of aurally and thematically resonant expressions, expressions that ramify in significance even as they impress themselves reiteratively upon the ear, contributing to what G. B. Shaw, writing of *Othello,* termed "the splendor of its word music" (135).[1] One is reminded of such expressions by the collocation whose occurrence, and recurrence, draw the attention of this essay, namely, "the state." On the face of it, to be sure, the interpretative possibilities annunciated by "the state" seem modest. Lacking the ironic power that builds in the numerous variations we hear on the word "honest," and less susceptible to the revealing paranoumasic dissonances that Patricia Parker has heard in "delate" and "dilate," references to "the state" seem to be what their contexts suggest: collectively an ellipsis for Venice the city-state, metonyms for the Venetian polity, for Venice in its governing authority and power. Indeed, context would seem to render it difficult to hear in the phrase a reference to "state" as "condition"; we do not hear anyone complain that there is something rotten in, or with, the state of Venice. Nor is the word "state" paired off against its etymological and phonological kin, "estate," which does not occur in the play. Instead, with the long vowel of its iamb giving it insinuatingly easy *entree* to the rhythms and sound of both prose and verse,[2] references to "the state" make the domain and claims of public affairs audible and rather talismanic presences in the opening act of the play and in its closing minutes: the claims of "the state" set the geographical agenda of the play; the recollection of service done "the state" brings the play to its "bloody period"; the intent to "relate" what has happened to "the state" brings the play to its smoothly rhyming close.

"The state" occurs more frequently in *Othello* than in *Hamlet,* with its princely protagonist and "statist" preoccupations; it occurs more often than in Shakespeare's earlier "Venetian" play, *The Merchant of Venice,* where a spate of references to "the state" clustered in the "trial" scene intones what Venice is legally exacted to permit and what it is legally permitted to exact (4.1.222, 312, 354, 365, 371, 373; also, 3.2.278; 3.3.29).[3] Indeed, references to "the state" occur more frequently in *Othello* than in any other of Shakespeare's plays except *Coriolanus,* a coincidence that would seem anomalous. For, however one assesses the various topical political readings that have been offered for *Coriolanus, Coriolanus* is still a play whose fable centrally concerns "the state," something that would seem less self-evidently true about *Othello.* In *Coriolanus* "the state" of Rome is part of the focal agon of the play, making Coriolanus and undoing him quite, its presence sustained and citations of it evenly distributed over the five acts of the play; in *Othello,* on the other hand, the role of "the state" and the Venice it represents seem thematically relegated to the margins they help spatially and aurally to define, the public sphere they evoke in acts 1 and 5 muted in and displaced by the domestic and claustrophobically private action of acts 2, 3, and 4. In short, "the state" seems integral to the subject of *Coriolanus,* but not to that of *Othello.*

Or so at least we might infer from Verdi and his librettist, Boito, who, locating the operatic center of the play in, in fact, the heavily domestic and claustrophobically private action on Cyprus, effectively mute references to "the state" by excising Shakespeare's entire first act along with Venice and "the state." In doing so, however, Verdi and Boito are only subtracting what Shakespeare appears to have added, at least if we follow Geoffrey Bullough's lead in taking as the principal source for *Othello* Cinthio's story of the "Moorish Captain." In Cinthio Shakespeare would have found references to the Signoria (Bullough, 242; 252)—which he absorbs (1.2.17)—but not to "the state." What difference does the addition of "the state" make? Most obviously, the presence of "the state," with its foreign strategic concerns and its debate over whether it is Rhodes or Cyprus that is likely to be in danger, brings into the discourse of the play the threat of the Turk, "the angrie Turke" whom "of all others," Richard Knolles wrote (1603) "that understanding and provident State" of Venice "most dread" (Bullough, 262). How potent was the

Othello, Desdemona, and attendants in Act IV, sene iii of Othello.

fear of "turning Turk" or forced conversion to the infidel for an early modern English audience has been interrogated recently by Daniel J. Vitkus ("Turning Turk in *Othello*"), and it may have had an especial immediacy for the original audience of *Othello,* who, as Virginia Mason Vaughan has suggested, were likely to have known about the fall of the historical Cyprus to the Turk some years before the play, and might have seen in the ruination of Venice's chosen general an admonition for the Christian West (34). Less obvious, perhaps, is the effect the presence of "the state" has upon the definition of the general himself. At the very least, to make Othello the most significant servant of the *mysterium* of Venetian power invests Othello and his story with a tragic *gravitas* that his counterpart in Cinthio's fiction—a fiction that evokes those steamy "enchantments of Circe" Roger Ascham derides in Italian *novelle* (67-68)—simply does not have. The repeated reference to Venice in act 1 as "the state" elevates Othello from mere employee of the city to savior of the nation—or at least part of its commercial empire—someone so vital that "the state" "[c]annot," as Iago remarks, "with safety cast him" (1.1.148).

Yet references to "the state" do more than provide a courtesy upgrade to this tragedy without a crowned head. Rather, in what is to follow I would suggest that "the state" and Othello are tied to each other in a relationship both mutually exploitative and mutually revealing, one that leads Othello to define himself by his reading of "the state," and that makes "the state" an interested participant in Othello's tragedy. Moreover, even as a number of recent analyses have invaluably drawn our attention to the culturally charged images in the play of disclosure, to the darknesses that whet the obsession within the play with "ocular proof" (Patricia Parker, *Shakespeare from the Margins;* Michael Neill, "Unproper Beds: Race, Adultery, and the Hideous in *Othello,* Issues of Death, 141-67; and Arthur L. Little, Jr.), a consideration of the role of "the state" complicates our appreciation, not simply of the discursive in the play, but of the sense in which the play draws attention to discourse, and to its medial and ultimately repressive relationship with the visual. It is for "the state" that certain accounts get delivered; it is with the intent of "relating" things to "the state" that the stage is cleared and the sight blocked off of "the tragic loading" of the bed. Indeed, though Richard Helgerson's caution against reading the early modern notion of "state" through anything even as little removed in time as a Hobbesian lens (295) makes us cautious in treating "the state" as an abstraction of political theory, still, the discursive interaction of protagonist and "state" in *Othello,* with "the state" vetting discourse and Othello shaping discourse on "cue," evokes the relationship of two powerful institutions whose negotiation was an ineluctable reality of Shakespeare's existence: the state—or the crown with which the state was identified—and the theater.

But what is "the state" in *Othello,* and would a contemporary audience have heard in the term anything but a transparent marker for Venice? Though it is unlikely that the audience would have felt invited to ponder the term as an abstraction, surely even an early Jacobean audience was not unfamiliar with efforts to describe the workings of "the state," or its equally familiar—if less prosodically commodious—synonym, "the commonweal." "Amongst many the great and deepe deuices of worldly wisedome, for the maintenance and preseruing of human societies (the ground and stay of mans earthly blisse) the fairest, firmest, and the best, was the framing and forming of Commonweales . . ." So Knolles alliteratively opines at the outset of a work he produced not long after his *The Generall Historie of the Turkes,* his translation (1606) of Jean Bodin's *The Six Bookes of a Commonweale* ("To the Reader," iv). Still, in *Othello* the reiterated appearances of "the state" have the effect of underscoring Venice in the exercise of its governing power and leaving unstated anything that would suggest that large complex organism Bodin and Knolles thought of as the "commonweal"; when, after all, Othello refers to "the state" as anything but "the state" or Venice he chooses a transliteration for the Venetian version of an executive council, "the signiory" (1.2.17).

And, to be sure, in this case any hint of mystery and abstraction that builds in the repetition of "the state" may well have reminded the audience how little they understood Venice itself. After all, as editors have observed, it is not clear that the playwright himself had fully mastered the *technicalities* of various Venetian governmental offices (Saunders, 64; n. 1.2.14; Honigmann 128, n. 1.2.13-14)—perhaps a reason in itself for referring to matters of state as often as possible by the umbrella term . . . "the state"! Nor if, as has been frequently suggested, the playwright looked at Lewis Lewkenor's translation of Gasparo Contareni's *The Commonwealth and Gouernment of Venice* (1599), would he have found the picture it presented of the intricate formulation of the Venetian system of government uniformly lucid, either in the model of government produced, or in the means that produced it.[4] "Shakespeare saw Venice as part of his world," E. A. J. Honigmann has observed, "but not so Cyprus" (11), a valid distinction if on no other grounds than that by the time of the play Cyprus had succumbed to Ottoman invasion, while Venice was still at least in the Christian orb. And the sense that Venice, for all its celebrated, or notorious, opulence was nonetheless culturally familiar has been helpful to a reading of the play that would parse it in culturally oppositional terms, with Othello the "outsider" and "extravagant and wheeling stranger" and Venice, or "the state," the establishment, indeed, a reading to which Brabantio, Roderigo, and Iago all in various ways find it convenient to subscribe: "This is Venice; / My house is not a grange" (1.1.105-106). Still, a glance at the commentary Lewkenor provided at the outset of his translation suggests that for this Englishman at least, unblushing purveyor, as Vaughan has noted, of the myth of Venice (17), "the state" of Venice was best appreciated as an exciting, "culturally broadening" conundrum. From the preface "To the Reader" to Lewkenor's translation of Contareni it is Venice itself that emerges as the "extravagant and wheeling stranger." Recalling that Homer especially praises Ulysses for the breadth of his travels, for the fact that *Multorum mores vidit & urbes*" (Ad), Lewkenor—who might have agreed with the Duke that Othello's adventurous "tale would win my daughter too"—offers a paean to the difference that is Venice in which two notes predominate: the "strangeness" of everything connected with Venice—its history, its government, its prosperity, its physical situation; "wonder" at having observed these things. Venice, the veritably floating signifier? Lewkenor signifies the intensity of his wonder at the thought by employing as an adverb of "otherness" a word we hear repeatedly in *Othello* to suggest moral hideousness: "what euer hath

the worlde brought forth more monstrously strange, then that so great & glorious a Citie should be seated in the middle of the sea. . . . ?" (A3v).[5]

Not, of course, that "the state" remains an abstraction throughout the play, and, indeed, it is in its selective moments of demystification that "the state" and the Venice it represents come to be drawn into the play as actors, at least as proximate occasions, in the circumstances that shape Othello's tragedy. In no scene are the officers and workings of "the state" rendered more humanly recognizable than in the momentous council scene (1.3), and particularly in the first forty-five lines, where we come upon the Duke and two senators attempting to puzzle out the sense of conflicting reports they have received on the Turks' intentions (1-43), a scene that seems especially demystified when compared with the description of the Great Council of three thousand described by Lewkenor, that body which deliberates so efficiently, and with so divine a peaceableness, and so without all tumult and confusion," Lewkenor gushes, "that it rather seemeth to bee an assembly of Angels, then of men" (A2d). Decidedly more sublunary, the effort of the three officers of "the state" at disambiguation puts "the state" in the business of reading signs and thus gives "the state" something in common with numerous enigma-pondering characters throughout the play, with the notable difference that the Duke and his colleagues actually manage to reason their way to a correct answer.[6] Nor is it the only time in the play at which "the state" turns out to refer to personages or collectivities. In an instance we noted earlier, Iago, who has already displayed a knack for demystifying august Venetian institutions—parrying Brabantio's charge, "Thou art a villain," with "you are a Senator" (1.1.117)—and can always be relied upon to "demystify" anyone or, in this case, thing by attributing to it a recognizably humanly self-serving motivation, and follows hard upon Roderigo's hendyadic invocation of "the state" as some abstract guarantor of justice—"the justice of the state" (9⟨1⟩.1.139) to predict, correctly, that "the state" will find Othello too valuable to "cast him" (1.1.147). Brabantio, anxious to assert his importance at a moment when that importance seems to have been disregarded, makes the state a fraternity to which he belongs, certain that the Duke or any of his "brothers of the state" would feel his grievance (1.2.96). And in its most impersonated form, "the state" "becomes a "they," when Othello reminds those about to lead him away that he had "done the state some service, and they know't" (5.2.354).

Still, when read in the diverse contexts in which it is cited, "the state" as an entity appears something of a chimera, less a thing or concept with definable terms than a rhetorical inflection. We encounter it as an affiliative tag-on that enables Brabantio both to flash his influence and ground his personal outrage and complaint in a presumption of socio-political empathy: "The Duke himself, / Or any of my brothers of the state, / Cannot but feel this wrong as 'twere their own" (1.2.95-7). We hear it invoked to justify why something is to be done, not done, or done later; a piece of allusion and illusion central to praeteritive devices of which Iago is only the most malevolent, not the sole, practitioner. "What if I do obey?" asks Othello, of course rhetorically, when Brabantio orders him to prison. "How may the Duke be therewith satisfied, / Whose messengers are here about my side / Upon some present business of the state / To bring me to him?" (1.2.87-91). And having enabled Othello to elude detention at the beginning of the play, the discourse of "the state" serves Othello at the end as well in the literally breathtaking praeterition with which Othello takes his leave, putting his "bloody period" to a lively demonstration of the sort of service to "the state" that he had begun this nineteen-line, "word or two" speech by reminding the assembled emissaries of the state that he would not continue to remind them of: "I have done the state some service, and they know't—No more of that" (5.2.339-40). "The state" occupies the final rhyme and image of the play, but its concluding centrality as the authority offstage to which Lodovico will "[t]his heavy act with heavy heart relate," not to mention the nature of the report it is likely to receive, are complicated by the image onstage of the tragically loaded bed, the "object" which "poisons sight," and which Lodovico orders to be "hid." In the final piece of praeterition perpetrated in the play "the state" is kept in shadow: the audience is invited to pass over what it has seen and is not likely to forget; to look forward to a report it will never hear to an entity it cannot see; instead of enjoying a privileged position as the repository of what has happened, "the state" is relegated to an alternative realm of report, a realm and report rendered necessarily more shadowy in the degree to which they are to be denied the fullness of sight, a realm and report associated through the words of Lodovico with suggestions of repression and censorship.

Shadowy as the representation of "the state" may be, things still get done in its name; indeed, it is an insight of the play into the paradox of Venetian power, and perhaps the power of states in general, that we never discern the power of Venetian authority so much as when we do not see it. When, for example, Lodovico exercises his authority to announce to Othello after his murder of Desdemona has been discovered that "Your power and your command is taken off, / And Cassio rules in Cyprus" (5.2.331-32), we may initially feel that we are in the presence of Venetian justice, until we recall that what sound like penalties meted out to Othello for his crime are performative statements of administrative actions that "the state" had already taken, news of which, it is supposed, Lodovico had brought to Othello in the letter from Venice (4.1.225). Since Othello had only arrived in Cyprus in act 2, clearly "the state" had wasted no time, or, rather, operated offstage and by its own "dilatory" time to remove the Moor once, presumably, it had somehow ascertained that the military threat to Cyprus had passed. Othello's transgression only allowed "the state" to give a punitive articulation and formality to actions intended to be muted in the silences of the epistolary form.

Yet as the visit of Lodovico to Cyprus can by itself only hint, the nature of "the state" in *Othello* is most fully on display in the complexities of its relationship with its "all in all sufficient" general. That Shakespeare seems to have conned the notion that aliens were permitted, even encouraged, to contribute their talents and services, artisanal, commercial, or military, to the Venetian state is evident, and A. D. Nuttall makes a useful observation when he declares that for Shakespeare Venetian tolerance, indeed, use of the exotically different would merely have been a reflection in its political culture of the exoticism and difference that defined Venice's physical environment. "Venice," Nuttall remarks, listing just a bit towards the *coloratura*, "is for Shakespeare an anthropological laboratory. Itself nowhere, suspended between sea and sky, it receives and utilizes all kinds of people" (141).

That Shakespeare was aware that the Venetian state *received* "all kinds of people," at least as business traders, was clear in *The Merchant of Venice* (3.3.27). His sense—and his character Othello's sense—of how Venice *utilized* "strangers" could only have been complicated by exposure to Contareni, who at once celebrates the welcome aliens received, while giving clues of the limits the Venetian state placed on its inclusiveness, particularly in its relationship with aliens it retained to address its military affairs. In Lewkenor's translation of Contareni one finds, for example, an accounting of the special legal processes instituted to expedite suits brought by "strangers," with the ostensibly benign rationale that they "should not be molested and lingred off with long delayes, but quickly come to an ende of their suites" (105). Implicit, of course, in the very attention paid to the benign and genuinely more than just treatment of "strangers," is the fact that aliens normally remain aliens and outside the citizenship reserved for "Venetians," natives of "the state," and far from all of those. One thinks of the norm when Contareni duly notes a significant exception, an exception for merit, one that echoes memorably in Othello's parting *apologia*—even in its association, by proximity, of "the state" with a plural pronoun. It happens, Contareni observes, that "some forrain men and strangers haue beene adopted into this number of citizens, eyther in regard of their great nobility, or that they had beene dutifull towardes the state, or else had done vnto them some notable seruice" (18). "[S]ome notable seruice," naturally, could refer to the deeds done by those mercenary generals who tend to Venice's military foreign policy, by the likes of Othello and, perhaps, the as yet unidentified Marcus Luccicos, for whom the Duke sends along with "the valiant Moor" (1.3.45-8). Yet a scan of Contareni's comments on the attitude of "the state" towards affairs and personages military reveals an ambivalence that would render any mercenary general's hold on public esteem precarious. With an early modern nod to the policy of preparedness, leaders are encouraged to cultivate "the offices of warre," but only "for the cause of peace" (9), while a historical aside reminds the reader that the founders of "the state" "alwaies with greater regard and reckoning applyed their minds to the maintenance of peace then to glorie of warres" (15). So much for "the plumed troop, and the big wars / That make ambition virtue" (3.3349-50); to thrive in Venice Othello's occupation might indeed be gone, or rather, the cast of mind that could find "content" (348) in battle might well be distrusted. That distrust surfaces, as it were, in a Venetian law that gives ancient Roman practice a nautical twist and prohibits any returning "Generall, Legate, or Captaine of a nauie" from bringing his war gallies into the city of Venice, and obliges him to disband at a point about a hundred miles away from Venice. And though, as Honigmann reminds us (7), Lewkenor's translation mentions that the "Captaine Generall" of the Venetian army is always a "straunger," the text adds the significant qualification that the "Captaine Generall" "hath no authority to doe or deliberate any thing without the aduice of the Legates," the political officers "who neuer stirre from the side of the Captaine Generall" (132). In *Othello* this anti-militarism attributed to the Venetian state goes unvoiced, conveniently displaced by the threat posed by the Turk, not to Venice itself, but to a colonial and commercial vital interest, and a threat not unacknowledged. Yet the cultural anxieties that, as Emily Bartels has shown, a Western audience was likely to have brought towards a Moorish protagonist may only have been reinforced by the peculiar symbiosis of Venice and its military factotums. Read in this context, the determination arrived at offstage by "the state" to have Othello replaced for unspecified reasons by Cassio—a change that seems all the more peremptory to an audience that has not been given any reason to believe that a substantial amount of time has elapsed in the play— seems merely to give dramatic emphasis to the uncertain position of the warrior and the stranger in Venice recorded in Contareni and Lewkenor.

That Othello reflects the uncertainty of the soldier's and stranger's position in the Venetian state helps, of course, to define the vulnerability that is his undoing with Iago in act 3. My concern here, however, is not to revisit the psychic dynamics of that scene, and ask why Othello falls or falls so rapidly in it, but to consider the role "the state" has in shaping the vulnerable self that Othello exhibits in the play, in the beginning and at the end. We observed above that Othello's memorable

protest, at "the end," that "I have done the state some service—and they know it" recalls closely the section in Lewkenor's translation that describes how "forrain men and strangers" can attain citizenship by "Notable seruise," by merit and deeds. The recollection is worth noting because Othello's outcry very much sounds like the protest of injured merit, or of merit unrecognized, or, rather, of someone who believes that "the state" about to cart him away would be susceptible to arguments from merit—"and they know it." The particular line Othello employs here to buy time with which to dictate his statement and do away with himself is interesting. For one thing, we had not been acutely aware that Othello was suffering the pangs of injured or unrecognized merit, and the circumstances seem hardly propitious for raising questions of merit. On the other hand, however, the tack Othello takes here reminds us of Othello's first appearance in the play, when Othello dismisses the concerns Iago so helpfully raises about the harm the enraged Brabantio may do, on the grounds that "[My services which I have done the signiory / Shall outtongue his complaints" (1.2.18-19). Michael Neill has referred to the "civil self" of Othello from which Iago strips away the fabric to expose the "dark" secrets Iago "has taught the audience to expect"(*Issues of Death,* 167). In Othello's comment to Iago in this first appearance we get a hint of what the fabric of that "civil self" may consist. Othello stakes his survival and advancement on the very Venetian notion of a meritocracy; that is, he defines himself according to what he believes "the state" will recognize and reward. In doing so, however, he chooses to suppress another part of himself, or, indeed, another version of himself, that part "'Tis yet to know," the lineage of "royal siege," of which, in the first piece of praeterition in which he engages in the play, he at once brags while claiming he will not brag of it until bragging is in vogue (1.2.19-23). Praeterition it is, but it is a piece of praeterition that ultimately gets nullified, in that that other self Othello claims he will suppress for awhile actually stays suppressed. "Men in Great Fortunes", Bacon claims in the essay that provides one of the epigraphs to this essay, "are strangers to themselves" (42). Othello has not defined himself by his fortune, but he follows the path Bacon sees men "Of Great Place," who are enslaved to "the state," following to self-alienation. Small wonder that in his final speech, just when he has ensured himself a captive audience and can say anything he might want to say about himself, his sense of subjectivity should lead him to reenact an episode from his *vita* and subsume, indeed, extinguish himself in deeds done for "the state."

Still, as Othello tells Iago, it is not exactly his deeds that Othello claims will redeem him with "the state," but the ability of his deeds to "outtongue" Brabantio's complaints. At a glance one might take this to be Othello's appeal to meritocracy and a deprecation of rhetoric, an assertion that his deeds "speak for themselves," or that "actions speak louder than words." Yet as the scene in the council meeting unfolds, "outongue" proves, of course, to be less metaphoric, or closer to personification than one at first supposes. For rather like "the state" itself, Othello's deeds in the play exist as rhetorical fodder, allusions to accomplishments designed to make points for or about Othello. It is not, we know, Othello's deeds as such that lead the Duke to "think" that "this tale would win my daughter too" (1.3.171), or even the tale itself, but a metatale, Othello's telling of how he had been accustomed to telling it, or as James Calderwood has described it, "a voice telling about himself telling about himself" (294). In approving that voice, "the state" does more than vet the rhetoric in which Othello fashions himself; rather, "the state" helps to define that self as rhetorical.

And well might "the state" claim some authority at judging rhetoric, since "the state" itself proves attentive to rhetoric, if ultimately transparent at its use, when it serves its interests. Nowhere is this more on display than in the council scene, where Shakespeare gives "the state" its fullest personification in the play and gives most audible voice to the celebrations of Venice's deliberative wisdom he might have found in Contareni and Lewkenor. That "the state" has interests is dramatically underscored when its spokesmen come to perceive those interests to be threatened, when in rapid succession the Duke and the senators deduce the threat to Cyprus only to hear Brabantio bring charges of witchcraft against their best hope at resisting that threat. "We are very sorry for't," the response of "All" to Brabantio's accusations (1.3.73) is heartfelt, even though the sentiment it embodies probably transcends fraternal regard for the injury suffered by their "brother of the state," Brabantio. And, indeed, it is a measure of their moral sense, or at least of their desire to live up to the moral reputation of the Venetian state, that its representatives on stage should feel an ethical dilemma at the possibility that defending Cyprus and avenging Brabantio might not be compatible goals, a dilemma that is made all the more embarrassing by the firm pledge of judicial severity the Duke issues—"yea, though our proper son / Stood in your action" (1.3.69-70)—immediately before he learns who the accused is. When "the state" is spared the necessity of condemning its military champion, it is, of course, still left with the dilemma of reconciling itself, and Brabantio, to the marriage of the fair skinned Desdemona and the dark-skinned Moor. Wooed by Othello's own rhetoric and bound by Venice's reputation of toleration towards strangers, especially strangers that are to help it defend its possessions against the Turk, "the state" in the cloying balm of the Duke's rhymed couplets, employs a trope to deny the seemingly undeniable fact of skin color, in the process endorsing the sort

of color-coded metaphysics that, as Neill has demonstrated, ultimately enables Othello to demonize Desdemona by demonizing himself (*Issues of Death*, 144-44):

> If virtue no delighted beauty lack,
> Your son-in-law is far more fair than black.

(1.3.289-90)

What the Duke so fecklessly does here, Lodovico will much more effectively do later, in fact ending the play in the process. That is, both align the authority of "the state" and rhetorical discourse to deny nothing less than the evidence of sight: the Duke formally bolsters the authority of his rank with the authority of rhymed couplets to claim that black can really be white; Lodovico, as we have noted before, forcibly averts everyone's glance from the sight-poisoning bed and diverts attention to a narrative to come, the narrative to be "related." In the process, the invention of "the state," its extrapolation on Shakespeare's putative source in Cinthio, provides a vehicle by means of which *Othello* appears to tame the narrative it has staged, devising strategies of domestication, familiarization, and ultimately recuperation while calling attention to the ways in which that narrative ultimately eludes control. Indeed, we get a hint of this in the scene in the council meeting when the Duke first calls for and then blesses Othello's account of how he used to account for his past and its adventures. Again, what wins Othello sympathy in this speech, before Desdemona arrives to exonerate him formally, is as much the performance of the speech as its content, its collection of wild and unfamiliar things and experiences harnessed within Othello's recognizably and sonorously attractive delivery. The Duke's prompt, "Say it, Othello" (1.3.126), or what Honigmann calls an unusual turn of phrase" (143, n.1.3.128), does not so much command Othello to speak as cue him to perform, and exemplifies both the way in which "the state" domesticates Othello's "extravagant strangeness" and part of the "service" through which Othello ingratiates himself with "the state." In "Othello Furens" Robert S. Miola has charted a number of instances in which Othello's language is suffused with recollections of Seneca's *Hercules Furens*, a possible source of the argot that Iago claims is laden with "bumbast circumstance / Horribly stuff'd with epithites of war" (1.1.13-14). Invested with a familiarly theatrically wild, heroic language that, much to Iago's stated chagrin, is part of the winning persona Othello wears in "the state," Othello and "the state" demonstrate the terms of their peculiar, mutually cultivating, mutually exploitative relationship. Indeed, that moment so central to Othello's need for ocular proof, the scenario Iago stages with Cassio for Othello's benefit (4.1.103-68), only demonstrates the way in which the imposition of a conventional dramatic form can hide sight and misinform, since Othello becomes enraged, less at what he sees than by the words he thinks he hears, the script from familiar plays he is imaginatively writing into what he sees before him, with Cassio a swaggering stage Roman: "Do [you] triumph, Roman? Do you triumph?" (4.1.118).

Finally, Lodovico's determination at the end of the play to hide the bed and what it reveals and his announcement of his intention to "relate" what had happened to "the state" enlist "the state" in a recuperative strategy that attempts to rewrite what has happened in familiarly, manageably, and conventionally tragic terms, terms that exempt us from having to pose or cope with the harder questions the events onstage force. To Iago, now conveniently demonized as "O Spartan dog" (5.2.361), incomprehensibly evil but, then, beyond the need to comprehend because undeniably inhuman, is shifted all of the responsibility for "the tragic loading of this bed; / This is thy work" (5.2.363-64). Simultaneously Othello emerges as a tragic icon and victim: his suicide provides a theatrically familiar demonstration that "he was great of heart" (5.2.361), and spares "the state" the burden of having to learn from his own testimony "the nature of [his] fault." In the degree to which the recuperative strategy doesn't work, leaving in our sight the bed and the questions it provokes, underscoring as a strategy of denial the narrative Lodovico will present to "the state," and affiliating "the state" itself with the agency of censor, *Othello* presents as an undomesticatable form drama itself.

Notes

1. See Granville-Barker, 130; Moisan; Parker, "Shakespeare and Rhetoric: 'dilation' and 'delation' in *Othello*, 54-74, *Shakespeare from the Margins* 229-72; Shaw.

2. So "the state" slips seems to slip formulaically into the rhythm of an editorial gloss by Kittredge on the name Marcus Luccicos, who Kittredge surmises is "[d]oubtless some foreigner in the service of the Venetian state" (16, n.1.3.44).

3. Unless otherwise stated, references to Shakespeare's text are from *The Riverside Shakespeare,* ed. G. Blakemore Evans, 2d ed. (Boston: Houghton Mifflin, 1997). References to "the state" are not affected by the notorious variations between Folio and Quarto.

4. So, for example, we have Contareni's account of Venice's "great counsell"—the Duke's voting powers on which Shakespeare has been said to have misrepresented—wherein "the shew of a popular estate" is seasoned, somehow, by just enough of "entermixture of the gouernment of the nobility" to ensure a meritocracy, a salutary hybridity that draws the marginal gloss, "The commonwealth of Venice is neither a popular estate, nor an Olygarchy, but a wel tempered gouernment betweene both" (33-4).

5. Kenneth Muir (187) has detected resemblances between Lewkenor's language and the language of the play in the Council Scene (.3), including the parallel between the modesty *topos* with which Othello prefaces his defense against Brabantio's accusation (1.3. 81-2)

6. Vaughan (20-21) cites speculation, or as she dubs it, "wild surmise," that the representation of the deliberations of the Venetian Senate in 1.3 could have had a topical significance and coincided with a visit by Venetian ambassadors to the English court around the time when *Othello* was first performed.

7. Indeed, as the play unfolds, Othello's standing with "the state" continues to be, in modern bureaucratic parlance, "performance based," but his "performance" is measured by criteria other than his military prowess, which, after all, becomes moot once nature intervenes to destroy the Turkish fleet. When Lodovico's arrival in Cyprus triggers Othello's outburst against Desdemona, Lodovico's indignant question, "Is this the noble Moor whom our full Senate / Call all in all sufficient" (4.1.264-5), suggests that "the state" reserves the right to define "sufficiency" by a number of criteria, including the decorum of one's public behavior. When Lodovico rebukes Othello for striking Desdemona by invoking Venice as an arbiter, "this would not be believ'd in Venice" (4.1.242), "the state" emerges as much as an aesthetic and theatrical critic as a moral censor.

Works Cited

Bacon, Francis. *Essays*. London. Oxford University Press, 1966.

Bartels, Emily C. "Making More of the Moor: Aaron, Othello, and Renaissance Refashionings of Race." *Shakespeare Quarterly* 41 (1990): 433-54.

Bodin, Jean. *The Six Bookes of a Commonweale: A Facsimile Reprint of the English Translation of 1606. Ed. And Introduction by Kenneth Douglas McRae.* Cambridge. Harvard University Press, 1962.

Calderwood, James L. "Speech and Self in *Othello*." *Shakespeare Quarterly* 38 (1987): 293-303.

Contareni, Gasparo. *The Commonwealth of Venice.* Trans. Lewis Lewkenor (1599) Amsterdam: De Capo Press, 1969.

Granville-Barker, Harley. *Prefaces to Shakespeare.* 2. Princeton: Princeton University Press, 1947.

Helgerson, Richard. *Forms of Nationhood: The Elizabethan Writing of England.* Chicago: The University of Chicago Press, 1992.

Little, Jr, Arthur L. "'An essence that's not seen': The Primal Scene of Racism in *Othello*." *Shakespeare Quarterly* 44 (1993): 304-24.

Miola, Robert S. "Othello *Furens*." *Shakespeare Quarterly* 41 (1990): 49-64.

Moisan, Thomas. "Repetition and Interrogation in *Othello*: 'What needs this Iterance?' or, 'Can anything be made of this?'" *Othello: New Perspectives. Ed.* Virginia Mason Vaughan and Kent Cartwright. London: Associated University Presses. 48-73.

Muir Kenneth. *The Sources of Shakespeare's Plays*. New Haven: Yale University Press, 1978.

Neill, Michael. "Unproper Beds: Race, Adultery, and the Hideous in *Othello*." *Shakespeare Quarterly* 40 (1989): 383-412.

————. *Issues of Death: Mortality and Identity in English Renaissance Tragedy*. Oxford: Oxford University Press, 1997.

Nuttall, A. D. *A New Mimesis: Shakespeare and The Representation of Reality*. London: Methuen, 1983.

Parker, Patricia. *Shakespeare from the Margins: Language, Culture, Context*. Chicago: The University of Chicago Press, 1996.

Parker, Patricia, and Geoffrey Hartman. Ed. *Shakespeare & The Question of Theory*. New York: Methuen, 1985.

Shakespeare, William. *Othello*. Ed. George Lyman Kittredge. Rev. Irving Ribner. New York: John Wiley & Sons, 1969.

————. *Othello: The New Cambridge Shakespeare*. Ed. Norman Sanders. Cambridge: Cambridge University Press, 1984.

————. *Othello: The Arden Shakespeare*. Ed. E. A. J. Honigmann. 3rd Edition. London: Thomas Nelson & Sons, 1997.

————. *The Riverside Shakespeare*. Ed. G. Blakemore Evans. 2nd Edition. Boston: Houghton Mifflin, 1997.

Shaw, John. "'What is the Matter' in *Othello*?" *Shakespeare Quarterly* 17 (1966): 157-61.

Vaughan, Virginia Mason. *Othello: A Contextual History*. Cambridge: Cambridge University Press. 1994.

Vitkus, Daniel J. "Turning Turk in *Othello*: The Conversion and Damnation of the Moor." *Shakespeare Quarterly* 48 (1997): 145-76.

FURTHER READING

Criticism

Bartels, Emily C. "Making More of the Moor: Aaron, Othello, and Renaissance Refashionings of Race." *Shakespeare Quarterly* 41, no. 4 (winter 1990): 433-54.

Probes the Renaissance racial discourse that informs Shakespeare's characters Othello and Aaron, the Moor in his drama *Titus Andronicus*, as exotic threats to the social order.

Caro, Robert V. "Ignatian Discernment and the World of *Othello*." *Cross Currents* 44, no. 3 (fall 1994): 332-44.

Applies the concept of spiritual discernment and analysis of spiritual disintegration proposed by St. Ignatius to an understanding of Othello's murder of Desdemona in *Othello*.

Ghazoul, Ferial J. "The Arabization of *Othello*." *Comparative Literature* 50, no. 1 (winter 1998): 1-31.

Surveys the reception of *Othello* in the Arab world through translation, interpretation, and literary adaptation.

Hunt, Maurice. "Predestination and the Heresy of Merit in *Othello*." *Comparative Drama* 30, no. 3 (fall 1996): 346-76.

Explores *Othello* as a Christian morality play in which the traditional Catholic theology of free will and temptation clashes with the Reformed Protestant doctrine of predestination.

Kaul, Mythili, ed. Othello: *New Essays by Black Writers*. Washington D.C.: Howard University Press, 1997, 223 p.

Collection of fourteen essays by various contributors on issues of theatrical, literary, or academic interest in regard to *Othello*, with a general emphasis on the racial aspects of Shakespeare's drama.

Kolin, Philip C., ed. Othello: *New Critical Essays*. New York: Routledge, 2002, 458 p.

Comprised of twenty contemporary, interpretive essays on *Othello* from a range of scholars, preceded by a survey of critical, stage, and filmic interpretations of the drama by the volume editor.

Slights, Camille Wells. "Slaves and Subjects in *Othello*." *Shakespeare Quarterly* 48, no. 4 (winter 1997): 377-90.

New historicist assessment of *Othello* that considers the drama as it exposes attitudes toward slavery and selfhood in early modern England.

Vanita, Ruth. "Men Beware Men: Shakespeare's Warning for Unfair Husbands." *Comparative Drama* 28, no. 2 (summer 1994): 201-20.

Examines Renaissance plays, including *Othello* and other works by Shakespeare, that incorporate a chastity theme and dubious tests of honor to the detriment (or in extreme cases, fatality) of innocent wives.

Pericles

INTRODUCTION

Pericles (ca. 1607), Shakespeare's first romance, has been considered by some critics to be one of his least satisfying works. In this play, introduced by the choric narrator Gower, Shakespeare used a fairy-tale style to recount the misfortunes of Pericles, prince of Tyre, who is exiled and separated from his wife and daughter. Pericles is grief-stricken and wanders at sea until he is happily reunited with his loved ones at the play's end. Scholars have identified several causes for their dissatisfaction with *Pericles*: its disjointed, episodic construction; its weak characters, inconsistent dialogue, and implausible plot twists; and—perhaps most vexing—its suspect heritage. Critics have long questioned whether Shakespeare is the sole author of the play, with the general consensus being that he wrote most of the final three acts whereas other writers were responsible for the first two. Despite these long-standing aesthetic and textual concerns, *Pericles* has received a substantial amount of attention in the last century. Indeed, recent critics have been drawn to the play for some of the same reasons that it was once scorned. In addition to debating the extent to which Shakespeare was involved in creating the drama, critics have analyzed the stylistic deviations in *Pericles* for clues to larger shifts in the literary, religious, and political landscape during Shakespeare's lifetime.

Several literary scholars have examined the playwright's narrative technique and distinctive mode of presentation in *Pericles*. Many of these discussions center on the play's choric narrator, Gower—a fictional recreation of the fourteenth-century English poet John Gower—who frequently addresses the audience and comments on the story. Walter F. Eggers (1975) identifies Gower as an "authorial presenter" who serves to distance the audience from the illusion of the play. Eggers maintains that Gower's limited viewpoint of the dramatic events allows the audience to place the representational aspect of the play in its proper perspective and instead focus on the basic story. Similarly, Kenneth J. Semon (1974) demonstrates how Gower's archaic moral perspective influences the dramatic events of *Pericles*. Semon speculates that Shakespeare intentionally underscored Gower's strict moral opinions in an effort to persuade the audience to identify more closely with the wonder-filled reactions of the other characters in the play. F. David Hoeniger (1982) asserts that Gower's archaic observations and language are a means for Shakespeare

to ridicule literary styles which he considered to be outdated, a technique that previously had been employed by Geoffrey Chaucer. Richard Hillman (1985) is less concerned with the character of Gower than with the work of the real-life poet. It has long been acknowledged that *Pericles* was inspired in part by a tale related in Gower's *Confessio Amantis* (1385-93); Hillman points out additional links between the two works.

Though popular with audiences during Shakespeare's time and well into the seventeenth century, *Pericles* later fell into disfavor and was almost completely absent from the stage during the eighteenth and nineteenth centuries. However, the play experienced a revival in the twentieth century. D. J. R. Bruckner (1998) notes that *Pericles* is a play that has everything, including "murder, kidnapping, drowning, lost children, resurrections, political intrigue, divine vengeance, a bordello redeemed by a virgin, admired rulers whose sex lives would arch Satan's eyebrow, pimps, homicidal jealousy, labor induced by a hurricane, birth onstage and eternal love." Bruckner gives high praise to the Kings County Shakespeare Company production of the play, directed by Jonathan Bank, for its ability to pull all the elements of the play together and create "irresistible entertainment." Charles Isherwood's 1998 review of the Joseph Papp Public Theater/New York Shakespeare Festival production, directed by Brian Kulick, is not so favorable. The critic faults the weak cast and stylistic treatment, and contends that the production lacked a "humanizing touch"; however, the critic grants that the "convoluted saga" presented in the play contributed to the production's failure. Also reviewing Kulick's production, John Simon (1998) strongly criticizes virtually every aspect of the play, especially the director's staging of the play as a farce. Lois Potter (2002) gives a positive review of the Royal Shakespeare Company production of *Pericles,* directed by Adrian Noble. The critic praises both the cast and the production's visual and musical splendor.

In recent years, a number of critics have maintained that Shakespeare imbued *Pericles* with a subtle commentary on the compelling social, political, and religious issues that England faced in the Elizabethan and Jacobean periods. Margaret Healy (1999) suggests that *Pericles* can be interpreted as a veiled criticism of the efforts of King James I to arrange marriage links between the English and Spanish royal families. Caroline Bicks (2000) detects references in *Pericles* to the tension surrounding the practice of traditional Catholic rituals in the Anglican church decades after the

Protestant Reformation of the mid-sixteenth century. In particular, Bicks points out dramatic episodes that echo the controversy over church ceremonies involving women after childbirth. Peter Womack (1999) asserts that *Pericles* shares similarities with earlier dramas that venerated saints, most notably the play *Mary Magdalen.* The critic discusses the two plays in the context of the changing critical, political, and religious sentiment in England during the 1500s and 1600s, which denigrated improbable and miraculous stories because of their connections to Catholicism. Heather Dubrow (2002) analyzes the dynamic involving parents and children in *Pericles,* positing that Shakespeare's treatment of familial relationships reflected a widespread apprehension about parental loss in Elizabethan and Jacobean society. According to Dubrow, Shakespeare manipulated the anxiety surrounding this cultural issue not merely to dramatize the emotional toll that parental loss took on children, but also to expose a flawed social convention in which unscrupulous guardians of orphaned children took advantage of the process of inheritance.

OVERVIEWS AND GENERAL STUDIES

F. David Hoeniger (essay date winter 1982)

SOURCE: Hoeniger, F. David. "Gower and Shakespeare in *Pericles.*" *Shakespeare Quarterly* 33, no. 4 (winter 1982): 461-79.

[*In the following essay, Hoeniger outlines the plot of* Pericles, *noting the play's appeal to live audiences and paying special attention to the figure of Gower. The critic maintains that at certain points in the play, Shakespeare attempted to create a burlesque that mocked antiquated literary conventions.*]

In this essay I wish to propose an entirely new approach to *Pericles* which arises from the conviction that critics have not yet grasped the play's highly unusual character and technique. Because large parts of the play, particularly its first two acts, seem to critical readers so obviously defective and crude, both in style and in dramaturgy, we may be surprised by the evidence that in Shakespeare's own time and for a generation after, the play was highly popular. The First Quarto of 1609 speaks of it as "The late, And much admired Play . . . diuers and sundry times acted by his Maiesties seruants, at the Globe on the Banck-side." Other references from the time tell us of large crowds flocking to see it, and of both the Venetian and French ambassadors watching an early performance. Between 1610 and 1631 it was revived several times, not only at the Globe, but on one occasion at Whitehall before distinguished guests; it was also performed by a traveling company in the country. Moreover, the Quarto text was reprinted no less than five times, thus confirming the unusual interest in the play. By 1635, the date of the Sixth Quarto, very few other plays had appeared as often in print. We know, of course, that in Shakespeare's time other plays of little dramatic subtlety and of far less literary merit than the best scenes in *Pericles* could produce a great stir. Yet it does seem strange, especially in view of the play's fate on the stage from Dryden's time to the 1920s and even later, that a work which appears so dismally written and undramatic in its first two acts could experience such a success on stage, and that there was so much demand for it by readers.

But what should surprise us most is that after producers hardly ever risked staging the play for centuries, and then only in major adaptations, several impressive revivals of it during the past thirty years have demonstrated that *Pericles* can hold modern audiences throughout—and more, that watching it can be an enchanting experience. If these audiences had been prepared simply to accept, for better or worse, the opening parts for the sake of the Shakespearean scenes in the later acts, we could understand this response quite easily. But the audiences were those that go to Stratford-upon-Avon and Stratford, Ontario, or the summer festival at Ashland, Oregon, and their like. A large proportion of them did not know the play or any criticism of it before seeing it. They were eager to see a work by Shakespeare that until then they had only vaguely heard about. Moreover, several people who experienced these productions told me, when I questioned them, how much they enjoyed the play from Gower's first appearance on, and that they were not particularly conscious of a marked change in the third act when Shakespeare's voice, with its rich and lively resonance, is first heard in Pericles' address to the storm on board ship. Readers at this point may well exclaim "Shakespeare, at last," but audiences of a good production evidently do not, though surely the poetry and increased life of the characters make them prick up their ears. These productions have also made us more fully aware than before how much the choric presenter, John Gower, contributes to the play's atmosphere and overall effect, besides confirming how deeply moving the scene of Pericles' reunion with Marina can be.

This new knowledge of how well the whole play works in the theatre should make us reflect on whether the traditional negative explanations that seek to account for the marked incongruity in quality of the play's scenes are at all convincing. We may well doubt that part of the play is the product of a very inferior collaborator; or that the printed text of the Quarto, the only form through which the play has reached us, was so badly corrupted by reporters that in large sections the Shakespearean original was obscured beyond recognition. The questions I will raise about both of these views familiar in criticism are not meant to ignore the clear evidence that the Quarto was badly printed, contains many manifest errors, and at points is so seriously corrupt that editors cannot hope to restore the true text with assurance. Some of the defects must be blamed on the compositors, others on their inability to understand clearly a difficult manuscript copy, which moreover was itself imperfect and evidently unauthorized by either Shakespeare or his company. Nor is it essential to my interpretation to rule out entirely the idea of collaboration.

But the notion that late in his career Shakespeare collaborated with such a hackwriter as George Wilkins (or even Wilkins together with the slightly more gifted John Day) is, on the face of it, difficult to credit. And the suggestion that a rough play composed by Wilkins and associates landed on Shakespeare's desk, and that as he perused it he became so fascinated by the possibilities of the story in the later parts that he largely redrafted them (but only them) before the whole was successfully staged, should be ruled out as preposterous. Could one imagine a Mozart or a Brahms responding to an inferior composer's quartet by rewriting only parts of its third and fourth movements, and then be happy to see the work performed?

As for the theory of extreme corruption of the text by reporters, one trouble with it is that we can infer the extent of corruption only from the Quarto itself, since no better and authorized text is available for comparison, as is the case of all other Shakespearean bad quartos, for instance those of *Hamlet* and *Romeo and Juliet.* Not knowing what the original was like, how can one deduce with any assurance the extent of a reporter's desperate improvisations? We need to remind ourselves that the only times we are on really safe ground in concluding that a text is corrupt is when it either does not make sense or errors are manifest. Clearly, for instance, something has gone very wrong in the text and even in the order of events in the first half of the second scene of *Pericles,* and also in the opening dialogue of V.i. But the idea that a reporter resorted to complete improvisation in most of the first two acts, as well as in parts of later scenes, is difficult to reconcile with the evidence of how they work on the stage. Moreover, if textual corruption was extreme, then the play's early printing history furnishes an instance unique in Jacobean drama. We do know, of course, that Heminge and Condell chose not to include the play in the First Folio, but we do not know why, and as the King's Men revived the play more than once, they must have owned a text that they were sufficiently satisfied with. But we also know that the First Quarto text was reprinted five times over a period of twenty-six years,

without any move by Shakespeare or his company to replace it by a more reliable text, as they did every previous time when an unauthorized and corrupt version of a Shakespearean play appeared—with the sole exception of *The Merry Wives,* which, however, was printed only once, and was followed by the authentic version in the First Folio. All of these considerations encourage me to assume that in spite of some evident defects and corruptions, the text of the First Quarto does in essence convey the original with some justice even in its first two acts. In short, although the original has been badly distorted in some places, the Quarto does not obscure for us the very character and style of large parts.

I

The play opens with Gower's extraordinary appearance and speech. Comparison between Gower and the Chorus of *Henry V* merely serves to emphasize their unlikeness. The Chorus of *Henry V* operates as a spokesman for his company and is dressed in their garb. He speaks vigorous Shakespearean blank verse that whets our appetite for the heroic action of the history play. He strives to infect us with his nationalistic enthusiasm and urges us to assist the actors with our imagination. Pleasing as he is in his vigor of expression, there is yet nothing about him particularly unusual, at least in a Shakespearean drama. But if we have not been prepared for it by reading *Pericles* before seeing it, we are surprised by the very sight of the medieval poet John Gower, with his quaint, archaic, moralizing lines. The effect he produces will not be forgotten, for in the course of the play he reappears seven times. Even when the play's action seems to be over, he enters once more, in order to summarize it, moralize in his characteristic manner about the characters, and wish the audience joy before announcing that the end of the play has really come. There is no parallel for such a character or effect anywhere else in Shakespeare.

Fortunately, we know from a contemporary woodcut in Wilkins' *Painful Adventures,* a prose narrative based on the play, what Gower probably looked like on stage during the play's first performance. Evidently old, with a dark and graying beard, he appeared stout and rather short, dressed in a long plain coat, an old-fashioned cap protecting his head against raw weather, and wooden shoes. In one hand he held a staff, in the other a branch of laurel marking him as a renowned poet. Gower's stiff figure has stepped out of a world of long ago. The Elizabethans knew him as "moral" Gower, and contrasted him with his more lighthearted contemporary, Chaucer. He tells us in his opening lines that he has returned "From ashes . . . Assuming man's infirmities" for the sake of narrating once more a "song" that many generations ago regaled "lords and ladies" who "read it for restoratives."[1] He expresses his hope that it may still be found acceptable by his new listeners, "born in these latter times, / When wit's more ripe." But of course he introduces it in his own archaic style and verse. He speaks with the conviction of a poet who is accustomed to be listened to with rapt attention:

> The purchase is to make men glorious
> *Et bonum quo antiquius eo melius.*
>
> (I. Chorus 9-10)

Gower was a learned poet, as the audience knew, and the Latin befits his authority. The line confirms that the story too is antique. Probably only a few members of the audience knew that it forms part of Gower's own *Confessio Amantis.* But this is unimportant, since the speech clearly conveys that he is the story's teller. We gather that the very idea of reviving the medieval poet on the stage and having him present his own ancient story was meant to appeal to an audience that had developed a liking for things old-fashioned and antiquarian. It was the time of Camden and the Society of Antiquaries. The audience could thus relish the quaint humor of the logic that the older a good thing is, the better it must be.

The effect of the opening chorus is not only striking but splendid. We become enchanted with Gower's poetry. That is attested to by our eagerness to learn at least part of the speech by heart. However heavily moral and stiff Gower appears, the impression is lightened by his song-like rhythm and by the very air of telling a story, which endow his lines with their peculiar charm. In his other seven speeches, the style and manner remain fundamentally consistent, even if not entirely uniform. I once wrote that

> The predominantly end-stopped tetrameter lines of the first two choruses yield to a freer handling of the verse, with more pentameter lines and lines of nine or eleven syllables, and with significantly more syncopation and variation in the use of caesura. . . . The change in style is accompanied by a difference in attitude towards the audience. The later choruses, especially that of IV.iv, remind us more of the Chorus in *Henry V.* Gower no longer merely presents the scenes to our eyes and judgment: he asks us to cooperate imaginatively with the actors.[2]

But while this description may be sound in detail, it requires strong qualification if it is not to produce a misleading impression. The changes in some of Gower's later speeches amount, it should be stressed, to no more than small adjustments in his characteristic manner of speech. Once the audience had become accustomed to the reincarnation and manner of speaking of the medieval poet, the playwright wisely introduced a little more freedom into his lines. But he took care not to depart from Gower's initial manner and rhythm, and in the chorus of V.ii he even returned to the stiff tetrameter rhymes of Gower's opening speeches. Gower's archaic style was allowed to vary only enough to ensure that it would remain interesting. And as sheer poetry, Gower's opening speech is certainly no less impressive than the rest.

When audiences first see and hear Gower, they readily accept the illusion that indeed "from ashes ancient Gower is come"; in fact they relish the very conception. But seated as they are in a theatre, they are not surprised when after a brief introduction Gower calls upon actors to present the story. Yet the impression never leaves us as the scenes develop that he controls the presentation of the whole play, which merely presents his own narrative in the adaptation suitable for a revival in a theatre. The actors merely serve him as appropriate tools and aids, and not even all the time, for Gower returns again and again to narrate pieces of the story mixed with moral commentary. Further, in the acted episodes themselves, the mode only now and then becomes fully dramatic—and, as we know, more fully in the later than in the early acts, but even then not consistently. All the way through, the mode and impression remain those of a consciously episodic adaptation of narrative to stage representation.

This method of dramatization, so very unlike that of any other Shakespearean drama, is confirmed by our realization that Shakespeare, or whoever designed the play, chose to follow the order of Gower's original narrative and his characters most of the time with singular subservience. We know that Shakespeare usually took great liberties when he used a story for the plot of his comedies and romances, and that he even did so in his English chronicle plays. Thus, for the first part of *Henry IV* he changed the Percy of history into a youth no older than Hal himself, and found a place in the action for the totally original character of Falstaff. For *Pericles,* on the other hand, Shakespeare decided to maintain the pattern of numerous short episodes that follow one another, with frequent changes in locale as the tale hops from one Aegean island to the next. The result is anything but concentrated drama. It is rather a series of "adventures" and spectacles, more like Dekker's *Old Fortunatus* or even Marlowe's *Tamburlaine* than like any other Shakespearean play. Only near the end are we given slightly more complex and drawn-out episodes: the final scene of nearly 200 lines in the Mytilene brothel, and the famous scene of 262 lines showing Pericles' reunion with Marina in V.i. But even these scenes are much shorter than the longest of any other Shakespearean play. And after them, the manner reverts to its loose episodic design, true to Gower's original tale. The structure of the whole play has thus been fitted to the dramatist's conception of Gower's character and role. The story takes the form of a show of colorful episodes, introduced and linked by narrative with commentary.

II

We are now ready to consider Gower's effect on the play in greater detail, but I will begin with the final act, where by general consent Shakespeare's own voice is much in evidence, and only then turn to the opening scenes, where Shakespeare appears hardly present. Act V opens, like the previous acts, with Gower:

> Marina thus the brothel 'scapes, and chances
> Into an honest house, our story says.
> She sings like one immortal, and she dances
> As goddess-like to her admired lays.

A great deal has happened to Marina since the ending of the previous scene. The story has moved on rapidly, as so often before, from extreme predicament and crisis to happiness. "Our story says": we are once more reminded that what we are watching and hearing is Gower's own tale. He continues:

> Here we her place
> And to her father turn our thoughts again,
> Where we left him on the sea.

> (V. Chorus 11-13)

His ship, he tells us, is now anchored off the port of Mytilene, and as the following scene opens we learn from the dialogue that Lysimachus, having sailed with companions on a barge to the vessel, has asked for permission to step on board. In the Quarto the speech headings and text of this opening dialogue are so unclear that editors have found it difficult to sort it out. But fortunately we can trust most of the rest of the scene, which presents Marina's reunion with her father, the play's most famous episode, often praised for being in Shakespeare's best late manner. The scene reminds one both of Lear's reunion with Cordelia and of reunion scenes in the later romances. But the reader need not be told how deeply moving this episode becomes. I will merely observe how its effect is ensured by the way the episode is drawn out, with Pericles at first not reacting at all to Marina's song. Only very slowly as she persists in speaking to him does it begin to dawn upon him that she must be the daughter he had been led to believe was dead. This strategy—and of course the Shakespearean poetry—achieve the effect. But the scene concludes rapidly after Pericles' vision of Diana. When he awakes he announces that, after brief refreshments, he will proceed to Ephesus at the goddess' command. When Lysimachus asks for the hand of his daughter, he assents immediately.

We are not shown the happy celebration and meal at Mytilene. Instead Gower enters once more to tell us:

> Now our sands are almost run;
> More a little, and then dumb.

> (V.ii.1-2)

His speech has reverted to tetrameters very much like those of his opening choruses. He asks us to imagine

> What pageantry, what feats, what shows,
> What minstrelsy, and pretty din,
> The regent made in Mytilin
> To greet the king.

> (ll. 6-9)

"What minstrelsy": the entertainment is typically medieval, of a kind Shakespeare's audience had read about in stories of old, not what they were familiar with in Jacobean England.

The final scene of Pericles' reunion with Thaisa at Ephesus follows. While the language seems Shakespearean, this second recognition can hardly be expected to move us as deeply as the first. Rather, the audience sits back, watching how the story concludes. The dramaturgy of the double recognition has therefore often been criticized, especially by contrast with how boldly and effectively Shakespeare solved the problem in the final scenes of *The Winter's Tale*. But any inference that Shakespeare was not aware from the beginning of how to make a double recognition more dramatic seems surely unwarranted. Once more, the order of events in Gower's original narrative was deliberately allowed to override considerations of immediate dramatic effectiveness. In fact this whole final episode is conveyed with notable perfunctoriness. I have noted how in the earlier scene Marina, ignorant that her patient is her father, has to persist for quite a while before Pericles begins to stir, and how long it then takes Pericles before he becomes convinced that Marina must really be his daughter. At Ephesus, on the other hand, Thaisa as high priestess recognizes Pericles as soon as he speaks, and it then takes only another twenty-five lines for Pericles to have proof that she indeed is his lost wife. We are very much aware that the play's story is close to conclusion, and the playwright avoids distracting us with further drama. When Pericles speaks his last lines, they appear to conclude the play in the characteristic manner of Shakespearean comedy:

> Yet there, my queen,
> We'll celebrate their nuptials, and ourselves
> Will in that kingdom spend our following days.
> Our son and daughter shall in Tyrus reign.
> Lord Cerimon, we do our longing stay
> To hear the rest untold: sir, lead's the way.

> (V.iii.79-84)

We would feel prompted to applaud as the actors leave the stage had Gower not once more appeared. For the play really to conclude, the teller of its tale needs also to take his leave. Once more he makes us see this story from his own perspective, driving home the moral, though with merciful brevity:

In Antiochus and his daughter you have heard
Of monstrous lust the due and just reward.

(Epilogue 1-2)

His summary account of what the action and characters represent even includes a reference to Helicanus, a minor character whom the audience only faintly remembers, since he has had no part in the action since the second act: "A figure of truth, of faith, of loyalty." Nor do we really care about Cleon and Dionysa's fate, but Gower evidently feels that we should know how they are punished for their crimes. When he wishes us goodbye, "our play" really "has ending."

This description of the development of Act V shows how much its structure and overall effect depend on the interplay between Gower and Shakespeare. Gower enters three times. And as in the rest of the play, so here only part of the action is staged. Much of it continues to be narrated in Gower's archaic rhymes. The writing of the two staged scenes is wholly or largely Shakespearean, but the dramaturgy betrays Shakespeare's brilliance more in the first scene than the last. The characters, especially Marina and Pericles, come to life as individuals far more than they do in either the source story or the play's opening acts. We become, in the first scene, absorbed with their immediate experience and feelings with an intensity we are accustomed to in Shakespeare, though less so in the scene of Pericles' reunion with Thaisa. There is therefore some real drama, not merely story and a series of pictorial effects accompanied by stylized dialogue and a sense of patterned experience representative of our essential human condition. Yet the play's pattern insists on reasserting itself, as does Gower with a perspective that is his own, quaint in its oldfashionedness and simplicity, stodgy yet charming. Such an interplay produces a unique effect in Shakespearean drama.

III

What we have learned from our study of the fifth act may help us as we turn back to consider Acts I and II. But there, of course, we face a different style. One cannot speak here of an interplay between Gower and Shakespeare. Neither the crude dramaturgy nor the quality of writing would warrant it, with the possible exception of some of the prose by the fishermen in II.i. The humdrum verse of the play's opening scene, and indeed of most of the two acts, does indeed smack of a hackwriter: as drama the scene is singularly weak. And yet the early scenes work much better in the theatre than critical-minded readers of the text have assumed. The main reason, I think, is that Gower's opening chorus prepares us for a manner and style in the staged episodes which follow that are quite unlike those we are accustomed to in Shakespeare. After Gower's introduction of his ancient story in quaint archaic

rhymes, the audience does not expect the characters who enter to speak like those in *Antony and Cleopatra* or *Twelfth Night*. If the staged episodes between Gower's opening chorus and his second speech had been conveyed in Shakespeare's characteristic blank verse and splendid dramatic manner, the effect, I think, would have been jarring. When the dramatist thought about how to fit the whole technique and manner of writing of the play to the unusual device of its archaic narrator, it appears that he concluded that in the early scenes the adjustment needed to be extreme; only when the audience had become completely used to the play's peculiar mood and style could he afford to compromise in the interest of liveliness. At first, Gower as presenter largely had to determine the play's style. Yet of course, it would hardly have been sensible to make the characters of the acted scenes speak in Gower's own pseudo-Middle English and sing-song rhythm—the Jacobean audience at the Globe would rapidly have wearied of it. Rather, a form of speech and dialogue was needed that was old-fashioned and in some ways similar to Gower's, yet more familiar and normal for the actors. And we know the form it took.

The chief differences between the verse of Gower's opening chorus and that by the characters in the play's first staged episode, at Antiochus' court, are that the characters speak in a more contemporary idiom and use prevailing pentameter lines. But much in their speeches does remind one of Gower's manner: the stiffness of the lines, the frequent moralizing, the kind of imagery, and the rhythm. A high proportion of the characters' lines are rhymed. At times the similarity becomes particularly marked, as in Pericles'

> One sin, I know, another doth provoke;
> Murder's as near to lust as flame to smoke.
> Poison and treason are the hands of sin,
> Ay, and the targets to put off the shame.

(I.i.138-41)

"As flame to smoke": Gower might use exactly the same image and expression. The great liberty taken with the rhyme "sin/shame" can be paralleled in Gower's second chorus, where he rhymes "sin" with "him" and "ship" with "split." The moralizing, too, is Gower-like; there is a great deal of it in the first two acts. Every opportunity for moral comment is seized. For instance, Pericles concludes his dialogue with Helicanus in the second scene:

> I'll take thy word for faith, not ask thine oath;
> Who shuns not to break one will crack both.
> But in our orbs we'll live so round and safe,
> That time of both this truth shall ne'er convince,
> Thou showedst a subject's shine, I a true prince'.

(I.ii.120-24)

When in II.ii some of Simonides' lords scoff at Pericles' rusty armor, the King responds:

Opinion's but a fool, that makes us scan
The outward habit by the inward man.

(II.ii.55-56)

There is more of the same in II.iv, the scene showing Helicanus with other lords of Tyre. The rhymes turn the conventional morals into tags that Gower would wish us to remember, tags that strike us as naive in their simplicity and patness, as do his own.

Our first impression of Pericles is that of a prince singularly bold. The display of the heads of precious suitors provides gruesome warning that failure to solve the riddle means certain death, yet Pericles is not frightened. But when Pericles reads out the riddle's lines aloud, we find that far from hiding their secret they give it away:

I am no viper, yet I feed
On mother's flesh which did me breed.
I sought a husband, in which labour
I found that kindness in a father.
He's father, son, and husband mild;
I mother, wife, and yet his child:
How they may be, and yet in two,
As you will live, resolve it you.

(I.i.65-72)

The first four lines reveal the meaning, the rest seem hardly needed. Yet anyone who concludes that the riddle is either inappropriate or improvised by the reporter will thereby merely show his ignorance of a folktale convention. Sensing by then, as we should, the nature and spirit of Gower's tale, we can accept it without question, untroubled by all those previous suitors who failed to see the obvious. The riddle's jingle is authentic, and continues the air of naive artistry established by Gower. Whoever composed the riddle showed a sense of decorum.

Thirty lines later occurs an image which some critics have liked so much that they have attributed it to Shakespeare:

The blind mole casts
Copped hills towards heaven, to tell the earth is
    thronged
By man's oppression, and the poor worm doth die
    for't.

(ll. 101-3)

Yet the image was a commonplace of the time, and what matters is that the lines are congruent with the rest of the scene. They do justice to Gower's fame as a poet. But in the main the scene continues in this measured, stiff way of writing until Pericles' exit. After that, the style loosens up and includes even some prose, but without gaining in distinction.

The second scene does not lend itself to the purpose of my discussion, since, as both Philip Edwards and I have shown (in my edition of the play), its text is manifestly corrupt, especially in the first half. In the original, Pericles may well have had more dialogue with the Lords at the beginning, followed by his monologue in a state of depression, and in turn by his encounter with Helicanus. In the defective text of the Quarto, Pericles' monologue begins with several lines that are markedly irregular in rhythm, and while most of his speech is unrhymed, it includes three couplets that repeat one or even two words, and that stand out awkwardly even in the writing of the early scenes: done/done (ll. 15-16), honour him/dishonour him (ll. 21-22), being known/be known (ll. 23-24). In the scene's second half, more than once a line seems to have been lost, but its overall style and rhythm resemble those of the opening scene.

The third scene, which presents Thaliard's arrival at Tyre, is lucid, unproblematical, and swift-moving. Thaliard's opening monologue in prose is quite lively and half comic. The rest is in the kind of verse we have by now become accustomed to. Thaliard uses three asides, and as that technique is used still more abundantly in Act II, I will comment on it then. Helicanus, as we now see, deserves Pericles' trust, for he is not only honest but also astute. While most of the verse is unrhymed, Thaliard breaks out into a lighthearted tag when he realizes that Pericles has escaped:

But since he's gone, the king's ears it must please,
He 'scaped the land, to perish at the seas.

(ll. 27-28)

The same or a closely similar rhyme occurs twice more in the play, and at short intervals. When in his second chorus Gower comments on Pericles' voyage after leaving Tharsus, he remarks:

He, doing so, put forth to seas,
Where, when men been, there's seldom ease.

(II. Chorus 27-28)

And four scenes hence, Helicanus resists the pressure of the lords of Tyre to assume the throne with

Take I your wish, I leap into the seas,
Where's hourly trouble for a minute's ease.

(II.iv.43-44)

As Gower's lines fit perfectly into his speech, one might be suspicious about the two other rhymes and blame them on the feeble invention of a reporter. But they do not jar in the least in their context, and they represent only a minor example in a play that is marked by a great deal of repetition. Gower will repeat a point whenever he likes it, however well we know it already. And during the play Pericles travels so often from island to island that by the time we hear of his fifth or sixth voyage, the effect becomes somewhat comic. (Indeed in one production I have seen, it was turned into farce by having a ship painted on cardboard carried across the stage each time.) Further, the rhymed tags are, like other features of the play's language and style of presentation, a spillover from Gower into the enacted episodes.

As the play's fourth scene, which shows Cleon and Dionyza commenting on the famine at Tharsus, is also marked by signs of major textual corruption, I will merely point out how it contrasts in mood and color with the surrounding scenes, and how in it the action stands entirely still for the first fifty-five lines, while Cleon and Dionyza echo each other's lament, until the lord enters announcing the sight of Pericles' ship. We watch Cleon and Dionyza as part of a tableau rather than a drama, the dialogue serving as an accompaniment to what we take in through our eyes. That technique, as we will see, marks several later episodes of the play.

Gower's second chorus first summarizes the contrast between Antiochus' incestuousness and Pericles' goodness, then invites the audience to wait patiently until he shows how "those in troubles reign, / Losing a mite, a mountain gain," before he narrates the ensuing action up to the point of the opening of the next scene. In meter, rhythm, and idiom, the speech is like his previous one. This time, however, he chooses to convey in mid-speech some of the happenings in the highly stylized form of a dumbshow. He does so again at the opening of Act III, and in the middle of Act IV. The old-fashioned semi-dramatic device, popular in plays two generations earlier, suits Gower and his ancient rambling tale perfectly. The three dumbshows, of which two occur in the later, "Shakespearean" acts, provide, like some of the other devices, bridges between the play's archaic presenter and an audience familiar with a subtler and more complex drama.

The prose dialogue of the fishermen Pericles encounters in II.i is, as has generally been agreed, of a higher quality than the surrounding verse. The fishermen's lively wit certainly comes as a welcome change in a play which at this point stands in need of more vigorous and earthy expression if it is to hold the audience's attention. And yet these fishermen are as much a part of the play's story world as the other characters. They are quaintly conceived. Vividly and fancifully as they express themselves, they have no counterpart in life. And Pericles' responses aside as he overhears them suit the play's conventions:

3. FISH.

> . . . Master, I marvel how the fishes live in the sea.

1. FISH.

> Why, as men do a-land: the great ones eat up the little ones. I can compare our rich misers to nothing so fitly as to a whale: a' plays and tumbles, driving the poor

fry before him, and at last devours them all at a mouthful. Such whales have I heard on a' th' land, who never leave gaping till they swallow'd the whole parish, church, steeple, bells, and all.

PER. (ASIDE)

> A pretty moral.

3. FISH.

> But master, if I had been the sexton, I would have been that day in the belfry.

2. FISH.

> Why, man?

3. FISH.

> Because he should have swallow'd me too; and when I had been in his belly, I would have kept such a jangling of the bells, that he should never have left till he cast bells, steeple, church, and parish up again.

· · · · ·

PER. (ASIDE)

> How from the finny subjects of the sea
> These fishers tell the infirmities of men!

(II.i.26-49)

Such light moralizing on what for Jacobean audiences was a familiar comparison between the commonwealth of man and that of fish suits the spirit of a play in whose scenes the action is often made to stand still so that we can take in the new situation and picture. On the modern stage the technique was revived by Brecht.

We noted how both in the scene of the fishermen and in the earlier one at Tharsus, a large part serves not to advance the action but merely to present us with a new tableau in a new setting and with new characters whose dialogue, in cooperation with what we see, establishes the episode's new mood. Only in the later part of these scenes does the action begin to move. But between the scenes, off stage, it moves very swiftly. Therefore, it is not merely Gower's reappearances and his narration of some of the story's events, but also the choice and techniques of the staged episodes, their frequent change in locale from one Mediterranean island to another, and our sense of how much Pericles moves about between the scenes that produce the impression that what we are witnessing is Gower presenting his story mainly in the form of a guided progression of selected shows rather than as a drama. This basic manner of the play holds essentially for its entire length, however much it is qualified by the livelier dramatization of some of the later episodes.

By the opening of II.ii, we find ourselves at Pentapolis, where, on a public way leading to the lists, six knights are passing one by one by a pavilion where King Simonides and his daughter Thaisa are seated. The first five knights, in splendid array, are accompanied by their squires, who hold their shields and hand them to the princess. Each time, she describes the device and reads aloud the motto before passing it on to her father, who, sometimes with a brief comment, returns it through her to the squire. But the entrance of the sixth knight, Pericles himself, comes in sharp contrast, for he wears rusty armor and is unaccompanied. He bears a simple device but presents it, as Simonides comments, with "graceful courtesy." It is a highly colorful but, apart from the obvious contrast, undramatic scene. It happens to be the only episode of the play for which there was no suggestion in the source. Yet a more suitable addition to Gower's story during its revival in 1607 can hardly be imagined. The vogue of tournaments was reaching its high point in popularity at the time. Knights parading past King James's or Queen Anne's pavilion before entering the lists, and presenting to them their elaborately adorned shields with emblematic devices and mottoes, were a frequent spectacle. Sometimes the shields of painted paper were exhibited long after the tournaments. In connection with the scene in *Pericles,* a surviving record from 1613 is all the more intriguing. It tells us that Shakespeare and Burbage received handsome payments of over forty-five shillings each for preparing and painting what were called *imprese,* with emblems and mottoes, for the Earl of Rutland, for use at the tilts on the King's anniversary day of accession. Did Shakespeare paint some of the knights' shields for *Pericles*?

We note the brevity of this scene and, especially, how quickly it ends. The first knight passes by the pavilion after line 16, and by line 46 Simonides has commented on the "pretty moral" of Pericles' device. Then follow merely a few comments by the lords in attendance, answered by the King, which indicate to us sketchily and in stylized form that, unlike them, the King does not underestimate Pericles' worth because of his drab appearance. This takes a mere twelve lines more before the scene ends with shouts from the lists off stage signaling that the tilt is over and Pericles the victor. While the characters on stage talk leisurely, an action of surely more than an hour's length occurs off stage. Such a technique fits both the story, with its multiple "adventures," and the manner of its presentation.

Of the last three scenes of the second act, it could well be said that brevity, ensuring quick movement from one episode to the next, is their only redeeming feature. Any attempt to defend them as literature would be absurd, for they offer little delight to the critical reader. Yet here too, even what seems worst does not seem to prevent them from being quite tolerable theatre. Both their kind of verse and some of their crude dramaturgical devices resemble those of previous scenes, though the sheer whimsicality of King Simonides in the third

and especially the fifth scene is a new element. Both scenes include no fewer than four asides, not all of which are needed for the audience's understanding, a method encountered before in the play. The moralizing and the imagery in Simonides' following lines addressed at his daughter remind one both of Gower and of earlier speeches in the play:

> Princes in this, should live like gods above,
> Who freely give to every one that come to honour
>   them:
> And princes not doing so are like to gnats
> Which make a sound, but kill'd are wonder'd at.
> Therefore . . .
>
> (II.iii.60-63)

The audience should be by then well used to this manner of speaking by characters who, as it were, extend Gower's didactic purpose.

The third scene, in particular, is marked by its several brief and quaint comparisons. It also furnishes an instructive example of how repetition is used in the play. When Pericles is entertained during the banquet, he has not yet revealed his name or background. Simonides therefore asks Thaisa to find out from him who he is. Pericles answers her:

> A gentleman of Tyre; my name Pericles;
> My education been in arts and arms;
> Who, looking for adventures in the world
> Was by the rough seas reft of ships and men,
> And after shipwreck driven upon this shore.
>
> (II.iii.81-85)

The audience notes Pericles' caution in describing himself simply as a gentleman, not as Tyre's prince. Then, however, follows a speech of a kind that dramatists normally do their best to avoid. Returning to her father, Thaisa communicates to him Pericles' answer, shortening it by only a third:

> He thanks your grace; names himself Pericles,
> A gentleman of Tyre,
> Who only by misfortune of the seas
> Bereft of ships and men, cast on this shore.
>
> (II.iii.86-89)

And yet the cumbersome-seeming repetition, with only slight variation, seems appropriate in *Pericles.* The same device had been employed abundantly in Peele's *Old Wives Tale* to deliberative purpose. There as well as here, it suits the manner in which the tale is told.

But what are we to make of Simonides' whimsical pretenses, once he senses how attracted Thaisa is by Pericles, in this and even more in the fifth scene? When the latter scene opens, Simonides informs us in a monologue that he has rid himself of the other knights and that Thaisa has sent him a letter revealing her affection for Pericles. The unlikelihood of a daughter who lives in the same palace as her father communicating with him that way is consistent with the nature and spirit of the story. Simonides welcomes her choice and assertiveness: "Not minding whether I dislike or no." Yet when Pericles enters, Simonides decides to "dissemble it," and over fifty lines of melodrama follow. He begins by praising Pericles, who has still not revealed that he is a prince, as a musician. Pericles reacts to this by slighting his artistic skill with a deference befitting a servant. When Simonides then asks him whether he finds Thaisa attractive, Pericles persists in cautious, noncommittal answers until the King thrusts her letter angrily into his hands. Now the melodrama starts in earnest, with Pericles falling on his knees and protesting innocence while Simonides pretends to become still more irate. When Pericles finds himself called a villain and a traitor, however, he rouses himself to a response worthy of a nobleman, yet only to catch himself short at the thought that Simonides is both the King and Thaisa's father:

> Even in his throat—unless it be the king—
> That calls me traitor, I return the lie.
>
> (II.v.55-56)

Whereupon Simonides expresses in an aside how pleased he is with the response: "Now, by the gods, I do applaud his courage." But he has not done yet; he continues his act after Thaisa arrives, and with yet another aside when he takes her harshly to task:

> Yea, mistress, are you so peremptory?
> *Aside.* I am glad on't with all my heart.—
> I'll tame you, I'll bring you in subjection.
>
> (II.v.72-74)

Another ten lines, and Simonides asks them to join hands and to kiss.

The two chief characteristics of this extraordinary episode are the arbitrary whimsicality of the King's act and the interruption of the act by asides which the audience does not need, knowing as it does from the start that the King is dissembling, and requiring no reminder. The King's conduct looks like a piece of crude and desperate characterization for the sheer sake of achieving some excitement in what has been a singularly static, undramatic play. But as we are made all the more conscious of the crudity of dramatic technique by the series of supererogatory asides, the effect may well be intentionally burlesque. I suggested earlier that Shakespeare's audience was particularly attracted by the antiqueness of Gower as well as of his story. But an audience whose "wit's more ripe" and is used to sophisticated Jacobean drama must have been bemused by the naive simplicity of Gower's outlook and art.

Because his tale and manner are so ancient, *antiquius,* they are not therefore better, *melius.* So the dramatist, aware that this was bound to be part of their response, made a point of catering to it directly from time to time, though of course not so much that they would miss the tale's real enchantment and moving moments. As for ourselves, the sense that the play as a whole reflects on fundamental human experience should not make us overlook all its sheer comedy. At any rate, the sheer corniness of the scene just discussed can have its appeal for actors.

IV

The end of Act II is an obvious point for an intermission. For the action of *Pericles* falls clearly into two parts. During the first two acts, Pericles' fortunes reach a low point when, escaping from his own country, he is shipwrecked and deprived of both companions and means, but from then on they rise rapidly up to his betrothal to the beautiful Thaisa. Similarly, in the second part, Pericles' fortunes sink to their nadir. He loses first his wife in childbirth, and later also his daughter, which causes him to fall into a chronic state of depression. But the final act presents his happy reunion with both Marina and Thaisa. Gower's comment, "I'll show you those in troubles reign, Losing a mite, a mountain gain," applies alike to both parts of his story. The opening of Act III therefore comes almost like a new beginning. And we happen to know that on an early occasion, in 1619, the play was staged at Whitehall in two parts, with the French guests enjoying refreshments before the third act.

This act opens, of course, once more with Gower and his archaic tetrameters. But then, as everyone knows, the style changes startlingly, when Pericles on shipboard addresses the storm. The reason is that Shakespeare's voice is clearly heard for the first time and continues to sound through much of the remainder of the play. Whether in the blank verse of Pericles' own speeches or in the comic and salacious, "realistic," prose of the Mytilene bawds in the fourth act, or in the poetry of the reunion scene with Marina, the new vibrancy, richness of expression, and variety of rhythm infuse the episodes and their characters with life. No longer are they just pasteboard or pantomime, but living human beings. And after the change occurs, we can assume that at least some of the time the audience move forward in their seats toward the actors—even though, as I pointed out near the beginning, a theatre audience is not startled into immediate consciousness of the change, as readers are when they first read the play.

In any event, one should beware of thinking the change to be larger and more absolute than it actually is. If we set Pericles' opening lines in Act III against some typical lame speech from Act I or Act II, the impression is certainly one of sharp contrast. But when we watch the play, the change occurs smoothly. And there are several reasons for this. The action of the first two acts holds its audience by its sheer spectacular quality, and by the speed with which it moves from one episode to the next. Its mode, as I have tried to show, is fitted to Gower, whose speeches and manner establish the atmosphere. He and the very nature of the story lure the audience to be content for a while with watching a series of scenes written in a manner and style that does not bring the characters to full life. The second reason is that the change is far from complete. For neither in dramaturgy nor in style are the play's last three acts consistently "Shakespearean." As was indicated earlier, this is not the case in the final act. For Gower re-enters from time to time, and the style in the acted scenes varies—thrilling at some moments as only Shakespeare can be, flat at others. In Act III, the new vigor of speech, characterization, and drama which marks its opening scene does not continue uniformly. The verse shows greater flexibility, yet at times the former, stiffer mode returns. In each of scenes ii, iii, and iv, what one would proclaim as Shakespearean writing with confident assurance is intermittent while the accustomed highly episodic presentation of the story continues, the scenes moreover remaining very short; III.iii has 41 lines, III.iv a mere seventeen. Act IV seems still more decidedly Shakespearean and benefits both from its new subject matter with Marina and from its contrasts in style. Marina's lyrical poetry in IV.i is followed by the comic lively talk of Pandar, Boult, and Bawd in the second scene. Yet during this rather longer act, Gower makes sure that we do not forget him. He even directs yet a further dumbshow. Now, however, his speech and show are set in sharp contrast with the surrounding scenes, particularly that which follows. Gower concludes:

> . . . while our scene must play
> His daughter's woe and heavy well-a-day
> In her unholy service. Patience, then,
> And think you are all in Mytilen.
>
> (IV.iv.48-51)

As he leaves, two gentlemen enter from the brothel:

1. Did you ever hear the like?
2. No, nor never shall do in such a place as this, she being once gone.
1. But to have divinity preached there! Did you ever dream of such a thing?
2. No, no. Come, I am for no more bawdy-houses. Shall's go hear the vestals sing?

(IV.v.1-7)

From Gower's narrative, this dialogue takes us right into Shakespeare's London, though not for long. For when in the next scene (scene vi) Lysimachus meets Marina, we are, though still in the same setting, back in the world of sheer story. In deference to Gower, Shake-

speare transformed the story only part way, producing thereby a singular effect.

We are happy that from the third act on Shakespeare did give more of a hand to Gower, and produced a livelier, more complex, and more profound drama. If he had not, the play might well have been doomed to a place in his apocrypha. It may then seem idle to think of reasons why he chose to do so rather than have the play continue in its earlier manner throughout. Perhaps he realized that two such short acts were enough; that the play would be sure to hold its audience only if he endowed some of its later action with greater vibrancy; and that the resulting interplay between Gower's style and manner of telling and his own afforded him with the opportunity of indulging in an intriguing theatrical experiment.

V

Close to the beginning of this article I stated that the two standard theories which serve to account for the marked incongruity in the sheer quality of style in *Pericles* deserve our skepticism. But however valiantly I may have argued my alternative thesis, most readers may well react to it with even greater disbelief. If they enjoy my reasoning at all, they will likely take it to be a *jeu d' esprit*, not a view to be taken seriously. I can imagine the response: "I will accept this only if you can tell me of a similar instance where a great writer or artist resorted for a large part of or an entire work to a style so unworthy of his own." The reader knows well that I cannot furnish him with any such instance from Shakespeare's other plays. Nor am I able to produce a similar case from any major Elizabethan or Jacobean or other drama. But fortunately, Gower's famous contemporary, Chaucer, comes to my rescue.[3]

Chaucer included himself among the storytellers of his *Canterbury Tales*. But when his turn comes, he starts with the silly tale of Sir Thopas in jingling rhymes, which appears to go nowhere until the Host interrupts with disgust and calls an end to it:

> 'Namoore of this, for goddes dignitee,'
> Quod oure Hooste, 'for thou makest me
> So wery of thy verray lewednesse
> That, also wisly God my soule blesse,
> Myne eres aken of thy drasty speche;
> Now swiche a rym the devel I biteche!
> This may wel be rym dogerel', quod he.
> 'Why so?', quod I, 'why wiltow lette me
> Moore of my tale than another man,
> Syn that it is the beste rym I kan?'
> 'By God', quod he, 'for pleynly, at a word,
> Thy drasty rymyng is nat worth a toord; . . .'[4]

"Rym dogerel" would serve well enough to describe some of Gower's own as well as some of the play's couplets, and the Host's sentiment, especially that of the last two lines, has been echoed by many commentators on the first two acts of *Pericles*. Chaucer appropriated for his *Rime of Sir Thopas* lines and phrases from several "romances of prys" composed by common rhymesters, and he wove them into a nonsense that evidently becomes too much for the sophisticated and "modern" Host, who is so irritated by the jogtrot that he misses the intent, which is pure burlesque. That, of course, makes Chaucer's approach to his tale fundamentally different from that of the author of *Pericles*. But we have seen how Shakespeare too may be winking at his audience in some of the play's most absurdly devised episodes, for instance in II.v. And if all the play had been written in the manner of its first two acts, a producer might well be justified in thinking that it could only succeed on stage as burlesque. Indeed I saw a production of *Pericles*[5] in that spirit, which proved hilariously entertaining without persuading me that this is how the play ought to be staged. Yet if Shakespeare or whoever wrote the play's first two acts had a chance to respond to the likes of Ben Jonson and later critics who misunderstood their spirit and method and sneered at the "mouldy tale," might he not protest, like Chaucer to the host: "why wiltow lette me / More of my tale than another man, / Sin that it is the beste rym I can?"

After stopping Chaucer's doggerel, the Host of the *Canterbury Tales* permits the pilgrim to redeem himself, but insists that his new tale be without "drasty" rhymes and include "some mirthe or som doctryne." Chaucer obliges with "a litel thing in prose," which turns out to be *The Tale of Melibeus,* nearly a thousand lines long. It contains no mirth whatever, but repetitive doctrine *ad infinitum.* Mockingly, Chaucer satisfies the needs of a more serious-minded audience. Though this second effort is equally burlesque, the Host is this time so pleased that he wishes his wife could have heard the story and been suitably instructed by it. The fun for the reader, of course, arises from his awareness of the contrast, both in style and in narrative artistry, between Chaucer's own two tales and those he wrote so splendidly for his other pilgrims. Again, the case of *Pericles* is obviously different. And yet the play was performed by Shakespeare's company, and it seems probable that many of those who saw it on the Jacobean stage thought that the creator of Falstaff and Hamlet was at least in large part responsible for it, in spite of all its "rym dogerel" and the moldiness of its tale. Nevertheless Heminge and Condell may have been wise to omit the play from the First Folio, sensing as they did that readers of future generations would be prone, without benefit of seeing the play performed in its original spirit, to misunderstand its technique and intent.

Robert French's comment on Chaucer's tale of Sir Thopas, which could be likewise applied to the tale of Melibeus, may help us to understand why in one of Shakespeare's last plays the art is so very different from that of his other work, and in a large part seems so grossly inferior to it:

> *The Rime of Sir Thopas* belongs unquestionably to a late period in Chaucer's career. Only the master craftsman can appropriate the ineptitudes of an inferior art and turn them to ridicule so effectively. The very unevenness of the meter is evidence that the poet has attained such mastery over his medium that he could trifle with the laws of rhythm.[6]

French was answering Skeat, who speculated that Chaucer in his youth may have "tried his hand at such romance writing in all seriousness." Today we are convinced that Shakespeare worked on *Pericles* late in his career, but Skeat's unwarranted guess about Chaucer's tale reminds one of Dryden's claim that "Shakespeare's Muse her Pericles first bore." From the very beginning of his career, Shakespeare's plays were remarkably experimental and innovative. That is clear from both his earliest comedies and history plays as well as *Titus Andronicus.* But only the mature Shakespeare would have seriously considered writing or rewriting a play based on a story so episodic and therefore unsuited to dramatic adaptation, using moreover ancient "moral" Gower as presenter and adhering closely to the narrative's own order. Only then was he prepared to compose a play whose style and dramaturgy were deliberately adapted to an "inferior art."

Yet the work he then created is still far more extraordinary than Chaucer's burlesque tales. And it suggests that when Shakespeare was turning after his tragedies once more to works of an entirely new kind, the romances, his imagination and experimentation took a dazzling turn so great that most producers and critics have failed to understand what happened. We know that after the episodic and simple-seeming *Pericles,* Shakespeare devised for his next romance, *Cymbeline,* a form so extremely complex that it has perplexed critics and producers who regard the play as interestingly experimental but not a success. Among the play's extraordinary features are: the intermingling of stories and characters from ancient Britain and Renaissance Italy; the grotesquely ironic treatment of Imogen, the romantic heroine, when she mistakes the headless body of Cloten for that of her husband; the scene of Posthumus' dream, so unusual in style and content, where the ghosts of his family berate Jupiter for his unfair treatment of their noble descendant; and the long final scene with its series of revelations and submission by Cymbeline to Rome, in spite of his victory. These make *Cymbeline* a play almost as different as *Pericles* from any that Shakespeare had written before. *Cymbeline* was followed by another "tale" in two parts, *The Winter's Tale,* remarkable too for its techniques, though more tightly constructed and dramatic than *Pericles*. Leontes' jealousy, unlike Othello's, arises with a sudden violence, as surprising to his companions as to us, though some critics and psychoanalysts have offered dubious explanations. The stage direction, *Exit, pursued by a bear*, has no parallel elsewhere in Shakespeare, marking as it does the shift in the play's mood from tragedy to comedy, even though we soon learn that Antigonus did not manage to escape. But what, for Shakespeare, is above all surprising in this play is the way he deceives the audience about Hermione's death, and yet, in spite of the trickery, turns the revival of her statue in the final scene into a moving experience. *The Winter's Tale* was followed by *The Tempest*, the most poetic and richly inventive of Shakespeare's romances, with a story that is as mere a tale as the others, but this time resonant with echoes of the immediately contemporary accounts of the experiences by voyagers to America, and fettered by a tight classical construction.

The romances recreate old tales, and it appears that when Shakespeare turned to this new form of drama he realized that for the sake of creating their proper atmosphere he needed to experiment with styles and techniques boldly different from those of his other plays. Further, he decided as he set out that it was desirable to begin by imitating the very manner of early storytellers and plays and even, though of course only part way, their lack of sophistication and crudity of devices and writing. So he revived Gower and his tale, and had him retell it for a while largely in his own manner before making his own presence and art felt. Then, in the plays which follow *Pericles,* Shakespeare step by step discovered the ways of creating a new art entirely his own.

Notes

1. All passages from the play are quoted from the text in my own New Arden edition (London: Methuen, 1963), except that I have conveyed past tense "ed" in the normal modern unelided form.

2. *Pericles,* New Arden ed., p. lv.

3. It was Professor Judith Kennedy who alerted me to this.

4. Cited from F. N. Robinson's edition of *The Complete Works of Geoffrey Chaucer,* Student's Cambridge Edition (Cambridge, Mass.: Houghton Mifflin, 1933), p. 200.

5. Toronto, summer 1971, at the Studio Theatre of the Centre for the Study of Drama; directed by Stephen Katz.

6. Robert French, *A Chaucer Handbook* (New York: F. S. Crofts, 1929), pp. 243-44.

CHARACTER STUDIES

Kenneth J. Semon (essay date spring 1974)

SOURCE: Semon, Kenneth J. "*Pericles*: An Order Beyond Reason." *Essays in Literature* 1, no. 1 (spring 1974): 17-27.

[*In the following essay, Semon argues that* Pericles *conveys a world where moral rules do not apply and where most of the characters respond to events with a sense of unexplained wonder. According to the critic, the only exception to this rule is Gower, who offers a strictly moral perspective that is inadequate in explaining the play's unusual events.*]

Like the tragedies, Shakespeare's last plays work toward evoking the dramatic effect of *admiratio,* or wonder.[1] But the effect of wonder in the tragedies depends upon the actions of a central character, usually those leading to the suffering and death of a great man; whereas, in the last plays, wonder derives from the fantastic and unexpected nature of events. The experience of wonder unique to *Pericles* derives not only from the nature of events but more specifically from the tension between the structure and content of the play—between Gower's mechanical understanding of the actions as he presents them, and the fantastic events which defy such a mechanical understanding.

The world of *Pericles* is morally inscrutable, and the audience, like the characters, can only respond with admiration for the fantastic reconciliations at the end of the play. Gower, who tells a tale of the trimph of the virtuous and the destruction of the vicious, tries and fails to impose a moral on those actions.[2] And during the course of the play many of the characters, besides Gower, seek to impose some kind of formula or rational explanation upon the fantastic events. All of their attempts fail. Only when one accepts the events without trying to explain or control them does one come to some kind of understanding; and that understanding is always beyond any rational explanations.

In *Pericles* one finds a number of scenes in which Shakespeare defines how things happen, and one also finds that how things happen cannot be explained with any consistency by resorting to the various conventional ways of explaining causality. The audience cannot respond to the events with Gower's dull piety but responds with wonder like that of various characters within Gower's presentation. "What world is this?" and "Is not this strange?"[3] seem altogether more appropriate than Gower's long moralistic Epilogue. The wonder expressed within the play, as opposed to Gower's "authorial" statements, shapes and controls the audience's experience of wonder at the end of the play.

I

Throughout *Pericles* occur references to the commonplace ideas of order in the world: for example, the king stands above all men in his kingdom as the gods stand above all men. Simonides expresses this idea when speaking to Thaisa: "for princes are / A model which heaven makes like to itself" (II.ii.10-11). At the banquet following the tournament Pericles observes this same idea of order operating in the court of Simonides:

> Yon king's to me like to my father's picture,
> Which tells me in that glory once he was;
> Had princes sit like stars about his throne,
> And he the sun, for them to reverence.

> (II.iii.37-40)

Earlier, while in Antiochus's court and after having read the riddle, Pericles addresses the king:

> Kings are earth's gods; in vice their law's their will;
> And if Jove stray, who dares say Jove doth ill?

> (I.i.104-05)

The proper response to a king is obedience, whether one believes the king is right or wrong, and this response is parallel to the proper response to the gods.

During the storm scene Pericles is told of Thaisa's death, and like a tragic hero he rails against his fate:

> O you gods!
> Why do you make us love your goodly gifts,
> And snatch them straight away? We here below
> Recall not what we give, and therein may
> Use honour with you.

> (III.i.22-26)

His question is central to Shakespearean tragedy where the commonplace notions of order seem to work, but inappropriate in this play where the stated notions of order do not work consistently. One idea of order in the play is clearly based on the analogy that the gods rule over men as kings rule over kingdoms. The relation between kings and men is clear enough and can be shown to be operating in the play: for example, Pericles is aware of Antiochus's sin, but he is also aware of the necessity for political order and makes no attempt to violate it ("And if Jove stray, who dares say Jove doth ill?"). In the same way causal relations in the temporal order are clear and may be demonstrated: Antiochus, for example, knows that Pericles has discovered the answer to his riddle, hence his desire to have Pericles murdered. But the causal relations between gods and men are not clearly represented; they may only be posited, not observed. Helicanus attributes the death of Antiochus and his daughter to the wrath of the gods (II.iv); but one cannot state that such is unequivocally the case—it may just be one of those fantastic events

which take place so frequently in this play and are beyond any understanding. Even more difficult to reconcile is the fact that according to the commonplace notion expressed in the play that the stars somehow govern our lives, the death of Antiochus's daughter is an impossibility. We learn in the first scene of the play that Antiochus's daughter was born while

> The senate-house of planets all did sit
> To knit in her their best perfections.

> (I.i.11-12)

She was born at the "most propitious time," Hoeniger notes, "and would thus all her life remain under the beneficial influences of the planets." Yet, she is struck by the same lightning bolt as her father.[4] The events in *Pericles,* then, are unlike the events in a tragic structure; there can be no ultimate answers given to questions of why things happen as they do—things simply happen as they do and they happen in an unpredictable way. There is no answer to the question Pericles raises; there is no rational explanation for his suffering. He has not sinned, and in the context of the play it would be difficult, if not ludicrous, to say that the gods are testing his virtue.

By the last act of the play it is clear that as a result of his experience Pericles has come to a new understanding. Like one of the fishermen who helps him in II.i, Pericles learns that "things must be as they may" (l. 112), and that there is no other explanation, no other consolation. When he discovers Thaisa in Diana's temple he expresses his thankfulness:

> You gods, your present kindness
> Makes my past miseries sports. You shall do well,
> That on the touching of her lips I may
> Melt and no more be seen.

> (V.iii.40-43)

The audience cannot see his past miseries as "sports," but still his new found joy overshadows his past suffering. He no longer questions but simply accepts. His response is one of wonder; he does not ask the gods how this has come to be but directs his questions towards Thaisa, who *may* be able to explain things:

> Now do I long to hear how you were found,
> How possibly preserv'd, and who to thank,
> *Besides the gods,* for this great miracle.

> (ll. 56-58. Emphasis mine.)

In this world no possibility is closed, no explanation final, and what is lost may be found again. The restoration of his wife and daughter is wondrous to Pericles and to the audience: wonder is finally the only response to events of this magnitude and in this kind of world. Although they are beyond expectation, they are a part of the wondrous order of things as that order is expressed in the play.

II

In most plays with a chorus figure the relationship between the chorus and the action is simple and without irony. His vision is necessarily more complete and more accurate than that of any of the characters who move within the bounds of his presentation: the chorus controls the action, presents what he wants his audience to see, and summarizes action of little dramatic importance. Consequently the audience's point of view depends significantly upon the things he shows and tells them, and in every instance the audience remains in harmony with him. Shakespeare used such a figure conventionally in *Henry V.* But in *Pericles* he fashioned a chorus unlike most others; for Gower is unable to understand, except in a limited way, the nature of things in the world of the play. The words he uses to describe the action are inadequate, and he fails to perceive the essentially wondrous order that pervades the play.[5] Whereas Pericles learns by the end of the play that the nature of events cannot be understood rationally, Gower persists in his attempts to impose his own moralistic order and meaning on events.

At the beginning of the play Gower calls on the audience not only to use its imagination in viewing the play, but also to judge his "cause":

> What now ensues, to the judgment of your eye
> I give my cause, who best can justify.
>
> (I.Chor.41-42).

Thus we are to judge the credibility of the story and the validity or truth as it applies to "reality." Gower is concerned with teaching, and it is clear that he serves as a guide who is able to "stand i' th' gaps to teach . . . / The stages of our story" (IV.iv.8-9), and as a moral instructor.[6] But in fulfilling his responsibilities as a moral instructor he is limited by the inability of his narrow moral statements to explain events represented in poetry. At several points in his narrative he presents us with his own judgments, but never with more vigor than in the Epilogue.[7] In *Pericles,* he tells us, we have seen "Virtue" "assail'd with fortune fierce and keen," "preserv'd from fell destruction's blast" (Epilogue 4-5), and we have heard how "wicked" Cleon and his wife came to ruin for their "cursed deed." One does not question the validity of Gower's judgments so much as one questions their ability to explain either the characters (it is too easy to call Cleon wicked, for example) or the significance of the characters' actions. Gower's comments are inappropriate (just like Pericles's "tragic question") except to his own limited perspective. His comments are not true to our more complicated response to the actions of the play. The effect of his summary is merely to emphasize his own lack of imagination and to strengthen our response of wonder to the fantastic events at the end of the play.

His summary works as a foil by suddenly returning us to the "common sense" rationality of the world outside the play where every event would *seem* to have a moral explanation.

We may compare the conflict between Gower's inadequate summary and the emotional force of the play with the tension between the structural and emotional movement of a Shakespearean tragedy. Structurally, the tragedies move from chaos to order. But the fact that Fortinbras is to rule Denmark is no compensation for the loss of Hamlet and all which that loss signifies. Fortinbras, then, functions as one way of structurally "rounding off" the play, and some have argued that we are to rejoice that the political order has been reestablished. Yet the audience is awe-stricken. Fear and sorrow have led them to admiration, to wonder, and that response is much too strong to be mitigated by a set speech. Similarly, at the end of *King Lear,* although the state may now enjoy the benefits of renewed order, we, like Kent, remain awed by the magnitude of the suffering we have witnessed: "The wonder is he hath endur'd so long" (V.iii.316). The contrast between our sense of wonder and the insignificance of the "proper" structural response heightens our initial response of wonder. In the same way, Gower's obsession with rationality—he is the only one in the play who doesn't learn—and with morality (in its most limited sense), leads us to experience more fully the wonder of the play.

Gower's purpose is to teach and to delight (I.Chor.7-16), and in order to accomplish that purpose he feels it necessary to supply the audience with his own judgment. He has emphasized our responsibility to use our imagination and judge the action, and in doing so we find his moralistic judgments inadequate: they cannot explain our wonder at the fantastic turn of events. Other characters within the play attempt to impose meaning and structure on events, and except for Marina, they fail to find a significant explanation.

At the beginning of I.iv. Tarsus is in the midst of a famine. Cleon, the Governor, laments the condition of his city. In searching for a way to deal with his desperate situation he resorts to a rather morbid rationalization in which he would ease his own sorrow by thinking upon the sorrow of others (ll. 1-3). Yet Dionyza points out the inconsistency of his position; to think on the sorrows of others would only intensify his own grief. Then Cleon describes his city's fall from a thriving place in which "towers bore heads so high they kiss'd the clouds, / And strangers ne'er beheld but wond'red at" (ll. 24-25), and recounts the terrible plight which has befallen the city. He does not seek reasons for the misfortune Tarsus suffers. Rather he deals with his situation by holding forth in a manner reminiscent of "moral Gower":

O, let those cities that of plenty's cup
And her prosperities so largely taste,
With their superfluous riots, hear these tears!
The misery of Tharsus may be theirs.

(ll. 52-55)

He acts as if he were presiding over a *de casibus* story in the *Mirror for Magistrates* and searching for something meaningful, or beneficial, for his audience. Yet the immediate context of his pronouncement is not that of a moral tale, and thus it is no more than a cry of anguish in an apparent void. He can make no sense of his condition.

Directly after his expression of despair a group of ships is sighted heading for Tarsus. When Cleon hears of the ships, he states, reasonably, that when a country is weak, another country will invade and conquer; Cleon is unable to imagine any other motive, and he feels his thinking is unassailable. When he is told that the ships are flying white flags and seem to come in peace, he reasonably states another commonplace: "Who makes the fairest show means most deceit" (l. 75). If one has drawn any moral lesson from the first episode of the play (in which Pericles learns this lesson at the court of Antiochus), it would justify Cleon's belief in this instance; and so it is ironically apparent when Pericles greets Cleon and proclaims his good intentions, that such lessons are not of any great value:

And these our ships, you happily may think
Are like the Trojan horse was stuff'd within
With bloody veins expecting overthrow,
Are stor'd with corn to make your needy bread. . . .

(ll. 92-95)

Pericles acknowledges Cleon's fear that things may not be as they seem, and in context his point is ironic: that things are what they seem, though not as they had seemed to Cleon. Like Gower's moralizing, Cleon's quasi-rational assumptions about events lead him to false conclusions—conclusions which do not account for the essentially wondrous nature of things in the world of *Pericles*. The pattern of unexpected and seemingly miraculous deliverance from suffering first begins to take shape in this scene. In a sense this pattern teaches us more than Gower can about how to respond to the events of the play. Cleon has exhausted his rational abilities, and when he learns of Pericles's mission he is speechless. His reaction is to drop to his knees, and he never questions Pericles's generosity or the reasons behind that generosity.

Along with the examples of Gower and Cleon, one finds other instances of ironic rationality or the ineffectiveness of quasi-rational efforts at understanding within the play. Perhaps the most obvious case occurs in II.i, the scene in which the fishermen discover Pericles after he has been shipwrecked. The first fisherman, a man of worldly wisdom, uses one of his friend's statements as a cue for some homespun philosophy:

3 FISH.

Master, I marvel how the fishes live in the sea.

1 FISH.

Why, as men do a-land: the great ones eat up the little ones. I can compare our rich misers to nothing so fitly as to a whale: a' plays and tumbles, driving the poor fry before him, and at last devours them all at a mouthful. Such whales have I heard on a' th' land, who never leave gaping till they swallow'd the whole parish, church, steeple, bells, and all.

PER. [*ASIDE.*]

A pretty moral.

3 FISH.

But, master, if I had been the sexton, I would have been that day in the belfry.

2 FISH.

Why, man?

3 FISH.

Because he should have swallow'd me too; and when I had been in his belly, I would have kep such a jangling of the bells, that he should never have left till he cast bells, steeple, church, and parish up again.

(II.i.26-43)

Pericles's comment, which I take to be spoken seriously (he is too exhausted for irony), as well as the metaphor the first Fisherman uses, are undercut by the absurd reasoning of the third Firsherman. Though based upon a too literal understanding, his reasoning is sound enough and makes a travesty of the first Fisherman's metaphor. The metaphor by which the first Fisherman seeks to explain a fact in life is simply limited in application: for example, it cannot accout for Simonides's actions. Like Gower's summary in the Epilogue and Cleon's conclusions about "seeming," the metaphor cannot withstand experience because it is too exclusive. I would not say there is no element of truth in the elder Fisherman's "pretty moral"; but his metaphor does not explain as much as either he or Pericles seems to think. The world does not operate according to proverbs.

Pericles himself is subject to the limits of reason in II.v, when Simonides presents him with a letter in which Thaisa speaks of her love for "the knight of Tyre." In some respects the situation is parallel to that of I.i. Pericles reads the letter as he had read the riddle, and fears for his life. He first pleads his innocence, and when the king calls him a traitor he rallies his courage and almost gives the king the lie. From his previous experience in the court of Antiochus, and his inability to see that the king is toying with him, Pericles misunderstands his situation. He really need not fear that he is too low to marry Thaisa; he need only inform Simonides of his true rank. The problem is resolved comically when Thaisa enters and Pericles asks her to

> Resolve your angry father, if my tongue
> Did e'er solicit, or my hand subscribe
> To any syllable that made love to you.

THAI.

> Why, sir, say if you had, who takes offence
> At that would make me glad?

(ii.v.67-71)

Thus, for Pericles, as well as for other characters in the play, that which seems clearly to be the case is not always so. Past experience and common knowledge cannot always be relied upon in order to explain either the present situation or the way in which one should deal with it. This is not to say that experience and knowledge have no value, merely that their value is limited in developing a true understanding of the world.

In contrast to the other characters in the play, Marina never tries to impose a false order on the events of her life. She alone seems to intuit the wondrous nature of the play's world. Her birth, in contrast to the birth of Antiochus's daughter, takes place under the worst possible conditions. When Lychorida first presents the infant to Pericles she tells him: "Here is a thing too young for such a place, / Who, if it had conceit, would die" (III.i.15-16), and Pericles expresses a similar opinion about Marina's poor start in life. When we first see Marina "full-grown" at Tarsus, we learn that she too reflects upon the storm at her birth and views it as a fitting metaphor of her life, at least up to this point:

> Ay me! poor maid,
> Born in a tempest, when my mother died,
> This world to me is as a lasting storm,
> Whirring me from my friends.

(IV.i.17-20)

Like Pericles in the storm scene, she laments her existence, and like him she is subject to intense suffering and injustice throughout the action of the play. Except for the scene with Pericles on board the ship, she appears on stage only when her life is threatened: by a murderer, by pirates, and in a brothel. But the tone of her lament is more gentle than that of Pericles at the nadir of his fortunes; and it is at once a recognition and an acceptance of her situation. She neither rails against the gods nor seeks reasons for her misfortunes; Marina does not give up, as Pericles does.

> I am a maid,
> My lord, that ne'er before invited eyes,

> But have been gaz'd on like a comet; she speaks,
> My lord, that, may be, hath endur'd a grief
> Might equal yours, if both were justly weigh'd.

(V.i.84-88)

Even as she faces her father and has gained the "conceit" Lychorida spoke of, she does not consider death. She perceives her life differently from the way Pericles perceives his, and she seems to possess a quality which sets her off from all of the other characters in the play.

Gower notes this quality in Marina, and in the prologue to Act IV he mentions that she is the source of "general wonder" (IV. Chor. 11).[8] Even the unimaginative Gower becomes lyrical when he speaks of her accomplishments:

> She sings like one immortal, and she dances
> As goddess-like to her admired lays.
> Deep clerks she dumbs, and with her neele composes
> Nature's own shape, of bud, bird, branch, or berry,
> That even her art sisters the natural roses;
> Her inkle, silk, twin with the rubied cherry. . . .

(V. Chor. 3-8)

Gower describes the quality related to her acceptance of her existence as the element of wonder, and we are moved to admiration when we see her acceptance of "awkward casualties" in the same way the people of Tarsus are moved by her grace and "deep clerks" are moved by her accomplishments.

Marina's ability to evoke wonder in those around her is directly responsible for her "escape" from the brothel. In IV.v, two gentlemen who are leaving the brothel vow that they are "for no more bawdy-houses," and they set off to hear the vestals sing. The comic use of hyperbole in this brief scene emphasizes Marina's special quality; that the scene verges on hilarity in no way detracts from the effect. The hyperbole functions to approximate, perhaps even to set an outermost limit upon, the quality of her character and her ability to move others to wonder.

Marina's ability to evoke wonder is most clearly (and seriously) illustrated during the recognition scene on Pericles's ship. Pericles has not spoken to anyone for three months, since the time Cleon had told him of Marina's "death." Lysimachus, the Governor of Mytilene, describes Marina's powers to Helicanus and assures him that she will "make a batt'ry through [Pericles's] ports" (V.i.46). The audience by this time in the play has witnessed the association between healing and music in Cerimon's restoration of Thaisa (III.ii), and Gower has told of Marina's musical abilities which, "when to th' lute / She sung . . . made the night-bird mute" (IV. Chor. 25-26). We are prepared for Marina's song to restore Pericles's mental state, but at the end of that song Pericles only stirs and pushes Marina back. After she says that she too "hath endur'd a grief / Might equal yours" (V.i.88-89), Pericles begins to come to his senses. He responds to her presence and begins to question her. Marina replies:

> If I should tell my history, 'twould seem
> Like lies, disdain'd in the reporting.
>
> (ll. 118-19)

Pericles protests:

> Falseness cannot come from thee, for thou look'st
> Modest as Justice, and thou seem'st a palace
> For the crown'd Truth to dwell in. I will believe thee,
> And make my senses credit thy relation
> To points that seem impossible; for thou look'st
> Like one I lov'd indeed.
>
> (ll. 120-25)

>   Tell thy story;
> If thine consider'd prove the thousandth part
> Of my endurance, thou art a man, and I
> Have suffer'd like a girl; yet thou dost look
> Like Patience gazing on kings' graves, and smiling
> Extremity out of act.
>
> (ll. 134-39)

Pericles recognizes not only that "My dearest wife / Was like this maid" (ll. 106-07) but also the quality particular to Marina herself. She is able not only to stir him from his melancholy but also to evoke a response that moves from the physical action of pushing her away to a confused verbal action ("My fortunes—parentage—good parentage—/ To equal mine—was it not thus?" ll. 97-98), to a moment of wondrous joy:

> O Helicanus, strike me, honour'd sir!
> Give me a gash, put me to present pain,
> Lest this great sea of joys rushing upon me
> O'erbear the shores of my mortality,
> And drown me with their sweetness.
>
> (ll. 190-94)

Her honesty, her endurance, her parentage all prove a source of wonder to Pericles, and the scene itself evokes wonder in the audience.[9]

III

The pattern we first witnessed with Cleon and Pericles, a movement from sorrow to questioning, from questioning to wonder, is repeated several other times during the process of the play. And during those other episodes the audience is taught to respond appropriately to the world of the play.

One of the many fantastic events is narrated by Helicanus:

> Antiochus from incest liv'd not free;
> For which, the most high gods not minding longer
> To withhold the vengeance that they had in store,
> Due to this heinous capital offence,
> Even in the height and pride of all his glory,
> When he was seated in a chariot
> Of an inestimable value, and his daughter with him,
> A fire from heaven came, and shrivell'd up
> Their bodies. . . .
>
> (II.iv.2-10)

Escanes, who has been listening to the narration, presumably responding in awe, anticipates our own reluctance to believe that such things can happen: "'Twas very strange" (l. 13). Since he can react this way within the play, we are more willing to accept the event, and we agree that, indeed, it *was* very strange.[10]

The world of wondrous events which most fully embodies the order of things in this play is apparent in Ephesus, where Cerimon works his magic and where Thaisa awaits Pericles. After the stormy night when Thaisa dies and is cast off the ship, her coffin is washed upon Ephesus's shore and brought to Cerimon. The coffin is "wondrous heavy" and from it pours forth a "delicate odor," and the whole scene is, as the Second Gentleman observes, "Most strange!" Even more miraculous is that the possibility for recovery exists. As Cerimon returns Thaisa to life our response to the scene is carefully guided by the observers on stage:

> The heavens, through you, increase our wonder,
> And set up your fame forever.
>
> (III.ii.98-99)

2 GENT.

> Is this not strange?

1 GENT.

> Most rare.
>
> (ll. 108-09)

Though Cerimon seems confident of his power to restore her, and assures the gentlemen who watch him that such events may be within the realm of possibility ("I heard of an Egyptian / That had nine hours lien dead, / Who was by good appliance recovered," ll. 86-88), he too responds with wonder at Thaisa's fantastic beauty:

>   She is alive!
> Behold, her eyelids, cases to those
> Heavenly jewels which Pericles hath lost,
> Begin to part their fringes of bright gold.
> The diamonds of a most praised water
> Doth appear to make the world twice rich. Live,
> And make us weep to hear your fate, fair creature,
> Rare as you seem to be.
>
> (ll. 99-106)

And like Thaisa, having witnessed the first miraculous event on stage, we ask, "What world is this?" (l. 107)

Thaisa's question is central to the play. One cannot divide the play into several worlds as one can with *The Merchant of Venice* where one speaks of the "world of Belmont" and its relationship to the "world of Venice," or in *Romeo and Juliet* where one speaks of the "world of the lovers" and the "world of society"; wondrous things happen in Antioch, Tarsus, Pentapolis, Mytilene, and Ephesus. The "world" of the play is constant and is a world where the best explanation of events seems to be that things happen because they do; no amount of questioning can delve any further. When the characters meet their proper and respective moral rewards, we are as satisfied as Gower; the way their ends are achieved causes considerable surprise and satisfaction, even though Gower assures us early in his narration that

> I'll show you those in troubles reign,
> Losing a mite a mountain gain.
>
> (II. Chor. 7-8)

Just as the world of the play is constant, so is our response to that world. We are filled with wonder at Thaisa's restoration; we are filled with wonder for Marina; and the recognition scene between Marina and her father, and later, between Pericles and Thaisa, affect us with the greatest awe. And though we have been presented with various explanations that seem, if only for a moment, to be valid, we cannot accept any of them as final. We return to our world with something of Marina's and Pericles's understanding that one can only note one's own suffering and joy, and never come to any final understanding. The morally inscrutable world we see on stage is deeply related to the inscrutable forces which shape our own lives.

Notes

1. For the importance of the idea of wonder in Shakespeare's tragedies see J. V. Cunningham, *Woe or Wonder: The Emotional Effect of Shakespearean Tragedy* (Denver: Alan Swallow, 1951). For the importance of wonder in the last plays see Joan Hartwig, *Shakespeare's Tragicomic Vision* (Baton Rouge: Louisiana State Univ. Press, 1972). Her introductory chapter and the chapter on *Cymbeline* are especially relevant, pp. 18-33, 61-103. Also, see my article, "Fantasy and Wonder in Shakespeare's Last Plays," forthcoming in *Shakespeare Quarterly.*

2. It is possible that Shakespeare inherited Gower from an earlier version of the play. However, such speculation is outside the scope of this essay. The best summary of the texual problems may be found in F. D. Hoeniger's New Arden edition (London: Methuen, 1963), pp. xxiii-lii, *passim.* J.

P. Brockbank, in a recent article, felt the need to bring up the matter of the text but gracefully entered into a critical reading of the play, saying, "In what follows I have expressed a disposition but abstained from arguing a case," in "'Pericles' and the Dream of Immortality," *Shakespeare Survey,* 24 (1971) 106. I follow suit. For another discussion of the problem see Hartwig, pp. 181-83.

3. *Pericles,* ed. F. D. Hoeniger (London: Methuen, 1963), III.ii.107 and 108. All references to the text are to this edition.

4. Compare the conditions surrounding Marina's birth:

> For a more blusterous birth had never babe. . . .
> Thou hast as chiding a nativity
> As fire, air, water, earth, and heaven can make,
> To herald thee from the womb.
>
> (III.i.28, 32-34)

If astrology were a reliable indication of the state of affairs, Antiochus's daughter would have had better fortune and Marina would never have lived to share in the reconciliations and wonder at the end of the play.

5. See John Arthos, *The Art of Shakespeare* (London: Bowes and Bowes, 1964), for an opposite view of Gower's understanding. Arthos feels that Shakespeare uses Gower to "tell us what this strange succession of adventures means, and what, especially, it means to him, an ancient poet brought back from death to put the play on" (p. 147). It would be interesting to compare Gower's perception of "his play" with the view of the Chorus in *Dr. Faustus.*

6. This function, of course, is conventional.

7. See also II. Chor. 1-4, and IV. Chor. 37-45.

8. One should distinguish between Gower's use of wonder as an attribute, and my use of wonder as a dramatic response.

9. Though Marina is a source of general wonder both to the characters in the play and to the audience, she never becomes an abstraction. This is partly because of her more "worldly" knowledge, her ability to get out of a difficult situation (the brothel, for example, where she uses what the bawd calls "virginal fencing"), and the fact that of all the characters in the play her immediate motivation is the most clearly drawn; she is paradoxically the most "realistic."

10. Cf. Hippolyta's "story of the night" speech in *A Midsummer-Night's Dream,* V. i, or the Gentlemen in *The Winter's Tale,* V.ii.

Walter F. Eggers, Jr. (essay date spring 1975)

SOURCE: Eggers, Jr., Walter F. "Shakespeare's Gower and the Role of the Authorial Presenter." *Philological Quarterly* 54, no. 2 (spring 1975): 434-43.

[*In the following essay, Eggers focuses on the character of Gower as an "authorial presenter," a dramatic role common during late 1500s and early 1600s. The critic suggests that this convention gives the play authority by linking it to the past and by providing the audience with a different perspective on the story.*]

In 1606, the prologue to a private-theater play declared, "Inductions are out of date, and a Prologue in Verse, is as stale as a black Velvet Cloak, and a Bay Garland."[1] These lines testify to the popular fashion of presenters in Elizabethan and Jacobean drama, a fashion that persisted in the public theater despite this private-theater caveat. Within the next two years, one of the most popular public-theater plays, *Pericles*, featured a presenter who spoke in archaic tetrameters, wore the traditional cloak, and carried bays.[2] The presenter in *Pericles* is the author of the story behind the play, "ancient" Gower. In the vividness of his characterization, Gower is one of a kind, but as an "authorial presenter" he is also the epitome of a well-established conventional role.

The convention of the authorial presenter has not adequately been explored, and for this reason the special complexities of Gower's character are unrecognized. Any presenter distinguishes himself from ordinary "inductions" and "prologues" by being characterized, by appearing frequently throughout the play, and by speaking directly to the theater audience. An authorial presenter is a more radically presentational device: he provides the audience not only a framework but, through his character as an author, a special perspective on the play proper. Some critics have speculated on the remote origins of the general role of presenter.[3] F. D. Hoeniger, in the introduction to his New Arden edition of *Pericles*, finds exclusive precedents for Gower in two contemporary plays.[4] But the following list shows that the role of the authorial presenter has roots deep in the history of Elizabethan drama and that (probably because of the popularity of *Pericles*) its greatest vogue was in the public theaters during the years after it was ridiculed on the private stage:

*Lydgate in *2 The Seven Deadly Sins* (Tarleton? 1585?).

Venus in Greene's *Alphonsus, King of Aragon* (1587-88).

Ate in *Locrine* (Peele? Greene? 1591-95).

Truth in Yarington's *Two Lamentable Tragedies* (1594-ca.98).

*Skelton in Chettle and Munday's *The Downfall of Robert, Earl of Huntington,* and *The Death of Robert, Earl of Huntington* (both performed in 1598).

Tragedy in *A Warning for Fair Women* (Heywood? ca. 1598-99).

St. Dunstan in Haughton's *Grim, the Collier of Croydon* (performed in 1600).

*Guicciardini in Barnes' *The Devil's Charter* (1607).

Fame in Day, W. Rowley, and Wilkins' *The Travels of the Three English Brothers* (1607).

*Gower in Shakespeare's (and another?) *Pericles* (1606-08).

*Homer in Heywood's *The Golden Age* (1609-11), *The Silver Age* (1609-12), and *The Brazen Age* (1610-13).

*Bardh in *The Valiant Welshman* (Armin? Anton? 1610-15).

*Raynulph Higden in Middleton's (and W. Rowley?) *Hengist, King of Kent, or, The Mayor of Queenborough* (1615-20?).

*Josephus in Markham and Sampson's *Herod and Antipater* (ca. 1619-22).[5]

This list distinguishes full-fledged authorial presenters (marked with asterisks) from presenters of a vaguely authorial character. As we see, authorial presenters can be found as early as in the fifteen-eighties. Considering the enormous quantity of lost popular dramatic romances from even earlier in the period,[6] the true prototype of this group of characters may never be found. The question is, what was the value of this conventional role? When the convention was most popular, the audience had certain expectations of the role, and it was the playwright's business to make use of those expectations. What did the popular audience expect of a character like Gower? A survey of examples should enable us to determine typical features of the authorial presenter, and on that basis we can consider the special achievement of Shakespeare's Gower.

I

A presenter's position on stage always carries special prominence and "authority": he stands alone between the play proper and the audience, at some distance from both. "Authorial" presenters typically appear often enough to seem to exercise continuous control over the presentation of their plays. Several deliver prologues and epilogues and make regular appearances between acts; Gower makes an exceptional eight appearances in *Pericles*.[7] Certain authorial presenters effect major structural transitions. Lydgate apparently holds several different playlets together in *2 The Seven Deadly Sins* (we have only the "plot" of this play to go by); in the middle of *The Death of Robert*, Skelton concludes the tragedy of Robin Hood and introduces the tragedy of Matilda with a long narrative and three dumbshows; in one of Gower's narrative choruses in *Pericles*, the audience must imagine that Marina has matured from an infant to a young woman; seventeen years pass between the first two acts of *The Golden Age*, and each act of

The Brazen Age is a separate playlet, all of which Homer tries to unify.[8] (Considered as a group, the Ages-plays have an immense narrative scope, but Homer provides some continuity among the plays in which he appears.)

If the single function of these presenters were to expedite the narrative, there would be little reason for their sometimes vivid characterization. The more familiar figure of the nameless chorus can perform a narrator's function less obtrusively. But the presenters on our list are not only narrators but didactic expositors, and this second function is more important as the presenter's authorial character is more conspicuous.

The presenter's position on stage calls attention to the play as a play, and when he moralizes from that position, the framework of the play is manifestly didactic. Guicciardini describes the various scenes of *The Devil's Charter* as "the visible and speaking shewes, / That bring vice into detestation" (3.5, ll. 1696-97);[9] and in this framework it is not inappropriate for the hero himself to turn to the audience and declare his story to be exemplary: "Learne wicked worldlings, learne, learne, learne by me / To saue your soules, though I condemned be" (5.6, ll. 3246-47). Between each act of *A Warning for Fair Women,* Tragedy presents dumb-shows containing allegorical representations of characters' motives, turning those characters into examples.[10] In *Two Lamentable Tragedies,* Truth draws a lesson from the revulsion of the audience when Merry hacks Beech's body and stuffs it into a sack: "All you the sad spectators of this Acte . . . oh be farre of, to harbour such a thought, / As this audacious murtherer put in vre."[11] Then, to stop our tears, he reminds us that "this deede is but a playe" (sig. E2[v]). Perhaps the most overtly didactic of these related plays is *Locrine,* in which, between each act, Ate presents dumbshows which are not explicitly related to the plot but function as visual emblems of Latin mottos; Ate is the expositor of these emblems and relates their lessons to the play by analogy. Twice in *Locrine,* once in a chorus and once in the dialogue (sigs. E3[v] and K2[r]), the broad lesson is drawn which enforces all these others: "our play is but a tragedy."[12]

There is an in an inherent didactic value in the characterization of "authorial" presenters, and the authority of their lessons is enhanced by a special feature of characterization which most of them share, antiquity. This explains the traditional cloak and archaic verse.[13] In the prologue to the first of the Ages-plays, Homer demands our attention and respect as only the original of all authors can:

> I was the man
> That flourish'd in the worlds first infancy:
> When it was yong, and knew not how to speake,

Leonine, Marina, and pirates in Act IV, scene i of Pericles.

> I taught it speech, and vnderstanding both
> Euen in the Cradle: Oh then suffer me,
> You that are in the worlds decrepit Age,
> When it is neere his vniuersall graue,
> To sing an old song . . .
>
> (*The Golden Age,* 1.1)[14]

Venus, the presenter of *Alphonsus, King of Aragon,* says she is compelled to take the role of author because there are no more Homers to sing the praises of her hero;[15] in *The Valiant Welshman,* Fortune claims that the story of her hero merits Homer's pen and so calls on the Welsh Bardh "That long hath slept."[16] Often the idea of a "revival" is explicit. At the end of that last play, the Bardh returns to his tomb expecting to be revived for a sequel; in *Hengist, King of Kent,* Raynulph Higden's *Polychronicon* "raiseth him, as works do men, / To see long-parted light again."[17] In this way, Homer's argument that the world continues to degenerate from its original perfection is appropriate even in unclassical contexts: the Prologue to *Herod and Antipater* explains the revival of Josephus in the same terms:

> Wit hath runne
> In a Zodaicall Circle, like the Sunne,
> Through all Inuention; which is growne so poore
> She can shew nought, but what has been before.[18]

The lesson is that "Ancient stories have been best" (*Hengist*, 1. Prol. 10) and that their original authors can tell them with most authority.

The moral values which the authorial presenter inculcates in the audience are thus the heroic values of an older generation or an earlier age—what moves Skelton to present the legend of Robin Hood is that "poets laureate . . . from their graves, / See asses and knaves."[19] This aspect of the authorial presenter's role is typified by two allegories, Fame in *The Travels of the Two English Brothers* and Truth in *Two Lamentable Tragedies*. The presenter keeps the memory of his hero alive in fame,[20] and he enacts the role of Truth in the familiar allegory of *Veritas temporis filia*.[21] This association is made explicit in at least two plays from this period, in *Herod and Antipater*—

> Times eldest Daughter (Truth) presents our Play;
> And, from forgotten Monuments of clay,
> Calls up th' Heroicke Spirits of old Times . . .
> And with Her owne Tongue, and owne Phrase, to tell
> The actions they have done
>
> (sig. A4ᵛ)

—and quite elaborately in the framing induction of Dekker's *The Whore of Babylon* (ca. 1606-07).

The didacticism of these plays is never somber and not usually even consistent. Homer demands a profound respect for himself and his story, as we have seen, but sometimes he elicits an almost jeering incredulity from the audience—"Gods will be gods," he says, summing up one episode and introducing the next (*The Golden Age*, 4.1, p. 53). Some of the most frivolous plays we have examined make the strongest claims that their stories have an ennobling effect on the audience.[22] Still, the role of the presenter as narrator and expositor is a potentially serious one. Homer's didacticism can be understood as a reflection of Heywood's own intention "to mooue the spirits of the beholder to admiration," "to new mold the harts of spectators and fashion them to the shape of any noble and notable attempt."[23] At least in respect to the wonders that these plays dramatize, the presenter speaks for the author in claiming the audience's attention. This brings us to Gower's role in *Pericles*.

II

Gower was at least partly Shakespeare's conception, and *Pericles* was the most popular Elizabethan play with a presenter. For these reasons critics continue to discuss Gower's individual character. Gower is also the authorial presenter whose conventional role is most fully developed. We have observed that he exercises almost continuous control over the presentation of the play, appearing more frequently than any other presenter on our list, and that his archaic language and costume help to characterize him uniquely. Shakespeare (or his collaborator) not only adopts the conventional role in its fullest form but turns it to a special purpose. As we shall see, the interplay between Gower and the play proper is a significant interpretive problem from the beginning to the end. Gower comes on stage seeming not to know what to claim for the presentation that follows; by the end, the wonders that have been dramatized have outstripped his narrow view, and his simple moralizing epilogue seems inadequate. The special complexities of Gower's role can best be understood in light of the conventions we have examined.

In the prologue to the opening scene, Gower ascribes apparently opposite purposes and effects to *Pericles*. First he calls his story an "old song" that

> hath been sung at festivals,
> On ember-eves and holy-ales;
> And lords and ladies in their lives
> Have read it for restoratives.
>
> (5-8)[24]

In the sense of these lines, the "restorative" is a kind of physic; as an old story, easy to digest, it restores health to the spirits of those in the audience who will take it straight. With the proper frame of mind, the audience's enjoyment should be simple and immediate, and here Gower encourages the audience not to be too critical. With the very next lines, however, Gower describes a different kind of "restoration":

> The purchase is to make men glorious,
> *Et bonum quo antiquius eo melius.*
>
> (9-10)

In this second perspective, the story-teller who restores life to a "mouldy tale" like *Pericles* is seen to effect nothing less than a renewal of modern culture. For this purpose, the older and ruder the tale—and, by implication, the more critical the audience—the better.

These apparently opposite views of the play's effect do accord with Gower's conventional role as narrator and expositor, for it is Gower's idea that theatrical presentation helps him enforce the didactic lessons of his story—however artistically inept the resulting drama may be. He recognizes that the drama is incapable of representing his story faithfully to a modern audience, first because no theater can contain its epic proportions and second because the story and Gower himself are antique, separated from the modern audience by a great gulf of time. On both accounts he is apologetic, but for his didactic purposes the double measure of "patience" required of his audience is doubly valuable.

Usually when Gower solicits the patience of the audience it is to make one of the great leaps in time and space which his story requires from one episode to the next:

> Be attent,
> And time that is so briefly spent
> With your fine fancies quaintly eche . . .
>
> (3. Ch. 11-13)

> The unborn event
> I do commend to your content;
> Only I carried winged time
> Post on the lame feet of my rime;
> Which never could I so convey,
> Unless your thoughts went on my way.
>
> (4. Ch. 45-50)

(See also 4.4.1-4, 5. Ch. 21, 5.2.15-20, and Epil. 17.) On the basis of this kind of language, Gower has been compared with the Chorus in *Henry V*,[25] where it is clear what serious purpose such language serves. By calling attention to the audience's role in sustaining the play imaginatively, the Chorus in *Henry V* invites the audience to participate directly in the celebration of the hero. The incapacity of the Chorus, speaking on behalf of the author or the company, to represent the hero as truly "like himself" (Prol. 6) is a measure of the greatness of the hero's story. Choric reminders about the inadequacy of dramatic representation are no way to induce a "suspension of disbelief" in the audience, but Shakespeare seems to intend a different effect: in *Henry V*, active "belief" on the part of the audience has positive didactic value.[26] Likewise, Gower's serious claim that he "restores" his audience is a tribute to the constructive power of the audience's imagination.

Gower's attitude is further clarified by how he expects the antiquity of the story to affect the audience, and in this respect particularly he seems to speak for his fellow authorial presenters as well. The antiquity of the story is reason for Gower to fear that it might not entertain a modern audience; yet on this account, too, he is confident that the presentation of the story will carry didactic value, for the antiquity of the story is what gives his lessons strong authority. The story is older than Gower himself, as he reminds us when he insists that we credit its improbable plot—"I tell you what mine authors say" (1. Ch. 20); "it is said / For certain in our story" (4. Ch. 19-20); "Marina thus the brothel scapes . . . our story says" (5. Ch. 1-2). The historical time which separates "ancient" Gower from the audience and makes his tale seem "mouldy" also testifies to its enduring didactic value, and any dramatic awkwardness on account of the antiquity of the story only confirms that value.

By this reasoning, the play needs no apology, but Gower delivers an epilogue in which he spells out the lessons of his story one by one and blesses the audience for its "patience." With this final gesture, Gower once more calls attention to the relationship between the story and its presentation, between the antique world of the play proper and the world of the modern audience, and this has two effects which Gower recognizes: the audience celebrates the hero and takes the lessons represented in the story to itself. From Gower's standpoint, the simple advantage of dramatizing a story is that seeing is believing—

> What now ensues, to the judgment of your eye
> I give, my cause who best can justify
>
> (1. Ch. 41-42)

—but "belief" is no end in itself. Drama can illustrate the lessons of *Pericles* more vividly than mere narrative can, but Gower must be there to point up the lessons; unless the audience has distance enough to recognize the story as an illustration, the lessons of the play might be lost. What Gower (and his fellow presenters) require of the audience is deliberate participation in recreating the story as drama.

In the special case of *Pericles,* this final claim of didactic value may be an ultimate complication of the authorial presenter's role. The wonders of reunion and reconciliation in the last scenes of this play cannot be reduced to facile couplets about the rewards of virtue.

> In Antiochus and his daughter you have heard
> Of monstrous lust the due and just reward.
> In Pericles, his queen and daughter, seen,
> Although assail'd with fortune fierce and keen,
> Virtue preserv'd from fell destruction's blast,
> Led on by heaven, and crowned by joy at last.
> In Helicanus . . .
>
> (1-7)

If this kind of moralizing seems patently inadequate as a conclusion, then in this play the device of the authorial presenter has been made to work ironically, requiring an additional critical perspective in the audience. Gower has once again used his "authority" to enforce some simple lessons, but this story is more significant than the "author" knows.

An authorial presenter is the image of the playwright's difficulties in turning fiction into drama and conveying the significance of his story, but an authorial presenter is also one of many fictional devices by which a playwright can distance his audience from the illusion of the play proper. With Gower and the others as presenters, none of the plays on our list can be understood as simply representational. In most of these plays, an emphasis on presentation has didactic value, and the authorial character of the presenter lends authority to the lessons presented. In *Pericles,* the audience attains distance on the presenter himself, finally, and

Gower's limited perspective makes his story seem the more profound. An emphasis on presentation is evident in Shakespeare's later romances, especially *The Winter's Tale,* and the special complexity of Gower's role in *Pericles* may provide an insight into the romances as a group. Shakespeare returns to the rudiments of drama—the presentation of a simple story—to mark the limits of dramatic representation and transcend them.

Notes

1. Beaumont, with Fletcher, *The Woman-Hater,* ed. A. R. Waller, *The Works of Francis Beaumont and John Fletcher* (Cambridge U. Press, 1912), X, 71.

2. See the drawing of Gower on the title-page of George Wilkins' *The Painfull Aduentures of Pericles Prince of Tyre* (1608), ed. Kenneth Muir (Liverpool U. Press, 1953).

3. The authorial presenter has been related to the *poeta* of the miracle or Saints' plays and the expositor of the moralities—see especially Howard Baker, *Induction to Tragedy* (Louisiana State U. Press, 1939), pp. 141-42; F. D. Hoeniger (ed.), *Pericles,* New Arden edition (London: Methuen, 1963), pp. lxxxviii-xci; and Howard Felperin, "Shakespeare's Miracle Play," *SQ, [Shakespeare Quarterly]* 18 (1967), 151-66. Enid Welsford argues that the influence of masques was decisive in *The Court Masque: A Study in the Relationship between Poetry and the Revels* (Cambridge U. Press, 1927), p. 276 ff. Dieter Mehl stresses the influence of civic pageantry and shows in *The Elizabethan Dumb Show: The History of a Dramatic Convention* (London: Methuen, 1965), pp. 8-9.

4. Hoeniger concludes that "the dramatic convention of the loose travelogue or romance narrated by a choric figure was begun by Barnes and so successfully developed in *Pericles* one or two years later that Heywood was persuaded to apply the same technique in his plays on the *Ages*" (p. xxiii).

5. Throughout this essay, attributions of date and author will follow the *Annals of English Drama,* ed. Alfred Harbage and Samuel S. Schoenbaum (U. of Pennsylvania Press, 1964). Texts will be cited in individual notes.

6. See especially Lee Monroe Ellison, *The Early Romantic Drama at the English Court* (Menasha, Wis.: George Banta, 1917), and Betty J. Littleton, *Clyomon and Clamydes: A Critical Edition* (The Hague: Mouton, 1968), Appendix B.

7. Additional plays in which a presenter makes regular appearances between acts include *Alphonsus, King of Aragon,* Peele's *Battle of Alcazar* (1588-89), *Locrine,* Shakespeare's *Henry V* (1599), and *The Devil's Charter.*

8. The chorus in the anonymous *The Thracian Wonder* (1590-ca.1600) "beguiles" time by turning an hourglass between acts; the Prologue in *The Weakest Goeth to the Wall* (Dekker in part? ca.1599-1600) effects a transition between generations with a dumbshow at the beginning of the play; in Shakespeare's *The Winter's Tale* (ca.1610-11), Time himself takes the stage to let sixteen years pass between Acts Three and Four. The most radical example of a presenter's control is Fame's in *The Travels of the Three English Brothers,* whose separate plots never converge until the stage itself is split into three locations for a concluding dumbshow which Fame narrates.

9. Ed. R. B. McKerrow, *Materialien zur Kunde des älteren Englischen Dramas,* 6 (Louvain: A. Uystpruyst, 1904).

10. Ed. John S. Farmer, *Tudor Facsimile Texts* (1912; rpt. New York: AMS, 1970), see sig. I3^r. These dumbshows function in a similar way to the "causal induction," a feature of some Elizabethan plays which is directly related to the role of "authorial" presenters in *2 The Seven Deadly Sins* and *Two Lamentable Tragedies*—see Robert Y. Turner, "The Causal Induction in Some Elizabethan Plays," *SP [Studies in Philology],* 60 (1963), 183-90.

11. Ed. John S. Farmer, *Tudor Facsimile Texts* (1913; rpt. New York: AMS, 1970), sig. E2^v.

12. The idea of *theatrum mundi* is frequent in Elizabethan and Jacobean drama as a means of making the audience take the lessons of a play to itself. See T. B. Stroup, *Microcosmos: The Shape of the Elizabethan Play* (U. of Kentucky Press, 1965), pp. 7-36.

13. The most distinctive characterizing verse is Skelton's old skeltonics in the two *Robert, Earl of Huntington* plays; both Gower in *Pericles* and Higden in *Hengisi, King of Kent* usually speak in archaic tetrameters.

14. *The Dramatic Works of Thomas Heywood* (London: John Pearson, 1874), III, 5-6.

15. Ed. W. W. Greg, *The Malone Society Reprints* (1926; rpt. New York: Russell & Russell, 1964), 1.1.8 ff.

16. Ed. Valentine Kreb, *Münchener Beiträge,* 23 (Erlangen and Leipzig: A. Deichert, 1902), 1.1.17-23.

17. *The Works of Thomas Middleton,* ed. A. H. Bullen (1885; rpt. New York: AMS, 1964), II, 1. Prol. 3-4.

18. London, 1622 (Folger Shakespeare Library, copy 1).

19. *The Death of Robert, 2.2—A Select Collection of Old English Plays Originally Published by Robert Dodsley,* ed. W. Carew Hazlitt, 4th ed. (London: Reeves and Turner, 1874), VIII, 136.

20. Guicciardini in *The Devil's Charter* descends "from the Christall Palace of true *Fame*" (Prologue. 11). Bardh tells the story of Caradoc the Valiant Welshman "that succeeding times, / In leaves of gold, may register his name, / And reare a Pyramys vnto his fame" (1.1.145-47; see also 2.2.8, 4.4.28-32)—*The Works of John Day,* ed. A. H. Bullen (London: Chiswick Press, 1881).

21. See Morris Palmer Tilley, *A Dictionary of the Proverbs in the Sixteenth and Seventeenth Centuries* (U. of Michigan Press, 1950), T580. The broad history of this allegory is discussed by Fritz Saxl in "Veritas Filia Temporis," *Philosophy and History: Essays Presented to Ernst Cassirer,* ed. Raymond Klibansky and H. J. Paton (New York: Harper & Row, 1963), pp. 197-222.

22. See, for example, "To the Ingenuous Reader," *The Valiant Welshman,* and *The Devil's Charter,* 1.2.190-94.

23. *An Apology for Actors* (1612), ed. Richard H. Perkinson (New York: Scholars Facsimiles and Reprints, 1941), sigs. B3ᵛ, B4ʳ.

24. All references to the text of *Pericles* use Hoeniger's New Arden edition, cited above.

25. Several echoes suggest to Hoeniger that *Pericles* is directly indebted to *Henry V* for the language of the choruses—see p. xx and notes to 3.Chorus.13; 4.Chorus.7, 18-19.

26. J. Dover Wilson describes the Chorus in *Henry V* as like "a priest leading his congregation in prayer or celebration" with "persuasive tones of eager entreaty from the playwright's own lips"—*Henry V,* New Cambridge edition (Cambridge U. Press, 1949), p. xv.

Richard Hillman (essay date winter 1985)

SOURCE: Hillman, Richard. "Shakespeare's Gower and Gower's Shakespeare: The Larger Debt of *Pericles.*" *Shakespeare Quarterly* 36, no. 4 (winter 1985): 427-37.

[*In the following essay, Hillman compares* Pericles *to John Gower's* Confessio Amantis. *The critic maintains that the character of Pericles shares many traits with the character Amans in the* Confessio *and undergoes a similar journey of self-discovery.*]

Shakespeare's Gower used to embarrass with his quaintness; nowadays, as often as not, he dazzles with his theatrical *savoir faire.* His choric role is increasingly recognized as an effective part of *Pericles'* dramatic method, while the effects themselves have become the chief subject of debate, most of which concerns the issue of mediation: does the Chorus create alienation or engagement, and exactly how?[1] The proliferation of aesthetic arguments parallels a welcome tendency to approach the play, whatever the circumstances of composition, as an artistic whole for which Shakespeare at least made himself responsible. Abetted, no doubt, by Gower's considerable appeal as a character—we warm to him, despite his moralizing, as we do not to the members of the romance plot itself—the momentum of appreciation has carried commentary well beyond the simple issue of his presence.

Yet a reappraisal of that issue, this time premised on Gower's success as a dramatic device, may be in order. It is nice to feel as comfortable with Gower as he evidently feels with us, but we may also be lulled into neglecting a significant aspect of the play's originality. In seeking precedents and parallels, editors and critics have naturally focused on other choric figures in Renaissance drama. A number of more or less instructive instances have been examined, with Shakespeare's own *Henry V* the inevitable starting point. In a few analogues, the choric figures are poets but not sources;[2] in what may be the closest one, *The Divil's Charter* by Barnabe Barnes, he is a source but not a poet. Indeed, despite the undoubted similarities discovered by F. D. Hoeniger,[3] Guicciardine, the Italian historian, is a far cry from John Gower, the widely read and greatly admired figure who was part of a living tradition of English poetry. In the end, Shakespeare's approach emerges as unique, less because of what Gower does than because of who he is. To assume that the creation of Gower simply followed from an artistic need for a chorus is to reverse this emphasis. What confronts us in *Pericles* is not merely an unusually sophisticated choric function, but the most sustained literary allusion to be found in Shakespeare. I believe that approaching the role of Gower in these terms can illuminate both the playwright's handling of his principal source and the final achievement of the play itself.

Not that the debt to Book VIII of the *Confessio Amantis* has been neglected. John Dean, in particular, goes beyond more mechanical comparisons to emphasize the close affinity in "style and spirit."[4] He also relates Gower's use of the Apollonius story as an *exemplum* of unnatural love to the thematic movement in the play from destructive passion to chaste creative love, from Priapus to Diana.[5] Nevertheless, as long as only that part of the *Confessio* is considered which substantially furnished the plot[6]—and, tellingly, Dean cites the work in the excerpts printed in Geoffrey Bullough's compendium of sources[7]—Gower's influence is bound to seem mainly superficial. What is most obviously missing is a precedent for Shakespeare's use of love themes as a means of exploring larger issues of human spirituality and self-realization. Taken as a whole, the *Confessio* strikingly furnishes such a precedent.

I

In the fictional structure of the poem, the story of Apollonius is not Gower's at all, but the final *exemplum* by which Genius, in his role as confessor, helps to restore the afflicted Amans-Gower to spiritual equilibrium. The key to this process is indeed the distinction between vain and selfish *amor,* bound up with self-delusion, and the *caritas* through which the sufferer finally becomes reconciled to himself and reintegrated into the human community. The tale's concern with what is natural in love and with the proper response to adverse fortune lends it a resonance appropriate to its climactic position. However, the focus is still relatively narrow, the tone straightforwardly moralistic, and the impact partial. The cure of Amans requires further direct advice from Genius and an appeal from Amans to Venus for his liberation. In evincing his spiritual growth, his new realism and perspective, that request reflects the work's broader themes.

It is unmistakably a question of identity. When, in Book I, Venus asked Amans who he was, he had replied, "'A Caitif that lith hiere . . .'" (I.161);[8] now, to the same query, his response is simply "'John Gower'" (VIII.2321).[9] And it is a question of accepting the basic terms of human existence, particularly mortality and the passing of time. The reminder of these realities—"'Remembre wel hou thou art old'" (VIII.2439)—plunges him into the trance, "Ne fully quik ne fully ded" (VIII.2451), in which he has his vision of lovers past and finally receives his cure. In Venus' mirror he sees his true position in nature's cycle of creation and destruction:

> And thanne into my remembrance
> I drowh myn olde daies passed,
> And as reson it hath compassed,
> I made a liknesse of miselve
> Unto the sondri Monthes twelve.

> (VIII.2834-38)

His vain passion, which had involved defiance of time, has been dissipated. He awakes, Reason returns (VIII.2862 ff.), and, "sobre and hol ynowh" (VIII.2869), Gower redirects his energy, his impulse for love, in the direction Venus indicates:

> Bot go ther vertu moral duelleth,
> Wher ben thi bokes, as men telleth,
> Whiche of long time thou hast write,
> For this I do thee well to wite,
> If thou thin hele wolt pourchace,
> Thou miht noght make suite and chace,
> Wher that the game is nought pernable.

> (VIII.2925-31)

Her injunction to "'preie hierafter for the pes'" (VIII.2913), together with the motto "*Por reposer*" (VIII.2907) on the beads she gives him, highlights the interdependence of the poet's future efforts on behalf of others and his continuing inner peace. It is a lesson he himself seems thoroughly to have learned, and there is profound satisfaction in it:

> And in my self y gan to smyle
> Thenkende upon the bedis blake,
> And how they weren me betake,
> For that y schulde bidde and preie.
> . . . . .
> Homward a softe pas y wente,
> Wher that with al myn hol entente
> Uppon the point that y am schryve
> I thenke bidde whil y live.

> (VIII.2958-70)

The *Confessio,* then, is far more than a loose collection of tales—"mouldy"[10] or otherwise—and not at all narrowly moralistic in its intellectual scope. This has been amply recognized by such admirers of the work as Derek Pearsall, who identifies its central concern as nothing less than the "art of living" and comments: "Love is the theme because it reveals man's moral nature under greatest stress."[11] Viewed in this context, Gower's redaction of the Apollonius story—not obvious raw material for drama, as has been observed[12]—begins to acquire more plausibility as a fitting source for the first of Shakespeare's romances. In particular, we can see that some of the departures from that source, even as they affiliate *Pericles* with the other romances, also bring it more closely into line with the central pattern of the *Confessio* as a whole, the tortuous psychic voyage of Amans toward self-discovery.

II

The most fundamental change concerns the nature of the fictional universe. Hoeniger points out that "In neither Twine nor Gower is there any attempt to find meaning in human suffering."[13] The good are ultimately rewarded, the evil punished, but the operations of fortune are independent and irrational:

> Fortune hath evere be muable
> And mai no while stonde stable:
> For now it hiheth, now it loweth,
> Now stant upriht, now overthroweth,
> Now full of blisse and now of bale . . .

> (VIII.585-89)

Even the dramatic reversal of the hero's misfortune, well-earned by any standard of justice, is pointedly made capricious:

> Fro this day forth fortune hath sworn
> To sette him upward on the whiel;
> So goth the world, now wo, now wel.

> (VIII.1736-38)

The most positive conclusion Genius can manage is that proper behavior at least offers a chance of happiness, while nothing good can come of wickedness:

> Fortune, thogh sche be noght stable,
> Yit at som time is favorable
> To hem that ben of love trewe.
> Bot certes it is forto rewe
> To se love ayein kinde falle,
> For that makth sore a man to falle.
>
> (VIII.2013-18)

There is a set of moral laws to which man may cling, but not a spiritual framework actively enfolding him.

Such a framework is implicit in the pattern of suffering and redemption in *Pericles*—a pattern universally perceived, however variously interpreted. To judge from the Chorus' formulaic allusions, which are very much part of the pseudo-medieval flavor, fortune itself is no less arbitrary:

> . . . fortune, tir'd with doing bad,
> Threw him ashore, to give him glad.
>
> (II.Chor.37-38)[14]

> . . . fortune's mood
>   Varies again. . . .
>
> (III.Chor.46-47)

> Let Pericles believe his daughter's dead,
> And bear his courses to be ordered
> By Lady Fortune. . . .
>
> (IV.iv.46-48)

But as the last of these references indicates, with its explicit distinction between Pericles' belief and our better knowledge, fortune's operations are firmly contained within a structure that is not arbitrary. The character of Gower, from the beginning of the play, is the chief means of establishing this structure and keeping us aware of it. He virtually stretches a safety net beneath the hero, thus enabling us to view tribulations and relief in the proper perspective. His supplying of a moral and spiritual context assures us that there is a point to growth, change, and response:

> Be quiet then, as men should be
> Till he hath pass'd necessity.
> I'll show you those in troubles reign,
> Losing a mite, a mountain gain.
>
> (II.Chor.5-8)

The change in Pericles' fortunes occurs with recognition of his daughter and is associated with the principle she embodies: ". . . thou dost look / Like Patience gazing on kings' graves, and smiling / Extremity out of act" (V.i.137-39). Various commentators, following the lead of G. Wilson Knight, have seen the achievement of some sort of transcendence through patience as an essential burden of the play.[15] The power of patience over fortune was a Renaissance commonplace with a venerable Stoic lineage. Its previous use by Shakespeare ranges from the often-compared ". . . like Patience on a monument, / Smiling at grief" (*Twelfth Night,* II.iv.114-15)[16] to the more dramatically functional lines of Cordelia:

> For thee, oppressed king, I am cast down,
> Myself could else out-frown false Fortune's frown.
>
> (V.iii.5-6)

In the universe of *King Lear,* as in life, such an attitude cannot alter circumstances; indeed, this seems to be part of Shakespeare's point in showing Cordelia lost by a hair's breadth. But the world of *Pericles,* a potently symbolic world where the music of the spheres can be heard, responds in kind. Even when she cannot actually deter "extremity"—as, for example, she converts Lysimachus in the brothel—Marina's spiritual power over fortune is reflected in the action. Thus, when Leonine will not be put from his bloody intention, fortune, in the form of the pirate raid, intervenes to save her. The purposeful higher powers of the play—the gods, Providence—ultimately serve the premise that man's fortune varies with his attitude toward life and that in one way or another he gets what he deserves.

This concept of fortune and of the working of the universe—developed through Shakespeare's Gower, yet foreign to the Apollonius tale—is part of the framework of the *Confessio.* The confessional basis of the work implies an ongoing relation between the supernatural and the spiritual state of Amans-Gower. In contrast with Gower's Apollonius, the gods take a serious active interest in his case. The initial inward discord of Amans generates a series of corrective lessons; in response to his awakening self-knowledge, Venus and Cupid vouchsafe his cure. In the Prologue, the poet universalizes the moral of this method in terms which might have been intended for *Pericles:*

> For after that we falle and rise,
> The world arist and falth withal,
> So that the man is overal
> His oghne cause of wel and wo.
> That we fortune clepe so
> Out of the man himself it groweth.
>
> (Prol.544-49)

This is far from the fatalistic shrug of Genius over Apollonius: "So goth the world, now wo, now wel."[17]

III

Moreover, Gower's belief in mankind's collective responsibility for the state of the world, his sense of the individual as contributing his own peace or discord to the human community at large, is far closer to *Pericles* than to Genius' tale. In the latter, the focus is strictly upon Apollonius as an individual—and, of course, as an *exemplum.* Even his wife and child are developed as characters only insofar as they bear directly on his loss and recovery of happiness. Not only does Shakespeare's dramatization spread our emotional involvement more broadly, but the reunions give us the sense of harmony—figured forth in the music of the spheres—that extends well beyond the participants. The role of Helicanus, developed from a negligible figure in the Apollonius tale, reinforces the social and political dimension of the pattern. The suggestion of a new order premised on spiritual renewal, achieved through exaltation of the good and purging of the wicked, brings the play in line with the typical Shakespearean romantic movement. But such a conclusion is also sanctioned by Gower's enfolding of Apollonius' mechanical ups-and-downs ("Fortune hath evere be muable / And mai no while stonde stable") within a larger vision of man's potential for generating an harmonious collective destiny:

> . . . upon divisioun
> Stant, why no worldes thing mai laste,
> Til it be drive to the laste.
> And fro the ferste regne of alle
> Into this day, hou so befalle,
> Of that the regnes be muable
> The man himself hath be coupable,
> Which of his propre governance
> Fortuneth al the worldes chance.

(Prol.576-84)

Again, Gower stresses the interdependence of macrocosm and microcosm, for human nature itself is the fundamental embodiment of discord—discord which makes us individually subject, not only to fortune, but to death itself:

> It may ferst proeve upon a man;
> The which, for his complexioun
> Is mad upon divisioun
> Of cold, of hot, of moist, of drye,
> He mot be verray kynde dye:
> For the contraire of his astat
> Stant evermore in such debat
> Til that o part be overcome,
> Ther may no final pes be nome.
> . . . . .
> Bot for ther is diversite
> Withinne himself, he may noght laste.

(Prol.974-89)

This is commonplace medieval science and theology, but Gower makes more than conventional use of it in developing the healing of Amans as a paradigm that may lead to collective peace. It is a paradigm based on compromise, in that the frailty of the human condition, including its mortality, is acknowledged: "Remembre wel hou thou art old." But through that acknowledgment, painful as it is, comes transcendence.

IV

This brings us to the overtones of rebirth and resurrection associated with Pericles' change of fortune. The basic structure has been carried over intact from the tale of Apollonius, who also moves both literally and symbolically "out of his derke place / . . . into the liht" (VIII.1740-41). But significant details form a stronger link with the experience of Amans-Gower. The first of these is the condition from which the characters are revived. Apollonius is merely a stylized embodiment of extreme grief, an active rather than a passive figure: his weeping is emphasized, both before and during his encounter with his daughter (VIII.1605, 1688). Pericles, on the other hand, has entered a trancelike state closer to the swoon of Amans, "Ne fully quik ne fully ded." This is far more effective for stage purposes, but there is also a telling difference in the spiritual condition it reflects. Pericles has passed beyond the simple pain of Apollonius into a state of spiritual death. His grief signifies abject surrender of selfhood in the face of death's overwhelming power. Amans describes his collapse, when confronted with his own subjection to mortality, in terms of a similar onset of existential despair:

> Tho wiste I wel withoute doute,
> That ther was no recoverir;
> And as a man the blase of fyr
> With water quencheth, so ferd I;
> A cold me cawhte sodeinly,
> For sorwe that myn herte made
> Mi dedly face pale and fade
> Becam, and swoune I fell to grounde.

(VIII.2442-49)

Shakespeare, moreover, invests the awakening of his hero with a spiritual significance reminiscent of the healing of Amans. There is no suggestion of this in the case of Apollonius, whose mellowing toward his unknown daughter comes merely from being "so sibb of blod" (VIII.1703). By contrast, Pericles is not only opened to revelation by her example of patience, but opened to that example by an initial impulse of pity, as she cites her own misfortunes:

> . . . she speaks,
> My lord, that, may be, hath endur'd a grief
> Might equal yours. . . .

(V.i.86-88)

It is highly characteristic of Shakespeare to mark a movement toward spiritual maturity by a character's new ability to feel for others: Lear's concern for the Fool and his prayer for the "poor naked wretches" (III.iv.28 ff.) comprise the *locus classicus,* but the pattern runs throughout his work, from the deposed Richard II's parting with his Queen to Prospero's decision to forgive his enemies. Certainly, the choric Gower's final praise of Helicanus ("A figure of truth, of faith, of loyalty" [Epil.8]) and Cerimon (". . . The worth that learned charity aye wears" [l. 10]) confirms the centrality of selflessness in the play's moral scheme. In the *Confessio,* such selflessness is explicitly a condition of the renewal of self experienced by Amans-Gower.

Indeed, in making his hero's spiritual state more clearly the issue, Shakespeare introduced another more specific parallel. What sets the seal on Pericles' recovery of identity is his declaration, "I am Pericles of Tyre" (V.i.204), when Marina asks his "title" (l. 203). The thematic significance of the statement coincides with its dramatic impact: since we are equally engaged in Marina's feelings, it forms the natural emotional climax of the scene. In the Apollonius story, as recounted by Gower (as well as Twine), there is no such questioning of father by daughter, no comparable affirmation. Only the reply of Amans to Venus, his resumption of the identity of "John Gower," furnishes a model. And it is a more exact model because of the parallel between the female figures. Marina's restorative power, after all, is ultimately the power of human love. Through that power, supported by the convention of immortality through children, she becomes "another life to Pericles thy father" (l. 207).[18]

V

From the vantage point of a comparison between Pericles' spiritual renewal and that of Amans-Gower, it is possible to see more clearly into a problematic feature of the play. While the redemption of Pericles is clearly the deserved gift of the gods, and easy enough to associate with the triumph of patience over fortune, it is hard to accept his previous suffering as having been brought on himself. Pericles' behavior seems morally impeccable from first to last. To argue, as Knight was the first to do,[19] that he is tainted by the incest from which he instantly recoils, is to import an incongruous theological premise. In refuting this argument Hoeniger finds it sufficient that the suffering in the play, like Job's, becomes meaningful through human responses to it.[20] Yet Job's sufferings, if equally undeserved, are never meaningless: they possess the intrinsic justification of proceeding from the divine will. In *Pericles,* we are still left with the difficulty of accepting a universe that is first arbitrarily hostile, then purposefully benevolent.

The parallel with Amans-Gower highlights the issue of Pericles' reconciliation to the human condition itself, including the limitation of mortality. The new sense of meaning and identity to which both Amans and Pericles awake is associated with a spiritual triumph over death premised on acceptance of death's power over physical life. This is a vital dimension of Pericles' patience. After all, the blows he has endured have been direct manifestations of death's power, stripping him of his wife and child, who had furnished him with a sense of

self: Thaisa's love transformed him from anonymous knight, bereft of all but his father's armor, to heir-apparent; the birth of his daughter, symbolic instrument of both her mother's immortality and his own, enabled him to cope with Thaisa's loss. Again, a modification of the Apollonius tale sharpens the thematic focus: in Genius' redaction, it is not by itself the supposed death of his daughter that plunges the hero into despair; his initial stoical reaction ("Bot sithe it mai no betre be, / He thonketh god and forth goth he . . ." [VIII.1589-90]) gives way only in the face of another storm at sea.

Amans is in need of existential redirection because his selfish love flies in the face of the realities of age and time. It constitutes, in effect, a false claim to immortality. Once we realize that Pericles, morally innocent though he is, may be making a similar claim through his emotional investment in the lives of others, his dependence upon them for his sense of self, then his persecution by fortune no longer seems so arbitrary. Nor does the mainspring of the action—his initial encounter with what Genius presents as the ultimate example of love acting self-indulgently and contrary to nature.

It is important to take Pericles at his word when he describes his purpose in courting Antiochus' daughter:

> . . . I went to Antioch,
> Whereas thou know'st, against the face of death
> I sought the purchase of a glorious beauty,
> From whence an issue I might propagate,
> Are arms to princes and bring joys to subjects.
>
> (I.ii.70-74)

The imagery of the episode, beginning with the vivid spectacle of the previous suitors' heads, insists upon the connection between gaining his object and defying death.[21] So thoroughly transported is he that he can

> . . . with a soul
> Embolden'd with the glory of her praise,
> Think death no hazard in this enterprise.
>
> (I.i.3-5)

Her goddess-like entrance, accompanied by music (the false forerunner of the music of the spheres), helps to convey Pericles' imaginative transformation of her into a virtual symbol of immortality. His prayer at this point is not only selfish and self-deluded, but evasive in making the gods responsible for his passion:[22]

> You gods, that made me man, and sway in love,
> That have inflam'd desire in my breast
> To taste the fruit of yon celestial tree
> Or die in the adventure, be my helps,
> As I am son and servant to your will,
> To compass such a boundless happiness!
>
> (I.i.20-25)

This has little to do with Apollonius, but it has much in common with the initial position of Amans:

> O Venus, queene of loves cure,
> Thou lif, thou lust, thou mannes hele,
> Behold my cause and my querele,
> And yif me som part of thi grace. . . .

>   (I.132-35)

The strong paradisal overtones of the "fruit of yon celestial tree" point up the role of Antiochus as diabolical tempter and destroyer. He tempts Pericles not only directly, by stage-managing his daughter's appearance and exalting her attractions, but indirectly, by reminding him, with supposed concern for his welfare, of the fate that waits on failure. Pericles' response to this warning sheds further light on his existential motive:

> Antiochus, I thank thee, who hath taught
> My frail mortality to know itself,
> And by those fearful objects to prepare
> This body, like to them, to what I must;
> For death remember'd should be like a mirror,
> Who tells us life's but breath, to trust it error.

>   (I.i.42-57)

The reminder of death is an incitement, not a deterrent, because it conveys the meaninglessness of life in the shadow of mortality. Pericles, like Amans, is at odds with the most fundamental condition of existence. Ironically, his attempt to project himself beyond mortality dramatically renews the threat of death. In solving the riddle of incest, he is confronted with a disillusioning but necessary truth—that there exists a secret and sinister alliance between death's destructive power and the meretricious hope of escape. The enmity of Antiochus has a very long reach, the power to deprive him, in essence, of his identity. He is thus started on the painful journey toward the rebuilding of selfhood and a transcendence of death premised on recognized acceptance of it.

VI

The audience already has its assurance that transcendence is possible.[23] The miraculous appearance of John Gower pointedly combines, Phoenix-like, the conquering of death and the resuming of mortality:

> To sing a song that old was sung,
> From ashes ancient Gower is come,
> Assuming man's infirmities . . .

>   (I.Chor.1-3)

And if, as we have argued, the playwright has summoned him not only as mouthpiece but also as muse, even this has a precedent of sorts in the *Confessio*. There the poet invokes the transforming power of a yet more ancient singer—the ability of Arion, who also by his song was saved from death, magically to create universal harmony:

> And every man upon this ground
> Which Arion that time herde,
> Als wel the lord as the schepherde,
> He broghte hem alle in good acord;
> So that the comun with the lord,
> And lord with the comun also,
> He sette in love bothe tuo
> And putte awey malencolie.

>   (Prol.1062-69)

Gower's own route toward what he clearly hopes will be a similar achievement must take his human limitations into account:

> I may noght strecche up to the hevene
> Min hand, ne setten al in evene
> This world, which evere is in balance.

>   (I.1-3)

His solution is to become his own most comprehensive, and extremely human, *exemplum*. It is this previous incarnation that most clearly qualifies Shakespeare's Gower to present his tale as a source of "restoratives," whose "purchase is to make men glorious" (I.Chor.8-9). In view of the profound tribute implied by the larger debt of *Pericles,* we should not be surprised by the Chorus' spiritual generosity, his willingness to interrupt his "final pes." Nor should we mistake it for anything less than the cost—and the reward—of mortally aspiring to Arion's luminous role: "I life would wish, and that I might / Waste it for you like taper-light" (ll. 15-16).

Notes

1. Recent studies include F. D. Hoeniger, "Gower and Shakespeare in *Pericles,*" *Shakespeare Quarterly,* 33 (1982), 461-79, and Richard Paul Knowles, "'Wishes Fall Out as They're Will'd': Artist, Audience, and *Pericles*'s Gower," *English Studies in Canada,* 9 (1983), 14-24, who usefully discusses previous criticism taking this approach.

2. Skelton in *The Downfall of Robert Earl of Huntingdon,* by Henry Chettle and Anthony Munday, cited by John Dean, *Restless Wanderers: Shakespeare and the Pattern of Romance,* Elizabethan and Renaissance Studies, 86, ed. James Hogg (Salzburg: Universität Salzburg, 1979), pp. 178-79; Homer in Heywood's plays of the three ages, which evidently postdate *Pericles*—see F. D. Hoeniger's Introduction to his Arden *Pericles* (London: Methuen, 1963), p. xxi.

3. Hoeniger, ed., pp. xxi-xxiii.

4. Dean, p. 171.

5. Ibid., pp. 174-75 and 271-77.

6. Commentators agree that the influence of Lawrence Twine's *The Patterne of Painefull Aduentures* was relatively small—see Hoeniger,

ed., pp. xiv-xvi. In none of the instances examined in this study have I found it necessary to take Twine's version into account.

7. *Narrative and Dramatic Sources of Shakespeare,* VI (London: Routledge & Kegan Paul, 1966).

8. The *Confessio Amantis* is cited throughout in the edition of G. C. Macaulay, *The Complete Works of John Gower* (Oxford: Clarendon Press, 1901), II-III.

9. This point is made by Russell A. Peck in the Introduction to his (abridged) edition of the poem (New York: Holt, Rinehart and Winston, 1968), pp. xxvii-xxviii. Peck similarly emphasizes the spiritual reorientation of Amans as the structural principle of the work.

10. Ben Jonson's notorious jibe at *Pericles* (in his "Ode to Himselfe") is not indicative of his opinion of Gower, who is one of the chorus of great poets in *The Golden Age Restored* and, as Peck points out (p. v), the author most frequently cited in the *English Grammar.*

11. "Gower's Narrative Art," *PMLA,* 81 (1966), 476.

12. Hoeniger, ed., p. xvi.

13. Ibid., p. xvii.

14. All references to *Pericles* are from Hoeniger's Arden edition.

15. See G. Wilson Knight, *The Crown of Life* (1947; rpt. London: Methuen, 1969), pp. 65-67; Hoeniger, ed., pp. lxxxiii-lxxxv; Derek Traversi, *Shakespeare: The Last Phase* (1955; rpt. Stanford: Stanford Univ. Press, 1965), pp. 32-41; Joan Hartwig, *Shakespeare's Tragicomic Vision* (Baton Rouge: Louisiana State Univ. Press, 1972), pp. 56-60; G. A. Barker, "Themes and Variations in Shakespeare's *Pericles,*" *English Studies,* 44 (1963), 407-10 and 413-14; and J. M. S. Thompkins, "Why Pericles?" *Review of English Studies,* NS 3 (1952), 317-18.

16. References to Shakespearean plays other than *Pericles* are to *The Riverside Shakespeare,* gen. ed. G. Blakemore Evans (Boston: Houghton Mifflin, 1974).

17. Gower's attack on fortune and emphasis on human responsibility are stressed by George R. Coffman, "John Gower in his Most Significant Role," in *Elizabethan Studies and Other Essays in Honor of George F. Reynolds,* Univ. of Colorado Studies, Ser. B, Vol. II, No. 4 (Boulder: Univ. of Colorado, 1945), pp. 52-61.

18. There is compelling evidence for the widely accepted emendation, first proposed by Mason, of the 1609 Quarto's "like" to "life"—see Hoeniger, ed., V.i.207 n.

19. Knight, pp. 38-40. See also Barker, pp. 401-14; Howard Felperin, *Shakespearean Romance* (Princeton: Princeton Univ. Press, 1972), p. 149, and "Shakespeare's Miracle Play," *SQ,* [*Shakespeare Quarterly*] 18 (1967), 366; W. B. Thorne, "*Pericles* and the 'Incest-Fertility' Opposition," *SQ,* 22 (1971), 43-56; and John P. Cutts, "Pericles' 'Downright Violence,'" *Shakespeare Studies,* 4 (1968), 275-93.

20. Hoeniger, ed., pp. lxxxi-lxxxvi.

21. The death-motif in this scene has been stressed mainly by critics tracing the "tainting" of the hero—e.g., Knight, p. 38; Felperin, *Shakespearean Romance,* pp. 147-49; and Cutts, pp. 275-76. Several commentators see Pericles as seeking some sort of spiritual fulfillment involving self-knowledge and transcendence of humanity. See Traversi, who speaks of a "search for an ideal expressed in terms of devotion to chivalrous love" (p. 20), and John Arthos, *The Art of Shakespeare* (London: Bowes, 1964), pp. 140-42.

22. Knight, p. 38, makes a similar point.

23. On Gower's as the first of the play's restorations, see Knowles, pp. 17-18, and Douglas L. Peterson, *Time, Tide and Tempest* (San Marino: Huntington Library, 1973), p. 73.

PRODUCTION REVIEWS

D. J. R. Bruckner (review date 19 August 1998)

SOURCE: Bruckner, D. J. R. "Hopscotching from Hilarity to Mourning, with Groundlings in Thrall." *New York Times* (19 August 1998): E5.

[*In the following review of the Kings County Shakespeare Company production of* Pericles, *directed by Jonathan Bank, Bruckner praises the wide range of emotional responses that the play elicited from the audience and notes the "disorderly" nature of the plot.*]

If it's not in *Pericles,* maybe it isn't possible in theater. This wonderful old bag of tricks has everything—murder, kidnapping, drowning, lost children, resurrections, political intrigue, divine vengeance, a bordello redeemed by a virgin, admired rulers whose sex lives would arch Satan's eyebrow, pimps, homicidal jealousy, labor induced by a hurricane, birth onstage and eternal love. The opening scene portrays father-daughter incest so vividly that television would have to warn you to shield your children from it. What a play!

Of course, it is a little disorderly, taking place in six ancient cities and at sea over about 30 years and involving 40 characters. Shakespeare's name is usually attached to it since the members of his theater company registered it as theirs in 1607, and he probably did write a couple of striking scenes. But its language tells you it was composed by at least a few hands over many years; some lines are almost as medieval as the underlying wildly romantic story, brought from the Continent into English by the poet John Gower in the 14th century. And if the most sophisticated playwrights and actors around Shakespeare knew his greatest plays were Olympian while *Pericles* was pulp, *Pericles* was wildly popular with the crowds down in the pit.

The production directed by Jonathan Bank for the Kings County Shakespeare Company, part of the troupe's three-show festival at the Picnic House in Prospect Park, lets you know why. Ten actors revolving through all the roles—occasionally pausing to tell the audience where they are as the action hopscotches across the Mediterranean—carry viewers from helpless laughter to rigid apprehension to mourning and back to mirth with scarcely a moment of emotional disorientation.

It is remarkable to see people gleefully cheering as a pander, his house madam and a pimp are thwarted and then defeated by a teen-age girl of terrifying virtue in an episode as funny as any in Elizabethan theater, and then, minutes later, to shed tears as Pericles, deprived of his wits by hopeless loss, recognizes that this girl is the daughter he believed had perished at birth in a storm—a scene that embodies a poem as perfect as any in the language.

Mr. Bank has been working on this play for 10 years, and he and this cast exploit the text as they ought to—shamelessly and with an eye to irresistible entertainment. They trim excessive or murky speeches, borrow lines from a contemporary book that we would now call a novelized version of the play and do not hesitate to let the audience know how much they enjoy their work, especially when they can seize the villainous roles. It had to be like this in Shakespeare's time: no story stays at the top of the charts for 200 years without devotees who know how to make people feel happy to hear it over and over.

Charles Isherwood (review date 16-22 November 1998)

SOURCE: Isherwood, Charles. Review of *Pericles. Variety* 373, no. 1 (16-22 November 1998): 42-3.

[*In the following review of the Joseph Papp Public Theater/New York Shakespeare Festival production of* Pericles, *directed by Brian Kulick, Isherwood faults the* weak cast and stylistic treatment, but grants that the "convoluted saga" presented in the play contributed to the production's failure.]

Shakespeare's late romance *Pericles* is a kind of hymn to the cycles of life, in which wrongs are miraculously righted, wounds healed, demises undone, so it's a pity indeed that Brian Kulick's new production at the Public Theater is so deadly. A chilly ceremonial style adds a distancing layer to a play that already contains enough disjunctions and fantastic reversals to give audiences pause. What's needed is a humanizing touch to bring to the fore the beauty in the play's conception of life as a series of storms over which only purity of heart can ultimately triumph. That's absent here, due to the stylized production and, more crucially, a cast that is simply not up to the demands of the text.

The talented young designer Mark Wendland has created an imposing set that probably seemed like a good idea on the page. It's a two-story metal contraption that slides back and forth, featuring various glowing gold panels that create distinct playing spaces. A giant blue wall slides out to symbolize the sea. It certainly looks grand under Mimi Jordan Sherin's lighting, but like the play itself, it's overcomplicated, and requires a lot of distracting labor from stagehands.

But perhaps it's a viewer's lack of involvement with the drama it supports that makes the set seem distracting. This is not entirely the fault of the production. *Pericles,* believed to be only partially written by Shakespeare, concerns the convoluted saga of the title character, the Prince of Tyre (Jay Goede), whose travails begin when he guesses the incestuous secret shared by King Antiochus and his daughter.

Fearing revenge, Pericles takes to the sea, an element that here symbolizes fate's mercurial hand. From the sea Pericles brings succor to the starving kingdom of Cleon, the first stop on his journey. But it is he who needs charity when a shipwreck casts him up on the shores of Simonides' kingdom, where he ultimately wins the hand of the king's daughter Thaisa.

His wedded happiness is undone when a storm during his journey home brings the apparent death of his wife in childbirth, and he must leave his newborn daughter Marina with Cleon and his wife before returning to lead his kingdom. The rest of the play, in which Shakespeare's hand becomes increasingly felt, concerns the saga of Marina (Miriam A. Laube), as the play skips forward to reveal her as a grown woman of pure heart who faces trials of her own before being reunited with her father in the play's most famous scene.

In this scene, Marina coaxes her father from his wounded silence by telling of her own woes. Their relationship is revealed, and the poisonous father-daughter relationship that began the play is supplanted by a pure one.

In this moving encounter Shakespeare rewrites the final meeting between Lear and Cordelia, supplying the happy ending that the dark vision of that play could not accommodate. In the right hands, it can have an equally powerful impact, but here it brings on no rush of emotion because the performers never succeed in conveying the depths of feeling required.

Goede declaims his lines from start to finish in an admirably comprehensible style that never seems to connect with anything in the character's heart. He comes easily by the wide-eyed boyishness of early scenes, but doesn't begin to suggest a man numbed and chastened by his tortuous journey at the end, brought back from the edge of despair by a miracle of fate. Laube's sweetly dreamy Marina is no more convincing as a wounded spirit who has endured a series of misfortunes. (And the hectoring tone she takes at the beginning of this scene is dismayingly inappropriate.)

They, and much of the rest of the cast, seem to be constantly aware that they're reciting Shakespeare's text, something we must not be conscious of if the play's spell is to take hold. Indeed, save for a couple of exceptions, it's better to pass over the rest of the multiracial cast's performances entirely, except perhaps to unhappily observe that the problem with doubling roles is that it allows an actor who might make a bad impression in a single role to make a bad impression in two or three.

The exceptions are Sam Tsoutsouvas, who gives authoritative and variegated performances in a trio of roles, and Gail Grate, whose performance as Thaisa is touching in its sad simplicity.

With a stronger cast, Kulick's clear and elegant staging might serve merely to streamline a complex text, instead of striking the cool, uninviting tone it does here (although I doubt I'd ever warm to some of the stylized touches, such as having a glass-enclosed miniature ship wheeled on and off to signify sea voyages). In *Pericles* Shakespeare painted a ruminative (if sketchy) picture of humanity at sea in an ever-changing world, but it's the actors who are at sea in this production.

John Simon (review date 23 November 1998)

SOURCE: Simon, John. "Parlous *Pericles*." *New York* 31, no. 45 (23 November 1998): 87-8.

[*In the following review of the Joseph Papp Public Theater/New York Shakespeare Festival production of* Pericles, *directed by Brian Kulick, Simon strongly criticizes the director's staging of the play as a farce.*]

Pericles is so imperfect a play that scholars postulate either a collaboration with a lesser dramatist responsible for the first two acts or, likelier, a revision of a lost earlier play by a hack, to which Shakespeare warmed only in the latter part as his involvement grew. It is based presumably on a likewise lost Hellenistic novel about Apollonius, Prince of Tyre, hugely popular through many medieval and Renaissance versions. But in no version is this tale about the whims of fortune, the endurance of trials, and miraculous events a farce. For that, it took Brian Kulick, artistic associate of the Public Theater, to place himself, squarely and foolishly, beyond the pale.

Pericles reaches the heights of poetry in several scenes, but even the other ones are based on the wondrous, the spectacular, the awesome. Kulick turns almost everything into the farcical, and navigates even the deeply moving into those shallows. Visually, his notion of presenting the play largely in gilded boxes of various sizes suggests that the Bard's collaborator was Godiva Chocolatier. Playing a goodly chunk on a steeply inclined plane, with actors performing feats of equilibrium or comically sliding down, suggests a further collaboration with Ringling Brothers. Tone-deafness to the music of verse and tongue-tiedness in its delivery bespeak untrained actors and a blockhead director.

As the poetical is clearly beyond Kulick's ken, the political becomes primary on the agenda. Kulick revels in casting black actors as the daughters of whites even where the text explicitly calls for blondeness, and, by way of escalating perversity into swinishness, deliberately picking actors whose looks and demeanor offend in roles demanding comeliness. It may be that he sees these gimmicks as marketable mainstays of Theater of the Ridiculous, but pandering to supposedly or actually subliterate audiences, instead of trying to educate them, is not only artistically but even politically self-defeating.

True, there may be some space and cost problems in staging a seafaring spectacle that requires a large cast and magical stage effects. But in a needless attempt to economize, Kulick double- and multi-casts recklessly, and diddles with two ship models—one small and portable, one large inside a glass container wheeled about on casters to and fro—instead of giving us one decent shipboard set. Even a competent actor such as Sam Tsoutsouvas is overused and undereffective in triple exposure, but damage can be done with less: Viola Davis confuses Shakespeare with August Wilson, Francis Jue plays the brutish Leonine as a girlish Leontine, and Miriam A. Laube turns Marina, the paragon of maidenly grace consigned to a brothel, into an ill-spoken gypsy romping through her caravan.

Mark Wendland's sets and Anita Yavich's costumes wallow in absurdity; Mimi Jordan Sherin's would-be prettifying lighting is chicken soup to a corpse. Mark Bennett's "original music" is rather too original to pass for music, and Naomi Goldberg's choreography is more appropriate to puppets, with which she has often worked. This peregrinating Pericles, forced from his home in Tyre, becomes the Prince of Tiresome.

Lois Potter (review date 12 July 2002)

SOURCE: Potter, Lois. "Songs of Excess." *Times Literary Supplement,* no. 5180 (12 July 2002): 19.

[*In the following excerpted review of the Royal Shakespeare Company production of* Pericles, *directed by Adrian Noble, Potter praises both the cast and the production's visual and musical splendor.*]

Eminent theatre directors who turn from Shakespeare to musical comedy, like Trevor Nunn and Adrian Noble, have an obvious precedent in Shakespeare himself. *Pericles* was a famous crowd-pleaser in its own time: scholars and directors, baffled by its uneven, possibly collaborative, text, have usually concentrated on the themes that it shares with other "late plays"—suffering, loss and reunion—and on the tense poetry of the hero's farewell to his dead wife, about to be buried at sea, or his tremulous reunion with his long-lost daughter, miraculously spared after attempted murder, kidnapping, and imprisonment in a brothel. Though Noble's production, his farewell to the Royal Shakespeare Company, follows *The Winter's Tale* and *The Tempest* at the Roundhouse, he makes a good case for seeing *Pericles* not as late play but early musical.

Taking his cue from the plot's emphasis on the wheel of fortune and the moving spheres, Noble emphasizes the Roundhouse's shape both aurally and visually. Sounds and music surround the spectators, from the buzzing flies on the severed heads in the first scene to the bells ringing round the theatre at the end to evoke the music of the spheres. When Pericles compares the king to the sun, with other kings "like stars about his throne", he is describing what we see—a small circular acting area in the centre, with a hanamichi occupied by musicians, concentric circles radiating from it and beautiful Middle Eastern lanterns giving light from above. The theatre's height allows for spectacular descents: the heads of the unsuccessful suitors at the beginning, Diana (a circus performer twirling in mid-air) near the end. Below the stage space, some spectators sit on Persian carpets. Belly-dancers and acrobats entertain. The *Arabian Nights* atmosphere is perhaps a celebration of (safely remote) Islamic culture.

Because of its narrative framework, with the medieval poet Gower as presenter, *Pericles* is sometimes treated as a play within a play. In this case, it is more like a song (which is what Gower initially calls it); at times it seems as if the actors exist simply to supplement the

bouzouki, gaida, flutes and keyboard. Especially in the heavily cut first half, most characters (including Brian Protheroe's graceful, well-spoken Gower) are almost indistinguishable, with only Thaisa (Lauren Ward) and Cerimon (Jude Akuwudike) making much impression.

If the auditorium could have revolved, it would have provided a still better analogy for the Ptolemaic cosmos, the characters' sense of being carried away by fate, and the passivity induced in the audience itself by the visual and musical splendour. Moments that seem to invite a response (like the presentation of emblematic shields and the series of single combats) do not get it and many of the best lines, though well-spoken, fail to make an impact; the same is true of attempts at contemporary relevance such as the scene in famine-stricken Tharsus with its warning to prosperous countries to learn from its example. But in the final scenes, where the writing gives everyone more help, the play comes into its own. The brothel scenes work as well as usual, and Ray Fearon's Pericles becomes human, affecting, and funny, helped by the presence of Kananu Kirimi as his principled (and surprisingly Scottish) daughter. Since Noble uses the Oxford text, both roles have acquired additional lines from a contemporary prose version of the story by George Wilkins. Even so, their most important words are neither Wilkins's nor Shakespeare's, but those of the recurring theme song (by Shaun Davey) that links father, mother and daughter in a dreamy meditation about the winds of fortune.

THEMES

Peter Womack (essay date winter 1999)

SOURCE: Womack, Peter. "Shakespeare and the Sea of Stories." *Journal of Medieval and Early Modern Studies* 29, no. 1 (winter 1999): 169-87.

[*In the following essay, Womack asserts that* Pericles *shares similarities with earlier dramas that venerated saints, most notably the play* Mary Magdalen. *The critic discusses the two plays in the context of the changing critical, political, and religious sentiment in England during the 1500s and 1600s, which denigrated improbable and miraculous stories because of their connections to Catholicism.*]

I

It was long ago discovered, by the industry which neglects no conceivable Shakespearean origin, that the main action of *Pericles* oddly resembles the King of

Marcylle episode in the fifteenth-century East Anglian play *Mary Magdalen*.[1] In both, a monarch is shown on a ship at sea with his wife, who dies in childbirth in the midst of a storm. The sailors, believing that it is fatally unlucky to have a corpse on board, insist that the dead woman be jettisoned; the monarch loses both wife and child, but later both are miraculously restored to him. The parallels are distinct enough to be interesting, but for what Stephen Greenblatt acidly calls "the conventional pieties of source study" they are an embarrassment rather than an illumination.[2] Since it is quite unlikely that the Magdalen play was performed later than the 1560s, and since it was not printed until the nineteenth century, any theory that requires Shakespeare to have been familiar with it involves implausible speculation. And in any case, the theory is not needed. The source which Shakespeare positively advertises— John Gower's *Confessio Amantis*—includes all the details Pericles shares with *Mary Magdalen*. The discovery of a stage precursor thus has the character of an ingenious solution where there was no mystery in the first place. An altogether different kind of continuity is in question, not expressible in the syntax of "influence."

The coincidence of plots is admittedly a matter of fairly conventional literary history, though not directly of Shakespearean "source studies." The story in *Confessio Amantis* is that of Apollonius of Tyre, which Gower found in the late-twelfth-century Pantheon of Godfrey of Viterbo, and which also appeared in the *Gesta Romanorum* and its numerous late medieval and Renaissance derivatives.[3] And the narrative source of the relevant parts of Mary Magdalen is the account of the saint in the thirteenth-century *Legenda Sanctorum of Jacobus de Voragine*—the "Golden Legend."[4] These collections were among the most copied and excerpted of all late medieval texts: thus the most cursory investigation of the sources of both plays leads into a network of transmitted, retold, summarized, and anthologized stories, a narrative reservoir for poets and playwrights alike, across Europe and over several centuries. It isn't quite a single network, of course: the *Gesta Romanorum* includes secular, pagan, and more or less overtly fictional tales, whereas the *Golden Legend* consists entirely of readings on the saints, whose fantastic details are consequently all presented as true. But the two spheres are not entirely disconnected either.

In the story of the King and Queen of Marcylle (Marseilles), the reason they are on the ship is that they are sailing to Rome, or to the Holy Land, in order to be baptized by St. Peter, having been converted to Christ by Mary Magdalen. The legend of Mary's missionary voyage to Marseilles probably emerged during the eleventh century to authenticate the Magdalen relics at Vezelay in Burgundy;[5] the episode of the King and Queen's voyage is presumably a slightly later supple-

Pericles and fishermen in Act II, scene i of Pericles.

ment.[6] If so, it is an appropriate one: the relics were making Vezelay into an important object of pilgrimage, and this is essentially a pilgrim story—the King and Queen "go the stations" in Jerusalem, having been protected on their hazardous journey by the influence of the saint.[7] Once the restored royal family returns, Magdalen's work is complete, and she retires to the wilderness to lead the life of a hermit, eventually being taken up to heaven in miraculous circumstances: in the details and iconography of this phase of the story there is evidently a crossover with an originally unconnected legend, that of Mary of Egypt, another sanctified *peccatrix quondam femina*.[8] The Magdalen legend, that is, is itself a compilation, bits having been added on to it from biblical and nonbiblical sources over more than a thousand years. This fact is inscribed on the surface of the English play Mary Magdalen in the form of its extreme stylistic heterogeneity.

The story of Apollonius is a good deal older. There is some scholarly uncertainty about whether it is a lost Greek romance or a Latin imitation of Greek romance, but either way it appears that the wanderings of Apollonius were proverbial by the sixth century.[9] And its diffusion is attested all over the place, not only in the Latin collections already mentioned: there is an Anglo-Saxon version from the eleventh century, and fourteenth- or fifteenth-century translations into all the main vernaculars of Europe.[10] It is likely enough, then, that the French monastic appropriation of the composite saint Mary Magdalen should have filled out its narrative iconography by borrowing from this widely known story. If so, it is that transfer that ironically surfaces, centuries later, in the rhyme between the Magdalen play and *Pericles.* It is not that *Mary Magdalen* influenced *Pericles,* but that the source of *Pericles* influenced the source of *Mary Magdalen.*

The transfer, though, is arguably less interesting than the transferability. The exchange of material between Hellenic romance and Christian hagiography can be shown to go back virtually to the beginning of both. Thus, for example, the second-century story of Thecla concerns a beautiful virgin who is converted by the preaching of St. Paul and braves various extremes of persecution and sexual harrassment in order to be by his side. The official genre is hagiography, and Thecla was indeed venerated as a saint, but the shape of the love story is unmistakable.[11] Earlier still, the biblical Acts of the Apostles can be read as a kind of Greek romance;[12] certainly Mary Magdalen's voyage to Marseilles borrows authority from St. Paul's journey to Rome, with its generically appropriate shipwreck, island, and miracle.

The Apollonius story itself offers a detailed instance of the system of exchange in the motif of the heroine's defense of her chastity. Apollonius's daughter Tarsia is captured by pirates and sold to the owner of a brothel; several clients are sent in to her, but her account of her sorrows so fills them with pity that they are unable to violate her.[13] On the one hand, this incident echoes saints' legends such as that of St. Agnes, who is sent to a brothel by the local prefect's son after she has spurned his advances; an angel meets her there and frightens away the clients with his radiance.[14] But one could also connect it with Antheia, the heroine of the *Ephesiaca of Xenophon,* who produces the same effect on her would-be ravishers by faking an epileptic fit.[15] The mechanism of the heroine's deliverance varies interestingly between these analogues: we may wonder at the heroine's faith, or at her resourcefulness, or at the force of her personality; and these differences are clearly a function of the story's moves into or out of a sacred context. But it is not possible, except on rather speculative dating evidence, to identify one of the versions as "original"—to say that St. Agnes is Antheia sanctified, or that Antheia is Agnes secularized. Even the equivocal comedy of the situation, which is made particularly obvious by dramatization, is not necessarily incompatible with its miraculous character. On the medieval stage, for instance, the Virgin Martyrs of Hrotsvitha plays a comparable story as a clown routine: the rapist's perceptions are divinely scrambled so that he mistakes the cooking pots for the object of his lust, and ends up satisfyingly covered in soot.[16]

This easy traffic between sacred and profane narratives is hardly a cultural accident. The basic structure of the few extant Greek "novels," after all, is the arbitrary separation of lovers, their quest for one another through episodes of abduction, shipwreck, and seeming death, their unshakeable devotion to one another, and their deserved reuniting by wonderfully fortunate means. Their secret mutual faith gives meaning to the random contingency of the story by turning it into a trial of love, and also empowers them to come through the trial unscathed. There is little difficulty in translating these tribulations into those that the saint experiences at the hands of a hostile world, seemingly cruel tests of faith under the ultimate supervision of a benign providence which eventually reunites the soul with Christ in recognition or martyrdom. The mechanisms that construct the hero and heroine as the pattern of love are identical with the mechanisms that construct the saint as the pattern of piety. One modern historian of Greek romance tersely and suggestively asserts that "[n] ovels and mystery religions flourished at the same time and in the same milieu";[17] and the connection between the two is amply represented by the most sophisticated of surviving classical "novels," *The Golden Ass.* But of course the most significant of the mystery religions turned out to be Christianity: if romance and hagiography blur readily into each other, it is because they were never entirely separate in the first place.

So if, as has more than once been suggested, *Pericles* is a Jacobean miracle play in secular disguise, there is more to the conjunction than a biographical collision, such as the hypothesis that Shakespeare was a crypto-Catholic,[18] or that he had seen a fugitive saint play in his youth.[19] The point is rather that romance and miracle are separable but not separate manifestations of a common repertoire of plots and plot devices—a langue, as it were, in relation to which *Pericles* and the legend of Mary Magdalen appear as instances of parole: a sea of stories.[20]

II

Perhaps the first impression that *Mary Magdalen* makes on a modern student of drama is one of technical incompetence. In the source story, Mary arrives in Marcylle and takes up lodging in a poor hut where she is without food until, prompted by angels, she appears to the King and Queen in a dream and orders them to offer her hospitality. The play stages this episode after it has shown Mary preaching to the King and Queen and destroying their heathen temple with fire from heaven; their neglect of so formidable a visitor is therefore puzzlingly absentminded. Later, when the Queen dies in childbirth on the voyage to the Holy Land, the storm, which is essential to the story, is alluded to in a couple of lines and then instantly forgotten. Then the King bizarrely deposits not only his dead wife but also his living child on a rock in the sea; then, instantly, he is shown disembarking at Jerusalem and paying off the sailors, a transaction that takes as long as his last farewell to his family did. He then proceeds to his baptism and pilgrimage as if nothing had happened, not so much as mentioning the tragedy when he introduces himself to St. Peter.[21]

And so on. We no longer believe the whiggish literary historians who depicted the fifteenth century as the infancy of English drama, from which it grew through its Tudor adolescence to Shakespearean maturity. But contemplating this exasperating mixture of redundancy and discontinuity, it is futile to pretend that we can't see what they meant. And of course, there is no reason to rule out the possibility that the writer of *Mary Magdalen* was just not a good dramatist, or even that dramatists of the later fifteenth century, like those of, say, the early nineteenth, were confronted by culturally posed problems of form which were not fully soluble under prevailing conditions.

That was certainly the light in which humanist writers viewed the state of drama during the 1570s and 80s—the decades when *Mary Magdalen,* like much of the medieval repertoire, dropped out of live theatrical use.[22] In 1578 George Whetstone, in his brief sketch of the dramatic shortcomings of various nations, declares English playwrights to be "most vaine, indiscreete, and out of order";[23] what he means by that is that they have no regard to probability, or to the unity of time and place. Sidney rehearses the same objections in the *Apologie for Poetry* a few years later. In such interventions there is more at stake than the fashionable promulgation of the "rules" of Italian neo-Aristotelianism. They coincide, after all, with the polemical and administrative attack on the London playhouses during the decade following the establishment of the Theater in 1576. Both Whetstone and Sidney are well aware of this context: Whetstone's dedication is an anxious defense of the moral legitimacy of comedy, addressed to the Recorder of London; and Sidney is in explicitly performed debate with assorted "Poethaters."[24] For both, the lamentable state of English playwriting is a serious embarrassment; Sidney does praise the language and morality of Gorboduc, but with a slight air of clutching at straws. Clearly this case would be easier to make if one could adduce some artistically respectable native drama.

Thus Thomas Lodge, replying to Stephen Gosson's Schoole of Abuse in 1579, concedes that contemporary theater poets "apply their writing to the people vain,"[25] and tries to distinguish the abuses of drama from drama itself so that he can argue for the reformation of the former instead of the abolition of the latter. This puts him in the fragile position of defending the theater for what it could be rather than for what it is, and Gosson,

returning to the attack in 1582, vigorously exploits this weakness. Lodge has said, claiming the authority of Cicero, that plays are the "Schoolmistresse of life; the lookinge glass of manners; and the image of trueth." Even if Cicero did say that (which Gosson doubts), can the sentiment really be applied to these plays?

> Sometime you shall see nothing but the aduentures of an amorous knight, passing from countrie to countrie for the loue of his lady, encountring many a terible monster made of broune paper, & at his retorne, is so wonderfully changed, that he can not be knowne but by some posie in his tablet, or by a broken ring, or a hand-kircher, or a piece of a cockle shell, what learne you by that?[26]

Here is the sea of stories again, contemplated this time with weary distaste. Lodge's mimetic formula, reasonably convincing as a rationale for Roman comedy which conforms to the principles of the Ars Poetica, provides only very patchy cover for a popular theater dominated, as all these writers agree it is, by wandering chivalric romance. Controversialists may disagree about the lawfulness of drama in general, but they all agree that the current practitioners are no good at all. There is, to put the case at its most neutral, a lack of fit between the actually existing theater and the language available for discussing it.

What if this anomaly—this gap between theory and practice, if you like—reflects not simply artistic failure on the part of the playwrights, but the existence of a different model of theater, unarticulated in comparison with the one confidently derived from Aristotle, Horace, and Castelvetro, and, evidently, incompatible with it? If so, we might articulate something of this converse aesthetic by taking the most conceptually agile of the neoclassical theorists, Sidney, and reading him backwards.

Like Gosson, he makes merry with the conventions of dramatic storytelling:

> Now ye shall have three Ladies walke to gather flowers, and then we must beleeue the stage to be a Garden. By and by, we heare newes of shipwracke in the same place, and then wee are to blame if we accept it not for a Rock. Vpon the backe of that, comes out a hidious Monster, with fire and smoke, and then the miserable beholders are bounde to take it for a Caue.[27]

The humor turns on the arbitrary demands the play places on the audience's belief—"we must beleeue," "we are to blame if we accept it not," "the miserable beholders are bounde to take it. . . ." The condition of the spectators seems to get more wretched as the list goes on: every concession they make is met with a further demand, more extravagant than the one before, and conflicting with it, until at last they are reduced to a state of indiscriminate credulity, having been effectively talked out of their senses. The requirement implicit in the mockery is that the show should reduce its demands on the spectator's belief to a minimum, by establishing its imaginary time and place once and then not undermining them with whimsical subsequent changes. In short, that the world of the play should be one.

There is enough detail in Sidney's comic sketch to make it clear that his target, like Gosson's, is secular romance.[28] However, after what has been said about the crossover between romance and hagiography, it comes as no surprise to note that his argument is an equally conclusive condemnation of the dramaturgy of *Mary Magdalen*. It does indeed feature a garden, a rock, and a hideous smoking Monster (though the last is in a heathen temple rather than a cave). And it inhabits a multiplicity not only of times and places but even of dramatic modes, being a moral allegory and a passion play and a miracle play. Not content with dividing its action between Palestine and France, it positively rubs our noses in this geographical extravagance by having a property ship travel, presumably on wheels, across the playing area from one country to the other, not once but three times.[29] So that we are at fault, you could say, if we do not conceive the *platea* to be the Mediterranean, and a few minutes of trundling over a flat ground to be a fortnight's voyage.

Mary Magdalen, then, is paradigmatic of the kind of drama Sidney regards as absurd and indefensible. The play sank into oblivion without finding an apologist in its turn. However, having decided to invent one, we can surely think of things for him to say. One is that the first dramatic purpose of *Mary Magdalen,* obviously, is to embody and animate the image of the saint. Unity is conferred upon the play's extreme stylistic and structural miscellaneity only by this central figure. And a saint is by definition a mediator between worlds: to realize this idea on stage absolutely requires that one shatter the unity of time and place, because it is constitutive of the saint's identity that she exists both in heaven and on earth, in time and in eternity, in Jerusalem and Provence and, if it comes to that, Chelmsford. Even if the makers of the drama had been familiar with the rule that one should only ask the spectators to believe in one dramatic world, they would have been obliged to transgress it by the very nature of their object of representation.

And then secondly, the primary means of dramatizing the saint's identity, at least in the legendary section of the play, is the representation of miracles. The destruction of the idol, the survival of the child, the raising of the dead mother—each significant episode is centered on the audience's witnessing an astonishing event that discloses divine power. The improbability of these actions—their arbitrary eruption through the earthly texture of causes and effects—is precisely the point of their enactment. One of the basic criteria for the recognition of a miracle, after all, is that it should be *contra naturam;*[30] consequently, anything in its presentation helping to reconcile it with the natural course of events would have the effect of blurring its outlines. To object that the play asks too much of the spectators' capacity for belief is beside the point, since to nourish that capacity is the very *raison d'etre* of the spectacle.

In other words, this is a theater in which the Aristotelian criteria of formal unity and probability are not merely not observed, but necessarily and militantly negated. It is not that the play fails to be probable and consequential, but that it fully intends to transcend consequence and baffle probability. To Gosson's sarcastic observation that the hero is so "wonderfully changed" that nobody can recognize him, it implicitly retorts that wonderful changes are the essential business of the performance.

At this point, however, we need to remember who Sidney was really arguing with: not the exponents either of saints' plays or of chivalric romances, but fellow Puritans who needed to be convinced that poetry in general, and theater in particular, had any place at all in a reformed and godly commonwealth. As Patrick Collinson has argued, the familiar denunciations of the stage—Northbrooke, Gosson, Stubbes—are documents from a "second phase" of the English Reformation, one marked by increasing hostility, not only to images directly representative of the Catholic past, but to images in general.[31] Thus Gosson's attack on improbable romances is not really the cry of an outraged Aristotelian, but an opportunistic debating point in the course of a very differently grounded argument to the effect that all plays are evil, because "every play to the worldes end, if it be presented vp on the Stage, shall carry that brand on his backe to make him knowne, which the devil clapt on, at the first beginning, that is, idolatrie."[32]

Theater is idolatrous in its first beginning because it originated in the worship of pagan gods. But it is also idolatrous in its essential nature because it works by setting up false images with the intention that they should be taken for truths. This line of attack makes it clear how consciously the condemnation of theater is part of the Reformation. To describe plays as incorrigibly idolatrous is to conflate them with late medieval Catholic culture as it appeared to those who destroyed it in the 1530s: the pageantry of the saints, the magical bones and phials of dubious blood, the theatricality of the liturgy, the superstitious populace—an impure mixture of magical belief, deception, and buffoonery, including, for Gosson, "the corruption of the Corpus Christi Playes that were set out by the Papistes . . . where some base fellowe that plaide Christe, should bring the person of Christ into contempt."[33] However assiduously it proclaims Protestant doctrine, the theater is still a Catholic kind of thing in its suspect reassigning of substance: a brown paper effigy is a dragon; some base fellow is Christ; wine is blood. Reforming drama in the manner of Bale or Wager doesn't begin to meet this case, because the popery it denounces is a matter, not at all of content, but of form.[34]

Sidney's implicit program can be seen in this context as a strategy for decatholicizing the theater. By proscribing arbitrary transubstantiations of the stage properties, he draws a clear dividing line between dramatic illusion and pseudo-miracle. By drastically restricting the demands placed on the spectator's credulity, he establishes a parallel difference between theatrical belief and superstition. And by insisting on a single stage world, he effectively calls for a secularized theater, devoid of heaven, hell, allegory, theophany, and magic.

Such a program of purification entails, as we have seen, a reimagining of the theater's relationship with story. This becomes clearer when Sidney is anticipating some practical objections to his neoclassical rigor:

> But they will say, how then shal we set forth a story, which contains both many places and many times? And doe they not knowe that a Tragedie is tied to the lawes of Poesie, and not of Historie? not bound to follow the storie, but, having liberty, either to faine a quite newe matter, or to frame the history to the most tragicall conueniencie. Againe, many things may be told which cannot be shewed, if they know the difference betwixt reporting and representing.[35]

This extends Sidney's armory of binary oppositions with two thoroughly Aristotelian distinctions—between tragedy and history (in tragedy the form is mandatory and the "matter" is freely disposable, whereas in history it is the other way round); and between diegesis and mimesis (one can be here and talk about Peru, and then change the subject to Calicut without difficulty, whereas to move between these places "in action" one needs "Pacolets horse"—that is, the magical repertoire of romance).

The first of these—the opposition between tragedy and history has the effect of dissociating drama from the category of referential truth, and so disposing of the accusation that its images, like those of idolatrous religion, are false. The story told by a play is required by Aristotle to be probable; it is not required to be true. If it is improbable, it is no defense to say that it is true: improbable things do sometimes happen, but that does not make them probable, and so does not make them suitable subjects for drama. Once again, *Mary Magdalen* offers an exact mirror image: in the saint play, it is positively required that the story should be improbable and true. The hagiographer is "bound to follow the storie," and the play's lumpy, undermotivated progress from one miraculous "point" to the next is, among other things, the sign that it is doing just that.

And then this explicit secondariness, this conspicuous deference to the authority of the story, undermines the distinction between "reporting and representing." Which, for example, is this: the moment when the Queen dies in childbed on the ship?

REGINA.

> An hevy departyng is betwyx vs in syth,
> Fore now departe wee!
> For defawte of wommen here in my nede,
> Deth my body makyth to sprede.
> Now Mary Mavdleyn, my sowle lede!
> In manus tuas, Domine!

REX.

> Alas, my wyff is ded!
> Alas, this is a carefull chans!

(1760-67)

This is certainly enactment: the King and Queen are aboard the property ship with the sailor and his boy, and the Queen's last line clearly cues a physical representation of dying. But the decisive speech acts are narrative ones: "now departe wee," "deth my body makyth to sprede," "my wyff is ded." The actors are not being asked to enter the world of the characters, but to show the events of the story—verbally and gesturally—to the audience. The conditions of performance are necessary context here: almost certainly this is an outdoor amphitheater performance on a festival occasion. The spectators are thus highly present—visually, in that they wholly or partly surround the playing area and define its limits; and culturally, in that their having assembled is an integral part of the event. The performance thus has the character of a public demonstration; the performers are not in the business of creating the illusion of a present experience; rather, they are telling an old story in a mode which includes "doing the actions." Passing instantly from one significant action to the next is therefore no more problematic than turning a page or saying, "Then the King did this." In other words, the stage action has the narrative character which Sidney reserves for verbal discourse. The representing is a kind of reporting.

One could put it this way: Mary in the play is already a saint. The devotional discourse which attaches to her is no less part of her stage being than the events of her life: what is staged is not a person about whom there will later be a legend, but the legend itself. It is consistent with this that many of the lines are not interlocutory dialogue, but general announcements, sermons, or prayers to God or the saints—that is, they are words which can be uttered as validly and appropriately in Suffolk on the day of the performance as in Marcylle on the day of the historical event. Even the dialogue often has this transhistorical character. For instance, when the King and Queen are welcomed home by Mary, they kneel to her, and the Queen says:

Heyll, thou chosyn and chast of wommen alon!
It passyt my wett to tell thi nobyllnesse!
Thou relevyst me and my chyld on the rokke of ston,
And also savyd vs be thi holynesse.

(1943-46)

Again, this is a dramatic interchange in a way. The Queen arrives home and greets her friend and teacher. But the communicative acts—kneeling, hailing her, naming her, rehearsing her goodness—are those of prayer: the discourse also belongs to a late medieval devotee of St. Mary Magdalen. So that "the rokke of ston," although it is a reference to a specific location in the world of the story, also sounds like a generalized emblem of hardship, and the Queen's "death" on it a universal experience. The story takes place in a performative present, dissolving Sidney's opposition between here and elsewhere, now and then, a thing done and a thing reported.

On all these central questions, then—time, space, unity, history, and representation—*Mary Magdalen* is informed by a coherent model of theatrical communication which is the antithesis of the neo-Aristotelian model proposed in the *Apologie*. Moreover, this antithetic model is fundamentally and inextricably Catholic: if the theater is to be rendered fit for performance in a godly commonwealth, the form of a play like *Mary Magdalen* has to be rejected—consigned to the past, to the "undramatic," and to the cultural dustbin of the "popular." To some extent this is indeed what happened: although the "unities" have long been as archaic as the dramaturgy they were seeking to reform, Sidney's underlying assumptions about what constitutes drama still survive in the form of common sense—which is why *Mary Magdalen* strikes us as incompetent. But the program of reform, like others in the Elizabethan settlement, only went so far. In 1614, when Shakespeare had already retired, Ben Jonson, as the conscious inheritor of Sidney's poetics, was still finding it necessary to denounce the theater of rambling and miraculous storytelling, as represented by those who continued to "beget Tales, Tempests, and such like drolleries."[36] "Renaissance drama" was persistently haunted by its pre-Reformation alternative: Sidney and Jonson constructed a theoretical embankment between the theater and the sea of stories, but it leaked.

III

So when Jonson, writing in 1629, famously dismissed Pericles as a "mouldy tale," noun and epithet were both carefully weighed.[37] Not only is this particular story extremely old, but also the type of story (voyages, shipwrecks, arbitrary separations, and reunions across years and countries) is exactly the kind of thing we saw being excluded from drama proper in the 1580s—the episodic stringing together of devices from that collective medieval repertoire which I have called the sea of stories, but which Jonson less picturesquely describes as "Scraps, out of every dish, / Thrown forth and raked into the common tub." Moreover, the play's mode of presentation, switching between enactment and gauche choric links, subordinates the stage action to the logic of narrative, breaking up, all over again, the unity and completeness of the dramatic image. Jonson's immediate context is a diatribe against the vulgarity and ignorance of audiences, and it is not hard to see how the success of Pericles seems, from a "Sidneian" point of view, to prove his point. In fifty years the theatergoing public had apparently learned nothing and forgotten nothing.

A curious set of records enables us to locate this obstinacy within a wider conservatism. In 1610, when the performance of saints' plays had effectively been illegal for decades, a show about St. Christopher was allegedly presented at Gowthwaite Hall, the home of a Yorkshire recusant named Sir John Yorke. The allegation was investigated by a commission of the Star Chamber, who questioned the principal actors, also themselves recusants. Part of their complicated and sometimes contradictory defense was that they always played from printed books, and one of them added that the plays they had in fact taken to Sir John Yorke's and other gentlemen's houses at the time in question were "Perocles prince of Tire" and "king Lere."[38]

These are formidable plays for a company of semiprofessional, provincial strolling players of dubious legal status, and John L. Murphy, in his study of these materials, plausibly suggests that the actors may have had some sort of sponsorship from the Jesuit mission to England, which was certainly active among exactly this network of Catholic Yorkshire gentry. We know that the English Jesuit college at St. Omer occasionally performed sacred plays, and that in 1619 its library, which mostly consisted of devotional and controversial works, possessed a copy of *Pericles*.[39] It starts to look as if the play was, so to speak, leading a double life.

To understand the capacity of the script to do this, we could start with the little scene which rounds off the role of Thaisa in the first half of the play. Having "died" in childbed at sea, like the Queen of Marcylle, she is cast overboard in her coffin, and then miraculously revived by the physician Cerimon. She explains to him:

That I was shipp'd at sea
I well remember, even on my eaning time;
But whether there deliver'd, by the holy gods,
I cannot rightly say. But since King Pericles,
My wedded lord, I ne'er shall see again,
A vestal livery will I take me to,
And never more have joy.

(III, iv, 4-10)

If Jonson ever inspected the play in detail, this is the kind of thing to which he will have taken exception. Thaisa has no recollection of whether her child was safely delivered or not; and the situation as she is aware of it gives her no reason to suppose that Pericles is dead, or that if he is alive, he has done anything except return sorrowfully to Tyre, where it would surely be feasible to send him a message. So why does she declare that she will never see him again? Because the "mouldy tale" requires her to stay out of the way while Marina grows up so that father, mother, and daughter can all have their wonder-filled reunion in the fifth act. Thaisa's improbable incuriosity about the people she is supposed to love is a symptom of the blind subordination of the dramatic action to the story.

This reductive answer is not absurd. As the play's most recent editors point out at length, the play positively insists on its status as a kind of storytelling: it not only executes, but self-consciously dramatizes, the primacy of narrative.[40] But there is another, less general way of interpreting Thaisa's strange gesture. When she was first revived, she asked, "What world is this?" (III, ii, 107). And when she says that she will never see her lord again, she is holding a scroll, addressed from him to whoever finds her, asking them to give her burial. In other words, it is not so much that she supposes her husband and child to be dead; rather, it is as if she herself had died. Her "terrible childbed," her burial at sea, the grief of Pericles, and the motherless childhood of Marina—these things amount to the story of Thaisa's death, so the Thaisa we see on stage obeys the logic of that story, even though there is also another story in which she has survived. Dead and living at once, she enters a liminal state, represented by her withdrawal from the world into Diana's temple. There cannot be a question about the probability of her actions, because she is not in the world where action takes place. As in the saint play, the journeying, episodic plot and the dislocated temporality are the sign and condition of access to multiple worlds.

Saints' legends are made up of four basic possible gests: conversion, martyrdom, miracle, and withdrawal from the world. They are fairly freely combinable: *Mary Magdalen,* a very rich example, contains all of them except martyrdom; some of the shortest of the stories in the *Golden Legend* focus on only one. The impact of the Reformation on this combination was selective. The miracle was redefined as idolatrous, as we have seen; and the withdrawal from the world was identified with monasticism—both of these therefore became signs of popery rather than of holiness. Conversion and martyrdom, on the other hand, not only retained their validity, but acquired new intensity from their special Protestant meanings. Thus Foxe's *Actes and Monuments* is constructed almost entirely around the gest of martyrdom, and Lewis Wager's Protestant dramatization of the

Mary Magdalen legend (1566) drops both the miraculous story and the eventual sanctification in the wilderness, leaving what is essentially a play about conversion.[41] The effect on these developments of the late-sixteenth-century secularization of the stage was consequently an ironic one. The gests of conversion and martyrdom were still sacred and therefore excluded from the theatrical repertoire. But the other two—miracle and withdrawal—had been desanctified and were therefore available, so to speak, for secular dramatic use. It is hard to think of plays that exploit this somewhat inadvertent and asymmetrical opportunity as fully as the Yorkshire recusants' selection: *King Lear* and *Pericles.*[42]

In her elegantly structural account of early saints' narratives, Alison Goddard Elliott distinguishes between hagiographic epic and hagiographic romance. Epic centers on martyrdom: it is about the saint's death, it takes place *in foro,* amid human institutions, and it is agonistic, pitting good against evil; it therefore entails assertion on the part of the saint. Romance centers on ascetism: it is about the saint's life, it takes place in the wilderness, among angels, demons, and animals, and it is gradational, charting a progression from sanctity to greater sanctity; it therefore entails submission on the part of the saint. "One of the most significant contributions of hagiographic romance," then, "was the enshrining of the concept of liminal space."[43] Between the world where we live and the world to which we go when we die, there is the place belonging to both and neither: the desert, the forest, the island. Sometimes the saint even joins with this environment to the point of becoming less or more than human: hairy, naked, buried in the earth, or communing with strangely amiable lions and bears.

It is easy to see how this binarism corresponds with the opposition I have suggested between reformable and unreformable saintly gests. The elements of "epic" hagiography are the Protestant ones, conversion and martyrdom: they happen in this world. Those of romance are the gests of Catholic sainthood, miracle and withdrawal: they intimate an encounter between this world and another, fracturing the unity of the dramatic image. It is as romance, then, that the theater of saints penetrates Elizabethan and particularly Shakespearean drama. Thaisa in her lightly paganized nunnery; Pericles on the sea, unkempt, unwashed and wordless; Marina, living incognito far from her imposing tomb at Tarsus—all inhabit varieties of liminal space, providentially relieved, you could say, on the rock of stone, none of them engaged in anything Aristotle would recognize as an action, all awaiting a miracle which outruns the category of action because it does not belong to any of them, but to the legend that contains them. When Pericles recognizes Marina

O, come hither,
Thou that beget'st him that did thee beget;
Thou that wast born at sea, buried at Tharsus,
And found at sea again

(V, i, 194-97)

the moment is theophanic. His rehearsal of the elements of her life—birth, burial, finding—makes it sound as if they were the fulfillment of a prophecy, as if he had discerned a divinely composed design in what had seemed until this moment to be meaningless contingencies. In fact there is no such prophecy in Pericles;[44] the mystery of which he becomes ecstatically aware in this moment is more diffused than that. It is, precisely, a formal illumination: Pericles realizes that what is happening to him is a story.

It is easy to imagine, then, how Sir John Yorke's Christmas guests, watching *St. Christopher* one night and *Pericles* the next, could have felt themselves to be in the same dramatic world. The saint play had found its way through a complicated set of internal and external determinants to a post-Reformation form, at once displaced, popular, and sophisticated. To suppose this, it is not necessary to think of *Pericles* as a crypto-Catholic *pièce à clè*, a saint play in protective disguise. The likelier story is vaguer but more interesting: that the decatholicizing of theater was only ever partly feasible, because the codes of miracle playing were carried into Protestant English drama in the formal structures of plays and their performances. It therefore remained possible for a Catholic audience to reconnect with sacred drama just by the way it watched these legally published plays about things that are lost and then return.

Notes

1. William Shakespeare, *Pericles,* ed. F. D. Hoeniger, Arden edition (London: Methuen, 1963), xc. References to *Pericles* are to this text; those to *Mary Magdalen* are to Donald C. Baker, John L. Murphy, and Louis B. Hall Jr., eds., *The Late Medieval Religious Plays of Bodleian MSS Digby 133 and E Museo 160,* EETS o.s. 283 (Oxford: Oxford University Press, 1982). The "Marcylle" sequence, which is my focus of interest, occupies lines 1349-1956.

2. Stephen Greenblatt, *Shakespearean Negotiations: The Circulation of Social Energy in Renaissance England* (Oxford: Clarendon Press, 1988), 94.

3. Geoffrey Bullough, *Narrative and Dramatic Sources of Shakespeare,* 8 vols. (London: Routledge and Kegan Paul, 1957-75), 6:351-54.

4. Jacobus de Voragine, *The Golden Legend: Readings on the Saints,* trans. William Granger Ryan, 2 vols. (Princeton: Princeton University Press, 1993), 1:374-83.

5. Louis Reau, *Iconographie de l'art chretien,* 3 vols. in 6 (Paris: Presses Universitaires de France, 1955-59), 3:846-48.

6. Both parts of the story were sufficiently established by the thirteenth century to feature in the windows of chartres. See Joseph Szoverffy, peccatrix quondam femina: A Survey of the Mary Magdalen Itymns," *Traditio* 19 (1963): 84.

7. The Golden Legend version actually refers to the King as "the Pilgrim" once the Holy Land episode is under way.

8. *Golden Legend,* 1:227-29; Reau, *Iconographie,* 3:855.

9. Laura A. Hibberd, *Medieval Romance in England* (New York: Burt Franklin, 1960), 164-73.

10. Bullough, *Narrative and Dramatic Sources,* 6:353.

11. The story is summarized, and discussed in these terms, in Tomas Hagg, *The Novel in Antiquity* (Berkeley: University of California Press, 1983), 154-62; and Alison Goddard Elliott, *Roads to Paradise: Reading the Lives of the Early Saints* (Hanover, N.H.: University Press of New England, 1987), 48-50.

12. Stephen P. Schierling and Maria J. Schierling, "The Influence of the Ancient Romances on Acts of the Apostles, *The Classical Bulletin* 54 (1978): 81-88.

13. Told in this way, for example, in Gower, *Confessio Amantis,* Book VIII, lines 1431-39, in Bullough, *Narrative and Dramatic Sources,* 6:407.

14. *Golden Legend* 1:101-4. Bullough, *Narrative and Dramatic Sources,* 6:352, points out the connection.

15. See Hagg, *The Novel in Antiquity,* 32, 147-53.

16. In *The Plays of Hrotsvit of Gandersheim,* trans. Katharina Wilson (New York: Garland, 1989).

17. Hagg, *The Novel in Antiquity,* 104.

18. The biographical case for Shakespeare's Catholic background is set out in, for example, E. A. J. Honigmann, *Shakespeare: "The Lost Years"* (Manchester: Manchester University Press, 1985).

19. Howard Felperin, *Shakespearean Romance* (Princeton: Princeton University Press, 1972), 145, 166.

20. The image is Salman Rushdie's. In his children's story *Haroun and the Sea of Stories* (London: Granta Books with Penguin, 1991), the sea is not merely whimsical; it represents the heteroglot tradition that sustains the art of the hero's father, a

professional storyteller. The culture of such performers, in which the storyteller's distinction consists of his ability to retell and combine stories rather than to make them up, is analogous to the one within which Shakespeare, Gower, and the makers of *Mary Magdalen* all meet.

21. The source in the *Golden Legend* makes better sense of some of these points: the events at Marcylle are in the right order; the baby is left with the mother on a coast, where there is some prospect of its finding succor; and the King relates his misfortune to St. Peter, who comforts him.

22. If John Coldewey's conjectures are correct, the last known performance was at a summer festival at Chelmsford in 1562. See John C. Coldewey, "The Digby Plays and the Chelmsford Records," *Research Opportunities in Renaissance Drama* 18 (1975): 103-21. The subsequent history of the script is pursued in Baker, Murphy and Hall, eds., *The Late Medieval Religious Plays of Bodleian MSS Digby 133 and F Museo 160,* x-xiv. In 1574 the playbook was still being held by the churchwardens, presumably with the possibility of occasional performances in mind. Some time after that they must have concluded that the script was not going to be of any further use, and it seems that it passed into the possession of Myles Blomefylde, who was the keeper of the churchwardens' accounts between 1582 and 1590, and died in 1603. From his collection it traveled by an unreconstructable route to that of Sir Kenelm Digby, where it arrived at some point between 1616 and 1633. It is difficult to pinpoint the moment in this somewhat speculative narrative when the manuscript ceased to be a functioning playscript and became an object of antiquarian curiosity; the best guess is some time during the 1580s.

23. Dedication to *Promos and Cassandra,* in G. Gregory Smith, ed., *Elizabethan Critical Essays,* 2 vols. (London: Oxford University Press, 1904), 1:59.

24. Ibid., 1:181.

25. Ibid., 1:83.

26. Stephen Gosson, *Playes Confuted in Five Actions,* in Arthur E Kinney, *Markets of Bawdrie: The Dramatic Criticism of Stephen Gosson,* Salzburg Studies in English Literature: Elizabethan Studies 4 (Salzburg: Institut fur Englische Sprache und Literatur, 1974), 161.

27. Smith, *Elizabethan Critical Essays,* 1:197.

28. The extant example which comes closest to the description is Sir Clyomon and Sir Clamydes; it is discussed as such by Brian Gibbons in A. R.

Braunmuller and Michael Hattaway, eds., *The Cambridge Companion to English Renaissance Drama* (Cambridge: Cambridge University Press, 1990), 207-12. The play itself is accessible as *Clyomon and Clamydes* (Oxford: Malone Society Reprints, 1913).

29. John Coldewey flirts with the idea of a waterway ("The Digby Plays," 117) but thinks it impracticable in Chelmsford. Glynne Wickham is similarly noncommittal while canvassing Ipswich in "The Staging of Saint Plays in England," Sandro Sticca, ed., *The Medieval Drama* (Albany: State University of New York Press, 1972), 112. A floating boat is not out of the question-unambiguous Continental examples are cited in Peter Meredith and John E. Tailby, eds., *The Staging of Religious Drama in Europe in the Later Middle Ages* (Kalamazoo, Mich.: Medieval Institute Publications, 1983), 98-99. But it seems less likely than a wheeled pageant, and, in any case, an artificial pond would if anything draw attention to the non-identity of theatrical signifier and oceanic signified even more brutally than dry land.

30. A fifteenth-century formulation, cited in Ronald C. Finucane, *Miracles and Pilgrims: Popular Beliefs in Medieval England* (London: J. M. Dent, 1977), 54.

31. Patrick Collinson, *The Birthpangs of Protestant England: Religious and Cultural Change in the Sixteenth and Seventeenth Centuries* (London: Macmillan, 1988), 98, 112-14.

32. Kinney, *Markets of Bawdrie,* 179.

33. Ibid., 178.

34. See Peter Happe, "The Protestant Adaptation of the Saint Play," in Clifford Davidson, ed., *The Saint Play in Medieval Europe* (Kalamazoo, Mich.: Medieval Institute Publications, 1986), 205-40.

35. Smith, *Elizabethan Critical Essays,* 1:198.

36. Ben Jonson, *Bartholomew Fair,* Induction, line 115, in vol. 4 of the *Complete Plays,* ed. G. A. Wilkes (Oxford: Clarendon Press, 1982). The affiliation to Sidney is more clearly seen in the prologue to *Every Man in His Humour,* which was probably written at about the same time.

37. Ben Jonson, "Ode to Himself," in *The Complete Poems,* ed. George Parfitt Harmondsworth: Penguin, 1975). 282.

38. The commission records are summarized in John L. Murphy, *Darkness and Devils: Exorcism and "King Lear"* (Athens: Ohio University Press), 93-118; and less reliably in C. J. Sisson, "Shake-

speare's Quartos as Prompt-Copies with Some Account of Cholmeley's Players and a New Shakespeare Allusion," *Review of English Studies* 18 (1942): 129-43.

39. Willem Schric, "'Pericles' in a Book-list of 1619 from the English Jesuit Mission and Some of the Play's Special Problems," *Shakespeare Survey* 29 (1976): 21-32.

40. *Pericles, Prince of Tyre,* ed. Doreen Delvecchio and Antony Hammond, New Cambridge Shakespeare (Cambridge: Cambridge University Press, 1998), 27-36.

41. Lewis Wager, *The Life and Repentaunce of Marie Magdalene,* ed. E J. Carpenter (Chicago: University of Chicago Press, 1902).

42. They were arguably remiss in failing to pick up *Timon of Athens.*

43. Elliott, *Roads to Paradise,* 204.

44. A prophecy of this kind, of course, is fulfilled at the corresponding point in *The Winter's Tale.*

Margaret Healy (essay date 1999)

SOURCE: Healy, Margaret. "*Pericles* and the Pox." In *Shakespeare's Late Plays: New Readings,* edited by Jennifer Richards and James Knowles, pp. 92-107. Edinburgh, Scotland: Edinburgh University Press, 1999.

[*In the following excerpt, Healy asserts that in* Pericles *Shakespeare presented a veiled criticism of the efforts of King James I to wed his children to members of the Spanish royal family.*]

Louis MacNeice's poem *Autolycus* (1944-7) gives aptly magical expression to the dominant apprehension of Shakespeare's late plays in our century. *Autolycus* evokes a picture of the Bard at the sunset of his career mysteriously moving away from the 'taut plots and complex characters' of the major tragedies, conjuring instead 'tapestried romances . . . / With rainbow names and handfuls of sea-spray', and from them turning out 'happy Ever-afters' (ll. 3-6). MacNeice's words capture a certain ambivalence towards this Shakespearean sea change: indeed, the romances, with their emphasis on the production of wonder, their tendency towards straggling plots and emblematic representation, and their preponderance of 'childish horrors' and 'old gags' (*Autolycus* ll. 14, 15), are often experienced as charming but enigmatic and not altogether satisfying puzzles—even as regressive aberrations. The latter is most true of the 'unwanted child' *Pericles,* a play of suspect parentage, excluded from the First Folio, and only available to us through what most editors agree is a particularly

bastardised quarto and its numerous offspring (it was printed six times to 1635, including twice in one year, 1609—an unusual occurrence).[1]

Frequently vilified and rarely performed today, *Pericles* has been the focus of considerable bewilderment: why, critics repeatedly ponder, was this play so acclaimed and popular in the Jacobean age when it has proven so relatively unappealing in ours?[2] The title page of the first quarto of 1609 describes it as 'The Late, and much admired Play . . . As it hath been divers and sundry times acted by his Majesties Servants, at the Globe'; and contemporary references suggest that it was a huge box-office success in London playhouses, a favourite for private house production, and for court performance, too.[3] It was, moreover, one of two Shakespearean plays—the other being *King Lear*—put on by a professional company with recusant sympathies (Sir Richard Cholmeley's Players), which toured Yorkshire in 1609.[4]

When *Pericles* was performed by the RSC in 1990, however, one theatre critic, dismissing the play 'as just a far-fetched fairy tale', could only explain its early seventeenth-century appeal in the following derogatory terms:

> It is fanciful to think that business had been flat at the Globe, and Burbage suggested that something with more sex and violence would pull audiences in. 'Incest and brothels will,' he might have said, 'do the box-office a power of good.'[5]

Steven Mullaney reached much the same conclusion in his important book, *The Place of the Stage.* Contesting the popular thesis that this is an experimental play which evolved to suit the new context of the Blackfriars theatre, Mullaney argues that *Pericles* rather 'represents a radical effort to dissociate the popular stage from its cultural contexts', a shift into 'pure' aestheticism, and that its subsequent literary fortunes testify to 'the limits of any work that seeks to obscure or escape its historical conditions of possibility'.[6] For Mullaney then, this was an experiment of a different kind which went badly wrong. For him, *Pericles* is unalloyed aestheticism pandering to the tastes of emergent liberal humanism—any quest for dissonant voices will get short shrift here.

Sandra Billington's *Mock Kings in Medieval and Renaissance Drama* obliquely reinforces this perspective. In her view the character of Pericles represents kingly perfection; he is 'an ideal courtly lord and effective prince, whose virtue does not waver despite the effects of the plot on it'. She finds *Pericles* an 'exception' in the world of plays from this period dominated by depictions of dubious and tyrannical monarchs, possibly, she suspects, because 'the devil has the most dramatic plots'.[7] Frances Yates and Glynne Wickham, and more recently Jonathan Goldberg and David Bergeron, also forestall a more questioning reading of the play when they argue that *Pericles* contains a thinly veiled likeness to James VI and I in the figure of its hero.[8] Indeed the majority of commentators are admiring of 'patient' king Pericles and if they read James, his family, and the events of his reign into the play, it is almost inevitably viewed as a eulogy to James and a celebration of his rule.[9] Such readings appear to be endorsed by the fact that the text of *Pericles* resonates with James's own aphorisms in his voluminous writings about kingship, a prime example from the beginning of the play being its hero's utterance, 'kings are earth's gods' (i, 146)—arguably the monarch's favourite tenet. Thus, once again, Shakespearean drama is construed as shoring up royal absolutism. This play's undisputed 'happy ending' bears witness to this: the royal marriage which allies two kingdoms is understood as a particularly fortuitous and positive outcome, the topical analogy being the projected peaceful Union of England and Scotland through James's mediation. The latter was a highly topical matter in 1607, and one which had achieved extravagant courtly representation in January of that year in *The Lord Hay's Masque* to celebrate the betrothal of a Scottish favourite and the daughter of an English lord. The masque opens with a fulsome address to 'Gracious James, King of Great Britain':

> O then, great Monarch, with how wise a care
> Do you these bloods divided mix in one,
> And with like consanguinities prepare
> The high and everliving Union
>   'Tween Scots and English. Who can wonder then
> If he that marries kingdoms, marries men.[10]

The 'marriage' of kingdoms was certainly a subject close to the king's heart throughout this decade.

The English-Scottish 'marriage' was not, however, the only one preoccupying James and exercising his patience c.1606-7 when *Pericles* was probably written. The king was simultaneously engaged in plans to ally Britain with Spain, and this projected 'marriage', for the majority of his subjects, was undoubtedly more pressing and more controversial. In fact, 'the Spanish Match' was unlikely to have won widespread public approval: James's repeated attempts to marry his son Henry to the Spanish Infanta and his daughter Elizabeth to the Duke of Savoy would hardly have been construed by the bulk of the populace (for whom Spain was the epitome of the Antichrist) as desirable, or as the stuff of happy endings and fairy-tale romance.[11] Building on this perspective, this chapter will argue that *Pericles*' ending, in particular the betrothal of Marina to Lysimachus, is far from suggestive of uncomplicated 'happy Everafters', and that analysis of this play's representations of early modern syphilis (the Pox), and its medicomoral politics, provides new contexts and substantial support for more dissonant readings.

My focus will be on the last two acts of *Pericles,* and in particular on the brothel scenes where discussion of

the Pox and its consequences are rife and nauseatingly explicit. I should point out that there are no references to syphilis or its consequences in either of the play's two reputed sources: John Gower's *Confessio Amantis* (Book 8) and Lawrence Twine's *The Patterne of Painfull Adventures* (a translation of the 153rd story of the *Gesta Romanorum*). Interestingly, too, George Wilkins' novel of the play, *The Painfull Adventures of Pericles Prince of Tyre* (1608), erases all references to the Pox, recuperates Lysimachus as a healthful and virtuous governor, and concludes by assuring its readers of the fruitfulness and happiness of this union.[12]

I will begin, though, by reminding you where we are at this stage in the action. The first three Acts of *Pericles* portray its hero being tossed impotently around the exotic world of the eastern Mediterranean, a prey to forces greater than himself, yet—in the manner of romance—managing to fall in love, marry and beget a child, Marina, in the process. Life is cruel but virtue flourishes in hardship: Marina, for all intents and purposes an orphan, grows up to be a paragon princess—beautiful, talented and saintly. Her tragic destiny, however, catches up with her, and her wicked guardian Dionyzia threatens her with murder at the hands of a servant just at the point she is mourning the death of her beloved nurse. Marina's suffering seems unremitting; she escapes murder through being captured by pirates, only to be sold by them to a brothel and to a fate—in her opinion—worse than violent and sudden death ('Alack that Leonine was so slack, so slow. / He should have struck, not spoke' (xvi, 61-2)).

Meanwhile the audience is introduced to Pander, Bawd and Bolt bewailing the poor state of their trade, caused not through a lack of customers ('gallants'), but rather through the 'pitifully sodden' condition of their prostitute wares (xvi, 18). The comic potential of this scene is undermined by the tragic import of the discussion, which would not have been lost on a Jacobean audience. For early modern playgoers child prostitution and syphilis were very real and allied diseases. The audience learns how the Pox is the inevitable fate of the Bawd's poor 'bastards', but in this subterranean world of inverted moral values the sympathy expressed is solely for an adult lecher (the 'poor Transylvanian' (xvi, 20-1)) who has lain with a 'little baggage'—an exhausted commodity grown 'rotten' with 'continual action' (xvi, 8-9). Is this to be the Princess Marina's fate?

Installed in the Mytilene brothel Marina bewails her plight, only to be consoled by Bawd with the knowledge that she will 'taste gentlemen of all fashions'—a far from edifying prospect (xvi, 75). Whilst Boult, Bawd and Pander banter about the Spaniard's mouth watering at Marina's description, at Monsieur Veroles (the French word for syphilis) cowering 'i' the hams' (xvi, 101)—in other words Jacobean society's foppish foreigner stereotypes of the diseased—it is native 'gentlemen' and 'the governor of this country' (xix, 58) who actually arrive at the brothel to threaten Marina's well-being. One by one Jacobean society's comforting stereotypes of the disease's victims and polluters are being undermined, 'safe boundaries' for the representation of the Pox are being trangressed: young children and an innocent woman are at risk from 'gentlemen' in this murky play world.[13]

But Marina's eloquent powers of persuasion prove more than a match for Mytilene's lecherous gentlemen, whose wayward morals she reforms in the very brothel.[14] The dramatic climax of the brothel scenes is undoubtedly the arrival and conversion of none other than the 'Lord Lysimachus', governor of Mytilene. Bawd announces that there's no way to be 'rid on't' (Marina's maidenhead) but, as she puts it,

> by the way to the pox.
> *Enter Lysimachus, disguised*
> Here comes the Lord Lysimachus disguised.
>
> (xix, 23-5)

Whilst it is never directly stated or implied by any of the characters that Lysimachus has the Pox, the language of the scene conspires to sow strong seeds of suspicion that he does. The proximity of the words 'pox' to 'it' (Marina's virginity) and the foregrounding of Lysimachus' disguise—disguise being intimately associated in early modern discourse with the Pox, which was also known as the great 'masquerader', the 'secret' disease—begin the process.[15] Lysimachus requests Boult find him some 'wholesome iniquity' (xix, 32) with which to do 'the deed of darkness' (xix, 37). He hides his dishonourable intentions in a cloak of euphemistic language, but the audience is not to be hoodwinked, for Bawd replies 'Your honour knows what 'tis to say well enough' (xix, 39). Furthermore the brothel's mistress is 'bound' (xix, 60), as she says, to this governor; by implication Lysimachus is a regular customer, all too familiar with the iniquitous business in hand. This established, Bawd's words serve to highlight Lysimachus' supreme status in Mytilene society; finally she declares 'Come, we will leave his honour and hers together' (xix, 69). There is, of course, a pun on 'honour' here. Marina later appropriates Bawd's terms and upbraids Lysimachus with them. She challenges:

> And do you know this house to be a place
> Of such resort and will come into it?
> I hear say you're of honourable blood,
> And are the governor of this whole province.
>
> (xix, 81-4)

Thus Lysimachus' honour is thrown seriously into question, and he increasingly resembles one of the hypocritical types, like Iniquity and Infidelity, who would have

been familiar to many amongst the original audiences as stock vices from the morality plays. Tail between legs, the governor leaves the brothel claiming that Marina's speech has altered his 'corrupted mind' (xix, 128). Lysimachus' mask may have been temporarily lifted, his vice exposed, but he appears to go quite unpunished for his misdeeds; indeed, he even seems to be rewarded, for Marina's princely father eventually betroths her to this nobleman of dubious honour and health.

But is this not taking the stuff of romance, emerging from a make-believe world, rather too seriously? What may seem just good bawdy and fun to a modern audience, however, is fraught with serious implications for contemporary playgoers familiar with other stage representations of fornication and disease.[16] This play, it has been repeatedly observed, returns to an emblematic form of theatre which invites spectators to search critically for understanding. The audience witnesses a series of emblematic tableaux, is called upon to make sense of the wooing knights' 'devices' on their shields, and listens to riddles, mottoes and endless aphorisms, especially ones about the abusive operations of power and kingship. Frequently there is a disparity between the morals the characters tritely recite and the action the audience observes on the stage. Thus sham morality, hypocrisy, is repeatedly exposed. Through these theatrical structures the audience is encouraged to observe the action with a heightened sceptical consciousness, and to be especially alert to emblematic representations.

Pericles is particularly partial to trotting out mottoes and adages about kingship (much like King James himself), but there is one that he omits which educated Jacobean playgoers may well have been thinking about when witnessing Pericles' rather casual consignment of his daughter to Lysimachus' care. As Gower relates, Lysimachus entertains the king with 'pageantry', 'feats', 'shows', 'minstrelsy and pretty din', which so impresses Pericles that he rewards the governor of Mytilene with a wife—his daughter, the heir to the throne of Tyre (xxii, 6-12). It is my contention that many among the original audiences of *Pericles* would have responded with horror to this marriage outcome, to this 'unequal match', because of their familiarity with the horrors of contracting syphilis and the intense and prolonged suffering associated with the most dreaded chronic disease of the Renaissance. Those with at least a grammar-school education would have been familiar, too, with widely disseminated Erasmian views on such hazardous 'matches', and some spectators would undoubtedly have seen a popular emblem which illustrated a 'Nupta contagioso'.

This emblem first appeared in a collection by Andrea Alciato (*Emblemata*) published in 1550; it was subsequently adapted, translated and distributed widely throughout Europe. It depicts a king on a dais oversee-ing a man and woman being bound together on the floor with a rope. As the accompanying poem describes, this is a savage deed comparable to that committed by a cruel Etruscan king who was in the habit of punishing his victims by tying them to a corpse. It reveals that for a dowry this king has purchased a son-in-law seared by the Gallic scab, apparent in the dreaded sore on his face: through self-interest he has committed his daughter to a living death, a 'Nupta contagioso'. This horrific emblem about the Pox was undoubtedly influenced by an Erasmian colloquy published in 1529 entitled *The Unequal Match* or *A Marriage in Name Only,* which was among the dramatic dialogues that English peda-gogues recommended all boys should read.[17] Erasmus' colloquies were a tool to teach schoolboys colloquial Latin but they were also intended, in Erasmus' own words, to impress on 'young people . . . [the] safe-guarding of their chastity'.[18]

The two participants in *The Unequal Match,* Gabriel and Petronius, discuss, with horror, how a beautiful, talented girl with winning manners has just been mar-ried off by her father to a rotting corpse—unmistakably a chronic syphilitic—because of his title. This wayward nobleman's dicing, drinking, lies and whoring have ap-parently earned him this 'living death' which will now be inflicted upon his young wife. Gabriel's words are hard-hitting. He exclaims:

> But this outrage—than which you could find nothing more barbarous, more cruel, more unrighteous—is even a laughing matter with the governing class nowadays, despite the fact that those born to rule ought to have as robust health as possible. And in fact, the condition of the body has its effect on mental power. Undeniably this disease usually depletes whatever brains a man has. So it comes about that rulers of states may be men who are healthy neither in body nor mind.
>
> (p. 407)

This colloquy thus functions as a powerful rebuke to parental, and especially princely parental, selfishness, greed and folly.

Pericles, I wish to argue, is a satirical play with the same cautionary message as *The Unequal Match.* The potential polluter of a beautiful young woman is a luxurious gentleman who abuses the privileges that his nobility favours him with. Through marriage, an in-nocent young woman will be placed at his disposal by the very person who should most seek to protect her—her father. Marina's response to the intended match is articulate silence. It is informative to read this outcome in relation to Petronius' condemnation of the 'unequal match' in Erasmus' dialogue: 'Enemies scarcely do this to girls captured in war, pirates to those they kidnap; and yet parents do it to an only daughter, and there's no police official with power to stop them!' (p. 408).

Marina has escaped rape and murder at the hands of her enemies, has survived her passage with her pirate-captors intact, and then just when the audience is relax-ing, thinking her safely delivered to the protection of her family, her father subjects her to an 'unequal match'. As Gabriel declares in the dialogue, such dubious matches reflect badly on the parents and have important implications for the commonwealth and its government: '[a]s private individuals, they're disloyal to their fam-ily; as citizens, to the state' (p. 408). Irresponsible father-rulers are putting both the health of their offspring and the state in jeopardy through this 'madness'.

The medico-moral politics of *Pericles* depend to some extent on the audience's experience of this tragic and widespread disease of the Renaissance—its unsightly, disfiguring, disabling and painful progress—and on their knowledge of popular humanist texts surrounding it. The Pox was in fact the most widely written-about disease in the Renaissance. These contexts are clearly not readily available to modern audiences and conse-quently the potential serious import and impact of *Pericles'* late scenes have been considerably watered down, even erased.

However, yet further Renaissance contexts require amplification before modern readers can appreciate the range and density of meanings and resonances circulat-ing, often in partially submerged form, in this richly layered play. Whilst reforming intellectuals like Eras-mus worried and wrote about the savage effects of this disease and called for preventive health measures to combat it, they were also not averse to utilising knowledge about its painful and horrific effects for propaganda purposes. Intent on foregrounding what he viewed as the corruption and decay of the Catholic Church, Erasmus began to disperse images of syphilitic priests throughout his writings. His message was that the clergy had grown so corrupt their fornication was spreading the new disease among them, to their in-nocent victims, and throughout the globe. Lutheran reformers seized upon Erasmus' powerful metaphor of church corruption, and English polemicists like John Bale, John Foxe, Lewis Wager and William Turner quickly appropriated the emblematic syphilitic body for the Protestant cause.

The mid sixteenth-century Edwardian stage displayed spotted, decaying and disabled 'Pocky' bodies lament-ing their disease and proclaiming it to be the conse-quence of fornication encouraged by Catholic Vices such as Infidelity and Iniquity, who inevitably disguise their corruption and hypocrisy under their religious vestments. The early Protestant dramatists clearly rec-ognised and exploited the compelling theatrical value, the tantalising erotic and comic possibilities, of sin: 'godly myrth' was extremely bawdy. As John King has argued, in the Protestant interlude fornication tends to become 'a composite symbol for the seven deadly sins'.[19] He cites as the main reason for this John Bale's development and popularisation for the English context of the Lutheran identification of the Whore of Babylon of Revelation with the Church of Rome: dramatic bawdry thus came to symbolise 'the spiritual fornication' of Roman ritualism.

When, therefore, the audience witnessed the seduction and fall of young virgins in the Protestant interludes, they were simultaneously engaging with the plays' allegorical levels of meaning, in which, according to the Protestant reformers' version of history, the True, undefiled Church was sullied and temporarily superseded by the corrupt False Church of Antichrist. Naturally the harlot Church, like her lascivious priests, had a special imagined affinity with venereal disease. In his propaganda pamphlet, provocatively entitled *A New Booke of Spirituall Physik for Dyverse Diseases of the Nobilitie and Gentlemen of Englande* (1555), the Marian exile William Turner reconstrues the origins of the 'pokkes' in a 'noble hore' of Italy: 'Ther was a certeyne hore in Italy, whych had a perillus disease called false religion . . . all the kynges and nobilitie of the earth . . . they committed fornication wyth her . . . and caught the Romishe pokkes.'[20]

This symbolism and allegorising surrounding the Pox, fornication and the Romish church was alive and flourishing in the first decade of the seventeenth century. Thomas Dekker's play *The Whore of Babylon,* staged by Prince Henry's Men probably about a year before the first production of *Pericles,* bears strong witness to this. Indeed *The Whore of Babylon* provides an important additional context to illuminate some of the fading emblematic resonances in *Pericles.* As the preface to the text explains, *The Whore of Babylon* is designed to lay bare the 'blody stratagems, of that Purple whore of Roome' in the reign of Elizabeth I.[21] However, its real thrust was undoubtedly to persuade Jacobean spectators that the iniquitous forces of Antichrist continued to pose a substantial threat to England and the Reformed Church, and to encourage a more militant stance against Rome. It features the lustful harlot the Empresse of Babylon, alias Rome, strumpet to her slaves, the kings of Spain, France and the Holy Roman Empire, and her Cardinal entourage. She is also served by her Bawd, Falsehood, who wears the garb of Truth (a gown of sanctity) but whose hypocrisy is evidenced by her red pimples—she, like her mistress, as Plain Dealing informs us, has a bad case of the Pox. Babylon's design is none other than to 'swallow up the kingdome of Faiery' (IV, iii, 37), whose queen is Titania (Elizabeth I), served by spotless Truth and her fairy lords.

The Empress's first stratagem is to send her kings off to woo Titania/Elizabeth. When they arrive at her court Titania asks them if they've come to 'strike off a poore

maiden-head' (I.ii.85), that is to rape her. The sexual manoeuvres and language of this play have the political meanings common to sixteenth-century Protestant discourse: raping a virgin signified a state adhering to the Reformed, true faith being engulfed forcibly by a Romish power. Rome is a rapist as well as a harlot in Protestant polemics. However, the kings reassure Titania that marriage rather than ravishment is their aim, but it does not matter which of the three Titania chooses because their desire is simply to please the Empress by wedding the forces of Babylon to those of Fairyland. Thankfully, Titania is not fooled by this suspect marriage proposal. She declares (and I think these words will throw a very important light on the marriage proposal in *Pericles*):

> When kingdoms marrie, heaven it selfe stands by
> To give the bride: Princes in tying such bands,
> Should use a thousand heads, ten thousand hands:
> For that one Acte gives like an enginous wheele
> Motion to all.
>
> (I, ii, 162-6)

The marriage alliance rejected, Babylon and her followers turn grisly: the Spanish Armada is sent into action and a plot is hatched to murder Titania with the aid of recusant spies. At the close of the play the forces of Truth triumph but, importantly, Babylon is not eradicated, just temporarily subdued: the Poxy threat persists.

Many among the original London audiences would probably have shared Dekker's perspective on the threat posed by Popishness and Spanish ambitions; and the Shakespearean play, as represented by the virtually identical 1609 quartos, is undoubtedly engaging in a more subtle way with the same concerns. This is how Pericles addresses Marina in the recognition scene:

> Prithee speak.
> Falseness cannot come from thee, for thou look'st
> Modest as justice, and thou seem'st a palace
> For the crowned truth to dwell in.
>
> (xxi, 108-11)

Pericles' words identify his daughter as an embodiment of Truth: Truth which the audience has observed being captured by a pirate with the same name, Valdes, as one of the Spanish Armada captains in *The Whore of Babylon;* whom they have seen threatened with but fending off rape; and who is about to be betrothed to a probably Poxy spouse by her negligent father. Pericles certainly does not use 'a thousand heads' in choosing his son-in-law.

All of this has important negative implications for how we read the character of Pericles in the Jacobean context. Pericles is a prince who is seldom in his own state (Tyre is a troubled kingdom 'without a head' (viii, 34));[22] who flees from danger rather than confronting it;

who readily commits his young daughter to the care of rather dubious others; whose wallowing in self-pity comes dangerously close to incurring a charge of effeminacy ('thou art a man, and I / Have suffered like a girl' (xxi, 125-6)); and who, through betrothing Marina to a potentially diseased son-in-law, is putting both her health and his future princely heirs' at stake. He may, unwittingly, through neglect and poor government, be introducing 'corruption' into the virgin body of his daughter and his kingdom.

Indeed, on the latter points King James himself had been nothing if not voluble in his treatise of advice to his son Henry, *Basilikon Doron* (1599), which specifically warns about the dangers of bodily pollution:

> First of all consider, that Mariage is the greatest earthly felicitie or miserie . . . By your preparation yee must keepe your bodie cleane and unpolluted, till yee give it to your wife . . . For how can ye justly crave to bee joyned with a pure virgine, if your bodie be polluted? Why should the one halfe bee cleane, and the other defiled?[23]

The *Basilikon Doron*'s constructions resonate with Erasmian maxims, and the above illustration suggests that James may well have been familiar with one of the numerous reproductions of Alciato's emblem. The treatise proceeds to rail against lust and fornication, reminding the young prince that the right end of sexual appetite is 'procreation of children', and stressing monarchical duty: 'Especially a King must tymously Marie for the weale of his people . . . in a King that were a double fault, as well against his owne weale, as against the weale of his people [to] . . . Marie one of knowne evill conditions' (p. 35). Crucially, there then follows a protracted discussion about religion, marriage and monarchy, in which James advises Henry, 'I would rathest have you to Marie one that were fully of your owne Religion', and warns about the hazards of 'disagreement in Religion'. The betrothal of two princely 'members of two opposite Churches' can only 'breed and foster a dissention among your subjects, taking their example from your family' (p. 35).

If the neglectful manner of rule of Pericles' royal protagonist bore resemblances to James VI and I's style of administration c.1607-9, some pointed comments about Jacobean power politics are thinly concealed in this play. James's management of the country was being heavily criticised in this period; not least because his instinct and drive was to make peace with Spain, exercise a policy of leniency towards recusants, and seek Catholic Spanish marriages for his devoutly Protestant children, Henry and Elizabeth. The Venetian ambassador to London confided to the Doge and Senate in 1607, that: 'His majesty . . . loves quiet and repose, has no inclination to war . . . a fact that little pleases many of his subjects . . . The result is he is despised

and almost hated.' Furthermore, throughout 1607 the Venetian ambassador (Zorzi Giustinian) sent anxious reports to his masters about the unsettled British populace, who 'would clearly like to, on the excuse of this rumour of a Spanish Armada', disturb 'the calm'. His dispatches repeatedly lamented: 'They [the populace] long for a rupture with Spain.'[24] Meanwhile their monarch was negotiating marital alliances with the enemy, which could well lead to 'dissention' (see above quotation from *Basilikon Doron*) among his subjects. It seems that James, like Pericles, was an expert purveyor of adages about kingship, but for many of his subjects he too seldom put them into action. He would have done well to take note of the emblem and motto of the fifth knight in *Pericles*: 'an hand environèd with clouds, / Holding out gold that's by the touchstone tried' and '*Sic spectanda fides*' (vi, 41-3), which might be rendered as, 'the trial of godliness and faith is to be made not of words only, but also by the action and performance of the deeds'.[25]

But all this begs the question of why a Yorkshire company of players with recusant sympathies should choose to stage *Pericles* in 1609. Perhaps it was for counter-propaganda purposes? The very fact that an Erasmian text is glanced at in this play would make it a prime target for appropriation by both sides of the religious divide. The preface to William Burton's translations of seven of the *Colloquies* (1606) is illuminating in this respect, for it reveals a religio-political intent partly motivating his project: readers will readily perceive, he declares in his preface, 'how little cause the Papists have to boast of Erasmus as a man of their side'. Ownership of Erasmus (with all the authority that implied) was hotly contested by English Catholics and Protestants in this period. Furthermore, Cholmeley was accused in 1609 of staging anti-Protestant plays, and the Star Chamber trial documents lend strong support to the view put forward by Sissons in 1942, that the company interpolated and omitted scenes, and improvised, according to 'the religious colour of their audience'.[26] This should perhaps serve as a timely reminder that plays are highly slippery art forms, and that ultimately their meanings reside with their equally unstable audiences. There is no way of knowing, for example, how closely a version of *Pericles* played at the Globe resembled the Yorkshire version(s) or, indeed, a production at Whitehall before distinguished guests: but it is easy to see how with a little fine tuning *Pericles* in performance could be construed as a pro-Jamesian play.

What can be said with certainty is that with its roots deep in the Jacobean cultural context, and engaging critically but obliquely with its power politics, *Pericles*—as represented by the 1609 quartos—has been wrongly consigned to the scrapheap of unalloyed aestheticism and 'happy Ever-afters'. *Pericles* is not a bastion of royal absolutism, though to discern its heterodox perspectives we need to penetrate its mirror-like surface, which appears to be reflecting Jamesian orthodoxy. As *Pericles* reminds its audiences, this was an age in which kings were 'earth's gods' (i, 146), one in which saying 'Jove doth ill' (i, 147) was fraught with danger. Indeed, as Philip Finkelpearl reminds us in an important essay on stage censorship, 'from 1606 it became a crime to speak against dignitaries even if the libel were true'.[27] Criticism of the reigning monarch was certainly best kept partially occluded, and, in skilful hands, the emblematic characterisation, straggling plots, exotic locations and make-believe worlds of romance were perfect structures for 'artistic cunning' and veiled comment.[28] Pocky bodies, medico-moral politics and dubious marriages were, I have argued in this chapter, powerful stage vehicles for coded dissent: *c.*1607-9 men could not say the king 'doth ill' but they could seek to reveal it, or at least gesture towards it, through dramatic representation.

Notes

1. Shakespeare probably collaborated with at least one other playwright in writing *Pericles*—the second writer remains a matter for speculation. I can see no justification for the designation of Q1 as a particularly corrupt, 'bad' quarto.

2. For a taste of this 'vilification' see theatre reviews for April 1990 (Royal Shakespeare Company) and May 1994 (Royal National Theatre) in *London Theatre Record.*

3. Hoeniger, 'Gower and Shakespeare', p. 461.

4. Sisson, 'Shakespeare quartos', pp. 136-7.

5. Shulman, 'Review of *Pericles* (RSC)', *Evening Standard,* 17 April 1990.

6. Mullaney, *The Place of the Stage,* pp. 147-51.

7. Billington, *Mock Kings,* p. 238.

8. Wickham, 'From tragedy to tragi-comedy', p. 44; Goldberg, *James I;* Bergeron, *Shakespeare's Romances,* p. 23; see also Tennenhouse, *Power on Display,* pp. 182-3.

9. Two notable exceptions are Dickey, 'Language and role', and Relihan, 'Liminal geography'.

10. Campion, *The Lord Hay's Masque,* ll. 15-20.

11. See Gardiner, *History of England,* vol. I, p. 343; in July 1605 Spain suggested that if Prince Henry married the eldest daughter of the King of Spain, Spain would surrender to the young couple its claims to a large portion of the Netherlands. Spain later retracted the offer, raising objections to the Infanta marrying a Protestant. Also Gardiner, *History of England,* vol. II, pp. 22-3; in 1607 the

abortive scheme for the marriage was renewed, together with a demand for the conversion of Prince Henry to Catholicism. The offer was refused because of the latter demand. However, in October of the same year James suggested an alternative plan: that his daughter Elizabeth be married to the son of Philip's brother-in-law, the Duke of Savoy. See also *Calendar of State Papers: Venetian, Vol. XI,* 15 August 1607: 'the Ambassadors of Spain are putting it about that by a matrimonial alliance and the death of the Archdukes the States might well come under the dominion of the King of England' (p. 23).

12. Gower's, Twine's and Wilkins' texts are in Bullough, *Narrative and Dramatic Sources,* vol. VI.

13. On safe boundaries for the representation of syphilis see Helms, 'The saint in the brothel', and Gilman, *Disease and Representation.*

14. On syphilis and declamation, see Helms, 'The saint in the brothel'.

15. See Davenport-Hines, *Sex, Death and Punishment,* p. 21.

16. The topic of my forthcoming monograph, 'Fictions of Disease: Bodies, Plagues and Politics in Early Modern Writings'.

17. See Watson, *English Grammar Schools,* pp. 328-9, and Clarke, *Classical Education,* p. 47.

18. Erasmus, 'De Utilitate Colloquiorum', *Colloquies,* p. 629, quoted by Thompson in the same edition, p. 154.

19. King, *English Reformation Literature,* p. 283.

20. Turner, *A New Booke,* fol. 74^r.

21. Dekker, *The Whore of Babylon,* p. 497.

22. On this matter one of Erasmus' adages famously declared: 'Sheep are no use, if the shepherd is not there . . . the common people are useless unless they have the prince's authority to guide them', *Adages,* II, vii, 26.

23. James VI and I, *Basilikon Doron,* p. 34.

24. *Calendar of State Papers: Venetian, Vol. X,* p. 513; and *State Papers: Venetian, Vol. XI,* pp. 17, 27, 39.

25. *Pericles,* ed. Hoeniger, II, ii, 38n. (p. 56), citing Claude Paradin, *Devises Héroiques,* trans. P.S. (London, 1591), sig. O3 (p. 213).

26. See *Star Chamber Proceedings,* PRO, STAC 19/ 10; 12/11. Sisson, 'Shakespeare quartos', p. 142.

27. Finkelpearl, '"The comedians' liberty"', p. 123. Finkelpearl suggests that 'the employment of arcane codes mastered by the cognoscenti' may

have operated in Jacobean England, p. 138. See also Annabel Patterson, *Censorship and Interpretation*. Indeed satire against the king had led to Jonson, Chapman and Marston being imprisoned in 1605 for their parts in *Eastward Ho!*; and in 1606 'sundry were committed to Bridewell' for producing *The Isle of Gulls*.

28. The expression is Finkelpearl's, '"The comedians' liberty"', p. 138.

Bibliography

PRIMARY

Bullough, Geoffrey, ed. *Narrative and Dramatic Sources of Shakespeare*, 8 vols (London and Henley: Routledge and Kegan Paul, 1957-75)

Campion, Thomas, *The Lord Hay's Masque* (1607), in David Lindley (ed.), *Court Masques* (Oxford: Oxford University Press, 1995)

Dekker, Thomas, *The Whore of Babylon,* in *The Dramatic Works of Thomas Dekker,* ed. F. Bowers (Cambridge: Cambridge University Press, 1953-61), vol. II (1955)

Erasmus, Desiderius, *The Colloquies of Erasmus,* ed. and trans. Craig R. Thompson (Chicago and London: University of Chicago Press, 1965)

Erasmus, Desiderius, *Collected Writings of Erasmus: Adages, II.vii.1 to III.iii.100,* trans. M. M. Phillips (Buffalo and London: University of Toronto Press, 1982)

James VI and I, *Basilikon Doron,* in *Political Works of James I,* ed. Charles Howard McIlwain (Cambridge, Mass.: Harvard University Press, 1918; repr. New York: Russell and Russell, 1965)

Shakespeare, William, *Pericles,* ed. F. D. Hoeniger (Methuen: London, 1963)

State Papers, *Calendar of State Papers: Venetian, Vol. X: 1603-1607,* and *Vol. XI: 1607-10,* ed. H. Brown (London: HMSO, 1900 and 1904)

Turner, William, *A New Booke of Spirituall Physik for Dyverse Diseases of the Nobilitie and Gentlemen of Englande* (n.p., 1555)

SECONDARY

Bergeron, David M., *Shakespeare's Romances and the Royal Family* (Lawrence, Kans.: University of Kansas Press, 1985)

Billington, Sandra, *Mock Kings in Medieval and Renaissance Drama* (Oxford: Clarendon Press, 1991)

Clarke, M. L., *Classical Education in Britain, 1500-1900* (Cambridge: Cambridge University Press, 1959)

Davenport-Hines, Richard, *Sex, Death and Punishment* (London: Collins, 1990)

Dickey, Stephen, 'Language and role in *Pericles*', *English Literary Renaissance,* 16 (1986), 550-66

Finkelpearl, Philip J., '"The comedians' liberty": censorship of the Jacobean stage reconsidered', *English Literary Renaissance,* 16 (1986), 123-38

Gardiner, Samuel R., *History of England from the Accession of James I to the Outbreak of Civil War, 1603-42,* 10 vols (London: Longman, 1905)

Gilman, Sander, *Disease and Representation: Images of Illness from Madness to Aids* (Ithaca, N.Y., and London: Cornell University Press, 1988)

Goldberg, Jonathan, *James I and the Politics of Literature: Jonson, Shakespeare, Donne, and their Contemporaries* (Baltimore and London: Johns Hopkins University Press, 1983)

Helms, Lorraine, 'The saint in the brothel: or, eloquence rewarded', *Shakespeare Quarterly,* 41 (1990), 319-32

Hoeniger, F. David, 'Gower and Shakespeare in *Pericles*', *Shakespeare Quarterly,* 33 (1982), 461-79

King, John, *English Reformation Literature: The Tudor Origins of the Protestant Tradition* (Princeton, N.J.: Princeton University Press, 1982)

Mullaney, Steven, *The Place of the Stage: License, Play, and Power in Renaissance England* (Chicago and London: University of Chicago Press, 1988)

Patterson, Annabel, *Censorship and Interpretation* (Madison: University of Wisconsin Press, 1984)

Relihan, Constance C, 'Liminal geography: *Pericles* and the politics of place', *Philological Quarterly,* 71 (1992), 281-99

Shulman, Milton, 'Review of *Pericles* (RSC)', *Evening Standard,* 17 April, 1990

Sisson, Charles J., 'Shakespeare quartos as prompt-copies', *Review of English Studies,* 18 (1942), 129-43

Tennenhouse, Leonard, *Power on Display: The Politics of Shakespeare's Genres* (London: Methuen, 1986)

Watson, Foster, *The English Grammar Schools to 1660* (London: Frank Cass, 1968)

Wickham, Glynne, 'From tragedy to tragi-comedy: *King Lear* as prologue', *Shakespeare Survey,* 26 (1973), 33-48

Paul Dean (essay date April 2000)

SOURCE: Dean, Paul. "Pericles' Pilgrimage." *Essays in Criticism* 50, no. 2 (April 2000): 125-44.

[*In the following essay, Dean contends that* Pericles *is a pilgrimage tale, and outlines several literary works that may have influenced Shakespeare's creation of the drama, including two from the Bible: the tale of Jonah and the Acts of the Apostles.*]

Had it been printed in the First Folio, *Pericles* (1608) might well have appeared among the comedies, with *The Winter's Tale* and *The Tempest,* rather than among the tragedies, with *Cymbeline,* which was perhaps placed there out of a feeling that it was more akin to the Roman plays or to *King Lear.* There was, as we know, no formal category of romance drama in Shakespeare's time.[1] Nor did he invent the kind of play whose absurdities and improbabilities were already being derided by Sidney in the 1580s[2] and which, as Leo Salingar has shown in detail,[3] are themselves lineal descendants of medieval dramatic romances.

Given such uncertainties, and the relatively modern coinage—dating, it seems, from the 1870s[4]—of 'romances' as a descriptive category for Shakespeare's later work, the question 'What kind of play is *Pericles?*' still seems a reasonable one to ask, and it is reopened by a lively and provocative new edition of the play, by Doreen DelVecchio and Anthony Hammond (Cambridge, 1998, hereafter DVH). They point out that, while *Pericles* marks a new direction in Shakespeare's writing, it also looks back as far as *The Comedy of Errors* which also takes its *dénouement* from Gower, as well as *A Midsummer Night's Dream, Twelfth Night,* and, substantially, *King Lear* and *Macbeth* (DVH notes on III. 0. 6, III. 1. 6, V. 1. 134-41, 209, IV. 3). They pinpoint the innovativeness of *Pericles* by saying that 'what Shakespeare dramatises' in that play is *'the story-telling process itself'* (DVH, p. 8, original italics; cf. pp. 27-36). It inaugurates a specific concern with the credibility of 'tales', scrutinising narrative technique with what now seems a modernist self-consciousness. (This is developed into *The Winter's Tale* with its comment that 'a sad tale's best for winter', II. i. 25, and its calling attention to its own improbability: 'so like an old tale that the verity of it is in strong suspicion', V. ii. 28-9, 'like an old tale still', V. ii. 60, 'hooted at / Like an old tale', V. iii. 116-17). It is true that *Pericles* is a descendant of late medieval classicism, syncretic in approach, as was the protean story of Apollonius itself,[5] displaying affinities both with new comedic romance in its character-types, symbolic voyages, locations and properties, and with Senecan tragedy whose *furor* it seems almost to parody.[6] But the central innovation—the onstage presence, as both source and character, of Gower—is not classical, and whatever one's views on the authorship of *Pericles* it is hard to believe that anyone except Shakespeare could have devised or sustained that. The technique is closest to Chaucer's manipulation of the framing fiction of the Canterbury pilgrimage. By making Gower narrate his own story, Shakespeare can play off different styles and perspectives against one another, in a development of the technique he had used for the Chorus in his previous play with a character named Gower: *Henry V.*[7] The effect would surely have been striking to an audience at the Globe, where *Pericles* was first staged, since they

only had to walk round the corner to Southwark cathedral to see Gower's tomb, yet here he is, a Phoenix reborn 'from ashes' (Prologue, l. 2), a character in a story which is both later than the past which he is retelling, and earlier than those to whom he now tells it. As Anne Barton has noted, the archaic quality of Gower's speech paradoxically makes him more remote from his auditors despite his mediating role, while at the same time making the story he presents seem closer: 'By turning the frame inside-out in this way, planes of reality are made to shift and blur in a fashion characteristic of the late plays'.[8] In Book VIII of the *Confessio,* where he tells the tale of Apollonius, Gower pays ritual homage to Godfrey of Viterbo, his 'authority' (ll. 271-2, 547, 1152, 1326),[9] but his relationship to his sources is not made as imaginatively powerful as Shakespeare's is to him.

Shakespeare is also likely to have learnt from Chaucer's sense of tale-as-game, and from his overarching device of the tale-telling competition which is also 'a game with its own rules'.[10] As the Host reminds the Clerk, 'what man that is entred in a pley, / He nedes moot unto the pley assente' (*CT* IV. 10-11). *Pericles* exists in a nexus of puns: to tell a tale (to recount an account) is to 'give an account' (of oneself, for instance), to be a 'telltale' (narrator/revealer of secrets), maybe even a kind of fibber, 'telling tales' (hence, perhaps, Sidney's high-minded unease); to 'play the game', however, is to keep to the rules, observe the shared conventions, be honest and not cheat. *Pericles* insists that only through the tale—only by becoming participants in its creation through lending it our credulity—can we have access to anything approaching 'truth'. This calls into question Anne Barton's further statement that the romances strive to 'distinguish the fictional from the "real", art from life, tales from truth'.[11] The 'truth' of *Pericles* resides precisely in its being a tale. But a tale of what kind?

Undramatic though the structure of Gower's own *Confessio* may be, the progressive examination of Amans' conscience by the confessor-figure Genius has a teleological impetus towards new life and a fresh start which is also possessed by *Pericles,* and Gower's own imagery of play has a richness by which Shakespeare may well have been struck. When Apollonius flees Tyre the city goes into mourning: 'There was no lif which leste plaie' (l. 486); in Tharse Apollonius learns of Antiochus' pursuit of him when he has gone out 'to pleie' (l. 572); he arrives at Pentapolis in time to take part in the 'comun game' which was 'pleid' before the king (ll. 678, 692), and, as one who 'of every game couthe an ende' (l. 697), wins renown by his skill. At the subsequent feast he is comforted in his melancholy by the harp-playing of the king's daughter, just as Saul is by David (1 Samuel 16: 14-23), but outdoes her performance and later gives her music lessons: 'of hire

Harpe the temprure / He tawhte hire ek' (ll. 832-3). This is appropriate to his name, as Shakespeare's other major source, Laurence Twine, explicitly says: 'he seemed rather to be Apollo then Apollonius'.[12] Having wooed the girl so that 'what in ernest and in game, / She stant for love in such a plit' (ll. 856-7), Apollonius marries her, and on the wedding night 'as thei pleiden hem betwene, / Thei gete a child' (ll. 972-3). There is none of this kind of language in Twine, whose Apollonius 'accomplished the duties of marriage'[13] in a highly respectable, almost Victorian, manner. Later, in the brothel, the child (whom Gower names Thaisa) is invited to a quite different kind of 'play', which she resists in such a saintly way that the pimp sent to deflower her weeps penitent tears rather than pursue the 'game' (l. 1445).

In the reunion with her father, Thaisa strives 'To glade with this sory man' (l. 1662) just as her mother had done (l. 759), drawing the mute stranger back to life with her playing of the harp. This is not just a matter of musicianship, however: the episode has magical overtones. Thaisa rises from the 'underworld' of the brothel only to descend into the underworld of Apollonius' subconscious, and, in Orphean fashion, sings him back to harmony. Shakespeare takes over these suggestions, associating Marina with Ovid's Proserpina and placing her in opposition to Tellus, the earth-goddess (IV. i. 13-17).[14] He also develops the character Cerimon as a thaumaturge, calling not only upon Apollo (III. ii. 66) but on his son Aesculapius (III. ii. 106) who had learned how to raise the dead. In both Gower and Shakespeare, Marina's would-be killers construct a sham tomb for her, which Pericles is shown, so that her reappearance must indeed seem like a resurrection to him: and, of course, for Gower's readers as for Shakespeare's audience an *empty tomb* could mean only one thing.

If, then, the romance tale is a kind of game, it is also a kind of quest; its art is the means of psychological and spiritual metamorphosis, a route to, rather than a diversion from, truth and reality. Gower knows this just as much as Shakespeare, and employs some unforced yet profound symbolism which clearly stuck in the latter's mind. Gower's Apollonius 'lith in so derk a place / That ther may no wiht sen his face' (ll. 1641-2), and Prince Athenagoras has to climb down a ladder on board ship to see him (l. 1644), a significant descent into the nether regions which is imitated by Thaisa. When her attempts to reawaken his intellect by philosophical discussion fail, and he cries to be left alone,

> Bot yit sche wolde noght do so,
> And in the derke forth sche goth,
> Til sche him toucheth.
>
> (ll. 1690-2)

Words are insufficient; she must venture forth 'in the derke' and touch him. In return he strikes her, only to realise his mistake. Their loving mutual recognition a few moments later redresses a pattern of wicked parent/ child relationships in the tale, of which Antiochus and his daughter are the paradigm.[15] Both fathers are bereaved, one actually, the other in imagination, but whereas Antiochus in his loneliness turns to his daughter as a replacement wife (ll. 283-5), Apollonius passes through psychic death to restoration; prompted by 'sibb of blod' (l. 1703) he 'loveth kindeley' (l. 1707). Gower has Antiochus' daughter complain to her nurse that

> Thing which mi bodi ferst begat
> Into this world, onliche that
> Mi worldes worschipe hath bereft.
>
> (ll. 329-31)

Shakespeare turned this into the unforgettable 'Thou that begetst him that did thee beget' (V. i. 190), so that a physical violation becomes a spiritual regeneration.[16]

Gower's episode concludes nobly:

> This king hath founde newe grace,
> So that out of his derke place
> He goth him up into the liht.
>
> (ll. 1739-41)

Apollonius learns about the need for patient submission to the will of Providence, but also about how to play the game of familial and social relations, or as Gower sums it up, how to be 'wel grounded' (l. 1992), a metaphor of musical, social and cosmic stability. Our natural feelings are also reverberations of the profoundest rhythms of being. Shakespeare carries this point to the extreme of having Pericles hear 'the music of the spheres' (V. i. 223) just before the theophany of Diana, to the consternation of the other onstage characters, who hear nothing.[17]

Gower's powerful imagining of the psychology of redemption contrasts with his lack of interest in explaining it. He offers a medley of conventional causalities: the fickleness of Fortune (ll. 585-91, 642-4, 2013-15), the wrath of Neptune (ll. 622-3), the benevolent oversight of Providence (ll. 628-9) or God (ll. 1158-60, 1788-9), poetic justice (l. 1962), even a shoulder-shrugging *che sera sera* (l. 1172)—all are pressed into service at one time or another. The tale, with its journeys across undulating seas, appears simply mimetic of the revolutions of Fortune's Wheel, the sudden changes of destiny and the caprices of human feeling. *Pericles* has often been slightly criticised as similarly episodic. Yet the journeys in Gower's tale are pilgrimages, and there is a destination, a moment of resolution, however well and long it may be concealed. Gower recognises that the best response to a contradictory universe is contradictory behaviour. When Apollonius is shown what he believes to be his daughter's tomb,

He curseth and seith al the worste
Unto fortune, as to the blinde . . .
Bot sithe it mai no betre be,
He thonketh god and forthe goth he.

(ll. 1584-5, 1589-90)

This perfectly sensible reaction is the same as that of the sailors when they throw Thaisa's coffin overboard, trusting that 'the corps shal wel aryve' (l. 1139). Gower's tale, with its recurring claustrophobic interiors from which liberation always comes (the ships' cabins, the coffin, the brothel, the mock-tomb, Apollonius' hiding-place), presents a Boethian world in which contingency subserves the purposes of destiny. Faced with the absence of a single explanation for why things happen as they do, the one imperative is to be open to fresh experience, all of which, including suffering, can be a means of growth. We may feel we are riding chaos, but we cannot know where we will be thrown ashore.

Shakespeare, in incorporating Gower into his play, supplies a guarantee of ultimate control, and so a means of detachment; Pericles' 'courses', Gower the character assures us, are 'ordered / By Lady Fortune' (IV. iv. 47-8). Yet he also emphasises darker patterns of history and society, for example the predatoriness of humanity in the First Fisherman's parable (II. i. 27-8), the depredations of Time who is 'the king of men: / He's both their parent, and he is their grave' (II. iii. 44-5), or the inexorability of 'We cannot but obey the powers above us' (III. iii. 10), or the helplessness expressed by Marina when she calls the world 'a lasting storm / Whirring me from my friends' (IV. i. 20). The closeness, noted earlier, of *Pericles* to *Lear* is important; so near allied are disaster and joy, a feather will turn the scale. Paradoxically, the play's most moving moment, the reunion of Pericles and Marina, is one of utter stillness: 'On a ship that does not move, the greatest journey is thus travelled in an instant's recognition' (DVH, p. 61). Yet the ship *never* 'moves': indeed, 'the ship' does not exist; it is our job, as Gower bids us, 'In your imagination' to 'hold / This stage a ship' (III. 0. 58-9). This is an audacious metadramatic injunction, but it makes it impossible for us to hold back from participating in the psychological and spiritual journeys of the protagonists. To assent to the rules of this particular game is to enact its logic in our own minds and lives. If we will not play God, as Puck and Prospero in their closing speeches also tell us, there can be no miracle.

John F. Danby long ago argued that *Pericles,* again like *Lear,* is in some sense a play about Christian patience.[18] That theme is not explicitly addressed by Gower in the *Confessio,* although Twine describes Lucina (his name for Shakespeare's Thaisa) as 'having learned the true trade of patience' (Bullough, VI. p. 473) through her service in Diana's temple. Pericles is patient in that he waits, and in that he suffers: his waiting is his suffering, and he suffers the more in that his suffering has no cause. Gower prays for us that 'On your *patience* evermore attending, / New joy *wait* on you' (Epilogue, ll. 17-18, my italics)—a very deep pun. Pericles, echoing Viola to Olivia, tells Marina that she looks 'like Patience, gazing on kings' graves, and smiling / Extremity out of act' (V. i. 135-6). Everything comes to him or her who waits, though we cannot predict whether the coming things will be welcome or unwelcome.

Normally one would think of Job in the context of patience, but at least one medieval writer, the *Gawain*-poet, thought of Jonah. No-one would claim *Patience* as a Shakespearean source, but it is an illuminating exercise to read it alongside *Pericles*. At the height of its storm the sailors call upon 'Diana deuout and derf [dread] Neptune' (l. 166).[19] Neptune is not surprising (cf. Gower, ll. 623, 1595, 1614), but Diana is. Neither is in the biblical book of Jonah, but that tale, which Shakespeare certainly knew, seems pertinent to his play. When Jonah, disobeying God's command to denounce the wickedness of Nineveh, flees from Joppa on a boat to Tarshish, God raises a storm at sea. The sailors invoke their gods, and awake Jonah, who had 'gone down into the sides of the ship' (1: 5)[20] to sleep, commanding him to call upon his god. A divination by lots indicates that his presence has caused the storm, and the others are not slow to act on his suggestion that he be thrown overboard. At once the storm ceases, and they give thanks. Jonah is swallowed by a 'great fish', as prearranged by God, and he spends three days and nights inside it, at the end of which he utters a prayer expressing confidence in God's deliverance, whereupon the fish vomits him up onto dry land. Making his way to Nineveh he delivers the divine message; the king and people fast and pray, and God forgives them. Jonah, apparently irritated at being made to look a fool, retires to sulk in the desert. To protect him from the pitiless heat, God shades him with a miraculous tree, which he then causes to be devoured by worms the following night. Next day, assailed by wind and sunshine, Jonah says he would be better off dead. He never accepts, not even at the end, that God knows best. But God points out that, if Jonah thinks him wrong to have destroyed one tree, how much more wrong it would have been to have destroyed a city of 120,000 people.

There the story abruptly stops. It is a weird little tale, full of puzzles and symbols. Jesus refers to it as a prefiguration of his own story: 'For as Jonas was three days and nights in the whale's belly; so shall the Son of Man be three days and three nights in the heart of the earth' (Matthew 12: 40), i.e. in the interval between the Crucifixion and the Resurrection, the period during which, traditionally, the Harrowing of Hell took place.[21] To walk the length of Nineveh takes Jonah three days and three nights (3: 3), reinforcing the parallel. The processes of descent and ascent are prominent in Jonah as in Gower and Shakespeare; Jonah 'goes down into' the ship, then further down into its sides, then further still into the 'sides' of the fish, and makes his prayer as from 'the belly of hell' (2: 2); his supposed escape is a cul-de-sac, a descent into Sheol, the underworld.[22] His sleep during the storm would recall, for a Christian reader, the similar action of Jesus (Mark 4: 35-41; Matthew 8: 23-7), except that Jonah's sleep, like Pericles' inertia, 'suggests paralysis rather than faith'.[23] Moreover, as F. D. Hoeniger noted in his edition of *Pericles,* Pericles' prayer, 'Thou god of this great vast, rebuke these surges' (III. i. 1), uses the same verb which Mark (4: 39) and Matthew (8: 26) use of Jesus' action towards the storm.

The poem *Patience* also uses this typology. Jonah imagines himself crucified, like Jesus, in Nineveh, 'On rode rwly to-rent with rybaudes mony' (l. 96); the whale is a 'warlow', the Devil (l. 258), its maw like Hell-mouth in the mystery plays or in medieval wall-paintings.[24] Jonah is not allowed to stay in the ship or the whale; his feelings of safety in those places are delusions, which he must see as such. He feels insecure in Nineveh, where he is perfectly safe, but learns no lesson from the penitence of its inhabitants, who adopt the traditional death-symbols of sackcloth and ashes. 'Whereas Jonah's disobedience precipitated his descent to the world of the dead, Nineveh's symbolic death is part of a return from its evil way'.[25] God's destruction of the tree by a 'worm', recalling the serpent in the Garden of Eden,[26] shows that Jonah can expect no external security, and should emulate the divine pity rather than feeling personally aggrieved. James S. Ackerman has attractively proposed that the book of Jonah be seen as a kind of satire on inappropriate human expectations of God, analogous to the classical satire being written contemporaneously in the Mediterranean region.[27]

Pericles seems to allude to the story of Jonah in a number of places. We might think of Pericles' initial desire 'To taste the fruit of yon celestial tree' (I. i. 22, a line Milton surely remembered), Antiochus' daughter, whom her father likens to a 'fair Hesperides, / With golden fruit, but dangerous to be touched' (I. i. 28-9). His immediate reaction to the threat posed by Antiochus is flight to Tarsus, Jonah's intended destination, and his ultimate discovery is Jonah's too: 'We cannot but obey the powers above us' (III. iii. 10). Like Jonah, Pericles addresses the celestial powers who have 'thrown' him 'from your watery grave', craving only 'death in peace' (II. i. 10-11); instead he meets three fishermen whose king is Simonides. As Marion Lomax has argued, this is surely meant to make us think of Simon Peter, and of Jesus' commission to the disciples to be 'fishers of men' (Matthew 4: 19, Mark 1: 16).[28] The scene (II. i) is reminiscent of Jonah's story too: the behaviour of humans is like that of fish, 'the great ones

eat up the little ones' (II. i. 27-8), and the Third Fisher-man says that if he had been inside the belly of the whale he would have made such a commotion that the whole parish would be vomited up (II. i. 34-40 and DVH note). The Sailors' plea to Pericles to cast his wife's corpse overboard (III. i. 48-52) echoes Jonah 2 (DVH note on III. i. 50) and a few lines later Pericles imagines 'the belching whale' keeping her coffin company (III. i. 62). When the coffin is thrown ashore, Cerimon remarks, 'If the sea's stomach be o-ercharged with gold, / 'Tis a good constraint of fortune it belches upon us' (III. ii. 53-4). But, like the leaden casket in *The Merchant of Venice,* this coffin contains a human rather than an inanimate treasure.[29]

There is a further link with the Jonah story, although a more elusive one, in Shakespeare's use of the name 'Marina'. His way with names in this play is typically tantalizing. The etymology of the sea-born girl is insisted upon (III. iii. 13, V. i. 154, 191-3), although she is never named during the Mytilene episodes but only recovers her name when she recovers her father.[30] Gower called Apollonius' daughter Thaisa; Twine called her Tharsia. Shakespeare transferred the name Thaisa to her mother whom Gower left nameless and Twine called Lucina—the name of the Abbess of the Temple of Diana in Gower (l. 1849). Lucina is also the name given to Juno in her role as goddess of childbirth, and Pericles invokes her when Marina is born (III. i. 10). 'Marina' itself is not a name Shakespeare invented. F. D. Hoeniger sought to align *Pericles* with the medieval miracle play, particularly the late fifteenth century Digby *Play of Mary Magdalene* (see his edition of *Pericles,* pp. lxxxviii-xci).[31] This features a woman giving birth during a storm, the husband's mistaken belief that both mother and child are dead, their casting overboard, and their subsequent miraculous preservation and reunion with the husband. Hoeniger's case is not finally persuasive, since the play dramatises episodes from the *Golden Legend,* which Shakespeare could read independently (it was first printed in 1483 with several subsequent editions), and in any case the tone and atmosphere of the two plays are quite different. Nevertheless, there is sense in seeing the Marina sections of *Pericles* in terms of the saint's-life genre, and perhaps in terms of this specific group of plays; as has been noted, the Digby play of the Conversion of St Paul is presented by a character called Poeta, as *Pericles* is presented by Gower.[32] Hoeniger observes that St Marina, also known as St Margaret, St Pelagia, and the Pearl of the Sea, was a virgin martyr of Antioch, but adds, 'it seems improbable that Shakespeare had heard of her' (p. 4). Does it? The coincidence of name, character and location is, at least, remarkable. Moreover, not only was Marina/Margaret one of the most popular saints in medieval England, she was also the patron saint of childbirth,[33] and the subject of a major medieval prose work, the thirteenth century *Seinte Marharete,* one of the so-called 'Katherine Group' of hagiographical texts which, like the Digby plays, draw upon the *Golden Legend.* The most celebrated episode has Margaret swallowed by a devil in the shape of a dragon, whose belly then bursts asunder.[34] It would be rash to insist too much on connections between this legend and *Pericles:* Marina is not vowed to perpetual virginity. Yet her saintly resistance to temptation to lose it prematurely associates her with her namesake, as also with St Agnes who spent some time in a brothel without being defiled (cf. Bullough, p. 352). She is clearly presented as a holy figure, like her mother a votaress of Diana (IV. ii. 121), who persuades the brothel's clientele to 'go hear the vestals sing' (IV. v. 7) and defies the Governor of Mytilene as Margaret defied Olibrius, the Governor of Antioch; Boult reports with comic dismay that 'she sent him away as cold as a snowball, saying his prayers too' (IV. v. 128).

Like Jonah, St Marina was preserved in the midst of her enemies, and swallowed by a demonic monster only to be vomited up again. The monster, like the fish in the biblical book, was all the time under God's control, and could do her no harm. In Shakespeare's play, Marina is similarly protected, but is only one of several characters who enact Jonah's symbolic death and resurrection. Her story, like Jonah's in the medieval poem, is an exemplum of patience, the suffering waiting which is rewarded with fulfilment. Shakespeare's Christian treatment of this subtext is thrown into relief if one compares it with a play which he almost certainly did know, Lodge and Greene's *A Looking-Glass for London and England* (c. 1588), which dramatises the Jonah story among much other material in order to preach repentance to Elizabethan England, lest it be visited by the wrath of God. The concluding lines of this play, spoken by Jonas, are as follows:

> Repent O London, lest for thine offence,
> Thy shepherd fail, whom mighty God preserve,
> That she may bide the pillar of his Church,
> Against the storms of Romish Antichrist:
> The hand of mercy overshade her head,
> And let all faithful subjects say, Amen.[35]

For Shakespeare, the story of Jonah is not the occasion for scoring sectarian points. Like the fisher-disciples, he casts his net wider than that.

Mention of the disciples recalls another biblical pilgrimage narrative which has long been recognised as an influence on *The Comedy of Errors* and may also have been formative for *Pericles:* the Acts of the Apostles.[36] The earlier play's description of Ephesus as a town

> full of cozenage,
> As nimble jugglers that deceive the eye,
> Dark-working sorcerers that change the mind,
> Soul-killing witches that deform the body,

Pericles and Lychorida in Act III, scene i of Pericles.

> Disguised cheaters, prating mountebanks,
> And many such-like liberties of sin

> (I. ii. 97-102)

derives from Acts 19, in which Ephesus is populated by 'exorcists' (v. 13), practitioners of 'curious arts' (v. 19) and worshippers of Diana, whose image in the temple they believe 'came down from Jupiter' (v. 35). Paul has gone to spread the gospel in Ephesus (leaving behind in Corinth, incidentally, a disciple named Apollos). Disputes arise about his preaching, which threatens the trade in trinkets and statues of the goddess, so that 'the whole city was full of confusion' (v. 29). In *The Comedy of Errors,* Shakespeare supplies Christian colouring, replacing Diana's Temple by a priory whose abbess is Egeon's long-lost wife, yet, as confusions multiply, he also strongly suggests the dark powers which rage through the city. When *Pericles* reinstates Diana's Temple, it also returns to Acts.

Shakespeare could hardly fail to notice that Acts combines third-person narrative with some first-person, the so-called 'we-sections' (chapters 16, 20, 21 and 27, describing St Paul's voyages) which have traditionally been seen not only as salvation-history but also as autobiography,[37] although, intriguingly, other scholars have discerned purely literary debts to Hellenistic romance.[38] Such a combination of reported and dramatised material chimes with Shakespeare's technique in *Pericles*. There is also some shared geography: in Acts 20: 14 the ship arrives at Mytilene, in 20: 16 it skirts Ephesus, in 21: 3 it calls at Tyre. In 27: 14 the voyagers run into difficulties caused by 'a stormy wind, called Euroclydon', or as the Vulgate has it *Euroaquilo, a* name which the poet of *Patience* remembered.[39] The writer of Acts seems to be deliberately reversing the story of Jonah, substituting Paul whose presence not only saves the ship and its inhabitants but is essential to their preservation, fulfilling rather than avoiding God's intentions, as is confirmed by Paul's vision of an angel who tells him, 'thou must be brought before Caesar' (27: 24). Shakespeare, as it were, combines Jonah and Acts into a single action. Gower had given Apollonius an 'Avisioun' (l. 1801) in which 'he that wot what schal betide, / The hihe god' (ll. 1788-9), commands him to go to Ephesus; Twine's Apollonius is visited by 'an Angell in his sleepe' (Bullough, p. 471) with similar instructions. Shakespeare brings Diana herself onstage, perhaps descending from the heavens, like Jupiter in *Cymbeline,* as DVH suggest (in support of this we might recall the Ephesians' belief that her image 'came down from Jupiter'). Marina is a kind of angelic visitor, whom Pericles compares to Juno (V. i. 107) and fears may be the messenger of 'some incensed god' (V. i. 140), but, as she insists, she is 'mortally brought forth' (V. i. 99). With a fine irony, Pericles' fear that her appearance is a 'dream' (V. i. 158) is doubly disproved: the greatest reality is reserved for the moment of vision. This is quite different from what we find in *The Comedy of Errors,* where, although the Temple of Diana happens to be the scene for the final recognitions and reunions, there is a strong sense of providential direction, but no theophany. Glyn Austen has related the resolution of *Errors* to the doctrine of the 'new man' created by grace in the Epistle to the Ephesians.[40] This idea is increasingly prominent in *Pericles,* which presents the reunited family as a restoration of wholeness and an expansion of being, a rebirth which is also a resurrection (cf. DVH, pp. 75-8). Marina twice states her belief that her mother's death coincided with her own birth (V. i. 155-6, 206-7), so that her reappearance provokes that of her mother; Pericles' 'O come hither, / Thou that begetst him that did thee beget' is later counterpoised by:

PERICLES:

O come, be buried a second time within these arms.

MARINA [KNEELS]:

My heart leaps to be gone into my mother's bosom.

PERICLES:

Look who kneels here: flesh of thy flesh, Thaisa
. . .

(V. ii. 41-3)

Not only does this echo the Prayer Book marriage service and the text from Ephesians which underpins it, 'For this cause shall a man leave his father and mother, and shall cleave to his wife, and they twain shall be one flesh' (5: 31), but it also harks back to the encounter between Jesus and Nicodemus in St John's Gospel:

> Jesus answered and said unto him, 'Verily, verily, I say unto thee, Except a man be born again, he cannot see the kingdom of God.' Nicodemus said unto him, 'How can a man be born which is old? Can he enter into his mother's womb again [AV has 'the second time'], and be born?' Jesus answered, 'Verily, verily, I say unto thee, except a man be born of water and of the Spirit, he cannot enter into the kingdom of God. That which is born of the flesh is flesh: and that which is born of the Spirit is spirit. Marvel not that I said unto thee, Ye must be born again. The wind bloweth where it listeth, and thou hearest the sound thereof, but canst not tell whence it cometh, and whither it goeth: so is every man that is born of the Spirit'.

(John 3: 3-8)

The echoes in Shakespeare ('a second time . . . my mother's . . . flesh . . . flesh') are noteworthy, and Nicodemus, who comes to Jesus 'by night', embodies the darkness in which, in the Prologue, John says the light shines. Literal-minded, he has to be instructed, in Frank Kermode's words, that 'the knowledge which belongs to generation, genesis, flesh, becoming, is irrelevant to the being of eternal life'.[41] The wind bloweth where it listeth, as Pericles, Marina and Thaisa discover. Safely in harbour, Thaisa can hear of her father's death (V. iii. 74) and belong wholly to Pericles, Marina can leave her father and mother and cleave unto Lysimachus, and all can quit Diana's Temple in an un-Pauline spirit, ready to forsake chastity and the cloister for possibly higher virtues.

I have been arguing that the 'medieval' element in *Pericles* extends beyond the use of Gower—that, without the need of positing yet more, and more improbable, Shakespearean 'sources' we nonetheless gain by reading the play in a pre-Reformation literary and scriptural context. It is not then surprising to learn that, as a still under-explored document attests, *Pericles,* together with *King Lear,* was acted by Sir Richard Cholmeley's Players, a troupe of Catholic recusants, at Gowthwaite Hall, Nidderdale, in Yorkshire on the feast of Candlemas (2 February) 1609.[42] The players were brought before the Court of Star Chamber on a charge of sedition because they had acted a play on the life of St Christopher; it looks very much as though they thought of the two Shakespeare plays as belonging to the same category. We know exasperatingly little about this, but it seems likely that the choice of *Pericles* related in some way to the feast.[43] Candlemas, as the commemoration of the Purification of Mary and the Presentation of Christ to Simeon, brings together a virgin-mother, a miraculous child, and a temple. The pre-Reformation proper Mass of the feast began with words from Psalm 47, 'We wait for thy loving-kindness, O God, in the midst of thy temple'.[44] This psalm also says, of the earthly rulers whose power over Jerusalem God will bring to an end: 'Fear came there upon them, and sorrow, as upon a woman in travail. As with an east wind thou breakest the ships of Tarshish, so were they destroyed' (vv. 6-7). Candlemas was the last great feast of the Christmas season; its juxtaposition of the aged Simeon and the infant Jesus underscored the themes of renewal and regeneration, while the elaborate processions involved each parishioner carrying a candle, symbolising the holy child, which was blessed and regarded as an aid against the forces of darkness.[45] Cholmeley's Players, one may reasonably suggest, divined something in the miraculous patience of *Pericles* which has been obscured to modern eyes.

Notes

1. Stanley Wells, 'Shakespeare and Romance', in John Russell Brown and Bernard Harris (eds.), *Later Shakespeare* (1966), p. 49.

2. Sidney, *An Apology for Poetry,* ed. Geoffrey Shepherd (1965), p. 134.

3. Leo Salingar, *Shakespeare and the Traditions of Comedy* (Cambridge, 1974), pp. 28-75.

4. See Edward Dowden, *Shakspere* (1877), pp. 55-6, cited in *The Winter's Tale,* ed. Stephen Orgel (Oxford, 1996), pp. 2-3.

5. Salingar, *Shakespeare and the Traditions of Comedy,* pp. 62-6.

6. Robert S. Miola, *Shakespeare and Classical Comedy: The Influence of Plautus and Terence* (Oxford, 1994), pp. 143-55, and *Shakespeare and Classical Tragedy: The Influence of Seneca* (Oxford, 1992), pp. 194-9.

7. *Henry V,* ed. T. W. Craik (1995), notes on III. vi. 25 that Pistol's use of 'buxom' in its medieval sense, in Captain Gower's first scene, is paralleled in Shakespeare only in Gower's Prologue to *Pericles,* l. 23.

8. Anne Barton, '"Enter Mariners Wet": Realism in Shakespeare's Last Plays', in her *Essays, Mainly Shakespearean* (Cambridge, 1994), p. 202.

9. Quotations, with references in text, are from *The English Works of John Gower,* ed. G. C. Macaulay, vol. ii (EETS ES 82, Oxford, 1900).

10. W. A. Davenport, *Chaucer and his English Contemporaries: Prologue and Tale in 'The Canterbury Tales'* (1998), p. 71.

11. Anne Barton, 'Leontes and the Spider: Language and Speaker in Shakespeare's Last Plays', *Essays, Mainly Shakespearean,* p. 178.

12. Twine, 'The Patterne of Painefull Adventures' (1594?), reprinted in Geoffrey Bullough, *Narrative and Dramatic Sources of Shakespeare,* vol. vi (1966), p. 438. Metrically, the first use of the name in Gower, 'Appolinus the Prince of Tyre' (l. 375), requires accentuation on the second syllable, bringing out the echo. Cerimon invokes Apollo in *Pericles,* III. ii. 66.

13. Bullough, *Narrative and Dramatic Sources,* p. 444. Subsequent references to Bullough are given in the text.

14. Jonathan Bate, *Shakespeare and Ovid* (Oxford, 1993), pp. 220-1.

15. Arestratus of Pentapolis and his daughter, who becomes Apollonius' wife, foreshadow Apollonius and Thaisa, while Dionysa and Strangulio, who plot Thaisa's murder, are Antiochus-like figures.

16. See C. L. Barber, '"Thou that beget'st him that did thee beget": Recognition in *Pericles* and *The Winter's Tale*', *Shakespeare Survey,* 22 (1969), 59-68.

17. Whether we, the audience, hear it too, as DVH assume ('music must be played here', V. i. 218 (s.d. n.) and supplementary note, p. 196) is open to question. A stage direction for music was first inserted by Dyce in his edition of 1857. DVH argue that we are privileged to share Pericles' special insight, but an at least equally mysterious effect could be obtained if we remained as deaf as Pericles' companions.

18. See Danby, *Poets on Fortune's Hill* (1952), reprinted as *Elizabethan and Jacobean Poets* (1965), pp. 87-103.

19. Quotations are from *Patience,* ed. J. J. Anderson (Manchester, 1969), who emends the manuscript's 'Nepturne' which he attributes to confusion with Saturn.

20. Quotations (spelling modernised) are from *The 1599 Geneva Bible,* a facsimile reprint (Ozark, M., 1990).

21. Anderson, p. 18, compares the reference to Jonah in the Cappers' Play in MS Harley 2124 of the Chester cycle. See *The Chester Mystery Cycle,* ed. R. M. Lumiansky and David Mills (EETS SS 3, 9), 2 vols. (Oxford, 1974, 1986), i. 478, ll. 345-60.

22. The three days and three nights Jonah spends in the fish's belly are 'the traditional time it takes to reach the underworld' according to James S. Ackerman, 'Jonah', in Robert Alter and Frank Kermode (eds.), *The Literary Guide to the Bible* (1987), p. 237.

23. Ibid., p. 236.

24. Noted in *The Poems of the Pearl Manuscript,* ed. Malcolm Andrew and Ronald Waldron (1978; revised edn., Exeter, 1987), on *Patience* 258.

25. Ackerman, 'Jonah', p. 239.

26. Ibid., p. 241, where Ackerman also notes that the name 'the Lord God' (4: 6) is the same in Hebrew as that used of God in Genesis 2.

27. Ackerman, 'Jonah', p. 242.

28. Marion Lomax, *Stage Images and Traditions: Shakespeare to Ford* (Cambridge, 1987), p. 81.

29. The parallel with *Merchant* is noted by Lomax, *Stage Images,* pp. 47-8, who also sees allusion to Pandora's box.

30. Anne Barton, *The Names of Comedy* (Oxford, 1990), pp. 148-9. Lomax, *Stage Images,* p. 52, sees analogies with Venus Anadyomene and with the Christian *Maria maris stella.*

31. The play is included in *The Late Medieval Religious Plays of Bodleian MSS Digby 133 and E Museo 160,* ed. Donald C. Baker, John L. Murphy and Louis B. Hall (EETS OS 283) (Oxford, 1982); for the date, see p. xl. Recently, Piero Boitani has interpreted the reunion of Pericles and Marina as a theophanic recognition recalling the meeting between Jesus and Mary Magdalen in St John's Gospel, ch. 20; see Boitani, *The Bible and its Rewritings* (Oxford, 1999), pp. 160-72.

32. The link was made independently by Howard Felperin, 'Shakespeare's Miracle Play', *Shakespeare Quarterly,* 18 (1967), 365, and David L. Jeffrey, 'English Saints' Plays', in Neville Denny (ed.), *Medieval Drama* (1973), p. 73. But the Digby plays' provenance is East Anglia (Baker, Murphy and Hall, pp. ix-xv) and Hoeniger sensibly stopped short of insisting that Shakespeare must have known them.

33. David Hugh Farmer, *The Oxford Dictionary of Saints* (Oxford, 3rd edn., 1992), p. 318, s.v. 'Margaret of Antioch (Marina)'.

34. *Seinte Marharete,* ed. Frances M. Mack (EETS OS 193) (Oxford, 1934), p. 24, ll. 7-19.

35. *A Looking-Glass for London and England,* ed. W. W. Greg (Oxford, 1932), ll. 2404-9, with spelling modernised. Cf. Lomax, *Stage Images,* p. 81.

36. *The Comedy of Errors,* ed. R. A. Foakes (1963), pp. xxix, 113-15.

37. F. F. Bruce, 'Acts of the Apostles', in Bruce M. Metzger and Michael D. Coogan (eds.), *The Oxford Companion to the Bible* (Oxford, 1993), pp. 6-10, esp. p. 7.

38. James M. Robinson, 'Acts', in Alter and Kermode (eds.), *The Literary Guide to the Bible,* p. 469.

39. God summons the winds 'Ewrus and Aquiloun' against Jonah (*Patience,* l. 133 and Anderson's note). Tyndale, in his translation of 1534, cuts the names, but his word for the wind, 'a flaw' (*Tyndale's New Testament,* ed. David Daniell (Yale, 1989, 1995), p. 204), is also used by Pericles at III. i. 40.

40. Glyn Austen, 'Ephesus Restored: Sacramentalism and Redemption in *The Comedy of Errors*', *Journal of Literature and Theology,* 1/1 (1987), 62. This epistle contains matter relevant to *Pericles* too, notably the statement that the ascended Christ 'descended first into the lowest parts of the earth' (4: 9), a text which is often interpreted as referring to the Harrowing of Hell and, by analogy, to Jonah. There is also much use of imagery of darkness and light (5: 8-14), and teaching on the mutual responsibilities of married couples and their children (5: 22-6: 4).

41. Frank Kermode, 'John', in Alter and Kermode (eds.), *The Literary Guide to the Bible,* p. 450. Boitani, *The Bible and its Rewritings,* also insists on the importance of the Johannine themes of *becoming* and *being* in *Pericles:* see especially pp. 152-5, 166-9.

42. C. J. Sisson, 'Shakespearean Quartos as Prompt-Copies, with some Account of Cholmeley's Players and a New Shakespeare Allusion', *Review of English Studies,* 18 (1942), 138. W. Schrickx, '*Pericles* in a Book-List of 1619 from the English Jesuit Mission and some of the Play's Special Problems', *Shakespeare Survey,* 29 (1976), 21-32, speculates that the play was in the repertory of the Jesuit theatre at St-Omer.

43. *Twelfth Night,* also acted at Candlemas in 1602, draws on some of the same liturgical material as *Pericles:* see Paul Dean, 'The Harrowing of Malvolio: The Theological Background of *Twelfth Night,* Act 4, Scene 2', *Connotations,* 7/2 (1997/98), 203-13.

44. Eamon Duffy, *The Stripping of the Altars: Traditional Religion in England 1400-1580* (New Haven, 1992), pp. 15-16.

45. Ibid., pp. 15-18. The episode is dramatised in all the extant mystery cycles and also in the Digby *Killing of the Children,* the play presented by Poeta. In the cycles the play is followed by, or merged with, that of the child Jesus astonishing the doctors in the Temple with his wisdom, much as Marina does the citizens of Tarsus in *Pericles* IV. 0. 5-29.

Caroline Bicks (essay date 2000)

SOURCE: Bicks, Caroline. "Backsliding at Ephesus: Shakespeare's Diana and the Churching of Women." In Pericles: *Critical Essays,* edited by David Skeele, pp. 205-27. New York: Garland Publishing, 2000.

[*In the following essay, Bicks detects references in* Pericles *to the tension surrounding the practice of traditional Catholic rituals as practiced in the reformed Church of England in the early 1600s. In particular, Bicks points out dramatic episodes that echo the controversy over church ceremonies involving women after childbirth.*]

> *Our lodgings, standing bleak upon the sea,*
> *Shook as the earth did quake;*
> *The very principals did seem to rend,*
> *And all to topple. Pure surprise and fear*
> *Made me to quit the house.*
>
> (*Pericles*, 3.2.14-18)[1]

> *Such an ordinarie service as yours is for every private woman . . . hath, in my opinion, neither legges nor foundation to stande on.*
>
> (*Certaine Questions . . . concerning Churching of Women,* 1601)

When Shakespeare's Thaisa awakens from her burial at sea to find herself on the shaken shores of Ephesus, her first words are to that city's goddess: "O dear Diana, / Where am I? Where's my Lord? What world is this?" (3.2.104-105). Except for her invocation of Diana, her words echo *verbatim* those of John Gower's heroine from the *Confessio Amantis,* the literary ancestor of the tempest-tossed Thaisa. This addition of Diana is a persistent feature of *Pericles:* Shakespeare refers to the goddess over a dozen times in the play, whereas Gower's work and Laurence Twine's *Patterne of Painefull Adventures,* his immediate sources, name her only twice.[2]

Critics generally read *Pericles'* oft-invoked Diana as a goddess of virginity and consider her Ephesian temple a site of maternal purification. From this perspective, Thaisa's enclosure in the goddess's temple and her reunion with husband and daughter fourteen years later are acts of compliance that reinforce male constructions of power based on the ideal of a chaste female body contained within a stable set of cultural rituals.[3] This reading has its roots in certain early modern conceptions of Diana and Ephesus. Arthur Golding popularized her as an asexual deity in Shakespeare's time when he translated Ovid's *Metamorphoses* and instructed his readers to understand her as representative of "maydens chaste."[4] Another common story in the early modern period claimed that the Virgin Mary had accompanied Saint John to Ephesus and lived her last years there, for

the city was also known as the site where Saint Paul established the new church—one of seven founded in Asia and central to the conversion mission.[5]

Ephesus and its goddess, however, were rich in mythical and pseudo-historical associations that went far beyond these chaste and often Christian-inflected parameters. The Temple of Diana, a vast marble monument built in the sixth century B.C., had been financed by the pilgrims and tourists seeking oracles from the goddess. Once built, the temple—revered as one of the seven wonders of the ancient world—also became central to the city's economic success and its consequent reputation as a nest of vice and luxury.[6] The Greek travel writer Pausanias memorialized the city for future generations when he remarked on its fame—"the size of the temple, which is the largest building in the world, the prosperity of the city of Ephesus, and the distinction which the goddess there enjoys."[7]

Although seventeenth-century Ephesus was a poor town whose famed Temple of Diana had sunk twenty feet into the silt, its reputation as an ancient thriving center of pagan worship and excess survived to be vividly narrated by early modern writers. Legends connecting the Amazons to the site compounded these illicit associations and competed with stories of the early Christian presence in Ephesus. In 1616, the Protestant minister Sampson Price dwelt more on the temple than the church:

> *Ephesus* is fallen; one of the most famous Cities of the world, the *Metropolis* of little *Asia,* the glory of *Ionia,* built in the 28. yeare of David, either by the Amazons or one called *Croesus.* . . . Heere *John* and the *Virgin* lived. *Ephesus* was renowned for the great temple of Diana, one of the wonders of the World, 425. feet long, 220. broad, having 127. pillars the workes of so many Kings, 220. yeares in building.[8]

Ancient writers consistently named the Amazons as the founders of this famous goddess's temple and claimed that the women were the first devotees to dedicate an image of her at Ephesus.[9] Thomas Heywood and Walter Ralegh were among the early modern writers to perpetuate the association.[10] In many of these texts, the Amazons who worship at Diana's Ephesian temple are not subdued vestal virgins, but rather relentlessly maternal and aggressive bodies: Heywood explains that "they had mutuall congression with their neighbor nations: the men children they slew, the female they nourced."[11]

As Price's and Heywood's texts suggest, stories of pagan worship, excess, and the sexually free-ranging Amazons threatened to eclipse references to the early Christian church. Price was not alone in lamenting that Ephesus—a city that became synonymous with the Protestant Church of England and its post-Reformation conflicts—"is fallen." To an early modern audience, the Church of England rested on shaky pagan foundations; Ephesus exemplified its struggle to resist backsliding into the idolatrous (i.e., Catholic) past on which it was built.

These troubling associations with idolatry and sexuality were aggravated by the fact that Diana was a scion of a pre-Hellenic fertility/mother goddess whose cult was centered in Ephesus and flourished throughout the Eastern Mediterranean. By the time she reached the early modern period, she was a constellation of contradictions. She had many names, each of which denoted a different function, but all of her incarnations found their way back, through centuries of tale-telling, to the Ephesian goddess's temple. As the Greek Artemis and the Roman Diana, she protected virginity; as Hecate, she embodied the mysteries of female power; her association with the procreative Amazons and the ancient fertility goddess led to her formulation as Luna, goddess of the moon, and Lucina, the Roman goddess of childbirth.[12]

The seventeenth-century midwife Elizabeth Cellier, confident that her readers would easily equate the Ephesian Diana with reproduction, made her the lynchpin of her argument for midwifery education: "here in London were Colledges of Women about the Temple of Diana, who was goddess of midwives here, as well as at Ephesus."[13] The mention of Diana in her Ephesian context evokes the goddess's function as midwife—Lucina and Diana are virtually indistinguishable. Shakespeare similarly conflates the figures in the climactic storm scene that ends with Thaisa's unhallowed descent into the ocean's ooze. Pericles makes Lucina central to his wife's survival, crying out to the goddess to help Thaisa in her "terrible child-bed" (3.1.56); in the next scene, Thaisa calls out to Diana on the shores of Ephesus. In Shakespeare's tale, then, Diana returns to her ancient reproductive function and foundation—invoked by a mother who will enter her temple and (paradoxically, it would seem) be her chaste votaress.

This conflation of the asexual Diana who protects the purity of women's bodies and the reproductive Lucina who attends to their procreative activities, however, far from being a textual inconsistency, is a central feature of the play itself. Shakespeare repeatedly summons Diana's incarnation as a fertility/midwife goddess in the midst of Thaisa's chaste devotion to her. Twine enacts a similar merger when he names his protagonist's wife Lucina and summarizes his first chapter at Ephesus with "*How Lucina was restored to life*" and placed "*in the temple of Diana.*"[14]

What I ultimately will argue here is that Diana's Ephesian temple and its connections to pagan mysteries and procreative women figured a heated religious debate of Shakespeare's time that centered on the maternal body and concerned the place of Catholic ritual in Protestant practice: the churching of women after childbirth. Originally a Jewish purification of the new mother, the ceremony continued as a Catholic ceremony in which the new mother returned to church with her birth attendants, after a prescribed time at home, to be cleansed by the priest and so readmitted to the congregation. In its English Protestant form, the ritual lost its purifying function when it was renamed the Thanksgiving, or churching of women after childbirth in 1552. With this change, reformers meant to erase the superstitious transformation of the new mother into an asexual, almost virginal figure reminiscent of the Holy Mother. The procreative female body, now distanced from any original polluted associations by this doctrinal shift, retained its physical maternal function while demanding the attention of a holy congregation. The result was the troubling entrance of a celebrated female sexuality into church doctrine and practice.

Like the Ephesian Diana and her votaresses, the churching community of mother, midwife, and friends affirmed both the miraculous *and* material process of birth. By retaining the ritual, but eliminating evocations of the Virgin, reformers had inadvertently set the pagan Mother goddess loose in their own church. Although misogynist satire focused on the financial burden that the ceremony placed on the beleaguered and displaced husband, it was in fact this public and hallowed acknowledgment of the material maternal experience that provoked the most anxious responses and brought the new church closer than ever to its pagan foundations.[15]

Religious opponents of the ritual felt it should not be present at all in the reformed Protestant Church precisely because of the ceremony's idolatrous associations: a Puritan Admonition to Parliament in 1572 complained that "Churching of women after childbirthe, smelleth of Jewishe purification: theyr other rytes and customes in their lying in, & comming to church, is foolishe and superstitious."[16] At the same time, they were troubled by the privileged position that the churching ceremony afforded mothers and that their own reformed church had promoted. Henry Barrow complained that "this particular and ordinarie (though miraculous) matter, more than all other strange actes . . . should be made a publique action of the church, an especial part of the publique worship."[17] His parenthetical acknowledgment of the "(miraculous) matter" of birth points to a paradox within the Protestant reworking of the ceremony: The maternal body contained both ordinary, earthly matter and a miracle deserving of reverence. To some reformers, this retention of the Jewish/Catholic ritual and elevation of everyday matter threatened a dangerous backsliding into pagan idolatry and exposed the new church's doctrinal instability—its ironic reliance on the very religious practices against which it was meant to define itself.

When Protestant ministers preached to their congregations against slipping back into Popish ways, they equated the Church of England's return to Catholicism with an early Christian Ephesus tottering on the brink of paganism. Ephesus, like Catholicism, was part and parcel of the foundational Judeo-Christian tradition from which the new church was toiling to emerge; at the same time, these foundations were tainted by superstitious associations. The shaking Ephesus that Thaisa first encounters, then, epitomizes the struggle of the reformed Church of England to negotiate its Popish/pagan past while constructing a new Protestant theology—one that was inescapably founded on idolatrous rituals and traditions. As one fictional debater in a 1601 work complains to the chancellor who pressures her to be churched: "such an ordinarie service as yours is, for every private woman such as my self, hath in mine opinion neither legges nor foundation to stande on."[18]

This ambivalent and sometimes hostile reception of the churching ceremony by church and lay fathers alike suggests new ways of exploring early modern portrayals of Diana, her Ephesian temple, and the cults of women who operated within it. Jeanne Roberts, in her important analysis of abortive birth rituals in Shakespeare's plays, notes that "the necessary transition from sexual abstinence to fertility is fraught with dangers, attested to repeatedly in Shakespeare, of incorporating 'whore,' chaste wife, and mother into one female figure."[19] Both Diana at Ephesus and the Protestant churching ritual allowed this uneasy incorporation of sanctity and sexuality in the figure of the mother. She became, then, the embodiment of the Church of England's own uneasy relationship to its pagan (Catholic) past. Her sexuality represented these illicit beginnings, while her sanctity was figured as the promise of a new Christian (Protestant) redemption at Ephesus.

In Shakespeare's works, Diana and her votaresses sometimes do appear as holy virgins;[20] however, the women who worship in the temple are also portrayed as fertile Amazons, widows, unwed mothers, and defiant daughters. In *A Midsummer Night's Dream,* for instance, Hermia would rather throw herself on "Diana's altar to protest / For aye austerity and single life" than obey her father and marry Demetrius (1.1.89-90). This aggressive pledge to the single life later is rendered far from austere by the sexual Titania (an alternative name for Diana), who revels in her Indian votaress's pregnancy.[21]

These conflicting visions of Diana and her Ephesian sanctuary clearly inform *Pericles,* where Shakespeare grapples with a maternal body that, thanks to Protestant revisions, was sacred *and* procreative—a reminder of the Great Mother and the magical rituals that surrounded her both in Catholic and pre-Hellenic practice. C. L. Barber has argued that *Pericles* is notable for the way its "symbolic action, centered on the recovery of lost bonds in a human family, is used to meet needs that, in different circumstances, are met in Christian worship of the Holy Family."[22] In post-Reformation England, however, the virginal Holy Mother was a troubling component of this family. Barber's claim that women's problematic position in Shakespeare's plays "reflects the fact that Protestantism did away with the Cult of the Virgin Mary" is particularly relevant to our exploration here of the maternal body's ritualistic movements in the reformed church and in *Pericles.*[23] When Shakespeare brings the new mother to Ephesus and scripts both her invocation of Diana and her movement to the goddess's temple, he aggravates all of the cultural and religious tensions that accompanied the Protestant Church's attempts to build a new doctrine of the maternal body on idolatrous foundations. Although it is tempting to interpret Thaisa's enclosure within the Temple of Diana as a patient withdrawal of the waiting wife before her smooth ritual return to husband and society, the complex associations of the temple with mysterious ritual and the sexual female body demand a more complicated reading of the Ephesian site in early Protestant theology and Shakespeare's late romance.

The Protestant Church of England, with its insistence on distancing doctrine from its idolatrous associations, did not quite know what to do with Ephesus. On the one hand, the city was a site of pagan mysteries and heathen Turks;[24] on the other hand, it epitomized the possibility of conversion to the "true" Christian church. William Caxton's *Golden Legend* narrates how Saint John "converted to Christ's faith 12,000 Gentiles" after his prayers toppled the temple, "so that the foundement turned up so down, and the image of Diana all-to dashed and destroyed."[25] Most famously, Acts 19 depicts Saint Paul's confrontation with the Ephesian silversmith Demetrius, who incites a pagan crowd to cry out "Great is Diana of the Ephesians!" In both these texts, the image of Diana stands for the paganism that must be annihilated in order for Christianity to thrive; ironically, however, her city comes to represent the potential for a model Christian community. Once she has been destroyed, the city of Ephesus goes on to become the site of the most powerful Christian church in Asia Minor.

With roots in both pagan and Christian tradition, Ephesus exemplified England and its post-Reformation conflicts. John's address to the church at Ephesus in his Revelation (2:1-7) expresses his concern for her loss of Christian enthusiasm. As we have seen, the Ephesus of John's text was often used in Protestant sermons to figure the Church of England's backsliding away from the reformed church and toward idolatrous Catholic practice. John Prideaux, rector of Exeter College, delivered a sermon in 1614 entitled *Ephesus Backsliding Considered and Applied to these Times* in which he explicitly connects England's religious laxity to that of the early Christian Ephesus: "*Hee that hath an eare to heare, let him harke what the spirit saith unto the Churches; to the Churches as well of Great Brittaine, as of those of little Asia.*"[26] Prideaux expresses displeasure with the Church of England's loss of religious enthusiasm and employs John's reprimanding letter to Ephesus as an analogy:

> For the best may grow remisse, and need dayly inciting. As *Ephesus* here, the *Metropolis* of *little Asia* and glory of *Ionia*, famous amonst the *gentils* for her *situation, & temple,* which (as *Pliny* reports) was 220 years in building, famous amongst *Christians*, for *S. Johns residence*, and *S. Pauls epistle* unto them; nay, which our *Saviour* here commends . . . for her *forwardnesse* in *labour*, for her *constancie* in patience, for *her zeale in reforming manners*, for her *discretion in dismasking heretiques.* . . . *Nevertheless I have somewhat against thee, because thou hast left thy first love.*[27]

In his interpretation of John's Revelation, Prideaux conflates paganism and Catholicism. His goal is to encourage his congregation to "hate the abominations of Poperie (as the Ephesians did here the deedes of the Nicolaitans)" (37). He wants his church to have the same "zeale in reforming manners" as Ephesus had shown in its early days under Saint Paul's influence, and he praises King James for being "so able & resolved to withstand Popery" (36). At the same time, he warns his congregation not to backslide as Ephesus apparently had.

Prideaux emphasizes Ephesus's ties to both a pagan and a Christian past: in his text, the Temple of Diana is equal in fame to the residence of Saint John. The goddess and her house seem to eclipse the "Angel" (the church) of Ephesus. Prideaux chastises the latter for falling from grace and leaving her "first love" of Jesus.[28] It is here, as he turns the church into a feminized creature easily seduced away from Christ, that the line between the Angel and the goddess begins to vanish: "hast thou not began in the *spirit,* and now art sinking *backe* to end in the flesh?" (3). His words recall the multivalent Ephesian Diana, who was both a Greco-Roman goddess of virginal purity and an ancient goddess of the flesh. Prideaux does not name Diana, but he uses the image of the moon, her most noted symbol, to elaborate on her city's, and England's, ecclesiastical errancy:

> It is usual with the *Fathers* to *compare* the *church* to the *moone,* in regard of her visible changing, like to the others *waxing* and *waning*. But the similitude holds as well, in respect of her borrowed light, and spotted face. . . . Her selfe acknowledgeth so much, *Cantic. I. 5. I am blacke but comely.*[29]

Although here Diana is the cherished beloved of Canticles, in other texts she is a Popish whore. In 1644, John Vicars described her as the "Romish-Catholicks Sweet-Heart"—"Babylons Beautie."[30] As Vicars's words and the destruction of Diana's statue by Saint John illustrate, the Ephesian goddess was often figured as either a Catholic or pagan enemy of the "true" church. Like her city's citizens, however, she also embodied the possibility of conversion. She and the struggling reformed church she came to epitomize could be all things to all men; both her temple and the Church of England wax and wane with the moon's vagaries—a fact that complicates any dyadic sacred/profane interpretation of the site and its goddess in early modern literature.

Before she was the Roman Diana of Reformation rhetoric, the Ephesian goddess was the Greek Artemis. The grove of Ortygia near Ephesus was the fabled place of Artemis's birth.[31] Callimachus, in his *Hymn to Artemis,* tells how she assisted with her twin brother Apollo's birth. He describes the role she subsequently took on as celestial midwife: "the cities of men I will visit only when women vexed by the sharp pangs of childbirth call me to their aid—even in the hour when I was born the Fates ordained that I should be their helper."[32] Legend claimed that Artemis was performing her duties as a midwife at the birth of Alexander the Great in 356 B.C. when Herostratus burned the temple to the ground.[33] As the midwife goddess, Artemis was associated with Eileithyia, and later with the Roman goddess Lucina.

Long before these Greco-Roman incarnations, however, she was an Anatolian mother goddess. She often merged with other such figures: Gaia, Rhea, Isis, Kybele, Kore, and Demeter. This connection to Demeter, and then to Persephone, queen of the underworld, fueled her later associations with darkness and witchcraft—hence her incarnation as Hecate. The maternal goddess's multibreasted statue was preserved in the sanctuary of the great temple at Ephesus.[34] This form of the goddess was familiar enough to have inspired a polymaste statue of her made for the Villa d'Este at Tivoli in the sixteenth century.[35]

These associations of Diana with female mysteries and sexuality, then, were familiar to Shakespeare and his contemporaries through both textual and visual representations. Centuries earlier, Chaucer had foregrounded these associations of the goddess with fertility when he created his Temple of Diana in *The Knight's Tale*. Far from being a site of corporeal purity, it is decorated with pictures of uncontainable metamorphoses and houses a laboring woman who cries wildly for "Lucyna."[36] Like Chaucer's Diana, the pre-Hellenic goddess was known for the animalistic forms she took. In the numismatic tradition, for instance, her polymaste image often appeared with a stag or a bee until it was replaced by the head of the virgin huntress after Alexander the Great's conquest.[37]

It is this ancient and untamed form of the Ephesian goddess who appears in one of the earliest known literary tales of Britain's foundation: Geoffrey of Monmouth's *Historia Regum Britanniae* narrates Brutus's encounter with Diana, who comes to him in his dreams and tells him where to found the English nation. Brutus describes Diana as *Diva potens nemorum terror silvestribus ac spes. Cui licet anfractus ire per ethereos infernasque domos* ("Powerful goddess, terror of the groves and hope of the forest beasts. To whom it is permitted to traverse the airy paths and the hellish homes").[38] Although Geoffrey situates the temple on an island called Leogetia, he is likely referring to Ortygia, the site in Ephesus of Artemis's mysteries.[39] In any case, the description of the goddess allies her with the ancient Ephesian goddess who had temples devoted to her throughout the Eastern Mediterranean.[40] Geoffrey's wild goddess who walks through heaven and hell is much closer in spirit to the deity who was rooted in the mysteries of birth and death than to the Hellenized and virginal Diana. Furthermore, as she guides Brutus toward England's future, she enacts one of the Ephesian goddess's most famous and enduring roles: As the Protestant minister Edward Chaloner described the city in 1618, it was "renowned for the Oracles of the Goddesse."[41]

With these powerful pagan and Christian associations of the goddess with prophetic speech, national foundation, and female sexuality, it is significant that Shakespeare uses Ephesus, and its echoes of the cult of the Great Mother, to explore the gendered and religious conflicts inherent in the Protestant retention and revision of Catholic rituals, particularly those surrounding birth. The Temple of Diana and the Christian church already threatened to merge at times in Protestant texts; churching completed this process by opening the doors of the church to a sexual maternal body and allowing the pagan goddess, surrounded by her votaresses, to enter in.

As a ritual that brought mothers and their birth attendants together within a holy space, the churching of women after childbirth provides an analogue to the sexual activities of the pre-Hellenic Diana's worshippers.[42] Like this pagan community, the maternal and midwiving bodies who were caught in the middle of the early modern churching debates occupied a multivalent space. Bringing to life the "spotted" goddess of Prideaux's sermon, *Ephesus Backsliding,* texts explaining the churching ritual portrayed the churched mother as tottering on the edge of institutional infidelity because of her time spent confined at home and away from an organized Christian community. As one such text by

Thomas Comber averred: "She is now joyned again to the Assembly of the Faithful, and we pray she may ever remain among that number, never forsaking her Principles, nor her holy Faith by Apostasie and *Backsliding*" (emphasis mine).[43] The maternal body here represents the potential of all true Christians to fall. She *is* Ephesus backsliding and, in a certain light, Diana herself. The 121st Psalm that was part of the ritual exhorted that "the sun shall not smite thee by day, nor the moon by night"; with the churching ritual's new emphasis on the sacred and sexual body of the mother, the pagan, fickle moon goddess and her "borrowed light" (to recall Prideaux's phrase) threatened to spot the body of the Protestant mother and the reformed church that celebrated it, sending both backsliding into idolatrous superstition.

As we have seen, Prideaux reproached his congregation for backsliding like its Ephesian ancestor: "hast thou not began in the *spirit,* and now art sinking *backe* to end in the flesh?" (3). As Jacqueline de Weever notes in her study of Diana of Ephesus, such a division of spirit and body would not have been applied to the goddess before the early modern period: "The Great Mother and the chaste goddess seem to exist side by side in classical and medieval mythographers."[44] In the nightmares of Shakespeare's religious contemporaries, however, the balance could tip: What "began in the spirit" of purity might sink back "to end in the flesh" of the great and pagan Mother.

Grounded in ancient Hebraic and Catholic tradition, the churching ritual, like those surrounding the Ephesian temple, provoked conflicted responses when placed in the context of the reformed Church of England. Both the ritual and the goddess had particularly pagan yet foundational associations: One could not simply topple them without destabilizing the foundation of England and its new church. A close look at Puritan objections to the churching ritual reveals a concern both with this lack of separation between the church and its past and with the transformation of a Protestant sanctuary into a privileged female space. Henry Barrow offers his critical commentary on the ritual:

> The weoman's monethlie restraint and separation from your church, her comming after that just tyme wympeled, vealed [veiled], with her gosips and neighbors following her, her kneeling downe before and offring unto the priest, the prieste's churching, praying over her, blessing her from sonne and moone, delivering her in the end to her former vocation, shewe somewhat besides giving of thankes.[45]

Barrow implies that the privileging of the maternal body's experience during churching was an intrusion into and appropriation of a sacred male space. His objection to the ritual is not, as some modern critics arguing for Puritan feminism put forward, a result of his respect for the processes of childbirth, but rather of his distaste for the special recognition accorded to the entire birthing community—the "gosips and neighbors" who accompanied the mother to church.[46] The fictional chancellor who debates churching with his kinswoman similarly objects to "the Ceremonie of it, as the Tyme, and th'Attyre, the companie of women . . . and the feasting of neighbours and friends."[47]

The time before the churching, consisting of the birth itself and the month of the mother's confinement—the lying-in, as it was called—at home, already provided a unique social space for the mother, her female friends, and her midwife. Churching, then, was the final and most public of these childbirth ceremonies. Far from being a ritual imposed upon women by a sexist culture, churching has been redefined by scholars in the past twenty-five years as a ceremony that women willingly upheld despite public religious conflicts.[48] Adrian Wilson, working from Natalie Zemon Davis's argument that the all-female ceremonies of childbirth placed women "on top" of their husbands, notes the popularity of the churching custom across religious and class divides "because it legitimated the wider ceremony of childbirth."[49] In addition, it was a time for midwives to advertise themselves as successful birth attendants.[50]

The need in Jewish/Catholic doctrine to cleanse the mother's body had been eliminated from the ceremony; this meant that she and her attendants could enter the church in celebration, not shame. The mother now knelt at the ritual center of the church and no longer had to wait "nygh unto the quier doore" until the priest sprinkled her with holy water and led her inside, as the purification ceremony had required.[51] The churching ritual allowed that "the woman shall come into the churche, and there shall knele downe in some convenient place, nigh unto the place where the table standeth."[52] As David Cressy asserts, such "minor adjustments . . . were enormously significant. They transformed the woman from a penitent to a celebrant (or 'gratulant'), from a petitioner at the margin to the focus of community attention."[53] Gail McMurray Gibson has argued that the older purification ritual afforded women an equivalent sense of empowerment: "the symbolic and ritual center of this drama was a woman's body—and the privileged body of women who had served as childbed attendants in the exclusively female space of the childbirthing room."[54] Even with Catholicism's desexualizing approach to the procreative female body, then, the ceremony brought women together as active agents within the church. Although the priest was officially responsible for the woman's reentry into society, the women who accompanied her created the impression of an empowered female society on public display.

When the ritual made its way into the reformed Church of England, it not only carried this strong idolatrous

community forward into Protestant practice, but it officially recognized its identity as a group that supported female sexuality. The new church itself had conflated the sacred and the procreative by speaking out against the idea of a polluted maternal body. Reformed doctrine, eliminating the Catholic priest's purifying role, pointed instead toward the woman's material powers and her direct relationship with God. The language of the churching ceremony made God the midwife to the thankful new mother: The closing prayer addresses "almightie god, whiche hast delyvered this woman thy servant from the greate paine and peryl of child birth."[55] Thomas Comber makes the analogy even more explicit in his explanation of the ritual: "our Creator . . . not only makes us in our Mother's Womb, but brings us also as wonderfully from thence. Thou art he (saith the *Psalmist*) that took me out of my Mothers Womb, *Psal.* xxii.9."[56]

Although this replacement of the midwife by God can be read as a textual removal of the mother's attendant within the church, it is more significant for its elision of the gap between maternal body and holy spirit that rendered the priest less significant in his own authorized realm. Bishop Bonner asked in 1554 whether there were any women who "by themselves or by sinister counsel have purified themselves after their own devices and fantasies, not coming to the church according to the laudable custom . . . where the parish priest would have been ready to do it, and some of the multitude to have been witnesses accordingly?"[57] This image of women anointing their own bodies graphically epitomizes the threat that the ceremony, steeped in an idolatrous past, posed to the Protestant Church's constructions of a new religious order. In an attempt to disempower the women who might interfere with this order, instructions were given to ministers that they should ensure "the midwife go not before the woman, that is to give her thanks, into the church and so up to the Communion table."[58]

These injunctions speak to some of the tensions that the female body and its community of attendants provoked when granted a place of honor within a traditionally male space. Robert Herrick brings this concern for maintaining a gendered order within the church to the level of the marital home when he describes Julia's churching:

> Put on thy *Holy Fillitings,* and so
> To th' Temple with the sober *Midwife* go.
> Attended thus (in a most solemn wise)
> By those who serve the Child-bed misteries.
>   . . . . .
> All Rites well ended, with faire Auspice come
> (As to the breaking of a Bride-Cake) home:
> Where ceremonious Hymen shall for thee
> Provide a second *Epithalamie.*[59]

(lines 1-4; 9-10)

The time of confinement before churching was a time of sexual abstinence as well as female gathering; churching was the last stage before the husband regained his rights over his wife and home. It was all well and good, therefore, for a woman to go to church and perform "Child-bed misteries" in the "Temple" with her midwife (words that recall the Ephesian cult of the Great Mother), as long as she came home to be bedded like "the breaking of a Bride-Cake" by her husband. Herrick's reference to these pagan details foregrounds the ritual's mysterious and female-centered past and reminds us of its troubled status within the reformed Church of England. Interestingly, his poem is entitled "Julia's Churching, *or* Purification" (emphasis mine)—an engagement, perhaps, with the unstable foundations of sexual female power and idolatrous backsliding upon which the Protestant ritual (and the church that created it) tottered.

Critics who have located traces of the churching ritual in *Pericles* and other Shakespearean plays tend to focus on how the maternal body is cleansed and returned to the husband so that family and nation—along with the religious and cultural structures that support them—can be restored. The victory of the husband (who has gone through a period of Christian-inflected redemption and salvation) over his once-procreative wife thematizes the patriarchal church's rescue from female sexual contamination. Janet Adelman, for example, suggests that "in the withdrawal and sanctified return of mothers after they give birth, Shakespeare found a dramatic equivalent for the customs surrounding churching."[60] She discusses the ritual in terms of its desexualizing and controlling power, pointing to "the cost of sacredness to the women made to bear its burden."[61]

Richard Wilson similarly reads both Thaisa's and Hermione's confinements and reunions with their husbands as an imitation of the churching ritual and reads that ritual as an ordering force. His analysis, however, leaves out the rich history of ambivalence and conflict that surrounded this movement of the Catholic/pagan past—with its cults of the Mother—into a Protestant present. He concludes that "science and religion had little to fear, it seems, from a *rite de passage* that reinstated the husband's claim to his wife's body; as Leontes 'will kiss her' when 'the curtain' is drawn from the face of Hermione."[62] Gail Kern Paster points to this ending of *The Winter's Tale* as well, but finds a critique rather than a celebration of patriarchy within it: "the ritualistic character of her unveiling symbolizes its function as a reminder of the churching ceremony that Leontes' trial prevented."[63] But even this approach to the ritual delegates the maternal body too easily to a position of compliance to a larger male-defined order. Paster reads

Hermione as "diminished," no longer a sexual being, but a "living statue [who] is herself the subject of an evidently successful, self-imposed discipline of shame."[64]

Thaisa's physical renewal after death in childbirth and her chaste confinement in the Temple of Diana at times do echo aspects of the purification ritual's superstitious and magical cleansing of the female body. But when Shakespeare recalls this older Catholic/Jewish form of the ceremony and evokes the pagan Temple of Diana—not only in *Pericles,* but in *The Comedy of Errors* and *The Winter's Tale* as well—he troubles rather than calms the waters of contemporary theological debates surrounding churching.[65] Surely Hermione as "living statue," for example, embodies some of the goddess's contradictions. An early tradition of the church claimed that the holy martyr Hermione, daughter of the Apostle Philip, was one of the three women who, with John the Evangelist, blessed Ephesus after the church was founded there by Paul's disciple Timothy.[66] This tradition must have affected Shakespeare's choice of names as he constructed the relationship between Paulina and Hermione. These Christian associations coexist with the Temple of Diana's pagan ones as Hermione and her apostle (who is called a "midwife" by Leontes in 2.3.160) perform an all-female ritual that reunites mother and daughter within Paulina's "chapel" (5.3.86). Aemilia, the displaced wife and mother of *Errors,* similarly presents a theological paradox: She is the abbess of the Temple of Diana. As Aemilia performs her healing mysteries, the Ephesian Diana is present in both her physical and sacred functions: She uses both earthly "drugs and holy prayers" (5.1.104). With all of these competing incarnations, it is important to be alert to the ambiguities surrounding Diana's temple—and Diana herself—when reading Shakespeare's Ephesus-inflected dramas. Clearly, more is happening inside Shakespeare's Temple of Diana than a nunlike cloistering in readiness for the wife's untroubled return to her Lord.

As Jeanne Roberts argues, "actual births are all conspicuously clouded, and the rituals . . . are truncated or aborted" in Shakespeare's plays.[67] These abortive moments are particularly apparent in *Pericles,* a play that separates mother and newborn at the moment of birth: Marina is separated untimely from her mother's body when Thaisa dies at sea. Previous to the family's journey, the female community surrounding birth had been intact. The first time Thaisa enters "*with child*" she is also "*with Lychorida, a nurse,*" and later her midwife (3.Cho.stage dir.). Beginning with her unhallowed burial at sea, however, the play truncates the rituals surrounding birth—fulfilling neither the Catholic nor Protestant ceremonial forms, but rather juggling both churches' treatments of the maternal body and ultimately leaving it in an unresolved and unincorporated state.

While Thaisa is in labor, Pericles calls out to Lychorida and Lucina, invoking and conflating both with his cry: "Lychorida!—Lucina, O / Divinest patroness and midwife gentle" (3.1.10-11). In his version of this scene, Twine makes no mention of the midwife, divine or otherwise, but simply states that Lucina "was weakened, that there was no hope of recoverie, but she must now die."[68] Gower similarly names no goddess and does not bring Lychorida into the action. Shakespeare, however, highlights and conflates both figures as Pericles prays to Lucina: "make swift the pangs / Of my queen's travails!—Now, Lychorida!" (3.1.13-14). This connection of the earthly Lychorida with the celestial Lucina momentarily elevates the midwife to a quasi-divine status that mirrors her role in the Protestant churching ceremony.

The moment Thaisa dies giving birth, however, the mother's helper and the maternal body slide from the sacred to the suspect as Catholic-inflected beliefs begin to determine the action of the play. Lychorida, now distanced from Lucina, is no longer the revered attendant. She gives Pericles his daughter with the words: "Take in your arms this piece of your dead queen" (3.1.17-18). In this scene, the midwife can only deliver death. As for the maternal body, Thaisa must be buried at sea because of a superstitious custom that attributed storms to the presence of the unburied dead. As Pericles debates with the sailors, he resembles a Puritan minister addressing a Popish congregation.

1. SAIL:

> Sir, your queen must overboard. The sea works high, the wind is loud, and will not lie till the ship be clear'd of the dead.

PER:

> That's your superstition.

1. SAIL:

> Pardon us, sir; with us at sea it hath been still observ'd, and we are strong in custom; therefore briefly yield 'er, for she must overboard straight.

(3.1.47-53)

Gower's Appolinus quickly sees the sailors' reasoning, and Twine's Apollonius resists because he cannot bear to throw his beloved overboard. Shakespeare's dialogue, however, is particularly steeped in the rhetoric of Popish/pagan "superstition" that informed the churching debates of his time.

The ritual of clearing the dead from the ship in order to calm the seas graphically enacts the backsliding that religious reformers feared. Pericles ultimately gives in to "custom," and Thaisa is sent into the muck:

> . . . Th'unfriendly elements
> Forgot thee utterly, nor have I time

> To give thee hallow'd to thy grave, but straight
> Must cast thee, scarcely coffin'd, in the ooze.

(3.1.57-60)

Custom is upheld for the sake of cosmic order and monarchical safety: But that ritual here leaves the mother in an unsanctified state. Thaisa's descent into the ocean's ooze can be read as a return of the maternal body to the polluted associations that supported the need for the Jewish/Catholic purification ritual. Pericles, by saying "A priestly farewell to her" (3.1.69), participates in this religious tradition, but does not succeed in rendering the custom "hallow'd."

If we are to read this scene as engaging with the superstition associated with churching's idolatrous foundations, then we must examine the simultaneous earthquake that shakes Ephesus. A gentleman of that city describes how "The very principals did seem to rend, / And all to topple" (3.2.16-17) as Thaisa's body is first thrown overboard and then borne by the stormy seas to Ephesus. This image of foundational instability—of "principals rend[ing]" and buildings "toppl[ing]"—recalls contemporary descriptions of the church's tottering state, of religious doctrine in disorder and decline. The custom of sacrificing the body is meant to calm the storm, but Ephesus—an original site of Christian conversion—shakes along with the unsettled and unhallowed Thaisa. Ephesus and the new mother appear to topple because they are backsliding into an idolatrous ritual that has no "legges or foundation" of its own in the new Protestant Church.

At the same time, the maternal body—the "spotted" goddess—must be recovered at Ephesus in order for familial reunion and salvation to occur. She is still a foundational figure for England and its church. When Thaisa washes up on the shores of Ephesus, she is given a second chance to properly rejoin the community. As Lord Cerimon brings her back to life, she resembles the churched woman exhorted by Comber to

> stand upon the shore, . . . to cast your eyes back upon the raging and tempestuous Sea, on which you were lately tost, and in which you were likely to be swallowed up; for if you forget the evil past, you will not be so thankful for that good state which God hath now put you in.[69]

As discussed earlier, Comber feared that the newly recovered mother might "forsake her principles . . . by Apostasie and backsliding." By bringing this new mother to a shaking and backsliding Ephesus, Shakespeare aggravates these concerns and unsettles the shore of safety that Comber and other Protestant leaders envisioned for their theology's new foundation.

Consequently, there is no one consistent way to read Thaisa's ritual revival; it recalls many of the superstitious elements that reformers preached against, but the text presents it as both authorized and illicit. Cerimon's name implies sacred ritual, but his arts recall the more Popish, magical elements of purification: he uses "fire and cloths" and "rough and woeful music" to raise Thaisa from the dead (3.2.87-88). After watching Cerimon revive Thaisa, one gentleman reveres Cerimon's powers as god-sent: "The heavens, / Through you, increase our wonder, and sets up / Your fame forever" (3.2.95-97). At the same time, Cerimon's engagement with the "secret art" of physic (3.2.32) allies him with the pagan practitioners of "magic arts" whom Paul humbled at Ephesus. At times, he resembles Gower's Cerymon, a "leche" who is rooted in a tradition of earthly medicine;[70] at others, however, Shakespeare's Cerimon recalls the Christian deity Comber described as working His wonders upon the delivering woman "to bring Life out of Death."

Thaisa's first words upon revival, her "O dear Diana," evoke the pagan Mother goddess and temporarily disrupt whatever Christian powers Cerimon had embodied. Restored to health, however, Thaisa does not remember the moment of Marina's birth over which Diana Lucina had authority: "That I was shipp'd at sea I well remember / Even on my eaning time, but whether there / Delivered, by the holy gods / I cannot rightly say" (3.4.5-8). She vows to dedicate herself to chastity, and Cerimon recommends the Temple of Diana, now a sanctuary of asexuality, "Where you may abide till your date expire" (3.4.14). This turn of phrase suggests a prescribed time of confinement similar to the lying-in period before churching. The fourteen years during which she is solely in the company of other women do represent a version of this lying-in month; her attendants, however, are not the experienced women (often mothers themselves) who would have assisted the new mother through her physical recovery, but rather chaste women devoted entirely to the spirit. Soon after Thaisa's retreat to the temple, we learn that "Lychorida, our nurse, is dead" (4.Cho.42).

Although the earthly midwife and mother have been removed at this point in the text, Diana's figure continues to complicate any clear-cut categories of the sacred and the sensual, the Christian and the pagan, for she next appears in her most bodily incarnation—as a visible oracle to Pericles:

> My temple stands in Ephesus, hie thee thither,
> And do upon my altar sacrifice.
> There when my maiden priests are met together
> Before the people all,
> Reveal how thou at sea didst lose thy wife.
>
> (5.1.240-244)

Her bidding brings Pericles to his wife and Thaisa to her daughter. Gower gives this role to "The highe God which wolde him kepe,"[71] and Twine casts "an Angell."[72]

Shakespeare's decision to replace these Christian messengers with the pagan Diana, making her the agent of familial reunion, demands a reading that resists seeing the play's ending at Ephesus as a compliant maneuvering of the female body back into the structures of a Christian-inflected order.

This "Celestial Dian" (5.1.250), insisting upon the intactness of genealogy, recalls the prophetic and wild goddess of Geoffrey's *Historia*. Her appearance here reminds us of Diana's foundational status, not only for Ephesus, but for England. She returns us to the "powerful goddess," the "terror of the glades and hope of the forest beasts" who appeared to Brutus long before the Greeks had incorporated and transformed her into the virgin goddess. This guidance by the ancient Mother toward female ritual, one that will occur within her temple, underscores churching as an inadvertant celebration of the procreative female body and of the ceremony's pagan past.

As the ritual reunion of husband and wife unfolds, the juggling of ceremonial traditions continues. Thaisa, *"standing near the altar, as high priestess"* (5.2.stage dir.), achieves a divine status that parallels the new mother's central role in the revised Protestant ceremony while recalling the pagan priestess who orchestrated the mysteries of Diana's temple.[73] Furthermore, her accompaniment by *"a number of virgins on each side"* illustrates a stripping of the sexual body from the ritual, a return to Jewish/Catholic purification. The direct relationship of the mother to God that the churching text allowed is compromised by Cerimon who acts as the priestlike intermediary. He reintroduces Thaisa to her husband: "This is your wife" (5.3.18). Similarly, when Pericles addresses Cerimon, he points to his powers of divine midwifery: "Reverent sir, / The gods can have no mortal officer / More like a god than you. Will you deliver / How this dead queen lives?" (5.3.61-63). In his next line, however, Pericles blesses "Pure Dian," an actual deity who needs no simile to achieve divinity (5.3.68). Gendered and religious tensions continue as Cerimon insists upon his central role in Thaisa's ritual return: He tells Pericles that he "recovered her, and plac'd her / Here in Diana's temple" (5.3.24-25), like the purifying Catholic priest who determined the appropriate moment of her entrance into the sacred space; fourteen years later, however, it is the untamed goddess who initiates her ritual release at Ephesus.

Pericles will "offer / Night oblations" to Diana (5.3.69-70), an act that recalls her associations with the dark mysteries of nature and reminds us that she was far more than a virgin goddess who purified women's bodies for a greater patriarchal and—thematically speaking—Christian good. As Kenneth Muir suggests, such a tribute relegates him to the role of an idolatrous Ephesian facing off with Saint Paul: "He might well cry, in scriptural phrase, 'Great is Diana of the Ephesians!'"[74] Thaisa's words upon seeing her husband similarly confound any consistent reading of the reunion as a restoration of a new sacred order: "If he be none of mine, my sanctity / Will to my sense bend no licentious ear" (5.3.29-30). He is, of course, her husband and *must* be in order for the family to approach salvation; but this truth goes hand in hand with the unsettling fact that she will forever listen to her "sense" and indulge the "licentious" leanings of her "sanctity." Her time in the Temple of Diana, then, has not stripped her of her sensuality.

It has, however, denied the husband—and the religious and cultural structures that upheld his rights over the female body—the promise of endurance.[75] As critics have noted, Shakespeare departs from his sources in failing to include Gower's and Twine's closing comments that the couple will have more children. There will be no "second *Epithalamie*" upon the churched mother's return from the "Temple" in this tale. Although one can read this final dramatic engagement with the Temple of Diana at Ephesus and the Protestant church-ing ritual as a successful ritualistic taming of the reproductive female and the paganism it represented, the play's inconsistent treatment of the maternal body suggests that we read the ending as a failure of the new church to find its own legs to stand on. Rather than playing her part in the drama of familial salvation, Thaisa will, as Pericles himself affirms, "be buried / A second time within these arms" (5.3.43-44). Their reunion evokes the superstitious muck of Thaisa's burial at sea—a final commentary, perhaps, on the reformed English church's unsuccessful attempts to build its new doctrine on idolatrous foundations. Burying herself in her husband's arms, Thaisa embodies more than ever the backsliding goddess and her temple that colored the rhetoric of Protestant ideology and figured its own top-pling church. Neither Thaisa, the church, nor the temple that an early modern audience knew had sunk into the marshy ooze are ever fully recovered from the darkness of their Ephesian pasts: "the ruines of that wonder," preached one of Shakespeare's Protestant contemporar-ies, "are intombed within the entrails of the Earth."[76]

Notes

1. All references to Shakespeare's plays are from *The Riverside Shakespeare,* ed. G. Blakemore Evans (Boston: Houghton Mifflin, 1974).

2. F. D. Hoeniger notes this pattern and comments that Shakespeare's departure from his sources on this point "may be significant." See his commentary on the *Dramatis Personae* in his edition of *Pericles,* The Arden Edition of the Works of William Shakespeare (London: Methuen, 1963), 4. Kenneth Muir notes the repeated invocation of Di-ana as well and argues that Thaisa's enclosure is a

form of atonement for taking her name in vain. See his *Sources of Shakespeare's Plays* (London: Methuen, 1977), 255.

3. See, for example, C. L. Barber and Richard Wheeler, *The Whole Journey: Shakespeare's Power of Development* (Berkeley: University of California Press, 1986), 327; Richard Wilson, "Observations on English Bodies," in *Enclosure Acts: Sexuality, Property and Culture in Early Modern England,* eds. Richard Burt and John Michael Archer (Ithaca: Cornell University Press, 1994), 142-144; and Janet Adelman, *Suffocating Mothers: Fantasies of Maternal Origin in Shake-speare's Play, Hamlet to the Tempest* (New York: Routledge, 1992), 196-198.

4. Arthur Golding, preface to *The XV Bookes of P. Ovidius Naso, Entituled Metamorphoses* (London, 1565).

5. W. M. Ramsay traces the legend back to the fourth century A.D. in his detailed study, "The Worship of the Virgin Mary at Ephesus," in *The Expositor,* vol. 12, 6th ser., ed. W. Robertson Nicoll (London: Hodder and Stoughton, 1905), 81-98.

6. For more on ancient Ephesus's attractions and visitors, see Bluma L. Trell's "The Temple of Ar-temis at Ephesos," in *The Seven Wonders of the Ancient World,* eds. Peter A. Clayton and Martin J. Price (London: Routledge, 1988), 84-86.

7. Pausanias, *Description of Greece,* trans. J. G. Frazer (London: Macmillan and Co., 1913), 4.31.6. All citations of Pausanias are to this translation. Pliny also describes the grandeur of the Temple in his *Natural History* 36.21.

8. Sampson Price, *Ephesus Warning before Her Woe* (London, 1616), 19. The Lydian king Croesus is now acknowledged as the historical builder of the monumental temple.

9. See, for instance, Callimachus, *Hymn to Artemis,* line 237. Pliny describes how artists competed to make the best statues of the Amazons, which were then dedicated in the Temple (*Natural History* 34.19.54).

10. Heywood claims that the Amazons "built Ephe-sus" in his *Gynaikeion* (London, 1624), 221. In an unusual reversal of the legend—and an effort to cast the Amazons in a destructive light—Ralegh claims that the Amazons "sackt Ephesus, and burnt the Temple of Diana" in his *History of the World* (London, 1614), 196.

11. Heywood, 220-221. The scholarship on Amazons in the early modern period is extensive: see Ce-leste Turner Wright's foundational essay, "Ama-zons in Elizabethan Literature," *Studies in Philol-*

ogy 37.3 (1940): 433-456; for a discussion of positive and negative allusions to the Amazons, see Gabriele Bernhard Jackson, "Topical Ideology: Witches, Amazon's and Shakespeare's Joan of Arc," *English Literary Renaissance* 18.1 (1988): 40-65.

12. For more on this complicated genesis of Diana's many forms, see Allen Jones, "Artemis," Chap. 4 of *Essenes* (Lanham, MD: University Press of America, 1985); also Jacqueline de Weever, "Chaucer's Moon: *Cinthia, Diana, Latona, Lucina, Proserpina*," *Names* 34.2 (1986): 154-174.

13. Elizabeth Cellier, *To Dr.—, An Answer to his Queries, concerning the Colledg of Midwives* (London, 1688), 6.

14. Twine, introduction to Chap. 9 of *The Patterne of Painfull Adventures* (London, 1594). All citations of Twine are to this version.

15. For examples of such satire surrounding the birth community, and churching in particular, see "The Humor of a Woman Lying in Child-Bed," Chap. 3 of *The Bachelor's Banquet* (London, 1615), and *A Crew of Kind Gossips all Met to Be Merrie* (London, 1613).

16. *Puritan Manifestoes: A Study of the Origin of the Puritan Revolt with a Reprint of the Admonition to Parliament, 1572*, eds. W. H. Frere and C. E. Douglas (1907; reprint, New York: Lenox Hill, 1972), 28.

17. *The Writings of Henry Barrow, 1587-1590*, Elizabethan Nonconformist Texts 3, ed. Leland Carlson (London: Allen and Unwin, 1962), 463.

18. *Certaine Questions by way of Conference betwixt a Chauncelor and a Kinswoman of his concerning Churching of Women* (London, 1601), 60.

19. Jeanne Addison Roberts, "Shakespeare's Maimed Birth Rites," in *True Rites and Maimed Rites: Ritual and Anti-Ritual in Shakespeare and His Age*, eds. Linda Woodbridge and Edward Berry (Chicago: University of Illinois Press, 1992), 131.

20. In *The Two Noble Kinsmen*, for example, Diana is a "sacred, shadowy, cold, and constant queen, / Abandoner of revels, mute, contemplative, / Sweet, solitary, white as chaste, and pure / As wind-fann'd snow," and Emilia is her "virgin" (5.1.137-140, 145).

21. Ovid names Diana "Titania" in his *Metamorphoses* 3.173.

22. Barber and Wheeler, 325.

23. C. L. Barber, "The Family in Shakespeare's Development: Tragedy and Sacredness," in *Repre-*

senting Shakespeare: New Psychoanalytic Essays, eds. Murray M. Schwartz and Coppèlia Kahn (Baltimore: Johns Hopkins University Press, 1980), 196.

24. For a detailed account of both positive and negative early modern English attitudes toward the Turks, see Samuel Chew's "The Present Terror of the World" and "The Great Turk," Chaps. 3 and 4 of *The Crescent and the Rose* (New York: Oxford University Press, 1937). For an analysis of these attitudes' contribution to Shakespeare's geographic choices in *Pericles* and of the "ambivalence toward the political and familial structures it asks us to accept," see Constance C. Relihan, "Liminal Geography: *Pericles* and the Politics of Place," *Philological Quarterly* 71 (1992): 281-299.

25. Jacobus de Voragine, vol. 2 of *The Golden Legend: or Lives of the Saints as Englished by William Caxton*, ed. F. S. Ellis (London: J. M. Dent, 1928), 169.

26. John Prideaux, *Ephesus Backsliding Considered and Applyed to These Times* (London, 1614), 5.

27. Ibid., 3.

28. Prideaux uses the term "Angell" to describe the church in his opening address. For a detailed study of John's Revelation text and a comparison of Ephesus's portrayal to that of the other six churches of Asia, see W. M. Ramsay, "The Letter to the Church in Ephesus," Chap. 18 of *The Letters to the Seven Churches of Asia* (New York: A. C. Armstrong and Son, 1905).

29. Prideaux, 7.

30. Both phrases appear in the title of John Vicars's diatribe against Diana of the Ephesians, *Babylons Beautie . . .* (London, 1644).

31. See, for example, Strabo, *Geography* 14.1.20.

32. Callimachus, *Hymns and Epigrams*, trans. A. W. Mail (1921; reprint, Cambridge: Harvard University Press, 1989), 63.

33. Ralegh repeats the tale in his *History of the World*, 168, as does Cellier in her letter *To Dr—*, 6.

34. There is no universal agreement as to what these shapes on the cult figure's chest are. Michael Camille, for instance, argues that it was a vest of fruits, "mistaken for breasts by early Christians" in his *Gothic Idol: Ideology and Image-Making in Medieval Art* (Cambridge: Cambridge University Press, 1989), 108. Other theories claim that they are bull scrotum or pouches to hold amulets.

35. An ancient legend explains how this polymaste cult image of the goddess may have spread beyond the eastern Mediterranean via Marseilles when the

Phocaceans sought her guidance on where to settle: The Greek geographer Strabo describes how the goddess commanded one of Ephesus's women "to sail away with the Phocacaeans, taking with her a certain reproduction which was among the sacred images; . . . in the colonial cities the people everywhere do the goddess honours of the first rank and they preserve the artistic design of the 'xoanon'" (vol. 2 of *The Geography of Strabo,* trans. H. L. Jones [Cambridge: Harvard University Press, 1960], 4.1.4). "Xoanon" is used in the text to mean "reproduction." The cult image also may have reached Europe via tapestries and manuscript illuminations brought back by eleventh-century Spanish Crusaders. Trell makes this argument and adds that in the thirteenth century a Spanish group, the Catalan Grand Company, ruled in Ephesus and may have brought back images of the temple (97). A marginal note to Acts 19 in the Genova Bible of course deplores this tale of the image's perpetuity, claiming that "Antiquitie & the covetousness of the Priests broght in this superstition."

36. Joseph Harrison connects Diana's changing and volatile associations to the pictures on the temple's walls in his "'Tears for Passing Things': The Temple of Diana in *The Knight's Tale,*" *Philological Quarterly* 63.1 (1984): 108-115.

37. See Ramsay, *Letters to the Seven Churches,* 219-222.

38. The Latin text is taken from Geoffrey of Monmouth, *The Historia Regum Britanniae,* ed. Acton Griscom (London: Longmans, Green and Co., 1929), 238-239.

39. Mary Lefkowitz and Hugh Lloyd-Jones researched this point and conveyed it to me in conversation, 20 May 1999.

40. In his *Description of Greece,* for example, Pausanias mentions sanctuaries of the Ephesian Artemis in Alea (8.23.1), Scillus (5.6.4), and Corinth (2.2.5). He writes that "all cities recognize Ephesian Artemis, and some persons recognize her privately above all the gods" (4.11.6).

41. Edward Chaloner, *Ephesus Common Pleas. Handled in a Sermon before the Judges in Saint Maries, at the Assises held at Oxford, An. 1618* (London, 1623), 116.

42. For detailed descriptions of these orgiastic rites, see Jones, *Essenes,* 86-87.

43. Thomas Comber, *The Occasional Offices of Matrimony, Visitation of the Sick, Burial of the Dead, Churching of Women, and the Commination, Explained in the Method of the Companion to the Temple: Being the Fourth and Last Part* (London, 1679), 536.

44. De Weever, 164.

45. *The Writings of Henry Barrow, 1590-91,* Elizabethan Nonconformist Texts 5, ed. Leland H. Carson (London: George Allen and Unwin, 1966), 77.

46. William Coster, for instance, argues that these Puritan objections countered the "very low opinion of sex, childbirth, and women in early modern England" that the ceremony seemed to promote. See his "Purity, Profanity, and Puritanism: The Churching of Women, 1500-1700," Studies in Church History 27, *Women in the Church,* eds. W. J. Sheils and Diana Wood (Oxford: Basil Blackwell, 1990), 384-386.

47. *Certaine Questions,* 19.

48. David Cressy argues, for instance, that "an alternative case can be made that women normally looked forward to churching as an occasion of female social activity, in which the notion of 'purification' was uncontentious, minimal or missing" ("Purification, Thanksgiving and the Churching of Women in Post-Reformation England," *Past and Present* 141 [1993]: 110). Jeremy Boulton notes the popularity of the practice in his study of a seventeenth-century London suburb, showing that 92.3 percent of women who survived birth went to be churched. See his *Neighborhood and Society: A London Suburb in the Seventeenth Century* (Cambridge: Cambridge University Press, 1987), 276-279. Susan Wright's study of a late Elizabethan "chrisom-book" reveals a 75-93 percent churching-rate. See her "Family Life and Society in Sixteenth- and Early Seventeenth-Century Salisbury" (University of Leicester Ph.D. thesis, 1982), 333-335.

49. Adrian Wilson, "The Ceremony of Childbirth and Its Interpretation," *Women as Mothers in Pre-Industrial England,* ed. Valerie Fildes (London: Routledge, 1990), 92. He is working from Davis's essay "Women on Top," in *Society and Culture in Early Modern France* (Stanford: Stanford University Press, 1975). Gail Kern Paster offers a different opinion, stating that the ceremony's enduring popularity among women "may argue just as forcefully for their internalization of shame and embarrassment as for their pride, relief, and self-congratulation." See *The Body Embarrassed: Drama and the Disciplines of Shame in Early Modern England* (Ithaca: Cornell University Press, 1993), 195.

50. Cressy, 114.

51. *The First and Second Prayer Books of Edward VI* (London: Dent, 1964), 278. All references to the purification and churching ritual are from this edition, unless otherwise noted.

52. Ibid., 428.

53. Cressy, 119-120.

54. Gail McMurray Gibson, "Blessing from Sun and Moon: Churching as Women's Theater," Medieval Cultures 9, *Bodies and Disciplines: Intersections of Literature and History in Fifteenth-Century England,* eds. Barbara Hanawalt and David Wallace (Minneapolis: University of Minnesota Press, 1996), 149.

55. *First and Second Prayer Books,* 429.

56. Comber, 512.

57. Qtd. in Cressy, 121.

58. W. P. M. Kennedy, *Elizabethan Episcopal Administration,* Alcuin Club Collections 27 (London: A. R. Mowbray, 1924), 3: 148-149. It is interesting to note that there were local clergy who refused to follow some of the injunctions for fear of community disruption. Peter Rushton points out that they "could easily be persuaded to church women (and baptise their children) without presenting them before the courts or exacting any prior penance" ("Purification or Social Control? Ideologies of Reproduction and the Churching of Women after Childbirth," *The Public and the Private,* eds. Eva Gamarnikow et al. [London: Heinemann, 1983], 123).

59. "Julia's Churching, or Purification," vol. 3 of *The Poetical Works of Robert Herrick* (London: The Cresset Press, 1928), 115.

60. Adelman, 347n. Although Roberts notes that "Shakespeare may have shared Protestant uneasiness at the idea of the need to purify women after childbirth," she concludes that are "no clear traces of this rite in his work" (136).

61. Adelman, 198.

62. Richard Wilson, 142.

63. Paster, 278.

64. Ibid., 279.

65. For an extended discussion and analysis of Ephesus and the Temple in *Comedy of Errors,* see Laurie Maguire's "The Girls from Ephesus," in *The Comedy of Errors: Critical Essays,* ed. Robert S. Miola (New York: Garland, 1997), 355-391. I am grateful to her for drawing my attention to her research.

66. Clive Foss, *Ephesos after Antiquity: A Late Antique, Byzantine and Turkish City* (Cambridge: Cambridge University Press, 1979), 33.

67. Roberts, 128.

68. Twine, Chap. 8.

69. Comber, 516.

70. Gower describes his healing as follows: "with the craftes which he couthe / He soghte and fond a signe of lif." References to *Confessio Amantis* are from *Tales of the Seven Deadly Sins, Being the Confessio Amantis of John Gower,* ed. Henry Morley (London: Routledge, 1889).

71. Gower, 428.

72. Twine, Chap. 19.

73. For a description of the priestess's role at Ephesus, see Guy M. Rogers, *The Sacred Identity of Ephesos* (London: Routledge, 1991), 53-55.

74. Muir, 255.

75. Adelman gives an illuminating reading of this ending as an unsatisfying loss of generativity in her *Suffocating Mothers,* 197.

76. Chaloner, 123.

Lisa Hopkins (essay date 2000)

SOURCE: Hopkins, Lisa. "'The Shores of My Mortality': *Pericles'* Greece of the Mind." In Pericles: *Critical Essays,* edited by David Skeele, pp. 228-37. New York: Garland Publishing, 2000.

[*In the following essay, Hopkins considers the treatment of geographical locations in* Pericles, *concluding that the travels depicted in the play are symbolic of an exploration of the characters' identities.*]

In *Pericles, Prince of Tyre,* the eponymous hero undertakes a convoluted series of travels which take him from Tyre to Antioch, back to Tyre, thence to Tarsus, next to Pentapolis, back to Tarsus again (en route for Tyre), to Mytilene, where he meets his long-lost daughter, who has been brought up in Tarsus, and finally to Ephesus, where he is reunited with his wife. These fantastic peregrinations may seem to align the play with some of the other narratives of travel that had proved so popular on the English stage, such as *The Three English Brothers* or the heroic journeyings of Tamburlaine or Faustus, but in fact the locations of *Pericles* are realized and represented in ways very different from the careful correspondence to the map that marks Marlowe's imagined space, or the personal experience of exotic locations that informs *The Three English Brothers.*[1] What we find in *Pericles* is not so much a Greece of the atlas as a Greece of the mind.

It used to be assumed that Shakespeare's representations of geographical locations were habitually careless: Bohemia in *The Winter's Tale* is gaily endowed with a seacoast, and characters in *The Two Gentlemen of Verona* improbably take ship from Verona to Milan.[2] Recently, however, growing interest in "local" or topical reading has prompted new appraisals of the degree of Shakespeare's knowledge of his foreign settings. R. W. Desai, for instance, has argued that the Sicily and Bohemia of *The Winter's Tale* are not so remote from reality as has been supposed,[3] and the degree of local color and local knowledge displayed in *Hamlet* has also often been remarked.[4] *Pericles,* however, seems to be characterized neither by notable ignorance or notable accuracy about geographical fact, but by an indifference to the particularities of location and atmosphere that might well be thought surprising in a play so centred on travel.[5] In *Pericles,* the true borders and the true journeys are of the mind, and for all the imagery of the sea, the most important shores are those that lap at the self—those that Pericles himself so memorably terms "the shores of my mortality."[6]

At the outset of the play, Gower announces:

> This Antioch, then, Antiochus the Great
> Built up this city, for his chiefest seat,
> The fairest in all Syria; I tell you what mine authors
>   say.
>
>   (1.Chorus.17-20)

There is a marked lack of interest here in the specificities of Antioch. The information, in keeping with the medieval reverence for authority and authors that is being so closely imitated, is avowedly secondhand; concrete description is limited to the bland and honorific superlatives "chiefest" and "fairest." Most telling, though, is the close association between place and person: Playing the nomenclature game so often found in connection with place names, Gower presents Antioch as virtually an extension of Antiochus's own identity—even the term "seat" can be appropriately applied to a part of the body. Moreover, personal identity and geographical identity are bound together even more closely, since, for us, Antioch is defined primarily as a place where riddles are set, and, as Frederick Kiefer points out, the riddles are inherently associated with identity: "a riddle usually defies immediate comprehension; it requires the challenger to pause and ponder—in this instance the relationship between the 'I' of the riddle and someone else."[7]

Antiochus himself goes on to employ much the same technique when he presents his daughter (who, suggestively, has no name of her own, and is thus seen as a dependent of her father in much the same way as his city is): "Before thee stands this fair Hesperides" (1.1.28). Less a person than a place, the daughter is figured as containing within herself an entire garden, though it will be well worth Pericles' while to remember that the Garden of the Hesperides contained apples,

symbol of the temptation and the Fall.[8] Thus, while we may learn little about Antioch, we receive a very clear introduction to the personalities who dominate it, and thence to a play in which geographical locality will be persistently subsumed in personal identity.

Tyre is treated with much the same minimality of detail as Antioch, as we see in Thaliard's bald statement "So this is Tyre, and this the court" (1.3.1)—an assertion quite devoid of any atmosphere or particularity. On his return home, Pericles is disturbed to find that his mood continues uneasy, even though, as he observes,

> danger, which I feared, is at Antioch,
> Whose arm seems far too short to hit me here.
> Yet neither pleasure's art can joy my spirits,
> Nor yet the other's distance comfort me.
>
>   (1.2.7-10)

Antioch here is quite clearly a place rather than a person: It has an arm, and it governs the relative pronoun "whom" rather than "which" (though Shakespeare, as has been much oberved in the recent debates over the authorship of the *Funeral Elegy for William Peter,* is by no means always consistent on this point). However, "the other's distance"—suggestive phrase—cannot "comfort," because Pericles has in effect internalized his own Antiochus:

> The great Antiochus,
> 'Gainst whom I am too little to contend,
> Since he's so great can make his will his act,
> Will think me speaking, though I swear to silence;
>   . . . . .
> With hostile forces he'll o'erspread the land,
> And with the ostent of war will look so huge
> Amazement shall drive courage from the state,
> Our men be vanquished ere they do resist,
> With care of them, not pity of myself,
> Who am no more but as the tops of trees
> Which fence the roots they grow by and defend them,
> Makes both my body pine and soul to languish,
> And punish that before that he would punish.
>
>   (1.2.16-33)

The fear of Antiochus's punishment makes Pericles punish himself; Antiochus bulks large indeed in his mind, overspreading the whole land; while Pericles himself reaches only to the tops of the trees. It is abundantly clear that, as in the play's descriptions of place, these are terms that reflect psychic rather than physical realities of size and proportion. It is also clear that in this play, what has effectively happened is that places do not stay in one place: Indeed Constance Relihan argues that "Tyre . . . becomes identifiable with Antioch, and its ruler, Pericles, becomes analogous to Antiochus,"[9] while Alexander Leggatt suggests that all Pericles' later relationships are "touched by shadows from Antioch."[10]

Helicanus's solution to Pericles' difficulties is that he should travel. At the same time, though, Helicanus also reasserts the strength of the person-place bond in his assurance that should Antiochus attack while Pericles is away, "We'll mingle our bloods together in the earth, / From whence we had our being and our birth" (1.2.113-114). The ease of "mingling" and the bringing of the sentence to rest on "being" and "birth" make this ostensible image of death a strangely soothing part of the cycle of personal identity, and the same soothing note is heard even more strongly in Pericles' reply:

> I'll take thy word for faith, not ask thine oath;
> Who shuns not to break one will sure crack both.
> But in our orbs we'll live so round and safe
> That time of both this truth shall ne'er convince,
> Thou showedst a subject's shine, I a true prince.
>
> (1.2.120-124)

It may well be objected that there is something palpably amiss with either the author of this speech or its transmission: The verse seems uncommonly regular, even plodding, for late Shakespeare, and what is "a subject's shine"? Nevertheless, one part of it is absolutely of a piece with this play's consistent imagings of space: Pericles counterpoises his talk of breaking and cracking with the extraordinary, lulling evocation of the two round, safe orbs, a foreshadowing of the transcendent reassurance of a supernatural order of things that will be afforded when he later hears the music of the spheres. The idea of the "orb" links to the speech's main thrust of confirming Helicanus's temporary sovereignty, of which an orb is the symbol, but it also confirms our growing sense of the extent to which, in this play, every man is his own world.

Immediately after Pericles' departure, Thaliard, the would-be assassin sent by Antiochus, arrives. Discovering that his intended prey has eluded him, Thaliard is resigned: "since he's gone, the King's seas must please; he 'scaped the land to perish at the sea" (1.3.26-28). For Thaliard, the sea is the king's—his king's—and he thus continues the imaging of Antiochus as huge, outstretching. Pericles, meanwhile, is on his way to Tarsus, which, for all its distance, will turn out to be, in many ways, almost interchangeable with the places he has left: Indeed Constance Jordan comments that "[at] Tharsus, Pericles contends with the economic consequences of Antioch,"[11] and many other recent critics have similarly observed the elaborate system of correspondences and equivalences which structures a play once thought fragmentary. Ruth Nevo observes the extent to which so many aspects of the play "possess a degree of unity bordering on the obsessive,"[12] and this is particularly true of its representation of its geographical locations. Although Tarsus is currently differentiated by the famine from which it is suffering, Cleon points out that this is a characteristic which could well prove purely temporary:

> O, let those cities that of plenty's cup
> And her prosperities so largely taste
> With their superfluous riots, hear these tears!
> The misery of Tarsus may be theirs.
>
> (1.4.52-55)

The one thing that sets Tarsus apart from the cities we have so far encountered could, then, become instead an attribute of theirs, and the potential for geographical displacement is further emphasized when Cleon refers vaguely to the danger posed by "Some neighbouring nation" (1.4.64) rather than naming a specific one.

We certainly hear of nothing else to help us register the specificity of Tarsus. Dionyza, wife of its governor, speaks of landscape early in the scene, but it is in purely metaphorical terms: "For who digs hills because they do aspire / Throws down one mountain to cast up a higher" (1.4.5-6). The governor himself does characterize the town, but it is in notably bland terms:

> A city on whom plenty held full hand,
> For riches strewed herself even in her streets,
> Whose towers bore heads so high they kissed the clouds,
> And strangers ne'er beheld but wondered at.
>
> (1.4.22-25)

All we really learn from this is that Tarsus was splendid and had high towers; and these are not particularizing or distinguishing details—indeed, John Pitcher argues that the lines "cannot but remind us, grimly, of the suitors who had tried in vain to solve the incestuous riddle, and whose heads were left impaled on the walls of Antioch."[13] Equally, the emphasis on the height of the towers could well seem to have been borrowed from the standard description of Troy. This is a suggestion which is perhaps reinforced when Pericles reassures Cleon that his ships are not "like the Trojan horse" (1.4.93), but even that likeness is undone when the grateful inhabitants of Tarsus respond by blessing Pericles with "The gods of Greece protect you!" (1.4.97): If his identity is so securely perceived as Greek, why might he have been acting like a Trojan?

These twinned references to the Trojan horse and to the gods of Greece might at first suggest that the play is exploiting the resonances of that other journey around the Mediterranean in quest of a wife and a child, the Odyssey—we do, after all, hear of a character called Nestor (3.1.65).[14] However, any such development is rapidly aborted, for our next port of call is Pentapolis. Kiefer notes that "when Pericles arrives in Pentapolis, he finds himself in a world resembling Antioch,"[15] but there is at least one difference, for in Pentapolis the fishermen speak not of the gods of classical Greece but of "bells, steeple, church, and parish" (2.1.42)—a set of terms that in fact serve to take us straight back to England. (We may indeed already have thought of England in this play when Gower invites us to look at severed heads [1.Chorus.40] just like those on London Bridge, while the law made by Antiochus to "Keep men in awe" [1.Chorus.35] may have reminded us of the alleged heresies of Marlowe.) Moreover, Pentapolis, like those cities that have preceded it, proves to have a strange reluctance to define an exclusive identity for itself— Constance Relihan notes that "Pentapolis is typically imagined as 'a group of five cities on the northern coast of Africa,' but their exact location remains obscure."[16] Pericles, like a curious traveller, inquires of the fishermen about local customs—"Why, are your beggars whipped then?" (2.1.90)—but the Second Fisherman answers him not in local terms but in general, quasi-transcultural ones: "O, not all, my friend, not all, for if all your beggars were whipped, I would wish no better office than to be beadle" (2.1.91-93). Taking "all" in the sense in which Hamlet employed it when he spoke to Horatio of "your philosophy," the Second Fisherman drains it of any specific applicability to Pentapolis; he simply assumes that he and Pericles, wherever the latter may come from, inhabit a shared world.

When we move on to the tournament, we discover that Pentapolis is in fact a strikingly cosmopolitan society. The first knight we see comes from Sparta, "And the device he bears upon his shield / Is a black Ethiop reaching at the sun" (2.2.20-21); the second is from Macedon, and his shield bears a motto in Spanish (2.2.27); the third, from Antioch, has his motto in Latin (2.2.30), as do the unidentified fourth and fifth, and Pericles himself, who makes the sixth. Even more to the point, the entire event transports us well away from Greece to the heart of the court culture of Renaissance England, just as the Pentapolis fishermen echo English rustics.[17] This court/country polarity—the first we have encountered—is further developed when Simonides, pretending to disparage Pericles, calls him "a country gentleman" (2.3.33). Pericles, in turn, thinks Simonides is "like to my father's picture" (2.3.37), which further confirms our impression that, however noticeable the divide between court and rustic culture, kings of any country are largely interchangeable. Simonides does, however, go on to provide one of the play's very few indications of geographical particularity when he says that "I have heard you knights of Tyre / Are excellent in making ladies trip" (2.3.101-102), though this might well be thought to be a nonce-view occasioned by Pericles' person and Simonides' developing plans for him.

As Pericles progresses toward marriage with Thaisa, it seems that his travels will now come to an end. Even before we learn that they will not, however, a new motif of travel is introduced as Pericles' lords resolve to seek him. The terms of their decision are in line with the "small world" depicted by the play as a whole: The First Lord declares "If in the world he live, we'll seek him out" (2.4.29). Helicanus persuades them to defer their journey, and when they agree he closes the scene with "When peers thus knit, a kingdom ever stands" (2.4.58): Again personal and national identity are inextricably interwoven. The visual image created by Helicanus and the three lords holding hands is soon echoed verbally in Gower's description of "the four opposing coigns / Which the world together joins" (3.Chorus.17-18). The Third Chorus seems to me in general a masterly piece of writing, catching the flavor both of Gower's speech and of the panic of the sea voyage, and I take the architectonic concreteness with which the round world's corners are imagined to be a very deliberate part of its archaicizing strategies, which may well shed light on why, throughout this play, the author is so patently uninterested in more contemporary geographical perspectives and information.[18]

With the storm that diverts Pericles' ship from Tyre to the Ephesian coast and thence to Tarsus, it first seems that now, at least, the facts of the physical world are exercising a decisive influence over the characters and their fates. In many ways, however, that initial impression is not an entirely accurate one, for the storm can clearly operate as a symbolic manifestation of the birth throes of Thaisa, as well as of the great life changes that the birth of a baby represents; Marina suggests something similar later when she says, "This world to me is as a lasting storm, / Whirring me from my friends" (4.1.19-20). Moreover, the diversion caused by the storm is also a symbolic as much as a physical one, since it takes Pericles back both to a place he has revisited and also, effectively, to an earlier stage in his life, before he had a wife. It is, then, fitting that the child who is born in the storm is given a name that elides personal and geographical identities: In a change from Shakespeare's sources, where the daughter was called Tarsia or Thaise, she is named Marina, a name that associates her not with where she grows up but where she was born.[19] From now on, "the sea" will be, in one sense, wherever Marina is, and in the same way the influence of Ephesus, which now enters the play, will also not be confined to the geographical location of Ephesus itself. Ephesus was a setting that Shakespeare had used before, in *The Comedy of Errors,* and there he makes much of the town's traditional associations with witchcraft, with Diana, and (like Tarsus) with St Paul. These resonances appear to be drawn on again when Thaisa comes to herself and exclaims, "O dear Diana! / Where am I?" (3.2.103-104). Her question virtually answers itself: She is in Diana's land—but the physician who treats her there models his practice not on anything indigenous but, at least in some versions of the text, on what he has heard of Egypt (3.2.83). Moreover, Pericles in Tarsus also invokes Diana (3.3.28), and so, later, does Marina in Mytilene (4.2.142)—the symbolism being underlined by the Bawd's scoffing response, "What have we to do with

Pericles, Thaisa, and attendants in Act V, scene iii of Pericles.

Diana?" (4.2.143). The atmosphere of Ephesus spreads far beyond Ephesus, an effect further enhanced when Gower's reference to Marina's "mistress Dian" (4.Chorus.29) is almost immediately followed by his comparison of her with a "dove of Paphos" (4.Chorus.32): Paphianism and Ephesianism are both, it seems, to be found as much in Tarsus as in their respective home territories.

At the same time, though, the play does seem to register a sharper sense of geographical differences from act 4 onward, perhaps partly as a consequence of a greater immediacy and fewer overtones of myth in Marina's perils than in Pericles'. Dionyza tells her guest, "I love the king your father and yourself / With more than foreign heart" (4.1.32-33), and the wordplay works only if we are prepared to accept, for the first time in the play, a concept of foreignness that assumes it to be hostile. This is followed by Marina and Leonine discussing which way the wind blows (4.1.51-52), which invites us to register, again in a way that is new, the specific location of Tarsus and the importance, to a

maritime population, of wind direction. Historical Tarsus is, though, unlikely to have been plagued by a pirate called Valdes (4.1.97), any more than historical Mytilene provides a credible home for a Transylvanian (4.2.20)—not to mention the improbability of its having chequins as its currency (4.2.25). Here we are back to an indifference to national distinctions that is also figured in Gower's broadly general "bourn to bourn, region to region" (4.4.4). Indeed Gower in this speech deliberately downplays difference, prefiguring the alienation effect as he casually remarks that "We commit no crime / To use one language in each several clime / Where our scene seems to live" (4.4.5-7)—a point that is neatly underlined when, with a typically English insouciance about the correct pronunciation of foreign names, he rhymes "Mytilene" with "then" (4.4.50-51).

In the scene when Marina confronts Lysimachus, the blurring of person and place takes on new point. The Bawd tells Marina that Lysimachus is "the governor of this country, and a man whom I am bound to" (4.6.50-

51); Marina replies, "If he govern the country, you are bound to him indeed, but how honourable he is in that I know not" (4.6.52-53). Surely implicit here is a pun on "cunt"; Marina may indeed doubt Lysimachus's honor if he is responsible for the government of the collective "cuntry" of the brothel, and Boult seems to play on the same meaning when he tells her that her "peevish chastity . . . is not worth a breakfast in the cheapest country under the cope" (4.6.120-121). Boult also images Marina herself as a country when he resolves to deflower her: "An if she were a thornier piece of ground than she is, she shall be ploughed" (4.6.142-143).

If Marina is a thorny piece of ground for Boult, she appears very different to Pericles, when they are finally reunited; even before he is sure of her identity, he says "thou seemest a palace / For the crowned truth to dwell in" (5.1.121-122).[20] He wants to know her parentage, but he is also insistently inquisitive about her geographical affiliations: "What country-woman?" (5.1.101); "Where do you live?" (5.1.113); "Where were you bred?" (5.1.115). His final question, though, shows that, once more, what is at stake is less an interest in national than in personal identity: "Where were you born? / And wherefore called Marina?" (5.1.155-156). When Marina answers "Called Marina / For I was born at sea" (5.1.5-6), and then adduces additional proofs of her parentage, the landscape of this play becomes its most definitively that of the mind as Pericles fears "Lest this great sea of joys rushing upon me / O'erbear the shores of my mortality / And drown me with their sweetness." (5.1.193-195).

The close of the play continues to show this. After Gower once again breaks the illusion to transport us, as in *Henry V,* on a journey that is overtly mental rather than physical (5.2.19-20), the governance of the various countries that have now fallen under Pericles' purview is arranged with fairy-tale indifference to realpolitik: Marina is to marry Lysimachus at Pentapolis and then reign in Tyre, while Pericles and Thaisa are to stay in Pentapolis—an arrangement which leaves neither of the two rulers, Pericles and Lysimachus, in their original states, and which leaves Mytilene completely rudderless, as also are both Antioch and Tarsus.[21] Pericles' exchange of Tyre for Pentapolis and Lysimachus's of Mytilene for Tyre, though, do no more than confirm the deliberate flattening of geographical difference that has all along so consistently marked the play. Even racial difference seems to count for little—Antiochus sleeps in "his bed of blackness" (1.2.89), which may well seem like a pointed displacement of racial marking, and Marina is promised "the difference of all complexions" (4.2.76), but this "difference" turns out to be no more than that between a Frenchman and a Spaniard. This is indeed a world where accidents of geographical

particularity have little impact compared with the force of the storm that blows inside the mind; within the shores of his mortality, each man is an island, in Tyre, of itself.

Notes

1. For the connection between *Pericles* and *The Three English Brothers,* see H. Neville Davies, "*Pericles* and the Sherley Brothers," in *Shakespeare and His Contemporaries* (Manchester: Manchester University Press, 1986), 94-113. Davies points to "significant similarities" between the two plays (98-99), but also argues that "the two plays are worlds apart" (112).

2. For other such instances, see Ton Hoenselaars, "Europe Staged in English Renaissance Drama," *Yearbook of European Studies* 6 (1993), 85-112.

3. R. W. Desai, "'What Means Sicilia? He Something Seems Unsettled,'" *Comparative Drama* 30:3 (Fall, 1996), 311-324.

4. See, for instance, Keith Brown, "Hamlet's Place on the Map," *Shakespeare Studies* 4 (1956), 160-182; Barbara Everett, *Young Hamlet: Essays on Shakespeare's Tragedies* (Oxford: Clarendon Press, 1989); Martin Holmes, *The Guns of Elsinore* (London: Chatto & Windus, 1964); Gunnar Sjogren, "A Contribution to the Geography of Hamlet," *Shakespeare Jahrbuch* 100-101 (1964-1965), pp. 266-73; and my own "Discovered Countries: Hamlet and Europe," *Q/W/E/R/T/Y* 6 (October, 1996), 39-45.

5. For a very vigorously developed argument to the contrary, though one which I do not ultimately find convincing, see Constance C. Relihan, "Liminal Geography: Pericles and the Politics of Place," *Philological Quarterly* (Summer, 1992), 71:3, 281-299.

6. William Shakespeare, *Pericles,* ed. Philip Edwards (Harmondsworth: Penguin, 1976), V.i.194. All further quotations from the play will be taken from this edition and reference will be given in the text. Although I am aware of the various speculations about the presence of a second author in *Pericles,* the pattern and nature of images of place seems to me consistent throughout the play, and I have not therefore engaged with issues of attribution.

7. Frederick Kiefer, "Art, Nature, and the Written Word in *Pericles,*" *University of Toronto Quarterly* 61:2 (1991-1992), 207.

8. See Alexander Leggatt, "The Shadow of Antioch: Sexuality in *Pericles, Prince of Tyre,*" in *Parallel Lives: Spanish and English National Drama 1580-1680,* ed. Louise and Peter Fothergill-Payne (Lewisburg: Bucknell University Press, 1991), 167-179.

9. Relihan, "Liminal Geography," 286.

10. Leggatt, "The Shadow of Antioch," 174.

11. "'Eating the Mother': Property and Propriety in *Pericles*," in *Creative Imitation: New Essays on Renaissance Literature in Honor of Thomas M. Greene* (Binghampton: Medieval & Renaissance Texts & Studies, 1992), 345.

12. Ruth Nevo, "The Perils of *Pericles*," in *The Undiscover'd Country: New Essays on Psychoanalysis and Shakespeare,* ed. B. J. Sokol (London: Free Association Books, 1993), 150-178, 151. On similar lines, Anthony Lewis argues that the whole of *Pericles* "enacts one theme" ("'I Feed on Mother's Flesh': Incest and Eating in *Pericles*," *Essays in Literature* 15 [1988], 147-163,); Neville Davies comments on the play's symmetricality (Davies, "*Pericles* and the Sherley Brothers," 110); and W. B. Thorne remarks on its circularity ("*Pericles* and the Incest-Fertility Opposition," *Shakespeare Quarterly* 22 [1971], 43-56), as does Douglas L. Peterson (*Time, Tide and Tempest: A Study of Shakespeare's Romances* [San Marino: The Huntington Library, 1973], 80-81).

13. John Pitcher, "The Poet and Taboo: The Riddle of Shakespeare's *Pericles*," *Essays and Studies* 35 (1982), 16-17. Pitcher is very illuminating in general on equivalences and doublings in the play. For other such patterns and repetitions, see Maurice Hunt, "*Pericles* and the Emblematic Imagination," *Studies in the Humanities* 17:1 (1990), 1-20.

14. Sara Hanna similarly suggests similarities between Antiochus's daughter and Helen ("Christian Vision and Iconography in *Pericles*," *The Upstart Crow* 11 [1991], 95).

15. "Art, Nature, and Language in *Pericles*," 212.

16. Relihan, "Liminal Geography," 290.

17. On the links between this scene and English court culture, see Alan R. Young, "A Note on the Tournament Impresas in *Pericles*," *Shakespeare Quarterly* 36 (1985), 453-456, 454, and F. David Hoeniger, "Gower and Shakespeare in *Pericles*," *Shakespeare Quarterly* 33 (1982), 461-479.

18. Richard Hillman, however, sees Gower not as an archaicizing figure but as one reminiscent of the historian Guicciardine—another analogy that undoes particularities of nationality ("Shakespeare's Gower and Gower's Shakespeare: The Larger Debt of *Pericles*," *Shakespeare Quarterly* 36 [1985], 427-437).

19. On the sources' names, see Elizabeth Archibald, "'Deep Clerks She Dumbs': The Learned Heroine in Apollonius of Tyre and *Pericles*," *Comparative Drama* 22:4 (Winter 1988-89), 293.

20. For discussion of this emblem see Deborah Willis, "The Monarch and the Sacred: Shakespeare and the Ceremony for the Healing of the King's Evil," in *True Rites and Maimed Rites: Ritual and Anti-Ritual in Shakespeare and His Age,* ed. Linda Woodbridge and Edward Berry (Urbana: University of Illinois Press, 1992), 164.

21. For comment on this see Relihan, "Liminal Geography," 291.

Heather Dubrow (essay date 2002)

SOURCE: Dubrow, Heather. "'This Jewel Holds His Building on My Arm': The Dynamics of Parental Loss in *Pericles*." In *In the Company of Shakespeare: Essays on English Renaissance Literature in Honor of G. Blakemore Evans,* edited by Thomas Moisan and Douglas Bruster, pp. 27-42. Madison, N.J.: Fairleigh Dickinson University Press, 2002.

[*In the following essay, Dubrow analyzes the dynamic involving parents and children in* Pericles, *positing that Shakespeare's treatment of familial relationships reflected a widespread apprehension about parental loss in Elizabethan and Jacobean society.*]

I

Festschriften and romance are cognate literary genres in that the bonds between generations impel and inform both of them. But if those bonds are celebrated in collections like this one, they are variously celebrated and contaminated, lost and recovered, rejected and reinterpreted, in romance. More specifically, whereas many critics are prone to associate that genre with the loss of children, the death of parents and its consequences are no less central to romance in general and Shakespearean romance in particular.

The events surrounding parental loss are, indeed, among the principal sources of danger and defeat in *Pericles* and among the principal sources of recovery for Pericles. The consequences of such deaths impel most of the major episodes of the play, and those effects are glossed in the extraordinary scene in which the hero recovers his armor. Hence both the cultural anxieties and the more personal preoccupations motivating Shakespeare's recurrent references to the early loss of parents emerge especially clearly in this play: so often and so rightly described as the genre of wish-fulfillment, romance here reveals the wishes and the fears associated with the early death of parents throughout Shakespeare's canon and throughout his culture, too. In so doing it also reveals the imbrication of generic conventions and questions about gender central to contemporary work in cultural studies.

The consequences of the loss of parents in early modern England were vast, with the impact typically encompassing not only emotional trauma but also material consequences.[1] In particular, many of those effects stemmed from the presence of stepparents and other surrogate guardians. A Renaissance translation of Petrarch, his *Phisicke against Fortune,* conflates such dangers with the devastation of fire: "Who so having children by his first marriage, bringeth a Stepmother among them, he setteth his house afire with is [*sic*] owne handes."[2] More immediate to the early modern period are the warnings about stepparenthood in William Gouge's highly influential marriage manual *Of Domesticall Duties* (1622); emphasizing the responsibility of stepparents, he expresses the intense fear that they would instead prove irresponsible and exploitative. Tales of such exploitation appear in many other contemporary texts, such as the account of the eponymous hero's problems with his stepfamily, including a diminution of his projected inheritance and internecine discord, in *Memoirs of the Life of Colonel Hutchinson.*[3] Ilana Krausman Ben-Amos's *Adolescence and Youth in Early Modern England* issues a shrewd warning about the accuracy of accounts of such issues written long after the event even as it acknowledges the pervasive traumas occasioned by parental loss.[4] But whether or not one challenges the reliability of a given account like the Hutchinson memoir, it is clear that in the early modern period, as today, what are currently described as "blended families" could threaten both the domestic tranquillity and the financial stability of the child who had lost a parent.

Stepparenthood involves semiotic and semantic threats as well; it signals the complexities of representation in general and of substitution in particular and in so doing carries with it implications for arenas ranging from the workings of rhetorical tropes to the problematics of gender. Surrogate parents both are and are not the parents they represent; if the dead are absent presences, so too in this sense are the living stepparents. Thus on one level they draw attention to the vulnerability of the individual family members they replace while on another testifying to the longevity of family roles. The mother is dead, long live the mother—an emotionally charged statement whether maternity is perceived as beneficent, as suffocating, or as both at once. And such assertions are further destabilized in that the death of one mother reminds one of the vulnerability of her substitutes as well.

But bereaved children were liable not only to, as it were, wicked stepmothers and stepfathers but also to many other apparently well-meaning guardians. The records of the Court of Orphans testify to the machinations of not only unscrupulous stepfathers but also other male relatives.[5] Uncles clearly had many opportunities for such exploitation, and it is telling that the villain in

the popular ballad "The Children in the Wood" is one—as are his analogues in *Hamlet* and *Richard III*. Given the emphasis on threatening male relatives in these and other renditions of parental loss, the focus on stepmothers rather than stepfathers in so many literary texts, notably *Pericles* itself, provides a particularly telling instance of the gendering of anxieties.

In addition, many abuses resulted from the wardship system, which deserves more attention than it has yet garnered from students of early modern literature.[6] In brief, if the head of an affluent household died, his minor children legally became wards of the crown, although the monarch's prerogatives and responsibilities could be and often were sold to another party. Lucy Hutchinson's biography of her husband reports that her father-in-law suffered so badly from his wardship arrangement that he sued his guardian—an action that resulted in that protector's attempt to murder his charge.[7] Though the accuracy of this account is, again, not beyond dispute, the prevalence of complaints stemming from wardship practices is indisputable. Developed by the Tudors as a source of revenue, that system exemplifies the pragmatic efficiency of those monarchs. Wardship, which was based on medieval conceptions of financial obligation and of marriage practices, again demonstrates the need to nuance generalizations about protocapitalism with the recognition that feudal practices survived—and were skillfully deployed—in the laws regulating wardship no less than in land law. And most germane to this study is its profound effect on the material as well as the affective consequences of parental loss. Fathers sometimes attempted to avert those sorry effects through such devices as passing on property while they were still alive, but nonetheless the potentially abusive system continued to flourish.[8]

Whereas the monarch might benefit financially by retaining a wardship, it was through their sales that most benefit accrued to the crown. And it was through such sales that a number of abuses indisputably arose. Ascertaining just how corrupt the national administrators of the system were remains problematical. Lord Burghley, Master of Wards between 1561 and 1598, took gifts, but so too did many other Tudor officials; weighing the evidence against him, the historian Joel Hurstfield does not wholly exonerate him but persuasively asserts that he was generally fair and judicious.[9] Whether or not one seconds that verdict, however, it could not be pronounced on many of the guardians created by the wardship system. Anticipating the antics of twentieth-century ambulance chasers, they were known to file petitions in anticipation of the death that would turn a child into a ward. It is clear that most of these guardians were more concerned with the financial profit they could gain from their ward than the child's education or spiritual well-being; witness among many other examples the marriages into which wards were often forced.

Moreover, both the policies of the wardship system and the practices of individual guardians intensified the displacement associated with parental death. The surviving mother received little if any preference in the assignment of wardships, but the temptation merely to read this as yet another instance of the disempowerment of women needs to be qualified by the recognition that when male relatives sought to become guardians, their relationship to the child did not necessarily ensure that they would succeed. In the reign of Edward VI, only one-fifth of wardships were sold to the mother, to a relative, to trustees chosen by the father, or to the ward him- or herself; during Mary's reign the figure came close to one in three, but in the opening years of Elizabeth's reign, it declined again to one in four. In 1587-90 one third of all grants went to such parties, an improvement but hardly a reversal of a disturbing pattern.[10] Because of it, a child who suffered the loss of a parent might well be forced to move far from home and in effect lose the other parent as well, thus suffering another loss. If wardship was another source of displacement, the unscrupulous guardians who benefited from it were another instance of invaders of a home, and their manipulations could turn the mourning child from the subject who pitches the reel in the game Freud termed *fort-da* to that object itself.

The emotional consequences of parental loss of course varied depending on the closeness of the parent and child, the child's age, and so on. But there is a clear and present danger in the current critical climate that the circus animals of cultural history will distract us from the foul rag-and-bone shop of grief. Shakespeare wrote in, to, and for a nation of mourners. Moreover, arguably in one important respect Protestantism compromised the trajectories of mourning: practices connected with Purgatory were curtailed in the course of the sixteenth century. Anthony Low finds in *Hamlet*'s repression of references to Purgatory an enactment of that radical change.[11] "The emotional and psychological consequences of the abolition of the doctrine of purgatory and curtailment of prayers for the dead," the social historian Ralph Houlbrooke observed, "constituted one of the great unchartable revolutions of English history."[12] Yet another reminder of regionalism, the survival of older Roman Catholic customs in northern and western areas, delimits but does not deny the significance of that revolution.[13] Houlbrooke goes on to speculate, persuasively enough, that this rejection of Catholic mourning rituals might decrease fear of suffering in the next world; but Joshua Scodel's suggestion that the same change emphasized the barrier between

the dead and the living is equally persuasive and more significant to an analysis of early parental loss.[14] *Pericles,* as we shall see, attempts to remove that barrier.

II

The Antiochus episode models the challenges of discerning the traces of these and many other questions in *Pericles.* To begin with, the likelihood that Shakespeare was only partly, if at all, responsible for the first two acts of the play complicates any critical analyses based on traditional concepts of authorship and intentionality, and even the alternative move of positing the culture as author does not of course resolve the textual problems that bedevil critical commentary on the play. But whoever had a hand in this episode, and however its cruxes are resolved, it relates closely to the treatment of parental death in sections of the play widely acknowledged as Shakespeare's. Like Marina, Antiochus's daughter is imperiled by the loss of her mother; like Dionyza, Antiochus perverts a parental relationship (tellingly, his victim and creature is given no name save "Antiochus's daughter"). As the riddle demonstrates, incestuous parents, no less than thieves, may create a category crisis, blurring the lines between daughter and wife and between father and husband; transgression typically announces its own etymology by crossing boundaries.

Shakespeare's Gower mentions the loss of the evil king's wife a few lines before he refers to the incest, generating the speculation that the first event facilitated the second both by removing a potential protector and by denying the king the most appropriate channel for his desires. Though the evidence for the often asserted presence of incestuous drives in Shakespeare's other romances is inconclusive enough to mandate caution, the possibility of such concerns in plays that focus on the loss of parents remains suggestive.[15] Arguably anxieties about increased opportunities for incest, anxieties all the more powerful for remaining largely unspoken, intensify fears of early parental death in early modern England. In any event, it is clear that as *Pericles* itself progresses, the link implied in the opening act between such losses and incest synecdochically comes to foreshadow a broader issue about parental death: *Pericles,* like *Richard III* and many other Shakespearean texts, repeatedly demonstrates that such events are dangerous less because of the gap they create than because of the unscrupulous people who may attempt to fill the gap.

If the reader practices the close reading skills that earlier suitors fatally lacked, not only the meaning of the relatively transparent riddle but also the relationship of this episode to the rest of the play and to Shakespeare's other analyses of parental loss becomes clearer. Whether or not Shakespeare himself actually wrote the line in question, when Pericles observes that the object of his desires is "apparelled *like* the spring" (I.i.12; italics added),[16] he again draws attention to the dangers of the surrogacy that is variously realized in metaphoric language and in the metaphoric familial relationships of the daughter who tragically plays at wife and the guardian who assumes the role of mother. The daughter-wife in question is like the spring in the beauty and freshness of her apparel, but that clothing involves a deceitfulness amd corruption not customarily associated with the season in question. Hence this reference prepares us for the preoccupation with the deceitfulness of other kinds of surrogacy, especially that of Dionyza, and for the interest in linguistic representation culminating in Pericles's recovery of his father's armor. In so doing the line also reminds us that clothing may bestow either the protection symbolized by that armor or the illegitimate veiling associated with Dionyza's apparent good will.

A "loss more than can thy portage quit / With all thou canst find here" (III.i.35-36), Marina's apparent deprivation of her mother sparks and shapes the development of the narrative. Born at sea, Marina describes herself as living "where I am but a stranger" (V.i.114): she dwells with people who betray her, and the brothel is a demonic parody of home. Here as in other romances, that protean symbol the sea is associated both with the loss of parents and with the recovery of them in the episode of the armor. Because, as Constance Jordan has demonstrated, shipwrecks can signal political upheaval, including tyranny, it is not surprising that the storms that occasion them can symbolize as well the wrecking of families through death and the resulting exposure to the abuses of power practiced by Dionyza and the mavens of the brothel.[17]

If the near-miraculous return of Thaisa at the end of the play unmistakably exemplifies wish fulfillment about parental loss, her parallel rebirth under the skilled ministrations of Cerimon does so more subtly. Both the burial ceremonies and Cerimon's ritualistic healing of her (borrowed from the sources, the name he bears in this deeply conservative drama fortuitously suggests "ceremony") repeatedly refer to the preservation of her body. Witness the insistent emphasis on odor when the coffin is first opened:

CER.

    It smells most sweetly in my sense.

2. GENT.

    A delicate odor

CER.

    As ever hit my nostril.

                (III.ii.60-62)

Though these lines explicitly refer to the spices, implicitly they counter fears of bodily decay and its distinctive smell. And the play proceeds to refer again to the spices with which she is buried, with Cerimon exclaiming shortly afterwards, "look how fresh she looks!" (79).

Northrop Frye observes that romance typically pits an idealized situation against its demonic parody, and the sweet-smelling Thaisa is thus contrasted with Antiochus's daughter, who is described as a "glorious casket stor'd with ill" (I.i.77) and whose dead body smells foul.[18] This contrast, though typical of the genre, is also embedded in contemporary conditions. If Donne "saw the skull beneath the skin" with more intensity than many of his contemporaries, he was hardly alone in seeing it; recent studies of death in early modern England disagree among themselves about the extent to which theological doctrine and social ritual could control fears of that event, but references to bodily decay appear with undeniable frequency in the texts of early modern England.[19] Commonplace doctrinal contrasts between the immortal soul and the corrupt and corrupting body no doubt intensified awareness of such decay, as did the infectiousness of victims of the plague, a subject to which I will return shortly. *Pericles* responds to such anxieties by staging not only the wish that parents who have seemed to die will be miraculously reborn but also the wish that their bodies be miraculously preserved.

Lychorida's life and death draw attention to other forms of preservation. Here, as in the sources, she assumes the parental role of protecting Marina, and her death, like the treachery of Dionyza and the hypocrisy of the governor who does not govern his own lusts, represents the failures of protection that are associated with loss in this play. Moreover, in a genre that delights in repetition and reduplication and a play that mirrors its own action through choric summaries and dumb shows, the death of this surrogate mother echoes that unfortunate daughter's loss of her biological mother, much as she in effect loses a father too because of Pericles's travels and travails.

If *Pericles* opens on the distorted surrogacy of Antiochus's wife-daughter, Dionyza perverts the maternal role of Thaisa and Lychorida. "Have you / A nurse of me" (IV.i.23-24) she implores, recalling the no less villainous Claudius's suggestion that Hamlet see his uncle as a second father.[20] In the same speech Dionyza chillingly expresses concerns for her charge's health—"Walk with Leonine, the air is quick there / And it pierces and sharpens the stomach" (27-28)—as a ploy in the plot to murder her. Here, as so often in Shakespeare's canon, loss is associated with a failure or perversion of the responsibility to protect.

Though Dionyza is not of course Pericles's wife, her behavior unmistakably recalls that staple of romance and fairy tale, the evil stepmother. Yet we have repeatedly observed how the play dovetails the transcultural meanings sometimes attributed to romance with the distinctive cultural and social conditions of early modern England; in this instance, the detail that the bodies of Antiochus and his daughter stink despite the purgative force of fire, which is not present in the sources, again recalls fears of infected bodies in a time of plague.[21] Similarly, Dionyza's behavior demonstrates as well how those ahistorical plot devices may be deployed as at once commentary on and construction of local historical situations. Following Bruno Bettelheim's analysis, readers often assume that the contrast between the good mother and the wicked stepmother expresses a child's bifurcated image of his female parent.[22] Perhaps. But in early modern culture other valences were as powerful—arguably even more powerful—in shaping interpretations of that odd couple the mother and stepmother. Children fearing that the woman their widowed father had married would exemplify the depraved figure variously delineated in fairy tales and the hortatory passages of marriage manuals might be pleasantly surprised by a supportive addition to the family; interpretations of the actions of a stepmother might seesaw between constructing her as villain and as savior. Hence, I suggest, when *Pericles* and other texts in early modern England juxtapose a saintly mother and a villainous stepmother figure, they present not only two perspectives on the mother but also two constructions of a stepmother, with the latter of particular interest in a country whose mortality crises had generated a large number of stepmothers. Once again generic norms interact in complex and surprising ways with cultural and social history, drawing on, as it were, the familial unconscious. Once again, too, the figure of the stepmother expresses gendered ambivalences.

But gender is more deeply and more immediately implicated in the presentation of Dionyza. In Gower's version, Dionyse arranges the murder but her husband willingly participates in the cover-up; in Twine's *Patterne of Painefull Adventures* (1594?), Dionisiades is responsible and Cleon's counterpart, Stranguilio, abhors her action but nonetheless participates in the cover-up and eventually dies for the crime; in George Wilkins's *Painfull Adventures of Pericles Prince of Tyre* (1608), the husband is also innocent of the murder but nonetheless executed for it without remark. Shakespeare's *Pericles* similarly offers inconclusive and unstable evidence about who is responsible for the attempted murder, but it further confounds the degree of Cleon's guilt. His involvement in the scheme is nowhere suggested in Gower's prologue or in the original dialogue between Leonine and Dionyza. The would-be murderer explains his motivation as "To satisfy my lady" (IV.i.71). Later, in a replay of dialogues between Mac-

beth and his unladylike lady, Shakespeare's Cleon, like his counterparts, expresses scruples; it is not completely clear, however, whether or not he had any part in the planning of it, and Dionyza's anticipation of his complicity after the fact if not before ("yet I know you'll do as I advise" [IV.iii.51]) hints at a culpable degree of moral cowardice and weakness. In any event, the epilogue nowhere suggests that he does not deserve to be executed. One explanation for these confusions is that the play merely follows those of its sources. Yet Shakespeare reshaped and added to those texts in accordance with his interests; witness above all the speech about Pericles's armor. Here he retains the ambiguities of the sources, I suggest, because they play out the ambivalences in his own gendering of evil. Shakespeareans have traced a diachronic shift in his canon between intense loathing and rejection of the female in general and the mother in particular in a number of plays, notably the tragedies, and a reconciliation in the romances.[23] The slippages between blaming only Dionyza and shifting some of the guilt to her husband enact synchronically a cognate pattern within *Pericles* itself.

The interaction between the generic and the cultural in the relationship between mother and stepmother is manifest as well in Dionyza's motivations. Like her analogues in the sources and like Duke Frederick, she is driven by a competitive urge: Marina outshines her daughter, and the literal hunger she describes in her first appearance is no sharper than the hunger for reflected glory. Rivalry dominated and indeed in a sense defined many arenas in early modern England: the struggles that could occur in a blended family, the challenges of literary imitation, the jostling of a patronage system that was as much a buyer's market as the academic job market in the 1990s. Moreover, throughout this study we have seen how rivalry inflects loss, though Shakespeare's own interest in that subject still has not received the attention it deserves from Shakespeareans. His sonnets demonstrate both his preoccupation with rivalry and his strained attempts to transcend that obsession. In *Pericles,* I suggest, he deflects his own competitiveness onto a figure indisputably presented as evil, thus at once expressing and repressing it.

But it is the episode in which the eponymous hero recovers his father's armor—a scene absent from the sources and hence all the more revealing—that best demonstrates the interplay between generic norms and immediate historical conditions that shapes this play. Although the authorship of this section of the play is again not beyond dispute, the concerns of the scene are bodied forth in language in which one critic finds "an authentic Shakespearean ring"[24]; and Pericles's speeches here echo patterns of loss and recovery we have been tracing throughout this study, increasing the likelihood that Shakespeare wrote or rewrote the scene in question.

Losing a gift from a dead parent is particularly painful because it duplicates the loss that is death; if the dead threaten not to stay in place, the missing object realizes the threat. And conversely, finding that talismanic legacy may be experienced as the magical recovery of the deceased, as it is here:

> An armor, friends? I pray you let me see it.
> Thanks, Fortune, yet that after all thy crosses,
> Thou givest me somewhat to repair myself;
> And though it was mine own, part of my heritage,
> Which my dead father did bequeath to me,
> With this strict charge, even as he left his life,
> "Keep it, my Pericles, it has been a shield
> 'Twixt me and death"—and pointed to this brace—
> "For that it sav'd me, keep it. In like necessity—
> The which the gods protect thee from! may defend
>   thee."
> It kept where I kept, I so dearly lov'd it,
> Till the rough seas, that spares not any man,
> Took it in rage, though calm'd have given't again.
> I thank thee for't. My shipwrack now's no ill,
> Since I have here my father gave in his will.

(II.i.120-34)

The pattern of speech acts in these lines implicitly enacts the very process of material and emotional recovery that the passage explicitly describes: the shift from questions and requests to declarations, whose authority is buttressed as well by the shift to couplets, stages Pericles's recovery of power by means of the type of armor tellingly called a "brace" (127). The couplet form also serves to mime the events being described: like parent and child and like Pericles and his armor, its two lines are bound together. Loss, as we have seen throughout this study, is typically associated with a loss of control, and here the literal recovery of an object enables the recovery of control manifest in Pericles's speech. The armor will allow him to seek and marry a king's daughter not only because it is de rigueur for the well-dressed knight, not only because it signals his social status, but also because it permits a restoration of confidence.

Pericles proceeds to request the armor from the fisherman, with his assurance "I know it by this mark" (138) linking it to the identifying birthmarks that figure so prominently in romance. In so doing he also implicitly contrasts the evidentiary certainty and epistemological clarity that the armor both permits and represents with the threats to categories (alive vs. dead; fish vs. man) that the sea effects. But lest we become too charmed by the reassurances associated with the armor, the fishermen's promptings about financial compensation for it yet again introduce the quotidian.

Shortly afterwards, our eponymous hero encapsulates the significance of the brace:

> By your furtherance I am cloth'd in steel,
> And, spite of all the rapture of the sea,

> This jewel holds his building on my arm.

(154-56)

In the first line of this passage, which again emphasizes protection, the literal and metaphoric cling to each other as closely as the armor encases the arm: Pericles wears sturdy metal and in so doing figuratively wears his father's strength. At the same time the image of the jewel functions proleptically: the jewel-like armor will allow its wearer to gain the hand of Thaisa, who is repeatedly associated with jewels and who, like the armor, will herself be lost at sea and recovered.

How, then, does this scene gloss parental loss in *Pericles* and the many imbricated questions about gender and subjectivity? To begin with, the workings of armor here draw attention to the valences of protection throughout the genre of romance. On the characterological level, its hero protects, and the magical accoutrements so often associated with him, whether they be Pericles's brace or the extraordinarily equipped wristwatches that "hold their building" on James Bond's arm, in turn protect him. Not the least contrast between the heroes and the villains in these black-and-white woodcuts is that the latter are often associated with the perversion of protection, whether that action takes the form of a Dionyza who threatens her charge or an Archimago who revealingly offers shelter. On the level of plot, what is often described as a movement from loss to recovery could instead be recast as a shift from the loss to the restoration of shields, literal and otherwise, or from absent or false protection to the genuine article. And on the level of genre, romance itself protects its plots from tragic closure. All this explains why the genre is so well suited to represent both the deepest fears and hopes connected with parental death.

Protection is also more immediately relevant to this play and its valuation of the armor. It literally protected Pericles's father in battle and may protect our hero in that way as well, but in addition it figures the stability and shielding that home should provide but too often does not—notice the repetition of "keep" and its cognates (126, 128, 130), as well as the resonances of a phrase that appears shortly afterwards, "holds his building" (156). The armor enables Pericles to become a knight, a role often associated with guarding others, and in so doing it guards him as well.[25] In short, here as in *King Lear,* recovering from loss involves recovering the ability to protect and be protected.

On one level, this conservative genre here celebrates conservative sources—in several senses of the adjective—for that recovery. Thus here, as in *The Rape of Lucrece,* Shakespeare demonstrates that the ideologies of protection may screen the desire to dominate. The reference to the "strict charge" (125) of a dying man draws attention to the authority of his father, suggesting that the armor is the material equivalent, the outward and visible sign as it were, of the spiritual armor forged by parental advice in the mother's manuals and the strictures of the *ars moriendi*. As analyses by Coppélia Kahn and other psychoanalytic critics would suggest, the armor is clearly implicated in a struggle for masculine identity.[26] Arguably, too, the stress on masculine power here, however it is problematized, may well represent a recoil from the gendering of power in the figure of Dionyza. And there is no question but that the emphasis on the father's "strict charge" (125) draws attention to the danger that an absent parent will continue to dominate, a threat that recurs throughout Shakespeare's canon.

Yet the scene primarily suggests that Pericles is controlling that threatened authoritarianism: in placing the armor on his arm Pericles in a sense dominates the symbol of potential domination. Compare the ambiguous and unstable shifts of power back and forth when a knight wears his lady's favor, or the late twentieth-century commodification and inversion of that event, the trophy wife displaying jewelry purchased by her husband.[27] In all three instances, the apparent subordinates who display a token of someone else's power at the same time augment their own, in part by demonstrating they are, as it were, attractive enough to attract such a gift. Moreover, in the passage at hand, the armor delimits parental power even while it is established: if the dead are frightening, and frighteningly powerful, precisely because they may not stay in place but instead keep coming back, this episode insists that the synecdochic representation of the father will be firmly and stably located in a clearly defined section of the body. Thus Pericles controls the return of his father—and does so by placing the brace on the bodily part associated with his own agency. In regaining and positioning the brace, Pericles asserts control over death and over the father who is in some sense attempting to control him.[28]

These paradoxes can be glossed with one of the most important additions to the classical Freudian analyses of mourning, the influential recent work of Nicolas Abraham and Maria Torok, which has been supplemented by the writing of their English language editor and collaborator, Nicholas Rand.[29] Their books mime their own subject matter by at once challenging and reaffirming connection with the author of "Mourning and Melancholy." Building on the work on introjection developed by Freud himself, by Sandor Ferenczi, and by Nicolas Abraham's predecessor Karl Abraham, Nicolas Abraham and Maria Torok develop a distinction between introjection, a healthy process that involves assuming some characteristics of the dead person, and incorporation, its pathological analogue characterized by a secret

internalization of the dead. Thus they extend the problematical hierarchy of normal and distorted mourning.

The buried secret, which shapes not only other writings by Abraham and Torok but also Torok's collaborative venture with Nicholas Rand, the book *Questions for Freud*,[30] is arguably a less common component of mourning than the proponents of this thought-provoking theory at some points imply; but the theoretical framework provided by Abraham, Torok, and Rand explicates how wearing the armor restores power to Pericles. In theorizing the relationship of space and place, Yi-Fu Tuan, among other writers, associates the former with uncontrolled amorphousness and the latter with specificity.[31] A textbook instance of introjection, Pericles's act of donning the brace creates, as it were, a chain of links to the past, hence performing the temporal equivalent of turning space into place in Yi-Fu Tuan's sense. Pericles acknowledges and glories in his relationship to his father and the past that progenitor represents, so to speak wearing his heart together with his armor on his sleeve.

I have been stressing power struggles between father and son; but in another sense the armor also marks the limits to the power of both its original owner and his son. However firmly positioned it may be, the brace is rusty. Much as Hermione must have her wrinkles and Paulina must settle for a second husband in a play that, despite all its other miraculous restorations, does not bring back her first one, the rustiness of the armor hints that the strategies for recuperating from parental loss, like other forms of restoration of romance, are limited. *Fort-da*, here played with a reel that miraculously returns itself rather than being cast away by the child, is a game whose victories involve not total mastery but partial control.

Representation and symbolization are, however, among the surest strategies for success in *fort-da*, and the armor restores power, though limited, to Pericles not only because of what it literally is and does but also because of what it symbolizes. And indeed, it represents representation itself in that it is not the recovered father but a signifier of and surrogate for him. Earlier psychoanalytic readings that position this episode as a stage in its hero's maturation should be further revised to acknowledge that here he encounters the Law of the Father in several intertwined senses: the strict commandment of his father, the association of masculinity with heroic enterprise—and the realm of symbolization. Entering that realm, he plays *fort-da* according to Lacan's rules in that the armor that is reeled in stands for the very act of substituting a representation of the father for that warrior himself. But much as the threats suggested by the father's "strict charge" (125) seem less potent than the power provided by the restoration of his armor, so too language empowers more than it limits in this recovered symbol. If parental death challenges representation in the ways detailed above, the restoration of the part restores representation as well.

If on some level the armor represents language, it also represents the genre of *Pericles*. The brace is found by fishermen, and romance is connected with folk traditions rather than sophisticated literary practices. The brace is an object from the past that has been restored, and romance is a literary form associated with the past, an association in this case intensified by the choric function of Gower, an author who returns from the past and speaks what might justly be called a rusty language. More specifically, indeed, romance comes back from the tumultuous ocean of Shakespeare's canon, which has included its anticipations in *A Comedy of Errors* and *King Lear*. And in the romances the effects of parental death, one of the most persistent of Shakespeare's revenants, return yet again from their earlier incarnations in *All's Well That Ends Well, As You Like It, Love's Labour's Lost,* and so many other texts in the canon.

The ending of *Pericles* is not without its troubling undercurrents; in particular, though Lysimachus attempts to distance himself from the miasma of the brothel, reminding one of nothing so much as his latter-day incarnations who claim to read *Playboy* for the interviews, that atmosphere leaves a cloud around his name. Nor does *Pericles* completely erase the threat of parental death: in a version of the message from Marcade, we learn in the last few moments of the play that Thaisa's father is dead. But Pericles's response signals the distance the play has travelled:

> Heavens make a star of him! Yet there, my queen,
> We'll celebrate their nuptials, and ourselves
> Will in that kingdom spend our following days.
> Our son and daughter shall in Tyrus reign.

> (V.iii.79-82)

This speech reminds us how different the effects of losing a parent can be when the child is established in life: Marina is all at sea when her mother apparently dies, while Thaisa faces that event fortified with a supportive family and evidence that the line will continue. Thus parental death is associated not with the violent and untimely "rapture" (II.i.155) but with orderly succession and the inheritance of a throne. If each Jack has his Jill at the end of romantic comedy, here each royal couple has its crown. In short, as at the end of *Cymbeline*, doubts and dangers are not absent, but neither are they intrusive.[32] The emphasis remains on restoration, including the fulfillment of a fantasy no doubt held by the many members of the audience who had lost a parent: the missing mother is restored to her

husband and daughter. During most of the play, interpretive certainties are buffeted, if not shipwrecked, by a storm of indeterminacies, but the play concludes on dry land. And as we survey that terrain, we realize that this is no country for poststructuralists.

III

Pericles, then, gestures toward the perspectives on parental loss that recur throughout its author's canon. Such deaths are perilous less because they leave canyons of emptiness in the lives of children than because unscrupulous guardians like Richard III and the Queen in *Cymbeline* are all too ready to fill such abysses. Those evil figures characteristically manifest their untrustworthiness above all by their distortions of protectiveness. But if the surrogacy of a stepparent or an ironically named Lord Protector demonstrates the perils of losing a parent, other forms of surrogacy, whether staged by more trustworthy parental figures such as the Countess of Rossillion or by language itself, can bring resolution and reconciliation—on some but by no means all occasions and in some but by no means all genres. And in yet other instances, the emotional upheavals of losing a parent are mimed by the moral instabilities created by guardian figures like Falstaff and Titania, whose behavior toward their charges demands complex and shifting judgments.

As we have observed, *Pericles* explores these and other questions about parental loss by rooting the norms of romance in the soil of early modern England. Sometimes the social and cultural pressures connected with the early loss of parents appear in the play only very indirectly—"the mnemonic flicker / Of the wave of lost particulars," as the modern poet Amy Clampitt writes of dreamwork ("The Burning Child," 1-2).[33] But Clampitt also acknowledges that "[t]he dream redacted cannot sleep; it whimpers / So relentlessly of lost particulars" (14-15), and at a number of points in *Pericles,* particularly passages engaging the fear of dangerously self-serving guardians, the specificities of cultural anxieties unmistakably emerge, neither whimpering nor whispering but rather firmly enjoining us to recognize their complex imbrication with the plot of the play.

Notes

Portions of this essay appeared in *Shakespeare and Domestic Loss: Forms of Deprivation, Mourning, and Recuperation,* published by Cambridge University Press. Kind permission to reprint is gratefully acknowledged.

1. For a more detailed discussion of this issue, see my book *Shakespeare and Domestic Loss: Forms of Deprivation, Mourning, and Recuperation* (Cambridge: Cambridge University Press, 1999), chap. 5.

2. Francesco Petrarch, *Phisicke against Fortune,* trans. Thomas Twyne (London, 1579), sig. Nviii^v.

3. Lucy Hutchinson, *Memoirs of the Life of Colonel Hutchinson,* ed. James Sutherland (London: Oxford University Press, 1973), 24-25.

4. Ilana Krausman Ben-Amos, *Adolescence and Youth in Early Modern England* (New Haven: Yale University Press, 1994), 49-50.

5. See Charles Carlton, *The Court of Orphans* (Leicester: Leicester University Press, 1974), esp. 44.

6. For a useful overview of wardship, see H. E. Bell, *An Introduction to the History and Records of the Court of Wards and Liveries* (Cambridge: Cambridge University Press, 1953); Joel Hurstfield, *The Queen's Wards: Wardship and Marriage Under Elizabeth I,* 2nd ed. (London: Frank Cass, 1973). Exceptions to the neglect of this system by students of early modern literature include the brief but useful commentaries on wardship and inheritance in Lisa Jardine, *Still Harping on Daughters: Women and Drama in the Age of Shakespeare* (Brighton, England: Harvester Press and Totowa, N.J.: Barnes and Noble, 1983), 80-84; Marilyn L. Williamson, *The Patriarchy of Shakespeare's Comedies* (Detroit: Wayne State University Press, 1986), 61-64.

7. Hutchinson, *Memoirs,* 16.

8. The *ante mortem* passing on of property is the central thesis of Lloyd Bonfield, "Normative Rules and Property Transmission: Reflections on the Link between Marriage and Inheritance in Early Modern England," in *The World We Have Gained: Histories of Population and Social Structure,* ed. Lloyd Bonfield, Richard M. Smith, and Keith Wrightson (Oxford: Basil Blackwell, 1986).

9. Hurstfield, *The Queen's Wards,* chaps. 10, 12, 13.

10. Bell, *Court of Wards,* 115-16.

11. Anthony Low, "*Hamlet* and the Ghost of Purgatory: Intimations of Killing the Father," *ELR,* 29 (1999): 443-67. I thank the author for making his manuscript available to me before it appeared in print.

12. Ralph Houlbrooke, "Death, Church, and Family in England Between the Late Fifteenth and the Early Eighteenth Centuries," *Death, Ritual, and Bereavement,* ed. Ralph Houlbrooke (London: Routledge in association with the Social History Society of the United Kingdom, 1989), 36.

13. On that survival, see Clare Gittings, *Death, Burial and the Individual in Early Modern England* (London: Croom Helm, 1984), 45; and David Cressy, "Death and the Social Order: The Funerary Preferences of Elizabethan Gentlemen," *Continuity and Change* 5 (1990): 102.

14. Joshua Scodel, *The English Poetic Epitaph: Commemoration and Conflict from Jonson to Wordsworth* (Ithaca: Cornell University Press, 1991), 21.

15. Many critics have argued for allusions to incest throughout the romances. See, for example, C. L. Barber and Richard P. Wheeler, *The Whole Journey: Shakespeare's Power of Development* (Berkeley: University of California Press, 1986), 301, 312-13; Ruth Nevo, *Shakespeare's Other Language* (London: Methuen, 1987), esp. 59, 93-94.

16. I cite Gwynne Blakemore Evans, ed., *The Riverside Shakespeare* (Boston: Houghton Mifflin, 1974).

17. See Constance Jordan, "'Eating the Mother': Property and Propriety in *Pericles,*" in *Creative Imitation: New Essays on Renaissance Literature in Honor of Thomas M. Greene,* ed. David Quint, Margaret R. Ferguson, G. W. Pigman III, and Wayne A. Rebhorn (Binghamton, NY: Medieval and Renaissance Texts and Studies, 1992), 346.

18. On the contrast between idealizations and their demonic parodies, see Northrop Frye, *A Natural Perspective: The Development of Shakespearean Comedy and Romance* (New York: Columbia University Press, 1965), 110.

19. The many recent studies of responses to death in the period include James L. Calderwood, *Shakespeare and the Denial of Death* (Amherst: University of Massachusetts Press, 1987); Bettie Anne Doebler, *"Rooted Sorrow": Dying in Early Modern England* (Rutherford, N.J., and London: Fairleigh Dickinson University Press and Associated University Presses, 1994); Robert N. Watson, *The Rest Is Silence: Death as Annihilation in the English Renaissance* (Berkeley: University of California Press, 1994).

20. Compare Anthony J. Lewis's observation that the play contrasts good and bad nurturing ("I Feed on Mother's Flesh: Incest and Eating in *Pericles,*" *Essays in Literature* 15 [1988]: 154).

21. George Wilkins's *Painfull Adventures of Pericles Prince of Tyre* (1608) offers a partial parallel, however, in that the guilty couple is struck by lightning and their countrymen disdain to bury them.

22. Bettelheim argues that aggression originally intended for mothers is redirected toward stepmothers, in *The Uses of Enchantment: The Meaning and Importance of Fairy Tales* (New York: Alfred A. Knopf, 1976), esp. 66-73.

23. For an influential and nuanced version of this argument, see Barber and Wheeler, *The Whole Journey;* they also note the survival of gendered antagonism in some romances (see, for example, 335).

24. Derek Traversi, *Shakespeare: The Last Phase* (London: Hollis and Carter, 1954), 24.

25. Douglas L. Peterson suggests that both the father's armor and Marina's presence draw attention to Pericles's responsibility to protect legacies *(Time, Tide, and Tempest: A Study of Shakespeare's Romances* [San Marino, Calif: Huntington Library, 1973], 95).

26. See Coppélia Kahn, *Man's Estate: Masculine Identity in Shakespeare* (Berkeley: University of California Press, 1981), 211-14.

27. I am indebted to Gwynne Blakemore Evans for the parallel with knighthood.

28. For a different but not incompatible argument about the genealogical significance of the armor, see David M. Bergeron, *Shakespeare's Romances and the Royal Family* (Lawrence: University Press of Kansas, 1985), 131. Bergeron suggests that the armor represents the royal family as well as Pericles' own heritage and that its rustiness may be an emblem of peace. Constance Jordan also relates the armor to the imperiled royal heritage and notes that it was rescued by subordinates, the fishermen *(Shakespeare's Monarchies: Ruler and Subject in the Romances* [Ithaca: Cornell University Press, 1997], 52).

29. See two studies written by Nicolas Abraham and Maria Torok and translated by Nicholas T. Rand: *The Shell and the Kernel,* vol. 1 (Chicago: University of Chicago Press, 1994); *The Wolf Man's Magic Word: A Cryptonymy,* Theory and History of Literature, vol. 37 (Minneapolis: University of Minnesota Press, 1986).

30. Nicholas Rand and Maria Torok, *Questions for Freud: The Secret History of Psychoanalysis* (Cambridge: Harvard University Press, 1997).

31. See Yi-Fu Tuan, *Space and Place: The Perspective of Experience* (Minneapolis: University of Minnesota Press, 1977), esp. chap. 1.

32. For an opposite view of the ending that stresses its instability, see Clifford Leech, "The Structure of the Last Plays," *Shakespeare Survey* 11 (1958): 22-23.

33. I cite Amy Clampitt, *The Kingfisher* (New York: Alfred A. Knopf, 1983).

FURTHER READING

Criticism

Abraham, Lyndy. "Weddings, Funerals, and Incest: Alchemical Emblems and Shakespeare's *Pericles, Prince of Tyre.*" *Journal of English and German Philology* 98, no. 4 (October 1999): 523-49.
　　Argues that *Pericles* is a non-Christian miracle play that conveys its meaning through the use of alchemical emblems.

Arthos, John. "*Pericles, Prince of Tyre*: A Study in the Dramatic Use of Romantic Narrative." *Shakespeare Quarterly* 4, no. 3 (July 1953): 257-70.
　　Analyzes the construction of *Pericles* to determine how Shakespeare was able to combine romantic material with the dramatic techniques he had developed in his comedies and tragedies.

Fawkner, H. W. *Shakespeare's Miracle Plays:* Pericles, Cymbeline *and* The Winter's Tale. Rutherford, N.J.: Fairleigh Dickinson University Press, 1992, 194 p.
　　Book-length study of three plays from the final phase of Shakespeare's career which seeks to illuminate their "mysterious, almost hermetic, quality."

Marks, Peter. "High Jinks on the High Seas, and a Little Shakespeare, Too." *New York Times* (10 November 1998): E5.
　　Reviews a production of *Pericles* at the Joseph Papp Public Theater in New York, concluding that the play suffered from poor performances and an overemphasis on visual effects.

Relihan, Constance C. "Liminal Geography: *Pericles* and the Politics of Place." *Philological Quarterly* 71, no. 3 (summer 1992): 281-99.
　　Surveys the geographical locations of *Pericles* and maintains that Shakespeare's use of such places "undermines interpretations of the play that see it affirming both James I's reign and time's ability to heal and restore."

Spradley, Dana Lloyd. "*Pericles* and the Jacobean Family Romance of Union." *Assays: Critical Approaches to Medieval and Renaissance Texts* 7 (1992): 87-118.
　　Views *Pericles* as a parody of King James I's attempts to unite England and Scotland.

Venus and Adonis

For further information on the critical history of *Venus and Adonis,* see *SC,* Volumes 10, 33, 51, and 67.

INTRODUCTION

Venus and Adonis, an erotic poem published in 1593, is believed by some critics to be Shakespeare's first poem, and perhaps his first published work. Inspired by a mythological tale found in Book X of Ovid's *Metamorphoses,* the poem centers on the refusal of a beautiful youth, Adonis, to submit to the amorous advances of Venus, the goddess of love. The poem concludes with Adonis's death after he is gored by a wild boar. Additional sources of the work include Ovid's erotic poems, *Ars Amatoria,* from which Shakespeare may have derived his version of Venus's conquest of Mars and Adonis's contention that he is too young to love. Despite the strong presence of Ovidian material in the poem, contemporary critics have noted that Shakespeare largely departed from his sources with his depiction of a willfully resistant Adonis and his brilliantly dramatic characterization of Venus. Although very popular in Shakespeare's day, *Venus and Adonis* suffered a lengthy interlude of critical neglect from the mid-seventeenth to nineteenth centuries, but was rediscovered in the twentieth century. Many contemporary scholars find *Venus and Adonis* to be an accomplished work in which Shakespeare transcended the limited conventions of Renaissance sensual poetry by addressing serious philosophical issues. Modern commentators are frequently captivated by the figure of Venus, and have studied the poem's allegorical and moral elements, as well as its masterful display of rhetoric and its complex study of desire.

Shakespeare's depiction of character, especially of Venus, has continued to be one of the most compelling areas of critical interest in *Venus and Adonis.* While traditional assessments of the goddess have tended to be unfavorable, emphasizing her lustful aggressiveness toward Adonis, her reluctant paramour has frequently been viewed as a static figure, immobile in his resistance to Venus's sensuous advances. John Doebler (1982) considers the title characters of the poem in light of Renaissance pictorial depictions of these mythic figures. In particular, Doebler compares the paintings of Adonis and Venus by Italian Renaissance painter Titian with Shakespeare's rendering of these mythological figures in his poem *Venus and Adonis.* The critic explores the

possibility that Titian's paintings were a source for Shakespeare's poem, and also examines how both artists altered Ovid's original myth in their works. Heather Dubrow (1987) underscores resemblances between the central figures of *Venus and Adonis* and the complex characters found in Shakespearean drama. She argues that Shakespeare depicted his Venus as a flattering love poet, at various moments forceful or tender, depending on the shifting dictates of her rhetorical mode. Delving into Venus's psychological makeup, Dubrow highlights the goddess's volatile nature and potential to variously elicit the reader's sympathy or moral aversion. Dubrow also probes the psychological motivations of Adonis, whom she sees as an entrapped figure, imprisoned by his own unsettled emotional responses and conflicting moral obligations—making him a tragic foil to the voracious Venus. Finally, considering Adonis's death, Dubrow suggests that its apparent randomness stresses Shakespeare's thematic interest in the capriciousness of fate.

Traditional critical approaches to theme in *Venus and Adonis* have generally tended to explore the poem's allegorical and moral elements, as well as Shakespeare's masterful display of rhetoric and complex study of desire in the poem. Eugene B. Cantelupe (1963) explores the structure and imagery of Venus and Adonis, viewing the work as an Ovidian poem that satirically contrasts Love and Beauty and features a strong moralizing element. The critic concludes that the work is a cautionary tale on the dangers of extreme lust. Robert P. Miller (1959) comments on Shakespeare's ironic use of Ovidian moral themes associated with the mythological love affair of Venus and Mars, which is recounted by Venus as she attempts to woo Adonis. Miller examines Shakespeare's stylistic deviation from Ovid's version of the myth, and contends that despite his deviations Shakespeare's poem engages in typically Ovidian moral ambiguity by emphasizing a complex juxtaposition of the seemingly opposed ethical concepts of lust and virtue. W. R. Streitberger (1975) considers a complementary moral theme in his study of *Venus and Adonis.* For Streitberger, Adonis personifies an ethical choice between responsibility and neglect in the context of romantic courtship; by rejecting the erotic advances of Venus, the critic claims, Adonis makes a moral choice in favor of constancy to duty. Anthony Mortimer (see Further Reading) identifies rhetoric as the poem's fundamental concern and principal theme. He traces a thematic link between rhetorical display, self-knowledge, moral relativity (in, among other things, the potential continuity between love and lust), and the expression of sensual desire. Richard Halpern (1997) explores *Venus and Adonis* as a misogynist work directed toward female, rather than male, readers. The critic examines its "slightly grotesque portrayal of female sexual desire" and maintains that the poem is concerned with female sexual frustration and places Venus in the symbolic role of the feminine reader.

OVERVIEWS AND GENERAL STUDIES

Eugene B. Cantelupe (essay date spring 1963)

SOURCE: Cantelupe, Eugene B. "An Iconographical Interpretation of *Venus and Adonis*, Shakespeare's Ovidian Comedy." *Shakespeare Quarterly* 14, no. 2 (spring 1963): 141-51.

[*In the following essay, Cantelupe examines the structure and imagery of* Venus and Adonis, *viewing the work as an Ovidian poem that satirically contrasts Love and Beauty and features a strong moralizing element in its lust motif.*]

Italian Renaissance painters and English Renaissance poets knew that Ovid's Venus ardently wooed an Adonis who was more interested in hunting than in love-making. This is how Shakespeare and Titian portray them. But here the resemblance between the greatest and most influential of literary and pictorial versions of the Ovidian myth ends.[1]

In Titian's *Pardo Venus,* in the Louvre, the goddess reposes peacefully in an idyllic forest because her beloved, a young Italian courtier, indulges his love for the noble sport by hunting a gentle stag; and in the version in the Prado Museum, Venus desperately clutches at a handsome Greek athlete because he is forsaking her to hunt the ferocious boar. Veronese, preferring to emphasize the love that Adonis, according to Ovid, did not entirely scorn, features in two paintings in the Kunsthistorisches Museum in Vienna a shy lad who lifts the hand of Venus from his thigh, and in the other version, an aggressive youth who fondles her breast. Both Venetians create pastoral settings, reminiscent of the Golden Age, for their paragons of physical beauty, but neither they nor such artists as Sebastiano del Piombo and Cambiaso, who were also attracted to the myth, depict as outrageously comic a couple as Shakespeare in his *Venus and Adonis.*[2] Far from an Arcadian meadow, in the English countryside parched from the sun's "purple-coloured face",[3] a love-sick Amazon immediately gathers the reins of Adonis' horse over one arm, and under the other easily tucks, like a sack of beans,

. . . the tender boy,
Who blush'd and pouted in a dull disdain,
With leaden appetite, unapt to toy,
She red and hot as coals of glowing fire,
He red for shame, but frosty in desire.

(ll. 32-36.)

The icy, petulant Adonis is an English gentleman who, handsome and naive as Marlowe's Leander, is identified with Beauty, the bait for Love; and Venus, although distressingly muscular, is the incredibly beautiful—the reader has her oft-repeated word for it—goddess of love. But like Marlowe's Mercury, who fails at seduction because he ironically substitutes earthly gymnastics for Olympian eloquence, Venus also fails because she insists upon underlining her persuasive arguments with excessive snatching, pawing, and crushing. Both Marlowe and Shakespeare, trying their hand at the new erotic-mythological poem, pull out all the rhetorical stops at their command—amorous dialectic, subtle puns and ingenious conceits, original mythological embroidery, and sexual humor ranging from the witty to the farcical—to prove themselves sophisticated gentlemen-poets as well as commercial dramatists. Like Lodge and Thomas Edwards, they also make the erotic, Italianate qualities of the genre more palatable to English taste by means of comedy.[4]

Shakespeare very probably wrote *Love's Labour's Lost* and *Venus and Adonis* at the same time, the play for an audience as emancipated in its literary taste as the talented young Earl of Southampton, to whom the poem is dedicated. Whereas in the play the courtly lovers display the folly of denying love, only to be punished by Cupid with its opposite, that of doting upon it, in the poem Adonis laughs at and scorns love, and Venus dwells upon it *ad nauseam*. Either form of behavior was considered excessive and unreasonable by the Elizabethans, and for the dramatists it was a subject for comedy. For Shakespeare, who considered love primarily a subject for comedy, such foolish extremes demanded the comic mode.[5]

Coleridge first noticed that *Venus and Adonis* consists of a series of sharply etched scenes rendered in dialogue that are relieved occasionally by stage business and stitched by a "never broken chain of imagery, always vivid and, because unbroken, often minute."[6] In other words, Shakespeare creates a simple, dramatic structure which supports an enormous weight of rhetorical embellishment and reveals, quickly and effectively, the characters of the heroine and hero.

The time scheme is twenty-four hours, from the first morning when Venus plucks the ruddy-faced boy from his horse, to the following morning when she finds his gored body. The first morning passes in lengthy lectures by Venus on her beauty and his responsibility to beget children, and an exemplum of her escapade with Mars (ll. 1-259); at noon, a breeding jennet distracts the horse of Adonis, and by nightfall, Venus has won no more for her brilliant and exhausting sermons and her clever but strenuous acrobatics than one quick, reviving, and one long, swooning kiss—which does not end in consummation but, ironically, in another sermon, this time delivered by Adonis (ll. 260-825). The second morning, when the gentle lark "From his moyst cabinet mounts upon hie", includes her apostrophe to Death, her discovery of her beloved's body, and her final lament that sorrow shall ever attend upon love (ll. 853-1194). Thus, the first twelve hours consist mainly of lectures delivered by Venus, and the last six of her soliloquies.[7]

Shakespeare, of course, gives the stellar role to Venus, and his casting her as an aggressive and practised siren who pursues an innocent and adolescent boy—he knew of Lodge's and Greene's less effective attempts, and of the reversal of the roles in Marlowe's popular poem—demanded an exploitation of the sensuous and erotic as well as the satirical and farcical.[8] Moreover, he makes doubly certain that the basic situation in which he places them provide for every possible irony. The virile, handsome Adonis, who loves hunting—"but loue he laught to scorn"—possesses a sweating palm which attests to his "pith and livelihood"; but he grows more scornful and resistant as Venus, who is "Loue . . . loues, and yet is not lou'd", grows more desperate and frenzied. He emerges as a self-indulgent, at times irritatingly obtuse but disarmingly naive male; and she a voracious, extravagantly absurd yet immensely comic and sympathetic female. Her never flagging efforts to fire the passive youth with either the procreative arguments that comprise Shakespeare's first eighteen sonnets or with glowing descriptions of her physical beauty and sexual prowess not only reveal her self-confidence, insatiable appetite, and wit, but also beget sympathy through rollicking, robust humor. Adonis is the inverse of Romeo and Troilus, and Venus the obverse of Juliet's Nurse and Falstaff.

One of Shakespeare's most happy touches is the goddess's proclivity for self-praise, often wild and hyperbolic but always amusing and entertaining.[9] The most effective of these self-laudatory passages is her recital of the conquest of Mars, an exemplum which should not only instruct the youth woefully ignorant of amatory lore but also impress him with the reputation of the woman who so desperately begs his attention. Shakespeare renders the scene as a magnificent medieval pageant. After Venus tells Adonis that Mars became her captive and slave who begged for that which the boy can have without asking, she describes the war god as prancing across a tented field on a caparisoned stallion, his "churlish drumme" beating an accompaniment to each victory—except that of love. To it he makes the supreme sacrifice. Over her altar, Venus boasts, he

> . . . hung his lance,
> His batter'd shield, his uncontrolled crest,
> And for my sake hath learn'd to sport and dance,
> To toy, to wanton, dally, smile and iest . . .
> Making my arms his field, his tent my bed.
>
> (ll. 104-109)

This stanzaic picture contrasts with Spenser's portrayal of a languid Acrasia and an impassive Verdant in the Bower of Bliss, but compares with a Venus and Mars painting by Francesca Cossa. The resemblance to Cossa's pictorial version, in the astrological cycle that decorates one of the rooms of the Palazzo Schifonia at Ferrara, depends upon the last image of the passage, which is one of the most engaging in the poem and one of Shakespeare's original details in his telling of this legendary romance. Venus emphasizes her triumph over Mars by adding that she then led him "prisoner in a red-rose chain".[10] This image alludes to her planetary grace and amiability, which are stronger than the physical prowess of the planet Mars, a power which Cossa depicts by placing Venus on a chariot with Mars, in full armor, kneeling before her, his waist encircled by a chain attached to her throne.

This passage not only summarizes the contemporary iconographical tradition in both the literary and graphic media but also illuminates the delicately lyrical, yet the smotheringly possessive qualities of Venus. This illustration, which Venus draws literally from the heights of Olympus and the heavenly spheres, succeeds merely in moving the youth, locked within the goddess's embrace, to complain

> . . . Fie! no more of loue:
> The sunne doth burn my face. . . .
>
> (ll. 187-188)

Even this childish rebuff fails to daunt her. Immediately, and ingeniously, she converts her arms, "this circuit of . . . iuory pale", into protecting borders around the park of her body, which includes hills, valleys, and a delightful plain with fountains,

> Sweet bottom-grass . . .
> Round rising hillocks, brakes obscure, and rough,
> To shelter thee from tempest, and from raine:
> Then be my deare, since I am such a parke,
> No dog shal rowze thee, though a thousand bark.
>
> (ll. 236-240)

Such conceits, worthy of a Biron or a Mercutio, only bring a smile of disdain to the cheeks of the boy, whose dimples ravish the goddess anew.

Shakespeare carefully balances her astonishing eloquence with physical dexterity and cunning. The more witty and clever her arguments, the stiffer the resistance they arouse in Adonis. This causes her to steam, sweat, and indulge in amorous gymnastics that are as bawdy and comical as her speeches. The late evening scene with the two kisses and the two fainting spells offers the best illustration. When Venus compensates for lack of physical union by indulging in a banquet of sense (ll. 435-450), her frustration sends her into a faint that he, conscience-stricken, attempts to erase with a brotherly peck and then a vigorous rubbing, clapping, and pinching of her anatomy. She revives, purring

> O, where am I . . . in earth or heaven,
> Or in the ocean drencht, or in the fire?
> What hour is this? or morn or weary even?
> Do I delight to die, or life desire?
>
> (ll. 493-496)

When he informs her that he cannot meet her the next morning to continue "the match" because he is going boar hunting with friends, she so trembles with terror that she grabs him around the neck—making certain that when they sink to the ground this time, "He on her belly falls, she on her back."

A forbidding note of death strikes across this uproarious scene—like that struck by the toy apple that an earthly Madonna often hands to a bouncing Christ Child in many Renaissance paintings—but Shakespeare muffles its sound by the superbly funny picture of this Mae Westian woman, who, like a military strategist, has at last maneuvered the enemy into a vulnerable position. Although Adonis again slips away, she, indestructible and indefatigable, counters with more verbal fireworks, pointing out the dangers of hunting the hideous boar, and the rewards of chasing the timorous hare, with which she ironically identifies herself, thus inviting Adonis for the hundredth time, surely, to pursue her instead.

The focus, of course, is upon Venus, not Adonis, who is not at all as interesting or appealing. His male beauty and youth serve mainly to incite Venus to words and acts that burlesque Renaissance styles, romantic literary conventions, and Neoplatonic notions of love. Yet he, too, is a comic character, manifesting the ridiculous naiveté and annoying priggishness that accompany virtually complete disinterest in and ignorance of love and sex. He makes a perfect foil, like Hal to Falstaff.

This "rose-cheek" male is no sooner pulled to the ground by the aggressive female than he pouts and blushes like a guilty child. When she fumes like a furnace, he squirms in her fiery embrace like a school boy whose uncomfortable plight becomes increasingly amusing because of his complete lack of awareness that he has inspired in her such consuming passion.[11] Bewildered and self-pitying, his only responses to the flattery, pleadings, and exertions of Venus are—

> . . . Let me go;
> My day's delight is past, my horse is gone,
> And 'tis your fault I am bereft him so. . . .
>
> (ll. 379-381)

> Fie, fie, you crush me: let me go;
> You have no reason to withold me so. . . .
>
> (ll. 611-612)

His longest and most famous speech on lust and love—it is delivered after a strenuous day with a talkative and perspiring gymnast who has lectured and coaxed, bounced and crushed him—comes as a surprise, even a shock. Undoubtedly the most serious passage in the poem, it utilizes one of the key images, that of gluttonous feeding, to link consuming human passion with the voracious appetite of caterpillars that devour "the tender leaves".[12] Adonis then concludes with an analogy between these polar emotions and the seasons. The atmospheric images not only review the hot and animalistic landscape the lovers inhabit but also describe their respective emotional states.

He dares not say more because "the text is old". It is also sentimental and trite—

> Love's gentle spring doth always fresh remain,
> Lust's winter comes ere summer half be done . . .
>
> (ll. 800-801)

and, coming from him, a bit cloying. Yet the fact remains that the "orator too green" has soundly delivered three pointed stanzas that moralize the actions and words of Venus. That he mouths Elizabethan clichés on the difference between frenzied and reasonable love neither diminishes his stature—a case could be made for its being suddenly increased—nor augments the comic tone. His stinging retort, like Venus' prophecy that Adonis will die by the tusk of the boar, rolls across the landscape—only to mingle with the frustrated groans of the abandoned goddess, which, in turn, curiously blend with realistic sounds from "shrill-tongued tapsters".

Yet the faintest echo of these forbidding notes hovers at the edges of the closing section of the poem when Adonis, comic foil to Venus, no longer appears. Shakespeare attempts to mute their sound and blunt the pathos implicit in the Ovidian myth first by having Venus, in soliloquies of ingenious burlesque, exclaim against such frustrating forces in the world as Jealousy and Nature—conventional Elizabethan complaints to which Spenser's Malbecco and Sidney's Sonnet LXXVIII attest;[13] and second, by avoiding the death scene.

He immediately establishes firm ground when the cool morning finds Venus furiously cursing, then sweetly flattering, Death in the same manner and tone that she did Adonis the morning before, and her emotional reaction to their separation is formed into imagery as grotesque as that depicting her response to their embrace. Whereas the long kiss that "drew his lips' rich treasure dry" made her face "reek and smoke, her blood . . . boil" and her lust engender "a desperate courage", the pain of separation and the fear for his death so fill her with despair that

> She vail'd her eyelids, who, like sluices, stopt
> The crystal tide that from her two cheeks fair
> In the sweet channel of her bosom dropt;
> But through the flood-gates breaks the siluer rain,
> And with his strong course opens them again.
>
> (ll. 957-961)

Suddenly a "huntsman hollo" turns the tide of her tears, which become imprisoned in her eyes "like pearls in glass".

> Thy weal and woe are both of them extremes;
> Despair and hope make them ridiculous . . .
>
> (ll. 987-988)

Shakespeare pauses to say of the goddess of love.

Rhetorical luxuriance and excess also rescue, from the edge of pathos, the scene where she discovers Adonis' body. The sight of the boar crashing through the underbrush, its "frothy mouth, bepainted all with red", sends her into semihysterical meanderings through the forest where she witnesses the aftermath of the boar's fury—a group of hounds howling, bleeding, and licking their wounds. Then she spies the "foul boar's conquest" of Adonis, and her eyes withdraw from the sight like "stars ashamed of day" and like the snail,

> . . . whose tender horns being hit,
> Shrinks backward in his shelly cave with pain. . . .
>
> (ll. 1034-1035)

Finally they roll back into "the deep-dark cabins of her head". These delicate and elaborate images of stars, fish, shell, and skull establish an emotional and imaginative correspondence with the goddess' sensitive and instinctive recoil from the scene of carnage, yet their ingenuity and sharp realism so call attention to themselves that the reader realizes but does not feel the emotions of Venus.[14]

The gory sight now dries her tongue, that had spouted advice and warning like a fountain, and also blurs her vision. This enables Shakespeare to describe her reaction to the beauty of the dead hero by indirect means, and he creates a *pietà* as sentimental and diverting as the earlier mural of Venus' conquest of Mars was martial and arrogant. Over the mangled body, Venus mourns the effect his absence will have upon human and animal nature. No one need fear wind- and sunburn,

since the sun will now scorn and the wind hiss humanity. Aside from the interesting contradiction, the reader immediately remembers that Adonis fretted, while locked in her arms, of too much sun in his eyes and on his face. Venus continues: the lion, tiger, and wolf will no longer be considerate enough to conceal their fury as they did for Adonis, lest they frighten him—a dubious tribute to the sportsman who preferred the most dangerous game. Shakespeare permits Venus a final turn of the screw when she concludes, finally, that had she been "tooth'd" like the boar, which meant, really, to nuzzle rather than gore the groin of the delightful youth, she would have killed the boy first with kisses.

There is nothing for her to do now but prophesy

> Since thou art dead . . .
> Sorrow on love hereafter shall attend . . .
>
> (ll. 1134-1135)

but she does so not in the imperious manner of an Olympian but rather the childish and egoistic manner of Adonis when he pouted

> My day's delight is past, my horse is gone,
> And 'tis your fault I am bereft him so. . . .
>
> (ll. 370-371)

Moreover, her sorrow and distress stem, really, not from his death so much as from the fact that

> . . . never did he bless
> My youth with his; the more am I accurst. . . .
>
> (ll. 1120-1121)

Her lament ends in the sudden metamorphosis of Adonis into a purple and white flower, the stalk of which she quickly and roughly

> . . . crops . . . and in the breach appears
> Green-dropping sap, which she compares to tears. . . .
>
> (ll. 1175-1176)

Crushing it to her breast where her "throbbing heart shall rock . . . [him] day and night", she carries him off to her temple at Paphos, which, considering the English country-side, seems to be located in the Channel.

This final bit of stage business brings the dramatic action of the poem to full circle. What Venus carries away at the end of the poem is the metamorphosed body of Adonis which she plucked from the horse and carried under her arm when the poem opened.[15]

Indeed there is very little of divinity and even less of mythology about Venus. Although she laments to Jove that Adonis

> . . . being dead, with him is beauty slain,
> And Beauty dead, black chaos comes again . . .
>
> (ll. 1019-1020)

there is not so much as a shred of Platonic ennoblement and spirituality in her feeling for him. Certainly there is only revulsion in his feelings for her. And this is the theme of the poem. Their names connote love and beauty, which they also personify, just as the events in the poem retell their Ovidian romance. Yet these facts do not prevent Shakespeare from parodying not only the myth but also its traditional presentation, literary and pictorial. Thus the rhetorical burlesque and the comic characterization of the legendary lovers travesty Neoplatonic notions of love, which were as current and popular then as Freudian concepts are now.[16]

Adonis' rejection not of love but

> . . . your [Venus'] device in love,
> That lends embracements unto euery stranger,
> You do it for increase: O strange excuse
> When reason is the bawd to lust's abuse . . .
>
> (ll. 789-792)

echoes the "Two loves . . . of comfort and despair" of Sonnet CXLIV, the central poem of the group devoted to the Dark Lady. The "bad angel" which Shakespeare identifies with a "woman colour'd ill" is what Adonis sees in Venus. This demon is lust, and the tragic awareness of its power informs the Dark Lady series,[17] just as it shadows the episodes of the Ovidian poem.

This sudden and biting distinction made by Adonis—it is prefaced by Venus' prophecy of his death—comprises the one brief, momentary shift in tone from the comic and satirical to the serious and the tragic. And the shift is intentional. Like Marlowe's Leander, Adonis is an innocent youth who finds himself in a new situation—except that it is one of Leander's own choosing—and both, unexpectedly, become mouthpieces for wise aphorisms on love. But whereas Marlowe utilizes Leander mainly as a focal point for mythological invention, which depends upon legend and pictorial images to comment on the tragic fate awaiting the young couple, Shakespeare uses Adonis as a mask to express ambivalent attitudes concerning aspects of love, particularly the physical. The settings both poets create for their characters illuminate this difference in attitude and function. Leander makes love to Hero in a romantic-mythological landscape of golden, sea-washed cities with a crystal temple and a stone tower, and Venus pursues Adonis in a humid, tangled wood filled with wild, predatory animals. The dream quality of Marlowe's setting, which is rendered as sharply and clearly as a landscape by Dali, is appropriate for wistful lovers toward whom Marlowe entertains an hilarious but also a gently humorous attitude, just as the ominous, abrasive

quality of Shakespeare's realistic woods is proper for the voracious, perspiring Amazon and the annoyed, reluctant sportsman. Finally, Shakespeare's is a natural setting to which the solicitations of Venus and the responses of Adonis are continually referred, and both, in themselves and in relation to each other, are at strife.[18]

The most important element of "nature with her selfe at strife" are the animals, which not only share the same human passion but also evaluate human emotions. Aside from the fact that the desire of Venus is described in images of the eagle (l. 55) and the hawk (l. 547), and the reactions of the Adonis to those of birds either tangled in a net (l. 67) or tamed by excessive fondling (l. 560), Shakespeare does not choose to establish a consistent dichotomy of the "vulture thought" of the goddess and the "unripe thought" of the hunter. The animal images are so ambivalent that the protagonists are identified with the same animal, at one and the same time.

The coupling of the horses, which illustrates the fire and frenzy of the generative passion, is an exemplum for Venus' afternoon lecture to Adonis, during which she begs him to learn a lesson in love-making from his courser. Then he should play that role, with her as the breeding jennet. Yet from the moment she gathers the reins of Adonis' horse over her arm, she has played the part of the stallion; but she also must be identified with the mare since she assuages male fury, as in her victory over Mars.[19]

On the other hand, Adonis, who prefers to hunt wild game, is not like his horse, because he is too passive and unassuming. He can never play an aggressive role any more than Venus can be like the mare that

> Being proud as females are, to see . . . [the courser]
> woo her,
> She puts on outward strangenesse, seemes unkinde;
> Spurnes at his loue, and scorns the heat he feels,
> Beating his kind imbracements with her heeles.
>
> (ll. 307-310)

Therefore Venus, already associated with birds of prey, is like the stallion, and Adonis, compared to timid birds, is like the mare. Ironically, total abstinence, not excessive love, has rendered him effeminate, just as indulgence has made her masculine.

The same division characterizes the hare and the boar. Shakespeare does not present the hare, the conventional attribute of the goddess of love, as a furry, docile animal, sheltered in the boudoir or a sunny bower, but as frightened, wretched "poor Wat", who must forever dodge, feint, and flee from blaring horns and baying hounds. The traditionally amorous animal of Venus appears as the bewildered victim of furious pursuit, like scowling Adonis in the arms of steaming Venus.[20]

The boar, with its "bristly pikes" and "short, thick neck", is armed with offensive and defensive equipment to fight hunters, as is Mars, the "direful god of war", to combat an enemy.[21] Yet Venus, victor over Mars, is as incapable of vanquishing the loathsome boar as Adonis, who states that he cannot know love "Unless it be a boar, and then I chase it". This "churlish swine" that Venus predicts will consume the beauty of her beloved as surely as he "roots the mead", is another image of gluttony,[22] like the caterpillars that consume the tender leaves, the eagle that gorges on "feathers, flesh and bone", and the stallion that devours, in his rage, the iron bit in his teeth. These images cluster around the person and appetite of Venus. And Adonis, who insists on tracking the boar, is destroyed by it on the second morning, as he was virtually consumed by Venus on the first.[23]

The divisive, yet synthesizing, ambivalence of the animal images amplifies the theme of the poem. Shakespeare satirizes Neoplatonic love because the relationship that it insists upon among love, beauty, procreation, and the spirit—thematic, with slight variation, in the poetry of Dante, Petrarch, the poets in Ficino's Academy, the English sonneteers, and particularly in Spenser, Drayton, and Chapman—is unrealistic and absurd. The comic characterization, humorous actions, and witty speeches express this theme. But it has an accompanying, amplifying motif. The pursuit of love on earth not only follows a path around or under the Neoplatonic ladder that leads to an intellectual, heavenly window—if the ladder ever existed—but also involves the individual, inevitably, in "Th'expense of spirit in a waste of shame". This motif of propelling and repugnant lust is implicit in the images of animals and gluttonous feeding, just as the theme is explicit in the dialogue and dramatic action. Theme and motif meet in Venus, whose panting, heaving bosom Adonis finds as offensive as the "melting buttock" of the stallion. Therefore, he delivers his one and only sermon on two kinds of love, but only the moment before he disappears into the night and from the narrative, because his "text", which he could, but dares not, develop, is not the matter for comedy but tragedy—*The Rape of Lucrece, Troilus and Cressida,* and *Antony and Cleopatra.*

This motif demolishes the Neoplatonic formula that the theme pokes fun at. Adonis-Beauty and Venus-Love should be complementary and sequential, but they are opposed and contradictory. Indeed, Beauty is the antagonist of Love. Therefore, the Neoplatonic circuit by which loving-procreating individuals return to God is broken before it can operate.

Lastly, the lust motif enables Shakespeare to make of his poem not only something delightful but also didactic, these dual aims which all Elizabethans, poets and readers, believed poetry must realize. It also fulfills the second requirement of the Ovidian genre—that of moral didacticism as well as warmth and sensuousness.[24] Moreover, it strikes that note of seriousness which always intrudes upon Shakespeare's comedies—like Aegeon's suffering in *The Comedy of Errors,* and the death of the Princess' father in *Love's Labour's Lost.* Like *Hero and Leander,* its brilliant Ovidian twin, *Venus and Adonis* is also a tragi-comedy of love.

Notes

1. For the most detailed analysis of the Ovidian myth and its treatment not only in Shakespeare but also in other English poets, see T. W. Baldwin, *On the Literary Genetics of Shakespeare's Poems & Sonnets* (Urbana, Illinois, 1950), pp. 1-93. For comparisons of Shakespeare's Venus with paintings by Titian, Rubens, Botticelli, and others—all of them exaggerated and inaccurate—see *Shakespeare: The Poems, A New Variorum Edition,* ed. Hyder Edward Rollins (Philadelphia and London, 1938), pp. 486, 499, 502.

2. Shakespeare's comic treatment of the Ovidian myth has been convincingly demonstrated in two articles by Rufus Putney, "'Venus and Adonis:' Amour with Humor", *Philological Quarterly,* XX (1941), 533-548, and "Venus 'Agonistes'", *University of Colorado Studies,* IV (1953), 1-9. Most other critics complain of such discordant elements as a conceited, artificial style that functions more for decoration than sense, a too realistic setting for mythological lovers, and an ambiguous tone that wavers between the comic and the serious—see Douglas Bush, *Mythology and the Renaissance Tradition in English Poetry* (Minneapolis, 1932), pp. 142-149; W. B. C. Watkins, "Shakespeare's Banquet of Sense", in *Shakespeare & Spenser* (Princeton, 1950), pp. 3-35; and Hallett Smith, *Elizabethan Poetry* (Cambridge, Massachusetts, 1952), pp. 84-90. Franklin M. Dickey, in *Not Wisely but Too Well* (San Marino, California, 1958), pp. 46-53, considers it an "allegory of love" in which lawful love opposes sweating lust.

3. The purple of the sun and the rose of Adonis' cheeks occur in the various accounts of the myth by Bion, Marlowe, and Thomas Cooper. Some say Venus turned Adonis into a rose, others into the purple anemone. See T. W. Baldwin, pp. 9-10. Hereward T. Price, in "Imagery in 'Venus and Adonis'", *Papers of the Michigan Academy of Science, Arts and Letters,* XXXI (1945), 292-295, analyzes the color symbolism and associates purple with red, the color of life-giving blood. Don C. Allen, in "Symbolic Color in the Literature of the English Renaissance", *Philological Quarterly,* XV (1936), 89, finds Greene using purple as an emblem of faith and wisdom, and Lyly as "a

symbol of fast love". Certainly the intensity of purple and the warmth of rose help Shakespeare create an atmosphere of uncomfortable, humid heat.

4. Rufus Putney, in "'Venus and Adonis:' Amour with Humor", pp. 534-546, establishes the comic tradition to which Shakespeare contributed his poem.

5. Franklin M. Dickey, Ch. IV, discusses this topic, yet, curiously enough, finds only "implicit humor" in Shakespeare's portrayal of an adolescent Adonis. See p. 48.

6. See *Biographia Literaria*, II (1817), 15-17.

7. Rufus Putney, in "Venus 'Agonistes'", p. 58, suggests a five-act structure for the poem.

8. For the influence of Marlowe's *Hero and Leander* upon Shakespeare's poem, see Douglas Bush, pp. 145-146.

9. Rufus Putney, p. 59, emphasizes this point as one of Shakespeare's original contributions to the Ovidian myth.

10. Cf. T. W. Baldwin, p. 15, who, after hunting with his usual energy in Homer, Ovid, Anacreon, and Ronsard for the source of this image, concludes that it "might well be as original with Shakespeare himself as such things can be."

11. Cf. Rufus Putney, "Venus 'Agonistes'", p. 59.

12. Franklin M. Dickey, pp. 50-51, believes that Shakespeare, through Adonis, points out the flaws in the reasoning of Venus. "She has misapplied valid arguments against celibacy as a mere cover for lust."

13. Cf. Douglas Bush, pp. 148-149, n. 21.

14. Cf. W. B. C. Watkins, pp. 5-6, who finds this passage an example of Shakespeare's rhetorical brilliance but one which illustrates how the rhetoric in the poem "does not seem to be always intentional or under full control".

15. Hereward T. Price, p. 295, overstates his case when he calls this gesture a butchering of Adonis and an example of the "savage irony" of the poem.

16. Cf. Erwin Panofsky, *Studies in Iconology* (Oxford University Press, 1939), Ch. V, and Nesca Robb, *Neoplatonism of the Italian Renaissance* (London, 1953), Ch. VI.

17. See Paul N. Siegel, "The Petrarchan Sonneteers and Neoplatonic Love", *Studies in Philology*, XLII (1945), 182.

18. Hereward T. Price, pp. 287-290, stresses the importance of the natural imagery which functions "to present nature at work on man". W. B. C. Watkins, p. 8, finds only incongruity between the realistic setting and the Ovidian lovers.

19. Most critics fail to see this ambivalence. For example, T. W. Baldwin, p. 26, calls the mare "the true symbol of Venus", and Hereward T. Price, p. 292, calls the courser "a convincing picture of the power of lust in Venus".

20. Baldwin's elaborate source hunting, pp. 33-38, in Ovid, Virgil, and Golding reveals the association of Venus with such timorous creatures as rabbits, does, and harts; and Price, p. 292, establishes an association of the hare with Adonis—both victims of lust.

21. T. W. Baldwin, pp. 33-37, cites Ovid, Golding, and A. Brooke's *Romeus and Juliet* as sources for Shakespeare's description of the boat. Baldwin, p. 36, claims that Shakespeare was particularly interested in Brooke's use of the boar to describe the fury of Romeus. The association of the boar with *ira* has been traced by Morton W. Bloomfield, *The Seven Deadly Sins* (East Lansing, Michigan, 1952), p. 60, from late antiquity through the Middle Ages.

22. See Bloomfield's Index, pp. 456, 474, for the emphatic association of the boar with swine, and both with guttony.

23. *Ibid.,* pp. 229-230. The author describes a scene from Guillaume de Deguileville's *Pelerinage de la vie humaine* in which Venus, riding on a boar, conspires with Gluttony, an old hag, to defeat the pilgrim. Although there is no indication that Shakespeare utilized this poem as a source—not even its various English translations, one of which is by Lydgate—still it indicates a well-known representation of one of the Sins, the lists of which were well known not only throughout Europe but also Elizabethan England. See pp. 105-106.

24. Cf. Franklin M. Dickey, pp. 147-148, who insists that the Ovidian genre demands allegorical interpretations of the poem even though it is not an allegory in form.

CHARACTER STUDIES

John Doebler (essay date winter 1982)

SOURCE: Doebler, John. "The Reluctant Adonis: Titian and Shakespeare." *Shakespeare Quarterly* 33, no. 4 (winter 1982): 480-90.

[In the following essay, Doebler compares Renaissance pictorial representations of Adonis and Venus with Shakespeare's rendering of these mythological figures in his poem Venus and Adonis.*]*

> Dost thou love pictures? We will fetch thee straight
> Adonis painted by a running brook,
> And Cytherea all in sedges hid.

These words describe one of the "wanton" pictures the drunken tinker from *The Taming of the Shrew* (1593-94) can expect to enjoy as a lord (Induction, ii. 49-51). The subject of this article is Shakespeare's *Venus and Adonis* (1593), where the paragon of male beauty betrays no more interest in the goddess of love than he does in the picture offered Christopher Sly. Although Cytherea is hidden from view in the painting, she is anything but unrevealed when she turns up as Venus in the narrative poem. The reluctance of Adonis in the poem to pity so ravishing a Venus has challenged those who have studied Shakespeare's sources. The major source, universally accepted, is Ovid's celebration of the contended love of Venus and Adonis (*Metamorphoses*, X). The usual explanation for the reluctant Adonis is the conflation of one or two other stories from Ovid.[1]

The tale of Salmacis and Hermaphroditus (*Met.*, IV) is most frequently cited, but the tale of Echo and Narcissus (*Met.*, III) is also mentioned. In both of these stories death concludes the refusal of an attractive fifteen- or sixteen-year-old male to answer the erotic pleas of a woman. Echo is too shy to initiate conversation (as we are led to expect from her name); she never actually touches Narcissus; and, once rejected, she hides in shame. But Salmacis steals reluctant kisses from Hermaphroditus and clings to him in the water until he drowns. The love-sick goddess hiding by the running brook in *The Taming of the Shrew* passage may also derive from the Salmacis story.

In *Venus and Adonis* Shakespeare lowers the age of Ovid's Adonis (*iam vir*) to that of a bare adolescent: "red for shame, but frosty in desire" (l. 36). Adonis even comes close to saying that he is not yet capable of the act of love. He tells Venus to measure his "unripe years," comparable to a green plum, difficult to pluck and sour to the taste (ll. 524-28). When Venus finally drags Adonis on top of her, "All is imaginary" (l. 597). Shakespeare stresses the physical maturity of Venus in her size and strength and underlines her erotic experience in the passage recalling her mastery over Mars. Despite invincibility in war, Mars is the foolish captive led in triumph at the end of a red-rose chain by love and beauty (ll. 97-114).

Venus, the misleader of grown manhood, is all the more dangerous as the temptress of youth. Among Shakespeare's most comic effects, often observed by critics, is a Venus who tucks a "tender boy" under her arm after plucking him from his horse (ll. 30-32).[2] Ovid describes the comedy of Venus, for that matter, not in the episode with Adonis, but in her adultery with Mars, cited by Venus in Shakespeare. What Shakespeare's Venus leaves out, however, is the well-known conclusion to the story: the exposure of both lovers to the laughter of the gods by her husband Vulcan (*Met.*, IV). Renaissance variations on the story of that triangle include Tintoretto's comic ridicule of Vulcan, more in the medieval tradition of the *Merchant's Tale* of January and May than that of the classical sources beginning in Homer (*Odyssey*, VIII). [A] Tintoretto painting creates a dramatic scene, with a dog barking at the poorly hidden Mars.[3]

The emblem tradition of Venus as temptress of youth, furthermore, creates that striking disparity of scale that provides Shakespeare with so many comic possibilities. See, for instance, the woodcut in Guillaume de la Perrière's *La Morosophie* (Lyons, 1553), no. 3.[4] The accompanying emblem poem underscores the idea that the young man is just coming into adolescence. Don Cameron Allen, who writes of Adonis as caught between the hard hunt of life and the soft hunt of love, calls Shakespeare's Venus "a forty-year-old countess with a taste for Chapel Royal altos." Referring back to Ovid, Allen says "that in tone, purpose, and structure the two poems have little to share. . . . Shakespeare's intent and plan are as different from that of Ovid as his Venus . . . is from the eternal girl of the Velia."[5]

The greatest difference is in the restrained sexuality of the Venus in Ovid. Dressed as a virginal Diana hunting harmless game, she is content to haunt the presence of Adonis. They finally sit upon the lawn in the shade of a tree so that she may tell him the cautionary tale of Atalanta and Hippomenes. Her head resting gently upon his breast, Venus combines words with kisses. The tale over, she leaves at once, believing Adonis fully convinced of the dangers of hunting savage prey. The digression told by Venus is a double warning. Atalanta and Hippomenes, driven wild by lust on consecrated ground, are turned by the offended Cybele into raging lions. The lions are yoked to the chariot she rides as the Great Mother of all creatures. Shakespeare eliminates this digression for the sake of describing the antics of a stallion and a mare in heat, an episode used by Shakespeare's Venus to endorse erotic fulfillment.

Ovid, furthermore, sets the tone for the tragedy by a recounting of Adonis' incestuous ancestry as the child of Myrrba and Cinyras. Adonis is the offspring of his sister and his grandfather, a seduction of father by daughter, the son conceived in darkness, cursed, and wept over. The fate of Adonis completes a cycle of retribution arising from illicit passion. Venus, more than anything, is trying to arrest the fateful process. Her love is protective, reserved, and maternal, in no way rapacious. Ovid's Venus, dressed as a chaste Diana, is closer to the Heavenly Venus in *The Symposium*, the Celestial Venus of the Neoplatonists, and even the idealized

Venus in Titian's *Sacred and Profane Love*[6] than she is to the heaving creature we find at the beginning of Shakespeare's poem. Whether he would wish to do so we have no way of knowing, but the Adonis in Ovid has no need to protect his chastity.

The critical issue in our understanding of Shakespeare's art, therefore, is not so much the reluctance of his Adonis as it is the rapacity of his Venus. The painfully shy Echo in Ovid is totally different, but not even Ovid's Salmacis can account for the degree of change Shakespeare is making when he casts Venus as a frenzied older woman driven by comic lust for a very young man barely emerging from boyhood.

A number of other suggestions for the changes have been made by literary scholars. Often cited are two songs from works by Robert Greene: *Perimedes the Black-Smith* (1588) and *Never Too Late* (1590). The songs, both saccharine and mildly comic, stress a naive, indeed callow, Adonis. In the one, Venus pleads for the pity of a beloved who dares not even look at her; in the other, "Wanton *Adonis*" sits "toying on her knee," he blushes when she kisses him, and she argues that his youth justifies taking pleasure in love.

It is more likely that Shakespeare deferred to Spenser rather than to Greene, who attacked Shakespeare in *Groatsworth of Wit* (1592). The first three books of *The Faerie Queene* were published in 1590, just three years before Shakespeare's poem. Spenser's description of The Garden of Adonis (*FQ*, III.vi.29 ff.) owes much to the tradition of the mythographers, who stressed the resurrection of Adonis in the spring by Venus as an Earth Mother, after his death caused by the boar as a symbol of winter.[7] Earlier in Book Three is Spenser's account of the tapestries in "*Castle loyeous*" (*FQ*, III.i.34-38). The costly "clothes of *Arras* and of *Toure*," hanging in the long chamber, depict a number of scenes: Venus overcome with desire, Venus wooing Adonis, "the boy" asleep in a bower and bathing in a fountain, her plea to forgo the hunt, Venus mourning his death, and his metamorphosis into "a daintie flowre." Spenser says that Venus "Entyst the Boy" with "sleights and sweet allurements," but the poet concludes that she "did . . . steale his heedelesse hart away."

Another reference to Venus and Adonis based on visual representation, also rendered in cloth, is the fleeting description of the embroidery on the sleeve of Hero in Marlowe's epyllion:

> Her wide sleeves green and bordered with a grove,
> Where Venus in her naked glory strove
> To please the careless and disdainful eyes
> Of proud Adonis that before her lies.
>
> (I. 11-14)

Hero and Leander was written in 1593, the year *Venus and Adonis* was published, and a number of scholars

have conjectured that Shakespeare might have seen in manuscript the Marlowe poem, so like his own in genre.

Nor has it escaped the attention of literary scholars that a considerable amount of Renaissance art is devoted to Shakespeare's subject. Painters and graphic artists who have rendered the attraction of the goddess of beauty to one of the most beautiful men in mythology include Tintoretto (1518-94), Cambiaso (1527-85), and Veronese (1528-88),[8] to say nothing of the countless representations of Venus alone or with her other companions.

The artist most frequently mentioned by students of *Venus and Adonis,* however, is Titian. He treated the subject both in the *Pardo Venus* at the Louvre and in the Prado *Venus and Adonis*. In the Louvre canvas Adonis hunts a gentle stag while Venus appears to be sleeping. The Prado painting shows Adonis trying to break away from a clinging Venus, and it is thus more closely related to the circumstances of Shakespeare's poem. The first to suggest a parallel between the Prado version and Shakespeare's reluctant Adonis was the editor A. H. Bullen, in 1905; but the painting has been mentioned by students of literature a number of times since, and it is extensively discussed as a source by Erwin Panofsky in his posthumous *Problems in Titian* (1969).[9] Panofsky cites a letter written by the artist to Philip of Spain in 1554, reporting the shipment of *Venus and Adonis*. The painting was sent by way of Madrid to London, where Philip was living briefly as the consort to Mary Tudor, and the canvas stayed in England for many years after Philip left for the Continent in 1555. The original finally ended up at the Prado, but many contemporary copies were made on canvas. One of the earliest, which may have been the copy Titian kept for himself, is now in London, at the National Gallery since 1824. The original apparently stayed in the Royal Collection of England until after the writing of *Venus and Adonis*. It was perhaps there even as late as 1636, when it is first reported in Spain. Even if Shakespeare, whose plays were increasingly honored by command performances at court, had no access to the original canvas, he may have known one of the several copies, or at least the widely distributed prints. Prints were executed by both Guilio Sanuto (dated 1559) and Martino Rota (ca. 1520-83).[10]

In the letter from Titian, the artist suggested that his royal patron hang *Venus and Adonis* as a companion piece to *Danaë in a Shower of Gold,* also by Titian and already in Philip's collection. The artist observed that the female nude is seen from the front in his *Danaë* and from the back in his *Venus and Adonis*. Other aspects of the female body are promised in two projected paintings, one of Perseus and Andromeda and the other of Jason and Medea. According to Panofsky, Titian's turning about of his nude in *Venus and Adonis* for the sake of delighting in a woman's back meant a rewriting of the myth, for which he was criticized by Raffaello Borghini in 1584. In Ovid's account, it is only after the departure of Venus for Cyprus that Adonis ignores her warnings and resumes the hunting of dangerous animals. He does it after her back is turned in another sense.

Other Renaissance pictures usually show one of two scenes: Adonis happy in the lap of Venus, as in the Veronese at the Prado; and Venus lamenting his death, as in several works by Cambiaso.[11] The mutual attraction of the lovers is particularly stressed in an engraving by Jacob Matham (1571-1631). In the Matham, Venus wears the magic girdle that makes her irresistible.[12] In the episode painted by Titian, however, Adonis tears himself away from the embrace of Venus in order to pursue the hunt. The artist here revives a motif of antique art known as the Leave-Taking of Adonis. This motif occurs, for instance, in the high relief from a second century A.D. Roman sarcophagus in the Lateran Museum.[13] The Ovidian episode of the Leave-Taking of Venus is thus converted and dramatized by Titian into the Flight of Adonis, with Cupid impotently asleep. Panofsky concludes that Titian's Prado version of *Venus and Adonis* is the source that inspired Shakespeare's reluctant Adonis.

But Titian is also consistent with Ovid in a way that Shakespeare is not. He retains the emphasis upon the conflict as vocational rather than erotic. The hunt is the center of disagreement, as in Ovid. Titian rewrites his myth only slightly. He extends the visit of the goddess of beauty until her conflict with Adonis can become physical as well as verbal. Titian provides the basis for a Mannerist treatment stressing physical movement, rather than a High Renaissance presentation of static loveliness. As for the back of Venus, the sorely disappointed Philip complained to the artist of the way its paint was damaged in transit. Titian's own interest in this detail of anatomy probably reflects in part his continuing concern with the Renaissance *paragone* debate between painting and sculpture. In several of his other pictures Titian goes to considerable lengths to answer the claim of the sculptors that they alone can render a figure from several points of view.[14]

An aspect of the painting seemingly overlooked by art historians, but suggesting comparison with Shakespeare's poem, is the use of animals as a symbolic comment on the central figures. The three dogs tied to the left arm of Adonis seem to restate the conflict implied within him. His powerful torso twists from the embrace of Venus, but his expressive eyes are turned back upon her pleading beauty. Two of the dogs, fangs bared, strain on their cords, eager for the hunt; but the third turns in hesitation, as if unsure of the day's plan. The conflicts are both internal and external in more ways than one. The right hand of Adonis grips the boarspear; the left hand restrains the dogs. In common with almost all

Renaissance representations of Adonis is the way Titian combines an athletic male body with a head erring toward soft femininity. Shakespeare retains this conventional tension between male firmness and an undercutting aesthetic appeal,[15] but he forgoes conflict within Adonis for the sake of external debate. The closest Shakespeare comes to creating the narrative moment rendered by Titian is in the lines immediately following Adonis' refutation of Venus' deliberate confusion between procreative love and mere lust:

> With this he breaketh from the sweet embrace
> Of those fair arms which bound him to her breast,
> And homeward through the dark laund runs apace;
> Leaves love upon her back deeply distress'd.
>
> (ll. 811-14)

Shakespeare does use the technique of animals as a comment on the main action, but in other than a subjective way. In the digression of the stallion and the breeding jennet, animal activity parallels or contrasts with the external behavior of the goddess and her beloved. Instead of Ovid's elaborate story of Atalanta and Hippomenes, which concludes with a brief transition back into the original narrative through the metamorphosis of the lovers into savage lions, Shakespeare substitutes a consistently relevant but much shorter episode. The precise relevance of the stallion and the breeding jennet to Venus and Adonis, however, has been much debated. One critic thinks the unbridled stallion a symbol of the animal lust which Adonis wisely rejects; another finds a parallel between the jennet and Adonis as a male coquette. But most interpreters agree that the digression corrects or mirrors the main narrative action in some way; and no one has suggested that it restates a conflict within either Venus or Adonis.[16] Perhaps Shakespeare himself provides the clearest artistic link between this digression and the rest of the poem. Venus uses the example of the runaway stallion to encourage Adonis in love: "Let me excuse thy courser, gentle boy, / And learn of him, I heartily beseech thee, / . . . / O learn to love . . ." (ll. 403-7). Adonis replies by contrasting the maturity of the horses to his own youth, comparable to ". . . the bud before one leaf" unfolds (l. 416). The rhetoric is pointed toward the factual surface rather than toward psychological or philosophical depths. The poem is more material than the painting, and the painting more subjective than the poem.

We will probably never know whether Shakespeare knew the Titian design. Even if it could be documented that he did, we would still debate whether or not the painting should be elevated into a source for the poem. What we do know is that two Renaissance artists of the first rank chose the same subject: the explicit rejection of Venus by Adonis. A comparison of poem and painting—analogues at least—brings us to a number of conclusions.

Neither artist shows any hesitation in altering the details of the original narrative in Ovid in order to serve a new artistic effect. Each draws upon a form outside of Ovid, in the case of Shakespeare the epyllion, used by Lodge only a few years earlier, and in the case of Titian the Leave-Taking of Adonis, found in antique designs.[17] Titian seems to have introduced a conflict within Adonis to augment the physical tearing away from Venus. Shakespeare draws upon the comedy associated with the name of Venus, turning that less toward the coyness of a reluctant Adonis than in the direction of a frenzied Venus, whose emotions are driven first by lust and then by grief. Both artists are "Mannerist" in their focus upon conflict. The conflict in Titian twists bodies and communicates irresolution; the more theatrical conflict in Shakespeare pits body against body and rhetoric against rhetoric.

Notes

1. Useful summaries of scholarship on the sources of the poem are Hyder E. Rollins, ed., *New Variorum Poems* (Philadelphia: I. B. Lippincott, 1938), pp. 390-405; and T. W. Baldwin, *On the Literary Genetics of Shakespeare's Poems and Sonnets* (Urbana: Univ. of Illinois Press, 1950), pp. 1-93 (the reluctance of Adonis, pp. 87-92). Geoffrey Bullough, *Narrative and Dramatic Sources of Shakespeare,* 8 vols. (London: Routledge and Kegan Paul, 1957-75), I, 161-76, confines the sources to Ovid.

   The edition used for Ovid in this article is the Loeb *Metamorphoses,* 2 vols. (London: William Heinemann, 1916); the text I quote for *Venus and Adonis* is the New Arden edition of the *Poems,* ed. F. T. Prince, 3rd ed. (London: Methuen, 1960).

2. The comedy in the behavior of both Venus and Adonis is stressed by Rufus Putney in two articles: "*Venus and Adonis:* Amour with Humor," *Philological Quarterly,* 20 (1941), 533-48, and "Venus Agonistes," *University of Colorado Studies in Language and Literature,* 4 (1953), 52-66. For Adonis as the primary object of Shakespeare's ridicule, compare J. D. Jahn, "The Lamb of Lust: The Role of Adonis in Shakespeare's *Venus and Adonis,*" *Shakespeare Studies,* 6 (1970), 11-25.

   The continuing debate about the tone of *Venus and Adonis* is summarized by J. W. Lever, "The Poems," *Shakespeare Survey,* 15 (1962), 19-22; and Norman Rabkin, "*Venus and Adonis* and the Myth of Love," in *Pacific Coast Studies in Shakespeare,* ed. Waldo F. McNeir and Thelma N. Greenfield (Eugene: Univ. of Oregon Press, 1966), pp. 20-32. The critical consensus seems to be that the poem combines a serious moral content with amusing sexuality, and that the two aspects are not necessarily reconciled. "Ambivalence" has been the critical term applied with increasing frequency.

3. The canvas by Tintoretto, *Mars and Venus Surprised by Vulcan,* was owned by the English painter Sir Peter Lely (d. 1682), who probably acquired it from the estate of the Earl of Arundel. Bought by the Bavarian state in 1925, it now hangs at the Pinakothek. See Wolf-Dieter Dube, *The Pinakothek, Munich* (New York: Harry N. Abrams, 1970), p. 174. Thomas Howard, Second Earl of Arundel and Surrey (1586-1646), was the first great English art collector and patron.

   The Mars and Venus myth is a good example of how the classical stories were interpreted both *in malo* and *in bono. In bono* is one of the versions suitable to *Antony and Cleopatra* and *The Faerie Queene,* esp. Bk. II, where the lovers symbolize *discordia concors.* See Raymond B. Waddington, "Antony and Cleopatra: 'What Venus Did with Mars,'" *Shakespeare Studies,* 2 (1966), 210-27; and Robert Kellogg and Oliver Steele, eds., *Books I and II of "The Faerie Queene," the "Mutability Cantos" and Selections from the Minor Poetry* (New York: Odyssey Press, 1965). The story *in malo,* with moralized English commentary from the mythographic tradition, was published a year before *Venus and Adonis.* Abraham Fraunce, *The Third Part of the Countess of Pembroke's Yvychurch* (1592, rpt. New York: Garland Press, 1976), fols. 31^v-32^r.

4. Arthur Henkel and Albrecht Schöne, *Emblemata: Handbuch zur Sinnbildkunst des XVI. und XVII. Jahrhunderts* (Stuttgart: J. B. Metzler, 1967), col. 1751, illustrate this emblem.

5. Don Cameron Allen, *Image and Meaning: Metaphoric Traditions in Renaissance Poetry,* 2nd ed. (Baltimore: The Johns Hopkins Press, 1968), pp. 42-43. (Allen's essay on *Venus and Adonis* first appeared in 1959.)

   A useful critical article on the general subject of Ovid and Elizabethan poetry is Caroline Jameson, "Ovid in the Sixteenth Century," in *Ovid,* ed. J. W. Binns (London: Routledge and Kegan Paul, 1973), pp. 210-43.

6. See Erwin Panofsky, *Studies in Iconology: Humanistic Themes in the Art of the Renaissance* (1939; rpt. New York: Harper Torchbook, 1967), esp. pp. 129-69. Panofsky argues that the Titian should be retitled "The Twin Venuses," the nude one on the right Celestial, the clothed one on the left a Venus Genetrix. Venus Genetrix is the honorable procreative love called *amor vulgaria* by Ficino in his *Convito.* Ficino thinks lust a madness and unworthy of the name of Venus.

Franklin M. Dickey, *Not Wisely But Too Well: Shakespeare's Love Tragedies* (San Marino, Calif.: Huntington Library, 1957), pp. 47-48, argues strongly that Shakespeare's Venus is in part Ficino's *amor vulgaria,* but Dickey thinks her vulgar in the common sense as well. Dickey concludes: "Adonis is not ripe for either sort of passion." The fourth poem in *The Passionate Pilgrim,* whether by Shakespeare or not, probably describes the situation intended in *Venus and Adonis* as well as any other attempt. "But whether unripe years did want conceit, / Or he refused to take her figured proffer," he "would not touch the bait."

As for the argument of Shakespeare's Venus to procreate, it is probably meant to be viewed as hypocrisy (in sharp contrast to the same theme in the first seventeen *Sonnets*). Venus is driven by simple lust at this point in the poem.

7. See George Sandys, *Ovid's Metamorphoses Englished, Mythologized, and Represented in Figures,* ed. of 1632, ed. Karl K. Hulley and Stanley T. Vandersall (Lincoln: Univ. of Nebraska Press, 1970), pp. 490-94.

Shakespeare, of course, used Arthur Golding's translation (1567), but Sandys is an important record of iconographic commonplaces contemporary with both Golding and Shakespeare. Most scholars seem to agree that Shakespeare knew both Ovid's Latin and Golding's translation. I rely on Ovid, not only because I find no significant differences between the two but also because Ovid is the source shared by all the Renaissance artists I discuss.

For an account of Ovid and the mythographers, see Don Cameron Allen, *Mysteriously Meant: The Rediscovery of Pagan Symbolism and Allegorical Interpretation in the Renaissance* (Baltimore: Johns Hopkins Univ. Press, 1970), Chap. 7. Allen (p. 186) calls Abraham Fraunce (note 3 above) the "conspicuous English precursor of Sandys." Fraunce's account of the meaning of the Venus and Adonis story (fols. 43ᵛ-45ʳ) is substantially the same as Sandys': a fertility myth.

An article relating the poem to the mythographic tradition in terms other than the fertility myth of Venus and Adonis is S. Clark Hulse, "Shakespeare's Myth of Venus and Adonis," *PMLA,* 93 (1978), 95-105.

8. See Andor Pigler, *Barockthemen: Eine Auswahl von Verzeichnissen zur Ikonographie des 17. und 18. Jahrhunderts,* 2 vols. (Budapest: Verlag der Ungarischen Akademie der Wissenschaften, 1956), II, 239-40. Pigler lists at least five versions of the subject by Cambiaso, six by Veronese or atelier, etc.

9. Bullen (1905) is quoted in Rollins' *Variorum* ed.: "Titian's famous picture . . . affords sufficient proof that Shakespeare was not the first to depict Adonis' coldness" (p. 397). The two Titian paintings are discussed, among others, by T. W. Baldwin (note 1 above), p. 92; and by Eugene B. Cantelupe, "An Iconographical Interpretation of *Venus and Adonis,* Shakespeare's Ovidian Comedy," *Shakespeare Quarterly,* 14 (1963), 141. The fullest application of Titian thus far, however, is Erwin Panofsky, *Problems in Titian, Mostly Iconographic* (New York: New York Univ. Press, 1969), pp. 150-55. Panofsky cites the *Variorum,* but he leaves the very strong impression that he is the first to mention Titian as an explanation of the reluctant Adonis in Shakespeare (p. 153). The Panofsky theory is cited as if seminal by Judith Dundas, but rejected: "Style and the Mind's Eye," *The Journal of Aesthetics and Art Criticism,* 37 (1979), 327.

10. An extant copy of the print by Sanuto is in the Print Collection of the British Museum, in the Titian (Myth) portfolio (Sloane Collection, XI-93), along with contemporary graphics of the same Titian by at least two other Renaissance printmakers (Sloane Collection, XI-95; and 1950-2-11-156). The Rota is listed in Adam Bartsch, *Le Peintre-graveur,* 21 vols. in 17 (Vienne: J. V. Degan, 1803-13), XVI, 282.108.

11. Panofsky, *Problems* (note 9 above), p. 152, and Baldwin, p. 13. The works by Cambiaso are illustrated by Bertina Suida Manning and William Suida, *Luca Cambiaso: la vita e le opere* (Milan: Casa Editrice Ceschina, 1958), figs. 121, 123, 124, and 128.

12. The Jacob Matham is listed by Bartsch, III, 229.16.

13. William Keach, *Elizabethan Erotic Narratives: Irony and Pathos in the Ovidian Poetry of Shakespeare, Marlowe, and their Contemporaries* (New Brunswick: Rutgers Univ. Press, 1977), p. 55, ill. p. 57. Keach is correcting Panofsky, who states that Titian is the first artist to render Adonis leaving Venus. Titian, at least, seems to have been the first artist in the Renaissance to revive the classical motif, and he establishes the highly dramatic prototype imitated by many artists, including Rubens. (Keach reports 1636 as the year of the first documentation of the original painting in Spain, p. 242, n. 12.)

14. See especially Titian's *Saint Sebastian* (Brescia), where both the front of the body and the entire back of the shoulders are shown. The painting is illustrated by David Rosand, *Titian* (New York: Harry N. Abrams, 1978), pp. 92-93. The standard

catalogue raisonné is Harold E. Wethey, *The Paintings of Titian,* 3 vols. (London: Phaidon Press, 1969-75). For information about the London version of *Venus and Adonis,* see Cecil Gould, *National Gallery Catalogues: The Sixteenth Century Venetian School* (London: The National Gallery, 1959), pp. 98-102.

15. The concept of vigorous young manhood destined for accomplishment amid hardships, but distracted or threatened by the powerful aesthetic attraction it exerts upon others, is a theme shared by the paintings of Venus and Adonis (or Mars), Shakespeare's narrative poem, and his *Sonnets.*

16. Robert P. Miller, "Venus, Adonis, and the Horses," *ELH,* 19 (1952), 249-64, believes that the digression serves three intentions: the comic ridicule of the romantic love claimed by Venus by using the horses to reveal such courtship as mere lust; a contrast of the run-away stallion with Adonis, to the moral advantage of Adonis; and a contrast of the breeding jennet, serving the natural law of propagation, with the base motives of Venus, who seeks only pleasure. A similar approach is that of Panofsky (*Problems,* p. 118 and n.), who believes that the digression equates the unbridled horse to unbridled passion. In sharp contrast is Jahn (note 2 above, pp. 21-22), who calls Adonis a coquette, to whom the jennet is at first similar. In the end, however, she is more "honest" than Adonis for relenting to the sexual excitement she has aroused in the stallion.

17. See Elizabeth Story Donno, ed., *Elizabethan Minor Epics* (New York: Columbia Univ. Press, 1963), "Introduction." Donno (p. 6, n. 3) suggests that "epyllion" is primarily a nineteenth-century (rather than a classical) term, but she acknowledges its usefulness in describing the Renaissance "erotic-mythological verse narrative" as a minor epic.

Heather Dubrow (essay date 1987)

SOURCE: Dubrow, Heather. "'Upon Misprison Growing': *Venus and Adonis.*" In Venus and Adonis: *Critical Essays,* edited by Philip C. Kolin, pp. 223-46. New York: Garland Publishing, 1997.

[*In the following essay, originally published in 1987, Dubrow interprets the behavior and motivations of Venus and Adonis, and examines the ways in which Shakespeare dramatized the psychological elements of their characters.*]

Readers have long acknowledged certain similarities between Venus and some of Shakespeare's dramatic characters: she shares, we are told, the earthiness of Falstaff, the sensuality of Cleopatra, and the determination of comedic heroines like Rosalind.[1] Yet we have been slow to admit that the sophisticated techniques through which she is characterized represent yet another link between Venus and her counterparts in the plays. And we have been equally slow to admit the many regards in which her behavior mimes that of actual people.

I do not mean that Shakespeare's portrait of Venus is mimetic in every sense of that term. Few women could literally tuck a young man, however slim and "hairless" (487) he might be, under their arms, fewer yet react to the death of their beloved by flying into the air. And the characterization of Venus does lack one type of complexity that we encounter even in Shakespeare's earliest plays, as well as in *The Rape of Lucrece:* the poem does not explore the relationship between a temperament and a social milieu. Moreover, we never wholly forget her symbolic significance: she is not only a lover acting in very human ways but also the abstract force of Love itself. Indeed, for all of Venus' follies the figure of Venus Genetrix evidently lies behind her. Yet facts like these need not, of course, preclude a portrait that is mimetic in broader senses of the word—a portrait that mirrors the ways actual people think, feel, and talk—any more than the allegorical significance with which Cordelia or Britomart are weighted precludes their being representational as well.[2]

Venus plucks Adonis from his horse at the beginning of the poem just as, symmetrically, she plucks the flower that represents him at the end (in the world of *Venus and Adonis,* as in the *Metamorphoses,* one may be literally as well as symbolically carried away by love). It is evident, then, that Venus connects loving Adonis with controlling him, mastering him; indeed, so deep is the connection as to make us suspect that even had he been less reluctant her impulse would have been to assert sovereignty by grasping and entrapping him. Yet her concern for mastery is more pervasive than it might at first appear: that concern shapes how she perceives many situations and how she reacts within them.

The goddess of love, like that other impresario Prospero, is prone to describe events, especially those involving love, in terms of mastery. She narrates her relationship with Mars in those terms:

> Yet hath he been my captive and my slave,
>
> (l. 101)

> Thus he that overrul'd I oversway'd,
> Leading him prisoner in a red rose chain:
> Strong-temper'd steel his stronger strength obey'd,
> Yet was he servile to my coy disdain.
> Oh be not proud, nor brag not of thy might,
> For mast'ring her that foil'd the god of fight!
>
> (ll. 109-114)

That extraordinary line "Leading him prisoner in a red rose chain" (l. 110) draws attention to the moral ambiguities we so often find in her behavior: on the one hand, a chain of roses charms us more than it troubles us, and yet even in this image Venus is stressing her own power and control (notice, for instance, that she chooses the verb "leading" rather than "making"). Similarly, Adonis is called "love's master" (l. 585). When she sings of the effects of love, she describes "How love makes young men thrall, and old men dote" (l. 837). (It is suggestive, too, that the subject of this ditty is the power of women over men even though the most recent events in Venus' own past have illustrated how love makes *women* thrall and makes them dote.)[3] Even when she is soliciting agreement from Adonis, the verb she chooses suggests domination: "But if thou needs wilt hunt, be rul'd by me" (l. 673). And it is telling that this same phrase, "be ruled by me," is used by other Shakespearean characters enamored by power, notably the Bastard in *King John* (II.i.377).[4] In other words, in a few instances Venus' preoccupation with power is manifest in her desire to submit to that of Adonis; but more often she is concerned to assert her own power.

The troubling undertones in the passages we have been examining lead us to reflect on how Venus' character has been shaped, and misshaped, by her tendency to see love not as "mutual render" (Sonnet 125.12) but rather as an aggressive struggle for domination. And since her vocabulary of mastery and captivity is drawn from the stock language of love poetry, our reflections on her aggressiveness generate literary questions as well. On one level, it is merely amusing to encounter a putative goddess who sounds like an Elizabethan sonneteer, much as we enjoy Leander's predilection for the tones of a university orator. But on another level the frequent echoes of Elizabethan poesy are disturbing: we again think about the underlying assumptions of that literary system (or, more precisely, systems) and in so doing wonder in particular whether it breeds in its speakers, fictional or otherwise, the tendency to conjoin and confound the sexual and the aggressive that we find in Venus. That tendency provides, as we shall see, a more intimate link between *Venus and Adonis* and *The Rape of Lucrece* than we generally acknowledge.[5] In both a central character connects passion and power; in both the conventions of love poetry express—and, more disturbingly, perhaps encourage—that connection.

Many of Venus' habits, whether they are linguistic gestures or psychological patterns, are a way of achieving and asserting domination. Writing in a genre that traces metamorphoses of all kinds, Shakespeare characteristically focuses on the transformations his heroine performs through her words: much as she appropriates Adonis, so she appropriates language itself. And much as her assertions of power over Adonis often

VENVS AND ADONIS.

EVEN as the funne with purple-colourd face,
Had tane his laft leaue of the weeping morne,
Rofe-cheekt Adonis hied him to the chace,
Hunting he lou'd, but loue he laught to fcorne:
    Sick-thoughted Venus makes amaine vnto him,
    And like a bold fac'd futer ginnes to woo him.

Thrife fairer then my felfe, (thus fhe began)
The fields chiefe flower, fweet aboue compare,
Staine to all Nimphs, more louely then a man,
More white, and red, then doues, or rofes are:
    Nature that made thee with her felfe at ftrife,
    Saith that the world hath ending with thy life.

Vouchfafe thou wonder to alight thy fteed,
And raine his proud head to the faddle bow,
If thou wilt daine this fauor, for thy meed
A thoufand honie fecrets fhalt thou know:
    Here come and fit, where neuer ferpent hiffes,
    And being fet, Ile fmother thee with kiffes.
                                                                B

Title page of Venus and Adonis *(1593).*

generate subtle reminders of his power over her, so her attempts to impress language into her service often lead us to recognize that she is herself imprisoned by it, once again a captive victor.

It is suggestive, to begin with, that she talks as much as she does: of the 1,194 lines in the poem, 537 are spoken by the goddess of love. The only analogues to this garrulity that we can find in other epyllia are passages anchored in the complaint tradition, such as the laments intoned by Lodge's Glaucus and Heywood's Oenone. But Venus is not delivering a complaint: she is cajoling, insisting, insinuating. Her talkativeness, like that of the Wife of Bath, reflects her desire to impose her presence, to dominate the conversation just as she dominates in so many other ways.

Assuming Adam's function, this postlapsarian Eve repeatedly names—or, more to the point, renames—the objects around her:[6]

    With this she seizeth on his sweating palm,
    The precedent of pith and livelihood,

And trembling in her passion, *calls it* balm,
Earth's sovereign salve to do a goddess good:

(ll. 25-28; italics added)

Panting he lies and breatheth in her face.
She feedeth on the steam as on a prey,
And *calls it* heavenly moisture, air of grace.

(ll. 62-64; italics added)

To name something is to assert one's power over it—as Hal recognizes when he festoons Falstaff with epithets and as Petruchio acknowledges when, in one of his most subtle but most effective gestures of domination, he insists that his future wife be called not Katherine but Kate. Another function of Venus' naming, however, is to attempt to change the nature of sweat and breath. The earthiest of heroines, she is transforming both into something more ethereal, a habit in her to which I will return shortly. The ambiguity of "calls it" emphasizes the same issue we encountered in the deer park stanzas: does she believe in the transformation she is effecting, or is it merely another way of flattering Adonis? The fact that we cannot know for certain reflects, I would suggest, a telling confusion in Venus herself: she, no less than Richard II, is prone to become carried away by her own words.

In the second passage I quoted, the dramatist who wrote *Venus and Adonis* plays two voices against each other in one of the ways nondramatic poetry permits: he establishes a dialogic tension between the speaker's "as on a prey" (l. 63) and the goddess' "And calls it heavenly moisture" (l. 64). That speaker's honest appraisal of the situation contrasts with her self-serving one. It is suggestive, too, that the more honest and more objective of the observers relies on a simile, "*as* on a prey": rather than transforming the steam into something else, he is respecting and retaining its individuality, its identity. In a sense, then, Venus substitutes a metonymic approach for the speaker's metaphoric one: unlike him, she attempts to change the identity of the breath as totally as Petruchio tries to change his Kate.

Venus' predilection for renaming the world typically assumes one form in particular: she tries to transform the material into the spiritual. The poem in which she appears insistently bodies forth the details of the natural world: people sweat and lust, aggressive eagles demonstrate that nature is indeed red in tooth and claw, and divedappers and rabbits remind us that it includes gentleness and frailty as well. Against this complex vision of the physical world is played Venus' distortion of it.[7] We have already observed the ways she uses language in an attempt to effect transformations, turning steamy breath into "heavenly moisture" (l. 64). And she attempts to reshape her own image along similar lines. This earthy goddess unpersuasively insists on the spirituality of love and on her own virtual lack of corporeality:

Love is a spirit all compact of fire,
Not gross to sink, but light, and will aspire.

Witness this primrose bank whereon I lie:
These forceless flowers like sturdy trees support me.
Two strengthless doves will draw me through the sky
From morn till night, even where I list to sport me.

(ll. 149-154)

Attuned to this habit in her, we find its analogue in her repeated descriptions of the earth as Adonis' lover:

And therefore would he put his bonnet on,
Under whose brim the gaudy sun would peep:
The wind would blow it off, and being gone,
Play with his locks; then would Adonis weep.

(ll. 1087-1090)

And she interprets the boar's attack as a kiss: "If he did see his face, why then I know / He thought to kiss him, and hath kill'd him so" (ll. 1109-1110). While in these instances she is not spiritualizing the natural world, she is performing a comparable travesty by idealizing it and by attributing her own emotions to it.

Such travesties serve as a commentary not only on Venus' artifices but also on Shakespeare's art. For many of her conceits exemplify one of his most familiar tools of trade, the pathetic fallacy. By placing it in Venus' mouth rather than that of a narrator, the poet leads us to evaluate that rhetorical technique more critically than we would otherwise do (in fact, in the lines from the poem in Theocritus' *Sixe Idillia* that may have influenced Shakespeare, the speaker, not Venus, attributes an amatory motive to the boar).[8] We recognize, in other words, that the pathetic fallacy may reflect the pathetic self-centeredness of its proponent. Shakespeare is dramatizing a rhetorical pattern by associating it with a psychological one, a habit we shall observe repeatedly in his major poems. And in so doing he is also problematizing a literary convention that is uncritically adduced in many other epyllia—an approach to genre that we will also meet many times in *The Rape of Lucrece* and the sonnets.

Another way in which Venus uses language to create a fictitious and factitious world is by telling stories—her habit of naming and renaming writ large. Like the improvisator figure whom Stephen Greenblatt has anatomized for us,[9] she turns the facts about her relationship with Mars into a scenario more attractive to herself—and more amenable to her aim, persuading Adonis to succeed the god of war in her bed. Thus she defines the relationship in terms of mastery—but then, as if realizing that this may not be the best strategy for wooing Adonis, she ends on a suggestion that the roles have been reversed, that he has mastered her: "Oh be not proud, nor brag not of thy might, / For mast'ring her that foil'd the god of fight!" (ll. 113-114). Most

320

revealing, however, is her omission of the humiliating conclusion of her liaison with Mars: they were both mastered, both caught in a net.[10] And by alluding to that type of trap in a different context only forty lines earlier ("Look how a bird lies tangled in a net" [l. 67]), Shakespeare subtly reminds us of the very fact Venus is attempting to conceal: the net result, as it were, of her involvement with Mars. Later, too, the goddess of love is characterized as a storyteller: her song is compared to the "copious stories" (l. 845) of all lovers, she whispers "a heavy tale" (l. 1125) to the dead Adonis, and, of course, she recounts the story of Wat.

But if Venus is a narrative poet, she is also a lyric one: her delivery of an elegy on Adonis is the appropriate culmination of her recurrent tendency to adopt the conventions of Elizabethan art, especially the traditions of love poetry. As many readers have observed, she repeatedly deploys hyperbole, the figure that Puttenham terms the "loud lyar":[11] "More white and red than doves or roses are" (l. 10), "A thousand kisses buys my heart from me" (l. 517), and so on.[12] And her courtship of that "lifeless picture, cold and senseless stone" (l. 211) evidently parallels the situation of the Petrarchan lover—with the important difference, of course, that the sex roles are reversed. We may suspect that the exaggerations of her language not only reflect but also encourage the unhealthy emotiveness of her own character—yet another reminder that rhetoric can be as dangerous for its speaker as its victim. Moreover, we never forget how self-serving her poesy is: Adonis' accusation that her speeches are "full of *forged* lies" (l. 804; italics added) underscores the link between the artistic and fraudulent connotations of that adjective.

Venus' aim, like that of other love poets, is less *educere* or *delectare* than *permovere,* and much of her language is directed toward persuading Adonis by flattering him. Because her initial words in the poem are devoted to such flattery, just as *The Rape of Lucrece* opens on Collatine's tributes to his wife, the reader's attention is immediately focused on the problems of praise:

"Thrice fairer than myself," thus she began,
"The field's chief flower, sweet above compare;
Stain to all nymphs, more lovely than a man,
More white and red than doves or roses are."

(ll. 7-10)

The first of Venus' many attempts to seduce Adonis, this passage reminds us how much of her behavior is in fact self-centered and self-serving. That self-centeredness is especially evident in her line, "Thrice fairer than myself" (l. 7): she is really lauding her own beauty even while seemingly concentrating on his, presenting herself as the measure of all loveliness. In another sense, too, the passage, like Venus' other compliments, reverses the hierarchies that it ostensibly

establishes and in so doing fulfills a function opposite from the one it apparently assumes. If on the most overt level her paeans are a tribute to the power of Adonis—he is beautiful enough to evoke such glowing tributes—on another level they are, as we have observed, an attempt to assert power over him. In short, Venus is preoccupied with mastery even when delivering lines that are seemingly self-effacing.

Nor is it an accident that, though the passage labels Adonis "sweet above compare" (l. 8), it in fact incorporates no fewer than three explicit comparatives: "Thrice fairer than myself" (l. 7), "more lovely than a man" (l. 9), and "More white and red than doves or roses are" (l. 10). Furthermore, behind the epithet "The field's chief flower" (l. 8) lie comparisons with other flowers that have been found wanting in contrast to Adonis, just as "Stain to all nymphs" (l. 9) establishes his superiority over those maidens. Venus' preoccupation with mastery, we come to realize, encourages her to cast relationships in terms of competition. We find allusions to competition, too, in some of the conventional imagery of the poem, such as, "To note the fighting conflict of her hue, / How white and red each other did destroy!" (ll. 345-346). And of course two actions in the physical world—the hunt for the boar, and Wat's attempts to escape—involve the competition between hunter and hunted. Venus' predilections, then, are mirrored in the world she inhabits. And they also find echoes in the competitive behavior of the characters in Shakespeare's other major poems.

We observed earlier that some of her tributes to Adonis unpersuasively claim to be self-effacing. Other compliments she delivers, however, are not even nominally self-effacing: she blatantly flatters herself as well as Adonis. In Fletcher's *Venus and Anchises,* for example, the goddess of love is praised by the narrator, whereas in Shakespeare's poem Venus describes her own beauty: "My eyes are grey and bright and quick in turning" (l. 140), and so on. Though such tributes may well be objectively true, they make us uneasy. The oddity of complimenting oneself alerts us to the general problems involved in compliments, and we have more reason to distrust Venus' rhetoric than that of Fletcher's speaker. Hence the passage from *Venus and Adonis,* unlike the blazons in *Venus and Anchises* and other epyllia, again draws our attention to the moral dangers of flattery.

Given how characteristic a mode flattery is for Venus, we should not be surprised that she not only opens on it but also returns to it in a moment of crisis: fearing for Adonis' well-being, she attempts to insure his future by flattering death:

And that his beauty may the better thrive,
With death she humbly doth insinuate;

Tells him of trophies, statues, tombs, and stories
His victories, his triumphs and his glories.

(ll. 1011-1014)

The jingly feminine rhyme in the final two lines reflects the mechanical quality of her compliments.

If Venus' compliments to Adonis function centripetally, directing our attention to the nuances of her own psyche, so too do they move centrifugally, highlighting the broader social ramifications of her epideictic mode. A number of scholars have recently demonstrated that Elizabethans were keenly aware of the parallel between courtiership and courtship.[13] Shakespeare activates that awareness by comparing his heroine to a "bold-fac'd suitor" as early as line 6 of the poem, and a subsequent allusion to a "suit" (l. 336) reinforces the parallel. One effect of these references is to underscore Venus' ambiguous and tenuous grasp on power. In the first quotation, "suitor" (l. 6) evidently suggests the efforts of the powerless to ingratiate themselves with the powerful, while "bold-fac'd" is the earliest of many indications in the poem that the goddess of love cannot or will not acknowledge that in certain regards she is indeed powerless. But the lines also serve to comment on the nature of romantic love and its analogue of courtly service: coming to see Venus' flattery as courtly in several senses of the term, we are reminded that the compliments delivered by courtiers are as self-serving as those delivered by lovers. In both instances flattery functions as an implicit bargain—"I will give you praise in return for your favors"—a function very different from the nobler one of inspiring virtue assigned to it by classical rhetoricians.[14]

We encounter lines that introduce these issues, notably Venus' initial tributes to Adonis, very shortly after we read the author's own sally into courtiership, his dedication to Southampton. Perhaps the necessity of praising a patron encouraged the young Shakespeare to think further about the issues raised by flattery. But if biographical experiences lie behind his interest in those issues, so too do literary ones; he repeatedly, perhaps even obsessively, explores flattery in his plays. In particular, in the personages of that triad Bushy, Bagot, and Green we find the clearest embodiment of a dramatic convention and political problem that runs throughout the other history plays as well: kings are susceptible to the compliments of bad advisers, prone to be infected by "the monarch's plague, this flattery" (Sonnet 114.2).

We are now in a position to address a question that has long troubled readers of the poem: why did its author make Venus the aggressor? Though that decision may have been influenced by pictorial or literary treatments of the story (scholars have enumerated parallels ranging from Titian's *Venus and Adonis* to Abraham Fraunce's

Amintas Dale to putative hints of a reluctant Adonis in Ovid himself),[15] the mere presence of such models cannot, as some have asserted, explain Shakespeare's reinterpretation of the goddess of love. After all, also accessible to him were a far greater number of versions in which the two lovers retain traditional sex roles.

Certain answers lie instead in the same impulse that, as we will see, led other epyllion writers to create aggressive women: the aim of commenting on the chaste heroines of Elizabethan love poetry. And politics in the narrower sense of the word lies behind the sexual politics of the poem: Venus' assertions of power may well reflect resentment of Elizabeth herself.[16] The sexually forward women in sixteenth-century epyllia reverse the customary roles of man and woman, much as a female monarch reverses those same roles. Hence in this epyllion, as in many others, ambivalence about an unsuccessfully manipulative heroine encodes ambivalence about a brilliantly manipulative queen.

Yet in this instance—as in many other recent scholarly discussions of the interplay between social history and literature—the vocabulary of encoding is potentially misleading: it can imply that all meanings save the covert political one are mere decoys. The political resonances that I am attributing to *Venus and Adonis* and other epyllia are no doubt present, but they do not subsume the more obvious significances of the poem. In this case, while Shakespeare's preoccupation with powerful women may initially have been sparked by the Britomart on England's throne, it is also likely that he had a deep and sustained interest in such temperaments for other reasons as well. In Venus we encounter a preliminary study of a character type that, as his later works testify, intrigued him: the heroine who, refusing to be daunted by literal or metaphoric shipwrecks, energetically attempts to take control of her destiny. But the obvious contrasts between the realization of that figure in Rosalind or Portia and in Venus herself indicate yet another facet of Shakespeare's interest in this plot. Accustomed to her power, evaluating experience in terms of it, Venus is confronted by her own powerlessness, engendered first by the unwilling Adonis and then by the willful boar. She reacts by desperately adducing the strategies that have helped her to assert and maintain her power before, such as renaming the objects around her and flattering his opponents. Shakespeare's concern with the powerlessness of the erstwhile powerful, a preoccupation embodied in the phrase, "She's love, she loves, and yet she is not lov'd" (l. 610), recurs in the other nondramatic poems as well and, of course, in many of the plays, testifying to his attraction to this situation.

Venus' most characteristic speech mannerism is one that critics have neglected, her reliance on conditionals:

If thou wilt deign this favour, for thy meed
A thousand honey secrets shalt thou know.

(ll. 15-16)

If thou wilt chide, thy lips shall never open.

(l. 48)

If they burn too, I'll quench them with my tears.

(l. 192)

But if thou needs wilt hunt, be rul'd by me.

(l. 673)

In addition to this list—and one could extend it—Venus formulates many sentences that are implicit conditionals. "Is thine own heart to thine face affected? . . . Then woo thyself" (ll. 157, 159), for example, can be transformed into "If thine own heart is to thine own face affected, then woo thyself." "Give me one kiss, I'll give it thee again" (l. 209) implies the conditional formulation, "If you give me one kiss. . . ."

Venus' conditional mode is the syntactical manifestation of habits of mind that emerge in many other ways as well: her propensity for establishing bargains and her closely related tendency to see one action as a payment for another. As "Give me one kiss, I'll give it thee again" (l. 209) would suggest, she uses kisses as counters in her bargains. Similarly, when she tries to arrange another meeting with Adonis, she selects a phrase that has connotations of bargaining: "wilt thou make the match" (l. 586). And she bargains even with death, in effect proffering the boar as a target for his rage.

The tendency we are observing, like so many of Venus' other predilections, is not wholly negative. In a sense, in fact, Venus' conditionals assume the function of the etiological myths that Shakespeare, unlike other practitioners of his genre, virtually omits: they symbolize a world of order, of rules—a world that is played against the irrational sphere of the boar, who respects no rules at all. Hence Venus' ability to shape sentences into conditionals—and the ability to promulgate rules, to predict patterns that it implies—breaks down when she fears Adonis' death: "If he be dead,—O no, it cannot be" (l. 937).

In practice, however, this speech mannerism generally manifests the darker, more dangerous tendencies in the goddess of love. First of all, it again signals the issue of power: when her conditionals involve a threat ("If thou wilt chide, thy lips shall never open" [l. 48]), they are evidently an attempt to dominate, to manipulate. This aspect of bargaining becomes explicit in an allusion to ransom that figures in the most negative description of Venus that we find in the whole poem:

Now quick desire hath caught the yielding prey,
And glutton-like she feeds, yet never filleth.
Her lips are conquerors, his lips obey,
Paying what ransom the insulter willeth.

(ll. 547-550)

And if Venus' conditionals in theory attest to at least a modicum of trust and communication between her and her listener, in fact they more often manifest the dissolution of both social and linguistic norms. For example, "If thou wilt deign this favour, for thy meed / A thousand honey secrets shalt thou know" (ll. 15-16) not only implies that Adonis has the choice of doing the favor or not but also stresses his authority and autonomy through the strikingly courtly, humble formula, "If thou wilt deign." But in truth he has no choice at all: without even giving him a chance to reply, Venus drags "the tender boy" (l. 32) from his horse.

Other conditionals rank as infelicitous speech acts in the sense Austin and Searle have defined: they violate one of the essential conditions for promising. In Searle's schema, one of the preparatory rules for promising is: "*Pr* is to be uttered only if the Hearer H would prefer S's doing A to his not doing A and S believes H would prefer S's doing A to his not doing A."[17] Often, however, Venus promises something that Adonis does not want at all. Thus in "Here come and sit, where never serpent hisses, / And being set, I'll smother thee with kisses" (ll. 17-18), her promise to kiss him must in fact seem more of a threat to her listener.[18] Nor would he necessarily welcome the promise she bestows on him later: "If they burn too, I'll quench them with my tears" (l. 192).

The violation of the normal rules for promising reflects the instability of a world in which generic and other stylistic rules break down as rapidly and as unpredictably as social ones. We may recall 2 *Henry IV*, where Prince John's violated pledge to the rebels is merely the most overt manifestation of a society in which Diogenes would grow cold and weary roaming the streets. But Venus' untrustworthy promises also serve to reflect her characteristic self-centeredness: unable to admit that Adonis is radically different from herself, she cannot recognize that he will not appreciate the sexual favors she promises him. The same type of self-centeredness is reflected in the rhetorical questions on which she so often relies: "Then why not lips on lips, since eyes in eyes?" (l. 120) and "Is thine own heart to thine own face affected?" (l. 157). Sentences like this imply that their answer is obvious—but Adonis would not in fact give the answer that Venus wants.

The self-centeredness of Venus' linguistic mannerisms is mirrored throughout the poem. We have already observed that her first words measure her beloved against her own beauty: "Thrice fairer than myself" (l.

7). As many readers have noticed, her repeated conceits about the earth and the boar kissing Adonis also represent a kind of self-centeredness: here, as in her conditionals and her rhetorical questions, she is refusing to acknowledge the Other, metonymically making the world over in her own image. And, as petulant and vengeful as an Ovidian god, after Adonis' death she prophesies that all lovers will suffer as she has done: "It shall be fickle, false and full of fraud" (l. 1141). The echoes with which she is surrounded the night before Adonis dies are an externalization, a bodying forth, of her tendency to live in a house of mirrors.

Venus' deceptive rhetoric exemplifies one of the broadest—and deepest—issues in the poem: failures of speech and of language itself. *Venus and Adonis* is concerned with faulty or failed communication, as well as faulty or failed perception; the one isolates us from the people around us, the other from the world we inhabit. The significance of communication in the poem is reflected in the fact that here, as in Shakespeare's other major poems and, indeed, in the *Metamorphoses,* the inability to speak repeatedly symbolizes other losses, other griefs; Adonis' initial silence aptly represents his loss of power, and even Venus herself is temporarily rendered speechless, first by impatience and then by grief.

One reason communication is problematical, Venus' behavior reminds us, is that language can serve multiple and often contradictory ends. In particular, its expressive and its persuasive aims may be at odds; in describing her love for Adonis the goddess of love in fact weakens her case, repelling rather that persuading him. And the poem plays on the paradox that Adonis' demurrals actually render him more, not less, attractive, much as Elizabeth Bennet finds that her most serious protests are merely interpreted as the coquetry of an elegant female. The failure of words to say what the speaker intends is one more breakdown in expectations and one more collapse of social codes in a poem that depicts so many of these failures. But if verbal signs cannot always be trusted to communicate as intended, neither can their gestural equivalent. The gestures of the horses, their tailwaving, stamping, and biting, effectively prevent a nascent breach between them. Yet in the human semiotic system gestures can be misleading in much the same way as words: though the red and white hues of Adonis' face in fact express his shame and grief, Venus finds them attractive.

Sexual gestures, too, can be an antithesis to communication rather than an extension of it:

> And kissing speaks, with lustful language broken,
> "If thou wilt chide, thy lips shall never open."
>
> (ll. 47-48)

> He saith she is immodest, blames her miss;
> What follows more, she murders with a kiss.
>
> (ll. 53-54)

On one level, of course, we should not take all this too seriously: Venus is again indulging in playful sexual games, and one would have to be as "unmoved, cold, and to temptation slow" as Adonis himself wholly to disapprove. The word "murders" (l. 54), however, reminds us that serious issues are at stake. The way kissing interrupts language in these instances is a microcosm of the way sexuality bars genuine communication between Venus and Adonis throughout the poem.

But much as Venus' aggressiveness does not preclude tenderness, so the violence that she inflicts on language does not preclude her using it with more respect and to more respectable ends.[19] Venus approaches rhetoric much as she approaches people: overwhelmingly, disturbingly, and yet with a type of vitality and verve that qualify the negative judgments we are tempted to make. As we saw, the deer park episode reflects not only her intention of manipulating Adonis but also the delighted and delightful fluency of her imagination. It is, however, the Wat incident that best exemplifies the positive uses to which she can put language. Though the iconographic association between Venus and hares may explain some of her interest in the unfortunate Wat,[20] in her precisely realized, sympathetic observations we find the very ability to transcend her own interests, look beyond her own mirrors, that she elsewhere lacks:

> By this, poor Wat, far off upon a hill,
> Stands on his hinder-legs with list'ning ear,
> To hearken if his foes pursue him still.
> Anon their loud alarums he doth hear.
>
> (ll. 697-700)

It is the process of storytelling, elsewhere used for self-serving ends, that here allows both Venus and her listeners to empathize with Wat. In fact, so involved are we with her descriptions that even after repeated readings we are startled when we are reminded of the framing story of Venus and Adonis by the line: "Lie quietly, and hear a little more" (l. 709).

The acuity of Shakespeare's portrayal of Venus is manifest not only in the broader psychological patterns we have been sketching but also in more isolated reactions. As one editor has noted, the multiple images of Adonis that she sees are a recognizable symptom of hysteria;[21] since the incident reminds us also that she has never seen him clearly, it functions symbolically as well as psychologically. At one point she is so involved in her own world that she forgets what she is saying ("'Where did I leave?' 'No matter where,' quoth he" [l.

715]), a moment that may well remind us of our own responses to stress. Also acute are Venus' rapid transitions from depression to anger. Grieving at Adonis' death, she vents her spleen by mocking the rest of the world:

> Bonnet nor veil henceforth no creature wear:
> Nor sun nor wind will ever strive to kiss you.
> Having no fair to lose, you need not fear.
>
> (ll. 1081-1083)

A little later her sorrow is transformed into the anger of her prophecy: "The bottom poison, and the top o'erstraw'd / With sweets that shall the truest sight beguile" (ll. 1143-1144).

If Venus' opening words aptly introduce her, her concluding ones are equally characteristic. So revealing is the final passage in the poem, in fact, that it demands to be cited in full:

> She bows her head, the new-sprung flower to smell,
> Comparing it to her Adonis' breath,
> And says within her bosom it shall dwell,
> Since he himself is reft from her by death.
>   She crops the stalk, and in the breach appears
>   Green-dropping sap, which she compares to tears.
>
> "Poor flower," quoth she, "this was thy father's guise,—
> Sweet issue of a more sweet-smelling sire,—
> For every little grief to wet his eyes;
> To grow unto himself was his desire,
>   And so 'tis thine; but know, it is as good
>   To wither in my breast as in his blood.
>
> "Here was thy father's bed, here in my breast;
> Thou art the next of blood, and 'tis thy right
> Lo in this hollow cradle take thy rest;
> My throbbing heart shall rock thee day and night:
>   There shall not be one minute in an hour
>   Wherein I will not kiss my sweet love's flower."
>
> Thus weary of the world, away she hies,
> And yokes her silver doves, by whose swift aid
> Their mistress mounted through the empty skies,
> In her light chariot quickly is convey'd,
>   Holding their course to Paphos, where their queen
>   Means to immure herself and not be seen.
>
> (ll. 1171-1194)

The repetition of "compare" in the first stanza I quoted draws our attention to the fact that Venus, like Richard II, is responding to grief by assuming the role of poet. Unlike that monarch, however, she also reacts with violence, plucking the flower much as she had plucked Adonis. In the next stanza, she develops the conceit that the flower is Adonis' son, an image that evidently reflects her maternality. But that maternality involves little genuine concern for the flower and less yet for the truth. When, for example, she claims that it is the flower's "right" (l. 1184) to wither in her breast, she is making the same mistake that marked and marred her promises to that fair flower Adonis: she implies that the blossom is grateful to have the right, that it would wish to wither in her breast. In another way, too, she is twisting facts: if her breast was Adonis' "bed" (l. 1183), he allowed it to be so only very briefly and unwillingly. But if our reactions up to this point have been negative, the assertion "There shall not be one minute in an hour / Wherein I will not kiss my sweet love's flower" (ll. 1187-1188) confounds our responses by increasing our pity for her. On the one hand, we have learned by now to distrust Venus' promises, and the hyperbolic vocabulary of this one makes it seem especially unreliable. Yet in this case we also feel that the extravagance of her language reflects the depth of her emotion, and we sympathize with her in her grief.

It is instructive to read through the ending of *Venus and Adonis* twice, once pretending that its penultimate stanza in fact terminates the poem and the second time including the actual ending. The difference is striking. First of all, had Shakespeare ended on "Wherein I will not kiss my sweet love's flower" (l. 1188), our final reactions to Venus would have been involvement and sympathy, though a sympathy laced with distrust of her hyperboles. The actual conclusion, however, distances us from her and in so doing enforces more negative moral judgments, a seesawing between sympathy and judgment that characterizes the whole poem. Moreover, by including the final stanza the poet reinforces certain points about Venus' temperament that have emerged throughout the poem. She is enacting her ability to avoid realities she does not wish to face; having escaped into an airy world of words earlier, now she is quite literally escaping into the air. And if her desire to "immure herself" (1194) once again testifies to her genuine sorrow, the preceding phrase in the line, "means to," surprises us by its ambiguity. It can, of course, merely function as a neutral announcement of her intentions— but as we read about her flying away we reflect that the intentions of this, as it were, highly volatile character are not always to be trusted. We may even suspect that her immuring herself is the last of many vows she does not keep, conditions she does not meet.

But these doubts necessarily cannot be confirmed: the poem is over. Hence our responses to the ending are uncertainty and even dismay, reactions all the more intense because they conflict with the aesthetic finality we associate with closure; the text no less than Venus is breaking a promise.[22] Venus' statements and actions represent an unreliable form of closure, an assertion of finality that jars against the irresolution introduced by "means to" (l. 1194). We react rather as we do at the end of *Measure for Measure*, where the sense of finality that the comedic conclusion offers conflicts with our expectations about how Isabella would really respond to the proposal. In short, then, Shakespeare is conjoining an aesthetic and a psychological problem here, as he so often does elsewhere in the poem: he is examining the issue of closure by associating that literary question with his heroine's sensibility.

Venus' inability to effect a satisfactory conclusion to her experiences is in fact foreshadowed a few stanzas earlier in one of the most revealing changes Shakespeare makes in his sources. In both Ovid and Golding, Venus wills the flower into being and in so doing creates an apt symbol for her grief as well as an apt ending for the story. Here, however, the blossom merely springs up unaided:

> By this the boy that by her side lay kill'd
> Was melted like a vapour from her sight,
> And in his blood that on the ground lay spill'd,
> A purple flower sprung up, checker'd with white.
>
> (ll. 1165-1168)

If we cannot trust the actions and reactions of Venus, those of Adonis are also problematical. Though he is less fully realized than Venus, his behavior manifests some of the same intriguing ambiguities.[23] In other epyllia, the few ambiguous moments we encounter typically reflect simple hypocrisy—Hero says *"Come thither"* (l. 358) because she is more interested in sex than she cares to admit—while in the case of both of Shakespeare's title characters such moments reveal more complex ethical and psychological problems. Adonis' youthfulness is a case in point. Emphasized by Shakespeare's repeated references to him as a boy (for example, ll. 32, 95, 344), his immaturity represents a striking deviation from the sources. Though Golding once calls his Adonis a "tender youth" (l. 634), elsewhere he indicates that he has reached manhood, and Ovid explicitly states that he was "iam iuvenis, iam vir" ("now a youth, now man," *Metamorphoses* X.523).[24] On the one hand, the youthfulness of Shakespeare's Adonis breeds sympathy for him, encouraging us to cast him as a victim of a scheming older woman and, in particular, providing at least a partial explanation for his reluctance. On the other hand, however, his chronological age also reflects his emotional immaturity, the callowness manifest in such dialogue as his comically petulant excuse, "Fie, no more of love! / The sun doth burn my face, I must remove" (ll. 185-186).

But we cannot rest satisfied that his youthfulness justifies his rejection of Venus; like the goddess of love herself, we are confused by his behavior. For one thing, that rejection is explained too frequently and too contradictorily: here, as with the plethora of motives that Iago announces, the very abundance of rationales leads us to distrust all of them—and to distrust the character who is so profusely offering them. In the open-

ing stanza, the narrator clearly announces that "love he laugh'd to scorn" (l. 4), while later in the poem Adonis himself as firmly asserts, "I hate not love, but your device in love / That lends embracements unto every stranger" (ll. 789-790). Similarly, he declares that he hates love because "it is a life in death" (l. 413) but only a few lines later implies that it is not the nature of love but rather his own youthfulness that impels him to scorn it (ll. 415-420). Recognizing that Adonis does not fully understand his own behavior, we begin to suspect subterranean motives that he cannot or will not face, such as the narcissism of which Venus accuses him. The poem nowhere confirms those suspicions—Venus, herself narcissistic, is not the most reliable of judges on this issue, as on so many others—but they remain a troubling undertone as we read.

Evaluating Adonis' ethical position is as complicated as assessing the reasons he assumes it. There is no question but that his coy, petulant tone leads us to distrust his moral stance.[25] At times asyndeton contributes to the impression of abruptness and churlishness:

> You hurt my hand with wringing, let us part,
> And leave this idle theme, this bootless chat;
>   . . . . .
> Dismiss your vows, your feigned tears, your flatt'ry,
> For where a heart is hard they make no batt'ry.
>
> (ll. 421-422, 425-426)

Like the academicians in *Love's Labour's Lost,* he sounds a little too smug and self-righteous when he dismisses love's "batt'ry" (l. 426).

The smugness finds its rhetorical equivalent in the aphorisms that characterize his speech:

> The colt that's back'd and burden'd being young,
> Loseth his pride, and never waxeth strong.
>
> (ll. 419-420)

> Love comforteth like sunshine after rain,
> But lust's effect is tempest after sun;
> Love's gentle spring doth always fresh remain,
> Lust's winter comes ere summer half be done.
>
> (ll. 799-802)

As we read these lines, we sense a tension between their neatness, the sense of intellectual and poetic stasis that they convey, and the rapidly moving, unpredictable world we encounter elsewhere in the poem.[26] As we will see, the couplets in Shakespeare's sonnets function in much the same way. The fact that Adonis' sentiments were Elizabethan truisms does not prove that Shakespeare was endorsing them, as some readers have assumed; rather, the author of the poem is holding these conventional "forms" up for our scrutiny, a scrutiny that would become all the more charged for a reader who had accepted and even repeated such aphoristic sentiments unthinkingly. Nor, however, should we assume that Shakespeare is merely mocking the conventional wisdom of his culture. Venus, surely a "tempest" (l. 800) as well as a temptress, exemplifies many of the points Adonis is making. And however suspicious his neat truisms may make us, they clearly provide him with an important bulwark against her attacks.

Where other epyllia typically assign aphorisms to an undramatized, vaguely defined narrative voice, Shakespeare places them in the mouth of one of his principal characters. Similarly, the hyperbolic language in which the narrators in other epyllia revel is here primarily associated with Venus. By dramatizing linguistic behavior in this way, he is highlighting the psychological traits that it reflects—an issue that he was, of course, exploring at roughly the same time in *Love's Labour's Lost* and in so many of his later works.[27] Both in the plays and in *Venus and Adonis* itself, one effect of this dramatization is to encourage us to question patterns of speech and thought that we might otherwise too readily accept; similarly, it is precisely because they are spoken by a Jaques or a Polonius that we reconsider our attitudes to the moral truisms those characters convey.

However antithetical the ethical positions of Shakespeare's two title characters may be, Adonis adopts some of the linguistic patterns we also found in Venus, demonstrating that here, as in *The Rape of Lucrece* and the *Sonnets,* the lovers share deeper affinities than they themselves would care to admit. Adonis too is very concerned with naming and misnaming: "Call it not love, for love to heaven is fled, / Since sweating lust on earth usurp'd his name" (ll. 793-794). Our first impression may be that he, unlike the huntress who pursues him, is assigning names correctly. But in him as well as her the process is self-serving in its aims, deceptive in its effects. Though lust is Venus' primary motive, it is by no means her only one and by no means an adequate label for her behavior: tender maternal love is commingled with her lust, as certain images testify ("Like a milch doe, whose swelling dugs do ache, / Hasting to feed her fawn, hid in some brake" [ll. 875-876]). And Adonis too makes and breaks promises, though not as frequently as Venus:

> So offers he to give what she did crave,
> But when her lips were ready for his pay,
> He winks, and turns his lips another way.
>
> (ll. 88-90)

> Now let me say good night, and so say you;
> If you will say so, you shall have a kiss.
>
> (ll. 535-536)

It is by subtly but significantly recasting his sources that Shakespeare develops another facet of Adonis: he is figured as entrapped, enclosed—sometimes by Venus

but sometimes by his own chastity. When recounting the story of Salmacis and Hermaphroditus, Ovid writes, "in liquidis translucet aquis, ut eburnea si quis / signa tegat claro vel candida lilia vitro" (IV.354-355). Golding renders this as, "As if a man an Ivorie Image or a Lillie white / Should overlay or close with glasse" (IV.438-439).[28] But in Shakespeare's hands the image becomes:

> Full gently now she takes him by the hand,
> A lily prison'd in a gaol of snow,
> Or ivory in an alabaster band.
>
> (ll. 361-363)

The charged word "prison'd" (l. 362) serves to develop the imagery of entrapment that runs throughout the poem (compare the deer park stanzas with which we began: "Since I have hemm'd thee here / Within the circuit . . . Within this limit" [ll. 229-230, 235]).[29] Later in the poem, however, Adonis speaks of a very different type of enclosure:

> Lest the deceiving harmony should run
> Into the quiet closure of my breast,
> And then my little heart were quite undone,
> In his bedchamber to be barr'd of rest.
>
> (ll. 781-784)

Here the protective custody of the breast displaces imprisonment. While Shakespeare does not recur to these figures or the implicit relationship between them elsewhere in *Venus and Adonis,* it is telling that they were present in his imagination this early in his career. They surface in the other nondramatic poems (as well as in several plays), and there they assume a more central role.

However we interpret Adonis' behavior, it is difficult to consider the boar a fitting punishment for it.[30] Those readers who have argued that the natural world is punishing him for his rejection of naturalistic love neglect the fact that the poem is ambivalent about that rejection. In any event, the punishment does not seem to fit the crime, even if we concentrate on its symbolic ramifications. Its inappropriateness is, I would suggest, the very point: Shakespeare is stressing the randomness, the injustice of fate. There is at times no providence in the fall of a sparrow. That randomness renders Venus' and Adonis' efforts to order experience, whether by renaming it or forcing it into the mold of aphoristic or conditional utterances, all the more understandable— but also all the more foolish.

Though they are alike in that "blessed rage for order," Venus and Adonis evidently differ from each other in their approach to morality. In anatomizing that difference, Shakespeare once again couples the formal and the psychological. Adonis not only subscribes to the conventional pieties, he repeatedly expresses them in a series of sententiae that would make even *A Mirror for Magistrates* look like an exemplar of amoral naturalism by comparison. What results is a poem in which one character bodies forth an amoral delight in sexuality, while the other both symbolizes and expresses a rejection of it in the name of higher philosophical verities. Hence *Venus and Adonis*—and Venus and Adonis themselves—dramatically enact a tension in the generic potentials of Ovidian mythological poetry. Venus stands for the amoral eroticism so common in the mythological narratives of Ovid himself, while Adonis represents the pieties of *Ovide moralisé*. The tension between Venus and Adonis is in effect also a tension between two possible ways of imitating and adapting Ovid, two potential metamorphoses of the *Metamorphoses:* the amoral, Italianate narrative and the pious commentary on human follies. Rosalie Colie has shown us how often Shakespeare's plays envision literary problems in terms of human psychology;[31] the same is no less true of his Ovidian narrative. By thus relating the literary to the psychological in *Venus and Adonis,* he deepens the resonances of his characters—we become aware that they represent distinctive responses to literary dilemmas as well as nonliterary ones—and also enlivens and dramatizes the questions raised by his genre. To be sure, other sixteenth-century Ovidian epyllia are packed with sententiae, but their truisms are normally assigned to the narrator, not one of the personages. Since these narrators are not fully realized characters, the conflict between the two approaches to Ovid is not enacted dramatically as it is in Shakespeare's poem. Shakespeare is, in other words, interpreting his genre and its mode very differently from the way his contemporaries do.

Notes

1. For such parallels see, e.g., Adrien Bonjour, "From Shakespeare's Venus to Cleopatra's Cupids," *Shakespeare Survey,* 15 (1962), 73-80; Robert Grudin, *Mighty Opposites: Shakespeare and Renaissance Contrariety* (Berkeley: U of California P, 1979), pp. 171, 207; Prince, "Introduction," p. xxxii.

2. For an opposing view, see Clark Hulse, *Metamorphic Verse: The Elizabethan Minor Epic* (Princeton: Princeton UP, 1981), p. 155. Also compare Lennet J. Daigle, "Venus and Adonis: Some Traditional Contexts," *Shakespeare Studies,* 13 (1980), 31-46, on the combination of realistic and allegorical elements in her character. James J. Yoch ("The Eye of Venus: Shakespeare's Erotic Landscape," *SEL,* [*Studies in English Literature, 1500-1900*] 20 [1980], 59-71) discusses characterization in terms of Venus' approach to the landscape.

3. William Keach notes in a different context that Shakespeare realizes that the wooer is really more dependent than the person being wooed (*Elizabethan Erotic Narratives: Irony and Pathos in the Ovidian Poetry of Shakespeare, Marlowe, and Their Contemporaries.* [New Brunswick: Rutgers UP, 1977], p. 59).

4. All citations from Shakespeare's plays are to William Shakespeare, *The Complete Works,* ed. Alfred Harbage (Baltimore: Penguin, 1969).

5. Though his psychoanalytic reading of the poem is on the whole unconvincing, Alan B. Rothenberg offers the interesting observation that *Venus and Adonis, The Rape of Lucrece,* and *The Taming of the Shrew* all involve types of rape ("The 'Speaking Beast': A Theory of Shakespearean Creativity," *Psychocultural Review,* 3 [1979], 239).

6. On naming in the plays, see, e.g., Joseph A. Porter, *The Drama of Speech Acts: Shakespeare's Lancastrian Tetralogy* (Berkeley: U of California P, 1979), esp. pp. 12-19.

7. Lucy Gent also observes this habit in Venus but interprets it differently, concentrating particularly on the use of hyperbole ("Venus and Adonis: The Triumph of Rhetoric." *MLR,* [*Modern Language Review*] 69 [1974], 721-29).

8. Theocritus, *Sixe Idillia* (London, 1588), "The XXXI Idillion," 27-31.

9. Stephen Jay Greenblatt, *Renaissance Self-fashioning from More to Shakespeare* (Chicago: U of Chicago P, 1980), pp. 227-228.

10. Compare Robert P. Miller, "The Myth of 'Mars' Hot Minion in *Venus and Adonis.*" *ELH,* 26 (1959), 470-481.

11. George Puttenham, *The Arte of English Poesie,* ed. Gladys Doidge Willcock and Alice Walker (1936; rpt. Cambridge: Cambridge UP, 1970), p. 191.

12. Though Venus' rhetoric has been neglected by most readers, a few have commented sensitively on it from perspectives different from my own. See Gent; Richard A. Lanham, *The Motives of Eloquence: Literary Rhetoric in the Renaissance.* New Haven: Yale UP, 1976), pp. 82-94. The latter analysis, though useful, is limited by its exclusive emphasis on the negative aspects of her rhetoric.

13. See esp. Arthur Marotti, "'Love Is Not Love': Elizabethan Sonnet Sequences and the Social Order," *ELH,* 49 (1982), 396-428; Leonard Tennenhouse, "Sir Walter Raleigh and the Literature of Clientage," in *Patronage in the Renaissance,* ed. Guy Fitch Lytle and Stephen Orgel (Princeton: Princeton UP, 1981).

14. On attitudes to epideictic oratory, see O. B. Hardison, Jr., *The Enduring Monument: A Study of the Idea of Praise in Renaissance Literary Theory and Practice* (Chapel Hill: U. of North Carolina P, 1962), chap. 2.

15. On these precedents, see Bush, *Mythology and the Renaissance Tradition,* p. 143; Keach, pp. 53-56.

16. The ways Elizabeth I affected literature have, of course, been exhaustively studied, both by traditional literary critics and by proponents of the "new historicism." On the tensions generated by the presence of a powerful female monarch, see esp. Louis Adrian Montrose, "'Shaping Fantasies': Figurations of Gender and Power in Elizabethan Culture," *Representations,* I (1983), 61-94.

17. John R. Searle, *Speech Acts: An Essay in the Philosophy of Language* (Cambridge: Cambridge UP, 1969), p. 63.

18. Jerome Schneewind argues that we must distinguish offers and promises ("A Note on Promising," *Philosophical Studies,* 17 [1966], 33-35); in the case of a promise, he contends, the promiser must have good reason to think the promisee wishes the act to be done. Even if one accepts this delimitation of the speech act of promising, however, my general argument about Venus remains valid: rather than suggesting that her infelicitous speech act reflects her self-centeredness, one could maintain that her inability to recognize that Adonis does not want what she promises, her unwillingness to distinguish offer from promise, itself demonstrates self-centeredness.

19. Compare Coppélia Kahn's point that Venus' sexuality itself is both healthy and destructive ("Self and Eros in *Venus and Adonis,*" *Centennial Review,* 20 [1976], pp. 360-364). An abbreviated version of the article appears in *Man's Estate: Masculine Identity in Shakespeare* (Berkeley: U of California P, 1981), with the relevant section on pp. 33-34.

20. On the iconographical connections between Venus and the hare, see, e.g., Don Cameron Allen, "On *Venus and Adonis,*" in *Elizabethan and Jacobean Studies Presented to Frank Percy Wilson* (Oxford: Clarendon, 1959), pp. 109-110.

21. Prince, p. 57.

22. For an overview of poetic closure, see Barbara Herrnstein Smith, *Poetic Closure: A Study of How Poems End* (Chicago: U of Chicago P, 1968).

23. Most studies of Adonis interpret him allegorically rather than psychologically. For a psychological reading different from my own but not incompat-

ible with it, see Kahn, "Self and Eros in *Venus and Adonis*"; this article focuses on his narcissism.

24. All citations from Ovid are to *Metamorphoses,* trans. Frank Justus Miller, 2nd ed., 2 vols. (Cambridge, Mass. and London: Harvard UP and Heinemann, 1966).

25. On this and other faults in Adonis, cf. J. D. Jahn, "The Lamb of Lust: The Role of Adonis in Shakespeare's *Venus and Adonis,*" *Shakespeare Studies,* 6 (1970): 11-25. Norman Rabkin suggests that the imagery associating him with animals, as well as his own perspiration, belie his attempts to escape the flesh (*Shakespeare and the Common Understanding* [New York and London: Free Press and Collier Macmillan, 1967], p. 161). For an earlier version of this chapter, see "*Venus and Adonis* and the Myth of Love," in *Pacific Coast Studies in Shakespeare.* ed. Waldo F. McNeir and Thelma N. Greenfield (Eugene, OR: U of Oregon P, 1966). These and other arguments about Adonis' faults call into question G. P. V. Akrigg's assertion that Shakespeare's epyllion compliments Southampton by implicitly rebutting the portrait of him in John Clapham's *Narcissus* (*Shakespeare and the Earl of Southampton* [Cambridge, Mass.: Harvard UP, 1968], pp. 33-34, 195-196). Other possible connections between *Narcissus* and *Venus and Adonis,* however, deserve more attention than they have received.

26. Lanham (pp. 82-94) argues that he is being criticized for his aphoristic rhetoric; Franklin M. Dickey, in contrast, maintains that he speaks "rather nobly" (*Not Wisely but Too Well: Shakespeare's Love Tragedies* [San Marino: Huntington Library, 1957] p. 50). This chapter suggests that the truth lies somewhere in between.

27. On attitudes to language in *Love's Labour's Lost,* see esp. William C. Carroll, *The Great Feast of Language in "Love's Labour's Lost"* (Princeton: Princeton UP, 1976).

28. All citations from Golding are to *Shakespeare's Ovid, Being Arthur Golding's Translation of the Metamorphoses,* ed. W. H. D. Rouse (Carbondale, Ill.: Southern Illinois UP, 1961).

29. For a different but not incompatible reading of the image, see M. C. Bradbrook, *Shakespeare and Elizabethan Poetry: A Study of His Earlier Work in Relation to the Poetry of the Time,* (London: Chatto and Windus, 1951), p. 64.

30. The significance of the boar has been discussed by many readers. The thesis of Don Cameron Allen's "On *Venus and Adonis*" is that Shakespeare is contrasting the soft hunt of love with the

hard hunt for the boar; A. C. Hamilton interprets that destructive beast as the forces that threaten beauty ("*Venus and Adonis,*" *SEL,* 1 [1961], 13).

31. *Shakespeare's Living Art,* esp. chap. 2.

THEMES

Robert P. Miller (essay date December 1959)

SOURCE: Miller, Robert P. "The Myth of Mars's Hot Minion in *Venus and Adonis.*" *ELH* 26, no. 4 (December 1959): 470-81.

[*In the following essay, Miller comments on Shakespeare's ironic use of Ovidian moral themes associated with the mythological love affair of Venus and Mars recounted in* Venus and Adonis.]

I

An interesting departure from the source of *Venus and Adonis* (*Metamorphoses* X, 503-559, 705-739) is Shakespeare's "reference," as it has been called,[1] to the fable of Venus and Mars in a passage (sts. 17-19) which has received surprisingly little attention from critics of this "first heire" of Shakespeare's "inuention." Although Venus' exemplum is clearly introduced "by way of contrast to her present experience with Adonis,"[2] the function of her argument, much less its total effect, is inadequately described simply by calling it a contrast. Rather, Shakespeare ingeniously develops Venus' persuasive autobiographical excursion as a piece of delightful dramatic self-revelation. The goddess reveals more of herself than she realizes; and, whether he smile with Adonis in coy disdain, or savor the humor less morally, the reader is invited here to enjoy the amusing logical (as well as dramatic) ironies in which she rushes to involve herself. The solemnity with which her argument has been viewed has remained a chief obstacle to an appreciation of the nature of "Loue" dramatized by Venus. Much of the verbal and philosophical sport in this passage, however, arises from Shakespeare's manipulation of assumptions conventionally associated, in his day, with the fable used here. Only when the stanzas are read in the context of such assumptions does the special quality of "wit" characteristic of Shakespeare's "Ovidian" narrative become available to us.

Venus' escapade with Mars was well-known to the audience addressed by the poem, not only in its Classical versions,[3] but as the subject of a definite mythographic tradition.[4] Many, at least, who cut their literary teeth on schoolboy Ovids, must have been prepared to appreciate the special point of view implied in her management of the facts and in her "application" of this tale. The story of adultery and exposure, in Ovid (as Spenser read him) so humorous "That all the Gods with common mockerie / Might laugh at them, and scorne their shameful sin,"[5] it appears, is even more humorously misemphasized by Shakespeare's goddess as a reflection of her special scheme of values. To assume impartiality on her part is to miss a prime value of the passage:

> I haue been wooed as I intreat thee now,
> Euen by the sterne, and direfull god of warre,
> VVhose sinowie necke in battell nere did bow,
> VVho conquers where he comes in euerie iarre,
>   Yet hath he bene my captiue, and my slaue,
>   And begd for that which thou vnaskt shalt haue.
>
> Ouer my Altars hath he hong his launce,
> His battred shield, his vncontrolled crest,
> And for my sake hath learnd to sport, and daunce,
> To toy, to wanton, dallie, smile, and iest,
>   Scorning his churlish drumme, and ensigne red,
>   Making my armes his field, his tent my bed.
>
> Thus he that ouer-ruld, I ouer-swayed,
> Leading him prisoner in a red rose chaine,
> Strong-temperd steele his stronger strength obayd.
> Yet was he seruile to my coy disdaine,
>   Oh be not proud, nor brag not of thy might,
>   For maistring her that foyld the god of fight.

Her account, especially its central stanza, is (with the suppression of the unflattering adjective *insanus*) virtually an expansion of Ovid's *Ars Amatoria* II, 563-564:

> Mars pater, insano Veneris turbatus amore,
> De duce terribili factus amator erat.

But there are even more obvious omissions. Ovid recounts not only the adultery but the exposure and shaming of the lovers in Vulcan's net. Since, indeed, the exposure emphasizes the point of both Ovidian versions,[6] it is especially noteworthy that Venus has neglected to mention the sameful denouement of this experience, and has, rather, presented her action, in obvious contrast to the familiar facts of the fable, as one involving an enviable pleasure without retribution: a proposal of temporal prosperity as the chief good and market of man's time.

II

Venus' view of this exploit is the more extraordinary when we realise that it also represents a direct contradiction of a substantial tradition of commentary upon the fable. For the renaissance, as for the medieval, reader, a fable *meant* something; and in this instance the mythographers, without substantial discrepancy from Fulgentius (c. 500) to George Sandys (1640), find the relation of Venus and Mars to illustrate a highly conventional "moral": the impossibility of concealing a *virtus corrupta libidine* (i. e., the corruption of an inner *virtus,* symbolized by the "warrior" Mars, by an inordinate desire, or lust). For example, the appropriate section in Fulgentius' gloss states:

> Perstant nunc in nostra vita de hac fabula certa admodum testimonia: nam virtus conrupta libidine, sole teste adparet. unde & Ovidius in Metamorphoseon [IV, 172] ait: *Vidit hic deus omnia prius.* Quae quidem virtus conrupta libidine, turpiter catenata fervoris constrictione tenetur.[7]

The Fulgentian "moral" is preserved by the French humanist, Pierre Bersuire, in his view that the fable "potest allegari contra eos qui malo amore se diligunt et cathena male consuetudinis: et carnalis delectationis ita adherent tenaciter."[8] And the immensely influential *Mythologiae* of Natalis Comes further emphasizes the significance of the all-seeing sun, and considers Vulcan's net to symbolize the just revenge of God (through Providence) on such corruption:

> Vulcanus ligauit Martem ac Venerem in rete, nempè claudus celerem, & inualidus fortissimum bellorum Deum: quia nullae vires iniquum hominem possunt à iusta vindicta Dei protegere. Quare per haec etiam homines hortabantur ad integritatem & ad innocentiam, & ab omni turpitudine reuocabant.[9]

These representative explanations show the consistent disposition to regard this Classical myth as hiding a moral truth beneath the veil of allegory. The fact is that the tale aptly fits one of the standard patterns of conflict which so preoccupied medieval and renaissance writers—a pattern which received Scriptural sanction in such seductions as those of Adam by Eve and Samson by Delila, and which proliferated in literary works in such situations as Rinaldo's bondage to Alcida in Tasso's *Gerusalemme Liberata* and Spenser's adaptation of this, Verdant's enslavement to Acrasia. Like Ulysses, these warriors—or "knights"—encounter antagonists who overthrow them, paradoxically, with soft blandishments rather than strong-tempered steel.

In none of these cases is the story primarily concerned with the type of domestic relationship which a simpler realism might propose. Rather, as the mythographers' glosses suggest, a deep moral issue is symbolized by such willing defeats. Regardless of what may have been originally intended by the Classical authors, the "source" from which Shakespeare drew this episode involved moral commitments which could not be ignored. The Venus-Mars story illustrated the essential conflict of Christian life—the tempting allurements of the flesh against the rational "manliness" of the spirit—a conflict described in the Pauline Epistles as "the Christian warfare," and epitomized in Gal. v, 17: "For the flesh lusteth against the Spirit, and the Spirit against the flesh: and these are contrary the one to the other: so that you cannot do the things that ye would."[10]

It can be seen that the glossators emphasize the significance of a number of figures traditional to Scriptural expression, which coincidentally occur in the Classical renditions of the fable. They stress the corruption of "strength" (*virtus*) or "manliness" into "effeminacy," and center upon the revealing "Sun" and the "net" to support their interpretations, bringing Christian values to bear on the pagan tale. Mars, the strong and manly warrior, is defined as *virtus* (literally, physical "strength" appropriate to the "*vir fortis*"). As an image in the moral psychomachia the strength appropriate to the outer man is transferred to the inner man to signify spiritual strength, or "virtue." In either case *virtus* may be expressed as "love"—on the one hand the rational love characteristic of the spirit and on the other the *amor sui* typical of sensuality, to which Bersuire refers. An approximate equivalence is hence seen between Mars and the male figure of Adam who was, by a common tropological gloss, understood to represent the reason and expected to control sensuality in the ideal order, but who, in submitting to Eve, made himself "effeminate."[11] Venus was consistently treated by mythographers as a specifically sexual force which *coniunctiones animalium quaerit*[12] and which, operating excessively in human nature, is identified as *carnis concupiscentia* "*quia omnium fornicationum mater est.*"[13] In the moral readings of this episode she is defined as *libido, luxuria, inordinata concupiscentia,* and *turpitudo.* The psychomachic pattern of "interior warfare" thus underlies the mythographic view of the fable. Reason battles sensuality; the spiritual strength of the inner man struggles with the powers of carnal concupiscence; the spirit contends with the flesh for the soul of man.[14]

The love affair between Venus and Mars was thus traditionally viewed as a mythological reenactment of man's fall to sin. Ovid was supposed, by virtue of the denouement, to have morally condemned it. A renaissance schoolboy could find Vulcan's net explained as a figure for the bondage of passion (*fervoris constrictio*) or carnal delight (*carnalis delectatio*) by which *virtus* is shamefully fettered (*turpiter catenata*)—the bonds of bad habit (*cathena male consuetudinis*) or "lascivious thoughts and pleasures." Arnulf d'Orléans specifies the embracement (*amplexus*) of Venus as that which binds and "dissolves" moral strength. The exposure of the entrapped lovers by the Sun is likened to the operation of the all-perceiving justice of God;[15] since such "bondage" is itself the punishment for sin, God's "revenge" was thought by Comes to be illustrated. The laughter of the gods ridicules the folly of lust when it is brought "to light." Shakespeare's own view of the fable is indicated by his exclusion of "Mars's hot minion" from the proper marriage celebrated by the epithalamium masque in *The Tempest* (IV, i, 86 ff.).

The "interior warfare" illustrated in Shakespeare's "source" for Venus' exemplum was, finally, the subject of a highly complex, if conventional, elaboration. The worlds of the flesh and the spirit, being mutually exclusive in the broad Pauline opposition, operated in analogous, though absolutely opposed, ways. Victory from the viewpoint of the flesh seems defeat to the spirit, and vice versa.[16] *Militiae species amor est,* said Ovid (*Ars Amat.* II, 233); but as there are two opposed "loves" in the Christian view, so there are two antithetical "warfares," which motivate military imagery in literary works. The *militia Christiana*—or the *exercitio* of the "knightly" spirit—and the *militia Veneris* are contraries which result from these opposed attitudes toward the "internal warfare" in man's spiritual life.[17] Mars is the more "manly" in Venus' eyes when he indulges in the *virtus* (the figure is here sexual), or love, which she values, and when he, by "conquering" her, becomes her vassal. But to do this he must abandon his proper *virtus* and, so to speak, lay aside his armor like Verdant; he must surrender his knightly "exercise" in "sloth" in order to engage in "exercise" on Venus' terms. This is what Shakespeare's Venus is made to imply when she says she overcame by "Making my armes his field, his tent my bed." What Venus represents cannot be defeated on its own terms, for in the "battle" between *virtus* and *libido* the strength of the former lies in the "mortification" represented by negation or self-denial; but since original sin has weakened man's abilities to resist the seductive importunities of his lower nature, even the mythographers were realistic enough to admit that *in hac pugna est victoria rara.*[18]

III

Against this background Shakespeare achieves a remarkably rich texture of verbal and philosophical wit in his treatment of the episode in *Venus and Adonis,* chiefly by an amusing reversal of the point of view of his source. When Ovid's account is retold by its protagonist for her own purposes[19] a wealth of ambiguity and irony is made possible. Thus Venus holds out as a desirable analogy to Adonis' present situation an affair which the reader could be expected to recognize as emblematic of the psychological state in which excess of passion leads to irrational turpitude; and illustrates the end she desires with a story which exemplified the seduction of the spirit into *amor sui* by the felicity of temporal prosperity. The dramatic virtue in permitting Venus to recount the tale herself has been ignored by critics of *Venus and Adonis.* As self-revelation the passage is similar in effect to the revealing eye of the sun in the fable, and involves about the same ludicrous results. The attitude capable of applying this incident to these purposes is equally capable of citing the efficacy

of "coy disdaine" as an argument against coyness,[20] and of concluding a rather self-flattering picture of its own power with the moral admonition "brag not of thy might."[21] Venus is just not on speaking terms with the values commonly thought to reside in the tale; she cannot see why Adonis should not be delighted to accept the rewards granted Mars, who "begd for that which thou vnaskd shalt haue."[22] The substitution of her attitude simply turns the accepted moral order upside down.

Hence themes of the traditional gloss appear in a humorously reversed form in her rendition. While Adonis' passivity in the dramatic context suggests the "self-denial" characteristic of spiritual *virtus*—resistance to the importunities of lust—, Venus thinks this unmanly. She seeks to convert him by telling him of Mars. What the Fulgentian tradition labeled as "corruption" reappears as "civilizing" from a kind of "churlish" barbarism to a courtly sophistication. The dissolution of "manliness" into "effeminacy" is described as the acquisition of the "graces" of the romantic lover[23]— qualities more proper to a "man" in Venus' eyes. In this conversion Mars puts off his armor, in an image of re-dedication;[24] his "tent" becomes the "bed" of Venus.[25]

Imagery of bondage recurs in a similarly obverted form, even though Venus excludes Vulcan's net from her account. Mars, who was "shamefully fettered" in the bonds of carnal concupiscence, does not appear to suffer an undesirable fate as her "captiue," though Venus makes him her "slaue," "Leading him prisoner in a red rose chaine."[26] Her images of governance support and recommend, in an appropriately charming way, the upside-down order of sin in which the spirit is "led by" the flesh.

We are not meant to forget, however, that Venus' account is essentially a romantic glorification of man's fall. Spiritual "effeminacy," typified here by the ludicrous picture of a "courtly" Mars, occurs when, under the instruction of corrupt instincts, the spirit makes what Chaucer by a bawdy pun described as the "queynte" things of the world the object of devotion. To hang one's "launce" on Venus' "Altar"[27] is to dedicate *virtus* to the flesh—to accept the philosophy proposed by the goddess. Venus glorifies *adulterium* (the term itself was frequently used to denote sin in general) by eliminating the Ovidian—and more obviously the Christian—reward of such action. It is the pleasure of the moment, without reference to future results, which is of supreme importance to her: the Epicurean philosophy later urged in "Take aduantage on presented ioy" (st. 68) and vividly illustrated in her concentration on the immediate joys presented.

Verbal ironies, finally, reflect the philosophical point at issue, especially when Venus who, like a wrestler, has thrown her weaker opponent and pinned him as with an eagle's talons, concludes,

> Oh be not proud, nor brag not of thy might,
> For maistring her that foyld the god of fight.

In any sense, the verb *foil* cannot be completely complimentary to Venus' concept of love. For despite the apparently intended sense of "overcome"[28] or "baffle,"[29] the context of physical struggle suggests victory in actual combat between warriors. Appropriate to the situation, another meaning of *foil* refers to throwing down an opponent in wrestling,[30] a sense supported by the verb *master*.[31]

The image of wrestling, moreover, is a commonplace alternative for that of the "internal warfare" and is thus applicable throughout this early section of *Venus and Adonis*. "Those that be true Christians," according to a popular manual, "do always wrestle with vices, and fight with concupiscence and lust; they endeavor to bridle wicked affections."[32] In this "wrestling" Venus "foyld" Mars, according to the mythographers. If Venus is thought of, after the mythographic tradition, as representing the "animal" motions of the flesh (cp. n. 12, above), we may find appropriate also the sense of *foil* which expresses the animal act of trampling underfoot,[33] while *master* may also apply technically to the control of animals.[34] These senses perhaps prefigure the implications of the Courser-Jennet episode, but a final sense of *foil* is immediately recommended by the force of convention: i. e. to "foul, defile, pollute."[35] A more particularized sense is cited by the NED as "to dishonor; *esp.* to deflower (a woman), to violate (chastity)."[36] Albeit unwittingly, Venus is therefore made to echo the Fulgentian moral, *virtus conrupta libidine,* when she concludes that she "foyld the god of fight."

IV

Though Venus may be said to parody the moralized version of her affair with Mars, even her point of view presents it as a conflict. I do not suppose that Shakespeare intends us to *choose between* Venus and a sober Fulgentius. We are meant, rather, to delight in the playful ironies and wit which result from the interplay of two opposed attitudes. But in any case the conflict remains—the battle of attitudes which informs the entire poem. The *militia* is, of course, an Ovidian trope, but Shakespeare's Ovid was a renaissance Ovid and *Venus and Adonis* is a renaissance poem. *What* Shakespeare is treating and *how* he treats it should not be confused. What he deals with in *Venus and Adonis* is the psychomachic "interior warfare" between the two contradictory aspects of human nature defined and elaborated in a thousand ways by his contemporaries. The relationship of the antagonists could be described by a number of metaphors, none of which, because of traditional

reiteration, was particularly original. Hence Shakespeare can reflect his narrative context with the commonplace analogy of the horse-and-rider,[37] or as a *militia amoris* which may be contested "in the verie lists of loue" anatomically defined in st. 100. He chooses to vary the trope with the homiletic image of "wrestling" in the early part of the poem, and we are supposed to appreciate the way he manipulates the doctrinal commonplace for humorous effects. Indeed we miss out on the fun if, unaware of such moral values in Elizabethan idiom, we do not recognize this interpenetration of meanings.

Louis R. Zocca follows the view of Douglas Bush when he finds that mythological poetry towards the end of the sixteenth century "shook off the bonds of a too strict morality, thus freeing the Ovidian myths of their layer of moralization."[38] This liberation conveniently frees Shakespeare and Marlowe from the contamination of moral ideas, and the idea has been used to support the reduction of these poets to the level of naive eroticism. Such conventions as those illustrated in the moralizations of the myth of Venus and Mars, however, do not necessarily produce sermons. In our own solemnity we tend to forget the delights of irony. Without the mythographic tradition, indeed, much of the sophisticated "Ovidian" wit and polish Meres (and how, we may well ask, did Meres read *his* Ovid?) recognized in Shakespeare's mythological narrative would be lost, the playful ambiguities darkened by a shallow literalism. Golding, Spenser, Shakespeare—each makes use of "Christianized" mythology to suit his own degree of moral fervor. Shakespeare, I submit, strove to emulate the clever and delightful ironies which he found in the Ovid of his day—and considered this spirit, too, something to be imitated from his "source."

Notes

1. J. A. K. Thomson, *Shakespeare and the Classics* (London, 1952), p. 42.

2. T. W. Baldwin, *On the Literary Genetics of Shakspere's Poems & Sonnets* (Urbana, Ill., 1950), p. 15.

3. Three Classical renditions of the fable are of major importance: Homer's *Odyssey* VIII, 266 ff., retold by Ovid in *Ars Amatoria* II, 561 ff. and reduced to briefer form in *Met.* IV, 171 ff. "Notum pueris adulterium Martis cum Venere," said a late mythographer, Francisco Pomey, in his *Pantheum Mythicum* (7th edn., Ultrajecti, 1717), p. 66.

4. Representative accounts of the fable may be found in the following works: Fulgentius, *Mythologiarum,* ed. A. van Staveren in *Auctores Mythographi Latini* (Amstelaed, 1742), pp. 682-3; Giovanni del Virgilio, *Allegoriae Librorum Ovidii Metamorphoseos,* ed. Fausto Ghisalberti in *Il Giornale Dantesco* XXXIV (1933), p. 55; Arnulf d'Orléans,

Allegoriae super Ovidii Metamorphosin, ed. Ghis-alberti in *Arnolfo d'Orléans, un cultore di Ovidio nel secolo XII* (Milano, Ulruo Hoepli, 1932), p. 210; Petrus Berchorius [Pierre Bersuire], *Metamorphosis Ouidiana Moraliter . . . explanata* [Paris, 1515], fol. xliiʳ; Boccaccio, *Genealogiae Deorum* (Venice, 1494), fol. 68ʳ; Natalis Comes, *Mythologiae* (Francofvrti, 1596), pp. 152, 155, 1020; Abraham Fraunce, *The Third part of the Countesse of Pembrokes Yuychurch: Entituled, Amintas Dale* (London, 1592) [MLA Rotograph, no. 75], p. 39; George Sandys, *Ovids Metamorphosis Englished, Mythologiz'd and Represented in Figures* (London, 1640), p. 77. Though I depart from his view of Shakespeare's use of fable, the best single account of the mythological tradition is still that of Douglas Bush: *Mythology and the Renaissance Tradition in English Poetry* (Minneapolis, 1932).

5. Spenser, *Muiopotmos,* 372-3. See *Metamorphoses* IV, 188.

6. *Ars Amat.* II, 561-2; *Met.* IV, 171-2. Both versions begin with reference to the lovers' shame. Sandys (p. 77) explains that "morally adulteries are taxed by this fable: which how potent soever the offenders, though with never so much art contrived, and secrecy concealed, are at length discovered by the eye of the Sun, and exposed to shame and dishonour." Compare lines 111-2 of the *Epistle* to Golding's *Ovid,* ed. W. H. D. Rouse (London, 1904), p. 3.

7. *Mythologiarum,* II, 10 (pp. 682-3). Medieval glossators perpetuate Fulgentius: as, e.g., Arnulf d'Orléans (p. 210): "Mars Venerem dicitur amasse, quia aliquando vir fortis in venerem dissolvitur, id est virtus aliquando corrupta amplexu Veneris id est libidinis Sole teste apparet id est in veritatis iudicio rea esse cognoscitur. Que quidam virtus prava consuetudine illiciti fervoris quasi cathena constringitur." Cp. Virgilio (p. 55): "Nam per Martem et Venerem intellige homines virtuosos, qui tamen aliquando decipiuntur per luxuriam. Quia in hac pugna est victoria rara."

8. Fol. xliiʳ. Boccaccio's view is equally moralized: "Verum dum in contrarium feruor inordinatae concupiscentiae fertur: fit ut occultis uniculis .i. cogitationibus atque delectationibus lasciuis artius alligetur incipiens: a quibus effoeminatus solui non possit: & iam palam factis obscoenis commixtionibus a sapientibus rideatur" (fol. 68ʳ).

9. *Mythologiae,* p. 1020. Compare pp. 152, 155, 162.

10. Gal. v commences with one of numerous Pauline references to the paradox of freedom and (a spiritual) bondage to sin: "Stand fast therefore in the liberty wherewith Christ hath made us free, and be not *entangled again with the yoke of bondage.*"

11. "Manliness" in renaissance usage strongly suggests man's essential nature: his rationality. See, for example, *Romeo and Juliet* III, iii, 109 ff.: "Art thou a man? Thy form cries out thou art; / Thy tears are womanish; thy wild acts denote / The unreasonable fury of a beast. / Unseemly woman in a seeming man. . . ."

12. The phrase is Comes' (p. 394). He commences his discussion of the goddess by stating. "Nihil est autem Venus, quam occultum coitus desiderium a natura insitam ad procreandum" (p. 391), and calls her *cupiditas procreandi* (p. 392). In his *Imagines Deorum* (Lyons, 1581) Vincenzo Cartari refers to Venus as a "vim . . . ad procreandum" (p. 240).

13. The phrase here is that of Bernard Silvestris in the *Commentum Bernardi Silvestris super sex libros Eneidos Virgilii,* ed. Riedel (Gryphiswaldae, Abel, 1924), p. 9. I purposely simplify the complicated philosophical treatment Venus receives in the mythographic tradition.

14. Typical expressions of this commonplace may be found in Eph. vi, 10-18, the Baptismal Service where "knightly" action is enjoined, Erasmus' *Enchiridion militis Christiani*—a kind of "military" manual, and Spenser's *Letter* prefixed to the *Faerie Queene.*

15. Tropologically the Sun was thought to represent *mens et ratio hominis* (Virgilio, p. 55). Neptune, who finally released the lovers, represented those "waters" which quench lust's fires (as in Boccaccio, fol. 68ʳ): "Neptunus autem qui solus pro captiuis interponitur: lasciuo feruori contrarius effectus est: quo uti ab aquae ignis sic ignominiosus amor extinguitur: & dum uelit qui patitur cathenata . . . relaxatur." Compare *Venus and Adonis,* line 94.

16. A similar basis for paradox exists in the other oppositions: manliness and effeminacy, strength and weakness, freedom and bondage.

17. The opposition is clearly drawn in the *Faerie Queene,* II, vi, 34.

18. Such a view of Venus and Mars occurs in the *F.Q.* III, xi, 44. In Chaucer's *Complaint of Mars,* Venus "brydeleth" the god, and "as a maistresse taught him his lessoun" Shakespeare's Venus also tries to "teach" Adonis a set of values, the implied metaphor surfacing in st. 68.

19. In Shakespeare's source Venus also tells Adonis a story of her past prowess, as a thinly-veiled threat showing the uselessness of resisting her. This is the fable of Atalanta and Hippomenes, which breaks the continuity of the "Venus and Adonis" in the *Metamorphoses.* It is introduced by the line

sic ait ac mediis interserit oscula verbis, literally translated by Shakespeare in line 47. (Shakespeare's Venus uses autobiography in an attempt to exact a "kisse" from Adonis.) Christian commentaries of course conclude that the story illustrates points opposed to those Venus claims in the Ovid; so that when Shakespeare read his Ovid he had a model for the ironic technique he adopts in imitation. Even without Christian coloring, it is quite obvious that Ovid structured the incident to make use of dramatic irony.

20. The three stanzas are introduced by the line "'Tis but a kisse I beg, why art thou coy?" Venus' "coy disdaine" is later parodied by the Jennet (st. 52).

21. Here, as in other spots in the poem, the reader is supposed to visualize the situation. In the fifth stanza "desire doth lend her force / Courageously to pluck him from his horse"; in the sixth she holds him under her arm; in the seventh "Backward she thrust him, as she would be thrust, / And govern'd him in strength, though not in lust." Here she warns him not to brag "For maistring her."

22. Ambiguity as to whether "vnaskd" modifies *which* or *thou* adds to the humor of her statement.

23. Mars' courtly achievements strongly suggest the qualities generally ascribed to the "Italianate" Englishman, who never fares well in Shakespeare's works. The characteristics of the romantic lover are later significantly parodied; see R. P. Miller, "Venus, Adonis, and the Horses," *ELH* XIX (1952), pp. 251-255.

24. The "armor" of Mars is intended to suggests that of the Christian knight described in Rom. xiii, 12; 2 Cor. vi, 7; Eph. vi,11-17; etc. Mars has thus figuratively given up the "shield of *faith,*" the "helmet of salvation" (*hope*), and the "launce" of the Spirit (*charity*), to the "Altars" of Venus.

25. The image of the "bed" suggests the *torum* in which Ovid's Venus tells the tale of Atalanta (*Met.* X, 556). The bed is coincidentally a Scriptural image for the seat of perfect marriage, as the *thalamus* of Cant. iii, 1. The "bed" Venus offers is, of course, an obverse figure. The conversion of the "tent" (symbolic of the "warfare" against the desires of the flesh) to Venus' "bed" (the battleground of fleshly warfare against the spirit) illustrates Shakespeare's precise use of significant imagery.

26. The source of this figure is not Ronsard but a commonplace tradition expressed by Boethius as the *rosea catena* of temporal delights (*de consolatione Philosophiae* III, met. x, 1-3.) See Virgil Whitaker, *Shakespeare's Use of Learning* (San Marino, Calif., 1953), p. 118. Conventional defini-

tion of Venus' "bondage" is conveniently gathered by Baldwin (p. 15). The metaphor, however, is a virtual platitude in the tradition of Christian literature. "Wicked wights," says Spenser, "knit themselves in *Venus* shamefull chaine" (*F. Q.* I, ii, 4). In Prudentius' *Psychomachia* Luxuria binds the virtues in chains of flowers (lines 351-7). Alexander Ross, in his *Mystagogvs Poeticvs* (2nd edn., London, 1648), p. 408, says of Venus that as she "was painted with fetters at her feet, so no men are tyed with such strong fetters, as they who are held with the fetters of loue." Compare Francis Thynne, *Emblemes and Epigrames,* ed. F. J. Furnivall (*EETSOS* vol. LXIV, London, 1876), pp. 12, 85.

27. Here as elsewhere Venus' sexual version (in this case of dedication) of an opposite ideal, is apparent. See E. Partridge, *Shakespeare's Bawdy* (New York, 1948), p. 138.

28. *NED, s.v. Foil,* v[1], 4, generalized. Cp. *Foil,* sb[2], 2: and cf. *3 Hen. VI,* V. iv, 42; *Troilus and Cressida* I, iii, 372.

29. NED, *s. v. Foil,* v[1], 5.

30. NED, *s. v. Foil,* v[1], 4 *spec.* Wrestling. Cp. *Foil,* sb[2], 1: and cf. *As You Like It* I, i, 135; I, ii, 199; II, ii, 14.

31. NED, *s. v. Master,* v[1], 1.

32. John Woolton, *The Christian Manual; or, Of the Life and Manners of True Christians* (1576) (Parker Society edn., Cambridge, 1851), p. 10. In his *Sermons* (ed. G. E. Corrie for the Parker Society, Cambridge, 1844) Bp. Hugh Latimer states that "all those which be in the kingdom of God must wrestle, strive, and fight with the devil" (p. 361) and "we must wrestle with sin" (p. 549). See Eph. vi, 12 and its context.

33. NED, *s. v. Foil,* v[1], 1, 2; sb[3]: "What is trampled underfoot; hence, Manure, dung." Cf. *F. Q.* V, xi, 33, line 8. Cp. *Venus and Adonis,* lines 311-2. The concept of the *homo animalis* is discussed in "Venus, Adonis, and the Horses," pp. 259 ff.

34. NED *s. v. Master,* v[1], 2. Adonis, in line 319, in his Courser's "testie maister," and in line 914 the "maister" of his hounds. The flesh is commonly symbolized by the horse: hence the frequent image of "bridling."

35. NED, *s. v. Foil,* v[1], 6.

36. NED, *s. v. Foil,* v[1], 7. Partridge does not record this usage.

37. Analyzed in detail in "Venus, Adonis, and the Horses." The humorous quality of *Venus and Adonis* has been emphasized by Rufus Putney, *"Venus Agonistes,"* Univ. of Colorado Studies, Series in Lang. and Lit., No. 4 (1953), pp. 52-66.

38. *Elizabethan Narrative Poetry* (New Brunswick, 1950), p. 230.

W. R. Streitberger (essay date summer 1975)

SOURCE: Streitberger, W. R. "Ideal Conduct in *Venus and Adonis.*" *Shakespeare Quarterly* 26, no. 3 (summer 1975): 285-91.

[*In the following essay, Streitberger stresses the moral themes of* Venus and Adonis, *and views Adonis as the embodiment of the young nobleman faced with a dilemma between duty and the temptation to neglect responsibility.*]

Although the sonnets in *The Passionate Pilgrim* (IV, VI, IX, XI) represent, as T. W. Baldwin observed, "a kind of first handling of the Venus and Adonis story, out of which the poem of *Venus and Adonis* grew,"[1] Don Cameron Allen has pointed out that the narrative poem takes an entirely different position. The substitution of the courser and jennet episode for the legend of Atalanta and Hippomenes indicates that Shakespeare's plan is as different from Ovid's "as his Venus—a forty-year-old countess with a taste for Chapel Royal altos—is. . . ." Professor Allen notes that the imagery associated with Venus, the "emptie eagle" given to "vulture" thoughts, points to her as the hunter, and that the imagery associated with Adonis, the bird "tangled" in Venus' "net," the deer in Venus' "parke," points to him as her prey. He goes on to connect the hare imagery with Venus, noting that she was often represented accompanied by a hare as the symbol of generative love, and traces the notion of love as a hunt from its classical origins to Shakespeare's Orsino who could "hunt the hart." Equating Venus' attempt to persuade Adonis to hunt the hare with her attempt to seduce him, Professor Allen establishes that Adonis, in refusing to be won by her arguments, rejects the love hunt and embraces the fierce animal hunt. Thus, the poem can be partially explained in terms of a timeless hunt: "Venus, the amorous Amazon . . . hunts with her strong passions; the hunted Adonis lives to hunt the boar; and the boar is death, the eternal hunter."[2]

While helping to resolve many of the troubling aspects of the poem, the interpretation has specific limitations. First, Venus attempts to persuade Adonis to hunt, not only the hare, but also the fox and the deer, and Professor Allen attaches no more than a general significance to the hunting of these animals. Further, no explanation of Venus' extreme reaction to Adonis' death is provided. Finally, the significance of Adonis' youth and the fact that he is too young for love is not explained. Obviously, if Adonis is too young to be tempted by love, identifying the encouragement to hunt easy animals

solely with the love hunt does not entirely clarify the situation. There is a great deal more to the poem than Adonis' rejection of Venus—too much, as Allen admits, to be reconciled under the theme of the timeless hunt alone. Shakespeare has synthesized his material from at least three sources, and the poem contains several seemingly disparate episodes. Unless we are willing to give the poem up as defective, the key to a unified interpretation must lie in a theme which satisfactorily relates all of its elements.

A consideration of the two major episodes—the seduction attempt and the hunt—and the background for them indicates that, while in general the action moves in terms of a timeless hunt, on a more specific level the concern in the poem is centered on conduct which leads to a moral, healthy, and heroic life. Adonis acts as the adolescent in training who concerns himself with proper preparation which will lead him to the ideal of noble manhood. Venus presents the temptations—not merely to lust, but to neglect of duty—to succumb to the easy pleasures and endeavors of life, and exhibits in her actions the results of giving in to those temptations. The major opposition in the poem develops between an ideal of conduct and action and the approximation of that ideal which leads to an unheroic existence. Success in pursuing proper training for manhood opens the way not only for a heroic life but also for a moral and healthy one.

Critics in the past have tended to assume that, as a serious work, the poem is defective.[3] More recent reviewers have attempted to circumvent the charge of defectiveness by suggestions that the poem is humorous or that Shakespeare is satirizing various conventions.[4] To deny that the poem is humorous or satirical is not to deny that there are elements of humor or satire in it. Indeed, Professor Allen observes that under the fabric of the epyllion "one hears the faint murmur of an inverted pastourelle, [and] of a mythological satire."[5]

The problems that critics have faced in connection with this poem are similar in certain respects to those encountered in *The Two Gentlemen of Verona*. Both works come fairly close together in Shakespeare's early period; both works have long been considered defective; and both, at times, have been defended against the charges of defectiveness by suggestions that Shakespeare intended to satirize the conventions he employed. "When *The Two Gentlemen of Verona* is performed nowadays the surrender of Sylvia is cut. . . . We leave it out because that special convention which Shakespeare was trying to satirize no longer exists and therefore we do not understand the passage."[6] It has also been argued that in *Venus and Adonis* Shakespeare changed Ovid's legend for essentially comic purposes and that "It is far better to possess a flawless trifle than a superannuated failure."[7] But these arguments do not take sufficient account of the backgrounds against which the works are set.

Shakespeare appears to have taken the conventions that he had to work with in his early period rather seriously and attempted to deal with them in terms of the problems they presented to the age. The evidence that critics have amassed concerning the male friendship convention, for example, indicates that Shakespeare worked out a perfectly orthodox solution for *The Two Gentlemen of Verona*. L. J. Mills has demonstrated that the concern in Sonnets 40, 41, 42, 133, and 144 is the resolution of tension between love and friendship.[8] R. M. Sargent has pointed out that tension between love and friendship developed through the clash of the medieval courtly ethic, which placed women at the center of the male/female relationship, and the classical idea of friendship as it was revived during the Renaissance.[9] The resolution of this tension, suggested by Sir Thomas Elyot and adapted by Lyly before Shakespeare, was that constancy in friendship held as the cornerstone of a personal morality was a necessary prerequisite for true love between the sexes.[10] From this perspective, the tension between clear moral duty dictated by the friendship convention and irresponsible passion centers in the character of Proteus in *The Two Gentlemen of Verona*. Once one is aware of the background it becomes clear that the play, far from being a satire, is a perfectly orthodox handling of the theme (whether or not it is good theater is another question). Similarly, in *Venus and Adonis* a tension centers in Adonis that we are unable to appreciate without an understanding of the background against which the poem is set.

The framework of the poem is certainly the erotic, mythological narrative in the vein of Lodge's *Scylla's Metamorphoses*. Using ornate imagery and the erotic tone of the genre, Shakespeare, as indicated by the dedication, is making a bid for acceptance into the sophisticated literary world. The audience here could be counted on to be receptive to a range of sophisticated allusions, and the prefatory couplet should suggest that we be careful in taking the poem too lightly:

> Vilia miretur vulgus: mihi flavus Apollo
> Pocula Castalia plena ministret aqua.[11]

Shakespeare drew on three sources from Ovid's *Metamorphoses* for the poem. In the story of Venus and Adonis (*Met.* X, 585-651; 826-63),[12] Ovid describes Venus' love for Adonis. She pleads with him to give up the hunt of the boar and the lion and relates the story of Atalanta and Hippomenes, who were changed into lions for defiling the garden of Cybele with their love-making. After Venus leaves him, Adonis is fatally wounded while hunting the boar. Adonis in this story exhibits none of the reluctance of Shakespeare's protagonist. For this dimension Shakespeare drew on

two other Ovidian sources. He takes Venus' forwardness, Adonis' blush (ll. 49-50; 76-78), the debate over the kiss (ll. 84-89; 115-28), the embrace (ll. 52-72; 225-30), and Adonis' reluctance (ll. 379; 710) from the story of Salmacis and Hermaphroditus (*Met.* IV, 347-481).[13] The third source is the story of Echo and Narcissus (*Met.* III, 427-542; 635-42), from which Shakespeare draws the accusation of self-love which Venus uses as an argument in her attempt to seduce Adonis (ll. 157-62). In addition there are suggestions throughout of other sources in the Ovidian corpus.[14]

If Shakespeare was merely looking for erotic material he could certainly have gotten enough from the Venus and Adonis story. The fact that he chose two other sources from Ovid for a reluctant Adonis indicates that he was working toward other ends. It does not follow, however, that those ends were necessarily humorous. The story of Echo and Narcissus might provide humor enough, and the question of why Shakespeare chose the story of Venus and Adonis arises. Other than providing a structure for the poem, the story provides the warning of Venus against the hunting of fierce animals and, an element overlooked by commentators, Adonis' insistence that he not be swayed from his purpose: ". . . manhood by admonishment restreyned could not bee" (*Met.* X, 832).[15] A consideration of the courser and jennet episode, the virtues considered important in a young nobleman, and Venus' attempt to persuade Adonis to hunt the fox, deer, and rabbit will show that there is a real dramatic situation in the poem and that Venus is, in fact, tempting Adonis.

R. P. Miller takes the courser and jennet episode in the poem to be an early ironic treatment of the romantic courtship theme.[16] Perhaps there is the dimension of irony here, but more obviously and more importantly in light of Professor Allen's suggestions and the Ovidian source it is a double-edged *exemplum*. Venus points to the situation as an allegory, proof that lust is natural, and attempts to entice Adonis. As Miller notes, she praises the courser's rebellion in crushing the bit with his teeth, "Controlling what he was controlled with" (l. 270). At this point, however, the narrator helps us with the interpretation of the line. He observes that the horse is a noble creature, but lacks "a proud rider on so proud a back" (l. 300). Professor Allen has perceptively drawn the parallel between this horse and Plato's passionate horse in the *Phaedrus*, but concludes that Venus' lesson is blunted by Shakespeare's description of the mare as a "breeding jennet."[17] This description of the horse in Plato, however, is part of his description of the soul, composed of the passionate and docile horses and the charioteer.[18] Shakespeare's sophisticated readers could hardly have missed seeing the reverse of Venus' allegory—the bit and rider as morality and reason abandoned for passion. Even if his readers did not get the point from reading Plato, they could have gotten it in a more complete form in Sir Thomas Elyot's *The Book Named The Governor*. If Shakespeare was familiar enough with *The Governor* to use it as a source for *The Two Gentlemen of Verona*, it seems reasonable to suppose that he was familiar enough with the rest of the work to use it as a background for *Venus and Adonis*, especially since the two works come so close together in Shakespeare's early period.

In Book III of *The Governor*, Elyot provides a discussion of the virtues that must be fostered in a young nobleman in order to produce the necessary constancy and stability which will make him a fit governor. He notes that in the training of youth "it ought to be well considered that the cement wherewith the stones be laid be firm and well binding. . . . Semblably, that man which in childhood is brought up in sundry virtues . . . be not induced to be alway [sic] constant and stable, so that he move not for any affection, grief or displeasure, all his virtues will shortly decay."[19] In Book I, Elyot sets out in detail the kind of cement the stones of the nobleman's personality ought to be laid with in order that he not swerve from his duty. He points out that in infancy only virtuous women should attend the child and that no wanton words should be spoken in front of him. He counters the charge that an infant does not know good from evil by asserting that "in the brains and hearts of children, which be members spiritual, whiles they be tender and the little slips of reason begin in them to burgeon, there may hap by evil custom some pestiferous dew of vice to pierce the said members and infect and corrupt the soft and tender buds."[20] The basic principle of Elyot's notion of virtue, Platonic in origin, is that virtue exists as a potential in the soul, but that it must be nourished and practiced so that, finally, virtuous action will follow from a knowledge of the right.[21] From the foregoing account it is clear that despite the fact that Adonis is too young for love—"Measure my strangeness with my unripe years (l. 524)"—he is still in moral danger. Indeed, Elyot points out that the chief enemy of virtue throughout man's life is lust: "nothing so sharply assaileth a man's mind as doth carnal affection, called (by the followers thereof) love."[22] Adonis is old enough to recognize Venus as a threat, and responds to her procreation argument in terms suggestive of Elyot: "Call it not love, for Love to heaven is fled, / Since sweating Lust on earth usurp'd his name" (ll. 793-94).

Throughout the debate Adonis acts as an ideal Renaissance schoolboy who has learned his lesson well. Indeed, he is in the second of the seven ages of man, noted by Jaques in *As You Like It* (II. vii. 143-66). He rejects Venus' procreation argument in terms reminiscent of the grammar school debate. T. W. Baldwin observes that Erasmus recommends the subject as good for the development of rhetorical technique, and that it was quite common for schoolboys to debate the pros and cons of procreation via marriage.[23] In the Sonnets Shakespeare took seriously the idea of gaining immortality through procreation, but that project belongs to men in the third stage of development, not the second to which Adonis belongs.[24] He has learned his lessons well and reproves Venus with an effective grammar school counter:

> What have you urg'd that I cannot reprove?
> The path is smooth that leadeth on to danger.
> I hate not love, but your device in love,
> That lends embracements unto every stranger.
> You do it for increase: O strange excuse,
> When reason is the bawd to lust's abuse!
>
> (ll. 787-92)

Adonis, although in moral danger according to Elyot's theory, is too young to be actually tempted to incontinence in pleasure. The temptation that Venus presents is to neglect of duty. She attempts to persuade him to give up the hunt of the boar for the rabbit, the fox, and the deer. Elyot maintains that hunting in the manner of the ancients is a "laudable exercise." He gives the chief animals that the ancients hunted as the lion, leopard, wild swine, and bear, and claims that "therein is the very imitation of battle, for not only it doth show the courage and strength as well of the horse as of him that rideth . . . but also it increaseth in them both agility and quickness, also sleight and policy."[25] After praising several famous Classical hunters, Elyot goes on to clarify why it is that Adonis must reject Venus' invitation to hunt these timid animals. Elyot states that "I dispraise not the hunting of the fox with running hounds, but it is not to be compared to the other hunting in commodity of exercise. . . . Hunting of the hare with greyhounds is a right good solace for men that be studious, of them to whom nature hath not given personage or courage apt for the wars. And also for gentlewomen. . . . Killing of deer with bows or greyhounds serveth well for the pot. . . . But it containeth therein no commendable solace or exercise, in comparison to the other forms of hunting."[26]

Quite clearly Venus attempts to persuade Adonis to reject everything that a young noble must train for. But Adonis is a good student and a firm and constant young man on his way not only to a noble life but to a healthy one. Adam in *As You Like It*, despite his almost fourscore years, claims that

> . . . in my youth I never did apply
> Hot and rebellious liquors in my blood,
> Nor did not with unbashful forehead woo
> The means of weakness and debility;
> Therefore my age is as a lusty winter.
>
> (II. iii. 48-52)

Of course, Adam does not refer to a nobleman's training, he is merely a servant; but if proper training and discipline in youth leads to a healthy life for a servant it will accomplish at least the same for a nobleman.

Venus' reaction to Adonis' death graphically exemplifies the inconstant and unstable behavior that is generated by succumbing to passion and the easy pleasures of life. In contrast to Elyot's contention that a nobleman must be constant in the face of "affection, grief, or displeasure," Venus shifts from groundless jubilant hope to excessive grief and despair. Of course, it is a woman's grief and this must be taken into account. But Elyot's suggestion that the easy hunt of the hare is fit sport for a gentlewoman or for men who do not have courage apt for war paves the way for a comparison of the youth who neglects his training to Venus. She vividly portrays the passions to which Adonis would be subject in the event that be responded to her arguments and neglected his training and purpose.

I conclude, then, that the courser and jennet episode is a double-edged *exemplum,* that Venus presents a moral threat to Adonis despite the fact that he is too young for love, that her attempt to persuade him from the noble to the easy hunt would destroy his virtues and make him an unfit gentleman, and that the striking similarities between Elyot's and Shakespeare's treatments of the material point to the fact that the seduction attempt is of real dramatic interest and is not merely an example of Shakespeare playing with literary conventions. Venus' temptations to neglect of duty are not merely part of an *argumentum* which sets her and Adonis off as representatives of particular qualities. Tension between clear duty and the temptation to neglect it centers in Adonis and is, like the tension in Proteus of *Two Gentlemen,* unrecognizable without an awareness of the background against which the work is set.

Professor Allen speculates that Shakespeare was fascinated "as young men often are, by innocent and unmerited death in youth."[27] Perhaps he was; but Adonis in rejecting Venus embraces constancy to duty, the only choice proper to a young nobleman. It seems relevant here to recall that the poem is dedicated by a struggling young artist, who claims in that dedication to embrace his own form of constancy to duty, to a promising young nobleman who, it is hoped, will answer "the world's hopeful expectations." And I suspect that the irony and poignancy of the death of a promising youth in the pursuit of duty would have been appealing to both men at this point in their careers. Shakespeare has succeeded admirably with this poem. For, while he manages to retain the erotic tone of the genre, he presents on another level an essentially moral struggle, one which his sophisticated readers were not likely to miss.

Notes

1. T. W. Baldwin, *On the Literary Genetics of Shakespeare's Poems and Sonnets* (Urbana: Univ. of Illinois Press, 1950), p. 44.

Frontispiece to a 1714 edition of Venus and Adonis.

2. D. C. Allen, "On *Venus and Adonis,*" in *Elizabethan and Jacobean Studies in Honour of F. P. Wilson,* ed. H. Davis and H. Gardner (Oxford: Oxford Univ. Press, 1959), pp. 100-105.

3. Hazlitt's assessment is that the poems "appear to us like a couple of ice-houses. They are about as hard, as glittering, and as cold. The author seems all the time to be thinking of his verses, and not of his subject,—not of what his characters would feel, but of what he shall say; and as it must happen in all such cases, he always puts into their mouths those things which they would be the last to think of, and which it shews the greatest ingenuity in him to find out. . . . The images, which are often striking, are generally applied to things which they are the least like: so that they do not blend with the poem, but seem stuck upon it." *Collected Works,* ed. A. R. Waller and A. Glover (London: J. M. Dent, 1902), I, 358-59. See also Hyder Rollins, *New Variorum, Poems,* pp. 390-405; 447-523.

4. R. Putney, *"Venus and Adonis:* Amour with Humor," *PQ,* [*Philological Quaterly*] 20 (1941), 533-48, suggests that Shakespeare omits the description of the death of Adonis and focuses on Venus' reactions for humorous purposes: "She merely finds the body. Thus a scene potentially painful is avoided. Then Venus' grief spurs her to such heights of absurdity that we are first incredulous, then amused." R. P. Miller, *"Venus and Adonis* and the Horses," *ELH,* 19 (1952), 249-64, takes the courser and jennet episode as an ironic treatment of the romantic courtship theme.

5. Allen, p. 101.

6. H. T. Price, "Shakespeare as a Critic," *PQ,* 20 (1941), 390-99.

7. Putney, p. 548.

8. L. J. Mills, *One Soul in Bodies Twain* (Bloomington: Indiana Univ. Press, 1937), pp. 239-43.

9. Cicero claimed that "friendship is nothing else than an accord in all things, human and divine, conjoined with mutual goodwill and affection, and I am inclined to think that, with the exception of wisdom, no better thing has been given to man by the immortal gods." *De Amicitia,* trans, W. Falconer (London: William Heinemann, 1923), pp. 130-31. See R. M. Sargent, "Sir Thomas Elyot and the Integrity of *The Two Gentlemen of Verona,"* *PMLA,* 65 (1950), 1166.

10. This is suggested in his story of Titus and Gisuppus from *The Governor.* L. J. Mills, p. 407, points out that there are many similarities between this story and *TGV* [*Two Gentlemen of Verona*] (see also Bullough, I, 203-17). Lyly adopted this resolution in two of his works. In *Endymion,* Eumenedes, having been counseled by Geron at the sacred fountain, elects the friendship of Endymion over his love for Semele. All works out for the best and he is reunited with Semele. There is little doubt that Shakespeare knew this play; he uses the subplot for his own subplot in *LLL* [*Love's Labour's Lost.*] Lyly's *Euphues: The Anatomy of Wit* deals with a variation of the theme. Euphues learns about the convention the hard way. He entices Philautus' love away only to be betrayed by her for another.

11. All quotations from Shakespeare are from *The Complete Plays and Poems of William Shakespeare,* ed. W. A. Neilson and C. J. Hill (Cambridge, Mass.: Houghton Mifflin, 1942).

12. The line references are to Golding's translation. See Geoffrey Bullough, *Narrative and Dramatic Sources of Shakespeare* (London: Routledge and Kegan Paul, 1957), I, 166-76, for the text and Latin line equivalents.

13. Allen, pp. 106-7, suggests that Adonis is a remaking of Hippolytus.

14. See Bullough, I, 161-65.

15. Bullough, I, 168.

16. Miller, op. cit. in footnote 4.

17. Allen, p. 108.

18. "Now when the charioteer sees the vision of his Love and his whole soul is warmed throughout by the sight and he is filled with the itchings and prickings of desire, the obedient horse, giving in then as always to the bridle of shame, restrains himself from springing on the loved one; but the other horse pays no attention to the driver's goad or whip, but struggles with uncontrolled leaps, and doing violence to his master and teammate, forces them to approach the beautiful and speak of carnal love" (*Plaedrus,* 254a).

19. Sir Thomas Elyot, *The Book named the Governor,* ed. S. E. Lehmberg (London: J. M. Dent, 1963), pp. 205-6.

20. Elyot, p. 16.

21. John M. Major, *Sir Thomas Elyot and Renaissance Humanism* (Lincoln: Univ. of Nebraska Press, 1964), pp. 241-69.

22. Elyot, p. 204.

23. T. W. Baldwin, op cit., pp. 183-86; and *Small Latin and Less Greek* (Urbana: Univ. of Illinois Press, 1944), II, 339-40.

24. Professor Allen observes that "hunting became first the proper preparation for knighthood and, later, for the forming of a gentleman" (p. 105). He goes on to point out that King Alfred was famous as a skilled hunter at twelve years of age. It seems then that Adonis should be taken at his word when he insists that he is too young for love and it should be clear that he belongs to the second, not the third, age of man.

25. Elyot, p. 66.

26. Elyot, p. 68. See also Allen, p. 105.

27. Allen, p. 111.

Richard Halpern (essay date 1997)

SOURCE: Halpern, Richard. "'Pining Their Maws': Female Readers and the Erotic Ontology of the Text in Shakespeare's *Venus and Adonis.*" In Venus and Adonis: *Critical Essays,* edited by Philip C. Kolin, pp. 377-88. New York: Garland Publishing, 1997.

[*In the following essay, Halpern focuses on* Venus and Adonis *as a misogynist poem concerning female sexual frustration that places Venus in the symbolic role of the feminine reader.*]

The prefatory material to Shakespeare's *Venus and Adonis* is a study in disingenuousness and misdirection, beginning with the epigraph from Ovid's *Amores:* "Vilia miretur vulgus: mihi flavus Apollo / Pocula Castalia plena ministret aqua."[1] ("Let cheap things dazzle the crowd; may Apollo serve me cups filled with water from the Castalian spring"). In what is at once a change of genre and a change of vocation, these lines apparently signal Shakespeare's conversion from popular playwright to classicizing poet.[2] (In Sonnet 111 he would similarly disparage his playwrighting as "public means which public manners breeds.") But of course his abandonment of the stage was hardly voluntary; he turned to writing Ovidian verse in 1593 not because he heard a higher calling but because the theaters had been closed on account of the plague.[3] Moreover, *Venus and Adonis* bears more than a little resemblance to the plays that Shakespeare seems to be rejecting. The poem divides rather neatly into comic and tragic halves, and the former of these explores issues central to Shakespeare's early romantic comedies. By depicting the sexual fascination exerted by a beautiful and androgynous young man, Shakespeare draws on the appeal that the boy-actors added to his crossdressing plays. Indeed, Venus' frustration at the sight of a physically compelling but sexually unforthcoming youth foreshadows Olivia's plight when confronted with the disguised Viola in *Twelfth Night.* Despite the Apollonian pretensions of its epigraph, *Venus and Adonis* is neither nobler nor purer than Shakespeare's "cheap" plays.

The suggestion that Shakespeare wanted to abandon a popular literary form for a more elite one is reinforced by the poem's dedication to the Earl of Southampton. Having deserted the crowd, Shakespeare apparently tries to accommodate the cultural tastes of the aristocracy. Yet if *Venus and Adonis* was meant to perplex and annoy the vulgar, it failed miserably. The poem was, in fact, immensely popular, going through sixteen editions by 1640.[4] If the Earl of Southampton read it, so, according to contemporary accounts, did tapsters and courtesans.[5]

Shakespeare misidentifies not only the class composition of his audience but also its gender. The dedication to Southampton suggests an ideal or intended reader who is not only aristocratic but male. Recent critics of English Ovidian verse have had relatively little to say about the composition of its readership, but there seems to be a general if sometimes unstated assumption that such verse was written for, and read by, men. And there is good reason to think so. The humor of *Venus and Adonis,* like that of much Ovidian verse, is intensely and often viciously misogynist. Moreover, the English tradition of Ovidian poetry was fostered in the universities and the Inns of Court,[6] exclusively male bastions that cultivated a homosocial style.[7]

While plausible, however, the hypothesis of a predominantly male readership is contradicted by most of the early references to *Venus and Adonis.* Contemporaries tended to depict Shakespeare's poem as the reading matter of courtesans, lascivious nuns, adulterous housewives, or libidinous young girls.[8] In Thomas Middleton's *A Mad World My Masters* (1608), the jealous Harebrain confiscates his wife's copies of *Venus and Adonis* and *Hero and Leander,* declaring: "O, two luscious marrow-bone pies for a young married wife!" Conversely, in Thomas Heywood's *The Fair Maid of the Exchange* (1607), Bowdler tries to seduce Mall Berry by reading passages aloud from *Venus and Adonis.*[9] Young women were often imagined as hiding copies of the poem about their persons or rooms, and imbibing loose morals or illicit sexual pleasures from it. The most vivid portrait of the poem and its readers comes from John Davies' *Paper's Complaint* (1610-11):

> Another (ah Lord helpe) mee vilifies
> With Art of Love, and how to subtilize,
> Making lewd *Venus,* with eternall Lines,
> To tye *Adonis* to her loves designes:
> Fine wit is shew'n therein: but finer twere
> If not attired in such bawdy Geare.
> But be it as it will: the coyest Dames
> In private read it for their Closet-games:
> For, sooth to say, the Lines so draw them on,
> To the venerian speculation,
> That will they, nill they (if of flesh they bee)
> They will think of it, sith *loose* Thought is free.
>
> (ll. 47-58)[10]

Davies himself, like the women he imagines, is rather coy here, for the very vagueness of his language prompts "venerian speculations" in the reader. What exactly are "closet games," and what is the "it" about which female readers find themselves compelled to think (the poem? the sexual act?)? By implicating *Venus and Adonis* in an autoerotic, possibly masturbatory scene, Davies may tell us more about the way men fantasized female readers than he does about the fantasies of those readers; yet his lines reflect widely expressed anxieties about the effects of *Venus and Adonis* on women.

The reactions of Davies and other contemporary moralists and playwrights underscore the ironies of Shakespeare's epigraph from Ovid. While *Venus and Adonis* announces itself as an Apollonian exercise as pure as the Castalian spring, it is in fact a piece of soft-core pornography. While it distinguishes itself from "cheap" drama, moralists feared it would provoke the same kinds of lascivious desires and acts as did stage comedies. And while it poses as an offering to a male, aristocratic readership, it actually appealed to a broadly popular and (to judge by contemporary accounts) a largely if not predominantly female audience. As I shall argue, however, the ironies of the poem's reception are by no means accidental. *Venus and Adonis* is largely "about" the paradoxical status of Ovidian verse, which is at once a high literary form and a source of pornographic thrills. It is also intensely self-conscious about the effect of such verse on female readers.

John Davies' lines on *Venus and Adonis* open the way to a reading of the poem by suggesting parallels between female readers and Shakespeare's Venus. Just as Venus is captured or overcome by Adonis' beauty, so the female readers of Shakespeare's text are depicted as the victims of a somewhat involuntary eros generated by the poem itself: the poem's lines "*draw* them on / To the venerian speculation," so that "will they nill they . . . they will think of it." Moreover, the phrase "venerian speculation" indirectly compares the readers' imaginations and Venus' more literal "speculation" or act of looking at Adonis. Shakespeare's Venus is, in fact, a prisoner in the realm of speculation or vision. Overcome by Adonis' charms but frustrated by his lack of sexual response, she can do nothing more than gaze at him. "Be bold to play," she urges, "our sport is not in sight" (l. 124). Later, she invokes one of a series of interlocked Ovidian allusions by comparing Adonis in all but name to Pygmalion's statue:

> Fie, liveless picture, cold and senseless stone,
> Well-painted idol, image dull and dead,
> Statue contenting but the eye alone,
> Thing like a man, but of no woman bred!
>
> (ll. 211-214)

Adonis is, according to Ovid, the great-grandson of Pygmalion and the transformed statue. Venus' phrase "of no woman bred" may thus refer not only to Adonis' birth from the myrrh tree but to his more distant descent from a piece of female sculpture.

In John Marston's poem "The Metamorphosis of Pygmalion's Image," Pygmalion actually attempts to make love to his statue; he kisses it, rubs its breasts, and lies against it: "Yet viewing, touching, kissing (common favour,) / Could never satiate his loves ardencie."[11] This scene depicts the power of the artwork as its capacity to frustrate the viewer—to provoke, yet not fulfil, an erotic desire. Here the viewing subject is male, and when Pygmalion berates his uncooperative beloved as "relentless stone," it is clear that she simply materializes the spiritual qualities of the traditional Petrarchan mistress. Shakespeare's innovation with respect to the Pygmalion myth—as in *Venus and Adonis* generally—is to explore the "comic" possibilites of reversing this situation. Hence he places Venus in Pygmalion's place, lusting hopelessly after an unresponsive image—a situation which is highly ironic, since it was Venus who granted Pygmalion's prayers by transforming the statue into a real woman. Here she proves unable to effect a similar change, and the failure of her erotic power is thus matched by the failure of her metamorphic power. Ironically, the first half of Shakespeare's Ovidian poem depends on the denial of a wished-for "metamorphosis."

The interest of John Davies' analogy, with which I began, is that it is subject to reversal: that is to say, Venus' sexual frustration at the hands of an arousing but unresponsive artwork allegorizes the plight of the female reader of Shakespeare's erotic text. As a mildly pornographic poem, *Venus and Adonis* is meant to generate some kind of sexual thrill or tension. But since it is, in the end, only a book, the female reader, like Shakespeare's Venus, must content herself with "venerian speculation" alone. The theological gap that separates Venus from the merely mortal Adonis stands in for the ontological gap between the female reader and the empty imaginations generated by the poem.

The misogynist humor of *Venus and Adonis* centers on Shakespeare's debasing and slightly grotesque portrayal of female sexual desire. The resentment of every male sonneteer who ever wooed a lady in vain doubtless found satisfaction in the spectacle of Venus, the very embodiment of female sexual power, grovelling helplessly before a beautiful, androgynous man. But Shakespeare considerably deepens this troubling strain by extending it allegorically to his female readers. *Venus and Adonis,* in other words, is not only a poem about female sexual frustration; it is meant to produce such frustration. Just as Adonis' beauty arouses Venus but refuses to satisfy her, so Shakespeare's poem aims to arouse and frustrate the female reader. If Shakespeare was himself no Adonis, his art produced a similar though somewhat mediated effect.

This somewhat peculiar allegory of reading becomes unmistakably evident in the three stanzas that occupy the numerical center of the poem. Adonis has announced his intention to hunt the boar, whereupon Venus, overcome with both sexual frustration and fear for his life, faints, pulling Adonis on top of her as she falls:

> "The boar!" quoth she, whereat a sudden pale,
> Like lawn being spread upon the blushing rose,
> Usurps her cheek; she trembles at his tale,
> And on his neck her yoking arms she throws.
> 　　She sinketh down, still hanging by his neck,
> 　　He on her belly falls, she on her back.
>
> Now is she in the very lists of love,
> Her champion mounted for the hot encounter;
> All is imaginary she doth prove,
> He will not manage her, although he mount her,
> 　　That worse than Tantalus' is her annoy,
> 　　To clip Elysium and to lack her joy.
>
> Even so poor birds, deceiv'd with painted grapes,
> Do surfeit by the eye and pine the maw;
> Even so she languisheth in her mishaps,
> As those poor birds that helpless berries saw.

> The warm effects which she in him finds missing
> She seeks to kindle with continual kissing.
>
> But all in vain, good queen, it will not be!
>
>   (ll. 589-607)

Commentators on Shakespeare's poem have scrupulously avoided this tasteless passage. Venus' sexual pratfall, her vain attempts to coax Adonis into an erection by kissing him, and the crude sexual innuendo behind the figure of the useless grapes, are both socially offensive and erotically unappealing. Nevertheless, these lines offer a rather complex statement on the relation between eros and art, and manage in some sense to move through, if not quite beyond, their own misogyny.

At least three classical references, all of them more or less implicit, organize this passage: the Ovidian myths of Pygmalion and Narcissus, and Pliny's story of the competition between the painters Zeuxis and Parrhasios. All three, moreover, pertain to Shakespeare's extended allegory of the female reader of the erotic text. Pygmalion returns in the general problem of the appealing and unresponsive image, but in reversing the genders of Ovid's tale Shakespeare anatomically specifies the failure of the artwork: it lacks the phallus. The female reader who is somehow aroused by Shakespeare's poem will find herself in Venus' position, missing the member which, this poem assumes, provides the only possible satisfaction for female sexual desire.[12] I think it is safe to assume two things here. First, while Shakespeare meant his poem to be mildly titillating, he could not possibly belive that it would produce the kind of desperately intense desire experienced by Venus. Second, he surely knew that in the unlikely event that any female reader of the poem found it seriously arousing, she possessed the means to satisfy her own needs, and did not require the magical incarnation of an imaginary phallus. Nevertheless, the strategic absence of Adonis' erection locates the ontological lack structuring the literary artwork, and particularly the erotic artwork. The point is that literary imagination, without some sort of physical intervention, lacks the means to satisfy erotic desire.

This moral is reinforced by the allusion to Pliny's famous story of the Greek artist Zeuxis, whose painted grapes were so realistic that they fooled birds into trying to eat them. Zeuxis, who thinks he has thus won his competition with the painter Parrhasios, nevertheless finds that he has lost when he tries to part the veil covering Parrhasios' painting and discovers that the veil *is* the painting. The point of this little parable is missed, I think, if it is read as suggesting that the power of art rests solely in mimesis or illusion. For Pliny's tale suggests that the power of mimesis depends in turn on its ability to *frustrate* the viewer, to arouse a desire which it then does not fulfill. The force of art lies not its capac-ity to grant some kind of aesthetic satisfaction, but precisely in its capacity to deny satisfaction and thus assert its mastery over the viewer.

The tale of Zeuxis and Parrhasios offers a stunning riposte to a Platonic ontology of art. For Plato, the mimetic work of art is a mere simulacrum, an empty shadow of the real. The painting of a grape is an ontological nullity in comparison with a real grape, just as the shadows on the wall of the cave are nothing in comparison with the real objects that cast them. Pliny's tale also contains a moment that manifests the merely simulacral status of the image. But now to reveal the image's emptiness is precisely to confirm its power. Zeuxis' temporary victory occurs when his grapes prove unable to feed the birds; and Parrhasios' ultimate victory comes when he subjects Zeuxis in his turn to the emptiness of the image. Indeed, a kind of metamorphic inversion occurs between viewer and object, for the unsatisfied hunger of the birds indicates *their own emptiness* in relation to the image, which is complete unto itself. In the paradoxical ontology of the artwork, it is the real birds who are hollow and the painted grapes that are full.

In Shakespeare's poem, of course, it is not birds but women who "surfeit by the eye [but] pine the maw." Caught in the toils of the erotic text, the female reader is presumed to be afflicted with need, mastered by the mimetic power of a poem that renders her unsatisfied, empty. Earlier, the text seemed ontologically hollow in relation to the reader because it lacked the phallus. Now the text is full and the reader is empty. It is not the text but the reader—particularly the female reader—who represents the void of castration.

This ontological reversal is represented within the poem by the fact that Adonis, a mere mortal, triumphs over the divinity of Venus. I say "triumphs" because, paradoxically, in this episode of sexual failure or uninterest it is Venus, not Adonis, who appears more ridiculous. Adonis' presumed incapacity is balanced by his emotional self-containment, while Venus is made risible by the intensity of her unsatisfied need. Like the birds in Pliny, she is left absurdly pecking at a painted grape. Venus' "pining maw" has become the poem's primary signifier of lack.[13]

I remarked earlier that this episode provides an allegory of reading, but it is more accurate to say that its allegory concerns textual consumption. After all, the birds in Pliny do not "read" the grapes, they try to eat them. Earlier in the poem, Venus is likewise depicted as trying to "consume" Adonis sexually:

> Even as an empty eagle, sharp by fast,
> Tires with her beak on feathers, flesh, and bone,
> Shaking her wings, devouring all in haste,

Till either gorge be stuff'd, or prey be gone;
Even so she kiss'd his brow, his cheek, his chin,
And where she ends, she doth anew begin.

(ll. 55-60)

Venus as eagle is a frighteningly powerful magnification of Pliny's delicate birds. Her frenzied efforts at sexual consumption make her precisely into an image of the consumer of a pornographic text. Such a consumer does not "read" in the academic sense, insofar as this activity suggests some attention to the literary or figurative status of the text. Rather, pornography requires, at least at some level, a naive submission to the representational claims of the work. *Venus and Adonis* is, as I shall argue later, intensely aware of the mimetic claims of pornography. If Pliny's bird is to represent the frustrated consumer of the text, the text itself must aspire to the condition of a perfectly painted grape, a pure mimetic surface without textual depth.

While the passage I have have been interpreting is ostensibly organized by Pliny's tale of Zeuxis, it is also more subtly permeated by another, Ovidian, tale: that of Narcissus. Various commentators have noted the importance of Narcissus to Shakespeare's poem, but they invariably identify Adonis as the poem's Narcissus-figure. In so doing they are following Venus' lead, for she herself berates Adonis by comparing him to the self-absorbed youth:

Is thine own heart to thine own face affected?
Can thy right hand seize love upon thy left?
Then woo thyself, be of thyself rejected;
Steal thine own freedom, and complain on theft.
Narcissus so himself himself forsook,
And died to kiss his shadow in the brook.

(ll. 157-162)

One of the ironies of the passage I have been addressing is that Venus, not Adonis, now occupies the narcissistic position. For it is she who attempts to kiss a shadow or empty image in the reluctant Adonis. Like Narcissus, who wastes away while peering at his reflection, Venus "surfeits by the eye and pines the maw."

In one sense, Narcissus just rounds out the cast of mythological characters who unsuccessfully attempt to embrace an image. In his *De Pictura*, Leon Battista Alberti employs the myth of Narcissus to depict art's attempt to grasp the world of alluring surfaces: "Consequently, I used to tell my friends that the inventor of painting, according to the poets, was Narcissus, who was turned into a flower; for, as painting is the flower of all the arts, so the tale of Narcissus fits our purposes perfectly. What is painting but the art of embracing by means of art the surface of the pool? (*Quid est enim aliud pingere quam arte superficiem illam fontis amplecti?*)"[14] Like Pygmalion, who makes love to a statue, or the birds in Pliny who peck at the painted grapes, Narcissus falls prey to the power of the image and mistakes it for the real. He thus represents once more the ontological and sexual dilemmas of Shakespeare's imagined female reader.[15] Yet Narcissus diverts the problem of frustration into new directions. In the story of Pygmalion, the spectator's desire eventually wins out over the coldness of the image when the statue is metamorphosed, with Venus' aid, into a real woman. But the tale of Narcissus reverses this plot, for here the image remains intransigently empty, and it is the viewer himself who is therefore transformed by his own desire. In Golding's translation of Ovid (1567), Narcissus perfectly reverses the Pygmalion story by becoming like a piece of sculpture: "Astraughted like an Ymage made of Marble stone he lyes, / There gazing on his shadowe still with fixed staring eyes."[16] Narcissus' tale differs from that of Zeuxis' birds as well, for after his initial mistake, Narcissus comes to understand that what he loves is his own reflection. But he is no less captured for having recognized the emptiness of the image, and he continues to adore it until he dies and is metamorphosed into a flower. Pliny's birds, one assumes, eventually abandon the painted grapes once they come to learn that they cannot be eaten. The birds, that is, are temporarily fooled by an illusion. But the desire of Narcissus survives even this moment of disillusionment and remains impossibly attached to its object. If Pliny's birds are captured by some ontological misrecognition, Narcissus' desire absorbs into itself the ontological discrepancy between spectator and image.

This difference between human and animal desire occupies Jacques Lacan at the opening of his famous essay on the mirror stage, where he contrasts the responses of a monkey and a human child when confronted with their images in a mirror: "This act, far from exhausting itself, as in the case of the monkey, once the image has been mastered and found empty, immediately rebounds in the case of the child in a series of gestures in which he experiences in play the relation between the movements assumed in the image and the reflected environment, and between this virtual complex and the reality it duplicates—the child's own body, and the persons and things, around him."[17] In this moment, which constitutes the birth of the imaginary, the child moves through the emptiness of the image, thereby incorporating the simulacrum as such into the structure of its desire. The power of the image no longer resides exclusively in its capacity to "dupe" the spectator, to make a monkey of him or her.

It is in this Lacanian and anachronistic sense that one must read the word "imaginary" in Shakespeare's line: "All is imaginary she doth prove." Like Pliny's birds, Venus is duped into hoping for real sustenance from a mere image. But unlike the birds, she does not abandon the image once it is ascertained to be empty. Her impossible love for Adonis survives even this decisive proof that she can expect nothing from him in the way of sexual satisfaction. Here we discover the difference between an erotic ontology and a philosophical one. Desire sustains the reality of its object even when that object has proven disappointing or frustrating.

If Venus' continued attachment to Adonis, beyond any hope of sexual consummation, signifies a kind of enslavement and hence a continued degradation, the tone of her representation nevertheless undergoes a change. After this episode she takes on an increasing grandeur, becoming less a comically failed suitor than a tragically failed protector. Just as the unresponsiveness of his reflected image provokes a metamorphosis in Narcissus as spectator, so Adonis' unresponsiveness causes a change in Venus. It is as if these stanzas, occupying the very center of the poem, were the mirroring pool in which the two halves engage in a chiastic and transformative reflection.

The erotic ontology of the text, which sustains it beyond the exhaustion of its sexual use-value, also transforms Venus' role as symbol of the female reader. For the frustration of sexual need has enabled the emergence of a desire which accords more harmoniously with the nature of the poetic object. The failure to receive physical satisfaction from the text passes over into a state in which the text is desired *as* a simulacrum. In effect, then, this episode registers the birth of the aesthetic from the sexual. And none too soon, for from this point on the poem offers nothing in the way of erotic pleasure or titillation. As the poem metamorphoses from a comically erotic to a tragic mode, so Venus as representative of the female reader evolves from the frustrated consumer of a pornographic text to the subject of an (aesthetic) desire which incorporates the death or emptiness of its object. I am not claiming that this movement in any way mitigates the misogyny of *Venus and Adonis*. It may even be said to deepen it. The best that can be said here is that Venus transcends her own degradation. Like Narcissus' image, she is not depleted by being emptied out.

Notes

1. Ovid, *Amores*, I.xv.35-36. All quotations of Shakespeare's works are from *The Riverside Shakespeare*, ed. G. Blakemore Evans, Harry Levin et al. (Boston: Houghton Mifflin, 1974).

2. In *Amores* I.xv, Ovid gives thanks for the privacy and leisure needed for lyric poetry. Early in that poem he thanks Envy for not "prostituting my voice in the ungrateful forum" ("me / Ingrato vocem prostituisse foro") (5-6), thus clarifying what he later means by the "vilia" that please the crowd. Ovid, *Les Amours*, ed. and trans. Henri Bornecque (Paris: Société d' Edition des Belles Lettres, 1968). This reference to public oratory makes it

even likelier that Shakespeare takes "vilia" to refer to public theater.

3. See, e.g., Leeds Barroll, *Politics, Plague, and Shakespeare's Theater: The Stuart Years* (Ithaca: Cornell UP, 1991), 17.

4. Heather Dubrow, *Captive Victors: Shakespeare's Narrative Poems and Sonnets* (Ithaca: Cornell UP, 1987), 15.

5. In George Peele's *Merry and Conceited Jests*, Shakespeare's poem is read by "a tapster . . . much given to poetry." *Dramatic and Poetical Works of Robert Greene and George Peele*, ed. Alexander Dyce (London: Routledge, [n.d.]), 619. *Venus and Adonis* is listed as part of the courtesan's library in Thomas Cranley, *The Converted Courtezan* (1639) sig. E4ᵛ.

6. William Keach, *Elizabethan Erotic Narratives: Irony and Pathos in the Ovidian Poetry of Shakespeare, Marlowe, and their Contemporaries* (New Brunswick: Rutgers UP, 1977), 31-33.

7. See Arthur F. Marotti, *John Donne, Coterie Poet* (Madison: University of Wisconsin Press, 1986), 25-37: "The Inns of Court as a Socioliterary Milieu."

8. See the references to *Venus and Adonis* in volume one of *The Shakespere Allusion-Book: A Collection of Allusions to Shakespere From 1591 to 1700*, 2 vols. (London: Oxford University Press, 1932).

9. *Shakespere Allusion-Book*, 1: 189, 177.

10. *The Complete Works of John Davies of Hereford*, ed. Alexander B. Grosart, 2 vols. (New York: AMS, 1967).

11. John Marston, "The Metamorphosis of Pigmalions Image," *Elizabethan Minor Epics*, ed. Elizabeth Story Donno (New York: Columbia UP, 1963), stanza 20.

12. The image of the phallic text appears in Richard Brathwait's *The English Gentlewoman* (1631), which warns women against reading Shakespeare's poem: "*Venus* and *Adonis* are unfitting Consorts for a Ladies bosome. Remove them timely from you, if they ever had entertainment by you, lest, like the *Snake* in the fable, they annoy you" (139; quoted in *The Shakespere Allusion-Book*, 354). In Brathwait's imagination, Shakespeare's Ovidian poem undergoes something very like a metamorphosis. Brathwait's image of the snake at the bosom recalls Shakespeare's Cleopatra and her phallic "joy o' the worm." (Cleopatra, it should be recalled, fashions herself after Venus in Shakespeare's play.) Paradoxically, then, Brathwait's warning constitutes a virtual

wish-fulfillment for Venus, since the text becomes the living phallus that she longs for. The danger of the poem is precisely its capacity to produce pleasure.

An interesting inversion of this problem occurs in Sonnet 20, which compares Shakespeare's "master-mistress" to the painting of a woman: "A woman's face with Nature's own hand painted / Hast thou. . . ." (1-2). Here, however, it is the presence, rather than the absence, of a penis which inhibits sexual consummation:

> And for a woman wert thou first created,
> Till Nature as she wrought thee fell a-doting,
> And by addition me of thee defeated,
> By adding one thing to my purpose nothing.
> 　　But since she prick'd thee out for women's pleasure,
> 　　Mine be thy love, and thy love's use their treasure.
>
> 　　　　　　　　　　　　　　　　　(9-14)

The image of Nature as an artist or sculptor who "fell a-doting" over her creation recalls Venus' position as female Pygmalion.

13. The association of Venus and castration is made explicit by sonnet IX of *The Passionate Pilgrim:*

> Fair was the morn when the fair queen of love,
> 　　　　　. . . . .
> Paler for sorrow than her milk-white dove,
> For Adon's sake, a youngster proud and wild,
> Her stand she takes upon a steep-up hill.
> Anon Adonis comes with horns and hounds;
> She, silly queen, with more than love's good will,
> Forbade the boy he should not pass those grounds.
> "Once," quoth she, "did I see a sweet fair youth
> Here in these brakes deep-wounded with a boar,
> Deep in the thigh, a spectacle of ruth!
> See in my thigh," quoth she, "here was the sore."
> 　　She showed hers, he saw more wounds than one,
> 　　And blushing fled, and left her all alone.

14. Leon Battista Alberti, *On Painting and On Sculpture,* trans. and ed. Cecil Grayson (London: Phaidon, 1972), II.26. Leonardo da Vinci probably has Narcissus' pool in mind, although he does not directly mention it, in the section of his *Treatise on Painting* entitled "How the mirror is master of painters": "The painting is intangible insofar as that which seems round and detached cannot be surrounded [*circondare*] with the hands, and the same is true of a mirror" (Leonardo da Vinci, *Treatise on Painting,* trans. A. Philip McMahon, 2 vols. [Princeton: Princeton UP, 1956], 1:160).

15. The ontological dilemmas of the reader are suggested by Shakespeare's apostrophe to Venus at the end of the above-quoted passage: "But all in vain. Good Queen, it will not be!" (l. 607). It is no accident that the pretense of direct address to a fictional character occurs just at the end of a passage depicting the non-responsiveness of the work of art. Here, I think, Shakespeare imitates Ovid's apostrophe to Narcissus in *Metamorphoses* III.432-436, which in turn anticipates Narcissus' vain address to his own image in lines 477-479. Ovid, *Metamorphoses,* trans. Frank Justus Miller, 2 vols. (Cambridge: Harvard University Press, 1921).

Shakespeare has in effect "split" the attributes of Narcissus between his two protagonists. Adonis embodies the problem of self-love while Venus represents desire for the image.

16. *Shakespeare's Ovid, Being Arthur Golding's Translation of the Metamorphoses,* ed. W. H. D. Rouse (Carbondale: Southern Illinois UP, 1961), III.523-524.

17. Jacques Lacan, *Écrits: A Selection,* trans. Alan Sheridan (New York: W.W. Norton, 1977), 1.

Gary Kuchar (essay date September 1999)

SOURCE: Kuchar, Gary. "Narrative and the Forms of Desire in Shakespeare's *Venus and Adonis.*" *Early Modern Literary Studies* 5, no. 2 (September 1999): 4.1-24.

[*In the following essay, Kuchar examines the rhetorical and intertextual elements of* Venus and Adonis *and demonstrates "that the poem's frustrating effects are largely a product of its rhetorical design."*]

Recent articles by Catherine Belsey, Richard Halpern, and James Schiffer have shifted the critical focus of Shakespeare's *Venus and Adonis* from questions of what the poem means, to how it means, from its moral allegory to its erotic and literary effects. For Belsey, this transition arose from her sense that readers of Shakespeare's epyllion who seek a "moral center that would furnish the work with a final meaning, a conclusion, a definitive statement" (262) tend to be interpreted by the poem in the very effort made to interpret it. *Venus and Adonis,* Belsey contends, "prompts in the reader a desire for action it fails to gratify. Meanwhile, the critical tradition in its turn, tantalized by the poem's lack of closure, has sought to make something happen, at least at the thematic level" (262).[1] Likewise, Halpern asserts that "*Venus and Adonis* is not only a poem about female sexual frustration; it is meant to produce such frustration. Just as Adonis' beauty arouses Venus but refuses to satisfy her, so Shakespeare's poem aims to arouse and frustrate the female reader" (381). Similarly, Schiffer argues that the poem dramatizes a Lacanian conception of desire to the extent that it reveals "desire can never be truly satisfied, because desire is always for absence, for lack, for what is not there" (369).

Although I agree that the poem aims to inspire a sense of frustration in its reader through its unrealized promise of satisfying closure, I do not think adequate attention has been paid to the rhetorical and intertextual elements that work to effect a reader's frustration. This paper aims, then, to demonstrate that the poem's frustrating effects are largely a product of its rhetorical design, the fact that a substantial portion of the narrative's comic-tragic trajectory is constructed through patterns of opposition, resolution, and subsequent disunion. Moreover, a closer rhetorical and intertextual analysis of *Venus and Adonis* reveals that the poem's "erotic ontology" (Halpern 383) does not, as Halpern suggests, restrict its frustrating effects to early modern female readers. Instead, the poem's reversal of gender norms enables a complex and unstable series of identifications that betray any straightforward assertion that a male reader is less likely to sympathize with Venus's cause than is a female reader; or, on the other hand, that a female reader is necessarily prone to identify with Venus over and against Adonis. Indeed, one of the primary effects of the poem's gender reversal is to complicate the process of identification so essential to literary response, making the identificatory process itself an issue for the reader, rather than something operating in terms of gender alone.

Part of the complexity involved in how a reader responds to the poem's use of reversals results from the way that Shakespeare organizes the symbolic oppositions through which the text is constructed. S. Clark Hulse understands the iconographic and imagistic oppositions in the poem less in terms of sustained narrative deferral, than as an expression of the poem's mythic and existentially *mediating* design:

> Shakespeare's sophisticated reworking of a literary myth [in *Venus and Adonis*] comes suprisingly close to recovering the function that Levi-Strauss suggests for primary myth: 'to bridge the gap between conflicting values through a series of mediating devices, each of which generates the next one by a process of opposition and correlation.'

> (Hulse 172-3, Levi-Strauss 213-23)

For Hulse, "Shakespeare's manner of paradox making has the characteristics of a persistent personal syntax. Indeed, if we think of myth as a conceptual form rather than as a content, we might call it Shakespeare's personal myth, a way of perceiving and reconciling the paradoxes of experience" (173). Although the poem's imagistic and rhetorical design, its "mediating devices" as it were, clearly orbit the mythic concerns of existential and ideological antagonisms, Shakespeare's text makes no claim, as does primary myth, to "explanatory totality" (Levi-Strauss 213-23). *Venus and Adonis,* in other words, has no pretensions of reconciling "the paradoxes of experience"; it dramatizes such paradoxes

and, as Belsey argues, it problematizes certain conflicting values—but it offers no answers. To this extent, Shakespeare's poem makes explicit what Jacques Derrida sees as the latent unending deferral operating in all mythic structures of thought. For Derrida the

> themes [in myth] duplicate themselves to infinity. When we think we have disentangled them from each other and can hold them separate, it is only to realize that they are joining together again, in response to the attraction of unforeseen affinities. In consequence, the unity of myth is only tendential and projective; it never reflects a state or moment of the myth

> (526)

Unlike primary myth, which aims explicitly towards a complete mediation of existential and ideological oppositions, *Venus and Adonis* purposefully resists the state of closure, the point of full reconciliation of opposites. In this sense, Shakespeare's poem makes dramatically explicit what Derrida locates as an implicit feature of mythic thought in general.

By choosing the sixain form of Thomas Lodge's epyllion *Scillaes Metamorphosis* over the heroic couplets of Marlowe's minor epic *Hero and Leander,*[2] Shakespeare is able to create a sense of narrative deferral through the use of repetition offered by the smaller narrative units of the sixain pattern. Indeed, when we compare the opening stanza of *Venus and Adonis* with the opening of Marlowe's poem, for instance, we notice that Shakespeare emphasizes action and movement rather than description and imagistic detail. The sense of movement achieved in the opening of Shakespeare's poem occurs through a series of implied similes that are contiguously linked. Marlowe, on the other hand, begins by describing the Ovidian world of *Hero and Leander.* In particular he draws on the Ovidian ekphrastic tradition in his description of Hero's garments. Such extended detail so early in the poem focuses less on dramatic action than on the narrator's witty rhetorical displays and his capacity for evoking lush visual imagery:

> At Sestos, Hero dwelt; Hero the faire . . .
> The outside of her garments were of lawne
> The lining, purple silke, with guilt starres drawne,
> Her wide sleeves greene, and bordered with a grove
> Where Venus in her naked glory strove.

> (7-11)

In Shakespeare's poem, however, we get neither extended physical description nor anything approaching narrative aside until the ekphrasis at line 259 when Adonis fails to mount his "trampling courser." Instead, we are immediately presented with Venus' wooing of Adonis through a series of contiguous images that creates tension and movement:

> Even as the sun with purple-colored face
> Had ta'en last leave of the weeping morn,

> Rose-cheeked Adonis hied him to the chase;
> Hunting he loved, but love he laughed to scorn.
> Sick-thoughted Venus makes amain unto him,
> And like a bold-faced suitor 'gins to woo him.
>
> (1-6)

These opening six lines present the reader with three movements of pursuit and one clear instance of abandonment. The larger narrative movement of pursuit and abandonment in the poem is thus encapsulated in this opening stanza as the first six lines initiate a movement towards resolution but conclude by simply emphasizing further pursuit. The proleptic image of the sun leaving the "weeping morn" frames both Adonis's and Venus' respective pursuits, establishing the poem's pattern of endless seeking, a pattern which fails to cease even at Adonis' death. In this case the pattern evolves through a series of contiguously associated implied similes that develop from the sun and morn to Adonis and the chase, to Venus and her erotic hunt. Shakespeare spends little time describing the mythic world that his characters inhabit; instead, he employs the image of the sun to establish the theme of temporality and the cycle of loss and dissatisfaction to which Venus and Adonis are prisoners. The chiasmus in line four introduces a rhetorical reversal that mirrors the gender reversal of the sexual combatants; such reversals, and the oxymoronic rhetoric they are often figured through, are central to establishing the sense of opposition characteristic of the poem and the subsequent sense of postponement such opposition inspires.

From the very beginning of the poem the key axis upon which the narrative moves is not the totalizing motion of metaphor, but a series of delayed and incomplete contiguous or metonymic relationships. The beginning of *Venus and Adonis,* which already alludes to its own unsatisfying end, begins a pattern or cycle of unfulfillment that repeats throughout the text. This repetition of unfulfillment constitutes the narrative's postponement or detour which sustains the sense of tension that is usually accented by the "middle section" of the narrative and then resolved at the end.[3] In *Venus and Adonis,* however, the beginning, middle, and end all play a role in enhancing the sense of postponement and delay. By dividing the first 810 lines of the poem into four narrative movements each constituting (with the exception of the ekphrasis) a pattern of pursuit, ostensible resolution and subsequent opposition, it becomes clear that the poem is *experienced* as an over-determined series of unresolved patterns of sexual pursuit intertwined with moments of apparent, but finally unrealized union. Lines 1-258 constitute the first main narrative pattern which is followed by the "breeding jennet" episode (259-324). Subsequently, lines 325-545 renew Venus' momentum lost at the end of the first section. This third movement concludes with the kiss at 545, but rather than satiating Venus the kiss leads to yet another intensification of her

desire: "Now quick desire hath caught the yielding prey / And glutton like she feeds, yet never filleth" (547-8). This intensification of desire and the unbearable sense of frustration it inspires reaches its climax at the poem's centre when it becomes apparent to the reader, if not to Venus, that "All is imaginary . . . / He will not manage her, although he mount her" (597-8). Venus follows this with an impassioned, if "over-handled," speech that Adonis be ruled by her rather than Cynthia[4] and Cynthia's subordinate, the boar. This takes us up to the tragic movement of the poem which furthers Venus' sense of loss and dissatisfaction through Adonis' death and the eventual "cropping" of the anemone. These larger narrative units within the first section of the poem contain a series of smaller narratives, as well as imagistic and metynomic patterns that develop the pattern of cyclic unfulfillment. Such sequences of images and the intertexts they evoke work in combination to develop the ceaseless detour and postponement of sexual and narrative resolution.

Lines 1-254 constitute the first extended narrative pattern of pursuit, imaginary resolution, and subsequent opposition. This narrative segment begins with the opening stanza that initiates Venus' hunt of Adonis and it moves towards the imaginary resolution of her attempt to "hemm [Adonis] here / Within the circuit of this ivory pale" (228-9). Venus' desire to imaginatively alter Adonis' perception of the world in her favour is then foiled when the narrator intervenes: "her words are done, her woes the more increasing / The time is spent, her object will away / And from her twining arms doth urge releasing" (254-6). Adonis then breaks from her arms and chases after his "trampling courser," allowing the major narrative cycle to repeat while the sub-plot of the horses portrays the quenching of previously thwarted desire. The primary sequence of pursuit and failure is over-determined within this first narrative unit through a series of imagistic and intertextual patterns that repeat the narrative cycle of unfulfillment. Between lines 55-90, for instance, the narration moves from the predatory eagle imagery of stanza 10 to Adonis' coy escape when "her lips were ready for his pay / He winks, and turns his lips another way" (89-90). This movement away from Venus breaks the ostensible union established through the imaginary "truce" where "one sweet kiss shall pay this comptless debt" (84). This early and failed attempt at seduction initiates a common rhetorical play on paradoxical images that insinuate incommensurability while ostensibly expressing a sense of sensual reciprocity.

Although the narrator indicates the possibility of union through the anxiously awaited kiss, his use of market language reveals that such desire is "comptless," hence unpayable. This rhetoric of monetary exchange accentuates the incommensurability between a Goddess and a human; its irony and humour arise through an unlikely figure in which Adonis is presented as infinitely wealthy and Venus as an impoverished investor in the market of love. Although the narration seems to sympathize with Venus to the extent that "she cannot choose but love" while Adonis remains uninterested, the patterning of imagery consistently implies a constitutional sense of dissension set between them. Line 81, for instance, introduces another proleptic image that looks forward to Venus' lament for Adonis when he is prosopopeically figured by the anemone: "And by her fair immortal hand she swears / From his soft bosom never to remove" (81-2). This image is reversed at the poem's tragic end when she holds the flower in the "hollow cradle" of her breast. Venus' desire never to be removed from Adonis' breast, and the previous image of Adonis "fastened" in her net, evoke the false, or in Northrop Frye's terms, *demonic* union[5] of Ovid's "Salamacis and Hermaphrodite." Salamacis, like Venus, grapples her lover/foe as she

> [catches] him fast betweene hir armes for ought that he could do
> Yea maugre all his wrestling and his struggling to and fro
> She held him still, and kissed him a hundred times and mo
> And willde he nillde he with hir handes she toucht his naked breast
> And now on this side now on that (for all he did resist
> And strive to wrest him from hir gripes) she clung unto him fast
> And wound about him like a Snake, which snatched up in hast
> And being by the Prince of Birdes borne lightly up aloft
> Doth writhe hir selfe about his necke and griping talants oft,
> And cast hir taile about his wings displayed in the winde.
>
> (Golding trans. 442-52)

The dramatization of this violent union leads up to the poem's tragic finale in which "Salamacis and Hermaphrodite" merge "in one form and face," completing Hermaphrodite's emasculation. The intertextual relationship between Salamacis and Venus is ambiguous at this point because on the one hand Venus is the Goddess of love and thus she offers Adonis the possibility of manhood rather than posing any threat to his masculinity, yet on the other a clear parallel is drawn between her and Salamacis through the similarity of their predatory images. What is unambiguous about the Ovidian intertext at this point is that it indicates a sense of unresolved or at least unsatisfying union. Indeed, Venus and Adonis' relationship is aligned very early on with the negative Ovidian transformations of dissension and false union rather than narratives which dramatize full reciprocity.

If we trace the imagistic patterning of lines 55-90 we notice that they follow our sequence of opposition,

imaginary union, and subsequent conflict. In stanza 10 Venus is figured as an "empty eagle" gluttonously feeding on her prey. The final couplet of the stanza plays on the Sisyphian or Tantalean nature of her desire: "Even so she kissed his brow, his cheek, his chin / And where she ends she doth anew begin" (60). The end couplet of the next stanza momentarily resolves this oppositional image of predatorial feeding by representing Venus' imaginary and hypothetical hope for satisfaction. Just as Venus will ostensibly resolve this first major narrative pattern through images of potential reciprocity in which she imagines her body as a park that contains Adonis who is transformed into a deer, she resolves this minor sequence by "Wishing her cheeks were gardens full of flowers / So they were dewed with [his breath's] distilling showers" (65-6). Here again the imaginary and hypothetical nature of Venus' imagery of reciprocation masks the predatory action which the narration had just presented. In the following stanza the narrator reverses Venus' wish fullfilling flower and rain imagery into its dialectical opposite, turning the garden full of flowers into a "river that is rank / Perforce will force it overflow the bank" (72-3). Thus we move from an image of opposition that the narrator presents in stanza 10, to an image of reciprocation that comes from Venus in the following stanza, back to an image of opposition that reverses Venus' hope for union. The same pattern then repeats over the next two stanzas as lines 73-8 introduce the oppositional colour motif of red and white which is momentarily resolved in the couplet of the following stanza where "one sweet kiss shall pay this comptless debt" (84). The sense of sexual combat and the tension which provokes it is bodied forth through the narrator's heavy use of medial caesura and the repetition of terms such as "still" and "entreats" which overtly express a sense of frustration:

> Still she entreats, and prettily entreats
> For to a pretty ear she tunes her tale
> Still is he sullen, still he low'rs and frets
> 'Twixt crimson shame and anger ashy-pale.
> Being red, she loves him best; and being white
> Her best is bettered with a more delight.
>
> (73-8)

The colour imagery which expresses Adonis' combination of fear and anger recalls us again to a similar passage in Golding's translation of "Salamacis and Hermaphroditus":

> This sed, the Nymph did hold hir peace, and therewithall the boy
> Waxt red: he wist not what love was: and sure it was a joy
> For in his face the color fresh appeared like the same
> That is in Apples which doe hang upon the Sunnie side:
> Or Ivorie shadowed with a red: or such as is espide

Of white and scarlet colours mixt appearing in the
Moone.

(Golding 400-6)

One of the most distinguishing features of Shakespeare's variation on this Ovidian passage results from
the metrical patterning of the sixain stanza which
naturally lends itself to a closing couplet that develops
or reverses the sense of the previous lines. The closing
couplet of stanza 13, for instance, plays on the sense of
desire's incapacity for fulfillment that closed out the
previous stanza with the river imagery. This sense of
Venus' insatiability is then repeated in the following
stanza through the trope of the comptless debt. Such
imagistic patterning and rhetorical reversals, which are
usually accomplished in the final couplet of the sixain,
are more fully exploited in Shakespeare than in Ovid.
Moreover, within this minor narrative and imagistic unit
of lines 55-90 we see that the closing couplets of stanzas
10, 12, 13, and 15 express the constitutional impossibility of Venus satisfying her desire for Adonis, while
stanzas 11 and 14 present an imaginary sexual resolution. Shakespeare thus adopts much of Ovid's imagery
in order to dramatize the sexual combat between Venus
and Adonis at the same time as he exploits a series of
rhetorical reversals in order to create the sense of an irreconcilable gap between the characters' perception of
one another.

Because Venus' sensuality is highly verbal as well as
deeply physical, she has far greater success achieving a
union of words than of bodies. Her failure to entice
Adonis reaches a brief and comic climax in lines 85-9
which completes this minor narrative pattern while
developing the water and flood imagery that re-appears
when Adonis sets off to meet the boar mid-way through
the poem. Line 86 embellishes the flood imagery
introduced in the couplet of stanza 11 as Adonis "like a
divedapper peering through a wave . . . / ducks as
quickly in: / So offers he to give what she did crave,
But when her lips were ready for his pay / He winks,
and turns his lips another way" (86-9). This comic
disappearing act is tragically replayed at line 819 as
Adonis vanishes in the waves of a "merciless and pitchy
night." The flood imagery takes on more profoundly
tragic dimensions as the shift in tone from the comic to
the mournful is initiated with the image of Adonis being swallowed into the darkness of approaching death:

. . . after him she darts, as one on shore
Gazing upon a late-embarked friend
Till the wild waves will have him seen no more
Whose ridges with the meeting clouds contend.
    So did the merciless and pitchy night
    Fold in the object that did feed her sight.
Whereat amazed, as one that unaware
Hath dropped a precious jewel in the flood . . .

(816-34)

The imagery of the rising and devouring waves contending with the limits of sky expresses a sense of tragic
foreboding that extends beyond Adonis' particularity.
This sense of the world becoming increasingly tragic in
tone is realized more fully when Venus bewails the loss
of true beauty that dies with Adonis. "Alas, poor world,
what treasure hast thou lost / What face remains alive
that's worth the viewing? / . . . The flowers are sweet,
their colors fresh and trim, / But true sweet beauty lived
and died with him" (1075-80). The patterning of flood
imagery embellishes and repeats the cycle of loss and
unfulfillment throughout the smaller narrative sequences
as well as the larger shift from the comic to the tragic.
This pattern overdetermines the profound sense of
frustration that Venus eloquently, if unsuccessfully,
strives to resolve.

The erotic rhetoric intensifies towards the end of the
first major narrative pattern (lines 1-258) as Adonis
arouses greater and greater frustration in his pursuer.
The carnal and even violent crescendo of the narrative
at this point is marked by a cyclic movement of
metonymic images which propels the sense of narrative
and sexual postponement. The sequence of images from
lines 240-53 moves through a metonymic logic that
concludes as it began, taking us through an imagistic
variation of the cyclic pattern of incommensurability,
union, and subsequent opposition. These lines immediately follow Venus' wish-fulfilling and imaginary
transformation into a park; they begin by reversing the
sense of union proposed by the park imagery and then
re-introduce it, only to undo it yet again:

At this Adonis smiles as in disdain
That in each cheek appears a pretty dimple;
Love made those hollows, if himself were slain
He might be buried in a tomb so simple
    Foreknowing well, if there he came to lie
    Why, there love lived, and there he could not die.
These lovely caves, these round enchanting pits,
Opened their mouths to swallow Venus' liking
Being mad before, how doth she now for wits?
Struck dead at first, what needs a second striking?
    Poor queen of love, in thine own law forlorn,
    To love a cheek that smiles at thee in scorn!

(241-53)

The patterning of images in these two stanzas illustrates
the sort of narrative negotiation between Venus' desire
and the reality principle of Adonis' refutations that
constitutes much of the poem's structural motion. The
metonymic sequence begins with Adonis' dimple
metamorphosing into a "tomb so simple" where Cupid
may lie "if himself were slain." Here again, the poem's
paradoxical rhetoric balances a latent sense of impending tragedy while manifestly expressing the young boy's
remarkable beauty. As the narrative focus shifts from
Cupid to Venus, Adonis' tomb like dimples transform
again into "lovely caves round enchanting pits . . .

[which] opened their mouths to swallow Venus' liking" (247-8). This transformation introduces one of the most explicit and sensual images of Venus' masculine position in the poem. The highly charged euphemism of Venus penetrating Adonis' "dimple" gives way as the narrative shifts from Venus' perception of the situation to the actual distance placed between her and Adonis: "Poor queen of love, in thine own law forlorn / To love a cheek that smiles at thee in scorn." Here the narrative moves away from Venus' perception of Adonis' dimple as a sexualized and penetrable object to a more sober and less erotic view of the situation. The patterning of imagery, here, is cyclic in motion, moving from dimple to tomb, to cave, to pit, to mouth, to cheek again. Such patterning creates a sense of movement towards quiescence while continually frustrating its realization. Moreover, Venus' imaginary and metaphoric transformations are continually undermined by the narration's redeployment of her own rhetoric, revealing that there is not "relief enough" within her limits.

The reversal of gender roles in *Venus and Adonis,* as in Ovid's "Salamacis and Hermaphrodite", plays an integral role in the necessarily frustrating conclusion the relation is driven towards. Venus' masculine role bodied forth in lines 55-90 is complemented in the third narrative section (lines 325-545) as Adonis unwittingly tropes himself in effeminate and emasculating terms. In an attempt to counter Venus' *carpe diem* argument, Adonis displays wisdom beyond his years, at the same time as he expresses an unwitting effeminacy and immature narcissism that undermines his argument:

'Who wears a garment shapeless and unfinished
Who plucks the bud before one leaf put forth?
If springing things be any jot diminished
They wither in their prime, prove nothing worth.
  The colt that's backed and burdened being young
  Loseth his pride, and never waxeth strong.
You hurt my hand with wringing; let us part
And leave this idle theme, this bootless chat;
Remove your siege from my unyielding heart;
To love's alarms it will not ope the gate.
  Dismiss your vows, your feigned tears, your flatt'ry;
  For where a heart is hard they make no batt'ry.'

(415-26)

In line 417 Adonis implicitly reintroduces the absent and/or flaccid phallus theme with unintentionally humorous results. Then in line 423, through another unfortunate choice of images, he portrays himself as the assailed virgin striving to keep the female phallus from his unyielding gate. Finally he adds insult to his own injury when he reveals that the only "hard" thing about him is his unbattered heart. Adonis' self-emasculating choice of images weakens his position in the poem, indicating an unnatural fear of intimacy that leads some readers to sympathize with Venus' reproach of the coy and unyielding boy.

It is the insistent absence of a satisfying male presence in *Venus and Adonis,* according to Halpern and Schiffer, which accounts for much of the poem's frustrating effect. Halpern reads this absence in the context of the poem's misogynistic and male centered vision of Venus' sexuality. Challenging the assumption that Shakespeare's audience was predominantly male, Halpern cites a variety of sources from the period to show that *Venus and Adonis* was often characterized as the reading material of "courtesans, lascivious nuns, adulterous housewives, or libidinous young girls" rather than the "sophisticated" readers alluded to in the Ovidian epigraph (377). Halpern's case regarding the poem's misogyny and its intention to frustrate primarily female readers is overstated to the extent that it underestimates the poem's capacity to titillate readers representing any number of gender and sexual differences, as is indicated by Titan's position in the poem:

By this the lovesick queen began to sweat
For where they lay the shadow had forsook them
And Titan, tired in the midday heat
  With burning eye did hotly overlook them
  Wishing Adonis had his team to guide
So he were like him, and by Venus' side.

(175-80)

Titan's evocation here accentuates the poem's lack of a satisfying male presence, and his wish parallels that of a male reader frustrated with Adonis's coyness. Titan manifests a heterosexual male reader's desire within the poem, marking out a definite textual site that invites a reader to play out his desire through identification with a powerful, yet finally absent, male presence in the narrative. Such passages indicate that Shakespeare's text does not discriminate in its capacity to titillate and amuse as well as frustrate its readers; if it did, its popularity in the sixteenth and early seventeenth centuries would be even more difficult to explain than is already the case.

As we saw in the poem's first narrative sequence (1-259), the poem's Tantalean structure moves through a series of images that express an apparent but unrealized union. This initial sequence establishes the imagistic and structural basis upon which the rest of the poem is then based. Within the larger narrative patterns of the poem there are smaller imagistic sequences, intertextual elements, and rhetorical forms that develop the dissension between Venus and Adonis while manipulating the reader's desire for a resolution to this dissension. These patterns also constitute the structural form of the third narrative pattern (lines 325-545) which begins by making explicit the Ovidian theme that unexpressed desire leads to dire consequences. Developing on the river and flood imagery introduced in lines 70-90, the narration moves from the ekphrasis (259-324) which expresses the fulfillment of desire to the mounting tension of Venus' lust and Adonis' growing impatience:

An oven that is stopped, or river stayed,
Burneth more hotly, swelleth with more rage;
So of concealed sorrow may be said
Free vent of words love's fire doth assuage;
    But when the heart's attorney once is mute
    The client breaks, as desperate in his suit.

(331-6)

The narrator establishes the ensuing debate (lines 368-450) between Venus and Adonis through a complementary set of images that ostensibly compare the two while further distancing them. Lines 331-6 imply that Venus burns to express her desire for Adonis, while in line 338 Adonis is figured as a burning coal whose anger revives with her return. "He sees her coming and begins to glow / Even as a dying coal revives with wind" (338-9). This imagistic chiasmus concludes with another illusory union between Venus and Adonis as "Taking no notice that she is so nigh / For all askance he holds her in his eye" (339-40).

The erotic distance between the two becomes even more palpable in this momentary unification in which Adonis "holds her in his eye" while he tries to hide from her in a solipsistic gesture of concealment. The gaze according to Renaissance theories based in Plato's *Phaedrus* saw staring as the beginning of intimacy; in this case it signifies a reluctant beginning that moves nowhere. This indication of a potential sexual union without its realization complements the patterning of imagery surrounding it which also evokes the sense of sexual union while suspending its actualization. Thus, action and image, plot and rhetoric, form and content move in analogous patterns of opposition and ostensible union, teasing but never fulfilling the text's and the subsequently the reader's desire for closure and completion.

The dialectic play of colour imagery in lines 353-364 shifts into a series of rhetorical and conversational reversals that begin the intense verbal combat of lines 368-450. The rhetorical chiasmuses which begin this sequence give the debate a dynamic, dramatic quality that retains a clear sense of playfulness, while at the same time developing Venus' increasing frustration:

Would thou wert as I am, and I a man,
My heart all whole as thine, thy heart my wound!
        . . . . .
'Give me my hand' saith he. 'Why dost thou feel it?'
'Give me my heart,' saith she, 'and thou shalt have it.
O, give it me lest thy hard heart do steel it,
And being steeled, soft sighs can never grave it.
    Then love's deep groans I never shall regard
    Because Adonis' heart hath made mine hard.

(369-78)

Venus here develops the earlier image of Adonis' imprinted cheek. This motif of "engravement" plays proleptically on Adonis' death in which the boar's tusk will "trench" (1052) itself in his thigh; when Venus laments that she will not witness "love's deep groans" she unwittingly parallels the "groans" of love with the "groans" of pain during Adonis' agonized and violent demise. For further on at line 950 when Venus chides death she ironically, and tragically asks "What may a heavy groan advantage thee?" thus returning our focus to the absent and long awaited coitus scene passed over in favor of the "hard hunt."

Shakespeare ends the third sequence (325-545) with a unique and highly ironic variation on Adonis' death, which in traditional mythic readings tends to signify the "dead time of the year, whether winter or the late summer drought" (Frye *Code* 69).[6] Shakespeare sets up a comic play on the mythic death and rebirth element underlying the narrative by having Venus faint (464) and then quickly revive with expectations for sexual gratification (482). This variation further develops the ontological and erotic distance between the two as we see Adonis comically kissing and poking Venus in an attempt to arouse her from her feigned sleep. "He bends her fingers, holds her pulses hard / He chafes her lips; a thousand ways he seeks / To mend the hurt that his unkindness marred. / He kisses her; and she, by her good will, / Will never rise, so he will kiss her still" (476-80). These unsatisfying kisses finally lead to the very thing Venus has been waiting for: "Her arms do lend his neck a sweet embrace; Incorporate then they seem; face grows to face; . . . / Till breathless he disjoined, and backward drew / . . . He with her plenty pressed, she faint with dearth, / Their lips together glued, fall to the earth" (540-5). These lines offer the clearest example of the poem's capacity to tease a reader with a sense of fulfillment while sustaining a dramatic sense of incompleteness. The ostensibly sensuous term "Incorporate" indicating the possibility of full physical union is qualified and thus undone by the disappointing "seem." Following the term "incorporate" Shakespeare alludes to the imagery of Corinthians I 13:12, expressing a sense of reciprocity which is consistently undermined: "For now we see through a glass, darkly; but *then face to face:* now I know in part; but then shall I know even as also I am known". This passage expresses precisely the sense of intimacy and knowledge of the other the poem seems to move towards without ever achieving. Finally, after drawing on this powerful Pauline image of reciprocity the narrator teases us further, relating how, "Their lips together glued." Even this moment of apparent union is permeated with comic and ironic overtones as the word "glued" indicates the struggle Venus had to undergo and which she must sustain in order to simply kiss the elusive boy-hunter.

The proximity the two achieve in the end of the third section is dramatically undone in the first three stanzas (547-564) of the fourth sequence. In the first of these stanzas the narration repeats three of the main rhetorical images of incommensurability we saw developed in the first sequence between lines 55-90. The first two lines of the stanza return us to the bird of prey motif indicating the unequal and predatory nature of the sexual rapport: "Now quick desire hath caught the yielding prey / And glutton-like she feeds, yet never filleth" (547-8). The third line repeats the military or combative image of master and slave implicit throughout much of the poem: "Her lips are conquerors, his lips obey," (549). And the fourth line returns us to the rhetoric of monetary exchange: "Paying what ransom the insultor willeth" (550). The repetition of such images indicates that Venus and Adonis have returned to their original state of disunion.

The most indicative feature of Shakespeare's concern with expressing the frustration and antinomies of passion, rather than any sense of symbolic union achieved through Adonis' death, is the way that Shakespeare reconfigures the significance of the anemone as it appears in Ovid. In Shakespeare's version, Adonis' body does not undergo the sort of active and ritualistic metamorphosis into an enduring reminder that we see in Ovid; instead, it is transformed by a power that remains unspecified and it is then quickly "cropped" by Venus in another aggressive act that perpetuates rather than resolves her desire. In Book X of Ovid's *Metamorphoses* Venus reproaches the fates and then immediately transforms Adonis' body into an anemone:

> She rent her garments . . .
> . . . and springing down
> Reproached the fates: "Even so, not everything
> Shall own your sway. Memorials of my sorrow
> Adonis, shall endure; each passing year
> Your death repeated in the hearts of men
> Shall re-enact my grief and my lament. . . .
> And with these words she sprinkled nectar
> Sweet scented, on his blood, which at the touch
> Swelled up, as on a pond when showers fall.

(Melville trans. 724-37)[7]

Shakespeare's ending is decidedly lacking the theme of recurrence and resurrection that characterizes Ovid's version, placing in its stead, a continued sense of dissension:

> By this the boy that by her side lay killed
> Was melted like a vapor from her sight
> And in his blood, that on the ground lay spilled,
> A purple flower sprung up, check'red with white,
>   Resembling well his pale cheeks and the blood
>   Which in round drops upon their whiteness stood.
> Comparing it to her Adonis' breath,
> And says within her bosom it shall dwell, . . . /
> She crops the stalk, and the breach appears
> Green-dropping sap which she compares to tears.

(1165-76)

Some critics, most notably Robert Merrix, have ignored or overlooked the term "crops", which clearly implies a

sense of being "cut short", in order to read the ending in more Ovidian terms of union and resurrection. Merrix cites lines 1183-5, "Here was thy father's bed, here in my breast; / Thou art next of blood, and 'tis thy right. Lo in this hollow cradle take thy rest;" in order to show that "[w]ith the transformation of Adonis into the anemone . . . the two composites are united, forming a sexual resolution, a synthesis in which the major attributes of each are embodied in the other" (345). Yet, even here we are invited to read against Venus' choice of images at the same time we are encouraged to sympathize with her. First of all, the image of the hollow cradle recalls us to her intense and insatiable desire that propels the poem's narrative motions; it indicates a sense of emptiness that has not yet been filled; and second by drawing attention to her throbbing heart we do not get a sense that she feels any release or resolution; but rather we sense a feeling of deepening sadness. We might also recall that at line 945 Venus accuses death of the very thing she is later guilty of, introducing an unintentional and unfortunate proleptic warning of the eternal dissension set between her and Adonis: "The Destinies will curse thee for this stroke / They bid thee crop a weed; thou pluck'st a flower" (945-6). In Shakespeare's version Venus becomes the procurer of her own worst fears.

It is also important to notice that the only line indicating close proximity between the ill fated two is spoken indirectly by Venus herself, creating a gap between the actual event as it is narrated and her own interpretation of it: "Comparing it to her Adonis' breath, and *says within* her bosom it shall dwell" (1172). William Keach has noted that the repetition of the word "compares" and the shock of the word "crops" in this final sequence makes it clear that the flower functions prosopopeiacally, rather than indicating the promise of return. Venus, Keach notes, realizes that "Adonis is not reincarnated in the flower . . . She . . . 'crops' the stalk and 'compares' . . . the drops of sap to the tears which came to Adonis' eyes (ll. 1175-1176). Venus' realization that the flower is not Adonis contributes to the pathos of her comparisons and, in a sense, mitigates the shock of her 'cropping' the flower" (82-83).

Part of the narrative dynamic of frustration being played out in this fourth narrative sequence, as well as the poem as a whole, consists of what Catherine Belsey, following Lacan, terms the *trompe l'oeil* motif. Because the poem constructs what Belsey refers to as a "promise of . . . presence it fails to deliver" (261), it is structurally analogous to the scopic or visual effect known as *trompe l'oeil*. Just as a visual representation might appear to be the thing-as-such, Shakespeare's poem represents an apparent but finally unrealized union. This withholding of aesthetic fulfillment suggests that the poem is based on an "erotic rather than philosophic ontology" (Halpern 383). Both Halpern and Belsey point to the poem's allusion to Pliny's story of artistic competition between Zeuxis and Parrhasius, based as it is on the principle of the *trompe l'oeil* (ll. 601-6), as a lucid example of this erotically charged aesthetic:

> Even so poor birds, deceived with painted grapes
> Do surfeit by the eye and pine the maw;
> Even so she languisheth in her mishaps
> As those poor birds that helpless berries saw.
> The warm effects which she in him finds missing
> She seeks to kindle with continual kissing.
>
> (601-6)

This passage, which occurs directly after the allusion to Tantalus, offers a pictorial analogy for the dynamic of frustrated desire the poem dramatizes. This "pictorial" analogy not only offers a meta-commentary on Venus' unrealized desire, it also reflects the aesthetic ontology with which the reader is engaged. For the reader, like Venus, is tantalized by a promise of narrative and sexual fulfillment that remains unfulfilled. Catherine Belsey summarizes Lacan's insights into the deceitful pleasures this *trompe-l'oeil* dynamic offers a reader or viewer:

> In order to enjoy the *trompe-l'oeil* we have to be convinced by it in the first instance and then to shift our gaze so that, seeing the object resolve itself into lines on a canvas, we are no longer convinced; we have to be deceived and then to acknowledge our own deception.
>
> (262)

For Lacan, the essence of tragic anagnorisis is the recognition of one's lack-of-being (*manque-a-etre*).[8] Venus is driven to such a recognition through her failed attempts to have Adonis return her desire. She expresses this negative recognition with a combination of humor and pathos, tragedy and melodrama we have come to expect from Shakespeare's Queen of love. "O, where am I? . . . in earth or heaven / Or in the ocean drenched, or in the fire? / What hour is this? or morn or weary even? / Do I delight to die, or life desire? / . . . / O, thou didst kill me, kill me once again!" (492-499). The pun on sexual satisfaction, mixed as it is with cosmological references, expresses a sense of total absence, loss, and lack. Venus' agonized recognition of her emptiness is appropriately expressed as a question, indicating the deep uncertainty she feels as a result of Adonis' refusals. This passage sets up the even more dramatic moment when she falls to the ground with Adonis on top of her only to realize "he will not manage her, although he mount her" (597).

Venus' recognition of her lack stems from her perception of Adonis as being full and complete unto himself. This same structural relation exists between the reader of the poem and the text; for just as Venus feels herself absent before a self-sufficient Adonis, the reader experiences a sense of lack in relation to a text that appears complete. Richard Halpern articulates the paradoxical nature of the poem's desire-based ontology by recognizing that

> to reveal [an] image's emptiness is precisely to confirm its power. . . . Indeed, a kind of metamorphic inversion occurs between viewer and object, for the unsatisfied hunger of the birds indicates their own emptiness in relation to the image, which is complete.
>
> (383)

This "metamorphic inversion," in which the viewer feels empty in the presence of an object that appears full and self-sufficient, occurs throughout the poem in a number of varying forms. The first instance of this occurs at lines 211-16 when Venus alludes to Pygmalion as she bewails Adonis: "Fie, lifeless picture, cold and senseless stone / Well-painted idol, image dull and dead, / Statue contenting but the eye alone, / Thing like a man, but of no woman bred!" (211-14). Here, as in the Pliny allusion, Venus' psychosexual struggle is expressed through an aesthetic analogy in which the object viewed inspires a heightened sense of lack in the viewer. Her object contents "but the eye alone", evoking rather than fulfilling desire. Where the reader is confronted with the fact that "the signifier precisely defers, supplants, relegates the imagined presence it sets out to name" (Belsey *Desire* 64), Venus is confronted with the fact that her object is unattainable and unrealizable. Venus' growing frustration over this intolerable situation expresses itself through her aggressive and cruel allusion to Adonis' unnatural origins. "Thing like a man, but of no woman bred!" (214). This erotic/aesthetic ontology in which Adonis is full and self-sufficient while Venus languishes in her lack is reversed in lines 235-40 when Venus imagines herself as a park upon which Adonis feeds himself. The fulfillment that Venus seeks thus demands a reversal of the unreciprocal mode of perceiving presented in lines 211-16: in order to achieve a sense of momentary fulfillment she imagines being self-sufficient, full, and generative. The same dynamic occurs even more explicitly at line 370, "Would thou wert as I am, and I a man / My heart all whole as thine, thy heart my wound!" Venus' only power against Adonis' refusals lies in such rhetorical gestures; for as Richard Halpern observes, Venus "must content herself with 'venerian speculation'" (Halpern 380). Halpern, moreover, sees an analogy between Venus' plight and the reader's relation to the text insofar as "[t]he theological gap that separates Venus from the merely mortal Adonis stands in for the ontological gap between the . . . reader and the empty imaginations generated by the poem" (380). Thus part of the process of reading the poem consists of imaginatively re-enacting or reproducing its dramatization of unfulfilled desire.

A further example of the *trompe l'oeil* dynamic occurs during the ekphrasis, when Adonis' horse is described in complete detail, playing on this ontological relationship between viewer and object:

> Look when a painter would surpass the life
> In limning out a well proportioned steed
> His art with nature's workmanship at strife
> *As if the dead the living should exceed*
> So did this horse excel a common one
> In shape, in courage, color, pace and bone . . .
>
> Look what a horse should have he did not lack
> Save a proud rider on so proud a back.
>
> (my emphasis 290-300)

The density of this passage lies in its long, careful description of the horse which functions like the close and mimetically accurate brush-strokes of a Renaissance painter filling in every conceivable detail in order to convey a sense of totality and completeness within the image:

> Round-hoofed, short-jointed, fetlocks shag and long,
> Broad breast, full eye, small head and nostril wide
> High crest, short ears, straight legs and passing strong,
> Thin mane, thick tail, broad buttock, tender hide.
>
> (295- 300)

Although some readers may find this passage somewhat tedious, its unusually dense and exaggerated description paradoxically reminds us as viewers that it is description and not real. Shakespeare's description presents a kind of wholeness while at the same time making it clear to a reader that the fullness is an effect and not the thing itself. Passages such as this offer a complex and subtle meta-commentary on the relationship between the reader and the text; for just as the description of the horse is a "full-representation" and not the thing itself, the text is an "unresponsive artwork" intended to "generate some kind of sexual thrill or tension" without being able to actually fulfill the desire it is capable of evoking (Halpern 380). Thus Shakespeare's poem presents an unusual self-awareness of the relationship between the text and the reader, revealing the ways in which the text is the site upon which the reader's own desires are manipulated, frustrated, and enjoyed. As much of the critical history of the poem reveals, it is extraordinarily difficult, perhaps even impossible, to interpret the poem without repeating some of the dramatic motions it represents.[9] To see the text as an allegory against lust is to repeat Adonis' position in the poem; to unabashedly enjoy its erotic and verbal play is to align oneself with Venus; to become frustrated with Adonis' refusals is to take up Titan's place in the poem. Thus the structure of the poem—with its repetition of ostensible moments of resolution, enticing and humorous rhetorical displays and its highly erotic aesthetic ontology—opens up an interpretive space that allows a reader to identify his or her own desires within its frame.

Notes

1. Belsey traces these tendencies in the critical tradition of *Venus and Adonis* from Coleridge to Lu Emily Pearson through to Heather Dubrow. See Samuel Taylor Coleridge, "Shakespeare's *Venus and Adonis*," in *Venus and Adonis: Critical Essays,* ed. Philip C. Kolin (New York: Garland, 1997), 69-72; Lu Emily Pearson, "Shakespeare's Philosophy of Love," in *Venus and Adonis: Critical Essays,* 103-7; and Heather Dubrow, *Captive Victors: Shakespeare's Narrative Poems and Sonnets* (Ithaca: Cornell UP, 1987).

2. It is generally understood that Marlowe's poem was written before Shakespeare's and that Shakespeare had some knowledge of it before publication. William Keach notes that "although Marlowe's epyllion was not entered in the Stationers' Register until 28 September 1593, almost five and a half months after Shakespeare's (18 April), and of course not published until 1598, it must have been written by the spring of 1593, since Marlowe was killed at Deptford on 30 May of that year" (85).

3. See Peter Brooks' "Freud's Masterplot: Questions of Narrative." *Literature and Psychoanalysis: The Question of Reading Otherwise* (Baltimore: Johns Hopkins UP, 1982), 94-207, for a discussion of the role of metonymy and desire in narrative.

4. Goddess of the moon, the hunt, and chastity.

5. The demonic erotic relation, according to Frye, "becomes a fierce destructive passion that works against loyalty or frustrates the one who possesses it" (*Anatomy* 149).

6. See Abraham Fraunce, *The Third Part of the Countesse of Pembrokes Yvychurch* (Northridge: California State UP, 1976), for a mythic reading of the poem by one of Shakespeare's contemporaries.

7. Golding's translation follows Ovid in making Venus explicitly responsible for the metamorphosis of Adonis into a flower (848-54).

8. For a discussion of Lacan's views on tragedy, particularly in relation to Hegel's reading of *Antigone* and Freud's views on catharsis, see *The Ethics of Psychoanalysis: Seminar VII* (243-311).

9. For readings that clearly identify with Adonis over against Venus see David N. Beauregard, "Venus and Adonis: Shakespeare's Representation of the Passions," *Shakespeare Studies* 8 (1976), 1-23, and C. S. Lewis, *English Literature in the Sixteenth Century, Excluding Drama* (Oxford: Oxford UP, 1954). See also Katherine Duncan-Jones, "Much Ado with Red and White: The Earliest Readers of

Shakespeare's *Venus and Adonis*," *Review of English Studies* 44 (1993), 479-501, for a discussion of William Reynolds' idiosyncratic response to the poem. For a reading that valorizes Venus see Nona Fienberg, "Thematics of Value in *Venus and Adonis*," in *Venus and Adonis: Critical Essays,* ed. Philip C. Kolin (New York: Garland, 1997), 247-58. For a discussion of the poem that seeks to symbolically unify Venus and Adonis see Robert P. Merrix, "'Lo, in This Hollow Cradle Take Thy Rest': Sexual Conflict and Resolution in *Venus and Adonis*," in *Venus and Adonis: Critical Essays,* 341-358.

Works Cited

Beaumont, Francis. "Salmacis and Hermaphroditus." *Elizabethan Minor Epics.* Ed. Elizabeth S. Donno. New York: Columbia UP, 1963.

Belsey, Catherine. *Desire: Love Stories in Western Culture.* Cambridge: Blackwell, 1994.

———. "Love As Trompe-L'Oeil: Taxonomies of Desire in *Venus and Adonis*". In *Venus and Adonis: Critical Essays.* Ed. Philip C. Kolin. New York: Garland, 1997.

Beauregard, David N. "Venus and Adonis: Shakespeare's Representation of the Passions." *Shakespeare Studies* 8 (1976): 83-98.

Brooks, Peter. "Freud's Masterplot: Questions of Narrative." In *Literature and Psychoanalysis: The Question of Reading Otherwise.* Baltimore: John Hopkins UP, 1982. 94-207.

Derrida, Jacques. "Structure, Sign, and Play in the Discourse of the Human Sciences." In *Criticism: Major Statements.* Ed. Charles Kaplan, and William Anderson. New York: St. Martin's Press, 1991.

Dubrow, Heather. *Captive Victors: Shakespeare's Narrative Poems and Sonnets.* Ithaca: Cornell UP, 1987.

Duncan-Jones, Katherine. "Much Ado with Red and White: The Earliest Readers of Shakespeare's *Venus and Adonis.*" *Review of English Studies* 44 (1993): 479-501.

Fienberg, Nona. "Thematics of Value in *Venus and Adonis.*" In *Venus and Adonis: Critical Essays.* Ed. Philip C. Kolin. New York: Garland, 1997. 247-58.

Fraunce, Abraham. *The Third Part of the Countesse of Pembrokes Yvychurch.* Northridge: California State UP, 1976.

Frye, Northrop. *Anatomy of Criticism: Four Essays.* Princeton: Princeton UP, 1957.

———. *The Great Code: The Bible and Literature.* Toronto: Penguin, 1983.

Greene, Thomas M. *The Light in Troy: Imitation and Discovery in Renaissance Poetry.* New Haven: Yale UP, 1982.

Halpern, Richard. "'Pining Their Maws': Female Readers and the Erotic Ontology of the Text in Shakespeare's *Venus and Adonis*". *Venus and Adonis: Critical Essays.* Ed. Philip C. Kolin. New York: Garland, 1997.

Hulse, Clark. *Metamorphic Verse: The Elizabethan Minor Epic.* New Jersey: Princeton UP, 1981.

Keach, William. *Elizabethan Erotic Narratives: Irony and Pathos in the Ovidian Poetry of Shakespeare, Marlowe, and Their Contemporaries.* New Jersey: Rutgers UP, 1977.

Lacan, Jacques. *The Ethics of Psychoanalysis: Seminar VII 1959-60.* Trans. D. Porter. New York: W.W. Norton, 1986.

———. *The Four Fundamental Concepts of Psychoanalysis.* Trans. A. Sheridan. Penguin books, 1977.

Levi-Strauss, Claude. *Structural Anthropology.* Trans. Claire Jacobson and Brooke G. Schoepf. New York: Basic Books, 1963.

Lewis, C. S., *English Literature in the Sixteenth Century, Excluding Drama* (Oxford: Oxford UP, 1954).

Marlowe, Christopher. "Hero and Leander." In *Elizabethan Minor Epics.* Ed. Elizabeth S. Donno. New York: Columbia UP, 1963.

Merrix, Robert P. "'Lo in this Hollow Cradle take Thy Rest'": Sexual Conflict and Resolution in *Venus and Adonis*". In *Venus and Adonis: Critical Essays.* Ed. Philip C. Kolin. New York: Garland, 1997.

Ovid. *Metamorphoses.* Trans. A. D. Melville. Oxford: Oxford UP, 1986.

Ovid. *Shakespeare's Ovid Being Arthur Golding's Translation of the Metamorphoses.* Ed. W.H.D. Rouse. New York: W.W. Norton, 1961.

Schiffer, James. "Shakespeare's *Venus and Adonis*: A Lacanian Tragicomedy of Desire". In *Venus and Adonis: Critical Essays.* Ed. Philip C. Kolin. New York: Garland, 1997.

Shakespeare, William. *The Sonnets and Narrative Poems: The Complete Non-Dramatic Poetry.* Ed. Sylvan Barnet. New York: Signet, 1988.

Lauren Shohet (essay date winter 2002)

SOURCE: Shohet, Lauren. "Shakespeare's Eager Adonis." *Studies in English Literature, 1500-1900* 42, no. 1 (winter 2002): 85-102.

[*In the following essay, Shohet illuminates the distinctive oppositional modes of desire articulated by the title characters of* Venus and Adonis.]

In Shakespeare's *Venus and Adonis,* when Venus solicits Adonis, he famously turns away. Venus entreats:

"Vouchsafe, thou wonder, to alight thy steed,
And rein his proud head to the saddle-bow;
If thou wilt deign this favor, for thy meed
A thousand honey secrets shalt thou know."[1]

Adonis rebuffs her, because "Hunting he lov'd, but love he laugh'd to scorn" (line 4). The critical tradition has discussed in great detail Adonis's refusal to love.[2] But, importantly, this line does not begin with a refusal. Rather, it introduces Adonis with a positive predicate: he "loves" hunting. Moreover, the "but" that conjoins his predilection for hunting with his antipathy to love has dialectical overtones: Adonis would seem to scorn "love" more as an alternative to the hunt than as an independent proposition.

The two characters thus articulate distinct forms of "love" that present competing models of desire. Furthermore, the poem provocatively interrelates models of desire and language. In the stanza cited above, if Adonis alights, Venus will reward him with "'a thousand honey secrets.'" Not only does Venus promise the linguistic reward of "'secrets'" for erotic surrender, but her proposal of "'honey secrets'" as "'meed'" ("reward," punning on "mead" [honey liquor]) also intertwines these linguistic treats with the honeyed sexual "'secrets'" also on offer ("'honey'" denoting moreover sexual bliss).[3] And while Adonis straightforwardly "loves" hunting, he does not simply "scorn" Venus—as grammatical parallelism would have him do—but rather "*laugh[s] to* scorn" her (my emphasis). Metrical contingency aside, this doubled verb adds a layer of complexity to Adonis's response to "love." Whereas hunting elicits an unmediated affective response ("hunting he loved"), the poem's evocation of eros emphasizes the mode through which Adonis (unlike Venus) distinctively expresses his response of Affective withdrawal.

Such intersections of desire and discourse have been remarked in various literary contexts—commentators include Michel de Montaigne and Michel Foucault—and have occasioned innumerable provocative analyses in criticism of the last two decades. Relatively less explored in Shakespeare studies have been the questions of whether different kinds of desire require different poetics, and whether, conversely, different modes of discourse produce different kinds of desire.[4] I propose that we might fruitfully read Shakespeare's *Venus and Adonis* as addressing just these questions: as considering multiple and competing discourses of desire, and exploring how different poetic and erotic modes might inflect one another.

Previous criticism of *Venus and Adonis* certainly has remarked on the poem's engagement with love on the one hand and language on the other. But most scholarship on *Venus and Adonis* focuses either on questions of desire and subjectivity or on issues of language and representation.[5] More significantly, the limited number of analyses that bring these areas together tend to take only one of the two categories as a complex and multiple field. In considering the poem's "taxonomy of desire," for example, Catherine Belsey argues that the poem innovatively distinguishes between the concepts of love and lust. But while her focus on the difference between these terms has discursive implications, Belsey's interest lies in contrasting modes of desire, not modes of representation. Similarly, Heather Dubrow connects Venus's "linguistic" and "psychological" habits, but relies on a unified notion of "language itself," whereas I would propose that the poem encompasses multiple and competing notions of what language is.[6] In one further example, James Schiffer remarks (in passing) that the poem illustrates the interdependence of economies of language and desire in Lacanian analysis ("Venus' prophecy-curse also reminds us of the relationship throughout the poem between language and desire"), but Schiffer distinguishes neither among kinds of desire (as Belsey does) nor kinds of language.[7]

In this essay, by contrast, I want to focus particularly on the range of disagreements between Venus and Adonis—sexual, linguistic, and representational—to explore how these contrasting views come together into distinct (if asymmetrically articulated) discursive models of poetic subjectivity. Venus's amorous eagerness is met with Adonis's disdainful withdrawal; Venus's heteroerotic desire for Adonis with his homoerotic desire for the hunt; Venus's invocations of a mythic realm of abstraction, personification, and analogy with Adonis's emphasis on the historical realm of particular experience; Venus's reliance on literary convention with the narrative innovation of Adonis's erotic refusal. Wryly dissociating the seduction and "venery" ("hunting") linked in traditional puns and mythography, the poem distinguishes between Venus's views of language, desire, and selfhood—largely consonant with the dominant Elizabethan models Jane Hedley characterizes as "static, synchronistic, and centripetal"—and Adonis's desires, which sketch out a tentative exploration of alternatives.[8] The vagueness of my last locution reflects the difficulty of definitively discerning Adonis's desires in a text largely controlled by the opposition. For Shakespeare's poem rearticulates the traditionally fecund venus genetrix in Venus's extraordinary volubility: she gushes forth stanza after stanza of erotic desire, hampering intrusions by her interlocutor or even, it seems, the narrator. Rather like the copious production of panegyric by Elizabeth's court, Venus's linguistic facility leaves little room for alternatives, effectively preventing Adonis's admittedly rather inchoate desires from coming fully into focus. Yet, as I shall argue below, the open-endedness of Adonis's aims is an important part of what makes them distinctive.

For Adonis does formulate positive aims. To be sure, Adonis's first direct speech in the poem (not granted him until line 185) is "'Fie, no more of love!'"; the next line adds to this wholesale rejection the intransitively negative "'I must remove.'"(line 186). Adonis is, however, fleeing toward something as well. He actively removes—re-moves—to the homosocial alternative of the boar hunt. He prefers keeping faith with his male hunting band to tarrying with Venus: "'I am,' quoth he, 'expected of my friends'" (line 718). And, as we have seen, the poem's very first claim about Adonis reports, "Hunting he lov'd" (line 4). Although it might be possible to interpret "hunt-love" here as an ironic aggregation opposed to the second phrase's "love" ("love he laugh'd to scorn"), Adonis protests in other lines as well that he does indeed "love" hunting, or perhaps the hunt, or even the deadly boar himself: "'I know not love,' quoth he, 'nor will not know it, / Unless it be a boar, and then I chase it'" (lines 409-10).[9]

Adonis's desire differs from Venus's both in its target and in the way it relates subject to object. Whereas Venus desires an eros that merges lover and beloved, Adonis desires the hunt, which depends upon boundaries between subject and object (albeit contingent and perhaps temporary ones). Adonis's desire fits somewhere along a homosocial-homoerotic continuum that is distinct in both its ends and its means from Venus's desires, as shown by three elements of his preference: Adonis's attraction to the boar itself, his allegiance to the masculine hunting band, and the ways in which the hunt suggests patriarchal order. The poem's presentation of the boar is, of course, quite phallic. Unlike Venus's suggested alternatives of foxes, hares, and roes (which Adonis spurns), the boar has tusks, a "'battle set / Of bristly pikes'" (lines 619-20), and a grave-digging snout. Adonis's keen interest in the boar hunt and simultaneous disdain for innocuous quarries betray some attraction to the deadly possibility of being penetrated by the boarish tusk.[10] More significant than this genitally suggestive imagery are the abstract qualities linking the boar not merely to the penis but to the phallus, with the full weight of cultural privilege which that term connotes. For the poem emphasizes the boar's powers of intention, resolution, invulnerability, and efficacy. As Venus fearfully describes him,

> "Being mov'd, he strikes, what e'er is in his way,
> And whom he strikes his crooked tushes slay.
> His brawny sides, with hairy bristles armed,
> Are better proof than thy spear's point can enter;
> His short thick neck cannot be easily harmed;
> Being ireful, on the lion he will venter.
> The thorny brambles and embracing bushes,

> As fearful of him, part, through whom he rushes."

> (lines 623-30)

Moreover, Adonis's desire draws him to the more abstractly phallic order of the hunt: an activity that develops identity—what Lacan calls the "social I"—by projecting the power, knowledge, and autonomy that the subject hopes to gain onto the ever-receding Other who putatively commands this mastery (who, in Lacanian terms, possesses the phallus).[11] Hence, whereas in discussing the boar as the "locus of the missing phallic impulse" William Sheidley uses "phallus" more or less synonymously with "penis," the Lacanian notion that the "phallus" is always illusory would suggest that the hunt itself, rather than the boar, embodies the "phallic impulse" that constitutes masculine self-realization.[12] In the poem (as in culture generally), the compensation for the impossibility of these young men ever attaining full mastery—because no subject ever realizes complete autonomy—is nothing other than patriarchy: a fraternal band, excluding women and children by the nature of its mission, linked in the bonds of a common purpose made all the more permanent because the goal never can be definitively accomplished (i.e., because patriarchy operates without authentic patriarchs). "'Expected of my friends,'" Adonis is not only awaited by his friends, but also, partitively, expected to become "of" his friends: part of a masculine order based on perpetual quest.[13]

Significantly, the poem articulates Adonis's desire not as finding, overcoming, or killing the boar, but rather as "chasing" him: "'I know not love,' quoth he, 'nor will not know it, / Unless it be a boar, and then I chase it.'" (lines 409-10). It is pursuit itself that attracts Adonis: a relation that depends upon preserving distance between desirer and object. By its nature, the ever-receding object of his desire is constitutively ungraspable. By contrast, Venus's erotics specifically seek to vanquish this distance; as Coppelia Kahn notes, Venus desires the "blurring of boundaries, an anonymous merging of eyes and lips."[14] Merging and boundlessness characterize Venus's version of erotic idyll: "'My smooth moist hand, were it with thy hand felt, / Would in thy palm dissolve, or seem to melt'" (lines 143-4).[15] Significantly, these same qualities prove fatal to Adonis, culminating in the images of commingling surrounding his death. The boar's mouth is painted with red, "Like milk and blood being mingled both together" (line 902); as the wound breaches Adonis's bodily boundaries, "No flow'r was nigh, no grass, herb, leaf, or weed, / But stole his blood, and seem'd with him to bleed" (lines 1055-6). Congruently, whereas Venus's erotics suspend time at the moment of consummation, pursuit rather than capture is endless in Adonis's "chase." (Accordingly, one of Adonis's two moments of erotic engagement with Venus comes at a point when he believes her to be similarly unattainable, in her deathlike swoon [lines

475-80]; in the other, he teases Venus with a kiss proffered and retracted [lines 88-90]). The proximity and the breaching of boundaries that constitute infinite and ecstatic fulfillment for Venus are inherently fatal in the hunt, an opposition emphasized by Venus's use of "'kiss[ing]'" to describe the boar's mortally wounding Adonis (line 1114). Indeed, the successful approach of hunter to quarry necessarily signals the end of the hunt, usually accompanied by the death of one or more participants.

Associated with these different modes of desire are different modes of poeisis. Venus's hermeneusis relies on mythic/conventional presentation; Adonis tends toward the palpable and the particular. Venus seeks to inscribe Adonis into an archetypal tale of seduction, speaking as the goddess of love who advocates eros and procreation as general principles:

> "Upon the earth's increase why shouldst thou feed,
> Unless the earth with thy increase be fed?
> By law of nature thou art bound to breed,
> That thine may live, when thou thyself art dead."
>
> (lines 169-72)

Near silent for most of the poem and dead at the end, Adonis struggles less than articulately to assert a character whose volition is undetermined by tradition or myth. Venus serves, perhaps, as the "straight" reader of Ovid, following the mythic script. Adonis resists this, but the sophisticated, ironic, self-reflective Ovid of the elite Elizabethan reader does not seem fully available to him either. Instead, eschewing both elegant rhetoric and erotic action, Adonis refuses to be written into the timeless seduction scene and insists on his present, idiosyncratic discomfort and lack of interest: "Fie, no more of love! / The sun doth burn my face, I must remove" (lines 185-6). In Adonis's narrative, particularity makes Venus and Adonis into personae with some degree of agency, rather than inherited figures whose desires are determined by the metatextual drama they enact.

The poem renders the mythic and realistic modes emphatically incompatible; indeed, the pointedly ridiculous effect of realistically narrating mythic action creates the poem's humor.[16] Comically, the mythic/conventional narrative relishes a poetic eloquence that the realistic eschews. The meter of the poem's opening lines is unapologetically elegant:

> Even as the sun with purple-color'd face
> Had ta'en his last leave of the weeping morn,
> Rose-cheek'd Adonis hied him to the chase;
> Hunting he lov'd, but love he laugh'd to scorn.
>
> (lines 1-4)

The stanza's concluding couplet, on the other hand, introduces the seduction theme in a burlesque rhyme: "Sick-thoughted Venus makes amain unto him, / And like a bold-fac'd suitor gins to woo him" (lines 5-6). The second stanza reverts to the stylishness of the first four lines, but in the third stanza, when Venus ceases lauding Adonis and begins soliciting him, singsong meter and comically overblown feminine rhyme return ("'Here come and sit, where never serpent hisses, / And being set, I'll smother thee with kisses'" [lines 17-81]). When Venus finally takes decisive action, in couplet lines, the metrical reinforcement of the plot is farcically pat: "Being so enrag'd, desire doth lend her force / Courageously to pluck him from his horse" (lines 29-30). The caesura trumpets dramatic suspense; the iambic regularity of the fast-reading, five-foot, mostly monosyllabic line 30 underlines the physical ease with which Venus accomplishes her kidnap, the melodramatic acceleration in tempo pointing up the ludicrousness of sweatily embodying the Goddess of Love.

More significantly, the poetic and narrative effects of the two discourses work to opposite ends. Venus's linguistic and erotic initiatives alike impede the diegetic progress of the suspended hunt narrative that Adonis desires to resume. For, although language serves many needs for Venus, narrative momentum is not one of them. Her discourse winds along digressive paths shaped by the figurative logic of her images or the forensic logic of her conventional arguments, interrupting the progression of the plot. In the opening stanzas discussed above, Venus addresses Adonis for three and a half figure-laden stanzas before seizing him. By contrast, the poem's so-called "action"—Adonis's sporadic bursts of motion away from Venus and toward the hunt—moves briskly forward precisely whenever Venus stops talking. Even Adonis's most extended speech, the seven stanzas that culminate in his narratively decisive departure,

> With this he breaketh from the sweet embrace
> Of those fair arms which bound him to her breast,
> And homeward through the dark laund runs apace,
>
> (lines 811-3)

seems terse and active in comparison to the preceding twenty-five stanzas of Venus's attempts to dissuade him—a passage that confuses even Venus, who must ask in the middle "Where did I leave?" (line 715).

As judged by capaciousness, poetic versatility, facility, and claims on the reader's attention—i.e., by the standards of humanist sprezzatura—it is Venus who owns language in the poem.[17] The poem associates Adonis's silences with his refusal of Venus's erotics; inverting this link, Venus's language is inextricably intertwined with the passion governing and governed by the goddess. Language and desire produce and magnify one another. . . .

Even the ruptures in Venus's speech—the kisses that render her "'lustful language broken'"—do not impede language so much as disperse it. Greedily inserting itself everywhere, Venus's language operates in an economy of lust that utterly overcomes Adonis's volition. When Adonis tries to articulate his refusal of Venus's arguments, her kiss prevents him: "He with she is immodest, blames her miss; / What follows more, she murthers with a kiss" (lines 53-4). "Murthers" figuratively realizes the earlier threat that disobedient lips "shall never open'" (line 48); "'smother[ing]'" Adonis (line 18), her kisses deny him both oxygen and argument.

Through conventional rhetorical strategies, Venus's discourse blurs temporal and rhetorical boundaries as well, to ends equally antipathetic to Adonis. Substitution of the figurative for the literal permeates Venus's arguments. She assures Adonis:

> "The kiss shall be thine own as well as mine.
> What seest thou in the ground? hold up thy head,
> Look in mine eyeballs, there thy beauty lies;
> Then why not lips on lips, since eyes in eyes?"
>
> (lines 117-20)

Departing from the Neoplatonic axiom that beauty lies in the beholder's eye, Venus advances a formal argument for acknowledging through action the commensurability between lips and eyes already established by conventional logic and by analogy. Erasing substantive difference between gazes and kisses, Venus's argument—like Scholastic or indeed Petrarchan reasoning—treats "eyes" and "lips" as interchangeable subjects of formal manipulation. This congruence rhetorically anticipates concession, further eroding distinctions between logic and volition, suggestion and acquiescence, wish and fulfillment. Furthermore, love's language propels its speakers out of narrative temporality into the timelessness of the mythic: "copious stories, oftentimes begun, / End without audience, and are never done" (lines 845-6). Accordingly, Venus's first declaration of passion for Adonis violates temporal boundaries by serving as prophecy, articulating the future in the present. The floral—and, incongruously, also apocalyptic—images she addresses to Adonis prefigure his eventual transformation in death: he is, ominously, "'more lovely than a man'" (line 9). Furthermore, "'Nature, that made thee with herself at strife, / Saith that the world hath ending with thy life'" (lines 11-2). As metaphoric comparison that also serves as literal prediction, this language of desire likewise dissolves the semantic distinction between vehicle and tenor.[18]

Venus's reasoning from analogy, together with her characteristic equation of distinct categories, thus exemplifies what Foucault calls "analogical" thought, distinct from the "modern" disjunctions between words and things and among kinds of things. "Analogic" thought ponders a world that "fold[s] in upon itself, duplicate[s] itself, reflect[s] itself, or form[s] a chain with itself so that things can resemble one another"; this language "par takes in the world wide dissemination of similitudes and signatures."[19] Whereas Venus's discourse is predicated on proximity and analogy, Adonis's is more invested in separation and substitution—in Foucault's terms, with "modern" signification: that is, the "ordering of things by means of . . . fabricated signs" for a "knowledge based upon identity and difference."[20] The poem figures Venus's affect through pathetic fallacies: her thoughts leach into nature as troubled "neighbor caves" murmur her longing (line 830) and "shrill-tongu'd tapsters" share her anxiety (line 849). Adonis's death, by contrast, is represented by signifiers requiring interpretation: the "sad signs" (line 929) the narrator associates with "apparitions . . . and prodigies" (line 926). Adonis's hunting hounds are saddened by his death, but not with the same kind of pathetic sorrow that Venus's caves express. Whereas the caves ironically participate in Venus's affect (in Roman Jakobson's sense of "icons" as signifiers that represent a signified by sharing its essence), the hounds suggest a signifying narrative.[21] In their silence, wound licking, and scowling (lines 914-7), the hounds present information that is interpretable but not transparent, emphasizing disjunctions and incommensurabilities where the caves and tapsters emphasize continuities. Hence the hunting hounds do not share a language with Venus, but rather preserve distinctions among species of discourse: "here she meets another sadly scowling, / To whom she speaks, and he replies with howling" (lines 917-8).

Adonis's death and metamorphosis further link him to semiotic habits associated with separation, distinction, and mediated "signification," as opposed to comparison, analogy and iconicity. The flower that Adonis becomes functions not as an icon but as a sign. To be more precise, it is a sign in the terms of his story; the meanings of the metamorphosis—indeed of metamorphosis in general—diverge significantly in the two logical frameworks. Venus attempts rather desperately to impose an analogical likeness onto the blossom: in her vision of the dead Adonis, the flower "Resembl[es] well his pale cheeks" (line 1169), and Venus informs the flower that it shares a kinship tie with Adonis: "'Here was thy father's bed'" (line 1183). But despite her insistence on the filial continuity between bloom and man, the point of view we can infer from Adonis's words as well as his representation in the poem makes the flower function as an incommensurable stand-in—like a sign—for the young man made absent by death. For existence as a flower, immobile and delicate, is utterly incompatible with existence as a hunter. Despite herself, Venus betrays the gap between Adonis and the flower by disingenuously suggesting that she has won the amorous contest. Claiming that her breast was "'thy father's bed' and announcing with a certain compensatory triumph that "There shall not be one minute in an hour / Wherein I will not kiss my sweet love's flow'r" (lines 1187), Venus glosses over a crucial inversion of agency: she had begged for the live Adonis to kiss her. The conventional association of flowering with completion or fulfillment casts further ironic light on the phrase "'my sweet love's flower'"; Adonis's transformation hardly constitutes Venus's love come to flower, but rather its final frustration. Soon to wither, deprived of the potential to grant the acquiescence Venus craves, the blossom escapes Venus's erotics despite its imprisonment in the "'hollow cradle'"—we might emphasize "'hollow'"—of her breasts (line 1185).

Metamorphosis directly engages questions of contiguity and separation, sameness and difference, the object as *Ding an sich* and the object as contingent and mutable manifestation of first matter, ideal form, or similar early modern notions of the cosmic relatedness of all things. In its play on form as stable, autonomous identity versus form as signifier of other potential or erstwhile states, metamorphosis provides the poem another arena for working through the differences between the mythic/conventional and the historical/particular modes of narrative, desire, and subjectivity. Like the actual metamorphosis that closes the tale, other metamorphoses figuratively invoked earlier in the poem provide double interpretative possibilities. These transformations contrast metamorphosis as the transcendent instantiation of analogy (similarity among things) to metamorphosis as destruction (the annihilation of a thing, alienated when a profoundly different form overcomes it). As part of her seduction argument, for example, Venus suggests an extended analogy between Adonis and a deer. . . .

Within the logic of Venus's poetics, the deer figure allows Adonis to be both himself and something else. That is, Venus proposes a metaphor that provides an alternative lexical framework for actions—whether grazing or caressing—that are equally possible for a man or a deer. The easy continuity in Venus's discourse between vehicle and tenor underlines the full congruence between Venus-as-body and Venus-as-park, conveying the wholesomeness, the delightful variety, and the naturalness of habitat (she maintains) for hart and lover alike. Adonis's transformation into a fragile flower, whose inevitable demise Venus rudely hastens, retroactively suggests a dissenting view of this same image: the deer metamorphosis that Adonis refuses would transform the young man into an entity inimical and fatal to his self—in fact, into quarry for his proper self. The echoes of Actaeon in the metamorphosis Venus offers heighten the opposition Adonis seems to see between heteroerotic seduction and hunting. Such alienation would certainly follow from a deer grazing/gazing on a goddess: Actaeon's transformation turned him from hunter to hunted, and Adonis wants no part of it.

Adonis's metamorphosis simultaneously realizes and frustrates both Venus's and Adonis's aims. Adonis escapes Venus's logic only to be returned helplessly to her bosom; Venus finally sees Adonis's scrupulously defended boundaries breached only to render him incapable of satisfying her passion. In its traditionally tragic end, the myth of Venus and Adonis explores the impossibility of erotic satisfaction when mortals are involved; Shakespeare's text distills this aspect of the tale into Venus's version of the story. This poem's reluctant Adonis renders another kind of fulfillment impossible—a pleasure that depends on escaping Venus. The entire narrative has shown the two figures' desires to be incompatible; analyzing Adonis's metamorphosis shows that the mere existence of each desire undermines the other's conditions of possibility. On one side, Adonis's distaste for Venus's proposals, together with the ways the poem pokes fun at Venus's excesses, suggests her limitations. On the other, Venus's use of mythic logic, her assertions of infinite analogy, and her own identity as the personification of love operate as inherently self-evident and universal: hence, they cannot accommodate compromise.[22] Notably, however, Adonis offers objections rather than alternatives: Venus's poetic dominance makes positively articulating other erotics, poetics, or values impossible.

Thus, whereas Peter Erickson and Patrick Murphy have interpreted the poem's cautiousness in representing alternatives to Venus's views as mere political circumspection, I would argue that the poem's recourse to indirect suggestions of vaguely delineated choices indicates more than strategic self-censorship.[23] Adonis's hesitations also gesture toward emergent paradigms of subjectivity and semiotics that are not sufficiently manifest to be clearly represented: something akin to what Francis Barker characterizes as the "incipient modernity" of Hamlet's "anachronistic" longing for a more modern subject position than his historical moment permits.[24] If we were to characterize the poem's competing modes of desire and representation historically, then, my understanding of Adonis's (proto) subjectivity would lead in the opposite direction from Nona Fienberg's conclusions. Fienberg associates Adonis with an aristocratic "fixity," "absoluteness," and "patriarchy" that she characterizes as essentially medieval, while her Venus evidences a "mutability and diversity" that "provid[e].. a way to reevaluate patriarchy."[25] While I agree to an extent that the poem associates Adonis's desires with "fixity" and "patriarchy," I would argue that these do not, as Fienberg claims, constitute the status quo in the poem—nor, entirely, in its historical context. Rather, the Venus whom Fienberg argues to be fluid and "dynamic" uses this "flexibility" only instrumentally, within traditional humanist rhetorical practice, to ingeniously and irrefutably perpetuate paradigms based on rhetorical analogy, ontological continuity, and the authority of mythic and literary-conventional tradition. Whereas Fienberg (in a move medievalists might find oversimplifying) characterizes

Adonis as "a relic of the time before the commercial and humanist revolutions, when value was a given"[26] who "holds on to his old ways of measuring time, growth, maturity, and value," I would argue that through inclining in both his desires and his semiotics toward deferral, separation, and idiosyncrasy, Adonis emerges as something of a figure for protomodernity, or at least for resistance to the values Venus espouses.[27] It is semiotic absoluteness, autonomous identity, and social patriarchy, I think, that the poem presents as constituting a departure.[28]

The poem's simultaneous representation of different discursivities and subjectivities might, however, give pause to the project of firmly historicizing these modes (a Foucauldean version of the Whiggish march to modernity). It might be more frutiful, and more accurate, to consider what I have called the poem's protomodern and nonmodern modes as simultaneous aspects of a typically mixed cultural moment. Indeed, particularly intriguing about this poem (and its milieu) are the differences between the modes and interests here aligned as congruent (femininity/status quo/speech, for example, versus masculinity/marginality/silence) with our more expected aggregations. This is not to say that the poem celebrates a happy heteroglossia of Elizabethan culture. By confining its represented action to what Venus witnesses, and by demonstrating the limitations of her practices, the poem thematizes the difficulty of representing competing models (whether we trace this difficulty to an authoritarian queen, the poetic demands of generic convention, a watershed moment in the history of subjectivity, covert cultural contests between masculinist poetic culture and propagandists for the Cult of Elizabeth—or concede it to be overdetermined). The hunting band provides the locus for alternatives to Venus's authority, in a way that may have been particularly satisfying for the primary 1590s (male) readership at the Inns of Court or indeed the royal court—but precisely what these alternatives would be remains pointedly oblique.[29] In the end, the poem draws much of its energy from this obliqueness, creating an epyllion about what Ovidian poetry cannot represent—a gushing epideictic on an overbearing queen, a camp triangulation of a Venus who does not realize she is in a poem, an Adonis who half realizes and does not want to be, and a reader who smugly knows the score. And in this obliqueness, I suggest, Adonis's positions come closest to a kind of realization, insofar as the poem's silences draw the reader into fleshing out what the text occludes. Venus argues her familiar positions all too thoroughly, leaving the reader no task but assent. But drawing the reader into chasing an alternative that is not fully visible, traceable from two steps behind through prints left between the lines, does not the poem invite the reader into the oppositional hunting band?

Notes

1. William Shakespeare, *Venus and Adonis,* in *The Riverside Shakespeare,* ed. G. Blakemore Evans (Boston: Houghton Mifflin, 1974), pp. 1705-19, lines 13-6. All subsequent references to *Venus and Adonis* will be to this edition and will appear parenthetically in the text by line number.

2. For the range of interpretations particularly focused on Adonis's reluctance, see T. W. Baldwin's Neoplatonic reading in *On the Literary Genetics of Shakespeare's Poems and Sonnets* (Urbana: Univ. of Illinois Press, 1950); S. Clark Hulse's and John Doebler's discussions of iconography in, respectively, "Shakespeare's Myth of Venus and Adonis," *PMLA* 93, 1 (January 1978): 95-105, and "The Reluctant Adonis: Titian and Shakespeare," *SQ* [*Shakespeare Quarterly*] 33,4 (Winter 1982): 480-90; J. D. Jahn's analysis of Adonis's moral failings in "The Lamb of Lust: The Role of Adonis in Shakespeare's *Venus and Adonis,*" *ShakS* [*Shakespeare Studies*] 6 (1970): 11-25; Coppelia Kahn's psychoanalytic account of Adonis's hesitation in *Man's Estate: Masculine Identity in Shakespeare* (Berkeley: Univ. of California Press, 1981); Catherine Belsey's taxonomy of desire in "Love as Trompe-l'oeil: Taxonomies of Desire in Venus and Adonis," *SQ* 46, 3 (Fall 1995): 257-76; Patrick M. Murphy's discussion of the poem as advice literature on negotiating competing obligations in "Wriothesley's Resistance: Wardship Practices and Ovidian Narratives in Shakespeare's *Venus and Adonis,*" in *Venus and Adonis: Critical Essays,* ed. Philip C. Kolin (New York: Garland Publishing, 1997), pp. 323-40; and A. D. Cousins's argument that Adonis is feminized by his refusal, in "Towards a Reconsideration of Shakespeare's Adonis: Rhetoric, Narcissus, and the Male Gaze," *SN* [*Studia Neophilologica*] 68, 2 (1996): 195-204. Although Karen Newman argues for a "shift in perspective from Adonis's unwillingness to Venus's desire" (p. 254), she shares these critics' understanding of a reluctant Adonis: see the important but seldom cited "Myrrha's Revenge: Ovid and Shakespeare's Reluctant Adonis," *Illinois Classical Studies* 9, 2 (Fall 1984): 251-65. Recently, Robert P. Merrix and, briefly, Bruce R. Smith have considered what does interest Adonis as well as what repels him, in Smith's *Homosexual Desire in Shakespeare's England: A Cultural Poetics* (Chicago: Univ. of Chicago Press, 1991) and Merrix's "'Lo, in This Hollow Cradle Take Thy Rest': Sexual Conflict and Resolution in *Venus and Adonis,*" in Kolin, pp. 341-58. An unusual earlier reading that acknowledges Adonis's desire is A. Robin Bowers, "'Hard Armours' and 'Delicate Amours' in Shakespeare's *Venus and Adonis,*" *ShS* [*Shake-

speare Survey] 12 (1979): 1-23. However, Bowers bases this argument on Adonis's single kiss, failing to account for the distaste Adonis demonstrates in the rest of the poem.

3. See Frankie Rubinstein, *A Dictionary of Shakespeare's Sexual Puns and Their Significance,* 2d edn. (New York: St. Martin's Press, 1995).

4. An important exception here is Joel Fineman's *Shakespeare's Perjured Eye: The Invention of Poetic Subjectivity in the Sonnets* (Berkeley: Univ. of California Press, 1986).

5. Influential examples of the former include Kahn, *Man's Estate,* and Nona Fienberg, "Thematics of Value in *Venus and Adonis," Criticism* 31, 1 (Winter 1989): 21-32. On the latter, see particularly Lucy Gent, "'Venus and Adonis': The Triumph of Rhetoric," *MLR* [*Modern Language Review*] 69, 4 (October 1974): 721-9; Hulse; and Jonathan Hart, "'Till Forging Nature Be Condemned of Treason': Representational Strife in *Venus and Adonis," Cahiers Elisabethains: Etudes sur la Pre-Renaissance et la Renaissance Anglaises* 36 (1989): 37-48.

6. Heather Dubrow, *Captive Victors: Shakespeare's Narrative Poems and Sonnets* (Ithaca: Cornell Univ. Press, 1987), p. 27. Conversely, Goran Stanivukovic examines rhetoric "as a cognitive mode which suggests the early modern conceptualisation of desire in *Venus and Adonis,"* in "Troping Desire in Shakespeare's *Venus and Adonis," FMLS* [*Forum for Modern Language Studies*] 33, 4 (October 1997): 289-301, 290 (my emphasis).

7. James Schiffer, "Shakespeare's *Venus and Adonis:* A Lacanian Tragicomedy of Desire," in Kolin, pp. 359-76, 372.

8. Jane Hedley, *Power in Verse: Metaphor and Metonymy in the Renaissance Lyric* (University Park: Pennsylvania State Univ. Press, 1988), p. 22.

9. Most interpretations of Adonis's Venus/boar opposition pair "love" and Venus together as an alternative to the boar hunt, rather than following the verse's syntactically implied opposition of Venus-love and boar-love. See D. C. Allen on hunting and love as alternative but complementary forms of pursuit ("On *Venus and Adonis,"* in *Elizabethan and Jacobean Studies Presented to F. P. Wilson,* ed. Herbert Davis and Helen Gardner [Oxford: Clarendon Press, 1959], pp. 100-11), and Norman Rabkin on the characters' arguments for and against sensual love, in *Shakespeare and the Common Understanding* (New York: Free Press, 1967). Exceptions to the tendency of opposing hunting and love include A. T. Hatto's "Venus and Adonis—and the Boar," *MLR* 41, 4 (October

1946): 353-61, which depicts the boar as "overbearing masculinity" that rivals Venus, and Kahn's notion of the boar as the repository of Adonis's projected fantasy/fears about Venus. Other interpretations making substantial use of this line include William E. Sheidley, "Unless It Be a Boar': Love and Wisdom in Shakespeare's *Venus and Adonis," MLQ* [*Modern Language Quarterly*] 35, 1 (March 1974): 3-15, and William Keach, *Elizabethan Erotic Narratives: Irony and Pathos in the Ovidian Poetry of Shakespeare, Marlowe, and Their Contemporaries* (New Brunswick NJ: Rutgers Univ. Press, 1977).

10. J. W. Lever notes the relevance here of Theocritus's idyll, translated in 1588, in which the boar declares his love for the young shepherd, see "The Poems," *ShS* 15 (1962): 18-22, 21.

11. See Jacques Lacan, "The Signification of the Phallus," in *Ecrits: A Selection,* trans. Alan Sheridan (New York: W. W. Norton, 1977), pp. 281-92.

12. Sheidley, p. 10.

13. As this discussion indicates, I disagree with Peter Erickson's claim that the dynamics of the hunting band are entirely opaque and thus irrelevant ("In theory, Adonis's hunt is not a solitary activity, as his allusions to his [male] friends . . . indicate . . . [but] . . . since they never actually appear, they are for practical purposes nonexistent"): see Erickson's *Rewriting Shakespeare, Rewriting Ourselves* (Berkeley: Univ. of California Press, 1991), p. 43.

14. Kahn, P. 36.

15. Likewise, Fienberg cites "The sea hath bounds, but deep desire hath none" (line 389) to illustrate that "Venus's desire is unlimited, multiple" (p. 25).

16. The contrast fails to amuse some commentators; for instance, Hallett Smith remarks that "the celebrated description of the horse, the account of the coursing of the hare, and the images of the dive-dapper, the snail, and the lark . . . [are] difficult to harmonize with the elements of classical myth" (introduction to *Venus and Adonis,* p. 1704). Others contend that the realistic and mythic modes are compatible; for example, Douglas Bush comments that rare "natural" images "heighten" the overall effect of Ovidian artifice; see *Mythology and the Renaissance Tradition in English Poetry* (Minneapolis: Univ. of Minnesota Press, 1932), p. 147. A more recent take on the same problem comes in Hart's claim that the work foregrounds the "friction between mimetic and supplemental art" (p. 37). Dubrow provides an important counterargument to these kinds of binary analyses,

arguing against "an absolute split between the rhetorical and the mimetic" (p. 16).

17. In remarks relevant to my linking Venus's discourse with specifically humanist mastery, Dubrow notes the poem's association of Venus with Elizabethan aesthetic convention; M. L. Stapleton intriguingly casts Venus as a rhetorical pedagogue ("Venus as Praeceptor. The *Ars Amatoria* in *Venus and Adonis*," in Kolin, pp. 309-21); Sheidley identifies Venus's language as that of the sonneteer; and Christy Desmet notes that "Venus is an orator . . . [whose] weapons are those commonly found in the schoolboy's arsenal" (*Reading Shakespeare's Characters: Rhetoric, Ethics, and Identity* [Amherst: Univ. of Massachusetts Press, 1992], p. 138).

18. Dubrow emphasizes a different aspect of this tendency in her discussion of Venus "renaming the world" by "transform[ing] the material into the spiritual" (p. 29); Gent discusses the same habit as "hyberbole," and Katharine Eisaman Maus notes the consistently violent results of collapsing metaphor in "Taking Tropes Seriously: Language and Violence in Shakespeare's *Rape of Lucrece*," *SQ* 37, 1 (Spring 1986): 66-82.

19. Michel Foucault, *The Order of Things: An Archaeology of the Human Sciences* (1966; rprt. New York: Vintage Books, 1973), pp. 25-6, p. 35.

20. Foucault, pp. 59, 63 (my emphasis).

21. See particularly Roman Jakobson's "A Glance at the Development of Semiotics," in *Selected Writings*, ed. Stephen Rudy, 8 vols.- (Gravenhage: Mouton, 1962-), 7:199-218.

22. Logically enough, psychoanalytic as well as archetypal interpretations of the poem reproduce Venus's reasoning. To give a twentieth-century psychoanalytic example: for Kahn, Venus is love, heterosexual erotics provide a requisite rite of passage, and Adonis's reluctance constitutes a refusal to embrace mature male identity. Ovidian commentators of late antiquity, who associate the myth with seasonal change and ritual renewal, work in a similarly definite framework.

23. Erickson remarks—and I would agree—that "Venus's domination evokes Elizabeth's control, and this undercurrent helps to account for the poem's unstable tonal mixture of defensive jocularity and general alarm" (p. 41). Murphy argues that the poem offers Henry Wriothesley counsel on his negotiations with the crown.

24. Francis Barker, *The Tremulous Private Body: Essays on Subjection* (London: Methuen, 1984), pp. 27, 37 (my emphasis).

25. Fienberg, p. 21.

26. Fienberg, p. 23.

27. Fienberg, p. 27.

28. Like mine, Belsey's argument aligns Adonis's position with historical change, insofar as Adonis is the figure who articulates the distinction between love and lust. This distinction "brings an emergent taxonomy into conjunction—and conflict—with a residual indeterminacy" (p. 275). Without making historical claims, Merrix and Smith both associate Venus with the fixity of social proscription and domestic confinement. Merrix argues that "[t]he conflict between Venus and Adonis . . . concerns conflicting lifestyles, one domestic, fruitful and secure, and the other exotic, sterile, and dangerous" (p. 343). Smith addresses the poem's participation in an Elizabethan paradigm shared by romance narratives and folk plays, which "strike . . . [a balance] . . . between positive and negative controls . . . Both, for a season, valorize' polymorphous passion. Both, in the end, take that value away" (p. 127.

29. Detailing the dynamics of these readerships lies beyond the scope of the present paper. Briefly, both these venues constitute circles of male power, subject to the greater authority of the queen, but internally exclusively male. Significantly, both the Inns of Court and the royal court are subject to far more frequent and regular assertion of the queen's authority—particularly, of course, the latter—than such analogous male bastions as the universities or the church, since they operate in such geographic proximity to Elizabeth's quotidian routines. Exploring how this poem functions in these circles would perhaps serve to flesh out what might be entailed in the "homosocial style" Richard Halpern enigmatically invokes without specification: 'The English tradition of Ovidian poetry was fostered in . . . exclusively male bastions that cultivated a homosocial style" ("'Pining Their Maws': Female Readers and the Erotic Ontology of the Text in Shakespeare's *Venus and Adonis*," in Kolin, pp. 377-88, p. 378). On Inns of Court readership of *Venus and Adonis*, see Keach; Philip J. Finkelpearl, *John Marston of the Middle Temple: An Elizabethan Dramatist in His Social Setting* (Cambridge MA: Harvard Univ. Press, 1969); and Arthur F. Marotti, John Donne, Coterie Poet (Madison: Univ. of Wisconsin Press, 1986). On Venus and Elizabeth, see also Kirby Farrell, *Play, Death, and Heroism in Shakespeare* (Chapel Hill: Univ. of North Carolina Press, 1989), pp. 125-30.

FURTHER READING

Criticism

Butler, Christopher, and Alastair Fowler. "Time-Beguiling Sport: Number Symbolism in Shakespeare's *Venus and Adonis*." In Venus and Adonis: *Critical Essays,* edited by Philip C. Kolin, pp. 157-69. New York: Garland Publishing, 1997.

> Stresses the presence of numerological patterns as significant thematic and structural components in *Venus and Adonis.*

Froes, João. "Shakespeare's Venus and the Venus of Classical Mythology." In Venus and Adonis: *Critical Essays,* edited by Philip C. Kolin, pp. 301-21. New York: Garland Publishing, 1997.

> Argues that the mixture of maternal and sexual love demonstrated by Shakespeare's Venus in *Venus and Adonis* coincides with, rather than contradicts, classical depictions of the Roman goddess.

Greenfield, Sayre N. "Allegorical Impulses and Critical Ends: Shakespeare's and Spenser's Venus and Adonis." *Criticism* 36, no. 4 (fall 1994): 475-97.

> Focuses on allegorical critical approaches to Shakespeare's *Venus and Adonis* and Book Three of Edmund Spenser's *The Faerie Queene.*

Kolin, Philip C. "Venus and/or Adonis among the Critics." In Venus and Adonis: *Critical Essays,* edited by Philip C. Kolin, pp. 3-65. New York: Garland Publishing, 1997.

> Surveys the critical reception and principal areas of scholarly debate regarding *Venus and Adonis.*

Mortimer, Anthony. "Rhetoric, Myth, and the Descent of Venus." In *Variable Passions: A Reading of Shakespeare's* Venus and Adonis, pp. 1-35. New York: AMS Press, 2000.

> Concentrates on the rhetorical methods of *Venus and Adonis* and surveys modern critical debate regarding the poem.

Murphy, Patrick M. "Wriothesley's Resistance: Wardship Practices and Ovidian Narratives in Shakespeare's *Venus and Adonis*." In Venus and Adonis: *Critical Essays,* edited by Philip C. Kolin, pp. 323-40. New York: Garland Publishing, 1997.

> Topical reading of *Venus and Adonis* that draws upon historical material related to Henry Wriothesley, the third Earl of Southampton, and his refusal to marry an heiress while still a youth and ward.

Shakespearean Criticism
Cumulative Character Index

The Cumulative Character Index identifies the principal characters of discussion in the criticism of each play and non-dramatic poem. The characters are arranged alphabetically. Page references indicate the beginning page number of each essay containing substantial commentary on that character.

Ariel
The Tempest **8:** 289, 293, 294, 295, 297, 304, 307, 315, 320, 326, 328, 336, 340, 345, 356, 364, 420, 458; **22:** 302; **29:** 278, 297, 362, 368, 377; **72:** 302, 318; **75:** 237

Armado
Love's Labour's Lost **23:** 207

Arthur
King John **9:** 215, 216, 218, 219, 229, 240, 267, 275; **22:** 120; **25:** 98; **41:** 251, 277; **56:** 345, 357; **78:** 26

Arviragus
Cymbeline See **Guiderius and Arviragus**

Audrey
As You Like It **46:** 122

Aufidius
Coriolanus **9:** 9, 12, 17, 19, 53, 121, 148, 153, 157, 169, 180, 193; **19:** 287; **25:** 263, 296; **30:** 58, 67, 89, 96, 133; **50:** 99

Autolycus
The Winter's Tale **7:** 375, 380, 382, 387, 389, 395, 396, 414; **15:** 524; **22:** 302; **37:** 31; **45:** 333; **46:** 14, 33; **50:** 45; **68:** 297

Banquo
Macbeth **3:** 183, 199, 208, 213, 278, 289; **20:** 279, 283, 406, 413; **25:** 235; **28:** 339

Baptista
The Taming of the Shrew **9:** 325, 344, 345, 375, 386, 393, 413; **55:** 334

Barnardine
Measure for Measure **13:** 112; **65:** 30

Bassanio
The Merchant of Venice **25:** 257; **37:** 86; **40:** 156; **66:** 63, 135

the Bastard
King John See **Faulconbridge (Philip) the Bastard**

Beatrice and Benedick
Much Ado about Nothing
ambivalent portrayal of **67:** 155
Beatrice's femininity **8:** 14, 16, 17, 24, 29, 38, 41, 91; **31:** 222, 245; **55:** 221
Beatrice's request to "kill Claudio" (Act IV, scene i) **8:** 14, 17, 33, 41, 55, 63, 75, 79, 91, 108, 115; **18:** 119, 120, 136, 161, 245, 257; **55:** 268; **78:** 70, 92, 101, 127
Benedick's challenge of Claudio (Act V, scene i) **8:** 48, 63, 79, 91; **31:** 231
Claudio and Hero, compared with **8:** 19, 28, 29, 75, 82, 115; **31:** 171, 216; **55:** 189; **67:** 108; **78:** 70
general discussion **78:** 140
marriage and the opposite sex, attitudes toward **8:** 9, 13, 14, 16, 19, 29, 36, 48, 63, 77, 91, 95, 115, 121; **16:** 45; **31:** 216; **48:** 14; **67:** 134, 163

mutual attraction **8:** 13, 14, 19, 24, 29, 33, 41, 75; **48:** 14; **78:** 92
nobility **8:** 13, 19, 24, 29, 36, 39, 41, 47, 82, 91, 108
popularity **8:** 13, 38, 41, 53, 79; **78:** 65, 92
transformed by love **8:** 19, 29, 36, 48, 75, 91, 95, 115; **31:** 209, 216; **55:** 236; **67:** 134
unconventionality **8:** 48, 91, 95, 108, 115, 121; **55:** 221, 249, 268; **67:** 108
vulgarity **8:** 11, 12, 33, 38, 41, 47
wit and charm **8:** 9, 12, 13, 14, 19, 24, 27, 28, 29, 33, 36, 38, 41, 47, 55, 69, 95, 108, 115; **31:** 241; **55:** 199; **67:** 163; **78:** 92

Belarius
Cymbeline **4:** 48, 89, 141

Benedick
Much Ado about Nothing See **Beatrice and Benedick**

Berowne
Love's Labour's Lost **2:** 308, 324, 327; **22:** 12; **23:** 184, 187; **38:** 194; **47:** 35; **77:** 98

Bertram
All's Well That Ends Well
characterization **7:** 15, 27, 29, 32, 39, 41, 43, 98, 113; **26:** 48; **26:** 117; **48:** 65; **55:** 90; **75:** 2, 57
conduct **7:** 9, 10, 12, 16, 19, 21, 51, 62, 104; **50:** 59; **55:** 143, 154
physical desire **22:** 78
transformation or redemption **7:** 10, 19, 21, 26, 29, 32, 54, 62, 81, 90, 93, 98, 109, 113, 116, 126; **13:** 84

Bianca
The Taming of the Shrew **9:** 325, 342, 344, 345, 360, 362, 370, 375
Bianca-Lucentio subplot **9:** 365, 370, 375, 390, 393, 401, 407, 413, 430; **16:** 13; **31:** 339; **64:** 255; **77:** 273

the boar
Venus and Adonis **10:** 416, 451, 454, 466, 473; **33:** 339, 347, 370

Boleyn (Anne Boleyn)
Henry VIII **2:** 21, 24, 31; **41:** 180; **61:** 119, 129; **72:** 36

Bolingbroke
Richard II See **Henry (King Henry IV, previously known as Bolingbroke)**

Borachio and Conrade
Much Ado about Nothing **8:** 24, 69, 82, 88, 111, 115; **78:** 80

Bottom
A Midsummer Night's Dream
awakening speech (Act IV, scene i) **3:** 406, 412, 450, 457, 486, 516; **16:** 34; **58:** 181; **70:** 123
folly of **46:** 1, 14, 29, 60
his dream **60:** 142
imagination **3:** 376, 393, 406, 432, 486; **29:** 175, 190; **45:** 147; **70:** 172
self-possession **3:** 365, 376, 395, 402, 406, 480; **45:** 158

Titania, relationship with **3:** 377, 406, 441, 445, 450, 457, 491, 497; **16:** 34; **19:** 21; **22:** 93; **29:** 216; **45:** 160; **58:** 203, 215; **70:** 105, 123, 193
transformation **3:** 365, 377, 432; **13:** 27; **22:** 93; **29:** 216; **45:** 147, 160; **70:** 105, 123

Brabantio
Othello **25:** 189

Brutus
Coriolanus See **the tribunes**
Julius Caesar **50:** 194, 258
arrogance **7:** 160, 169, 204, 207, 264, 277, 292, 350; **25:** 280; **30:** 351
as chief protagonist or tragic hero **7:** 152, 159, 189, 191, 200, 204, 242, 250, 253, 264, 268, 279, 284, 298, 333; **17:** 272, 372, 387
citizenship **25:** 272
funeral oration **7:** 154, 155, 204, 210, 350
motives **7:** 150, 156, 161, 179, 191, 200, 221, 227, 233, 245, 292, 303, 310, 320, 333, 350; **25:** 272; **30:** 321, 358; **74:** 167
nobility or idealism **7:** 150, 152, 156, 159, 161, 179, 189, 191, 200, 221, 242, 250, 253, 259, 264, 277, 303, 320; **17:** 269, 271, 273, 279, 280, 284, 306, 308, 321, 323, 324, 345, 358; **25:** 272, 280; **30:** 351, 362; **74:** 113
political ineptitude or lack of judgment **7:** 169, 188, 200, 205, 221, 245, 252, 264, 277, 282, 310, 316, 331, 333, 343; **17:** 323, 358, 375, 380; **50:** 13
self-knowledge or self-deception **7:** 191, 200, 221, 242, 259, 264, 268, 279, 310, 333, 336, 350; **25:** 272; **30:** 316; **60:** 46
soliloquy (Act II, scene i) **7:** 156, 160, 161, 191, 221, 245, 250, 253, 264, 268, 279, 282, 292, 303, 343, 350; **25:** 280; **30:** 333
The Rape of Lucrece **10:** 96, 106, 109, 116, 121, 125, 128, 135

Buckingham
Henry VIII **22:** 182; **24:** 129, 140; **37:** 109

Bushy, Bagot, and Greene
Richard II **58:** 259

Cade (Jack [John] Cade)
Henry VI, Parts 1, 2, and 3 **3:** 35, 67, 92, 97, 109; **16:** 183; **22:** 156; **25:** 102; **28:** 112; **37:** 97; **39:** 160, 196, 205

Caesar
Antony and Cleopatra **65:** 270
Antony, relationship with as leader **48:** 206
Julius Caesar **50:** 189, 230, 234
ambiguous nature **7:** 191, 233, 242, 250, 272, 298, 316, 320; **74:** 136, 167
ambitious nature **50:** 234; **74:** 136
arrogance **7:** 160, 207, 218, 253, 272, 279, 298; **25:** 280
idolatry **22:** 137
leadership qualities **7:** 161, 179, 189, 191, 200, 207, 233, 245, 253, 257, 264, 272, 279, 284, 298, 310, 333; **17:** 317, 358; **22:** 280; **30:** 316, 326; **50:** 234
as tragic hero **7:** 152, 200, 221, 279; **17:** 321, 377, 384
weakness **7:** 161, 167, 169, 179, 187, 188, 191, 207, 218, 221, 233, 250, 253, 298; **17:** 358; **25:** 280

74, 79, 96, 111, 129; **37**: 283; **50**: 99; **64**: 25, 40, 79; **75**: 92

traitorous actions **9**: 9, 12, 19, 45, 84, 92, 148; **25**: 296; **30**: 133

as unsympathetic character **9**: 12, 13, 62, 78, 80, 84, 112, 130, 157; **64**: 79

the courser and the jennet

Venus and Adonis **10**: 418, 439, 466; **33**: 309, 339, 347, 352

Cranmer

Henry VIII

prophesy of **2**: 25, 31, 46, 56, 64, 68, 72; **24**: 146; **32**: 148; **41**: 120, 190; **56**: 196, 230, 248, 273

Cressida

Troilus and Cressida

as ambiguous figure **43**: 305

inconsistency **3**: 538; **13**: 53; **16**: 70; **22**: 339; **27**: 362

individual will vs. social values **3**: 549, 561, 571, 590, 604, 617, 626; **13**: 53; **27**: 396; **59**: 234, 272

infidelity **3**: 536, 537, 544, 554, 555; **18**: 277, 284, 286; **22**: 58, 339; **27**: 400; **43**: 298

lack of punishment **3**: 536, 537

as mother figure **22**: 339; **71**: 287

objectification of **43**: 329; **59**: 323; **65**: 290

her silence **78**: 254

as sympathetic figure **3**: 557, 560, 604, 609; **18**: 284, 423; **22**: 58; **27**: 396, 400; **43**: 305; **59**: 234, 245; **71**: 236

as a Trojan **59**: 257

Cymbeline

Cymbeline

characterization **61**: 54; **73**: 19

Dark Lady

Sonnets **10**: 161, 167, 176, 216, 217, 218, 226, 240, 302, 342, 377, 394; **25**: 374; **37**: 374; **40**: 273; **48**: 346; **51**: 284, 288, 292, 321; **62**: 121; **75**: 280, 297, 307

the Dauphin

Henry V See **French aristocrats and the Dauphin**

Desdemona

Othello

as Christ figure **4**: 506, 525, 573; **35**: 360

complexity **68**: 95; **79**: 151

culpability **4**: 408, 415, 422, 427; **13**: 313; **19**: 253, 276; **35**: 265, 352, 380

death of **68**: 180

innocence **35**: 360; **43**: 32; **47**: 25; **53**: 310, 333; **68**: 95

as mother figure **22**: 339; **35**: 282; **53**: 324

passivity **4**: 402, 406, 421, 440, 457, 470, 582, 587; **25**: 189; **35**: 380

spiritual nature of her love **4**: 462, 530, 559

staging issues **11**: 350, 354, 359; **13**: 327; **32**: 201

Diana

Pericles

as symbol of nature **22**: 315; **36**: 233; **51**: 71; **66**: 236

Dogberry and the Watch

Much Ado about Nothing **8**: 9, 12, 13, 17, 24, 28, 29, 33, 39, 48, 55, 69, 79, 82, 88, 95, 104, 108, 115; **18**: 138, 152, 205, 208, 210, 213, 231; **22**: 85; **31**: 171, 229; **46**: 60; **55**: 189, 241; **78**: 80

Don John

Much Ado about Nothing See **John (Don John)**

Don Pedro

Much Ado about Nothing See **Pedro (Don Pedro)**

Dromio Brothers

Comedy of Errors **42**: 80; **54**: 136, 152; **66**: 1

Duke

Measure for Measure

as authoritarian figure **23**: 314, 317, 347; **33**: 85; **49**: 274, 300, 358; **65**: 19, 30, 45, 80, 100; **76**: 111; **78**: 249

characterization **2**: 388, 395, 402, 406, 411, 421, 429, 456, 466, 470, 498, 511; **76**: 111 **13**: 84, 94, 104; **23**: 363, 416; **32**: 81; **42**: 1; **44**: 89; **49**: 274, 293, 300, 358; **60**: 12; **65**: 30

as dramatic failure **2**: 420, 429, 441, 479, 495, 505, 514, 522

godlike portrayal of **23**: 320; **65**: 14, 91

noble portrayal of **23**: 301; **65**: 53; **76**: 111

speech on death (Act III, scene i) **2**: 390, 391, 395

as spiritual guide **66**: 300

Othello **25**: 189

Duke Frederick

As You Like It

as tyrant figure **69**: 30

Duncan

Macbeth **57**: 194, 236; **69**: 318

Edgar

King Lear **28**: 223; **32**: 212; **32**: 308; **37**: 295; **47**: 9; **50**: 24, 45; **72**: 235, 263

Edgar-Edmund duel **22**: 365

Edmund

King Lear **25**: 218; **28**: 223

Edmund's forged letter **16**: 372

Edmund of Langley, Duke of York

Richard II See **York**

Egeon

The Comedy of Errors **77**: 29, 54

Egeus

A Midsummer Night's Dream **70**: 105, 140

Elbow

Measure for Measure **22**: 85; **25**: 12

Elbow (Mistress Elbow)

Measure for Measure **33**: 90

elder characters

All's Well That Ends Well **7**: 9, 37, 39, 43, 45, 54, 62, 104

Eleanor

King John **68**: 45, 50

Elizabeth I

Love's Labour's Lost **38**: 239; **64**: 166, 179

Emilia

Othello **4**: 386, 391, 392, 415, 587; **35**: 352, 380; **43**: 32; **68**: 135, 180

The Two Noble Kinsmen **9**: 460, 470, 471, 479, 481; **19**: 394; **41**: 372, 385; **42**: 361; **58**: 322, 338, 345, 356, 361

Enobarbus

Antony and Cleopatra **6**: 22, 23, 27, 43, 94, 120, 142; **16**: 342; **17**: 36; **22**: 217; **27**: 135

Evans, Sir Hugh

The Merry Wives of Windsor **47**: 354

fairies

A Midsummer Night's Dream **3**: 361, 362, 372, 377, 395, 400, 423, 450, 459, 486; **12**: 287, 291, 294, 295; **19**: 21; **29**: 183, 190; **45**: 147; **70**: 186, 193

Falstaff

Henry IV, Parts 1 and 2

characterization **1**: 287, 298, 312, 333; **25**: 245; **28**: 203; **39**: 72, 134, 137, 143; **48**: 117, 151; **57**: 120, 156; **69**: 128, 178

as comic figure **1**: 287, 311, 327, 344, 351, 354, 357, 410, 434; **39**: 89; **46**: 1, 48, 52; **57**: 120; **69**: 147, 148

as comic versus tragic figure **49**: 178

as coward or rogue **1**: 285, 290, 296, 298, 306, 307, 313, 317, 323, 336, 337, 338, 342, 354, 366, 374, 391, 396, 401, 433; **14**: 7, 111, 125, 130, 133; **32**: 166

as deceiver deceived **47**: 308

diminishing powers of **47**: 363

dual personality **1**: 397, 401, 406, 434; **49**: 162

female attributes **13**: 183; **44**: 44; **47**: 325; **60**: 154

Iago, compared with **1**: 341, 351

as Jack-a-Lent **47**: 363

Marxist interpretation **1**: 358, 361; **69**: 128

moral reformation **60**: 26

as outlaw **49**: 133

as parody of the historical plot **1**: 314, 354, 359; **39**: 143; **69**: 100

as positive character **1**: 286, 287, 290, 296, 298, 311, 312, 321, 325, 333, 344, 355, 357, 389, 401, 408, 434

rejection by Hal **1**: 286, 287, 290, 312, 314, 317, 324, 333, 338, 344, 357, 366, 372, 374, 379, 380, 389, 414; **13**: 183; **25**: 109; **39**: 72, 89; **48**: 95; **57**: 147; **66**: 256; **69**: 140, 148, 150

as satire of feudal society **1**: 314, 328, 361; **32**: 103

as scapegoat **1**: 389, 414; **47**: 358, 363, 375; **57**: 156

stage interpretations **14**: 4, 6, 7, 9, 15, 116, 130, 146; **47**: 1

as subversive figure **16**: 183; **25**: 109

Henry V **5**: 185, 186, 187, 189, 192, 195, 198, 210, 226, 257, 269, 271, 276, 293, 299; **28**: 146; **46**: 48; **60**: 26; **79**: 20

Posthumus

Cymbeline **4:** 24, 30, 53, 78, 116, 127, 141, 155, 159, 167; **15:** 89; **19:** 411; **25:** 245, 319; **36:** 142; **44:** 28; **45:** 67, 75; **47:** 25, 205, 228; **61:** 34, 45, 76; **73:** 6, 19

Prince Henry

King John See **Henry (Prince Henry)**

Prospero

The Tempest

characterization **8:** 312, 348, 370, 458; **16:** 442; **22:** 302; **45:** 188, 272; **61:** 307; **72:** 325, 328

as God or Providence **8:** 311, 328, 364, 380, 429, 435

magic, nature of **8:** 301, 340, 356, 396, 414, 423, 458; **25:** 382; **28:** 391; **29:** 278, 292, 368, 377, 396; **32:** 338, 343; **61:** 272; **72:** 3443

psychoanalytic interpretation **45:** 259; **69:** 212

redemptive powers **8:** 302, 320, 353, 370, 390, 429, 439, 447; **29:** 297; **61:** 326, 338; **68:** 244; **72:** 363; **75:** 203; **78:** 169

as revenger **68:** 254

as ruler **8:** 304, 308, 309, 420, 423; **13:** 424; **22:** 302; **29:** 278, 362, 377, 396; **61:** 315; **75:** 237

self-control **8:** 312, 414, 420; **22:** 302; **44:** 11; **72:** 302

self-knowledge **16:** 442; **22:** 302; **29:** 278, 292, 362, 377, 396; **72:** 302, 334, 352

as Shakespeare or creative artist **8:** 299, 302, 308, 312, 320, 324, 353, 364, 435, 447; **61:** 280, 288; **72:** 319, 329, 343, 352

as tragic hero **8:** 359, 370, 464; **29:** 292

Proteus

The Two Gentlemen of Verona **6:** 439, 450, 458, 480, 490, 511; **40:** 312, 327, 330, 335, 359; **42:** 18; **54:** 325, 332

Puck

A Midsummer Night's Dream **45:** 96, 158; **70:** 105

Queen

Cymbeline **73:** 19

Quickly (Mistress Quickly)

Henry V **5:** 186, 187, 210, 276, 293; **30:** 278

Regan

King Lear **31:** 151; **46:** 231, 242; **61:** 160

Richard (King Richard II)

Richard II

artistic temperament **6:** 264, 267, 270, 272, 277, 292, 294, 298, 315, 331, 334, 347, 368, 374, 393, 409; **24:** 298, 301, 304, 315, 322, 390, 405, 408, 411, 414, 419; **39:** 289; **70:** 282

Bolingbroke, compared with **24:** 346, 349, 351, 352, 356, 419; **39:** 256; **52:** 108, 124; **58:** 275

characterization **6:** 250, 252, 253, 254, 255, 258, 262, 263, 267, 270, 272, 282, 283, 304, 343, 347, 364, 368; **24:** 262, 263, 267, 269, 270, 271, 272, 273, 274, 278, 280, 315, 322, 325, 330, 333, 390, 395, 402, 405, 423; **28:** 134; **39:** 279, 289; **52:** 169; **58:** 229, 241, 253, 259, 267, 307; **70:** 231, 282

dangerous aspects **24:** 405; **58:** 253

death of **60:** 21

delusion **6:** 267, 298, 334, 368, 409; **24:** 329, 336, 405

homosexuality **24:** 405

kingship **6:** 253, 254, 263, 272, 327, 331, 334, 338, 364, 402, 414; **24:** 278, 295, 336, 337, 339, 356, 419; **28:** 134, 178; **39:** 256, 263; **52:** 169; **58:** 241, 275; **70:** 202

language and imagery **58:** 301

loss of identity **6:** 267, 338, 368, 374, 381, 388, 391, 409; **24:** 298, 414, 428

as martyr-king **6:** 289, 307, 321; **19:** 209; **24:** 289, 291; **28:** 134

nobility **6:** 255, 258, 259, 262, 263, 391; **24:** 260, 263, 274, 280, 289, 291, 402, 408, 411

political acumen **6:** 263, 264, 272, 292, 310, 327, 334, 364, 368, 374, 388, 391, 397, 402, 409; **24:** 405; **39:** 256; **70:** 202

private vs. public persona **6:** 317, 327, 364, 368, 391, 409; **24:** 428; **70:** 202

role in Gloucester's death **52:** 108, 124

role-playing **24:** 419, 423; **28:** 178

seizure of Gaunt's estate **6:** 250, 338, 388

self-dramatization **6:** 264, 267, 307, 310, 315, 317, 331, 334, 368, 393, 409; **24:** 339; **28:** 178; **60:** 21

self-hatred **13:** 172; **24:** 383; **39:** 289

self-knowledge **6:** 255, 267, 331, 334, 338, 352, 354, 368, 388, 391; **24:** 273, 289, 411, 414; **39:** 263, 289; **60:** 21, 46; **70:** 282

spiritual redemption **6:** 255, 267, 331, 334, 338, 352, 354, 368, 388, 391; **24:** 273, 289, 411, 414; **52:** 124; **60:** 21, 46

Richard (King Richard III, formerly Richard, Duke of Gloucester)

Henry VI, Parts 1, 2, and 3

characterization **3:** 35, 48, 57, 64, 77, 143, 151; **22:** 193; **39:** 160, 177; **74:** 3, 32

as revenger **22:** 193

soliloquy (3 *Henry VI*, Act III, scene ii) **3:** 17, 48

Richard III

ambition **8:** 148, 154, 165, 168, 170, 177, 182, 213, 218, 228, 232, 239, 252, 258, 267; **39:** 308, 341, 360, 370, 383; **52:** 201, 223

attractive qualities **8:** 145, 148, 152, 154, 159, 161, 162, 165, 168, 170, 181, 182, 184, 185, 197, 201, 206, 213, 228, 243, 252, 258; **16:** 150; **39:** 370, 383; **52:** 272, 280; **62:** 104; **73:** 186

credibility, question of **8:** 145, 147, 154, 159, 165, 193; **13:** 142

death **8:** 145, 148, 154, 159, 165, 168, 170, 177, 182, 197, 210, 223, 228, 232, 243, 248, 252, 258, 267

deformity as symbol **8:** 146, 147, 148, 152, 154, 159, 161, 165, 170, 177, 184, 185, 193, 218, 248, 252, 267; **19:** 164; **62:** 110; **73:** 150, 174, 196, 210

inversion of moral order **8:** 159, 168, 177, 182, 184, 185, 197, 201, 213, 218, 223, 232, 239, 243, 248, 252, 258, 262, 267; **39:** 360; **52:** 205, 214; **73:** 210

as Machiavellian villain **8:** 165, 182, 190, 201, 218, 232, 239, 243, 248; **39:** 308, 326, 360, 387; **52:** 201, 205, 257, 280, 285; **62:** 2, 60, 78, 110; **73:** 154, 207

as monster or symbol of diabolic **8:** 145, 147, 159, 162, 168, 170, 177, 182, 193,

197, 201, 228, 239, 248, 258; **13:** 142; **37:** 144; **39:** 326, 349; **52:** 227, 272; **66:** 286; **73:** 174

other literary villains, compared with **8:** 148, 161, 162, 165, 181, 182, 206, 213, 239, 267

role-playing, hypocrisy, and dissimulation **8:** 145, 148, 154, 159, 162, 165, 168, 170, 182, 190, 206, 213, 218, 228, 239, 243, 252, 258, 267; **25:** 141, 164, 245; **39:** 335, 341, 387; **52:** 257, 267; **62:** 78; **73:** 186, 208, 210

as scourge or instrument of God **8:** 163, 177, 193, 201, 218, 228, 248, 267; **39:** 308; **62:** 60

as seducer **52:** 223, 227; **62:** 91, 104; **73:** 206

self-esteem **52:** 196; **62:** 78; **73:** 207, 208

as Vice figure **8:** 190, 201, 213, 228, 243, 248, 252; **16:** 150; **39:** 383, 387; **52:** 223, 267; **62:** 78; **73:** 154, 164

Richard Plantagenet, Duke of York

Henry VI, Parts 1, 2, and 3 See **York**

Richmond

Richard III **8:** 154, 158, 163, 168, 177, 182, 193, 210, 218, 223, 228, 243, 248, 252; **13:** 142; **25:** 141; **39:** 349; **52:** 214, 257, 285; **66:** 286

the Rival Poet

Sonnets **10:** 169, 233, 334, 337, 385; **48:** 352; **75:** 322

Roman citizenry

Julius Caesar

portrayal of **7:** 169, 179, 210, 221, 245, 279, 282, 310, 320, 333; **17:** 271, 279, 288, 291, 292, 298, 323, 348, 351, 367, 374, 375, 378; **22:** 280; **30:** 285, 297, 316, 321, 374, 379; **37:** 229

Romeo and Juliet

Romeo and Juliet

characterization **65:** 159; **76:** 273

death-wish **5:** 431, 489, 505, 528, 530, 538, 542, 550, 566, 571, 575; **32:** 212; **76:** 258

first meeting (Act I scene v) **51:** 212

immortality **5:** 536

Juliet's epithalamium speech (Act III, scene ii) **5:** 431, 477, 492

Juliet's innocence **5:** 421, 423, 450, 454; **33:** 257; **65:** 201

maturation **5:** 437, 454, 467, 493, 498, 509, 520, 565; **33:** 249, 257; **65:** 159

rebellion **25:** 257; **73:** 113; **76:** 298, 305

reckless passion **5:** 419, 427, 431, 438, 443, 444, 448, 467, 479, 485, 505, 533, 538, 542; **33:** 241; **76:** 227

Romeo's dream (Act V, scene i) **5:** 513, 536, 556; **45:** 40; **51:** 203

Rosaline, Romeo's relationship with **5:** 419, 423, 425, 427, 438, 498, 542, 575; **76:** 258

Rosalind

As You Like It **46:** 94, 122

Beatrice, compared with **5:** 26, 36, 50, 75

charm **5:** 55, 75; **23:** 17, 18, 20, 41, 89, 111; **69:** 43

disguise, role of **5:** 75, 107, 118, 122, 128, 130, 133, 138, 141, 146, 148, 164,

Shakespearean Criticism
Cumulative Topic Index

The Cumulative Topic Index indentifies the principal topics of discussion in the criticism of each play and non-dramatic poem. The topics are arranged alphabetically. Page references indicate the beginning page number of each essay containing substantial commentary on that topic. A parenthetical reference after a topic indicates that the topic is extensively discussed in that volume.

324; **25:** 347; **36:** 295; **42:** 301; **45:** 297, 344, 333; **50:** 45; **57:** 278, 285, 319, 347

language versus action
Titus Andronicus **4:** 642, 644, 647, 664, 668; **13:** 225; **27:** 293, 313, 325; **43:** 186; **62:** 225; **68:** 204; **73:** 306, 324

Law and Justice (Volume 49: 1, 18, 23, 27, 37, 46, 60, 67, 73)
Henry IV **49:** 112,116,123,133,137
Henry V **49:** 223, 236, 260; **79:** 72
Henry VIII **61:** 92
Measure for Measure **49:** 274, 286, 293
The Merchant of Venice **53:** 169; **66:** 180
Othello **53:** 288, 350

law versus passion for freedom
Much Ado about Nothing **22:** 85

laws of nature, violation of
Macbeth **3:** 234, 241, 280, 323; **29:** 120; **57:** 242, 263; **65:** 226; **69:** 298, 367

legal issues
King Lear **46:** 276

legitimacy
Henry VI, Parts 1, 2, and 3 **3:** 89, 157; **39:** 154
Henry VIII **37:** 109; **56:** 209, 220, 230; **69:** 194, 249
Macbeth **60:** 340

legitimacy or inheritance
King John **9:** 224, 235, 254, 303; **13:** 147; **19:** 182; **37:** 132; **41:** 215; **56:** 325, 335; **60:** 295, 329; **68:** 19, 64, 73, 77; **78:** 26, 35

liberty versus tyranny
Julius Caesar **7:** 158, 179, 189, 205, 221, 253; **25:** 272

love
See also **ideal love**
All's Well That Ends Well **7:** 12, 15, 16, 51, 58, 67, 90, 93, 116; **38:** 80; **51:** 33, 44; **75:** 36
As You Like It **5:** 24, 44, 46, 57, 79, 88, 103, 116, 122, 138, 141, 162; **28:** 46, 82; **34:** 85; **69:** 2, 39, 58, 87
King Lear **2:** 109, 112, 131, 160, 162, 170, 179, 188, 197, 218, 222, 238, 265; **25:** 202; **31:** 77, 149, 151, 155, 162; **61:** 220, 237
Love's Labour's Lost **2:** 312, 315, 340, 344; **22:** 12; **23:** 252; **38:** 194; **51:** 44; **77:** 141
The Merchant of Venice **4:** 221, 226, 270, 284, 312, 344; **22:** 3, 69; **25:** 257; **40:** 156; **51:** 1, 44; **66:** 63, 127; **77:** 154
sacrificial love **13:** 43; **22:** 69; **40:** 142
A Midsummer Night's Dream
passionate or romantic love **3:** 372, 389, 395, 396, 402, 408, 411, 423, 441, 450, 480, 497, 498, 511; **29:** 175, 225, 263, 269; **45:** 126, 136; **51:** 44; **58:** 175

Much Ado about Nothing **8:** 24, 55, 75, 95, 111, 115; **28:** 56; **51:** 30; **78:** 127, 135
Othello **4:** 412, 493, 506, 512, 530, 545, 552, 569, 570, 575, 580, 591; **19:** 253; **22:** 207; **25:** 257; **28:** 243, 344; **32:** 201; **35:** 261, 317; **51:** 25, 30; **53:** 315; **54:** 119
The Phoenix and Turtle **10:** 31, 37, 40, 50; **38:** 342, 345, 367; **51:** 145, 151, 155; **64:** 209, 211, 217
Sonnets **10:** 173, 247, 287, 290, 293, 302, 309, 322, 325, 329, 394; **28:** 380; **37:** 347; **51:** 270, 284, 288, 292; **62:** 153, 170; **75:** 297, 307, 333
The Tempest **8:** 435, 439; **29:** 297, 339, 377, 396
Twelfth Night **1:** 543, 546, 573, 580, 587, 595, 600, 603, 610, 660; **19:** 78; **26:** 257, 364; **34:** 270, 293, 323; **46:** 291, 333, 347, 362; **51:** 30; **52:** 57; **62:** 297; **74:** 188
The Two Gentlemen of Verona **6:** 442, 445, 456, 479, 488, 492, 494, 502, 509, 516, 519, 549; **13:** 12; **40:** 327, 335, 343, 354, 365; **51:** 30, 44
The Two Noble Kinsmen **9:** 479, 481, 490, 498; **41:** 289, 301, 355, 363, 372, 385; **50:** 295, 361; **58:** 345, 356, 371; **70:** 302
The Winter's Tale **7:** 417, 425, 469, 490; **51:** 30, 33, 44

love and friendship
See also **friendship**
Julius Caesar **7:** 233, 262, 268; **25:** 272

love and honor
Troilus and Cressida **3:** 555, 604; **27:** 370, 374; **59:** 251, 257, 337

love and passion
Antony and Cleopatra **6:** 51, 64, 71, 80, 85, 100, 115, 159, 165, 180; **25:** 257; **27:** 126; **47:** 71, 124, 174, 192; **51:** 25, 33, 44; **58:** 2, 41, 105; **60:** 179, 222

love and reason
See also **reason**
Othello **4:** 512, 530, 580; **19:** 253

Love and Romance (Volume 51: 1, 15, 25, 30, 33, 44)
Pericles **51:** 71
The Phoenix and Turtle **51:** 145, 151, 155
Romeo and Juliet **51:** 195, 203, 212
Sonnets **51:** 284, 288, 292; **65:** 277
Venus and Adonis
The Rhetoric of Desire **51:** 345, 352, 359, 368

love and time
Antony and Cleopatra **65:** 235
Romeo and Juliet **65:** 235; **76:** 277, 286, 339

love, lechery, or rape
Troilus and Cressida **43:** 357

love versus fate
Romeo and Juliet **5:** 421, 437, 438, 443, 445, 458; **33:** 249

love versus friendship
See also **friendship**
Romeo and Juliet **65:** 142
The Two Gentlemen of Verona **6:** 439, 449, 450, 458, 460, 465, 468, 471, 476, 480; **40:** 354, 365; **54:** 295, 307, 325, 344; **74:** 312

love versus lust
Sonnets **65:** 277
Venus and Adonis **10:** 418, 420, 427, 434, 439, 448, 449, 454, 462, 466, 473, 480, 489; **25:** 305; **28:** 355; **33:** 309, 330, 339, 347, 357, 363, 370; **51:** 359; **67:** 286, 297, 320, 327

love versus reason
See also **reason**
Love's Labour's Lost **54:** 225, 234
Sonnets **10:** 329

love versus war
Troilus and Cressida **18:** 332, 371, 406, 423; **22:** 339; **27:** 376; **59:** 234, 251, 257

Machiavellianism
Henry V **5:** 203, 225, 233, 252, 287, 304; **25:** 131; **30:** 273; **60:** 304; **79:** 81, 101
Henry VI, Parts 1, 2, and 3 **22:** 193; **60:** 304
King John **60:** 304
Macbeth **52:** 29; **57:** 236

Madness (Volume 35: 1, 7, 8, 24, 34, 49, 54, 62, 68)
Hamlet **19:** 330; **35:** 104, 117, 126, 132, 134, 140, 144; **59:** 31; **75:** 222
King Lear **19:** 330
Macbeth **19:** 330
Othello **35:** 265, 276, 282
Twelfth Night **1:** 554, 639, 656; **26:** 371

Magic and the Supernatural (Volume 29: 1, 12, 28, 46, 53, 65)
The Comedy of Errors **1:** 27, 30; **54:** 215; **66:** 22; **77:** 29, 54
Macbeth
supernatural grace versus evil or chaos **3:** 241, 286, 323; **69:** 269
witchcraft and supernaturalism **3:** 171, 172, 173, 175, 177, 182, 183, 184, 185, 194, 196, 198, 202, 207, 208, 213, 219, 229, 239; **16:** 317; **19:** 245; **20:** 92, 175, 213, 279, 283, 374, 387, 406, 413; **25:** 235; **28:** 339; **29:** 91, 101, 109, 120; **44:** 351, 373; **57:** 194, 242; **69:** 322
Measure for Measure
supernatural grace versus evil or chaos **48:** 1
A Midsummer Night's Dream **29:** 190, 201, 210, 216
The Tempest **8:** 287, 293, 304, 315, 340, 356, 396, 401, 404, 408, 435, 458; **28:** 391, 415; **29:** 297, 343, 377; **45:** 272; **61:** 326, 356
Sonnets
occult **48:** 346
The Winter's Tale
witchcraft **22:** 324

male discontent
The Merry Wives of Windsor **5:** 392, 402

Topic Index

Shakespearean Criticism
Cumulative Topic Index, by Play

The Cumulative Topic Index, by Play identifies the principal topics of discussion in the criticism of each play and non-dramatic poem. The topics are arranged alphabetically by play. Page references indicate the beginning page number of each essay containing substantial commentary on that topic. A parenthetical reference after a play indicates which volumes discuss the play extensively.

All's Well That Ends Well (Volumes 7, 26, 38, 55, 63, 75)

appearance versus reality **7:** 37, 76, 93; **26:** 117

audience perspective **7:** 81, 104, 109, 116, 121

bed-trick **7:** 8, 26, 27, 29, 32, 41, 86, 93, 98, 113, 116, 126; **13:** 84; **26:** 117; **28:** 38; **38:** 65, 118; **49:** 46; **54:** 52; **55:** 109, 131, 176

Bertram

characterization **7:** 15, 27, 29, 32, 39, 41, 43, 98, 113; **26:** 48; **26:** 117; **55:** 90; **75:** 2, 57

conduct **7:** 9, 10, 12, 16, 19, 21, 51, 62, 104; **50:** 59; **55:** 143, 154

desire **22:** 78

transformation or redemption **7:** 10, 19, 21, 26, 29, 32, 54, 62, 81, 90, 93, 98, 109, 113, 116, 126; **13:** 84

comic elements **26:** 97, 114; **48:** 65; **55:** 148, 154, 164; **75:** 36, 57

conclusion **38:** 123, 132, 142; **54:** 52; **55:** 148, 154, 170; **75:** 62

dark elements **7:** 27, 37, 39, 43, 54, 109, 113, 116; **26:** 85; **48:** 65; **50:** 59; **54:** 30; **55:** 164, 170; **75:** 9, 31, 32, 53

Decameron (Boccaccio), compared with **7:** 29, 43; **75:** 36, 72

desire **38:** 99, 109, 118; **55:** 122

displacement **22:** 78

education **7:** 62, 86, 90, 93, 98, 104, 116, 126

elder characters **7:** 9, 37, 39, 43, 45, 54, 62, 104

family, theme of **73:** 58

gender issues **7:** 9, 10, 67, 126; **13:** 77, 84; **19:** 113; **26:** 128; **38:** 89, 99, 118; **44:** 35; **55:** 101, 109, 122, 164

genre **48:** 65; **75:** 36, 57

Helena

as agent of reconciliation, renewal, or grace **7:** 67, 76, 81, 90, 93, 98, 109, 116; **55:** 176; **75:** 36

as dualistic or enigmatic character **7:** 15, 27, 29, 39, 54, 58, 62, 67, 76, 81, 98, 113, 126; **13:** 66; **22:** 78; **26:** 117; **54:** 30; **55:** 90, 170, 176

as "female achiever" **19:** 113; **38:** 89; **55:** 90, 101, 109, 122, 164

characterization **75:** 21, 36, 57

desire **38:** 96; **44:** 35; **55:** 109, 170

pursuit of Bertram **7:** 9, 12, 15, 16, 19, 21, 26, 27, 29, 32, 43, 54, 76, 116; **13:** 77; **22:** 78; **49:** 46; **55:** 90; **75:** 21

virginity **38:** 65; **55:** 131, 176

virtue and nobility **7:** 9, 10, 12, 16, 19, 21, 27, 32, 41, 51, 58, 67, 76, 86, 126; **13:** 77; **50:** 59; **55:** 122

implausibility of plot, characters, or events **7:** 8, 45

irony, paradox, and ambiguity **7:** 27, 32, 58, 62, 67, 81, 86, 109, 116

King **38:** 150; **55:** 148; **75:** 62

language and imagery **7:** 12, 29, 45, 104, 109, 121; **38:** 132; **48:** 65; **75:** 2, 14, 62, 72

Lavatch **26:** 64; **46:** 33, 52, 68; **55:** 143

love **7:** 12, 15, 16, 51, 58, 67, 90, 93, 116; **38:** 80; **51:** 33, 44; **75:** 36

merit versus rank **7:** 9, 10, 19, 37, 51, 76; **38:** 155; **50:** 59

"mingled yarn" **7:** 62, 93, 109, 126; **38:** 65

morality plays, influence of **7:** 29, 41, 51, 98, 113; **13:** 66

mythic or mythological elements **60:** 169

naturalism **60:** 169

opening scene **54:** 30

Parolles

characterization **7:** 8, 9, 43, 76, 81, 98, 109, 113, 116, 126; **22:** 78; **26:** 48, 73, 97; **26:** 117; **46:** 68; **55:** 90, 154; **75:** 9, 14

exposure **7:** 9, 27, 81, 98, 109, 113, 116, 121, 126

Falstaff, compared with **7:** 8, 9, 16

reconciliation **7:** 90, 93, 98; **51:** 33

religious, mythic, or spiritual content **7:** 15, 45, 54, 76, 98, 109, 116; **66:** 335

romance or folktale elements **7:** 32, 41, 43, 45, 54, 76, 104, 116, 121; **26:** 117; **75:** 36

sexuality **7:** 67, 86, 90, 93, 98, 126; **13:** 84; **19:** 113; **22:** 78; **28:** 38; **44:** 35; **49:** 46; **51:** 44; **55:** 109, 131, 143, 176; **75:** 72

social and political context **13:** 66; **22:** 78; **38:** 99, 109, 150, 155; **49:** 46; **75:** 9

staging issues **19:** 113; **26:** 15, 19, 48, 52, 64, 73, 85, 92, 93, 94, 95, 97, 114, 117, 128; **54:** 30; **75:** 30, 31, 32, 34, 35

structure **7:** 21, 29, 32, 45, 51, 76, 81, 93, 98, 116; **22:** 78; **26:** 128; **38:** 72, 123, 142; **66:** 335; **75:** 2, 53, 57

words versus deeds **75:** 62

youth versus age **7:** 9, 45, 58, 62, 76, 81, 86, 93, 98, 104, 116, 126; **26:** 117; **38:** 109

Antony and Cleopatra (Volumes 6, 17, 27, 47, 58, 70)

allegorical elements **52:** 5

All for Love (John Dryden), compared with **6:** 20, 21; **17:** 12, 94, 101

ambiguity **6:** 53, 111, 161, 163, 180, 189, 208, 211, 228; **13:** 368

androgyny **13:** 530

Antony

characterization **6:** 22, 23, 24, 31, 38, 41, 172, 181, 211; **16:** 342; **19:** 270; **22:** 217; **27:** 117; **47:** 77, 124, 142; **58:** 2, 41, 118, 134; **70:** 2, 66, 94

Cleopatra, relationship with **6:** 25, 27, 37, 39, 48, 52, 53, 62, 67, 71, 76, 85, 100, 125, 131, 133, 136, 142, 151, 161, 163, 165, 180, 192; **27:** 82; **47:** 107, 124, 165, 174

death scene **25:** 245; **47:** 142; **58:** 41; **60:** 46

dotage **6:** 22, 23, 38, 41, 48, 52, 62, 107, 136, 146, 175; **17:** 28

nobility **6:** 22, 24, 33, 48, 94, 103, 136, 142, 159, 172, 202; **25:** 245

political conduct **6:** 33, 38, 53, 107, 111, 146, 181

public versus private personae **6:** 165; **47:** 107; **58:** 41; **65:** 270

self-knowledge **6:** 120, 131, 175, 181, 192; **47:** 77

as superhuman figure **6:** 37, 51, 71, 92, 94, 178, 192; **27:** 110; **47:** 71

as tragic hero **6:** 38, 39, 52, 53, 60, 104, 120, 151, 155, 165, 178, 192, 202, 211; **22:** 217; **27:** 90

audience response **48:** 206; **58:** 88

Caesar **65:** 270

Cleopatra

Antony, relationship with **6:** 25, 27, 37, 39, 48, 52, 53, 62, 67, 71, 76, 85, 100, 125, 131, 133, 136, 142, 151, 161, 163, 165, 180, 192; **25:** 257; **27:** 82; **47:** 107, 124, 165, 174

characterization **47:** 77, 96, 113, 124; **58:** 24, 33, 59, 118, 134; **70:** 14, 24, 66, 94

Topic Index, by Play

Topic Index, by Play

Measure for Measure (Volumes 2, 23, 33, 49, 65, 76)

Italian comedy, influence of **59:** 105
jealousy **5:** 334, 339, 343, 353, 355, 363; **22:** 93; **38:** 273, 307
Jonsonian humors comedy, influence of **38:** 319; **59:** 105
knighthood **5:** 338, 343, 390, 397, 402; **47:** 354
language and imagery **5:** 335, 337, 343, 347, 351, 363, 374, 379; **19:** 101; **22:** 93, 378; **28:** 9, 69; **38:** 313, 319; **59:** 89
male discontent **5:** 392, 402
marriage **5:** 343, 369, 376, 390, 392, 400; **22:** 93; **38:** 297; **51:** 44; **59:** 95
mediation **5:** 343, 392
morality **5:** 335, 339, 347, 349, 353, 397; **59:** 132
Neoclassical rules **5:** 332, 334; **71:** 115
Page, Anne **47:** 321
Page, Mistress Margaret **47:** 321
pastoral elements **59:** 132
play and theatricality **47:** 325
play-within-the-play, convention of **5:** 354, 355, 369, 402
poaching **71:** 160
realism **38:** 313
reconciliation **5:** 343, 369, 374, 397, 402
revenge **5:** 349, 350, 392; **38:** 264, 307; **71:** 127
as satire or parody **5:** 338, 350, 360, 385; **38:** 278, 319; **47:** 354, 363
schemes and intrigues **5:** 334, 336, 339, 341, 343, 349, 355, 379
setting **47:** 375 **59:** 89, 139
sexual politics **19:** 101; **38:** 307; **59:** 95; **71:** 143
social milieu **18:** 75, 84; **38:** 297, 300; **59:** 132, 139, 144
sources **5:** 332, 350, 360, 366, 385; **32:** 31; **59:** 123
stage history **18:** 66, 67, 68, 70, 71; **59:** 123
staging issues **18:** 74, 75, 84, 86, 90, 95; **71:** 141, 142
structure **5:** 332, 333, 334, 335, 343, 349, 355, 369, 374; **18:** 86; **22:** 378; **59:** 89, 111; **71:** 104
unnatural ordering **22:** 378
wit **5:** 335, 336, 337, 339, 343, 351
women, role of **5:** 335, 341, 343, 349, 369, 379, 390, 392, 402; **19:** 101; **38:** 307; **71:** 143

A Midsummer Night's Dream (Volumes 3, 12, 29, 45, 58, 70)

adaptations **12:** 144, 146, 147, 153, 280, 282
ambiguity **3:** 401, 459, 486; **45:** 169
appearance, perception, and illusion **3:** 368, 411, 425, 427, 434, 447, 459, 466, 474, 477, 486, 497, 516; **19:** 21; **22:** 39; **28:** 15; **29:** 175,190; **45:** 136
Athens and the forest, contrast between **3:** 381, 427, 459, 466, 497, 502; **29:** 175
autobiographical elements **3:** 365, 371, 379, 381, 389, 391, 396, 402, 432
Bottom
    awakening speech (Act IV, scene i) **3:** 406, 412, 450, 457, 486, 516; **16:** 34; **58:** 181; **70:** 123
    his dream **60:** 142
    folly of **46:** 1, 14, 29, 60
    imagination **3:** 376, 393, 406, 432, 486; **29:** 175, 190; **45:** 147; **70:** 172
    self-possession **3:** 365, 376, 395, 402, 406, 480; **45:** 158
    Titania, relationship with **3:** 377, 406, 441, 445, 450, 457, 491, 497; **16:** 34; **19:** 21; **22:** 93; **29:** 216; **45:** 160; **58:** 203, 215; **70:** 105, 123, 193
    transformation **3:** 365, 377, 432; **13:** 27; **22:** 93; **29:** 216; **45:** 147, 160; **70:** 105, 123

brutal elements **3:** 445, 491, 497, 511; **12:** 259, 262, 298; **16:** 34; **19:** 21; **29:** 183, 225, 263, 269; **45:** 169; **70:** 105, 123, 193
capriciousness of the young lovers **3:** 372, 395, 402, 411, 423, 437, 441, 450, 497, 498; **29:** 175, 269; **45:** 107
ceremonies, rites, and rituals, importance of **58:** 189
the changeling **58:** 162, 167
chastity **45:** 143
class distinctions, conflict, and relations **22:** 23; **25:** 36; **45:** 160; **50:** 74, 86
colonialism **53:** 32
as dream-play **3:** 365, 370, 372, 377, 389, 391; **29:** 190; **45:** 117; **58:** 181; **70:** 157
dreams **45:** 96, 107, 117; **70:** 186
duration of time **3:** 362, 370, 380, 386, 494; **45:** 175
Egeus **70:** 105, 140
Elizabethan culture, relation to **50:** 86; **58:** 220; **70:** 119
erotic elements **3:** 445, 491, 497, 511; **12:** 259, 262, 298; **16:** 34; **19:** 21; **29:** 183, 225, 269; **58:** 194
fairies **3:** 361, 362, 372, 377, 395, 400, 423, 450, 459, 486; **12:** 287, 291, 294, 295; **19:** 21; **29:** 183, 190; **45:** 147; **70:** 186, 193
farcical elements **58:** 169
feminist interpretation **48:** 23
gender **53:** 1; **58:** 215
Helena **29:** 269; **58:** 194
Helena and Hermia, relationship between **60:** 142
Hermia **29:** 225, 269; **45:** 117; **58:** 194
Hippolytus, myth of **29:** 216; **45:** 84
homosexuality **60:** 142
identity **29:** 269; **58:** 215
imagination and art **3:** 365, 371, 381, 402, 412, 417, 421, 423, 441, 459, 468, 506, 516, 520; **22:** 39; **70:** 164, 172, 186
language and imagery **3:** 397, 401, 410, 412, 415, 432, 453, 459, 468, 494; **22:** 23, 39, 93, 378; **28:** 9; **29:** 263; **45:** 96, 126, 136, 143, 147, 169, 175; **48:** 23, 32; **58:** 181, 186, 194
the lovers **58:** 151, 169
male domination **3:** 483, 520; **13:** 19; **25:** 36; **29:** 216, 225, 243, 256, 269; **42:** 46; **45:** 84; **58:** 203, 220; **60:** 142
marriage **3:** 402, 423, 450, 483, 520; **29:** 243, 256; **45:** 136, 143; **48:** 32; **51:** 1, 30, 44; **58:** 175
metadramatic elements **3:** 427, 468, 477, 516, 520; **29:** 190, 225, 243; **50:** 86
Metamorphoses (Golding translation of Ovid) **16:** 25
mimetic desire **60:** 172, 245
Minotaur, myth of **3:** 497, 498; **29:** 216
music and dance **3:** 397, 400, 418, 513; **12:** 287, 289; **25:** 36
mythic or mythological elements **58:** 194 **60:** 172, 245, 259; **70:** 157, 193
Oberon **58:** 151, 162, 167, 203; **60:** 142; **70:** 105
    as controlling force **3:** 434, 459, 477, 502; **29:** 175
Ovid, influence of **3:** 362, 427, 497, 498; **22:** 23; **29:** 175, 190, 216; **60:** 172
parent-child relations **13:** 19; **29:** 216, 225, 243; **69:** 212; **70:** 140
passionate or romantic love **3:** 372, 389, 395, 396, 402, 408, 411, 423, 441, 450, 480, 497, 498, 511; **29:** 175, 225, 263, 269; **45:** 126, 136; **51:** 44; **58:** 175
patriarchy **60:** 259
Pauline doctrine **3:** 457, 486, 506; **70:** 123
Platonic elements **3:** 368, 437, 450, 497; **45:** 126
politics **29:** 243; **70:** 172
power **42:** 46; **45:** 84; **58:** 151

psychoanalytic interpretations **3:** 440, 483; **28:** 15; **29:** 225; **44:** 1; **45:** 107, 117; **58:** 167
Puck **45:** 96, 158; **70:** 105
Pyramus and Thisbe interlude **3:** 364, 368, 379, 381, 389, 391, 396, 408, 411, 412, 417, 425, 427, 433, 441, 447, 457, 468, 474, 511; **12:** 254; **13:** 27; **16:** 25; **22:** 23; **29:** 263; **45:** 107, 175; **50:** 74
race **53:** 1, 32
reason versus imagination **3:** 381, 389, 423, 441, 466, 506; **22:** 23; **29:** 190; **45:** 96; **70:** 186
reconciliation **3:** 412, 418, 437, 459, 468, 491, 497, 502, 513; **13:** 27; **29:** 190; **70:** 140
reversal **29:** 225; **60:** 245
Romeo and Juliet, compared with **3:** 396, 480
rustic characters **3:** 376, 397, 432; **12:** 291, 293; **45:** 147, 160; **70:** 172
sexuality **22:** 23, 93; **29:** 225, 243, 256, 269; **42:** 46; **45:** 107 **53:** 32; **58:** 203, 215, 220
sources **29:** 216; **60:** 259; **70:** 152; **70:** 123, 157, 193
staging issues **3:** 364, 365, 371, 372, 377; **12:** 151, 152, 154, 158, 159, 280, 284, 291, 295; **16:** 34; **19:** 21; **29:** 183, 256; **48:** 23; **70:** 140, 147, 149, 150, 152
structure **3:** 364, 368, 381, 402, 406, 427, 450, 513; **13:** 19; **22:** 378; **29:** 175; **45:** 126, 175; **58:** 186, 189; **70:** 119, 164
textual issues **16:** 34; **29:** 216; **58:** 151; **70:** 105, 140
Theseus **51:** 1
    characterization **3:** 363; **58:** 151, 220; **70:** 172, 193
    Hippolyta, relationship with **3:** 381, 412, 421, 423, 450, 468, 520; **29:** 175, 216, 243, 256; **45:** 84; **70:** 105
    as ideal **3:** 379, 391
    "lovers, lunatics, and poets" speech (Act V, scene i) **3:** 365, 371, 379, 381, 391, 402, 411, 412, 421, 423, 441, 498, 506; **29:** 175
    as representative of institutional life **3:** 381, 403; **70:** 172
Titania **29:** 243; **58:** 151, 162, 167, 203; **70:** 105
tragic elements **3:** 393, 400, 401, 410, 445, 474, 480, 491, 498, 511; **29:** 175; **45:** 169; **58:** 175, 186; **70:** 186
as a transgressive play **60:** 142
unity **3:** 364, 368, 381, 402, 406, 427, 450, 513; **13:** 19; **22:** 378; **29:** 175, 263; **70:** 164
unnatural ordering **22:** 378

Much Ado about Nothing (Volumes 8, 18, 31, 55, 67, 78)

appearance versus reality **8:** 17, 18, 48, 63, 69, 73, 75, 79, 88, 95, 115; **31:** 198, 209; **55:** 259, 268; **67:** 163; **78:** 65
battle of the sexes **8:** 14, 16, 19, 48, 91, 95, 111, 121, 125; **31:** 231, 245 **55:** 199; **78:** 70
Beatrice and Benedick **78:** 140
    ambivalent portrayal of **67:** 155
    Beatrice's femininity **8:** 14, 16, 17, 24, 29, 38, 41, 91; **31:** 222, 245; **55:** 221
    Beatrice's request to "kill Claudio" (Act IV, scene i) **8:** 14, 17, 33, 41, 55, 63, 75, 79, 91, 108, 115; **18:** 119, 120, 136, 161, 245, 257; **55:** 268; **78:** 70, 92, 101, 127
    Benedick's challenge of Claudio (Act V, scene i) **8:** 48, 63, 79, 91; **31:** 231

Topic Index, by Play

colonialism **13:** 424, 440; **15:** 228, 268, 269, 270, 271, 272, 273; **19:** 421; **25:** 357, 382; **28:** 249; **29:** 343, 368; **32:** 338, 367, 400; **42:** 327; **45:** 200, 280; **53:** 11, 21, 45, 67; **61:** 297, 307; **72:** 293, 309, 318, 327
compassion, theme of **42:** 346
conspiracy or treason **16:** 426; **19:** 357; **25:** 382; **29:** 377
dreams **45:** 236, 247, 259
education or nurturing **8:** 353, 370, 384, 396; **29:** 292, 368, 377; **78:** 169
exposition scene (Act I, scene ii) **8:** 287, 289, 293, 299, 334
family, theme of **73:** 127
father-daughter relationship **69:** 212
Ferdinand **8:** 328, 336, 359, 454; **19:** 357; **22:** 302; **29:** 362, 339, 377
freedom and servitude **8:** 304, 307, 312, 429; **22:** 302; **29:** 278, 368, 377; **37:** 336; **72:** 288, 343
gender **53:** 64, 67
Gonzalo **22:** 302; **29:** 278, 343, 362, 368
Gonzalo's commonwealth **8:** 312, 336, 370, 390, 396, 404; **19:** 357; **29:** 368; **45:** 280; **72:** 352
good versus evil **8:** 302, 311, 315, 370, 423, 439; **29:** 278; 297; **61:** 338, 362; **72:** 302, 329
historical content **8:** 364, 408, 420; **16:** 426; **25:** 382; **29:** 278, 339, 343, 368; **45:** 226; **53:** 21, 53; **61:** 297
incest, motif of **69:** 212
the island **8:** 308, 315, 447; **25:** 357, 382; **29:** 278, 343
language and imagery **8:** 324, 348, 384, 390, 404, 454; **19:** 421; **29:** 278; **29:** 297, 343, 368, 377; **61:** 280, 288; **78:** 169
love **8:** 435, 439; **29:** 297, 339, 377, 396
magic or supernatural elements **8:** 287, 293, 304, 315, 340, 356, 396, 401, 404, 408, 435, 458; **28:** 391, 415; **29:** 297, 343, 377; **45:** 272; **61:** 272, 356
the masque (Act IV, scene i) **8:** 404, 414, 423, 435, 439; **25:** 357; **28:** 391, 415; **29:** 278, 292, 339, 343, 368; **42:** 339; **45:** 188; **72:** 293, 334; **75:** 203
Miranda **8:** 289, 301, 304, 328, 336, 370, 454; **19:** 357; **22:** 302; **28:** 249; **29:** 278, 297, 362, 368, 377, 396; **53:** 64
Montaigne's Essais, relation to **42:** 346
morality **52:** 43; **61:** 338
music **8:** 390, 404; **29:** 292; **37:** 321; **42:** 339; **61:** 315; **72:** 288; **75:** 159, 190, 203, 237, 251
mythic or mythological elements **75:** 251
nature **8:** 315, 370, 390, 408, 414; **29:** 343, 362, 368, 377; **61:** 362
Neoclassical rules **8:** 287, 292, 293, 334; **25:** 357; **29:** 292; **45:** 200
politics **8:** 304, 307, 315, 353, 359, 364, 401, 408; **16:** 426; **19:** 421; **29:** 339; **37:** 336; **42:** 327; **45:** 272, 280; **52:** 43; **61:** 315; **75:** 251
Prospero
    characterization **8:** 312, 348, 370, 458; **16:** 442; **22:** 302; **45:** 188, 272; **61:** 307; **72:** 325, 328
    as God or Providence **8:** 311, 328, 364, 380, 429, 435
    magic, nature of **8:** 301, 340, 356, 396, 414, 423, 458; **25:** 382; **28:** 391; **29:** 278, 292, 368, 377, 396; **32:** 338, 343; **61:** 272; **72:** 343
    psychoanalytic interpretation **45:** 259; **69:** 212
    redemptive powers **8:** 302, 320, 353, 370, 390, 429, 439, 447; **29:** 297; **61:** 326, 338; **68:** 244; **72:** 363; **75:** 203; **78:** 169
    as revenger **68:** 254

as ruler **8:** 304, 308, 309, 420, 423; **13:** 424; **22:** 302; **29:** 278, 362, 377, 396; **61:** 315; **75:** 237
self-control **8:** 312, 414, 420; **22:** 302; **44:** 11; **72:** 302
self-knowledge **16:** 442; **22:** 302; **29:** 278, 292, 362, 377, 396; **72:** 302, 334, 352
as Shakespeare or creative artist **8:** 299, 302, 308, 312, 320, 324, 353, 364, 435, 447; **61:** 280, 288; **72:** 319, 329, 343, 352
as tragic hero **8:** 359, 370, 464; **29:** 292
providential order **52:** 43
race **53:** 11, 21, 45, 53, 64, 67; **72:** 309
realism **8:** 340, 359, 464
reality and illusion **8:** 287, 315, 359, 401, 435, 439, 447, 454; **22:** 302; **45:** 236, 247; **72:** 319, 326, 334, 343, 352; **75:** 203
reconciliation **8:** 302, 312, 320, 334, 348, 359, 370, 384, 401, 404, 414, 429, 439, 447, 454; **16:** 442; **22:** 302; **29:** 297; **37:** 336; **45:** 236; **72:** 288
religious, mythic, or spiritual content **8:** 328, 390, 423, 429, 435; **45:** 211, 247; **61:** 280; **72:** 363
revenge **68:** 254
romance or pastoral tradition, influence of **8:** 336, 348, 396, 404; **37:** 336; **72:** 293
sexuality **53:** 45; **61:** 288; **69:** 212; **75:** 237
Shakespeare's other plays, compared with **8:** 294, 302, 324, 326, 348, 353, 380, 401, 464; **13:** 424; **68:** 254
silence **78:** 169
spectacle versus simple staging **15:** 206, 207, 208, 210, 217, 219, 222, 223, 224, 225, 227, 228, 305, 352; **28:** 415
sources **45:** 226; **61:** 326; **72:** 293
staging issues **15:** 343, 346, 352, 361, 364, 366, 368, 371, 385; **28:** 391, 415; **29:** 339; **32:** 338, 343; **42:** 339; **45:** 200; **54:** 19; **61:** 297; **72:** 318, 319, 325, 326, 327, 328
Stephano and Trinculo, comic subplot of **8:** 292, 297, 299, 304, 309, 324, 328, 353, 370; **25:** 382; **29:** 377; **46:** 14, 33
structure **8:** 294, 295, 299, 320, 384, 439; **28:** 391, 415; **29:** 292, 297; **45:** 188; **65:** 264; **72:** 329
subversiveness **22:** 302; **75:** 237
The Tempest; or, The Enchanted Island (William Davenant/John Dryden adaptation) **15:** 189, 190, 192, 193
The Tempest; or, The Enchanted Island (Thomas Shadwell adaptation) **15:** 195, 196, 199
time **8:** 401, 439, 464; **25:** 357; **29:** 278, 292; **45:** 236; **65:** 235, 264, 311; **68:** 244
tragic elements **8:** 324, 348, 359, 370, 380, 408, 414, 439, 458, 464; **68:** 254
trickster, motif of **22:** 302; **29:** 297
usurpation or rebellion **8:** 304, 370, 408, 420; **25:** 357, 382; **29:** 278, 362, 377; **37:** 336; **72:** 309
utopia **45:** 280; **72:** 288
wonder **72:** 343, 352

***Timon of Athens* (Volumes 1, 20, 27, 52, 67, 78)**

Alcibiades **25:** 198; **27:** 191; **67:** 242, 264; **78:** 297, 309, 320
alienation **1:** 523; **27:** 161
allegorical elements **67:** 223, 230, 253; **78:** 327
Apemantus **1:** 453, 467, 483; **20:** 476, 493; **25:** 198; **27:** 166, 223, 235; **67:** 264; **78:** 297, 309
appearance versus reality **1:** 495, 500, 515, 523; **52:** 311, 329
Athens **27:** 223, 230; **67:** 264

authorship controversy **1:** 464, 466, 467, 469, 474, 477, 478, 480, 490, 499, 507, 518; **16:** 351; **20:** 433
autobiographical elements **1:** 462, 467, 470, 473, 474, 478, 480; **27:** 166, 175
economics **78:** 315
Elizabethan culture, relation to **1:** 487, 489, 495, 500; **20:** 433; **27:** 203, 212, 230; **50:** 13; **52:** 320, 354; **67:** 247
friendship **67:** 242, 247, 253, 264; **78:** 327
genre **1:** 454, 456, 459, 460, 462, 483, 492, 499, 503, 509, 511, 512, 515, 518, 525, 531; **27:** 203; **67:** 212
homoerotic elements **78:** 320
as inferior or flawed play **1:** 476, 481, 489, 499, 520; **20:** 433, 439, 491; **25:** 198; **27:** 157, 175; **52:** 338, 349; **78:** 297, 330
King Lear, relation to **1:** 453, 459, 511; **16:** 351; **27:** 161; **37:** 322
language and imagery **1:** 488; **13:** 392; **25:** 198; **27:** 166, 184, 235; **52:** 329, 345, 354; **67:** 212, 242
language and philosophy **52:** 311
as medieval allegory or morality play **1:** 492, 511, 518; **27:** 155; **78:** 326
misogyny **78:** 337
mixture of genres **16:** 351; **25:** 198; **78:** 309, 315
nihilistic elements **1:** 481, 513, 529; **13:** 392; **20:** 481
pessimistic elements **1:** 462, 467, 470, 473, 478, 480; **20:** 433, 481; **27:** 155, 191; **78:** 325, 329
Poet and Painter **25:** 198; **52:** 320; **78:** 297, 320
politics **27:** 223, 230; **50:** 13; **67:** 264
religious, mythic, or spiritual content **1:** 505, 512, 513, 523; **20:** 493
satirical elements **27:** 155, 235
self-knowledge **1:** 456, 459, 462, 495, 503, 507, 515, 518, 526; **20:** 493; **27:** 166
Senecan elements **27:** 235
Shakespeare's other tragedies, compared with **27:** 166; **52:** 296; **78:** 297
sources **16:** 351; **27:** 191; **52:** 301; **78:** 286
staging issues **20:** 445, 446, 481, 491, 492, 493; **67:** 239, 240, 241; **78:** 325, 326, 327, 329, 330
structure **27:** 191; **52:** 338, 345, 349; **67:** 212, 242; **78:** 309, 315
Timon
    comic traits **25:** 198
    death of **60:** 46
    as flawed hero **1:** 456, 459, 462, 472, 495, 503, 507, 515; **16:** 351; **20:** 429, 433, 476; **25:** 198; **27:** 157, 161
    generosity **67:** 230, 242, 247, 253; **78:** 309, 320, 337
    misanthropy **13:** 392; **20:** 431, 464, 476, 481, 491, 492, 493; **27:** 161, 175, 184, 196; **37:** 222; **52:** 296, 301; **67:** 223, 230, 264; **78:** 286, 309, 320, 331
    as noble figure **1:** 467, 473, 483, 499; **20:** 493; **27:** 212
    psychological motivation **67:** 223, 230; **78:** 309, 329, 331
    wealth and social class **1:** 466, 487, 495; **25:** 198; **27:** 184, 196, 212; **50:** 13; **78:** 331

***Titus Andronicus* (Volumes 4, 17, 27, 43, 62, 73)**

Aaron **4:** 632, 637, 650, 651, 653, 668, 672, 675; **27:** 255; **28:** 249, 330; **43:** 176; **53:** 86, 92; **73:** 251, 260, 273
amputations, significance of **48:** 264
appearance versus reality **73:** 301
authorship controversy **4:** 613, 614, 615, 616, 617, 619, 623, 624, 625, 626, 628, 631, 632, 635, 642; **62:** 208, 254; **73:** 301

ISBN 0-7876-7009-X